WE THUNDERED OUT

WE

200 YEARS OF

THUNDERED OUT

THE TIMES 1785-1985

by Philip Howard

Research by Jack Lonsdale

Times Books London

First published in Great Britain by
TIMES BOOKS LIMITED
16 GOLDEN SQUARE, LONDON W1R 4BN

Design Ivan Dodd
Editorial direction Pauline Batchelor
Newspaper facsimile photography Tessa Musgrave
Picture consultant and research Ann Gould
Editorial assistant Rosemary Wilkins

British Library Cataloguing in Publication Data
Howard, Philip
'We thundered out——': 200 years of *The Times*, 1785–1985
1. Times, The
I. Title
072'.1 PN129.L7T5
ISBN 0-7230-0266-5

Printed in Great Britain

ACKNOWLEDGEMENTS

The author and publishers would like to thank the following for their help and cooperation on various aspects of this book: Anne Piggott, Archivist, *The Times*; Michael Roffey, Manager, *The Times* Picture Library; Colin Wilson, Chief Librarian, *The Times*; John Westmancoat, British Library (Newspaper Division), Colindale; John Frost, Historical Newspaper Service.

The Times on microfilm can be obtained from Research Publications, P.O. Box 45, Reading.

Illustrations and photographs are reproduced by kind permission of: BBC Hulton Picture Library, p. 162a; British Library, pp. 50a, b, 52a, b, c, d; British Museum, pp. 13a, 17a, 27a, 28a, 30a, 32a, 35a; Camera Press, p. 75b; Evening Standard, and Centre for the Study of Cartoons and Caricature, University of Kent, Canterbury, p. 109b; Guildhall Library, pp. 10b, 18b, 134a, b, 136b; Louis Heren, p. 144c; Imperial War Museum, pp. 40b, 88a; National Army Museum, p. 49c; National Portrait Gallery, pp. 66c, 158b; The Clothworkers' Company, p. 166a; The Illustrated London News Picture Library, pp. 62a, 65a, 76b; The Mansell Collection, pp. 16a, b, 18c, 36b, 42a, 55b, 58a, 59b, 70b, 130b, 146a, b, 158a, 170a; United Press International (UK) Ltd, p. 120a; Wellcome Institute for the History of Medicine, p. 87b. Frontispieces: British Museum; Mel Calman; New Statesman; Pictorial Press, London; The Mansell Collection; MShott. All other photographs are © *The Times* and are reproduced with permission of *The Times* Picture Library.

Every effort has been made to trace and acknowledge the original sources of the illustrations. In the case of any omission, please inform the publishers, who will correct and acknowledge in any further printing.

CONTENTS

NEWSPAPERS are, by definition and name, ephemeral. What matters about them is tomorrow's issue. Yesterday's sev'n thousand issues are wrapping for fish and chips, except that this ancient practice is now prohibited by clean food legislation. Not many good books or other fictions have been written about the perpetual evanescent hurly-burly of daily journalism: *Towards the End of the Morning*, about the old *Manchester Guardian*, by Michael Frayn; *The Front Page*, that hard-boiled Broadway comedy by Hecht and MacArthur; but not many others leap to mind.

Nevertheless, there is a curious fascination in old newspapers, which is clearly felt by those outside the trade. You have only to look at the scrapbooks of newspaper cuttings in attics and cellars around the country. Life is fleeting. Newspapers are the only cheap record easily available to most people. *The Times* is the paper of record, and the oldest daily newspaper in English. Its back numbers are a rich source of two hundred turbulent years of history, life frozen in newsprint, signposts *à la recherche du temps perdu*, memorials of the English idiosyncrasy.

They are not quite what you might expect. There is a misapprehension widely spread among those who do not read *The Times* that it is a pompous though endearing voice of the British Establishment, which represents the official view. National institution, yes; voice of Establishment, no. You have only to read this tiny fraction of sheets from *Times* past to recognize that *The Times* has had its finest hours when it has been a radical, campaigning, bloody-minded paper, questioning established wisdom, and when necessary blasting down governments with its thunderbolts.

In its early days, *The Times* had to pioneer the freedoms of the press that we take for granted, in the teeth of obstinate and ferocious opposition from the Establishment and ruling classes. In the political storm of the nineteenth century, *The Times* led the middle classes to a share in the government, and opened the road to today's mass democracy.

The cure for thinking of *The Times* as a deferential voice of the Establishment is to read what it wrote about George IV on the morning after his death, or what Queen Victoria wrote about the vile rag to her Prime Ministers. The finest hours of *The Times* in the nineteenth century came when its political stance was a little left of centre, thundering for reform. Its bad times have been when it stood too close to the Prime Minister in Downing Street, and forgot that the right posture for *The Times* is the high and mighty one that the centre of the world runs through Printing House Square.

The cure for thinking of *The Times* as stuffy is to read its account of some sensational event, for example the Jack the Ripper murders, which cannot be rivalled for ghastly, almost prurient, detail, and reveals something not altogether pleasant about the taste of the Victorian clubman: I turn pale and swallow nervously to read it. The cure for thinking of *The Times* as remorselessly high-minded is to read its accounts of the bloody old prize-fights; or its charming fashion columns for Jane Austen's contemporaries; or the way it would have no mention of Shelley in the paper, on the grounds that he was a trendy lefty; its tendency to review a new novel by Dickens extravagantly harshly – a fact that may be not entirely unconnected with the fact that Dickens was the editor of *A Daily Other Newspaper* that was rising to challenge the monopoly of *The Times*. The cure for thinking of *The Times* as respectable is to read the account of some of the financial, editorial and political skulduggery that has gone on behind the solemn facades of Printing House Square. The

FOREWORD

two hundred years of history which you are about to enter is a period rich in disasters, terrible with world wars, torn by civil political struggles, turbulent even in peace. It was also the period in which the United Kingdom and its Empire became the greatest power in the world, and *The Times* became the greatest newspaper in the world.

The story of *The Times* over two hundred years, as shown by its back numbers, is also, in parts, hilariously funny, grotesquely eccentric, and on occasions quite incredible. And here is a paradox for you. For most of this period the identity of the men and women who wrote *The Times* was a closely guarded secret. There were no bylines, and employees were sometimes operating on the shady side of the law. They could, and sometimes did, go to prison if they were identified. Yet what comes strongly out of this tiny selection of pages is the identity of the person known in the office as 'a *Times* man'.

This protean character wears many faces. He is the great war correspondent, the gregarious Irishman Billy Russell, and that plausible Bohemian rascal, Henri de Blowitz. He is the secret Thomas Barnes, and the open John Thadeus Delane. He is a series of John Walters extending over the whole of the nineteenth century, good old English country gents on the make, and rather surprised by the prodigious baby that they had produced in Printing House Square. He is sometimes a woman, like the clever, crusading Flora Shaw, the first female executive in the inky business. He sometimes becomes a General in a war he is supposed to be reporting, like Ferdinand Eber. He is sometimes murdered in the line of duty to Printing House Square, like poor young Frank Power. He sometimes goes magnificently native, like Walter Harris. He occasionally works for the Secret Service on the side. Sometimes he suffers from Napoleonic megalomania, like Lord Northcliffe. He is adventurer and don, hack and essayist, Government Minister secretly writing for Printing House Square, and full-time leader writer thundering daily.

And many *Times* men and women there be, that have no memorial, except the yellowing pages of back numbers of the paper to which they gave their lives. They were a mixed bunch. But what they had in common was a passionate belief that *The Times* was the greatest newspaper in the world, and a determination to get the news first, and get it right.

Pages from old newspapers may not look much of a memorial and you may need a magnifying glass to read some of the more ancient ones. But these once shook the world, and shaped our lives today. We descendants of this astonishing family stretching back two centuries have a great tradition to live up to. We shall do our best. But now, as always in Printing House Square, what matters is tomorrow's paper.

PHILIP HOWARD

The founding father

Done at the
Lgogographic Office,
Printing-House Square,
BLACK-FRIARS,
December, 1788.

Top Portrait of John Walter I, 1783-4, by an unknown artist; now in *The Times* Board Room.

Above Imprint from a handbill produced by John Walter in 1788, to promote his logographic process.

Below Map engraved by John Prine and John Tinney in 1746 showing Printing House Yard (later Square).

This is the front page of issue number 1 of *The Daily Universal Register*, shortly to be renamed *The Times*. It appeared on 1 January 1785, a Saturday, never a good day for newspaper subscriptions, and sold about a thousand copies at 2½d each. Only one copy of this first issue survives. It had been ordered in advance by the Rev. Dr Charles Burney, father of the novelist and diarist Fanny Burney, an energetic collector and 'one curious in newspapers'. It is now in the British Library.

The Daily Universal Register was started by John Walter I (1739–1812) as a by-product of his new Logographic Press, which printed by 'logotypes' – blocks of syllables or complete words – instead of single and separate letters. Its format was the conventional one for daily newspapers of the period: a single sheet folded once to produce a four-page paper in folio 12¼ inches × 18¾ inches. Each page was made up in an arrangement of four columns, with little in the way of headlines or crossheads.

In his prospectus addressed 'To the Public' in the first issue, John Walter explained the purpose of his publication:

> A News-Paper ought to be the Register of the times, and faithful recorder of every species of intelligence; it ought not to be engrossed by any particular object; but, like a well covered table, it should contain something suited to every palate: observations on the dispositions of our own and of foreign courts should be provided for the political reader; debates should be reported for the amusement or information of those who may be particularly fond of them; and a due attention should be paid to the interests of trade, which are so greatly promoted by advertisements.

It was the ambition of newspaper proprietors then as now to fill the paper with advertisements.

The founder also promised the readers of his new journal that it would contain nothing that would wound the ear of delicacy or corrupt the heart, and that it would abstain from unfair partisanship and scandalous scurrility.

The first issue devoted three of its columns to news and three to the prospectus. There were ten columns of advertisements, including a back page puff for *The Register* itself signed 'Gregory Gazette'. It was a businesslike sheet, aimed at City businessmen. There was no leading article, no political news or commentary. The column of foreign intelligence was preceded by ten lines of Court News, and an Ode for the New Year by Thomas Whitehead, the forgotten Poet Laureate, which, it announced, 'will be sung in the great Council Chamber'. Then came a paragraph on new 'Protecting Duties' on British exports to Ireland. A Guildhall examination of a bankrupt was given almost a column.

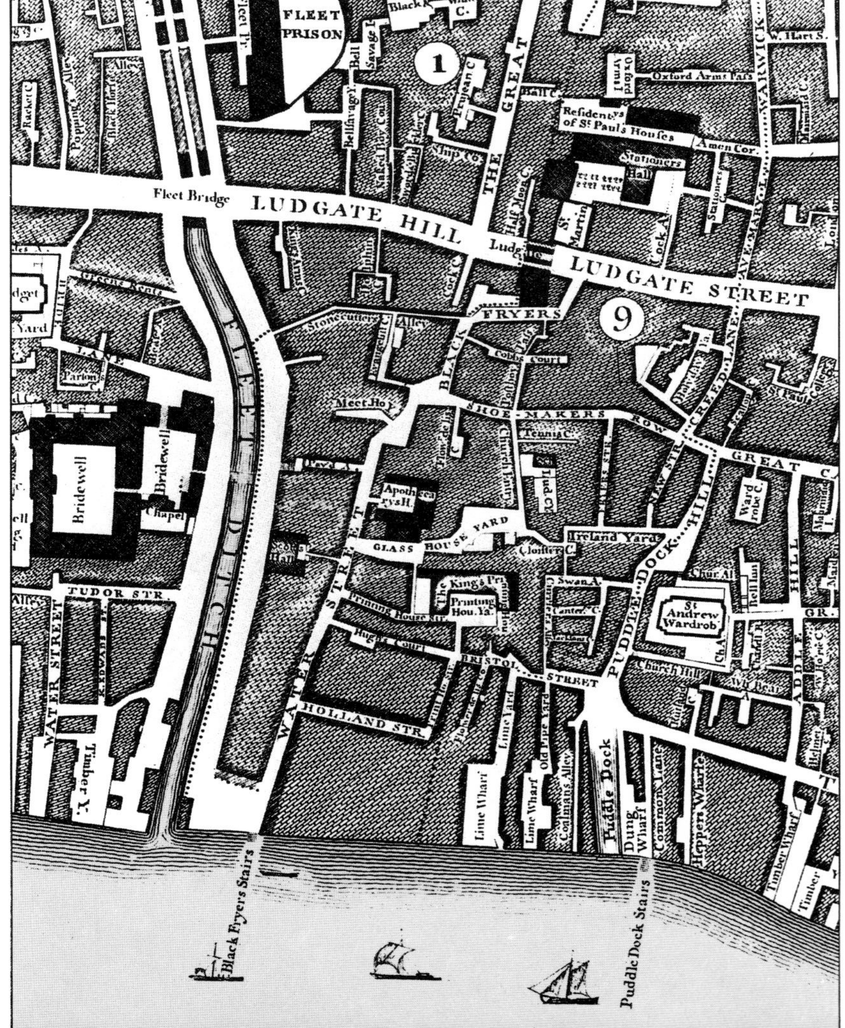

The first issue was attended by production difficulties, not for the last time in newspaper publishing. The logographic principle was responsible for its share of mechanical troubles. John Walter had announced in his prospectus that publication would take place every morning at six o'clock. On that first morning it was so late that the hawkers, already on the streets with the other journals, would not wait for their copies of *The Daily Universal Register*. Accordingly Walter thought it proper to repeat his long manifesto in the second issue, for 'his numerous friends and others according to promise' who had missed it on the first day.

The logographic printing process was not a great success. Walter complained: 'The journeymen caballed and refused to work at the invention without I paid the prices as paid in the common way'. But the newspaper intended originally as an advertisement for the logographic process survived. It came into existence at a time when there was no free expression of opinion in the press. Newspapers were in the pay of parties or individuals, and journalists were hacks who wrote paragraphs in or against the interest of a political party or personage. By its eventual commercial success John Walter's paper pioneered the idea that a newspaper could be independent and free to express its opinions in the national interest, without fear or favour.

The name was clumsy, and confused with other *Registers*, so on 1 January 1788 it was changed to *The Times*. This makes it the oldest paper in the English language with a record of continuous daily publication. It became the best-known newspaper in the world, and the pre-eminent national journal and paper of daily historical record. Its most important achievement was to establish, in the political struggles of the nineteenth century, the principle that the press could be free, and the fourth estate of the realm.

John Walter was the son of a coal merchant in the City of London. He succeeded to his father's business, and played a part in the establishment of the Coal Exchange. He also started underwriting ships engaged in shipping coal. American privateers, French men-of-war, and a hurricane in Jamaica ruined him, but it was an honourable bankruptcy in which he managed to pay all his creditors in full. He had to find a new job, and for a time looked for 'some respectable post under Government'. Walter then became interested in logography, an invention of Henry Johnson, a London printer. He was encouraged in his interest by Benjamin Franklin, who had also experimented to simplify the printing process.

Walter purchased the old King's Printing Office in Printing House Square, Blackfriars, and set up as a printer and publisher. These were stormy times for publishers and journalists. John Walter I had two spells in Newgate and had to pay numerous fines for criticism of the authorities. One of his offences was the statement (no doubt true, but judged libellous) that the then Prince of Wales and other royal princes had by their misconduct incurred the just disapprobation of King George III.

John Walter was moderately successful as a publisher and a printer; as an inventor and innovator he was sanguine and somewhat visionary; as a journalist he was unlucky. But he gave *The Times* the germ of the character it has since maintained. In 1795 he gave up the management of the business, and retired into the country at Teddington, 'intending to enjoy the few years that I have to live in *otium cum dignitate*'. His eldest son William was a bad businessman and had been involved in his father's libels. Accordingly he was succeeded by a younger son, John Walter II (1776–1847), who in 1803 took sole charge of the business.

The front page of the first issue of THE DAILY UNIVERSAL REGISTER. John Walter's intentions are laid before his readers in columns 3 and 4, and he concludes (on the next page, not illustrated) that he 'hopes that it will appear to the public deserving of their encouragement'.

1 JANUARY 1785

NUMB. 1.] SATURDAY, JANUARY 1, 1785. [Price Two-pence Halfpenny.

The SIXTH NIGHT.
By His MAJESTY's Company

AT the THEATRE ROYAL in DRURY-LANE, this preſent SATURDAY, will be performed

A New COMEDY, called
The NATURAL SON.

The characters by Mr. King, Mr. Parſons, Mr. Benſley, Mr. Moody, Mr. Baddeley, Mr. Wrighten, and Mr. Palmer. Miſs Pope, Miſs Tidſwell, and [Miſs Farren.
With new Scenes and Dreſſes.
The Prologue to be ſpoken by Mr. Banniſter, jun.
And the Epilogue by Miſs Farren.
After which will be performed the laſt New Pantomime Entertainment, in two Parts, called
HARLEQUIN JUNIOR;
Or, The MAGIC CESTUS.
The Characters of the Pantomime, by
Mr. Wright, Mr. Williamſon, Mr. Burton, Mr. Staunton, Mr. Williames, Mr. Palmer, Mr. Waldron, Mr. Fawcett, Mr. Chaplin, Mr. Phillimore, Mr. Wilſon, Mr. Alfred, Mr. Spencer, Mr. Chapman, and Mr. Grimaldi. Mrs. Burnet, Miſs Burnett, Miſs Tidiwell, Miſs Barnes, Miſs Cranford, and Miſs Stageldoir.
To conclude with the Repulſe of the Spaniards before
The ROCK of GIBRALTAR.

To-morrow, by particular deſire, (for the 4th time) the revived Comedy of the DOUBLE DEALER, with the favorite Maſque of ARTHUR and EMMELINE.

On Tueſday the Tragedy of VENICE PRESERVED: Jaffier by Mr. Brereton, Pierre by Mr. Benſley, and Belvidera, by Mrs. Siddons: And on Friday the Carmelite. Maſſinger s Play of the MAID of HONOUR, (with alterations and Additions) is in Rehearſal and will ſoon be produced.

NINTH NIGHT. FOR THE AUTHOR.

AT the THEATRE-ROYAL, COVENT-GARDEN, this preſent SATURDAY, January 1, 1785, will be performed, a New Comedy, called
The FOLLIES of a DAY,
Or, The Marriage of Figaro.
With new Dreſſes, Decorations, &c.
The principal characters by Mr. Lewis, Mr. Quick, Mr. Edwin, Mr. Wilſon, Mr. Wewitzer, Mr. Bonnor, Mr. Thompſon, and Mrs. Martyr; Mrs. Bates, Mrs. Webb, Miſs Wewitzer, and Miſs Younge.
With a new Prologue, to be ſpoken by Mr. Davies.
To which will be added, for the the ſixth time,
A new Pantomime, called,
The MAGIC CAVERN,
Or, VIRTUE's TRIUMPH.
With new Scenery, Machinery, Muſic, Dreſſes, and Decorations.
The Scenes chiefly deſigned by Mr. Richards, and executed by him, Mr. Carver, Mr. Hodgins, and Aſſiſtants.
The Overture, Songs, Choruſſes, and the Muſic of the new Pantomime, and compoſed by Mr. Shield.
Nothing under full Price will be taken.
The Words of the Songs, &c. to be had at the Theatre.

MR. WALTER returns his thanks to his Friends and the Public for the great encouragement and generous ſupport he has already received from them to his new improvement in Printing, by the readineſs with which they have ſubſcribed to his intended publication of the works of ſome eminent Authors; and whilſt he ſolicits a continuance of their favours, begs leave to acquaint them that by
The middle of January will be publiſhed,
In One Volume 12mo,
MISCELLANIES IN VERSE AND PROSE,
Intended as a Specimen of his Printing Types at the Logographic Office, Printing-Houſe Square, Blackfriars.—And by the beginning of February, his firſt volume, containing Watts's Improvement of the Mind, with an Introduction written on the occaſion, will be ready to be delivered to the ſubſcribers.

This Day is publiſhed, Price 6d.

PLAN of the CHAMBER of COMMERCE, King's-Arms Buildings, Cornhill, London; which is open every day, for Conſultation, Opinion, and Advice (verbal or in Writing) Mediation, Aſſiſtance, Arbitration, &c. in all *Commercial, Maritime,* and *Inſurance* Affairs, and matters of *Trade* in general; and the *Laws* and *Uſages* relating thereto.——The Addreſs is, To the Director of the Chamber of Commerce, as above.

To be had of Richardſon and Urquhart, Royal Exchange; J. Sewell, Cornhill; T. Whieldon, Fleet-ſtreet; W. Flexney, Holborn; and at the aforeſaid Chamber.

Where may alſo be had, in one Volume Folio;
Mr. Weſkett's COMPLETE DIGEST of the THEORY, LAWS and PRACTICE of INSURANCE; an entire new and comprehenſive work, including all the adjudged Caſes extant, with ſeveral never before printed; Extracts from the Statutes, foreign Ordinances, and marine Treaties; accounts of all the Inſurance Companies the MaritimeCourts, the commercial and maritime Laws, the Law of Nations, &c. the whole forming (alphabetically) a new *Lex Mercatoria.*

☞ "This Work has been compiled with great Care and Induſtry, by one who is evidently a Maſter of the Subject. It abounds with Proofs of extenſive Reading, as well as mature Reflection, and judicious Remarks; and if the completeſt Syſtem of Inſurance that has hitherto been compoſed be entitled to Praiſe, the preſent uſeful Digeſt muſt meet with the Approbation of the commercial World." Crit. Rev. Vol. 52, p. 443.—All the other Literary Journals ſpeak in ſimilar Terms of this Book; which had already been tranſlated abroad.

This Day is publiſhed, in 3 Vols. Price 9s. ſewed.
By the LITERARY SOCIETY,

MODERN TIMES: or The ADVENTURES of GABRIEL OUTCAST. A Novel, in Imitation of Gil Blas.
"Qui capit ille facit."
Printed for the Author, and ſold by J. Walter, Printing-houſe Square, Black-friars; where may be had, gratis, the Plan of this Society, aſſociated for the Encouragement of Literature, who propoſe to print and publiſh at their own Riſk and Expence ſuch original Works as they may approve of, and give their Authors all Profits ariſing from the ſame.

MRS. KING begs leave to acquaint her Friends ſhe opens her SCHOOL at CHIGWELL in ESSEX, on Monday, the 10th of January, for the EDUCATION of YOUNG LADIES: as ſhe has always been accuſtomed to watch and improve the opening mind, hopes to give ſatisfaction to thoſe who truſt her with ſo important a charge.

Till the 10th of January Mrs. King may be ſpoke with at Mr. Kerr's, Bit-maker to his Majeſty, in the Mews, Charing-croſs.

N. B. Wanted an Apprentice and Half-boarders.

SHIP-PING ADVER-TISEMENTS

For NICE, GENOA, and LEGHORN,
(With Liberty to touch at One Port in the Channel,)
The NANCY.
THOMAS WHITE, Commander,

BURTHEN 160 Tons; Guns and Men anſwerable. Lying off the Tower, and will abſolutely depart on Saturday the 8th inſtant.

The ſaid Commander to be ſpoken with every morning at Sam's Coffee-houſe, near the Cuſtom-houſe; at Will's Coffee-houſe, in Cornhill; and at Exchange hours on the French and Italian Walk; or
WILLIAM ELYARD, for the ſaid Commander, No. 16, Savage-Gardens.

Direct for LISBON,
The NANCY.
JOHN RACKHAM, Commander,

BURTHEN 300 Tons, Men anſwerable. Lying off Horſlydown Chain; Seven-eighths of her Cargo abſolutely engaged, and is obliged by Charterparty to depart on Saturday the 8th inſtant.

The ſaid Commander to be ſpoken with every morning at Sam's Coffee-houſe, near the Cuſtom-houſe; at Will's Coffee-houſe, in Cornhill; and in Exchange hours in the French and Italian Walk; or
WILLIAM ELYARD, for the ſaid Commander, No. 16, Savage-Gardens.

For NICE, GENOA, and LEGHORN.
(With Liberty to Touch at One Port in the Channel.)
The LIVELY,
ROBERT BRINE, Commander,

BURTHEN 200 Tons, Guns and Men anſwerable. Lying off Iron Gate.

The ſaid Commander to be ſpoke with every Morning at Sam's Coffee-houſe, near the Cuſtom-houſe; at Will's Coffee-houſe in Cornhill; and in Exchange Hours in the French and Italian Walk; or
WILLIAM ELYARD, for the ſaid Commander, No. 16, Savage-Gardens.

For CONSTANTINOPLE and SMYRNA, or SMYRNA and CONSTANTINOPLE,
(With Liberty to Touch at One Port in the Channel,)
The BETSEY,
ROBERT LANCASTER, Commander,

BURTHEN 200 Tons, Men anſwerable. Lying at Iron-Gate. Two-thirds of her Cargo engaged, and is obliged to depart by Charterparty, in all the preſent Month of January.

The ſaid Commander to be ſpoke with every Morning at Sam's Coffee-houſe, near the Cuſtom-houſe; at Will's Coffee-houſe in Cornhill; and in Exchange Hours in the French and Italian Walk; or
WILLIAM ELYARD, for the ſaid Commender, No. 16, Savage-Gardens.

N. B. No Goods to be taken on Board the Veſſel without an Order from the Broker.

NEW NOVELS.

This Day are publiſhed, (in two Volumes, price 5s. ſewed,)

THE YOUNG WIDOW; or, the HISTORY of Mrs. LEDWICH.

The HISTORY of Lord BELFORD and Miſs SOPHIA WOODLEY, 3 vol. 9s. bound.

Printed for the Editor, and ſold by F. Noble, in Holborn;
Where may be had lately publiſhed,
St. Ruthin's Abbey, a Novel, 3 vols. 9s. bound.
The Woman of Letters; or, Hiſtory of Fanny Belton, 2 vol. 7s. bound.
A Leſſon for Lovers; or, Hiſtory of Col. Melville and Lady Richly, 2 vols. 7s. bound.
Literary Amuſements; or, Evening Entertainer, 2 vol. 7s. bound.
Adventures of a Cavalier, by Daniel Defoe, 3 vols. 9s bound.

T. RICKABY, PRINTER,
No. 15, Duke's Court, Drury Lane;

REſpectfully informs his Friends and the Public in general, that the Partnerſhip between him and Mr. Moore being entirely diſſolved, he now intends to carry on every branch of the PRINTING BUSINESS upon his own account;—and having purchaſed a complete aſſortment of the neateſt and beſt materials, is determined to purſue a Mode of Printing which he hopes will meet with the approbation of his employers.

N.B. Cards, Hand-Bills, Circular Letters, and all articles of the kind, accurately printed at a few hours notice, in a manner particularly neat, and at the loweſt prices.

*** An Apprentice wanted.

To the Readers of the London Medical Journal.
This day is firſt publiſhed, price 1s.

SYMPATHY DEFENDED; or, the State of MEDICAL CRITICISM in London; written to improve the Principles and Manners of the Editor of the London Medical Journal: To which are added the Contents of the Treatiſe on Medical Sympathy, and a Poſtſcript, on account of a premature Review in a late Number of the London Medical Journal.
By a Society of Faculties;
Friends to the Public and Enemies to Impoſition.
"Cum tua non edas, carpis mea carmina, Laeli,
"Carp re vel noli noſtra, ede tua."
MART. Epig.

This pamphlet has been hitherto diſtributed gratuitouſly. The repeated applications for them, particularly from the country, have become ſo numerous, that the Society feel themſelves under the neceſſity of putting them into the hands of a publiſher.
Sold by J. Murray, Bookſeller, Fleet-ſtreet.

Nondum lingua ſuit dextra, peregit opus.
MART.

SHORT-HAND, on the lateſt and moſt approved Principles taught by J. LARKHAM, No 11, Roſe Alley, Biſhopſgate Street.

It would exceed the limits of an advertiſement merely to mention the various errors either in the *plan* or the *execution* of the different ſchemes of Short-hand hitherto made public, or to point out the peculiarities and excellencies of the preſent: Mr. L. therefore only begs leave to obſerve, that the approbation of many gentlemen well known in the literary world, and well verſed in the *Theory* and *Practice* of Short-hand, expreſſed in ſtronger terms than delicacy will permit him to repeat, warrants him in ſaying *his* will be found a ſyſtem of ſhort and ſwift writing; more *eaſy* to acquire and retain, more *expeditiouſly*, more *legible* and more *regular* than any ever yet offered to the Public.

The terms of teaching *one* Guinea, the *uſual* time of learning *ſeven* leſſons.

To the Public.

TO bring out a New Paper at the preſent day; when ſo many others are already eſtabliſhed and confirmed in the public opinion, is certainly an arduous undertaking; and no one can be more fully aware of its difficulties than I am: I, nevertheleſs, entertain very ſanguine hopes, that the nature of the plan on which this paper will be conducted, will enſure it a moderate ſhare at leaſt of public favour; but my pretenſions to encouragement, however ſtrong they may appear in my own eyes, muſt be tried before a tribunal not liable to be blinded by *ſelf-opinion*: to that tribunal I ſhall now, as I am bound to do, ſubmit theſe pretenſions with deference, and the public will judge whether they are well or ill founded.

It is very far from my intention to detract from the acknowledged merit of the Daily Papers now in exiſtence; it is ſufficient that they pleaſe the claſs of readers whoſe approbation their conductors are ambitious to deſerve; nevertheleſs it is certain ſome of the beſt, ſome of the moſt reſpectable, and ſome of the moſt uſeful members of the community, have frequently complained (and the cauſes of their complaints ſtill exiſt) that by radical defects in the plans of the preſent eſtabliſhed papers, they were deprived of many advantages, which ought naturally to reſult from daily publications. Of theſe ſome build their fame on the length and accuracy of parliamentary reports, which unqueſtionably are given with great ability, and with a laudable zeal to pleaſe thoſe, who can ſpare time to read ten or twelve columns of debates. Others are principally attentive to the politics of the day, and make it their ſtudy to give ſatisfaction to the numerous claſs of politicians, who, bleſſed with eaſy circumſtances, have nothing better to do, than to amuſe themſelves with watching the motions of miniſters both at home and abroad; and endeavouring to find out the ſecret ſprings that ſet in motion the great machine of government in every ſtate and empire in the world. There is one paper which in no degree interferes with the purſuits of its cotemporaries; it looks upon parliamentary debates as ſacred myſteries, that cannot be ſubmitted to vulgar eyes without profanation; political inveſtigations it apprehends to be little ſhort of treaſon, and therefore *loyally* abſtains from them; it deals almoſt ſolely in advertiſements; and conſequently, though a very uſeful, it is by no means an entertaining paper. Thus it would ſeem that every News-Paper publiſhed in London is calculated for a particular ſet of readers only; ſo that if each ſet were to change its favourite publication for another, the commutation would produce diſguſt, and diſſatisfaction to all; the politician would then find nothing to amuſe him but long accounts of petty ſquabbles about trifles in Parliament, or panegyrics on the men and meaſures that he moſt diſliked; or libels on thoſe whom he moſt revered. The perſon to whom parliamentary debates afford unſpeakable delight, would find himſelf bored with political ſpeculations about the meaſures that the different courts in Europe might probably adopt; or diſguſted with whole pages of advertiſements, in which he felt no concern;—whilſt the plain ſhop-keeper who wanted to find a convenient houſe for his buſineſs, and the ſervant who purchaſed his paper in hopes of ſeeing in it an advertiſement directing where he might find a place to ſuit him, would have their labour for their pains, in peruſing publications, filled with ſenatorial debates, or political eſſays and remarks, which would direct them to nothing leſs than the houſe or place they wanted.—A News-Paper, conducted on the true and natural principles of ſuch a publication, ought to be the Regiſter of the times, and faithful recorder of every ſpecies of intelligence; it ought not to be engroſſed by any particular object; but, like a well covered table, it ſhould contain ſomething ſuited to every palate: obſervations on the diſpoſitions of our own and of foreign courts ſhould be provided for the political reader; debates ſhould be reported for the amuſement or information of thoſe who may be particularly fond of them; and a due attention ſhould be paid to the intereſts of trade, which are ſo greatly promoted by advertiſements.—A paper that ſhould blend all theſe advantages, and by ſteering clear of extremes, hit the happy medium, has long been expected by the public.—Such, it is intended, ſhall be the UNIVERSAL REGISTER, the great objects of which will be to facilitate the *commercial* intercourſe between the different parts of the community, through the channel of *Advertiſements*; to record the principal occurrences of the times; and to abridge the account of debates during the ſitting of Parliament.

It is no leſs the intereſt of the proprietors of News-Papers, than of the public, that every encouragement ſhould be given to advertiſing correſpondents; yet this private intereſt of the proprietors is frequently ſacrificed to the rage for parliamentary debates, to the great injury of trade; for the extreme length of theſe debates ſo greatly retards the publication of the New-Papers which are noted for detailed accounts of them, that the advantages ariſing from this ſpecies of intelligence, though highly acceptable in itſelf, are frequently over-balanced by the inconvienences occaſioned to people in buſineſs by the delay. Theſe inconveniences are great and many; it generally happens, that when either Houſe of Parliament has been engaged in the diſcuſſion of an important queſtion till after midnight, the papers in which the ſpeeches of the Members are reported at large, cannot be publiſhed before noon; nay, they ſometimes are not even ſent to preſs ſo ſoon; conſequently parties intereſted in *ſales* are eſſentially injured, as the advertiſements, inviting the public to attend them at *ten* or *twelve* o'clock, do not appear, on account of a late publication, till ſome hours after.—From the ſame ſource flows another inconvenience; it is ſometimes found neceſſary to *defer* ſales, after they have been advertiſed for a particular day; but the notice of putting them off not appearing early enough, on account of the late hour at which the papers containing it are publiſhed, numbers of people, acting under the impreſſion of former advertiſements, are unneceſſarily put to the trouble of attending.—It will be the object of the *Univerſal Regiſter* to guard againſt theſe great inconveniences, without depriving its readers of the pleaſure of learning what paſſes in Parliament.—It is intended, then, that the debates ſhall be regularly reported in it; but on the other hand, that the publication may not be delayed to the prejudice of people in trade, the ſpeeches will not be given on a large ſcale; the *ſubſtance* ſhall be faithfully preſerved; but all the unintereſting parts will be omitted. I ſhall thus be enabled to publiſh this paper at an early hour; and I propoſe to bring it out *regularly* every morning at *ſix* o'clock. The *Univerſal Regiſter* will therefore have this advantage over the *Daily Advertiſer*, that, though publiſhed as early, it will contain a ſubſtantial account of the proceedings in Parliament the preceding night, which is never to be found in that paper; and compared with the other morning papers it will be found to have the merit of containing in ſubſtance, what they give in long detail (which men in buſineſs cannot well ſpare time to read) and, nevertheleſs, of being publiſhed much ſooner. Theſe circumſtances, it is hoped, will give the *Univerſal Regiſter* at leaſt an *equal* claim to public favour with the parliamentary papers, and the *trading* part of the metropolis, it is preſumed, will find it their advantage to give it the preference.

An eſſential part of the plan of this new paper is, that, for the convenience of advertiſing correſpondents, their favours ſhall, *to a certainty*, be inſerted on the very day that they ſhall direct; provided they deliver them at the office in due time. For the *ſtrict* obſervance of this rule, the credit of the paper ſhall ſtand pledged; and its pretenſions to public countenance will be renounced, if this fundamental principle in its inſtitution ſhall ever be violated, except in caſes of abſolute neceſſity, which human prudence cannot prevent.—And here I beg it may be underſtood that I do not make uſe of the word *neceſſity* as a reſerve, under colour of which, I may, whenever I think fit, be released from my engagements; I mean by that word a neceſſity ariſing from accidents that ſometimes happen in the printing buſineſs, and from which, the moſt careful man cannot, at all times, be ſecure. But ſo far from wiſhing to ſhrink from my engagements, I intend, whenever the length of the Gazette, Parliamentary Debates, &c. ſhall render it impoſſible for me to inſert all the advertiſements promiſed for the day, in *one* ſheet, to print an additional half ſheet, and publiſh it with the ordinary paper without any additional charge to my cuſtomers.—From the difficulty that people experience in procuring the inſertion of their advertiſements even in the *Daily Advertiſer*; and particularly from the impoſſibility of obtaining an *early* inſertion at ſome periods of the year, it may be preſumed that this regulation will greatly recommend the UNIVERSAL REGISTER to public notice, and procure it ſupport.

Theſe, though in my opinion good, are not the *only* grounds on which I build my hopes of ſucceſs. I flatter myſelf, I have ſome claim to public encouragement, on account of a great improvement which I have made in the art of printing. The inconveniences attending the old and tedious mode of compoſing with letters taken up *ſingly*, firſt ſuggeſted the idea of deviſing ſome more expeditious method. The cementing of ſeveral letters together, ſo as that the type of a *whole word* might be taken up in as ſhort a time as that of a *ſingle letter*, was the reſult of much reflection on that ſubject. But the bare idea of cementing was merely the opening, not the accompliſhment or perfection of the improvement. The fount conſiſting of types of words, and not of letters, was to be ſo arranged, as that a compoſitor ſhould be able to find the former with as much facility as he can the latter. This was a work of inconceivable difficulty. I undertook it however, and was fortunate enough, after an infinite number of experiments, and great labour, to bring it to a happy concluſion. The whole Engliſh language is now methodically and ſyſtematically arranged at my fount: ſo that printing can now be performed with greater diſpatch, and at leſs expence, than according to the mode hitherto in uſe.

In bringing this work to perfection, I had not my own advantage ſolely in view; I wiſhed to be uſeful to the community; and it is with pleaſure I ſee that the public will derive conſiderable benefit from my induſtry; for I have reſolved to ſell the REGISTER *One halfpenny* UNDER the price paid for ſeven out of eight of the morning

1785 1789

1804 1804

1815 1815

Above Newspaper duty stamps, designed according to the instructions of the Inland Revenue, and stamped on every newspaper produced.

Below Satirical print by Rowlandson, published by Tegg of Cheapside, April 1810. Caricaturists had long enjoyed their freedom to ridicule and comment without fear of prosecution, but journalists and newspapers, in particular the radical press, were subject to frequent legal action for any adverse comments. Rowlandson's burlesque of the Libel Hunters features two recent prosecutions: against Perry of the Morning Chronicle for an article on the King; and Sir Francis Burdett, sent to the Tower for his manifesto in Cobbett's Political Register, challenging Parliamentary powers to "imprison the People of England". Riots followed his arrest, Cobbett was charged with sedition, and prosecutions against other journalists followed.

In the beginning

When John Walter launched *The Daily Universal Register* on 1 January 1785, he launched it into a primitive sea of journalism, and darkness was upon the face of the deep. You can trace the origins of newspapers back to pamphlets produced during the English Civil War (1642–5). Landmarks in newspaper history include the journals of Steele and Addison, Samuel Johnson's biweekly *The Rambler* and his weekly *The Idler*, and John Wilkes's *North Briton*, which broke the shackles on free expression of opinion. By 1772 the right to publish parliamentary reports had been established.

It was an age of pullulating Corantos, Diurnalls, Passages, Mercuries, Posts and Intelligencers. It was a short life and a merry one for the inchoate press: when press censorship was finally abandoned in 1693, the *Postboy* was founded as a daily newspaper, and lasted four days. The court was at Oxford in 1665 because of the plague, when Henry Muddiman, the most famous journalist of the age, published the first volume of the biweekly *Oxford Gazette*. In the following year it became the *London Gazette*, and has appeared ever since on Tuesdays and Fridays as the official organ of government.

The first publication recognizable as a daily newspaper was *The Daily Courant*, which burst upon an astonished world on 11 March 1702. It cost a penny, and contained foreign news translated from Continental newspapers. Like its contemporary weekly and biweekly journals, it sold its opinions and conscience to the highest bidder, Whig or Tory. It lasted until 1735.

Grub Street was a grotty and venal trade. Sam Johnson, who had started his career there, and knew the inky trade, described these early journalists and pamphleteers in 1758: 'Of those Writers who have taken upon themselves the Task of Intelligence, some have given and others have sold their Abilities to one or other of the Parties that divide us; and without a Wish for Truth, or Thought of Decency'.

By the time John Walter launched his little daily, there were eight rather shaky London morning newspapers; the oldest was *The Daily Advertiser*, founded in 1730, the newest *The Morning Herald*, founded in 1780. There were nine London evening papers, published on Tuesdays, Thursdays and Saturdays. Of these the *Chronicle* had the largest circulation, but *The Public Advertiser* carried the most political influence, particularly during the years in which it published the Letters of Junius. It contained home and foreign news, and correspondence, mainly political, from writers of all shades of opinion. Wilkes and Tooke fought a famous dispute in its columns.

Of the morning papers only one, apart from Walter's, survived into the twentieth century. This was *The Morning Post*, founded in 1772 and amalgamated with the *Daily Telegraph* in 1937.

The papers had much in common. They contained extracts from the official *London Gazette* (a summary of parliamentary business), Court news, paragraphs on Society affairs (the primitive gossip columns), judgments from the law courts, accounts of ghastly murders, and commercial and financial intelligence.

All of them received secret subsidies from one or other of the two political parties. In his first year in office William Pitt spent more than £1,000 on supporting various newspapers. During the French Revolution he budgeted about £5,000 a year, under the counter, to fix the press. Some of it went to *The Times*. In addition individual journalists tended to be on the private payrolls of the Government or the Opposition, in return for writing the right sort of articles.

In 1785 the price of these early papers ranged from 2d to 3d each. But not all of this went into the pocket of the proprietor. Until the second half of the nineteenth century newspapers had to pay special taxes, described polemically as 'taxes on knowledge'. These were divided into three parts: there was a newspaper stamp duty, first levied by Parliament in 1712 at a penny a sheet of paper; there was a duty on each advertisement; and a paper duty.

The advertisement tax set in 1712 was a shilling for every advertisement appearing in 'any printed paper, such paper being

The front page of the first issue of the newspaper after it was renamed THE TIMES. It then cost threepence, equivalent to almost a pound today.
1 JANUARY 1788

NUMB. 940. TUESDAY, JANUARY 1, 1788. (Price Three-pence.)

Theatre-Royal, Drury-Lane,

By his MAJESTY's COMPANY,
THIS EVENING,
Will be presented the Tragedy of
JULIA:
OR, THE ITALIAN LOVER.
The principal Characters by
Mr. KEMBLE, and Mrs. SIDDONS,
The Prologue to be spoken by Mr. Kemble;
And the Epilogue, by Mrs. Siddons.
With new Dresses, Decorations, &c.
To which will be added
The DESERTER.
Henry, Mr. KELLY; Skirmish, Mr. BANNISTER, jun.
And Louisa, by Mrs. CROUCH.

Tomorrow, (by Desire) The Wonder, with, the 6th Time, Harlequin, jun. On Thursday the Tragedy of Percy; Elwina, Mrs. Siddons.

BY COMMAND OF HIS MAJESTY,

And under the same DIRECTORS as the CONCERT of ANTIENT MUSIC,

THE Oratorios of SOLOMON, ALEXANDER's FEAST with the CHOICE of HERCULES, JOSEPH, ACIS and GALATEA, with DRYDEN's ODE, ESTHER, and MESSIAH, will be performed on the Six FRIDAYS in LENT, at the CONCERT ROOM in TOTTENHAM-STREET.

Subscriptions taken at Messrs. Longman and Broderip's Music Shops, in the Haymarket and Cheapside; and at Mr. Ashley's, No. 4, Pimlico; at Three Guineas each, the Tickets NOT transferable.

ROYALTY THEATRE,

WELL-STREET, NEAR GOODMAN's FIELDS.
THIS EVENING
An OCCASIONAL ADDRESS,
By Mr. PALMER,
In the Character of Christmas.
A Musical Entertainment, called
THOMAS and SUSAN Or,
The GENEROUS TAR.
For the 3d Time, a New Pantomimic Entertainment, called,
The DESERTER of NAPLES:
Or, ROYAL CLEMENCY.
Under the Direction of Mr DELPINI.
The Airs, Duets and Chorusses, composed by Mr. REEVE,
The DESERTER by Mr. PALMER.
The other Characters by
Mr. W. Palmer, Mr. Cooper, Mr. L'Estrange, Mr. Hudson, and Mr. DELPINI.
Mrs. Delpini, Madems. Bitthemer, and Mrs. GIBBS.
End of the first Part, a Grand Representation of MOUNT VESUVIUS, at the Time of Eruption, with the Flowing of the Lava.
The Dances by Mr. Holland, Mad. Bitthemer, and Mad. Constance; composed by M MALTER.
A SONG by Master BRAHAM.
The Whole to conclude with (37th time) a new Pantomimic Entertainment, called
HARLEQUIN MUNGO;
Or, A PEEP INTO THE TOWER.
Harlequin, Mr. RAYNER, jun.
Mungo Harlequin, Mr. BOURKE;
Pantaloon, Mr. FOLLETT, sen.
Keeper of Wild Beasts and Warder of the Tower, (with a Chaunt) Mr. GRACE.
Captain, Sailor, and first Waterman (with Songs), Mr. ARROWSMITH;
Clown, Mr. FOLLET, jun.
Planter's Wife, Mrs. BURNETT;
And Columbine, Mrs. GIBBS.
In Part First, a Dance of Slaves, by Messrs. Holland, Bourke, Menage, &c.
To conclude with a grand Ballet,
By Monf. Malter, Mr. Holland, Mad. Bithemer, and Mademoiselle Constance.
Boxes 5s. Pit 3s. First Gall. 2s. Second Gall. 1s.

Places for the Boxes to be taken of Mr. Clark, at the Stage Door of the Theatre.

The Doors to be opened for the future at Half past Five, and to begin precisely at Half past Six o'Clock.

*** No Money will be returned after the Curtain is drawn up; nor will any Person be admitted behind the Scenes. Vivant Rex & Regina.

N. B. No King under 1 oz will be taken.

TO BE LETT OR SOLD,

EXTENSIVE Premises in the Neighbourhood of Cheapside.
Apply at No. 9, Cheapside.

A CAUTION to prevent IMPOSITION.
SHARP's CONCAVE RAZORS

ARE made of the very best Steel that can be possibly procured in this or any other country, tempered and finished with the greatest nicety and circumspection. Their superior excellence above all others, has made them more esteemed, than any Razor now in use; the consequence of which is, that some persons have offered, and still do offer, an inferior article under their name.

C. SHARP, Perfumer and Razor-Maker to his Royal Highness the Prince of Wales, at No. 131, Fleet-street; and No. 57, Cornhill,

Most respectfully intreats the public to observe, that his Concave Razors are not sold at any other places in London, but at his shops as above, Sharp stamped on the blade of the Razors; all others are counterfeits.

Sharp's Metalic Razor Strops, which keep the Razor in good order, without the use of a Hone or grinding, are not to be equalled; but the above articles are too well esteemed to need any thing being said in their behalf.— His Alpine Soap for shaving, is by far the best adapted for that purpose of any yet invented; it never causes the least smarting sensation, but a perfectly soft, sweet and pleasing. Likewise, his curious Cyprian Wash-balls. Great variety of shaving cases and pouches, that hold all the implements necessary for shaving, dressing, &c.

Sharp's sweet, hard, and soft pomatums, are remarkable for keeping good in any climate, longer than any other. His Lavender Water drawn from the flowers, his warranted Tooth-brushes, and the Prince of Wales's Tooth Powder, are articles worthy the attention of the public.

Combs, soaps, wash-balls, and every article in the Perfumery branch, wholesale, retail, and for exportation.

N. B. Families, &c. who take any of Sharp's articles by the dozen, save considerably.

A complete Dressing-case, fitted up with razors, combs, &c. for 10s. 6d.

KING's THEATRE, Haymarket.

By PARTICULAR DESIRE, on Thursday next, January 3, 1788.
WILL BE PRESENTED THE SERIO-COMIC OPERA, called
IL RE TEODORO in VENEZIA.
Or, THEODORE, KING OF CORSICA, AT VENICE.
The Principal Characters by
Sig. MORELLI, Sig. MORIGI,
Sig. BALELLI, Sig. CALVESI,
And Sig. FINESCHI,
Signora SESTINI, and Signora STORACE.
The Music composed in his best stile, by the celebrated Mr. PAESIELO,
Under the Direction of Sig. MAZZINGHI.
And Leader of the Orchestra, Mr. CRAMER.
Painter and Machinist, Sig. GAETANO MARINARI.
Inventor and Maker of the Dresses, Sig. LUPINO.
The Doors to be opened at Six, and begin precisely at Half past Seven o'Clock.
Pit 10s. 6d. First Gallery 5s. Upper Gallery 3s.
Tickets to be had, and Subscriptions paid, as usual, at Messrs. Ransom, Moreland, and Hammersley's, Bankers, No. 57, Pall-Mall.

End of Act I. a New DIVERTISSEMENT, composed by Monf. CHEVALIER, and performed by Monf. VESTRIS, Monf. COULON, And Monf. CHEVALIER; The two Miss SIMONETS, Signora BEDINI, And Mad. COULON.

End of the Opera, a New BALLET, composed by Monf. NOVERRE, called,
LES OFFRANDES A L'AMOUR.
And performed by
Monf. VESTRIS, Monf. COULON, And Monf. DIDELOT, Miss HILLESBERG, Mad. VEDIE, And Mad. COULON.
The other Characters by
Messrs. SAUNLIER, COULON, HENRY, SALA, Mademoiselles GRENIER, &c. &c.
And MEZIERRES.

N. B. For the better accommodation of the Subscribers, the office is removed back to Union-court, Haymarket.

The Nobility and Gentry are requested to take notice, that the first Masqued Ball will be given at this place, on Monday, the 4th of February, 1788.

NEW MUSIC.

This day is published,
By LONGMAN AND BRODERIP,
Music Sellers, and Musical Instrument Makers to his Royal Highness the PRINCE of WALES,
No. 26, Cheapside, and No. 13, Haymarket.

Authors		£	s.	d.
J. Haydn,	THREE SYMPHONIES for a Grand Orchestra, dedicated to his Royal Highness the Prince of Wales, Op. 51.	0	10	6
Ditto,	A Set of QUARTETTS for two Violins, Tenor and Violoncello expressive of the Passion of our Saviour, Op. 48.	0	8	0
Mozart,	Two SYMPHONIES for a Grand Orchestra, Op. 8 and 9, each	0	6	0
Ditto,	Six QUARTETTS, dedicated to Mr. Haydn, Op. 10.	0	15	0
Ditto,	QUARTETT for the Harpsichord	0	3	0
Storace,	CARE DONNE CHE BRAMATE, sung by Signora Storace, in Il Re Teodore in Venezia	0	2	6
Pleyel,	Two SONATAS for the Harpsichord, with an Accompaniment for a Violin, Op. 9.	0	4	0
Ditto,	TRIOS for a Violin, Tenor, and Violoncello, Op. 11.	0	6	0
Giordani,	Three GRAND DUETS for the Harpsichord, from the works of Haydn	0	7	6
Chalon,	Three DUETTS for the Harpsichord, Op. 7.	0	7	6
Barthelemon.	COMPLETE INSTRUCTIONS for the Pedal Harp, with Airs, Arpegios, and Sonatas, and an easy method for tuning	0	10	6
Percy,	Six ITALIAN ARIETTAS in the Venetian stile, for the Voice and Piano Forte, Op. 5.	0	5	0
Starkel,	Three SONATAS for the Harpsichord, with Accompaniments, Op. 22.	0	7	6
Millico,	A Fourth Set of Six ITALIAN CANZONETS, dedicated to Lady Louisa Hervey.	0	5	0
Bishop,	Six MINUETS, and Twelve COUNTRY DANCES, for the year 1788.	0	2	6
Jones,	Ditto, ditto, ditto.	0	2	6
Shield,	The FARMER, a Comic Opera, for the Voice and Harpsichord.	0	6	0

NEW MUSIC.

This Day are published,
By J. BLAND, No. 45, Holborn,

THE SONGS in Robin Hood, of "Charming Clorinda," and "When generous Wine," sung by Mr. Bowden, 1s. each. "When ruddy Aurora," and "The Trump of Fame," each 6d. Aurora, a ballad, 1s. He vow'd to have me, Goodwin, cantata; O thou wert born to please me, a duet; Ye woods and ye mountains, an elegy; each 6d. Bland's 13th and 14th ladies glees, each 1s. 6d. Ditto, first vol. of ditto, bound, 18s. Periodical Ital. song, No. 35. 2s. 6d; ditto No. 36, 2s. 6d. Pleyl's Sonatas composed for the harpsichord, op. 7. 4s. C. I. L. T. Sonatinas, dedicated to Dr. Burney, 5s. Mozart's Terzette, 2s. 6d. Bland's Harpsichord Collection, No. 1. to 6, each 5s. Hoffmeister's Duets, for violin and violoncello, op. 6. or 13. 4s. Ditto Flute Trios; 6s. Ditto Flute Quartetts, 10s. 6d. and a variety of new publications.

OIL AND LAMP WAREHOUSE.

No. 5, New-street, Covent-Garden.

GEORGE DOWNING, Oil Merchant, proprietor of the above Warehouse, begs leave to offer the most proper tender of his grateful acknowledgments to the Nobility, Gentry, and public in general, for the repeated favours conferred on him, the respectfully informs his friends, that the OIL and LAMP TRADE continues to be transacted on the same liberal terms, that first recommended him to their particular attention.

N. B. Orders for town and country executed with punctuality.

New-street, Covent Garden, Jan. 1, 1788.

CALEDONIAN MACABAU SNUFF.

JOHN YOUNG, Manufacturer and Vender of the Hibernian high dried or Lundy Foot's Snuff, presents his respects to the Nobility, Gentry, &c. with his Caledonian Macabau Snuff, which upon trial he is convinced will be found deserving the estimation his Irish Snuff has so justly acquired. Orders sent to his Snuff Manufactory, No. 73, in Drury-Lane, near Russel Court, will be attended to with the highest respect and gratitude.

N. B. Snuffs and Tobacco in the highest perfection.

STATIONARY.

ADAM THOMPSON, at his Paper Manufactory Warehouse, Hind-Court, Upper Thames-street, begs leave to return his Friends sincere thanks for all past favours; and as he is now well stocked with a general and choice Assortment of Writing, Printing, Wrapping, Sugar and Blue Papers, summer made, shall be happy to receive their further orders, which shall be duly attended to on the most moderate terms. Notes and Bills taken in payment, at one, two, and three months.

N. B. Has also about fifty reams French Mezzotinto Bay, to be sold 20 per cent. below current price.

NEW MUSIC.

This Day is published,
By LONGMAN and BRODERIP, No. 26, Cheapside, No. 13, Haymarket; and at their Manufactory in Tottenham Court Road.

MUSICAL INSTRUMENT MAKERS, AND SELLERS, TO HIS ROYAL HIGHNESS THE PRINCE OF WALES;

THE New Comic Opera, now performing at Covent-Garden Theatre with great applause, called the Farmer, composed and compiled by Mr. Shield, 6s. Pleyel's two grand Sonatas, op. 7. for the Piano Forte, 4s. Pleyel's three Trios Concertante op. 11. for a violin, tenor, and violincello 6s.; Percy's Italian Arietts, op. 5th, 5s.; Mozart's Harpsichord Quartett, 2s. 6d.; complete Instructions for Pedal Harp, with a Selection of favourite Songs and Sonatas, by Mr. Barthelemon, 10s. 6d. Stockel's three Sonatas, op. 22, with accompanyments 7s. 6d; Thomas and Susan, or the Fortunate Tar, performed at the Royalty Theatre, 3s 6d.; Chalon's three Duets for the piano forte, op. 7th, 7s. 6d.; Mozart's Airs, with Variations for the piano forte, each 2s.; Breval's easy Solos for the violincello, op 28th, 7s. 6d.; Clementi's Sonata, op. 20, 3s.—Lately imported from the Continent, great variety of Harp Music, by the most eminent masters; together with the most distinguished new works of the following authors, consisting of Simphonies, Concertes, Quartetts, Trios, Duets, Solos, and Harpsichord Sonatas, by Haydn, Pleyel, Kozeluch, Mozart, Breval, Trickler, Fodor, Devieme, Vanhal, Sirkel, Viotti, &c.—Also the Overture and Songs of Tarare, and select Collections of the most favourite Songs from the latest French operas, for the Harpsichord.—Where may be seen, their new-improved grand and small Piano Fortes, and Mr. Corri's new-invented Harpsichord Desk, with a Dictionary of Musical Terms, Examples, &c.—Also, his new-invented Piano Forte Board, with Dictionary, &c. Each one Guinea.

THE OPERA FANS.

To the Subscribers and Frequentors of the
KING's THEATRE,
Last Saturday were published, according to Act of Parliament.

THE delivery, however, was put off till the re-opening of the Opera House, next week, for the purpose of presenting them in the best state of improvement.

These FANS, calculated to present, at one view, both the number of boxes, including the additional ones, names of Subscribers, &c. have been carefully compared with the plan of the House, as kept at the Office, and will be sold only by the Proprietors,

Mrs. H. M. No. 81, Hay-Market,

Where she will receive, with respectful gratitude, any commands from the ladies, and wait on them if required.

HANDEL's SUBSCRIPTION.

Dedicated by Permission to His MAJESTY,
This day is published,

THE ELEVENTH NUMBER of HANDEL's WORKS. The Four First Numbers, comprehending the compleat Score of the Oratorio of Athalia; the four following the whole of Theodora, and the remainder a large portion of the Messiah. The elegant Apothesis of Handel will be delivered to subscribers only, with the Twelth Number.

Subscriptions are received by Dr. Arnold, No. 480, Strand; Messrs. Longman and Broderip, No. 13, Haymarket; and Birchall and Co. New Bond-street.

This day is published,
Price 2s. 6d separately, or 4s. 6d. together,

AN ABRIDGMENT of the MEMORIAL addressed to the KING of FRANCE.
By M. DE CALONNE,
Minister of State.
In FRENCH and ENGLISH.
TRANSLATED from the French by W. WALTER.

Printed at the *Logographic Press*, by J. WALTER, Printing House Square, Blackfriars; and sold by Messrs. Robson and Clarke, and T. Hookham, New Bond Street; P. Elmsley, Strand; Messrs. Egertons, Charing-Cross; and W. Richardson, Royal Exchange.

This day is published,
Price One Shilling,

CRAZY KATE; A FAVOURITE BALLAD;
Taken from Cowper's Task,
Set to Music, with Accompaniments,
By JOHN MOULDS
THE FEAST OF APOLLO, No. IV.
Price One Shilling,
Containing a Favourite Overture for the Piano Forte,
"Sans Vous Ma Chere," a Favourite Song.
"The Sailor he fears not the Roar of the Seas," ditto.
London: Printed for G. Goulding, Haydn's Head, No. 6, James-street, Covent Garden.
Where may be had,
LA FEVRE,
Taken from STERNE,
A Favourite SONG, set to Music by HAYDN,
Price only Sixpence.
"The Sailor he fears not the Roar of the Seas,"
A Favourite SONG, set to Music with Accompanyments by RELFE, Price One Shilling.
SANS VOUS MACHERE,
A Favourite SONG, sung by Mr. INCLEDON at Bath.
Composed by MOULDS. Price Sixpence.

Theatre-Royal, Covent-Garden.

THIS EVENING,
Will be presented the revived Tragedy of
The ROMAN FATHER
Horatius, Mr. Farren; Tullus Hostilius, Mr. Aickin Valerius, Mr. Davies; and Publius, Mr. Pope. Valeria Mrs. Morton; and Horatia, Miss Brunton.
In Act V. will be introduced a Roman Ovation.
To which will be added, (6th time) a New Pantomime called
THE DUMB CAKE:
Or, the REGIONS OF FANCY.
With new Music, Scenery, Dresses, Machinery, and Decorations.
N. B. Nothing under full price will be taken.

To-morrow, (not acted this Season) The Suspicious Husband; Ranger, Mr. LEWIS, and Clarinda, Mrs. ABINGTON.

PROPAGATION OF A LIE.

W. DICKINSON, Bond-Street, has this Day published a Print from an original Drawing, by H. Bunbury, Esq. representing the Propagation of a Lie, being a companion to the much admired print of the Long Minuet.

Likewise just published,
An Academy for grown Horsemen, containing the compleatest instructions for

Walking,	Galloping,
Trotting,	Stumbling, and
Cantering,	Tumbling.

Illustrated with Copper-plates, and adorned with a Portrait of the Author, by Geoffry Gambado, Esq. Riding-master, Master of the Horse, Grand Equerry to the Doge of Venice.

Where likewise is published all Mr. Bunbury's elegant and caricature Prints.

FESTIVAL OF ANACREON.

This day is published, price 3s. 6d.
A New Edition, of

THE FESTIVAL of ANACREON: Containing the Songs of Capt. Morris, Mr. Hewerdine, and other Lyric Writers, as sung at the Anacreontic Society, the Beef-Steak, and Humbug Clubs.

Published by William Holland, No. 50, Oxford-street, near Berner's-street, removed from No. 66, Drury-Lane.

Of whom may be had, just published,

A Portrait of Kitty Cut-a-Dash; a Dilly setting out from King's Place with a Guard; History of Modern Flagellants, in seven distinct works, each of which may be had separate; Comtesse de Barre's Whim; the Pretty Nursery Maid; My Aunt; Hal's Looking Glass; and a large Collection of Books, Pamphlets, Paintings, Drawings, and Prints, for the Cabinets of the Moralist, the Politician, and the Bon Vivant.

☞ Pæans of Pleasure, and Memoirs of Kitty Cut-a-Dash, will be speedily published.

This day is published,
Price Six Shillings in Boards,

MEDICAL COMMENTARIES for the Year 1787, exhibiting a concise View of the latest and most important Discoveries in Medicine and Medical Philosophy; collected and published by
ANDREW DUNCAN, M. D. F. R. & A. S. Edin. &c.
Decade Second.—Volume Second.

Printed for C. Elliot, T. Kay, and Co. opposite Somerset-Place, Strand, London; and C. Elliot, Edinburgh.

Of whom may be had,

Complete SETS of DECADE FIRST, from 1773 to 1785, inclusive. Ten vols. 8vo. price 3l. in boards, and 3l. 10s bound.

ALSO,—Vols. 8, for 1781-2, Vol. 9, for 1783-4, Vol. 10, for 1785, and Vol. 1. Decade II. for 1786, at Six Shillings each in boards.

N. B. As above may be had gratis,—C. Elliot, T. Ray, and Co.'s Catalogue of Books in all the different branches of Medicine for 1788, with the lowest prices affixed.

This Day are published,
Printed in One Volume Octavo, on a superfine Medium Paper, price 6s. in Boards,

I.

FAMILIAR and FRIENDLY CORRESPONDENCE of FREDERICK the SECOND, KING of PRUSSIA, with U. F. DE SUHM, Counsellor to the Elector of Saxony.

II.

Handsomely printed in 2 vols. large Octavo, on a Superfine medium Paper, price 12s. in Boards,

A SELECTION from the WORKS of FRANCIS LORD BACON, Viscount St. Alban; consisting of his ESSAYS on Civil, Moral, Literary, and Political Subjects: the Advancement of Learning, System of Moral Philosophy, Theology, &c. and his celebrated History of Life and Death; together with his own Life, by Dr. WILLYMOTT.

III.

In 2 Vols. 8vo. on a superfine Medium Paper, Price 12s in Boards, illustrated with Copper-plates,

A new and elegant Edition of

DR. DERHAM's PHYSICO and ASTRO-THEOLOGY: the first contains a Demonstration of the Being and Attributes of God, from his Works of the Creation; the second, a General Survey of the Heavens; with considerable Notes, and many curious Observations.

IV.

In Three Volumes, price 9s. sewed,
The MINIATURE PICTURE;
OR,
PLATONIC MARRIAGE.
A NEW NOVEL.
By Mrs. CARTWRIGHT.

This Lady displays, throughout the work, a perfect Knowledge of the human passions, and the characters are pourtrayed in the most chaste and elegant language.

V.

Elegantly printed in a small Pocket Volume, on superfine Writing Paper, Price 1s. 6d. sewed in Marble Paper,

A New Edition, being the Third, of

LETTERS which passed between an ILLUSTRIOUS PERSONAGE, and a LADY of HONOUR at Brighton.

London: Printed at the *Logographic Press*, by J. Walter, Printing-House-Square, Blackfriars; and sold by T. Longman, Paternoster-row; Robson and Clarke, New Bond-street, and W. Richardson, under the Royal Exchange.

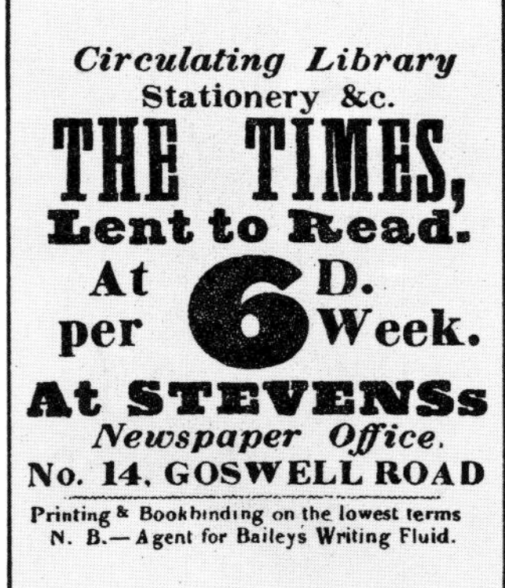

Top WAITING FOR THE TIMES by Benjamin Haydon, 1831, purchased for £200 in 1947 from Charles Morley. Now in the Editor's office at THE TIMES.

Above THE TIMES/Circulating Library label, 1831.

dispensed or made public weekly or oftener'. By 1785 the tax on each advertisement, whatever the length, was 2s 6d. The revenue stamp was impressed on each sheet of paper. When stamp duty was first imposed, Addison wondered whether to throw down his pen 'as an author that is cashiered by Act of Parliament'.

On 1 January 1785, Walter's new *Daily Universal Register* cost 2½d, stamp duty being 1½d. The duty on paper was 3d a pound, or about a farthing a sheet. In return for stamp duty, newspapers got the privilege of being sent post free through the mails.

The rates of these taxes varied over the years. The highest stamp duty was levied in 1815 at 4d, forcing *The Times* to put its price up from 6½d to 7d. Owning a newspaper was a speculative enterprise, then as now, my masters.

Over the years strong and influential opposition grew to these newspaper taxes. The Association for Promoting the Repeal of Taxes on Knowledge was formed in 1849. The tax on advertisements was the first to go in 1853. In that year stamp duty was only a penny, but the Government was reluctant to dispense with it entirely, since it gave them some sort of financial control over the growing power of the press. Cobden fulminated: 'So long as the penny lasts, there can be no daily press for the middle or working class. The governing classes know that the stamp makes the daily press the instrument and servant of the oligarchy.' In 1855 stamp duty was abolished. In 1861 the press was untied from the last of Nanny's apron strings with the repeal of the tax on paper.

In 1785 newspapers were sold by booksellers and hawkers. The hawkers collected bundles of newspapers hot off the presses, and delivered them to coffee houses and other resorts of the reading and arguing classes. The famous painting by Benjamin Haydon shows a man waiting on tenterhooks for his turn to read *The Times* for the latest news of Bonaparte or the Reform Act. The custom of an individual having his personal copy of *The Times* delivered started in the middle of the nineteenth century.

In 1787 the Government set up a Newspaper Office. The publishers delivered their papers in bulk there, and Clerks of the Roads distributed them from there to postmasters around the country. Postage was free, in return for stamp duty. After the repeal of stamp duty, newspapers started having to pay postage, though at a special low rate.

The owner goes to prison

When John Walter I turned to printing and journalism, William Pitt the Younger (not merely a chip off the old block, but the old block itself) had recently become Prime Minister. Pitt was a protégé of George III and an ally of the Tories. In those days, as now, newspapers could not survive without subsidies. It was natural that the rising young statesman should seek the support of the rising young newspaper, which claimed to be a better interpreter of public opinion than all its rivals. John Walter's *Daily Universal Register*, soon renamed *The Times*, proclaimed its support for the new administration. As the sort of *quid pro quo* that used to be given between Ministers and newspaper proprietors – and still is, for example in honours – John Walter was appointed Printer to His Majesty's Customs in 1787, and two years later was granted a subvention of £300 a year, despite his professed intentions of political independence.

This alliance was threatened by the King's recurrent bouts of insanity. It was generally assumed that if the King were declared incapable of ruling, as eventually he was, the Prince of Wales would become Regent, dismiss Pitt and ask Fox to form a Ministry. The Whigs looked forward to a Regency, and the Whig newspapers to the pickings of government.

In February 1789 the doctors certified that the King's mind was as sane as it had ever been. There was an outburst of national, and particularly Tory, jubilation. *The Times* crowed in article after article, attacking the partisans of the Prince of Wales. The reader was asked 'To determine to which Paper he ought to give credit – to The TIMES which, through the whole of this important and melancholy state of the Kingdom, had preserved its fidelity to its Sovereign, and its character for AUTHENTIC INFORMATION to the Public – or to those low, scurrilous, misinformed Opposition Prints'.

On 21 February John Walter published in *The Times* two unsigned paragraphs, which had been supplied to him by Mr Steele, Secretary of the Treasury, in accordance with his agreement with the Government:

> The Royal Dukes, and the leaders of opposition in general, affect to join with the friends of our amiable Sovereign, in rejoicing on account of His Majesty's recovery. But the insincerity of their joy is visible. Their late unfeeling conduct will forever tell against them; and contradict the artful professions they may think it prudent to make.
>
> It argues infinite wisdom in certain persons, to have prevented the Duke of York from rushing into the King's apartment on Wednesday. The rashness, the Germanick severity, and the insensibility of this young man, might have proved ruinous to the hopes and joys of a whole nation.

Below FILIAL PIETY, Satirical print by Thomas Rowlandson 1788. There was widespread comment and scandal about the Prince of Wales' unruly behaviour and disputes with his parents. Rowlandson depicts the Prince, with his friends Sheridan and Hanger, bursting in to the King's sick room in a drunken frolic, declaring 'Damme, come along . . . I'll see if the Old Fellow's ___ or not ___.'

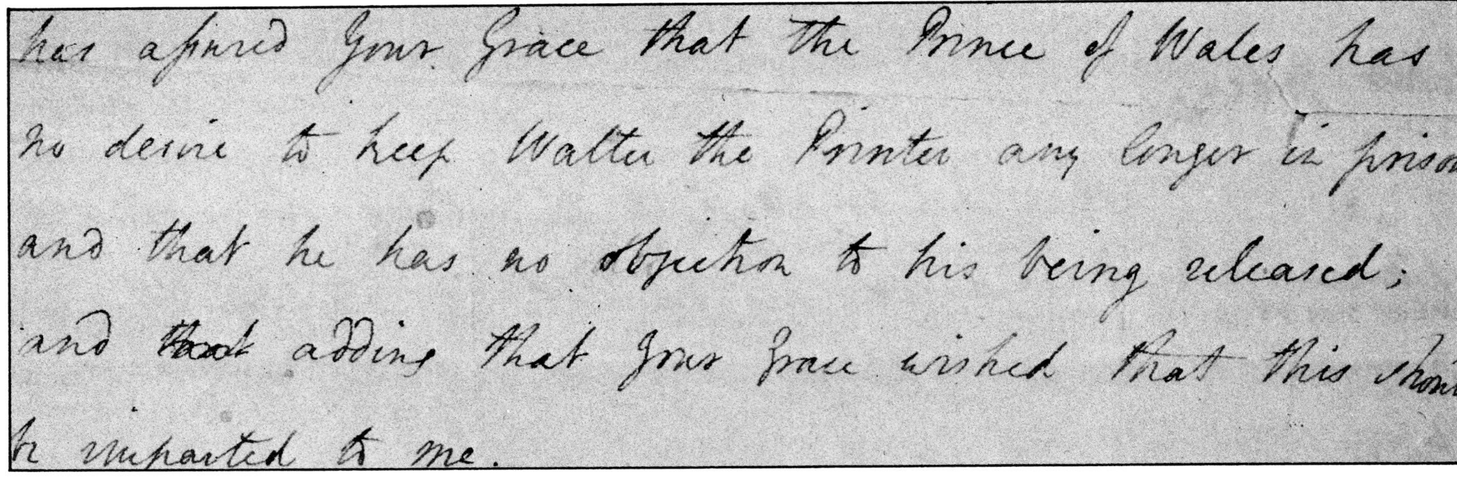

has assured Your Grace that the Prince of Wales has
no desire to keep Walter the Printer any longer in prison
and that he has no objection to his being released;
and ~~that~~ adding that Your Grace wished that this should
be imparted to me.

Right Extract from a letter from Lord Grenville to the Duke of Leeds pleading for John Walter's release from prison.

Below A later photograph of the prisoners' walkway from the cells to the courtroom at Newgate. The building had changed very little since John Walter's imprisonment.

Bottom A contemporary eighteenth-century view of the exterior of Newgate Prison.

A few days later a similar statement was published criticizing the Prince of Wales. There was more truth than tact in the tiny articles. The public triumph of the Prince and Duke, of the Opposition magnates and the Whig ladies, during the King's illness had been a public scandal, at any rate for the Tory press.

In June both Princes indicted Walter for libel. *The Times* at once published a justification, charging the Whigs, rather than the Princes, with attacking the liberty of the press: 'Temptation often held out its golden prospects to make us desert the King, and support his Opponents; and when Bribes were found ineffectual, Threats were used as Compulsory Arguments'.

The Duke of York's action came to trial in July. John Walter defended himself as the representative of *The Times*, not as author, printer or publisher of it or of the offending paragraphs. There was prudence in the anonymity of the press in those turbulent times. Walter pleaded guilty to libel, but submitted a plea of extenuation: the haste and hurly-burly of producing a daily newspaper induced unwitting error. The proprietor could not control or read every detail. The libellous paragraphs 'were inserted at a time of dreadful tumult and confusion, at a period in which moderation was considered as a contemptible virtue'. Unless newspapers published comments that the temper of the day required, they would be read by nobody but the printer.

The court was not impressed by this defence. The prosecuting counsel remarked: 'If he had sworn that he was misled to insert this unprincipled and infamous calumny, the Court must have sent him to Bedlam instead of a prison'.

John Walter refused to name his sources, thereby setting a precedent for a robust journalistic attitude. The effect of his heroic stand is somewhat lessened, firstly in that everybody who was anybody guessed that he had been given the paragraphs by the Government, and secondly by Walter's expectation that his political friends would help and recompense him.

On the first libel he was fined £50, sent to Newgate Prison for a year, sentenced to stand in the pillory at Charing Cross for an hour, and ordered to give £500 security for his good behaviour for seven years. The pillory was remitted, but Walter went to Newgate. As soon as he had served his term, he started another twelve-month sentence for libel of the Prince of Wales.

Walter wrote to his political contacts from prison, hinting that he had held his tongue 'expecting remuneration', and complaining about conditions:

> Newgate was undoubtedly a receptacle for felons, though it is the fashion of the Court at present to extend it to misdemeanours by which means we are subject to more solitary confinement than felons guilty of murder. Though I am confined to what is called the State side, and, paying for a room, have one to myself, the same entrance leads likewise to the felons and whenever any are brought into the jail, the outward door is shut and they are fettered in the common passage, so that it discourages my friends from access – such is the audacity of the turnkeys that they will frequently keep them and those who bring my provisions an hour at the door, even when they are lolling in their chairs in an adjoining room, because several people shall collect together; and what is still worse at 8 o'clock I am locked up every evening in common with the felons after which time no soul is permitted to have a person with him.

Release came not from his friends and patrons, but ironically through the intervention of the Prince of Wales. John Walter was freed in March 1791 before the completion of his sentence. In the following year Pitt's Secret Service accounts record: 'Mr Walter a Gift of £250' – compensation, no doubt, for services and sufferings rendered.

John Walter's libel set important precedents. Newspapers have a duty to tell the truth, afflict the comfortable and attack the mighty when the mighty are wrong. And all hacks have reverence and affection for a newspaper proprietor who went to prison rather than betray his journalists.

A report of the libel case against John Walter. Despite the privations Walter suffered during his sixteen months in Newgate, he continued to draw his £500-a-year salary from the Government.

15 JULY 1789

SAILING MATCH.

Yesterday evening at high water the following boats sailed for the Annual Vauxhall Cup, or more properly, met at Blackfriars for the purpose of sailing:

The Phœnix,	The Adventure,
The Mercury,	The Duchess of Cumberland,
The Æolus,	The Venus,
The Nancy,	The Eagle,
The Cumberland,	The Griffin.

But out of this list the Phœnix, Mercury and Æolus were the only contending boats. The Eagle did not like the high wind, the Griffin wetted her sails before starting, the Cumberland did not sail, and the Nancy and Venus mixed with the crowd, merely to observe how things went, and not to fatigue themselves by any contention.

The *Phœnix* took the lead at starting, and kept it till she came to the *goal*. She was pushed hard by the Æolus as far as Ranelagh, where the Mercury passed her by on the starboard tack, and came within four minutes of the *Phœnix*, at turning round the stationary boat at Pultney. Having gained so much way, she endeavoured to get a-head of the winning boat, but the very excellent manœuvring of the Phœnix baffled every attempt; and the Mercury saved her credit by coming in just two minutes later than her leader.

The Cup therefore was adjudged to the Phœnix, the owner of which is Mr. Parkins of Vauxhall.

The Mercury is accounted the best sailing boat on the river, and must have won, had there been as much attention paid to the rudder, as to the company.

Such was the disposition of the public on the occasion, that the Thames exhibited one of the most beautiful scenes which can be conceived —a floating assemblage that covered the whole surface of the river.

In going up the river the boats were obliged to lie within four points of the wind, and the contest in the tacks was fine entertainment to the nautical people.

Yesterday arrived the mail from Holland.

The principal news which it brings is to the following effect:

A battle has been fought between the SWEDES and RUSSIANS, on the frontiers of Finland, near two villages on the extremity of the province of Savolax.

The Russians having, on the 11th of June passed the frontiers to the number of 6000 men, attacked the post of St. Michael, where a magazine was lodged. They were opposed by a very inferior number of Swedes, under the command of *Colonel Stedingk*, who fought them with small arms during the space of 17 hours, when the Russians were obliged to retire to *Christina*, leaving 250 men dead on the field, besides several officers taken prisoners. They were under the command of GENERAL MICHELSON.

At the close of the action, the Swedish regiment of *Ostro Bothnie* arrived with six pieces of cannon. It behaved in a very exemplary manner, having marched six Swedish miles and an half in one day, and the two last miles they ran, to be in time for the action.

In a battle fought since, near Parasalmi, the Russians had 700 men killed and wounded, two carriages laden with stores, 258 musquets, &c. taken. The Swedish loss was 43 killed and wounded.

The KING has created *Colonel Stedingk* a Knight of the Grand Cross of the Order of the Sword. His Majesty was by the last accounts at Borgo.

The Swedish army and navy are both badly off for provisions, having lost several vessels laden with corn, on their passage across the Baltic.

Prayers have been offered up in the Swedish churches on account of this victory.

The SWEDES have published a declaration the same as Russia, assuring the safety of all neutral vessels trading in the Baltic.

The French have for a considerable time been feeding the Russian *Boars* with white bread and flattery, for which they are themselves now put to very short allowance of black bread, with the *hope* only of a double allowance of liberty and licentiousness; they would fain cajole England to furnish them with flour and corn, merely for the purpose of feeding the Russians. There is not a scruple of doubt, but they will effect their wishes through the means of Guernsey and Alderney, from Southampton, the Isle of Wight, and Gosport, unless Ministers keep a most excellent look out, and a keen eye upon every little creek between the Downs and the Land's end.

We never understood that the common course of Mr. Louton's practice led him to employ clerks to seek for informations,—it cannot be to serve the purposes of Party.

Mr. SHERIDAN is a much better *Orator* than *Arithmetician*—for let him *dot*, at the character of the Minister as a financier, ever so much, it has been proved beyond all doubt, that he cannot *carry one!*

A private loan is now subscribing in the City, to the amount of *one hundred thousand pounds*, by the way of Tontine, said to be for the use of *three young gentlemen* at the West end of the town, to be paid off when either shall arrive at his paternal inheritance.

The medium terms of the above loan are seven years purchase; and one gentleman in the City has already bought in seven hundred a year for seven thousand pounds.

A race was on Monday run at Hampton Court between Powell, the famous walker, and a boy. The distance was one mile. The boy ran three-fourths of a mile in five minutes, Powell at that time wanted only 123 yards of having performed the mile.—The bet was for Twenty Guineas.

Yesterday morning at one o'clock, a fire broke at the house of Mr. Browne, Cabinet-maker, on the South side of St. Paul's Church-yard, which consumed the same, and damaged the adjoining houses; it was got under about three o'clock.

LAW REPORT.

WESTMINSTER-HALL.

COURT OF KING'S BENCH.

Saturday, July 11.

Before Lord Kenyon and a Special Jury.

The KING *against* Mr. WALTER,

BOOKSELLER OF PICCADILLY.

For publishing in a Daily Paper called the Times, two Paragraphs stated to be a Libel on his ROYAL HIGHNESS THE DUKE OF YORK.

Mr. Silvester opened the pleadings, vide, *The Times of the 16th of June last.*

Mr. Erskine's address to the Jury on the part of the prosecution.

Gentlemen of the Jury,

I am Counsel for this Prosecution which is brought before you by His Royal Highness the Duke of YORK, in the ordinary course of the criminal law of England, as it is handed down to us from the most antient times. And although I am one of those who think that an information filed by the Attorney General, would in this case have been perfectly legal, yet his Royal Highness the Duke of York has been pleased to spare it, and comes before you as if he were the meanest man in the kingdom, to vindicate his character from an aspersion that has been cast upon it, not availing himself of that high rank and dignity which belongs to him as the Son of the Sovereign.

The Grand Jury has found the bill. You have now heard it read. The time at which this publication appeared, was a season in which I should have thought that any person not lost to every principle of humanity, which this author must have been, must have felt that the mind of his Royal Highness the Duke of YORK was sufficiently afflicted with the unhappy situation of his family, without attempting still more to wound the peace of his mind, by that indignity and contempt which has been thrown on his head. Many ignorant people, at a distance, might be induced to have believed it. It is impossible for language to convey matter more offensive, more cruel, or more shocking.

The Royal Dukes must mean his Royal Highness the Duke of Gloucester, his Royal Highness the Duke of Cumberland—and his Royal Highness the Duke of York, *who prosecutes this Indictment*. At this time his Majesty's third son was not called up to the House of Peers, and therefore the Royal Dukes could only mean the three Royal Dukes, whom I have just mentioned, "And the leaders of Opposition in general, affect to join with the friends of our amiable Sovereign (meaning our said Lord, the present King) in rejoicing on account of his Majesty's Recovery, meaning the said recovery of our said Lord, the King from his said sickness and malady.) But the insincerity of their joy (meaning the joy of the said Dukes and the Leaders of Opposition in general) is visible (thereby meaning and insinuating that the said Dukes were disaffected to his Majesty's person, and did not sincerely rejoice on account of his said Majesty's recovery, but had assumed a false and counterfeit appearance of joy for such recovery.) Their late unfeeling conduct (meaning the conduct of the said Dukes, and of the Leaders of Opposition in general, upon occasion of the said sickness and recovery of our said Lord the King, and that such conduct denoted a want of affection and regard to his said Majesty) will for ever tell against them, (meaning the said Dukes and the Leaders of Opposition in general) and contradict the artful professions they (meaning the said Dukes and the Leaders of Opposition in general) may think it prudent to make."

Now, Gentlemen, with regard to the Leaders of Opposition no inuendo is put concerning them. What they thought and felt is nothing to the present purpose, and I trust they have that magnanimity not to regard any thing thrown out out on them in common newspapers. Not so with the Duke of York. He stands in a very different situation. Before I consider whether this is a libel on the Duke of York, reflect whether it would not be a libel upon any of you.

His Majesty is the Father of his People, the Sovereign of the country, and the free constitution of the country, and every thing dear and valuable to us, depends very much on the Successor to the Crown. We are to look up to the Sovereign as the source of all our happiness and prosperity, and every man ought to feel for his welfare. His Majesty was then suffering as the Father of his Family, and that man must have been brutal not to have rejoiced at an event at which *we have all since rejoiced.*

The Duke of York stood in a nearer relation, which rendered him infamous for ever unless you can suppose him to have had the most heart-felt satisfaction at the King's recovery. What must a parent have felt to have read in this Paper, that "Their late unfeeling conduct will for ever tell against them, and contradict the artful professions they may think it prudent to make." This applies to the three Royal persons, and individually to every one of them. It peculiarly affects the Duke of York, who stands so nearly connected with the family of the Sovereign, and attacks him as a son, as a Christian, and as a man.

The Royal Family of England are the children of the people—they are the children of the country; and we all know how important it is to the Constitution of these kingdoms, that their characters should be held sacred. Who can tell, if it should please God in his Providence to cast the Crown on the Prince who prosecutes this indictment, how much it might alienate the subjects of these kingdoms, because in former periods he stood disgraced in the newspapers, which are circulated through every part of this kingdom, and perhaps through all Europe. It would be wasting your time to say more on this subject—It would be an insult to your understandings. The simple question is, whether this is, or is not, a foul calumny on his Royal Highness the Duke of York.

There is another paragraph, "It argues infinite wisdom in certain persons to have prevented the Duke of YORK, &c." This was at a time when his Majesty was recovering from a violent disposition, and when it prudent or indelicate conduct rendered it most brutal not to have attended to the delicate situation of a parent. Yet it, seems the sick King was not safe in receiving the congratulations of his own family. He was not safe in the embraces of his own children, who ought to be most dear to him, but must depend on the prudence of those persons who surrounded him. He ought not to rely on the friendship of his son, whose brutality, Germanic rashness, and insensibility must have proved ruinous to the hopes of a whole nation, by a conduct so indiscreet, so dangerous, so devoid of all sensibility, as to have thrown his Majesty into that state which would have disappointed those hopes, which we trust are now well founded.

To persons of your description, it is unnecessary to say more. His Royal Highness comes here with no enmity against this paper. What mitigation of punishment this defendant, who is the publisher, may be able in future to shew, I neither know nor anticipate. I with others, think it a paper of so much malignity, that I hope the defendant will receive that punishment which he deserves. But all this is foreign to the present subject. I shall prove by a witness, that the defendant is the publisher of this paper. What degree of guilt has been incurred, will hereafter be considered and is not matter for to-day. Receiving like men of your sense, your opinion in point of law from the Judge trying this cause, if you think it no libel on a son to say he is treacherous to his own parent, and does acts which would disgrace any man, however unconnected in blood, and standing only in the common relation of a subject, I shall not contend the defendant is guilty; but if you think this is a libel, then your verdict be for the crown.

You have only to pronounce guilty or not guilty.

Henry Kelly, examined by Mr. Chambre.

When did you buy that Newspaper?

I bought it on the 21st of February, at Mr. Walter's, Piccadilly, in a public shop.

What was the Number?

I do not recollect the Number, but believe it to be No. 169.

What name was there over the door?

The name of WALTER was written over the door.

Did you know Mr. Walter before the time when you bought this paper?

I have seen him in the shop before, and since the time I bought this paper, *behind the counter with his hat off.* †

From whom did you receive this paper?

I received it from a servant, and paid him for it.

Cross examined by Mr. Dallas.

What are you Mr. Kelly?

I am Clerk to Mr. Lowton *

Mr. Lowton here read the two paragraphs in the Paper of 20th February, upon which the indictment was founded.

Mr. Erskine.—My Lord, we have Mr. Dundas, apothecary at Kew, here to prove the state in which his Majesty was when these libels were written.

Mr. Dallas—My Lord, I will not put Mr. Erskine to any such proof.

FOR THE DEFENDANT.

Mr. DALLAS,

"*Gentlemen of the Jury,*

"I have the honour to address you as counsel on behalf of the defendant, who stands charged with the publishing of the two paragraphs, which have been read to you, and which are alledged to contain libellous matter. And I conceive, under my Lord's direction, there are but two questions for you to try.

1st. Whether or not in point of fact, the defendant did publish the paragraphs in question?

The second is, supposing he did publish them, whether they bear the meaning imputed to them by the indictment?

I conceive these to be the only questions you have to try.

Whether or not in point of law these paragraphs amount to libels, is that which you will receive from his Lordship's directions. With regard to the first of these, whether the defendant did publish the paper in question, it would be idle and silly in me to contend the contrary. Most undoubtedly the fact of publishing does seem to me to be proved. With regard to the second, what construction is to be put upon these paragraphs, it is your province to determine. I shall leave this for you to decide. The only instructions I have received from my client, are those which are perfectly agreeable to my own judgment and my own feelings—to abstain from making any observations which might be construed to have the most remote tendency, indirectly to shew, that which directly I should not be allowed to justify. These paragraphs I leave to you, to put that construction on them, which, as men of sense, and as men upon your oaths, you suppose they bear. I shall not at present enter into any observations, to examine the degree of guilt which may arise, if this publication shall be found to be a libel—I shall not waste his Lordship's time, as I shall have a fit opportunity of making some remarks on this circumstance on a future occasion.

Lord KENYON's address to the Jury.

Gentlemen of the Jury,

The questions have been very accurately and properly stated to you by the counsel for the defendant.—The publication and the inuendos, are the only two points you have to ascertain.—The publication has been proved. The other point is, whether the Royal Dukes mean their Royal Highnesses the Dukes of Gloucester, Cumberland, and York. Any thing which the defendant can alledge to shew this is not a libel, may be moved in arrest of judgment. The punishment for the offence is an after consideration. Every man's feelings tell him these are paragraphs which ought by no means to have been sent abroad among the public.—GUILTY.

† *We think Mr. Kelly not accurate in the evidence, as will hereafter be particularly noticed.*

* *Mr. Lowton is Clerk at Nisi Prius.*

BEFORE LORD KENYON.

THE KING *v.* WILKES.

Tuesday, July 14.

This was an indictment for a libel on Mrs. FITZHERBERT, with which we shall not shock the ears of our readers.

Mr. *Erskine* was counsel on the part of the prosecution.

Mr. *Dallas* made an excellent speech on the part of the defendant.

After Lord *Kenyon* had, in a manner infinitely to his honour both as a man and a judge, given his charge to the Jury, they immediately found the defendant GUILTY.

☞ The grounds of the above Trial were sent us six months since with some references, but the respect and good opinion we ever entertained of the lady in question, made us not hesitate to reject the publication of the contents.

PLYMOUTH,

July 12.

Orders came down yesterday, after post, to countermand the fitting out of the Culloden and Bombay, and to order the getting ready for sea the following guardships, now lying at Hamoaze:

The Carnatic, 74 guns, Captain Ford.

The Cumberland, 74 guns, Captain M'Bride, And Orion, 74 guns, Captain Chamberlayne.

This morning they were ready, owing to the exertions of their Officers and Men, and would have gone down into the Sound, had the wind been fair; but it has been squally, mostly at S. W. and a great swell. If the wind should shift, there is not any doubt of their getting down this evening, or to-morrow morning: they are to sail for Spithead.

The following is a more particular account of the melancholy circumstance which happened in Whitechapel on Sunday morning:—Two eminent carcase butchers, Mr. Tyler and Mr. Edis, were next door neighbours, and intimate friends. Mr. Edis was married about six months ago; since which a sister of Mr. Tyler, a beautiful girl of sixteen, having quitted school, came to reside with her brother. On Saturday last Mr. Tyler supped with Mr. Edis; and, having been informed that too familiar an intercourse subsisted between Mr. E. and his sister, he expostulated with him on the subject, and warned him to desist from the pursuit, intimating that a contrary conduct would inevitably be attended with the most fatal consequences to himself. Mr. Edis assured him his suspicions were ill founded, and that his conduct would be so circumspect in future, as to give him no cause of complaint; in consequence of which they parted friends.

It unfortunately happened that the information Mr. Tyler had received was too well founded, and he paid no credit to Mr. Edis's assertions.—Supposing, or having heard, that Mr. E. visited his sister after the family were gone to rest, he obliged her to exchange apartments with him. About two o'clock on Sunday morning, Mr. Edis was entering the chamber window; Mr. T. fired at him, shot him through the head, and he fell dead into the apartment.

Monday, at five o'clock, the Coroner's Inquest met at the Crown and Magpie, Aldgate High Street. The Jury, after a minute investigation of all the circumstances that preceded the melancholy catastrophe, brought in their verdict, at five o'clock yesterday morning, *Self Defence.*

The ——, Sikkes, from Rotterdam to Petersburgh, is taken by a Swedish cutter, and carried into Carlscroon.

The Good-Intent, Murray, from London to Marseilles, is put into Lisbon, having thrown part of her cargo overboard.

Captain Poindestre of the Harriot, from Honduras, spoke the following ships, lat. 39, 40, N. lon. 59, 24, W. spoke the Maryland, from Bourdeaux to Maryland, lat. 43, 25, N. lon. 52, 20, W. spoke the Ant, from Newfoundland to Dominica.

The Prince of Piedmont, Persumo, which arrived from India the 5th of last month, having a considerable quantity of salt-petre on board, by some accident caught fire in the harbour of Ostend, the 11th instant, and communicating to the Powder Magazine, the vessel was blown up, two people killed, and several wounded. No other vessel injured.

The Polygraphic Exhibition will close this evening. Those who wish to become purchasers will do well not to omit the only opportunity for this season, of comparing the copies with the originals.

DIED.

On Sunday Morning, at his house in Welbeck Street, James Brydges, Esq. son of the late Honourable and Rev. Henry Brydges, brother to the first Duke of Chandos.

Yesterday se'nnight, at his seat at Fenham, near Newcastle, in the 37th year of his age, William Ord, Esq. He served the office of High Sheriff for the county of Northumberland, in the year 1771.

MEETINGS OF CREDITORS TO-MORROW AT GUILDHALL.

	Meet. Hour.
John Thrupp, Colchester (second)	11
W. Davis, Fleet Market, Staffordshire Warehouseman	10

ERRATUM.—In Yesterday's Paper, in the Advertisement of "Wants a Place as Butler,"—for No. 77, South Moulton street—read No. 47.

PRICE OF STOCKS.

BANK STOCK, 180 1-half a 181

3 per cent. reduced 73 a 1-4th

3 per cent. Consol. shut, 77 1-8th a 78 1-4th with div.

Ditto 1726 shut

4 per cent. Consol. 97 3-4th a 7 1-8th

Navy 5 per cent. shut

Bank Long Ann. 22 13-16ths a 7 8ths

Ditto Short 1778 and 1779 13 5-8ths

INDIA STOCK, 170 1-half

Ditto bonds 89 a 90s. pr.

SOUTH SEA STOCK, 87 1-half

New Ann. shut

3 per Cent. 1751 shut

New Navy 1 1-half dis.

Tontine 104 3-4ths a 105

2339

Revolution in France

Here is a dramatic account of one of the most dramatic and terrible news stories in history: the execution of Louis XVI, King of France. The breathless style, the dramatic present and the *pointillisme* of colons and semicolons indicate that it is the work of our grand old *philosophe*-historian, Thomas Carlyle.

He advances to the edge of the Scaffold, 'his face very red', and says: 'Frenchmen, I die innocent: it is from the Scaffold and near appearing before God that I tell you so. I pardon my enemies; I desire that France —' A General on horseback, Santerre or another, prances out, with uplifted hand: '*Tambours!*' The drums drown the voice. 'Executioners, do your duty!' The Executioners, desperate lest themselves be murdered (for Santerre and his Armed Ranks will strike, if they do not), seize the hapless Louis: six of them desperate, him singly desperate, struggling there; and bind him to their plank. Abbé Edgeworth, stooping, bespeaks him: 'Son of Saint Louis, ascend to Heaven.' The Axe clanks down; a King's Life is shorn away. It is Monday the 21st of January 1793. He was aged Thirty-eight years four months and twenty-eight days.

Executioner Samson shows the Head: fierce shout of *Vive la République* rises, and swells; caps raised on bayonets, hats waving: students of the College of Four Nations take it up, on the far Quais; fling it over Paris. D'Orléans drives off in his cabriolet: the Townhall Councillors rub their hands, saying, 'It is done, It is done'. There is dipping of handkerchiefs, of pike-points in the blood. Headsman Samson, though he afterwards denied it, sells locks of the hair: fractions of the puce coat are long after worn in rings. And so, in some half-hour it is done; and the multitude has all departed.

The Times was lucky to be born when there was a lot of news around. Another way of putting it is that the intense drama of the last decades of the eighteenth century and the first decades of the nineteenth created a public hunger for the latest news that made something like *The Times* inevitable. Moralists may deplore it, but battle, murder and sudden death sell newspapers. The British public were fascinated by the French Revolution: some saw it as a threat, others as hope; all as terrible and fascinating,

TAKING PHYSICK OR NEWS FROM SWEDEN, published 11 April 1792. Gillray's caricature shows George III and Queen Charlotte rising from the royal privy in consternation as Prime Minister Pitt dashes in with the news of the shooting of the King of Sweden: 'Another Monarch done over!' At this time the crowned heads of Europe lived in fear of the spread of revolution and of assassination.

THE TIMES recounts the execution of King Louis XVI of France.
25 JANUARY 1793

THE TIMES.

LONDON.

☞ Conversion of St. Paul.—*A Holiday at all the Public Offices.*

The present moment is of all others the most favourable for declaring war against France, and we have pretty sure grounds for believing, that it will be proposed in Parliament on a very early day in the ensuing week (probably on Monday). It has been perhaps a matter of sound policy to delay this declaration to the present moment; and we will venture to say, that no war was ever undertaken with the more general concurrence of the people, than that in which we are about to engage.

By the same letter which brings us the account of the King's execution, we learn that in the violent storm which happened in the Mediterranean, it is feared that almost the whole of the French fleet, under the command of Admiral *Truguet*, has been destroyed. The *Larguedoc* of 80 guns, which is dismasted, is arrived in the Bay of Naples, and is the only ship that has been heard of. Who can say, that this dreadful calamity may not have been inflicted by Divine Providence, as a scourge on those villains, whose only project was to visit the defenceless towns on the coast of Italy, to plunder and assassinate the innocent inhabitants of them.

Yesterday at half past twelve o'clock, a message was received by Lord Onslow at St. James's, from the King at Buckingham House, that there would be no Drawing Room at St. James's on that day.

The King will have a Levee at St. James's this day at twelve o'clock, after which his Majesty will hold a Council.

Yesterday a Board was held at the Admiralty Office, when the Illustrious of 74 guns was put into commission, and the command given to Captain Frederick.

Yesterday at one o'clock the King held a Cabinet Council at Buckingham House, which was attended by Mr. Pitt, the Duke of Richmond, the two Secretaries of State, and Lord Amherst.

Lord St. Helen's will set out this day or to-morrow, on his return to his Embassy at Madrid. His Lordship goes by the way of Lisbon.

Setting aside the horror and infamy of the deed, the death of Louis the XVIth, under the circumstances of his confinement, will be of political advantage to Europe. Monsieur will now be instantly acknowledged by the Powers of Europe—Regent of France; and we have some reason to believe, that the Court of Great Britain will be among the first to acknowledge him as such.

The event, in respect to many Morning Papers, publishing an account of the murder of the unfortunate Louis, turned out just as we expected. Those papers which depend upon speculation for the authority of early intelligence, knowing that the Act of Regicide was to take place, gave it to the Public, as a fact done before any account of its execution arrived. Indeed, the time at which these papers asserted the fatal event to have taken place, and that at which it really happened, sufficiently proves the fallacy of their intelligence; which was not until yesterday morning.

The National Convention had in the first instance decreed, that the Murder of Louis the XVIth, should be executed on the Sabbath day;—a day consecrated to religious duties, and on which all other nations occupy themselves in actions of religious worship towards their Creator. The sentence was postponed to the Monday morning, from no other motives than those of apprehension, least a tumult should ensue.

Thus do the French glory as much in offending their God, as they rejoice in murdering their King—as if they set the vengeance of Heaven, and the execration of Mankind, at equal defiance. And yet the savages talk of *fraternity* with the world!

The *ci-devant* Duke of Orleans, Mr. *Equality*, in dooming his nephew to death, reminds us of *Richard the Third*, giving orders for the murder of his brother's children. The uncles were educated with similar ideas of humanity, and equal sentiments of justice.

Having now got rid of their lawful Sovereign in France, the dispute for Sovereignty will be between his murderers—Shall the King or Ruler be a *Jack Cade* or a *Wat Tyler*? This will be hardly fought at Paris, and many streams of blood shall flow in the contest. But as it is the interest, so it is the intention of Europe, to destroy both of these savage parties; and the ensuing campaign will, we trust, bring the murderers to condign punishment.

Spain will now most probably unite her force with the other Powers armed against the Conventional Tyrants of France; and for the sake of humanity, we hope that one campaign will be amply sufficient to crush those vipers, and bring the murderers of Louis XVI. to the most exemplary punishment.

Our intelligence in this day's Paper, concerning the execution of the unhappy King of the French, we have received it from indisputable authority; and though we are happy at all times to give the best information to our Readers, we must say that this is the most melancholy task we ever performed. We find it new to the mind; and in a country where compassion flows round every heart,—from the cottager to the Peer,—even the bare recital freezes the warm blood of nature with a kind of horror, that almost arrests the very power of utterance.

Lord Amherst has received his appointment as Chief of the Staff of the British Army.—He is to execute the functions of Commander in Chief without the title.

BRUSSELS.

January 19.

Our Representatives are reduced to a small number, since the retreat of many who had been elected. The electors nominated in the Primary Assemblies the 29th December, assembled notwithstanding the prohibition of the provisional Representatives. Some were arrested, but were released after two days.

The people of Brabant complain loudly, that instead of the liberty held out to them, they experience nothing but the tyranny of a small faction, and that instead of promised independance, they groan under the afflicting despotism of foreign military.

All quarters of Belgia re-echo with complaints against the decree of the 15th December. Although the provisionary representatives of Namur were slighted by the Convention, the representatives of Malines have not been intimidated from protesting in the most emphatic manner against the same decree, as an attack upon the Sovereignty of the people of Malines. They state in a letter to the Convention, *that their conduct is a tyranny of which history exhibits no example, and which has yet no name.* Even Flanders, where the French principles had made greater progress, has revolted at seeing France prescribing laws, and preparing under the hitherto unknown authority of revolutionary power, to unite this province with herself, and has succeeded in admonishing all persons against the designs of a nation which promised to give Liberty, and Independance to the Belgians.

Frankfort on the Main, Jan. 5.

The Prussian and Hessian troops, whose head quarters are at Wickert, surround the works which the French have thrown up round Cassel on all sides, in a manner almost impregnable. Hostheim is the only fortified post which they hold on the other side the Rhine, except the fortress of Konigstein; 120 French of the garrison of this latter place, endeavouring to make a *sortie* on the 29th, were compelled by the besiegers to re enter.

January 8.

On the night between the 5th and 6th, the French, straitened in their position, endeavoured to attack Hockiem; upon which the King of Prussia marched at the head of his troops. A heavy cannonade was heard, which continued till nine in the morning. The Prussians took 12 cannons and 160 prisoners; one Colonel and several French, who endeavoured to escape, were killed.

During the action, the Hereditary Prince de Hohenlohe, posted at Visbaden, fell upon the flank of the French, and compelled them to retreat to their entrenchments in Cassel, where they are very narrowly shut up, particularly since the ice upon the Rhine has obliged them to remove the bridge which secured the communication with Mayence. Some state the number of French killed to be 300, others 700; the loss of the Prussians only 52. Fourteen Hessians were wounded by the blowing up of a powder carriage.

It is believed, that if it had not been for the treachery of a Prussian Hussar, who deserted during the march, all the French army would have been surprised, surrounded, and made prisoners.

Lord Lauderdale greatly regrets, that his eagerness to be the first messenger to the English Jacobins, with the joyful intelligence of the condemnation of Louis, should have induced him so soon to quit Paris. Had any of his friends in the Convention informed him, that the *humanity* of that collection of savages would so speedily have brought their King to the block, he certainly would have remained a few days longer, to have dropped some *tears of iron*, over the corpse of a *Tyrant*.

Such Englishmen as are now in that *Land of Freedom*, France, we conceive will act wisely in quitting it as fast as possible; for in the event of a war, little dependence can be placed on such wretches as now rule France, paying any respect to the laws of Nations.

There will, no doubt, be a *Court Mourning* on account of the murder of his Christian Majesty, which most probably will be followed up by a general one. The Regicides are mistaken in the principles of Englishmen, and to their cost they will find the hatred of this country manifested in the course of the ensuing campaign.

Every bosom burns with indignation in this kingdom, against the ferocious savages of Paris, insomuch that the very name of Frenchman is become odious. A Republic founded on the blood of an innocent victim must have but a short duration. This fact was tried by *Oliver Cromwell*, and proved by the Restoration of Charles the Second.

Shutting the Theatre in the Haymarket yesterday evening, on account of the barbarous murder of the late King of France by a set of Conventional Butchers, does the highest honour to Mr. Kemble. It was a mark of respect to the memory of the unhappy Louis, with which the whole British nation must be pleased. It must likewise be considered as a proof of the great deference Mr. *Kemble* pays to the opinion the King had plainly expressed, by not going to the Theatre the preceding evening.

Louis XVI. of France, was murdered for the same *crime*, for which Agis, the Lacedemonian, was put to death by his ignorant rebel subjects; in fine, for wishing to revive the reign of Liberty and Justice, among a People, incapable of knowing the intrinsic value or blessing of either.

The Republican Tyrants of France have now carried their bloody purposes to the uttermost diabolical stretch of savage cruelty. They have murdered their King without even the shadow of justice, and of course they cannot expect friendship nor intercourse with any civilized part of the world. The vengeance of Europe will now rapidly fall on them; and, in process of time, make them the veriest wretches on the face of the earth. The name of Frenchman will be considered as the appellation of savage, and their presence be shunned as a poison, deadly destructive to the peace and happiness of Mankind. It appears evident, that the majority of the National Convention, and the Executive Government of that truly despotic country, are comprised of the most execrable villains upon the face of the earth.

EXECUTION OF LOUIS XVI.

King of the French.

By an express which arrived yesterday morning from Messrs. *Fector* and Co. at Dover, we learn the following particulars of the King's execution:

At six o'clock on Monday morning, the King went to take a farewell of the Queen and Royal Family. After staying with them some time, and taking a very affectionate farewell of them, the King descended from the tower of the Temple, and entered the Mayor's carriage, with his confessor and two Members of the Municipality, and passed slowly along the Boulevards which led from the Temple to the place of execution. All women were prohibited from appearing in the streets, and all persons from being seen at their windows. A strong guard cleared the procession.

The greatest tranquillity prevailed in every street through which the procession passed. About half past nine, the King arrived at the place of execution, which was in the *Place de Louis* XV. between the pedestal which formerly supported the statue of his grandfather, and the promenade of the Elysian Fields. Louis mounted the scaffold with composure, and that modest intrepidity peculiar to oppressed innocence, the trumpets sounding and drums beating during the whole time. He made a sign of wishing to harangue the multitude, when the drums ceased, and Louis spoke these few words. *I die innocent; I pardon my enemies; I only sanctioned upon compulsion the Civil Constitution of the Clergy.*—He was proceeding, but the beating of the drums drowned his voice. His executioners then laid hold of him, and an instant after, his head was separated from his body; this was about a quarter past ten o'clock.

After the execution, the people threw their hats up in the air, and cried out *Vive la Nation!* Some of them endeavoured to seize the body, but it was removed by a strong guard to the Temple, and the lifeless remains of the King were exempted from those outrages which his Majesty had experienced during his life.

The King was attended on the scaffold by an Irish Priest as his Confessor, not choosing to be accompanied by one who had taken the National oath. He was dressed in a brown great coat, white waistcoat and black breeches, and his hair was powdered.

When M. de *Malsherbes* announced to Louis, the fatal sentence of Death. "Ah!" exclaimed the Monarch, "I shall then at length be delivered from this cruel suspense."

The decree imported that Louis should be beheaded in the *Place de Carouzel*, but reasons of public safety induced the Executive Council to prefer the *Place de la Revolution*, formerly the *Place de Louis* XV.

Since the decree of death was issued, a general consternation has prevailed throughout Paris;—the Sans Culottes are the only persons that rejoice.—The honest citizens, immured within their habitations, could not suppress their heart-felt grief, and mourned in private with their families the murder of their much-loved Sovereign.

The last requests of the unfortunate Louis breathes the soul of magnanimity, and a mind enlightened with the finest ideas of human virtue. He appears not to be that man which his enemies reported. His heart was sound—his head was clear—and he would have reigned with glory, had he but possessed those faults which his assassins laid to his charge. His mind possessed the suggestions of wisdom; and even in his last moments, when the spirit of life was winged for another world, his lips gave utterance to them, and he spoke with firmness and with resignation.

Thus has ended the life of Louis XVI. after a period of four year's detention; during which, he experienced from his subjects every species of ignominy and cruelty which a people could inflict on the most sanguinary tyrant. Louis XVI. who was proclaimed at the commencement of his reign the friend of the people, and by the Constituent Assembly, the restorer of their liberties—Louis, who but a few years since was the most powerful Monarch in Europe, has at last perished on the scaffold. Neither his own natural goodness of heart, his desire to procure the happiness of his subjects, nor that ancient love which the French entertained for their Monarch, has been sufficient to save him from this fatal judgment.

Long in the habit of supporting the virtues of this unhappy Victim of savage Republicanism; and, steady in persevering to declare, that his highest ambition was the happiness of his people, we hold ourselves justified, from the universal indignation which has marked this last act of cruelty exercised against him, to pay our sorrowing tribute to his memory, and join with the united millions of Europe, in supplicating the wrath of Heaven, and the vengeance of Mankind, to extend to his unnatural murderers the most exemplary punishment.

Posterity, in condemning those infamous Judges who have sacrificed Louis to the fury and ambition of the vilest of men, will extend their censures yet further; and in the warmth of virtuous indignation, will not refrain from blasting the memory of that Minister (Necker), who, to gratify a selfish vanity, directed the Royal victim to make the first step towards that precipice, from the brink of which he is now precipitated.

Posterity will condemn those Members of the Constituent Assembly, who allured by the meteor of false philosophy, madly burst asunder the bonds of popular subordination; tore down the pillars of Monarchy and Religion, and left Louis defenceless, forsaken, and abandoned to those hordes of Monsters, who under the different appellations of Legislative Assemblies, Clubs, and Sections, have inflicted upon their miserable victim a thousand agonizing deaths and apprehensions, before they delivered him up to the axe of the executioner.

The perpetrators of such crimes may proceed in their career, till they draw down the same punishment on themselves. The virtuous of every country will bedew with sensibility, the memory of a good and pious King; whilst the tardy tears of the first Revolutionists shall blend themselves with the hypocritical complaints of the new Republicans upon the precipitancy of the King's execution.

Unquestionably, the blood of this unfortunate Monarch will invoke vengeance on his murderers. This is not the cause of Monarchs only, it is the cause of every nation on the face of the earth. All potentates owe it to their individual honour, but still more strongly to the happiness of their people collectively, to crush these savage Regicides in their dens, who aim at the ruin of all nations, and the destruction of all Governments. It is not by feeble efforts only, that we can hope to exterminate these inhuman wretches. Experience has proved them to be ineffectual. Armed with fire and sword, we must penetrate into the recesses of this land of blood and carnage. Louis might still have been living, had neighbouring Princes acted with that energy and expedition, which the case required.

Letter from the Chevalier D'Ocariz, Charge d'Affaires *from the* Court *of* Spain *to* France. *Addressed to the* President *of the* National Convention.

[*It may be remembered that this letter was refused to be received by the Convention, because it was known to intercede in the King's behalf.*]

"The new orders which I have received, and the urgency of the circumstances, authorise me not to omit any means in which I can manifest the anxiety which his Catholic Majesty feels on the occasion of the trial which is so near to end, and in so fatal a manner to the unfortunate head of his family. I, therefore, take the speediest opportunity to repeat to you in his Majesty's name, his instant solicitations and his most ardent entreaties, to the French nation and their representatives. I think that the new considerations which I am going to lay before you, will appear to you to deserve a particular attention; I entreat you to communicate them to the National Convention.—I am convinced that the French People are destined, by their character, and by the nature of the situation of the country they inhabit, to preserve a great existence in Europe, as well as vast relations with other countries, and that the Assembly of their Representatives cannot quite have shut their ears against all reflections of political prudence which have been offered to them by several of their Members. I shall not presume to add to them. But, Sir, the importance of the cause, and the interest which the King of Spain takes, and ought to take in it, is such, that I hope I shall not be disowned, when I come to intreat you by this letter, to obtain from you the time to desire his intervention and good offices, to establish peace between France and the other Belligerent Powers. If this step, being, at the same time, useful to the French, could also soften and ameliorate the fate of his unhappy relative, I may confidently expect the approbation of his Majesty, that in the manner in which my offer shall have been accepted, the King, my master, shall think himself bound and engaged to enter into negociations, the success of which will be so important to humanity. I very ardently wish that the proposal I am making, may be accepted of, and in the case it should, I require no more than strictly the time necessary for the going and return of a courier.

"I have the honour to be, with the sentiments of the most distinguished consideration,

(Signed) "The Chevalier D'Ocariz."

☞ The outline of the propositions made by Government to the East India Company for the renewal of their Charter is founded on nearly the same principles as the existing charter. The conduct and management of the territorial revenues of the country are to remain with the Directors, as well as the continuation of their exclusive trade.

From the great importation of coals last year, and a fresh supply arriving at market, coals are reduced to the prices of 32s. to 37s. in the Pool;—39s. to 44s. delivered to housekeepers.

General Anselme has been arrested at Apte, his native place; he left Avignon on the 30th of December. He has been conducted to Paris by an escort of the Gendarmerie, who are relieved from place to place.

On Friday, the 18th instant, the Anniversary of her Majesty's Birth Day was observed with great loyalty at Finlayston, the seat of the Earl of Glencairn; on which occasion all his Lordship's Tenants were entertained with the ancient hospitality of that family. In the evening bonfires, music and illuminations concluded a day in which all persons present testified their attachment and respect for the illustrious Family on the Throne, and the happy Constitution of the Country.

and something that they must read all about as soon as possible.

The Times carried its own report of the execution of Louis XVI – maybe not as dramatic as Carlyle's, but dramatic enough, and anticipating him by forty-four years. In those pristine days when daily journalism was struggling to develop its techniques, foreign news was obtained either by translating foreign journals or literally from correspondents, people in foreign cities who sent letters to Printing House Square relating the latest news. Hence professional foreign reporters are still called correspondents, even though these days they communicate with Printing House Square more briskly than by letter.

John Walter sensed the public hunger for news, particularly of the French Revolution. In 1792 he wrote 'Continental affairs are so engrossing', and announced new arrangements for getting the news first:

> We have established a new correspondence both at Brussels and Paris, which we trust will furnish us with the most regular and early intelligence that can possibly be obtained. Our communications will not be confined to the ordinary conveyance by the Foreign Mails only, as we have taken such measures as will enable us to receive Letters from abroad on those days when the Foreign Mails do not become due. Our new Correspondence commences this day. The foreign Gazettes which chiefly guide the other Morning Prints are become so extremely partial, that they aggravate or suppress almost every material fact, as suits the purpose of their several parties.

Establishing its own private network, independent of foreign mails and foreign gazettes, was one of the things that made *The Times*. It worked, though it was very expensive. 26 June 1792: 'We have some reason to be proud of our Foreign Correspondence in this Day's paper. *The Brussels Gazette* has been stopped from being printed since the French troops entered Flanders. From this disappointment we are led to believe that none of the other Morning Papers of this Day will have any news from Flanders.'

The Times started to scoop the world, breaking the news before anybody else in Britain. For example on 3 August 1792 it published exclusively the anti-revolutionary declaration of the Duke of Brunswick. But there were difficulties. In September *The Times* took its readers into its confidence on the subject:

> It is a matter of great vexation to us, that the plans we had laid for obtaining the most early correspondence from Paris and Bruxelles [sic] should have been so frequently obstructed, by the interruption of letters in the Post-offices abroad. We had taken the most certain measures to procure a Daily Correspondence from both these places, by having Agents at the Out-ports to forward our letters; but from the circuitous channels which they must now pass through, and from the frequent stoppage of all kind [sic] of correspondence from France, which is not tinctured with the spirit of rebellion, we have been subject to daily disappointments.
>
> The Declaration of the Duke of Brunswick which first appeared in this paper, should have reached us a week sooner than it did; . . . The Manifesto of the Confederate Powers we now learn, was sent to us four days after its first publication, but has never yet been received.

Above A revolutionary medal struck in 1791, bearing the slogans 'To live free or to die', 'Let us swear to uphold the constitution'.

Below right Engraving and medal feature emblems and slogans. Among the allegories and images adopted in the commemorative prints and medals, the Roman *Fasces* was defined in the 'Loi du 9–15 avril, 1791' as the symbol of unity and armed force.

The establishment of this network of foreign correspondence was the most expensive item on the editorial budget. The postage of a single letter from any part of Holland, France or Flanders to Printing House Square was 10d; from Spain 18d. Walter spoke of its 'immense cost'. But if *The Times* was going to survive and profit as a newspaper, it had to get the news first and more reliably than its competitors. There were others in the field, feeding the public hunger for news about the French Revolution. For example, there was John Bell, the most energetic as well as the most fashionable bookseller of the day, and Walter's great rival. Bell made a special journey abroad in the spring of 1794 for the express purpose of establishing a regular chain of Continental agents to continue his series of dispatches. *The Times* denounced him as 'a vagabond Jacobin', and published a puff for its own news of the Revolution, expounding the novel Printing House Square axiom for daily journalism that it is not worth getting it first unless you also get it right. Referring to the unreliability of foreign news in all other newspapers, we declared:

> Not one of [them] contained an article of news respecting the events now passing in West Flanders, to which it could speak as a positive fact. It is not, however, to be wondered that such contradictory and false rumours should be circulated, when those who write them from the Continent are for the most part vagabond Jacobins, who report as a fact every thing they hear; which is farther aggravated on this side the water by all the virulence of disappointment and malignity. We have offered these remarks, because we feel it impossible to keep pace with the intelligence of the many expresses which these communicative purveyors of news receive, according to their own account, every hour. Of the Correspondence of this Paper the public are to judge for themselves. We shall merely state, that on Monday night, though it was at a late hour, we received all the Newspapers printed at Brussels on *Saturday last*; and we had a letter from Ostend dated on *Sunday afternoon*. We do not contend for any greater expedition!

You can see other symptoms of the rush for news of the portentous events in France in the advertisements for assistants in the Foreign Department of *The Times*. For example, 27 August 1792:

> Wanted immediately, A Gentleman who is capable of translating the French Language. In order to prevent trouble, he must be a perfect Master of the English Language, have some knowledge of the Political State of Europe, and be thoroughly capable of the situation he undertakes. His employment will be permanent and take up a considerable share of his attention; for which a handsome salary will be allowed. Apply at the office of this Paper between the hours of Five and Six this Evening, or Tomorrow morning, between Eleven and Twelve o'clock.

In the storm of the century *The Times* was born. There was a huge demand for fast, accurate news, instead of the official version deemed suitable by the Establishment for ordinary people to know. The French Revolution was fuelled by an immense pile of manuscript newspapers, street ballads, brochures, a paper-storm of print. Newspapers were bound to come anyway. Reports of such great events as the day they cut off a King's head were the sensations that brought *The Times* to birth.

In column 4 is a vivid eye-witness account of Louis XVI's execution. Newspapers at this time obtained most of their foreign news from 'correspondents' – literally, letter-writers who chanced to be at the scene of a notable event. The name has stuck.
28 JANUARY 1793

FATE of His Most Christian MAJESTY LOUIS the XVIth.

PROPOSALS for Publishing by Subscription, a Print of the above Important Event, from a Picture now Painting by MATHER BROWN, Historical Painter to their Royal Highnesses the Duke and Duchess of York. The Sketch to be seen by the Subscribers, and subscriptions received by Mr. Brown, Cavendish-square.

Mr. Brown's large Picture of Lord CORNWALLIS receiving the HOSTAGE PRINCES, containing upwards of 100 Figures, will in a few days be publicly exhibited.

At the same time will be likewise exhibited the State Muzhned, which was used by Tippoo at full Durbar, and which was taken from the Sultaun at Bangalore.

This Day are published, Price 3s. 6d. in boards,

DE MORBIS QUIBUSDAM COMMENTARII.

Auctore CLIFTON WINTRINGHAM, Baronetto, M. D. Colleg. Medic. Londinens. et Pariliens. Socio, Societatis Regiæ Sodali, Exercitus Britannici Medico primario, et Medico Regio. Tom II.

Apud T. Cadell.

This Day is Published, price 1s. 6d.

THE Necessity of a SPEEDY and EFFECTUAL REFORM in PARLIAMENT, addressed to the "Friends of the People."

By GEORGE PHILIPS.

Printed for J. Johnson, in St. Paul's Church-Yard; and Falkner and Co. Manchester.

This Day is published,

In One Volume Octavo, Price 6s. in Boards,

Dedicated to the Right Hon. Sir James Sanderson, Knt. Lord Mayor, the Aldermen, Common Council, and Citizens of London.

THE CHARTERS of LONDON complete; also MAGNA CHARTA, and the BILL of RIGHTS. With Explanatory Notes and Remarks.

By JOHN LUFFMAN, Citizen and Goldsmith of London.

London: Printed for J. Luffman, No. 5, Windmill-street, Finsbury-square, Moorfields; and T. Evans, No. 46, Paternoster-Row.

This Day is published,

The Third Edition, Price 3s. 6d. in Boards,

THE FESTIVAL OF LOVE: Being a Collection of warm yet elegant Poems, including many Original Pieces, never before published, by the first Wits and Bonvivants of the present time; also Translations from Musæus, Coluthus, Anacreon, Sappho, &c.

Printed for C. and G. Kearsley, No. 46, Fleet-street.

Where may be had,

The Fifteenth Edition, Price 3s. 6d. of

The FESTIVAL of WIT; selected by G—— K——, Summer Resident at Windsor; and carefully copied from the Common-place Book, with the Names of the Parties who introduced them to the R— E—.

Just published, Price 1s. 6d.

TAXATION of COALS, considered in an ADDRESS to the Inhabitants of the Cities of London and Westminster, and all places supplied with Coals from the Port of London. By DAVID HARDIE.

Sold by J. Debrett, Piccadilly; W. Richardson, Royal Exchange; J. Strahan, No. 67, Strand, and D. Offerd, No. 21. Great Russel-street, Bloomsbury.

Last Session the City of London presented a Petition to the House of Commons, praying a Repeal of the local Duty at the Port of London of 3s. 4d. per Chaldren, and Mr. Hardie has authority to say, that the proper measures are now taking for a renewal of that application on the first Meeting of the Common Council.

TRIAL of PAINE.

This day is published, a new Edition, price 3s. 6d.

THE PROCEEDINGS at large on the TRIAL of THOMAS PAINE; containing the Evidence, exact Copies of all the Letters, and the Speeches of Mr. Attorney-General and Mr. Erskine.

Taken in Short-hand by JOSEPH GURNEY.

Sold by Martha Gurney, Bookseller, No. 128, Holborn-hill; and Mr. Stockdale, Piccadilly.

N. B. This Publication is entered at Stationers'-hall, and if any person presume to print any part of it, they will be prosecuted.

Of the same Booksellers may be had, 11th Edition.

Mr. GURNEY's SYSTEM of SHORT-HAND, dedicated with Permission, to the King.

This Book is a sufficient Instructor of itself, but if any difficulties occur, they shall be removed upon Application to the Author without any additional Expence.

NEW RIVER SCENERY.

In this Month will be published,

Eight AQUATINTA PRINTS, engraved by F. JUKES, from Drawings by R. M. BATTY; being the First Number of

A SERIES of VIEWS on the NEW RIVER and its VICINITY. Each Number will contain Eight Prints on quarto imperial Paper, and short Historical Observations of the Views and the River, will be given in the course of publication. Price 15s. each number plain, or 30s. printed in colours.

In this Collection particular attention has been paid to the Scenery of Amwell, celebrated by the late Mr. Scott, in his Poems.

To the Right Hon. Lord Romney, President, and to the rest of the Society for the Encouragement of Arts, Manufactures and Commerce, these Views on the New River and its Vicinity, are, with the greatest respect and gratitude, inscribed by their most obliged and obedient Servant,

FRANCIS JUKES.

No. 10, Howland-street,

Jan. 1, 1793.

Speedily will be published, Price 2s. 6d.

THE CONFESSIONS of the COUNTESS of STRATHMORE,

WRITTEN by HERSELF!

These Confessions contain a very interesting and undisguised History of Lady Strathmore's Life, from the Age of Eleven Years; and also many curious Particulars of the following Persons, viz.

Late Earl of Strathmore,	Rt. Hon. C. J Fox,
A. R. Bowes, Esq.	Mr. Scott,
George Gray, Esq.	Mr. James Graham,
Duke of Buccleugh,	Mr. Chaloner,
Earl of Bute,	Mr. Mayne,
Hon. Mr. Lyon,	——— Fernandez, the Jew,
A Venetian Marquis,	Mr. Matra,
George Dempster, Esq.	Mr. D. Graham,
Mr. Pianta,	G. Walker, a Footman—and
Rev. Mr. Pennick,	Duchess of Northumberland,
Rev. Mr. Palograve,	Countess of Bute,
Rev. Mr. Stephens,	Mrs. Montague, &c. &c. &c.

Printed for W. Locke, No 12, Red Lion-street, Holborn; and sold by the Booksellers in Paternoster-row and Piccadilly.

This Day is published, in Two Volumes, Quarto, Price Two Guineas and a Half, in Boards,

A DIGEST OF THE STATUTE LAW: Being an Abridgment of all the public Acts of Parliament in force, and of general use from Magna Charta, in the Ninth Year of King Henry III. to the Thirtieth Year of his present Majesty King George III. inclusive.

By THOMAS WALTER WILLIAMS,

Of the Inner Temple, Barrister at-Law.

The Editor submits to the attention of the Public a very copious, and, as he conceives, accurate Abridgment of all the Acts of Parliament now in force, so arranged as to exhibit at one view, under proper titles, a consolidated and perspicuous display of the whole Statute Law. And as the operative words of every Act have been carefully attended to and preserved, together with the prescribed Forms of Oaths, Convictions, and other proceedings, he farther flatters himself that this Book, exclusive of its general utility, must be particularly convenient to the Magistrates, the Lawyer, the Merchant, and every other person immediately concerned in the operation of the Statutes.

Printed for G. G. J. and J. Robinson, No. 25, Paternoster-row; and C. and G. Kearsley, No. 46, Fleet-street.

Where may be had, by the same Author, in 4 vols. 8vo. price 1l. 8s. bound, a New Edition of

ORIGINAL PRECEDENTS in CONVEYANCING; settled by the most eminent Conveyancers, with the Opinions of Counsel.

The cheapest and most useful Book to young Men ever printed.

This day is published, price 1s. 6d.

The eleventh Edition, beautifully printed by Hodson, Bell-yard, on a new Letter, and fine wove demy Paper.

NATURE's ASSISTANT to the Restoration of HEALTH.

The Utility of this publication is best evinced by its rapid and encreasing sale amongst people in all ranks of life, some thousands being sold of it annually. This Tract should be read by persons of all ages, ranks and conditions, there being scarcely an individual who is not interested in some part of it. An early attention to the latter part may serve to guard youth from a fatal rock on which thousands have split, and be the means of preserving their minds, their bodies, and all their faculties from destruction. It is, therefore, recommended to the young nobility and gentry, and particularly to all those who receive their education at any of the great schools or popular seminaries, as a perusal thereof may guard them against certain fashionable follies and imprudent habits, which tend to plunge them into a state of misery and woe.

Sold by Deighton, in Holborn; Matthews, Strand; and all Booksellers in Town and Country.

Mr. FOX's LETTER.

This Day is Published, price 1s.

A LETTER from the Right Honourable CHARLES JAMES FOX, To the Worthy and Independent ELECTORS of the City and Liberty of WESTMINSTER.

Printed for J. Debrett, opposite Burlington House, Piccadilly.

For GENTLEMEN going to HOT COUNTRIES.

This Day is published, in 8vo. price 6s. in boards.

NATURE and EFFECTS of EMETICS, PURGATIVES, MERCURIALS, and LOW DIET, in Diseases of Bengal, and similar Latitudes.

By JOHN PETER WADE, M. D

Of the Hon. East India Company's Bengal Establishment.

London: Printed for J. Murray, No. 32, Fleet-street,

Where may be had,

1. Select Evidences of a successful Method of treating Fever and Dysentery in Bengal. By the same Author, 8vo. Price 6s. in Boards.

2. A Paper on the Prevention and Treatment of the Disorders of Seamen and Soldiers in Bengal, presented to the Hon. Court of East India Directors in 1791. By the same Author. 8vo. Price 3s. 6d. in Boards.

3. Observations on the Diseases which prevail in Long Voyages to Hot Countries, particularly to those in the East Indies, and on the same Diseases as they appear in Great Britain. By John Clark, M. D. Fellow of the Royal College of Physicians, at Edinburgh; Physician to the Infirmary and Dispensary at Newcastle, &c.

*** The Parts of this Work which give an Historical Account of the Diseases which usually occur in long Voyages, which prevail in various places of Asia, and which treat of the means of Prevention, are intended for the Perusal of Gentlemen in General, but more especially of Officers, on whom the Health of the Men depends. These subjects are, therefore, treated in as perspicuous a manner as possible, and all technical Terms avoided.

In the Press, and speedily will be published by Subscription, by J. Murray, No. 32, Fleet-street,

THE TRIAL of AVADAUNUM PAUPIAH BRAMIN, (Dubash to John Hollond, Esq. late Governor of Fort St. George, and his Brother Edward John Hollond, Esq. late Member of the Council thereof) of AVADAUNUM RAMAH SAUMY BRAMIN, (Brother to Avadaunum Paupiah Bramin) SUNKARAPORAM VINCATACHILLAH CHITTY and APPEYINGAR, BRAMIN, for a Conspiracy against David Haliburton, Esq; a Senior Merchant in the service of the East India Company, under their Presidency of Fort St. George; by which Conspiracy he was removed in Sept. 1789, during the Administration of Messrs. Hollond, from his station of Member of the Board of Revenue and Persian Translator.

Of this Conspiracy they were all convicted at the Quarter Sessions held at Fort St. George, the 11th, 12th, and 13th days of July, 1792, after a Trial which lasted above 27 hours.

To the Trial is prefixed an Address to the Public by Mr. Haliburton, detailing all the particulars which led to this Conspiracy, as also the subsequent proceedings of and correspondence with Government, to the time an enquiry was set on foot in Feb. 1792, which traced this Conspiracy to its source, and enabled Mr. Haliburton to prosecute the Conspirators to Conviction.

☞ Subscribers are requested to give in their Names to J. Murray, Fleet-street.

FOR GENTLEMEN GOING TO INDIA.

BOOKS printed for J. MURRAY, No. 32, Fleet-London, London.

And recommended by the Hon. the Court of Directors to their Governors, Councils, and other Servants abroad.

This Day is published,

Very handsomely printed at the Clarendon Press, Oxford, in Two large Volumes in Folio, Price Ten Guineas, bound.

A DICTIONARY: Persian, Arabic, and English; and English, Persian, and Arabic.

By JOHN RICHARDSON, Esq. F. S. A.

Of the Middle Temple, and of Wadham College, Oxford.

Where may be had,

I. A Grammar of the Arabic Language, 4to. Price 13s. bound. By the same.

II. A Grammar of the Persian Language, by Mr. Jones, 4to.—Price 13s. bound.

III. Institutes of Timour, improperly called Tamerlane, translated from the Persian by Major Davy and Mr. White; with Notes and Cuts, Persian and English, 4to. 1l. 11s. 6d. boards.

IV. Dr. Clark's Observations on the Diseases which prevail in long Voyages to warm Countries, particularly to the East Indies; a new Edition, enlarged, in two Volumes, price 10s. in boards.

V. Letters and Essays of the Diseases in the West Indies, 8vo. boards, 4s.

VI. Dr. Bell's Enquiry into the Causes and Means of preventing Diseases in the Army in the West Indies, 8vo. 3s. 6d. boards.

VII. Dr. Jackson's Treatise on the Fevers of Jamaica, &c. 8vo. boards, 6s. 6d.

VIII. Dr. Robertson's Observations on Fevers, and other Diseases, which occur in Voyages to Africa and the West Indies, 4to. 12s. boards.

IX. Bontius's Account of the Diseases which prevail in the East Indies, 8vo. 5s. bound.

X. Dr. Blane's Observations on the Diseases incident to Seamen, just published, large 8vo. 7s. bound.

XI. The English Review for January, 1793, and all the preceding Numbers, 1s. each.

*** At No. 32, Fleet-street, Gentlemen going to India may be supplied with a proper Assortment of valuable Books and new Publications, adapted to the Country and the Voyage.

CHELSEA HOSPITAL,

Jan. 25, 1793.

THESE are by Order of the Right Hon. the Lords and others Commissioners for managing the Affairs of the Royal Hospital at Chelsea, to give Notice, that his Majesty has been pleased to order that all Out Pensioners (the Cavalry, Lettermen, such as by the Hospital Books are upwards of fifty years of age, those who have served twenty-five years in the Army, previous to their discharges, as well as all those who may be blind, or have lost their limbs excepted) belonging to the said Hospital, and residing in London, or within the distance of twenty-five miles thereof, do personally and regimentally appear at the said Hospital on the several respective days as are undermentioned, and appointed for them, and when and where attendance will be given from nine o'clock in the morning, till three in the afternoon, in order to be examined by a Board to be held, for the purpose of their being sent to Garrison only.

Notice is also given, that every man found fit for duty, on his arrival at the Garrison to which he shall be sent, shall be entitled to a Bounty of One Guinea, or so much thereof as shall remain after supplying him with proper necessaries, and that he be accounted with for his subsistence as an Invalid for the number of days deemed requisite for his journey, from the place of his residence to his appointed Garrison; and those who, on examination are found unfit for Duty, are to be dismissed with proportionate subsistence to carry them back to their homes.

And it is further notified, that all such of the said Out-Pensioners (except such as are above excepted) who shall not appear and shew themselves at the said Hospital, as hereby directed, will be considered as otherwise provided for by Government, or Dead, and will accordingly be struck off the Books of the said Hospital.

THURSDAY, JANUARY 31, 1793.

The Pensioners from the First and Second Regiment of Foot Guards.

FRIDAY, FEBRUARY 1.

The Third Regiment of Foot Guards, as also those from the First Regiment of Foot, to the Tenth Regiment, inclusive.

SATURDAY, FEB. 2.

Those from the Eleventh Regiment of Foot, to the Thirty-fifth of Foot, inclusive.

MONDAY, FEB. 4.

Those from the 36th Regiment of Foot, to the 66th of Foot, inclusive.

TUESDAY, FEB. 5.

Those from the 67th Regiment of Foot, to the 119th, inclusive; as also the Pensioners from Lord Strathaven's, Major Waller's, Elford's, and Fish's Corps, the Royal Garrison Battalion, Loyal, Irish, Queen's Rangers, Fencibles in North Britain, Cinque Ports, and Lancashire Volunteers, with all the American and other Corps the Pensioners from the Marines, and Independent Companies, those from the Militia, and those who have been In-Pensioners of Chelsea Hospital.

SAMUEL ESTWICK, Secretary and Register.

SCHINNER'S RHEUMATIC PILLS.

THE number of extraordinary Cures that have been performed by the use of these Pills, have long established their reputation as a sovereign and specific remedy for the Rheumatism, Rheumatic Gout, Spasms, Sciatica, Lumbago, and all other Rheumatic Complaints, however obstinate, or in whatsoever part they may be situated.

They are perfectly safe and easy in the operation, and need no other confinement than is usual with a common dose of physic. One box in general relieves, and frequently so as to restore the patient to perfect health and vigour, though the complaint may have been of several years standing.

They are sold, Wholesale and Retail, only by FRANCIS NEWBERY, at the Warehouse for Dr. James's Powder, No. 45, the East End of St. Paul's, a few Doors from the Corner of Cheapside, London, Price 3s. 6d. a Box, Duty included. And all Purchasers will observe that the Name of "F. Newbery," is engraved in the Stamp, as the most certain mark of authenticity. Sold also Retail, by his Appointment, by Mr. Steers, No. 10, Old Bond-street; Mr. Burchell, No. 79, Long-acre; Mr. Wape, No. 163, Fleet-street; Mrs. Randall, at the Royal Exchange Gate; Mr. Clarke, No. 169, Borough High-street; and by Messrs. Freake and Fallofeild, No. 3, Tottenham-court-road.

From the LONDON GAZETTE, January 26.

THE QUEEN'S HOUSE, JAN. 24.

The King was this day pleased, by his Majesty's Order in Council, to direct that Monsieur Chauvelin, late Minister Plenipotentiary from the Most Christian King, should depart the realm, on or before the 1st day of February next.

WHITEHALL, JAN. 26.

The King has been pleased to order and direct the Lord Lieutenant of the county Palatine of Lancaster to embody the whole of the Militia forces of the said county Palatine.

LORD CHAMBERLAIN'S OFFICE, JAN. 25.

Orders for the Court's going into mourning on Sunday next the 27th instant, for his late Most Christian Majesty, viz.

The Ladies to wear black silk, fringed or plain linen, white gloves, necklaces, and ear-rings, black or white shoes, fans, and tippets.—Undress, white or grey lustrings, tabbies or damasks.

The Gentlemen to wear black full trimmed, fringed or plain linen, black swords and buckles.—Undress, grey frocks.

The Court to change the mourning on Sunday the 3d of February next, viz,

The Ladies to wear black silk or velvet, coloured ribbons, fans, and tippets, or plain white, or white and gold, or white and silver stuffs, with black ribbons.

The Gentlemen to wear black coats, and black or plain white, or white and gold, or white and silver stuff waistcoats, full trimmed, coloured swords and buckles.

And on Thursday the 7th of February next, the Court to go out of mourning.

THE AVERAGE PRICE OF SUGAR,

Computed from the Returns made in the week ending the 23d of January, 1793, is 54s. 7¾d. per Hundred Weight, exclusive of the Duty of Customs paid or payable thereon, on the Importation thereof into Great Britain.

BANKRUPTCIES ENLARGED.

John Pain, of Watling-street, Merchant, to surrender Feb. 23, at ten, at Guildhall,

William Inglis, late of Bloomsbury Square, Tea-dealer, to surrender March 12, at ten, at Guildhall.

BANKRUPTS.

Richard Mulford, of Bristol, Grocer, to surrender Feb. 13, 14, and March 9, at five, at the White Hart, in Broad-street, Bristol. Attorney, Messrs, G. and T. Pearson, Pump-Court, Temple.

David Davis, of Monmouth, Mercer, to surrender January 28, and March 8 and 9, at ten, at the Beaufort's Arms, Monmouth. Attornies, Messrs. Hill and Meredith, No. 15, Gray's Inn, London.

Peter Sharples, Thomas Bennett, and William Halstead, of Copthurst, Lancaster, and Thomas Knipe, of Manchester, Callico Printers, to surrender Feb. 11, 12, and March 9, at four, at the Star Inn, Manchester. Attorney, Mr. Foulkes, Hart-street, Bloomsbury Square.

Thomas Smith, late of Fleet-street, Haberdasher, to surrender Jan. 30, and Feb. 13, and March 2, at ten, at Guildhall. Attorney, Mr. Day, No. 1, Pump Court, Temple.

Timothy Brown, late of Marlborough, Wilts, Innholder, to surrender Feb. 8, 9, and March 9, at eleven, at the Bear and Castle Inn, Marlborough. Attornies, Messrs. Mayo and Ford, Old City Chambers, Bishopsgate-street.

John Cleaver, the younger, of St. George's Fields, Surry, Victualler, to surrender Feb. 2, 16, and March 9, at ten, at Guildhall. Attorney, Mr. Davies, Great St. Helen's, Bishopsgate-street.

James Banks, of East Smithfield, Haberdasher, to surrender Feb. 2, 16, and March 9, at eleven, at Guildhall. Attorney, Mr. Loxley, Bucklersbury, London.

William Young, of Poole, Rope-Maker, to surrender Feb. 11, at four, and 12, at eleven, and March 2, at four, at the New Antelope Inn, in Poole. Attornies, Messrs. Allen, Clifford's Inn.

Thomas Bennett, now or late of Copthurst, Township of Whittle in the Woods, Lancaster, Callico-printer, to surrender Feb. 1, 2, and March 9, at eleven, at the New Black Bull Inn, Blackburn, Attornies, Messrs. Shawe and Phillips, New Bridge-street, London.

Thomas Cood, of Gracechurch-street, Haberdasher, to surrender Feb. 2, 5, and March 9, at ten, at Guildhall. Attorney, Mr. Toulmin, Walbrook.

John Pike, of Fleet-street, Taylor, to surrender Feb. 2, at ten, and 16, at eleven, and March 9, at ten, at Guildhall. Attornies, Messrs. Tunnard and Sadler, Bucklersbury, London.

Thomas Clarke, now or late of Lyme Regis, Dorsetshire, Mealman, to surrender Feb. 5, 12, and March 9, at ten, at Mr. Alpin's, the George Inn, in Lyme Regis. Attorney, Benjamin Follett, of the Temple, London.

Robert Dobinson, of Duke-street, St. James's, Westminster, Money Scrivener, to surrender Feb. 2, at eleven, and 5, at six, and March 9, at four, at Guildhall. Attorney, Mr. Barren, Scotland Yard, or No. 11, James-street, Westminster.

Giles Dean, of Dean's Buildings, Walworth, Surry, Builder, to surrender Feb. 2, at twelve, and 5, at six, and March 9, at four, at Guildhall. Attornies, Messrs. Lane and Edmunds Hatton-street, London.

John Hopwood, late of Castle-street, Southwark, Surry, Glove Manufacturer, to surrender Jan. 30, Feb. 13, and March 9, at ten, at Guildhall. Attornies, Messrs. Crowther and Peale, Guildhall Yard, London.

George Donadieu, of Hatton-street, Brandy Merchant, to surrender Feb. 2, at twelve, and Feb. 9, at six, and March 9, at four, at Guildhall. Attornies, Messrs. Pender and Syms, Wardrobe Place, Doctors Commons, London.

DIVIDENDS.

Feb. 16. James Syme, of London, Merchant, at eleven, at Guildhall.

Feb. 16 Thomas Hervey, late of Blackheath, Lewisham, Kent, Dealer, at ten, at Guildhall.

Feb. 16. George Walker, late of Greetham, Rutlandshire, Innholder.

Feb. 19. James Robertson and James Hutchison, of Fleet-street, Oilmen, at eleven, at Guildhall.

Feb. 6. Matthew Wiggins, of Market-street, St. John the Evangelist, Westminster, Brewer, at twelve, at Guildhall,

Feb. 16. Thomas Row, of Newcastle upon Tyne, Ship Owner, at eleven, at Guildhall.

Feb. 16. Thomas Harrison, of the Hamlet of Ratcliffe, St. Dunstan, Stepney, Coal Factor, at ten, at Guildhall.

Feb. 15. Edward Wilmott, of Claverham, Yatton, Somersetshire, at eleven, at the Bush Tavern, in Corn-street, Bristol.

March 9. Thomas Smith, late of Sweeting's Alley, Cornhill, Stationer.

Feb. 20. William Dirrick, of Westmorland Buildings, Aldersgate-street, Watchmaker, at ten, at Guildhall.

Feb. 16. William Pearcey, late of St. Saviour, Southwark, at eleven, Guildhall.

CERTIFICATES

To be granted on or before the 16th of February.

Anna Cheslyn and John Thomas Cheslyn, of Aldgate, High street, Ironmongers.

Thomas Hoare, of Holborn, Cutler.

William Wakelin, of Windmill-street, Haymarket.

John Turney, of Pudding Lane, Apothecary

James Newby, late of St. Martin's Lane, Money Scrivener.

Floyd Clay Peck, of Chelmsford.

THE TIMES.

LONDON.

Business in Parliament for the Week, as it now stands:

HOUSE OF LORDS.

MONDAY.—Lord GRENVILLE to deliver a Communication from the KING, of an intention to increase the National Forces.

TUESDAY.—Scotch Election Petitions.——The Judges to deliver their Answers to the Law Questions put to them last Sessions.——Committee on Johnstone's Name Bill.

HOUSE OF COMMONS.

MONDAY.—Mr. DUNDAS to deliver a Message from his MAJESTY, respecting an Augmentation of the Army.——The Land and Malt Taxes to be brought forward in the Committee of Ways and Means.

TUESDAY.—Mr. WILBERFORCE to move on the Subject of the Slave Trade.

FURTHER PARTICULARS OF THE *EXECUTION OF LOUIS XVI.*

EXTRACT OF A PRIVATE LETTER FROM PARIS, BY A GENTLEMAN WHO WAS A SPECTATOR OF THE EXECUTION OF LOUIS XVI.

"I have been a spectator of one of the most tragical sights that ever my eyes witnessed; but the circumstance was of too much importance to allow me to be absent from the spectacle. Upwards of 60,000 horse and foot were on duty.

"The Mayor's carriage being arrived at the place of execution, drew up close to the scaffold. The two executioners approached the coach. The King and his Confessor then got out of it. The King, on mounting the scaffold, instantly took off his stock himself, as well as his great coat, and unfastened his shirt collar. His hair had been clubbed up close like an Abbe's, in order that no indignity might be offered him, or that it should occasion delay by hanging loose. The executioner went to tie up his arms, which the King recoiled at; but it was soon done. —The executioner then took up a large pair of scissars to cut off his hair. The King appeared mortified at what was doing, and said, 'I have put all right'—The executioner, however, cut the hair off.

"His Majesty then said, 'I pardon my enemies—May my death be useful to the nation.' The executioners then placed him to be beheaded; the King recoiled, and said—'Another moment, that I may speak to the people. The *Aid de Camp* to the Commandant, *Santerre*, then said to *Henri Sauson*, the executioner, "Do your duty." The wedge then slipt, and his head was instantly off. Two minutes after the head was shewn to the people, and, with the body, thrown into a long basket, and taken to the Church-yard of St. Magdelaine, where it was immediately buried.

"The time of the arrival of the carriage at the scaffold, to the King's mounting, was precisely ten minutes, and six minutes after he was executed; for very particular orders had been given, that as little time as possible should be employed in the execution. In nine minutes after, the body was removed.

"From a particular acquaintance with some of the Municipal Officers, I learn, that, on the Thursday preceding the execution, the King was permitted to see the Queen, for the first time for a month. It was in the presence of six Municipal officers. LOUIS said to the Queen—'I am told the Convention has condemned me to death.—I exhort you to prepare yourself for the like fate. I pray you to bear up the minds of our children to meet the like sacrifice, for we shall all be victims.'

"A dead silence reigns in the public streets of Paris; but all the playhouses are open, and the city is illuminated every night, as if the French wished to make their wickedness more visible."

Yesterday morning THEIR MAJESTIES and the PRINCESSES attended Divine Service at St. George's Chapel, Windsor; the Sermon was preached by Dr. WILSON Canon in Residence. The Royal Family appeared in mourning for his late Most Christian Majesty.

On Thursday the QUEEN will have a Drawing Room at James's.

On Wednesday the LORDS SPIRITUAL and TEMPORAL will attend divine service at St. Margaret's Church, it being the Anniversary of the Martyrdom of CHARLES the FIRST.

Yesterday Lord RAWDON had an interview with his Royal Highness the PRINCE of WALES, at Carlton House.

His Royal Highness the Prince of WALES is appointed Colonel of the 10th regiment of Light Dragoons with the rank of a General in the Army, vice Sir WM. PITT.

A COUNCIL is summoned to meet this day at Lord GRENVILLE's Office, Whitehall.

This day both Houses of Parliament meet pursuant to their last adjournment, when it is supposed a message will be delivered from his MAJESTY, stating the necessity of an immediate declaration of war against France.

The PRINCE of WALES has given a very leading Gentleman of *Opposition*, and who has hitherto been supposed to be much in his Royal Highness's confidence, to understand, that his visits at Carlton-House would no longer be agreeable.

It would certainly have been becoming in the good LORD CHAMBERLAIN to have made the order for a general mourning a little more public, especially as the notice in the Gazette was necessarily obliged to be very short, and could only be generally known this day. Publishing a notice of such general importance in one or two obscure newspapers, is not paying that respect to the public convenience which ought to be done. If, out of such a large income, the trifling expence of an advertisement was an object, we should willingly have inserted it at our own cost. It is a very paltry saving.

On Saturday Earl HOWE received his commission as Commander in Chief of the Channel fleet.

On Friday the following ships were commissioned by the Admiralty:—The Berwick, of 74 guns, Sir JOHN COLLINS; St. Alban's, of 64, Capt. VASHON; Ulysses, of 44, Capt. ———; Beaulieu, of 40, Earl of NORTHESK, and Ariadne, of 20 guns.

It is said that the number of seamen to be voted this day is 30,000l.

It is said that a subscription is about to be opened by some patriotic Gentlemen, for the support of the WAR. It will give us very particular pleasure, to know of such a plan being carried into execution.

The DUTCH are under great apprehension, on account of the camp forming near Antwerp, composed of the disaffected people from Holland, who have established themselves under the title of STATES GENERAL, and assume to themselves the right of legislation.

The different reports about town of new murders in Paris, and also of the death of the Princess Royal, are wholly unfounded. We have letters from Paris of the date of last Thursday, which are silent on the subject. The Convention is much puzzled how to act, in respect to the Queen.

The Trafalgar edition

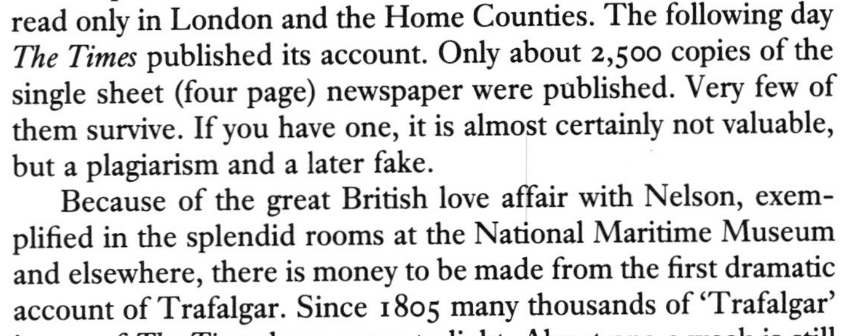

This account of the Battle of Trafalgar and the death of Nelson is one of the most famous front pages ever carried by *The Times*. The one opposite is a reproduction of the genuine article. Most of the thousands of others are fakes and forgeries.

It was a famous victory and a notable event in naval (and newspaper) history. 'The death of Nelson was felt in England as something more than a public calamity; men started at the intelligence, and turned pale, as if they had heard of the loss of a dear friend' (Robert Southey).

With Trafalgar *The Times* could not claim (as it often could) to have scooped the world with the news and to be ahead even of the official communiqué. The battle that removed any threat of an invasion of England and established British naval supremacy was fought on 21 October 1805. On 6 November the *London Gazette* published news of the Triumph and Tragedy, but it was read only in London and the Home Counties. The following day *The Times* published its account. Only about 2,500 copies of the single sheet (four page) newspaper were published. Very few of them survive. If you have one, it is almost certainly not valuable, but a plagiarism and a later fake.

Because of the great British love affair with Nelson, exemplified in the splendid rooms at the National Maritime Museum and elsewhere, there is money to be made from the first dramatic account of Trafalgar. Since 1805 many thousands of 'Trafalgar' issues of *The Times* have come to light. About one a week is still sent in to *The Times* for valuation. They are all the work of jobbing printers throughout the country publishing, without the authority of *The Times*, copies of or improvements on the original issue for sale to gullible tourists and such cattle.

The rip-off began not many years after Trafalgar; it was at its height in the late nineteenth and early twentieth centuries, when the Navy League used to organize the then ceremonious national anniversary on 21 October in Trafalgar Square. Hawkers did a good trade selling patriotic souvenirs, including pamphlets, broadsheets and books. Southey's *Life of Nelson* was very popular. But top of the pops and the annual best-seller was what purported to be a genuine issue of *The Times* of 7 November 1805.

At first the spurious issues were copies. Later printers grew careless, and gradually ludicrous attempts at verisimilitude, which could deceive nobody who had ever read the ancient organ, were being hawked around and bought by the simple-minded. The practice has continued till very recently.

What, then, are the distinguishing marks of the spurious copies? How can we recognize the real thing? These are not academic, bibliomane questions – we have to deal with them all the time at New Printing House Square. An attic is cleared. A dead man's possessions are sold. An old house is demolished. And sure enough, here is the story of the victory and the death of Nelson in the famous issue of *The Times*, proclaimed and published from London, from the provinces, and even from enterprising printing houses in the Commonwealth. Of the thousands that have been sent hopefully in to *The Times*, not one has yet been certified as genuine. This is not surprising. After bubbles and other hot air, of all materials newspapers are the most ephemeral. Even museums have been caught out displaying what was thought to be a blue-moon original Trafalgar *Times*.

It is not usually hard to detect a fake Trafalgar issue. If the front page has four columns of advertising, smell a rat: the genuine issue carried advertisements only in column 1; the Admiralty dispatch, because of the importance of the news, ousted ads and began in column 2. If the price is printed as 6d, it is a fake: the original spelt it out as sixpence. If the news of the victory is carried in the same issue as a poem on the death of Nelson, which actually appeared in the issue of 7 December, then that is a particularly blatant forgery.

If the copy of *The Times* does not carry the newspaper duty stamp, it is probably not genuine. In theory all newspapers of that period were stamped. In practice single sheets were sometimes missed in the stamping process, or the stamp may have been cropped when the sheet was bound into a volume. In general the absence of a stamp is yet another indication of forgery.

Anything that purports to be a Trafalgar issue of *The Times* must be looked at with beady and sceptical eyes. If it passes the tests already mentioned, we shall need to compare the coat of arms, the clock device, and then the typography with the original. The chances are, if you think that you have a Trafalgar issue, that you have struck not gold but a forgery.

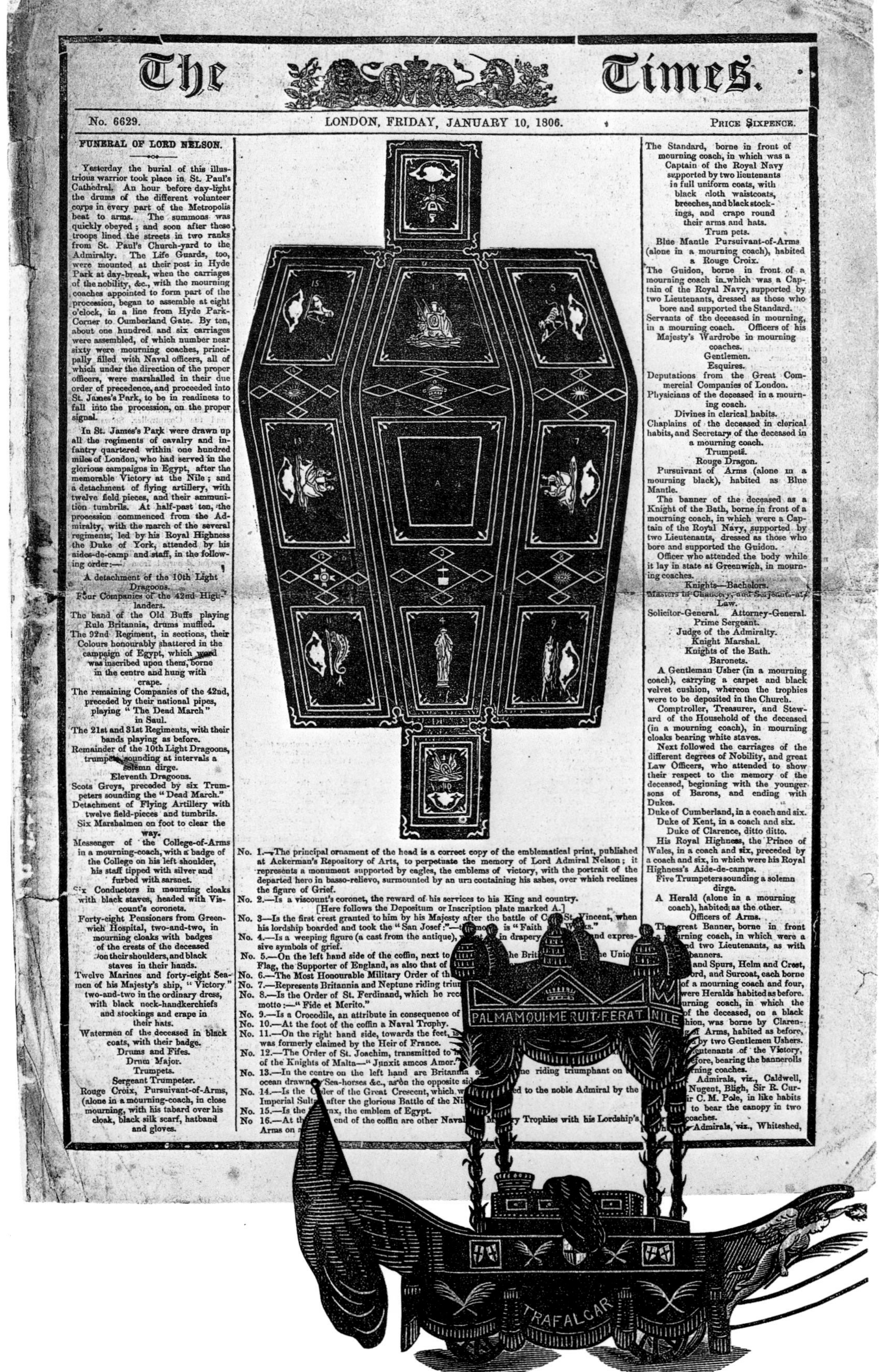

The Times.

No. 6629. LONDON, FRIDAY, JANUARY 10, 1806. PRICE SIXPENCE.

FUNERAL OF LORD NELSON.

Yesterday the burial of this illustrious warrior took place in St. Paul's Cathedral. An hour before day-light the drums of the different volunteer corps in every part of the Metropolis beat to arms. The summons was quickly obeyed; and soon after these troops lined the streets in two ranks from St. Paul's Church-yard to the Admiralty. The Life Guards, too, were mounted at their post in Hyde Park at day-break, when the carriages of the nobility, &c., with the mourning coaches appointed to form part of the procession, began to assemble at eight o'clock, in a line from Hyde Park-Corner to Cumberland Gate. By ten, about one hundred and six carriages were assembled, of which number near sixty were mourning coaches, principally filled with Naval officers, all of which under the direction of the proper officers, were marshalled in their due order of precedence, and proceeded into St. James's Park, to be in readiness to fall into the procession, on the proper signal.

In St. James's Park were drawn up all the regiments of cavalry and infantry quartered within one hundred miles of London, who had served in the glorious campaigns in Egypt, after the memorable Victory at the Nile; and a detachment of flying artillery, with twelve field pieces, and their ammunition tumbrils. At half-past ten, the procession commenced from the Admiralty, with the march of the several regiments, led by his Royal Highness the Duke of York, attended by his aides-de-camp and staff, in the following order:—

A detachment of the 10th Light Dragoons.
Four Companies of the 42nd Highlanders.
The band of the Old Buffs playing Rule Britannia, drums muffled.
The 92nd Regiment, in sections, their Colours honourably shattered in the campaign of Egypt, which word was inscribed upon them, borne in the centre and hung with crape.
The remaining Companies of the 42nd, preceded by their national pipes, playing "The Dead March" in Saul.
The 21st and 31st Regiments, with their bands playing as before.
Remainder of the 10th Light Dragoons, trumpets sounding at intervals a solemn dirge.
Eleventh Dragoons.
Scots Greys, preceded by six Trumpeters sounding the "Dead March."
Detachment of Flying Artillery with twelve field-pieces and tumbrils.
Six Marshalmen on foot to clear the way.
Messenger of the College-of-Arms in a mourning-coach, with a badge of the College on his left shoulder, his staff tipped with silver and furbed with sarsnet.
Six Conductors in mourning cloaks with black staves, headed with Viscount's coronets.
Forty-eight Pensioners from Greenwich Hospital, two-and-two, in mourning cloaks with badges of the crests of the deceased on their shoulders, and black staves in their hands.
Twelve Marines and forty-eight Seamen of his Majesty's ship, "Victory" two-and-two in the ordinary dress, with black neck-handkerchiefs and stockings and crape in their hats.
Watermen of the deceased in black coats, with their badge.
Drums and Fifes.
Drum Major.
Trumpets.
Sergeant Trumpeter.
Rouge Croix, Pursuivant-of-Arms, (alone in a mourning-coach, in close mourning, with his tabard over his cloak, black silk scarf, hatband and gloves.

No. 1.—The principal ornament of the head is a correct copy of the emblematical print, published at Ackerman's Repository of Arts, to perpetuate the memory of Lord Admiral Nelson; it represents a monument supported by eagles, the emblems of victory, with the portrait of the departed hero in basso-relievo, surmounted by an urn containing his ashes, over which reclines the figure of Grief.
No. 2.—Is a viscount's coronet, the reward of his services to his King and country.
[Here follows the Depositum or Inscription plate marked A.]
No. 3—Is the first crest granted to him by his Majesty after the battle of C[illegible] St. Vincent, when his lordship boarded and took the "San Josef:"—t[illegible] is "Faith [illegible] Works."
No. 4.—Is a weeping figure (a cast from the antique), [illegible] in drapery [illegible] and expressive symbols of grief.
No. 5.—On the left hand side of the coffin, next to [illegible] the Brit[illegible] the Unio[illegible] Flag, the Supporter of England, as also that of [illegible]
No. 6.—The Most Honourable Military Order of th[illegible]
No. 7.—Represents Britannia and Neptune riding triu[illegible]
No. 8.—Is the Order of St. Ferdinand, which he rec[illegible] motto:—"Fide et Merito."
No. 9.—Is a Crocodile, an attribute in consequence of [illegible]
No. 10.—At the foot of the coffin a Naval Trophy.
No. 11.—On the right hand side, towards the feet, is [illegible] was formerly claimed by the Heir of France.
No. 12.—The Order of St. Joachim, transmitted to [illegible] of the Knights of Malta—"Junxit amcos Amor."
No. 13.—In the centre on the left hand are Britannia a[illegible] riding triumphant on [illegible] ocean drawn by Sea-horses &c., as on the opposite sid[illegible]
No. 14.—Is the Order of the Great Crescent, which w[illegible] ed to the noble Admiral by the Imperial Sulta[illegible] after the glorious Battle of the Ni[illegible]
No. 15.—Is the [illegible]nx, the emblem of Egypt.
No 16.—At th[illegible] end of the coffin are other Naval [illegible] y Trophies with his Lordship's Arms on [illegible]

The Standard, borne in front of mourning coach, in which was a Captain of the Royal Navy supported by two lieutenants in full uniform coats, with black cloth waistcoats, breeches, and black stockings, and crape round their arms and hats.
Trum pets.
Blue Mantle Pursuivant-of-Arms (alone in a mourning coach), habited a Rouge Croix.
The Guidon, borne in front of a mourning coach in which was a Captain of the Royal Navy, supported by two Lieutenants, dressed as those who bore and supported the Standard.
Servants of the deceased in mourning, in a mourning coach. Officers of his Majesty's Wardrobe in mourning coaches.
Gentlemen.
Esquires.
Deputations from the Great Commercial Companies of London.
Physicians of the deceased in a mourning coach.
Divines in clerical habits.
Chaplains of the deceased in clerical habits, and Secretary of the deceased in a mourning coach.
Trumpets.
Rouge Dragon.
Pursuivant of Arms (alone in a mourning black), habited as Blue Mantle.
The banner of the deceased as a Knight of the Bath, borne in front of a mourning coach, in which were a Captain of the Royal Navy, supported by two Lieutenants, dressed as those who bore and supported the Guidon.
Officer who attended the body while it lay in state at Greenwich, in mourning coaches.
Knights—Bachelors.
Masters in Chancery, and Serjeants-at-Law.
Solicitor-General. Attorney-General.
Prime Sergeant.
Judge of the Admiralty.
Knight Marshal.
Knights of the Bath.
Baronets.
A Gentleman Usher (in a mourning coach), carrying a carpet and black velvet cushion, whereon the trophies were to be deposited in the Church.
Comptroller, Treasurer, and Steward of the Household of the deceased (in a mourning coach), in mourning cloaks bearing white staves.
Next followed the carriages of the different degrees of Nobility, and great Law Officers, who attended to show their respect to the memory of the deceased, beginning with the younger sons of Barons, and ending with Dukes.
Duke of Cumberland, in a coach and six.
Duke of Kent, in a coach and six.
Duke of Clarence, ditto ditto.
His Royal Highness, the Prince of Wales, in a coach and six, preceded by a coach and six, in which were his Royal Highness's Aide-de-camps.
Five Trumpeters sounding a solemn dirge.
A Herald (alone in a mourning coach), habited as the other.
Officers of Arms.
The great Banner, borne in front [illegible] mourning coach, in which were a [illegible] and two Lieutenants, as with [illegible] banners.
[illegible] and Spurs, Helm and Crest, [illegible]rd, and Surcoat, each borne [illegible] of a mourning coach and four, [illegible] were Heralds habited as before.
[illegible] mourning coach, in which the [illegible] of the deceased, on a black [illegible] cushion, was borne by Claren[illegible] of Arms, habited as before, [illegible] by two Gentlemen Ushers.
[illegible] Lieutenants of the Victory, [illegible] before, bearing the bannerolls [illegible] mourning coaches.
[illegible] Admirals, viz., Caldwell, [illegible] Nugent, Bligh, Sir R. Cur[illegible] Sir C. M. Pole, in like habits [illegible] to bear the canopy in two [illegible] coaches.
[illegible] Admirals, viz., Whitehed,

Below The front page of 10 January 1806 carried the account of Lord Nelson's funeral at St Paul's Cathedral on the previous day. The woodcut showed the coffin panels, engraved with various crests and allegorical figures related to Nelson's campaigns. The woodcut of the 'funeral car' that bore the coffin, printed on page 2 of the same issue, inset below.

The front page announcement of the death of Nelson at the Battle of Trafalgar. The report on page 3 of the same issue declared: 'There was not a man who did not think that the life of the Hero of the Nile was too great a price for the capture and destruction of twenty sail of French and Spanish men of war.'

7 NOVEMBER 1805

Times.

NUMBER 6572. LONDON, THURSDAY, NOVEMBER 7, 1805. PRICE SIXPENCE.

The LONDON GAZETTE EXTRAORDINARY.

WEDNESDAY, NOV 6, 1805.

ADMIRALTY-OFFICE, Nov. 6.

Dispatches, of which the following are Copies, were received at the Admiralty this day, at one o'clock A. M. from Vice-Admiral Collingwood, Commander in Chief of his Majesty's ships and vessels off Cadiz:—

SIR, *Euryalus, off Cape Trafalgar, Oct. 22, 1805.*

The ever-to-be-lamented death of Vice-Admiral Lord Viscount Nelson, who, in the late conflict with the enemy, fell in the hour of victory, leaves to me the duty of informing my Lords Commissioners of the Admiralty, that on the 19th instant, it was communicated to the Commander in Chief, from the ships watching the motions of the enemy in Cadiz, that the Combined Fleet had put to sea; as they sailed with light winds westerly, his Lordship concluded their destination was the Mediterranean, and immediately made all sail for the Streights' entrance, with the British Squadron, consisting of twenty-seven ships, three of them sixty-fours, where his Lordship was informed, by Captain Blackwood (whose vigilance in watching, and giving notice of the enemy's movements, has been highly meritorious), that they had not yet passed the Streights.

On Monday the 21st instant, at day-light, when Cape Trafalgar bore E. by S. about seven leagues, the enemy was discovered six or seven miles to the Eastward, the wind about West, and very light; the Commander in Chief immediately made the signal for the fleet to bear up in two columns, as they are formed in order of sailing; a mode of attack his Lordship had previously directed, to avoid the inconvenience and delay in forming a line of battle in the usual manner. The enemy's line consisted of thirty-three ships (of which eighteen were French, and fifteen Spanish), commanded in Chief by Admiral Villeneuve: the Spaniards, under the direction of Gravina, wore, with their heads to the Northward, and formed their line of battle with great closeness and correctness; but as the mode of attack was unusual, so the structure of their line was new; it formed a crescent, convexing to leeward, so that, in leading down to their centre, I had both their van and rear abaft the beam; before the fire opened, every alternate ship was about a cable's length to windward of her second a-head and a-stern, forming a kind of double line, and appeared, when on their beam, to leave a very little interval between them; and this without crowding their ships. Admiral Villeneuve was in the Bucentaure, in the centre, and the Prince of Asturias bore Gravina's flag in the rear, but the French and Spanish ships were mixed without any apparent regard to order of national squadron.

As the mode of our attack had been previously determined on, and communicated to the Flag-Officers, and Captains, few signals were necessary, and none were made, except to direct close order as the lines bore down.

The Commander in Chief, in the Victory, led the weather column, and the Royal Sovereign, which bore my flag, the lee.

The action began at twelve o'clock, by the leading ships of the columns breaking through the enemy's line, the Commander in Chief about the tenth ship from the van, the Second in Command about the twelfth from the rear, leaving the van of the enemy unoccupied; the succeeding ships breaking through, in all parts, astern of their leaders, and engaging the enemy at the muzzles of their guns; the conflict was severe; the enemy's ships were fought with a gallantry highly honourable to their Officers; but the attack on them was irresistible, and it pleased the Almighty Disposer of all events to grant his Majesty's arms a complete and glorious victory. About three P. M. many of the enemy's ships having struck their colours, their line gave way; Admiral Gravina, with ten ships joining their frigates to leeward, stood towards Cadiz. The five headmost ships in their van tacked, and standing to the Southward, to windward of the British line, were engaged, and the sternmost of them taken; the others went off, leaving to his Majesty's squadron nineteen ships of the line (of which two are first rates, the Santissima Trinidad and the Santa Anna,) with three Flag Officers, viz. Admiral Villeneuve, the Commander in Chief; Don Ignatio Maria D'Aliva, Vice Admiral; and the Spanish Rear-Admiral, Don Baltazar Hidalgo Cisneros.

After such a Victory, it may appear unnecessary to enter into encomiums on the particular parts taken by the several Commanders; the conclusion says more on the subject than I have language to express; the spirit which animated all was the same: when all exert themselves zealously in their country's service, all deserve that their high merits should stand recorded; and never was high merit more conspicuous than in the battle I have described.

The Achille (a French 74), after having surrendered, by some mismanagement of the Frenchmen, took fire and blew up; two hundred of her men were saved by the Tenders.

A circumstance occurred during the action, which so strongly marks the invincible spirit of British seamen, when engaging the enemies of their country, that I cannot resist the pleasure I have in making it known to their Lordships; the Temeraire was boarded by accident, or design, by a French ship on one side, and a Spaniard on the other; the contest was vigorous, but, in the end, the Combined Ensigns were torn from the poop, and the British hoisted in their places.

Such a battle could not be fought without sustaining a great loss of men. I have not only to lament, in common with the British Navy, and the British Nation, in the Fall of the Commander in Chief, the loss of a Hero, whose name will be immortal, and his memory ever dear to his country; but my heart is rent with the most poignant grief for the death of a friend, to whom, by many years intimacy, and a perfect knowledge of the virtues of his mind, which inspired ideas superior to the common race of men, I was bound by the strongest ties of affection; a grief to which even the glorious occasion in which he fell, does not bring the consolation which, perhaps, it ought: his Lordship received a musket ball in his left breast, about the middle of the action, and sent an Officer to me immediately with his last farewell; and soon after expired.

I have also to lament the loss of those excellent Officers, Captains Duff, of the Mars, and Cooke, of the Bellerophon; I have yet heard of none others.

I fear the numbers that have fallen will be found very great, when the returns come to me; but it having blown a gale of wind ever since the action, I have not yet had it in my power to collect any reports from the ships.

The Royal Sovereign having lost her masts, except the tottering foremast, I called the Euryalus to me, while the action continued, which ship lying within hail, made my signals—a service Captain Blackwood performed with great attention: after the action, I shifted my flag to her, that I might more easily communicate my orders to, and collect the ships, and towed the Royal Sovereign out to Seaward. The whole fleet were now in a very perilous situation, many dismasted, all shattered, in thirteen fathom water, off the shoals of Trafalgar; and when I made the signal to prepare to anchor, few of the ships had an anchor to let go, their cables being shot; but the same good Providence which aided us through such a day preserved us in the night, by the wind shifting a few points, and drifting the ships off the land, except four of the captured dismasted ships, which are now at anchor off Trafalgar, and I hope will ride safe until those gales are over.

Having thus detailed the proceedings of the fleet on this occasion, I beg to congratulate their Lordships on a victory which, I hope, will add a ray to the glory of his Majesty's crown, and be attended with public benefit to our country. I am, &c.

William Marsden, Esq. (Signed) C. COLLINGWOOD.

The order in which the Ships of the British Squadron attacked the Combined Fleets, on the 21st of October, 1805.

VAN.	REAR.
Victory,	Royal Sovereign,
Temeraire,	Mars,
Neptune,	Belleisle,
Conqueror,	Tonnant,
Leviathan,	Bellerophon,
Ajax,	Colossus,
Orion,	Achille,
Agamemnon,	Polyphemus,
Minotaur,	Revenge,
Spartiate,	Swiftsure,
Britannia,	Defence,
Africa,	Thunderer,
Euryalus,	Defiance,
Sirius,	Prince,
Phœbe,	Dreadnought.
Naiad,	
Pickle Schooner,	
Entrepenante Cutter.	

(Signed) C. COLLINGWOOD.

GENERAL ORDER.

Euryalus, October 22, 1805.

The ever-to-be-lamented death of Lord Viscount Nelson, Duke of Bronté, the Commander in Chief, who fell in the action of the twenty-first, in the arms of victory, covered with glory; whose memory will be ever dear to the British Navy, and the British Nation; whose zeal for the honour of his King, and for the interests of his Country, will be ever held up as a shining example for a British Seaman—leaves to me a duty to return my thanks to the Right Honourable Rear-Admiral, the Captains, Officers, Seamen, and detachments of Royal Marines serving on board his Majesty's Squadron now under my command, for their conduct on that day; but where can I find language to express my sentiments of the valour and skill which were displayed by the Officers the Seamen, and Marines in the battle with the enemy, where every individual appeared an Hero, on whom the Glory of his Country depended; the attack was irresistible, and the issue of it adds to the page of Naval Annals a brilliant instance of what Britons can do, when their King and their Country need their service.

To the Right Honourable Rear-Admiral the Earl of Northesk, to the Captains, Officers, and Seamen and to the Officers, Non-commissioned Officers, and Privates of the Royal Marines, I beg to give my sincere and hearty thanks for their highly meritorious conduct, both in the action, and in their zeal and activity in bringing the captured ships out from the perilous situation in which they were after their surrender, among the shoals of Trafalgar, in boisterous weather.

And I desire that the respective Captains will be pleased to communicate to the Officers, Seamen, and Royal Marines, this public testimony of my high approbation of their conduct, and my thanks for it. (Signed) C. COLLINGWOOD

To the Right Honorable Rear-Admiral the Earl of Northesk, and the respective Captains and Commanders.

GENERAL ORDER.

The Almighty God, whose arm is strength, having of his great mercy been pleased to crown the exertion of his Majesty's fleet with success, in giving them a complete victory over their enemies, on 21st of this month: and that all praise and thanksgiving may be offered up to the Throne of Grace for the great benefits to our country and to mankind:

I have thought proper, that a day should be appointed of general humiliation before God, and thanksgiving for this his merciful goodness, imploring forgiveness of sins, a continuation of his divine mercy, and his constant aid to us, in the defence of our country's liberties and laws, without which the utmost efforts of man are nought; and direct, therefore, that be appointed for this holy purpose.

Given on board the Euryalus, off Cape Trafalgar, 22d Oct. 1805

(Signed) C. COLLINGWOOD.

To the respective Captains and Commanders.

N. B. The fleet having been dispersed by a gale of wind, no day has yet been able to be appointed for the above purpose.

SIR, *Euryalus, off Cadiz, Oct. 24. 1805.*

In my letter of the 22d, I detailed to you, for the information of my Lords Commissioners of the Admiralty, the proceedings of his Majesty's squadron on the day of the action, and that preceding it, since which I have had a continued series of misfortunes; but they are of a kind that human prudence could not possibly provide against, or my skill prevent.

On the 22d, in the morning, a strong southerly wind blew, with squally weather, which, however, did not prevent the activity of the Officers and Seamen of such ships as were manageable, from getting hold of many of the prizes (thirteen or fourteen), and towing them off to the Westward, where I ordered them to rendezvous round the Royal Sovereign, in tow by the Neptune: but on the 23d the gale increased, and the sea ran so high that many of them broke the tow-rope, and drifted far to leeward before they were got hold of again; and some of them, taking advantage in the dark and boisterous night, got before the wind, and have, perhaps, drifted upon the shore and sunk; on the afternoon of that day the remnant of the Combined Fleet, ten sail of ships, who had not been much engaged, stood up to leeward of my shattered and straggled charge, as if meaning to attack them, which obliged me to collect a force out of the least injured ships, and form to leeward for their defence; all this retarded the progress of the hulks, and the bad weather continuing, determined me to destroy all the leewardmost that could be cleared of the men, considering that keeping possession of the ships was a matter of little consequence, compared with the chance of their falling again into the hands of the enemy; but even this was an arduous task in the high sea which was running. I hope, however, it has been accomplished to a considerable extent; I entrusted it to skilful Officers, who would spare no pains to execute what was possible. The Captains of the Prince and Neptune cleared the Trinidad and sunk her Captains Hope, Bayntun, and Malcolm, who joined the fleet this moment from Gibraltar, had the charge of destroying four others. The Redoubtable sunk astern of the Swiftsure while in tow. The Santa Anna, I have no doubt, is sunk, as her side was almost entirely beat in; and such is the shattered condition of the whole of them, that unless the weather moderates I doubt whether I shall be able to carry a ship of them into port. I hope their Lordships will approve of what I (having only in consideration the destruction of the enemy's fleet) have thought a measure of absolute necessity.

I have taken Admiral Villeneuve into this ship; Vice-Admiral Don Aliva is dead. Whenever the temper of the weather will permit, and I can spare a frigate (for there were only four in the action with the fleet, Euryalus, Sirius, Phœbe, and Naiad; the Melpomene joined the 22d, and the Eurydice and Scout the 23d,) I shall collect the other flag officers, and send them to England, with their flags, if they do not all go to the bottom), to be laid at his Majesty's feet.

There were four thousand troops embarked, under

Old Crabby: first foreign correspondent

Henry Crabb Robinson, *c.*1818.

If William Howard Russell was the greatest war correspondent, Henry Crabb Robinson of *The Times* was the first. His life ran from 1775 to 1867; he was educated at Jena University, and was one of those sociable, gabby, xenophile Englishmen who get on like a house on fire with all sorts and nationalities of men, and make an effort to speak languages other than English. He was a wanderer, a determined bachelor, the archetypal foreign correspondent, known in the office as 'Old Crabby'.

At the beginning of the nineteenth century news of the Napoleonic wars that were redrawing the map of Europe was supplied to England only from Continental newspapers. Such information was thin, spasmodic, unreliable and biased. John Walter II decided that *The Times* needed its own special correspondent to keep an eye on Napoleon, and appointed Old Crabby in 1807. He was stationed at Altona, the capital of Holstein, on the Danish border. The town was neutral, central, and packed with refugees from France.

In January 1807 the first professional foreign correspondent left Harwich for Altona. His journey was a suitable anticipation of the rigours of the trade: it included three days without food, some time in an open boat on the North Sea in mid-winter, and two days in an open carriage.

From Altona, under the romantic byline 'From the banks of the Elbe', Crabb Robinson reported the fall of Danzig, the Battle of Friedland in which Napoleon defeated the Russians at great cost to his own troops, and the subsequent Peace of Tilsit. His dispatches were analytic as well as descriptive. After the Battle of Friedland, he argued that Russia was too vast to occupy and too unwieldy to destroy, and pointed to the conditions that forced Napoleon to retreat from Moscow five years later.

After Britain intervened in Europe to stop Napoleon, Crabb Robinson had to go on the run in disguise from the police. The French almost caught him in Hamburg, but he escaped back to Printing House Square through Sweden. While he was back Walter made him editor for a spell. Crabb Robinson, typical reporter, was not happy about his increased responsibilities. He was a writer, and he feared that after the defeat of Napoleon he might disagree with his proprietor. For the moment he agreed to take on the boring duties because 'To oppose Buonaparte is the Sum and Substance of all our public duties'.

In 1808 Crabb Robinson was off on his travels again covering Sir John Moore's advance into Spain from Portugal to threaten the rear of Napoleon's invading army. He landed at Corunna in July 1808 and as usual quickly made friends with officials and other contacts for the latest news. In Altona he had had access to sources on both sides; at Corunna the French were missing.

Below Dispatches from France, *c.*1805. During the Napoleonic Wars, the Government tried to suppress THE TIMES's criticism by stopping at the ports the foreign packages addressed to it. John Walter II organised a cutter to run between France and England, and was thus able both to free the paper from Government interference and to publish important news even before the official intelligence reached the Government. The picture shows the news report being handed to a rider, while the cutter waits at anchor.

Like Russell's in the Crimea half a century later, Crabb Robinson's dispatches described inefficiency and cock-up in the British Army:

> The utter want of all preparations for promoting the march of that Army was seen with deep affliction by both British and Spaniards. No man pretends to fix the culpability upon any one; they can only judge of those who are privy to the negotiations which preceded the expedition. The sad effect, however, is very obvious.

He pointed out however, in characteristic analysis, that as an invading army the French could live off the land whereas the British had to respect the private property of their allies, and could not forage or commandeer supplies.

Robinson has been criticized by later generations of journalists for sitting in Corunna and filing second-hand reports of the campaign, instead of accompanying the army in the field to get first-hand accounts. Let us defend the old fellow. The Peninsular Campaign was fought over notoriously difficult terrain. Roads and transport, if there were any, were terrible. There were no fixed battle lines, only a confusion of march and countermarch, and unpremeditated engagement. If Crabb Robinson had marched with the army, he would have found himself in the position that every correspondent dreads above all others: having a big story, but no method of getting it away. At Corunna Crabb Robinson was able to piece together from his many contacts an overall view of the jigsaw war that he could never have discerned in the field. His reports are one of the primary sources for the history of the war.

Robinson is more justifiably criticized for baling out just before the battle that became famous for the death and burial of Sir John Moore:

> We buried him darkly at dead of night,
> The sods with our bayonets turning.

On 11 January 1809 he saw the whole retreating British Army digging into its lines around Corunna. He wrote 'This spot will most probably become the scene of a furious and bloody contest'. A few days later, while dining in his hotel, he observed that all the officers had left the room, 'not a redcoat to be seen'. The fleet was at hand for the evacuation:

> The last two days have materially changed the appearance of things. Yesterday evening, the fleet of transports, which had been dispersed in their passage from Vigo, began to enter the harbour, and the hearts of thousands were relieved by the prospect of deliverance. I beheld this evening the beautiful bay covered with our vessels, both armed and mercantile, and I should have thought the noble three-deckers, which stood on the outside of the harbour, a proud spectacle, if I could have forgotten the inglorious service they were called to perform.

That night he boarded ship to leave Spain. The final battle was about to start. I dare say that it was a prudent time to leave. Not many of the gungho, fire-eating modern correspondents remained in Saigon for the arrival of the North Vietnamese.

From his ship he heard the rattle of musketry. It was our cavalry shooting their horses before embarking. Then he heard the powder magazine being blown up:

> When the cloud of smoke which had been raised was blown away, there was an empty space where there had been a solid building a few moments before: but this was a less exciting noise than when, about one o'clock, we heard a cannonading from the shore at the inland extremity of the bay. It was the French Army.

The Times carried an eyewitness report of an early Dunkirk. Crabb Robinson's dispatches were the first professional newspaper reports of war in the history of journalism.

A report from Crabb Robinson, from the front line of the war against Napoleon.
5 SEPTEMBER 1807

PRIVATE CORRESPONDENCE.

"BANKS OF THE ELBE, July 18.

"The spirit of reasoning and suggesting is by no means destroyed by the knowledge that peace has been signed, since we are still in utter ignorance concerning the terms of it. The expectation of the public is, that England will be the victim of this amicable adjustment; that Buonaparte has granted conditions which have the shew of liberality towards Prussia, and are calculated to flatter the ambition of Russia in the East; with no other return, than at least unbounded liberty to pursue his projects against his sole remaining enemy; or, possibly, he may have effected a sort of league against those whom he is pleased incessantly to style the tyrants of the seas. But the field of political possibility is too wide to be seen by a single glance; and the policy of Buonaparte too recondite to be detected by first appearances. Whether the spirit of revolution has at last exhausted itself; whether the peace of Tilsit will form a new and lasting basis for the public law of Europe, like that of Westphalia, time only will shew. It will not be so, if the analogy of nature be preserved also here: that beings quickly generated and born, quickly die. Our papers have remarked, in this respect, the contrast between the two treaties of peace. When the famous Congress assembled, which ended in the peace of Westphalia, two years were spent in disputing about precedency; and, even then, the contest could be decided only by an ingenious contrivance: a little round room was built, containing twelve doors, leading to twelve seats; each Ambassador had of course his own, and they all went in together. We are exempt from the follies of a former age, but we have, alas! the crimes of our own.

"Without pretending to pierce the diplomatic cloud which hangs over the destiny of Europe, and which will be probably dissipated but gradually, I will only add, that it is said Dantzic is to be restored to its ancient place among the Hanse Towns; and that Swedish Pomerania will be one of the indemnifications given to Prussia. Others are apprehensive, that Prussia will also, in return for the loss of Poland and its Westphalian and Franconian provinces, be finally put in possession of the original source of the war, Hanover. On the one hand, it would gratify the malignant genius of the Conqueror, and be a new indignity cast upon the vanquished Monarch, to compel him to receive as a boon the spoils of those very Allies, by whom he hoped to be restored to his dominions. It would be a seed of new jealousy and hate; and having in the field lost all but honour, in the Cabinet he would be made to lose that too. Yet, on the other hand, it is the undoubted policy of France, that Hanover should be again restored to the King of England; a sort of vassalage, at least, would thus be established, and the easy means afforded of punishing any resistance to the will of the master. I have no means of judging whether your present Ministers are in danger of being the dupes of such a policy.

"On the 13th, the war was renewed in Pomerania. The army under Brune advanced, as I am informed from very good authority, with a force twice as numerous as that of the King of Sweden; 15,000 retreated in good order before 30,000. Pomerania was of necessity abandoned to the enemy, and Stralsund is again in a state of siege. The singular position of this fortress, and the power of inundating the environs, may prevent it long from falling into the hands of the enemy; but now that the war is at an end, it is not easy to imagine any service gained to—I was about to say—the common cause, having forgotten for a moment, that that cause is now annihilated. I know not how Sweden or England will be materially benefited by the possession of a place from which an attack might be made, when they have no power which can make the attack.

"General Blucher has left Stralsund, and has marched towards Colberg. You will be also not displeased to hear that the English were still on the Island of Rugen, when the army under Brune advanced, and were therefore unable to give any aid when the attack was made; they at least have not retreated before an army of invaders.

"We have at length received the French accounts of the Revolution in Constantinople; from which it results, that this bloody scene was a mere ordinary Turkish succession, such as the annals of the savage Ottoman Empire present in every age.

"It is said, that the farce of reconciliation between the ancient Sovereigns of the North and the new Emperor of Gaul, has been played by all the Imperial and Royal actors, with more or less grace. Alexander, according to private letters from Copenhagen, secured himself an affectionate embrace from Napoleon, by the hasty salutation of *Emperor*.

"When Buonaparte heard that the unfortunate but amiable Queen of Prussia, whom he had himself, a few months before, called contemptuously Madame de Strelitz, was on the road to Tilsit, he rode to meet her; and the rencontre took place several leagues from the head-quarters. He addressed her, as it is said, in these words:—' My dear Cousin, since your misfortunes, you have never ceased to occupy my thoughts!'"

STATE PAPERS.

CIRCULAR NOTE FROM THE COURT OF VIENNA TO THE BELLIGERENT POWERS.

"The Emperor Francis I. could not see, without the greatest regret, the revival of war last Autumn, between his Majesty the Emperor of the French and King of Italy, and his Majesty the King of Prussia; and he was soon after more deeply affected, to see hostilities extend, and fall upon a great part of Europe. If guided by a principle of strict and rigorous impartiality from the first, his Imperial, Royal, and Apostolic Majesty has had the good fortune to maintain in these stormy periods his system of neutrality, and to preserve his people from the misfortunes of war, he has not the less lamented the calamities which were multiplied around his dominions; and in his just fear for the tranquillity and security of his kingdom, he could not conceal from himself, either the perpetually recurring alarms on his frontiers, or the sinister effects experienced by several branches of its internal Administration. The Emperor, invariably animated by the same dispositions, had no other views from the commencement, and during the course of hostilities, than to labour to bring about a reconciliation, and to avail himself of every favourable opportunity to put an end to the misfortunes of war. He conceived, that the best mode of attaining this salutary object, was constantly to impress upon the Belligerent Powers his sentiments of moderation and conciliation, and studiously to endeavour to excite in them correspondent dispositions.

"The confidence which a prospect so consoling inspires, the general welfare and the interests of his own States, make it the duty of his Majesty to present to the Belligerent Powers his friendly interposition, and, in consequence, he does not hesitate to communicate to ———— the offer of his mediation and good offices.

"But, considering the extended and complicated nature of the present war, the Emperor would feel that he had but imperfectly expressed his ardent wishes for peace, and his hopes of its speedy and complete re-establishment, if he did not declare, at the same time, his firm conviction, that it can be only by the united attention of all the Powers concerned in the war, and by a general negociation which should comprehend their respective interests, that permanent tranquillity, and such a solid and durable peace as may, for the future, confirm the political relations of Europe, can be established. From this strong impression, which the frankness of his Majesty's character will not allow him to conceal, his Imperial Majesty feels it to be his duty to communicate this pacific overture to those Cabinets who are to take a part in the conferences; and, in consequence, he hastens equally to invite the Courts of St. Petersburgh, London, and the Thuilleries, to adopt the same views of conciliation, and to enter into negotiations for peace, in which the most important concerns of all the parties interested may be combined, as far as it is possible.

"The Emperor has expressed his earnest wish to see peace re-established. He will not allow himself to suggest the particular form of the negotiations, still less to anticipate the intentions of other Powers, or to express any opinion respecting the preliminaries which it may be necessary to lay down, in order to establish the principles of the first approximation between the Belligerents.

"His Imperial Majesty, notwithstanding, in the hope that the friendly offer of his interposition will be regarded in the manner that the rectitude of his intentions inclines him to think it will, hastens to propose, for the purpose of facilitating by his interposition the opening of the negotiations, such place in his dominions as, from its situation and locality, may be convenient to all parties, and which, on this account, should not be too contiguous to the theatre of war; and in this, as well as in all other points, the Emperor will feel the greatest pleasure in contributing to accelerate the period of so desirable an union."

"Vienna, April 3, 1807."

ANSWER OF THE COURT OF FRANCE.

"The Undersigned Minister for Foreign Affairs has lost no time in laying before his Majesty the Emperor and King, the Note which his Excellency General Baron de Vincent did him the honour of addressing to him on the 7th of this month.

"His Majesty the Emperor Napoleon accepts for himself and his Allies the friendly interposition of his Majesty the Emperor of Austria, to effect the re-establishment of peace, so necessary to all nations.

"His Majesty has only one fear; it is, that the Power who hitherto seems to have laid it down as a plan to found its elevation and greatness upon the divisions of the Continent, will endeavour to extract from the Congress which may be formed new subjects of irritation, and new pretexts for disagreement. However, a mode which holds out a hope of stopping the further effusion of blood, and of affording consolation to the bosoms of so many families, ought not to be rejected by France, who, as all Europe knows, was forced against her inclination into the present war.

"His Majesty the Emperor Napoleon finds, moreover, in this circumstance, a favourable opportunity of strongly expressing the confidence with which his Majesty the Emperor of Austria has inspired him, and the desire he has to see those connexions re-established between the two nations, which in other times produced their mutual prosperity, and which, at this day, could more than any thing else consolidate their tranquillity and happiness.

"The Undersigned, happy in the opportunity of expressing these sentiments in the name of his August Sovereign, renews to his Excellency General Baron De Vincent the assurances of his most high consideration.

(Signed) "C. M. TALLEYRAND,
"Prince of Benevento."

"Warsaw, April 19, 1807.

THE POST OFFICE.

Messrs. FREELING and STANHOPE have most certainly had the advantage of us, and they appear to be very proud of the circumstance. It is indeed true, that, in stating some abuses of the Post Office, we imputed a criminal conduct to them, which we were not qualified to justify in a Court of Law, and we suffered the award which our ill-digested attack upon them was thought to merit. By the advice of those who understood the law better than ourselves, we suffered judgment to go by default; but subsequent matters may have created in us some feelings of regret upon that subject.

We proceeded, perhaps, with too much haste, and with too little caution, to our examination of Post-Office abuses, from the general approbation which accompanied our design from the most respectable quarters, and the hope that some reform might be thereby produced in a department which is generally considered as imperiously requiring reformation. The popularity of the cause, as well as the ill-treatment we had received, seduced us from our usual caution. But, after all, the alarm excited by our zeal for reform in the Post Office, cannot be more fully proved, than by the pains Mr. FREELING has taken, and the expence he has employed, in extending our apology beyond the limits of our offence. The one was committed in *The Times*, and it was certainly understood by us, when we assented to the apology, that the other should be confined to it. Mr. FREELING, however, thinks his triumph, such as it is, of too much consequence, to appear only in one Paper, and in one day. An acknowledgment, that the charge of extortion could not be proved against him and Mr. STANHOPE was, in his opinion, too important; we will not suppose necessary to their characters, not to be blazoned for the information of the court and city, and town and country readers of the public prints.

The insinuating and very fascinating suavity of Mr. FREELING's application to the Newspapers, to forward his purpose, will appear in the following *billet-doux* from the Post-office:—

"Mr. FREELING presents his best compliments to Mr. ——, and will be much obliged to him to insert the enclosed in a conspicuous part of his Paper; and if Mr. —— will take the farther trouble to let Mr. FREELING know the expence of its insertion, he will most thankfully and readily pay for it.

"Mr. FREELING is desirous that it may appear in the *common type* in which the —— is printed; and he hopes Mr. —— will pardon the liberty which Mr. FREELING has taken, in addressing himself immediately to Mr. —— upon this subject.

"General Post-office, July 9."

Several of the public Papers, however, have thought proper to resist the Post-office influence, and its golden promises; and we cannot but express our surprize, that others of them, who have been as loud, though not quite so incautious as ourselves in the reprobation of its abuses, should have yielded to its persuasions on this occasion. We therefore think it a duty we owe to ourselves, to counteract any unfavourable opinion that might be raised against us, were we to suffer an insidious propagation of our apology, beyond its implied limitations, to proceed in its illiberal and purchased career, without observation.

COURT MARTIAL.

TRIAL OF CAPTAIN LAROCHE, FOR COWARDICE.

PORTSMOUTH, JULY 23.

On Monday and the three following days, a Court-Martial was held on board the *Gladiator*, to try Capt. Laroche, late commanding his Majesty's ship *Uranie*, for not doing his utmost to bring the enemy to action, on the 15th of May, and the 22d of June last. The Members composing the Court were:—

Capt. BRADLEY, (commanding the *Plantagenet*) President.

Captain IRWIN	Captain HOSTE
—— BOYLE	—— VESHAM
—— SCOTT	—— WOOLCOMBE

Lieutenant MORRISON, First Lieutenant of the *Uranie*, was the Prosecutor.

The Admiralty order for the trial was read, and then a letter from Lieutenant Morrison, and other Officers of the *Uranie*, and also a letter from part of the petty officers and ship's crew of the *Uranie*, to the Lords of the Admiralty, stating the conduct (as they alledged) of Captain Laroche, and the reports which prevailed to the disadvantage of the character of the *Uranie*, imputing cowardice to her on the above days, and demanding a Court Martial on Captain Laroche, to clear their fame, were severally read.

The Court being then sworn, they proceeded to the examination of witnesses.

The witnesses in behalf of the prosecution were—the Second Lieutenant, Master, Master's Mate, Carpenter, Pilot, Surgeon, Lieutenant of Marines, and a Seaman of the *Uranie*; who deposed, that four of the main deck guns were in the hold, when the enemy was first seen (on the 5th of May, when a corvette came out of Cherbourg, and having looked at the *Uranie*, ran in again); that they were not mounted on the main deck till the day after the enemy was seen a second time (on the 15th of May, when the corvette and a frigate came out, and, after a few movements, returned to port); that on the 22d of June, the frigate and corvette came out, and stood towards the *Uranie*; and that the *Uranie* wore from the enemy for some time, and was an hour before she was ready for action; that there was great confusion on board the *Uranie* during that time; that Captain Laroche betrayed symptoms of agitation, fear, and (one witness swore to a question put by the prosecutor) of cowardice; that he frequently changed colour; and was agitated in a manner that he never betrayed before or since; that the *Uranie* did not carry all the sail she could have done; that, if she had, and Captain Laroche had done his utmost to bring the enemy to action, he must have cut off the corvette, and must have brought the frigate to action, if she did not abandon the corvette; and that he passed the enemy's frigate within gun-shot (giving a broadside) and wore, and must have been in close action within a few minutes, if he had chased the frigate, and carried all sail.

The Surgeon (on cross-examination), said, that Captain Laroche had been ill three or four days of a bilious fever, and had taken medicine that morning—calomel and salts; and others admitted, he had not dined with his officers, from indisposition, for three or four days.

All the witnesses for the prosecution said, that Captain Laroche had lain at anchor close in the shore several times, and for a long time together, and had on one occasion, when the enemy's frigate was saluting the Governor of Paris, stood close in to the works, hove to, hoisted his colours, and fired at the frigate, by way of defiance. The witnesses admitted that Captain L. and his Officers were on ill terms: one witness said, that Captain L. was on ill terms with all at times, and with some at all times.

The case for the prosecution closed at ten o'clock on Tuesday, when Captain Laroche requested a short time to prepare his defence. In about two hours, the Court again opened, and Captain Laroche's friend read a very able defence, which insisted that his prosecutors were in a combination against him, from personal prejudice; that he had watched the enemy at anchor (except when the weather would not permit) incessantly; had frequently defied him, and that when the enemy came out, he had endeavoured to decoy him farther from under the batteries, and that the enemy's object was to decoy the *Uranie* under the batteries; that the enemy's frigate carried fifty 18-pounders, the *Uranie* only thirty-six 12-pounders; that the *Uranie* was foul in her bottom, and the enemy's frigate was a faster sailer, and could bring him to action when she pleased, and avoid an action at her pleasure; that he carried all the sail he could with safety to his Majesty's ship then on a lee shore, and close in with it; that caution the more behoved him, as, during this war, the *Minerva* frigate had been captured by running on shore at this very place. The defence paid a most elegant compliment to the bravery of his Majesty's Navy at this day; expressed a confidence they would but lightly believe evidence to prove cowardice against an officer who had the honour to command one of his Majesty's ships; it concluded by saying, Captain Laroche would call witnesses that could have no bias, to prove that he had done his utmost to bring the enemy to action, and had in no degree tarnished his Majesty's flag, or dishonoured the corps he was proud to belong to.

The witnesses for Capt. Laroche were, the Lieutenant commanding the gun-brig *Defender*, (in company with the *Uranie* on this occasion) and the other officers of that brig, and several of the *Uranie's* seamen, among which last were Captains of the tops and fore-castle: they all deposed, that Capt. Laroche did his utmost to bring the enemy to action; that, had the *Uranie* carried all the sail she could, and done every thing that could be suggested, it was impossible for her to bring the enemy to action while he avoided it, which he did; that the enemy could bring Captain Laroche to action when he pleased, and avoid it in like manner; that both forces were close in shore, and had Captain Laroche continued the pursuit when he fired and tacked, he might have fallen under the batteries, and greatly endangered the safety of the *Uranie*.

Two military officers, who had been on a cruize with Captain Laroche, as visitors, deposed, that he had always displayed the most undaunted courage, and tried every means to provoke the enemy to try his strength. Admiral Sir Isaac Coffin deposed, that Captain Laroche had, verbally and by letter, reported to him officially, that the *Uranie's* bottom was foul, and that she wanted to be docked; Mr. Diddams (builder in the dock yard) deposed, that the *Uranie* stood in need of several repairs, and that her bottom was very foul. The defence closed at ten o'clock on Thursday morning, and the Court were in deliberation till half past one o'clock.

The Court being again opened, the Judge Advocate read the sentence, which was, that "*the charge being in part proved, Captain Laroche is sentenced to be dismissed from the command of his Majesty's ship Uranie.*"

A whimsical circumstance actually occurred at Sadler's Wells, on Tuesday evening, during the representation of the Aquatic Spectacle. Three sailors, doubting the reality of the water, got on the stage, from which one of them actually plunged into the reservoir, and as he rose, exclaimed loudly to the audience, "D—n my eyes, it is real water;" and then swimming to the farther extremity of it, got out highly delighted with his experiment.

The new comic Pantomime of Telemachus, or Harlequin and Calypso, at ASTLEY's, was again witnessed yesterday evening, by a crowded overflowing and brilliant assemblage of the first characters in the kingdom. Loud and repeated plaudits accompanied the change of every scene, and it is but justice to say, that the sense of the house, on the fall of the curtain, was such as to promise, from the marks of admiration expressed, another overflowing audience this night.

Erratum.—In the Advertisement, yesterday, of Mr. Renny's Work, entitled "FREE TRADE TO THE EAST INDIES," instead of the words "our countrymen," read "our countrymen in general."

MARRIED.

On Thursday last, at Walcot Church, Bath, by the Rev. John Sibley, George Samuel Kett, Esq. of Seething-hall, Norfolk, to Miss Milford, only daughter of Richard Milford, Esq. of that city.

On Wednesday last, Mr. Benjamin Travers, jun. of Cateaton-street, to Miss Morgan, daughter of William Morgan, Esq. of Stamford-hill.

By the Rev. Mr. Smith, Chaplain to his Royal Highness the Duke of Kent, Richard Broad, Esq. Captain of the Royal Foot, and Brigade-Major of the Home District, to Miss E. A. Mair, of the Terrace, Kensington.

On Saturday evening last, at Lady Lismore's, in Charles-street, Berkeley-square, William Cavendish, Esq. to the Hon. Miss O'Callaghan, eldest daughter of the late Lord Lismore.

DIED.

On Thursday, after a lingering illness, Edmond James Moody, Esq. of the Navy office, aged 32 years, eldest son of Robert Sadleir Moody, Esq. Commissioner for Victualling his Majesty's Navy.

PRICE OF STOCKS.

Bank Stock, 228	India Bonds, 1s. dis. 1s. prem.
3 p. Ct. Red. An. 6[illegible]	Imp. 3 p. Ct. 61 [illegible]
3 p. Ct. Cons. An. 61 [illegible]	Exch. Bills, 2s. dis. par
4 p. Ct. 80 [illegible]	Omnium, 1 [illegible] dis.
5 p. Ct. Navy 94 [illegible] 95	English Tickets, 20l. 7s.
Long Ann. 17 [illegible] 11-16ths	Cons. for Acc. 63 [illegible]
India Stock, 172 [illegible]	

Last Price.—Cons for Mo. 61 [illegible].—Ditto for Ac. 62 [illegible].

HAZARD, BURNE, WARNER, and Co.
Stock-Brokers, No. 93, Royal Exchange.

'A newspaper should be free'

It takes more than wise editors and journalists of genius to build a great newspaper. They need a proprietor who believes in what they are doing. His passion for the truth must be above the passion for profit. He will have to stand up for his journalists against the politicians and the businessmen, the pressure groups and the old boy networks, the public attacks and the private influence that will try to deflect them from their chase. He needs to be brave and wise, adventurous and lucky. It helps if he is rich.

The founding proprietor of *The Times* was John Walter II (1776–1847), the second son of John Walter I. Without him the paper would have petered out early in the nineteenth century, like so many other primitive newspapers.

The actual founder was his father, who was not as awful as described by Henry Crabb Robinson, 'Old Crabby', his first foreign correspondent: 'As dishonest, worthless a man as I have ever known'. But John Walter I was a businessman of his time on the make. He saw nothing improper in asking for and taking subsidies and bribes from Government or Opposition politicians. He went to prison to protect his sources for his paper's libel on the royal Dukes – but he did so because he reckoned they would make it worth his while. He was not averse to taking money for keeping things out of the paper that his masters would prefer not to see there.

Below Portrait of John Walter II, donated to THE TIMES by a later John Walter, in 1930.

Bottom Printing House Square, watercolour, 1811, by G. Shepherd.

But his son John Walter II invented the remarkable principle that a newspaper should be free from government control, bribes, puffs, extortion, calumny and blackmail. He established this principle in *The Times* as a precedent for later newspapers all over the world.

He was educated at Trinity College, Oxford, that nurse of intelligent and civilized scholars. He left to join his father to carry on 'in partnership together in Printing House Square aforesaid the Trade, Art, Mystery or Business of Printers for their mutual and equal benefit'. It became clear that his elder brother William was not suited to be either the editor or the manager of a newspaper, so in January 1803 John Walter II, aged only 27, was given sole charge of all activities at Printing House Square. *The Times* was in a rocky state: circulation was only just over 1,500.

Journalism was regarded by officialdom and public as a scruffy trade carried out by Grub Street hacks, who wrote what they were told, or bribed, to write. John Walter changed all that. Crabb Robinson and then John Stoddart edited for a few years while the young man learnt the job. He then took over as editor as well as manager, until in 1817 he appointed another young man, Thomas Barnes, as editor. The foundations of *The Times* were laid by young eagles, not extinct volcanoes.

These were years of violent controversy. The notion of power passing to an independent press was considered offensive, dangerous and almost treasonable by the Establishment. Officialdom made life as difficult as possible for the revolutionaries at Printing House Square. The Post Office, through which all foreign news was passed, cut off its lifeline by withholding the mails. Government departments refused to place advertisements in *The Times*. And in 1805 Pitt's administration cancelled the newspaper's lucrative printing contract for His Majesty's Customs.

John Walter was combative and clever. He built up his own private network for obtaining news from the Continent. It was reliable, up-to-date news, often faster than the official version – note a letter of 1813 from the Under Secretary at the Foreign Office to Walter, saying that he was directed by Lord Castlereagh 'to request if [Mr Walter] will have the goodness to tell him if he has received any Intelligence of the reported defeat of the French near Dresden'. The Russian Ambassador asked Walter for information, 'since nobody here has better Correspondents than you'.

Circulation rose as the public bought *The Times* to learn the latest news of the revolutions and wars on the Continent. As circulation went up, so did the number and cost of advertisements. Walter had started to make his paper independent of government-funded advertising. Commercial independence is a necessary condition of editorial independence.

John Walter discussed his struggle for independence in a long article in *The Times* of 11 February 1810: 'The same practices [*sc.* blockading the editor's mails from abroad] were resorted to at a subsequent period. They produced the same complaints on the part of the editor; and a redress was then offered to his grievances provided it could be known what party in politics he meant to support. This, too, was declined as pledging the independence of this paper.'

Walter also declared the independence of *The Times* from the theatrical managers. The arrangement in those days was for the managers to place advertisements in the press. In return, editors were expected to write friendly puffs for the performances. Leigh Hunt described the arrangement in the *Examiner* of 1805: 'Puffing and plenty of tickets were the system of the day'. It is still a danger, and a disreputable practice. John Walter II wasn't having any of it. He insisted that his critics pay for their tickets and that their notices become objective – some complained, brutal. The author of one play was described in *The Times* as 'undoubtedly the lowest dramatist of this wretched day'. The theatrical managers were outraged. The public loved it. (It is a melancholy fact of human nature that the reviews remembered by the public are the rude ones: 'This is not a novel to be lightly tossed aside: it should be hurled with great force.')

It was *Sturm und Drang* on all fronts to establish those freedoms of the press that journalists in the lucky parts of the world take for granted today.

Industrial relations were as harsh and violent as the rest of life in these foundation days of *The Times*. In 1810 Walter's

In column 2, John Walter's leading article proudly announces the introduction of the steam-powered printing press, and vaunts its glories. This was the first issue to be printed by steam press.
29 NOVEMBER 1814

any gentleman, whether this qualification was not disre-
ed.

BATHURST observed, that by the recruiting from the mi- ..., this country had been enabled to make those exertions of ... we all now knew the result. That policy, therefore, could not be matter of regret. True it was, that the retaining part of ... ilitia embodied was not a systematic measure on the part of ... ment, but was dictated by the demands for the employment ... regular forces abroad.

... grant was then put, and carried.

... PALMERSTON moved a grant of 55,000l. for the mainte- ... of volunteer corps in Great Britain and Ireland, for a space ... days, commencing with the 15th of December.

... J. P. GRANT really thought there was an understand- ... a former night, that this vote should be withdrawn al- ... ; and he was now surprised to hear it brought forward ... the smallest preface.

... PALMERSTON acknowledged that the vote was with- ... at the suggestion of his right hon. friend (Mr. Vansittart); ... was only for reconsideration, and not with an intention to ... It had been reconsidered, and the estimate for England ... from 50,000l. to 30,000l., and that for Ireland to 25,000l. ... eduction from last year was still more considerable, when ... l. had been voted for the volunteer service in Eng- ... alone. This he conceived to be a species of force the ... nstitutional in its nature, the cheapest, and the least liable to ... on. It put arms into the hands of those least likely to abuse ... and who on any sudden emergency were best qualified from ... knowledge and influence to put down disorder, and to pre- ... he peace. In this view these corps were much more effec- ... an any regular troops.

... J. P. GRANT said he had expressed no jealousy of the ... er corps, but great jealousy of the management of the public ..., which the present ministers squandered on all hands with ... r and more lavish profusion than any administration with ... this country was ever cursed *(a laugh)*. He would repeat ... r profusion was a curse in the present state of our finances, ... was by far the most serious difficulty with which the coun- ... d to grapple.

... CHANCELLOR of the EXCHEQUER said, it was true ... suggested reconsideration to his noble friend on a former ... as 100,000l. struck him at the time as a very large sum to ... r the volunteers. It would be improper to put an end to ... corps all at once, and, above all, highly objectionable to dis- ... he Irish yeomanry.

... PEELE spoke strongly of the importance of the yeomanry ... nd. To rebut the charge of profusion brought by the hon. ... man, he would simply state to what an extent the Irish go- ... ent had reduced the estimates for the volunteer service. In ... was 348,000l., in 1814 it was 312,000l., and now it was re- ... to 58,000l.

... WHITBREAD admired the singular confession of the ... llor of the Exchequer. It struck the right honourable gen- ..., it seemed, when 100,000l. was first proposed, that it was ... sum, and deserved reconsideration. Now he had ... thought that the Chancellor of the Exchequer must ... iously consulted about every estimate; but now it appeared ... e Secretary at War had broke loose from all such trammels. ... ly, it was surprising, that in the midst of a profound peace ... e continent, it was thought necessary to keep up an armed ... n the country, with bayonets on their muskets, and broad- ... by their sides. Such things never had been before. ... corps had volunteered for the war,—that war had ceased, ... England at least he saw not the slightest occasion for their ... services. Still, however, the questions put the other ... n this very topic had saved 45,000l. to the public.

... PALMERSTON was sorry he could not congratulate the ... ttee on any such saving, as the present vote was only for half ... r. In illustration of the impropriety of disbanding the volun- ... at once, he said he had that day received a letter from a ... ndant of volunteer cavalry, stating great reluctance to be ... d on the part of the corps, as they had been induced to ... would be the case, from what had passed the other night in ... e. They begged, rather than be dismissed, to serve without ... wance.

... BARING said, his objection to the vote was from the ... which it entailed on the country. The truth was, we ... hasting ourselves by our expenditure even in peace. Do- ... ecurity at present would be best provided for by economy, ... lso, when war might again take place, would enable us to ... forts proportioned to the crisis. He was afraid that the dis- ... of many members of these cavalry corps, to retain them em- ... was merely that they might have an excuse to get ... from the tax upon horses and other taxes. ... reland, having no personal knowledge of that country, he ... not deny that the maintenance of the yeomanry corps there ... necessary, though he could not help looking upon it as the ... gross mismanagement on the part of the government of ... try, which made it necessary to put arms in the hands of ... rity to keep down an oppressed majority.

... FITZGERALD was astonished that the hon. gentleman, ... professed his ignorance of Ireland, should yet throw out a ... of gross mismanagement against its government.

... NEWPORT said, it was sufficient to look into the history of ... to be convinced it had been a misgoverned country for ... centuries, which circumstance alone rendered the continu- ... this force necessary.

... P. GRANT suggested, that the vote for England should be ... from that for Ireland, as many gentlemen who thought the ... necessary might vote for the latter.

... WHITBREAD wished to ask why the Secretary at War ... accept the proposal of the gallant volunteers, who had of- ... serve for nothing rather than be disbanded? No, he would ... this; he would rather force the acceptance of the money ...

... PALMERSTON replied, that the offer to which he had ... was founded merely on a contingency, which it was not ... of government should take place. It should be recollected, ... that the members of the different corps received ... the whole of the grant went to the maintenance of the staff ...

... WHITBREAD thought it would be desirable to do away ... ptions which the yeomanry cavalry at present enjoyed.

... some further conversation, an amendment was proposed for ... 45,000l. instead of 55,000l. and leaving out the words ... Britain." A division took place, when the amendment was ... d by 45 votes to 14.

... xt vote proposed was, that a sum not exceeding 6,706l. be ... for paying salaries and pensions of officers and other per- ... the superannuated list.

... TIERNEY commented on the list of pensioners before the ... e. He observed a retired apothecary in Ireland who had ... ar. There was also another, a retired treasurer, who had ... ar. Now he would appeal to the experience of a ... gentleman opposite, whether this man might not execute ... of a Treasurer up to a very late period of life, and yet it ... he had been superannuated these ten years. *(a laugh.)*

... OSE—"The right hon. gentleman is just as capable of giv- ... swer to that question as I am."

... NEWPORT then enquired whether the retired apothe- ... received this pension of 300l. a year was not the Dr. ... whose name was implicated in certain severities charged ... been exercised in Kilmainham jail. This introduced a ... of some length, in which Mr. P. Moore strongly ob- ... giving such a person any pension. On the other hand, ... clared by Mr. Wellesley Pole that the conduct of Dr. ... had been acquitted of the charges brought by the pri- ... report made by the judges on the subject. He confessed, ... that Trevor was chargeable with some severities of which ... approve.

... olution was then agreed to. Report to-morrow.

... ort on the Thread and Silk Lace bill was agreed to, and ... red to be brought in.

... PALMERSTON brought up a Return of the Battalions ... ular army disbanded since the 11th of May. Ordered to ... table.—Adjourned.

FRENCH PAPERS.

MADRID, Nov. 13.

... cular from the Minister of War announces the ... lishment of the old militia of this kingdom, on ... ng of 1808, to the amount of 42 battalions, ... en to eight hundred men each; to furnish re- ... the regiments of the line in time of war, and to ... up by fresh supplies in proportion to these ... It appears that his Majesty is resolved to ... espectable army.

... ations of the Clergy from different places have ... present addresses to his Majesty within these ...: at the head of one of them, for the town of ... we observed the Marquis of Santa Cruz and ... Castanos. This circumstance has dissipated ... reports current recently with respect to the ...

... al Miguel Alava is still in prison, and does not ... kely soon to go as Ambassador to the Hague, ... situation he was appointed. He is accused of ... e writer of some imprudent letters to the Editor ... riodical print, previous to the return of his Ma- ... his dominions. The intercession of the Am- ... r of a great Power calmed the resentment ex- ... the discovery of these first writings; but it is ... eged that fresh imprudences have produced ... ere resolution that has deprived him of his ...

The claim of the refugees for the repeal of ... questration imposed on their property has ... erred to the Council of Castille, which will re- ... his Majesty the measures proper to be taken. ... visional successor of M. Macanaz, as Minister ... e, is a Magistrate of known moderation, grown ... e study of the laws of his country. In the place ... ills, the knowledge of the laws of the country, ... accustomed forms of practice, is essentially ... y. M. Macanaz was very deficient in this ... tion, for he put his private signature to circu- ... which the most solemn legal forms were requi- ... is not ascertained whether this ignorance was ... fault. The rigour with which he is treated gives ... thousand conjectures.

... e recommendation of General Freire, the dis- ... of a Gold Cross has been granted to the officers ... d in the battle of the Bidassoa. The petty ... d privateers are also to have an honorary badge. ... ssued in the official *Gazette*, to leave no room ... of ignorance, enjoins all the Generals and ... employed in the expedition for Buenos Ayres, under General Murillos, to be at their post on the 20th instant, without fail.

BRUSSELS, Nov. 19.

We learn from a source which we deem authentic, that the union of Belgium to Holland will not be carried into effect in the mode hitherto supposed. These two countries will be governed by the same Sovereign: they will contribute in common to the public expenses, to the means of defence, of independence, and mutual prosperity; but they will be governed each by its own laws, and they will preserve separately the particular form of government and internal administration to which they have been accustomed.

PARIS, Nov. 25.

The sale of colonial productions which has taken place at Havre attracted a great number of French from the different departments, and Belgians, who profitted of that opportunity to form new connections with the merchants of that port, or to renew those which circumstances had long since dissolved.

CHAMBER OF DEPUTIES.—SITTING OF THE 24TH.

M. AUBERT, in the name of the Committee of petitions, made a report on a memoir addressed to the Chamber by Madame Montansier, widow of Sieur Bourdon Neuville.

The reporter set forth that Madame Montansier was formerly owner of the Versailles theatre. Imperious circumstances brought her to Paris, where she purchased the theatre of the Palais-Royal, which being found too small, Madame M. and her husband built another in the rue de Richelieu, to which they gave the name of the Theatre of Arts. They were soon after denounced to the Commune of Paris, as having built this theatre with the premeditated design of setting fire to the National Library. They were thrown into prison, and stripped of their property, for the purpose of establishing the Opera on the same spot. After the 9th Thermidor Mme. M. and her husband were compelled to sell the Theatre of Arts for 8 millions, payable in *assignats*, or in current money, by instalments at fixed periods. In pursuance of this clause, a part of the money ought to have been paid in specie, after the disappearance of paper money: this, however, never took place; and by a decree of the Consuls, in the year 10, it was ordered that the remainder of the money should only be paid in the same scale of proportion. The Committee, while they acknowledged the incompetence of the Chamber, proposed that the petition should be transmitted to Government.

M. SYLVESTRE DE SACY opposed the reference. He thought that the time of the Chamber was too frequently occupied with objects of trifling importance, and the jurisdiction of which belonged to the Administration. We ought to regard every thing which ought to come under the cognizance of the ministerial and judicial powers as foreign to our discussions.

M. DUMOLARD spoke with warmth against this principle. It tended to extinguish the salutary vigilance which the Chamber of Deputies ought to exercise for the public interest, and, according to constitutional forms, over the conduct of the judicial and administrative authorities. Nothing, he observed, which is capable of interesting the nation, can be foreign to its representatives. "I solemnly declare my opinion at this tribune, and I regard the declaration as of very high importance."

After some further conversation, the Chamber passed to the Order of the Day on the petition of Mademoiselle Montansier.

LONDON, TUESDAY, NOVEMBER 29, 1814.

Our Journal of this day presents to the public the practical result of the greatest improvement connected with printing, since the discovery of the art itself. The reader of this paragraph now holds in his hand, one of the many thousand impressions of *The Times* newspaper, which were taken off last night by a mechanical apparatus. A system of machinery almost organic has been devised and arranged, which, while it relieves the human frame of its most laborious efforts in printing, far exceeds all human powers in rapidity and dispatch. That the magnitude of the invention may be justly appreciated by its effects, we shall inform the public, that after the letters are placed by the compositors, and enclosed in what is called the form, little more remains for man to do, than to attend upon, and watch this unconscious agent in its operations. The machine is then merely supplied with paper: itself places the form, inks it, adjusts the paper to the form newly inked, stamps the sheet, and gives it forth to the hands of the attendant, at the same time withdrawing the form for a fresh coat of ink, which itself again distributes, to meet the ensuing sheet now advancing for impression; and the whole of these complicated acts is performed with such a velocity and simultaneousness of movement, that no less than eleven hundred sheets are impressed in one hour.

That the completion of an invention of this kind, not the effect of chance, but the result of mechanical combinations methodically arranged in the mind of the artist, should be attended with many obstructions and much delay, may be readily admitted. Our share in this event has, indeed, only been the application of the discovery, under an agreement with the Patentees, to our own particular business; yet few can conceive,—even with this limited interest,—the various disappointments and deep anxiety to which we have for a long course of time been subjected.

Of the person who made this discovery, we have but little to add. Sir CHRISTOPHER WREN's noblest monument is to be found in the building which he erected; so is the best tribute of praise, which we are capable of offering to the inventor of the Printing Machine, comprised in the preceding description, which we have feebly sketched, of the powers and utility of his invention. It must suffice to say farther, that he is a Saxon by birth; that his name is KŒNIG; and that the invention has been executed under the direction of his friend and countryman BAUER.

By the *Hamburgh* mail we learn, that a note which was understood to be of great importance was delivered into the Congress on the 10th inst. It was supposed to relate to the fate of Poland, and to be connected with the journey of the Grand Duke CONSTANTINE to Warsaw. It is long since this Prince was designated for a kingdom. In his very infancy his grandmother, whose thoughts were then turned towards Greece, caused medals to be struck with the inscription "Constantine, King of the Grecians." He is understood to be by no means so popular in Poland as his brother ALEXANDER; but the hope of recovering their national independence would easily reconcile the Poles to any Sovereign through whom such a boon was likely to be obtained. Some suspicion seems to be entertained in Germany that Bavaria inclines more toward the French interest than is quite compatible with German feelings: and the aggrandisement of Prussia is viewed the more favourably, on account of the patriotic spirit evinced by the Prussians in the late war.

The accounts from Spain in the *French* papers afford little prospect of an improvement in the state of affairs there. The expedition fitting out in the vain hope of reconquering Buenos Ayres seems to experience great backwardness on the part both of the men and officers. It is now asserted, that the union of Belgium with Holland will not be effected by placing both countries under the same internal system of government; but by preserving to each its local laws and regulations, under a common sovereign. This latter mode, as less likely to injure private interests, or to offend general prejudices, seems to promise greater strength and stability to the new state.

The right of petitioning has again come under debate in the Chamber of Deputies. It is not very surprising that these new Legislators, so long kept in leading-strings by the Despot before whom they trembled to speak, should entertain considerable difference of opinion among themselves on the extent and nature of the powers they ought to exercise under a beneficent and constitutional Sovereign. M. DUMOLARD, whose political education seems to have been of the popular kind, lays it down as a leading principle, that nothing which is capable of interesting the nation can be foreign to it's representatives, in which he evidently confounds what is *interesting* with what is *for the interest* of the nation. At one time, the worship of the Goddess of Reason, at another time the charlataneries of a military mountebank, may be very interesting to a nation like the French. Denunciations of *incivism* may be the order of the day at one period, and outcries against the *Emigrants* at another; but a wise and virtuous Legislator will disdain to be led away by these popular noises: he will not easily be diverted from his high and important functions—those of providing for great public emergencies, and framing permanent rules of conduct for the whole State; but when serious evils, for which the common course of the law presents no remedy befall individuals, he will then, and then alone, turn to the consideration of the particular case, and give to the petitioner that support which the constitution of the State does not elsewhere afford. Viewing the subject in this light, we think the Chamber erred alike in paying attention to the petition which we mentioned yesterday, and in rejecting that of which we have now to speak. The former evidently related to a trifling quarrel between two insignificant persons, exaggerated for purposes of mere faction; but the latter is the complaint of a lady, who having been robbed of her whole property by the injustice of the successive revolutionary governments, has no means of obtaining compensation by any legal process, and can therefore look to nothing but the national liberality. It affords a tolerable idea of the extravagant wickedness and absurdity to which the civic denunciators of those times (the CARNOTs and MEHEES of the day) pushed their accusations, when we find that Madame MONTANSIER, the person in question, was charged with having built a theatre in the Rue Richelieu, with the premeditated design of setting fire to the National Library!

THE CLOVEN FOOT.—The *Morning Chronicle*, not contented with asserting the authenticity of the libel published in France, under the false title of Protest of the Parliament of Paris, has at last taken upon itself to defend the notes appended to that infamous publication. These notes, it says, are "written in the glowing spirit of liberty." Glowing enough, GOD knows! Witness the sample produced by the worthy Editor in justification of the murder of LOUIS XVI.!! "Who, then, are the *Regicides*? Are they the entire nation who formed a convention to try LOUIS XVI.? &c." This is exactly what we should have thought "a true Jacobin" would have privately approved; but we did not expect that any one at this time of day would have braved public contempt by avowing that approbation.

It is no longer a mystery how or why the amiable LOUIS was murdered. He owed his death to a set of villains, who under the name of liberty and equality wished to plunder and tyrannise over their fellow citizens, and who stifled the opposition of the respectable part of France by the infuriated outcries of a blood-thirsty mob. The French nation never did form a Convention to try the King." On the contrary, many Members of the Convention refused to vote on that trial, upon the express ground that they were appointed to be Legislators and not Judges. The individuals who voted for his condemnation all strenuously resisted an appeal to the people, because they knew such an appeal would have saved his life. If the nation had, in fact, authorised the sentence, it would not the less have been a murder of the foulest kind; but the real regicides were they who, profaning the sacred judicial character, bawled with the fury of demons, *La mort et dans les vingt-quatre heures! La mort et sans appel!* Never did Englishman disgrace himself by becoming the apologist of those hell-hounds, until the Editor of *The Morning Chronicle* on Saturday first shewed the cloven foot.

EXTRACT OF A LETTER FROM PARIS.

"November 24.

"Much has been said by the newspapers lately relative to an arrest of a French General and others *for treason*. This latter part of the story must be a pure addition of the English tale-bearers:—there never was the slightest mention in Paris of General Dufour, and 40 associates, being taken up for an attempt to overturn the King's authority in France. There were two stories afloat: one that he had been engaged in procuring natives of Belgium, settled in France, or once in the French service, to join the Belgic armies under the Prince of Orange;—the other account was that he had busied himself in a similar way, to get French officers for the service of the *United States of America*. If the latter had been the case, the time and labour of the General would have been most foolishly thrown away: for I happen to know, as a matter of fact, *that several officers have returned to France, disappointed in their hopes* of employment in the American armies;—the republicans being so jealous of foreigners—so confident in their own strength—and, alas! in the feeble measures of their adversary, that they have refused to appoint any of these French gentlemen even to a serjeant's pike. But with regard to General Dufour's arrest, I can assure you that he was seen and spoken to by a friend of mine the day after that on which it was said to have happened. These mischievous statements prove only the malice of their inventors, but nothing whatever as to the state of France. You see by the arrival of the *Fingal* what I have long prophesied, that both parties in America have actually coalesced—and that if you wish to preserve the Canadas, or a foot of ground on the Northern Continent, you must put forth the whole strength of the British Empire.—God grant that even so you may succeed."

HAMBURGH, Nov. 18.

We learn, by a letter from Switzerland, that in various parts of that country, endeavours had been made to restore the Jesuits; but all efforts of this kind had been hitherto fruitless. The government of Freyburg, which was at first thought to be favourably inclined towards the reverend Fathers, has declared that it will have nothing to do with them. The governments of Lucerne and Soleure have given similar answers.

The following is an extract of a letter from Vienna, dated Nov. 10:—

"The departure of the Grand Duke Constantine for Warsaw is supposed to have a close connection with the decisions adopted respecting the affairs of Poland.

"Saxony will be wholly united to Prussia, and all intelligent German patriots rejoice in a measure so closely connected with the welfare of the whole. Its advantages may be thus classed: the first and greatest will be for Germany, the second for Saxony, and the third for Prussia.

"The French, on their part, become daily more active. The complicated relations of Germany present an abundant field for diplomacy: all the Cabinets are not equally German in their feelings, and the private advantage of one or two Princes, which is in marked opposition to that of the whole, always leads them back, either more or less, towards France; but so much the more strongly do all who have the repose of their common country at heart attach themselves to the State in which patriotic ardour is the most prevalent. Prince Hardenberg enjoys general confidence; and by his side stand the men most distinguished both in civil and military affairs.

"The activity which prevails here is extraordinarily great; and as the full powers are not yet authenticated, so there are only prolix private discussions, without any common connection. The German commission proceeds in its labours, but without having yet advanced any great steps in its progress. Many plans for the constitution of Germany have already been rejected. The smaller German Lords wished to share in these deliberations; but the *medial* Princes alone have hitherto formed a mutual union, to stand up for their common rights. It seems much less just to exclude those who suffered least from the French, than those who had to thank the French for their sovereignty. Prussia has taken considerable steps towards their satisfaction.

"The Commission for the arming of Germany and the defence of its frontiers has not yet assembled; there are still some difficulties in the way, which have been raised by Marshal Wrede in the name of Bavaria. Lieutenant-Colonel Ruhle will draw up the protocol.

"On the part of Russia, a very important declaration has been this day handed in. The journey of the Grand Duke Constantine appears to be connected with it."

General SMITH, it is said, is arrived in this country.

The Duke DE GUICHE arrived on Saturday from Paris.

The Duke of PORTLAND and several English of distinction are at Bourdeaux.

We understand that the principal brewers met yesterday fortnight, to consider the propriety of reducing the price of porter, when it was determined to continue the present price, but increase the strength. The publicans received notice of this yesterday.

Sunday night, the neighbourhood of St. Martin's-lane was thrown into alarm, by several *explosions*. The main sewer has been for some time opened, for the purpose of renewing the arch. The heavy rain has not only thrown down a considerable part of the new work, but the press of water has broke down the external walls of the cellars of two houses. The neighbourhood, from six o'clock till nine, was in dreadful uneasiness, from the noise of masses of brick which fell from time to time, the roaring of the water in the centre of the street, and the clamour of the workmen.

LAW REPORT.

COURT OF KING'S BENCH, MONDAY, Nov. 28.

VIVEASH V. BECHER.

Lord ELLENBOROUGH delivered the judgment of the Court in this case, which we reported at great length yesterday. In recapitulating the case, he observed, that the defendant's commission was not addressed to the sovereign of the state to which the consul was appointed, but to all persons whatsoever,—a kind of *sciant omnes*, requesting every one to recognise him as consul and agent for commercial relations, the duties of which office were pointed out in separate instructions. The Prince Regent recognised him "as consul as aforesaid," and notified his approval in the London Gazette. His commission authorised him to appoint vice-consuls in every port in England; it was questionable whether he was not so authorised to appoint a deputy in the port of London, where he lived, for that port was not specifically mentioned in the commission as that for which the defendant was to act as consul himself. If he was so authorised, no mischief would arise from his personal restraint, for he might delegate his authority. The functions pointed out in the defendant's instructions were purely commercial, and there was not one which could be called a state function, to be performed by the defendant, as representing the crown of the Duke of Oldenburg for public state purposes. In this case, the defendant was appointed *eo nomine* as consul, which distinguished it from that before Lord Talbot, where the defendant was called an "agent for commercial affairs," and part of the labour was to consider what his function was, Lord Talbot saying that he was "at most a consul." Here the defendant was so designated and denominated in the Commission. The defendant's affidavit stated, that there was no other minister or diplomatic agent for the Duchy of Oldenburg in this country, and that the defendant had acted as such diplomatic agent, but in what particulars distinct from those of a commercial nature was not stated. One function, it was stated, he had performed, viz. that of obtaining arms from the British government for the Duchy of Oldenburg. If the defendant had been in the habit of receiving directions from the Duke, he should have shewn the terms of his communication of them to our government. Why did not he state the terms of his application to our government for these arms? Such an obtainment did not require a public functionary. We all knew that the largest issue of arms, namely, that for the liberation of Holland, was obtained without the intervention of any person invested with a public function or character. In answer to the defendant's affidavit, the plaintiffs have sworn, that the defendant being a resident London merchant, having been a bankrupt, had lately stopped payment for 120,000l.; and that sheriffs were in the frequent habit of arresting consuls from foreign countries. The question was, what (if any) immunities the defendant had by the law of nations, and particularly whether he was privileged from arrest? And first, was he an "ambassador or other public minister of any foreign power" within the stat. of Anne? He certainly had some authority from a foreign power, but there was no writer upon the law of nations, however loose, who held that a consul was a public minister. But, then, it is said, that if a consul be not named or included in the words of the act, that statute is only declaratory of the common law of which the law of nations is part, and that the rights of a consul, by the law of nations, still remain untouched by the stat. True: but the Act of Anne is reciting all who by the law of nations are entitled to privileges; and the question was, whether a consul is a "public minister;" for the act industriously comprehended all who were thus entitled, and was a declaration not only of what is the law of nations, but of the extent of that law. But, supposing the defendant to be entitled independently of the description in the act, how does his title stand with the usage of the law of nations? In Vattel, b. ii, c. 2, s. 34, it is said, "Among the modern institutions for the advancement of commerce, one of the most useful is that of consuls, or persons residing in the large trading cities, and especially the sea-ports, of foreign countries, with a commission to watch over the rights and privileges of their nation, and to decide disputes between her merchants there. When a nation trades largely with a country, it is requisite to have there a person charged with such a commission: and as the state which allows of this commerce must naturally favour it, for the same reason also it must admit the consul: but there being no absolute and perfect obligation to this, the nation that wishes to have a consul, must procure this right by the commercial treaty itself." So that a consul is not at all like the ancient *legatus*, but a creature of modern commercial growth; and in Grotius's very learned and laborious chapter on *legati*, although Grotius may be considered for this purpose as a modern writer, the name of *consul* does not occur. Neither does it in Molloy. Any nation, whether amicable or hostile, may send a *legatus*; and he shall, by the law of nations, have all the privileges of an ambassador: but to the admitting the consul, Vattel says there is no absolute and perfect obligation, and the nation that wishes to have one must procure this right by a commercial treaty. "*The consul*," Vattel proceeds, "*is no public minister, and cannot pretend to the privileges annexed to such characters*: yet bearing his sovereign's commission, and being in this quality received by the Prince in whose dominions he resides, he is, in a certain degree, entitled to the protection of the law of nations. The sovereign by the very act of receiving him tacitly engages to allow him all the liberty and safety necessary to the proper discharge of his functions, without which the admission of the consul would be nugatory and delusive." He is entitled to the protection of the law of nations in a certain degree, and so is every man under a safe conduct: he is entitled to all that may enable him to discharge his functions; he is not to be insulted or disabled from performing them. The defendant is not a natural born subject, but he owes a temporal allegiance here; he has been a bankrupt here; and if by concealment of his effects or otherwise, he has incurred any of the penalties of the bankrupt laws, no doubt he is liable to them. And is he to be exempted from all this by the mere act of a foreign Prince appointing him his consul? His Lordship then read Vattel, b. iv. c. 6. s. 75. in which the mere private agents of foreign princes were held entitled to some attention. He was surprised that it had been so positively averred, that Vattel was an authority in the defendant's favour. In c. 8. s. 112. it is said, "A subject of the State may still continue its subject, notwithstanding his acceptance of a commission from a foreign Prince. His subjection is expressly established, when the Sovereign acknowledges him as a minister only, with a reserve that he shall remain a subject of the State. The States-General of the United Provinces, in a decree of the 19th of June, 1681, declare, that no subject of the State shall be received as ambassador or minister of another Power, but on condition that he shall not divest himself of his character as subject, even with regard to jurisdiction, both in civil and criminal affairs; and that whoever, in making himself known as ambassador or minister, has not mentioned his quality of subject of the State, shall not enjoy those rights or privileges which peculiarly belong to the minister of foreign Powers. Such a minister may likewise retain his former subjection *tacitly*; and then by a natural consequence drawn from his actions, state, and whole behaviour, it is known that he continues a subject." Lord Ellenborough said, he should be afraid of adopting that as law, for that would leave the minister the option of stripping the sovereign whose subject he might be of all dominion over him. "Thus, independently of the declaration abovementioned, those Dutch merchants who obtain the title of residents of certain foreign princes, and nevertheless continue to carry on their commerce, thereby sufficiently denote that they remain subjects. Whatever inconvenience may attend the subjection of a minister to the sovereign with whom he resides, if the foreign Prince chooses to acquiesce in such a state of things, and is content to have a minister on that footing, it is his own concern; and should his minister on any ignominous occasion be treated as a subject, he has no cause of complaint." This was directly in point to the present case of consul, who is in most countries a subject where he resides, and is appointed such from his knowledge of the language of that country: this was the case of a large proportion of the consuls in this kingdom. The authority of Vattel was therefore not against that of Wicquefort. In the case before Lord Talbot, it might have been convenient to soothe the King of Prussia at that time by our government paying the money; but the opinion of the Chancellor was strong against the privileges of consuls: and so was that of Lord C. J. Mansfield, in the late case in Common Pleas. It would be an enormous inconvenience to hold not only this defendant privileged, but all his vice consuls, of whom he had the power of appointing one in every port in the kingdom; and that the defendant should have a power of granting what the crown could not. It did not appear by the affidavits before the court, that the debts which were the subject of these actions were not contracted prior to the time of the defendant's being appointed consul. With every disposition to extend rather than narrow the decisions in favour of the law of nations, the Court could not but discharge the present rule.

Lord ELLENBOROUGH gave notice that the Court would sit on Wednesday, the 11th of January next, in Serjeant's Inn-hall, to hear the new trials of the present term, and the remainder of the special cases.

COURT OF CHANCERY, Nov. 28.

W. AGAR, ESQ. V. THE REGENT CANAL COMPANY.

Mr. BELL applied for an injunction to prevent the Company from carrying their works through the plaintiff's premises at Pancras, as they were deviating from the line described in the act.

Messrs. LEACH and WETHERELL contended on behalf of the Company, that the present application was not for the purpose of confining the Company to any particular line, but for that of completely excluding them from proceeding with the canal. They maintained, that Mr. Agar had been guilty of disrespect to the Court, to use the most lenient expression, in so far neglecting the decision of his Lordship in March last, as to resist the servants of the Company, thereby virtually annulling that decision. Mr. WETHERELL also held, that the plaintiff had no right to the injunction, as he had acquiesced in the decision of the Grand Jury of the county, which had awarded him a sum of 2,600l. for the ground wanted.

Sir SAM. ROMILLY, for the plaintiff, contended that he had never acquiesced in that verdict, nor received the money in question, it still remaining in the bank, where it was originally deposited, to await the ultimate decision of the affair. He trusted his Lordship would not be led by the representations of his learned friends, to think that Mr. Agar, who had been influenced merely by a laudable desire to defend his property from encroachment, had evinced the slightest disrespect for the Court.

His Lordship said, it appeared to him that the company had evinced no wish to do the plaintiff any injury; for when he had complained of the line they were taking through his grounds, they had proposed that he himself should fix upon the line described by the act. He could not, however, blame him for refusing to do this; but on the whole, he was inclined to think, that his most correct way of opposing them would have been an action for trespass. He signified his intention to postpone his final judgment.

PLYMOUTH, Nov. 26.

Arrived the *Royalist* brig from a cruise; the Edward, from Teneriffe, with wines, bound to London, was captured by the *Lawrence* American privateer, and recaptured by the *Glasgow*: the Blessing, from St. John's, Newfoundland, 16 days passage, sailed with the fleet under convoy of the *Comet* sloop, but parted two days after.

FALMOUTH, Nov. 25.

Yesterday arrived the Comus, William and Nancy, Aurora, &c. The above sailed from Portsmouth under convoy of the *Meander*, 38, brigs *Amaranthe*, 18, and *Badger*, 16; parted from them on the night of the 23d inst. off Berry Head, in a gale of wind; they were originally 70 sail. The Master of one of the vessels which arrived this day reports, that he saw the *Meander*, with about 20 sail in company, going into Plymouth.

YARMOUTH, Nov. 27.

Passed in the offing two ships of war to the westward, and a numerous fleet of coasters. The barracks in this town were sold by auction this week for 400l. The naval store at this port have received orders from their Board to send all the stores away, and the clerks to be discharged on the 30th instant. The commander of the signal station has also been discharged, and the officers of the Ordnance Department here are expected to follow the example soon.

DEAL, Nov. 27.

Sailed yesterday the *Nereus* frigate for the river. Came down from the river the *Clorinde*, and remains with his Majesty's ships *Bombay*, *Rosario*, *Vixen*, *Mercurius*, and *Wrangler*. Came down from the river several West Indiamen.

PORTSMOUTH, Nov. 27.

Arrived yesterday the *Comet* and *Challenger*, from Newfoundland. Came into harbour the *Stag*. The *Tortoise* went out of harbour. The West India fleet are at St. Helen's. Arrived the Trafalgar and Isabella transports, from Newfoundland. The brig Woodman is on shore on Warden Ledge, Isle of Wight.

RAMSGATE, Nov. 27.

The La Commune de Bourdeaux, with wine, brandy, cambric, silk, china, &c. was the night before last wrecked in the Godwin Sands; no part of cargo or vessel saved: crew landed safe at Broadstairs. Put in upwards of 20 sail for shelter.

The John Dixon, arrived in the Creek from Zante, spoke on the 11th instant the Emerald, from London to Trieste, and was informed, that four days before, about 120 miles west of the Barlings, she fell in with an American ship, a brig, and schooner, had a running fight for several hours, and escaped by superior sailing.

The Emerald was severely cut in sails and rigging, and received many shots in her hull.

The John Dixon spoke on the 11th instant, the Jane, from London to Amsterdam.

The Don Rodrigo, from London to Rio Janeiro, wilfully parted convoy from the *Duncan*, at sea, on the 5th inst. in lat. 40. 43. long. 15. 32.; and the Platus, from London to Teneriffe, disobeyed signals and parted company on the 3d inst.

Several of the *Meander*'s convoy, bound to Spain, Portugal, &c. have put into Falmouth.

By the latest accounts from the coast of America, the Constitution and Guerriere United States frigates had been victualled for twelve-months, and were waiting for an opportunity to put to sea; supposed destined for the East Indies.

BIRTHS.

On Monday last, at Duke-street, Westminster, Mrs. George Field, of a son.

On Sunday, the 27th inst. at Carshalton, the lady of James Ramsay, Esq. Old Broad-street, of a daughter.

At Montpelier, South Lambeth, Mrs. Tomkins, of a daughter.

MARRIED.

On Tuesday last, at Longdon Church, near Lichfield, by the Rev. Thomas Grove, Robert Henry Hurst, Esq. eldest son of Robert Hurst, Esq. of Horsham-park, Sussex, Member of Parliament for Horsham, to Dorothea, eldest daughter of John Breynton, Esq. of Haunch-hall, in the county of Stafford.

At Ipswich, on Saturday, the 26th inst. by the Rev. T. Cobbold, Robert Knipe Cobbold, Esq. of Eye, Suffolk, to Emily Mary, daughter of the late John Paul Smith, Esq.

DIED.

On Saturday morning, the 26th instant, Eva Beata, daughter of William Heyliger, Esq. aged two years.

On the 26th inst. at her house in Lower Seymour-street, Mrs. Brassey, widow of the late Nathaniel Brassey, Esq.

On Sunday morning, at his house in King's-road, Bedford-row, after a very long and severe illness, Anne, the wife of Joseph Sladen, Esq.

Nov. 25, aged 58, Thomas Walls, jun. of Nelson-square.

On Monday morning, at his house at Clapton, Wm. Bowman, Esq. of Lombard-street, banker.

At Ilford, at the house of his sister, Mrs. Stepple, on Saturday, the 26th inst. and in the 64th year of his age, Henry Stepple, Esq. From the integrity of his conduct, the clearness of his intellect, and correctness of his taste in literature and the arts, his memory will be long respected, and his loss regretted.

RETURN of WHEAT, from Nov. 14 to Nov. 19, is 12543 quarters,—Average, 67s. 8½d.—0s. 7½d. lower than last return.

RETURN of FLOUR, from Nov 12 to Nov. 18, is 16857 sacks.—Average, 68s. 8½d.—0s. 1½d. lower than last week.

COAL-MARKET, Nov. 28.

Ships at Market.	*Ships sold.*	*Price.*
10 Newcastle	8½	56s. 6d. to 66s. 9d.
½ Sunderland	½	61s. 0d.

PRICE OF STOCKS.

Navy 5 per Cent. 96½ ½ ⅛	India Bonds, 17 pr.
Irish 5 per Cent. 96½	Exchequer Bills, 1 4 pr.
4 per Cent. 80½ 81	Omnium, 2½ ½ dis.
3 per Cent. Red. 64¼ ⅜ ¼	Imperial Annuities, 5¾
3 per Cent. Cons. 65¾ ⅝ ¾ ⅝	Consols for Opening, 66½ ⅝ ½
Bk. L. A. 16½ 1-16th	State Lottery Tickets, 21l. 19s.

printers and compositors went on lightning strike for more money. Newspapers are peculiarly vulnerable to sudden strikes, because a lost issue can never be recovered. John Walter, who had done his apprenticeship as a printer, himself worked with some casual printers in the composing and press rooms for 36 hours without a break, and got the paper out on time. He then prosecuted his striking printers. When they were sent to prison, he petitioned the Regent for clemency. Thereafter *The Times* employed only non-union labour until the twentieth century. On the other hand, it was recognized in the trade as the house offering the best conditions for printers. These were savage times, my masters. John Walter II took the heretical but magnificent view that nothing matters more than getting tonight's issue out.

In addition to his splendid obsession with independence, Walter was a brilliant businessman, innovative, as sharp as a box of ferrets. He introduced the first steam press in Britain, printing 1,100 sheets an hour instead of 250 with the old hand presses. This Koenig and Bauer press was smuggled secretly into Printing House Square, to avoid alarm and Luddite demonstration from the printers of the ancient Mystery. Walter bluffed his workmen by keeping them on a bogus standby until 6 am on the morning of 28 November 1814. Then he entered the press room and announced dramatically: '*The Times* is already printed by steam'.

He promised the printers that the alarming new machines would not cause any redundancies. And they accepted the new technology, led newspapers into a new world and increased their wages hugely. John Walter II did not rest on this laurel. He never did. He continued his experiments to speed the print; and in 1828, with the brilliance of two British engineers, Applegarth and Cowper, he developed a new press capable of turning out 4,000 copies an hour.

After he had installed Barnes as editor in 1817, and trained him and supported him for his first few years, John Walter II began to retire gradually from the daily grind of journalism. When he took over *The Times* it had a circulation of under 2,000. When he retired it had risen to 30,000 and had become a real power in the land.

By then he was a widower. He married again, bought a big country house at Bearwood, Berkshire and took up a new life as a country gentleman. His period as a Member of Parliament, first for Berkshire and then for Nottingham, was as anonymous as *The Times* itself – but not so influential. He did not move in political or social circles. Personal ambition and vanity were foreign to his nature. Mary Russell Mitford, the contemporary bluestocking, found him 'the most bashful of men'. He was the archetypal newspaper proprietor, the founder of the press.

During his final illness, he moved back to London to be near his physician. It was appropriate that John Walter II died in the old private house at Printing House Square, annexed to the offices of the paper he had served so well, and, in a sense, created. R.I.P. – though peace was not an element in which he was content. Hallelujah. We shall not look upon his like again.

Below Bearwood in Berkshire, country home of John Walter II.
Bottom The Koenig and Bauer steam-powered press, the first in Britain, was installed at Printing House Square in 1814. It printed over 1,000 copies an hour.

'The most powerful man in the country'

Thomas Barnes was one of the founding fathers of nineteenth-century England. He turned *The Times* from an efficient newspaper into a mighty political instrument. His influence on political life was comparable to that of Nelson on the Navy, Peel on the police, and Arnold on the public schools. *The Times* was his life as well as his life's work. Apart from his newspaper, and its prodigious influence, we know very little about him.

He was born at Tenterden in Kent on 11 September 1785, the year in which *The Daily Universal Register* was first published. He was educated at Christ's Hospital where he was a contemporary of Leigh Hunt and Charles Lamb, and at Pembroke College, Cambridge. No biography of him has ever been written: there is not the material. The archives at Printing House Square contain nothing about Barnes, except the issues of *The Times* that he edited, which shook the world; and brief notes that he used to have his hair cut in the office by one of the compositors, and that he dined off tripe in his office.

Below Caricature by H.B., published by Thomas McLean, Haymarket, 1830 (the initials 'HB' preserved the incognito of the artist John Doyle for years). The publisher notes: 'John Bull led by the nose by THE TIMES newspaper. This probably is what THE TIMES meant when it assumed the title of "The leading journal of Europe".' Barnes himself wrote appreciative reviews of later publications of the *Political Sketches* of H.B.

Inset Portrait of Thomas Barnes by W. J. Newton, 1832.

Even death did not lift the veil from this very private man. After he had edited *The Times* for twenty-four years, his name was published there for the first time in May 1841, to announce his death: 'On the 7th inst., at his house in Soho-square, Thomas Barnes, Esq., in the 56th year of his age'. That was all.

Nearly a year later, commenting on a law case, *The Times* broke its Trappist reticence about its great editor by referring to Barnes as 'A gentleman connected with us who died last year and whose valuable services we must ever highly appreciate'.

John Walter II commissioned Barnes as a young man to report law cases, then Parliament, and then to review the theatre. He appointed him editor when Barnes was just thirty. Barnes was a good scholar and a young man of parts. If he had not become the thundering patriarch of journalism, he could have had a place in English literature or at Westminster. When he became editor, *The Times* consisted of one sheet of four pages. When he died it had become a paper of eight pages with frequent free supplements. Its circulation had risen to double the combined circulations of its three nearest competitors. Barnes and John Walter II had created the first newspaper to influence and reflect the public opinion that never had spoken yet.

Barnes would have approved the terse notice of his death. It was a memorial to his professional life. He believed in the potency of anonymous journalism and disliked the personality cult. A journalist had real power to influence events, but his name should be obscure or evanescent. In a leading article in 1835 he explained why: 'The public is a gainer because it obtains a free and full discussion without any mixture of that egotism and self intrusion which are almost inseparable from the composition of any individual writer in his personal character'.

Barnes created the authority and independence of *The Times*, without which it has no *raison d'être*. Northcliffe, no mean judge of the inky trade, said: 'The true founder of *The Times* was the second John Walter and its greatest editor, Thomas Barnes'. When Barnes became editor in 1817, *The Times* was just another journal among a Babel of others. When he left the chair, the voice of *The Times* was heeded by the great middle-class public and feared by governments. He said that his destiny was 'to arouse the public-spirited exertions of the middle-orders'.

He was lucky to have as his proprietor John Walter II, a man of strength of character, probity, fair-mindedness and liberal sympathies. Under John Walter I *The Times* had taken its share of bribes and subsidies: all newspapers did. Walter II and Barnes pioneered the notion that a newspaper could pay its way without them, solely by revenue from circulation and advertising.

Criticizing the Government was a hazardous as well as an unprecedented activity. Barnes's objectivity was put to the test early by the Peterloo Massacre. In 1819 at Saint Peter's Field, Manchester, cavalry charged a crowd of 60,000, killing eleven and injuring hundreds. *The Times* printed seven columns of devastating blow-by-blow account, and many more later in the year when the inquests were held.

Barnes was the son of a country solicitor. His family came from the London middle classes, 'citizens and clothworkers'. His great asset was his understanding of the middle classes – the professions, the men of property, the new industrial owners – who were about to lead the world in the industrial revolutions and the rise of empire. He disdained the aristocracy. And although he

Above Coloured lithograph (1829) of the office of THE TIMES, showing the public counter for placing advertisements and notices. In the foreground, an Englishman extols the paper to an American: 'Well Brother Jonathan, here we are in that Office from whence emanate the prototype of all Newspapers in this country. The most impartial, the most unchangeable and the most clever written paper ever published.' The American adds 'And I can see certainly the most Independent!!!' Barnes is seated in the box on the left, scanning galley proofs of News from the East, on the Russo-Turkish War. On the right, John Walter II, with an Owl on his chair-back, is being handed a purse by a Jew requesting him to rough-handle the Spaniards. Walter replies 'We are for the good of the good people', and promises an account of the Spanish expedition.

Below Extract from the diary of Charles Greville, recounting the Duke of Wellington's famous description of Barnes.

was in sympathy with the working classes, he did not direct his appeal to them, as did Cobbett with his *Political Register*.

By 1817 *The Times* already had an excellent service of foreign news: better than its rivals, often better than the Government. Barnes built up an equally omniscient service of home news. His network of intelligent, accurate and anonymous local correspondents around the country made *The Times* the ears and the tongue of public opinion. No man could judge the mood of the country better than Barnes. He could sense its change of direction uncannily. In following its master, the intelligent public, the newspaper was charged with inconsistency, and nicknamed 'The Turnabout'. Barnes replied that what mattered was 'Whether what we say *now* is true and just and to the purpose *now*'.

It was an age when journalists and pamphleteers did not mince their words. Barnes was no exception. His language was always vigorous, often violent, sometimes offensive. He declared that 'Newspaper writing is a thing *sui generis*; it is to literature what brandy is to beverage'.

He practised what he preached. Demanding Cabinet changes, he wrote: 'The rubbish must be wheeled away to the last barrowful. Good God! Are we to have another downright fraud passed upon the country?' He saw that the middle classes were timid and irresolute, and took it to be his duty to educate them in their rights and urge them forward. His leader of 29 January 1831 gave the message: 'Unless the people everywhere come forward and petition, ay, thunder for reform, it is they who abandon an honest Minister – it is *not* the Minister who abandons them'. 'Thundering for Reform' became the slogan of *The Times*. He once referred in print to an opponent as 'An unredeemed and unredeemable scoundrel, who has lied more foully than it could have entered into the imagination of the Devil himself to lie'.

No politician did more than Barnes to secure Catholic emancipation in 1829, and parliamentary reform. The Reform Bill of 1832 was a triumph for *The Times*, which had public opinion united behind Barnes's demand for 'The Bill, the whole Bill, and nothing but the Bill'. In 1834 Barnes literally laid down his terms for giving the support of *The Times* to Peel's new Government: the Lord Chancellor commented, 'Why, Barnes is the most powerful man in the country'. He was not joking.

Apart from his life in *The Times*, little is known. We can glean fragments from letters, diaries and the conversations of his friends. He was a good scholar, good at athletics, robust in mind and body, and a useful boxer. He was always on the side of the underdog; his passionate opposition to the Poor Law Bill of 1834, with its 'odious scheme of the workhouses', for once did not prevail. He acquired an unconventional and relaxed attitude to life at Cambridge, and never lost it. He was fond of wine, and in spite of his 'tripe in the office' could offer a good dinner table to his friends in Nelson Square and later Great Surrey Street. He was not married, but the lady he lived with from 1820 was known as Mrs Barnes and treated with remarkable respect by the stuffy society of the time. He was a great editor and a good man.

and he will again see the Duke & consider of
meeting one – He said "why Barnes is the most
powerful man in the country" – The Standard has
[illegible] to offer its support – the Duke said he had

Thomas Barnes's most famous leading article, in which he exhorts the people to 'thunder for reform' (column 5).
29 JANUARY 1831

From the LONDON GAZETTE, Friday, Jan. 28.

WHITEHALL, JAN. 26.

The King has been pleased to direct letters patent to be passed under the Great Seal of the United Kingdom of Great Britain and Ireland, granting to His Royal Highness the Duke of Sussex the offices of Chief Ranger and Keeper of Hyde Park and St. James's Park.

DOWNING-STREET, JAN. 26.

The King has been pleased to appoint the Right Hon. Robert John Wilmot Horton to be Governor and Commander-in-Chief of the Island of Ceylon.

PARTNERSHIPS DISSOLVED.

J. T., and J. K. Tillotson, Sheffield, merchants.—J. and T. Stringer, White Hart-place, Kennington-cross, surgeons.—J. Green, jun., R. Jordan, and H. Wartnaby, Ware, Hertfordshire, attornies; as far as regards J. Green, jun.—J. Upstone and J. Carlon, Gray's-inn-square, attornies.—T. Fryer and R. Warrington, Pontefract, Yorkshire, curriers.—Staniland and Garbutt, Kingston-upon-Hull, silk-mercers.—T. Redford and W. Stephenson, Kingston-upon-Hull, coal-dealers.—J. and W. Bradford, Thorney, Somersetshire, coal-merchants.—S. Hill and W. Pennycost, Portsea, Hampshire, coach-makers.—Cope and Taylor, Grocer's-hall-court, Poultry, merchants.—J. Labdon and R. Kelley, Exeter, coopers.—J. and J. J. W. Bowyer, Cheltenham, attornies-at-law.—Bee and Fullman, Harwood-street, Regent-street, milliners.—G. Popple, Sons, and Co. Growths, Yorkshire, saint and colour-manufacturers; as far as regards W. Todd.—R. Lakin and D. Wheldon, Dudley, Worcestershire, hatters.—T. Binney and J. Bailey, Sheffield, anvil-manufacturers.—Hall and Boult, Liverpool, wine-merchants.—D. Pennington and Co., Waterloo-bridge-road, livery-stable-keepers.

INSOLVENT.

Jan. 27.—Richard Hill, Lewes, Sussex, upholsterer.

BANKRUPTCY SUPERSEDED.

Abraham Lyon and Nathan Jacob Calisher, Birmingham and George-street, Jewry-street, wholesale jewellers.

BANKRUPTS.

Joseph Harrison, Hammersmith, coal-merchant, to surrender Feb. 8, 11, March 11, at 11 o'clock, at the Bankrupts' Court, Basinghall-street: solicitors, Messrs. Baddeleys, Leman-street, Goodman's-fields.

Arthur Wood, Great Tower-street, and Southampton-street, Camberwell, carpenter, Feb. 8, at 12 o'clock, Feb. 11, March 11, at 1, at the Bankrupts' Court, Basinghall-street: solicitor, Mr. Cawood, University-street, London University.

Hugh Lloyd, Palsgrave-place, Temple, scrivener, Feb. 4, 11, March 11, at 12 o'clock, at the Bankrupts' Court, Basinghall-street: solicitor, Mr. Fry, Cheapside, Trinity-square, Southwark.

Samuel Wilby, Aldermanbury, printer, Feb. 4, at 1 o'clock, Feb. 11, March 11, at 12, at the Bankrupts' Court, Basinghall-street: solicitors, Messrs. Wilkinson and Lawrance, Bucklersbury.

Thomas Griffin, Bridgwater, and Cross-place, Prince's-road, Lambeth, timber-merchant, Feb. 4, 8, March 11, at 1 o'clock, at the Bankrupts' Court, Basinghall-street: solicitors, Messrs. Rixon and Son, Jewry-street.

James Broadley and John Watson, North Moor, Lancashire, cotton-spinners, Feb. 18, 19, March 11, at 9 o'clock, at the York Hotel, Manchester: solicitors, Messrs. Milne and Parry, Temple.

Alfred Atkins, Glocester, merchant, Feb. 14, 15, March 11, at 11 o'clock, at the Red Lion Inn, Banbury, Oxfordshire: solicitors, Messrs. Lowe, Tanfield-court, Inner Temple.

William Fallows, Stafford, innkeeper, Feb. 18, 19, March 8, at 1 o'clock, at the Littleton Arms Inn, Penkridge: solicitors, Messrs. Chaves, Orme, and Wedlake, King's Bench-walk, Temple.

Henry Summers, Manchester, lace-manufacturer, Feb. 1, 2, March 11, at 11 o'clock, at the Albion Hotel, Manchester: solicitor, Mr. Nias, Copthall-court, Throgmorton-street.

James Munro, Liverpool, iron-founder, Feb. 15, 16, March 11, at 1 o'clock, at the Clarendon-buildings, Liverpool: solicitors, Messrs. Walmsley, Keightley, and Parkin, Chancery-lane.

Thomas Hall, Wigan, Lancashire, shopkeeper, Feb. 9, at 6 o'clock, Feb. 10, at 10, March 11, at 12, at the office of Mr. Leigh, Wigan: solicitors, Messrs. Adlington, Gregory, and Faulkner, Bedford-row.

Thomas Winn, Leeds, victualler, Feb. 7, 8, March 11, at 11 o'clock, at the Court-house, Leeds: solicitors, Messrs. Battye, Fisher, and Sudlow, Chancery-lane.

Robert Laskey, Exeter, haberdasher, Feb. 5, 12, March 11, at 11 o'clock, at the New London Inn, Exeter: solicitors, Messrs. Brutton and Clipperton, New Broad-street, city.

DIVIDENDS.

Feb. 22, S. Woods and G. G. Webb, George-yard, Lombard-street, woollen-drapers.—Feb. 22, C. Price, Strand, umbrella-manufacturer.—Feb. 18, J. Lane, Arundel, Sussex, corn-merchant.—Feb. 22, J., G., and J. L. Parker and T. Roberts, Birchin-lane, merchants.—Feb. 18, H. Kingsbury, Broad-street, Ratcliffe, builder.—Feb. 18, W. W. and J. M. Dunn, Sambrook-court, Basinghall-street, brokers.—Feb. 18, J. Fawley, Berwick-street, Oxford-street, ornamental painter.—Feb. 18, W. Richards, William's-court, Guildford-street, Southwark, measure-maker.—Feb. 18, W. Lunn, St. Mary-at-hill, slopseller.—Feb. 18, S. Lee, Church-row, Newington, master-mariner.—Feb. 18, W. H. Stamp and W. Nicholson, Milbank-street, Westminster, timber-merchants.—Feb. 26, C. Hankinson, Hale, Cheshire, tanner.—Feb. 18, J. Burraston, Hereford, coal-merchant.—Feb. 18, W. Offord, Colchester, cutler.—Feb. 19, P. Valentine, Bury, Lancashire, hardwareman.—Feb. 21, G. B. Watson, Rock-lodge, Durham, corn-merchant.—Feb. 19, W. Davis, Newbury, Berkshire, upholsterer.—Feb. 22, J. Richards, Wolverhampton, grocer.

CERTIFICATES to be granted, unless cause be shown to the contrary on or before Feb. 18.

T. Rogers, Shacklewell, boarding-house-keeper.—J. Mellor, Lingards, Yorkshire, dyer.—W. H. Fenn, Old Change, tea-dealer.—W. Hirst, Leeds, merchant.—T. Dalley, Nottingham and Beeston, lace-manufacturer.—W. Prince, Liverpool, tailor.—J. Fraser, Bath, perfumer.

SCOTCH SEQUESTRATION.

Alexander M'Kenzie, Stornoway, house-carpenter, Feb. 11, 28, at the house of Hugh M'Kenzie, Stornaway.

PRICE OF CORN.

General weekly average received in the week ended Jan. 21:—Wheat, 70s. 6d.; Barley, 40s. 2d.; Oats, 24s. 8d.; Rye, 42s. 11d.; Beans, 38s. 7d.; Peas, 41s. 6d.

Aggregate average of six weeks which governs duty:—Wheat, 68s. 6d.; Barley, 38s. 5d.; Oats, 24s. 3d.; Rye, 41s. 3d.; Beans, 39s. 1d.; Peas, 42s. 9d.

The average price of Brown or Muscovado Sugar, computed from the returns made in the week ending Jan. 25, is 24s. 6¼d. per cwt.

BRUSSELS PAPERS.

BRUSSELS, JAN. 24.

NATIONAL CONGRESS.—SITTING OF THE 24TH.

After the usual preliminary business, the Count d'Arschot, member of the Diplomatic Committee, ascended the tribune to communicate the following documents:—

"Paris, Jan. 23.

"TO THE COUNT D'ARSCHOT.

"Sir,—I received on the 21st the letter which you did me the honour to address me on the 19th. On the next day (the 22d) I sent a note, of which a copy is subjoined, to Count Sebastiani, who sent to me this morning an answer, which I transmit to you by express. I had foreseen that the term assigned was very near, and that it would be very difficult to comply with the wishes of the Congress by the 28th of this month. I think that I must wait for new orders to be able to fulfil the task which is imposed on me.

"I have the honour, &c.

"Count de CELLES."

"Paris, Jan. 22.

"TO COUNT SEBASTIANI.

[This note, from the Count de Celles, merely communicates the resolution of the Congress on the 19th, that the envoys who are at Paris, should send to the Congress as soon as possible, positive information respecting every thing concerning the choice of a Sovereign of Belgium; the territory, the commercial interests, or allowances, and that the Congress had fixed the 28th for the election of a Sovereign.]

"Paris, Jan. 23.

"TO COUNT DE CELLES.

"The undersigned Minister for Foreign Affairs has received a note, which Count de Celles did him the honour to address to him on the 22d. This communication is of such importance, and embraces questions of such high interest, since it regards the election of the Sovereign of Belgium, the extent of its territory, its commercial relations, and the nature of its alliances, that the undersigned cannot give an answer to it which shall offer the solution of all the questions comprehended in the resolution of the Congress.

"The choice of the sovereign is an act on which the future fate of Belgium will depend. Too much reflection, time, and deliberation, cannot therefore be given to it. Though the liberty of this choice is absolute, the Congress cannot, however, forget that Belgium, at the moment when it has become an independent state, and is going to occupy so important a place among the European powers, ought to show that it knows how to combine the exercise of its rights with the regard for other powers which a wise policy requires. The time which the Congress has fixed appears to me much too near to ensure the future happiness of the Belgians, and to remove every appearance of precipitation.

"The extent of the territory of the new state cannot be fixed without a concurrence of the Powers interested. France will never forget that the extent ought to be such as to secure to the Belgians natural frontiers, easy to be defended, and carefully to protect the interests of its agriculture, manufactures, and commerce."

The note concludes by declaring, that France will always consider Belgium as a member of the great French family, for which it has obtained all that was possible—viz. its separation from Holland. As for commercial questions, they are too complicated to be now discussed, but France will always secure to Belgium every advantage compatible with the interest of its own commerce and manufactures. As for new alliances, a new state ought not to be in a hurry to contract any.

(These papers were ordered to be printed.)

M. H. de Brouckere moved that the diplomatic committee should be called upon to inform the Assembly whether the Government of Maestricht had given orders, in consequence of the cessation of hostilities, to leave the navigation of the river free; to which M. d'Arschot answered, that the Government had sent a flag of truce to General Dibbetz, who had refused to receive it, that the diplomatic committee having no direct communication with Holland, is obliged to send its demands to the Hague through the envoys of the great Powers, which occasions delay in the negotiations.

M. Robaulx said,—If our flags of truce are not received, why do we withdraw our troops from the environs of Maestricht?

M. Lehon made some observations. He thought that the Governor of Maestricht might perhaps entertain some doubts on the subject. The retreat of our troops, he said, would not enable the garrison to obtain either fresh supplies of provisions, or reinforcements.

M. de Brouckere said,—We retire to the distance of two leagues and a half; consequently it will be easy to obtain supplies. We are duped again, for the Scheldt may be shut up again in 24 hours.

The galleries having loudly applauded, the President threatened to have them cleared.

M. Vilain XIV. required that the Government should make known the answer which it had given to the protocol of the 9th of January.

M. Lehon read the answer, which is in these terms:—

"VERBAL NOTE OF 19TH JANUARY.

"The President and members of the Committee of Foreign Affairs has had the honour to receive from Lord Ponsonby and M. Bresson, a copy of the protocol of a conference held at London, the 9th of January, by the Plenipotentiaries of the five great Powers.

"The Provisional Government of Belgium cannot consider the resolution taken, on the 9th of January, by the five great Powers, as any thing but a consequence of their desire to secure a reciprocal effect to the convention for the suspension of arms, and thus to complete the task which the Powers had undertaken for the sake of conciliation and humanity. In fact, it is only in this spirit that the mediation of the five great Powers was spontaneously offered to Belgium by the protocol of the 4th of November, and that it was accepted by the Provisional Government in the answers of the 10th and 21st of November and 18th of December. The Belgian Government, faithful to the word given, and on the faith of reciprocal execution, has caused all hostilities against Holland to cease on our part on the 21st of November, and has maintained this state of a suspension of arms for nearly two months past on almost every point, notwithstanding the permanent violation of it by Holland of its principal condition, by the prolonged blockade of the Scheldt, and notwithstanding the other evident acts of hostility against us, pointed out in the notes of the 3d, 8th, 18th, and 28th December.

"After these unequivocal proofs of good faith, the Provisional Government, however just may be its distrust of the intentions and promises of Holland, consents to give a new pledge of its moderation by ordering immediately—

"1. That on the 20th of this month at the latest the Belgian troops in the environs of Maestricht shall be withdrawn from that place so as to avoid opportunities for daily rencontres between the soldiers in and out of the place.

"2. That hostilities continue suspended on our side along the whole line, and that the troops shall resume the positions which they occupied on the 21st of November, 1830.

"As for the positions which they occupied within the undisputed limits of Belgium, the committee has judged that the faculty of changing them was left perfectly free to the two belligerent Powers. The Provisional Government, acting with the entire good faith, has a right to expect the complete execution of the engagements of Holland on the 20th of January.

"If this just hope should be again deceived,—if the Scheldt should remain closed after two months of vain complaints and expectations, it is the duty of the committee to declare that it would be extremely difficult to express the cries of the nation for war, and the enthusiasm of the army.

"On this subject the committee forbear mentioning here, that in the note delivered to Lord Ponsonby and M. Bresson, on the 24th of November, 1830, Belgium did not mean to bind itself towards the Powers by an engagement from which no circumstance could release it, and in particular, that it did not renounce the right, which belongs to every nation, to maintain itself by arms the justice of its cause, if the laws of justice should be violated or disregarded towards it.

"It appears to it besides incontestable, that every convention, the effect of which would be to determine questions of territory or finance, or to affect the independence or any other absolute right of the Belgic nation, is essentially one of the attributes of the National Congress, and that it alone has a right finally to decline. Accordingly, it is because the proposals of the Powers did not affect any of these rights or great interests, because they had for their object a situation merely temporary, and transitory as the nature itself of its attributes, that the Belgic Government has been able to give its assent to them. The committee will add, the very serious consideration that any other interpretation of the spirit of the negotiations that have hitherto been carried on, and of their results, would really transform the friendly proceeding of the Powers into direct and positive intervention in the affairs of Belgium,—an intervention, the principle of which the Congress has formally rejected, and which would appear to the committee no less incompatible with the general peace of Europe than with the independence of the nation."

M. Robaulx is not skilled in diplomatic language, but he thinks the pretext too feeble.

M. Le Hon.—On the 28th we will protest more energetically.

It was asked if Venloo was to be restored?

M. Le Hon said that that town will remain in our possession, as having been taken before the 21st of November.

The assembly then discussed some articles of the Constitution.—*Brussels papers*, Jan. 26.

(From the *Courrier des Pays Bas* of Tuesday.)

BRUSSELS.—SITTING OF THE CONGRESS OF JAN. 24.

The sitting commenced at half-past one, and the process-verbal of the former sitting was read and adopted.

The order of the day was the report of the Committee of Petitions.

The press of matter prevents us from giving an account of this part of the proceedings. We may, however, state that a report was made of the political declaration of more than 20,000 inhabitants of the Grand Duchy of Luxemburg, who protested against any arrangement which tended to separate their province from Belgium.

This document was deposited in the archives of the Congress in the following terms:—

"The Congress, having already decided that Luxemburg was an integral part of Belgium, directs that those acts of patriotism shall be deposited in the archives."

The unexpected arrival of M. d'Archot, a member of the Diplomatic Committee, who requested leave to make a communication to the Congress, interrupted the reading of the report of the commission.

Profound silence ensued, and much interest was excited amongst the assembly.

M. d'Archot mounted the tribune, and read the following letters:—

"Brussels, Jan. 23.

"Sir,—The National Congress having thought fit to consult the Government of His Majesty the King of the French, whose feelings of anxiety and friendship towards Belgium are well known, I hasten to communicate a despatch which I have just received from his Excellency Count Sebastiani.

"I remain, &c."

"Paris, Jan. 21.

"Sir,—The situation of Belgium has again attracted the attention of the King and Council. After a deliberate examination of all the political questions connected with it, I have been directed to inform you, in a clear and distinct manner, of the intentions of the King's Government. He cannot consent to the re-union of Belgium to France. He will not accept the crown for the Duke of Nemours, even were it offered to him by the Congress. His Majesty's Government is of opinion that the choice of the Duke of Leuchtenberg would be likely to interrupt the tranquillity of France. We have not the slightest idea of restricting the liberty of the Belgians in their choice of a sovereign, but we shall exercise our right in declaring, in the strongest manner, that we shall not recognize the election of the Duke of Leuchtenberg. No doubt the other Powers will not be very favourable to that choice; for our part, we are only influenced in this refusal by state reasons, to which every other consideration ought to yield, when it does not interfere with the rights of any individual. The close relation between France and Belgium, the interest his Majesty takes in its inhabitants, and the desire we entertain of preserving the strongest ties of friendship between the two nations, call on us to explain clearly and frankly to a people whom we respect and revere. No hostile feeling to the Duke of Leuchtenberg or his family, whom we highly esteem, influences this determination. The King's Government is solely guided by a love of peace, both at home and abroad. You are fully authorized to give an official intimation of this resolution of the King's Government, but with that frankness and respect which he is always desirous of maintaining with the Belgian nation. Believe me to remain, Sir, yours, &c.

"HORACE SEBASTIANI."

The reading of this letter was followed by cries of indignation. A member required that this document should be printed. ("No, no;" "Yes, yes;" from several.)

M. Lebeau insisted upon the necessity of printing the document, so that it might be known that the French Government disowned the principle of a free election of a sovereign. ("Bravo, bravo.") He should also suggest that it be mentioned in the proces verbal, that the Congress had no influence in the investigation which had been demanded.

M. Devaux supported the first resolution of M. Lebeau, and inveighed with much warmth against the answer of the French Cabinet. This refusal to recognize our King is nothing more nor less than an intervention. ("Yes, yes.")

M. Jottrand.—You must all have noticed that the note of M. Sebastiani speaks throughout of the Government of the King of the French. We know that these words mean the ministry. This is a doctrine a little contested in France, as it will be in this country, as soon as our new constitution shall be in full force. Well, then, this Government of the King of the French, which threatens not to recognize our choice, will probably be thought nothing of here in a few weeks. Other ministers will belong, in a few weeks, to that Government of the King of France. What has taken place between M. Sebastiani and us will hasten that change. You may now judge whether the interests of Belgium ought to be sacrificed to the opinion of a cabinet which will, in all probability, be dismissed on account of those very opinions.

M. Robaulx spoke with much energy against the answer of the Cabinet of the Palais Royal. If France excludes the Duke of Leuchtenberg at the present moment, to-morrow she will oblige us to accept the Prince of Orange as a ruler. ("Yes, yes; very true.")

M. Lebeau.—I do not believe that France wishes to force the Prince of Orange upon us. But France has some view in this; she is afraid to express it openly; in fine, she wishes to conquer us; it is through the ordeal of anarchy she wishes to lead us to the yoke which she is preparing for this nation. ("Hear, hear.")

The answer of the Cabinet of the Palais Royal was ordered to be printed.

At the very moment we are writing these lines, unanimous acclamations at the theatre of La Monnaie hail the accession of Augustus Beauharnois to the throne. 4,000 inhabitants of Brussels call for the election of this Prince in the most unequivocal manner. It is, in point of fact, a national fete; but why is it that the chief guest is absent?

Yesterday evening we witnessed an extraordinary scene at the theatre of La Monnaie, a scene which the people of Brussels can never forget. Between the acts the audience called for "La Beauharnaise," (a favourite air). M. Campenhout advanced to the front of the stage, and sung this melody, in the midst of the acclamations of the entire audience, who joined in the chorus. The bust of Augustus Beauharnois was exhibited, and was placed over the King's box, having been previously crowned by one of our wounded citizens. An extraordinary degree of enthusiasm prevailed throughout the theatre, and at the conclusion of the performance the audience retired with cries of "Long live Augustus Beauharnois!" "Long live the son of Eugene!"

The words "We wish to be the authors of our own liberty," in the piece entitled "*Napoleon at Schoenbrun and St. Helena*," were loudly applauded.

The portrait of the Duke de Leuchtenberg was installed at the Domino coffee-house, and was crowned amidst the acclamations of an immense concourse of people.

A petition in favour of the Duke de Leuchtenberg was deposited yesterday at the coffee-house of the Demy-Lune. The opinion of the inhabitants in favour of the Duke of Leuchtenberg is as strongly marked as that of the Congress.

TO CORRESPONDENTS.

We see no chance of being able to publish any letters for a long time to come, except the two or three which we have promised to insert.

☞ The publication of *The Times* commenced at 5 o'clock yesterday morning, and finished at 8.

LONDON, SATURDAY, JANUARY 29, 1831.

The French Government seems to have given great offence to the Congress at Brussels, and to the Belgic press, by objecting to the choice of the son of BEAUHARNOIS for their king. On this, as on other occasions of late, the stirring part of the Belgic nation are too eager to show their independence, and seem on the alert for insults never intended. The French Government does not interfere to prevent the election of the Duke of LEUCHTENBERG,—it merely declares what it intends to do in settling its relations with Belgium should that Prince be elected. Even such a declaration might be reckoned an interference, had it been gratuitously announced; but the French Government said nothing about its policy and intentions till its opinion as to certain nominations was asked. Deputation after deputation proceeded to Paris for the purpose of ascertaining the views of the Citizen King. A long list of candidates was discussed, and the opinion of the French Ministry on each was solicited. Was this meant to be an idle compliment, or was it intended that the sentiments of the party consulted should have some weight with the party consulting? If the application was a mere ceremony, why was the fact not so explained?—if it conferred the right of giving advice, and stating hypothetical resolutions, why are the Congress displeased with a result which they themselves provoked?

But if we can rely on a paragraph in one of the French papers, all this difficult deliberation on one side, and all this indignant alarm on the other, would be thrown away. That paragraph states that the young Duke of LEUCHTENBERG has written a letter to Paris, declaring that "he loves France too well to allow "his personal elevation to become a subject of anxiety "to the French Government," and that consequently he would not accept the crown of Belgium though it were tendered him. If this be the determination of the Prince, the ground of misunderstanding between the French and their Belgic allies is removed. The *nolo episcopari* will be more efficient in the case of a prince than a bishop.

The outrage lately offered to the Minister of Public Instruction and the Attorney-General, by some of the students, seems to have produced the effect that might have been expected from such a disgraceful transaction. The great body of the students have declared their horror at such conduct: the influence of the rioters is thus reduced to its real dimensions, and the hands of the University authorities are strengthened.

A journal entitled *l'Avenir* began to be published in Paris after the revolution in July. It is conducted entirely by priests, the chief of whom is the Abbé de LA MENNAIS. The Abbé and his followers belong to that fraction of the Catholic church which exalts the power of the POPE above all temporal authority. He, therefore, during the reign of the BOURBONS, called for severe laws against heretics, and opposed the rights of the Gallican Church as a kind of heresy. Since the revolution he has endeavoured to ally the most exalted claims of the spiritual power with the broadest principles of popular sovereignty. As the clergy cannot now direct the policy of the state in France, he thinks that he could increase their power by making them independent of it, and therefore proposes that they shall be supported by the offerings of the faithful instead of the ways and means of the budget.

But this is not the only singular notion of the learned Abbé. He has found out that none but Catholics are lovers of liberty, and cites the example of Belgium, Ireland, and Poland in proof of his discovery. Ireland is placed in the same category with the other two states, not only in its spirit of liberty, but in the certain issue of its supposed rebellion, and O'CONNELL is eulogized to the skies as its brave, *loyal*, and *patriotic* liberator. This jumble of doctrines and principles is not a little amusing. The Abbé, who is for the universal monarchy of the POPE, can have no sympathy with revolt, unless such a revolt as Popes formerly sanctioned. In the three cases where he extols the Catholics for their spirit of revolt, he found them subjected to rulers of a different faith. Hence the Poles, the Belgians, and the mobs of O'CONNELL, derive all the merit of their resistance. Were a Protestant people to resist the despotism of a Catholic Government, the Abbé's ideas of their merits would no longer be the same.

The following are a few extracts from the papers of Wednesday:—

(From the *Messager des Chambres*, dated Thursday).

"TOULON, JAN. 17.

"The *Syrene* frigate has arrived here from Algiers, whence it sailed on the 12th, with 600 men of different regiments. When it left Algiers all was quiet. The inhabitants do not appear to have any thing to fear from the partial evacuation which is now taking place. They depend on the 10,000 troops which will continue to occupy the country, and on the National Guard, which is being organized in all the towns which are under the French authority.

"PARIS, JAN. 26.

"There were some trifling disturbances yesterday morning in the College of Henri IV. The students of rhetoric and philosophy illtreated a sub-director, and barricaded themselves in their apartments: the other pupils, at the desire of the director, immediately went home to their families. At one o'clock the rebels, pressed by hunger, capitulated, opened their doors, and were delivered to their parents, who waited for them in the court-yard.

"The only motive assigned for this disturbance is, letters written by pupils expelled from other establishments to those of the College of Henri IV., reproaching them for not having yet had an insurrection.

"Duke Charles of Brunswick has returned to Paris, after having in vain sought the support of his relative the King of England, and then that of the Diet of Frankfort. His Serene Highness has formally protested against the resolution taken by the Diet on the 2d of December, 1830, by which Duke William is authorized to assume the Government till a family council shall decide the question of the sovereign.

"FORBACH, JAN. 23.

"It was reported to-day that the Belgian troops had blockaded the citadel of Luxemburg, in which there are 3,000 Prussians. (A reconnoissance by some detachments of Belgian troops in the Grand Duchy seems to have given rise to this very improbable report.)"

FRENCH FUNDS.—PARIS, Jan. 26.—Five per Cents., 93f. 60c. 70c. 65c. 75c. 80c. 75c.; Four per Cents., 78f. 75c.; Three per Cents., 61f. 50c. 45c. 50c. 55c. 75c. 65c. 75c. 50c.; Bank Stock, 1,500f. 1,495f.; Rente de Naples, 63f. 50c. 60c.; Rente d'Espagne, 14¾ ⅝ ½ ⅝; Royal Spanish Loan, 60⅛ ¼; Rente Perpetuelle d'Espagne, 46½ ¾ ½ ⅝ ½; Haytian Loan, 315f. Exchange on London, one month, paper, 25f. 10c.; money, 25f. 10c.; three months, paper, 25f.; money, 25f.—*Cours Authentique.*

Our readers will find, under the head of Brussels papers, copies of a curious correspondence between the Belgic and the French Governments, and accounts of the proceedings of the National Congress before whom the correspondence was laid. The Belgic Government like the Dutch has agreed to the armistice, under a similar protest. In the Congress there appear great bustle and little business,—noisy talk and indecisive conduct.

The naval preparations at Portsmouth, which occasioned some alarm in the city on Thursday, are, we believe, discontinued. At least the chief cause of them has ceased. When the King of HOLLAND showed an obstinate determination to blockade the Scheldt, it became, of course, necessary to be prepared with some of those cogent reasons for enforcing conviction which have been supposed to have most weight with monarchs. Since His Majesty has opened the Scheldt, there is no need of any appeal to this *ultima ratio*. We have reason to think that it will be found that there is no longer any extraordinary movement in any of our naval depots.

A pamphlet, entitled *Question of Reform Considered*, opens with an admission and an explanation of the difficulties which Ministers will have to contend with in their promotion of that great national good.

"The proposal of Parliamentary reform," says the author, "which Ministers are pledged to introduce "after the recess, is, unquestionably, one of the most "important measures that ever was submitted to a "deliberative assembly; and whether it shall obtain "the sanction of the whole Legislature, or be defeated "by the weight of interest, prejudice, and opinion, "arrayed against it, the consequences cannot be in"different to the public welfare and tranquillity. It "must be acknowledged, that Ministers have under"taken a task of predigious difficulty. They have to "encounter *the active, zealous, and disciplined hostility* "*of the whole host of the late disbanded Administration* "*and their connexions*,—of the 'general camp, pion"'eers and all,' who have grown up in the employ"ment of Government; they have, further, to combat "the interests of many powerful and respectable indi"viduals, and of the class to which they belong, who "have long enjoyed the personal benefit of engrossing "the actual nomination of a large portion of the mem"bers of the House of Commons."

The writer's anticipation of hostility from certain portions of the "late disbanded Administration," we have reason to believe is correct. There has been hatched, according to the best intelligence,—and in fact we have already denounced it,—a plan for thwarting the measure of reform at every stage of its progress through the House of Commons. Almost incredible as such an enterprise might appear, in the present state of public feeling and opinion throughout England, we are told that the thing is undeniable. The parties to this plot have agreed among themselves in a conclave, held lately at a certain country seat (it matters not where), to oppose Parliamentary reform to the uttermost, and to make their systematic stand on this opposition.

The parties express themselves (so profound is their knowledge of the state of Parliament and of the national temper and feeling) with a perfect assurance of success; reckoning on it as a necessary consequence of their victory that the present Cabinet must be dissolved,—that a new Administration will be formed by Sir R. PEEL himself,—(how must the Right Hon. Baronet have been amazed at this intelligence!)—and that, to reinforce still further the vast power of the conspiring potentates, some members of the existing Government will be solicited and persuaded to serve *under* Sir ROBERT PEEL!

We understand that one main reliance of the contracting parties is on those stanch and sturdy veterans, the members (miscalled representatives) for Scotland—a description of allies which must tend no doubt to enhance the popularity of the whole proceeding, and to facilitate a return to office of those Englishmen who avail themselves of such creditable agents for prolonging, in this part of the island, a system of representation, than which none but that of Scotland herself can be more execrably vicious.

As it seems desirable that all Members of Parliament, especially moderate and unsuspecting men, should be made acquainted with the tactics which are to be employed on this occasion, we think it right to announce as our conjecture, that, so far as the plotters now alluded to are concerned, no direct or open resistance will be made to the *principle* of reform. No, no! that would be too dangerous. But a wily and plausible course will be pursued; professions will be made of a full acquiescence in the abstract expediency of some reform; but ample vengeance will be taken for that unsavoury acknowledgment, by opposing, clause after clause, and syllable by syllable, all and every item in the *details* of the measure to be laid by Ministers before the House. In this way will the fight be conducted. The shadow will be spared, the substance massacred. The "principle"—worth nothing, because it is a mere word—will remain unmolested; and credit will be assumed by some of those who vote for it as if they were themselves reformers! but from behind the "principle," as a screen, the conspirators will attack the body and reality of reform, and will so contrive, if they can win over a credulous majority by thus exhibiting false colours, that the same House of Commons which glorifies itself for consecrating the abstract right of the country to a reformed Parliament, may effectually strangle every hope of improving the right into the possession. If Sir R. PEEL should, by some accident, not have learned the great tidings of all that is intended to be done for him, we would respectfully beg of Messrs. GOULBURN, TWISS, and one or two others, to acquaint the Right Hon. Baronet.

As for looking for any succour from the hard old Tories, we advise the agents of the PEEL party not to take labour in vain. The Tories, *par excellence*, hate Sir R. PEEL: they will have nothing to do with him—nothing to say to him, either towards badgering the present Ministry, or towards forming a new one; nor will the Duke of WELLINGTON be apt to serve under an old colleague whom his Grace is said to regard as but his own lieutenant.

But there is another party which may, perhaps unconsciously, cause as much mischief as the regularly organized opponents of reform: we mean the radicals, who, with their hopes excited by a reforming Ministry, aim at procuring by one stroke all those results which few but themselves think of paramount importance. We warn this party, whose intentions we believe to be good, but whose zeal we think too exacting, to be careful lest they fall into the snare already prepared for them by the Tory conspiracy: they would, we are sure, be the first to regret the ineffable mischief of upsetting an honest Cabinet, and would never forgive themselves for having contributed to such a catastrophe by their junction with men whose principles they abhor, and by whom they themselves would be laughed at and abjured as soon as the baneful victory should be achieved. It is, however, to the people we chiefly look: unless the people—the people every where—come forward and petition, ay, thunder for reform, it is they who abandon an honest Minister,—it is *not* the Minister who betrays the people. But in that case, reform, and Minister, and people too, are lost.

We are glad to see that the Grand Jury of Dublin have acted as became firm and upright men, and have found true bills against Mr. O'CONNELL and his followers. All honourable men, of all parties, are anxious to disclaim any participation with these mischievous disturbers of their country's peace,—these inveterate enemies to their country's happiness. It is with great pleasure that we are able to announce, that we have not received one well-written letter from any quarter, in defence of Mr. O'CONNELL, or in disapprobation of our own view of the subject. Bitter, and ferocious, and ruffianly abuse we receive from day to day, and we give the following letter as a fair specimen of the temper, taste, and sense of our opponents (anonymous, of course). It is needless to say what effect such compositions produce on our minds:—

"TO THE EDITOR OF EVERY THING THAT IS BAD.

"You grovelling, false, and rotten scribbler,—you inflammatory mass of contaminating corruption,—you vile and hell-doomed offspring of woman's womb,—you distorted supporter of human beings' wrongs,—you base forger of heavy chains for the persecuted frames of fellow-creatures,—you trampling oppressor upon human sufferers' rights,—you filthy scorn and disgrace from nature's meanest and lowest production,—you monstrous savage in deeds,—you poisonous viper in heart and soul,—withdraw from the wings of Time, by the command of honour, justice, and humanity, your unjust, your abominable, and monopolizing notions, your villainous insinuations, your gross misrepresentations of the admirable intentions and national wishes of 'Daniel O'Connell,' and his fellow countrymen,—O'Connell, the hero of his country,—the advocate of his country's rights and national independence,—the advocate and representative of all Ireland,—the everlasting admiration of the Irish,—the best and most sincere director of the people,—who are numerous enough to gorge their false-hearted foes in tuns of human blood, in the defence of that hero, of his liberty and just demands, and, moreover, in defence of their rights and national independence, against base and false-hearted foreigners, who wield an additional and despotic power over that which already binds down millions of the Irish beneath its forced weight, and cruel oppression. The voice of the Irish, from the Giant's Causeway to Cape Clear, proclaim these demands for that of which they have been so long most shamefully and maliciously deprived. The Irish shall be free from vile oppressors' cutting chains, from foreign foes, and from scribbling forgers' wrongs, and base and false representations, for they will be guided by none but Irish—

"HONOUR, JUSTICE, AND HUMANITY.

"London, Jan. 27."

On Monday Louis Philip I. gave a grand ball in the Palais Royal to 1,800 of the citizens of Paris. The party consisted of peers and deputies, merchants, artists, and manufacturers. The Queen and Princesses did the honours of the entertainment to the ladies, 600 of whom sat down to supper with the Royal Family.

[From a Correspondent.]—A society of artists, and one of artists and amateurs, have for some time existed at the west end of the town, and by their monthly meetings during the season have collected the most distinguished individuals at the Freemason's-tavern, and some of the finest specimens of living genius. We learn with pleasure, that an institution on a similar plan, and having the same objects in view, held its first meeting on Thursday evening last, at No. 10, Stationers'-hall-court, under the designation of "The City of London Artists' and Amateurs' Conversazione," which it is intended shall, in future, hold its meetings at one of the great city taverns. The meeting was numerously attended by individuals eminent for taste and talent. Among the contributions were the following productions:—Young in *Hamlet*; and a portrait of Bannister, by George Clint, A.R.A.; the *Family of Rembrandt*, by Stephanoff, the property of Mr. F. G. Moon; some exquisite drawings by E. T. Parris; busts of Dr. Stewart, Dr. Styles, Miss Bacon, and several others, by H. Behnes Burlowe; some portraits, by J. R. Wildman; some highly-finished academical studies and portraits, by John Wood; several studies, by Boxall; impression of medal-die of Lord Stowell, after W. Behnes, by Scipio Clint; Prince Leiningen and Lord Beresford, by Richard Rothwell.

Mr. Stanley, the Secretary for Ireland, was to leave Dublin on Wednesday for London.

We perceive by the Dublin papers, that an address to the Marquis of Anglesey, from the bankers, merchants, and traders of Dublin, expressing their confidence in his administration, and their determination to support the measures which may be necessary to restore the peace of the country and preserve the integrity of the united kingdom, is lying at the Royal Hotel, College-green. It has already received nearly 150 signatures, including the firm of Latouche and Co., which heads them.

RUN ON THE BANKS.—The following is an extract of a letter, dated Limerick, January 24, 3 o'clock p. m.:—"I have the pleasure to say that the run on the branches has ceased, and intimations were given by both, this day, of discounts, &c., being resumed as before."—*Dublin Evening Packet.*

It is rumoured in Leeds, that a riot took place at Carlisle on Monday last, and that five persons were killed by the military.—*Leeds Intelligencer.*

A county rate of three farthings in the pound has this week been levied on Middlesex, which amounts to 16,776*l.* The annual rental, as sworn at the last Michaelmas Clerkenwell sessions, is 5,368,408*l.*

DOVER, Jan. 27.—A fleet of about 150 sail, bound to London and the northward, which had collected in this roadstead during the late north wind, proceeded this morning. The *Echo* Dutch corvette sailed this morning for Flushing, her cruise having expired.

COURT CIRCULAR.

The Duke of Cumberland left town yesterday morning for the seat of Prince Leopold at Claremont. The Duke, Prince Leopold, and a select party, spent the day shooting in the neighbourhood of Claremont.

Count Flahaut, who has recently arrived in town from Paris, on a special mission from the King of the French, had a long interview yesterday with Earl Grey at the Treasury.

A Cabinet Council was held yesterday afternoon at the Foreign-office, which was attended by Earl Grey, the Marquis of Lansdowne, Lord Durham, Viscount Melbourne, Viscount Palmerston, Viscount Goderich, Viscount Althorp, the Right Hon. C. Grant, and Lord Holland.

The Council sat in deliberation two hours. The Earl of Carlisle was absent from the meeting, having left town for Brighton, in order to be present at the grand entertainment given by their Majesties last evening.

The Austrian, French, and Russian Ambassadors, and the Prussian Minister, were engaged in conference for some hours yesterday afternoon, at the Foreign-office, with Viscount Palmerston.

The American Minister had an interview yesterday with Viscount Palmerston, at the office of the Secretary of State for Foreign Affairs.

Viscount Palmerston and Viscount Goderich visited Earl Grey yesterday at the Treasury.

The Lord Chancellor entertained the Chancellor of the Exchequer and a select party to dinner yesterday, at his residence in Berkeley-square.

Earl Grey had a dinner party last evening at his residence in Downing-street.

MONEY-MARKET and CITY INTELLIGENCE.

Friday Evening.

The foreign exchanges having declined below par, though but in a trifling degree, attention has been directed in the city to that subject, and some persons seem disposed again to sound the alarm respecting a large exportation of gold. We doubt, however, whether any operations in that way, on a large scale, and founded on the profit of the transaction, have been entered into. Indeed, the advantage is so small in favour of the exporter, especially at this season when the steam-packets are not in use, that it could not be undertaken by any one purely as a commercial speculation. Whatever exportation is going on, therefore, must have some other object, and we think not unlikely, what we have heard surmised, that a speculation in grain is going on, and that gold is being sent to the continent as the most useful medium for the purpose. This, however, is a distinct affair from an exportation founded on profit, or on a higher price of gold on the continent compared with England, and the demand from such a source must be extremely limited. The gold sent to Ireland does not of course rank as "exportation," though it is extremely probable that the large amount sent over to counteract O'Connell's threatened run upon the banks has been the source in some degree of the alarm to which we have alluded. The Provincial Bank of Ireland, which has its head-quarters in London, and the agencies for the other banks, have all been actively engaged of late in forwarding the requisite supplies of gold to meet the run. By the most recent accounts from the various district banks, it appears, however, that they felt generally more secure, and considered the danger nearly at an end; so that in all probability no further supplies of gold will be required for protection, though a degree of caution with regard to advances, very injurious to the local interests, must for some time be adhered to.

There occurs nothing new in the Portsmouth letters to-day, and the writers seem to be of opinion that though there is an increase of activity in the Dock-yards, by the employment of the workmen six days in the week instead of five, and the preparations going on, which have already been stated, there is not such a degree of bustle as would indicate any definite object in view.

A meeting of subscribers took place at Lloyd's to-day, chiefly for the purpose of confirming the proceedings of the former meeting, at which it had been agreed that every measure proposed for altering any of the existing regulations of the establishment shall be decided by ballot. The minutes of the last meeting were confirmed, after which the question of the guinea fee to the committee, which had remained undecided in consequence of there having been an equal number of votes on each side, was again discussed. A proposition that a second ballot should take place on the subject was made, and lost by a considerable majority. The matter, therefore, remains *in statu quo*.

There was an almost entire suspension of business to-day at the Stock Exchange, and not the slightest fluctuation in Consols, the price during the whole day being 80½ to ⅝ for the account. In the foreign funds, though this was settling day, there occurred no fluctuation of the least importance.

Sydney papers to the 25th of August have been received to-day. They do not bring any intelligence of importance. It appeared from a recent arrival from New Zealand, with a cargo of [illegible], that trade with that island was increasing rapidly, and promised in a short time to become important to the New South Wales colonists. The principal articles of barter with the New Zealanders were muskets and gunpowder.

RUSSIAN BONDS.

TO THE EDITOR OF THE TIMES.

Sir,—In the beginning of the last year some Russian Bonds were purchased by myself and others, from the recommendation produced by the Russian Government having cancelled, in the year before, bonds to the amount of 84,000*l.*, viz., in June and October, 1829. To our surprise, during the last year, only one cancelling took place, viz., in April, to the extent only of 33,000*l.* How these bonds are cancelled, whether by purchase of them at the Stock Exchange, or in any secret way, is not known. Information on this subject will oblige a constant reader. VERITAS.

SOCIETY FOR THE SUPPRESSION OF VICE.

TO THE EDITOR OF THE TIMES.

Sir,—Observing an advertisement in your paper of the 25th instant from the Society for the Suppression of Vice, from which it appears that it is actively engaged in the laudable task of putting down the venders of obscene publications, and a paragraph in the same paper from you approving of and recommending the Society's exertions, in this respect, to the notice of the public, I herewith send you 5*l.* for the use of that Society. I have observed, with much gratification, your occasional reprobation of this infamous trade, and by sending this contribution through you, my motive is to show that I am duly influenced by the call of a journal whose respectability has secured that great and well-merited influence upon the public mind which it is generally acknowledged your paper possesses. From your constant reader,

A FRIEND TO PUBLIC MORALS.

Islington, January 27.

. The 5*l.* note has been sent to Mr. Pritchard, the Secretary of the Society.

THE COMET.

TO THE EDITOR OF THE TIMES.

Having twice availed myself of your kindness to distribute amongst such of your readers as take an interest in astronomical matters the place of the comet, of which the first notice was given by you in your journal of the 7th instant, it was not my intention to have troubled you any more on the subject, imagining as I did that the data then given were sufficient to enable any one to find it. Experience, however, shows me that such is not the case.

It was observed here on Wednesday and this morning. On the former occasion, it might by a person knowing well where to look for it, be with difficulty detected by the unassisted eye; this morning, certainly not. In either instance, with a very slight illumination of the field, it became invisible.

At 14h. 16m. 38sec. sidereal time of Tuesday, the 25th, its right ascension was 16h. 14m. 46sec. and 3-10ths; its southern declination was 6deg. 30m. and 0sec.; while at 14h. [illegible] 16sec. and 6-10ths sidereal time of yesterday, the 27th, its right ascension was 16h. 4m. [illegible], its southern declination 5deg. 45m. and [illegible]. Hence the daily diminution of right ascension in time, is about 5m. 20sec., and of southern declination, about 25m. [illegible].

The "lettered paragraph" in your paper of this morning gives its right ascension, January 25, at 14h. 16m. sidereal time, as 16h. 14m. and 54s.; and its polar distance, 96 deg. 35 min. and 40 sec. My observation [illegible] which, at least to one second of time, I am prepared to [illegible] reduced to that time, would give right ascension 16h. 14m. 38s.; differing no less than 16 seconds, a quantity equal to more than one hour's motion of the comet. If the two observatories are really so far asunder, is not for me to determine.

As for the polar distance assigned by your correspondent, as both observatories are nearly on the same meridian, it will place [illegible] sufficiently with my observation, "on lopping off 10 degrees from that which he has given us," and which doubtless is an error which he has committed in the reading his instrument. Whether the discrepancy between our observed right ascensions may be traced to the same cause, is not quite so easy to decide. J. S.

Observatory, Kensington, Jan. 28.

While Sir H. Davy was with Mr. Borlase, as an apprentice, it was his constant custom to walk in the evening to Marazion, to drink tea with an aunt to whom he was greatly attached. Upon such occasions, his usual companion was a [illegible], with which he procured specimens from the rocks on the beach. In short, it would appear that at this period he paid more attention to [illegible] that he thought more of the bowels of the earth when he should have been [illegible] his patients; and that [illegible] the sick, he was opening veins in the [illegible] surgery, he was [illegible]. Instead of preparing medicines in the [illegible] Mr. Tonkin's garret, which had now become [illegible] alchymical operations; and, upon more than one occasion, it is said that he produced an explosion which put the doctor and all his glass bottles in jeopardy. "This boy Humphry is incorrigible!" "Was there ever so idle a dog!" "He will blow us all into the air!" Such were the common exclamations of Mr. Tonkin; and then, in a jocose strain, he would call him "the philosopher," and sometimes, prophetic of his future renown, "Sir Humphry," as if [illegible].—*Paris's Life of Sir H. Davy.*

We regret to state, that a student of St. John's College ([illegible]) has been missing since Saturday last, and is supposed was drowned in the Cam, in the course of the preceding night, as his cloak and cap were found at the back of Jesus-green sluice-house, on the Chesterton side of the river, on Saturday morning. The body of the unfortunate gentleman has not yet been discovered.—(*Cambridge Chronicle.*

The Peterloo Massacre

Peterloo (named by analogy from Waterloo), or the Manchester massacre, was a politically controversial as well as a terrible event. Not for the first or the last time, *The Times* made news as well as reported it. Its account of Peterloo was by far the most complete, impartial and authoritative of all eye-witness accounts. It has become the historical record as well as a newspaper report.

A meeting was held on 16 August 1819 in St Peter's Field, Manchester to demand the reform of Parliament. It was to be addressed by 'Orator' Henry Hunt, the Radical reformer described by his opponents as 'a most unprincipled demagogue'.

The Times in 1819 was in sympathy with the movement for reform, without going the whole hog with Hunt. It denounced agitators but stigmatized as 'incendiaries' those (like Lord Liverpool's administration) who talked 'only of putting down by force every culpable, however pitiable, expression of popular suffering'. It denounced the intention of holding the assembly at Manchester; though, since the Radical reformers persisted in that intention, *The Times* expressed its hope that 'nothing will occur to divide the blame of any tumult with the parties who *prima facie* have provoked it'. And it sent one of its best reporters, John William Tyas, to St Peter's Field to record the meeting.

Tyas realized that he would have difficulty in hearing and reporting the speeches on 16 August because of the large crowd. He managed to see Hunt, who agreed to let the reporter have a seat on the platform. About 60,000 people turned out, including an unusually large proportion of women and children. They were unarmed and their behaviour was admitted to be wholly peaceful. Nevertheless the magistrates, who were in a nervous condition, ordered the Manchester Yeomanry cavalry to seize the speakers immediately after the meeting had begun. The Yeomanry, who were untrained and undisciplined businessmen, did not confine themselves to arresting the leaders but made a general attack on the crowd, crying 'Have at their flags', and cutting people down with the edge as well as the flat of their sabres.

The chairman of the magistrates, in the uproar, ordered the 15th Hussars and the Cheshire Yeomanry to charge the crowd also. Within ten minutes the field of Peterloo was cleared except for bodies, 'some still groaning, others with staring eyes, gasping for breath; others will never breathe more; all silent save for those low sounds and the occasional snorting and pawing of steeds'.

The numbers of casualties were disputed. But the best account states that eleven were killed and about six hundred wounded.

Tyas was arrested with the rest of the platform party. After a night in prison, he was released with polite apologies for the 'inconvenience' he had suffered. *The Times* wrote:

> Our readers will find amongst the names of the prisoners, that of a gentleman of the name of Tyas. Mr Tyas went down from London to take notes of whatever he should see and hear, and report it for *The Times*. He is a gentleman of talent and education; nephew to an individual of great respectability in the town of Manchester, and, so far as we can judge from his preceding conduct towards this journal, about as much a Jacobin . . . as is Lord Liverpool himself. Mr Tyas had been very seriously indisposed from the day of his arrival at Manchester. Anxious, however, to discharge in the most satisfactory manner, his duty to us and to the public, he determined to procure, if possible, a place near Hunt on the day of the meeting, for the sake of his own infirm health, and for the greater facility of sending us a complete report.

In spite of Tyas's arrest at Peterloo, the reports in *The Times* were remarkably full. Seven out of the twelve columns of reading matter in the issue of 19 August were given to the completest of all press accounts of the massacre. *The Times* broadcast its comments as well as its reports. It called its readers to acknowledge 'the dreadful fact that nearly a hundred of the King's unarmed subjects have been sabred by a body of cavalry in the streets of a town of which most of them were inhabitants, and in the presence of those Magistrates whose sworn duty it is to protect and preserve the life of the meanest Englishman'.

The reports in *The Times* were reproduced throughout the country, and increased the pressure for reform. John William Tyas did not leave a household name for the *Dictionary of National Biography*. But he had the real power of the Recording Angel at a turning-point in British history.

Tyas's eyewitness report of the Peterloo Massacre. Little is known of Tyas himself, except that he became one of the paper's senior parliamentary reporters and retired in 1864.
19 AUGUST 1819

Below Print of the Massacre at St Peter's Field, Manchester, by George Cruikshank, published September 1819. A crowd of 50,000 people had gathered to hear Henry Hunt and others speak on issues of Reform and the formation of Associations and Unions. The Yeomanry and Hussars were sent to arrest Hunt and break up the meeting. THE TIMES reporter Tyas was on the platform with Hunt, shown crying 'Shame, Murder, Massacre', as the troops set upon the crowd.

LONDON, THURSDAY, AUGUST 19, 1819.

We insert in our columns of this day, such details as have reached us since our last publication, relative to the deplorable transactions which took place during Monday's Manchester meeting. Whatever may have been the preliminary or accessory circumstances connected with that assembly—whatever may be our sense of the merits of those who promoted and presided at it—of their principles political and moral—of the predominant feelings and temper of their followers—of the unfitness of the season at which 50,000 people, half employed and half starved, were congregated to a single spot, there to be puffed up by prodigious notions of their strength, and inflamed by artful pictures of their grievances—whatever, again, an observant mind may suspect as to the real projects of the few who thus played upon the passions and misfortunes of a suffering multitude,—all such considerations, all such suspicions, sink to nothing before the dreadful fact, that nearly a hundred of the King's unarmed subjects have been sabred by a body of cavalry in the streets of a town of which most of them were inhabitants, and in the presence of those Magistrates whose sworn duty it is to protect and preserve the life of the meanest Englishman. In *The Times* of Monday we concluded an article which severely blamed HUNT as a moral agent, by expressing an anxious hope that no persons (thereby meaning the magistracy) would so conduct themselves as to *share* with that brawler the reproach of any evil consequences which might follow the assemblage of so large a body of discontented labourers, at a period teeming, like the present, with solicitude and alarm. The hope we expressed was an indirect, though sufficient intimation of the fears of which we could not divest ourselves on that subject; and our readers are now as well qualified as ourselves to form an opinion to what extent those melancholy forebodings have been justified. It appears by every account that has yet reached London, that, in the midst of the Chairman's speech, within *less than twenty minutes* from the commencement of the meeting, the Yeomanry Cavalry of the town of Manchester charged the populace sword in hand, cut their way to the platform, and with the police at their head, made prisoners of HUNT and several of those who surrounded him—seized the flags of the Reformers—trampled down and cut down a number of the people, who, after throwing some stones and brickbats at the cavalry in its advance towards the hustings, fled on all sides in the utmost confusion and dismay. Of the crowd, as we stated yesterday, a large portion consisted of women. About 8 or 10 persons were killed, and, besides those whom their own friends carried off, above 50 wounded were taken to the hospitals; but the gross number is not supposed to have fallen short of 80 or 100, more or less, grievously wounded. Such are the facts: we do not absolutely affirm that they cannot be defended, but we are still to seek their justification, not indeed in the newspaper descriptions of certain mottos inscribed on flags, (however foolish and inflammatory)—nor in the display of a cap of liberty, the model of which is borne before the sovereign of Great Britain, when he meets his Parliament—No, the advocate of the measures resorted to at Manchester, by the assembled magistrates and the armed force, must rest their defence on some *legal* principle; for if the justification should fail in law, we suppose it will not be attempted on grounds of good feeling or humanity.

A word on this part of the question, which concerns the capture of HUNT and those about him. Our readers will find amongst the names of the prisoners, that of a gentleman of the name of TYAS. Mr. TYAS went down from London to take notes of whatever he should see and hear, and report it for *The Times*. He is a gentleman of talent and education; nephew to an individual of great respectability in the town of Manchester, and, so far as we can judge from his preceding conduct towards this journal, about as much a Jacobin, or friend of Jacobins, as is Lord LIVERPOOL himself. Mr. TYAS had been very seriously indisposed from the day of his arrival at Manchester. Anxious, however, to discharge, in the most satisfactory manner, his duty to us and to the public, he determined to procure, if possible, a place near HUNT on the day of the meeting, for the sake of sparing his own infirm health, and for the greater facility of sending us a complete report. By what means he so unluckily succeeded in this purpose, as to be considered one of HUNT's party, we have yet no materials for conjecturing: but, greatly as we have been grieved for his sake by this accident, and severely as it has disappointed our hopes of affording more ample and perfect information to our readers, we mention the circumstance less as a subject of complaint with regard to our personal feelings, than as a mode of illustrating the manner in which those who acted for the magistrates thought fit to exercise the power, and to discharge the functions, assigned to them. Mr. TYAS, we have reason to know, was absolutely unacquainted with HUNT, at the moment of his entering Manchester: of what has since happened, we are as ignorant as the public at large.

But we revert to the more solemn question, of the legal and constitutional basis on which this seizure of persons and spilling of blood is to be justified by those who directed them. We speak not of the moral, but of the *legal* justification, and desire at present to be considered as referring to the latter alone.

The Riot Act, and the act against seditious meetings, both limit the magistrate's right of interference, to "unlawful assemblies," and no other. Was that at Manchester an "unlawful assembly?" Was the notice of it unlawful? We believe not. Was the subject proposed for discussion (a reform in the House of Commons) an unlawful subject? Assuredly not. Was any thing done at this meeting before the cavalry rode in upon it, either contrary to law or in breach of the peace? No such circumstance is recorded in any of the statements which have yet reached our hands. The *Courier*, indeed, labours hard to prove, that this was an adjourned, and therefore, by the Act of 1817, an unlawful meeting. But the fallacy of such an argument is clear from this,—that the former meeting was wholly given up, because it had been summoned for *an illegal* purpose; namely, for a usurpation of the elective franchise, and of the right of representation: whereas this was called for a professedly lawful purpose; and could not, therefore, be identified by those who administer the laws, with one which set those laws at defiance. HUNT's *dictum*, in his speech to the mob, has no influence on the question in a legal sense. Having said so much as to the legality of the cause of interfering, let us proceed to the legality of the *mode*. The Riot Act, some say, was read; some say otherwise—but all are agreed, that before an hour had elapsed from the reading of it, the soldiers attacked, and the people were cut down. Yet we pronounce not a final opinion upon this momentous proceeding. We have begged for information rather than uttered a decision; and happy shall we be to find, that while one party is charged with violating the laws of England, the opposite party may be able to prove that they have respected them.

Accounts from Manchester, up to 2 o'clock on Tuesday afternoon, reached us last night. At that hour nothing had occurred of a nature sufficiently serious to disturb the peace of the town. Compared with the tumultuous proceedings of Monday, tranquillity might be said to prevail; but indications of a forced submission on the part of the populace, of vindictive feelings suspended, but not suppressed, were too apparent not to cause alarm in those who carefully observed their motions, and listened to their discourse. The military who had patrolled the streets during the whole of Monday night, were equally vigilant on Tuesday morning; they were judiciously employed in checking, before they could become formidable, the first symptoms of riot and disorder. Small parties of cavalry rode through the principal streets; and if any of the populace were collected into a group, they were immediately dispersed. The shops and the lower part of the houses continued shut the whole morning. The temper of the Reformers, though thus prevented from displaying itself in action, was strongly manifested by an unbounded license of expression; and threats of revenge, directed more particularly against those members of the Manchester Yeomanry who were most active in the affair of Monday, and who, by residing in the town and being well known to the disaffected persons, became distinctly marked out as objects of their hatred. The female part of the multitude were not less conspicuous than on Monday for the share they took in what was going on, and were even more bitter and malignant in their invectives than their male associates. New-Cross, the place where the most dangerous rioting had occurred on Monday evening, was taken possession of during the morning of Tuesday, by companies of the 31st regiment of foot, who relieved each other in succession. An attempt was made by the very lowest of the populace to assemble there at the early hour of seven, but they were soon put to flight, and by nine o'clock every thing was tranquil in that quarter. A report (which appears to have been spread with the view of diverting the attention of the military) was circulated early in the morning, that a large body of the disaffected, armed with pikes, amounting in number to 15,000, were advancing to Manchester by the Oldham road. A party of the 15th Light Dragoons, with two pieces of artillery, were immediately stationed in Oldham-street; and the Cheshire Yeomanry, who were previously on duty at St. Peter's-green, were ordered to advance on the road to Oldham. This alarm proving to be unfounded, the troops and artillery were withdrawn by two o'clock. The exertions of the soldiery, though fully effectual in preventing any tumultuary assemblages, could not, however, so completely guard against individual outrage. A butcher in Oldham-street is stated to have been attacked and desperately wounded in the head by a small party of the mob, and carried to the Infirmary, with little hope of recovery. One of the special constables, a watchmaker, was marked out for a similar species of revenge. The latter was fired at by a pistol, and wounded, but not dangerously. Mr. J. HULME, the gentleman who fell in the first attack by the Manchester Yeomanry, was still alive when the accounts left the town; but the fracture of the skull which he had sustained was so severe, as to leave little hope of his recovery. HUNT, together with JOHNSON, and MOREHOUSE of Stockport, are said to have been brought up for examination on Tuesday, but *none of them were admitted to bail*; and it was even circulated, though on what grounds we are unable to state, that these three leading Reformers were under commitment to Lancaster Gaol on a charge of high treason. At all events they still remained in confinement. The proceedings of Monday have been already so minutely detailed, that little remains to be added to them; we cannot, however, forbear noticing an act of indiscretion committed by a member of the Yeomanry, and which, if correctly stated, will scarcely admit of palliation. This person was peculiarly active in the attack of Monday, and succeeded in personally seizing one of the insurrectionary flags, displayed by the Reformers on the hustings at St. Peter's-green. Not contented with the mere possession of this trophy, he thought proper to exhibit it from the window of his house, which stands in one of the most frequented streets and outlets of the town, in full view of the populace then retiring, indignant, though discomfited, from the scene of action. They took fire at this insult, and watching their opportunity, when the attention of the military was called off from that particular spot, completely demolished every window by a volley of stones and other missiles, and would probably have proceeded to more serious acts of outrage, but for the arrival of prompt assistance. The individual has himself alone to blame for the consequences of his indiscretion. In the existing temper of the mob, which we have described, it will create no surprise that threats have been unsparingly used, and that both the houses and factories of the more active members of the Yeomanry, have been marked out for destruction; but we are happy to state, that no instance of so formidable a species of revenge has hitherto occurred, and confidently hope that any calamity of such a nature may still be prevented.

EXPRESS FROM MANCHESTER.

Just as our paper was going to press, we received from the gentleman deputed by us to report the proceedings at Manchester, the following account. It comprises not only copious details of what took place on Monday, and brings up those of Tuesday to a late hour, but contains, besides, some very important occurrences in other parts of the great manufacturing district, to which we direct the serious attention of our readers.

DISPERSAL OF THE REFORM-MEETING AT MANCHESTER BY A MILITARY FORCE.

This meeting, which has caused such universal anxiety and trepidation throughout the whole of the country, took place on Monday last at Manchester.

The place appointed for the meeting was a large vacant piece of ground on the north side of St. Peter's Church, which is well known in Manchester by the name of St. Peter's-place. At half past 10 o'clock about 250 idle individuals might be collected within it. About half-past 11 the first body of Reformers arrived on the ground, bearing two banners, each of which was surmounted by a cap of liberty. The first bore upon a white ground the inscription of "Annual Parliaments, and Universal Suffrage;" on the reverse side, "No Corn Laws." The other bore upon a blue ground the same inscription, with the addition of "Vote by Ballot." After these flags had been paraded over the field for some time, it was thought fit by the leaders of the party which had brought them, that they should remain stationary. A post was accordingly assigned to the bearers of them, to which shortly afterwards a dung-cart was brought, into which the standard bearers were ordered to mount, and from which all the standards arriving afterwards were most appropriately displayed. Numerous large bodies of Reformers continued to arrive from this time to 1 o'clock, from the different towns in the neighbourhood of Manchester, all with flags, and many of them drawn up five deep, and in regular marching order. A club of female Reformers, amounting in number, according to our calculation, to 156, came from Oldham; and another, not quite so numerous, from Royton. The first bore a white silk banner, by far the most elegant displayed during the day, inscribed "*Major Cartwright's Bill, Annual Parliaments, Universal Suffrage, and Vote by Ballot.*" In one compartment of it was Justice, holding the scales in one hand, and a sword in the other; in another, a large eye, which we suppose was impiously intended to represent the eye of Providence. On the reverse of this flag was another inscription; but in the hurry of the day we found it impossible to decipher what it was, and can only say that there were upon it two hands, both decorated in *shirt ruffles*, clasped in each other, and underneath them an inscription, "*Oldham Union.*" The latter (i. e. the females of Royton) bore two red flags, the one inscribed, "*Let us* (i. e. women) *die like men, and not be sold like slaves;*" the other, "*Annual Parliaments and Universal Suffrage.*" The Radicals of Saddleworth brought with them a black flag to the field, on one side of which was inscribed, "*Taxation without representation is unjust and tyrannical; equal representation or death;*" on the other side, "*Union is strength.—Unite and be free. Saddleworth and Mosley Union.*" The Reformers from Rochdale and Middleton marched to the sound of the bugle, and in very regular time, closing and expanding their ranks, and marching in ordinary and double quick time, according as it pleased the fancy of their leaders to direct them. They had two green banners, between which they had hoisted on a red pole a cap of liberty, crowned with leaves of laurel, and bearing the inscription, "*Hunt and Liberty.*" Another band bore a banner, in which Britannia was represented with her trident, leaning on a shield, upon which was inscribed the motto borne by Sir William Wallace, "God armeth the Patriot."

In this manner the business of the day proceeded till 1 o'clock, by which time we should suppose that 80,000 people were assembled on the ground. During this period we found it impossible to approach the waggon, though very desirous to do so, as a young lad, not more than 17 or 18, was addressing the meeting with great vehemence of action and gesture, and with great effect, if we may judge from the cheers which he every now and then extracted from his audience, who were now beginning to be impatient for the arrival of Hunt, and the other orators who were to follow in his train, like the satellites which attend on some mighty planet.

The Reformers who had up to this time arrived in the field demeaned themselves becomingly, though a posse of 300 or 400 constables, with the Boroughreeve at their head, had marched in a body into the field about 12 o'clock, unsupported by any military body to all outward appearance. Not the slightest insult was offered to them. The people did indeed rush to behold them; but this was probably occasioned by an idea that they were another body of Reformers. As soon as they saw who they were, they turned away from them with a smile; and, attracted by a crowd which was advancing from another corner of the area, went to meet it, crying, "Let us keep peace and order, and go and welcome this body, which is one of ours."

As we stood counting the members of the Oldham Female Reform Club in their procession by us, and whilst we were internally pitying the delusion which had led them to a scene so ill-suited to their usual habits, a group of the women of Manchester, attracted by the crowd, came to the corner of the street where we had taken our post. They viewed these Female Reformers for some time with a look in which compassion and disgust were equally blended; and at last burst out into an indignant exclamation—"Go home to your families, and leave *sike-like matters as these* to your husbands and sons, who better understand them." The women who thus addressed them were of the lower order in life.

We had waited up to one o'clock on the field of action for the arrival of Mr. Hunt; but as he had not then made his appearance, we determined to go and meet the procession, which it was said was to attend the orator. We met it just by the Exchange, where the people were cheering most loudly, and Hunt and Johnson joining in the cheers. They were seated in an open landau, along with Carlisle, Knight, and others, and had moved in grand procession from Smedley-cottage, past New-cross, and Shude-hill, preceded by a large body of male, and followed by a scarcely less numerous body of female Manchester Reformers. Before them were carried two boards, on which were inscribed, "*Order, order;*" these were followed by two flags for annual Parliaments and universal suffrage, and also by Hunt's old flag and cap of liberty, of Westminster notoriety, "Hunt, and universal suffrage." This latter was held by a female Reformer, seated on the *dicky* of the landau, which had the honour of carrying the illustrious band of patriots whose name we have just mentioned. It was now to be exhibited in the last of its fields.

[It was just opposite to the Exchange, as was before mentioned, that the individual who furnishes this report met the procession in full march: from the numbers whom he had already seen collected on the field, and those whom he then saw proceeding to increase them, he felt convinced of the impossibility of getting into any position in which he could hear the proceedings of the day, unless he received some personal accommodation from Mr. Hunt himself. He had never previously spoken to that individual, nor would he have thought of addressing him upon this occasion, had he not known that every gentleman connected with the London press had gladly availed himself of similar assistance at the Smithfield meeting. As to espousing the political principles, or advocating the wild doctrines of radical reform, supported by Mr. Hunt, it is the very last thing, if he knows himself, that he should ever be induced to do; he holds them in as utter abhorrence as the most loyal subject of his Majesty possibly can hold them, and will always be ready to express that disgust in the warmest and most indignant terms. Mr. Hunt, on this individual's asking to be admitted, if possible, on to the hustings, immediately acceded to his request. He desired him to stand as close as possible to the landau in which he was riding, and promised to take care that every accommodation in his power should be paid to his convenience. He followed in the train of the Orator till he arrived in the field of action.]

The enthusiasm excited among the crowd by the presence of the Orator was certainly beyond any thing which we ever before witnessed; and the cheers with which he was hailed were loud and lasting. When he had taken his stand upon the hustings, which were formed of two carts lashed together, and boards spread over them, he expressed considerable disapprobation of the manner in which they were formed, and of the place in which they were situated. This will not excite surprise, when we state, that it was so arranged that the speaker had to talk against the wind; and also, that on Mr. Hunt's last appearance at Manchester, the hustings were so slightly built as to yield to the pressure of the superincumbent crowd, though fortunately no accident happened from their giving way. After the different persons who intended to address the multitude had taken their position upon them, and silence had been obtained, Johnson came forward, and proposed that Henry Hunt be appointed their Chairman. Here a short pause ensued, as if Johnson had expected that some person would have come forward to second his proposition. No person, however, doing so, Johnson proceeded to call upon them to carry the question by acclamation. The meeting did so, and Henry Hunt was declared Chairman, amid cheers of 3 times 3. The noise continuing longer than usual, Hunt found it requisite to entreat his friends to preserve tranquillity. He commenced his address by calling the assembly "gentlemen," but afterwards changed the term to "fellow countrymen." He had occasion, he said, to entreat their indulgence. (*Noise continued.*) Every man wishing to hear, must himself keep silence. (*Laughter, but no silence.*) "Will you," said he, addressing himself to the mob, "be so obliging as not to call silence while the business of the day is proceeding?" (*Silence was then obtained.*) He hoped that they would now exercise the all-powerful right of the people; and if any person would not be quiet, that they would put him down and keep him quiet. (*We will.*) For the honour which they had just conferred upon him, he returned them his most sincere thanks: and for any services which he either had or might render them, all that he asked was, that they would indulge him with a calm and patient attention. It was impossible for him to think that with the utmost silence he could make himself heard by every member of the numerous and tremendous meeting which he saw assembled before him. If those, however, who were near him were not silent, how could it be expected that those who were at a distance could hear what he should say? [A dead silence now pervaded the multitude.] It was useless for him to recal to their recollection the proceedings of the last 10 days in their town; they were all of them acquainted with the cause of the late meeting being postponed; and it would be therefore superfluous in him to say any thing about it, except, indeed, it were this—that those who had attempted to put them down by the most malignant exertions had occasioned them to meet that day in more than twofold numbers. (*Hear.*) (Knight here whispered something into Mr. Hunt's ear, which caused him to turn round with some degree of asperity to Knight, and to say, "Sir, I will not be interrupted: when you speak yourself, you will not like to experience such interruption." They would have perceived, that since the old meeting had been put off, and the present one had been called—though their enemies flattered themselves with having obtained a victory, they showed by their conduct that they had sustained a defeat. (*Long and loud applause.*) In the interval between the two meetings, two placards had been circulated, to which the names of two obscure individuals were attached: the first was signed by Tom Long or Jack Short, a printer in the town whom nobody knew.

At this stage of the business the Yeomanry Cavalry were seen advancing in a rapid trot to the area: their ranks were in disorder, and on arriving within it, they halted to breathe their horses, and to recover their ranks. A panic seemed to strike the persons at the outskirts of the meeting, who immediately began to scamper in every direction. After a moment's pause, the cavalry drew their swords, and brandished them fiercely in the air: upon which Hunt and Johnson desired the multitude to give three cheers, to show the military that they were not to be daunted in the discharge of their duty by their unwelcome presence. This they did, upon which Mr. Hunt again proceeded. This was a mere trick to interrupt the proceedings of the meeting: but he trusted that they would all stand firm. He had scarcely said these words, before the Manchester Yeomanry cavalry rode into the mob, which gave way before them, and directed their course to the cart from which Hunt was speaking. Not a brickbat was thrown at them—not a pistol was fired during this period: all was quiet and orderly, as if the cavalry had been the friends of the multitude, and had marched as such into the midst of them. A bugle-man went at their head, then an officer, and then came the whole troop. They wheeled round the waggons till they came in front of them, the people drawing back in every direction on their approach. After they had surrounded them in such a manner as to prevent all escape, the *officer* who commanded the detachment went up to Mr. Hunt, and said, brandishing his sword, "Sir, I have a warrant against you, and arrest you as my prisoner." Hunt, after exhorting the people to tranquillity in a few words, turned round to the officer, and said, "I willingly surrender myself to any civil officer who will show me his warrant." Mr. Nadin, the chief police officer at Manchester, then came forward and said, "I will arrest you; I have got informations upon oath against you," or something to that effect. The military officer then proceeded to say, that he had a warrant against Johnson. Johnson also asked for a civil-officer, upon which a Mr. Andrew came forward, and Hunt and Johnson then leaped from off the waggon, and surrendered themselves to the civil power. Search was then made for Moorhouse and Knight, against whom warrants had also been issued. In the hurry of this transaction, they had by some means or other contrived to make their escape. As soon as Hunt and Johnson had jumped from the waggon, a cry was made by the cavalry, "Have at their flags." In consequence, they immediately dashed not only at the flags which were in the waggon, but those which were posted among the crowd, cutting most indiscriminately to the right and to the left in order to get at them. This set the people running in all directions, and it was not till this act had been committed that any brick-bats were hurled at the military. From that moment the Manchester Yeomanry Cavalry lost all command of temper. A person of the name of Saxton, who is, we believe, the editor of the *Manchester Observer*, was standing in the cart. Two privates rode up to him. "There," said one of them, "is that villain, Saxton; do you run him through the body." "No," replied the other, "I had rather not—I leave it to you." The man immediately made a lunge at Saxton, and it was only by slipping aside that the blow missed his life. As it was, it cut his coat and waistcoat, but fortunately did him no other injury. A man within five yards of us in another direction had his nose completely taken off by a blow of a sabre; whilst another was laid prostrate, but whether he was dead or had merely thrown himself down to obtain protection we cannot say. Seeing all this hideous work going on, we felt an alarm which any man may be forgiven for feeling in a similar situation: looking around us, we saw a constable at no great distance, and thinking that our only chance of safety rested in placing ourselves under his protection, we appealed to him for assistance. He immediately took us into custody, and on our saying that we merely attended to report the proceedings of the day, he replied, "Oh! oh! You then are one of their writers—you must go before the Magistrates." To this we made no objection; in consequence he took us to the house where they were sitting, and in our road thither, we saw a woman on the ground, insensible, to all outward appearance, and with two large gouts of blood on her left breast. Just as we came to the house, the constables were conducting Hunt into it, and were treating him in a manner in which they were neither justified by law nor humanity, striking him with their staves on the head. After he had been taken into the house, we were admitted also; and it is only justice to the man who apprehended us to state, that he did every thing in his power to protect us from all ill-usage, and showed us every civility consistent with his duty. In the room into which we were put, we found the Orator, Johnson, Saxton, and some other individuals of minor note, among whom was another woman in a fainting condition. Nadin the constable was also there. Hunt and Johnson both asked him to show them the warrants on which they had been apprehended. This he refused to do, saying that he had information upon oath against them, which was quite sufficient for him. Hunt then called upon the persons present to mark Nadin's refusal. Shortly after this transaction, Mr. Hay, the chairman of the magistrates, came into the apartment, and asked Hunt if he was afraid to go down to the New Bailey; if he was, he himself would accompany him, and look after his safety. Hunt, who we forgot to mention had received a slight sabre wound on one of his hands, said, that he should have no objection to the Magistrate's company; he certainly did not like either a cut from a sabre or a blow from a staff, both of which had been dealt out to him in no small quantity. Mr. Hay shortly afterwards went out, having first made a reply to Mr. Hunt, which some riot out of doors prevented us from hearing. On casting our eyes at the place where the immense multitude had lately been assembled, we were surprised in the short space of ten minutes to see it cleared of all its former occupiers, and filled by various troops of military, both horse and foot. Shortly after this had occurred, a Magistrate came into the room, and bade the prisoners prepare to march off to the New Bailey. Hunt was consigned to the custody of Col. l'Estrange, of the 31st foot, and a detachment of the 15th Hussars; and under his care, he and all the other prisoners, who were each placed between two constables, reached the New Bailey in perfect safety. The staffs of two of Hunt's banners were carried in mock procession before him.

After these individuals had been committed to the custody of the Governor, they were turned into one common yard, where the events of the day formed the subject of conversation. Knight and Morehouse, who had been taken a short time after them, were afterwards added to their company. About 5 o'clock the Magistrates directed the Governor of the prison to lock each of them up in a solitary cell, and to see that they had no communication with each other. This was accordingly done.

The writer of this article was one of the parties thus imprisoned. Except that it was imprisonment, he has no reason to complain of the treatment which he received. He was in custody from 2 o'clock on Monday, till 12 o'clock on Tuesday. As soon as the magistrates were acquainted with the circumstances under which his apprehension had taken place, they immediately ordered his release, and expressed in very polite terms their regret for the inconvenience to which he had been subjected. When we were once more allowed to enjoy that freedom of which we had been for a moment deprived, we took a walk through most of the principal streets of Manchester, and found that they were at that time (12 o'clock) completely under military disposal. Soldiers were posted at all the commanding positions of the town, and were to be seen extended at full length on the flags in various directions. At three o'clock, they had, however, all of them returned to their quarters, and the town was to all outward appearance once more in a state of tranquillity.

At seven o'clock, when we quitted Manchester, all was quiet in the town. A report had, however, reached it that there was a serious riot at Oldham, and in consequence some troops of the Chester Yeomanry were sent to quell it.

In our road to Stockport, our attention was forcibly struck by the numerous groups of idle men, who were congregated together along it. They appeared ready for any wicked or desperate purpose; and we have reason to believe that before the evening was concluded they were engaged in an attack upon the magistracy of Stockport. About a mile from that place some hundreds of them were assembled near a petty public house. A new hat, a tea-kettle, and some other articles of little value, were displayed at the window, as is customary to display the prizes given at wakes or feasts in this part of the country. This was to serve as a pretext for their meeting together; but that it was only a pretext we learned to a certainty during our stay at Macclesfield.

On our entry into that town about 10 at night, we were met by several women, who flung themselves in the way of our chaise, and entreated us for God's sake not to enter it, as murderous work was going on within it. This was not, to be sure, pleasing information; but on consulting with our driver, he said that there could be no harm in our proceeding on as far as the Royal Hotel, which lies nearly at the entrance of the town as you come from Manchester. On arriving there, our horses were seized by some special constables, and we were advised not to proceed farther up the town, if we had any regard whatsoever for our lives. Of course we took their advice, and turned our horses into a yard, as they desired us. On inquiring into the cause of the anxiety which was depicted in all their faces, they informed us that the Reformers in their neighbourhood, irritated by the defeat which they had sustained at Manchester the day before, had assembled in a body of 2 or 3,000 men, and had been committing the most abominable acts of violence in different quarters of the town. In the market-place they had broken every window which looked into it, and in various other places had done similar acts of atrocity. They were emboldened in their villany by the knowledge that there were only a few military men in the town, and that in the custody of these men, were 300 stand of arms, and several thousand rounds of ball cartridge. The circumstance of these arms being so loosely guarded, filled the minds of the peaceable inhabitants with the utmost dread, especially when they found, on going to the guard-house, that out of the six soldiers stationed in the town, two were dead drunk, and one of them the sergeant at the head of the detachment. They were all, however, persuaded to stand to their arms, and being aided by several respectable inhabitants of the town, assumed so formidable an appearance that the rioters thought it unwise to attack them. This disinclination on their part gave fresh courage to the friends of order and tranquillity; and in consequence they made an attack on the rioters, and took several of them prisoners. In the meanwhile, an express was sent off to Stockport, desiring that one of the three companies of the 31st, which had marched from their quarters at Macclesfield to Stockport, might be sent back to the former place, or else a company of the Cheshire Yeomanry Cavalry, many of whom are inhabitants of the place, might be dispatched to the assistance of their townsmen. Whilst this scene was transacting in Macclesfield, it was said that bonfires had been lighted on all the hills which surround it, and it was surmised that these served as signals to the disaffected. The first lighted was on Blakeney-hill; this was answered by similar fires on all the hills, from thence up to Northern Laney there it stopped; but at another signal, fire-rockets were thrown up from it. Whether there was any meaning in these fires or not we are unable to say; but shortly after they appeared, the rioters resumed their attacks, having first taken the precaution to extinguish all the gas-lights in the town. This was attended by twofold advantage inasmuch as it did not leave them so open to detection, and therefore gave them a better opportunity of continuing their devastations. Still, with all these advantages, they never durst meet the small but resolute band of special constables; who, under the command of the Mayor, were every where ready to resist them. Some 8 or 9 gentlemen who had mounted themselves on horseback and armed themselves with swords, were of great utility in scouring the streets and bringing in prisoners, who were immediately placed in the custody of the soldiers of the 31st. We are happy to say, that in the struggles between the two parties, no serious personal injury was done to either of them. Some of the rioters got heavy blows from the staffs of the constables, and some of the constables awkward contusions from the brickbats hurled at them by their opponents; but no lives were either lost or endangered. When we left the town, which was at 4 o'clock in the morning, tranquillity was perfectly re-established; 30 or 40 rioters were in custody, and the gentleman who had gone with the express to Stockport, had returned with the intelligence, that, though a battle between the military and the rioters was momentarily expected, a troop of infantry had started from Stockport, and were when he left them within an hour's march of Macclesfield. At Stockport the magistrates were assembled at the Warren Bulkeley Arms, before which the soldiery was drawn out, as that was the first point against which the rioters had declared their intention of making an attack. Similar riots were expected at other places; almost all the military being stationed at Manchester.

THE RADICAL REFORMERS.

(From the *Manchester Mercury*.)

FATAL RESULTS OF THE RADICAL REFORM MEETING.

The events of yesterday will bring down upon the name of Hunt, and his accomplices, the deep and lasting execrations of many a sorrowing family, and of the well-affected members of society at large. With a factious perverseness peculiarly their own, they have set at open defiance the timely warnings of the Magistracy; and having daringly invited the attendance of a mass of people, which, as it respects yesterday's muster, may, with much reason, be computed at 100,000 individuals, they proceeded to address them with language and suggestions of the usual desperate and malevolent character.

That such a state of things has existed quite long enough must be admitted by every good man; and yesterday's proceedings showed, that the revolutionary attempts of this base junto were no longer to be tolerated.

It was not until near one o'clock that this fellow and his immense mob traversed the streets, by an indirect route, towards the place of meeting near St. Peter's Church. The first notable object in the procession was a board exalted above the crowd, bearing the specious inscription "*Order;*" next came a miserable band of musicians; and in about the centre of the phalanx, the odious instigators of the day's calamity, viz. Hunt, Johnson, Knight, and another *worthy*, carried in an open hackney-coach; upon the box was displayed an *amiable* specimen of the *female* branch of these *philanthropists*, who was very busy buffeting the air as she went along with a white handkerchief; the red cap of liberty held a prominent place in the procession, and several flags with the usual inflammatory sentences were displayed. They halted, as they have been accustomed, opposite the Exchange, while they astounded all ears with continued shouting and clapping of hands.

About half-past one, they arrived at the area appointed for their performances, and the leading characters ascended the hustings. Hunt was proposed and accepted as Chairman; and some preliminary business had been entered upon, altogether occupying about twenty minutes, when the bugle sounded, and the Manchester and Salford Yeomanry Cavalry, who, pursuant to instructions, had been in attendance about ten minutes, advanced in full charge through the multitude, and surrounded the *Orators* upon their own stage, who were all taken into custody, and consigned forthwith to the New Bailey prison. Hunt demurred, and said he would surrender to no one but a magistrate; a gentleman in the commission then appeared, and the whole were given up to the special protection of Mr. Nadin. The 15th Hussars and the Prince Regent's Regiment of Yeomanry Cavalry next approached, and routed the throng, with the utmost dismay, in all directions. The constituents of the meeting were formed of six divisions, to each of which was attached a red cap of liberty; and no less than 15 flags, with a variety of inscriptions, were exhibited.

Now ensues a most painful and melancholy part of our recital; the necessary ardour of the troops in the discharge of their duty has led, we lament to say, to some fatal and many very serious accidents. A respectable innkeeper, (Mr. Ashworth, of the Bull's Head,) who was officiating as a special constable, was rode over and mortally wounded; another young man, who is at present unknown, experienced the same fate; Mr. A. Tifford, innkeeper, has been most dangerously hurt; another unfortunate sufferer lies dead in the Infirmary, and several are without hopes of recovery; there are eighteen in-patients there, (principally from Oldham, Saddleworth, Middleton, &c.), and 32 out-patients; a considerable number have been taken, wounded, to their own homes. A most worthy and respectable young gentleman, a member of our Yeomanry, is lingering in the Infirmary, every moment expected to breathe his last: during the charge, he was assailed by a brick-bat, which brought him off his horse, when he was rode over, and had his skull fractured. The extent of injuries received is truly heart-rending; we fear what we have already stated will prove to be strictly within compass.

Mercury-office, 7 o'clock.

The Riot Act has just been read at the New-cross, in consequence of the windows of Mr. Tate, grocer, being entirely demolished by stones from the pavement. The town certainly wears an alarming aspect at the present moment; but we are well supplied with military protection, and their exertions and resolute conduct are truly praiseworthy, and a theme of general eulogium.

8 o'clock.

Our respected fellow townsman in the Infirmary, we are just informed, is now haplessly no more.

(From the *Manchester Herald*.)

We now come to the eventful Monday, August 16, to which so many persons resident, and so many at a distance, who have friends in Manchester, have looked forward with considerable anxiety.

Early in the morning the municipal authorities caused precautionary placards, of which the following is a copy, to be posted throughout the town:—

"The boroughreeves and constables of Manchester and Salford most earnestly recommend the peaceable and well-disposed inhabitants of those towns, as much as possible, to remain in their own houses during the whole of this day, Monday, August 16, and to keep their children and servants within doors."

By 10 o'clock a great body of special constables assembled in readiness in St. James's-square, and the different military corps were resting on their arms, prepared for the call of the Magistracy, if their services should be deemed requisite.

Soon after 12 o'clock, the Magistrates and a body of constables repaired to the ground, to which the brigaded Reformers had marched; and in consequence of depositions made before several of his Majesty's Justices of the Peace, by many of the most respectable inhabitants of the towns of Manchester and Salford, in which they stated their apprehension of riot and tumult, as the probable consequence of such an assemblage of persons from distant townships, marched thither under banners so explicit of rebellious intentions, the Riot Act was read; but it did not appear to be much attended to by the infatuated crowd, who continued to scowl and laugh at the constables, &c. in attendance.

At 1 o'clock another procession passed the Exchange, escorting Hunt to the place of meeting; for the Great Man, perhaps to enhance his consequence, made the would-be legislators wait for him, although their advertisement stated that the chair would be taken at 12 o'clock. The leader of this band bore a large club, and he was followed by some hundreds of men and boys, who marched in columns, with military step, to the music of a regular band, dressed in gray uniforms. By the colours which were displayed, the van, at least, were from Oldham. After them was borne a board elevated on a pole, and, as if in downright mockery, on both sides was painted "Order, Order." Almost immediately before the barouch in which Hunt rode, was borne the same flag and cap of liberty which were displayed on his first visit to Manchester. On the box of the carriage was seated a woman! bearing a flag; and in the open carriage stood the main pivot of mischief; several other persons were seated in it, but we did not learn

The Duke and THE TIMES

It is safe to say that the first Duke of Wellington was not a great fan of the British press. He shared the prejudices of his class and period against the wretched scribblers of Grub Street. Yet even Wellington came to recognize *The Times* as an independent and incorruptible new power in the realm. It took him a little while.

In 1810 he accused the London editors of 'stultifying England'. In 1826 *The Times* annoyed him in a personal matter. It reported that Wellington had taken his great and good friend, Mrs Arbuthnot, to a fancy dress ball dressed as a man. Mrs Arbuthnot claimed that she was in fact dressed as Mary Queen of Scots. Wellington threatened to sue, and described Barnes as 'an insolent, vulgar fellow'. On 2 May 1827 he complained in the House of Lords of 'the manner I have been treated by the corrupt Press in the pay of the Government'.

Paradoxically, *The Times* grew great on the exploits of the Duke of Wellington. It had an arrangement with his agents by which it was able to publish the first news of his campaigns, before the official report in the *London Gazette*. The coffee-house customer in Haydon's painting *Waiting for 'The Times'* (illustrated on p. 12) is probably waiting for news of the Duke's latest victory in the Peninsular Campaign, or his latest move in the political struggles for parliamentary reform or over the Corn Laws.

The Duke's military career reached its peak at Waterloo, from where he wrote: 'The attack succeeded in every point; the enemy was forced from his position on the heights, and fled in the utmost confusion . . . It gives me the greatest satisfaction to assure your Lordship, that the army never, upon any occasion, conducted itself better' (reprinted in *The Times* 22 June 1815).

When the Duke gave up campaigning and turned to politics, he had to start dealing with the press. In a letter to his crony John Wilson Croker, the Tory politician and *literato*, on 14 September 1828, the Duke put his fastidious view:

> My dear Croker,
> I hate meddling with the Press. The perpetual interference with the Press was one of the rocks on which my predecessors struck. But I am afraid we do meddle, that is to say the Secretary of the Treasury does;

Below POLITICAL SKETCHES by HB (John Doyle) (1829). The Duke reads out to George IV a report of their difference of opinion. Lady Conyngham, the King's mistress, is seated between them, her husband and Knighton, Secretary, confidant and physician to the King, stand beside his chair. Wellington told Mrs Arbuthnot that he spent half an hour laughing heartily over this caricature of himself.

READING THE TIMES.

The 'Official Bulletin', and leading article, on Wellington's victory over Napoleon at Waterloo. Despite the momentous news, it was kept to page 3 of the paper: only such events as the death of Nelson could oust advertisements and the Agony Column from the front page.
22 JUNE 1815

he justified his lamentation by considerations very similar to those urged in defence of military torture. He said there was something in the nature of Frenchmen which required it (a laugh). The hon. baronet, after a variety of further observations, concluded by remarking, that hope and fear were the grand instruments of human actions. If we were to trust our soldiers and seamen better, we should give them a motive very superior to the instigation of fear. He congratulated himself, however, on the progress the question had already made, and he trusted that in the next session it would be again introduced, and that the fullest information connected with it would be no longer withheld.

Mr. BABINGTON opposed the motion as unnecessary at present.

Lord PALMERSTON and Mr. M. SUTTON explained.

Mr. BENNETT then replied, after which the question was negatived without a division.

Mr. MELLISH moved for several papers respecting the public deposits and unclaimed dividends in the hands of the Bank.

The Lords' amendments to the East India Shipping Bill were read and agreed to.—Adjourned.

THEATRE ROYAL, DRURY-LANE.
THIS EVENING, RULE A WIFE AND HAVE A WIFE.
Leon, Mr. Kean.
To which will be added, CHARLES THE BOLD.

THEATRE ROYAL, COVENT-GARDEN.
THIS EVENING, ISABELLA.
Isabella Miss O'Neill
To which will be added, COMUS.

For the Benefit of Mr. BRANDON, Box-Book and House-keeper.
THEATRE-ROYAL, COVENT-GARDEN.
On FRIDAY, June 30, THE DUENNA.
Carlos, Mr. Sinclair, who will introduce 'Just like Love;' Clara, Miss Stephens.
In the course of the evening, 'Black Eyd Susan', and 'The Storm,' by Mr. Incledon
With a FARCE and other ENTERTAINMENTS.
Tickets and places to be taken of Mr. Brandon, at the Box-office.

ROYAL AMPHITHEATRE, (ASTLEY'S).
THIS EVENING, at half past six precisely, HORSEMANSHIP by Mr. Avery, and a comic Act, by the Clown, Mr. Brown. A New splendid Serio-Comic Equestrian Pantomime, with extraordinary preparations, called THE LIFE, DEATH, and RESTORATION of the HIGH-METTLED RACER; or, Harlequin on Horseback. In the course of twenty-one interesting Scenes will be introduced a REAL HORSE RACE, and a REAL FOX CHACE. A favourite comic Song by Mr. Herring. Equestrian Exercises, by Mr. W. Davis. After which, a Comic Musical Piece, called KING HENRY VIII. AND THE COBLER. To conclude with (16th time) THE SAILOR'S LOVE, or Constancy Rewarded. Second Price at half-past eight.

The last Week of the present Arrangements.—The Public are respectfully informed, that in consequence of the extraordinary expensive Preparations making for a Ship Launch on real Water, no Aquatic Scene can be exhibited this week.

SADLER'S WELLS.
THIS and 3 following EVENINGS only, a new Dance, called THE PLOUGH BOY; a Comic Song, by Mr. Sloman; a favourite pantomime, called THE MERMAID, Clown, Mr. Grimaldi. The Entertainments to conclude with a new Melo-Drama, called THE RED HANDS; or, Welch Chieftains. Box 4s.; Pit 2s.; Gal. 1s. Doors opened at half past 5, and begin at half past 6; places kept till half past 7. On Monday, June 26, will be produced a new Pantomime, which has been a long time preparing, called Harlequin Brilliant; or Clown's Capers; to conclude with a Ship Launch on real Water.

VAUXHALL.
Under the Patronage of his Royal Highness the PRINCE REGENT. TO MORROW Friday, June 23, will be a GRAND GALA, and brilliant EXHIBITION of FIRE-WORKS by Signor Bologna. Admission 4s.—Doors open at half-past seven, and the Concert begins at half-past 8.

LONDON, THURSDAY, JUNE 22, 1815.

OFFICIAL BULLETIN.

"DOWNING-STREET, JUNE 22, 1815.

"The Duke of WELLINGTON's Dispatch, dated Waterloo, the 19th of June, states, that on the preceding day BUONAPARTE attacked, with his whole force, the British line, supported by a corps of Prussians: which attack, after a long and sanguinary conflict, terminated in the complete Overthrow of the Enemy's Army, with the loss of ONE HUNDRED and FIFTY PIECES of CANNON and TWO EAGLES. During the night, the Prussians under Marshal BLUCHER, who joined in the pursuit of the enemy, captured SIXTY GUNS, and a large part of BUONAPARTE's BAGGAGE. The Allied Armies continued to pursue the enemy. Two French Generals were taken."

Such is the great and glorious result of those masterly movements by which the Hero of Britain met and frustrated the audacious attempt of the Rebel Chief. Glory to WELLINGTON, to our gallant Soldiers, and to our brave Allies! BUONAPARTE's reputation has been wrecked, and his last grand stake has been lost in this tremendous conflict. TWO HUNDRED AND TEN PIECES OF CANNON captured in a single battle, put to the blush the boasting column of the Place de Vendome. Long and sanguinary, indeed, we fear, the conflict must have been; but the boldness of the Rebel Frenchmen was the boldness of despair, and conscience sate heavy on those arms which were raised against their Sovereign, against their oaths, and against the peace and happiness of their country. We confidently anticipate a great and immediate defection from the Rebel cause. We are aware that a great part of the French nation looked to the opening of this campaign with a superstitious expectation of success to a man, whom, though many of them hated, and many feared, all had been taught to look on as the first captain of the age. He himself went forth boasting in his strength, and still more in his talents. He had for many years ridiculed CARNOT's plan of a Northern Campaign, and had openly avowed at Paris his intention to break through the centre of the Allied Armies, instead of moving round both their flanks. With as little reserve had he declared that he would open the campaign on the Meuse and Sambre. In short, by a refinement in finesse, he had exposed his true plan, imagining that nobody would believe that such was his real intention. We do not deny that his plan might have been one of considerable ability; but he did not take into the account that he was to be opposed by abilities superior to his own. That unpalatable truth his vanity would not allow him to believe, nor would it easily find credit with his admirers; but the 18th of June, we trust, will satisfy the most incredulous. Two hundred and ten pieces of cannon! When, where, or how is this loss to be repaired? Besides, what has become of his invincible guard, of his admired and dreaded cuirassiers? Again, we do not deny that these were good troops; but they were encountered by better. We shall be curious to learn with what degree of coolness, of personal courage, and self-possession, BUONAPARTE played this stake, on which he must have been well aware that his pretensions to Empire hung. It is clear that he retreated; nor are we prepared to hear that he fled with haste or cowardice; but we greatly suspect that he did not court an honourable death. We think his valour is of the calculating kind, and we do not attribute his surviving the abdication at Fontainebleau entirely to magnanimity.

To the official Bulletin we have as yet little to add. The dispatches, we understand, were brought by Major PERCY, Aide-de-Camp to the Duke of WELLINGTON; and we have heard, but we hope the statement is premature, that among the British slain was that gallant and estimable officer Sir THOMAS PICTON. But whoever fell on this glorious day cannot have fallen in vain. The fabric of rebellion is shaken to its base. Already, we hear, numerous desertions have taken place from the Rebel Standard; and soon, it is to be hoped, the perjured wretches NEY, and DESNOUETTES, and EXCELMANS, and LALLEMAND, and LABEDOYERE, and their accomplices in baseness and treason, will be left alone, as marks for the indignation of Europe, and just sacrifices to insulted French honour.

Those who attended minutely to the operations of the Stock Exchange yesterday, were persuaded that the news of the day before would be followed up by something still more brilliant and decisive. Omnium rose in the course of the day to 6 per cent. premium, and some houses generally supposed to possess the best information were among the purchasers. For our own parts, though looking forward with that confidence which we yesterday expressed, we frankly own this full tide of success was more than we had anticipated. We were very well satisfied that Mr. SUTTON's account, so far as it went, was correct,—that BUONAPARTE's grand plan had been frustrated, and that he had not only been prevented, from penetrating between the English and Prussian armies, but forced to fall back behind the Sambre. How far the Duke of WELLINGTON and Prince BLUCHER might have thought it prudent to pursue him, was a point on which we did not conceive ourselves warranted to form any decisive opinion from the evidence before us. We had no doubt that he would be harassed in his retreat, and perhaps ultimately be driven into his entrenched camp, or under the guns of his fortresses; but without some distinct official information, we repeat, that we could not have ventured to anticipate such a triumphant result as that on which we have now to congratulate our country and the world.

Among the rumours which obtained some credit in the city yesterday, was one of an insurrection in Paris. We are not much inclined to give credit to this, conceiving that the Parisians will not move until the tyrant's force in the field is broken. We know, however, that a spirit of hostility to his usurpation is very generally and very boldly expressed in the French capital. We have received from thence a paper which has obtained extensive circulation there, and which will be found in another of our columns. It contains an address to the inhabitants of the Fauxbourgs St. Antoine and St. Marceau, and a Declaration in the name of the Duke of ORLEANS. Both these documents are plainly and ably drawn up. The one successfully opposes the ferocious doctrines of the Jacobins, the other the more insidious views of those who seek to cover their criminality with the respect justly due to a brave and honourable Member of the House of Bourbon. Whether his Serene Highness has authorised this avowal of his sentiments, we know not; but it is one, which appears perfectly congenial with that fair and manly conduct which he has alway observed. The Duke of ORLEANS has never at any time given the least countenance to those criminal projects, which, under the specious pretence of attachment to himself, would as completely break down the principle of legal succession, as if a BUONAPARTE or a ROBESPIERRE were the object of election. That principle once violated, the faction assuming to-day the right of choosing any given Sovereign, might to-morrow, with equal authority, assume the right of cashiering him. Nothing would be permanent or secure. Neither King, nor Dynasty, nor form of Government, would be certain of lasting a twelvemonth; the intolerable perpetuity of change would necessitate the ultimate submission to despotism; and none would be more miserably the sufferers than those unfortunate personages who might be mocked with the capricious grant of a delusive sovereignty by the paramount authority of faction.

Yesterday his Royal Highness the PRINCE REGENT held a Council at Carlton-house, which was unexpectedly summoned. It was attended by the Lord President, the Lord Privy Seal, the First Lord of the Treasury, the Chancellor of the Exchequer, the First Lord of the Admiralty, the Master General of the Ordnance, the three Secretaries of State, the President of the Board of Control the Chancellor of the Duchy of Lancaster, the Master of the Mint, the Commander in Chief, &c.

Among other important proceedings, an Order in Council for reprisals and letters of marque against the French was agreed upon, and signed by all the members of the Council present, in consequence of hostilities having commenced.

His Royal Highness gave audiences to the Earls of LIVERPOOL, HARROWBY, Viscount SIDMOUTH, and Mr. BATHURST. The Rev. Dr. LUXMORE, the late Bishop of Hereford, did homage before the PRINCE, upon his being translated from the Bishopric of Hereford to the Bishopric of St. Asaph.

We have seen a gentleman who left Brussels on *Sunday evening*, at which time the people were manifesting the greatest joy for a decisive victory gained by the Duke of WELLINGTON on that day. The wounded were beginning to be brought in, in waggons, as this gentleman quitted Brussels.

Many of the British Officers present in the affair of the 16th, declared that they never witnessed more severe fighting in the Peninsula than that which took place on the plains of Fleurus and its vicinity. What made the fate of the 79th and 42d regiments so severe was their having been taken by surprise by a strong force of cuirassiers, who lay in ambush for them in a road, the sight of which was completely intercepted by fields of corn immensely high. With such fury was the 79th regiment attacked, that most of them were cut to pieces, and the whole were in danger of being destroyed, but for the coming up of the brave 42d. This latter regiment formed itself into a square, and five times were they broken. On the sixth attack they formed the plan of opening a passage to the enemy; and the moment he effected it, they changed their position, and so hemmed in the cuirassiers, that not a single man was suffered to escape: thus was the destruction of one of BUONAPARTE's finest regiments completed. Col. CAMERON, says our informant, was killed at the head of the gallant 42d. Next day, Saturday, when the 79th was mustered, the men amounted to no more than 54, and two officers. A few more were, however, expected to be brought in. General PICTON's division did wonders; and the gallant General himself fought at the head of it in a manner to astonish the greatest veterans. The Duke of WELLINGTON exposed himself as usual to imminent danger: the bullets, says our informant, were whizzing about him in every direction.

PRIVATE CORRESPONDENCE.

HAMBURGH, JUNE 13.

Yesterday the first column of our contingent of troops, consisting of a battalion of infantry and a squadron of cavalry, set out for the Netherlands, to join the army under the Duke of Wellington.

The Lubec contingent, destined also for the army of Wellington, arrived to-day at Hamburgh, where it was received with Hanseatic fraternity.

The following letter from Bremen of the 8th instant communicates farther information as to the march of the Hanseatic troops.

"On the 14th inst. our contingent will break up from hence for the army. On the 15th the first division of the Hamburghers will enter on the 18th the Lubeckers, and on the 19th the second division of the Hamburgh contingent. Their route is by Wildeshausen, Lingen, &c. for Antwerp."

Field Marshal Barclay de Tolly, with some thousands of Russian troops, attended the funeral of Marshal Berthier at Bamberg.

The public are anxious here lest too much time be given to the common enemy.

The following documents have been published at Paris:—

TO THE INHABITANTS OF THE FAUXBOURGS ST. ANTOINE AND ST. MARCEAU.

Good inhabitants of the Fauxbourgs, peaceful and laborious people! They deceive you: traitors mislead you, and endeavour to render you the imprudent victims of perfidy.

For whom do they exhort you to revolt and carnage? For a single man, become the terror as he is the hatred of France and the whole world: for a barbarian, who, in his rage to destroy, thinks with delight of the new torrents of blood which he is again about to shed; who smiles at the idea of the frightful calamities which an impotent and criminal resistance will inevitably bring on your city, your families, and yourselves; for a man who is no longer your Sovereign, who has no longer any right to you, not even that of interesting you in his fate.

Against whom do they excite your courage, and wish to arm you? Against your King, your father; against a King whom you love, because he is virtuous and good, and because you, like all true Frenchmen, are generous and feeling; against a father who made the care of your welfare his dearest study, and who never speaks without pleasure and emotion of *his good people of Paris*. Inhabitants of the fauxbourg St. Antoine, you in particular have seen that good king, that tender father, come to deposit among you, with expressions of his affection for you, the treasures of his mild beneficence. From that moment you gave him your hearts, and promised to him eternal affection. Will you now break your oaths? Consider that the more he is unfortunate and afflicted, the more you owe him consolation and fidelity; consider that he has given his royal word to employ the first moments of his return, in distinguishing and rewarding the *virtuous citizens who shall devote themselves to the good cause*; consider also that it will be so much the more honourable to be rewarded by him, inasmuch he will doubtless never have either the wish or the courage to punish you.

If, then, you must be armed, let it be for him and not against him; but let it be in a manner worthy of you and of him; let it be not to shed the blood of his servants, nor even that of his enemies and your's, but in order to watch with the brave and faithful national guards over the maintenance of order and respect to persons and property, to preserve to your fellow-citizens their goods and repose, and to your King his subjects and capital.

Thus will you shew yourselves worthy of the French name; thus will you acquire an eternal claim to the esteem and gratitude of the nation, as well as to the good will of your legitimate Sovereign.

S. M.

DECLARATION OF THE DUKE OF ORLEANS, FIRST PRINCE OF THE BLOOD OF FRANCE.

Frenchmen,—I am under the necessity of breaking the silence I had imposed on myself, and since some have had the audacity to connect my name with guilty wishes and perfidious insinuations, my honour dictates to me, in the face of all Europe, a solemn protest which my duties prescribe to me.

Frenchmen, they deceive, they mislead you; but those among you especially deceive themselves, who arrogate the right of choosing another master, and who outrage by seditious hopes, a Prince, the most faithful subject of the King of France, Louis XVIII.

The irrevocable principle or legitimacy is now the sole guarantee of peace in France and in Europe. Revolutions have only made its force and importance more strongly felt: consecrated by a warlike league and by a pacific congress of all the princes, this principle will become the invariable rule of reigns and successions.

Yes, Frenchmen, I should be proud to govern you, but solely in the event of my being unfortunate enough to have my seat on the throne opened to me by the extinction of an illustrious branch. It would be then only that I should also make known intentions far different perhaps from those which some ascribe to me, or which they choose to suggest to me.

Frenchmen, I address myself to none but a few misled men. Become yourselves again, and proclaim yourselves faithful subjects of Louis XVIII. and of his natural heirs, with one of your princes and fellow-citizens.

LOUIS PHILIP, Duke of ORLEANS.

LAW REPORT.

COURT OF KING'S BENCH, WEDNESDAY, JUNE 21.

SAMPSON V. CHAMBERS.

This was an action by a widow lady, residing in Harley-street, against some of the inhabitants of the Hundred of Ossulton, on the riot act 1 G. 1. st. 2, c. 5. s. 6. to recover damages on account of the partial demolition of her house by the rioters, on account of the corn bill. There being no doubt that this riot was a felony within the act, it being proved that the damage amounted to a beginning to demolish or pull down the house within the 4th section (See 5 T. R. 14. 7 T. 496), the Jury found their verdict for the plaintiff—Damages 55l. 5s. 5d.

SEBRIGHT, BART. V. KINSEY.

This was a similar action against two or more of the inhabitants of the hundred in which Curzon-street is situated, on account of damage to Mr. Ponsonby's house, of which the plaintiff is entitled to the reversion. The Attorney-General said, the public were indebted to any individual (however slight his damage) who set the example of taking this beneficial recourse to make the whole hundred pay for the damage of a lawless mob. Verdict for plaintiff—Damages 56l. 16s. 10s.

ROBERTSON, ESQ. V. HUTTON.

This was an action brought by Captain Robertson against an upholsterer in Mortimer-street, Cavendish-square, of whom he agreed to take furnished lodgings for himself and his lady, upon the term of being waited upon by the defendant's servant. The servant deposed that the agreement was, that *she* was to wait upon the plaintiff; but this servant was, during the occupation, dismissed by the defendant, who did not procure another to supply her place. The plaintiff accordingly engaged one himself, and now brought this action for this breach of agreement, and the defendant (who appeared to be suspicious of the marriage of the plaintiff, and anxious to get rid of him as a tenant) having further inconvenienced the plaintiff by taking away a table from his room, by blocking up the passage with goods, and by entering his room after he had gone to bed, to serve a notice to quit; these circumstances were put into the declaration as further breaches of the agreement, express or implied. Lord ELLENBOROUGH said he never recollected an action for such trivial injuries, but the law must recognise it. It appeared that the plaintiff had been deprived of the services of the defendant's servant 6 weeks, during one of which one of his workmen waited upon him and during the rest of the time he was put to the expense of hiring a servant of his own. This did seem to constitute some damage: but Lord ELLENBOROUGH left it to the Jury whether, the agreement being that *the witness* was to wait upon the plaintiff, when she was discharged the defendant was bound to provide another servant. As for the taking away the table, it appeared to have been afterwards replaced by another; the passage appeared to have been blocked up, in fulfilment of a threat on the part of the defendant that he would do so; but it did not appear that the defendant entered the plaintiff's *bed*-room to serve the notice. The Jury after retiring found their verdict for the defendant.

A weekly paper, entitled *The Sunday Monitor*, has, we learn, published, or does still publish, some letters with the signature of VETUS, intimating to its readers that they are the production of our valued correspondent, who used that signature. We do not know what kind of readers they are that may be imposed upon by such a fraudulent insinuation,—enlightened ones no doubt!—but we assert, with the utmost confidence, that the person whose designation is thus surreptitiously adopted, has never since written or suggested a line of polities to any other journal whatsoever than *The Times*.

The Proprietors of Covent-garden have, as a tribute of gratitude to Miss O'NEILL for her successful exertions, offered to her acceptance the profits of the revived tragedy of *Jane Shore*.

[Advertisement.]—NEW GALLERY, PALL-MALL.—We are desired to state, that this Gallery will be re-opened to the Public this day, with a splendid collection of Pictures, formed at a liberal expense, from many of the finest collections of Europe, and which contains many celebrated pictures by the most esteemed masters of the Italian schools, as Reffaelle, Correggio, Sebastian del Piombo, Tera. Bartolomeo, Titian, the Caracci, &c. From the many capital examples of the works of these masters which this collection possesses, it may be considered as a most interesting and valuable addition to the present exhibition at the British Gallery, to which it adjoins; that Gallery being for this year limited to the exhibition of the works of the Flemish and Dutch schools.

TIMES OFFICE, Thursday Morning, 8 o'clock.

We stop the press to insert the following letter, received this morning by the LORD MAYOR:—

(COPY.)

DOWNING-STREET, JUNE 22, 1815, 1, A. M.

MY LORD,—I have the greatest satisfaction in informing your Lordship, that the Hon. Major H. PERCY, is just arrived with dispatches from the Duke of WELLINGTON, dated Waterloo, the 19th instant, containing the account of a most decisive and glorious victory having been obtained over the whole of the French Army, by the Allied Forces, on the 18th instant, the result of which has been the overthrow of the French army, with the loss of more than 200 pieces of artillery, an immense quantity of ammunition, and a part of the baggage belonging to BUONAPARTE.

The loss of the British Army upon this occasion has unfortunately been most severe. It had not been possible to make out a return of the killed and wounded when Major PERCY left head-quarters, the names of the Officers killed and wounded, as far as they can be collected, are annexed.

I have the honour to be,
Your Lordship's most obedient humble servant,
BATHURST.

To the Right Hon. the LORD MAYOR.

BRITISH KILLED AND WOUNDED.

KILLED.

Duke of Brunswick Oels.
Lieutenant-General Sir Thomas Picton.
Lieutenant-General Sir H. Ponsonby.
Colonel du Plat, K. G. L.
Colonel Omphets, ditto.
Colonel Morrice, 69th Regiment.
Colonel Sir W. Ellis, 23d.
Lieutenant-Colonel Macara, 42d Regiment.
Lieutenant-Colonel Cameron, 92d Regiment.
Lt.-Col. Sir Alex. Gordon, K.C.B. A.D.C. to the Duke of Wellington.
Lieutenant-Colonel Canning.
Lieutenant-Colonel Currie, Lord Hill's Staff.
Major the Hon. Fred. Howard, 10th Hussars.
Major George Bain, Royal Artillery.
Major Norman Ramsay, ditto.
Major Cairnes, ditto.
Major Chambers, 30th Regiment.
Brigade Major Crofton, 5th Division.
B. Major Rosewiel, 2d Light Regiment.
Captain Bolton, Royal Artillery.
Captain Crawford, Guards.
Capt. the Hon. Curzon, A.D.C. to His R. H. the Prince of Orange.
Captain Chambers, A. D. C. to Lieut. Gen. Picton.
Captain Charles Ellis, 95th Regiment.
Captain Robertson, 73d Regiment.
Captain Kennedy, 73d Regiment.
Captain Shanman, 2d Lt. Bat. K.G.L.
Captain Halgeoman, 1st Ditto.
Captain Henry Marshal, 1st Ditto.
Captain Grohen, Ditto.
Captain Gumming, 10th Hussars.
Captain Grove, 1st Guards.
Lieutenant C. Manners, Royal Artillery.
Lieutenant Lister, 95th Regiment.
Ensign Lord Hay, Aid-de-Camp to General Maitland.
Ensign Brown, 1st Guards.

WOUNDED.

General His Royal Highness the Prince of Orange, K. C. B. severely.
Lieut.-General the Earl of Uxbridge, G. C. B. right leg amputated.
Lieut.-General Sir Charles Alten, K. C. B. severely.
Lieut.-General Cook, right arm amputated.
Lieut.-General Sir E. Barnes, K. C. B. Adjut.-Gen. severely
Lieut.-General Sir J. Kempt. K. C. B. slightly.
Lieut.-General Sir Colin Halkitt, K. C. B. severely.
Lieut.-General Adams, severely.
Lieut.-General Sir W. Dornbey, K. C. B. severely.
Colonel Sir J. Elley, K. C. B. slightly.
Colonel Harris, 73d regiment.
Colonel Quentin, 10th Hussars, slightly.
Colonel the Hon. Frederick Parnaby, severely.
Colonel Sir William De Lancy, severely.
Lieutenant-Colonel Lord Fitzroy Somerset, right arm amputated.
Lieutenant-Colonel Hay, 16th Light Dragoons, severely.
Lieutenant-Colonel Vigoureau, 30th.
Lieutenant-Colonel Abercrombie, A. Q. M. G. slightly.
Lieutenant-Colonel Hamilton, 30th regiment.
Lieutenant-Colonel Cameron, 95th, severely.
Lieutenant-Colonel Wyndham, 1st Foot Guards, severely.
Lieutenant-Colonel Bowater, 3d Foot Guards, slightly.
Lieutenant-Colonel Macklonell, Coldstream, slightly.
Lieutenant-Colonel Dashwood, 3d Guards, severely.
Lieutenant-Colonel Sir R. Hill, Royal Horse Guards Blue, severely.
Lieutenant-Colonel Hill.
Lieutenant-Colonel Schreider, 8th Line Battalion.
Lieutenant-Colonel Adam, 1st Guards, severely.
Lieutenant-Colonel Miller, 1st Guards, dangerously.
Lieutenant-Colonel Sir George Henry Berkeley, A. A. G.
Major Maclean, 73d.
Major Beckwith, 95th severely.
Major Jessop, Assistant Quarter Master General.
Major Burche, 1st Light Bat. K. G. L., right arm amputated.
Major Parkinson, 73d, severely.
Major Parker, R. H. Artillery, leg amputated.
Major Robert Ball, Royal Artillery, severely.
Major Hamilton, Aid-de-Camp to General Sir E. Barnes.
Major Lindsay, 69th regiment, severely.
Major Watson, 69th regiment, ditto.
B. M. Emem, dangerously.
L. Wilkins, 95th regiment, severely.
M. Miller, ditto ditto.
Capt. Smith, ditto ditto.
Capt. Taylor, Aid-de-Camp to Sir Thomas Picton, slightly.
Capt. Dance, 23d Light Dragoons.
Captain Johnston, 95th.
Captain Carmers, ditto.
Capts. Darney, Napier, A. M'Donald, Webber, Royal Artillery, severely
Captain Dumaresque, Aide de Camp Gen. Sir J. Byng, severely.
Captain Whynnates, Royal Artillery, severely.
Captain Barpes, Brigade Major, Royal Artillery, severely.
Captain the Hon. E. Daag, left arm amputated.
Captain A Daugton, A. D. C. to Lieut. Gen. Picton, severely.
Lieutenant Foster, Royal Artillery, severely.
Lieutenant Crome, ditto ditto
Lieutenant Robe, ditto ditto
Lieutenant Smith, ditto ditto,
Lieutenant Strangway, ditto ditto,
Lieutenant Homey, ditto, arm amputated.
Lieutenant Bloomfield, ditto, slightly.
Lieutenant Bruton, severely.
Lieutenant Forbes, ditto, ditto.
Lieutenant D. Crawford, ditto, slightly.
Lieutenant Harelock, Aid-de-Camp to Gen. Sir Charles Alten.
Lieutenant Pringle, Royal Engineers, slightly.
Lieutenant Hamilton, 46th Regiment, slightly.
Lieutenant Heise, 1st Veteran Battalion.
Lieuts. Gardiners Johnstone, Mottry, Simmons, J. Gardiner, Fitzmaurice, Shenley, Wright, 95th, severely.

MARRIED.

Yesterday, at St. Mary's, Lambeth, by the Rev. —— Barrett, Nicholas Geary, Esq. of Stakes-hill, Hants, to Elizabeth, second daughter of James Freshfield, Esq. of Reading, Berks.

On Tuesday, the 20th instant, by the Hon. and Rev. A. H. Cathcart, at St. Marylebone Church, East. George Clayton, Esq. second son of Sir Wm. Clayton, Bart. to Marianne Frances, eldest daughter of Charles Bishop, Esq. his Majesty's Procurator General.

On Tuesday, the 20th instant, at St. John's Church, Westminster, by the Rev. Robert Stevens, Prebendary of Lincoln, Walter Cosser, Esq. of Milbank-street, to Maria, second daughter of Charles Boynton Wood, Esq. of Upper John-street, and Hayes, Middlesex.

DIED.

On Monday, at his seat, at Swindon, Wilts, after a few days' illness, in his 89th year, Ambrose Goddard, Esq. formerly representative for that county during a space of 35 years.

On Sunday, the 18th instant, at Slades-place, Deptford, Mrs. Ferguson, aged 81 years, widow of Gilbert Ferguson, Esq. late surveyor of shipping to the Hon. United East India Company.

On Tuesday evening, at Dulwich, in the 44th year of her age, Susanna, wife of Thomas Latt, jun. Esq.

On Tuesday evening, in Great Portland-street, aged eight years, Charlotte Mary, eldest child of Wolfenden Kenny, Esq

On the 21st of June, at Oak-lodge, Southgate, Sarah, wife of Edward Smith, Esq.

On Sunday last, Mrs. Ann Sandell, wife of Mr. Nicholas Sandell, late of Little St. Thomas Apostle, solicitor.

PRICE OF STOCKS.

Navy 5 per Cent. shut.	India Bonds, 3 4 dis
4 per Cent. 60¾ 70 ½	Exchequer Bills, par 5 dis.
3 per Cent. Red. 54⅝ ¼ 5¼ ½	Cons. for Open. 56½ ¼ 7 6¾ 7⅛ ⅞
3 per Cent. Consols shut.	State Lottery Tickets 22l. 15.
B. L. A. 14 1-16th 5-16ths ½	

HORNSBY and Co. Stock-brokers, State Lottery-office, 26, Cornhill, where Tickets and Shares are on sale.

LETTERS of VERAX.—This day are published, price 2s.

LETTERS of VERAX, to the EDITOR of the MORNING CHRONICLE on the Question of a War to be commenced for the Purpose of putting an End to the Possession of the Supreme Power in France by Napoleon Bonaparte. By WILLIAM GODWIN. Printed for Longman, Hurst, Rees, Orme, and Brown, Paternoster-row. Of whom may be had, by the same Author, Lives of Edward and John Philips, Nephews and Pupils of Milton; including various Particulars of the Literary and Political History of their Times. Embellished with an Original Likeness of President Bradshaw, and two other Portraits, in 4to, price 2l. 2s. in boards.

WANT PLACES.—All Letters to be post paid.

AS HOUSEKEEPER, or Cook and Housekeeper, where a kitchen-maid is kept, a steady middle-aged Person, who can have an undeniable character from her last place. Direct to 5, Little Rider-street, St. James's.

AS HOUSEKEEPER to a single Gentleman, or as Upper Servant in a genteel family, or to attend upon 2 or 3 young Ladies, a middle-aged Person, who flatters herself she shall be able to give satisfaction in either capacity. Direct to C. D. at Mr. Williams's, cheesemonger, 18, Great Winchester-street, Broad-street.

AS LADY'S-MAID, or to wait on two young Ladies, a young Woman, who can have an unexceptionable character from her last place, where she lived seven years; no objection to go abroad. Direct to G. N. at Miss Kenan's, dress-maker, 26, Chapel-street, Grosvenor-square.

AS LADY'S-MAID, or to wait on two or three young Ladies, a respectable young Woman; has no objection to take an Upper Housemaid's place, she perfectly understands hair-dressing, can work well at her needle, and get up fine linen: can have a good character from the Lady whom she has just left. Direct to C. M. 15, Robert-street, Bedford-row.

AS WET-NURSE, a young Woman, aged 27; first child; has a good breast of milk, and can be well recommended. Direct to E. R. at 21, Paradise-row, Back road, Islington.

AS WET-NURSE, a Person, about 22 years of age, without any incumbrance, with a good breast of milk, having lost her first child: and can have a good recommendation: would have no objection to have one at home; but would prefer the former. Direct to C. W. 2, Mark street, Paul-street, Shoreditch.

A YOUNG PERSON, aged 23, to attend on one or two young Ladies, or as Upper Housemaid in a small family; can work well at her needle, and get up fine linen; no objection to travel. Direct to J. G. at 251, High Holborn.

A YOUNG WOMAN, of respectable connections, to attend upon an elderly Lady, or young Ladies; understands plain dress-making, getting up fine linen, and can have a good character from the Lady she has just left; no objection to travel. Direct to A. B. 35, Trinity-square.

AS COOK and HOUSEKEEPER, a Person, who perfectly understands her business in both branches, and can have an unexceptionable character from her last place, where she lived 2¼ years. Direct to A. H. 14, Great Chesterfield-street Marylebone.

AS COOK and HOUSEKEEPER to a single Gentleman, or in a regular genteel family, where the Lady is her own housekeeper, a sober, steady Person, who understands her business in all the branches of cookery, no objection to the country, and the care of a small dairy, where assistance is allowed in the kitchen; character undeniable from the family she has just left. Direct to A. B. 23, New Broad-street, city.

AS COOK, a steady Woman; has no objection to town or country, where no dairy is kept. Direct to S. S. 3, Collingwood-place, near Mile-end-turnpike.

AS good PLAIN COOK, where a Footman is kept, a steady active Woman, or to a single Gentleman in town or country; understands a dairy; can have a good recommendation from the place she has left. Direct S. R. 22, Marshal-street, Golden-square.

A PLACE-OF-ALL-WORK, a young Woman, in a small genteel Family, where there is no children: can have a good character. Direct to E. B. 71, Fetter-lane.

AS HOUSEMAID in a genteel family, a young Woman; she has lived 2¼ years in her last place. Direct to S. D. 76, Little Britain, Aldersgate-street.

AS NURSERY or HOUSEMAID, a young Woman, initiated in the dress-making, in a respectable family. Direct to C. P. at 61, Old Broad-street, City.

AS HOUSEMAID, or Upper Nurse in a genteel Family, a steady Woman, who can make herself useful in making up small linen, and work well at her needle, and whose character can bear the strictest enquiry. Direct A. W. 4, Charles-street, Long-acre.

AS HOUSEMAID, a steady young Woman, where a footman is kept; no objection to the country; can have a good character from her last place. Direct to M. P. 12, Gresse-street, Rathbone-place.

AS LAUNDRY-MAID, a Person, who understands her business, having always lived in that capacity; would prefer the country. Direct to F. J. 2, Little Pancras-street, Tottenham-court-road.

AS UNDER LAUNDRY-MAID, or Housemaid, in a family, a young Woman, who can be well recommended. Direct to C. L. 17, New Belton-street, Seven-dials.

AS KITCHEN-MAID in a respectable Family, or as Housemaid in a small family where a footman is kept; can have a good character from a respectable family where she lived last. Direct to C. S. Mr. Latham's, fishmongers, 28, Lime-street, Leadenhall-market.

A Single steady WOMAN, who can bear confinement, and has no followers, to live with a single elderly Lady or Gentleman, a Person who understands needle work and cooking well; her study will be to act with care and economy: no objection to a small regular family in town or country; her character will bear the strictest enquiry from her last place, where she lived two years. Direct to G. L. 36, Great Castle-street, Cavendish-square

A YOUNG GIRL, 14 years of age, in a family or nursery; can work well at her needle, and will make herself generally useful. Direct to A. B. at Mr. Taylor's, 11, Church-street, St. Saviour's Church, Borough. No office-keeper need apply.

AS BUTLER, a middle aged Man; can be well recommended from places he has lived in some years; would have no objection to go with a single Gentleman or family for the summer Direct to J. D. 7, Edward-street, Portman-square.

AS GARDENER, a young Man, 25 years of age, who thoroughly understands his business; can have an undeniable character from his last place, where he has lived 2 years and upwards. Direct to J. R. at Mr. Bull's, gardener, Highbury-place, Islington.

AS COACHMAN, a young Man, 27 years of age: no objection to town or country; can have a good character from his last place, where he lived 3 years. Direct to S. W. at Mr. Henderson's, 61, Old Broad-street, City.

AS COACHMAN, a single young Man, who can have a good character from his last place, where he lived 2 years. Direct to P. J. 21, Stephen-street, Tottenham-court-road.

AS COACHMAN, a married Man, about 27 years of age; lived upwards of 3 years in his last place; his reason for leaving was the death of his master, where he can have an undeniable character. Direct to Y. Z. 8, Benniter-street, near Tottenham-court-road.

AS UPPER FOOTMAN, in or out of Livery, a young Man, 26 years of age, who perfectly understands his business in every respect; and can have a good character from the place he has just left, where he has lived upwards of 2½ years. Direct W. D. at Mr. Haylett's, baker, 46, South-street, Berkeley square.

AS FOOTMAN, in or out of Livery, with a small regular family, or single Gentleman, a young Man, who perfectly understands his business; and can have a good character from the place he has left. Direct to S. D. 12, Harp-lane, Tower-street. No register office letters will be attended to.

AS FOOTMAN, a young Man, 18 years of age; perfectly understands his business; and can have a good character from his last place; and willing to make himself generally useful to his employer; a family in the City would be preferred. Direct R. H. 16, Cross-street, Wilderness-row. No office keeper need to apply.

AS GROOM, or Valet; has no objection to town or country. Direct to E. D. at Mr. Flack's, 1, Norfolk-place, Curtain-road, Shoreditch.

AS GROOM, a young Man: no objection to town or country; can have an undeniabe character from the Gentleman he is now with. Direct to W. W. at Mr. Dixon's, baker, Carter-lane, Doctors'-commons.

AS GROOM, or to look after a Horse and Chaise, or under a Coachman, or Groom in a Gentleman's Family, a young Man, aged 20: can have an undeniable character from his last place, where he has lived six years, and leaves in consequence of not wishing to go to sea. Direct to W. H. at Mr. Hammond's oilman, Brownlow-street, Holborn.

AS SERVANT, either in or out of Livery; has no objection to a travelling family; can have a good character from his last place. Direct to E. R. at Mr. Rouse's, grocer, Wigmore-street, Cavendish-square.

AS SERVANT to a single Gentleman, or in a small regular family, where one is kept, a young Man of colour; has no objection to travel to any part of England or to go abroad, understands well his business; and can have an undeniable character from his last place. Direct to W. D. at Mr Jones's, grocer, Carnaby-street, Carnaby-market.

AS VALET, or Groom and Valet, a young Man, aged 27; has no objection to town or country, or to go abroad with a Gentleman; can be well recommended from the Gentleman he has just left, with whom he has lived upwards of five years; would not object to live as In-door Servant in a small respectable family, to be out of livery, being perfectly acquainted with the sideboard and other requisites for an In-door Servant Direct to H. D. at Mr. Burn's, boot and shoemaker, 47, Piccadilly, or Mr. Tremens breechesmaker, Jermyn-street, St. James's.

AS PORTER in a Shop or Warehouse, a married Man, 30 years of age; can write a plain hand, and is willing to make himself useful to his employer; his character will bear the strictest enquiry. Direct to A. B. 3, Phit's-buildings Houndsditch

A YOUNG MAN, who has been in town about 3 months; would have no objection to look after a horse and chaise, as that is what he has been used to, or as Porter in a warehouse; would be willing to make himself useful to his employer. Direct to A. B. 63, Whitecross-street, City.

A Single, steady Man, in a small, genteel, regular family, in or out of livery, where only one man, or one man and a boy, are kept; perfectly understands his business in all its branches as complete domestic servant, hair-dressing, brewing, &c and can have all undeniable character from his last place, where he lived upwards of four years. Direct to H. Tucker, at Mr Cotton's, tea-warehouse, 111, High-street, Marylebone.

TO CORRESPONDENTS.

No notice can be taken of anonymous communications. Whatever is intended for insertion must be authenticated by the name and address of the writer; not necessarily for publication, but as a guarantee of his good faith.

The donation referred to by "A. B. C." was duly received, and applied as requested.

The publication of *The Times* commenced at a quarter to 7 o'clock yesterday morning, and finished at 20 minutes to 11.

LONDON, THURSDAY, DECEMBER 4, 1845.

The decision of the Cabinet is no longer a secret. Parliament, it is confidently reported, is to be summoned for the first week in January; and the Royal Speech will, it is added, recommend an immediate consideration of the Corn Laws, preparatory to their total repeal. Sir ROBERT PEEL in one house, and the Duke of WELLINGTON in the other, will, we are told, be prepared to give immediate effect to the recommendation thus conveyed.

An announcement of such immeasurable importance, and to the larger portion of the community so unspeakably gratifying, almost precludes the possibility of comment. No pen can keep pace with the reflections which must spontaneously crowd upon every thoughtful and sensitive mind. They who have long desired this change, and have long traced its manifold bearings on the welfare and happiness of the world, will in one moment see the realization of that fair prospect, and will hardly endure to be informed of what they already behold. The approaching event, therefore, which we this day communicate to our readers, must be left to speak for itself.

It is understood that until Parliament meets nothing is to be done. For the Legislature will be reserved the responsibility and the glory of opening the ports. We presume that none will quarrel with this brief appearance of delay, now that the resolution of the Cabinet is known. The moral certainty of an early opening will be equivalent in its operation to an immediate order in Council. It is enough for the merchant and the capitalist to know that by the end of January at the latest, the produce of all countries will enter the British market on an absolute equality with our own, excepting only those disadvantages which Nature itself has made, and which man cannot entirely remove. Any unnecessary appearance of haste would only create alarm, and might thus defeat, for a time at least, the very object of the measure. Happily there is no occasion for haste, even if haste were not almost certain to interfere with speed.

It is said that the decision has been made with that unanimity which perhaps the compulsion of circumstances alone can inspire. The reported exceptions are both insignificant and doubtful, and not of a sort to interfere with the construction of the Cabinet. There is, of course, one man who had it in his power to offer an enormous impediment and create a frightful collision; but experience coming to the aid of his own intuitive sagacity, has, we are told, taught him to retire from an eventually fruitless opposition, and to husband his strength for more attainable objects. Fortunately for the present peace, if not for the ultimate prosperity of the nation, he has long exemplified that which the chief writer on the British constitution has declared to be the most decisive and triumphant test of its soundness—viz., the absolute impotence of military greatness against the constitutional movements of the popular will. It is scarcely fair to imagine a contingency from which the possible author has himself most judiciously recoiled; but we feel very sure that the Upper House will be only too thankful to be spared an unequal and, perhaps, a disastrous conflict with the Ministers of the Crown and the representatives of the people.

It is evident that this is the only quarter from which the PREMIER's position has been seriously threatened. From that quarter he might have been overthrown if his assailants felt sufficient interest in their cause to wish to be buried in its ruins; but the British aristocracy feels no such injurious and suicidal ambition. It is either too good or too wise to strike with such force that its own life is spent in the blow. The PREMIER has not been blind to the security afforded by the alternative of a common destruction. He has set his political existence against the Lords, and won the stake. Our traditionary reverence for the first estate of the realm may lead us to regret that it should ever be thrown into a position involving defeat by so unequal a combatant. We may justly regret that it has not lately been more accustomed to draw on the known resources of hereditary wisdom—that it has allowed itself to be represented by a few, and has thus changed its broad aristocratical basis for the more manageable, and, therefore, less enduring, form of an oligarchy—and, above all, that it has delegated its credit and authority to leaders who are kind only in flattering its foibles, bold only in committing it to errors, and wise only in consenting to defeat.

The other parties with whom Sir ROBERT PEEL might have been called upon to measure his strength really, like some countries we see on the maps, have, at the present moment, rather a geographical than a political existence. In whatever way it has come to pass, so it is, the agriculturists have just now no more power than the animals they are industriously bringing to such magnificent proportions. What they wish, or hate, or fear, their interests and their grievances, have literally been dropped out of the calculation. The PREMIER, who has enjoyed their support, has a just sense of its value, and is at no pains to conceal that he can do without it. Whether his is the case of the steward who grows rich himself while his employer decays, we will not now inquire, but the result is the same. From this quarter nothing was to be feared, and to imagine a danger would have been simply a mistake. They, however, who expect to see us a nation of heroes and martyrs would probably have desired that the present patriotic surrender should have been the voluntary and gratuitous act of those at whose risk, if not at whose loss, it is done.

But if the Conservatives should be broken up, the Whigs would come in. Here was a substantial, a political, an historical foe, whom Sir ROBERT might remember and fear! Truly they are an historical foe—*magni nominis umbra.* The members of the party may survive and reign in another form; but the party itself is scattered and overthrown.

It is an unfortunate circumstance that so good a deed should literally go a-begging for an author. The nation has done it, but who is the instrument? It is in Sir ROBERT PEEL's hand, but is it his property? Nor have the Whigs much more claim to it. They only proposed to give up the Corn Laws when it was evident the peril of the experiment would be the inheritance of their successors.

Shall we, again, call the League the true hero of the crisis—the real SIMON PURE of free trade? Truth compels us to answer in the affirmative; but the idea is still somewhat distasteful, and human nature itself will cavil at a patriotism, the virtues of which were so closely allied with its interests.

The PREMIER appeals to the good sense and the growing intelligence of the nation. We are flattered by an appeal which assures us that we are wiser than our forefathers. Still, it is unusual to see those mutations of opinion which are usually spread over ages, and divided by successive generations, concentrated in one man. Grant that it is a piece of good sense, and wisdom, and intelligence, it is distressing to reflect how long we have been denied it. The appeal is next made to our experience. The sliding scale has been tried in every form, and every form has required a change. The last change has not been the most successful. Never since it began has it done any good to the farmer, till just now, when the country will not bear it. Grant that the experiment is a failure; but whose experiment was it? Some perhaps will not trust the same experimentalist again. The appeal to our condonation is the next resort. The nation is merciful, and Sir ROBERT has had too many proofs of its forgiving temper not to confide once more in that amiable element. But why are people to forgive when there is no help for it? It is mockery to carry a matter against a person's will and then ask his pardon. The truth is that it must be done. Necessity knows no laws. The sliding scale cannot, and will not, stand. Protection cannot be maintained. The country cannot be kept in a state of civil war, with the most fearful jealousies daily ripening and coming to a head. The thing must be done, and it is Sir ROBERT PEEL's common-sense and convenient view of the case that he is the actual Premier, and therefore bound to do it.

We have seldom had to deal with a series of such constant and aggravated misrepresentations as the statements which have been put forward to impugn the policy of the Government with reference to the affairs of the River Plate. The origin of these strange effusions may easily be traced to the private interests of certain parties connected with Buenos Ayres, which will probably suffer some temporary injury from the intervention of England and France for the purpose of pacifying both banks of the river. The attempts of ROSAS to destroy the commerce of Monte Video, and to intercept the passage of foreign merchandise to the provinces situated higher up the Uruguay and the Parana, have, doubtless, been popular among the Portenos and the foreign merchants established at Buenos Ayres, who desire nothing more than that the whole commerce of the River Plate and its tributaries should be sacrificed to the interests of that one port and city. Hence the outcry which has arisen even in the trading cities of this country, but more especially among a certain class of traders in Liverpool, against the measures of the English and French Governments, which have no object but the pacification of the country, the opening of the river, and the destruction of a species of monopoly most injurious to the commerce of the world. In all operations of war, even in those which are most necessary for the defence and protection of mercantile interests, certain mercantile interests must be temporarily put in jeopardy. But we have to choose between the evil of a short interruption of trade and risk of property during the continuance of these operations, or the permanent and complete destruction of foreign trade with Monte Video and with the upper provinces of the Plate. In their zeal to protest against a grievance which now lies at their own doors, these parties forget that ROSAS and his lieutenant, ORIBE, have for several years past been wantonly inflicting on the Banda Oriental and the British merchants trading with the north bank of the Plate the same hardships, in a far greater degree, which they declare to be intolerable when they encompass the port of Buenos Ayres; and they suppress the most important fact that it is in the power of ROSAS and the Argentine Government instantly to put an end to all these embarrassments, by withdrawing his army from a region which he has wrongfully invaded. That is all that the Powers have required of him; and if the state of war continues in the River Plate, which we shall lament as much as any one, it is solely attributable to the pride and obstinacy of the Dictator, who asserts, by force of arms, rights of conquest and command to foreign and independent States, over which he has no more just dominion than we have ourselves.

It is disgraceful to the English press that, either for want of proper inquiry into the facts, or for the contemptible objects of party strife, any of our contemporaries should lend his influence to the propagation of these distorted views, which are transmitted to him for the express purpose of being used in South America as evidence that the acts of Mr. GORE OUSELEY and the policy of the English Government are not sanctioned by public opinion in this country. This is no question of party politics at all; it is simply a matter of national, and especially of mercantile, interest. The mercantile interest most urgently and assiduously solicited the pacification of the River Plate, and the removal of those unlawful and unjust impediments to trade which had cost us millions of money and exposed our fellow-countrymen in Monte Video to total ruin in the event of the triumph of ORIBE's army. The mercantile interest has obtained the protection it sought; and, although this is not a matter which can confer any great honour or advantage upon the arms or political interests of Great Britain, it may be fearlessly asserted that the Government was bound to take measures to put an end to a state of things which destroyed the trade of the river and violated the treaties negotiated under our own auspices.

We are told that "these two neighbouring states, "which for years have been at war, *were at last on "the point of harmonizing;"* in plainer and truer language, ORIBE was on the point of consummating by the capture of Monte Video the subjugation of the Banda Oriental, and crushing a State, the independence of which England has expressly recognized, under the dictation of the implacable Dictator of Buenos Ayres. *Delenda est Carthago*—"Death to the savage Unitarians," is the cry of ROSAS, and his tools or adherents. Monte Video sheltered the fugitives from the opposite coast; Monte Video is a powerful rival of Buenos Ayres; Monte Video must be destroyed. The partisans of ROSAS in this country (for it seems that he has such, and where we should least have expected to find them—amongst the people who commonly deal most largely in freedom and philanthropy) have deliberately adopted the very system of policy towards the other states of the River Plate by which the Dictator of Buenos Ayres seeks to justify his oppression and his aggressions on his neighbours. His sole object is to crush all these independent provinces under the State of Buenos Ayres, and the State of Buenos Ayres under himself, in order to establish his absolute and sanguinary power over the whole of the ancient Viceroyalty of Spain in that region. We have no concern with the form of Government in these countries; and if the republics of the Plata can form a confederate state, such as was projected by the founders of their independence, it will readily obtain the countenance and good-will of England. But there is nothing in common between such a system of policy and the absolute subjugation of these fine provinces by the Gaucho who has already enslaved Buenos Ayres. They owe him no allegiance; they are resisting in arms his emissaries and his forces; they claim the common use of the great stream which waters their territories; and they are all of them actually at war with the Argentine Government. Paraguay has been too recently emancipated by death from the yoke of one execrable tyrant to consent to fall under the grasp of another, who, in addition to all the crimes of a FRANCIA, is a foreigner to the country and an enemy to its local interests. Corrientes requires the free navigation of the Parana, and the export of her own produce, which some of our countrymen were the first to bring into the market of Europe. The Banda Oriental is an independent state, placed under the protection of positive treaties with European Powers, and entitled to as much consideration as Buenos Ayres itself. There can be no solid or durable peace in the Plate until the Argentine Dictator has been compelled to recognize and respect the natural rights and the political independence of his neighbours. Those neighbours might easily become the allies of Buenos Ayres, but they will never be the subjects of ROSAS.

The French Opposition have attempted to base an accusation of double-dealing against M. GUIZOT upon a semi-official letter of that Minister, which it seems was taken out by a French agent (Captain PAGE), shown by him to the Argentine Government, and recently published in the *Buenos Ayres Gazette.* The substance of this letter is simply that France and England have no desire to attack or injure the Government of Buenos Ayres, but merely to restore peace on the shores of the River Plate. Nothing can be more absurd than to seek for any contradiction between the terms or spirit of this letter and the instructions and measures of the English and French Ministers on the spot. They are, in fact, identical. No attack whatever has been made on the Argentine Government or territory; and the blockade of Buenos Ayres, which has recently been proclaimed, is the only act of *quasi*-hostility against that state of which it can even complain—an act in itself of a precautionary, rather than an aggressive nature. Yet we are gravely told that the fact that the Argentine Government had given strict orders that no foreigner should be insulted in the slightest degree is a surprising proof of ROSAS's magnanimity. Actual war would not justify him in allowing acts of violence or insults to be offered to private individuals residing in the country; but as long as not a gun has been fired by the European Powers on the right bank of the river, and ORIBE's forces have only been attacked in positions which they had no right to occupy, any injury done to British subjects in Buenos Ayres would be an unwarrantable enormity, for which this country would certainly exact a heavy retribution.

It would be consolatory, under present circumstances, to see the numerous projects that are being brought forward to counteract the impending scarcity of food, if it were not for the awkward fact that the suggestions are merely speculative, and many of them of a wholly impracticable character. There are a number of ingenious persons who are fond of making experiments, and when any public question arises to which an inquiring mind may fairly apply itself with a prospect of getting some attention paid to its labours, there is always the very greatest activity among the persons alluded to. The potato is at present the pet subject with this very numerous class, who are devoting all their energies to the treatment of the disease which has affected this popular esculent. The *savans* have taken it in hand, and all sorts of operations are recommended for the cure of the afflicted vegetable. If any individual had the time and patience to follow the instructions that have been from time to time put forth, we should find him occupied twelve hours a-day in doctoring his potatoes upon some new system. One day he is told he should have "clamped them with earth, having straw chimneys "every two yards;" and then he is recommended to "bake them in an oven, and put "them into separate shallow baskets." It is not clear whether there should be a separate shallow basket for each potato; but we have no doubt that it is seriously intended there should be, for most of the proposed plans comprise difficulties and intricacies which could not be understood by ordinary people or carried out in ordinary establishments. Too many cooks, we know, spoil the broth, and too many experimentalists are likely to deprive us of what still remains to us of the potato. It is in danger of being destroyed by the over solicitude of zealous but injudicious friends, who are literally killing it with kindness.

We should not attach so much importance to the great potato movement which is now going on in the pseudo-scientific world, if we did not find that men who are looked up to as authorities in matters of the kind, are sending forth numberless puerilities on the subject of the threatened scarcity. Dr. BUCKLAND has rendered himself peculiarly prominent by a paper which he read very recently to the members of the Ashmolean Society at Oxford, from which we extracted somewhat copiously in our paper one day last week. The chief object of the document to which we allude is apparently to undermine the reputation of the potato, and destroy the character it has hitherto enjoyed as a wholesome and grateful nutriment. The Doctor sneers at the esculent upon which Sir WALTER RALEIGH founded part of his imperishable fame, and makes an endeavour to exalt the pea, the bean, and even the mangold-wurzel, above the article that has hitherto enjoyed so large a share of public favour. He pits a pint of peas against a given quantity of potatoes for the production of gluten and fibre; while he points to the restorative effect of "a "feed of beans" on a jaded hack or an exhausted racehorse, as an argument, we presume, in favour of our taking an occasional "feed of beans" to recruit our energies and satisfy our hunger. He tells us encouragingly, how pease were the food of the ladies in the time of HOLLINSHED, how Friar TUCK laid parched pease before his Prince as the first dish, and how Sir W. BETHAM found records of a vessel loaded with pease that was wrecked in the fifteenth century. It is not a question what the ladies ate in the time of HOLLINSHED, how Friar TUCK feasted his Prince, or whether the English soldiers were fond of pease in the fifteenth century, for though these are curious facts to the antiquary, they are worse than puerile when addressed to a nation keenly alive to the horrors of impending famine, and looking eagerly to the Government for the means of mitigating the suffering that there seems no chance of wholly escaping from. It is all very well to tell an Irishman that potatoes are not nutritious in proportion to their bulk, and that he will acquire more gluten, phosphorus, &c., from a pound of peas than from four pounds of potatoes. His answer will be, that he has relied upon his patch of potatoes, which have failed, and that he has neither pease, starch, mangold-wurzel, burnt bones, nor any other article in Dr. BUCKLAND's proposed bill of fare, to subsist upon. Some allowance also must be made for habit, and it is not such an easy matter to persuade the ignorant that they will derive proper nourishment from the food that their cattle have been hitherto exclusively fed upon. Mangold-wurzel, which has been grown for sheep, is recommended by Dr. BUCKLAND, who calls upon the farmers of England to sell it, as a boon to their poor neighbours, at the same price as potatoes. The flour of burnt bones is another of the substitutes for food which is strongly recommended in the document to which we have referred, and which apparently proceeds on the supposition that starvation will give human beings an appetite for almost anything. The case of the famished paupers at Andover was probably in the recollection of Dr. BUCKLAND when he proposed some of the articles which we find suggested as food for the poor during the approaching apprehended scarcity.

There are a few propositions in the paper to which we have alluded that are not objectionable on the ground of their being revolting to the tastes and habits of human beings, like most of the suggestions we have already called attention to. Dr. BUCKLAND talks about "a polar party that travelled for nearly "a fortnight without food, sustaining life by "drinking warm water and sleeping in blankets "with their feet round a fire." Such an expedient as this may have been necessary in the case of a polar party temporarily cut off from supply; but there is something monstrous in the proposition to put a whole nation upon warm water, to say nothing of that portion of the project which requires blankets and a fire that are not usually within the reach of a famished people. The "woman of Tutbury" is also cited as an illustration of how feeding may be accomplished in the absence of anything to eat, for we are told by Dr. BUCKLAND that this "woman of Tutbury" lived for days and weeks by sucking the starch out of her pocket handkerchief.

We can scarcely afford to smile at this trifling, when we consider the awful gravity of the subject to which it refers. We regret that a great national calamity should be met by nothing better than a series of scientific speculations that might serve as an entertaining pastime at any other period than the present. The crisis in which we now are is not a fit subject for ingenious calculations as to the relative quantities of gluten in peas and potatoes, nor for antiquarian researches into the question whether the people of England lived three hundred years ago upon peas-pudding. Dr. BUCKLAND has quoted a nursery couplet to prove the fact, and seems to think he has succeeded in finding a remedy for the dreaded evil when he refers triumphantly to the lines—

"Pease-pudding hot, pease-pudding cold,
"Pease-pudding in the pot nine days old."

It is time for practical men to put an end to all this delusive nonsense, by holding out some hope of practical measures of relief; and we should have a very bad opinion of the prospects of the country if we could expect no better from the Minister than from Dr. BUCKLAND.

Our ordinary French express had not arrived at the time of going to press.

The *Andria* of Terence will be performed this year by the scholars of St. Peter's College, Westminster. The representations will take place on Monday, Dec. 8; Thursday, Dec. 11; and Monday, Dec. 15.

COURT CIRCULAR.

The wet and unfavourable state of the weather on Tuesday afternoon prevented Her Majesty and Prince Albert and the Royal children from taking airings.

The Countess Desart arrived at Osborne-house on Tuesday afternoon. Her Ladyship has succeeded Lady Portman as the Lady in Waiting on Her Majesty. Lady Portman remains on a visit at Osborne-house.

Her Majesty and her Royal Consort walked on the sea-beach yesterday morning.

His Royal Highness the Prince of Wales was taken in a carriage to the beach yesterday forenoon.

Mr. M'Queen and Mr. Thomas Sturge had an interview with the Earl of Dalhousie yesterday.

Mr. Freshfield had an interview with the Chancellor of the Exchequer yesterday, at his official residence in Downing-street.

A numerous deputation from Marylebone, headed by Mr. Joseph Hume, M.P., had an interview with Sir James Graham yesterday at the Home-office.

The Ecclesiastical Commissioners for England had a general meeting yesterday at the office in Whitehall-place. There were present the Archbishop of Canterbury, the Bishop of London, the Bishop of Ely, the Bishop of Oxford, the Bishop of Rochester, and the Secretary of State for the Home Department.

The Duke of Buccleuch has left town for Ditton.

Mr. Hart Davis, Deputy-Chairman of the Excise, and Mr. Carr, Solicitor to the Excise, had an interview with the Chancellor of the Exchequer yesterday.

Mr. Montgomery Martin had an interview yesterday with the Earl of Dalhousie.

Despatches for the Governor-General of Canada, and also for the Governors of the other North American provinces, were sent off yesterday evening from the Colonial-office. Despatches were also sent off last evening from the Colonial-office for the Governor of New Zealand.

The GRAND DUKE CONSTANTINE of RUSSIA.

PLYMOUTH, DEC. 2.

His Imperial Highness, who embarked on the 25th ult. on board the Ingermanland, Captain Moffitt, has been by contrary winds detained in Plymouth Sound ever since. The weather during the last week has been very boisterous, the wind veering from south-west to south, accompanied by rain. The dulness of lying wind-bound was somewhat relieved this morning by those demonstrations of joy which annually record the return of the accession-day of His Imperial Majesty the Emperor of all the Russias.

At 11 o'clock the rigging of the Ingermanland, and that of the corvette Vaarshafsky, Captain Glassenap, was dressed in fancy colours, from the jibboom to the peak, and from the mast-heads to the bulwarks. On hoisting the Russian national standard at the main, Royal salutes were fired from both ships, and at 12 o'clock Her Majesty's ships the Queen and President, both at anchor in the Sound, honoured the Imperial flag with a similar compliment, which was repeated by Her Majesty's ship Caledonia in Hamoaze.

On board the Ingermanland the Grand Duke has resumed his place as First Lieutenant, and in that rank take his regular watch, and scrupulously performs the duties assigned to him.

His Excellency Baron Brunow, the Russian Ambassador, who is afflicted with rheumatism in the face, left Plymouth on the 29th ult. for London.

The Nimrod, 20, was commissioned here yesterday by Commander Dacres.

This morning the Avenger steam frigate arrived from the Thames.

LORD JOHN RUSSELL.—On the occasion of the Dowager Lady Holland's funeral the noble Lord came express from Scotland to attend the obsequies, and subsequently went to pay a short visit to the Duke and Duchess of Bedford, at Woburn Abbey. His Lordship has been in town a few days, and on Saturday left for Edinburgh, where Lady John Russell and family are residing. We regret to hear her Ladyship's health is not what might be desired. Mr. Rutherfurd, M.P., has given up his house near Edinburgh to the noble Lord and his family while in the north.—*Globe.*

RUBINI AND HIS TEMPTERS.—Mr. Lumley, who is still in Italy, has been on a short visit to Rubini, at his chateau at Romano, and has, it is understood, been endeavouring to tempt the *gran' tenore* to one more "last engagement" at Her Majesty's Theatre in London. The terms offered by this prince of *impresarii* to the prince of tenors are described as simply—a blank sheet of paper, to be filled up altogether by Rubini, on whatever terms he chose to propose—a truly regal mode of doing business. We have not yet learned the result.—*Galignani's Messenger.*

The will of the late Right Hon. John Charles Earl Spencer has been proved by his brother, the present Earl, the sole executor; the personal estate within the province of Canterbury was sworn under 100,000*l.* His Lordship has devised and appointed all his manors, &c., freehold, copyhold, or leasehold, in the counties of Nottingham, Lincoln, and York, to his brother, the present Earl (heretofore the Hon. Frederick Spencer), subject and chargeable with the payment of the legacies and annuities, and in exoneration of any mortgages or other encumbrances. He has left to the Rev. Christopher Nevill, and to his brother, George Nevill, Esq., 10,000*l.* each; to Dr. London, of Leamington, an annuity of 100*l.*; to his bailiff, John Hall, a legacy of 1,000*l.*, and all the short-horned cattle on the farm in Nottingham, or 2,000*l.*, should the present Earl wish to preserve the breed and to retain the same; and to John Elliot, his bailiff on his Northamptonshire estates, he has left a legacy of 2,000*l.*; liberal annuities to his principal servants, his huntsman, gamekeeper, gardener, butler, and annuities and legacies to other of his servants, male and female. The residue of his real and personal estate he leaves to his brother, the Right Hon. Frederick Earl Spencer. His Lordship's will, with a codicil, was made in the year 1840.—*Morning Post.*

THE WESTMINSTER COURT OF SEWERS.—A special general meeting of the Commissioners of the Westminster Court of Sewers took place yesterday at the Court-house, Greek-street, Soho, to receive from the special committee appointed by the Court on the 5th of September, a report of their observations upon Mr. Leslie's pamphlet, addressed to the representative vestries under Sir John Hobhouse's act, and to take such steps thereon as might be deemed advisable. The chair was taken at 1 o'clock by Mr. Edward Willoughby. The minutes of the appointment of the committee in compliance with the request of the Right Hon. Sir James Graham to be informed respecting the allegations in the pamphlet were read. The Right Hon. the Lord Mayor, as chairman of the committee, then rose, and, after briefly stating that every care and attention had been bestowed by them (the committee) to answer satisfactorily the inquiries submitted to them by the Home-office, his Lordship presented the report. This document was of great length, and was a real or attempted refutation of charges and statements nowise creditable to the acting commissioners, contained in Mr. Leslie's pamphlet. The report was received, and, on the motion of the Lord Mayor and Captain Bague, ordered to be transmitted to Sir James Graham forthwith. The minutes of the evidence upon which the committee based their refutation, were then called for. The chairman pronounced this motion not regular; however, after a somewhat stormy discussion, the Lord Mayor declared that he for one had no desire to avoid publicity, and his coadjutors concurring, the chairman said that he had no desire to keep back anything, but a discussion upon the minutes would come on with greater propriety at their next meeting. The minutes were then brought forward and read. Their details were ample, and the observations subsequently made upon them numerous. The report was ordered to be printed and circulated amongst the commissioners. The Court adjourned at a late hour.

FRIGHTFUL ACCIDENT.—On Thursday afternoon, about 3 o'clock, as Mr. John Lewis, of Maldon, horse-dealer, was on his way on horseback from Tilbury-fort to Brentwood, a man riding a second horse belonging to him by his side, when near the Cock, at Orsett, they were overtaken by Mr. W. Stephens, farmer, of Bulphan-fen, who was riding at a furious pace, and the horse, over which it was evident he had no control, came in contact with that upon which Mr. Lewis's man was mounted. Such was the violence of the collision that the man was thrown from his seat, but fortunately he escaped unhurt. Mr. Stephens was also precipitated to the ground, and his horse rolled over him. He was taken into Barrington's-farm, and Inspector Smith, of the police force, who was near the spot, with the greatest promptitude obtained the assistance of Mr. Corbett, surgeon, when it was found that Mr. Stephens was much injured upon the hip, and greatly bruised. The poor animals fell a sacrifice to the casualty, the one rode by Mr. Lewis's man expiring from the effects of the shock in about five minutes; and Mr. Stephens's being so much injured that its sufferings were necessarily put an end to with the knife half an hour after the occurrence. The latter, it appears, from some cause took fright at Chadwell, near Grays, from which time Mr. Stephens lost all power over him, the animal, we are informed, actually clearing by a leap a donkey and cart, which were upon the road. Mr. Lewis's horse is said to have been worth about 12*l.*, Mr. Stephen's 25*l.*—*Essex Herald.*

SOUTH-EASTERN RAILWAY.—Gross traffic receipts for the week ending Nov. 29, 1845:—

	£	s.	d.
Passengers	£2,985	12	9
Carrying account, special engine, and mails	1,052	8	4
Whitstable Railway receipts... ...	181	7	6
Folkestone-harbour dues	70	1	2
	£4,290	9	9
Greenwich Railway	907	17	2
	£5,198	6	11

GRETNA-GREEN MARRIAGES.—All young men and maidens who wish to follow the example of Captain Ibbetson and Lady Villiers, must do so speedily, for, by a recent act, all marriages similar to that recently performed at Gretna-green will cease to be legal after the 1st of January next.—*Berwick Advertiser.*

THE DUKE OF WELLINGTON AND THE CIGARS.—The general order against smoking in the army has occasioned a deep sensation in every mess-room in the kingdom, and created such a panic in the cigar market, that good cheroots were done at an unusually low figure, and the Manillas were done at a penny, which had been commanding three-halfpence, with a fair sprinkling of buyers, for the last eight months. The cabbage-growers are in despair, for the young officers had been the chief consumers of the hardy winter savoy, which must now be sold as food for the lower classes, instead of being packed in ivory cases for mess-room tables, as the best Havannahs, imported direct from Havannah by the Hammersmith 'bus. As to the military themselves, meetings are being called in every regiment, to consider whether the officers shall coolly submit to allow the Duke of Wellington to put all their pipes out. The Duke of Wellington has blown a cloud over the whole of the army by his inconsiderate endeavour to banish the cigar from the mess-room. The officers naturally ask what they are to do when they meet; for they are to be restrained from boxing, wrestling, leap-frog, blind-man's-buff, as well as prohibited from smoking, and they dread the possibility of being thrown upon their conversational resources, which must have a most dreary effect. Under their present trying position, we can offer no consolation to the inmates of the barracks, except such as they may derive from taking it by turns to read *Punch* aloud to the whole mess.—*Punch.*

ADVICE GRATIS.
AN ECLOGUE.

(From *Punch.*)

Paddy.—What's to be done at all, Misther Commissioner?
Here's a lot of praytees wouldn't plaze the pigs, Sir,
Earlies and Lumpers, cups and common taters,
Gone to the divil.

Commissioner.—Dig up your tubers, store them in a dry place,
Plenty of straw put underneath each layer,
Grind them to pulp, or, if you like it better,
Toast on a griddle.

Paddy.—Murdther alive, but where's the straw to come from?
Mill for to grind, or griddle for to toast 'em?
Divil the place I've got to keep myself dry,
Much less my praties.

Dr. Buckland.—Ignorant peasant, don't mind Kane and Playfair—
Starch is only gluten, therefore innutritious;
Steam your potatoes, and you'll find the fungus
Equal to mushrooms.

Mr. Tilley.—Chloride of lime is better, if you've got it—
Twopence a pound is all that it will cost you.
One pound of chloride, properly employed, saves
Two of potatoes.

All together.—But whate'er you do, Pat, keep your mind quite easy.
Science is at work examining the fungus;
Though, for the present, we confess that we know
Nothing about it.

[*Exeunt* COMMISSIONER, BUCKLAND, *and* TILLEY. PADDY, *with his hands in his pockets, looks after them bewildered.*

GAME LAWS.

TO THE EDITOR OF THE TIMES.

Sir,—Communications, written and verbal, since my last letter, which I beg to thank you for inserting, induce me to believe the subject of sufficient importance to excuse my again troubling you. I have been asked what preserves I alluded to. I feel no delicacy in stating that I mean the Royal preserves of Windsor forest.

Since my last I have received an intimation from a gentleman of the Royal suite (in not over courteous terms, bye-the-by, but let that pass), stating that no gamekeeper will be appointed in the forest near me, that a rabbit catcher has been placed there (a dozen would hardly be sufficient), and that such determination was come to some weeks ago, and not in consequence of my correspondence with the press. Be it so. Will this recompense me and my neighbours for the damage already sustained? Will it protect us from future inroads? and may not that determination be reversed at any future period as the law stands? The part of the forest aforesaid is merely the end of a long and extensive line of preserves, and contains not one acre of cultivated land, the property of the Crown, in it, and is and will be overrun by game and rabbits from the other parts. The establishment consists of a large body of gamekeepers and others, who, during the early part of the summer, are employed in procuring (I have known poor men punished for only possessing) pheasants' eggs, hatching them under common fowls, and rearing the chickens, and, before the harvest, turning them down, to the number of some thousands, to shift for themselves on the property of the neighbours; and wo to the unfortunate farmer who, not having the fear of statute 1 and 2 William IV., c. 32, before his eyes, but not liking to see his corn fields darkened with game as I have seen mine, should dare to protect himself and attempt to impound such trespassers "damage feasant"—him the justice, sessions, constabulary, and keepers would worry. We saw a short time ago some strong critiques on the new and un-English system of *battues.* The carnage about here is not less than elsewhere. After about two hours' firing, the game and rabbits being hemmed in by keepers to prevent escape, my information leads me to believe the amount of the slain generally exceeds 200,—some of which are sold at Egham, fattened by the neighbours. My contribution towards it (I mean this in the most literal sense of the words, and shortly mean to prove it by the oaths of competent witnesses) amounts this year to the entire rental of my estate.

Surely, Sir, it is extraordinary that the law should intrust such power of injury to any individual; more extraordinary still, that any one in the 19th century should so mercilessly exercise it. When England

"Lies at the proud foot of a conqueror,"

we may be called upon to submit to such a system; but meanwhile, and before that happens, I hope enlightened public opinion will pronounce judgment on the game laws.

I am, Sir,
Your obedient and humble servant,
JOHN FORBES, Captain R.N.,
Deputy-Lieutenant and Magistrate for Berks.

Winkfield-place, Windsor Forest,
Dec. 3.

THE LONDON WEATHER.

TO THE EDITOR OF THE TIMES.

Sir,—The past month has not borne out the usual character of the November fogs, although there has been a very damp and ungenial atmosphere without so much of the smoke, which is to be ascribed to the force of the upper currents. The vacillation of the barometer has fully borne out my last anticipations, and I believe that there will be no settled weather until the middle of this month, when I expect some fair and frosty weather will continue to the end of the year.

The comparative analysis of my observations of the past month present a diurnal average of increase in the temperature, although the cold downfall and aqueous state of the atmosphere have been conjointly very prejudicial. I find that my night thermometer at the coldest average of the past month was 42° 25″ of Fahrenheit, the highest in the shade 52° 93″, and in the S.W. aspect 62° 46″, making an increase relatively of 1° 09″, 4° 45″, and 66″. The highest degree of temperature in the shade was on the 6th ult., 61°, and that of the sun was, on the same day, 83°. The lowest, screened from the downfall, was on the 23d, 32°.

The barometer was on the 4th, 30′ 22″ as the extreme height, and on the 20th was 29′ 13″, making a difference of one inch and very nearly a-tenth. The average has been diurnally through November, 29′ 67″.

I am, Sir, your subscriber,
Bermondsey-square, Dec. 3. H. P.

FALL OF THREE HOUSES.—On Tuesday night, about 8 o'clock, an occurrence that at the time caused great excitement, and has since spread a gloom over the neighbourhood, took place in Cavendish-place, Wandsworth-road. It appears from the inquiries made by the reporter that Mr. Corrall, a builder, had recently erected four six-roomed houses with shop fronts, in Cavendish-place. They had been covered in, and the lathing and flooring had been completed, but there yet was some plastering, and other matters to be done. On the night in question Oliver Carroll, the son of the builder, who was only in his 20th year, his brother, and a labourer, were at work on one of the basement-floors of the houses, laying concrete, when, as it is supposed, the end wall of the house nearest the Cavendish Arms, bulged out, and in less than a minute the three houses separated from the fourth, which was apparently much more strongly built, and fell with a loud crash, burying in the ruins the two brothers, the labourer escaping with a few bruises from the falling bricks. An instant alarm was given, and in an incredibly short space of time a large body of men assembled, and commenced removing the bricks and timber with the sanguine hope of preserving the persons buried. In a few minutes one of the Carrolls was discovered, and brought out; he was alive, and owed his preservation to two pieces of timber falling crossway, and thus preventing the rubbish suffocating him. He was carried home by two men, suffering from some very severe contusions. In about ten minutes after the accident occurred, Sergeant Emmerson, 16 V, with a number of constables, arrived, and cleared away the mob that had assembled, so that the men might pursue their work uninterrupted. The men laboured unceasingly for three-quarters of an hour, when a sufficient opening was made for a man to creep in, who reported that he saw the deceased Oliver Carroll in a sitting position, about three yards distant from where he was. The men redoubled their energies, and in another ten minutes they cleared an enormous mass of timber and brick which were on the deceased, and Sergeant Emerson dragged him out. His head had been driven between his knees, and his back was apparently broken. He was, to all appearance dead, but, nevertheless, was conveyed with the utmost celerity to the Cavendish Arms, where Mr. Palmer a surgeon had been in attendance since the accident, so that he might be of service to the unfortunate sufferers. Mr. Palmer resorted to bleeding, the application of stimulants, &c., but although one or two drops of blood came there was no sign of life manifested, and the surgeon gave it as his opinion that the deceased must have been suffocated some time. One or two carpenters were in the act of leaving the building at the time of its falling, so that their escape may be considered miraculous. The materials of the houses were evidently of a very common description, the mortar especially seemed to have been made without that great essential lime, for there was scarcely a brick to which it adhered.

STATE OF TRADE.—MANCHESTER.—Although the market wore a very gloomy appearance yesterday, in consequence of the announcement of several failures, including those of two extensive concerns in London, there was, upon the whole, a little more disposition to do business than for some time past, and sales of cloth were more readily made, though at very low prices. Yarn, suitable for the East India market, was also in fair request, and a considerable amount of business was done at the full rates of last week. Other descriptions are still very heavy of sale, but there is no further change in prices.—*Manchester Guardian.*

York Herald
Lord President of the Council
Lord Archbishop of York
Lord High Chancellor
Lord Archbishop of Canterbury
In a Mourning Coach

Assistant Quarter-Master-General	Assistant Adjutant-General
Aide-de-Camp to the Deceased	Aide-de-Camp to the Deceased
Deputy Quarter-Master General	Deputy-Adjutant General
Qtr-Master-General	Adjutant-General

[At Temple-bar, the Lord Mayor, carrying the City Sword, will join in the procession]

His Royal Highness Prince Albert in a Carriage drawn by Six Horses; attended by the Lord Chamberlain of Her Majesty's Household, and the Groom of the Stole to His Royal Highness

A second Carriage with other Attendants

A Third Carriage with other Attendants

Herald

THE GREAT BANNER,

Carried by a Colonel, supported by two Lieutenant-Colonels on Horseback

Sergeant Trumpeter

[Here on reaching the Cathedral the Dignitaries of the Church, meeting the Body at the West Door, fall in]

FOREIGN BATONS.

Top THE FIELD OF BATTERSEA, coloured etching by 'Paul Pry', (Henry Heath) March 1829. Wellington challenged Winchilsea, opponent of the Catholic Emancipation Bill, to a duel. They both fired to miss, but the Prime Minister insisted on a written apology. 'Lobsterhead' was the colloquialism for the scarlet uniformed soldier; Wellington, as supporter of the Bill, is garbed in priest's habit.

Above Wood engravings from a broadsheet of the Duke of Wellington's funeral procession, September 1852.

but he does not attend to it; nor does he meddle with that degree of intelligence which might be expected of him. I must put this to rights.

Ever yours, etc.

WELLINGTON.

The Duke moved fast. His instinctive opposition to reform and to meddling with the press was softened by his high sense of public duty. He decided that Catholic emancipation, to relieve British Catholics of their political disabilities, was necessary to resolve the Irish Question, which was with us even then. The trouble was that George IV was even more opposed to Catholic emancipation than his father, and threatened to abdicate if the Duke pushed it. Two months after his letter to Croker announcing that he was taking up press relations, *The Times* carried a significant notice:

We rejoice to say again, what we made known some months ago – viz. that we have the very strongest reasons for attributing to the Duke of Wellington a fixed determination to introduce a Bill for the relief of the Catholics in the ensuing Session. We announce this, and we stand to it as our firm conviction, founded on intelligence from quarter alike incapable of being deceived itself, and of deceiving others.

That was not so much code as an illustrated billboard announcing that the Duke of Wellington had managed to overcome the King's objections, that the Cabinet had resolved upon emancipation and that the Duke had instructed Croker to pass the message to Printing House Square. *The Times* supported the Duke in the vehement struggle over emancipation. Both were blackguarded by the fanatical Protestant opposition. *The Times* was described as 'the Duke's Own' and 'the hireling of Popery'. The Duke fought a duel with Lord Winchilsea over the allegation that he was conspiring to bring back the Pope.

Within a year of the Catholic Emancipation Act, *The Times* was calling for the Duke's resignation. There was a general election as a consequence of the accession of William IV, and Wellington tried to form another administration. He was opposed to parliamentary reform, for which *The Times* was thundering. In his reply to the debate on the King's Speech, Wellington asserted that the legislature and system of representation possessed the full and entire confidence of the country. *The Times* disagreed, and forthwith informed its readers that the Duke must resign because of the differences between himself and his colleagues on the burning topic of the age. The Wellington Government was defeated on the Civil List, and fell. *The Times* said goodbye handsomely in a leader of 17 November 1830:

If the management of public affairs has been difficult during His Grace's Premiership, the difficulty has resulted more from petty perplexities than great affairs. When the Duke of Wellington made the declaration, to the effect that he was opposed to every species of Parliamentary reform, we saw that his fate was sealed. We do not know that he did not court it. Mr Canning made a declaration to the same purpose. But Mr Canning was loved by the people. Since the Catholic Emancipation the Duke has been hated by the Tory aristocracy with a bitterness equal to its injustice.

On 4 December 1845 *The Times* published a scoop that shook the political world. Its leading article started:

The decision of the Cabinet is no longer a secret. Parliament, it is confidently reported, is to be summoned for the first week of January; and the Royal Speech will, it is added, recommend an immediate consideration of the Corn Laws, preparatory to their total repeal. Sir Robert Peel in one house, and the Duke of Wellington in the other, will, we are told, be prepared to give immediate effect to the recommendation thus conveyed.

It was sensational news that the Grand Old Man of High Toryism was about to do a U-turn on Whiggish Free Trade, for which *The Times* was campaigning. And why had the scoop appeared in *The Times* instead of in one of the papers that supported the Government? The Prime Minister, Peel, wrote carefully to the Queen that the paragraph in *The Times* 'asserting that your Majesty's servants had unanimously agreed to an immediate and total repeal of the Corn Laws, is quite without foundation'. Every adjective and adverb in his letter pulled its full qualifying weight. And Peel made no public denial. The Government papers published categorical denials under such headings as: ATROCIOUS FABRICATION BY THE TIMES.

But the denials were non-attributable. And *The Times* stuck to its story. The fight in Cabinet was so fierce that Peel resigned. The Opposition could not form an administration, so Peel returned and duly repealed the Corn Laws.

The Times scoop had been right. The secret struggle in Cabinet had been leaked to Printing House Square by Lord Aberdeen, the Foreign Secretary. The Duke of Wellington, when told by Peel that his resignation over the Corn Laws would bring down the Government, had agreed to go along with the general view, and even use his influence to carry Free Trade through the House of Lords.

One of *The Times* moles at the heart of politics was Charles Greville, the diarist, who was Clerk of the Privy Council from 1821 to 1865, and was secretly writing leaders and passing information to Printing House Square all the time. He records that he once asked the Duke of Wellington if he had seen *The Times* that morning:

He said 'No'; and I told him there appeared in it considerable disposition to support the new Government, and I thought it would be very advisable to obtain that support if it could be done. He said he was aware that he had formerly too much neglected the Press, but he did not think *The Times* could be influenced.

It showed that Wellington had got the message about the rising power in the constitution, a paper that could not be influenced.

When the Great Duke died, *The Times* paid eloquent tribute in its obituary to its old adversary, who had stood on the other side of the battle in most of the political struggles that forged *The Times*: 'The Duke of Wellington had exhausted nature and exhausted glory. His career was one unclouded longest day.'

THE TIMES's scoop announcing Wellington's *volte face* over free trade, for which the paper had campaigned.
4 DECEMBER 1845

The Great Exhibition

'The Productions of All Nations about to appear at the Great Exhibition of 1851.' Figures from a sheet of woodcuts, printed by Elliot, New Oxford Street, price one penny.
From top: Specimen from the Sandwich Islands; Specimen from the Highlands; Specimen from Hong Kong – a Mandarin; Specimen from Amsterdam.
Below View of the Chinese section of the Great Exhibition, Hyde Park, 1851.

The Great Exhibition of 1851 was a portentous symbol of national pride and controversy. On one hand it was a proud demonstration that Britain had become the workshop of the world. On the other hand it caused ructions and strife. *The Times*, established as the national newspaper of the new Britain being celebrated in the great Crystal Palace in Hyde Park, joined enthusiastically in both celebration and controversy.

Its article on the opening of the Exhibition compared it, with a touch of hyperbole, to the concourse of all peoples on the Day of Judgment. For once Queen Victoria was pleased by something in *The Times*, complimentary to Albert's pet project. She cut out the article and wrote that the occasion seemed like her coronation over again, except that the continuous cheering made it more touching, 'for in a church naturally all is silent'.

In the face of fierce and sustained prejudice, not unmixed with personal abuse, the Prince Consort was the prime mover in the Great Exhibition. The result was a triumph for the Queen and Albert as much as for the nation. Neither had been particularly popular before, as the new Britain had fought its way to birth. The Great Exhibition was unexpectedly a national carnival celebrating Great Britain and the Empire; the Queen and Prince Consort were the symbolic stars of the show. A Continental visitor wrote: 'In England loyalty is a passion'.

The Great Exhibition was the grand advertisement for Free Trade and the Industrial Revolution. Samuel Smiles was the prophet of the mid-Victorian creed of meritocracy, the Prince Consort was its impresario, Paxton was its architect and *The Times* was its publicist.

On the central issue embodied by the Exhibition, the new power of industry and the middle classes, *The Times* was enthusiastically on the side of the new world: it had itself led the way into a new world of independent journalism and steam printing. This new world was opposed by the Old Guard, protectionists, and fashionables and fox-hunters from the shires, led by a Colonel Charles Sibthorp, who called down curses from heaven, including crystal-shattering hail, upon this new Tower of Babel.

During 1850 and 1851 pages and pages of the paper were devoted to the Great Exhibition. But it was not all puff. *The Times* has never been a courtierly paper. It described Sir Joseph Paxton's great crystal erection in minute detail, listed the exhibitors and visitors from the round earth's imagined corners, gave space to the event that seems inordinate today; but it reserved the journalist's irritating right to put the other side of the case, particularly if it is going to annoy somebody.

The site chosen for the Crystal Palace excited fierce controversy, gleefully reported and stirred up in *The Times*. Not only was the great temple of commerce high enough to enclose the great elm trees of Hyde Park, but it spread 1,600 feet, far enough to impede the smart riders in Rotten Row. Their complaints were aired and shot down in *The Times*. The Queen had no sympathy for them. How dared they endanger Albert's Exhibition 'merely for the sake of the Ride in Hyde Park about which people have suddenly gone quite mad?' Thackeray wrote a *May Day Ode* on the row. It started:

> But yesterday a naked sod,
> The dandies sneered from Rotten-row,
> And cantered o'er it to and fro;
> And see 'tis done!
> As though 'twere by a wizard's rod
> A blazing arch of lucid glass
> Leaps like a fountain from the grass
> To meet the sun.

The Exhibition caused uproar in foreign relations, fought out in the columns of *The Times*. On one hand, would the foreign exhibitors import into Britain revolution, political agitation, crime, rabies and other nasty foreign habits? Printing House Square was reassuring, on the whole. On the other hand, Prince Albert's Continental cousins from the old world were nervous about trusting themselves into the new world, haven of emigrés, radicals, constitutionalists and a free press. The Tsar refused passports to the Russian nobility, for fear of 'contamination' in London. King Bomba of Naples went further, and refused to allow Neapolitan goods to be sent to the Exhibition, in case even they might be contaminated by the British pox.

The King of Prussia wrote to Prince Albert at the last minute asking whether it was really safe for the Crown Prince and his family to come to London. Albert replied sarcastically that there was '*no* fear here'. But since he could not absolutely guarantee anybody's life, he would not invite the Prussians. Victoria wrote that this 'would cause a great sensation'.

Even the birds caused trouble. They roosted in the trees inside the Crystal Palace, and threatened to cover the Exhibition with more conspicuous contempt than the jealous Continental royalties had managed to do. Many remedies were suggested in the correspondence columns of *The Times* and elsewhere. It was left to the Duke of Wellington to hit upon the obvious: 'Try sparrow-hawks, ma'am', he suggested to the Queen.

Then the Prime Minister, Lord John Russell, caused trouble. He suggested that the proposed salute of guns by the Serpentine would certainly shatter the crystal dome. The guns should be fired at a safe distance, in St James's Park. The Prime Minister's advice was disregarded. The gunners banged away by the Serpentine. No glass broke.

It was one of the great popular events of the century, and vast crowds were expected for the opening. The Prince took fright that they would trample the Queen, so he altered the arrangements. Season-ticket holders would be admitted at one o'clock, not at 11 am as had been previously arranged; by one the Queen would be safely home from the Crystal Palace. *The Times*, which had by now adopted the Exhibition, was furious and thundered indignation. The Prime Minister wrote to Prince Albert: 'The fashionable society in London might be disregarded, but it would be a pity to alienate the manufacturers and the middle classes'. Season-ticket holders were let in at 11 am after all.

The Great Exhibition was the climax of the Victorian revolution. It epitomized the changes fought for and won over the previous fifty years. In celebrating this, *The Times* was also celebrating its own coming of age as a national institution.

A description of the exhibitors and categories of exhibits at the opening of the Great Exhibition. The diagram showing the layout of the Crystal Palace was most unusual: at this time, THE TIMES generally carried no illustrative material of any kind.
2 MAY 1851

THE GREAT EXHIBITION.

The inauguration of the Temple of the Industry of the World, an edifice as unexampled in its magnitude and materials as for the purposes to which it is applied and the collection it displays, will render yesterday for ever memorable as a great epoch in the progress of civilization. Erected at the exclusive cost and by the spontaneous subscription of the British people, it has been dedicated to the celebration of the triumphs of the useful arts throughout the globe. Its portals have been thrown open, without restriction or limit, to all nations, invited to meet there in amicable rivalry and on equal terms—an invitation which has been responded to in a spirit correspondent with that in which it was given. From the east and from the west, from the north and from the south, from the ardour of the tropics and the rigour of the poles, thousands have come to present their offerings at the common shrine—trophies collected in the victories of mind over matter—rich spoils carried away by man in his conquests over nature. The prisoners who follow the triumphal car of the victor are here the elements themselves, brought into subjection to the indomitable sway of the human will. Nothing in nature is so stubborn or intractable as to resist this power. The lightning dares no longer strike. It glides innocuous along a prescribed path, and is made to pass, as though in mockery of its impotence, over the objects which, being uncontrolled, it would have reduced to ruin. The wind and tide no longer obstruct the vessel which advances triumphantly against their force. Space and time are annihilated, and intelligence flies instantaneously between man and man at any distance, however great. Let those who take pleasure in such reflections, and delight to observe the means by which these and numerous other miracles of art are wrought, accompany us to the Crystal Palace, where they will find in every object a fruitful source of wonder and admiration. It will be our part from day to day to point out what is most worthy of attention, to explain and illustrate what may seem obscure, and to supply those links in the chain of useful and elevating information which may not always be suggested by the objects exhibited.

The plan appended will be found useful, not only as illustrating our remarks, but as a guide to the wonders of the collection.

According to the view of the Commission, the objects exhibited would be reducible to thirty principal divisions; four of which consist of RAW MATERIALS, six of MACHINERY, and the remaining twenty of FABRICATED ARTICLES.

Such a division is obviously enough in accordance with the operations of industry. The end to which all labour is directed is to effect such change of form and state upon the raw productions of nature as may adapt them to the uses of life. The industrial arts therefore naturally present the three subjects for examination and inquiry above-mentioned; that is to say, the matter upon which those changes are to be wrought, the means whereby they are to be effected, and the objects which result from them; in other words, MATERIALS, MACHINERY, and MANUFACTURES, each of these terms being used in their largest conceivable sense.

There is, indeed, a fourth principal class or division mentioned, which comprises certain objects of the fine arts, as sculpture, models, mosaics, enamels, and the like, considered as illustrative of the taste and skill displayed in the productions of human industry. But it appears to us that this supplemental division may be considered as fairly included (so far at least as this Exhibition is concerned) among the ornamental branches of MANUFACTURE in the large sense in which that term is here used.

The following, then, is a brief synopsis of the component parts of this vast collection classified in accordance with the principles just mentioned.

Under MATERIALS are comprised not only raw materials, properly so called, such as mineral ores and native metals, but also prepared materials, such as the pure metals supplied by the processes of metallurgy, and also all the varieties of machinery and instruments used in the processes by which they are obtained. Materials, in this sense of the term, are subdivided into four principal classes, as follows:—

I. MINING, QUARRYING, METALLURGIC OPERATIONS, AND MINERAL PRODUCTS.—This subdivision includes all the ordinary operations of mining, such as sinking shafts, cutting adits, driving levels, ventilation, illumination, and the means of communication between these subterraneous regions of industry and the surface, and transferring between them men and materials. It also includes the machinery applied for the purpose of pounding, dressing, roasting, smelting, and otherwise reducing the ore after it has been raised, for effecting those changes of state and form of particular metals so as to adapt them as materials for special purposes—such, for example, as the production of cast, malleable, sheet, and bar iron, steel, wire, alloys and their adaptation to special purposes in the arts, such as statuary, bronzes, fire-arms, bells, and telescope specula, those white alloys so extensively used in the arts under the titles of Britannia metal, German silver, pewter, type metal, sheathing metals, and so forth.

Among the non-metallic mineral products by far the most extensive in quantity and utility and in national importance are those minerals used as fuel, such as pit coal, which will be found in infinite variety in this museum. Next in importance under this head will come the mineral products used for building, such as stones, flags, and slates of every description.

Those classes of minerals adapted for ornamental and decorative purposes and for the fine arts follow, such as marbles, alabasters, porphyries, spars, &c. and constructive materials, cements and artificial stones, the calcareous and hydraulic cements, Puzzolanas, gypsum, &c. The classes of mineral materials are completed by a vast quantity of specimens of the earths used in the fabrication of porcelain and glass in all their varieties, from the rudest tiles to the most finished ornamental productions of the art, and the minerals used for peculiar ornament, for scientific and other miscellaneous purposes, such as the gems and precious stones.

II. CHEMICAL SUBSTANCES AND PROCESSES.—The second principal division of materials includes those products denominated chemical, and the expedients by which they are prepared, such as sulphur, phosphorus, the acids, the alkalies, the salts, from the mineral kingdom; pigments for dyeing and colouring from the vegetable and animal kingdoms; and a large catalogue of substances, mineral, vegetable, and animal, appropriated to medicine and pharmacy.

III. HUMAN FOOD.—To the third principal division of materials is assigned human food, vegetable and animal, the produce of the farm and the garden, comprising the varieties of grain, pulse, oil, &c., dried fruits, the materials for the production of fermented liquors, spices and condiments, starch, arrow-root, sago, &c., sugar from the cane, beet, maple, palms, birch, poplar, oak, ash, and the grape; animal food, especially such as it is artificially preserved; preserved meats, portable soups, caviare, trepang, Oriental food, such as fins, nests, honey, blood; and industrial products, such as gelatine, isinglass, glues, &c.

IV. SUBSTANCES, ANIMAL AND VEGETABLE, USED IN THE ARTS.—The vegetable materials comprised under this head include gums, resins, oils, acids, dyes, and colours, tanning substances, fibrous materials (such as cotton, hemp, flax, &c.), cellular substances (such as corks, barks, &c.), woods used for ornament or dyeing, and miscellaneous products (such as soaps, perfumes, &c.).

The animal substances included are extremely important and various, and supply the materials for vast branches of industry. They consist of wool, hair, silk, feathers, furs, skins, bones, horn, hoofs, ivory, pearls, shells, oils, tallow, wax, sponge, glue, isinglass, blood, certain dyes (such as cochineal and carmine, galls, cocoa, &c.).

Such is a view of the first principal division of the objects of exhibition, included under the extensive term MATERIALS.

Let us now turn to the second principal division, included under the comprehensive term of MACHINERY, which must be understood to apply not merely to machines properly so called, but to every mechanical agent, great or small, simple or complex, which can be imagined to be interposed between the human hand or any other moving power and the object to which force or motion is to be applied. In this sense, therefore, machinery includes every species of implement and tool.

This principal division is resolved into six subdivisions, as follows:—

I. MACHINES FOR DIRECT USE.—This class, besides all engines, machines, and apparatus of whatever description, for the purpose of locomotion, whether by land or water, aerial or submarine, and all machines whatever which may be regarded as moving powers, such as steam engines, wind and water mills. It also includes machines which, without being prime movers, are means of transmitting and modifying a moving force, such as pneumatic machines, air pumps, blowing furnaces, and blast engines; hydraulic machines, such as pumps, fire engines, water rams and presses; cranes adapted to jacks, windlasses, capstans, pile engines whether moved by animal or steam power, sawing machines, and pile extractors.

Under this subdivision is also included all the material employed in the construction of railways, such as the permanent way, rails, sleepers, chairs, switches, turn-tables, signals, and the accessories of the stations. In fine, there are included in the same subdivision instruments and machines for weighing, measuring, and registering quantities and magnitudes for commercial, but not for philosophical, purposes.

II. MANUFACTURING IMPLEMENTS.—This subdivision includes manufacturing machines, tools and implements employed in the production of spun, woven, felted, and laid fabrics and in the manufacture of vegetable and animal substances; all the varieties of machinery necessary for the production of the complete manufactured fabric from the following raw materials—cotton, wool, flax, hemp, silk, caoutchouc, gutta percha, and hair, paper-making, paper-staining, printing, and bookbinding.

It includes the vast range of manufactures in metal, such as the conversion of the raw metal into bars, rods, wire, sheets, the casting and polishing of metal, the cutting and working it by tools, such as machines for turning, planing, drilling, boring, slotting, sawing, stamping, shearing, rivetting, and punching, machines and implements used in the manufacture of gold, silver, and plated goods, and those for cutting nails, screws, pins, needles, buttons, and metallic pens, the machines and the implements used by locksmiths and die-sinkers, and in the preparation and working of every species of glass, stone, granite, alabaster, slate, and clay, and in the preparation, working, and polishing of gems and precious stones, in the preparation and working of wood, the grinding, crushing, or other preparation of vegetable substances, and working horn, bone, ivory, and other animal substances, and, in fine, in brewing and distilling, and in manufacturing chymistry.

III. CIVIL ENGINEERING AND ARCHITECTURE.—This subdivision includes the machines and implements used in hydraulic works, scaffoldings, and centerings, machines used in the construction of bridges and tunnels, and expedients for crossing rivers and ravines; docks, harbours, and rivers, and canal works; light-houses and beacons; of roofs covering large areas; of water-works and contrivances for the supply of towns with water; of gas-works and contrivances for the production and distribution of artificial light; of sewerage, cleansing, paving, and expedients connected with the sanitary condition of towns; and, finally, for the heating and ventilating of buildings.

This extensive subdivision of machinery comprises some of the most important and interesting monuments of art, among which may be found pile machinery, coffer dams, machinery for the construction of light-houses, diving-bells and diving apparatus, boring apparatus; scaffoldings and centerings, such, for example, as those used in structures like the Britannia Bridge; centerings and shields for tunnels; bridges of every form and material, docks and slips for the building and repair and the loading and unloading of ships; canal machinery, such as locks, gates, stop gates and sluices; harbours of refuge, breakwaters, jetties, wharves, and piers, dredging machines, hedgehogs, and in general machines used in harbour works; roofs like those over markets, railway stations, and theatres; fire-proof buildings, well sinking and boring.

IV. MILITARY AND NAVAL ENGINEERING, &c.—The objects of exhibition under this head include models of ship-building for purposes of commerce and war, with or without the application of steam power, pleasure vessels, yachts, rowing boats, fishing vessels, life boats, &c., also ships' rigging, anchors, windlasses, capstans, and in general all the accessories of shipping; army clothing and accoutrements, camp furniture, gunnery (military and naval), arms and projectiles of every description, apparatus for field operations, such as military bridges, pontoons, rafts, boats, and the apparatus for fortification.

V. AGRICULTURE AND HORTICULTURE.—To this subdivision are consigned agricultural and horticultural implements, consisting of those used in tillage, such as ploughs, harrows, scarifiers, crushers, rollers, digging and trenching machines; those used in drilling, sowing, manuring, and harrowing, such as presses, drills, dibbles, hoes; in harvesting, such as those used for cutting, tedding, and collecting grass and corn; barn machinery, such as threshing machines, straw machines, machines for rubbing, cleansing, crushing, and splitting, flour and meal mills, chaff cutters, machines for sowing and measuring corn, bruisers, cutters, and presses; machinery for the field, fold, and farm-yard, such as turnip cutters, root grating and squeezing machines, potato washing, steaming, and feeding apparatus, weighing machines for cattle, fire-engines, and watering machines; agricultural carriages and their appendages, implements for draining, and implements for the dairy.

VI. PHILOSOPHICAL, ARTISTICAL, AND PROFESSIONAL APPARATUS.—This subdivision includes philosophical, musical, horological, and surgical instruments.

Under philosophical instruments are comprised those whose purpose is to measure space, whether linear or angular, such as transit instruments, quadrants, circles, sectors, equatorials, sextants, &c.; astronomical and topographical instruments of illustration, such as globes, orreries, maps, charts, &c.; optical instruments, such as telescopes; surveying instruments, both topographical and hydrographical; instruments for the measurement of the effects of mechanical forces, and the illustration of the laws of mechanical and physical science; instruments showing the application of mechanical and physical science to special purposes, such as mechanics, acoustics, optics, heat, magnetism, and electricity, and, in fine, chemical and pharmaceutical apparatus in all their varieties, and musical instruments, in which, as might be expected, the Exhibition is especially rich.

Under horological apparatus is included the entire range of the art of watch, clock, and chronometer making. The objects exhibited comprise church, steeple, and public clocks, astronomical and naval chronometers, clocks applied to register particular phenomena—such as the changes of the barometer, the tides, and winds, clocks to check the vigilance of watchmen, to show the motions of the sun and moon, the recurrence of eclipses, the equation of time, the moon's age, the golden number, &c. In the same class is, of course, included time-pieces of every form for domestic purposes, ornamental clocks for rooms mounted in every variety of case, clocks possessing peculiar properties and escapements—such as that of going while being wound up, pocket watches in all their varieties, watches adapted for peculiar markets—such as those of Turkey and China, requiring peculiar cases and dials. In this subdivision is also included the important, extensive, and various instruments used in anatomy and surgery, classed according to the members to which their operations are respectively directed. Thus in one department will be found a collection of instruments for operations on the eye, another for operations on the ear, another on the nose and its adjacent regions, on the mouth, thorax, and respiratory organs, the alimentary canal, and in short all the other regions of human anatomy. In this subdivision is also included all species of philosophical instruments which have about them a special adaptation to surgical or medical use, such as microscopes, urinometers, thermometers, specula for examining internal parts, instruments in caoutchouc, water cushions and water beds, air mattresses, chairs, cradles, bandages, &c.

Such is a general view of the extensive class of objects exhibited under the title of machinery.

The last and largest principal division of objects exhibited includes all the finished products of human labour, under the general designation of manufactures.

This chief division consists of no less than twenty subdivisions, as follows:—

I. COTTON.—This class includes every fabric produced by the spinning frame and the loom. Among these we find yarns and threads, calicoes, cords, and beaverteens, muslins, plain and figured and fabricated, in the form of shawls, handkerchiefs, and dresses, dimities, quilts, counterpanes, table covers, sheets, hollands, diapers, and damasks; in fine, coloured goods, such as handkerchiefs for the pocket, head, neck, and shoulders, ginghams, checks, striped muslins, coloured diapers, striped jeans, derries, Hungarians, ginghams for umbrellas, dresses, scarfs, and zebras.

II. WOOL.—This class includes cloths, broad and narrow, quilts, blankets, woollen clothing, serges, tartans, worsted stuffs, fabrics composed of a mixture of wool, silk, and cotton, and of alpaca and mohair mixed with cotton or silk.

III. SILK.—Such as thread spun, thrown, and sewing, woven silk, plain and fancy, adapted for dresses, handkerchiefs, cravats, scarves, veils, aprons, &c.; velvets, plain and figured, plushes, gauzes and crapes, ribands, plain and figured.

IV. FLAX AND HEMP.—Such as flax fibre, yarn and thread, plain linen, bleached, unbleached, and dyed; damasks, diapers, drill, and other figured linens, bleached, unbleached, and dyed; cambrics, plain and embroidered, printed and dyed, printed linens and lawns; cordage, such as ropes, lines, nets, &c.

V. MIXED FABRICS.—Such as stuff composed of cotton shot with wool, mohair, linen, silk, or China grass, for dresses, damasks, shoes, shawls, scarfs, &c.; silk shot with wool, mohair, thread, or cotton, plain, watered, figured, or embossed; linens shot with wool, mohair, silk, or cotton, watered and figured; cotton and silk waifs shot with cotton, mohair, silk, worsted, or China grass; in fine,

shawls composed of mixed materials in all their varieties.

VI. LEATHER AND SKINS.—This subdivision includes leather tanned, curried, enamelled, and dyed, oil and white or alum leather; various skins for rugs, parchment and vellum, saddlery and harness; furs in all their varieties, such as the sable, the otter, the fox, bear, and beaver, the mink, buffalo, the lynx, racoon, ermine, and weasel, seal, rabbit, lamb, squirrel, chinchilla, musquash, cat, goat, lion, tiger, and all ferocious animals; feathers, such as those of the ostrich, marabout, rhea, osprey, emu, birds of paradise, heron, ibis, swan, peacock, pheasant, eagle, and all common birds; in fine, hair fabricated artificially as a substitute for human hair, also formed into ornaments, hair-cloth, and other articles for furniture.

VII. PAPER, PRINTING, AND BOOKBINDING.—Paper raw from the mill fit for packing, mill boards, printing, drawing, writing, tissue, and tracing; articles of stationery, such as envelopes embossed in fancy patterns; wedding and mourning stationery, wax, pens, ink, &c., pasteboards, cards, cartonnerie; printing in types, printing inks, and varnishes; bookbinding in cloth, vellum, leather, velvet, wood, papier maché, and metal; desks, cabinets, and in general the accessories of the bureau.

VIII. PRINTED AND DYED FABRICS.—Such as muslins composed of silk, wool, and alpaca mixture; Cashmere, barege, and balzarin, printed and dyed cotton or silk table covers, printed and dyed silks, such as corah bandannas, Indian and British twills; spun silks, cambrics, spun silk and corah dresses, printed calicoes, cambrics, muslins, velvets, and velveteens, printed shawls; dyed cotton goods, such as cambrics, morries, bastas, mull and book muslin, velvets and velveteens; and, finally, dyed and printed linen goods, and dyed and printed goods composed of leather, hair, fur, &c.

IX. TAPESTRY, LACE, AND EMBROIDERY.—This class includes carpets of every description, whether produced by machine or hand, such as Axminster, Brussels, and Kidderminster; mosaic tapestry and rugs, printed felt carpets, druggets, table covers, and curtains; cloth embroidered by machinery, for table covers and curtains, matting composed of hemp, corah-nut fibre, straw, reeds, and grasses; oilcloths for floors and tables, woven embroidery, crochet, and net work, ornamental tapestry of silk, linen, mohair, cotton, metallic wire, or any mixture of these—lace fabricated by pillow or machine, or partly by machine and partly by hand; trimming, laces, veils, falls, scarves, shawls, &c.; sewed and tamboured muslins, embroidery in threads of gold, silver, and glass, silk, Berlin wool, and embroidery by machinery; fringes in passementerie, fancy, and industrial works, such as Berlin work, needle-work, &c.

X. CLOTHING.—For the head, such as hats, caps, bonnets of silk, beaver, and other materials for men; and of straw, silk, chip, willow, grass, tuscan, plaiting, &c., for women; horse-hair trimmings, hosiery, cotton, woollen, linen, and silk gloves; boots and shoes of leather, skin, and other materials, and miscellaneous clothing for both sexes.

XI. CUTLERY AND EDGE TOOLS.—Such as knives and forks, pen and pocket knives, scissors, shears, razors, cork-screws, button-hooks, boot-hooks, knippers, &c., files and edge tools used by engineers, smiths, and workers in metal, for building by masons, bricklayers, and plasterers, for fine metallic work, such as watch and clock making, jewellery, engraving, modelling, and working in precious stones; for wood-work, as for carpenters, joiners, cabinet-makers, &c.; for leather, as for saddlers, shoemakers, bookbinders, &c.; finally for drawing, artistical and engraving instruments.

XII. IRON AND HARDWARE.—Manufactures in brass, copper, zinc, pewter, and general brazing; manufactures in iron, including domestic furniture, baths, ventilators, pipes, gutters, spades, shovels, &c., nails, screws, horse-shoes, gates, railings, &c.; manufactures in steel, such as tools, steel ornaments, fancy toys, steel pens, needles, fish-hooks and fishing tackle, buttons, wire gauze, pins, hooks and eyes, wire basketing, and wire rope.

XIII. PRECIOUS METALS, JEWELLERY, AND VIRTU.—Gold and silver plate for public and domestic purposes, electro-plating, Sheffield plating, gilt and ormoulu work, jewellery in all its departments, ornaments and toys in iron, steel, and other metals, such as steel chains, sword hilts, buckles, Berlin iron ornaments, chains, necklaces, bracelets, enameling, and Damascene work.

XIV. GLASS.—Such as crown, sheet, and blown glass, coloured sheet and flashed glass, ventilators and shades; enamelled, embossed, painted, and stained glass, for ornamental windows; cast plate glass, bottle glass, glass for chemical and philosophical apparatus; flint glass, white; coloured and ornamented for vases, &c.; flint and crown glass for optical instruments.

XV. PORCELAIN.—Of Oriental and foreign fabrication, statuary porcelain, soft or tender porcelain, English and French; stoneware, glazed and unglazed; earthenware, terra cotta vases, architectural ornaments, tiles, chimney pipes, bricks, &c.; ornamented or decorated porcelain painted by hand, or transferred colours on bisque or on the glaze, with imitations of metallic lustre, enamelling, gilding, &c., porcelain for architectural purposes.

XVI. UPHOLSTERY.—Decorations generally, imitations of woods and marbles, furniture and cabinet work in marqueterie, buhl, and inlaid wood, carved chairs, sofas, beds, &c., paperhangings, papier maché, pearl, tortoiseshell and japanned goods.

XVII. MANUFACTURES IN MINERAL SUBSTANCES FOR DECORATIVE ARCHITECTURE.—Manufactures in common stone, slate, cements, and artificial stone; marbles, granites, porphyries, alabaster, spar, &c., for useful and ornamental purposes, and internal and external decoration; inlaid work in stone, marble, and other mineral substances; ornamental work in plaster, composition, scagliola, and imitation marbles, combinations of iron and other metals with glass and other substances for architectural and miscellaneous purposes.

XVIII. MANUFACTURES IN ANIMAL AND VEGETABLE SUBSTANCES, NOT INCLUDED IN FORMER CLASS.—Articles in caoutchouc and gutta percha, productions in ivory, tortoiseshell, shells, bone, horn, bristles, and vegetable ivory; articles in wood, produced by turning, carving, cooperage, and basket-work; articles in straw, grass, and similar materials.

XIX. MISCELLANIES.—Perfumery, articles for the dressing room, travelling articles, artificial flowers, candles, confectionary, beads, and toys, umbrellas, fishing tackle, archery, &c.

XX. FINE ARTS.—Sculpture in gold and silver, copper, iron, zinc, lead; compound metals, such as bronze, electrum, &c.; simple minerals, as marble, stone, gems, clay, &c.; artificial materials, as glass, porcelain, &c.; wood and animal substances, such as ivory, bone, &c. Productions in die sinking and in intaglios, such as coins, models, gems, and seals; architectural decorations, mosaics, and inlaid work, enamels, encaustic and fresco painting; ornamental printing, lithography, zincography, and models in architecture, topography, and anatomy.

Such are the general features of this vast collection of the products of human industry.

In observing the proportions in which the various nations of the earth have contributed to it, we find, as might be expected, the several divisions of Europe the largest and most varied contributors, supplying for the most part the same products as are supplied by our native contributors. Those contributions which come from the greatest distance, and which are more limited in their quantity and variety, present, however, circumstances of peculiar interest.

Thus we find a large collection of productions, natural and artificial, have been supplied from the Islands of the Indian Archipelago. Among these we find birds'-nests, which constitute an article of food, and are stated to be highly esteemed in China for their nutritious and restorative properties. Various samples of this aliment, arranged in boxes, will be found in the Exhibition. Another large article of food received from this quarter of the globe are the fins of sharks, for which the Chinese have an especial taste.

Wax is exhibited, produced by the bee of these regions, the habits of which differ from those insects of the same tribe in Europe, inasmuch as they do not build in hives, but suspend their nests from the branches of a tree, where they may be seen forming in masses of great bulk. Certain trees become favourites with them, to which they adhere from year to year, and from generation to generation; and even though their nests be disturbed, they are soon reproduced. These trees, it is stated, become private property among the oriental tribes, and descend in hereditary succession. From the same quarter proceeds a vast collection of woods employed for furniture, not less than 28 specimens of which will be seen at the Exhibition. Among these is a fine specimen of the Lingoa wood, known as the Amboyna of commerce, a slab of which will be seen measuring nearly eight feet in length by upwards of five feet in breadth.

Among the textile materials and fabrics from the same quarter will be found a species of thread, remarkable for strength and durability, produced from the rind of a species of nettle called rami.

Threads are also exhibited produced from the fibres of the aloe, the pineapple, and the musa or plaintain.

This collection includes (besides a variety of fancy manufactures, fishing gear, agricultural and industrial implements, and miscellaneous articles) some curious models of the native vessels. One of these is a model of a pirate vessel of the first-class, adapted to carry a crew of about 100 men. In this form of vessel the tripod mast, of which the two after feet work on hinges, is converted into a bridge for the purpose of boarding a vessel which is attacked by it. In a smaller model of the second-class, adapted to a crew of about 50 men, a stage or platform is suspended at the mast, with grappling hooks attached to it, which is in like manner converted into a bridge for boarding.

CHINA.

An extensive collection of native productions has been received from China. Among these several will be regarded with interest as likely to become valuable for commerce. Of these may be mentioned a fine specimen of red copper from Japan, a peculiar species of wax, which is miscalled vegetable wax, being in fact not the product of the tree from which it is gathered, but of an insect which breeds in it.

A most interesting and complete collection of the various materials used at the great porcelain works of King Tih Chin, in the vicinity of Poyangdale, will be found in this collection, including the clay which forms the porcelain, and the materials with which it is coloured.

Among the productions of this class supplied by the East India Company are the dyes used for colouring green tea, which it appears is expressly dyed in the district of Hung Chou for exportation.

Among the articles in this collection will be found the original address, bearing the signatures of 770 merchants, presented to His Excellency Hwang on his appointment to the office of Deputy-Governor of Canton, in the reign of the Emperor Keen Lung, in the year 1720. This address measures nearly eight feet in length and six in width, and contains 2,320 Chinese characters, finely worked in gold on silk, and is lined with Chinese embossed velvet, with a gold border. Mr. Thoms, the printer, of Warwick-square, who exhibits this curiosity, has sent an English translation of it, from which we take the following extracts:—

"We, the undersigned, respectfully approach and pray that a blessing may descend on Tsincho (private name), our literary father Hwang, who, being of noble descent, may glory and honour attend him. The poets say that the tung tree, when agitated with the golden wind, not only sends forth its fragrance, but becomes more luxuriant, and with air more splendid and glorious. Such may be said of your Excellency; for when you filled inferior appointments one might as well endeavour to stop the ascent of vapour, the motion of the clouds, or pull the planets out of their courses, as to impede the promotion of you, our minister.

* * * * * * * * * *

"Unexpectedly you were appointed to preside over the western district of the city (that part where Europeans reside), when the respectable and honourable inhabitants assembled before your door, who resembled a covey of sparrows, which hop to and fro, anxious to give expression to their feelings, enjoyed what they had long desired, to offer you their congratulations on your coming among them; and now they thus address you.

"We, mean people, have long dreaded covetous magistrates, who have been compared to voracious tigers with wings. But brighter prospects now shine forth, for the felicitous Lin, with its horn, has come among us; while the Fung, the king of the birds, has also built his nest. Having both the Lin and the Fung, we know we shall have that which is just and correct.

* * * * * * * * * *

"The autumn is luxuriant, and the sun shines in full splendour. At such a time well might the man of letters, and the man that fills an important station, cement themselves together to offer praise to the Divine Powers. While the husbandman is singing in his field, the mechanic happy in his shop, and the merchant delighted with his speculations, the sire will beat time as the children dance and are regaled with a cup of tea or a glass of pleasant wine; and the eyes of the youthful will sparkle as they ascend the stately hall—for all mankind have a heart."

EGYPT.

The Egyptian Government has contributed a collection consisting of upwards of 380 articles of the artificial and natural productions of that country.

TUNIS.

The Regency of Tunis has also sent a collection of articles, consisting chiefly of clothing and other objects of domestic use, ornamental saddlery, and some animal, vegetable, and mineral productions.

GREECE.

From Greece we have a variety of marbles, among which will be especially noticed a piece of Cipolino marble brought from the old quarry which produced the marble of which the columns of Antoninus and Faustina, in Rome, were hewn. In the Curia Innocenziana there is a very large column composed of a single block of this marble.

The Prior of the Monastery of Pentelicon sends a block of white marble of the same description as that of which the Parthenon and other monuments in Athens were built and many of the ancient statues were sculptured.

Among the animal productions sent from Greece is a jar of honey from the celebrated Mount Hymettus, and a piece of comb of the same honey. This honey, so celebrated through all antiquity, owes its peculiar and highly esteemed flavour to the odoriferous vegetation of the surrounding country.

The Bishop of Eubœa sends also a jar of honey from Carysto, also long celebrated, and denominated Rhodo-meli, from its having the flavour of roses.

The nuns of the Convent of St. Constantine, in all their seclusion, have not forgotten the Great Exhibition, and have sent a variety of silk handkerchiefs and mosquito nets.

ROME.

If the Eternal City has not been profuse in its contributions, it has, nevertheless, sent several objects which will rivet the attention of the lovers of art, among which may be mentioned three sculptured groups by Benzoni, consisting of a Cupid and Psyche, Gratitude and Fidelity, and Innocence; several mosaics from the Royal manufactory of St. Peter, among which is especially deserving of notice a Square, copied from the celebrated S. Gio. Battesta by Guercino, 4 feet high by 3 feet wide, by Raffaele Castellini; a Medallion, the Portrait of Pope Bonifaccio II. copied from the picture by Sig. Roberto Bompiarri, each 5 feet in diameter, and intended to be placed in the new Basilica St. Paul's, by Raffaele Castellini; also two Mosaic Tables by Boschetti, 3 feet in diameter; Mosaics by Moglia, representing the Temple of Pæstum, St. George, the Roman Forum, and the Coliseum.

Savellini sends beautiful cameos, in pietra dura, representing Jupiter Tonans, and in shell, Venus, from a bas-relief by Gibson; and the Hours leading the Horses to the Chariot of the Sun, from a bas-relief by the same artist, cut for the Earl Fitzwilliam, as well as 10 other subjects not less striking.

RUSSIA.

The contributions from Russia are numerous, and consist chiefly of mineral productions proceeding from the several Imperial establishments. Thus, there are silver ores from the Barnaoulsk works in Siberia, copper ores from the Imperial works of Perm, iron stone from Goroblagodatsk, Kamensk, Koussinsk, Ninjne-Tourinsk, Verkhne-Barraut Chinsk, Verkhne-Tourinsk, besides various Imperial iron establishments in Poland and other provinces.

Prince Demidoff also sends various specimens of iron in the raw and reduced states, steel, malachite, copper in ore and ingots. The Prince also sends a single piece of native gold weighing upwards of 6lb., and a second lump weighing above 2lb., a piece of native platinum weighing 25½lb., and a second weighing 22½lb., and a third 21½lb.

SWEDEN AND NORWAY.

The contributions from Sweden and Norway consist chiefly, as might be expected, of iron, of which twenty fine specimens have been sent by one proprietor, including part of the rock in which the mine is situate, the leading stone, the mineral intermixed with the ore, the several ores, and their analyses, showing their constituents, the pig iron, the scoria, the blooms, and the bars. In this series are exhibited all the conditions of excellence which have long rendered the Swedish iron and steel so much celebrated. The magnetic iron and ore are found there in abundance, an ore which in England has only been found in two places—one near Penzance in Cornwall, and the other on Dartmoor, in Devonshire.

This ore, and the use of charcoal and wood in the process of smelting, are the chief sources of the excellence of the Swedish iron. Specimens of ore have also been sent from the celebrated Dannemora Mines, considered to afford the best Swedish iron.

The mining region for iron in Sweden occupies the whole breadth of the country from the frontier of Norway to the Gulf of Bothnia, its northern boundary being marked by a line drawn from Glommen through Lake Siljan to Soderham, and its southern boundary lying along the 59th parallel of latitude. The area of this district is about 16,000 square miles, and its annual produce in bar iron amounts to about seventy thousand tons.

The productions of the other countries of Europe, which appear in the Exhibition, being for the most part analogous to those presented by the exhibitors of the United Kingdom, it will be unnecessary to present here any synopsis of them. It will be sufficient to notice, as we shall do from time to time, such objects amongst them as present the strongest claims upon public attention. Meanwhile, it may be stated generally, that, after the United Kingdom, France is by far the largest contributor. Austria comes next; and nearly equal to it is the collection from the States of the Zollverein, including Prussia; Belgium and Russia follow next in order; after which come Switzerland, Spain, Holland, Portugal, Wurtemberg, and the lesser States.

(To be continued.)

'By Jove, I am Editor of THE TIMES!'

Top Portrait of John Thadeus Delane, 1862, by August Schiott.

Above Thomas Chenery, TIMES reporter in Constantinople during the Crimean War, who later became editor.

Right Delane's power is seen in this personal letter from Palmerston, obsequiously requesting him to refrain from political comment on the marriage of the Prince of Wales.

Delane was the second of the two great founding editors of *The Times*. Barnes made *The Times* a power in the land and the constitution. Delane spread its influence through the civilized world – though by the time he took over, *The Times* was already losing the monopoly it had established as purveyor of news and Thunderer of opinion.

John Thadeus Delane was born in London on 11 October 1817. He was educated at King's College, London and Magdalen, Oxford. He did not distinguish himself at his studies but devoted a great deal of his time to riding and hunting, activities that he pursued enthusiastically for the rest of his life.

Delane's father was financial manager of *The Times*. The son entered Printing House Square in 1840 and was engaged on parliamentary and general reporting. When Barnes died, Delane was appointed editor at the age of twenty-three. He burst into a friend's room shouting: 'By Jove, John, what do you think has happened? I am editor of *The Times*.' Years later he was asked whether he had been alarmed at taking such responsibility so young. 'Not a bit' he replied. 'What I dislike about you young men of the present day is that you all shrink from responsibility.'

Unlike Barnes, Delane was not an intellectual. He had little taste for literature or learning, and positively disliked poetry. Once, when asked whether he would publish a review of a poem by Shelley, he cried: 'Excrement! Excrement!' He was a sporting and sociable Irishman. He was married but his wife spent most of her life in an asylum under medical care. He was devoted to his mother and wrote to her every day if he did not manage to see her. John Walter II guided his young protégé for the first few years, but when Walter died in 1847 Delane took full control of the ship.

Under his editorship *The Times* was at the heart of the government of Britain. For example, in 1845 *The Times* made the sensational announcement that Peel's administration was about to repeal the highly controversial Corn Laws. The Tory press described the story as an 'atrocious fabrication'. But Delane's mole was Lord Aberdeen, the Foreign Secretary. And the story was true.

94 P[illegible], [illegible] 1862

My dear Delane

I should be very glad if in mentioning at any time the intended marriage of the Prince of Wales with the Danish Damsel you would avoid giving the connection a political character, as an alliance that is to bear

There is a legend about this scoop. It was gossiped that Delane got the information from Caroline Norton, the sexy granddaughter of Sheridan. She was said to have got it from Sidney Herbert, the Secretary of State for War. Mrs Norton, an occasional contributor to *The Times* (as was everybody who was anybody), was said to have sold the information to Delane for £500. The legend, romantically embellished in Meredith's *Diana of the Crossways*, has persisted into the twentieth century. Not true. Aberdeen was the source.

Delane pulled off another spectacular scoop in the crisis leading to the Crimean War. The war brought *The Times*, not for the first or the last time, into head-on conflict with the Establishment. Since its foundation, the paper has seldom been accused of warmongering or jingoism. But in the crisis leading up to the Crimean War it came near to it.

The ultimatum offering peace or war to Russia spent a number of days en route from London to St Petersburg. Delane got hold of the text and published it, so that the Tsar read it in *The Times* before he received the official ultimatum. Both Government and Opposition were enraged. *The Times* justified publication in terms that proclaimed its establishment as the fourth estate of the realm: 'We hold ourselves responsible . . . to the people of England, for the accuracy and fitness of that which we think proper to publish.'

The Times provided the first proper coverage of any war, not excepting even Thucydides. William Howard Russell, the greatest war correspondent, told it as it happened, not as the generals said it happened. Thomas Chenery (a future editor) covered the diplomatic angle from Constantinople. General Eber, the Hungarian freedom fighter, had a roving commission to cover the war. And Delane himself went out to the Crimea and saw the original landings.

The Times's coverage in the Crimea had more influence on the course of the war than anything done by the soldiers or the politicians. William Howard Russell told the world about the appalling chaos, the incompetence of the generals (who were still fighting Waterloo), the lack of medical facilities, the shortage of food, clothing and transport. Nobody had ever reported the truth about war so immediately. Delane blasted the Government with his leading articles.

The attitude of *The Times* provoked howls of indignation and cries of disloyalty from the Government and Palace. They spoke of 'the base, bloody, and brutal *Times*'. Delane was accused of publishing information so soon that it helped the enemy and imperilled our own boys. But the newspaper saved the Army and brought down the Government. In January 1855 Aberdeen's administration fell, and was replaced by Palmerston's. Lord John Russell, a former Prime Minister, commented on the political earthquake: 'If England is ever to be England again, this vile tyranny of *The Times* must be cut off'. The Duke of Newcastle said to the special correspondent of *The Times* in the Crimea: 'It was you who turned out the Government, Mr Russell'.

The paper did its job. Public opinion believed what it wrote, and was appalled. Money and gifts to support the Army and succour the wounded poured into Printing House Square. *The Times* sent its own commissioner of the Crimea to administer its funds. Florence Nightingale arrived on the battlefield because of the campaign in *The Times*.

Unlike Barnes, Delane was not a writing editor. We can identify only two or three leaders that he wrote himself during his thirty-six years in the chair. His strength lay in editing, cutting, amending, strengthening, and adding a touch of ginger to not only the leaders, but to every article and paragraph in the paper.

Heavy black rules were used as THE TIMES mourned the death of one of its greatest editors, John Thadeus Delane.
25 NOVEMBER 1879

likely to be undervalued. If, however, it be assumed that this is the light in which University reformers regard the decision of the Commissioners, the public will be greatly deceiving itself. So far the more adequate endowment of the University might be accounted simply supplementary to the collegiate system. Had contributions towards the support of the University been exacted by the Commission from the Colleges thirty years ago, that and nothing else would have been the effect. Either the legion of professorial recruits would have been merely gratuitous private tutors, or their lectures would have been merely, as it were, subscription College lectures. Since the appointment of the first Oxford and Cambridge Commissions a new theory altogether of the relation of University and Colleges has gained possession of both Universities. It is no longer taken for granted that the University is nothing more than the aggregate of the Colleges. The University is held to have a life of its own distinct from the Colleges, and functions they can never discharge. The Colleges hitherto have dwarfed the University, and compelled it to seal mechanically their decrees. Henceforward the University may be expected to resume its ancient independence. How that independence will assert itself, and in what directions the University as distinct from the collegiate existence will develop, can only at present be conjectured. The movement, under its ill-chosen appellation of the Endowment of Research, has involved itself in a certain degree of odium, which, it may be hoped, will be dispelled as it is better understood and better understands itself. The English public is not likely to feel much sympathy with schemes for the foundation of wealthy chairs in order that the occupants might give themselves to the leisurely accumulation of private wisdom. What, however, is really contemplated by the advocates of the doctrine that a University is something different from the total of the Colleges is the creation of an educational system in which the teacher's attention shall be directed first and foremost to the subject he teaches, but also, though secondarily, to his pupils. A College is a school of a high grade, and its lecturers are schoolmasters under a higher or a different title. It is their business to consider the particular circumstances, intellectual and moral, of their classes, and, as the constituents change, to change their mode of instruction too. A University professor must never close his eyes and ears to the fact that he is a professor, not at Jena or Berlin, but at Oxford or Cambridge. He must adapt his teaching to the genius of the place. But he must not, like the College lecturer, be constantly remembering that this or that member of his audience is about to enter this or that examination, or has failed to pass this or that test. He bends his faculties to the consideration of the branch of learning he professes, and allows his hearers to observe how his mind works. The lecturer studies his pupils; the pupils study their professor. There is the key to the difference between the use to which the Colleges will continue to put the revenues left at their disposal and that to which the University ought to apply those which the Commissioners propose to bestow upon it.

The restoration of the University, whether at Oxford or at Cambridge, to its old liberty of action necessarily implies curtailment or, at any rate, alteration in the province of the Colleges. It is not as if the University, having recovered from the Colleges its share of the inheritance, were about to migrate elsewhere. It is not even as if distinct persons represented the Colleges and the University. The Colleges and the University will remain indissolubly bound together, and actually the same persons will constitute both bodies. In these circumstances it can scarcely be but that the independence of the Colleges will be in time compromised by the overshadowing prerogative of the University. The University will henceforth do much which as yet the Colleges have been doing. Socially the meeting of Undergraduates from various Colleges at the University lectures will, by the operation of an influence already observable, tend to break down the high wall of partition which for centuries has separated one College companionship from another. In education College lecturers will tend more to do the work of private tutors. In discipline itself the power of the University may possibly, in course of time, make itself felt even inside the sacred asylum of a College quadrangle. College authorities have to consider how they can take advantage of being relieved through the University of part of their duties by concentrating themselves upon the rest. Possibly an inclination may manifest itself for a division of labour among themselves. At present each College is a kind of servant of all work. Its doors are open to all temperaments and capacities and careers. Were they to addict themselves severally to special portions of the field of higher education, the general work of academical training might be done far more successfully than now. We quoted on Saturday a statement by a weekly contemporary on the future destination of the institutions at Oxford termed Halls. According to this paragraph, one of the Halls is to be appropriated to the reception of native candidates for the Indian Civil Service. Whatever the authenticity of the rumour, it points to a change in the right direction. Distribution and concentration of labour are what Oxford and Cambridge Colleges need. They constitute a magnificent educational apparatus, of which the several parts are rather apt to get in one another's way. By commissioning the University to do a portion of the work, and by arranging among themselves what of the residue each shall undertake, the Colleges might double or treble the advantages they bestow on the country. If, however, at the present moment we have a fear, it is not so much of want as of excess of zeal in endeavouring to attain this end. The nation, it must always be recollected, is not so dissatisfied with its Universities, even as they are, as to desire to see them something else altogether.

In a letter which we publish to-day, Sir Henry Drummond Wolff gives an explanation of the statement respecting the German army to which Major von Vietinghoff, the Military Attaché to the German Embassy, has taken exception. It would seem that the former did not exactly tell his audience at Christchurch that German officers "without trial and on their own motion," sometimes struck their men on the face. He was misunderstood. What he said was that in some Continental armies, in which no summary punishments of a more lenient character than death are known, the officers punished their soldiers for minor offences with blows rather than expose them to the extreme penalty of military law; and he mentioned that the practice existed in the German army. Major von Vietinghoff, no doubt, knows best. He assures us that if an officer so far forgot himself as to strike a soldier, he would be sure to meet with a severe punishment. This is, of course, the true account of the matter, which could be at once proved by reference to particular articles in the military code. The German army is not what it was, a multitude of abject peasants officered by haughty nobles. A Prussian colonel who used his cane would be an anachronism. But it is only another proof of the tenacity of misconceptions as to nations that this is not universally understood. Many people fancy that the spirit of old Frederick William still rules in the Prussian army, that the cane is freely employed, and that the privates have no rights of their own. If an *opéra bouffe* were brought out in which a Prussian general figured, it would not be thought amiss if he were represented belabouring his subalterns when they were out of favour or in fault. When told of the growth of Russia's power, Heine hinted that he did not fear the reign of the knout, seeing some of his countrymen were familiar with the cane. Sayings of that sort are remembered long after they have ceased to be true. Prejudices against one's neighbours live amazingly long, and there are scores of educated people who would have been inclined to think that the fist or cane played much the same part in a Prussian regiment as the knout once did in Russia. It is a mistake, nevertheless. The statement gave an erroneous idea of German military law and discipline, which are, no doubt, as humane as Major von Vietinghoff says, but which have hitherto suffered from reports to their disadvantage. Reduced as Sir Henry Drummond Wolff's statement now is, it is, perhaps, not so very wide of the truth. The ineffable haughtiness of the Prussian officer to the private soldiers under him is notorious, and, it may be, necessary. Politeness might be thrown away where rough, stern usages are not merely borne, but win respect; and, like navvies, who are said sometimes to prefer and to work better under a swearing foreman than under one who is indulgent, German soldiers may even be pleased to serve under a fierce disciplinarian.

Englishmen are not solitary in making this class of mistakes. If attachés to our embassies abroad were to write to foreign journals every time that some mis-statement respecting English institutions appeared in print, they would lead a busy life. They would in these days have to correct seven times a week the notion, dear to some foreigners, that Ireland is somehow still treated as a conquered country, that it suffers from peculiar disabilities, and that it is drained of its wealth by England. We do not speak of purely vulgar prejudices to the disadvantage of this country, but of those which find an entrance into the minds of educated foreigners. How often is it alleged that our army is officered by gentlemen who feel themselves much too good for their profession and who take no interest in it! It is the firm belief of many Frenchmen and some Germans that Englishmen care nothing for what lies outside their own land, except so far as it affects buying and selling and other sordid interests; the fact being that no other country in modern times has engaged in so many chivalrous or quixotic expeditions beyond its borders. There is an illustration of this proneness to error as to national peculiarities in the comments of the German Press on the new Press regulations. They are spoken of with much gravity and sympathetic commiseration as forming a true *Maulkorbgesetz* quite as bad as, if not worse than, the gagging Bill passed to suppress Socialist journals. This is a strange mistake. The Germans have the historic genius in a marvellous degree. They can enter into and conceive for themselves the life of the past. No system of thought, no mode of existence, is too remote for some of their scholars not to get at the standpoint or kernel. But the limits of this capacity are manifest in the remarks of the German journals on the Press regulations. Some of them write as if there was no longer any love of freedom left in this country. All of them assume that correspondents will in practice be fettered by these absurd trammels. They do not know that in this country when ordinances come up to a certain degree of preposterousness it is certain that they will be put aside. The public look with apathy on regulations the puerility and ephemeral nature of which are written on their faces. If Germans imagine that English newspaper correspondents are henceforth to wear badges as cabmen or porters do; that "retired officers" are to be preferred as correspondents; and that they are all to be placed under a military censor, they are much mistaken. The regulations are unreasonable and foolish; they carry their own cure. We cannot wonder that German journalists, who find it gravely stated by the highest military authorities that "correspondents are not to be "allowed to go to the outposts without special "permission," and that they are to be encouraged by the promise that this permission "will not, "however, be generally granted," make the English Press the subject of commiseration. It may appear supremely ridiculous to a great military nation that our War Office should employ so much zeal in persecuting and worrying correspondents whose services truly great commanders are the first to own. It is not known that these regulations, as soon as they were disclosed, were condemned with one common voice, and that they cannot be long carried into effect. It is a pity that one is not able to deny the existence of these rules as Major von Vietinghoff denies the practice of striking private soldiers in the German army. But the foreign critics who send us condolence on our loss of freedom of speech may rest satisfied that the new code will soon be remembered only as a stupid blunder. Perhaps some high official will yet write in the frank spirit in which Sir Henry Drummond Wolff has done in regard to the erroneous statement attributed to him, and will disavow the miserable compilation.

The new rules have been commented upon in every country in Europe, and, read by themselves, they would give the idea that English generals are afraid to hear the truth told about them. The fact is that most of them, especially those who are capable, desire faithful chroniclers to be beside them. It is the interest of the private soldier that there should be some one to give expression to his wishes or to tell of his hardships. The public obviously gain by this. No one is any the worse, except the incompetent and the unsuccessful. In the days of the French Republic deputies or delegates often went to the camp to put the general into connexion with the outer world, and especially with the Government. No deputies go in these days to the seat of war, and a general is left free to carry out his plans in his own way. But newspaper correspondents do the work which they did, and do it better. They animate and nerve the soldier; they cheer and instruct him; they put him in communication with his distant country. People would find war far more intolerable than it is if they got scanty, uncertain news of the whereabouts or movements of their troops; and the soldier's motives to do his duty would be sensibly weakened if he knew that his deeds of gallantry might never reach the ears of his friends at home. For once that the Press has been the means of embarrassing a general in the field it has scores of times assisted him. If the foreign censors of the Press regulations bear in mind that all this is well recognized, they will understand that English journals regard the new code without much alarm. The rules are in flat contradiction to the spirit of our institutions; they can never be put in operation; and when the *Tagblatt* or the *Norddeutsche Zeitung* twits Englishmen with gagging correspondents in the field, it brings a charge which is as unpleasant to the former as it is for Germans to be told that their officers often strike their men.

The Prince of Wales.—The Prince of Wales last evening arrived at Melton Constable on a visit of a few days to Lord Hastings.

Princess Louise.—Princess Louise (Marchioness of Lorne) yesterday visited the Victoria Hospital for Children, Chelsea.

The Ministry.—Summonses were issued yesterday for a Cabinet Council to be held at the Prime Minister's official residence in Downing-street this afternoon at 4 o'clock.

Mansion-House.—Yesterday being the Lord Mayor's birthday, the Lord Mayor and the Lady Mayoress entertained a select company at dinner in the Long Parlour of the Mansion-house.

DEATH OF MR. DELANE.

The British public has finally lost one of the oldest, most devoted, and most meritorious of those who may be called its own special servants. Mr. Delane died on Saturday evening at his residence at Ascot, having not long completed his sixty-second year. In the summer of 1877 it became painfully evident to Mr. Delane's friends, and not less to himself, that near 40 years of incessant work had told on a vigorous constitution and powerful nerve, and that it would be well for him to seek rest while still able to enjoy it. The result showed that the determination was not arrived at too soon, and Mr. Delane has not survived more than two years his release from the continuous round of daily and nightly duties. Perhaps it is not more than public men have a right to expect. Soldiers and sailors, if on the one hand liable to be cut off in mid career, are much more generally rewarded with half a life of honourable rest and pleasant retrospection. But as a rule they who have once entered the political strife never quit it willingly or become deaf to the old challenges and familiar rallying cries. They would be ready to die in harness if they could only persuade their colleagues that the old is still better than the new.

John Thaddeus Delane was born at Bracknell, which all our readers may not know to be a pleasant spot, half town, half village, in the favoured and residential part of Berkshire, included so recently as the beginning of this century in Old Windsor Forest. While he was still in his boyhood his father, a solicitor, received from the late Mr. Walter an appointment in *The Times* Office. The conductors of this journal very early saw in young Mr. Delane the industry, the quickness of apprehension, the eagerness for information, and the accessibleness to new impressions and ideas which might qualify him for a place in its future management. He was educated, therefore, it may be said, for the purpose, and if Mr. Delane owed much to himself, few men have owed so much to favourable circumstances and to the kind and provident care of their friends. After learning about as much as boys usually learn at a private school, and perhaps more than is usually learnt at a private tutor's, in Lincolnshire, he was admitted to Magdalen Hall, in the University of Oxford, where the present Bishop of Chester was Tutor and Vice-Principal, under Dr. Macbride. Mr. Jacobson's thorough scholarship and genial temper converted not a few of his pupils, from very different schools, into attached friends, and Mr. Delane was one of them. Perhaps this and his friendship with Sir G. Dasent were the special gains of his University career which he ever most appreciated. Immediately on leaving Oxford, indeed before taking his degree, Mr. Delane was qualifying himself for almost any profession he might finally decide on, under good direction, with a view to the better discharge of the post eventually assigned to him. He walked the London hospitals for several terms, and, having a natural taste for the art of medicine and for operative surgery, he made more real progress than many who have no other aim than the exercise of the medical profession. He kept his terms at the Middle Temple, where he was called to the Bar. He reported both on Circuit and at the House of Commons, where for two years he took his turn in the gallery. There was no necessary training which he did not undergo with as much spirit as if his career was to begin and end there;—an example to those who imagine that important positions are to be jumped into or had for the asking, and that luck is the arbiter of eminence. When he entered the Editor's room he had the advantage of an able and accomplished chief, and of excellent instruction and advice as to the traditions and policy of this journal. As he did his work well, it grew in his hands till, by the successive deaths of two colleagues, he became in 1841 the recognized Editor of *The Times*, and so continued till the autumn of 1877.

After stating the special advantages and qualifications Mr. Delane had for his position, we shall be only adding to his merits when we allude to deficiencies which some would think insurmountable. He had not had the thoroughly classical education then to be obtained only in one of our old public schools. He was out of the "ring" which for a long time had claimed the monopoly of orthodox literature. What was more, he never was a writer; he never even attempted to write anything except what he wrote much better than most writers could do—reports and letters. These he had to do, and he did them well. He had a large staff of writers, and it was not necessary he should write except to communicate with them. This was, indeed, the greatest of his numerous advantages. He immediately started with a number of able and educated men, found for him by those who were, above all things, good judges of character. When it is considered that he was, at least in early years, younger than most of the men he had to deal with, and that while they were practised writers he was not, it is no slight testimony to his success in the discharge of his delicate office that none of these writers ever disputed the value of his criticisms, or failed to agree cordially in his revisions, alterations, and suppressions. Thousands of times when in the heat and haste of writing expressions had been employed which the writer had some little doubt about and felt to be weak points in his composition, he has found the Editor's pen falling with sure discernment on the faulty passage and justifying the writer's own suppressed misgivings. The advantage of this process was mutual. To criticize freely and to submit to criticism is to learn and improve. The greatest writers in our language, in this and in former ages, if they have not themselves admitted that they had published much which would have been the better for a previous censure, have at least left their readers to say it in stronger language. One of the greatest of living writers has often stated that every man ought to have a reviser. It is not without its cost to the person charged with the duty. The almost exclusive practice of critical revision is not favourable to original writing, for it developes fastidiousness. When Lord Beaconsfield said that critics were unsuccessful writers, he ingeniously inverted the natural order of the fact. It is too true that if a man's life work is criticism, it is likely to take away freedom and freshness of expression, except in those familiar utterances in which he is not trammelled by the obligations of style.

The work of an Editor can only be appreciated by those who have had the fortune to have had some little experience of it. The Editor of a London daily newspaper is held answerable for every word in 48, and sometimes 60, columns. The merest slip of the pen, an epithet too much, a wrong date, a name misspelt or with a wrong initial before it, a mistake as to some obscure personage only too glad to seize the opportunity of showing himself, the misinterpretation of some passage perhaps incapable of interpretation, the most trifling offence to the personal or national susceptibility of those who do not even profess to care for the feelings of others, may prove not only disagreeable, but even costly mistakes; but they are among the least of the mistakes to which an Editor is liable. As it is impossible to say what a night may bring forth, and the most important intelligence is apt to be the latest, it will often find him with none to share his responsibility, without advisers, and with colleagues either pre-engaged on other matters or no longer at hand. The Editor must be on the spot till the paper is sent to the press, and make decisions on which not only the approval of the British public, but great events, and even great causes, may hang. All the more serious part of his duties has to be discharged at the end of a long day's work, a day of interruptions and conversations, of letter reading and letter writing, when mind and body are not what they were 12 hours ago, and wearied nature is putting in her gentle pleas. An Editor cannot husband his strength for the night's battle with comparative repose in the solitude of a study or the freshness of green fields. He must see the world, converse with its foremost or busiest actors, be open to information, and on guard against error. All this ought to be borne in mind by those who complain that journalism is not infallibly accurate, just, and agreeable. Their complaints are like those of the Court lord who found fault with the disagreeable necessities of warfare.

Since Mr. Delane became Editor of this journal there have been 13 Administrations, all founded necessarily on some new concurrence of circumstances. At the beginning of this period Lord Melbourne was in power. Since his time Sir R. Peel was in power once, Lord Russell twice, Lord Derby three times, Lord Aberdeen once, Lord Palmerston twice, Lord Beaconsfield twice, and Mr. Gladstone once. Every one of these 13 Governments has been typical of some new phase of opinion, some new policy, or some new idea, and in every instance a new mass of particulars, amounting, as it were, to a new volume of political history, had to be accurately mastered, justly appreciated, and carefully kept in view. An Editor, it has often been said, sometimes not very seriously, must know everything. He must, at least, never be found at fault, and must be always equal to the occasion as to the personal characteristics, the concerns, the acts and utterances of those who are charged with the government of this great Empire. But this is only one of many points, some even more difficult, because more special and more apt to lie for a time out of the scope of ordinary vigilance. Since the year 1841 the world has seen unprecedented improvements in naval and military material and tactics, not slowly making their way as curiosities that might take their time, but forced into notice by frequent reminders of their necessity. Europe has seen not only two or three but many revolutions, wars unexampled for their dimensions, their costs, and their results; many dynasties overthrown, an Empire rise and fall, another all but finally dismembered amid a scramble over the spoil, and several re-unifications effected beyond even the hopes of former times. Scientific discovery in every department of knowledge has been more than ever active, and that in the practical bearings which claim the notice of the public from day to day. Never before have the earth and the sea so freely revealed their resources and their treasures. Continents supposed to be protected from intrusive curiosity by intolerable heat, by untameable savagery, or by national jealousy, have been traversed in all directions by explorers whose volumes have been as familiar as our Continental Handbooks. Within this period have been the gold discoveries and the new communities founded on them. It is commonly said that the English never really learn geography or history till forced upon their acquaintance by wars or other disasters. This shows how much has to be learnt if any one has to keep pace with events. The American Civil War, our own Indian Mutiny, and the occupation of France by the German Armies are events which the future student of history may find comprised in a few paragraphs, but the record and explanation of them day by day for many months involved particulars sufficient to fill many bulky volumes. With a large class of critics, a small mistake counts as much as a large one, but everybody is liable to make mistakes, and an Editor labours under the additional danger of too readily accepting the words of writers, some of whom will always be too full of their ideas to pay needful attention to such matters. These are days of Blue-books, of enormous correspondence, of tabular returns, of statistics twisted into every possible form, of averages and differences always on supposition to be carefully remembered, of numerical comparisons everybody challenges if they are not in his own favour, and of statements that if they possess the least novelty or other interest are sure to be picked to pieces. Reference has been made to the severe conditions under which all this work has to be done. It frequently happens that a long night's work has to be thrown away, including many carefully revised columns of printed matter, to make room for an over-grown Parliamentary debate, a budget of important despatches, or a speech made in the provinces by some one, may be, who did not love this paper, and to whom it owed nothing but public duty. Often has it been said at 2 in the morning that a very good paper has been printed and destroyed to make way for a paper that very few will read, none perhaps except a few Parliamentary gentlemen looking out for passages which, if they don't read well, must have been incorrectly reported. As an instance of what may happen to an editor the Quarterly Return of the Revenue once came with an enormous error, an addition instead of subtraction, or *vice-versa*. The writer who had to comment on it jotted down the principal figures, and the totals, which were unexpected, and returned the original for the printers. It was not till an hour after midnight that, on a sight of the Return in print, the error was perceived, and corrected, without a word of remark, by the paper. Of course, the comments had to be re-written and carefully secured from error.

It is not in man not to have a bias, personal as well as political, and this bias is even more inevitable where there is a considerable acquaintance with the subject or the person concerned. As with the Editor, so with his indispensable informants, subordinates, and other colleagues. Great as is the audacity of inner consciousness in these days, its place is not in an editor's room. For the materials, and, to a great extent, for the use made of them, he has to depend on others, and very often upon persons at a great distance, surrounded by influences amounting sometimes to a sort of compulsion. At high heat, the most honourable combatants or controversialists are conscious of nothing but their own case, and can tolerate no other. Partizanship has to be reduced to impartiality, rancour to fairness, and one-sided statements to approximate truth, in the editor's room. This delicate process has often to be performed after midnight, as a mere episode in the continual press of ordinary, but still exigent matters. How far "The man who worked *The Times*," as Mr. Delane would sometimes describe himself, for near 40 years has done this successfully is a point on which people will claim opinions of their own. It cannot be pretended, however, that any other person can be put in competition with him, as having had an equal task, as having been so long at it, and as having achieved such a preponderance of success. What is the measure and proof of that success? It is not far to seek. He is the best General, the Great Duke said, who makes the fewest mistakes. For the long period of time named above the British public took up what may be called their favourite "broadsheet" every morning, not expecting, or intending, or even wishing to agree constantly with what they found in it, yet with the utmost confidence that they would find the great questions of the day fairly and fully stated, that nothing would be added or left out from malice or carelessness, and that they were at least furnished with all the materials for forming opinions of their own. The great work in which Mr. Delane has borne the chief administrative part has not been done in a corner. It has been before the whole world. The course of this paper has been the course of this nation and of the world. If that course be a failure, if England is but the wreck of what it was 40 years ago, if it has lost wealth, happiness, grandness, and whatever else constitutions, governments, statesmen, patriots, and soldiers are made of, then Mr. Delane has assisted to lead public opinion the downward road of decline and decay. If, like most Englishmen, we believe the course of public affairs to have been upwards rather than downwards, we must credit our departed friend with a long and victorious service in a cause vastly more important than that of ordinary conquerors.

Mr. Delane had in a remarkable degree several qualities which are indispensable to success in all business of importance. He was capable of long application and concentrated attention. After hours of work, under harassing and perplexing circumstances, he had ample reserve of strength for those critical emergencies which make the greatest demand on the powers of apprehension and judgment. He could always seize on the main point at issue, and lay his hand on that upon which all the rest depended. It seemed a kind of intuition that enabled him to foresee at once the impending fate of a cause or the result of a campaign, but it was a practical and methodical power. He could distinguish between the relevant and the irrelevant in the calculation of probabilities as well as in the conduct of an argument. In a continual experience of mistakes and disappointments—for, as we have said, the nightly birth of the broadsheet is not without its agonies and mishaps—he maintained more equanimity and command of temper than most people do under the petty harasses of private life. Compelled as he was occasionally to be decisive even to abruptness, and to sacrifice the convenience of contributors and subordinates to the paramount interest of the public, he never lost the respect or affection of those who could sympathize with him in his work, make due allowance for his difficulties, and think less of themselves than of the great issues at stake. In these days a great man is expected to master a bulky report in one day and deliver it in flowing sentences the next; but the former process is performed in the quiet of a study, and the latter with the comfortable feeling that so long as the orator is on his legs he has possession of the audience. If he is not clear, he can be diffuse; if he misses the point himself, he can take care that his hearers miss it too; he can at least lead his foes a dance as well as his friends and admirers. Mr. Delane could always, at a moment's call, give a succinct epitome, in terse, telling English, of any speech or debate, any book, any correspondence he had read or listened to; and many a writer and speaker might have been thankful to learn from him, for the first time, the real purport and drift of all the sentences or facts they had been stringing together. He did this without being either tedious or slapdash, if we may use the word, for his was an honest attempt to do justice even to those with whom he did not agree. The facility with which he did this, and the sometimes marvellous manner in which he would present the real substance of addresses beyond the patience of ordinary hearers or readers, made him most welcome, almost too welcome, in every society in this country. The self-denying ordinance Mr. Delane had to submit to is not to be estimated simply by the usual repugnance to put business before pleasure, work before play, or by the natural and universal preference shown by educated men for what is called good society. There were features in Mr. Delane's character which made the sacrifice specially painful. He had the instincts of family affection almost to excess, for in no one was more exemplified the old saying that blood is stronger than water. A warm and, in this matter, almost impulsive nature found vent in friendships which lasted many years, and passed, in many instances, from the parents to the children, and embraced a widening circle. It cost no small management, as well as self-denial, to divide days and hours, body and soul, between friends and a country equally unwilling to take a denial. It is the ordinary martyrdom of public men in this country, but of even our best and greatest men few can estimate what it was for Mr. Delane to withdraw as unobservedly and as early as he could from the assembled guests, "before they had joined the ladies," to spend many hours selecting materials, pruning redundant paragraphs, fining down tedious narratives, deciphering manuscripts, correcting proofs, harmonizing discordant intelligence, discovering the sense of telegraphic riddles, and often finishing by sacrificing the editorial labour of many hours to make room for some bulky and important, but very late arrival, that must be published at whatever cost. It is curiously said that most Englishmen accept the glorious phenomenon of sunrise on the authority of the poets who describe it and the astronomers who prove it, for they have never seen it themselves, except now and then on the walls of the Royal Academy. For nearly half the year Mr. Delane saw it every morning, not after what it is a mockery to call his night's rest, but before it.

The most jealous rival would not venture to dispute that Mr. Delane did honour to his singular position as the chief of English journalists. He held his own amid temptations, solicitations, and interferences of a less gentle kind, and, though an affectionate friend and a pleasant companion, could deny the unreasonable requests incessantly made, in one form or other, to all who are believed to have anything to do with public opinion. As is universal with British statesmen and politicians, his one idea of dignified happiness was that of a country gentleman. For many years his delight was to go down on the Saturday and bury himself for a few hours in a rather dull cottage, in a corner of his native parish, and feel himself once more at home. Some 20 years since he bought one of two pieces of barren heath near Ascot that an enthusiastic freetrader had bequeathed to Mr. Cobden. Here he eventually built a mansion and reclaimed the surrounding sands with the usual economical results. A stranger who might see Mr. Delane here, surrounded by his relatives, and ready to enter into any question that might afford a topic of common interest and unite friends in pleasant companionship, would little suppose that he had been credited for years with a power as great as that of Governments and Legislatures. However that might be, he had borne his honours meekly and could easily bear to resign a burden of which none had known more than he the weight and anxiety. At Ascot-heath, within a short drive of his birthplace, surrounded by home associations, amid the fir plantations and evergreens that redeem the otherwise sterile waste, he looked back on 40 years of incessant toil, not without a sense of shortcomings and failures, and desiring no other record of him than that he had done his best.

LORD LIVERPOOL ON COINS.

TO THE EDITOR OF THE TIMES.

Sir,—With reference to your article on the bimetallic controversy and to your suggestion that the letter of Lord Liverpool on coins should be republished, I have to acquaint you that it is now being reprinted at the Bank of England.

I remain, Sir, your obedient servant,

Bank of England, Nov. 24. H. R. GRENFELL.

Arctic Exploration.—Last evening, at the second meeting for the present session of the Royal Geographical Society, held under the presidency of Lord Northbrook, a paper by Captain A. H. Markham, R.N., on "The Arctic Campaign of 1879 in the Barents Sea" was read, in the absence of the author, by Mr. Clement Markham, hon. secretary of the Society. The present year, the author said, would always be regarded as a very remarkable one in the annals of Arctic exploration, for during the last few months two important geographical problems had been successfully solved: The Swedish ship Vega, under the leadership of that persevering and energetic explorer, Nordenskjold, had completed her voyage from the Atlantic to the Pacific, by rounding the northern outskirts of the old world—a voyage which, even if it should not prove important in a commercial sense, would always rank as one of the greatest geographical feats of the present century—and a small sailing schooner had reached the hitherto inaccessible shores of Franz-Josef Land. A brief reference to what had already been accomplished in the Nova Zembla waters proved that the past summer, during which the Willem Barents made her memorable trip, was not an exceptionally favourable one, and that the only other time when Franz-Josef Land had been approached, namely, in 1872-3, when the Tegethoff was drifted thither, was a remarkably unfavourable ice year. Early in the present year the author accepted an invitation from Sir Henry Gore Booth to accompany him on a sporting trip to Nova Zembla, with the understanding that they should afterwards examine the ice in the Barents Sea and other localities, during what he considered to be the navigable season—namely, during the month of September. For the cruise he had hired the little Norwegian cutter Isbjørn, already rendered historical by her exploits under Payer and Count Wilczek. The Isbjorn was a vessel of 43 tons burden, 55ft. long, with a beam of 17ft. She was built in 1870, and made her first voyage in the following year with Weyprecht and Payer. The crew consisted of a skipper, mate, two harpooners, and five seamen. As the result of their voyage the highest latitude reached was 78deg. 24min., or six miles further north than that attained by the Dutch expedition last year. He trusted that a vessel would be sent out to Franz-Josef Land prepared to winter there, and from that starting point in the following season to attack the work of Arctic exploration. Count Bylandt, Sir Leopold M'Clintock, Sir George Nares, and Admiral Hamilton took part in the discussion which followed, and expressed their pleasure at the addition which the narrative of the cruise, as contained in the paper, had made to Arctic geography.

University College, Bristol.—Professor Marshall has withdrawn his resignation as Principal of this institution, the Council having made arrangements by which his work will be lessened, and it is hoped will enable the Professor long to continue to discharge the duties of his office.

The Bordesley Ritualistic Case.—Mr. John Perkins, Churchwarden, Holy Trinity, Bordesley, Birmingham, writes:—"As you have published the Bishop of Worcester's letter to me on the above case, I trust you will be good enough to insert the accompanying letter in reply. 'Birmingham, 14, Trinity-terrace, Camp-hill, November 22. —To the Right Rev. the Bishop of Worcester.—My Lord, —I have already had the honour to acknowledge the receipt of your letter of the 11th inst. In your letter your Lordship says:—"It has been represented to me that you produced for the examination of the Court some bread which had been consecrated for use in the Holy Communion, and that though you did not yourself obtain possession of the bread by pretending to communicate, you received it from a person who did so profane the Holy Sacrament, and, knowing how it had been obtained, made use of it for the purpose of the prosecution in which you were engaged, and thereby made yourself partaker of the profanation." I beg respectfully to deny this charge *in toto*, and distinctly to disclaim to your Lordship, both on my own part and on the part of those who have acted with me, any profanation, either in intention or in act. No bread was produced in court; what was produced in court was not 'bread, such as is usual to be eaten, the best and the purest wheat bread that conveniently may be gotten' (as the rubric enforces), but an illegal wafer. Consequently, your condemnation falls to the ground, as being entirely misdirected. I feel that it is not just for your Lordship to condemn me unheard, and upon *ex parte* statements which cannot be proved. I trust, therefore, that your Lordship will see fit, in justice to myself, to withdraw your condemnation, and that you will give the withdrawal the same publicity as has been given to your letter containing the condemnation.—I remain, my Lord, your obedient servant,—John Perkins, Churchwarden, Holy Trinity, Bordesley.'"

Fire at a Railway Station.—A fire broke out early yesterday morning in the chief offices of the Manchester, Sheffield, and Lincolnshire Railway, London-road, Manchester. The flames were first seen soon after 4 o'clock in one of the clerk's offices, which was soon destroyed. They next reached the private-secretary's room. The books of the company, being in a safe, were untouched; but a number of documents in other rooms were destroyed. The booking-office of the company, as well as that of the Midland Company, was entirely burnt down, and the refreshment-rooms were also greatly damaged. The fire was got under by 6 o'clock. The origin of the fire is unknown, but it is supposed to have arisen in the guards' room over the booking department.

Respite.—Thomas Dean, convicted of murdering his wife at Warton, near Devizes, and sentenced to death, has been respited, the Home Secretary having directed a commission to inquire into the state of his mind.

OBITUARY.

Mr. John Remington Mills, formerly M.P. for Wycombe, died on Saturday at Kingswood, his seat, near Tunbridge Wells, in the 82d year of his age. The third son of the late Mr. Samuel Mills, of Russell-square, London, by his marriage with Mary, daughter of Mr. Thomas Wilson, he was born in 1798, and was educated for a commercial career, his family having been largely interested in the silk trade. He was well known in Nonconformist circles as one of the wealthiest and most generous supporters of the charities of the Dissenting Churches and he was a large contributor to the erection of the great Memorial-hall in Farringdon-street. He sat in Parliament in the advanced Liberal interest for the borough of Wycombe from 1862 down to the general election of 1868, when he was defeated by the Hon. William Carington, the present member. On two occasions he contested Leeds and was also an unsuccessful candidate for Finsbury in 1861. Mr. Mills was a magistrate for Middlesex, Hertfordshire, and Kent. He married, in 1831, Louisa Matilda, daughter of Mr. Joseph Trueman, of Walthamstow, Essex, by whom he has left a family to lament his loss.

General John Hobson, late of the Bombay Staff Corps, whose death was yesterday announced, attained his first commission on March 1, 1820, and became lieutenant in the following June. He served in the Persian Gulf in 1821, and was present at the night attack of the Arabs on the camp at Zoar and in the action before Beniboo Ali. He served, also, with the force sent against Kolapore in 1826-27. He was made brevet-captain in March, 1835, and captain in September of the same year. He became brevet-major in 1846, and served with the Bombay Column in the Punjab campaign of 1848-49, receiving the medal with clasps; he became major-general, September 2, 1861; lieutenant-general, June 25, 1870; and general on the Retired List, July 11, 1877.

Mr. Henry Crawshay, the well-known ironmaster of the Forest of Dean, and the only surviving brother of Mr. Robert Crawshay, of Cyfarthfa, South Wales, died yesterday, at his family residence, Oaklands-park, near Newnham-on-Severn. The deceased gentleman had been dangerously ill for only a few days. The immediate cause of death was congestion of the lungs and heart disease. Mr. Crawshay had just attained his 67th year.

The Earl of Durham.—The Earl of Durham was attacked with serious illness on Thursday morning, and still remains in a precarious state at 39, Hill-street. Sir W. Jenner and Mr. W. Butt are in attendance.

The Irish Secretary.—The Right Hon. James Lowther, M.P., arrived in London yesterday morning from Dublin, and will remain in town a few days.

Wellington College.—The Wellington College Royal Commissioners have adjourned their next meeting, at 5, New-street, Spring-gardens, until Monday, the 1st of December, to afford an opportunity to officers interested in the subject of stating their views on the affairs of the college.

Overflow of the River Guadalquiver.—A Lloyd's telegram from Seville, under date November 23, reports:—"River Guadalquiver overflowing quay, but floods probably subsiding; no damage reported to shipping or merchandise."

The Vistula Railway Bridge at Graudenz.—The new railway bridge over the Vistula at Graudenz, which was commenced April 6, 1876, was this year finished so that the first train passed over it on the 25th of October last. The length of the structure is 1,143 metres. It rests on 12 piers, between each of which the distance is rather more than 94½ metres. The total weight of the iron forming the superstructure is 8,360,000 kilogrammes, or not quite 8,000 tons, while the total area of the surface is 27,000 square metres. The height of the rails above the general level of the water of the river is 12 metres.

The British Museum.—"A Disappointed Reader" writes under date November 24:—"In reference to the new arrangement at the British Museum with the electric light, permit me to offer my experience. I obtained a ticket and left the City an hour earlier than usual last week, intending to read from 5 to 7, but I was informed that no books were given out after 3 30 p.m., thus making the new rule practically useless."

Free Libraries.—A public meeting was held in the Masonic-hall, Camberwell New-road, last night, in connexion with the proposed Free Reference and Lending Libraries for Camberwell. The result of the poll taken was as follows:—Against, 1,306; for the opening of the libraries, 679—majority against 627.

Palmer's "Index to *The Times*."—Mr. Samuel Palmer, of Adelphi-house, Strand, has just brought out the second, or spring quarter, volume of his "Index to *The Times* of 1879, embracing the months of April, May, and June. It includes, *inter alia*, more than half of the details of our campaign in Zululand, which occupy nearly three columns. American, Turkish, Italian, and American affairs claim spaces ranging from one column to three. This present volume includes also a large proportion of the Parliamentary speeches of the past Session; and the usual amount of accidents, bankruptcies, deaths, criminal trials, murders, &c. Among the deaths is that of the Prince Imperial, and among the murders are those at Richmond and in Euston-square, for which Katherine Webster and Hannah Dobbs respectively were tried. The present volume, which forms the 61st of the series, is also of interest as recording some of the earliest stages of electric lighting, and of Mr. Edison's and other efforts in the introduction of the telephone.

Ritualism.—At a crowded meeting in Hope-hall, Liverpool, on November 18, resolutions in support of the Protestant character of the Church were unanimously passed, and the chairman (Mr. Hugh Evans) was instructed to forward them to the Premier and Lord Sandon, the senior member for the borough. The resolution addressed to the Premier called his attention to the fact that the Public Worship Act had not put down Ritualism or extinguished the 'mass in masquerade,' and prayed for such an amendment of the law as would put an end to the lawlessness prevalent within the pale of the national Church." The reply sent on behalf of the Premier merely acknowledged the receipt of the resolution. Lord Sandon wrote as follows.—"I am always glad to hear expressions of the determination of the country to maintain the Protestant Reformed Church of England, an object which is very dear to my own heart and for the promotion of which I shall continue to take advantage of every suitable opportunity and to adopt that course which appears to me to be best calculated to secure this great end."

The Patent Shaft and Axle-tree Company (Limited).—A special meeting of the Patent Shaft and Axle-tree Company (Limited) was held at Birmingham yesterday, when Mr. William Coath, the late defaulting secretary of the company, against whom a warrant was issued some months ago, unexpectedly put in an appearance, and attempted to address the meeting. Mr. Coath's solicitors, Messrs. Duignan and Co., of Walsall, announced a few days ago that their client would surrender himself at Wednesbury to answer all charges against him on the 2d of December, but for some unexplained reason Mr. Coath decided to forestall that appointment, and placed himself in the hands of the shareholders yesterday. The meeting, which was presided over by Mr. Walker, M.P., had been called to confirm the resolutions passed on the 3d inst., reducing the ordinary share capital, by a reduction of £3 per share, to £510,000, divided into 30,000 shares of £17 each. The resolutions having been moved and seconded, the chairman was about to put them to the meeting when Mr. Coath, who had entered the room some time previously and taken his seat among the other shareholders, rose and asked to be heard before the motion was put. A scene of considerable excitement ensued, every one standing up to catch a sight of Mr. Coath. The chairman then said he declined to allow the man who had risen to speak. He had succeeded in baffling the efforts of the police to apprehend him for some weeks. Mr. Coath said that was not true. The Chairman.—"I shall have you removed from the room. He has succeeded in passing a constable who holds a warrant to arrest him in the street. We have sent for the police, and he will be arrested as soon as they are brought in." Mr. Coath.—"Gentlemen, all I ask is fair play. I wish to place you in a proper position. The position you are in is a false one, and the directors know it perfectly well." The Chairman.—"The resolution is carried and the meeting is at an end." Mr. West, a shareholder, moved that Mr. Coath should be heard. A shareholder put the question to Mr. Coath, "Why did you go away?" Mr. Coath.—"I have never gone away from the company, and the directors could have laid hands on me at any moment if they liked. The balance-sheet is falsified to the extent of £130,000. I can prove it." A detective who had just entered the room then took Mr. Coath into custody and conveyed him to the police-court, where he was at once placed in the dock. Mr. Beale, who appeared for the Patent Shaft and Axle-tree Company, applied for a remand until Wednesday. Mr. Kynnersley, the stipendiary magistrate, remarked that as the prisoner was not charged with any offence committed in that district he must be discharged, which was accordingly done. On leaving the court Mr. Coath was followed by Superintendent Holland, who held a warrant for his arrest from the Wednesbury magistrates, and was again taken into custody. He will be brought up at Wednesbury to-morrow.

Pistol Accident.—On the morning of the 19th inst. Seymour Hawkesley Acheson, fourth son of Mr. J. Acheson, J.P. for the county of Wexford, took a rook pistol to have a shot at some birds from the roof of the house. On getting, however, through some narrow exit, the pistol by some mischance exploded and the ball passed through his body. Prompt surgical attention was afforded to the sufferer, but he lingered only 20 hours. The deceased was 17 years old.

A New Geographical Journal.—The forthcoming publication of a new journal of geography is announced from Vienna, under the title of *Zeitschrift für Wissenschaftliche Geographie*. It is intended as a sort of supplement to the *Mittheilungen* of the Vienna Geographical Society, which, of course, is mainly occupied with the proceedings of that body. The editor is Julius Iwan Kettler, who will be assisted by some of the best of the scientific geographers of Germany. Its programme is comprehensive, including—1, Method of Geographical Research and Geographical Education; 2, Mathematical Geography, Cartography; 3, Physical Geography in its widest sense; 4, Volkskunde, Geography of Culture and Commerce, Historical Geography; 5, History of Geography and Cartography. In Germany, France, and Italy there is quite a host of journals specially devoted to geography and exploration; in this country we have only the "Proceedings" of the Geographical Society, which, in spite of its new form, is still little more than the organ of that body. It seems strange that the greatest exploring nation of the world should be without any special organ in that department.

Above THE TIMES Press Room showing the Walter Printing Presses, *c.* 1868. Introduced under Delane, these presses were a remarkable innovation developed by MacDonald and Calverley of THE TIMES, using stereotype plates on cylinders which could print both sides of a page simultaneously. These machines continued in use until 1895.

Above, inset The camp at Sebastopol, photo by James Robertson, 1855.

He once noted: 'Not a column has been published in *The Times* which has not some of my handwriting in the margin'.

Delane was the complete professional journalist. National and international affairs were the staple fare of his paper. But he did not look down his nose at any event that would interest or entertain his readers: he wrote to his deputy 'That was a good murder you had last week'. His day was long and arduous. He would arrive at Printing House Square at ten o'clock at night, and leave about five in the morning, having seen, he said, 'more sunrises than any man alive'. He would rise at noon and after a meal, ride in the Park; then to his chambers, where he would work for a few hours before attending a social gathering or dinner party. At these dos he met Ministers and Opposition leaders, and talked to them at ease. His staff were gratified when he was seen riding down Whitehall with a duke walking on either side, talking to him. His connections with top people provoked Lord John Russell to write to Queen Victoria: 'The degree of information possessed by *The Times* with regard to the most secret affairs of state is mortifying, humiliating, and incomprehensible'.

Barnes was a secret man with a private life at home, or with his contemporaries of Christ's Hospital or Cambridge. Delane was a public man. His life was *The Times*, and in Society. The Prince of Wales was his friend. He never missed Ascot. Delane's list of regular correspondents in the archives of *The Times* reads like a *Who's Who* of the second half of the nineteenth century: Palmerston, Aberdeen, Wellington, Gladstone, Disraeli, Derby, Peel, and the rest of the top table. He seldom dined at home, and once complained: '"Swelling" is very laborious, and now having had five or six days of it, I shall be very glad of a day's rest'. When he retired, Disraeli asked 'But who will undertake the social part of the business? Who will go about the world, and do all that Mr Delane did so well?'

Barnes and Delane created public opinion as a force in government, and *The Times* as its loudspeaker. Barnes created the thunder of the paper, and Delane broadcast it to the Chancelleries of Europe and into the New World. When Delane took over in 1847, *The Times* usually had eight pages and a circulation of 32,000. When he retired in 1877, it regularly had sixteen pages, sometimes twenty, and a circulation of 62,000. Its political power was based on commercial success.

Delane gave his life to the paper. He died, worn out, two years after he laid down his editorial pen.

Palmerston and THE TIMES

The Times had become a power in the land, and it was a matter of consequence for the ambitious politician to have it on his side. This phenomenon is illustrated by the stormy relationship between Printing House Square and Lord Palmerston, the great Whig Foreign Secretary, Prime Minister and statesman.

In October 1855 Palmerston told the Queen: 'From the time when I first went to the Foreign Office, for some reason or other which I could never discover, *The Times* has been animated by undeviating hostility, personal and political, towards me'. Even as he wrote the words, a dramatic change was taking place in the relations between the two powers. On 6 October *The Times* wrote: 'It is but bare justice to say that at this period the country needed a man, and that it found in Lord Palmerston the man it needed'. It was a *volte face* as startling as a Trappist monk becoming a disc jockey. Its causes show the turbulence in which The Thunderer earned its name.

Pam was exaggerating when he told the Queen that *The Times* had been against him from the very beginning. When he first entered the Foreign Office he had the general support of the paper. It wrote: 'Lord Palmerston has had long experience at the head of a difficult department, and, if we may judge by his public speeches, is a man of liberal politics with regard to foreign affairs'. Soon it found him wanting in his support for struggling nationalities; nevertheless, Whigs were better than Tories.

Barnes then formed his alliance with Peel and *The Times* became an enemy of the Whigs, in one of those shifts of policy at Printing House Square that earned it the sobriquet of 'The Turnabout'. But the attacks on Palmerston exceeded the normal buffets of party polemics, even in those bare-fisted days. They were palpable for their personal acerbity. Pam was categorized in *The Times* as 'the simpering Secretary', habitually given to 'silly dandyism' and 'feeble facetiousness', the 'worn-out hack of a dozen Administrations' (the facsimile on p. 157 shows an example of such invective).

The bitterness was partly explained by noticing that *The Times* was fighting a circulation war with the *Morning Chronicle*, which was in Pam's pocket and received scoops and tip-offs from him. But Barnes personally disapproved of Palmerston as fundamentally 'frivolous'. And Palmerston had attracted the baleful attention of Henry Reeve, the most influential foreign leader writer ever to have sounded off from Printing House Square. Reeve was Clerk of Appeals to the Privy Council. He was introduced to *The Times* by his senior colleague, Charles Greville, Clerk to the Council, who was a great manipulator of press and politics behind the scenes. Greville wrote that he looked to Reeve to give to *The Times* 'a higher tone and on great occasions to render it an instrument of public good'.

Reeve took to journalism like a beagle to dustbins. He was nicknamed *Il Pomposo* by his colleagues at Printing House Square, and once solemnly wrote in his diary after watching *The Times* being printed: 'It gave me a strange and almost exciting sensation, for by this instrument my own thoughts and opinions are propagated and diffused over the habitable earth, with a power that seems at times irresistible'. He wrote the foreign leaders for *The Times* for fifteen years, calculating with characteristic vanity that he had written 2,482 articles, and received upwards of £13,000 for them. It was an odd position for a senior civil servant intimately concerned with the day-to-day running of government to be instructing his political masters and reproving them in public.

Reeve said that his principal duty as a writer for *The Times* was 'to punish the presumption of that man' (i.e. Palmerston). And he fulfilled his duty faithfully over the years. Of course there were political grounds for fighting Pam. Printing House Square was more alarmed by the menace of the Russian bear, 'the fierce tartar who now fills the throne of Russia', than Palmerston. Having started by finding Palmerston lukewarm on behalf of small nations, *The Times* came to attack him for meddling on behalf of insurgent nationalists throughout Europe.

But it is hard not to detect personal virulence in *The Times* whenever it wrote about the Foreign Secretary, which was most days. It described his writings as 'Dickens stuff', which was not intended as a compliment. When he published the dispatches about the Spanish marriages, Reeve wrote:

> If we were called upon, in the exercise of the ordinary functions of literary criticism, to pass a judgment on the style and merit of the English dispatches in this collection, we should complain that they are large without being vigorous, hasty without being energetic, coarse and inelegant without being strong.

Take the case of Don Pacifico as an example of the war in high politics. Don Pacifico was a Levantine Jew who had worked for the Portuguese Government, but was also a British citizen because he had been born in Gibraltar. At Easter 1847 the Greek Government banned the customary amusement of burning an effigy of Judas Iscariot, in deference to a visiting Rothschild, from whom they had expectations. The Athens mob burnt down Don Pacifico's house in revenge. He appealed to the British Government for redress. Palmerston took up his case with enthusiasm and off his own bat. The Navy blockaded the Piraeus in 1850, and there was nearly a European war.

The Times seized the opportunity to get at Palmerston, and, with a bit of luck, evict the intolerable old dandy from the Foreign Office. On 22 February it proclaimed that Palmerston had roused

Below Henry Reeve, foreign leader writer on THE TIMES, and Clerk of Appeals to the Privy Council.
Bottom Lord Palmerston, 1859.

'the indignation of the civilized world' . . . 'England may be disgraced, Europe exasperated, Greece oppressed – what matters if the whim of the Foreign Secretary be gratified, and if his Lordship's sovereign commands are obeyed?'

From then on there were Pacifico articles every day. In the last days of May there was a series of four special articles critically examining the whole controversy, and filling nine columns in all. The Prime Minister discussed with the Queen the advisability of moving Palmerston to some other post to get him out of the position of lightning conductor. A vote of censure in the House of Lords was carried by a majority of thirty-seven, a number that *The Times* described optimistically as 'overwhelming'.

On 24 June there was a general vote of confidence in the foreign policy of the Government. It produced one of the great debates of the century. Palmerston spoke for five hours, making his '*Civis Romanus Sum*' speech. In spite of powerful replies by Gladstone, Disraeli and Peel, he carried the day in the House and in the country. Lady Clarendon wrote in her diary: 'He has triumphed over a great mass of educated public opinion, over that mighty potentate *The Times*, over two branches of the Legislature, over the Queen and Prince and most of the Cabinet he sits in, besides all foreign nations'.

The Times saw itself as the reflector as well as the leader of public opinion, and was uneasy about its long vendetta with the Foreign Secretary, whose popularity was sweeping the country. Eventually, in the Crimea crisis, Delane came to recognize Palmerston as the Right Man in the Right Place. They met, and talked, and developed an understanding. *The Times* described Palmerston's speech on the capture of Sebastopol as manly, and admitting that it was spoken by somebody the paper had so often blamed, turned 'to that fraction of the community who cannot understand why we should now praise the policy of our ancient foe'.

Disraeli's weekly, the *Press*, noted the change of policy: 'Far more surprising than any of these marvels is the astonishing event that on Saturday, the 20th of September, a panegyric was actually fired off from *The Times* at Lord Palmerston. Well *that* is a wonderful event. Pam has now humbled his old enemy into being his trumpeter.' Pam explained to the Queen that *The Times* was probably behind him because of the paper's well-known readiness to support a winning cause. He was not too keen on her suggestion that journalists ought not to be received socially or mixed with:

> There is no Doubt some inconvenience in the Admission of Editors and writers of newspapers into general society; but if they happen to be in a Position of Life which would naturally lead to their being invited, it would not be easy to exclude them merely on account of their Connection with a newspaper.

But relations between Palmerston and *The Times* were always abrasive. He wrote to the Queen on one occasion: '*The Times*, in order to maintain its circulation, criticises freely everybody and everything'.

Henry Reeve, *Il Pomposo*, left *The Times* in 1855, the year in which the paper changed its mind about Palmerston. The occasion of his departure was a characteristically intemperate and vigorous article on the visit of Prince Frederick of Prussia to Balmoral 'to improve his acquaintance with the Princess Royal'. The King of Prussia was described as 'the degenerate successor of Frederick the Great'; the Prussian royal family were said to be connected in the minds of the Prussian people with 'foreign subjection and national degradation. The days of these paltry German dynasties are numbered.'

Lord Clarendon, a friend of Printing House Square, said that the article would be a dagger in the Queen's heart. She did not like newspapers anyway – and particularly not *The Times*. The piece caused trouble. Reeve resigned in a huff and Delane accepted his resignation somewhat reluctantly, recognizing the power that his leaders had brought to *The Times* for fifteen years. He had no alternative, unless he was going to hand over the entire foreign policy of the paper to a maverick outsider.

Reeve was a peacock and a prima donna. But then, in their different ways, so were Palmerston and Delane. They may not always have fought on the same side. But, by God, they produced good politics and exciting journalism; and did the best, as they saw it, for the country and for Printing House Square.

Top Their Royal Highnesses Prince Frederick William of Prussia and the Princess Royal of England, whose meeting caused Reeve's resignation from THE TIMES.

Above PUNCH cartoon by John Leech on the Don Pacifico affair, when Palmerston dispatched Admiral Parker to Piraeus in 1850.

The first column and a quarter contain, verbatim, the last part of Palmerston's famous five-hour speech to Parliament. Almost at the very end occurs the phrase '*Civis Romanus Sum*', by which the speech has come to be known.
26 JUNE 1850

HER MAJESTY's THEATRE.—The LAST GRAND CLASSICAL and DRAMATIC CONCERTED MUSICAL ENTERTAINMENT will take place on Wednesday Morning, July 10, and will unite the talents of Mesdames Sontag, Parodi, Catherine Hayes, Giuliani, Ida Bertrand, and Frezzolini; Signori Coletti, Belletti, Lorenzo, F. Lablache, and Lablache; Signori Gardoni, Calzolari, Baucarde, and Mr. Sims Reeves. The valuable assistance of M. Thalberg has been secured, who will execute some favourite pieces, and amongst others, an admired Concerto of Beethoven, accompanied by full orchestra. Conductor—M. Balfe. Selections will be made from the most classical and admired authors, and will include pieces not hitherto performed in this country. The whole resources of the establishment, vocal and instrumental, will be employed, and every effort will be made to justify the high character and patronage with which these performances have been honoured. Prices of admission:—Boxes, £2 2s.; pit stalls, 12s. 6d.; pit, 5s. 6d.; gallery stalls, 5s.; gallery, 2s. 6d. Application for boxes, stalls, and tickets to be made at the box-office of the theatre. The concert will commence at 2 o'clock precisely.

ROYAL ITALIAN OPERA, COVENT-GARDEN.—Morning Concert.—The Last of the Season.—On Monday, July 8, the LAST CONCERT of the Season will take place; on which occasion, in addition to a Miscellaneous Selection, will be performed Haydn's oratorio, The Creation, supported by the principal artistes of the establishment, the full band, and chorus. Prices of admission to the concert:—Boxes, £1 11s. 6d., £2 2s., £2 12s. 6d., £3 3s.; orchestra stalls, 10s. 6d.; pit, 5s.; amphitheatre stalls 3s.; front row 5s.; amphitheatre, 2s.

MRS. GLOVER's FAREWELL BENEFIT, under the patronage of his Grace the Duke of Devonshire, his Grace the Duke of Beaufort, the Earl Glengall, and other distinguished patrons of the drama, will take place at Drury-lane Theatre on Wednesday, July 10. Full particulars will be shortly announced. Subscriptions will be received by Mr. Leigh Murray, who has kindly consented to act as Honorary Secretary to the Committee, and who will attend at Drury-lane Theatre every day, between the hours of 3 and 5 p.m.

THEATRE ROYAL, HAYMARKET.—Mr. BENJAMIN WEBSTER, Sole Lessee and Director, begs to announce to his patrons that his ANNUAL BENEFIT is fixed for Monday, July 8, when will be presented a variety of Entertainments, embracing the entire strength of the company. Tickets and private boxes may be secured of Mr. Webster, at the theatre; and at the box-office. Further particulars will be duly announced.

MDLLE. RACHEL.—Monday next.—French Plays, St. James's Theatre.—Mr. MITCHELL respectfully announces that the PERFORMANCES of the eminent tragedienne, Mdlle. RACHEL, are definitively arranged to commence on Monday Evening next, July 1. It is also respectfully announced that the engagement of Mdlle. Rachel is positively limited to 12 representations, which cannot possibly be exceeded, owing to engagements entered into at Berlin and Vienna. The following order of representation will be adhered to as nearly as possible:—Monday, July 1, Racine's tragedy of Phèdre. Wednesday, July 3, Racine's tragedy of Bajazet. Friday, July 5 (for the first time in this country), Polyeucte, Martyr; Tragédie Chrétienne, by Corneille. In addition to a petite comedy, in one act, by Armand Barthet, entitled Le Moineau de Lesbie. The character of Lesbie by Mdlle. Rachel. Monday, July 8 (the first time in this country), a new play, in five acts, by MM. Scribe et Le Gouve, entitled Adrienne Lecouvreur (produced at the Théâtre Français, Paris, April, 1849, with unexampled success), Adrienne, Mdlle Rachel. The subsequent representations will be selected from Les Horaces, Marie Stuart, Virginie, Jeanne d'Arc, and Andromaque. The company engaged to support Mdlle Rachel has been selected from the leading theatres of Paris and the provinces. Subscriptions to the stalls, for any six consecutive performances, five guineas; or for the 12 representations, eight guineas; stalls by the night, one guinea. Subscribers who may be desirous of continuing their boxes or stalls for Mdlle. Rachel's representations are solicited to intimate their wishes as early as possible.—Royal Library, 33, Old Bond-street.

THEATRE ROYAL, HAYMARKET.—Legitimate Attraction.—La! Tempest! Ha!—Triumphant Success of the grand burlesque founded on The Tempest, written by two celebrated Scribes, entitled THE ENCHANTED ISLE; or, "Raising the Wind" on the Most Approved Principles, as Shakspeare "would have written it," will be repeated EVERY EVENING; with the successful comic drama of NONE BUT THE BRAVE DESERVE THE FAIR.

ADELPHI THEATRE.—Uproarious Success of Esmeralda.—THIS EVENING (in consequence of its great success), THE WEPT OF THE WISH-TON-WISH; the new burlesque of ESMERALDA, by the entire strength of the company, including novel scenic effects, the Truandaise, Danse de Fleurs, the Anticagitana, Pas de Fascination, Esmeralda's lucky bag and fine arts distribution of prizes, new gorgeous scenery, dresses, &c.; and JACK IN THE GREEN.

HER MAJESTY's THEATRE.—First Appearance of Signor Gardoni.—Mde. Frezzolini and Mdlle. Parodi.—I Capuletti e I Montecchi.—On Saturday next, June 29, will be produced (for the first time at this theatre) Bellini's celebrated opera, entitled I CAPULETTI E I MONTECCHI. Romeo, Mdlle. Parodi; Tebaldo, Signor Gardoni (his first appearance this season); Capellio, Signor Belletti; Lorenzo, Signor Lorenzo; and Giulietta, Mde. Frezzolini. With various Entertainments in the Ballet Department, in which Mdlle. Carlotta Grisi, Mdlle. Amalia Ferraris, and M. Charles will appear. Applications for boxes, stalls, and tickets to be made at the box-office of the theatre.

THE TIMES

BOARD of GREEN CLOTH.

ST. JAMES'S PALACE, June 25, 1850.

Notice is hereby given to the Ambassadors, the Foreign Ministers, the Members of Her Majesty's Most Honourable Privy Council, and the Officers and Ladies of the Royal Household, invited to Her Majesty's Ball, at Buckingham Palace, on Wednesday Evening, the 26th instant, that their Carriages are to enter St. James's-park by the Great Gate on Constitution-hill, pass along to the Arch in the North Wing of the Palace, set down at the Garden Entrance, and leaving the Garden by the Gate near the Riding House, are to turn to the right.

The empty Carriages are afterwards to proceed in like manner through Constitution-hill Gate into the Park, wait there till called to take up, and go away through Grosvenor-place.

The Carriages of all other persons invited to the Ball are to fall into line in St. James's-street, enter the Park by Stable-yard Gate, pass the front of the Palace and through Buckingham Gate, to set down at the Equerry's Door.

The empty Carriages are turn round, and passing down the Bird-cage-walk, are to cross the Parade opposite the Horse Guards, to wait in the Mall till called to the Equerry's Door; after taking up, they are to re-enter the Park by Buckingham Gate, and go away through Stable-yard Gate, up St. James's-street.

WESTMINSTER, Lord Steward.

HER MAJESTY'S THEATRE.
Grand Extra Night.
La Tempesta.

It is respectfully announced that a Grand Extra Night will take place To-morrow Evening (Thursday), June 27, when will be presented (for the ninth time) the highly successful new grand opera, by Halevy, the poem by Scribe, founded on The Tempest of Shakspeare, and composed expressly for Her Majesty's Theatre, entitled LA TEMPESTA. The incidental dances by M. Paul Taglioni; the scenery by Mr. Charles Marshall; the costumes executed under the superintendence of Mde. Copere. Dramatis personæ:—Alfonso (King of Naples), Signor Lorenzo; Prospero (Duke of Milan), Signor Coletti; Antonio (his Brother, the Usurper), Signor F. Lablache; Ferdinand (Prince of Naples), Signor Baucarde; Trinculo, Signor Ferrari; Stephano, Mdlle. Parodi; Sycorax, Mdlle. Ida Bertrand; Spirit of the Air, Mde. Giuliani; Ariel, Mdlle. Carlotta Grisi; Caliban, Signor Lablache; and Miranda, Mde. Sontag. Director of the Music and Conductor—Mr. Balfe. With various entertainments in the Ballet Department, in which will appear Mdlle. Carlotta Grisi, Mdlle. Amalia Ferraris, and M. Charles. Applications for boxes, stalls, and tickets to be made at the box-office of the theatre.

ROYAL ITALIAN OPERA, COVENT-GARDEN.
Fourth Night of Madame Viardot.
Fourth Night of Le Prophete.
Extra Night.

To-morrow Evening (Thursday), June 27, a Grand Extra Night will be given, when the fourth representation of Meyerbeer's grand opera, LE PROPHETE, will take place. Fides, Mde. Viardot; Bertha, Mde. Castellan; Jean of Leyden (the Prophet), Signor Mario; Count Oberthal, Signor Tagliafico; Sergeant, Signor Lavia; Peasants, Signori Rommi and Soldi; Giona, Signor Mariatti; Mathisen, Signor Polonini; Zaccaria, Herr Formes. The Choir in the Grand Coronation Scene of the third act will combine the powers of the full orchestra, the military bands, the chorus, and organ. The incidental Ballet in the Skating Scene will be supported by Mons. Alexandre and Mdlle. Louise Taglioni (as danced by them at the Grand Opera at Paris), and comprise the celebrated Quadrille des Patineurs. Composer, Director of the Music and Conductor—Mr. Costa. The performances commence at 8. Tickets for the boxes, stalls, or the pit may be had at the box-office of the theatre, which is open from 10 till 5; and at the principal musicsellers and libraries.

THEATRE ROYAL, HAYMARKET.
Mr. Benjamin Webster, Sole Lessee and Director.
THIS EVENING, SEPARATE MAINTENANCE.
Mr. Pennipother, Mr. Keeley; Mrs. Pennipother, Mrs. Keeley.
After which, NONE BUT THE BRAVE DESERVE THE FAIR.
To be followed by THE ENCHANTED ISLE.
To conclude with AN ALARMING SACRIFICE.

THEATRE ROYAL, ADELPHI.
Under the Direction of Madame Celeste.
THIS EVENING will be presented THE WEPT OF THE WISH-TON-WISH. Characters by Messrs. H. Hughes, Cullenford, Worrell, Boyce, Wright, O. Smith, &c.; Mde Celeste, Miss Woolgar, Mrs. Laws, &c. After which, ESMERALDA. To conclude with JACK IN THE GREEN; or, Hints on Etiquette.

NEW STRAND THEATRE.
Lessee and Manager, Mr. W. Farren.
THIS EVENING will be presented HEARTS ARE TRUMPS. Principal characters by Messrs. W. Farren, Leigh Murray, Compton, W. Farren, jun., and G. Cooke; Mesdames Stirling, Bartlett, and A. Phillips. After which, NOT TO BE DONE. To conclude with GWYNNETH VAUGHAN.

SURREY THEATRE.
Lessees, Messrs. Shepherd and Creswick.
THIS EVENING will be presented BRUTUS; or, The Fall of Tarquin. Brutus, Mr. Creswick; Titus, Mr. J. Coleman; Collatinus, Mr. T. Mead; Tullia, Mde. Ponisi; Tarquinia, Miss Jane Coveney. After which, MY WIFE'S OUT. To conclude with THE RED MAN; or, The Mariner and his Dogs.

ASTLEY'S ROYAL AMPHITHEATRE.
Proprietor and Manager, Mr. W. Batty.
THIS EVENING will be presented the magnificent spectacle of THE AFFGHANISTAN WAR; or, The Revolt of Cabul and British Triumphs in India. After which, an admired routine of Equestrian Wonders in the Scenes of the Circle. To conclude with a comic ballet, called LOVE IN THE HIGHLANDS.

TO CORRESPONDENTS.

We cannot undertake to return rejected communications. Whatever is intended for insertion must be authenticated by the name and address of the writer; not necessarily for publication, but as a guarantee of his good faith.

No notice can be taken of anonymous communications.

☞ The publication of THE TIMES commenced at 8 o'clock yesterday morning, and finished at a quarter past 9.

LONDON, WEDNESDAY, JUNE 26, 1850.

In the House of Lords last night the Royal assent was given by commission to several bills.

After some further complaints as to the working of the new postal regulations, the Leasehold Tenure of Land (Ireland) Act Amendment Bill passed through committee.

The Marquis of LONDONDERRY postponed until Thursday his motion respecting the abolition of the Irish Lord-Lieutenancy.

Their Lordships then adjourned.

In the House of Commons, on the order of the day for the resumption of the debate on the foreign policy,

Mr. OSBORNE said, the point for the consideration of the House was, how far the international principles of our foreign policy were to be guided by the established code of nations, and how far British commerce and British subjects were to be protected by the Government of this country; not whether every particular act of our Foreign Minister had been right, but whether his policy was hereafter to be regulated by the ideas of Ministers of other states, he being a mere automaton, and his moves governed by the wily and unseen agency of a foreign prompter. Mr. OSBORNE then passed some severe and sarcastic strictures upon the course taken by Sir F. THESIGER and Sir J. GRAHAM, who for four years past had either maintained a perfect silence, not disapproving, if not approving, the policy they now affected to view with so much alarm. This conduct, he observed, savoured rather of the jesuitical evasions of Muscovite chicanery than of the honest, open, and candid conflict of English political warfare. He then discussed the policy of erecting a Greek kingdom, whose financial maxim was, "Base is the slave that pays"; and, glancing at the salient points of M. PACIFICO's case, asked whether the House had not a shrewd suspicion that the envenomed hostility evinced towards Lord PALMERSTON could not be traced to his being identified on the Continent with responsible government, and regarded as an advocate of liberal opinions. Greece was a mere pretext; there was a conspiracy against him which had extensive ramifications, and the reversal of his policy would cripple British commerce, arrest the progress of civilization, and seal the humiliation of Great Britain. Believing her interests and those of the world to be at stake, he gave his support to the motion with pride and pleasure.

Lord J. MANNERS opposed the motion, because he believed that Cossack domination, which Mr. OSBORNE so much dreaded, would be promoted by the policy pursued by the Government. He denied both the propositions contained in the motion, and disputed the assertion of Mr. ROEBUCK, that the leading principle of our foreign policy had been to protect the commerce and the people of this country. If the ægis of England was extended over British subjects in every part of the world, why had a British subject in one of the States of North America been seized and cast into prison like a common malefactor without redress? In his conduct towards Greece Lord PALMERSTON could not have taken more effectual measures to extinguish British influence in the Levant and to extend that of Russia had he been really a foreign Minister. Reviewing his policy in the affairs of Switzerland and of Italy, he asked how that policy had conduced to the honour and dignity of England, or even to the extension of liberal principles. In the case of CHARLES ALBERT's invasion, Lord PALMERSTON and Mr. ABERCROMBY had manifested the spirit of keen partisans in that unjust encroachment upon Austria and Lombardy, the people of which were attached to their ruler, and when this iniquitous appeal to arms had failed Lord PALMERSTON endeavoured to secure Lombardy to CHARLES ALBERT by diplomacy. The practical result of these insurrections in the Italian peninsula was the extension of the Zollverein restrictions, to the prejudice of the commercial interests of this country.

Mr. ANSTEY found a preliminary difficulty in being unable to comprehend the motion. If it referred to the recent passages of our foreign policy since 1848 he should be prepared to vote for it, for, in a spirit of fair play towards Lord PALMERSTON, he was bound to say that he had erred rather on the side of moderation than of excess. He justified this opinion by a reference to the transactions in Italy subsequent to the election of PIUS IX.; to the affair of the Hungarian refugees, and the entrance of the British fleet into the waters of the Dardanelles. He also vindicated the proceedings of the noble lord in relation to the two Greek islands as well as to M. PACIFICO. As his approval of our foreign policy was confined to the latter part of it, he could not vote for the motion; at the same time, as he could not pronounce the whole policy as blameable, he would not vote against it.

Mr. COCHRANE said, he had charged Lord PALMERSTON with having spread revolutionary doctrines throughout Europe and tampered with the interests of this country; he now charged him, in addition, upon the authority of M. D'HAUSSONVILLE, with bad faith in connexion with Swiss affairs in 1847. After giving the details of this accusation, Mr. COCHRANE traced the proceedings of Lord MINTO in his Italian mission, which, he contended, had aided and abetted rebellion at Rome, and at Naples had widened the breach between the KING and his Sicilian subjects. These were grave charges against the foreign policy of the Government, which was anything but an English policy, being based upon oppression of the weak and concession to the strong.

Lord PALMERSTON began by insisting upon the importance of the question, which concerned not only the tenure of office by an individual or a Government, but involved principles of national policy, and the interests, honour, and dignity of this country. He observed that those who had thought themselves strong enough to try to take the Government by storm ought not to have been content with obtaining an expression of the opinion of the House of Lords; it was either their duty to have sent down the resolution for the concurrence of this House, or those connected with the party there should have proposed a confirmation of the resolution. However, the question now was whether this House would adopt the resolution, which involved the future and the past, laying down for the future a principle of national policy which he considered totally incompatible with the interests, rights, and honour of this country, and the happiness of other countries. The principle, which the person who moved it was obliged to modify, was that British subjects in foreign lands were entitled to nothing but the protection of the laws and tribunals of the country in which they might happen to be, and were not to look for any protection from their own country; and the House of Lords had not limited this principle to constitutional countries. He denied this doctrine, which was a doctrine upon which no English Minister had acted, and the people of England would never suffer any Minister to act upon it. He contended, however, for no such principle as that British subjects in foreign countries were to be above the laws. In the first instance, they were bound to have recourse to the laws of the land; but there might be cases in which the tribunals were not of a character to inspire confidence, and the rule would not apply to despotic or nominally constitutional Governments. The noble Lord then gave a short history of the Greek State, and described the nature of our relations with it. The object of this Government was to base the institutions of Greece upon the representative principle; but the advice and influence of the other Powers, France included, were adverse to our views. One evil of the absence of a Constitution in Greece was, that the whole system of the government was full of abuses. The police, in particular, practised tortures of the most revolting kind upon both sexes. There were in Greece a great number of persons, Maltese, Ionians, as well as British subjects, whom we were bound to protect; but it was the practice of the Greek authorities to make no distinction between Maltese, Ionians, and their own subjects. Lord PALMERSTON then detailed the alleged insults which had been offered to British subjects in Greece, and showed the moderation and reasonableness of the demands made for reparation; and with reference to the case of Mr. FINLAY, he justified his claim, which for 14 years the Greek Government had put aside with shuffling excuses, and which had not been, as asserted, finally and conclusively settled. With respect to the case of M. PACIFICO, whose character, whatever it might be, was no reason why he should be robbed with impunity by a mob, headed by the son of the Minister of War, he could get no redress, and we were, therefore, entitled to call upon the Greek Government for compensation, but they had denied the principle of the claim, so that it must either have been abandoned or enforced; and the course adopted of making reprisals was acted upon with great moderation. In these circumstances the French Government tendered, and we readily accepted, their good offices, the extent and conditions being distinctly understood, namely, that they were not to involve the negation of the principle of the demands. It was also understood between himself and M. DROUYN DE LHUYS that Mr. WYSE should not determine when the mission of M. GROS had failed, and if a difference of opinion occurred between M. GROS and Mr. WYSE on those points which the former was competent to discuss, the latter was to refer home for instructions. Lord PALMERSTON entered very minutely into the details and dates of the communications between the different parties in the negotiations, which had reached this point, that Mr. WYSE had consented to accept from the Greek Government the sum suggested by M. GROS, namely, 150,000 drachmas, when the latter raised a new objection on a point respecting which he was not competent to act, and withdrew from the negotiation. An impression had gone abroad that on the 24th of April M. GROS had received and communicated to Mr. WYSE the draught of the convention of London, which had not been proposed to him (Lord PALMERSTON) until the 15th, and not agreed on until the 18th, and that with a knowledge of this convention Mr. WYSE had renewed hostilities. This was totally untrue. Mr. WYSE received no information from M. GROS as to the draught of the convention until the 2d of May. He was sorry that the convention did not arrive at Athens until after the other arrangement had been made, but this was not his fault, and the negotiations had not been put an end to by Mr. WYSE, but by M. GROS himself, who had afterwards an opportunity of resuming them, but again declared that he had withdrawn. The negotiations between the English and French Governments had come to a satisfactory conclusion,

Responsible to the people of England

'The liberty of the press is the palladium of all the civil, political, and religious rights of an Englishman' wrote Junius a few years before *The Times* was founded. Much cant and fog are still generated about the freedom of the press. Governments and Parliament still threaten newspapers with D-notices, the Official Secrets Act and the Press Council. In reply newspapers declaim passages from John Milton's *Areopagitica*: 'Give me the liberty to know, to utter, and to argue freely, according to conscience, above all liberties.'

The British press is notably less free in some respects than, for example, the American. But its freedom from political control was won and defined in the nineteenth century by *The Times*. Before then newspapers depended on politicians for their news and licences to print. The Government or an opposition party gave the hacks a subsidy and titbits of convenient or suitably doctored news. In return the hacks supported their patrons and blackguarded the opposition. By its commercial success and its independent news-gathering service *The Times* freed itself and thereafter the rest of the press from such dependence on party politicians (pp. 25–7 describe the crusade for press freedom).

Occasionally the great change in journalism was defined by an almighty row. The first occasion arose when Prince Louis Napoleon assumed power in France in 1851, in a *coup d'état*. The Government broadly approved of him. *The Times* did not, and riddled him with a salvo of thunderous leaders. It described him as 'A man who has extinguished freedom among the most advanced nations of the continent'.

Louis Napoleon, who had spent a long time in England before his *coup*, understood the power of *The Times* to stimulate, to anticipate, and on occasions to organize British public opinion. His dislike of criticism in *The Times* became a personal matter. He tried bribery. His ambassador wrote directly to him explaining that *The Times* could not be bought: 'Venal in the sense that its policy can be influenced with money, that is absolutely false and I defy anyone to achieve that result even with a considerable sum of money'.

Accordingly Louis Napoleon tried bullying. He tried to frighten the British Government into muzzling *The Times*. In the Debate on the Address on 3 February 1852 both the Prime Minister and the Earl of Derby (Leader of the Opposition in the Lords) put the official case for limiting the freedom of the press with a decent restraint:

> If, as in these days, the press aspires to exercise the influence of statesmen, the press should remember that they are not free from the corresponding responsibility of statesmen, and that it is incumbent on them, as a sacred duty, to maintain that tone of moderation and respect even in expressing frankly their opinions on foreign affairs which would be required of every man who pretends to guide public opinion.

John Walter III and his editor Delane, still in his early thirties, saw this as a good opportunity to declare the principles of press freedom that they were creating. Walter wrote to Delane:

> A very good article might be written, pointing out the different functions of statesmen and journalists, and showing that although journalists may aspire to be statesmen, still their responsibility is due not to foreign governments, but to the British public, who will say what they think whether cabinets feel themselves hampered or not.

The Times published its counterattack in two leading articles on 6 and 7 February. It was as spectacular a defiance of the established opinion of traditional *bien-pensants* as the ninety-five theses on indulgences that Luther nailed to the church door in Wittenberg. It has become a sacred text of press freedom in the continual struggle between politicians and journalists.

The identity of the writer of a leading article in *The Times* is kept secret. The leader represents the corporate view of the newspaper. Anonymity protects the writer from pressure and lends authority to his opinions. Nevertheless the identity of the writers of every leader is recorded in a leather-bound book kept in the archives. The first blast of the trumpet on the freedom of the press was written by Robert Lowe and Henry Reeve, two of Delane's most powerful leader writers. Lowe wrote leaders for nearly twenty years, while also being a Member of Parliament and holding minor office. He stopped writing *Times* leaders reluctantly when he became Home Secretary and then Chancellor of the Exchequer. Reeve was Clerk of Appeals to the judicial committee of the Privy Council. He worked under Charles Greville, the Clerk of the Council, and was, accordingly, one of the best-informed men in the country on political secrets and Establishment gossip.

But the battle for the freedom of the press was not over – it has to be fought from generation to generation. Two years later, on the eve of the Crimean War, *The Times* caused a European sensation and scandalized politicians by publishing the British ultimatum offering peace or war to the Russians before the Tsar received it. The ultimatum was sent via Paris, and Delane got hold of the gist of it and published it before the courier arrived.

In the House of Lords, Lord Derby returned to the attack, accusing the Prime Minister of leaking. This was improbable and ironic: since *The Times* had gone over to the war party, Delane was hardly on speaking terms with Lord Aberdeen. Derby attacked directly: 'How is it possible that any honourable man, editing a public paper of such circulation as *The Times*, can reconcile to his conscience the act of having made public that which he must have known was intended to be a public secret?'

Delane was at the Bar of the House to hear this speech. *The Times* took up the challenge the next morning:

> We hold ourselves responsible, not to Lord Derby or the House of Lords, but to the people of England, for the accuracy and fitness of that which we think proper to publish. Whatever we conceive to be injurious to the public interests, it is our duty to withhold; but we ourselves are quite as good judges on that point as the leader of the Opposition.

It is the duty of politicians to run the country as best they can. It is the duty of the press to seek out the truth and publish it. These duties are bound occasionally to conflict. In the great political struggles of the nineteenth century *The Times* established this truth: 'A newspaper such as *The Times* is in the position rather to confer than receive favours, and rather to act as the umpire than the tool or the instrument of party'.

Above PUNCH cartoon of 1852.
Right Napoleon III in 1870.

A TIMES leader on press freedom, which it had pioneered, in response to a speech by the Earl of Derby supporting curtailment.
6 FEBRUARY 1852

TO CORRESPONDENTS.

No notice can be taken of anonymous communications. Whatever is intended for insertion must be authenticated by the name and address of the writer; not necessarily for publication, but as a guarantee of his good faith.

We cannot undertake to return rejected communications.

The publication of THE TIMES commenced at half-past 7 o'clock yesterday morning, and finished at 9.

LONDON, FRIDAY, FEBRUARY 6, 1852.

In the House of Lords last night,

The LORD CHANCELLOR, in reply to Lord LYNDHURST, stated that one of a series of bills founded on the recommendations of the Commission on Law Reform would be brought forward in the Lower House this evening.

The Marquis of WESTMEATH communicated to the House HER MAJESTY's reply to the address.

The Duke of WELLINGTON took that opportunity to express his approval of Sir HARRY SMITH's conduct while in command at the Cape. The only error in the operations against the Caffres was, in his opinion, the omission on the part of the General to open roads through the woods which formed the fastnesses of the barbarian enemy.

The Earl of ELLENBOROUGH gave notice that on Tuesday next he should ask questions with regard to the expiration of the East India Company's Charter, and to the state of our relations with the Court of Ava.

The LORD CHANCELLOR laid on the table the Common Law Procedure Amendment Bill, which he described as a measure which would dispense with or simplify all the forms and steps used at present, which would shorten the proceedings, and prevent the delays arising from the technicalities of the law.

Lord CAMPBELL hoped that provision was made in the bill for the diminution of fees.

The LORD CHANCELLOR replied that the bill would lead in a great measure to the diminution of fees.

After some further discussion the bill was read a first time.

Their Lordships then adjourned, after despatching some other business.

In the House of Commons, on the motion of Mr. MACKENZIE, the House went into committee to consider the law respecting public-houses in Scotland, when the Chairman was ordered to move for leave to bring in a bill for the better regulation of those houses.

Leave was given.

On the motion of Mr. FRESHFIELD leave was also given to bring in a bill to consolidate and amend the statutes relating to county rates in England.

After some other business the House adjourned, at 8 o'clock.

The Earl of DERBY remarked with considerable emphasis in his speech on the Address, that as in these days the English press aspires to share the influence of statesmen, so also it must share in the responsibilities of statesmen. If the first of these propositions be established, the second follows as matter of course; and we, of all men, are the least disposed to lower the proper functions or to deny the responsibilities of the power we may derive from the confidence of the public. But, be that power more or less, we cannot admit that its main purpose is to share the labours of statesmanship, or that it is bound by the same limitations, the same duties, the same liabilities as that of the Ministers of the CROWN. The purposes and the duties of the two powers are constantly separate, generally independent, sometimes diametrically opposite. The dignity and the freedom of the press are trammelled from the moment it accepts an ancillary position. To perform its duties with entire independence, and consequently with the utmost public advantage, the press can enter into no close or binding alliances with the statesmen of the day, nor can it surrender its permanent interests to the convenience of the ephemeral power of any Government.

The first duty of the press is to obtain the earliest and most correct intelligence of the events of the time, and instantly, by disclosing them, to make them the common property of the nation. The statesman collects his information secretly and by secret means; he keeps back even the current intelligence of the day with ludicrous precautions, until diplomacy is beaten in the race with publicity. The press lives by disclosures; whatever passes into its keeping becomes a part of the knowledge and the history of our times; it is daily and for ever appealing to the enlightened force of public opinion—anticipating, if possible, the march of events—standing upon the breach between the present and the future, and extending its survey to the horizon of the world. The statesman's duty is precisely the reverse. He cautiously guards from the public eye the information by which his actions and opinions are regulated; he reserves his judgment on passing events till the latest moment, and then he records it in obscure or conventional language; he strictly confines himself, if he be wise, to the practical interests of his own country, or to those bearing immediately upon it; he hazards no rash surmises as to the future; and he concentrates in his own transactions all that power which the press seeks to diffuse over the world. The duty of the one is to speak; of the other to be silent. The one expends itself in discussion; the other tends to action. The one deals mainly with rights and interests; the other with opinions and sentiments. The former is necessarily reserved; the latter essentially free.

It follows, therefore, from this contrast, that the responsibilities of the two powers are as much at variance as their duties. For us, with whom publicity and truth are the air and light of existence, there can be no greater disgrace than to recoil from the frank and accurate disclosure of facts as they are. We are bound to tell the truth as we find it, without fear of consequences—to lend no convenient shelter to acts of injustice and oppression, but to consign them at once to the judgment of the world. Statesmen, it is said, have duties of a nicer order; they are bound to repress the throb of indignation which will rise at the sight of evils and oppressions they cannot avenge; they are prone to pursue particular objects rather than to pledge themselves to general principles; they are forbidden to risk for an instant the important interests confided to their care; and, though the support of public opinion is essential to their success, it is only by rare and occasional efforts that they can attempt to guide it.

If the public writer shares in any degree the influence of the statesman, he shares at least few of those personal objects which constitute so large a part of ordinary statesmanship. He is not toiling or sacrificing the best years of his life and the best faculties of his nature in the pursuit of personal aggrandizement, for none can either reward or corrupt the obscure course of his labours. Even the triumph of his opinions is not accompanied by the applause of a party or the success of a struggle for patronage and power. Those opinions which he has defended, and, so to speak, created, slip from him in the moment of their triumph, and take their stand among established truths. The responsibility he really shares is more nearly akin to that of the economist or the lawyer, whose province is not to frame a system of convenient application to the exigencies of the day, but to investigate truth and to apply it on fixed principles to the affairs of the world.

The responsibility we acknowledge has therefore little in common with that of statesmen, for it is estimated by a totally different standard of rectitude and duty. Of all professions, statesmanship is that in which the greatest laxity of practice is tolerated by the usages of society. Concealment, evasion, factious combinations, the surrender of convictions to party objects, and the systematic pursuit of expediency, are things of daily occurrence among men of the highest character once embarked in the contention of political life. We know not if these be useful or essential parts of statesmanship, and we more than suspect that Lord GREY would confess, by his own experience that they are not so. But we know that they are absolutely destructive to the credit, the power, and the success of a public writer; and he who would traffic with his pen on such terms had better take refuge at once among those mercenary hacks who court the favours of every successive Government. Of all journals, and of all writers, those will obtain the largest measure of public support who have told the truth most constantly and most fearlessly.

Again, the eyes of a Minister are rivetted upon the interests of his own country, and his duties can scarcely be said to extend beyond it. The press owes its first duty to the national interests which it represents, but nothing is indifferent to it which affects the cause of civilization throughout the world. The press of England, standing, as it now does, alone in the enjoyment of entire freedom, would grievously neglect its exalted privileges if it failed to recollect how much is due to the common interests of Europe. It may suit the purposes of statesmen to veil the statue of Liberty, and to mutter some formulary of disingenuous acquiescence in foreign wrongs, dictated by their fears rather than by their convictions; but we prefer to await for our justification the day when the entombed and oppressed liberties of Europe shall once more start into life and array themselves under the standard to which we cling. For to what, after all, are the statesmen of England to look for strength and national power, if injuries and offences rise against us, but to the enlightened resolution of the people of England to uphold the principles on which our own polity and independence are founded? Far from thinking that language of too great energy and alarm has been employed to convey to our own countrymen a true and just impression of the political condition of the great nation which exists within a few miles of our own coasts, we fear that this sudden change in the state of France is still but imperfectly understood in all its formidable consequences to Europe, and possibly to ourselves. It is the unquestionable duty of Ministers to watch over the maintenance of our pacific relations with other States, and to disclaim all that might be erroneously construed into hostile intentions on our part, while they provide efficiently for the independence and security of Britain against all contingencies. But it seems to us the first duty of public writers is to take care that the people of England are not lulled into indifference to the destruction of liberty and the violation of political rights in such a country as France, since that liberty and those rights were the chief pledges of our pacific relations and our common interests. It is our duty to point out danger, however remote, whether it consist in the uncertain policy of a neighbouring State, or in our own disarmed condition; and a far heavier weight of responsibility than we now bear might be laid to our charge if we had neglected to describe the late occurrences in France in their true colours, or if we had affected to acquiesce, from a shortsighted and mistaken policy, in a revolution which calls for the utmost vigilance on the part of this country and of the rest of Europe.

Amid the excitement of Ministerial explanations, and the noise of national defences, the Earl of DERBY's speech on the Address might have slipped through without the notice which in some respects it deserved. But two days of Parliamentary inaction afford us an opportunity of reverting to it. The speech is a pleasing specimen of that serenity and moderation which are so often found or believed to prevail in the most elevated regions of the political atmosphere. While partizans are ready to tear one another to pieces, and know no words bad enough to express their mutual abhorrence, the chiefs have been known to mingle with as much respect and affection as if they felt a grudge to fate for separating such men. Nay, it is even credited that the captains to whom the vulgar ranks are ever looking to feed their antipathies and point their revenge, can meet in friendly intercourse and exchange a few smiles over the absurd, though profitable, enthusiasm of their respective dupes. The truth is such a belief finds a ready home even in the heart of the rude partizan. It is supposed by many that at the very poles, within a circle of impenetrable ice, there are verdant fields, and fluent seas, and warm-blooded men; that in the midst of the ocean, amid tornadoes and monsoons, there is an oasis of perpetual calms; that at the centre of this solid earth there is an open space and a luminous atmosphere; and that there are inhabitants even on the surface of the sun, whom a cool canopy of clouds protects from circumambient fires. Such sweet delusions, if delusions they be, might receive considerable countenance from Lord DERBY's speech, composed apparently with the benevolent design of avoiding the vitals of political controversy and inflicting no incurable wound. There was scarcely a hit in it which might not have been interchanged in the most amicable spirit between the members of the Government themselves, and certainly none that should preclude the hope of Lord DERBY's own ultimate cooperation. As such, of course, it proved an enigma to the most friendly as well as the most hostile understanding, and though his Lordship's supporters had enjoyed the benefit of attending a rehearsal of the speech that very morning, still they are at a loss to understand an antagonism so superfluously fine-tempered and keen.

We will just run over the chief heads of his Lordship's reply, in some such form as he might be supposed to have jotted them down to assist his memory. The arrangement of the Royal speech, he thinks, was rather higgledy piggledy. The prospects of agriculture have not brightened very much since last session. It is true that barley, oats, and stock fetch pretty good prices, but the latest average of wheat is only 39s. 3d.; and though that rise is not more than 5 per cent., the bakers, as if to bring the farmers into odium, have raised the price of bread 20 per cent. His Lordship is still of opinion that a slight duty ought to be laid on foreign corn for the sake of revenue to the State, protection to the grower, and security to the people. He considers that the history of the last four years has added to the probability that some day we shall find ourselves without corn of our own, and treacherously denied any relief out of the granaries of the world. Whether this apprehension is founded on the abundance of the foreign supplies, or on their deficiency, or, if on neither, on what other circumstance, his Lordship does not say. He thinks the treaty between Germany and Denmark a long time coming into execution. As all the Governments of France for the last 60 years have been usurpations, he thinks the tone of the press on the subject most injudicious, and even unjustifiable. It is perfect madness, perhaps treason, to provoke a powerful neighbour and publish our own weakness. LOUIS NAPOLEON, he believes, to be a well-intentioned and particularly peaceable man. As his peaceable intentions, however, may be overruled, it is better to prepare for the worst. The example of France, at all events, is conclusive against democratic institutions. The Cape is in a very unpleasant state, and has been, says his Lordship, for two years. This is the second Commander-in-Chief this Government has recalled. The Irish Government has not succeeded in getting a verdict against the alleged murderers of Mr. BATESON, and meanwhile there has been another attempt. The south of Ireland has been tranquilized, and, at the same time, thinned and wasted by emigration. The constitution of New Zealand has to be doctored once more before it can be put into motion. As to the condition of our people, it is true that many taxes have been repealed, but it is at the price of an income tax. Imports and exports have increased, but prices have not also risen; with larger returns the profits are less and the risks greater. The pledge of another Reform Bill was needless, and any more change in the direction of the former bill objectionable. Such is the nature and extent of the attack made upon Government by the chief of a formidable Opposition. How delightful it is to find with the strength of a giant the gentleness of a child. What with objections that are really sound, and what with those that are nothing to the purpose, what with badinage, and what with professions of sympathy, it is hard to say what place such a speech is to occupy in the science of Parliamentary tactics, and whether it is more designed to annoy the Government or to cajole its adversaries.

When a political chief, at the head of a party "verging on success," gets up on the first night of the session and takes a full survey of the Government, its fortunes, and its measures, it is generally supposed that he is bidding for power. The Earl of DERBY in fact is bidding for power, and the very moderation of his tone betokens a man already trembling with Ministerial responsibility. But we defy any auctioneer of political property to describe the exact terms of the bid in this instance. If the Protectionists have commissioned the Earl of DERBY for this office, we must beg to inform them that, though he has gratified the ears of a polite assembly, and won the praises of his rivals, he has not done the business with which he was charged. He has not yet told the House of Lords what he is prepared to do, and whether he is immediately prepared to do anything at all for the good of the agriculturists. All that he asks for his own followers is, leave to doubt whether, after a few years, it may not perhaps be advisable to levy a duty of 3s. or 4s. a quarter on foreign wheat. This possible, problematical *paulo-post futurum* expedient is the most solid and appreciable item in his budget, or rather the only one—the solitary crumb of hope left at the bottom of his political wallet. But if this is all he can do for his particular friends, what has he to offer the rest of the community? Should the Earl of DERBY and his embryo Cabinet scale the heights of power, the merchants of Liverpool and the manufacturers of Manchester, whose value in the scale of British interests his Lordship should be the first to acknowledge, will find that he has not wholly forgotten their interests. He will take care that their foreign trade shall not exceed the limits of safety. Increased buying and selling, especially with foreign customers, implies increase of credit on all sides, and increase of credit implies increase of risk, increased dependence on the honesty, the judgment, and the success of innumerable parties in the great circle of trade. With abundance, too, comes cheapness. If we export much we cheapen it; if we import much we cheapen it; and if we import and export much at one scale of prices the articles may possibly have to be got rid of at a lower. The Earl of DERBY has considered all this in his truly patriot mind. He has taken counsel of divers unfortunate merchants and manufacturers who knew not when to stop and went out of their depth. Possibly, it has been brought home to him in the non-payment of a few rents in his snug Lancashire property. So, if he ever comes into power, he will take the merchants and manufacturers in leading-strings, that they shall not go too far. He will construct dams and floodgates for the stream of foreign trade, that it shall flow as equably and quietly as the current of the Bridgewater Canal. A well regulated duty on all imports shall check the dangerous excesses of commercial enterprise, and teach the manufacturer to look more at home for the source of his profits. At home he cannot but know his customers better and be more secure. That is all the bid for power the Earl of DERBY makes to the representatives of the great commercial interests, happily in the same future tense and conditional mood as his bid to the agriculturists.

A certain body of men, with whom our readers are now pretty well acquainted as composing the Executive Council of the "Amalgamated Society," have at length issued a "declaration." This document is obviously put in circulation as a full confession of faith, and purports to inform the public of the true "demands and intentions" of the Society as contra-distinguishable from those which have been attributed to it. It is only at the eleventh hour of the dispute that such a manifesto has been extorted, and now that it has appeared, we can only say that it misstates the question before the public, and treats even its own misstatement with insincerity and evasion. They "think it necessary," they observe, "publicly to "declare what they have done, and what "they have not done." Nobody doubted, in the sense here implied, either one point or the other. It was perfectly well known that one notice, and one only, had as yet been served by the Society, in pursuance of its plans. It was perfectly well known that this notice contained only two demands; but it was also perfectly well known that these were only precursors of others, and that more were presently to follow. What the public is concerned with is not the particular precedence given to this or that demand in Mr. W. NEWTON's schemes, but the general character of a society commencing operations of this description. An organized association issues a certain notice to the members of a trade, in consequence of which the trade is brought to a standstill. The country, therefore, is interested in ascertaining not only what form is given to the notice in question, but with what views it has been served, and what is the character of the society which is thus acting. Everybody knows what the Society "have done," or, in other words, how far they have as yet proceeded in their designs. The points to be certified were the principles on which they went to work, and the length to which they intended to carry them.

But even their own declaration, limited as it is, is either falsely or evasively framed. It states that "they have not demanded the discharge of un"skilled workmen. They have not endeavoured "to throw the skilled operative, not belonging to "the Society, out of work, nor have they ever re"commended others to do so. Neither have they "countenanced a system of intimidation having "that object. They do not seek to fix or equalize "wages, but hold the doctrine that wages should "be settled by individual agreement. They do "not endeavour to prevent the introduction of "machinery, but by their skill and labour perfect "and multiply it. They do not attempt to bring "about any of these things, but in their circular "to their employers carefully limit themselves to "the questions of overtime and piecework." Now, in the first place, who are meant by "*they*?" On whose behalf, or in whose persons is this oath of abjuration proffered? Does the Executive Council speak strictly for itself, or for its individual members, or for the "Society" at large? That the "Council" have not yet arrived at the demand for the discharge of unskilled labourers, nobody requires to be told; but to say that the constituent members of the Society have not made this demand, or that its rules do not imperatively commit them to such a policy, or that the Council itself has not implicitly recognised it, is absolutely false.

As concerning this point, there are appended to the "declaration" certain "extracts from the "minutes of the Executive Council" intended to explain its proceedings in the now famous dispute between Messrs. HIBBERT and their men. Now, without reverting to the countless equivocations of Mr. NEWTON and his friends on this subject, we will simply remind the reader of the facts incontestably established. The workmen of Messrs. HIBBERT and PLATT, being mostly constituent members of the Amalgamated Society, disagreed with their employers. The disagreement related almost exclusively to the employment by Messrs. HIBBERT of "unskilled hands" at their machines. A deputation appointed by the Council for the express purpose of seeing that *their* views might be properly carried out, waited upon Messrs. HIBBERT and PLATT, and the result of *this* negotiation, conducted by the Society's nominees on behalf of the Society's members, and authenticated by the signatures of these very individuals, was that all the machines in the establishment should be placed at the disposal of "mechanics" exclusively—that is to say, that all unskilled labourers should be discharged—a respite of seven months in which to effect the arrangement being all the grace that could be obtained. We abstain on the present occasion from reproducing any of the documentary evidence which testifies so conclusively to the real "intentions" on this point of the Amalgamated Society. We merely request the public to observe the simple facts above quoted, and to form his own opinion as to the honesty of the present denial. Is it credible that the "Executive Council," being, as it avows itself, "the organ through which the voice of the "trade is expressed," could be in direct antagonism with what are the manifest opinions of its constituent members? Or if such a case could happen, is it credible that a deputation, selected by the Council for the very purpose of giving effect to its own particular views, could so have falsified its mission as to have signed those notorious terms at Messrs. HIBBERT and PLATT's? One of two things we must inevitably believe. Either Messrs. NEWTON and HEMM, being fully convinced of the injustice of the demand, and specially charged to carry out the like views of the Council, did nevertheless negotiate for the wholesale discharge of labourers, or they thoroughly sympathised in an agitation which they now repudiate. As to the direct action of the "Council" in the matter, it was of course not likely that they would formally prefer in the month of May a demand for which they considered the time to be not yet come in the month of December; but every page of their rules and transactions shows that they coincide in its spirit.

Exactly similar in character are their other disclaimers. They have not recommended, they say, that non-society men should be put out of work, or "countenanced any system of intimidation with that "object." What such men have "countenanced" it is of course very difficult to discover; but thus much is placed beyond reach of dispute, that the rules of the Society not only recommend but enjoin, under fixed penalties, that every man shall refuse to work for a non-society shop, and that an organization should be maintained by which all vacancies in workshops should fall to members first, while it is expressly announced that every operative not supporting the Society would find himself in an "isolated position." How far these plain, undeniable injunctions are consistent with the forbearance now professed, we leave the public to decide; but in respect of "wages," which the Council now declare they "do not seek "to fix or equalize, but leave to be settled by "individual agreement," there never was equivocation more shameless. Of course the point is not touched upon in the demands made by the Council's circular, but nothing can possibly be clearer than that Mr. NEWTON and his colleagues have for years past been perseveringly engaged in keeping up an artificial scale of wages by curtailing the natural supplies of labour, by enjoining workmen to rebate nothing of a certain sum, and by procuring, under threats, the dismissal of those who were willing to work for less. Instead of "holding the doctrine, that "wages should be settled by individual agreement" they have laboured to establish a system for regulating wages by arbitrary rule. They thrust themselves between masters and men to discover the terms of their engagements; they had the assurance to issue printed forms, to be filled up by the amount of wages then or previously received by independent workmen; they sent out their mandates in accordance with their information, and held up to public odium all those who refused to demand the prescribed increase of pay. Documents exemplifying these views, and signed with the names of Mr. NEWTON and his colleagues, are now lying before us.

On the question of overtime we can really tax public patience no more. So repeatedly have we printed what Mr. NEWTON professes, and stated, in his own words, what he actually means, that we cannot again go through the task of exposure. By whatever abuses the practice may be attended the Amalgamated Society have no title to speak. They never said or thought anything of the "overtasked workman" till it was deemed expedient to cheat the public into a misconception of their views. Their motives had reference exclusively to the operative with too little work; their speeches to the operative with too much. They pretended to be caring for the overworked artizan, when they were caring for the "Society man" out of employment. To demands thus insincerely advocated they now profess in their "declaration" to be rigidly "confining themselves;" whereas their own report, issued before the exposure of their schemes, openly acknowledges that these demands are only preliminary, and that "when "they shall have been secured, and secured "effectually," the Society would then proceed to ulterior measures for the "lasting social advan"tage" of its members. The "declaration" of the Council is too late. Their "intentions" are too plainly visible in their own published ordinances to admit of being disguised or qualified now. They may forego their designs and take the benefit of repentance, but they cannot recal their own words or disavow views which they were proclaiming with boastful confidence but six weeks ago.

It was a favourite saying with the late Sir WALTER SCOTT, that "there was nothing like a "good dinner for lubricating business." It may be a humiliating reflection to the more ardent psychologist, that the immortal essence of man should be clipped in its heavenward flight by a base subservience to the more appetites and cravings of our grosser animal nature. Still, we must take that mixed creature, man, as we find him—a compound of mind and matter; an immortal being, if you will, but yet a being who must dine once a-day during his brief sojourn upon earth. There is no need of argument to make good the position that any man who would conduct his affairs in a rational spirit must devote some little consideration to the condition of his digestive organs. Who can bring his mind to bear upon any subject with proper effect while his whole frame is in a state of nervous collapse from the want of proper sustenance at the accustomed hour? What a world of hallucinations and thick-coming fancies,—what an amount of peevishness and petty vexations, are not dispelled by a few spoonfulls of soup and a simple glass of sherry! If a politician had a point to gain or a favour to ask, would he urge his application just before or just after the dinner hours of his patron? What is true of individuals is true of assemblies in a still higher degree. It is idle to expect the attention of great numbers of hungry men to any proposition but one for adjourning to the dinner table with all convenient speed. Our greatest statesmen and orators in either House are so well aware of the fact, that they invariably reserve themselves for that genial hour when the digestion of noble lords and honourable gentlemen is in a certain degree elaborated. Then it is they will listen with complacency and attention to the most lengthy expositions of policy, or the most tedious array of tabulated figures. The House are in good humour. The set speech which would not have been tolerated three hours before is received with the most exemplary patience. Until about half-an-hour after midnight, if any exciting discussion be "on," as the phrase runs, all goes well. Beyond that time we cannot answer for consequences. There is something too much of truth in the complaint made by Colonel SIBTHORP on Wednesday last. "I myself," said the gallant member for Lincoln, "have seen millions "of money voted in this House, and on "some occasions only 15 members were present, 7 "of whom were asleep." The truth is, the interval between two meals has been thoroughly exhausted. The supper hour has arrived. Hon. gentlemen have stolen off from the fascinations of a finance committee to broiled bones and oysters, and probably from the supper-table to bed.

Now, what is the most appropriate method of reconciling these two great public objects? It is necessary that the members of the Legislature should be absent from their posts for as short a time as may be, and that they should dine, and dine well. Experience proves that if they are allowed to slip away about 6 o'clock to their clubs and private residences they are sometimes apt to forget the claim their country has upon their services during the remainder of the evening. After the experience of a few sessions, when the juvenile ardour of the young member has a little worn off, even the House of Commons loses something of its first attraction. He is apt to remain longer than he should do at the hospitable board of some congenial friend, or even to wile away the pleasant hours of early night among the syrens of the drawing-room. Nor, on the other hand, is it to be expected that hon. gentlemen should bring in their pockets a German sausage, or a case of ham-sandwiches, and devour them in their places. Even patriotism has its limits. What is the alternative? The wisdom of the Lower House has discovered that the secret of securing the attendance of members, notwithstanding these prandial difficulties, lies in the careful management of the refreshment-rooms attached to the department of the SERGEANT-AT-ARMS. A most exciting discussion upon this interesting topic occurred the day before yesterday. We confess that it adds not a little to our feeling of security when we see the attention of our senators so completely absorbed in questions of this description. The Gauls may be at the gate, but the Conscript Fathers at least feel no alarm. We find them discussing their chops rather than the dangers of their country. On Tuesday we had the speech from the Throne; on Wednesday the speech from the kitchen. Without the least inclination to speak lightly of dignities, we must frankly confess that, according to the printed reports, the culinary debate appears to have been conducted with more zest than even the discussion upon the Address. Lord MARCUS HILL, an excellent judge of such matters, opened the question to the House with singular ability. The noble Lord did not shrink from statistics, and, for a wonder, statistics were listened to with respect. We are informed that hon. gentlemen can have a portion of soup for 1s.; mutton broth and a chop, 1s.; fish—soles, whiting, and mackerel, 1s.; turbot and codfish, 1s. 6d.; salmon, with sauce, 2s. "Then as to the more sub"stantial parts of the repast—three cutlets, 9d., "&c."

In such fashion began the session of 1852. War may be raging at the Cape, agrarian crime is rife in Ireland, and well nigh the whole of Europe lies groaning under military despotism. The English Parliament meets, and the first subjects of serious discussion we find to be—mutton broth, cutlets, turbot, codfish, and salmon with sauce. The French Autocrat might take a hint from constitutional England for once. Let him convert his Legislative Assembly into a first-rate restaurant. Let his fame the energies of France with filets and matelotes, and saturate the representatives with the produce of the choicest vintages, and his Senate will give him but little cause for anxiety.

COURT CIRCULAR.

WINDSOR, FEB. 5.

The following were the additions to the Royal dinner party yesterday:—

Her Royal Highness the Duchess of Kent, the Marquis and Marchioness of Breadalbane, the Lady in Waiting to the Duchess of Kent, the Baroness de Speath, Lord Cowley, Lord Portman, and the Hon. Mrs. Grey.

The band of the Grenadier Guards attended in the Castle during dinner, and performed the following selection:—

[illegible]

Her Majesty's private band attended afterwards in the evening, and performed the following compositions:—

[illegible]

The Queen walked in the Home Park and Slopes this morning.

The Prince of Wales, the Princess Royal, and the Royal children took walking and pony exercise.

His Royal Highness Prince Albert went out shooting this forenoon, attended by Lieutenant-Colonel the Hon. A. Gordon.

The Marquis of Westminster, Lord Steward of the Household, arrived from London this forenoon at the Castle and had an audience of the Queen to present the address of the House of Lords in answer to Her Majesty's speech on the occasion of opening Parliament. Lord Marcus Hill, the Treasurer of the Household, also arrived from London and had an audience of Her Majesty to present the address from the House of Commons in answer to the speech from the throne on the opening of the present session of Parliament. The Queen was attended by Lord Waterpark, Lord in Waiting.

Invitations have been received by the following personages, who are expected to arrive at the Castle to-day:—The Marquis of Salisbury, the Marquis of Anglesey, the Earl and Countess of Minto, Viscount and Viscountess Mahon, Lord and Lady Ashburton, Lord Broughton, and the Right Hon. T. B. Macaulay.

Lord Cowley left the Castle this afternoon.

M. Van de Weyer, the Belgian Minister, transacted business yesterday at the Foreign-office. His Excellency had an interview with the Right Hon. Henry Labouchere yesterday at the office of the Board of Trade.

Mr. Abbott Lawrence, the American Minister, had an interview with Earl Grey yesterday at the Colonial-office.

Mr. Osborne had an interview with Lord John Russell on Wednesday at his official residence, in Downing-street.

A deputation, consisting of Lord Stradbroke, Sir Edward Gooch, Bart., M.P., Mr. Adair, M.P., and Mr. Peto, M.P., had an interview with Sir George Grey yesterday at the Home-office, on the subject of equalizing the county-rates of the county of Suffolk.

Major-General the Hon. G. Cathcart, Governor of the Cape of Good Hope, had an interview yesterday with Earl Grey. Mr. Cripps had also an interview yesterday with the noble Earl at the Colonial-office.

Mr. Rumbold, M.P., had an interview yesterday with the Right Hon. Henry Labouchere.

Mr. Mostyn, M.P., had an interview yesterday with Sir George Grey.

Despatches were received from the Governor of New South Wales yesterday at the Colonial-office.

INFLUENCE of FREE TRADE on PAUPERISM.

The number of adult ablebodied persons relieved under the Poor Laws on the 1st of January, 1852, is shown in a return made to the House of Commons on Wednesday.

This table is the best index we have to the condition of the labouring poor of the country. With want of employment the number of the adult ablebodied paupers increases most rapidly, while it decreases almost as rapidly with abundance of work, especially if food is cheap at the same time. The annual report from the Poor Law Board last year shows that the total decrease per cent. on the number of adult ablebodied paupers relieved on the 1st of January, 1850, as compared with the 1st of January, 1849, was 15.4; the 1st of January, 1851, as compared with the 1st of January, 1850, was 14.7. The return presented last night shows the decrease per cent. to be, on the 1st of January, 1852, as compared with the 1st of January, 1851, 11.2. Comparing the number of adult ablebodied persons in receipt of relief on the 1st of January, 1852, with the number of the same class in receipt of relief on the 1st of January, 1851, it will be seen by the annexed table that there was an increase in three English counties, and a decrease in 39, reckoning the Yorkshire Ridings as separate counties; and as regards the Welsh counties, an increase in 5 and a decrease in 7.

It may be well to look at the several counties, arranged according to their rates of decrease:—

DECREASE PER CENT.		DECREASE PER CENT.	
Hereford	25.4	Durham	[illegible]
Leicester	21.8	Monmouth	[illegible]
Warwick	21.6	Cambridge	[illegible]
Nottingham	20.0	Suffolk	[illegible]
Surrey	19.1	Cornwall	[illegible]
Salop	17.9	Essex	[illegible]
Dorset	17.5	Huntingdon	[illegible]
Derby	17.4	Lincoln	[illegible]
Middlesex	17.0	Sussex	[illegible]
Devon	16.1	Somerset	[illegible]
Cumberland	15.2	Oxford	[illegible]
Nottingham	14.5	Worcester	[illegible]
Glocester	14.2	York, W. R.	[illegible]
Norfolk	13.9	York, N. R.	[illegible]
Kent	13.2	Stafford	[illegible]
Lancaster	13.2	Bedford	[illegible]
Buckingham	12.5	Northampton	[illegible]
Wilts	11.7	Westmoreland	[illegible]
Hertford	11.4	Wales	[illegible]
Berks	11.3		
Northampton	10.5	Total decrease	11.2
INCREASE PER CENT.		INCREASE PER CENT.	
Chester	1.6	York, E. R.	2.3
Rutland	3.0		

KOSSUTH IN THE UNITED STATES.—Extract from a private letter, dated Baltimore, Jan. 6:—"We have had a very pleasant little excitement with your European adventurer Kossuth. He is certainly a clever talker, but, I fancy, nothing more, for his mistakes here have been of a very serious character. If he had acted with judgment, he might have given us trouble. Had he proceeded modestly and quietly to Washington on his arrival in the country, ingratiated himself with the leading members of Congress and with the Cabinet, he might, under colour of a provision for himself and his comrades in exile, have obtained a large appropriation of money, which he could have used for the purpose he has so much at heart, always supposing that his professions be sincere. But instead of doing this, he has begun by the most arrogant pretensions, personal and political; has made the most incendiary appeals to the people, in anticipation of the decision of Government on the question of intervention in European affairs; has assailed the settled policy of the United States, criticised the wisdom of Washington; and has ended by revolting the good sense of the country from his cause, and in a great measure from all sympathy with himself. Later than at the eleventh hour he has discovered that the American people, both in their private and public capacity, are a little more than a word, he has too fixed rather than shaken the non-intervention policy of the Government, whose course he did not think fit to consult. His power of disturbing is gone, and he has lost sympathy, and will be lucky if he can gain any respectable support."

DESTRUCTION OF THE BROADWALL SAW MILLS.—Yesterday morning, about 6 o'clock, a conflagration, attended with a great destruction of property, broke out in the Broadwall Saw Mills, the property of Messrs. Addison and Co., in Broadwall, Lambeth. The Lambeth Company's engine having yielded an abundant supply of water the engines were called into operation; but by that time the premises of Mr. Clarke, builder, adjacent, together with a [illegible] and stabling, were on fire, and the whole of the mills and the principal portion of the buildings would have been levelled with the ground. It was ascertained that a woman, named [illegible] Clarke, was in the upper room, over the gateway, and unable to effect her escape. Sergeant [illegible] and Police-constable Mahon, No. 28, at the risk of losing their lives, rushed into the building and succeeded in carrying the poor creature down stairs and conveying her to a place of safety. The firemen eventually succeeded in getting the flames subdued, but not until the entire premises, and serious damage done to the surrounding property, especially to those of Mr. Clarke, &c. Unfortunately the principal sufferers were uninsured.

MISS ANNIE ROMER.—The theatrical world has sustained a considerable loss by the sudden death of the young and rising vocalist, Miss Annie Romer, who was the chief supporter of the Haymarket burlesque, which was the permanent prime donne of that theatre. She had been married for about a twelvemonth to Mr. William Brough, the elder of the brothers who [illegible] the Surrey. Although also [illegible] [illegible]

William Howard Russell in the Crimea

Right Letter from Russell to John Thadeus Delane from Varna in June 1854.
Below Painting of Russell writing in his tent in the Crimea.

William Howard Russell's account of the Battle of Balaclava is one of the most famous reports ever to have been published in *The Times*. It brought the phrase 'the thin red line' into the English language – though what Russell actually wrote was: '*they dash on towards that thin red streak topped with a line of steel*'. This is what appeared in his dispatch on 25 October 1854, and what was reprinted in the book of his dispatches. It has suffered mutations, due chiefly to its author, who years later said that the word 'topped' should have been 'tipped'. The phrase 'thin red line' is inaccurate, arising possibly from confusion with Kinglake's 'slender red line'. But it became the cliché of Victorian jingoism, expressing the control and discipline of British riflemen in the face of Lesser Tribes without the Law, whose superiority in numbers could not outweigh the professionalism and valour of the thin red line.

William Howard Russell (1820–1907) was the first great war correspondent and one of the most influential newspapermen ever to have scribbled instant history. He was a reporter for *The Times* for nearly thirty years, covering many great events, including wars in four continents: the Crimean War, the Indian Mutiny, the American Civil War and the Franco-Prussian War.

Russell landed with the first troops at Gallipoli in the Crimea, almost forty years after Waterloo, since when the Army had basked in the memory of that victory, and grown rusty. It was ill-equipped and ill-led; few officers had battle experience, and a great number of them were noble amateurs who had purchased their commissions. From the outset of the campaign Russell's dispatches described in detail the appalling deficiencies of the military machine. Other newspaper correspondents came out to the Crimea, but they generally kept a safe distance from the action. Russell lived in camp with the Army, sharing the privations of the troops, and was often in personal danger. He saw the very last troops leave in 1856. His honest, factual and eloquent reports strongly influenced public opinion.

At this period *The Times* was rising to the height of its power. The new commercial middle classes – its readers – were taking the place of the aristocracy and demanding an increasing say in the running of the country. The profits that *The Times* made from its large sales and advertising revenue made it the first newspaper independent of political subsidy, and therefore free to take its own line for what it saw to be the good of the country. The Thunderer became not merely a recorder of events, but a political giant that influenced events.

John Thadeus Delane, the editor of *The Times*, supported Russell's criticisms of the Army in his leading articles. The Thunderer had a quick success when, following its trenchant argument for a single control of the Army, a new Secretaryship of War to do just that was established in June 1854. Russell's dispatches and Delane's concomitant thunderous leaders led the campaign for an inquiry into the conduct of the Crimean War. In January 1855 the Aberdeen Government fell and Palmerston became Prime Minister. *The Saturday Review* declared: 'No apology is necessary for assuming that this country is ruled by *The Times*'. Queen Victoria deplored the paper's 'infamous attacks'; and Prince Albert called Russell 'a miserable scribbler'.

Russell's writing was done in difficult as well as dangerous conditions. He had to write from his tent in the bitter cold, late into the night by the light of a candle. Paper was scarce, and he was driven to mix his own ink out of gunpowder. On one occasion a gale swept the headquarters staff area, which was beaten flat; Russell was 'pressed down and half stifled by the heavy folds of wet canvas which beat us about the head with the greatest fury'. In such circumstances and the hurly-burly of battle, we are not

Russell's first report, by telegraph, on the charge of the Light Brigade (column 5). On the same page is a leading article on the disaster (columns 1 and 2).
11 NOVEMBER 1854

Page 48
Russell's report (column 5) of Florence Nightingale's arrival in the Crimea. She undertook her mission of mercy as a result of Russell's description of the war in THE TIMES.
18 NOVEMBER 1854

TO CORRESPONDENTS.

No notice can be taken of anonymous communications. Whatever is intended for insertion must be authenticated by the name and address of the writer; not necessarily for publication, but as a guarantee of his good faith.

We cannot undertake to return rejected communications.

The publication of THE TIMES commenced at 5 o'clock yesterday morning, and finished at 11.

LONDON, SATURDAY, NOVEMBER 11, 1854.

We have received with much regret from our correspondent in the Crimea a telegraphic despatch which proves that the loss sustained by the allies in the encounter of the 25th on the heights of Balaklava was more serious than recent reports had led us to believe. According to this account the surprise of the Turkish position had to be redeemed by the loss of 600 cavalry and 400 light infantry. The loss of the cavalry must, according to Lord STRATFORD's account, have fallen almost entirely on the English army; as to the light infantry, we are as yet uncertain whether in that number is comprehended any part of the casualties of our allies.

A great nation in arms for a great cause must bear without repining the inevitable vicissitudes of war—neither elated by prosperity nor depressed by adverse fortune. The blood which has been shed has not flowed in vain. The brave soldiers we have lost nobly sacrificed their lives in arresting the course of an operation the success of which would have cut off our communication with our fleet, turned our position, and compromised the safety of the whole army. If the price paid has been heavy the result was worthy of so great a sacrifice. At whatever cost, the attack has been repulsed after its first most unexpected success, and the enemy have shown no inclination to renew it. Never was a more costly sacrifice made for a more worthy object. We trust before the publication of our next impression to be furnished with the fullest details, which will at any rate terminate the dreadful anxiety of families and friends, and put an end to the long and lingering torture endured by so many since Lord STRATFORD's despatch first informed us of the loss sustained in these severe skirmishes.

For ourselves, being unwilling to forestall by conjecture the sad details which we shall soon be in a condition to give from undoubted authority, we avail ourselves of this opportunity only to press upon the attention of Government some considerations as to our position in the Crimea, and the measures it suggests, which do not, indeed, depend upon the intelligence we have just communicated, but to which it lends additional force and urgency. We have never deluded ourselves with the notion that the enterprise we have undertaken was a slight or an easy one. Two vast fleets have swept our enemy's ships from the sea, and carried the English flag to regions it never visited before, beyond the limits of the Polar Circle to the north, and to the shores of the fabled land of JASON and MEDEA to the east. What might have been less expected from us, we have sent out an army, moderate in numbers, yet so admirably disciplined and equipped, that it has achieved, as soon as brought into contact with real war, successes to be expected only from the steadiness and discipline of veteran troops. So far, then, no one whose mind is free from party or personal bitterness can doubt that the efforts of this country have been in every way worthy of her past fame and her present position. Still it must be recollected that we have had to encounter difficulties and drawbacks which in their full magnitude no human foresight anticipated. The year has been one of sickness and mortality, spread with singular impartiality over the whole surface of the globe. Had our troops remained at home they would doubtless have contributed their tale of victims to the cholera; and of course the transfer to an eastern climate, with the adverse sanitary conditions of a life under canvass, were not likely to diminish the loss. Malignant fever, too, has done its work upon our little army; and it has also had to undergo that decimation which every army must bear in passing from peace to war, by the loss of a considerable number of soldiers whose constitutions are not sufficiently robust to withstand the fatigues and exposure of a campaign. We are carrying on our part of the siege of Sebastopol with an army which sickness, the bloody victory of the Alma, and the inevitable consumption of life by an army acting in the face of an enemy, have reduced to little more than one-half of the number with which we landed in the Crimea on the 14th of September. We are obliged to eke out the scanty numbers of our force by draughts from the fleet, and when our ships were called upon to attack the Russian forts their crews, weakened by cholera and by the numbers detached to serve in the siege, did not suffice to work the whole of their guns. The result of all these things is, that we have not a man too many in the Crimea—nay, that we are short-handed both on shore and afloat, and NEED LARGE REINFORCEMENTS.

We are aware that Ministers have not been unmindful of this necessity. We believe that about 4,000 men have been sent to reinforce Lord RAGLAN, and that, besides the Algiers, other ships are to be despatched to augment the power of our fleet. But these reinforcements are not made on a scale and with a promptness worthy of this great emergency. We are playing boldly for a stake of enormous magnitude. We need not point out the immense results which will follow success in the Crimea, nor the enormous evils which would result from even a partial check or failure. It would be almost impossible to exaggerate either the one or the other. We have, then, every motive to put forth our whole strength. Those "men in England "who do no work to-day" might be of the most inestimable service in the decision of this great contest. Our aim should be not only to reduce Sebastopol itself, but all the forts in its neighbourhood, and to compel the covering army of the Russians to evacuate the peninsula or to lay down their arms. For these purposes a far greater increase of force than our army or fleet have yet received is absolutely necessary, and ought, we contend, to be instantly supplied. Why should we leave in the Euxine a single sailing man-of-war to be driven helplessly about by the tempests which may soon be expected, and perhaps drifted on the coast of Asia Minor, at the very moment when her services are most needed in the Crimea? Why waste our men and stores in manning machines so obsolete in their construction and so useless in action? Why not send out the steam fleet as it arrives from the Baltic, to enable us to be masters of the Euxine during the stormy season of the year, and to keep up in every part of it the unintermitted terror of our arms? We believe we have some 20,000 soldiers at home, besides some thousands more who might be drawn from our garrisons in the Mediterranean, their place being supplied, if necessary, by militia, ready and willing to discharge this duty. Why should not all that is disposable of this force be thrown at once on the shores of the Crimea? Why should our soldiers and sailors be worn out with incessant fatigue by day and night in the effort to make 16,000 men discharge the duty which was intended for 30,000? The defence of Sebastopol has proved more obstinate than was expected, its forts are stronger, its artillery heavier, its powers of reparation far greater. Let our spirits and our efforts rise with the emergency, and, if we have been met by unexpected difficulties, let us encounter them with corresponding energy. In these happy islands we need not a single soldier to enforce obedience to the law, nor loyalty to the CROWN. It is our pride that the truncheon of the policeman would gain no additional power from the bayonet of the soldier. We fear no invasion from foreign countries, and, if we did, we have a force sufficient to defend our shores without the aid of a regular army. We have no motive to keep our soldiers here, and every conceivable inducement to send them to the East. Even if there were hazard, which there is not, in reinforcing Lord RAGLAN immediately with 15,000 soldiers and a whole fleet of steamships, that hazard is infinitely less than the risk of leaving an army whose efficiency is reduced so low by so many concurrent causes to achieve a tremendous siege, to be succeeded by another, and then, probably, by a winter campaign, without adequate reinforcements. The student of ancient history well knows that it was neither the sword of MARCELLUS nor the shield of FABIUS that forced HANNIBAL from the possession of Italy. It was the paltry policy of the envious Carthaginian Senate, in withholding succours till they were too late to turn the fortune of the war, that ruined the plans of that great general, exhausted by a hundred victories, and left to achieve the work he had so nobly begun with no other aid than the *prestige* of so many glorious, but enfeebling triumphs.

Two of the declarations made at the civic banquet on Thursday will command the hearty approval of the whole country. Lord HARDINGE acknowledged that every incident of the campaign in the Crimea attested the valour and discipline of the British army, while Lord ABERDEEN declared that HER MAJESTY's Ministers would never be found fainthearted or irresolute in the prosecution of the war. In these avowals the CZAR may read the feelings of the entire British nation. We cannot anticipate that the fortune of war will be always and invariably in our favour; we do not expect that battles are to be won without cost, or towns taken without effort; but we are resolved to do our duty without flinching, and we see good reason for confidence in the result.

Meantime the operations before Sebastopol appear to be surely but slowly advancing. If we are to trust Prince MENSCHIKOFF's report, no "visible result" had attended the exertions of the allies up to the evening of the 3d, but it is easy to see that this bulletin contains only a partial representation of the truth. We may so far believe in its announcements as to suppose that, up to the date specified, no regular assault had been made by the besiegers; but we know from unquestionable information that their operations had produced "results" of most material importance,—that the breaching batteries had been advanced within a short distance of the defences, that the town had been in flames, and that the Russian losses were enormous. Whether the fire of the English had really, as the bulletin proceeds to state, "become weaker," is a very doubtful point, but it is not impossible that the immense expenditure of ammunition may have suggested a slower and more deliberate order of firing. The stores of shot and shell originally sent out were large beyond example—twice as large, we believe, as the highest estimate of such requirements demanded—but the consumption has been also beyond precedent; and, though large supplies have reached Balaklava since the commencement of the siege, economy may, perhaps, have become advisable. The details of the combat of the 25th, in which, after a most severe loss of light infantry and cavalry on our side, the enemy was repulsed, are as yet imperfectly known. It appears that the Russians attacked in great force the Turkish redoubts near Balaklava, that they got possession of some of them, and that in the engagement which ensued our cavalry suffered much loss. It is also known that this attack was conducted by General LIPRANDI, probably at the head of the relieving army, but so much still remains obscure that it seems as yet hardly certain if the Russians have maintained any permanent footing in the works from which the Turks were expelled. According to some reports, though they were driven out of one or two of the redoubts, they retained possession of others, and to this assumption we must probably refer the telegraphic announcement that on the 27th "the allies attacked General LIPRANDI's "corps without effect." Such an operation would appear to imply that the Russian commander was still established somewhere in the neighbourhood of our position, and that we had vainly endeavoured to dislodge him. On the other hand, it is not easy to understand how the enemy, after having been fairly "repulsed," as, by all accounts, was the case, could have contrived to retain certain small earthworks, indifferently armed, in the very teeth of the allied forces assembled to repulse him. If the Russians could drive the Turks from these positions without a struggle, it is natural to presume that the French and English could, if the effort had been necessary, have dealt successfully with the Russians; and, indeed, we are assured by other accounts that General LIPRANDI had drawn off his troops and retired to Bakshiserai.

As far therefore as regards the general effect of LIPRANDI's attack, we think it plain, even from the Russian reports, that it was a failure, and that the operations of the siege were not disturbed by the attempt. We should be disposed to carry the inference still further, and to conclude that if General LIPRANDI had indeed effectually established himself in an offensive position on our flank, Prince MENSCHIKOFF would hardly be content with announcing to his Imperial master that "nothing "decisive" had occurred, and that the relative situations of the belligerents remained without change. If any position of importance had been really thus occupied by the Russians, it seems reasonable to suppose that between the 25th ult., when the occupation took place, and the 3d inst., up to which date our information from Russian sources extends, some attempts would have been made to dislodge the enemy, and fighting enough to demand a more particular notice have ensued. As it is, though the St. Petersburg bulletins still speak of two redoubts as being "retained and "fortified," we learn nothing, even from Russian accounts, except that something ineffectual was attempted on the 27th, while it is plainly acknowledged that for a whole week afterwards—*i. e.* up to the 3d inst., the operations of the allies against Sebastopol proceeded exactly as before.

With the progress of these operations there is no reason to be dissatisfied, though the public impatience is easily intelligible. It was conceived, for the moment, after the battle of the Alma, that our troops were in full pursuit of a beaten and demoralized army, retiring upon a panicstricken town. This, indeed, was little more than the truth, but sufficient regard was not paid to other circumstances telling strongly in favour of the enemy. Sebastopol, independently of its natural and external defences, contained one of the largest arsenals in the world, and an almost inexhaustible supply of the implements and munitions of war. Reinforcements of men, too, were close at hand, and when battalion after battalion had been poured into the place the result was a fresh army, strongly posted, ably led, and taught by skilful engineers how to improve to the utmost the extraordinary resources of the town. Accordingly, when we thought that our guns and our numbers would overpower those of the enemy, we found him as strong as ourselves, and we are now conducting the siege of this redoubtable fortress with resolution indeed to win, and with good prospect of such an issue, but with even fewer advantages than such operations are generally held to require.

The proper observance of Sunday is one of those things that must necessarily come under the law of the land. That has never been disputed by any reasonable person who thinks about the matter. As little can it be doubted that the nature of the observance must be dictated with a proper regard to the public convenience and the purposes of the day. Those purposes are, the periodical rest which experience shows man to require, both for the refreshing of his mental and bodily powers, and also an opportunity for those religious acts and meditations which cannot but be much assisted by quiet and freedom from the ordinary business of the world. Supposing that as a matter of fact everybody could go to church on Sunday as often as he pleased, as quietly as he pleased, and that no scandals or disorders of any kind occurred on the Sunday, then there would, perhaps, be no reason for imposing any restrictions on travelling, on trade, on the sale of refreshments and liquors, the opening of publichouses, or anything else thought allowable on a week day. The matter of fact, however, is, unfortunately, the other way, for the institution of Sunday, enforced as it is both by custom and by law, has led, particularly, as it appears, in the great cities of Scotland, to a lamentable amount of dissipation, drunkenness, disorder, and even crime. It is found that the greater part of the population of these cities seldom enter places of worship, and, having no taste for religious reading or meditation, must go out of doors for some means of filling up the Sabbatical void. Once out of doors, they find too many people catering without scruple for their pleasure, in the lowest sense of that word. What should therefore be, as it has been called, "the "rest of Heaven," is perverted into something quite the contrary; and the better class of people who have been taught by their forefathers, and not less by the State, that the Sabbath is a day to be observed with great sanctity, abstraction, and quiet, justly complain that they are not protected, but rather hindered, in the observance of a lawful institution. Viewing the law on one side, and the practice on the other, one cannot but be struck with a great inconsistency, pressing hard on those who desire to follow their duty and the law, and then find themselves discouraged, impeded, and even rendered ridiculous by standing few among many. Certainly this is a state of things that should not be endured. Conscience itself is not always consistent and strong, but it is a great evil when the law is still more illusive and weak. Indeed, the power of religion and moral obligation is altogether apt to be weakened by the spectacle of a State which does not know whether to say a thing or not; which lays heavy burdens on the tender-minded and scrupulous, and is itself the first to fly from the responsibility it has created or enforced.

We are not surprised, then, but rather we take it as a great proof of Scotch principle, Scotch consistency, Scotch fairness, and, so to speak, Scotch "hardness of head," that two thousand people met the other day in the northern metropolis for the purpose of reviewing the operation of the "FORBES MACKENZIE Act." That measure has been partly successful, partly unsuccessful, or, rather, it has done a great deal, and only has not done as much as it might reasonably be expected to do. In the city of Edinburgh it has caused a very great diminution of police cases evidently arising out of Sunday drinking. We published the important and satisfactory statistics of the question in a letter some time since, and every succeeding Sunday has added to the testimony in favour of the act. We shall not repeat the figures, because figures are always open to cavil, and we will only say that, without any predilection in favour of what is called the Puritanical Sabbath, and without any disposition to enforce Christianity by law, we are quite satisfied, on the evidence of the calculations given at the Edinburgh meeting, that the FORBES MACKENZIE Act has promoted temperance, public order, and morality on the sacred day of worship and rest. It was to be expected that it should do so, and it has done so. Undoubtedly many a poor creature turns into the gin-shop, or the grocer's shop—for they have long been identical in Scotland—simply because the suspension of work leaves him nothing else to do on Sunday. It is all very well to talk of families and homes, but many of these poor fellows have neither families nor homes, nor any other place where they can go, as one of ourselves goes to his library or the family fireside. Even those altars of the domestic affections that many of us spend a life in raising, and that figure so largely in the works of modern moralists, do not always sustain the charm with which we are wont to invest them. Gentlemen will often run away from their firesides on a Sunday to a club or a friend in the country, or to Brighton, or anywhere for change. The hard-worked working man has no such alternatives. The gin-shop is often his only chance of cheer, of company, of outward light and of inward refreshment. We are strongly of opinion that it ought not to be, and that in fact it ought to be closed, and other places of innocent resort found for him. But, as a first step, unquestionably the poor working man ought not to be forbidden to work and be shut out of shops on Sunday, and then, by a strange perversity, find the ginshop the only place open to him. This is, in fact, to encourage and sanction Sunday drinking with the utmost countenance of the law. The actual result of the act for closing the publichouses in Scotland is quite what we expected. We said, however, that the act had been partially unsuccessful. That is for a very sufficient reason. It has been only partially put in force. With the culpable connivance of the authorities the law has not been enforced within nearly two-thirds of the police bounds of the city of Edinburgh. Of course, it is but natural that crime, on the whole, should not be found much affected by a law not carried out in those very parts of the city and its suburbs where crime is chiefly concocted and matured, and where there are the most opportunities for its commission. While the magistrates within the Royalty carry out the act, they find themselves besieged by a circle of neglect, drunkenness, and crime outside the Royalty, pervading a population of nearly 100,000. At Glasgow, Paisley, and Brechin the act has fair play, and its results are less qualified.

Of course, we do not forget in these remarks that the Sabbath was made for man, and not man for the Sabbath. In our humble opinion Sunday observance is a matter for reasonable arrangement, and that any man absolutely needing locomotion, refreshment, and even moderate recreation on that day, has as much right to expect it as the ox or the ass to be drawn out of the pit, or the sick to be healed. Point out any case of necessity, and that case must be met, either by a special provision of the act, or by a dispensing power in the hands of the magistrates. We say that it must be met, simply because so long as it is not met it will give a character of extravagance and absurdity to any general enactment, and eventually lead to its repeal. When a gentleman is brought to a standstill within fifty miles of his dying child on a "Sabbath-eve," or when a man compelled by the inexorable public to work all Sunday night at an employment draining his strength, and requiring it to be continually recruited, cannot get a glass of the mildest stimulant, then a stigma and a scandal is brought upon law, for nature and common sense will not endure so tyrannical a discipline. The public convenience is the best rule in these questions, and, though individuals must continually be called on to sacrifice their advantage or their comfort to the general good, it will never be tolerated that a lawful, honourable, and necessary employment shall be accompanied with severe and unnecessary hardships, simply through the rigid application of a law. There can be no possible analogy between the case of a man hard at work in the way of a necessary calling, and that of an idle man seeking early in the day for a stimulus which he has no occasion for, and had better be without.

There is, of course, much practical difficulty in meeting particular cases without letting in large classes, or, in other words, devising exemptions which shall not be fatal to the measure. That is a difficulty. The application of common sense always is difficult, much more difficult than the application of a PROCRUSTEAN rule which shall convict itself of folly at once. For a hundred who can reason in an exact and mathematical manner only one can reason sensibly and wisely, and in that ratio is wise legislation more difficult than laws done by rule of three. Nevertheless, this is the only legislation that human nature will tolerate or that will endure.

A Cabinet Council was held yesterday afternoon at the Foreign-office, Downing-street. It was attended by the Earl of Aberdeen, Lord John Russell, the Lord Chancellor, the Duke of Argyll, Viscount Palmerston, the Earl of Clarendon, Sir George Grey, the Duke of Newcastle, the Chancellor of the Exchequer, Sir James Graham, Sir Charles Wood, the Right Hon. Sidney Herbert, Sir William Molesworth, and Earl Granville. The Council sat near three hours.

THE CIVIL SERVICE.—Board of Trade Department Register and Record-office, Custom-house, London.—Mr. Williamson, Senior Third-class Clerk, has been appointed Second-class Clerk, *vice* J. Akers, deceased; Mr. William Courtis, Second Division of Third-class Clerks, has been appointed Third-class Clerk, *vice* R. Garrett, deceased. Messrs. Alan, Stoneham, and Leaker, extra clerks, have been appointed Fourth-class Clerks. Customs—Mr. C. Smith has been appointed principal coast officer at Fareham; Mr. F. C. Hammond has been appointed extra clerk in London; and Mr. A. Thompson has been appointed clerk at Liverpool. A clerkship for general business is vacant at Liverpool, *vice* W. B. Poole, appointed clerk and searcher at Lancaster. Salary 70*l.* a-year. Mr. John Boyle, collector of Port Glasgow, has retired, after having completed 42 years of service, upon a superannuated allowance of 265*l.* per annum. The appointment of postmaster at Nottingham is vacant, caused by the death of Mr. O. J. Oldknow, salary 200*l.* per annum, the gift of the Postmaster-General. Mr. D. T. Groom, surveyor of taxes, Bristol, has been appointed surveyor at Liverpool, *vice* Cottrill. Mr. J. Sanderson, surveyor at Hull, has been promoted to be surveyor of Rochdale, Lancashire, *vice* Amery, promoted to Manchester. Mr. Yeates, surveyor at Truro, has been promoted to be surveyor at Bristol, *vice* Groom, promoted to Liverpool.—*Civil Service Gazette.*

THE CUSTOMS, London.—Mr. R. Woodifield, Inspector-General of the Imports and Exports at the Custom-house, after upwards of half-a-century's labour in the public service retires on his full salary of 900*l.* per annum. He has proved himself to be an invaluable public servant, and has gained the highest esteem from all parties with whom his official career has brought him in contact.—*Civil Service Gazette.*

SECOND EDITION.

THE TIMES-OFFICE, Saturday Morning.

THE ATTACK ON BALAKLAVA.

(BY SUBMARINE AND BRITISH TELEGRAPH.)

We have received from our correspondent at Marseilles the following despatch, which had reached that port by the French post steamer which left Constantinople on the 30th ult:—

"Your correspondent in the army before Sebastopol writes on the 28th that 607 light infantry were engaged in the affair of the 25th, and that only 198 returned.

"Eight hundred cavalry were engaged, of whom only 200 returned.

"Nine officers were killed, 21 wounded, and 4 were missing.

"The 17th Lancers were almost destroyed.

"We require reinforcements."

We have received the following from our correspondent at Vienna, dated Friday morning:—

"According to authentic advices of the 28th ult. from Balaklava, a council of war was held on the preceding day, when it was resolved not to attempt to storm Sebastopol until the effect of the siege guns had been fairly tried.

"It is considered highly probable that a battle will be fought with the Russians under General Liprandi before Sebastopol is stormed.

"The Russian reinforcements are estimated at 30,000 men."

VIENNA, FRIDAY EVENING.

The following telegraphic despatch has been circulated in Vienna. It must be received with the greatest caution:—

"CZERNOWITZ, Nov. 9.

"A most violent attack has been made on Sebastopol.

"There was a conflagration in the town, which the garrison could not extinguish.

"Prince Menschikoff had demanded an armistice of 12 hours, which was refused."

The *Journal de St. Petersbourg* of the 2d contains Prince Menschikoff's report of the above disastrous affair. It is as follows, and is dated the 25th of October:—

"His Majesty the Emperor has just received the following report from Aide-de-Camp-General Prince Menschikoff, dated the 25th of October:—

"'Our offensive operations against the besiegers began to-day, and were crowned with success.

"'Lieutenant-General Liprandi had orders to attack, with the division under his charge, the private intrenched camp of the enemy which defends the route from Sebastopol to Balaklava.

"'This operation was executed by him this morning in a brilliant manner. Four redoubts, in which we captured 11 pieces of artillery, are now in our possession.

"'The principal redoubt of the enemy, which was defended by the Turks, was carried by assault by the Azoff Regiment of Infantry, under the command of Major-General Semiakine, commander of the brigade, and the commander of the regiment, Colonel de Krudener, who distinguished himself in this affair.

"'The English cavalry also opposed our detachment. Under the command of Lord Cardigan, it charged with extraordinary impetuosity the brigade of Hussars of the 6th Division of Cavalry, but, taken in flank by four squadrons of the combined regiment of Lancers in reserve, and forced upon the cross-fire of shot of the artillery of the 12th and 16th Divisions of Infantry, and upon that of the men armed with carbines of the first brigade of the latter division, it suffered considerable loss.

"'The 1st brigade of the 16th Division, under the command of Major-General Jabokritsky in person, was pushed forward in advance to prevent the enemy from turning the detachment of General Liprandi. At the same time that it attacked our Hussars, the English cavalry rushed at a gallop upon the battery of position No. 3 of the Don, where some of the gunners were put to the sword.

"'The loss of our infantry in this affair does not exceed, as it appears to me, 300 men both in killed and wounded.

"'As to that of the cavalry and artillery, it is not yet known even by conjecture.

"'Major-General Khaletsky, commander of the regiment of Hussars of his Imperial Highness Prince Nicholas Maximilianovitch, was wounded by a sword on the ear and arm.

"'It is difficult to calculate with certainty the loss of the enemy, but it is nevertheless believed that the English cavalry lost 500 men. We made prisoners of about 60 English, including one superior and two subaltern officers.

"'Of the four redoubts captured from the enemy two will be demolished to-night, and the other two will be more strongly fortified, in order to maintain that position, from which an attack may be made upon the village of Kadekoi, where the route passes which leads from the enemy's camp to Balaklava. Up to this time the artillery of the ramparts of Sebastopol has not at all yielded to the batteries of the besiegers, but the shells and the incendiary projectiles of the latter have burnt 40 small houses in the locality of the artillery.

"'This preliminary report, and the information collected by me upon the spot, will be delivered to your Imperial Majesty by my aide-de-camp, captain of a corvette belonging to the crew of Baron de Willebrandt, who was with Lieutenant-General Liprandi.

"'I have the honour, in conclusion, to inform your Imperial Majesty that I took upon myself to thank, in your Majesty's name, upon the field of battle, all the troops who distinguished themselves on this day.'"

EXPRESS FROM PARIS.

The following is our Paris correspondent's letter, dated yesterday, 6 p.m.:—

I noticed yesterday the movement of bodies of troops in the south of France. I am now assured that orders have been given for the immediate embarcation at Marseilles and Toulon of two divisions for the Crimea. These two divisions would amount to about 30,000 men. It was rumoured some six or seven days ago that the question of altogether withdrawing the army from the Crimea was mooted by one of the Ministers during a Cabinet Council. This rumour has been repeated to-day, and the name of the Minister, who is not unlikely to have suggested such a measure, mentioned. I cannot vouch for the correctness of the report; but it is also affirmed that the Emperor at once cut the matter short, and stopped the mouth of the Minister by declaring that, if necessary, he would send 100,000 men more rather than give up Sebastopol. The order I have just alluded to proves that the war will be carried on with energy until this great object is attained.

This is the moment for the most disheartening rumours. They are circulated abundantly, and are believed with too fatal facility. It is said that the amount of reinforcements reported to have reached the Russian head-quarters is very considerable, and that despatches to that effect have been received by the Government. There is nothing extraordinary in the fact of the Russians receiving reinforcements, seeing that Perekop is still open to them. Why that door has not been shut up I have not seen satisfactorily explained. Whether the shallowness of the water prevents ships from reaching close to the shore, or that the Allied army could not afford to detach a sufficient force to that point, I know not, but it is certain that as long as Perekop lies open the Russian army can be constantly reinforced.

The same unmanly feeling of discouragement which I noticed yesterday still prevails among a certain portion of the Paris public, and I fear that the panic is encouraged by those who ought, on the contrary, to inspire hope in the prosperous issue of a cause so just as the one we are engaged in. It is difficult to discover any good grounds for such a state of things. The fable of the Tatar had deluded us into a belief that Sebastopol was not only taken, but even when the error was discovered, that it might yet be taken by a *coup de main*; and now when we are obliged to reduce it by the slow but certain process of a regular siege, we lament as if we had hitherto met with nothing but disaster and defeat; and in our absurd impatience we even forget that such a battle as the Alma has been fought and won. There is nothing really unsatisfactory in our position. We have, under enormous difficulties, and in the face of formidable fortresses, and liable to be harassed every moment by a large army, successively pushed our approaches close to the defences. Our losses are shown not to be so great as was supposed, and as might have been expected under the circumstances. We have beaten the Russians wherever we have encountered them, from the heights of the Alma to the last sortie from Sebastopol. We have proved ourselves superior to them with all our disadvantages; and, whether they met us in the open day, or stealthily approached us in the darkness of the night, we have invariably repulsed them. Much of the murmuring and discontent we now witness may, perhaps, be attributed to the fact of one date after another being fixed in the accounts published in the *Moniteur* for the taking of Sebastopol. The nervous public, finding that neither on the 23d, nor the 25th, nor the 28th October, nor, as recently announced, on the 1st or 2d of November, has the event taken place, are naturally disappointed, and begin to think either that the Generals are not equal to their task, or that the obstacles are too formidable to be overcome. A letter from a superior officer of the army, dated the 28th, before Sebastopol, which has reached Paris this day, speaks nearly in positive terms of the 2d instant as the day when it must fall; and this confident assurance has, like so many others, been disappointed. But nothing, not even the certainty of failure, can justify the feeling of despondency which has prevailed here for some days past.

A Hamburg letter of the 7th inst. says,—

"It appears positive that the two Grand Dukes Nicholas and Michael of Russia, who had first proceeded to Odessa and Kischenef, subsequently left for the Crimea, where they must have arrived at this moment. But the organic ukase of 1827, which fixes the supreme hierarchy as respects the members of the Imperial family, stipulating that the sons of the Emperor can never be placed under the command of a General, it may be inferred that the two Grand Dukes in undertaking a journey to the Crimea have no other object but to show themselves to the army, and to inquire into the real state of affairs at the seat of war."

We read in the *Sentinelle Toulonnaise* of the 7th inst.:—

"Orders arrived yesterday for the two ships Donawerth and Turenne to complete their armament and sail immediately for the East. All hands were put in requisition to expedite their departure. The Semillante and Vengeance are also to be despatched to the East without delay. The greatest activity prevails in this port. The Turenne took on board this morning 669 men, and the Donawerth, 559, making in all 1,228 men belonging to different corps."

The *Courrier de Lyons* of the 9th inst., gives the following:—

"The formation of the army at Sathonay is decided on. The number of troops to assemble there will amount to about 24,000. Having found that barracks answered much better in winter than tents the Government has entered into contracts for the timber necessary and a certain quantity of zinc, destined probably for the roofs."

The *Journal de Toulon* of the 7th inst. states:—

"The expedition to Bomarsund will have been the means of embellishing the Church of Muret with a trophy taken in that island. Within the precincts of the principal fort was a beautiful chapel, the top of which was placed a large gilt globe, surmounted by a brass cross. When the destruction of the fortress was resolved upon, and when the engineers were about to spring the mines, General Niel, being anxious to preserve this cross, ordered a few sappers to take it down. Five or six immediately ascended the roof, and by great skill and boldness managed to remove it uninjured. The General afterwards obtained permission to bestow it on the Church of Muret, his native town. The gift was received by his fellow townsmen with the liveliest satisfaction."

The Emperor has given orders to build six theatres at the Camp of Boulogne, and four at St. Omer. Mr. Pellegrin, former manager of the provincial theatres, is charged with this organization. All the expenses are to be defrayed by the Emperor's private purse.

The *Moniteur* publishes the following monthly debtor and creditor account of the Bank of France, made up to Thursday last:—

DEBTOR.	f.	c.
Capital of the Bank ...	91,250,000	0
Reserve of the Bank ...	12,980,750	14
Reserve of the Bank in Landed Property	4,000,000	0
Bank-notes in circulation ...	485,445,400	0
Ditto of the Branch Banks ...	149,287,000	0
Bank-notes to order ...	6,531,191	32
Receipts payable at sight ...	10,446,065	0
Treasury account current creditor ...	58,249,837	57
Sundry accounts current ...	110,613,281	1
Ditto with the Branch Banks ...	25,741,601	6
Dividends payable ...	647,577	25
Discounts and sundry interests ...	5,619,166	30
Commission on deposits ...	22,750	65
Re-discounted during the last six months	916,188	68
Protested bills...	219,008	43
Sundries ...	7,061,103	49
	969,034,212	15

CREDITOR.	f.	c.
Cash in hand ...	287,220,201	[illegible]
Cash in the Branch Banks ...	150,101,219	[illegible]
Commercial Bills overdue ...	434,121	7
Commercial Bills discounted, but not yet due, of which 59,858,308f. 31c. were received from the Branch Banks ...	118,647,311	[illegible]
Ditto in the Branch Banks ...	151,244,349	[illegible]
Advanced on deposit of bullion ...	982,160	0
Ditto by the Branch Banks ...	1,136,583	0
Advanced on French public securities ...	21,325,936	15
Ditto by the Branch Banks ...	3,934,940	0
Advanced on railway securities ...	47,520,600	0
Ditto by the Branch Banks ...	14,676,100	0
Advanced to the State on the treaty of June 30, 1848 ...	63,000,000	0
Discount of Treasury Bonds ...	39,000,000	0
Government Stock reserved ...	10,000,000	0
Ditto disposable ...	53,449,559	81
Hotel and furniture of the Bank ...	4,000,000	0
Landed property of the Branch Banks ...	3,823,719	0
Expenses of the management of the Bank	1,139,553	66
Sundries ...	74,047	[illegible]
	969,034,212	15

Certified by the Governor of the Bank of France,
d'ARGOUT.

It appears from these returns that the metallic reserve has diminished during the past month 38,770,464f. in Paris, and 981,117f. in the branch banks. The discount accommodation has increased both in Paris and in the departments; in the former 8,357,939f., and in the latter 6,117,751f. The advances on public securities have augmented in Paris 386,100f., and diminished in the departments 27,300f. The notes in circulation have decreased in Paris 995,400f., and augmented in the departments 3,155,350f. The Treasury account current has increased 12,907,244f.; the [illegible] officers killed and wounded between the 27th of October and the 1st of November.

Captain Maude, of the Horse Artillery, an excellent officer, is, I am assured, doing well.

I likewise enclose the naval return of casualties.

I have, &c.,

RAGLAN.

His Grace the Duke of Newcastle, &c.

RETURN OF CASUALTIES AMONG OFFICERS FROM 27TH OF OCTOBER TO 1ST OF NOVEMBER, BOTH DAYS INCLUSIVE.—NOVEMBER 2.

October 25.

Royal Artillery.—Captain G. A. Maude, wounded dangerously (omitted in the return from 22d to 26th).

October 28.

49th Regiment.—Major C. T. Powell, killed.

J. B. BUCKNALL ESTCOURT, Adjutant-General.

RETURN OF CASUALTIES FROM 27TH OF OCTOBER TO 1ST OF NOVEMBER, BOTH DAYS INCLUSIVE.

CRIMEA, November 2.

Artillery.—1 officer (Captain G. A. Maude), 1 sergeant, 5 rank and file, wounded.
Sappers and Miners.—1 rank and file wounded.
Coldstream Guards.—1 rank and file wounded.
7th Regiment.—1 rank and file wounded.
19th Regiment.—1 rank and file wounded.
20th Regiment.—1 drummer, 4 rank and file wounded.
21st Regiment.—2 rank and file killed.
49th Regiment.—1 officer (Major Powell) killed.
57th Regiment.—2 rank and file wounded.
63d Regiment.—1 rank and file killed; 1 rank and file wounded.
77th Regiment.—1 rank and file wounded.
88th Regiment.—1 rank and file killed; 1 sergeant, 5 rank and file wounded.
1st Battalion Rifle Brigade.—1 rank and file killed; 1 rank and file wounded.
Total—1 officer, 5 rank and file, killed; 1 officer, 2 sergeants, 1 drummer, 23 rank and file, wounded.

J. B. BUCKNALL ESTCOURT, Adjutant-General.

WAR-OFFICE, Nov. 17.

The Right Hon. the Secretary at War has received from his Grace the Duke of Newcastle the following list of casualties among the non-commissioned officers and privates in the forces under the command of General Lord Raglan, G.C.B., from the 22d of October to the 1st of November, 1854, both days inclusive:—

NOMINAL RETURN OF CASUALTIES IN THE FORCES UNDER THE COMMAND OF GENERAL LORD RAGLAN, G.C.B., FROM OCTOBER 22 TO NOVEMBER 1, BOTH DAYS INCLUSIVE.

OCTOBER 22.

ARTILLERY.

Killed.—Acting Bombardier William Fox; Gunner Alfred Element.

Wounded.—Bombardier John Blacker, slightly. Gunners John Bennett, severely; Samuel Cator, severely; Henry Sims, slightly; John Williams, slightly; James Mitchell, slightly; John Dugan, slightly; John Preslee, slightly.

1ST REGIMENT OF FOOT.

Wounded.—Private William Bristow, slightly.

7TH REGIMENT OF FOOT.

Wounded.—Privates John Shepherd, severely; James Robinson, slightly; Patrick Tyne, slightly; Thomas Kirk, slightly; John Ford, slightly.

20TH REGIMENT OF FOOT.

Wounded.—Private David Swan, slightly.

30TH REGIMENT OF FOOT.

Wounded.—Private J. Byng, slightly.

77TH REGIMENT OF FOOT.

Killed.—Private John Mason.

OCTOBER 23.

ARTILLERY.

Killed.—Gunners J. Hodgeson and R. Morrison.

Wounded.—Sergeant J. Mitchell, slightly. Acting-Bombardier W. Pinion, slightly. Gunners D. Walsh, slightly; W. Hannigan, severely; R. Coats, severely; and J. Death, severely.

1ST REGIMENT OF FOOT.

Wounded.—Private William Noonan, slightly.

47TH REGIMENT OF FOOT.

Killed.—Private C. Kerivan.

50TH REGIMENT OF FOOT.

Wounded.—Private J. Wait, severely.

OCTOBER 24.

ARTILLERY.

Killed.—Sergeants F. Taylor and J. Spiers.

Wounded.—Bombardier J. M. Manne, severely. Gunner W. Pemberton, dangerously.

Wounded on the 20th, omitted in last return.—Bombardier James Dundass, slightly. Gunners W. Cavanagh, slightly; E. Kench, slightly; and R. Russell, slightly. Bombardier W. Lane, slightly.

ROYAL ENGINEERS.

Wounded.—Privates J. Wheeler, slightly; and J. Bland, dangerously.

19TH REGIMENT OF FOOT.

Wounded.—Privates P. M. G. Gun, severely, since dead; Edward Keating, severely.

41ST REGIMENT OF FOOT.

Wounded.—Private M. Starkey, severely.

63D REGIMENT OF FOOT.

Wounded.—Private Robert Ives, slightly.

77TH REGIMENT OF FOOT.

Killed.—Corporal Charles Dermett.

1ST BATTALION RIFLE BRIGADE.

Wounded.—Private J. Carter, slightly.

2D BATTALION RIFLE BRIGADE.

Wounded.—Private W. Jackson, severely, since dead.

OCTOBER 25.

ARTILLERY.

Wounded.—Gunners William Davidson, Arthur Jackson, Joseph Gobsell.

ROYAL ENGINEERS.

Wounded.—Private James Dilling.

7TH REGIMENT OF FOOT.

Wounded.—Private Edwin Butler, severely.

20TH REGIMENT OF FOOT.

Wounded.—Private James Lynch, slightly.

28TH REGIMENT OF FOOT.

Wounded.—Private Edmund Flaherty, slightly.

44TH REGIMENT OF FOOT.

Wounded.—Private Benjamin Ford, slightly.

57TH REGIMENT OF FOOT.

Wounded.—Private A. McNamara, slightly.

68TH REGIMENT OF FOOT.

Killed.—Private Michael Gallivan.

Wounded.—Private Patrick Crawley, slightly.

1ST BATTALION OF RIFLE BRIGADE.

Wounded.—Private William Wright, slightly.

4TH DRAGOON GUARDS.

Killed.—Private Thomas Ryan.

Wounded.—Troop-Sergeant Major John Evans, slightly; Sergeant William Percy, slightly; Privates James Anchinclass, slightly; Henry Preece, slightly; and William Scanlon, dangerously.

5TH DRAGOON GUARDS.

Killed.—Corporal James Taylor and Private Bernard Callery.

Wounded.—Corporal Charles M'Keegan, severely; Privates Edward Malone, severely; Henry Herbert, severely; John M'Cabe, severely; William Wilson, severely; Charles Babbington, severely; Joseph Jenkings, severely; G. H. Dickson, slightly; and William Morris, slightly.

1ST DRAGOONS.

Killed.—Privates Charles Middleton, Thomas Shore.

Wounded.—Sergeant M. Noake, severely; Trumpeter George Stacey, severely; Privates, J. R. Astlett, severely; James Blake, severely; George Taylor, severely; B. Kennedy, slightly; Samuel Woodward, slightly.

2D DRAGOONS.

Killed.—Corporal A. P. Clifford and Private Henry Campbell.

Wounded.—Troop-Sergeant-Majors Mat. Brown, slightly; Jas. Dearden, slightly; Jas. Davidson, slightly. Sergeants Thomas Kneath, severely; John Wilson, severely; David Gibson, severely. Corporal Francis Campbell, severely. Privates Owen Ward, severely; Richard Foster, severely; William Jackson, severely; A. D. Gardiner, severely; William Johnston, slightly; Henry Lochrie, slightly; Thomas Goffey, slightly; James Hunter, slightly; Robert Kerr, slightly; William Heywood, slightly; Alexander Weir, slightly; John McNee, slightly; Charles Glancy, slightly; Robert Barnet, slightly; Thomas Langdon, slightly; James Taylor, slightly; Peter Burley, slightly; William Seggie, severely; William Hammond, severely; Robert Thompson, severely; George Alexander, slightly; William Davis, severely; William Caulfield, slightly; James Aitken, slightly; George Burns, slightly; William Donaldson, severely; James M'Pherson, slightly; James Hackett, slightly; James Bothwicke, severely; John Borland, slightly; Donald Davidson, slightly; Walter Fawke, slightly; A. S. Long, severely; Thomas Trail, severely; William Marshall, slightly; James Watson, slightly; William McPherson, slightly; William J. Allis, severely; James Allen, slightly; Richard Livingstone, severely; McAdam Galbraith, severely; William Conmell, slightly; Charles Currie, slightly; James Colter, slightly; John Knowles, slightly; and William Morrison, severely.

6TH DRAGOONS.

Killed.—Privates Robert Elliott and Alexander Latimer.

Wounded.—Troop-Sergeant-Major Alexander Shields, severely. Sergeants Richard Jeffreys, severely; Frederick Bolton, dangerously. Corporal John Kidney, slightly; Privates Michael Rourke, dangerously; Robert Turner, severely; Charles Clarke, severely; John McCanna, slightly; Robert Keane, slightly; James Backler, slightly; William Breadins, slightly; John Davis, slightly; William Lyons, slightly.

4TH LIGHT DRAGOONS.

Killed or Missing.—Troop-Sergeant-Major Francis Herbert; Sergeants Richard Lynch and Edward Campbell; Corporal Henry Spence; Trumpeters Edward Lovelock and Thomas Burns; Privates James Donaldson, Daniel Haxhall, Thomas Hutton, Charles Marshall, Thomas Moody, Michael Phelan, George Robinson, George Swan, Thomas Tomset, Charles Waight.

Wounded.—Troop-Sergeant-Major Henry Jennings, slightly; Corporal Denis Heron, slightly; Privates James Devlin, severely; James Olley, slightly; John Hughes, slightly; Thomas Armes, slightly; Joseph Carter, slightly; Edward Bradley, slightly; Joseph Phillips, slightly; William Sutcliffe, slightly; James Tyler, slightly; Frederick Downing, slightly; Thomas Herbert, slightly; George Croydon, slightly; Thomas Rogers, slightly; William Jones, slightly; Joseph Whitby, slightly; William Thorne, slightly; Peter Carroll, slightly; John Gray, slightly; Joseph Gosbell, severely; and William Keenan, slightly.

8TH HUSSARS.

Killed or Missing.—Troop-Sergeant-Major H. McCluer, Sergeants Michael Rielly and William Williams. Corporal William Donald. Privates Joshua Adams, John Barry, Michael Brennan, James Dies, Andrew Finnegan, Denis Haurahan, Thomas Heffron, Edmund Herbert, Matthew Keating, Martin Lemmion, Edward McDonald, George Morris, Charles Waterer, and John White.

Wounded.—Troop-Sergeant-Major — Clarke, slightly. Trumpet-Major William Gray, slightly. Corporal John Sewell, severely. Trumpeter John Dunn, severely. Privates Francis Bray, dangerously; John Brown, severely; Henry Cheshire, severely; James Clement, severely; Patrick Doolan, dangerously; William Fullon, slightly; R. O. Glendire, severely; Richard Kennedy, severely; Patrick Kiterick, slightly; Joseph Ross, severely; William Ryan, dangerously; Christopher Spain, slightly; and Thomas Tevamley, severely.

11TH HUSSARS.

Killed or Missing.—Sergeants T. Jordan and J. Jones. Corporal T. France. Privates R. Bubb, R. Levett, J. M. George, C. Allured, C. B. Cooper, W. Davis, R. Gwinnell, G. Horne, R. Lazell, J. Stephenson, J. Jackman, J. Larkin, D. Purcell, T. Shrive, D. Ward, H. Wakelin, W. Wareham, G. Wootton, J. Elder, L. Shoppee, W. H. Spring, and J. Brunton.

Wounded.—Sergeants R. Davies, slightly; W. Bentley, slightly; J. Lawson, severely. Corporals E. Hudson, slightly; J. Kilvert, slightly; C. Cork, slightly. Privates D. Andrews, slightly; H. Groome, slightly; H. Jewell, severely; W. Walker, slightly; T. Roberts, severely; W. H. Pennington, slightly; J. Glainster, dangerously; R. Martin, severely; S. Milburn, severely; J. C. Purvis, severely; G. Turner, dangerously; E. Wilcox, slightly; R. Young, severely; W. Firth, severely; W. Tayler, slightly; G. Jowett, slightly; J. Bingham, slightly; S. Samer, severely; T. Strutt, slightly; and H. Shergold, slightly.

13TH LIGHT DRAGOONS.

Killed or Missing.—Troop-Sergeant-Major John Webster. Corporal E. W. A. Smith. Privates Thomas Blackett, Charles Court, William Derell, Robert Fraser; A. Holliday, William Lawson, Thomas McGerrine, James Slattery, James Watson, and T. J. Williams.

Wounded.—Sergeant Frederick Peake, severely. Privates John Brooks, severely; John Ettridge, severely; John Keen, severely; Joseph Moore, dangerously; Henry Pegler, severely; Joseph Rhodes, severely; Richard Rowley, severely; William Sewell, severely; George Williams, severely; George Wilde, slightly. Sent on board ship without being seen by the Regimental Surgeon.—Serjeant Edward Martin. Private James Cameron, James Cunningham, Joseph Douglas, H. D. Naylor, James Naylor, William Nicholson, John Veitch, Thomas White, Edmund Wright, and Robert Evans.

17TH LANCERS.

Killed or Missing.—Sergeant Edward Talbot. Corporals James Hall and Cont. Wrigley. Privates Charles Aldows, William Baker, William Barker, John Bow, George Broom, Walter Brooks, Henry Carter, Thomas Corcoran, Richard Dollar, Patrick Dowling, George Flowers, Henry Gray, William Harrison, John Lees, Robert Ling, Frederick Melrose, Charles Mitton, Robert M'Neill, Robert Jackson, Henry Pearce, Johnson Sewell, James Stamage, and John Wilson.

Wounded.—Sergeant James Scarfe, severely; Corporals John Pyne, slightly; George Taylor, severely. Lance-Corporal John Brown (3d), slightly. Trumpeters William Brittain, dangerously; Martin Landfred, slightly. Privates John Andrews, severely; Peter Brown, severely; James Buck, slightly; Frederick Clifford, dangerously; William Doyle, slightly; Thomas Dudley, severely; John Duggan, severely; Patrick Fegan, slightly; James Friend, slightly; Thomas Foster, dangerously; John Hart, slightly; George Herriott, slightly; Thomas Magee, slightly; Thomas Mullen, dangerously; James Mustard, slightly; David M'Neill, severely; John Gravenor, slightly; James O'Gorman, slightly; John Payne, slightly; William Pearson, severely; William Phelan, severely; William Purvis, severely; Patrick Rafferty, severely; Benjamin Soley, severely; David Stanley, severely; John Stewart, severely; and James Watts, severely.

OCTOBER 26.

3D BATTALION GRENADIER GUARDS.

Wounded.—Private Matthew Lake.

1st REGIMENT OF FOOT.

Wounded.—Private Robert Kernan, slightly.

7TH REGIMENT OF FOOT.

Wounded.—Privates William O'Connell, severely; John Myland, severely; Edward Carney, severely; and William Hopes, slightly.

19TH REGIMENT OF FOOT.

Wounded.—Privates James Gomm, slightly; and William Crowley, slightly.

23D REGIMENT OF FOOT.

Wounded.—Private John Calville, severely.

30TH REGIMENT OF FOOT.

Killed.—Privates Charles Freeman, George Rose, Bryan Mathews, Thomas Jenkinson, Patrick Morris, George Smith, (4th), and Robert Hunter.

Wounded.—Sergeant Daniel Sullivan, slightly; Corporals Thomas Delany, slightly; John Sharp, (1st), severely; Privates John Evans, slightly; Archibald Fisher, slightly; John Tucker, severely; Edward Horgan, severely; David M'Cabe, dangerously; William Winimo, slightly; Bartholomew Regan, severely; Patrick Doody, slightly; William O'Brien, slightly; Francis Sturgeon, dangerously; John Smith, (4th), slightly; James Kerr, severely; Charles Reynolds, severely; David Bennett, severely; Michael Kennedy, severely; Edward Brennan, severely; John Law, slightly; Peter McGinn, slightly; and James Gibbins, dangerously.

41ST REGIMENT OF FOOT.

Killed.—Private John Martin.

Wounded.—Privates Robert Dudley, severely; Charles Light, severely; Roger Hanrahan, severely; John Clough, severely; Michael Grace, slightly; William Tilley, severely; Timothy Keeffe, severely; and Daniel Donovan, severely (since dead).

47TH REGIMENT OF FOOT.

Killed.—Private Frederick Pittman.

Wounded.—Corporal William Bowler, slightly; Privates Patrick Finlay, severely; Robert Mulligan, slightly; John Neill, slightly; John Cantrill, slightly; Patrick Mamard, slightly; and William Houlihan, slightly.

49TH REGIMENT OF FOOT.

Killed.—Private George Swayne.

Wounded.—Colour-Sergeant William Armstrong, severely; Corporals James Campbell, severely; Daniel Dunn, severely; Charles Henry, slightly; Drummer Eugene Sweeney, severely; Privates James Atherton, dangerously; William Brown, severely; James Cardiff, severely; Thomas Faby, severely; Thomas Fensome, severely; John Jones, dangerously; Samuel Jones, severely; Edward Jordan, slightly; John Lake, slightly; Michael Lyons, dangerously; Thomas Monaghan, severely; James Parker, severely; James Sable, severely; and Thomas Donahy, slightly.

88TH REGIMENT OF FOOT.

Killed.—Private James Kilden.

Wounded.—Privates Thomas O'Brien, slightly; Bartholomew Purcell, slightly; Michael Connolly, slightly; and John McMahon, slightly.

95TH REGIMENT OF FOOT.

Killed.—Private Charles Cardoe.

Wounded.—Sergeant-Major Roger Conner, slightly; Privates John Doody, slightly; Peter Ombley, slightly; John McElligott, slightly; George Clarke, slightly; George Elliott, slightly; Charles Legget, slightly; Thomas Baxter, slightly; and James Dalton, slightly.

2D BATTALION RIFLE BRIGADE.

Wounded.—Corporal D. Graham, slightly; Privates William Crouch, slightly; J. Rielly, slightly; and J. Waldron, slightly.

J. B. BUCKNALL ESTCOURT, Adjutant-General.

OCTOBER 27.

ROYAL ARTILLERY.

Wounded.—Sergeant John Mould, dangerously (omitted in return, 25th of October); Gunners William Wilson, slightly; and John Cliburn, slightly.

57TH REGIMENT OF FOOT.

Wounded.—Private Henry Mullen, slightly.

63D REGIMENT OF FOOT.

Wounded.—Private John Leonard, slightly.

OCTOBER 28.

7TH REGIMENT OF FOOT.

Wounded.—Private Francis Bretton, severely.

OCTOBER 29.

ROYAL ARTILLERY.

Wounded.—Gunners Robert M'Kee, slightly; James Morley, slightly; and William Williams, slightly.

20TH REGIMENT OF FOOT.

Wounded.—Drummer James Horsford, slightly; Private Samuel Pemberton, slightly.

57TH REGIMENT OF FOOT.

Wounded.—Private James Carson, slightly.

OCTOBER 30.

19TH REGIMENT OF FOOT.

Wounded.—Private James Flinn, wounded on the 21st, not returned before.

SAPPERS AND MINERS.

Wounded.—John Hutton, slightly.

OCTOBER 31.

1ST BATTALION RIFLE BRIGADE.

Killed.—Charles Lewis.

Wounded.—William Martin, slightly.

77TH REGIMENT OF FOOT.

Wounded.—James Long, slightly.

NOVEMBER 1.

COLDSTREAM GUARDS.

Wounded.—Private William Tooley, severely.

21ST REGIMENT OF FOOT.

Killed.—Privates Fenton Dumphey, John Wright.

63D REGIMENT OF FOOT.

Killed.—Private Joseph Brennan.

20TH REGIMENT OF FOOT.

Wounded.—Privates George Akins, mortally; William Seaford, severely; and Charles Humphries, slightly.

88TH REGIMENT OF FOOT.

Killed.—Private John M. Hugh.

Wounded.—Sergeant Edward Somers, slightly; Corporal William Knowles, slightly; Privates Thomas Kelly, dangerously; Alexander Anderson, severely; Michael Garaghty, severely; and John Downs, severely.

J. B. BUCKNALL ESTCOURT, Adjutant-General.

RETURN OF PRISONERS TAKEN BY THE RUSSIANS, THE 25TH OF OCTOBER, 1854.

WOUNDED.

4TH LIGHT DRAGOONS.—Troop-Sergeant-Major William Fowler, Corporal William Thomas, Privates Thomas Linser, Thomas Fletcher, Thomas Lucas, James Boxhall, and James Nermoyle.

8TH HUSSARS.—Cornet George Clowes, Corporal William Taylor, Privates John Berlin, William Perry, James Maccanon, Edward Turner, and John Fitzgibbon.

11TH HUSSARS.—Corporal James Williams, Privates William Sheppard, John Berry, Walter Hyde, and John Dryden.

13TH LIGHT DRAGOONS.—Troop-Sergeant-Major George Smith, Trumpeter William Howard, Privates William Martin, Christopher Haulon, A. Harris, John Maccan, William Duke, George Cooper, Thomas Cook, and William Benton.

17TH LANCERS.—Lieutenant John Chadwick, Privates Thomas Brown, Thomas Marshall, James McCallister, Henry Ellis, Henry Young, Thomas Sharp, Alfred Tanner, Robert Edge, James Wightman, William Kirk, and John Lyle.

PRISONERS NOT WOUNDED.—4TH LIGHT DRAGOONS.—Trumpeter Hugh Crawford, Corporal Joseph Armstrong, Privates James Bagshaw, Thomas King, Charles Frederick, Michael O'Brien, Samuel Parks, Robert Farquharson, and James Bolton.

8TH HUSSARS.—Privates Patrick Horan, Richard Palframan, and William Bird.

11TH HUSSARS.—Privates N. Henry and Henry Parker.

13TH LIGHT DRAGOONS.—Troop-Sergeant-Major John Lincoln. Private Charles Warren.

OFFICERS OF THE COMMISSARIAT.—Issuers Edmund Johnson and James Kerrs.

J. B. BUCKNALL ESTCOURT, Adjutant-General.

A RETURN OF THE KILLED AND WOUNDED IN THE NAVAL BRIGADE DURING THE THREE DAYS ENDING OCTOBER 31, 1854.

RODNEY.—Wounded.—Thomas Marlow, ordinary, slightly, October 29.

BRITANNIA.—Wounded.—John Williams, A.B., slightly, October 30.

Total wounded, 2.

STEPHEN LUSHINGTON, Captain Commanding Naval Brigade.

To the Military Secretary to his Excellency Lord Raglan, Commander-in-Chief of the Army.

A RETURN OF THE KILLED AND WOUNDED IN THE NAVAL BRIGADE ON THE 1ST OF NOVEMBER, 1854.

LONDON.—Wounded.—William Garrett, leading seaman, slightly.

ARETHUSA.—Wounded.—William Walker, A.B., slightly.

VENGEANCE.—Wounded.—Thomas Lemmon, A.B., slightly.

Total wounded, 3.

STEPHEN LUSHINGTON, Captain Commanding Naval Brigade.

To the Military Secretary to his Excellency Lord Raglan, Commander-in-Chief of the Army.

THE BLACK SEA FLEET.

(FROM OUR OWN CORRESPONDENT.)

OFF THE KATCHA, Nov. 1.

Since I wrote my last letter a great change has taken place, which may materially influence the activity of the fleet, and act the part of a powerful ally to the Russians; I mean the change of weather.

The steamer which carried my letter informing you of the continuance of the mild autumnal weather had scarcely departed when, after sunset, a strong breeze sprang up, which, during the night from Saturday to Sunday, gradually increased to a gale, and still continues with such violence that the communication with boats is entirely interrupted, and the ships are tossed about like playballs in the open roadstead. The wind is coming round to between north and east —a very fortunate circumstance, for it would be nearly impossible to keep at anchor with safety if the wind was from the west or north-west. The ground is, indeed, good for anchoring, but there would be great danger of the cables snapping if a blow from the west was to expose them to the whole fury of the Black Sea.

Of course, as long as this gale lasts there is no possibility for the vessels to make any attempt against the forts on the sea side. But there are other disadvantages besides this. For the last week the ships have been sending a considerable quantity of ammunition for the troops and guns on shore. There are still orders to prepare more, but as long as this gale continues it will be impossible to send it away in boats to the steamers, which carry it down to Balaklava.

Since the late attack on Balaklava several of the steamers have again gone to the latter place, so that now the Agamemnon, Sanspareil, Wasp, Cyclops, and Vesuvius are anchored partly outside, partly inside the bay, while the Firebrand, the Niger, the Beagle, and Arrow perform the office of couriers between the two portions of the fleet, bringing wounded and sick men and taking back ammunition.

Notwithstanding this daily communication, however, there is very little communicated of what is going on on shore. The French and English Admirals make after every arrival the usual signal of "Nothing new," and leave every individual free to use his imagination to construct news from the flashes and reports of the batteries and of the fortress.

I am rather surprised that no telegraphic line has as yet been established between the camp and the main body of the fleet off the Katcha. I think I told you that there is one between the camp and Balaklava, by means of four flagstaffs. It would be, I think, just as easy to communicate with the rest of the fleet by carrying a series of flagstaffs through the French camp down to the shore, and thence by a steamer cruising about to convey them to the flagship.

Yesterday we had two new arrivals—the Gladiator, direct from England, and the Emeu, with French troops from Constantinople. As the difficulties seem to be greater than was at first supposed, the 10,000 Frenchmen who are said to have arrived at Constantinople will be a timely reinforcement.

Nov. 2.

This morning the wind, although still very strong, has somewhat abated, so that there seems again a chance of the return of milder weather. Except on Sunday, when there were heavy squalls of rain and hail, the rest of the time we had a nearly cloudless sky, so that, however paralyzing this change of weather to the fleet, it was not unfavourable to the health of the troops.

The Stromboli has come in from Balaklava, bringing again sick and wounded. It is curious that the naval brigade suffers much more on shore than the army; it seems the latter has paid its tribute to cholera and fever, and is becoming more and more *aguerri*, while the change from a snug berth on board ship to a frail tent, unprotected from wind and weather, tells on the sailors. Fortunately, these latter can fall back on their ships, which, notwithstanding the want of assistant-surgeons, which is daily felt, are still far better off than the soldiers whom I saw foraging in Balaklava, not only for food, but likewise for medicine, which they could not get at the camp.

The following is an extract from a letter from an officer of the Guards, dated Nov. 3:—

"The Russians have lately appeared in considerable strength, and are seen constantly moving about in the plains below us, on our right flank. We have consequently been taken off all trench duty, to look after and strengthen our position. We have daily a battalion on picket, and working parties to erect redoubts and breastworks. We are hard at work at these now, not knowing from day to day from where we may be attacked. Our whole line from the Genoese Fort at Balaklava to the extreme left of the French line of attack is little less than 14 miles; and, as half the army is always occupied in carrying on the works of the siege, it leaves but comparatively few men for the defence of such extensive lines, if the Russians succeed in bringing many troops in our rear."

THE "AFFAIR" OF BALAKLAVA.

TO THE EDITOR OF THE TIMES.

Sir,—If you will give a conspicuous place in your columns to the following extracts from a letter written by the late Duke of Wellington on the 15th of May, 1811, its publication will not, I think, be deemed inopportune. It is to be found in the selections from the despatches and general orders of his Grace, published by Lieutenant-Colonel Gurwood, p. 479:—

"I entertain no doubt of the readiness of the officers and soldiers of the army to advance upon the enemy, but it is my duty, and that of every general and other officer in command, to regulate this spirit, and not to expose the soldiers to contend with unequal numbers in situations disadvantageous to them, and, above all, not to allow them to follow up trifling advantages to situations in which they cannot be supported, from which their retreat is not secure, and in which they incur the risk of being prisoners to the enemy they had before beaten.

"The desire to be forward in engaging the enemy is not uncommon in the British army, but that quality which I wish to see the officers possess who are at the head of troops is a cool, discriminating judgment in action, which will enable them to decide with promptitude how far they can and ought to go with propriety, and to convey their orders and act with such vigour and decision that the soldiers will look up to them with confidence in the moment of action, and obey them with alacrity.

"The officers of the army may depend upon it, that the enemy to whom they are opposed are not less prudent than they are powerful. Notwithstanding what has been printed in gazettes and newspapers, we have never seen small bodies, unsupported, successfully opposed to large; nor has the experience of any officer realized the stories which we have read, of whole armies being driven by a handful of light infantry or dragoons.

"I trust that this letter, copies of which I propose to circulate to the general officers commanding divisions, with directions to circulate it among the officers of the army, will have the effect of inducing them to reflect seriously upon the duties which they have to perform before the enemy, and to avoid the error which is the subject of it, which is really become one of serious detriment to the army and the public interest."

I am, Sir, your obedient servant,

J. O.

FOREIGN INTELLIGENCE.

[The following appeared in our second edition of yesterday:—]

(BY SUBMARINE AND BRITISH TELEGRAPH.)

We have received the following from our correspondent at Vienna:—

"VIENNA, FRIDAY MORNING.

"Three days ago the Emperor of Austria sent an autograph letter to the Emperor Napoleon, the sense of which is said to be, that 'if the Eastern question was not settled by the spring, Austria would no longer remain a passive spectator.'"

PARIS, FRIDAY MORNING.

The *Moniteur* publishes a decree re-constituting immediately the 6th company of the third battalion of each of the 100 regiments of the line.

FRANCE.

(FROM OUR OWN CORRESPONDENT.)

PARIS, THURSDAY, Nov. 16, 6 P.M.

A despatch from General Canrobert, dated the 3d, has not, I believe, as yet been made public. It announces that the trench works of the French camp were then at 140 metres from the *enceinte*, but that the difficulties of the soil precluded the possibility of their being pushed nearer. The *place d'armes* was about to be established where the attacking columns were to be assembled. The works were carried on under cover of the batteries on the right, which had opened their fire on the 1st. The cannonade was most energetic on both sides. The enemy was constructing incessantly new batteries behind the *enceinte*. The struggle was obstinate, but the fire of the besieged was commanded by that of the besiegers. The enemy's forces, whose number it was difficult to estimate, were fortifying themselves on the heights to the north-east of Balaklava, which they menaced on the left. The utmost vigilance of the allied Generals was directed to that point. The loss of the allies was of little importance in comparison with that of the enemy, which was known to be very considerable. The sanitary condition of the army was excellent. The weather was fine, though cold.

The following Russian despatch has also been received:—

"BERLIN, 15th, (ST. PETERSBURG, 15th).—Prince Menschikoff writes from the Crimea under date of the 8th:—The siege continues. We have repaired our damages with success. The enemy has strongly intrenched himself on the left flank of his position."

It would, then, appear from this despatch that, if on the 8th the assault had not yet taken place, neither had the Russians attempted any new attack against the allies. This appears to confirm the opinion of General Canrobert as to their inability for action for 10 days after the defeat of the 5th. That battle must indeed have been bloody when the enemy has not dared to interrupt, even once, by sorties or attacks on the flanks of the allied army, the siege works and the continued destruction of the town. The despatch adds that the allies were fortifying themselves strongly on their left. Such in fact is the system of the Generals, who are resolved not to be tempted by the manœuvres of the enemy to descend from the heights they occupy, and the natural strength of which they are adding to by art, so as to render any surprise or attack on the part of the Russians impossible. In the meantime the work of demolition is steadily progressing at Sebastopol. The bombardment does not cease; each day the breach is enlarged, and some of the defensive works of the city demolished, and when it is taken then it will be the turn of the allies to assume the offensive against Prince Menschikoff.

The letters received from Constantinople of the 5th bring news from the Crimea to the 3d. They announce that on the 30th of October and on the 1st and 2d of November the allies had each day to repulse the attacks of the garrison. On the 3d the breach was practicable, and the assault was imminent. The reason why it did not take place is explained by the combat of the 5th. The Russians are said to have abandoned a portion of the ground; and a part of the city, or rather of the ruins of the city, countermined by the allies, had, it was also said, been evacuated by the garrison, which had intrenched and fortified itself in the interior of the place. It was stated that the numerical force of the defenders of Sebastopol was diminishing, and that they were becoming more and more discouraged every day. The pictures which these letters present of the state of that doomed city is terrible. It is, in fact, one vast ruin; the dead strew the streets and public places, and the bodies remain without burial. Pestilence was said to have been engendered by that hideous accumulation of corpses; but the present letters make mention only of aggravated cholera, occasioned by the privations and terrible sufferings of a population so long given up to all the horrors of a siege—and such a siege. It was believed at Constantinople that the assault would take place on the 8th. The fire of our guns had occasioned fresh conflagrations, and the destruction of an hospital in which 2,000 sick and wounded perished in the flames is again noticed in these letters. The English Lancaster guns had sunk two Russian ships of the line. In a word, the injury done to the enemy is described as enormous; and it is difficult to imagine how the resistance of the besieged can be protracted much longer. From Constantinople 80 guns had been sent to the allies. The Egyptian reinforcements which the bad weather had delayed were about to leave for the Crimea. Reinforcements were also expected from Malta and from France, and the brigade of General Mayran had arrived from Athens.

The Marseilles journals of the 15th inst. announce that the 6th batallion of Chasseurs de Vincennes and two batteries of artillery were on the point of being embarked to join in the Crimea the 6th division, commanded by General Paté. By the arrival of that division the effective force of the French army before Sebastopol will be increased to 70,000 men. The Government has, besides, ordered the immediate departure of two other divisions for the East, commanded by Generals Dulac and De Salles. The division of General Dulac, which will form the 7th of the army of the East, will consist of two brigades. The first, under the orders of General Beusinger, is to be composed of the 17th battalion of Chasseurs de Vincennes, the 10th Regiment of Light Infantry, and the 57th of the line; the second, under General Bisson, of the 10th and 61st regiments of the line, two batteries of artillery, and a company of engineers. The first brigade is to embark this week at Toulon, and the other troops are to leave in succession, according as the transports are ready to receive them. The division of General De Salles is to occupy, in the camp of the South, the cantonments vacated by General Dulac, until the necessary preparations are made for its embarkation. That division, the 8th of the army, is to consist of two brigades—the first, commanded by General Faucheux, formed of the 10th battalion of Chasseurs de Vincennes, the 4th Regiment of Light Infantry, and the 18th of the line; the second, under General Duval, of the 14th and 43d Regiments of the line, two batteries of artillery, and a company of the 3d Regiment of Engineers. All those troops will have sailed before the end of the month. Those two divisions, it is believed, are not intended to operate in the Crimea. They are to land either at Trebizond, to strengthen the Turkish army at Kars, or at Batoum, to combine operations with Schamyl. "Whatever may happen," says the *Courrier de Marseilles*, "and however great and arduous may be the task undertaken by France, the means she has employed will be found fully adequate to it, and we may consequently await with calmness and confidence the result of a war so resolutely carried on by England and France." Indeed, it may be said that reinforcements for the army of the East are marching from all quarters. The 5th battery of the 1st Regiment of Artillery left Vincennes yesterday by rail for Lyons, on its way to the Crimea. A detachment of the 6th battalion of Foot Chasseurs, coming from Strasburg, arrived yesterday in Paris, and left in the evening for Toulon. The Minister of War has issued orders for all the depôts of the regiments now serving in the Crimea to send reinforcements to their respective corps with all possible despatch.

M. Guibert, a ship builder at Nantes, has received orders from the Government for the construction of gunboats and floating batteries. Boats of a similar description, but of iron, are now building at Creuzot, and we are told by very competent judges that it is difficult to form an idea of their powers of resistance. They are to be furnished with a screw propeller; their draught of water will be very small, and only sufficient room will be left above water-line for their batteries. The boats are to be painted green, to render them less remarkable; as they are to have smoke-consumers they will not be betrayed by that of the engine. Their crews will be provided with every possible comfort.

We read the following in the *Echo de Valenciennes* of the 14th:—

"The siege of Sebastopol has caused a kind of feverish impatience among the inhabitants of our city, from which those in the country districts, usually so calm, are not entirely free. Although very patriotic, this impatience is rather unreasonable, and must be attributed to their ignorance of military tactics. If the old inhabitants would tax their memories a little, they would remember that in the siege of 1793 our city was bombarded during 42 days and nights; that 160,000 projectiles, 48,000 of which were shells, had been thrown into the town; that two allied armies, as now at Sebastopol, were laying siege to the place; that Colonel Congreve, who invented the destructive rockets of that name, directed the fire of the English, and Baron de Unterberger that of the Austrians; finally, that 100,000 men carried on the siege, with 344 guns and mortars, and only 10,000 defended the town, with 175 pieces of cannon. What a difference between the two sieges! Here the ground the assailants had to work on was excellent; at Sebastopol it is rocky and uneven. The Imperialists of 1793 found abundance of provisions in the country; the allies of 1854 must get all their supplies by sea. Valenciennes was completely invested. Sebastopol has its communication open with the neighbouring country. With all the advantages of their position, the Duke of York and his allies were obliged to bombard the city for six weeks before it capitulated. We ought not to be astonished if Sebastopol, with an army and the crews of an entire fleet added to its garrison, does not fall as speedily as we desire. 20 days were required to take the citadel of Antwerp, which may be called an isolated fort. The attack on Sebastopol only commenced the 17th of October, and, admitting that it be taken in one month, the achievement will be considered one of the most glorious of the present age."

The Three per Cents. closed to-day at 71f. 90c. for the end of the month; the Four-and-a-Half per Cents. at 96f.; and the New Loan at 71f. 95c.; Orleans Railway Shares, 1,162f. 50c.; Rouen, 947f. 50c.; Havre, 535f.; Great Northern, 847f. 50c.; Strasburg, 780f.; New Shares, 623f. 75c.; Paris and Lyons, 987f. 50c.; Lyons and the Mediterranean, 843f. 75c.; Western of France, 640f.; Bordeaux and Cette, 595f.; Great Central of France, 510f.; Lyons and Geneva, 510f.; Bank of Crédit Mobilier, 717f. 50c.

Cours Authentique.—PARIS, Nov. 16.—Cash Prices.—Four-and-a-Half per Cents. (not reimbursable for 10 years), 96f. 96f. 20c.; ditto, New Loan, 96f. 10c.; Three per Cents., 71f. 95c. 90c. 72f. 71f. 95c. 90c. 95c.; ditto, New Loan, 71f. 95c.; Bank Actions, 2,980f.; Crédit Foncier, 575f.; ditto Obligations of 500f., 435f. 430f.; ditto of 1,000f., 942f. 50c.; ditto, Tenths, 96f. 25c.; Crédit Mobilier, 718f. 75c. 717f. 50c.; Discount Bank, 575f.; Piedmont Five per Cents., 84f. 50c.; Austrian Five per Cents., 82¾; Belgian Four-and-a-Half per Cents., 90¼; Rentes de Naples (Rothschild's), 105f.; Romans, 86 85¾ 85; Haytian Loan, 500f.; Spanish Interior Debt, 33½ ⅜ ½. Exchange on London, at sight, money, 25f. 7½c.; three months, money, 24f. 80c.

TURKEY.

(FROM OUR OWN CORRESPONDENT.)

CONSTANTINOPLE, NOVEMBER 5.

To-day the Vectis arrived, with Miss Nightingale and 37 nurses for the sick and wounded at Scutari. Although the unfortunate men who return from the Crimea are now much better cared for than when, in the last days of September, they were brought down in shiploads from Kalamita-bay, yet the assistance which can be rendered by the new-comers is most opportune, and the reception they have met with shows the sense entertained of their devotion and their probable usefulness. The Vectis suffered much from the tempests which have prevailed during the last few days; her bulwarks have been much injured, and two cabins on deck have been washed away; happily, however, no harm has occurred to any one on board, and, beyond the usual exhaustion of a sea voyage, there is nothing to prevent the ladies who have arrived from immediately commencing their useful labours. To-day the whole of them were established in their new quarters in the barracks of Scutari. Five rooms of large size have been set apart for the use of any general officer who might be brought down wounded or sick. The good fortune of the British army has as yet not been interrupted by any such calamity, and the rooms have been assigned, at least for the present, to the newly arrived nurses. They made their appearance on shore this afternoon, neatly attired in black, and formed a strong contrast to the usual aspect of hospital attendants. The subscription which the munificence of the British nation has raised for the relief of the sick and wounded will be applied with care to its proper objects. As yet it is impossible to give any statements as to the course which will be adopted; but it may be mentioned that the want of shirts and socks for the men has been represented to me by the commandant of the barracks, and the first step taken will probably be to provide a supply of those necessaries. The present state of the hospital is by no means unsatisfactory; the dreadful scenes which I described a month ago were the result of a sudden accumulation of sick and wounded after the landing in the Crimea and the battle of the Alma. Since then the arrivals have been fewer, and the fine weather experienced by the expedition till within the past week has prevented the hospitals from being overcrowded by a multitude of disabled men, while the transport service has been brought into some degree of order through the strong representations made to the authorities concerning those very incidents which some people at home, it seems, are bold enough to deny. There is reason, however, to suppose that any conflict like that of the Alma may be followed by a recurrence of what has so much shocked the public; and that such conflicts may be expected daily is almost certain. Further than this, the month of November is attended by winds and storms which harass and wear out troops more than the most active enemy. A large addition to the number of inmates at Scutari may be daily looked for, and, though every one is willing to do his best, the duties of the place may be again found beyond the powers of those who have charge of it. The large sum which the public has placed at the disposal of your journal will be found of the greatest service within the next few weeks, and in aiding the labours of the devoted women who have just landed; those who administer the funds collected will do their duty and, I think, satisfy the public.

The numbers in hospital at the present time are nearly 3,000. About 1,500 are placed in the great barracks, 800 in the hospital, and 500 or 600 in the Turkish line-of-battle ship moored off the Seraglio. This vessel was granted to the British authorities by the Ottoman Government for the use of convalescents, who may be seen on a fine day pacing the decks or lying about in the warm sun, refreshed by the sea breeze, and slowly recovering health and spirits. Two long wards are lined each with a double row of beds, and though they seem confined and ill-ventilated, yet they are clean, and the men are not uncomfortable. Within the last fortnight tressles have been provided for the beds to raise them off the cold ground. As the weather becomes more severe, the benefits of this improvement will be greatly felt. Another ward is being prepared for the reception of wounded, in accordance with an order just received. The commandant is directed to receive the wounded brought down from Balaklava after the 25th, and, furthermore, to provide accommodation for 1,000 others immediately, together with surgeons and dressers to attend upon them.

The wounded who arrived on the 30th, after the battle of the 25th, were not landed till yesterday. The violent winds and rains of the last few days entirely prevented any communication with the shore. Even for persons in health the crossing from Pera to Scutari has been no slight labour, and it might have cost many a wounded man his life to be rocked on the waves which rush round the base of the Asiatic shore. Although yesterday the wind had fallen, and the sea was comparatively calm, yet the celebrated current of the "Seven Brothers," where seven different streams unite, almost defied the exertions of the most practised rowers. The numbers landed were 193 from the Australian, 126 from the Echunga, and a small body from the Shooting Star. The officers were—Captains Morris, White, Webb (leg amputated yesterday), Maud, R.A., Ansell, and Campbell; Lieutenants Sir W. Gordon, Hartopp, Hon. G. Neville, Trevelyan, Houghton (slightly wounded, though returned killed), Clutterbuck; with Captain Brown, of the 44th.

The Shooting Star brought the following sick officers:—Major Coats, Vandeleur, Breedon, Byrn, and Marten.

We learn to-day from the Crimea that the French are making great progress, having mounted 64 guns. It is also said that they have mined the Russian position; but this is not to be believed, for the earth is extremely shallow, and there is scarcely enough for common siege operations. Sebastopol is planted on a rock, which defies the efforts of engineers to pierce it. If there be any truth in the assertion that mining has taken place, the operation must have been only partial. The agreeable tidings are somewhat damped by the news that sickness is increasing, and that the troops suffer dreadfully from the cold and frosty nights. Such news as this shows how opportune is the generous assistance of the public. To make good the necessary short-comings of the military arrangements is what the subscribers have had in view when they sent in their contributions, and in a few days we shall be able to announce in what way this new aid can be best applied.

The dreadful gales of the last few days have caused much damage to the shipping in the Black Sea. As far as can be learned, no great injury has been suffered by any French or English vessel, but a calamity has fallen on the Ottoman fleet in the loss of two ships out of its already diminished squadron. There can be little doubt that an Egyptian two-decker of 80 guns and a frigate of 28 were wrecked on the 30th, between the Bosphorus and Varna. The Capudan Pasha sent to Admiral Boxer yesterday, and informed him of the lamentable event, asking him to send out any steamer which might be ready to bring off the survivors and to learn the real extent of the disaster. The Admiral had previously despatched the Harpy up the coast, and another vessel followed her in the course of a few hours. These have not yet returned, but there seems little doubt that the vessels are entirely lost. It was at first supposed the Mahmoudie, of 134 guns, the largest ship in the Turkish navy, was also wrecked. She is a very old vessel, constructed after the models in use in the time of Rodney and Suffren, but of enormous size, and carrying 1,200 men. It was thought that she would hardly escape in such a tempest, but yesterday she made her appearance in Bujukdere Bay uninjured.

The Himalaya was much damaged by the storm in her passage from Varna, and is now unfit for sea. The Captain says that she was not in a safe state even before she left England with the Scots Grays, but that it was thought necessary to hurry out these to Turkey, although they subsequently remained six weeks in the barracks at Koulili. The Himalaya was ordered to take in French troops, but on the night of the 29th she lost her bowsprit and foremast, and injured her screw so much that she can only proceed to Malta by being towed. The Admiral expects to repair her here, but the facilities for the purpose are very few. The Trent, West India steamer, went on shore near Varna, but got off without damage. About 25 small craft have been lost, mostly Greeks and Sardinians.

Dr. Cumming, Inspector-General, Dr. Price, senior surgeon, and Dr. Mackleray, with 11 fresh surgeons, arrived in the Vectis. The steamer returns to-day. Stoves are wanted for the hospital. The medical officers have made requisition for 30, and more will be wanted as soon as the cold weather sets in severely. Last evening the landing of the wounded had to be discontinued at about half-past 6 o'clock, on account of the bitter cold of the night air. It will be concluded to-day.

THE BALTIC FLEET.

(FROM OUR OWN CORRESPONDENT.)

KIEL (HOLSTEIN), Nov. 13.

In my despatch of the 11th inst. I intimated that the state of the weather was such as to render it probable that the winter season had fairly set in with the severity peculiar to the Baltic regions. The present date is that on which, according to the average observations of more than 100 years, the ice on the Neva has formed to a sufficient extent to preclude the possibility of any vessel effecting a safe navigation to that locality. You may therefore assume that before another week has passed away the Russian fleet will be completely frozen in, both at Sweaborg and Cronstadt. The English fleet will therefore, on being apprised of that fact through the medium of one of the ships under the orders of Captain R. Watson, leave this port *en route* for England.

Even at this place, the latitude of which is several degrees to the southward of the enemy's ports in the Gulf of Finland, the cold has been more severe than is usual at this period of the year. The wind has gradually shifted during the past 48 hours from W.N.W. to N.N.E. It reached the latter quarter yesterday morning, blowing hard, when a heavy snow storm came on, which continued for upwards of three hours. The snow fell so thickly as to envelope every object within 50 yards' distance in perfect obscurity.

At 8 a.m. the thermometer in the open air indicated a temperature of 25° Fahrenheit, at noon the mercury had risen to 30°, towards evening it gradually fell, and at midnight it was 8° below the freezing point. The whole face of the country is covered with snow to a small extent, and, as the barometer, which has been very low for several days, has risen considerably, it may be conjectured that the frost which has set in will continue and increase in intensity.

The fleet remain in a state of complete inactivity, awaiting orders for its departure for England. Every ship is complete in provisions, stores, and necessaries up to the termination of the present year. Every possible opportunity is afforded to the officers of visiting the various towns of Germany which possess objects of interest. Very many have gone to Hamburg, and some to Berlin, while others were content to spend the leave allowed them in Kiel.

The seamen of the fleet are not allowed to go on shore, except on duty, owing to the very strict police regulations existing in this port, which have been enforced in consequence of the very great irregularities committed by a few to whom the indulgence was granted on the arrival of the ships, resulting in the death of one or two men, who defied the authority vested in the preservers of the public peace.

With the exception of the departure of the Rosamond, Commander G. Wodehouse, on the afternoon of the 11th inst., there is nothing to report as regards the movements of the fleet. Her destination is unknown, but supposed to be for the purpose of procuring pilots to conduct the various ships through the Great Belt.

The only arrival here during the past two days has been a Danish merchant steamer. The tradesmen are reaping a rich harvest from the numerous purchases which the officers have made.

The prices of everything have increased 50 per cent. within the past week, owing to the great demand for the necessaries of life, luxuries, &c. This however is not surprising, when it is considered that the numbers serving on board the fleet are nearly equivalent to the entire population of Kiel.

BELGIUM.

(FROM OUR OWN CORRESPONDENT.)

BRUSSELS, NOVEMBER 15.

A decree of the King, dated the 6th inst., declares that the day after the promulgation of the law, the following will be free of import duty:—Corn, wheat, beans, peas, barley, &c., and oxen, sheep, swine, &c. In consequence of the deficiency in the potato crop, which is considerably below an average one and of inferior quality, their exportation is prohibited.

Projects of law on—1, a commercial treaty between Belgium and Mexico; 2, a literary convention between Belgium and Great Britain; and, 3, on the prevention of desertion in the marine—have been presented to the Chamber by the Minister of Foreign Affairs. The two former will be examined by the sections, and the latter (on a proposition of M. Osy) by a special commission. MM. de Baillet and de Sécus, who were the Questors last year, have been unanimously re-elected. The numbers were, for M. de Baillet 57, and for M. de Sécus 48 voices.

Below PUNCH cartoon by John Leech, 1855, underlines public concern at the shortage of supplies at Balaclava.

Right Russell also covered the Austro-Prussian war. His sketch plan of the Battle of Sadowa (1866), was made from his observation point up a tower on the outskirts of the town, to view the battlefields across the Elbe and the retreat of the Austrian army.

Bottom Interior of the Redan, Sebastopol, after the Russian withdrawal in September 1855. Albumen photograph on glass by James Robertson.

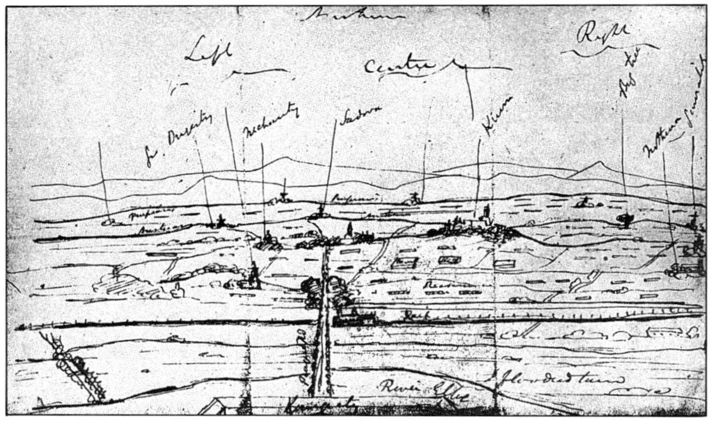

surprised when he writes: 'Looking at my own account [of the Battle of Alma], which was written literally on the field, I find I have made mistakes which I confess without a blush.' He made fewer mistakes than war correspondents then and since.

Russell had a grandstand view of the Battle of Balaclava, high on a ridge overlooking the scene, and for once reported in ideal conditions. He had his watch, notebook and spyglass, and there was plenty of time to keep notes during the frequent pauses in the action. He knew every British unit involved, and knew many of the officers personally. As a result he wrote one of the best reports of a battle ever written: comprehensive and accurate, colourful and compelling. He showed a remarkable gift, unavailable alas to the British generals, of grasping the nub of what was going on, and making instant but balanced judgments.

On the Charge of the Light Brigade he wrote, on the spur of the disaster: 'Don Quixote in his tilt against the windmill was not near so rash and reckless as the gallant fellows who prepared without a thought to rush on almost certain death'. The last sentence of his 'Letter' spoke of 'this melancholy day, in which our Light Brigade was annihilated by their own rashness'.

His dispatches bring to life the Crimean War: its muddle, its stink of death, its uselessness. At the same time his report from Balaclava reveals what he never criticized: the courage and dogged heroism of the British soldier. He was not the most elegant of war correspondents. His style was sometimes clumsy, and sometimes overblown. But it was clear and forceful. And even those readers who were outraged by his reports came to realize that they could trust his word and rely on his judgments. He was the first newspaper correspondent to turn the reporting of war into a serious profession.

In the crypt of St Paul's Russell's memorial is inscribed: 'First and greatest of war correspondents'. He could also have been described as a reformer. By his dispatches the War Department was brought kicking and screaming into the nineteenth century, and the conditions under which the soldier served were made more tolerable and humane. In 1882 Russell reflected: 'I wonder what would have come of it all had I followed the quiet path instead of noisy drums and trumpets'.

"WELL, JACK! HERE'S GOOD NEWS FROM HOME. WE'RE TO HAVE A MEDAL."
"THAT'S VERY KIND. MAYBE ONE OF THESE DAYS WE'LL HAVE A COAT TO STICK IT ON!"

The Indian Mutiny

Below The Billiard Room in the Residency at Lucknow shattered by shell-fire.

Bottom The ruins of the Residency. The European families and townspeople had taken refuge there during the siege. Sir Henry Lawrence, the Governor of Oudh, was fatally injured by a shell burst inside the building in July 1857.

The Indian Mutiny of 1857–8 took Printing House Square, almost as much as it took the Government, by surprise. The *Times* correspondent in Calcutta was Cecil Beadon, Home Secretary to the Indian Government. His identity was as closely guarded a secret as half way down the throat of a Bengal tiger, because servants of the East India Company (the agent of the British Government in India, until 1857) were forbidden to communicate with the press. Early in the year Beadon protested in *The Times* against the withdrawal of European troops from India for service further east. But in general he has been severely criticized by historians for not recognizing the storm that was about to break. Delane wrote a memo to his assistant in April ordering a piece about the news from India: 'It *looks* nasty, but I can't believe there is anything to be frightened about'. The Calcutta correspondent reported that the 19th Infantry Regiment was to be disbanded, 'but the Empire is in no danger. There is, so far as we know, no real disaffection among the great body of the Army.' The Mutiny broke out in May. In June the massacres started at Delhi.

By the autumn of 1857 Englishmen had at last realized that the Mutiny was a terrible threat to the Empire. *The Times* had until now thought it a little local difficulty, not worth sending out a special war correspondent to report. There was no shortage of copy: the national habit of writing to *The Times* was already so ingrained that officers in India, old soldiers in Britain, Anglo-Indians and Indian experts overwhelmed the paper with opinion and comment upon every aspect of the campaign. Most of it was vindictive, frightened and reactionary. William Howard Russell described one of the regular correspondents to *The Times* as 'the mad little Cromwellian theorist'.

The Times supported Lord Canning, the Governor General, in his policy of appeasement and clemency to the mutineers. The policy aroused howls of fury from the shellbacks and diehards, including most *Times* correspondents, who were typical Anglo-Indians. Printing House Square tried to get them to moderate their reports:

> Your views, you must allow me to say, are extreme. Perhaps I do you injustice, and do not make sufficient allowance for the feelings of an almost spectator, we at home being so far off as hardly to come within the range of enthusiasm. I try to make allowances for all this – and still you appear to me a little ultra. That the mutineers should be signally punished, blown from guns, bayonet [sic], hung – anything you please – all this of course – But afterwards – that is the real difficulty.

Delane at this point went off on his annual holiday, and his assistant promptly fell into line with rabid popular feeling. In October a leader declared: 'Every tree and gable-end in the place should have its burden in the shape of a mutineer's carcase. But between justice and these wretches steps in a prim philanthropist from Calcutta.' The prim philanthropist was the official sent to Cawnpore to ensure that Canning's merciful policy was observed. In Delane's absence, *The Times* turned its guns on the Governor General himself: 'We do not go along with the Calcutta Government in its absurd attempts to hamper the military commanders in the execution of justice upon the mutineers'.

Delane returned *The Times* to the sane policy in favour of Canning and moderation. And he decided to send out the paper's great war correspondent, William Howard Russell, to discover the truth about the reports of atrocities and to give an impartial account of what was going on, untainted by the ferocity of Anglo-Indian opinion.

After his reporting of the Crimean War, and the effects this had on the British Government and people, Billy Russell was a power to be reckoned with, by even the stuffiest top brass. The Governor General received him in Calcutta and undertook that his dispatches would be given top priority after service messages, and sent *The Times* correspondent off with an introduction to the Commander-in-Chief at Cawnpore. Russell did not really need an introduction since the Commander-in-Chief was his old friend from the Crimea, that fine old Highland warrior Sir Colin Campbell.

Sir Colin welcomed him warmly:

> Now, Mr Russell, I'll be candid with you. We shall make a compact. You shall know everything that is going on. You shall know all my reports and get every information that I have myself, on the condition that you do not mention it in camp or let it be known in any way, except in your letters to England.

Things had changed in the year since the Crimean War. The Army had recognized the power of Printing House Square. The rank and file had not forgotten their debt to William Howard Russell. And publication of military plans in England could do no harm, for the mutineers were not in telegraphic communication with Europe.

Russell's report of the fall of Lucknow to the British army.
20 APRIL 1858

INDIA.

[The following appeared in our second edition of yesterday:—]

THE CAPTURE OF LUCKNOW.

By the arrival of the Bombay mail we have received the subjoined graphic account of the siege of Lucknow from the pen of "Our Special Correspondent."

The telegraphic news received at Bombay, which we publish from our Bombay correspondent, completes the picture, with the news of the capture of Lucknow:—

HEAD-QUARTERS, CAMP, BIBIAPOOR, BEFORE LUCKNOW, MARCH 9.

I was compelled to close my last letter very hastily, owing to the march of the army, the order for which we received at 11 o'clock on the night of the 2d of March. There is now no time to revert to the many matters of interest which I was obliged to leave unnoticed, inasmuch as the events of each subsequent day have absorbed every moment. The conclusion of my letter dated the 2d of March was but a series of hurried transcripts from semi-illegible entries in my diary, relating mostly to personal experiences on the line of march. I have now subjects of great importance to deal with. We are before Lucknow, and, as I write, my tent is flapping to and fro at the vibration of our bombardment. As I do not know when I may be summoned to the final scene of the assault I shall waste no more time on introductory matter, but shall at once resume my narrative from the point at which I left off in the last letter.

You will recollect that the Cawnpore force, which I accompanied, left the camp there on the morning of the 27th February, and in three marches arrived at Bunthurah. Sir Colin Campbell left Cawnpore on the 28th, and in one day rode to Bunthurah, and thence on to the Alumbagh, whence he returned the same evening to his quarters, having ridden upwards of 50 miles in the day. On the 2d of March he started at dawn with the following force:—Two 24-pounders, two 8-inch howitzers of the Naval Brigade (elephant draught), with three troops of Horse Artillery, one a 9-pounder battery; two companies of Punjab Sappers; the head-quarters of the Cavalry Division, with the 1st brigade of Her Majesty's 9th Lancers; the 2d Punjab Cavalry, a detachment of the 5th Punjab Cavalry, a detachment of Wale's Horse, and the 2d Division of Infantry complete.

The first bugle sounded at 4 a.m., and at 5 the men were formed on the right of their camp. The advanced guard consisted of a troop of Horse Artillery, a squadron of Lancers, a squadron of Punjabees, and a regiment of infantry. The cavalry moved in two columns, one on each flank of the infantry and guns. A troop of Horse Artillery was on each flank of the infantry, and the heavy guns were put between the infantry brigades, the baggage being in rear of the column. The rear guard was composed of two Horse Artillery guns, two squadrons of cavalry, and half a regiment of infantry. Each soldier was provided with a loaf of bread before starting. The road proceeds in a straight line through a country which is as flat as a bowling-green, well cultivated, and covered with patches of thick groves and mango topes. The point to which the march tended was the south-east extremity of the environs of Lucknow, to the east of the position held by us at the Alumbagh; and as soon as our force had arrived within some mile or so of the Alumbagh, the head of the column inclined to the right by the fortress of Jellalabad, which forms the extreme point held by General Outram, and in which were stored large quantities of stores and material. Having thrown out skirmishers to the front the force advanced towards the Dilkoosha, a palace standing in a large enclosure, within a short distance of the banks of the Goomtee, in front of the Martinière. The enemy's Sowars were now visible, watching our troops, and as we proceeded a force of infantry and cavalry, with two guns, appeared, as if to dispute our progress, and the enemy's skirmishers began a long and feeble fire from the edges of the standing crops on our flanks. They were speedily silenced and obliged to retire before our men. Sir Colin gave them no time to collect themselves. He pressed them at once. Our cavalry and three troops of Horse Artillery, in the full speed of emulation between Bengal and Royal Horse Artillery, dashed across the broken ground at a gallop, the guns hopping and bounding over the dry ditches which intersect the fields as if they were made of caoutchouc, and the enemy fled, leaving one of their guns in our hands. A few matchlockmen and Sepoys kept up a running fire, which caused us no damage, and our forces occupied the enclosures, parks, and residences of the Bibiapoor and the Mahomed Bagh, and the Dilkoosha (or Dilkushah), with little or no opposition. Sir Colin reconnoitred the enemy's position, a portion of which is quite open to view from the Dilkoosha and the ground in front of it, and it then became evident that the enemy had availed themselves of the respite so unavoidably permitted them, and had thrown up works of astonishing strength, so far as the height and solidity of the parapets and batteries were concerned. As the Sepoys still lined an old wall from the river's bank along the front of the Dilkoosha, a few companies of Punjabees, supported by a party of the 38th Regiment, were sent to take it in the evening. Breaking into a run from the Dilkoosha, the Sikhs, with a loud cheer, went at the enemy with the bayonet, and, although the latter numbered 600 or 700, they fled after one discharge of their pieces, which caused only six or seven casualties in our ranks. The wall was at once seized, and the loopholes were used against the enemy, who fell back upon their trenches in front of the Martinière. As the enemy opened upon us from a light gun at the proper left of the Martinière, ground was selected for a battery on the right of the Dilkoosha ("Heart's content") to silence them, and arrangements were made to begin the attack on the vast city as speedily as possible. Orders were sent to Bunthurah for the rest of the army to march, which were received just as they were turning in for the night, and six guns of Peel's train were detailed to accompany them.

As to the general condition of the army you will best form an opinion from these simple facts:—The total of the Queen's troops with this army on the 28th of February numbered 16,347. The proportion of sick to well in that force, according to the weekly return, was 1 in 27 221-576; of deaths to strength, 1 in 3,229⅔; of deaths to sick, 1 in 117 4-5. On the advance to and occupation of the Dilkoosha, Bibiapoor, and Mahomed Bagh, we suffered the following losses:—

Killed.—Naval Brigade, 1 man.

Wounded.—Naval Brigade, 1 man; 9th Lancers, 1 officer, 1 man; 2d Punjabees, 1 man; 5th Punjabees, 1 man; 1st Sikh Punjab, 1 officer, 1 man; 34th Regiment, 1 man; 38th Regiment, 2 men; 42d Regiment, 1 man; 4th Punjab Rifles, 3 men. Total, 2 officers, 12 men.

Missing.—9th Lancers, 1 man.

Horses.—5 killed, 15 wounded, and 3 missing.

MARCH 3.

The moon lighted up our early march this morning along a road which bore frequent traces of rough usage and of the enormous traffic which follows in the wake of an Indian army. Mile after mile we passed the slow trains of the bullock carts of the Commissariat, which extended in one uninterrupted line from our late camping-ground to the rear guard of the troops. When morning broke we were in the rear of the Alumbagh, which was about a mile and a half in front of us, and we could just catch the report of the guns, engaged in their usual encounter with the enemy, and the white tops of some buildings inside the position. Thence the march deflected to the right towards the fort of Jellalabad, a square fortification with high and thick mud walls and bastions baked as hard as brick by the sun, but seamed, nevertheless, by the violent rains which have traced their course downs its sides. It was difficult to get on through the dense multitudes of men and animals, sailors, Highlanders, Sikhs, Pathans, Punjabees, bheesties, dooly-bearers, camp servants, bullocks, camels, horses, elephants, goats, cows, sheep, guns and carriages, which filled the plain for miles in front of us, but at length we managed to emerge from the dust and heat, and to come up with the advanced guard of the 7th Hussars, near whom were riding most of the head-quarter staff and heads of departments, who had been in the saddle from the previous midnight. As we crossed the plain there were abundant evidences that we were near the battle-grounds of the garrison of the Alumbagh and their enemies. In topes of trees were lying skeletons from which the dogs had torn the clothes and flesh, and out on the open were the same ghastly spectacles extended in fantastic attitudes, dried up by the sun and mummified, some with bits of their old Sepoy red jackets still clinging to their whitened bones. These were all that remained of the men cut up from time to time by the Military Train and Hodson's Horse, in their charges, whenever the enemy ventured out in the open. Having passed this plain, we approached a much closer country, covered with trees, thick corn fields, and walled enclosures. Here and there we could see the white-coated Sowars of the enemy watching us, but they were not numerous. It was, however, impossible to say what force might be hid in the cover and among the trees, and our men advanced along the road with due precaution. At length we came to another plain, cut up by nullahs, and in the distance, about a mile and a half away, we were told, was the Dilkoosha. The enemy had thrown up a parapet, with two embrasures to sweep this road, but they had not the courage to use them. A small body of the 7th Hussars was halted at the end of this road where it debouched on the plain. As we were waiting for orders to proceed, or possibly for a guide, a cloud of dust, above which rose a clump of lances, appeared in sight before us. It came nearer and nearer, and presently it resolved itself into an English officer riding hard and followed by an escort of Irregular Horse. As soon as he arrived, Captain Johnson (of the Quartermaster-General's Department) was kind enough to offer me the escort he had brought with him, and, as the enemy's horse were said to be on our left flank, I had no objection to the protection of eight stout Lancers well mounted and keeneyed. Captain Johnson proceeded to direct the march of our column, the officer who was more than my comrade on this march, having been guide, interpreter, and friend since I left Cawnpore, mounted on his fast dromedary, and we both rode for the Dilkoosha. The leader of our escort was a fine, handsome fellow—not darker than a Spaniard—with a free and open expression of face, white teeth, and a frank smile. His black beard, divided at the chin, was plaited in with his whiskers, and turned up over his ears so as to fasten in a knot under his turban at the top of his head. As to pistols, he had any number of them, not to mention a rifled carbine slung at his back, and a broad-bladed keen-edged sabre. He was dressed in a slate-coloured tunic of quilted silk, wadded with cotton, tight pantaloons of the same coloured calico, and long jack-boots. What lies this beau chevalier told us! How we had killed hundreds the day before—how we had taken the Martinière—how the Sikhs had bayoneted and chopped up whole battalions of Sepoys! All these lies he told us simply to make himself agreeable and to say something he thought we should like to hear. He led us by a detour across the plain to avoid the pot-shots of the enemy in the enclosures, and in about 20 minutes more we made out a small body of cavalry coming towards us, which at first our friend seemed to think might consist of hostile Sowars. "No," said he, after a keen look, "they are not, for, see! those men with the camels do not run away from them." This indication was beyond my seeing or comprehension, but he was quite right, for the body turned out to be the escort of another staff officer, and we learnt we were only half-a-mile or so from the enclosure of the Dilkoosha, in which the General had pitched his tents. The ground was soon passed over, and my companion, who had accompanied Sir Colin Campbell's force in the relief of the Residency, dismissed the escort as soon as we came in sight of a long brick wall, over which, amid the green trees, appeared white lines of tents, and the roofs and gilded pinnacles of the palace of the Dilkoosha. We were soon among bullocks and guns, and troops and ravines again, but, passing inside the boundary wall, I met Colonel Wood, the Brigadier of the Field Artillery, and he was kind enough to volunteer to show us the way, forgiving, and I hope forgetting, a little misunderstanding in times gone by in the Crimea. We wound through dry nullahs, cut by watercourses in the rainy season, inside to a park containing most delightfully shady trees, and soon espied the Commander-in-Chief's camp, pitched with its usual strictness of outline. The 42d Highlanders were just turning out to take duty in the Dilkoosha, and we were aware that we could not be very far from the enemy by hearing the whiz and plump of their round shots all around us. As soon as we had refreshed ourselves we rode to the palace, which stands on a slight elevation in front of the enclosure in which our camp was pitched, at the distance of 200 yards or so from the boundary wall. Emerging from the park, which put me, somehow or other, in mind of Greenwich Park during fair time, perhaps on account of the trees, the dust, and the noise, through an arched gateway in front, at a short distance stands the palace of the Dilkoosha, built evidently on an Italian model, with a flat-terraced roof, turrets covered with gilt ovals and spires, and mounted with plaster statues of Nymphs and clumsy Graces and Apollos. The line of rising ground on which it stands bounds the view in front, so that only the strange summits of the Martinière are visible, and on the right flows, in a clear bright stream, meandering in many curves through a wide expanse of corn-fields studded with groves of fruit and forest trees, the river Goomtee, which takes its name from its nature—*nomen ab re factum*—the "winding." As we approached the Dilkoosha inch after inch the Martinière comes in sight; behind it an expanse of trees and enclosures, shut in by a high bank of tawny earthworks, which is the first line of the enemy's defences. To the left this bank again appears, bounding another vast suburb, above the trees of which rise the domes and spires and minarets of a magnificent city. The whistling of round shot from the Martinière, which tear up the earth close at hand, warns us to get under cover, and so we make for the Dilkoosha, which we find strongly occupied by the 42d Highlanders. The hall retains traces of its departed splendour; the gilt frames of pictures and of huge mirrors still adorn its walls; our men are lying on a marble table with richly gilt legs, and the roof and sides of the room are bright with fanciful frescoes and colourings. One of the winding staircases of the turrets conducts us past many fine corridors and suites of rooms up to the roof, the parapets of which are lined with the Highlanders. I looked into some of these apartments, and I must own the style of the decorations surprised me. The chimneypieces of mosaic and marble, with gilded fretwork, the frescoed roofs, the ceilings covered with paintings of houris amid clouds, with medallion heads of short-waisted, befrizzled, and bebonneted English beauties, borderings of wild animals in chase, and representations of the various celebrities of the Indian zoology—the size and lofty dimensions of the rooms, the coloured glass of the shattered windows, all gave the place an air of taste and luxury which one scarce expected to find in a Lucknow palace, and which indicated very certainly the existence of an Italian architect and decorator, whose views had been controlled by an Asiatic. From the roof the summits of the Residency, of the Mess-house, of the Kaiserbagh, of the Secunderbagh, of the Shah Nujeef, and of many other places unknown to us, were visible in a widely-spread panorama on our left. This palace when last our men were here was surrounded by trees, but the enemy had cut them all down to clear their line, and we could see the inequalities of the ground thickly filled by Sepoys, who just at this moment began to open fire on the Dilkoosha. Our Highlanders soon sent their Enfield bullets whistling among them, and forced them to seek cover; but the Commander-in-Chief, who came up at the time, disapproved this desultory waste of powder, and the enemy were permitted to send their bullets up to the Dilkoosha with impunity, and to vary their amusements by throwing round shot over us into our camp. Who built the Martinière? It looks like the result of a competitive examination among a college of mad architects. But what most interested me in the Martinière was a black eunuch whom we could see through the glass, and who was busily engaged in rifle practice at us. The fellow was splendidly dressed in green silk, and he sat at one of the windows watching whilst one of his attendants loaded his rifle, and then he fired at any one he saw on the roof of the Dilkoosha. All his shots fell short, and it was unpleasant to find that ours in return did not reach this rascal. That he was what I have said I decided on two grounds: first, the Lucknow garrison are agreed in saying their greatest enemies during the siege were the eunuchs of the Court, and that they were the best shots in the place, and the most determined; secondly, there was a coolness about the fellow which showed he did not care much for life, and a malignity which proved that he hated all mankind. Our soldiers lining the wall, and the Sepoys in the trenches along the foot of the Martinière, kept up a brisk fire, but they were too well sheltered to do any harm to each other. After spending all day on the top of the palace I returned to camp only to find that the round shots were pitching among our tents and causing us some annoyance; as our guns are not yet up we cannot return their fire, and so we must submit till the time comes.

MARCH 4.

The effect produced on the inhabitants of Lucknow by the appearance of the British force on the banks of the Goomtee and in the Dilkoosha has been very depressing. They are described by our spies as being "like people without hearts," and we are told that they were flying in such multitudes to the two bridges that the sentries placed there to prevent egress were forced and overwhelmed. It is scarcely credible, but it is only too true, that, in addition to the 30,000 regular Sepoys of our mutinous regiments, and to the 50,000 or 60,000 men under arms of irregular levies and volunteers, there is a population of 300,000 men, women, and children within the walls of the city. Now, I have no sympathy with rebellion, murder, and mutiny, but I cannot refrain from expressing a most earnest hope that these unfortunate people, who are at most guilty of a forced neutrality, will not be handed over to a very excited and irritated soldiery, to the fierce Sikhs and to the wild Ghoorkas of Nepaul. The time for indiscriminate bloodshedding must cease, let all that the angry civilians of British India can say be said, with the punishment of the mutinous Sepoys and of those actually taken in arms against us. Justice and even vengeance must after a period rest satisfied. We cannot, and God forbid that the British people would if they could, put to death *all* who have at any time and under any circumstances taken up arms against us. We cannot, after the work of the bullet and the sabre has been done, put hundreds of thousands of people to death. To many tens of thousands we were unable to afford protection; these people were therefore forced to obey the orders of the authorities who reigned in our stead, and, though it may be very easy to say that they should have come over to us, it was not at all easy to do so at a time when the whole of the North-Western Provinces, except the Punjab, swarmed with our enemies, and when the British were only to be seen in a few beleagured posts. In the case of Lucknow all our difficulties will most probably be solved by the sword; but "there is an hereafter." Are the hundreds of thousands who must escape to be shut out from all hope? to be deliberately driven into desperate dacoitee and outlawry? Are we to look to the rope and the rifle as the only means of "reassuring the country," and of "restoring law and order?" Even as it is we are obliged to close the gates of mercy on many who would willingly enter if they had a chance, inasmuch as, for political reasons, they cannot be opened till the gates of Lucknow have been opened also. It is a positive fact that the Prime Minister of Oude—a man whose influence, it is true, has been diminished by that of the Begum's favourite, but who still holds a high position—has made overtures to Sir James Outram, to which that officer has been compelled to give an unfavourable reply. It may be very unpopular to say so, but I cannot refrain, nevertheless, from the expression of my own individual opinion, that much of the enmity which exists against us has been engendered by want of honesty, by trimming, and by a Laodicean policy, which has enabled the natives to charge us with the very subtleties and falsehoods for which they are themselves notorious. Let that be. The question is,—Are you now prepared for a new crusade? Is England determined to enter upon a holy war against the Hindoo and the Mussulman? Will she disclaim or accept the views of proselytism imputed to her, and will she, fresh from a sanguinary war, in which she supported the independence of a Mahomedan State against a Christian Power, do battle in the name of Heaven against Mahomed and the million foul deities of the Hindoo mythology, which, by too many treaties, she has bound herself to respect? Let us see how the natives think we have acted; let us mark and learn and digest the accusations which our present enemies, late our servants, our friends, our hired soldiers, do not hesitate to prefer against us in the face of all the world. Here are two documents which will repay perusal, and reward the profoundest attention of those who seek to divine the causes of this war. They are, as their title indicates, the bills of indictment preferred against us, on which juries of hundreds of thousands of armed men have returned a verdict of guilty. It is, after all, most gratifying to find that the charges which are tenable and provable are so light, but it is very distressing to observe that those charges which are utterly groundless are still urged against us with as much force and as if they were true. Were they true, would the case against us be worse? It is needless to say that, except in a very few isolated cases, there is no ground whatever for the statements that our soldiers committed any violence against women.

The following proclamation issued for the Mahomedan inhabitants of Oude, Kulhyr, Rampore, and Mooradabad, was posted on the gates of all police stations in Oude:—

"God says in the Koran, 'Do not enter into the friendship of Jews and Christians; those who are their friends are of them—*i. e.*, the friends of Christians are Christians, and friends of Jews are Jews. God never shows his way to infidels.'

"By this it is evident that to befriend Christians is irreligious; those who are their friends are not Mahomedans, therefore all the Mahomedan fraternity should with all their hearts be deadly enemies to the Christians, and never befriend them in any way; otherwise all will lose their religion and become infidels.

"Some people, weak in faith and worldly, think that if they offend the Christians they will fall their victims when their rule is re-established. 'God says of these people, Look in the hearts of these unbelievers, who are anxious to seek the friendship of Christians through fear of receiving injury,' to remove their doubts and assure their wavering mind. It is also said that 'God will shortly give us victory, or will do something by which our enemies will be ashamed of themselves.' The Mussulmans should therefore always hope, and never believe that the Christians will be victorious and injure them; but, on the contrary, should hope to gain the victory and destroy all Christians.

"If all the Mahomedans join and remain firm to their faith they would no doubt gain victory over the Christians, because God says that the victory is due to the faithful from Him; but if they become cowards and infirm to their religion, and do not sacrifice their private interest for the public good, the Europeans will be victorious, and, having subdued the Mahomedans, they will disarm, hang, shoot, or blow them away, seize upon their women and children, disgrace, dishonour, and christianize them, dig up their houses and carry off their property; they will also burn religious and sacred books, destroy the Musjids, and efface the name of Islam from the world.

"If the Mahomedans have any shame, they should all join and prepare themselves to kill the Christians without minding any one who says to the contrary; they should also know that no one dies before his time, and when the time comes nothing can save them. Thousands of men are carried off by cholera and other pestilence; but it is not known whether they die in their senses, and be faithful to their own religion.

"To be killed in a war against Christians is a proof of obtaining martyrdom. All good Mahomedans pray for such a death; therefore, every one should sacrifice his life for such a reward. Every one is to die assuredly, and those Mahomedans who would spare themselves now will be sorry on their death for their neglect.

"As it is the duty of all men and women to oppose, kill, and expel the Europeans for deeds committed by them at Delhi, Jhujur, Rewaree, and the Doab, all the Mahomedans should discharge their duty with a willing heart; if they neglect, and the Europeans overpower them, they will be disarmed, hung, and treated like the inhabitants of other unfortunate countries, and will have nothing but regret and sorrow for their lot. Wherefore this notice is given to warn the public."

The following proclamation issued for the zemindars, and all the inhabitants of the kingdom of Oude, was posted on each police station:—

"All the Hindoos and Mahomedans know that man loves four things most:—1, his religion and caste; 2, his honour; 3, his own and his kinsmen's lives; 4, his property. All these four are well protected under native rulers; no one interferes with any one's religion; every one enjoys his respectability according to his caste and wealth. All the respectable people—Syad, Shaikh, Mogul, and Puthan, among Mahomedans; and Brahmins, Chatrees, Bys, and Kaeths, among the Hindoos—are respected according to their castes. No low-caste people like Chumars, Dhanook, and Passees can be equal to and address them disrespectfully. No one's life or property is taken unless for some heinous crime.

"The British are quite against these four things—they want to spoil every one's caste, and wish both the Mahomedans and Hindoos to become Christians. Thousands have turned renegades, and many will become so yet; both the nobles and low caste are equal in their eyes; they disgrace the nobles in the presence of the ignoble; they arrest or summon to their courts the gentry, Nawabs, and Rajahs at the instance of a Chumar, and disgrace them; wherever they go they hang the respectable people, kill their women and children; their troops dishonour the women, and dig up and carry off their buried property. They do not kill the Mahajuns, but dishonour their women and carry off their money.

They disarm the people wherever they go, and when the people are disarmed, they hang, shoot, or blow them away.

"In some places they take in the landholders by promising them remittance of revenue, or lessen the amount of their lease; their object is that when their Government is settled, and every one becomes their subject, they can readily, according to their wish, hang, disgrace, or christianize them. Some of the foolish landholders have been taken in, but those who are wise and careful do not fall into their snares.

"Therefore, all the Hindoos and Mahomedans who wish to save their religion, honour, life, and property are warned to join the Government forces, and not to be taken in by the British.

"The Passees* should also know that the Choukeedaree† is their hereditary right, but the British appoint Burkundazes in their posts, and deprive them of their rights; they should therefore kill and plunder the British and their followers, and annoy them by committing robbery and thefts in their camp."

The nearest way of reaching the enemy's positions is by going round them. It has occurred to our engineers that by moving to the north side we may secure a good chance of taking their lines in enfilade, and Sir James Outram is ordered to take command of a force which will be detached to establish itself on the other side of the Goomtee, as the commencement of our attack on the enemy. Our materials, such as casks, fascines of dry wood, rope, and balks of timber for bridge-making, are all in readiness, and to-night, when the moon rises, we intend to throw two bridges across the river.

The greater portion of our combinations are developing themselves with order and precision. The first of these is the arrival of Brigadier-General Franks's column, which, after a very successful and extraordinary progress, in which it broke up immense masses of the enemy and took many guns, reached our position in the afternoon of this day. About 10 miles from this, however, on the Sultanpore road, the General had a small engagement, which was not so complete in its results as could have been desired. He was in full march to join Sir Colin Campbell, when he heard that a small body of the enemy were in position near him. With a portion of his force he at once attacked and defeated them, but the greater number of them took refuge in the citadel or interior work of one of those forts called Khoosagunge, in which Oude abounds. The Brigadier brought his light guns to bear on the gates, but they were strong, and the shot passed through without shattering them. In an attempt to take the place and blow in the gates Lieutenant Innes, of the Engineers, was severely wounded, and Lieutenant Brockhurst received a severe wound. As the General did not wish to delay his march, he did not consider it expedient to send for his heavy guns to batter down the place, and accordingly he marched off, leaving the enemy in the fort to claim, as they will, no doubt, the credit of having repulsed the British army. Another small success I must also record for our foe. They actually compelled us to shift the head-quarters camp to-day, and to move to Bibiapoor, by dropping and plumping long-range shots among our tents. Bibiapoor is the nearest enclosure to the park of the Dilkoosha, and the house contains six large rooms, some of which will be available for the Commander-in-Chief and his Staff, but his Excellency and General Mansfield will still live under canvass, and give up the rooms as offices. The shot came too near to be pleasant over and among our tents, and the change is, therefore, by no means disagreeable.

There is no chance of any immediate co-operation from Sir Hugh Rose's column, except from a distance, and he finds the difficulties of procuring supply and transport so great that he cannot promise to be with us till the 20th March, and then only in case he gets all that he wants. He is on his march to Jhansi, but he describes the country as being very formidable, and seems unwilling to trust his small force in the defiles and passes through which they must march, surrounded, as he appears to be, by a hostile population. The news of his approach has, however, been heard by the Calpee force, who believe he is close to Banda, and are proportionately alarmed. These "gallant Gwaliors" are held in complete check by Her Majesty's 32d and 88th Regiments, by some Irregular Horse, and Blunt's field battery, under the command of Colonel Maxwell, and they have done nothing to justify the expectations entertained of them by some of their friends at home. They have, indeed, hanged a spy sent in by one of the civilians at Cawnpore, but they have been well trounced by our gallant little ally, the Rajah of Churkaree, whose valiant adherence to our cause will, I hope, procure for him the special consideration of the Government. So little do we think of the Gwaliors, who are much disturbed by the news that Rose is advancing in our direction, that we are about to send for the 88th Regiment to join this force.

The following is a list of the casualties on the 3d and 4th of March, from which it will be seen how insignificant is the result of the enemy's firing. It does not include, however, the casualties of Franks's force:—

Wounded.—42d Regiment, 1; F troop Royal Horse Artillery, 1; 6th company 11th Battalion Royal Artillery, 1; 5th Punjab Cavalry, 2; Her Majesty's 34th Regiment, 1; 4th Punjab, 1; Bengal Fusileers, 1. Total, 8.

MARCH 5.

Late last night I went down to see the commencement of the process of bridging the Goomtee. It was bright moonlight, and the whole of the enemy's side of the river was plainly visible, our figures being cast into shade, so that any one at the opposite side could see us readily, but not a man fired a shot, not a wandering Sowar came down to find what was the cause of all the noise inevitable in such operations. There was the creaking of hackeries laden with the casks and planks necessary for the construction of the bridges, and the tumult of men and the rumble of artillery which came down to cover the working party in case of opposition. The river is about 40 yards broad, and flows with a gentle placid current between hard sandy shelving banks of seven or eight feet in height, so that it is favourable for the work. Major Hassard, R.E., and a party of Sappers and Miners were engaged all through the night, and when morning dawned I found one bridge nearly completed and the other advanced half way. Some unexpected delays had occurred in making the landing-places, but the first bridge was pronounced to be extremely firm, although it consisted of nothing more solid than porter casks lashed to crosspieces of wood with ropes, and floated off section after section till in a fit state to have the planking connected. The enemy now for the first time seemed to be aware of our tactics. We had already a picket of the 38th Regiment at the other side of the river, who lined the banks near the bridge, and occupied a small knoll on the left of it. In front of us was a wide plain, covered with corn-fields, and patches of dall and grain, and high grass, fringed by groves and clumps of trees. Through this plain the enemy's cavalry were riding in small groups, watching our proceedings in evident consternation. Their infantry came hurrying out of the city from the north side, and presently three guns were tugged out from the Fyzabad road, and were placed under clumps of trees so as to bear on the bridge. Had they attacked us with resolution at that moment they might have prevented the completion of the bridge for the time, and retarded the operation of turning their flank, and taking their whole line on their left in reverse, but the Sepoys seem to have no notion that such a movement exists, notwithstanding all the lessons they have received in this campaign. They construct batteries and trenches without any flanking fire, as if for the sole purpose of having them turned. As we were watching their movements a very gay cavalier rode out from under a mango tope, as if to inspect. He came down boldly, managing a handsome horse with ease and grace, and as he approached nearer and nearer he displayed a remarkable resemblance to the eunuch of the Martinière. After him came an escort of 16 regular Lancers—troopers of our only Lancer regiment. They came on till they were within 700 or 800 yards. Our soldiers who were lining the bank near me, unable to restrain themselves any longer, blazed away, and off went the Minié balls, picking up little tufts of dust as they bounded on the plain. You should have seen the change in our cavalier and his following. His head dropped at once to his horse's neck, down went his hands, and in went his heels sharp to the horse's flanks, and off, riding for life, he went, helter skelter, through corn, and over meadow, and across fence, as if he had the eyes of all Melton on him. His Lancers were no less expeditious in their retrograde movement. Not a man drew bridle till he had placed a good mile between himself and those wasplike missiles which had so disturbed their composure. Their guns now opened on the head of the bridge and the round shot flew over the heads of our men, and some crashed into our camp behind the bridge. At the same time the obstinate little gun which had been so long (two days or more) bothering us from the angle of the Martinière opened and tried to touch the bridge with a cross fire. Our artillery replied to the guns in the open, and the moment we got the range and burst a shell and sent one round shot near each they limbered up and retired out of sight. The Martinière gun still kept up its fire, and two of Peel's heavy guns were brought up to the bank to reply to it, but the range was too great for them, although not for the Sepoys, who fired at a reckless elevation, so that their shot fell dead and did not ricochet. The guns and howitzers in the battery on the right front of the Dilkoosha, near the river, gave five or six shots for every one fired by the Sepoys from the Martinière, but somehow or other they could not silence their gun or bring down the angle wall on the top of it. Some of our shell practice was not good, and more than once the shell burst on leaving the gun, to the great discomposure of our soldiers in front of the battery. I had almost forgotten to note Sir William Peel's coolness in bringing up his guns across the open to the Dilkoosha, to open on the Martinière. The enemy laid their guns well from the canal wall, and the shot tore up the ground again and again just at the rear of the guns, but the enemy was always too late, and shot behind his bird. Sir William, however, verges a little on rashness, and he seems to believe what he said to me when talking on the top of the Dilkoosha about the enemy's fire, "Oh, the fellows can't touch one at any distance: the very extreme range of a matchlock is 400 yards, and at that they can do no harm." Nevertheless, this day they flattened their bullets against the wall above our heads at 700 and 800 yards.

Sir James Outram, who came over from the Alumbagh, is to have the command of a strong column, which will cross the river to-morrow morning, and advance along the Fyzabad road to reconnoitre, and, if possible, to get a position whence to take the enemy's first line of defences in reverse. As the enemy's fire on the Dilkoosha has been rather hot, Sir Colin issued an order to the officer of the day on duty to prevent officers assembling on the top, and in consequence of some little irregularity, I presume, at the camp of Bunthurah, the following characteristic order was issued:—

"While a vigilant look out should be kept by all ranks it is indispensable to prevent false alarms.

"Staff officers when warning regiments to turn out will invariably seek the commanding officer of the corps or the senior officer in camp, but they are not to rush wildly about vociferating to regiments to turn out, and thereby causing panic."

At present Sir E. Lugard has his head-quarters in the Dilkoosha.

In the room in which we were breakfasting a round shot went right through one of the walls, which is a proof that the place is not calculated for domestic quiet.

Colonel J. P. Sparks, 38th Regiment; Lieut.-Colonel Kelly, 34th Regiment; Lieut.-Colonel L. Hay, 93d Regiment, are placed on the rolster as acting Brigadiers. Colonel Adrian Hope, 93d, and Colonel Horsford, Rifle Brigade, also act as Brigadiers.

The First Division, under Outram, part in garrison at the Alumbagh, consisting of the 84th, 1st Madras Fusileers, 5th Fusileers, 78th Highlanders, 90th Light Infantry, and Ferozepore Regiment, musters about 5,000 strong.

Lugard's (the Second Division), consisting of the 34th, 38th, 53d (3d brigade), and 42d, 93d, 90th, and 4th Punjab Rifles (4th brigade), presents a total of 5,350 men.

Walpole's Division (the 3d), which will be under the orders of General Outram to-morrow, consists of 4,300 infantry. The force will be accompanied by 30 pieces of field artillery and by 14 squadrons of cavalry.

Franks's Division (the 4th), consisting of a company of Madras artillery, with light field battery, detachments of Benares, Pathan, Lahore, and Sikh horse, the 10th, 20th, and 97th Regiments, with six battalions of Ghoorka Infantry, is just 4,800 strong.

The Engineer brigade consists effectively of 11 officers and 89 rank and file Royal Engineers; 25 officers and 26 men of Bengal Engineers; 19 officers and men Punjab Pioneers; 9 Pioneer Corps, all Europeans, to which are attached 1,522 native sappers and miners.

The Artillery division numbers 57 European officers, 42 non-commissioned officers, 957 rank and file, 411 horses, and 72 bullocks, effective—the details being, field artillery brigade, 339; siege artillery, 286; and Naval Brigade 431.

MARCH 6.

We have made another move on the board, and we have closed up one great outlet from Lucknow, and have dried up one large source of supply to the garrison and inhabitants. This morning early the force detached for the purpose, consisting of a full division of infantry, 14 squadrons of cavalry, and 30 guns, field battery and horse artillery, crossed the bridges which we constructed across the Goomtee, and, followed by an enormous number of baggage and ammunition animals, proceeded by a flank march to reconnoitre the enemy's position on the north-east of Lucknow, and to place themselves on our right flank across the Fyzabad road. I proceeded to view the operation from the top of the Dilkoosha, which commands a very extensive prospect over the wide plains of waving corn, now fast losing their early honours under the restless tread of war. The day was tolerably clear, and, as soon as the enemy perceived that our force was crossing, they were thrown into a state of great excitement. Their guns from the Martinière strove in vain to reach the bridges with certainty, and threw their shot over or short of the masses of men and animals which covered the ground for many thousand yards at each side of the stream. Meantime our glittering cavalry, the Bays conspicuous in their white-covered helmets and scarlet, the 7th Hussars in their blue and yellow, and the 9th Lancers with flagless lances glancing in the sun, the grand array of artillery, the swift squadrons of the Irregular Horse, and the sombre, solid, block-like battalions of our infantry, followed by camels, elephants, and an army of camp attendants, spread across the plain, and stretch in receding lines through an atmosphere of dust till they reach a road bordered with trees, and fall in upon it in order of march. I was sorry I could not go with them, but one must move with one's tent in India, and of course I could not strike mine and leave my quarters single-handed; nor have I succeeded in obtaining a horse up to a hard day's work, so I had to trust to a long shot with the telescope, and as it turned out I was better off than if I had gone out, and I saw more than nine-tenths of the force did. The country is well wooded, and in consequence our troops were speedily lost to view, and all we could see was the dust which rose above the topes marking the line of their progress. But the enemy were plainly visible. They could be seen coming out in irregular groups all over the cornfields, mostly in white, with cross-belts, but some in their old red Sepoy jackets. Their cavalry in more regular order, Lancers and light horse, poured along the road towards Fyzabad as if to fight for the right of way; troopers and brightly-clad cavaliers dashed through the long grass and corn, pointing, with lance and scimetar, towards our advancing troops. Some great people, on elephants, were also in sight, proceeding in much state to witness the discomfiture of the Infidel, and we could see also several bullock-guns taking up positions under shady groups of trees, so as to rake our columns. The Martinière was crowded with people as anxious but not as confident as ourselves. The yellow eunuch was too much occupied to fire. The line of the canal works, the Yellow House, and the Race-stand were filled with matchlockmen, and a strong body of horse and foot was stationed near the long bridge which by 11 arches crosses a nullah on the Fyzabad road, near the city, which the rains fill with a foaming torrent. This road appears like a ridge through the fields, open here and there through the trees, but for the most part shut from view by thick mangoes. Whilst we were waiting, the enemy, determined to annoy us, never ceased throwing cannon shot at the Dilkoosha, which flew over it, and dashed into the plain beyond, but, as they did not ricochet, owing to the distance, they hurt no one amid the crowd of soldiers below us. Sir Colin Campbell and General Mansfield came up to the Dilkoosha later in the day, and reconnoitred the enemy. It seemed evident, from the interest with which they regarded the works, that the Sepoys have got better defences than they expected to find when they sat down before the place, and that some modification in the plan of attack is in contemplation. I think it is pretty evident that the Alumbagh attack must be abandoned, and that our position there will be turned into a post, our major attack being made from the north side of the Goomtee, near the bridges which afford access to the city. We cannot afford to run any risk or to lose a single chance. The Commander-in-Chief is almost in air as it is, without any very decided base of operations, with an enormous number of non-combatants, prodigious *matériel* and stock to cover, and long lines of communication to keep open with Cawnpore, so that really he is deprived of half his force. He has not now much more available strength than when, with 5,000 men in light marching order, without tents, he relieved the garrison of the Residency. To be sure, there are the Ghoorkas. But it is almost dangerous to our prestige to avail ourselves of these gallant allies. Indeed, the authorities at Lucknow do not hesitate to tell their troops that the Nepaulese are coming to their aid; and the Sikhs are heard to say that we are dependent upon them and Jung for the safety of our empire and the punishment of the Poorbeahs. Besides, we fear that the Ghoorkas will bring in their train disease and disorder; they are known to be suffering from the smallpox. Sir Colin Campbell has, then, a most difficult rôle, and it is no wonder if he searches anxiously with that keen bright blue gray eye for the enemy's weak points, and

* A low caste numerous in Oude—pig-drivers, celebrated as fierce thieves when unemployed, but very faithful as servants.

† "Watchmen."

An album of photographs, found among the ruins of Lucknow, was given to Russell. The salt-print photographs were taken by the only local photographer, Ahmet Ali Khan, in 1856. The groups and portraits of families and officials are a unique record of the local inhabitants before the mutiny. Most of them are named, with rank and occupation; many bear additional notes as to their fate: 'Killed in siege', or 'Killed at Lucknow'. This album was presented to the India Office by Russell's daughter in 1922.

Right Mr Thomas Henry Kavanagh of the Indian Civil Service, and his daughter Blanche. Kavanagh was a hero of the siege. He escaped from the Residency disguised as an Indian, and guided the relief forces, led by Sir Colin Campbell, into Lucknow. He was awarded the V.C.

Below
Other photographs from the album.

Russell was with Campbell on the famous night march for the final capture of Lucknow. *The Times* maintained its strict rule on anonymity, laid down during Thomas Barnes's editorship, despite Russell's reputation. His report of the fall of Lucknow (see previous page) was accorded a special introduction: 'By the arrival of the Bombay mail we have received the subjoined graphic account of the siege of Lucknow from the pen of "Our Special Correspondent"'. The report was greatly admired at home. Delane wrote to Russell:

I have nothing but to congratulate you on the perfect success with which you have sustained your fame. I feel myself, and hear everybody saying, that we are at last beginning to learn something about India, which was always before a mystery – as far removed from our sight and which it was as impossible to comprehend as the fixed stars. The public feeling has righted itself more promptly than was to be expected, and we had before the recess a debate in which the most humane instead of the most bloodthirsty sentiments were uttered. The key to the savage spirit was the 'atrocities', and these seem to have resolved themselves into simple massacre.

Russell marched on with Campbell. At the end of April 1858 they crossed the Ganges at dawn. Russell was severely injured in the stomach and thigh while trying to save his horse from some uproarious stallions. He was carried in a litter, in great pain, but he continued to file his dispatches. The manager complained that his telegraph bill came to £5,000: 'It was, however, one of those occasions on which it would never have done for us to have been content with moving neck and neck with the penny papers'.

Leeches were applied to his leg. He was nearly cut down by mutinous cavalry at the Battle of Bareilly. It was hot and confusing business to report. But Russell continued to send his vivid, fair and scrupulously truthful dispatches. In particular, he found no evidence to substantiate the gruesome horror stories that had inflamed public opinion. Russell and *The Times* did a great deal to pacify the racialism and brutality of the British Raj. Russell

My letters have produced a most material effect on the tone of the Indian Press, and as to Society, though I undergo a good deal of quizzing, it is more than compensated when I hear one man threaten to break every bone in his bearer's skin held in check by the half serious, half-joking remonstrance, 'You had better not, or you will have *The Times* down on you.'

In its great days during the Age of Imperialism, under its great editor, with its great war correspondent, *The Times* was an influence for reason against rage, for humanity against exploitation, for truth against lies. Billy Russell wrote home to Delane at Printing House Square:

I believe that some great effort must be made to check the aggressive and antipathetic treatment of the natives. Our rule is now more secure in India than it has ever been before, and nothing but extreme oppression and injustice, and the misery and wretchedness and despair which may arise from these, can produce another rising; but, at the same time, there are more doubts as to our intentions, more suspicions of our motives, greater jealousy of our race, than there ever was before; and these feelings are mixed up with the animosities of a defeated nationality, such as it is, and with resentment against those who in their indiscriminate zeal and desire for vengeance punished the innocent with the guilty.

Russell was a wise and humane statesman as well as a marvellous descriptive writer. *The Times* is at its best when it is thundering on behalf of the weak against the mighty.

The American Civil War

Above Abraham Lincoln, elected President in November 1860.
Below William Howard Russell, photographed in Washington D.C., 1861.

The American Civil War, or the War between the States as the Americans prefer to euphemize it, was a grand missed opportunity for *The Times*. Relations between the United Kingdom and the United States were sour for a number of years after the conflict. We cannot doubt that the line doggedly followed by *The Times* throughout the Civil War embittered the sourness. In 1863, in the middle of the war, the historian Godwin Smith wrote of 'the enormous power which *The Times* has, its exclusive command of publicity, and its exclusive access to a vast number of minds'. A closer look at what went wrong may be instructive of how error can creep and spread in the daily policy of a newspaper, growing great from small mistakes.

The complacent Englishman in the middle of the nineteenth century knew little and cared less about the New World across the Atlantic. Writing in 1865, Leslie Stephen observed with more truth than poetry that 'the name of America, five years ago, called up to the ordinary English mind nothing but a vague cluster of associations, compounded of Mrs Trollope, *Martin Chuzzlewit*, and *Uncle Tom's Cabin*'.

Printing House Square was more interested and better informed about America than the general public. But there was prejudice in the office. The proprietor, John Walter III, nicknamed 'the Griff', short for griffin (or grim and unpredictable guardian), favoured the South in the impending struggle; but he was a narrow and fussy man who was unable to talk matters through with his journalists. Delane, the editor, had little sympathy with American institutions and aspirations. Mowbray Morris, the manager, had been born in the West Indies and could not shake off his innate sympathy for the South and slavery.

The paper did its best to cover American affairs fully and fairly. It kept regular correspondents in New York and San Francisco. In addition, visiting journalists filed reports from different parts of the country. In 1856 a reporter named Filmore toured many states, and filed sound and well-received reports. Also in that year Thomas Gladstone and Delane visited the States. Gladstone's pieces praised the North in comparison with the 'servile South'; the editor contributed nothing of value to the columns of *The Times*: Delane was a great editor, not a writer.

Lincoln was elected President in 1860. Slavery was the burning topic of the year. In December South Carolina seceded, and started the dominoes falling. In a leading article *The Times* put the blame on the South. But by the following spring, policy at Printing House Square had changed. There were two reasons for the change. First, the abolition of slavery was not the President's main target. In March he said 'I have no purpose, directly or indirectly, to interfere with the institution of Slavery in the states where it exists'; Lincoln's main aim was to preserve the Union. Second, the South favoured free trade, the North wanted a policy of protectionism. *The Times* viewed with alarm and hostility the disruption that protectionism would bring to the Lancashire cotton industry, which was dependent on supplies from the South.

The Times view was fundamentally and uncharacteristically ambivalent from the start: the coming war was about secession; *ergo* the North was legally in the right; but Lincoln was wrong in failing to recognize that the powerful Confederate states could not be kept in the Union against their will. It was not a moral but a commercial issue, in a faraway country between people of whom we knew little.

With the drums beating and war inevitable, *The Times* dispatched its best man towards the sound of the gunfire: William Howard Russell, of the Crimean War and the Indian Mutiny, sailed for America in March 1861. His reputation preceded him. Shortly after his arrival Lincoln received him in the White House and told him:

> Mr Russell, I am very glad to make your acquaintance, and to see you in this country. The London *Times* is one of the greatest powers in the world – in fact, I don't know anything which has much more power – except perhaps the Mississippi. I'm glad to know you as its minister.

Billy Russell wrote a marvellous colour piece about the President's appearance, concluding 'A person who met Mr Lincoln in the street would not take him to be what – according to the usages of European society – is called a gentleman'.

Russell left Washington and made a tour of the Southern States. He saw the slave market in operation, and was filled with loathing of the 'peculiar institution'. When war came, Russell's the danger. The late shiftings and changings in the Ministerial offices were apparently intended to precipitate the shock.

The House of Lords met yesterday afternoon at 2 o'clock.

Lord CLANRICARDE, in moving for a return of the number of civil bills and of ejectments in the Civil and Criminal Courts of Ireland, called attention to the report of the Office of Registry of Deeds, and hoped the Government would institute an inquiry into the condition of that office.

Lord STANLEY of ALDERLEY having stated that it was the intention of the Government to institute such an inquiry, agreed to the motion.

Lord SHAFTESBURY, on moving "that an humble Address be presented to HER MAJESTY, praying HER MAJESTY to give directions that an inquiry be made into the employment of children and young persons in trades and manufactures not already regulated by law," dwelt upon the benefits which had arisen from previous legislation on subjects of an analogous nature, and, while admitting that many evils pointed out by the Commission in 1842 had been mitigated, contended that abuses still existed of so aggravated a character as to demand the closest investigation. Quoting from the report of the Commission of 1840, he showed the terrible effects of too long hours of work, of defective workshops and factories, of night work, and of the treatment of the children by their employers, on their physical and social and moral condition, and concluded by stating that, in the opinion of Mr. SENIOR, the treatment of some of these children so employed was infinitely worse than that of the slave children on the worst managed plantation of America. The measures which had been already passed had done much to reconcile the working classes to their position in life, and to convince them that their interests were watched over in Parliament, and he therefore hoped that by assenting to the Address, their Lordships would give another proof of their solicitude for the working classes.

Lord STANLEY of ALDERLEY assented to the motion; and admitted that his former apprehension that legislation on such a subject was dangerous, had not been fulfilled.

After a few words from Lord MONTEAGLE the motion was agreed to.

Their Lordships adjourned at 5 minutes to 3 o'clock.

The House of Commons met at 2 o'clock yesterday, and, after a few petitions had been presented and one or two unimportant questions asked, adjourned till to-day, when the prorogation will take place.

COURT CIRCULAR.

OSBORNE, AUG. 5.

Her Majesty and his Royal Highness the Prince Consort, accompanied by Count and Countess de Lacroma, the Crown Prince and Princess of Prussia, Princess Alice, Princess Helena, and Princess Louise, embarked in the Fairy this morning at half-past 10 o'clock, and steamed towards Cowes.

Her Majesty held a Council afterwards, at which were present his Royal Highness the Prince Consort, Earl Granville the Lord Chancellor, Viscount Palmerston, the Duke of Newcastle, Earl Russell, the Right Hon. W. E. Gladstone, Chancellor of the Exchequer; the Right Hon. E. Cardwell, Chancellor of the Duchy of Lancaster; the Earl of St. Germans, Lord Steward; and Viscount Sydney, Lord Chamberlain.

At the Council the Royal Speech, on closing the Session of Parliament (this day), was submitted and approved.

Mr. A. Helps, the Clerk of the Privy Council, attended.

Earl Russell had an audience of the Queen.

His Excellency M. Musurus, the Turkish Ambassador, had an audience of the Queen and delivered his credentials. His Excellency was introduced by Earl Russell, Secretary of State for Foreign Affairs.

Viscount Palmerston had an audience of Her Majesty.

Mr. Roundell Palmer, Solicitor-General, was presented to the Queen at an audience by Earl Russell, one of Her Majesty's principal Secretaries of State, and received from the Queen the honour of knighthood.

The Chancellor of the Exchequer and Earl Granville had audiences of the Queen.

Her Majesty's Commissioners for the International Exhibition of 1862 have received an intimation that a Commission has been formed in the Netherlands to forward the interests of intending exhibitors in that country.

The Turkish Ambassador, Viscount Palmerston, the Duke of Newcastle, Earl of St. Germans, Viscount Sydney, the Chancellor of the Exchequer, the Right Hon. E. Cardwell, and the Solicitor-General, left London at a quarter before 9 o'clock yesterday morning, travelled by a special train on the South-Western Railway to Gosport, and crossed in the Fire Queen steamer to Osborne Pier. After attending Her Majesty's Court, the Turkish Ambassador, the Lord Chancellor, the Duke of Newcastle, Lords St. Germans, Palmerston, and Sydney, Mr. Gladstone, Mr. Cardwell, and the Solicitor-General recrossed to Gosport, in the Fire Queen, and returned to town by a special train. Earl Russell travelled with his colleagues from Osborne to London.

The Right Hon. W. Hutt has left London, for his residence, Gibside, near Gateshead.

Despatches were received yesterday at the Colonial-office, from the Governors of the North American Provinces, and the Lord High Commissioner of the Ionian Islands. Despatches were sent to the Governors of the Cape of Good Hope, Natal, and St. Helena.

The Chancellor of the Exchequer acknowledges the receipt of the second half of a bank-note for 5*l*., on account of Income-tax, from "J. D."; also of the second half of a bank-note for 10*l*., from "T. T. T."

PARLIAMENTARY CHANGES DURING THE SESSION.—There have been more than the average number of changes in the House of Commons during the Session which is now at its close. On the first evening of meeting (February 5) new writs were issued for South Wiltshire, vacant by the elevation of Mr. Sidney Herbert to the Peerage; for Bolton, vacant by the resignation of Mr. Crook; for Bradford, by the resignation of Mr. Salt; and for Aberdeenshire, by the succession of Lord Haddo to the Earldom of Aberdeen. For these constituencies the following gentlemen were subsequently elected:—South Wiltshire, Lieutenant-Colonel Bathurst; Bolton, Mr. Barnes; Bradford, Mr. W. E. Forster; and Aberdeenshire, Mr. Leslie. On the same evening Major Barttelot (who had been elected in the recess in the place of the Earl of March, who had become Duke of Richmond) and Mr. Lort Phillips (who had been elected for Pembrokeshire) took their seats. In a day or two afterwards Mr. Heygate took his seat for Leicester, in the room of Dr. Noble, deceased. By the death of Sir John Owen in February a vacancy was caused in the representation of the borough of Pembroke. To fill this vacancy Sir Hugh Owen was elected. By the death of the Duke of Sutherland the Marquis of Stafford was raised to the dukedom, and left a vacancy in the representation of Sutherlandshire. Sir David Dundas was elected to fill it. On the 28th of March Lord Palmerston was re-elected for Tiverton on his acceptance of the Wardenship of the Cinque Ports. Mr. Harvey Lewis succeeded Mr. Edwin James, Q.C., in the representation of Marylebone. By the death of Mr. David Pugh on the 29th of April a vacancy occurred in the representation of the Montgomery Boroughs. He was succeeded by his son-in-law, Captain Willes Johnson, who was returned without opposition. Just at this time Mr. Hugh Taylor resigned the representation of South Shields, and was succeeded by Mr. Hodgson; Major Gordon Duff resigned Banffshire, and was succeeded by Mr. R. W. Duff Abercromby. The Hon. Thomas Edward Mostyn Lloyd Mostyn died on the 7th of May. He was succeeded by Lord Richard Grosvenor, a son of the Marquis of Westminster. Mr. Locke was re-elected for Southwark on his appointment as Recorder of Brighton. In consequence of the elevation of Sir Richard Bethell to the Lord Chancellorship a vacancy took place in the representation of Wolverhampton. Mr. Weguelin, a director of the Bank of England, and formerly member for Southampton, was elected to fill it. Other results of Sir Richard Bethell's elevation were the re-election of Sir William Atherton, the new Attorney-General, for the city of Durham, and the election of Mr. Roundell Palmer, Q.C., the new Solicitor-General, for Richmond, in the room of Mr. Henry Rich, resigned. Colonel Luke White was returned for Longford in the room of Colonel White, who resigned. For Selkirkshire Lord H. Scott, a son of the Duke of Buccleuch, was elected in the room of Mr. Eliott Lockhart, who retired. In consequence of the elevation of Lord John Russell to the Peerage a vacancy in the representation of the City of London took place. After a sharp contest with the Lord Mayor, Mr. Western Wood was elected. Mr. H. B. Sheridan was returned for Andover, in the room of the Lord Mayor (Mr. Cubitt) who resigned for the purpose of contesting the city. Within the last few days Sir George Grey, Mr. Cardwell, and Sir Robert Peel have been re-elected for Morpeth, Oxford, and Tamworth, in consequence of Government changes.

SOUTHAMPTON, Monday.—The Union Company's steamship Cambrian, Captain W. Strutt, sailed hence this afternoon for the Cape of Good Hope, taking a full mail and 58 passengers, among whom are Brevet-Major and Ensign Rogers, Rev. E. Steward, Dr. Exton, Captain [illegible], R.N., the Hon. Mrs. Stewart and three children; Lieutenant Robertson, Cape Mounted Rifles; Dr. Landsberg and Dr. Albertyer.

[illegible] REPENTANCE.—The *Lombardo* of Milan publishes the following curious letter, addressed to the Pope by an old woman, once a celebrated dancer:—"At the advanced age of 78 I humble myself in the dust, and bitterly repent having occasioned many scandals by dancing in public during a period of 25 years, and having heaped up wealth and riches by the practice of that diabolical art. At this time, when the Roman Government is enduring such anguish, I venture, unworthy sinner as I am, to come to its aid with the trifling sum of 500 Austrian livres, which I offer as a contribution to St. Peter's penny, imploring at the same time his blessing and prayers for my deceased father, my daughter Charlotte, and her [illegible] and Elizabeth his wife, and all the children they have, and finally for all my children and posterity, and that the good may triumph and the wicked [illegible]. His Holiness' humiliated servant and sinner, [illegible] TALANDRA, Ex-first dancer of the Ancient Cisalpine Republic (*sic*)."

THE CIVIL WAR IN AMERICA.

THE DEFEAT AT MANASSAS.

(FROM OUR SPECIAL CORRESPONDENT.)

WASHINGTON, JULY 19.

The army of the North is fairly moving at last, and all the contending voices of lawyers and disputants will speedily be silenced by the noise of the cannon. Let no one suppose that the war will be decided in one or two battles, or conclude from any present successes of the Federalists that they will not meet with stern opposition as they advance. The Confederates uniformly declared to me after their failure to take either Faneuil-hall or the Capitol they would wait in Virginia and "entice" the Confederates into certain mysterious traps, where they would be "destroyed to a man." There is great reliance placed on "masked batteries" in this war, and the country is favourable to their employment; but nothing can prove more completely the unsteady character of the troops than the reliance which is placed on the effects of such works, and, indeed, there is reason to think that there have been panics on both sides—at Great Bethel as well as at Laurel-hill. The telegraph is faster than the post, and all the lucubrations of to-day may be falsified by the deeds of to-morrow. The Senate and Congress are sitting in the Capitol, within the very hearing of the guns and the sight of the smoke of the conflict which is now raging in Virginia. Senators and Congress men are engaged in disputations and speeches, while soldiers are working out the problem in their own way, and it is within the range of possibility that a disastrous battle may place the capital in the hands of the Confederates; and the news which has just come in that the latter have passed Bull's Run, a small river which flows into the Potomac below Alexandria, crossing the railroad from that place, is a proof that Fairfax Court-house was abandoned for a reason. It is stated that the Confederates have been repulsed by the 69th (Irish) Regiment and the 79th (Scotch) New York Volunteers, and as soon as this letter has been posted I shall proceed to the field (for the campaign has now fairly commenced) and ascertain the facts. If the Confederates force the left of M'Dowell's army they will obtain possession of the line to Alexandria, and may endanger Washington itself. The design of Beauregard may have been to effect this very object while he engaged the bulk of the Federalists at Manassas Junction, which you must not confound with Manassas Gap. The reports of guns were heard this morning in the direction of the Junction, and it is probable that M'Dowell, advancing from Centreville, has met the enemy, prepared to dispute his passage. There are some stories in town to the effect that General Tyler has met with a severe check on the right, but the advance of M'Dowell was very cautious, and he would not let his troops fall into the ambuscades against which they have been especially forewarned. Let speculation, which to-morrow's news must outstrip, cease here, and let us examine the composition of the forces actually engaged with the Confederates. The head of the naval and military forces of the United States is the President, in theory and in the practice of appointments, but Lieutenant-General Winfield Scott is "Commanding-in-Chief" of the United States' army. His staff consists of Lieutenant-Colonel E. D. Townsend, Assistant Adjutant-General, Chief of the Staff; Colonel H. Van Ransselaer, A.D.C. (Volunteer); Lieutenant-Colonel George W. Cullum, United States' Engineer, A.D.C.; Lieutenant-Colonel Edward Wright, United States' Cavalry, A.D.C.; Lieutenant-Colonel Schuyler Hamilton, Military Secretary.

The subjoined General Order gives the organization of the Staff and of the several Divisions of the army under Brigadier-General M'Dowell, now advancing into Virginia from the lines opposite Washington:—

"GENERAL ORDERS, No. 13.

"Head-quarters Department, N. E. Virginia.
Washington, July 8, 1861.

"Until otherwise ordered the following will be the organization of the troops in this Department:—

"STAFF OF THE DEPARTMENT COMMANDER.

"Adjutant-General's Department.—Captain James B. Fry, Assistant Adjutant-General.

"Aides-de-Camp.—First Lieutenant H. W. Kingsbury, 5th Artillery; Major Clarence S. Brown, N.Y. State Militia; Major James S. Wordsworth, N.Y. State Militia.

"Acting Inspector-General.—Major W. H. Wood, 17th Infantry.

"Engineers.—Major J. G. Barnard; First Lieutenant F. E. Prime.

"Topographical Engineers.—Captain A. W. Whipple; First Lieutenant Henry L. Abbott; Second Lieutenant Haldimand S. Putnam.

"Quartermaster's Department.—Captain O. H. Tillinghast, Assistant Quartermaster.

"Subsistence Department.—Captain H. F. Clarke, Commissary of Subsistence.

"Medical Department.—Surgeon W. S. King; Assistant-Surgeon David L. Magruder.

"FIRST DIVISION.

"Brigadier-General Daniel Tyler, Connecticut Militia, commanding.

"First Brigade.—Colonel E. D. Keyes, 11th Infantry, commanding. 1st Connecticut Regiment Volunteers; 2d ditto; 3d ditto; 4th Maine ditto; Captain Varian's Battery of New York 8th Regiment; Company B, Second Cavalry.

"Second Brigade.—1st Ohio Regiment Volunteers; 2d ditto; 2d New York ditto; Company E, 2d Artillery (Light Battery).

"Third Brigade.—Colonel W. T. Sherman, 13th Infantry, commanding. 69th Regiment New York Militia; 79th ditto; 13th ditto, Volunteers; 2d ditto, Wisconsin ditto; Company E, 3d Artillery (Light Battery).

"Fourth Brigade.—Colonel J. B. Richardson, Michigan Volunteers, commanding. 2d Regiment Michigan Volunteers; 3d ditto; 1st ditto Massachusetts; 12th ditto New York.

"SECOND DIVISION.

"Colonel David Hunter, 3d Cavalry, commanding.

"First Brigade.—Colonel Andrew Porter, 16th Infantry, commanding. Battalion of Regular Infantry (2d, 3d, and 8th Regiments); 8th Regiment New York Militia; 14th ditto; Squadron 2d Cavalry, Companies G and I; Company 5th Artillery (Light Battery).

"Second Brigade.—Colonel A. E. Burnside, Rhode Island Volunteers, commanding. 1st Regiment Rhode Island Volunteers; 2d ditto; 71st ditto New York Militia; 2d ditto New Hampshire Volunteers; Battery of Light Artillery, 2d Rhode Island Regiment.

"THIRD DIVISION.

"Colonel S. P. Heintzelman, 17th Infantry, commanding.

"First Brigade.—Colonel W. B. Franklin, 12th Infantry, commanding. 4th Regiment Pennsylvania Militia; 5th ditto, Massachusetts ditto; 1st ditto, Minnesota Volunteers; Company E, 2d Cavalry; Company I, 1st Artillery (Light Battery).

"Second Brigade.—Colonel O. B. Wilcox, Michigan Volunteers, commanding. 1st Regiment Michigan Volunteers; 11th ditto, New York ditto; Company D, 2d Artillery (Light Battery).

"Third Brigade.—Colonel O. O. Howard, Maine Volunteers, commanding. 2d Regiment Maine Volunteers; 4th ditto; 5th ditto; 2d ditto, Vermont ditto.

"RESERVE.

"FOURTH DIVISION.

"Brigadier-General T. Runyon, New Jersey Militia, commanding. 1st Regiment New Jersey Militia, three months' Volunteers; 2d ditto, ditto; 3d ditto, ditto; 4th ditto, ditto; 1st ditto, three years' Volunteers; 2d ditto, ditto; 3d ditto, ditto.

"FIFTH DIVISION.

"Colonel D. S. Miles, 2d Infantry, commanding.

"First Brigade.—Colonel Blenker, New York Volunteers, commanding. 8th Regiment New York Volunteers; 29th ditto, ditto; Garibaldi Guard; 24th Regiment Pennsylvania Volunteers.

"Second Brigade.—Colonel Davies, New York Volunteers, commanding. 16th Regiment New York Volunteers; 18th ditto, ditto; 31st ditto, ditto; 32d ditto, ditto; Company G, 2d Artillery (Light Battery).

"By command of Brigadier-General M'Dowell,
"JAMES B. FRY, Assistant-Adjutant General."

Some changes have been made since this order was published, and the Corps has been strengthened by the accession of two regular field-batteries. The effective strength of the infantry, under M'Dowell, may be taken at 30,000 and there are about 60 field-pieces at his disposal, and a force of about ten squadrons of cavalry.

The following is an approximation to the number of General M'Clellan's division in Western Virginia, with their positions previous to the late action. The numerical strength of his command is near 35,000, nearly all volunteers:—

"At Beverley, Laurel-hill, and Buckhannon.—Head-quarters of Major-General M'Clellan and Brigadier-Generals Rosecrans and Schleich.—3d Ohio Volunteers, Colonel J. H. Marrows; 4th ditto, Colonel Lorin Andrews; 6th Ohio, Colonel Bosley; 9th Ohio Volunteers, Colonel R. L. M'Cook; 10th ditto, Colonel W. H. Lytle; 14th ditto, Colonel J. B. Steadman; 17th ditto, Colonel J. M. Connell; 18th ditto, Colonel J. R. Stanley; 19th ditto, Colonel Samuel Bratty; 20th ditto, Colonel Thomas Morton; 8th Indiana ditto, Colonel W. P. Benton; 9th ditto, Colonel R. M. Milroy; 10th ditto, Colonel M. D. Manson; 15th ditto, Colonel G. D. Wagner; Chicago Dragoons, Captain W. Baker; Chicago Sturgiss Rifles, Captain W. Sturgiss; Coldwaters Artillery, Michigan, Captain T. W. Culp; Chicago Cavalry, Captain Barker; Flying Artillery, Captain Howe.

"At Cheat River.—15th Ohio Volunteers, Colonel G. W. Andrews; 16th Ohio Volunteers, Colonel J. Irvine; 1st Virginia Union Volunteers, Colonel ——.

"At Clarksburgh.—2d Virginia Union Volunteers, Colonel ——; 3d Virginia Union Volunteers, Colonel ——; Cincinnati Rover Dragoons, Captain W. H. Stevens.

"At Grafton.—Head-quarters of Brigadier-General Hill. —7th Indiana Volunteers, Colonel E. Dumont; Troop of Horse, Colonel ——; Regular Artillery, from Kansas, Colonel ——; Company L, 4th Artillery, Lieutenant Ward; 12th Ohio Volunteers, Colonel W. F. Smith; 5th Ohio Volunteers, Colonel Dunning.

"Phillippa.—Brigadier-General Hill.—6th Indiana Volunteers, Colonel Crittenden.

"Along Railroad from Parkersburgh to Grafton.—23d Ohio Volunteers, Colonel W. E. Gilmore.

"Glenville.—7th Ohio, Colonel E. B. Tyler.

"Ripley.—21st Ohio Volunteers, Colonel J. S. Norton.

"*En route* by the Kanawha.—Brigadier-General Cox. —8th Ohio Volunteers, Colonel Du Puy; 12th Ohio Volunteers, Colonel J. W. Lowe; 1st Kentucky Volunteers, Colonel W. Woodruff; 2d Kentucky Volunteers, Colonel W. G. Terrell.

"*En route.*—13th Indiana Volunteers, Colonel J. C. Sullivan; 14th Indiana Volunteers, Colonel N. Kimball; 17th Indiana Volunteers, Colonel Hascall."

The division under General Patterson is about 22,000 strong, and has three batteries of artillery attached to it; and General Mansfield, who commands the army of Washington and the reserve watching the Capitol, has under him a corps of 16,000 men almost exclusively volunteers. General M'Dowell has also left a strong guard in his intrenchments along the right bank of the Potomac, guarding the bridges and covering the roads to Alexandria, Fairfax, and Falls Church. The division in military occupation of Maryland under General Banks, most of which is concentrated in and around Baltimore, consists of 7,400 men, with some field guns. The corps at Fortress Monroe and Hampton, under General Butler, is 11,000 strong, with two field batteries, some guns of position, and the fortress itself in hand. General Lyon, who is operating in Missouri with marked success, has about 6,500 men. General Prentis at Cairo commands a division of 6,000 men and two field batteries. There are besides these forces many regiments organized and actually in the field. The army under the command of General Beauregard at Manassas Junction is estimated at 60,000, but that must include the reserves, and a portion of the force in the intrenchments along the road to Richmond, in the immediate neighbourhood of which there is a corps of 15,000 men. At Norfolk there are 18,000 or 20,000, at Acquia Creek 8,000 to 9,000, and Johnson's corps is estimated at 10,000, swollen by the *débris* of the defeated column. The railways from the South are open to the Confederates, and they can collect their troops rapidly, so that it is not at all beyond the reach of probability that they can collect 150,000 or 160,000 men in Virginia, if that number is not now actually in the State. In cavalry they have a superiority, but the country is not favourable for their operations till the armies approach Richmond. In field artillery they are not so well provided as the Federalists. They have, however, a great number of heavy batteries and guns of position at their disposal. Food is plentiful in their camps; the harvest is coming in. In general equipments and ammunition the Federalists have a considerable advantage. In discipline there is not much difference perhaps in the bulk of the volunteers on both sides, but the United States' forces have the benefit of the example and presence of the regular army, the privates of which have remained faithful to the Government. If we are to judge from what may be seen in Washington there are *mauvais sujets* in abundance among the United States' troops. The various foreign Ministers have been so much persecuted by soldiers coming to their houses, and asking for help, that sentries were ordered to be put at their doors. Lord Lyons, however, did not acquiesce in the propriety of the step, and in lieu of that means of defence against demands for money, a document called "a safeguard" has been furnished to the domestics at the various legations, in which applicants are informed that they are liable to the penalty of death for making such solicitations. General M'Dowell writes in his despatch from Fairfax Court-house:—"I am distressed to have to report excesses by our troops. The excitement of the men found vent in burning and pillaging, which, however soon checked, distressed us all greatly." What will take place at the close of a hardly contested action in the front of populous towns and villages? The vast majority of the soldiers are very well behaved, but it will require severe punishment to deter the evil-disposed from indulging in all the licence of war.

The energy displayed in furnishing the great army in the field with transport and ambulances is very great, and I have been surprised to see the rapidity with which waggons and excellent field hospitals and sick carts have been constructed and forwarded by the contractors. The corps in Virginia under M'Dowell may be considered fit to make a campaign in all respects so far as those essentials are concerned, and the Government is rapidly purchasing horses and mules which are not inferior to those used in any army in the world. These few lines must suffice till the despatch of the mail on Wednesday.

JULY 22.

I sit down to give an account—not of the action yesterday, but of what I saw with my own eyes, hitherto not often deceived, and of what I heard with my own ears, which in this country are not so much to be trusted. Let me, however, express an opinion as to the affair of yesterday. In the first place, the repulse of the Federalists, decided as it was, might have had no serious effects whatever beyond the mere failure—which politically was of greater consequence than it was in a military sense—but for the disgraceful conduct of the troops. The retreat on their lines at Centreville seems to have ended in a cowardly route—a miserable, causeless panic. Such scandalous behaviour on the part of soldiers I should have considered impossible, as with some experience of camps and armies I have never even in alarms among camp followers seen the like of it. How far the disorganization of the troops extended I know not; but it was complete in the instance of more than one regiment. Washington this morning is crowded with soldiers without officers, who have fled from Centreville, and with "three months' men," who are going home from the face of the enemy on the expiration of their term of enlistment. The streets, in spite of the rain, are crowded by people with anxious faces, and groups of wavering politicians are assembled at the corners, in the hotel passages, and the bars. If in the present state of the troops the Confederates were to make a march across the Potomac above Washington, turning the works at Arlington, the Capitol might fall into their hands. Delay may place that event out of the range of probability.

The North will, no doubt, recover the shock. Hitherto she has only said, "Go and fight for the Union." The South has exclaimed, "Let us fight for our rights." The North must put its best men into the battle, or she will inevitably fail before the energy, the personal hatred, and the superior fighting powers of her antagonist. In my letters, as in my conversation, I have endeavoured to show that the task which the Unionists have set themselves is one of no ordinary difficulty, but in the state of arrogance and supercilious confidence, either real or affected to conceal a sense of weakness, one might as well have preached to the Pyramid of Cheops. Indeed, one may form some notion of the condition of the public mind by observing that journals conducted avowedly by men of disgraceful personal character—the be-whipped and be-kicked and unrecognized pariahs of society in New York—are, nevertheless, in the very midst of repulse and defeat, permitted to indulge in ridiculous rhodomontade towards the nations of Europe, and to move our laughter by impotently malignant attacks on "our rotten old monarchy," while the stones of their bran new republic are tumbling about their ears. It will be amusing to observe the change of tone, for we can afford to observe and to be amused at the same time.

On Saturday night I resolved to proceed to General M'Dowell's army, as it was obvious to me that the repulse at Bull's Run and the orders of the General directed against the excesses of his soldiery indicated serious defects in his army—not more serious, however, than I had reason to believe existed. How to get out was the difficulty. The rumours of great disaster and repulse had spread through the city. The livery-stable keepers, with one exception, refused to send out horses to the scene of action—at least, the exception told me so. Senators and Congress men were going to make a day of it, and all the vehicles and horses that could be procured were in requisition for the scene of action. This curiosity was aroused by the story that M'Dowell had been actually ordered to make an attack on Manassas, and that General Scott had given him till 12 o'clock to be master of Beauregard's lines. If General Scott ordered the attack at all I venture to say he was merely the mouthpiece of the more violent civilians of the Government, who mistake intensity of feeling for military strength. The consequences of the little skirmish at Bull's Run, ending in the repulse of the Federalists, were much exaggerated, and their losses were put down at any figures the fancy of the individual item who was speaking suggested. "I can assure you, Sir, that the troops had 1,500 killed and wounded; I know it." I went off to the head-quarters, and there General Scott's aide informed me General M'Dowell's official report gave 6 killed and 37 wounded. The livery keepers stuck to the 1,500 or 2,000. The greater the number *hors de combat* the higher the tariff for the hire of quadrupeds. All I could do was to get a kind of cabriolet, with a seat in front for the driver, to which a pole was affixed for two horses, at a Derby-day price, and a strong led-horse, which Indian experiences have induced me always to rely upon in the neighbourhood of uncertain fighting. I had to enter into an agreement with the owner to pay him for horses and buggy if they were "captured or injured by the enemy," and though I smiled at his precautions they proved not quite unreasonable. The master made no provision for indemnity in the case of injury to the driver, or the coloured boy who rode the saddle-horse. When I spoke with officers at General Scott's head-quarters of the expedition, it struck me they were not at all sanguine about the result of the day, and one of them said as much as induced me to think he would advise me to remain in the city if he did not take it for granted it was part of my duty to go to the scene of action. An English gentleman who accompanied me was strongly dissuaded from going by a colonel of cavalry on the staff, because, he said, "the troops are green, and no one can tell what may happen." But my friend got his pass from General Scott, who was taking the whole affair of Bull's Run and the pressure of the morrow's work with perfect calm, and we started on Sunday morning—not so early as we ought, perhaps, which was none of my fault—for Centreville, distant about 25 miles south-west of Washington. I purposed starting in the beautiful moonlight, so as to arrive at M'Dowell's camp in the early dawn, but the aides could not or would not give us the countersign over the Long-bridge, and without it no one could get across till after 5 o'clock in the morning. When M'Dowell moved away he took so many of the troops about Arlington that the camps and forts are rather denuded of men. I do not give, as may be observed, the names of regiments, unless in special cases—first, because they possess little interest, I conceive, for those in Europe who read these letters; and, secondly, because there is an exceedingly complex system—at least, to a foreigner—of nomenclature in the forces, and one may make a mistake between a regiment of volunteers and a regiment of State militia of the same number, or even of regulars in the lower figures. The soldiers lounging about the forts and over the Long-bridge across the Potomac were an exceedingly unkempt, "loafing" set of fellows, who handled their firelocks like pitchforks and spades, and I doubt if some of those who read or tried to read our papers could understand them, as they certainly did not speak English. The Americans possess excellent working materials, however, and I have had occasion repeatedly to remark the rapidity and skill with which they construct earthworks. At the Virginia side of the Long-bridge there is now a very strong *tête de pont*, supported by the regular redoubt on the hill over the road. These works did not appear to be strongly held, but it is possible men were in the tents near at hand, deserted though they seemed, and at all events reinforcements could be speedily poured in if necessary.

The long and weary way was varied by different pickets along the road, and by the examination of our papers and passes at different points. But the country looked vacant in spite of crops of Indian corn, for the houses were shut up, and the few indigenous people whom we met looked most blackly under their brows at the supposed Abolitionists. This portion of Virginia is well wooded, and undulating in heavy regular waves of field and forest; but the roads are deeply cut and filled with loose stones, very disagreeable to ride or drive over. The houses are of wood, with the usual negro huts adjoining them, and the specimens of the race which I saw were well dressed and not ill-looking. On turning into one of the roads which leads to Fairfax Court-house and to Centreville beyond it the distant sound of cannon reached us. That must have been about 9.30 a.m. It never ceased all day; at least, whenever the rattle of the gig ceased the booming of guns rolled through the woods on our ears. One man said it began at 2 o'clock, but the pickets told us it had really become continuous about half-past 7 or 8 o'clock. In a few minutes afterwards a body of men appeared on the road, with their backs towards Centreville and their faces towards Alexandria. Their march was so disorderly that I could not have believed they were soldiers in an enemy's country—for Virginia hereabout is certainly so—but for their arms and uniform. It soon appeared that there was no less than an entire regiment marching away, singly or in small knots of two or three, extending for some three or four miles along the road. A Babel of tongues rose from them, and they were all in good spirits, but with an air about them I could not understand. Dismounting at a stream, where a group of thirsty men were drinking and halting in the shade, I asked an officer "Where are your men going, Sir?" "Well, we're going home, Sir, I reckon, to Pennsylvania." It was the 4th Pennsylvania Regiment, which was on its march, as I learnt from the men. "I suppose there is severe work going on behind you, judging from the firing?" "Well, I reckon, Sir, there is." "We're going home," he added after a pause, during which it occurred to him, perhaps, that the movement required explanation,—"because the men's time is up. We have had three months of this work." I proceeded on my way, ruminating on the feelings of a General who sees half a brigade walk quietly away on the very morning of an action, and on the frame of mind of the men, who would have shouted till they were hoarse about their beloved Union—possibly have hunted down any poor creature who expressed a belief that it was not the very quintessence of everything great and good in government and glorious and omnipotent in arms,—coolly turning their backs on it when in its utmost peril because the letter of their engagement bound them no further. Perhaps the 4th Pennsylvania were right, but let us hear no more of the excellence of three months' service volunteers. And so we left them. The road was devious and difficult. There were few persons on their way, for most of the Senators and Congress men were on before us. Some few commissariat waggons were overtaken at intervals. Wherever there was a house by the roadside the negroes were listening to the firing. All at once a terrific object appeared in the wood above the trees—the dome of a church or public building, apparently suffering from the shocks of an earthquake, and heaving to and fro in the most violent manner. In much doubt we approached as well as the horses' minds would let us, and discovered that the strange thing was an inflated balloon attached to a car and waggon, which was on its way to enable General M'Dowell to reconnoitre the position he was then engaged in attacking—just a day too late. The operators and attendants swore as horribly as Anna's warriors in Flanders, but they could not curse down the trees, and so the balloon seems likely to fall into the hands of the Confederates. About 11 o'clock we began to enter on the disputed territory which had just been abandoned by the Secessionists to the Federalists in front of Fairfax Court-house. It is not too much to say that the works thrown up across the road were shams and makebelieves, and that the Confederates never intended to occupy the position at all, but sought to lure on the Federalists to Manassas Gap, where they were prepared to meet them. Had it been otherwise the earthworks would have been of a different character, and the troops would have had regular camps and tents, instead of bivouac huts of branches of trees. Of course the troops of the enemy did not wish to be cut off, and so they had cut down trees to place across the road, and put some field-pieces in their earthworks to command it. On no side could Richmond be so well defended. The Confederates had it much at heart to induce their enemy to come to the strongest place and attack them, and they succeeded in doing so. But, if the troops behaved as ill in other places as they did at Manassas, the Federalists could not have been successful in any attack whatever. In order that the preparations at Manassas may be understood, and that General Beauregard, of whose character I gave some hint at Charleston, may be known at home as regards his fitness for his work, above all as an officer of artillery and of skill in working it in field or in position, let me insert a description of the place and of the man from a Southern paper:—

"Manassas Junction, Virginia, June 7.

"This place still continues the head-quarters of the army of the Potomac. There are many indications of an intended forward movement, the better to invite the enemy to an engagement, but the work of fortification still continues. By nature the position is one of the strongest that could have been found in the whole State. About halfway between the eastern spur of the Blue Ridge and the Potomac, below Alexandria, it commands the whole country between so perfectly that there is scarcely a possibility of its being turned. The right wing stretches off towards the head-waters of the Occoquan, through a wooded country, which is easily made impassable by the felling of trees. The left is a rolling table-land, easily commanded from the successive elevations, till you reach a country so rough and so rugged that it is a defence to itself. The key to the whole position, in fact, is precisely that point which General Beauregard chose for his centre, and which he has fortified so strongly that, in the opinion of military men, 5,000 men could there hold 20,000 at bay. The position, in fact, is fortified in part by Nature herself. It is a succession of hills, nearly equidistant from each other, in front of which is a ravine so deep and so thickly wooded that it is passable only at two points, and those through gorges which 50 men can defend against a whole army. It was at one of these points that the Washington Artillery (of New Orleans) were at first encamped, and though only half the battalion was then there, and we had only one company of infantry to support us, we slept as soundly under the protection of our guns as if we had been in a fort of the amplest dimensions. Of the fortifications superadded here by General Beauregard to those of Nature it is, of course, not proper for me to speak. The general reader, in fact, will have a sufficiently precise idea of them by conceiving a line of forts some two miles in extent, zigzag in form, with angles, salients, bastions, casemates, and everything that properly belongs to works of this kind. The strength and advantages of this position at Manassas are very much increased by the fact that 14 miles further on is a position of similar formation, while the country between is admirably adapted to the subsistence and intrenchment of troops in numbers as large as they can easily be manœuvred on the real battle-field. Water is good and abundant, forage such as is everywhere found in the rich farming districts of Virginia, and the communication with all parts of the country easy. Here, overlooking an extensive plain, watered by mountain streams which ultimately find their way to the Potomac, and divided into verdant fields of wheat, and oats, and corn, pasture and meadow, are the head-quarters of the advanced forces of the army of the Potomac. They are South Carolinians, Louisianians, Alabamians, Mississippians, and Virginians, for the most part; the first two, singular enough, being in front, and that they will keep it their *friends* at home may rest assured. Never have I seen a finer body of men—men who were more obedient to discipline, or breathed a more self-sacrificing patriotism. As might be expected from the skill with which he has chosen his position, and the system with which he encamps and moves his men, General Beauregard is very popular here. I doubt if Napoleon himself had more the undivided confidence of his army. By nature, as also from a wise policy, he is very reticent. Not an individual here knows his plans or a single move of a regiment before it is made, and then only the colonel and his men know where it goes to. There is not a man here who can give anything like a satisfactory answer how many men he has, or where his exact lines are. For the distance of 14 miles around you see tents everywhere, and from them you can make a rough estimate of his men; but how many more are encamped on the by-roads and in the forests none can tell. The new-comer, from what he sees at first glance, puts down the numbers at about 30,000 men; those who have been here longest estimate his force at 40,000, 50,000, and some even at 60,000 strong. And there is the same discrepancy as to the quantity of his artillery. So close does the General keep his affairs to himself that his left hand hardly knows what his right hand doeth, and so jealous is he of this prerogative of a commanding officer that I verily believe, if he suspected his coat of any acquaintance with the plans revolving within him, he would cast it off."

It was noon when we arrived at Fairfax Court-house—a poor village of some 30 or 40 straggling wooden and brick houses, deriving its name from the building in which the Circuit Court of the county is held, I believe, and looking the reverse of flourishing—and one may remark, *obiter*, that the state of this part of Virginia cannot be very prosperous, inasmuch as there was not a village along the road up to this point, and no shops or depôts, only one mill, one blacksmith and wheelwright. The village was held by a part of the reserve of M'Dowell's force, possibly 1,000 strong. The inhabitants were, if eyes spoke truth, Secessionists to a man, woman, and child, and even the negroes looked extra black, as if they did not care about being fought for. A short way beyond this village, Germantown, the scene of the recent excesses of the Federalists, afforded evidence in its blackened ruins that General M'Dowell's censure was more than needed. Let me interpolate it if it be only to show that General Beauregard and his rival are at least equal in point of literary power as masters of the English tongue:—

"Head-quarters Department of Virginia,
Fairfax Court-house, July 18.

"GENERAL ORDERS, No. 18.

"It is with the deepest mortification the General Commanding finds it necessary to reiterate his orders for the preservation of the property of the inhabitants of the district occupied by the troops under his command. Hardly had we arrived at this place, when, to the horror of every right-minded person, several houses were broken open, and others were in flames, by the act of some of those who, it has been the boast of the loyal, came here to protect the oppressed and free the country from the domination of a hated party. The property of this people is at the mercy of troops who, we rightly say, are the most intelligent, best educated, and most law-abiding of any that ever were under arms. But do not, therefore, the acts of yesterday cast the deepest stain upon them? It was claimed by some that their particular corps were not engaged in these acts. This is of but little moment; since the individuals are not found out, we are all alike disgraced. Commanders of regiments will select a commissioned officer as a provost marshal, and ten men as a police force under him, whose special and sole duty it shall be to preserve the property from depredations, and to arrest all wrongdoers of whatever regiment or corps they may be. Any one found committing the slightest depredation, killing pigs or poultry, or trespassing on the property of the inhabitants, will be reported to head-quarters, and the least that will be done to them will be to send them to the Alexandria gaol. It is again ordered that no one shall arrest, or attempt to arrest, any citizen not in arms at the time, or search or attempt to search any house, or even to enter the same without permission. The troops must behave themselves with as much forbearance and propriety as if they were at their own homes. They are here to fight the enemies of the country, not to judge and punish the unarmed and defenceless, however guilty they may be. When necessary, that will be done by the proper person.

"By command of General M'Dowell,
"JAMES B. FRY, Assistant-Adjutant-General."

The chimney stacks being of brick are the sole remains of the few good houses in the village. Here our driver made a mistake, which was the rather persisted in that a coloured chattel informed us we could get to Centreville by the route we were pursuing, instead of turning back to Germantown, as we should have done. Centreville was still seven miles ahead. The guns sounded, however, heavily from the valleys. Rising above the forest tops appeared the blue masses of the Alleghanies, and we knew Manassas was somewhere on an outlying open of the ridges, which reminded me in colour and form of the hills around the valley of Baidar. A Virginian who came out of a cottage, and who was assuredly no descendant of Madame Esmond, told us that we were "going wrong right away." There was, he admitted, a by-road somewhere to the left front, but people who had tried its depths had returned to Germantown with the conviction that it led to any place but Centreville. Our driver, however, wished to try "if there were no Sechesers about?" "What did you say?" quoth the Virginian. "I want to know if there are any Secessionists there." "Secessionists!" (in a violent surprise, as if he had heard of them for the first time in his life) "No, Sir-ree! Secessionists, indeed!" And all this time Beauregard and Lee were pounding away on our left front some six or seven miles off. The horses retraced their steps, the coloured youth who bestrode my charger complaining that the mysterious arrangement which condemns his race to slavery was very much abraded by the action of that spirited quadruped, combined or rather at variance with the callosities of the English saddle. From Germantown onwards by the right road there was nothing very remarkable. At one place a group of soldiers were buying "Secession money" from some negroes, who looked as if they could afford to part with it as cheaply as men do who are dealing with other people's property. Buggies and waggons (Anglicè, carriages) with cargoes of senators were overtaken. The store carts became more numerous. At last Centreville appeared in sight—a few houses on our front, beyond which rose a bald hill, the slopes covered with bivouac huts, commissariat carts, and horses, and the top crested with spectators of the fight. The road on each side was full of traces of Confederate camps; the houses were now all occupied by Federalists. In the rear of the hill was a strong body of infantry—two regiments of foreigners, mostly Germans, with a battery of light artillery. Our buggy was driven up to the top of the hill. The coloured boy was despatched to the village to look for a place to shelter the horses while they were taking a much required feed, and to procure, if possible, a meal for himself and the driver. On the hill there were carriages and vehicles drawn up as if they were attending a small country race. They were afterwards engaged in a race of another kind. In one was a lady with an opera glass; in and around and on others were legislators and politicians. There were also a few civilians on horseback, and on the slope of the hill a regiment had stacked arms, and was engaged in looking at and commenting on the battle below. The landscape in front was open to the sight as far as the ranges of the Alleghanies, which swept round from the right in blue mounds, the colour of which softened into violet in the distance. On the left the view was circumscribed by a wood, which receded along the side of the hill on which we stood to the plain below. Between the base of this hill, which rose about 150ft. above the general level of the country, and the foot of the lowest and nearest elevation of the opposite Alleghanies extended about five miles, as well as I could judge, of a densely-wooded country, dotted at intervals with green fields and patches of cleared lands. It was marked by easy longitudinal undulations, indicated by the form of the forests which clothed them, and between two of the more considerable ran small streams, or "runs," as they are denominated, from the right to the left. Close at hand a narrow road, descending the hill, went straight into the forest, where it was visible now and then among the trees in cream-coloured patches. This road was filled with commissariat waggons, the white tops of which were visible for two miles in our front.

On our left front a gap in the lowest chain of the hills showed the gap of Manassas, and to the left and nearer to us lay the "Junction" of the same name, where the Alexandria Railway unites with the rail from the west of Virginia, and continues the route by rails of various denominations to Richmond. The scene was so peaceful a man might well doubt the evidence of one sense that a great contest was being played out below in bloodshed, or imagine, as Mr. Seward sometimes does, that it was a delusion when he wakes in the morning and finds there is civil war upon him. But the cannon spoke out loudly from the green bushes, and the plains below were mottled, so to speak, by puffs of smoke and by white rings from bursting shells and capricious howitzers. It was no review that was going on beneath us. The shells gave proof enough of that, though the rush of the shot could not be heard at the distance. Clouds of dust came up in regular lines through the tree-tops where infantry were acting, and now and then their wavering mists of light blue smoke curled up, and the splutter of musketry broke through the booming of the guns. With the glass I could detect now and then the flash of arms through the dust clouds in the open, but no one could tell to which

T.C. 5 Dec. '61

My dear Russell

If there is war between England and America, the scene of your operations will, I presume, be Canada. Your principal object of course will be to place yourself in safety on board a British ship. I take for granted that Lord Lyons will allow you to attach yourself pro. tem. to his embassy. He, I should think, will go to Halifax unless his orders are

Above Letter to Russell from Mowbray Morris, 5 December 1861.

Right An engraving of the Retreat after the Battle of Bull Run, when the Federal troops were routed by the Confederates on 11 July 1861. Russell observed the battle – it was the subject of his first and last report of the Civil War.

sympathies, so far as a good foreign correspondent can have sympathies, were for Lincoln and the North. His sympathies were not shared at Printing House Square. John Walter III observed 'Why should we be so very anxious to see the Union preserved? What has it done to command our sympathy?'

Russell's first and last battle report was of the Battle of Bull Run, just outside Washington, on 21 July. Surrounded by ladies and members of Congress with their picnic baskets, he saw the untrained Federal troops break and run before the Confederate attack. His dispatch filled seven columns of *The Times* of 6 August 1861, and gave a detailed and professional account of the shambles and panic. On the following day a leading article castigated the American press for its euphemistic and eulogistic account of the battle.

When Russell's report (or, in some cases, garbled versions of it) reached New York, there was uproar. Only the *New York Times* considered it fair. He became known as Bull-Run Russell, and was sent to Coventry by both the military and civilians. Printing House Square advised him to seek sanctuary in the British Embassy. He was refused a pass to march south with the Federal Army, and, fed up with the whole war, Russell sailed for home. The Federal authorities made a great mistake: in forcing his return, they had lost an impartial reporter sympathetic to their cause; and they had persuaded the government at Printing House Square that the North was a bigoted regime.

Russell's only battle report of the American Civil War, on the Battle of Bull Run, at Manassas.
6 AUGUST 1861

Russell's replacement was Charles Mackay, not on *The Times* staff, and a fervent supporter of the South. He wrote: 'I disapproved of the policy of war, and disagreed with the logic of its Northern supporters'. Mackay's reports were not impartial. Even Mowbray Morris remonstrated: 'I ask myself whether any Government or set of men can be so wholly bad that not a single good word can be said for them'. In the South *The Times* appointed Francis Lawley as war correspondent, another partisan of the South.

Both correspondents were filing propaganda, not news, to *The Times*. Partly influenced by them the leading articles were equally biased. When New Orleans fell, *The Times* carried mourning borders. It suppressed the news that a Liverpool shipbuilder was constructing a Confederate warship, the commerce-raider *Alabama*: suppression of news is a sin against the Holy Ghost for a newspaper. When Lincoln made a proclamation on freeing the slaves in September 1862, *The Times* attacked him as 'a sort of moral American Pope', and called him 'Lincoln the Last'. In January of the next year it argued that the Bible justified slavery, and suggested that Negroes might feel they should refuse the proffered liberty. Not many Negroes seem to have been readers of *The Times*.

In spite of *The Times*, the words of the man who did not look like a gentleman were having an effect in Britain. The paper found itself being criticized and execrated at emancipation meetings around the country. Despite continual Federal successes, *The Times* stuck in the corner into which it had painted itself, and argued that the Union could not be restored by force. Probably with covert Government concurrence, it opposed a move for European intervention and a peace by compromise. Its view of the war was blurred by the unbalanced reports by its correspondents. In 1864 Sherman marched through Georgia to the sea, and Savannah fell. It was a bitter surprise to Delane, who had been prophesying emphatically that the march could not succeed.

The Times coverage of the American Civil War was unbalanced, disgraceful and wrong. It had built its opinion on prejudice, and on the foundation of painted smoke of reports by unprofessional correspondents. In the post mortem Mowbray Morris admonished Charles Mackay. He wrote to him: 'Your letters have been deficient in the qualities of a sound foreign correspondence. They have contained but few facts and a great deal of wild declamation. Every statement was one-sided, and every remark spiteful.' True. But who appointed Mackay, and swallowed his reports for three years?

Once the war was over, Delane recognized his mistake and accepted the future. After Lincoln's assassination, *The Times* at last admitted his great qualities in its account of his career and achievements. The mills of *The Times* grind slow, but they grind exceeding small, and get it right eventually. If you want to justify the line of *The Times* during the Civil War, you can argue that if Lincoln had declared from the outset that his object was to set the slaves free, and not simply to preserve the Union, his cause would have stirred Britain, and he would have carried with him the power of the Mississippi . . . Things would have been different if Russell had stayed on . . . But it is simpler and more manly to admit that *The Times* got it horribly wrong.

Paris by pigeon and balloon

It was during the Franco-Prussian War of 1870 that *The Times* found itself being scooped for the first time in the techniques it had taught the world. Younger rivals were getting their correspondents to the scene of the gunfire and printing the news first. During the siege of Paris, when post and telegraph were cut, communications between the French capital and Printing House Square were cut off more completely than at any time, even during the Napoleonic Wars.

The news must get through. *The Times* had recourse to that peculiarly French innovation, the hot-air balloon of the Mongolfier brothers; as Carlyle put it: 'So, riding on windbags, will men scale the Empyrean'. The new-fangled mail flew over the besieging Prussian lines and was then posted or telegraphed to London. By October *The Times* was publishing daily reports received by balloon post from Paris. And advertisements in French carried by balloon began to appear in the Agony Column, announcing births, marriages, deaths, and the other little disturbances of life that continue, war or no war. By the last few weeks of the siege, these French Agony announcements occupied the whole of the front page and most of the second.

Inside Paris they read the Agony Column by using pigeons. The front page of *The Times* was reduced to microscopic size, and the tiny print carried from Tours by carrier pigeon into Paris. There the messages were enlarged and distributed. Contemporary prints show the besieged Parisians turning to the source of authentic news, Printing House Square, even though it had to be brought to them by balloon, pigeon and the conventional methods of printing a daily newspaper, which are in their own way just as miraculous.

The Franco-Prussian War was Billy Russell's last big war. He marched with the German armies, and was, as usual, on familiar terms with the great captains and kings, a fact that he dropped disarmingly into his copy. Matthew Arnold sent the old war horse up:

> You know the sort of thing, he has described it himself over and over again. Bismarck at his horse's head, the Crown Prince holding the stirrup, and the old King of Prussia hoisting Russell into his saddle. When he was there, the distinguished public servant waved his hand in acknowledgement, and rode slowly down the street, accompanied by the *gamins* of Versailles, who even in their present dejection could not forbear a few involuntary cries of *quel homme*!

There was a little local difficulty over the Battle of Sedan. After Napoleon III had surrendered to the King of Prussia, various romantic and inaccurate accounts of the meeting between the two sovereigns were published. Wishing, he said, to correct these factions, the Crown Prince of Prussia gave Russell by word of mouth a detailed account of what actually happened. Russell published. Reuter's then sent a statement to all newspapers, purporting to be signed by Bismarck: 'The report of the conversation between King William and the Emperor Napoleon, given by Dr Russell, *The Times* correspondent, is founded throughout upon mere invention'.

Delane refused to publish this statement, having complete confidence in his star reporter. But Russell was shown it by a friendly colleague. He at once demanded, and got, an interview with Bismarck, who was by now installed in Versailles. The Iron Chancellor denied that he had signed any such statement, but he refused to publish a denial, and eventually admitted that the substance of the Reuter's statement had indeed been issued with his approval.

Bismarck was an old fox who used the press. He blamed Russell for indiscretion: 'I do not care if you published every word I said to you, but when you hear things from that dunderhead the Crown Prince you should know better'. Russell retorted: 'Do I understand I have your Excellency's permission to publish your opinion of the Crown Prince?'

Below and right THE TIMES on microfilm was sent by carrier pigeon to Paris where it was enlarged, and projected by magic lantern on to a screen. Clerks then copied it for distribution.

A PIGEON'S LETTER

A MEMENTO OF THE GREAT WAR OF 1870-1 WHEN PARIS, FOR SEVERAL MONTHS, DEPENDED SOLELY ON THE CARRIER PIGEONS FOR ALL INFORMATION FROM THE OUTER WORLD.

THE TIMES" CONTAINING SEVERAL COLUMNS OF FRENCH ADVERTISEMENTS &c., TO RELATIVES IN PARIS.

THIS PHOTOGRAPH WAS SENT TO M. GAMBETTA FOR TRANSMISSION BY PIGEON FROM BORDEAUX.

WHEN RECEIVED IN THE BUREAU AT PARIS, IT IS MAGNIFIED BY THE AID OF THE MAGIC LANTERN, TO AN ENORMOUS SIZE AND THROWN UPON A SCREEN. A STAFF OF CLERKS IMMEDIATELY TRANSCRIBE THE MESSAGES, AND SEND THEM OFF TO THE PARTIES INDICATED.

STEREOSCOPIC CO. COPYRIGHT

News from the Franco-Prussian War, including the proclamation of the Prussian King as Emperor of Germany, at Versailles. Bismarck awarded Russell the Iron Cross for his reporting services during the war.
20 JANUARY 1871

LATEST INTELLIGENCE.

[A portion of the following appeared in our Second Edition of yesterday:—]

THE EMPEROR OF GERMANY.

(BY TELEGRAPH.)

(FROM OUR SPECIAL CORRESPONDENT.)

VERSAILLES, JAN. 19, 9 A.M.

King William of Prussia was yesterday proclaimed Emperor of Germany in the Hall of Mirrors, in the Palace of the French Kings, and in the presence of all the German Princes who are under the standards of the army before Paris and surrounded by the representatives of the different regiments.

The diplomatists in Paris, except Mr. Washburne, have applied for leave to come out. It will be refused.

(REUTER'S TELEGRAMS.)

BERLIN, JAN. 19.

In to-day's sitting of the Lower House of the Prussian Diet, the address in reply to the Proclamation of the Emperor of Germany was voted, the Polish members alone dissenting.

JANUARY 19.

In to-day's sitting of the Upper House of the Prussian Diet the President announced that he had yesterday addressed a telegram to the Emperor, giving expression to the joyful assent of the Upper House to the King's acceptance of the title of Emperor, and stating that the Upper House would stand by the German Emperor as it had stood by the Prussian King. The President further announced that the Emperor had returned thanks to the Upper House by a telegraphic message, saying:—"May it be vouchsafed to me to lay for a united Germany the foundation stone of a glorious history such as Prussia can show to-day after a period of 700 years."

THE WAR.

(BY TELEGRAPH.)

(GERMAN ACCOUNTS.)

(FROM OUR OWN CORRESPONDENT.)

BERLIN, JAN. 19.

The Emperor-King has sent the following despatch to the Empress-Queen:—

"General Bourbaki, after three days' fighting, has withdrawn before the heroic resistance of General Werder, to whom, as well as to his valiant soldiers, the highest acknowledgments are due. General Werder maintained his entrenched position, which was strengthened by heavy batteries, and repulsed all attacks. Our loss in the three days' fighting was 1,200 men."

The following telegrams have also been received here:—

"VERSAILLES, Jan. 18, 1 a.m.

"Yesterday there was a renewed attack by Bourbaki on General Werder.

"The latter victoriously defended his position, which was entrenched, and strengthened by heavy guns, and repulsed all the attacks.

"Our losses in the three days' fighting were estimated at about 1,200 men."

"VERSAILLES, Jan. 18.

"The attempt to relieve Belfort having been frustrated by General Werder's three days' victorious combats, General Bourbaki's army is in full retreat.

"The bombardment before Paris is being continued with good results. Our loss to-day is two officers, one man killed, and one officer and 6 men wounded."

(REUTER'S TELEGRAMS.)

VERSAILLES, JAN. 18.

It is reported that M. Jules Favre has requested a safe-conduct to enable him to attend the London Conference.

The army of General Chanzy begins to show symptoms of dissolution.

Piercingly cold weather set in yesterday.

CARLSRUHE, JAN. 19.

The Minister of War has received the following telegram from General Glümer:—

"BREVILLERS, Jan. 18, Afternoon.

"On the 17th inst. the attacks of the enemy were victoriously repulsed along our whole line. The right wing under General Keller was chiefly engaged. To-day the enemy is retreating. Our losses are rather considerable. No details have as yet been received."

CARLSRUHE, JAN. 19, EVENING.

The Minister of War has just received the following telegram from General Glümer:—

"FRAHIER, Jan. 19, Noon.

"Our vanguard is pursuing the enemy to-day along the whole line. The 2d Baden Infantry Brigade, with two light field batteries and two cavalry squadrons, under Major-General von Degenfeld, are marching upon Beverne."

(FRENCH ACCOUNTS.)

BORDEAUX, JAN. 18.

According to an official despatch the army of General Bourbaki yesterday made a general attack on the enemy, who remained constantly on the defensive, but suffered serious losses. Owing to reinforcements which he received, and the strength of his position, he was able to resist all our efforts, and his line remained unbroken. The town of Avalon was bombarded on Monday, and about 20 houses more or less damaged. It was afterwards abandoned by the enemy.

JANUARY 19.

On the 17th a brigade of the Army of the North dislodged some battalions of Prussians from the wood of Buive, near Templeux; on the same day a corps of Prussians abandoned Vermand on the approach of the French from [name of place omitted]. On the morning of the 18th a French division was attacked by Prussians forming part of the corps of General Goeben, during the whole day, in a position before Vermand, where it maintained itself.

Yesterday skirmishes occurred near Gien and Tours. The enemy also appeared at Mont Louis, near La Haite. The Francs-Tireurs had a small engagement and held their ground against five or six times their number.

CHERBOURG, JAN. 18.

There is no material change in the state of affairs. The few thousand troops remaining here have received orders to prepare for an immediate advance.

It is stated that the mail service between here and Southampton by the London and South-Western Company's steamers will be removed to St. Malo, and a daily service each way will be carried on by the above packets between St. Malo and Southampton.

THE SIEGE OF LONGWY.

ARLON, JAN. 19.

The bombardment of Longwy was continued vigorously to-day; 300 shells have fallen in the town. The steeple of the church has been damaged and some houses have been destroyed by the bombardment. There have been a few killed and wounded. The garrison have made a sortie, and the fire of the besieged has dismounted one of the Prussian guns.

FIGHTING ON THE SWISS FRONTIER.

PRUNTRUT, JAN. 19, EVENING.

Yesterday afternoon the Germans captured the village of Abbevillers, which had been set on fire.

The French retired to the South on Blamont and Pont de Roide.

The German troops yesterday drove the French out of all French frontier posts, the population flying across the Swiss frontier at Dampvent.

FRANCE.

BORDEAUX, JAN. 10.*

The Minister of the Interior has received an address dated Strasburg, Dec. 12, from the French Government *employés* in Alsace, protesting against the Prussian assumption that they were disposed to retain their appointments under German rule. The *employés* declare they will accept no kind of Prussian service, either provisional or definitive.

The *Siècle* publishes a letter without date from Louis Blanc to Victor Hugo. Louis Blanc argues that even the Capitulation of Paris would in no way terminate the war, as France would still fight on. The Capitulation of Paris would therefore only terribly increase the material suffering there. It is not to be supposed the Prussians would allow egress from the city; the Parisians would then be even closer prisoners than before, and famine would become inevitable. The object of the armies operating in France must be to prevent the enemy from receiving supplies. "Hence," Louis Blanc concludes, "Paris cannot choose. There is but one way—counselled by wisdom, commanded by necessity. Paris cannot lag behind; her present inaction cannot continue, and the sole issue lies in a vigorous offensive, ably led."

*Delayed in transmission.

EVENING.*

A Ministerial circular requires the Prefects to telegraph before the 25th of January the number of persons liable to military service in their respective departments.

The *Moniteur* publishes the letter of Louis Blanc which has already been telegraphed.

An official census gives the population of Paris in December, including refugees, at 1,095,709, exclusive of the army, the Garde Mobile, and the sailors.

The *Gazette de France* publishes the protest of the Count de Chambord against the bombardment of Paris.

The *Siècle*, in reference to the rumoured capture of a French vessel by a Prussian corvette at the mouth of the Gironde, complains of the inaction of the French fleet, and demands to have cruisers sent to intercept the German packets between Bremen and New York.

*Delayed in transmission.

BELGIUM.

BRUSSELS, JAN. 19.

A balloon fell last night near Ruremonde, having left Paris at 3 in the morning. The bombardment continued without interruption on the forts as well as on several parts of the city, causing considerable damage and fires, which were, however, easily extinguished. Great difficulty was being experienced in grinding the corn. About 15 daily were killed through the bombardment.

LIEGE, JAN. 18.

The *Mémorial de Liège* of to-day says:—

"Travellers arrived here to-day state that an engagement had been fought near Roupy and Vermand, west of St. Quentin. Cannonading was heard faintly from 11 a.m. until 3 p.m., when it increased in intensity.

BAVARIA.

MUNICH, JAN. 19.

In to-day's sitting of the Chamber of Deputies the President announced that 68 new telegrams, giving in adhesions to the Treaties with the North German Confederation, had been received, in addition to those which had already arrived from municipalities and popular meetings. These telegrams were chiefly from districts in which Liberal members had been elected. One of the telegrams arrived from the inhabitants and the clergy of Frontenhausen.

4 45 P.M.

In the sitting of the Lower House to-day Count Bray, the Minister for Foreign Affairs, declared that he shared the hopes of one party, and not the fears of the other, with regard to the relations between Prussia and Austria, and he rejoiced that the first act of the new German Empire had been an approach to Austria. It had been said that no great weight ought to be attached to the recent exchange of despatches. "But," continued the Minister, "when the expressions of Governments are a reflex of the material interests of the nation, deeds follow words, and words themselves become deeds. Members should call to mind what was said in Count Beust's despatch with regard to the Austrian Emperor's view of the reconstruction of Germany. Such words coming from such mouths are in themselves facts of political moment. An alliance with Austria has hitherto been the only means of realizing the idea which many of us had inscribed on our banners, the idea of a great and united Germany. Within the federation we may carry it out; without its pale we are only an object of contention."

THE LONDON CONFERENCE.

BELGRADE, JAN. 19.

The Servian Government has sent the Head Director of the Ministry of Finance to represent the interests of Servia in a semi-official capacity at the London Conference.

HUNGARY.

PESTH, JAN. 19.

In yesterday's sitting of the Austrian Delegation the debate on the Budget of the Ministry for Foreign Affairs was resumed. All the clauses were voted, in conformity with the propositions of the Committee. The Secret Service money was likewise voted, as proposed by the Committee, after a warm discussion, in which Count Beust was specially attacked by Herr Carneri.

THE RUSSIAN BUDGET.

ST. PETERSBURG, JAN. 19.

The Budget for 1871 is made public to-day, and shows the revenue, as well as the expenditure, to be 489 million roubles; 10½ million roubles are devoted to the construction of railways.

AMERICA.

(BY CABLE.)

WASHINGTON, JAN. 18.

Congress finally passed to-day a supplemental Funding Bill authorizing the increase of the issue of Five per Cent. Bonds to $500,000,000, but providing that this shall be no increase of the total amount of Funding Bonds.

Senator Wade and two other San Domingo Commissioners sailed yesterday.

NEW YORK, JAN. 18.

The steamers leaving to-day for Europe take out $2,750,000 in specie.

COMMERCIAL INTELLIGENCE.

CLOSING PRICES.

Gold closed at 110⅝. The highest quotation during the day was 110¾, the lowest 110½.

Sterling exchange on London, 109½.

Five-Twenty United States' Bonds, 1882, 109⅝; ditto, 1885, 108⅞; ditto, 1867, 108; Ten-Forty United States' Bonds, 1867, 107⅞.

Illinois shares, 133½; Erie shares, 22.

Cotton—middling upland, 15⅝c.

Petroleum—standard white, 25c.

Flour—extra State, $6 40c. to $6 60c.

Corn—old mixed, 83c.

INDIA, CHINA, AND AUSTRALIAN MAILS.

BRINDISI, JAN. 18.

The Peninsular and Oriental Company's steamer Delta arrived at 8 a.m. to-day. The mails leave for London at 11 this morning.

ROUGH JUSTICE.—The committee elected to preside over the diamond diggers at Puiel, on the Vaal, had a puzzling case before them recently. A young lad picked up a diamond of 12 carats at a spot between two cradles. This piece of luck was not kept a secret by him or his relatives. Coming to the ears of one of the adjacent cradle owners, the diamond was claimed by him, on the ground that it must have been carelessly thrown out of his sieve. The father of the boy refused to give up the stone, and the affair was referred to the committee, who decided that the stone should be sold and the produce divided between the three parties—the finder and the two cradle owners. There seems to be no prison at the diggings. In November a German who had stolen money was put in the stocks for twelve hours, and then drummed out of the fields with "Thief" painted on his back, and informed that if he returned he would be flogged and kept to hard labour for a long term.

A SEA-GOING TURRET SHIP.

In *The Times* of the 15th of December we gave a short notice of a design prepared by Mr. Frank Haddan, of the Admiralty, by which he hopes to render a low freeboard ship like the Captain capable of cruising in a seaway under sail without danger. We now proceed to give further details as to the manner in which this result is expected to be attained.

Mr. Haddan proposes, in the first place, to extend the hurricane deck laterally to the full width of the vessel, since it has been proved in evidence that the Captain could not be handled quickly under sail on account of the insufficiency of her deck area. The sides of the hurricane deck, thus widened, will be made to push back under the central portion by means of sliding girders, and when drawn out they will receive and fix the upper part of rising sides or moving bulwarks, which are to be hinged to and raised from the fighting deck, or lowered and permitted to rest upon its surface. When these bulwarks are raised, and resting against the widened hurricane deck, they will give a freeboard of 17ft., instead of one of 6ft., and an angle of immersion of the upper deck of 35 degrees, instead of 14 degrees, thus greatly increasing the stability of the ship when under sail. When the ship is required for action, the bulwarks will fall upon the fighting deck, so that the guns may fire over them, and the sides of the hurricane deck will be pushed beneath the centre, so as to afford the usual low freeboard of a fighting Monitor.

Mr. Haddan further proposes to work the guns on a different method to that used in the Captain, and by this to diminish the height of the turrets above the fighting level; the weight thus saved compensating for that of the rising bulwarks and expanding hurricane deck. His plan is to arm the turrets with muzzle-pivoting guns mounted on the *barbette* or Moncrieff system, but so constructed that they and the turret can be bodily lowered to any required extent, thereby avoiding the necessity for the use of any form of ballast for cruising under sail. The lowering of the guns might also be usefully employed as a means of raising the sides and of widening the hurricane deck. By adopting the *barbette* system under turrets protection would be afforded to the guns when in the act of firing, and not only in the act of loading, as done by Moncrieff; while the gunners would also be screened from rifle shots. As the guns would be loaded below the fighting deck, the size of the turrets would also be reduced in diameter, and in this way weight would be again saved.

The chief novelty in Mr. Haddan's design is the mobility of the bulwarks, not their employment. A sum of over 15,000l. has been expended in merely fitting temporary bulwarks to enable the Cerberus to cross the ocean to Australia; and this sum will be entirely lost, as the bulwarks will be removed as soon as the ship reaches her destination. We hear that the falling bulwarks have been objected to upon the hypothetical grounds that they would be shaken to pieces when the guns were fired over them, and that they could not be made watertight when raised. These objections seem to us to have reference to matters of detail rather than of principle, and could probably both be obviated by the resources of modern engineering. To the second, especially, we should attach but little weight, since it would not matter how much water was shipped through bulwarks if it only found free exit as the vessel rose. The problem is of national importance, and we trust the Board of Admiralty will cause Mr. Haddan's suggestions to be thoroughly examined by the Shipbuilding Committee just appointed.

HOW FAMILIARITY BREEDS CONTEMPT.

TO THE EDITOR OF THE TIMES.

Sir,—In your columns of to-day much space is occupied to make the public believe that a scientific correspondent escaped from a terrific gale on board Her Majesty's ship Urgent on the 6th of December last.

I was a passenger on board Her Majesty's ship Urgent, and, as a sailor, feel it my duty to give my opinion, and wish to let the public know that there was nothing exceptional to be said about the gale we met off the coast of Portugal to warrant the liberty of taking up so much of people's time with a landsman's impression of his first gale at sea.

We were favoured with most beautiful weather from the moment of leaving Spithead all across the dreaded "Bay of Biscay O!" until we rounded Cape Finisterre, on the night of December 6. We had to struggle against a strong gale from the southward. It blew a strong gale for six hours. In the middle of the night the tiller ropes, which, being new, had stretched, required to be set up taut. In performing this operation the engines were stopped, and the ship fell off her course, which brought her broadside-on to the swell for a short time. Consequently the ship did roll; things which were not properly secured fetched way, some little water was shipped, and other every-day scenes of sea-life in a gale occurred; but I never could see any comparison between our position and that of Her Majesty's ship Captain, or any of the "awfuls" which your correspondent pictures.

My opinion is that the voyage was a very fine one, and lucky will be the passenger who will get the "clerk of the weather" to insure him a voyage to Gibraltar in the winter under the same favourable conditions of weather as we were so highly favoured with.

The case was that our scientific expedition was composed of about 30 gentlemen who were strangers to the freaks of Father Neptune. Everything was marvellous to their eyes, and some made copious notes of all they saw and were told. I never shall forget those note-books, at every turn of the deck there you saw being dotted down every minutiæ. I believe that every time the fishes were fed is recorded. Jack, who is fond of a joke, gulled the landsmen by telling them the gale was a hurricane, we were shipping heavy seas, ship making water, &c., until each landsman thought himself a hero; then came the practical joke of giving out that the sternpost was going, all this amid a smash of crockery and gentlemen without sea legs.

On the return voyage we had a worse gale. On rounding Cape Finisterre it was very satisfactory to observe what good weather the Urgent made of it, and made four knots against a gale right in her teeth.

But what I consider is more right and fitting that the country should know is that the Eclipse Expedition to Oran, Gibraltar, and Cadiz have reason for deep gratitude to the Government for the great liberality by which we were provided with the means of getting to Oran at the public expense, and most especially to the authorities at the Admiralty for selecting a very commodious and suitable ship, with everything necessary for our comfort; also for the kindness and patient attention shown us by the captain and officers of the Urgent.

I have the honour to be, Sir, your obedient servant,

ERASMUS OMMANNEY, Rear-Admiral.

6, Talbot-square, W., Jan. 18.

[We are sure no landsman will regret to have had the gale described by a fellow-landsman, instead of by a seaman so accustomed to the sea as to see nothing wonderful in anything. It is indeed the old story of "Eyes and No Eyes."]

FALL OF A HOUSE IN THAMES-STREET.—Last night the Bridge Coffee-house, in Upper Thames-street, a refreshment-house where a number of persons lived as lodgers, fell to the ground. Happily the creaking timbers gave a few minutes' warning, and the inmates, with the exception of three or four, managed to escape altogether free from injury, while of those who were buried in the ruins or caught by the falling materials two only were injured. The house was 193, Upper Thames-street, and it was in the occupation of a coffee-house keeper named Hawkins, who at the time of the accident was from home. Shortly before 8 o'clock, a French tailor who lived on the second floor heard a cracking in the woodwork, to which he at first paid little attention. But the noise increasing he warned those above him that the timbers were breaking. He at once seized his three children, and taking charge of three other children, belonging to a fellow-lodger, made haste out of the house, followed by his wife. The door fell to as he got out, and at that instant his wife was struck down. She was at once rescued, but her shoulder was dislocated. At the same time the action of the timbers had been observed in the ground floor, where Mrs. Hawkins was, for she called in the watchman of the house next door, which was in course of demolition, along with some adjoining houses in Garlick-hill. The watchman saw the walls moving, and saying that the house was falling darted out of the place. The house fell into the street, the materials knocking down and severely injuring a boy who was passing. In the top floor of the house No. 193 were a man and wife named Smith, both of whom were taken out without serious injuries. The three persons injured—namely, Mrs. Binder, Mrs. Hawkins, and the boy—were taken to St. Bartholomew's Hospital. The accident is attributed to adjoining houses being taken down without supports being put up in their place.

CHLOROFORM ROBBERIES.—How is it that only people who are mysteriously robbed can be rendered instantaneously insensible by chloroform or other anæsthetic vapours? Instantaneous means of producing anæsthesia by inhalation are unknown to men of science, and we are all aware that to produce anæsthesia by any known fluid evaporating from a handkerchief is a comparatively slow process, and one which is still more impeded when we have not the ready and intelligent co-operation of the subject except in children, whose loud cries lead to deeper inhalation and more rapid insensibility. It is hard to suppose that the thieves have compassed a secret beyond the skill of men of science.—*British Medical Journal.*

CONTAGION AND CONVEYANCE.

TO THE EDITOR OF THE TIMES.

Sir,—In connexion with the prevalence of infectious complaints, I observe frequent reports in your columns of a class of occurrences which strike me as very inexcusable. I refer to the cases in which patients suffering from the Smallpox or Scarlet Fever are forwarded from Hospital to Hospital, and are sometimes sent across London, before they find shelter. We are told of a man standing outside Westminster Hospital with the disease out upon him; he presents his ticket of admission, but is refused, and carries his infection elsewhere. Another is driven about in a cab from place to place. In a third instance, a child is taken in the parochial conveyance, by order of the doctor, from her house at the West-end to Hampstead, and thence to Highgate; the Hospitals are full at both places, and at last, after six hours' journeying, she is carried back to St. James's Workhouse. Your readers will recall many more such cases.

It is obvious, Sir, that such treatment is equally disadvantageous for the individual and for the public. It must tend to aggravate the patient's illness, and it must multiply indefinitely the risk of infection. I do not suppose any blame rests with the managers of the hospitals. They cannot receive patients if their wards are full, or if they have no wards adapted for the treatment of infectious complaints. But what surprises me is that doctors do not ascertain, before sending a case to a Hospital, that the managers are capable of receiving it. Where is the difficulty of using the telegraph for such a purpose? Why should a sick child be sent round to Hampstead and Highgate, when at the cost of three or four shillings a messenger might have taken the journey on her behalf?

When such facilities are available, this cruel and dangerous mismanagement is to me unaccountable. So far as Poor Law officials are responsible, it is a fit subject for the attention and the censure of the Poor Law Board, and they will, I hope, prohibit a repetition of such gratuitous neglect. As to unofficial doctors, it ought to be within the competence of the Medical Department of the Privy Council to restrain them; but I fear this offers another instance in which Mr. Simon's influence is restricted to mere advice. The case, however, appears so plain that a suggestion in your columns ought to be sufficient. Cabmen are liable to fine if they omit to disinfect their vehicles after conveying a patient with a contagious disease. It seems to me that doctors or visitors are equally culpable who, without the least necessity, send Smallpox patients through the streets on a fruitless errand.

I am, Sir, yours obediently,

J. R.

THE SMALLPOX EPIDEMIC.—Yesterday Dr. Bridges, Poor Law Medical Inspector, under direction of the Poor Law Board, attended the meeting of the Board of Guardians of St. Pancras, for the purpose of conferring with them upon the prevalence of smallpox in the metropolis. After referring to the circular of the Metropolitan Asylums Board and the progress of the epidemic in London, he said the number of cases reported to him in St. Pancras for the week ending the 7th of January was 26, all pauper cases for whom no accommodation could be found either at Highgate or Hampstead. He therefore advised the Board to do one of two things—either to rent an empty house sufficiently isolated and fit it up for the reception of cases, or to erect a temporary iron building on some vacant ground. St. Olave's Union had undertaken to erect such a shed of corrugated iron, 60ft. long and 20ft. wide, at a cost of 265l. Mr. Joseph Salter would ask Dr. Bridges if he could guarantee that the Poor Law Board would sanction the Guardians incurring the necessary expense. Dr. Bridges said it would most undoubtedly. Mr. Joseph Salter then said he would move, "That it be referred to the General Purposes Committee to carry out the views enunciated by Dr. Bridges, and that they have full power to procure a building, houses, medical staff, furniture, and whatever was required." This was seconded and carried. A report was also presented from the General Purposes Committee, recommending that the Vaccination Clerk be wholly employed in seeking out and reporting unvaccinated cases, and taking the necessary steps under the Act for enforcing the law. This report was moved by Mr. Parson and seconded by Mr. J. Smith. Mr. Salter said this step was most essential, as during the half-year ending the 31st of December last there had been no less than 2,140 cases in that parish in which the law had not been complied with in forwarding certificates of successful vaccination. There could be no doubt that this matter had not been followed up with proper vigilance. A case had only a day or two since been taken before the magistrate at Clerkenwell Police-court, but failed through the prosecution not being made within six months, in accordance with the law. The resolution having been carried, Dr. Bridges expressed his satisfaction at the steps taken by the Guardians in endeavouring to arrest the spread of the disease. He should, as a matter of course, report the readiness with which they had entered into his views to the Poor Law Board.

DESTRUCTIVE FIRE.—On Wednesday night, about 10 o'clock, a destructive fire broke out at the Ealing Refuge for Orphan Girls, by which a large amount of property was destroyed and the building itself considerably damaged. The Refuge at the present time contains upwards of 100 girls, and many of them are engaged in the laundry where the clothes belonging to the establishments in Broad-street and Queen-street are washed and prepared. The girls were on Wednesday engaged as usual in the laundry, and ceased work between 8 and 9 in the evening, when it was supposed all was left in safety. About a quarter before 10, however, one of the girls had occasion to enter the wash-house, when her attention was attracted by a light in the laundry on the next floor. The matron, Miss Frost, was at once apprised of the circumstance, and on proceeding to the laundry she discovered the place in a blaze. It was discovered that the main body of the fire was near the doorway, and quite away from the ironing stoves. The firemen were enabled to subdue the flames without the entire destruction of the laundry and washhouse, but, notwithstanding, a large amount of property was destroyed. The flooring of the laundry was burnt through, and the contents of the room—folding-boards, tables, and mangle, and between 400l. and 500l. worth of clothes—completely destroyed. It is calculated that it will require at least 100l. to restore the building, which was fortunately insured.

THE UNEMPLOYED.—Last night an adjourned conference was held in the Cowcross Mission-hall, White-horse-close, West Smithfield, to consider what can be done for the unemployed workmen who are starving in London, and to devise means to find them employment. Mr. Catlin, city missionary, occupied the chair. He said there were to his knowledge hundreds of skilled artisans idle who had pawned all their tools, and were gradually selling every article of furniture to purchase food, and in a few weeks many of them would be cast into the streets with their families without food or shelter. He did not wish long speeches, but practical suggestions. Mr. Hyde, Greenwich, said London was not a manufacturing city, but it had in past years a host of industries which gave work to working men and women. These were being gradually swept away, and no new field of labour was being opened up to them. Food was much dearer than in former years, and labour was paid at a higher rate; but there was nothing to do, owing to free trade. The corkcutters, who once numbered 5,000 in London, were now idle because the foreign corks were cut and brought into the English market at a less price than they could be manufactured at home. Other trades had proportionately suffered. They could never compete with the foreign market, as men there got 1s. 8d. a day, and could live better than the English mechanic who had 4s. a day. But the work-people on the Continent paid no local rates, while the English did. He concluded by moving, "That this meeting considers the want of employment and contingent distress among the industrial poor are caused by the introduction of foreign-manufactured goods free of duty, thus depriving a large number of persons of occupation; and this meeting further considers that the principle of one-sided free trade as established in England is prejudicial to the true interests of the nation, and especially injurious to the working classes." Mr. Brown seconded the resolution. Mr. Townsend Trench said there were many difficulties in the way of returning to Protection, as it was not a remedy to the evil of which they complained. Free-trade was for the advantage of England, and if 5,000 cork-cutters suffered by it, 1,000,000 other Englishmen were the gainers. The commerce of England had nearly doubled itself in some things since Free-trade was introduced, more especially the exports. As to the question of reclaiming land, he saw many difficulties in the way; for, allowing that the Government did take the matter in hand and reclaimed the waste lands, what was then to be done with the working men? The only remedy which presented itself to his mind was migration and emigration. The workmen should go from place to place, and on knowing that the trade was brisk in a certain district proceed there, and if it were found that the country was really overstocked, emigration could be resorted to. He moved as an amendment, "That this meeting wishes to see a system of migration and emigration adopted for the relief of the unemployed." Mr. Rowland seconded the amendment, and on the resolution and amendment being put to the meeting the latter was carried by a large majority. Mr. Richardson moved, "That a registry of names and addresses of unemployed mechanics and labourers be kept at the Mission-hall, and advertisements to that effect be inserted in the newspapers." Mr. Downie seconded the resolution, which was agreed to. Mr. Boon then addressed the meeting at great length, and attributed the present distress to the wealth of the aristocracy. Mr. Curtis moved "That they form a society to enable suitable persons to emigrate either to Canada or the United States." Mr. Jones seconded the resolution. Mr. Alsager Hill suggested that the name of the society should be the Cow-cross Employment Society, which was adopted. The resolution was, after some discussion, agreed to. The registry was then opened, and a numerous body of working men out of employment put down their names. The meeting closed with a vote of thanks to the chairman.

TENNYSON'S WORKS.—In the case of "Tennyson and Messrs. Strahan and Co. (his publishers) v. Forrester," for alleged piracy, Lord Gifford, in the Court of Session, Edinburgh, issued on Wednesday an interlocutor repelling the defender's plea against the competency of the action. The interlocutor was as follows:—"Edinburgh, Jan. 18, 1871.—The Lord-Ordinary having heard parties' procurators, and having considered the closed record, repels the first, second, and third pleas in law stated for the defender, and appoints an issue or issues for the trial of the cause to be adjusted on Thursday, the 26th curt."

THE VOLUNTEERS.

ST. GEORGE'S RIFLE VOLUNTEERS.

The regimental and other prizes gained by the winners in the annual rifle shooting competition of this corps were presented last night, in the theatre of the London University in Burlington-gardens. The prizes were distributed by Lieutenant-Colonel the Hon. C. H. Lindsay, M.P. The spacious hall was filled with members of the corps and their friends. There was an unusually large attendance of ladies. The challenge cups, tankards, goblets, and other pieces of plate, placed among the multifarious prizes, which were of an aggregate value of 800l., made a brilliant display.

Lieutenant-Colonel LINDSAY, in addressing the regiment, said that the building in which they had met on that occasion to take part in the annual ceremony of distributing the prizes won by the members of the corps during the year revived many associations connected with the Volunteer movement, and more especially with that regiment. It was in the gardens of Burlington-house that their first presentation of prizes was made, and this circumstance would bring to their recollection the causes which led to the formation of the Volunteers in 1859. They had good reason, he said, to be satisfied with the position which they then assumed, and had ever since maintained. They undertook a great national work, by nobody's order, but by their own free will, and the support given to the Volunteers by the Government of that day was of itself an acknowledgment of the necessity of their action. Every man who enrolled himself was eagerly armed by the State. The decision of a Royal Commission in favour of State aid was an important and tentative step in the right direction, but one which soon proved to be short of the mark. Notwithstanding the repeated declarations of commanding officers that the Government grant was wholly insufficient to meet the necessary expenses, the only concession which could be obtained was a proposal to increase the grant upon a calculation of 5s. per head all round upon the completed establishments of officers and sergeants; but, since those establishments were very far from being completed, this calculation was based upon a false and deceptive issue. (Hear.) He had found, by analyzing this calculation, that even if every officer and sergeant succeeded in obtaining a certificate the sum obtained would be very little more than 2s. 6d. a head. It would, he thought, be an error in judgment to mix up the valuable instruction now offered by Government with so paltry a concession, and thereby fetter it with such unpalatable conditions. So far as voluntary efforts and gratuitous services went, the Volunteer service had nothing to reproach itself with. The question of organization, however, must now be considered by the Government and House of Commons. It was not to be denied that the Volunteer service could not organize itself, and the absence of the requisite organization was obviously caused by want of moral courage to grapple with the question on the part of the Government. The Volunteer service did not possess a greatcoat, or a blanket, or any one article needed to go into camp with. The question of personal equipment was not, he ventured to say, a difficult one if the Government would take the trouble to grapple with it, and the country need not be put to the cost of a farthing until the crisis of an invasion was at hand. Let there be a general military or army pattern for every article, from the shako to the boot, and let a Volunteer store be established capable of equipping 300,000 men at the shortest possible notice. The army, which was always requiring equipment, might draw upon this store, care being taken to replace immediately what was used. Our artillery was a myth—200 guns where there ought to be 2,000—our cavalry was a farce, and our commissariat, medical staff, and land transport were inefficient because incapable of expanding themselves. The Militia was no doubt the great and reliable reserve of the army, and therefore every man between 20 and 40 should be liable to be drawn for it under the operation of the ballot. Then, and not until then, would England be in a position to part safely with one of her soldiers. He felt it his duty to refer to a question which had been raised within the last few days affecting the honourable discipline and position of the Volunteer service. He alluded to the proposition that Volunteers had a right to take part in political or other demonstrations when wearing their uniforms, provided they did not carry arms. Now, the uniform was intended to be used solely for the purpose of military training, and the oath of allegiance administered to every member on joining was a close and binding contract for no other object but that of his country's defence. He therefore deprecated the attitude which had been assumed as having a dangerous tendency to disturb the hitherto high tone and patriotic sentiment which had pervaded the Volunteer service. (Cheers.) Referring to the state of the regiment, he stated that the efficients at 30s. numbered 333 in 1870 as compared with 244 in 1869; the efficients at 20s. were 41 last year, against 113 in the previous year; the non-efficients 130, against 148 in 1869; making the total strength 504 in 1870, or one less than in the preceding year. The percentage of efficients was 74·20 in 1870, showing an improvement of 3·51 per cent.

The prizes were next distributed. First came the best shots in class firing—Private R. Andrews, of No. 2 Company (distinguished as the best shot of the battalion), Privates Rowe, Harrow, Pickwick, Ingram, and Sergeant Pocock. The St. George's Challenge Cup and gold medal were won by Private Taylor; the Turner Memorial Plate and silver medal, Private Harrow; the Ladies' Challenge Plate and silver medal, Private Torr; the Ortner Shield and facsimile, having been won for the third time by Private Rowe, now became his property.

The Rev. H. HOWARTH, rector of St. George's, Hanover-square, hon. chaplain to the regiment, proposed a vote of thanks to the hon. and gallant Colonel, which was accorded with acclamation, and the proceedings then terminated.

In addition to the list published in *The Times* of the 13th inst. several additional regiments and administrative battalions of Rifle Volunteers have since received their supply of Snider rifles. The distribution has now proceeded as far as "130" on the official list, and as the last number is "229," it will be seen that considerably more than half the force is now armed with the breechloader. Should the distribution continue at the rate at which it has already progressed, there is little doubt that all the Metropolitan Corps will possess the new weapon before the Easter Monday Volunteer Review. The additional regiments and administrative battalions which have received the rifles are the following:—Metropolitan.—3d City of London, 1st Administrative Battalion Tower Hamlets, and 28th Middlesex (London Irish). Provincial.—4th Administrative Battalion Cheshire, 3d West Riding York, 39th West Riding York, 2d Administrative Battalion Cornwall, 4th Administrative Battalion Lanark, 4th Administrative Battalion Lancashire, 105th Lanark, 1st Sussex (Brighton), 1st Administrative Battalion Roxburgh, 1st Administrative Battalion Banff, 1st Administrative Battalion Argyll, 47th Lancashire (St. Helen's), 5th Administrative Battalion West Riding York, 1st Administrative Battalions Notts, Ayr, Lincoln, Glamorgan, and Ross; 2d Administrative Battalion Renfrew, 1st Administrative Battalion Cheshire, 3d Administrative Battalion Suffolk, 2d Administrative Battalion West Riding York, 1st Administrative Battalions Inverness and Shropshire, 34th West Riding York (Saddleworth), 1st Administrative Battalion Berwick, 3d Administrative Battalion West Riding York, 1st Administrative Battalion Dumbarton, 3d Administrative Battalion Durham, 1st Administrative Battalion Somerset, 2d Administrative Battalion Hants, 15th Lancashire (Liverpool), 1st Administrative Battalion Denbigh, 5th Administrative Battalion Stafford, 2d Administrative Battalion Worcester, 1st Administrative Battalion Leicester, 1st Norfolk (Norwich), 2d Administrative Battalion Cheshire, 1st Administrative Battalion Worcester, 2d Administrative Battalion Forfar, 1st East Riding York (Hull), 8th Northumberland, 1st Administrative Battalion Warwick, 2d Administrative Battalion Cambridge, 6th Administrative Battalion Lancashire, 2d Administrative Battalion Glamorgan, 1st Administrative Battalion Flint, 1st Administrative Battalion Northampton, 29th West Riding York (Dewsbury), 3d Administrative Battalion Aberdeen, 1st Administrative Battalion Haddington, 1st Administrative Battalion West Riding York, 2d Administrative Battalion Monmouth, 1st Administrative Battalion Dumfries, 1st Administrative Battalion Wilts, 4th Administrative Battalion West Riding York, and 1st Administrative Battalions North Riding of York, Isle of Wight, Devon, and Brecon. By order of the Secretary of State for War, the provisions of Article 147 of the Volunteer Regulations, which are as follow, will be strictly enforced:—"The arms are to be deposited after drill in the armouries of the corps, except when the commanding officer may judge it expedient to permit members of the corps to keep their arms at their own houses, in which case a written permission is to be given by him to each member who is allowed to take his arms home. As the commanding officer is responsible to the Government for the condition of the arms issued to the corps, it will be his duty to give those permissions with care, and any of them may be withdrawn by him whenever he may consider it necessary. The arms retained in private custody will be subject to inspection at any time by the Assistant-Inspector of the district and the field-officer commanding any administrative regiment to which the corps may belong, and they are to be examined at least once in six months by the commanding officer of the corps or by some officer or officers appointed by him for that duty. In any case in which the arms are neglected the discretionary power granted to the commanding officer in this Article will be withdrawn."

RAILWAY ACCIDENT.—HARTLEPOOL, Thursday.—About a quarter to 7 o'clock last evening an accident to a passenger train, which nearly resulted in serious loss of life, occurred between Castle Eden and Hartlepool stations, on the North-Eastern Railway. The train in question, consisting of two third, one first, and one second class carriages, and a powerful break, left Ferryhill junction, with several passengers, at 6 10 p.m., and was due at Hartlepool at 7 5 p.m.; but after ascending a steep incline known as Hesleden bank, a portion of the train (fortunately not inclusive of the engine) left the rails, to the intense alarm of the passengers. Providentially, the accident occurred too soon after ascending the incline for the engine to have increased its speed to the usual rate; hence the couplings held, and the train was saved from going over the edge of the embankment, which could scarcely have occurred without loss of life. The carriages which ran off very luckily did not fall over, and, in consequence, their occupants, as well as those of the rest of the train, escaped with a severe shaking, and the very natural alarm which such a casualty would excite. Upon the arrival of the 6 15 p.m. train from Sunderland, which joins the Ferryhill line above Castle Eden, the passengers of the disabled train were transferred, and the train itself shunted past the Ferryhill one, so that they all safely arrived at Hartlepool before 8 o'clock. The supposed cause of the accident is either that the ballast had given way owing to the recent frost, or that the second carriage jumped the rails in passing the set of points by which the Sunderland train was enabled to shunt.

LOCOMOTIVES ON RAILWAYS.—The following railway companies each owned more than 100 locomotives at the close of 1869:—Great Eastern, 413; Great Northern, 493; Great Western, 903; Lancashire and Yorkshire, 477; London and North-Western, 1,549; London and South-Western, 280; London, Brighton, and South Coast, 256; London, Chatham, and Dover, 112; Manchester, Sheffield, and Lincolnshire, 270; Midland, 736; North-Eastern, 899; South-Eastern, 243; Caledonian, 514; North British, 396; Glasgow and South-Western, 184; Great Southern and Western of Ireland, 121.

UNIVERSITY INTELLIGENCE.

OXFORD.

An examination will be held in University College on Tuesday, the 14th of February next, and following days for two open Classical Scholarships, of the value of 80l. per annum during residence, and tenable for five years from election. Candidates, if already members of the University, must not have completed their eighth Term. Also for a Mathematical Exhibition, of the value of 50l. per annum, during residence, and tenable for 18 Terms from matriculation. Also for another Exhibition, of the value of 30l. per annum, tenable for the same period. Classical candidates will, unless they have passed responsions, be examined in arithmetic, and in either *Euclid*, Books I. and II., or in Algebra, as far as simple equations, inclusive. Candidates are requested to call on the Master on Monday, the 13th of February, with certificates of their baptism and testimonials from their Colleges or schools; and, if members of the University, certificates of their matriculation. At the same time, six vacancies for Commoners who wish to reside in the following Easter or Michaelmas Term will be filled up by competition. For these optional papers will be given in mathematics. Candidates are requested to communicate by letter with the Master, and to send certificates of their baptism and testimonials from their School before the 11th of February, and to call on the Master on Monday, the 13th. The examinations will commence at half-past 9 o'clock on February 14.

THE BOMBARDMENT OF PARIS.

A MONSIEUR LE DIRECTEUR DU TIMES.

Monsieur,—Ce n'est pas comme Français, mais comme disciple de la morale du Christ, et comme membre de la grande famille humaine, que je viens demander l'hospitalité de vos colonnes pour une idée qui honorera à jamais la nation Anglaise.

Votre Gouvernement, qui tient le premier rang parmi les pays civilisés, ne peut pas et ne doit pas souffrir que les Prussiens fassent la guerre aux femmes, aux enfants, aux vieillards, et aux malades. C'est pourtant là le crime qu'il commettent chaque jour en bombardant l'intérieur de Paris.

Il appartient à l'Angleterre de réclamer hautement par persuasion d'abord, et s'il y a lieu par une intervention active, la cessation de ce scandale qui déshonore l'Europe.

Lors du bombardement de Strasbourg, la petite république d'Helvétie n'a pas hésité à faire une démarche couronnée de succès. Une députation d'hommes vaillants a obtenu la sortie de la ville bombardée pour les femmes, les enfants, les vieillards, et les malades.

L'Angleterre n'aurait-elle pas un devoir semblable à remplir en ce qui concerne la population de Paris, j'entends celle qui est hors d'état de concourir à la défense?

Tous les peuples ont un égal intérêt à s'opposer aux actes de barbarie qui abaissent le niveau social, confié à l'honneur de tous les hommes qui veulent le règne de la justice et de l'humanité sur terre.

Confiant que cette demande trouvera bon accueil dans votre honorable journal, je vous prie d'agréer, Monsieur le Directeur, l'assurance des sentiments distingués de votre serviteur,

F. SANTALLIER, Directeur du *Havre*.

162, Boulevard de Strasbourg, Havre, 18 Janvier.

THE PRINCE AND PRINCESS OF WALES.—The meet of the West Norfolk hounds at Rudham on Wednesday was a brilliant affair. The party from Sandringham-house consisted of their Royal Highnesses the Prince and Princess of Wales, the Princess Mary of Cambridge and Prince Teck, the Danish Ambassador and Madame Bulow, the Earl of Leicester, Lord and Lady Downe, Lord Harris, the Marchioness of Carmarthen, General Sir W. K. Knollys, Lieutenant-Colonel Teesdale, Mr. F. Knollys, &c. The Royal party drove to Rudham, a distance of seven or eight miles, and the Prince of Wales and Prince Teck, having mounted their hunters, rode to the meet. After the Prince of Wales had chatted with Mr. A. Hamond, of Westacre, the popular master of the Hunt, and several of the leading members, the hounds were trotted off to the coverside, and a fox being soon found, a fair day's sport was enjoyed. The Royal party returned to Sandringham late in the afternoon. The Prince of Wales, with Prince Teck, Lord Harris, the Danish Minister, Lord Downe, the Earl of Leicester, and others went out shooting yesterday morning. The Princess of Wales and Princess Mary of Cambridge drove out. There will be a grand lawn "meet" at Sandringham of the West Norfolk hounds to-day.

MR. GLADSTONE AND HIS CONSTITUENTS.—A meeting was held last night at the Cambridge Hotel, Woolwich, in support of the requisition calling upon Mr. Gladstone to resign his seat for the borough of Greenwich. Admission was again regulated by ticket, as at the stormy meeting in the Greenwich Lecture-hall on Monday; but in most other respects nothing could well be more complete than the contrast presented by last night's tame and quiet assemblage and the tumultuous gathering of Monday. The room in which the proceedings were conducted could not have contained 100 persons, and the choice of it as a place of meeting showed that the organizers of the movement did not count on a popular demonstration. But scant as the accommodation provided was, there was room enough and to spare for all comers, for the entire muster, even including the reporters and some stock orators from London, did not exceed 60. The landlord of the house in which this select assembly met was pressed into the service as chairman, being supported by Mr. Henry Pook, Mr. T. O'Brien, and Mr. H. Mayhew—all gentlemen who, it may be recollected, figured rather prominently in the same *rôles* on Monday evening. The proceedings did not commence till some three-quarters of an hour beyond the appointed time, and the resolutions adopted were an exact reproduction of those proposed on all the previous occasions. The Chairman, in introducing the business, said he felt more grief than anger at the misery and destitution brought upon that locality by the wasteful conduct of the Government in destroying establishments on which millions of the public money had been expended. A number of his own houses in that neighbourhood were left unoccupied, owing to these reductions, and very many more were empty that belonged to other people. It was a very cruel and shameful thing that persons who had bought property, taken leases, and invested their capital in business, on the faith of that Government employment which had existed for centuries, should be robbed for the alleged benefit of the country, and left uncompensated for losses they were sustaining daily. He knew of most pitiable cases in which frugal and industrious people, who had scraped together enough to place them in independence in their old age, were now reduced to penury and want by the false and unfeeling economy of a pseudo-Liberal Ministry. Mr. Phillips, in moving the first resolution, demanding the surrender of Mr. Gladstone's seat, drew a distressing picture of the broken windows, untenanted houses, paralysis of trade, and general destitution prevalent in Woolwich, and also inveighed against the Premier's foreign and domestic policy. The motion having been seconded by Mr. Orchard and supported by Mr. Pook, was carried with only three dissentients. The next resolution, urging the electors to sign the requisition, was passed by a similar majority, inhabitants of Woolwich moving and seconding it, in response to an earnest entreaty from Mr. Pook that some local Curtius would throw himself into the gap. Mr. Lee, the gentleman whose public spirit prompted him to this effort, began by stating that he represented a little property, which was completely empty, owing to the action of their member; and then proceeded to complain of the insult which the Government had tamely allowed to be offered to our flag at Duclair—a thing which Lord Palmerston would never have tolerated. The local eloquence having been exhausted, Mr. O'Brien and Mr. Mayhew next supported the resolution, and a vote of thanks to the chairman closed the proceedings.

REPRESENTATION OF NORWICH.—(By Telegraph.)—NORWICH, Thursday Evening.—Mr. Colman has consented to offer himself as a Liberal candidate for the representation of Norwich, and his address will probably appear in a day or two, although it is not yet issued. Mr. G. Howell is also a candidate in the advanced Liberal interest; his address is not yet published, but it will be placarded to-morrow. Mr. Howell advocates a reform of the land laws, a reduction of taxation, the repeal of the game laws, a firm, conciliatory foreign policy, the establishment of Courts of Conciliation and Boards of Arbitration, and the furtherance of all movements leading to the development of intellectual and moral progress. He also declares in favour of County Financial Boards, and a reorganization of the military system.

PLYMOUTH, JAN. 19.—(By Telegraph.)—The ship Murray, of London, 902 tons register (belonging to the Orient line), Captain W. Begg, from Port Adelaide November the 3d, has passed up Channel for London. All well. She brings a full cargo.

THREATENED STRIKE.—(By Telegraph).—A collier strike is threatened. At a meeting of the Executive Committee of the Amalgamated Association of Miners, representing 30,000 men, held at Manchester yesterday, it was resolved,—"That this executive expresses its regret at learning that the employers in Lancashire, North Staffordshire, and North Wales have not acceded to the appeal recently sent by the miners for a 10 per cent. rise in their wages. We, therefore, recommend the miners in those places to send circulars immediately demanding an advance of 10 per cent. in wages, and if such advance be not conceded, this association determines to use every lawful means to secure the same."

EPIDEMICS.—The Registrar-General's return for the second week of 1871 shows a decline in the mortality from fevers. In the 17 large towns making weekly returns to his office the deaths from scarlet fever fell in that week to 153, viz.—77 in the metropolis, 25 in Liverpool, 11 in Leicester, 9 in Birmingham, 6 in Hull, 4 in Manchester and in Sheffield, 3 in Norwich, in Leeds, and in Bradford, 2 in Bristol, in Salford, and in Sunderland, and 1 in Nottingham and in Wolverhampton. Other fevers cut off 114 persons in the week, viz.—38 in the metropolis, 28 in Liverpool, 13 in Manchester, 10 in Sheffield, 5 in Birmingham and Hull, 4 in Leeds and in Portsmouth, 3 in Sunderland, and 2 in Bristol and in Newcastle-upon-Tyne. Mortality from smallpox is on the increase in several of the 17 towns, viz.—London, Liverpool, Manchester, Hull, and Newcastle. Hooping-cough was in the mortality returns of 13 of the towns, and measles in nine, the former causing 100 and the latter 86 deaths.

A PERSIAN MANUSCRIPT.—A Persian manuscript of great beauty, containing 60 full-page miniature illuminations, and profusely ornamented throughout in the highest class of ancient art, was recently sold by Messrs. Puttick and Simpson, of Leicester-square, for 205l.

CATTLE DISEASE.—A very alarming outbreak of the foot and mouth disease has occurred this week in Mr. Superintendent Young's division of Buckrose, East Riding. On one wold farm near Flixton no fewer than 23 straw yard beasts, all heifers, have taken the disease. In Kellington, also, the cows are attacked, there being three in one place. During the late storm the disease had disappeared.

WRECK.—TRURO, Thursday.—On Tuesday morning a French brig, name unknown, from Algiers for Cardiff, with sulphur ore, &c., went ashore about a mile west of St. Ives' Head, near Penzance, and has become a total wreck; crew of seven saved.

Above William I of Germany proclaimed Emperor at Versailles 18 January 1871. Painting by Anton von Werner.

More serious than the precise details of the meeting between the dynasty-makers was the fact that Russell was being scooped. Other papers were publishing the news first. The man from the *Daily News* later explained his methods. He got hold of advance plans from the Crown Prince of Saxony's staff (the hacks were travelling with the armies). He then made up premature and anticipatory articles based on these plans, sent them to London and instructed his office to hold them. When the plans started to go into action, he signalled London to release the message. It worked for the start of the bombardment of Paris. When the first gun went off, he telegraphed London to go ahead, and a vivid and imaginative account of the carnage astonished the world and infuriated Printing House Square. It is a chancy way to work: the critic who shirked going to the theatre and wrote a flattering and imaginary review, found next day that the theatre had burned down while he had assumed the play was being performed.

Russell, always a prima donna, nearly deserted the action, as he had after the Battle of Bunker Hill. He wrote to Delane:

> After much reflection I have come to the decision that I cannot, with regard to my own feelings on the subject and to your interests, remain here to chronicle a bombardment of Paris, a city of two millions of men, women and children. It is the bombardment of the City of Paris I object to. If the forts only are attacked that is not a horror for one's old age to remember.

Delane 'stroked' Russell (in the patronizing terms of modern management psychologists) and begged him to see the business through to the end. Prussians in London had assured him that because of the scandal they were not going to bombard Paris, only its fortifications.

Russell stayed. And he got a typical scoop about the end of the war. He went to the proclamation of the King of Prussia as German Emperor in the *Salle des Glaces* at Versailles, and wrote a graphic colour piece for *The Times* of 20 January 1871. A few days later, while he was walking in the streets of Versailles, he met one of his French friends:

> The Frenchman was much agitated. 'Tell me, for God's sake, what it is all about,' he exclaimed. 'Why should Jules Favre[1] be here? What can he be doing unless Paris is doomed?' 'Jules Favre here!' said Russell. 'That is impossible.' 'But I swear it. I know him as well as I know myself. Not five minutes ago he passed me in a carriage going towards the Rue de Provence.' This was news indeed. Keeping his information to himself, Russell hurried off to headquarters and had the news confirmed. He then sent off a telegram, and in *The Times* of the next day London read that the negotiations for the capitulation of Paris had begun.

The other sensational *Times* scoop of the Franco-Prussian War was its publication in 1870 of a proposed carve-up between France and Prussia, agreed in 1866. The French proposed that they would recognize a federal union between North and South Germany in return for Prussian support for their proposed invasion of Belgium. *The Times* published the document in the original French, with a leading article: 'We are satisfied that our information is correct, and that the project has recently again been offered as a condition of peace'.

The French Prime Minister immediately wrote a letter denying the story. The public and opposition press were delighted to mock the Grand Old Lady of Printing House Square. But the story was, of course, true. It had been leaked to Delane by the German Ambassador on the instructions of Bismarck. The uproar and outrage it caused must have gratified him, and performed valuable propaganda for the Prussian cause. The Prime Minister wrote to the Queen:

> Your Majesty will, in common with the world, have been shocked and startled at the publication in today's *Times* of a proposed project of Treaty between France and Prussia. A large portion of the public put down this document as a forgery, and indeed a hoax; Mr Gladstone fears it is neither.

The publication in *The Times* of the outrageous proposal led Britain to guarantee the neutrality of Belgium. And that, a generation later, was the issue on which Britain finally chose to enter the First World War.

[1] Vice-President and Minister of Foreign Affairs.

Blowitz scoops the world

Journalism is not a gentlemanly profession. One of the most flamboyant and successful journalists who ever worked for *The Times* was Henri Stefan Opper de Blowitz, who made himself Paris correspondent and eventually something like expatriate foreign editor.

Blowitz was a Bohemian immigrant to France, a tiny man with a big head and bushy side-whiskers. He spent most of his life as a teacher of German in French state schools, until he joined *The Times* at the age of 45. He was vain, preposterous, egotistical and a dreadful liar outside his trade. He wrote his dispatches in French, causing grief at Printing House Square, where somebody had to translate them. He was opinionated in his writing and careless about descriptive detail. He was no gent, no doubt. He was easy with women, and they told him things. He was one of the great foreign correspondents of journalism.

His exclusive report of the Treaty of Berlin, published as it was being signed, was one of the scoops of journalistic history. His account of it in his *Memoirs* reads like a Sherlock Holmes short story with a touch of Le Carré. It might have been entitled The Case of the Exchanged Hats.

In June 1878 the statesmen of Europe, with those of Russia and Turkey, came to Berlin to try to solve the Eastern Question, the debris left by the distintegration of the Ottoman Empire, 'that shifting, intractable and interwoven tangle of conflicting interests, rival peoples and antagonistic faiths'. Journalists of the world came too, to pick up what few scraps filtered through official channels as well as the drawing-room gossip. Blowitz led *The Times* team. He was determined to scoop the world by getting the text of the treaty into the paper on the day it was signed.

It was not an easy assignment. Bismarck disliked Blowitz because of his report that the war party in Germany was planning a pre-emptive strike against France. Security was tight. Blowitz complained bitterly: 'In Paris the fish talk. In Berlin the parrots are silent'.

Blowitz says that he persuaded a young foreign friend to insinuate himself as the unpaid private secretary of a foreign statesman who was likely to attend the conference. If this is true, he was one of the Turkish delegation. It may not be true: some of the incidents in Blowitz's *Memoirs* are clearly fictitious.

The young man was being watched. So Blowitz devised the plan that he should either lunch or dine at Blowitz's hotel every day, carrying his message in the lining of his hat. He would hang his hat on the rack. After the meal Blowitz and his spy would each pick up the wrong hat. It worked until one day a stranger took the loaded hat by mistake. Fortunately it fell down over his nose, and he came back and exchanged it for his own.

Blowitz had other sources also. By pretending to know more than he did, he squeezed information out of the diplomats at parties. His stream of exclusive reports was so accurate that at one of the conference sessions, Bismarck lifted up the tablecloth 'to see if Blowitz is not underneath'. The Iron Chancellor was so impressed that he gave Blowitz the only press interview he gave throughout the conference. It lasted five hours. 'Just as I was going out of the room', writes Blowitz, 'the Chancellor asked

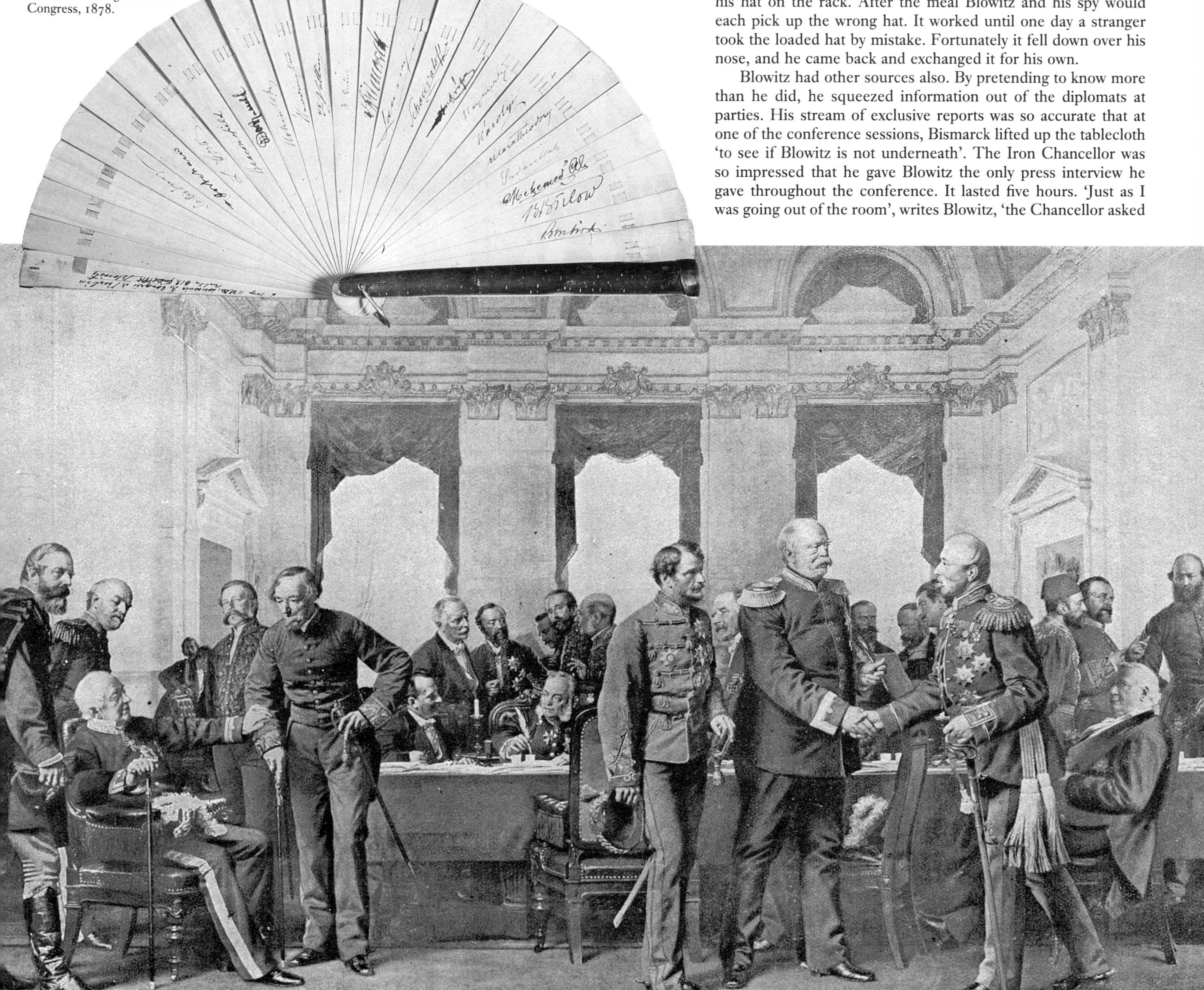

Below Blowitz's famous fan which he had signed by the principal participants at the Congress.
Bottom PEACE WITH HONOUR, painting by Anton von Werner of the Representatives of the European Powers attending the Berlin Congress, 1878.

CONTENTS OF THIS DAY'S PAPER.

LONDON, MONDAY, JULY 15, 1878.

On Saturday we placed the text of the Treaty of Berlin in the hands of the public at the very time when the Plenipotentiaries were affixing their signatures to it at Berlin, and to-day we republish the momentous document. It is certainly the most important international decree that has appeared since the treaties recording the labours of the Congress of Vienna. It would be of the highest political moment even if it did no more than record the arrangements by which the Great Powers have averted a war that might have spread from end to end of Europe. But it will also be a great historical landmark because it has transformed an Empire which contains the most coveted territory in the world, and which periodically threatens the general peace by its disorganization. It would be futile to deny that Turkey has been subjected to vast changes, and, indeed, the Plenipotentiaries would have condemned themselves if, in presence of so desperate a state of decay, they had wielded the amputating knife with a timid hand. They are open, however, to no such reproach. The changes they have made may be divided into several groups, and in the first may be placed those outlying provinces of the PORTE which were practically independent before the war. Roumania and Servia were linked to Constantinople by the frail tie of a tribute which in recent years they sometimes forgot to pay. Both provinces are now formally declared to be independent. Roumania, as the public knows, is to give back to Russia a portion of that Bessarabian territory which she received after the Crimean War; and in exchange she is to obtain the Dobrudja, with territory stretching from the east of Silistria to the south of Mangalia on the coast of the Black Sea. Although nothing can excuse the conduct of Russia in thus taking the land of a gallant little ally, Roumania has otherwise good reason to be pleased with what she has received in exchange. Servia also gets some additional territory. In the same group of changes may be classed the new position and boundaries of Montenegro. That little State has never acknowledged any fealty to the Sultan, and its independence is at last admitted by the PORTE and by the Powers of Europe. Thus ends a struggle which has been waged for centuries. A good deal of additional territory has been given to Montenegro, and in particular the port of Antivari, so that the energetic mountaineers will at last have an outlet for their scanty produce. On the other hand, the Congress has imposed some obligations on the States which have thus been freed from all connexion with the PORTE and enlarged at its expense. Montenegro and Servia will have to bear a part of the Ottoman Debt proportionate to the size of the new territory which they have received. No such burden has been laid on Roumania, because the Dobrudja is regarded, not as an addition, but as an exchange. The amount of the tribute hitherto paid by Servia and Roumania is to be capitalized, and thus an end will be put to all the pecuniary ties between those Principalities and the Turkish capital. The Congress has further laid a duty of high importance on Roumania, Servia, and Montenegro by stipulating that all the subjects of these States shall be totally free from religious disabilities. Such is the satisfactory reply to the just complaint of the Jews at the treatment which they have sustained in Servia and Roumania; and in the same provision the Congress has in view the rights of any Mussulmans who may choose to remain in the territory which has been separated from the PORTE. In Europe the last and most striking case of complete amputation is presented by Bosnia and Herzegovina. These provinces are dismissed in the brief phrase that they "shall be occupied and administered by Austria-Hungary." As they fall under the sway of a great civilized Power, the Congress assumes that it need lay down no rules for the toleration of religious minorities. It is also not stipulated that the occupied territory is to pay any tribute to the PORTE or to bear any portion of the Turkish Debt. The separation is absolute and unconditional. So is the surrender of the Asiatic territory which falls to the share of Russia, except in so far as she engages to make Batoum a commercial port.

The second zone of change is filled up by the new Bulgaria, which includes all the territory from the Danube to the Balkans except the part forming the compensation given to Roumania. Bulgaria is to be "an autonomous and tributary Principality" under the suzerainty of the Sultan. It is to have a Christian Government and a national militia. Its Prince is to be elected by the people, subject to the confirmation of the PORTE and the assent of the Great Powers, the only restriction on the freedom of choice being that he shall belong to none of the reigning dynasties of the Great Powers. There is to be a representative form of government and complete religious equality. The principality is to pay a fixed tribute to the PORTE, and to bear part of the Turkish Debt. On the other hand, all the Ottoman troops are to be withdrawn, and all the fortresses to be destroyed. The separation of Bulgaria from the PORTE will be complete in all but the name and the obligation to pay a fixed sum of money. Thus it will be in nearly the same position as that which Servia occupied before the war. But it will take some time to prepare the requisite changes, and meanwhile the provisional organization will be directed by a Russian Commissioner. He will be "assisted," however, and the "provisional organization" "controlled," by a Turkish Commissioner, as well as by Consuls to be appointed by the signatory Powers. Since the temporary Government is not to last for more than nine months, the action of the Russian Commission will be both closely watched and of short duration. Still, it may be thought, much room will be left for the growth of Russian influence subsequent to the final arrangements of the new Principality. The Government and the Militia, it may be said, will be controlled by Russian officials; and the gratitude of the Bulgarians, or, at least, a fear that they may again need the aid of Russia, may disincline them to protest. Such a danger is certainly not visionary. It is extremely likely that Russia would wield undue influence in Bulgaria if the treaty were regarded as self-acting. But treaties have to be enforced as well as made, and it will be the business of the Powers to see that no Government shall gain disproportionate authority over the new Principality. Austria in particular will be expected to watch the interests of Europe as well as of herself now that, by gaining Bosnia and Herzegovina, she has pushed herself forward into the Balkan peninsula.

A third group of changes begins to the south of the Balkans. East Roumelia will have a more formal connexion than Bulgaria with the PORTE. It is to have a Christian Governor-General, who will be chosen by the Sultan, with the assent of the Great Powers, and will remain in office for a term of five years. Practically, therefore, he will be appointed by them, and they may cause his tenure of command to be prolonged beyond the specified time if he should give exceptional proof of fitness. The administrative arrangements of the province have still to be determined by a European Commission, which will work in concert with the PORTE, and takes as its starting-points the propositions made at the eighth meeting of the Conference of Constantinople. If we may judge from those plans, the administrative independence of the province will be almost as complete as that of Bulgaria itself. The budget will be so settled that a definite part of the revenue will be reserved for the local expenses, and another definite part sent to Constantinople. Thus East Roumelia would, like Bulgaria itself, be practically a tributary State. Its freedom will also be assured by the stipulation of the Congress that internal order shall be kept by a native gendarmerie and a local militia, so recruited as to represent the religion of the districts over which they will watch. But it is provided that the officers of both these corps shall be appointed by the Sultan. Still more important is his right to raise fortifications and keep troops on all the frontiers of the province, and therefore on the Balkans as well as on the southern boundary. The Governor-General will also have power to call for Turkish troops if the internal or the external security of the province should be menaced. The decision of the PORTE must then be stated and justified to the representatives of the Great Powers at Constantinople. Practically, therefore, the court of final appeal for East Roumelia will be the assembled Ambassadors; and, on the whole, its position will not be unlike that held by Servia before the Turkish troops were withdrawn from Belgrade in 1867. In a fourth group of changes we may place the Island of Crete and "the other parts of Turkey "in Europe for which a special organization "has not been provided by the present treaty." So far as Crete is concerned, the PORTE promises to apply scrupulously the administrative plan which was formed in 1868, and to improve that law in any fashion which shall be deemed equitable. Hence, we presume, the Powers have still to review the causes of the discontent which keeps that island in a state of rebellion. They have also provided a good deal of further work by the stipulation that the PORTE shall form special commissions to prepare plans for the government of the provinces which the Congress has not passed under review. Thus the administrative schemes for what may be called West Roumelia have still to be framed, and the Plenipotentiaries have left part of their task undone. We have also still to learn the answer of the Porte to the proposal that a considerable amount of territory should be ceded to Greece. But it would be unreasonable to complain that the Congress has done too little. It has made changes which transform an Empire; it has removed long standing causes of discontent; it has pacified, we may hope, provinces which were torn by dissension and misrule; it has placed barriers between rival forms of implacable bigotry; it has stopped many avenues of foreign intrigue; and, if it has abridged the power of the PORTE, it has given peace to Europe.

The Congress is at an end, and the results of its many-sided labours are written down in the Treaty of Berlin. We hail the appearance of this important document with a feeling of satisfaction which is amply warranted by its contents. It is a settlement of the most complex and troublesome problem which has occupied the attention of statesmen in our time. The Eastern Question has now ceased to be, what it has been for some time, a menace to the public peace of Europe. We have gained, we may fairly hope, something more than a mere breathing space. If the treaty does what it is intended to do, and what we may not unreasonably expect from it, it will so change the condition of South-Eastern Europe that the Eastern Question can never again present itself in its old form. Its principal provisions are of a two-fold character. It brings a cure for the oppression and misgovernment in the provinces of European Turkey which have furnished in the past an excuse for Russian interference, and it admits thereby of the growth and development of a vigorous national life, which will be the surest barrier against all encroachments from without. We cannot as yet be sure how far this result will be attained, but the prospect is at least hopeful. The great difficulty with which the Congress has had to deal has been the poor nature of the materials it was compelled to work with. The swoop of Russia was irresistible, just because there was nothing sound to oppose to it. What the Congress has done has been to construct a framework within which a better state of things may grow up. Its completion must be the work of time. All that Europe can do is to make sure that it has a fair start. The Treaty of Berlin does all that we could expect in the way of securing this. The rest must be done by the regular ordered development which seldom fails to follow in due course where its conditions have been duly furnished. When we compare Eastern Europe as it was only a few months since and as it now promises to be, the contrast is enormous. Turkey was crushed and helpless. Russia was pressing on unopposed, and was already in virtual possession of the dominions of her vanquished neighbour. The excitement in this country, and not in this country alone, was so great as to endanger the preservation of peace. The Treaty of Berlin puts an end to all this. The course of Russian conquest is at least arrested. Turkey revives and enters on a new and more hopeful life. The principles of nationality and of political justice are recognized as they never have been before. The measured prose of the Treaty of Berlin appeals to the imagination, if we read it aright, with a force beyond that of poetry. It is the poetry of real life, the charter of hope and of national well-being to the peoples it frees and for whose future career it provides as far as such provision is possible.

We must acknowledge in detail the debt of gratitude we owe to the eminent statesmen who have taken part in the deliberations at Berlin. To Prince BISMARCK, as President, the first recognition must be given. The address of thanks he received from Count ANDRASSY in the name of the entire Congress, flattering as its terms were, did not go at all beyond the literal truth. Prince BISMARCK has made it his business to arrange the differences and to smooth down the susceptibilities which threatened from time to time to be fatal to the task of pacification which the Congress had before it. The general opinion of Europe will endorse all that Count ANDRASSY has said. The expression of gratitude is not more than has been fairly and fully earned by Prince BISMARCK'S important services. Nor must the French Plenipotentiaries be forgotten as having done good work in forwarding the common object. The professed policy of France was one, indeed, of inaction and of neutrality somewhat beyond the real needs of the case. Not the less has the Congress been aided in its task by the presence of the French representatives. Their extreme position as neutrals inspired confidence in them as referees on more than one important question, and their decision was accepted in some part from the mere fact that their own views had been pressed with so little pertinacity. Count ANDRASSY had, perhaps, the most difficult part of any to play. He represented a State which was far from united, and which had, or believed itself to have, conflicting interests of its own. By accepting the care of Bosnia and Herzegovina Austria has helped forward the general work of the pacification of Eastern Europe. Her own interests have not been sacrificed by this, and it is now understood that they have not been. Hungary is already beginning to acquiesce in a settlement to which she was once most strongly opposed, but which could not have been declined without grave danger to the regions which would have been left unprovided for. Of the work done by our own representatives we need not speak at length. Englishmen are not likely to be unmindful of it or ungrateful for it. We have gained by the Treaty of Berlin, if not everything we hoped for, at least as much as we could reasonably expect, and as the facts of the case admitted. It is for firmness in maintaining the interests of England and of Europe that Lord BEACONSFIELD has been most properly praised. But the firmness he displayed was as far as possible from the mere unyielding obstinacy with which he was credited by extreme partisans at home. He has thus secured, or largely helped to secure, a settlement with which England may be well satisfied. He has checked Russia, effectually to all appearance, and this he has done without the cost of a great war, the possible duration of which could not have been foreseen, and which might very well have spread over half Europe. We may doubt if England has ever, on a like occasion, been represented by a Plenipotentiary who has better deserved her thanks both for what he has done and for what he has avoided doing.

The work of having achieved peace is that with which the CROWN PRINCE of GERMANY most justly credits the late Congress. We may look with satisfaction on the means by which this has been attained scarcely less than on the end itself. That such grave and threatening questions as those with which the Congress of Berlin had to deal have been arranged without war is a distinct triumph for the cause of peace both now and hereafter. It is proof, in spite of much to the contrary, that Europe has advanced in public morality. Seldom has the outlook been darker than it was when the Congress of Berlin met, and seldom has it been brighter and clearer than it is now left when the Congress has finished its sitting. The Treaty of Berlin is an advance, too, upon previous treaties in the nature of the arrangements it has sanctioned. The States it has dealt with have been treated not as mere inert masses to be disposed of in any way that might seem to suit the general convenience. Ties of race have been duly taken into account, with all the tendencies and hopes and wishes and aspirations that follow from them. There is thus room left for expansion within the limits which the Treaty of Berlin has marked out. Its terms may even be modified, should the need arise, without any violent process of disruption. We will not be too confident or too hopeful as to the turn affairs may take. The new races are, so to say, on their trial, and they have yet to prove themselves worthy of the care which Europe has bestowed upon them. But we may remember that it is just two-and-twenty years since a settlement of the Eastern Question, far less promising than the present one, was made. If the arrangements of 1856 have endured so long, we may trust that the arrangements of 1878 will be at least equally vital. If so, the Eastern Question, solved or unsolved, will at least have been pushed on safely through the present century. The next century, if it is not satisfied with what has been done, may take the matter up afresh and deal with it in its own way. Some part, at least, of what we have gained is not likely to be taken from us. The growth of Russia has been felt distinctly as a peril not only to this country, but to civilization itself. It was like the progress of a huge glacier, slow, irresistible, and hopelessly crushing to all life that it spread over. It is no small relief that we are free from any present apprehension of this. If the danger is not finally averted, it is at least indefinitely postponed. The next generation must take care in its own way for the interest of itself and its successors. The Treaty of Berlin may fairly be looked upon as a sufficient achievement for one generation to have performed.

The Irish Intermediate Education Bill stands for second reading in the House of Commons this afternoon, and, as it is the first among the Orders of the Day, it will, no doubt, receive adequate discussion. The measure passed through the House of Lords without the slightest show of opposition, and almost without a word of criticism. It was not altered in committee. Lord O'HAGAN and Lord EMLY, the most conspicuous representatives of the Irish Roman Catholics among the Peers, eulogized the proposals of the Government without a hint of question or qualification, and Mr. BUTT publicly declared in favour not only of the principle of the Bill, but of the expediency of giving it every form of practical aid. The advanced section of the Home Rule party are for once inclined to defer to Mr. BUTT'S advice and guidance, and they will probably abstain from any course which might be called obstructive, because in this instance Irish opinion would look resentfully upon their attempts to obstruct. Hitherto, then, the Bill has met with none but favourable omens. Still it would be rash to assume that because the measure has passed through the House of Lords almost unchallenged it will not be criticized in the House of Commons. A Bill of this character is always handled with more knowledge of and taste for details by members of the popular branch of the Legislature, while the Peers are content to review and pronounce upon principles of policy. The classes for whose benefit a reform of intermediate education is intended can be only represented indirectly in the Upper House, but in the Lower House their aspirations and apprehensions find distinct and direct utterance. Moreover, the enthusiasm with which the proposals of the Government were at first hailed in Ireland has already, to some extent, cooled down. The Irish are not less pleased than they were three weeks ago at the prospect of a division among them of a million sterling, but some of them have begun to work themselves into a belief that the amount of the benefaction is insufficient, and others, having scrutinized the conditions of its distribution, have come to the conclusion that they ought to be modified or removed. Again, it may be expected that the peculiar form of Conservatism cherished in Protestant Ulster will find in the House of Commons the spokesmen it failed to find among the well-disciplined Ministerialists of the House of Lords. From this quarter, possibly, may come a direct attack upon the Bill, in which some of the most determined advocates of secular instruction among English politicians may join. But the open opposition to the Bill, if any such should be attempted at all, will be no more than the resistance of a minority content with the registration of a public protest.

It is by collateral movements that the Bill, which the House of Commons will undoubtedly read a second time, may be brought into jeopardy. The debate will, in all probability, bring to light a great deal of information about the views and wishes, the hopes and fears, of Irish parties in connexion with measures for reforming Irish education and for changing the destination of the Irish Church surplus. Much of this will be quite new to the House of Commons, and some of it may tend to disturb the equanimity of the Ministerial majority. Efforts may be made also to amend the Bill, to restrict or to enlarge its scope, to claim for it a greater share of the funds which it is admitted by the Bill may be applied to educational purposes, and to alter the conditions under which the Government grant is to be distributed. If there were any prospect of carrying grave changes of this kind, and if there were any intention on the part of the Ministry to accept or introduce amendments modifying the Bill in its vital parts, Parliament might fairly hesitate before taking up what would be substantially a new measure. It is likely that the Government will be pressed to assent to various changes of more or less importance, but it may be expected that Mr. LOWTHER will declare his inability to accede to any suggestions of that character. The Bill in its present form has an excellent chance of becoming law, but if it were to be materially altered its fortunes might be wrecked on shoals now unseen. Every proposed modification must be considered in the light of the fact that the Parliamentary Session has not more than four weeks of life remaining. The Bill as it stands, backed by the all but unanimous approval of the Upper House, is not likely to be defeated by the mere force of a protest against the application of the Irish Church surplus to educational purposes. But the protest which will doubtless be made by the representatives of the Orange party ought to elicit some curious explanations from eminent statesmen of both parties. It is not forgotten that the preamble of the Disestablishment Act designated certain purposes to which the surplus funds now being capitalized by the Temporalities Commission should be exclusively applied, and in the debates of that time the exclusion of educational purposes was assented to by the leaders of both parties. Mr. GLADSTONE ought to be able to offer an interesting and instructive criticism upon the present proposals of the Government from the point of view which he took up when he was advocating his great measure of disendowment in 1869.

But, though the project of drawing the funds needed for the working of the Intermediate Education Bill from the Church surplus will hardly pass unchallenged, it is improbable that the decision of the House of Lords upon this point will be seriously questioned. If, however, large and important changes were made in the other parts of the Bill, the disposal of the Church surplus would have to be reconsidered. In the debate on the second reading in the House of Lords it was hinted from the Conservative as well as the Liberal benches that the conscience clause might be dispensed with, and that result fees might be earned by masters of schools in which religious instruction was strictly compulsory. Lord CARLINGFORD, Lord MIDLETON, and Lord BELMORE urged this change, though they made no attempt to give effect to their views in committee. Several members of the House of Commons, however, are inclined to propose amendments removing the restraint of the conscience clause, and the Government will, no doubt, be asked beforehand in to-night's debate to sanction the omission. It must be pointed out, however, that the omission of the conscience clause would change the aspect of the proposal to distribute a part of the Church property among intermediate schools. From another point of view the threatened amendments would open up a wide and dubious controversy. It would be contended that the grant of public money in aid of intermediate schools unprotected by a conscience clause would establish a dangerous precedent which might be used to break down the safeguard of the elementary system of instruction in the National schools. The principle that public money will not now be granted by the State to any schools in which the rights of conscience are not effectually and visibly protected has been adopted in Great Britain as well as in Ireland, and the Government will not be disposed to acquiesce in amendments which would tamper with that principle. For other reasons it may be assumed that Mr. LOWTHER will turn a deaf ear to those who will contend that the amount of State aid ought to be increased, that a larger sum ought to be taken from the Church surplus, that the emoluments of the new scholarships and the scale of payments for results ought to be augmented. The Bill, it must be confessed, initiates an experiment, and a million sterling is enough to spend tentatively on what may prove a failure. The supporters of the Bill may exert themselves with advantage to dispel the doubts of those who do not believe that the distribution of a number of £20 scholarships among promising boys and of "result "fees" among schoolmasters will turn bad schools into good ones, or call schools into existence where they do not exist at present. The wretched condition of intermediate education in Ireland is admitted, and it would be a waste of time to dilate upon this point. It is more material to show that the stimulation which the Bill, when it passes, will provide is likely to be effectual. But Parliament and the Irish people must be warned against expecting that this or any other measure will work in a magical way and begin to produce visible effects immediately.

A Cabinet Council was held on Saturday in Downing-street. The Ministers present were the Lord Chancellor, the Duke of Richmond and Gordon, the Duke of Northumberland, Mr. Secretary Cross, the Right Hon. Sir M. E. Hicks-Beach, the Right Hon. Colonel Stanley, Viscount Cranbrook, the Chancellor of the Exchequer, the Right Hon. W. H. Smith, Lord John Manners, and Viscount Sandon.

THE COURT.—The Queen, accompanied by Princess Beatrice, and attended by the suite, is expected to leave Windsor Castle about Wednesday next for Osborne.

LORD BEACONSFIELD'S RETURN.—Lord Beaconsfield will arrive at Charing-cross Station at 4 45 p.m. on Tuesday. The South-Eastern Railway Company have on this occasion placed the station at the disposal of the Prime Minister's personal friends. Two hundred tickets have been issued for admission to the platform. The Prime Minister has accepted by telegraph an invitation to be present at a dinner which is to be given upon his return at the Carlton Club by the leading members of the Conservative party.—*Observer.*

AN EMIGRANT VESSEL ASHORE.—Lloyd's Correspondent at Shoeburyness reported by telegram on Saturday morning that a bark had gone ashore on the Maplin Sand, near the Admiralty Beacon, and that assistance had been sent to her. A steamer which arrived at Gravesend reported that she was high and dry. It was ascertained that the vessel was the Scottish Admiral, which left London on the 11th inst. for Brisbane, on her first voyage, having on board 500 emigrants. A later message reports that the vessel, having been towed off by two tugs, returned to Gravesend in tow.

CHURCH OF ENGLAND TEMPERANCE SOCIETY.—On Saturday morning an influential gathering of members and supporters of the Church of England Temperance Society assembled in the banqueting-room of St. James's-hall, Regent-street, to meet the Colonial and American Bishops, who had been invited by the society to discuss the subject of the "Duty of the Church in relation to the present prevalence of Intemperance." The chair was occupied by the Bishop of Glocester and Bristol, at whose right sat the Rev. Canon Ellison (Chairman of the Southern Executive Church of England Temperance Society), and others. The chairman, after a brief address of welcome to those assembled, called upon Canon Ellison, who explained fully the aims and progress of the parent society. The Bishops of Bloemfontein, Western New York, Adelaide, and Missouri; the Right Hon. Cowper-Temple, the Rev. Canon Farrar, the Rev. Ernest Wilberforce, and the Rev. S. Sturges took part in the discussion.

THE TREATY OF BERLIN.

The following text of nearly the whole of the Treaty signed on Saturday at Berlin was telegraphed by our Correspondent at Brussels, and appeared in our Second Edition of Saturday. The portions omitted have reference to lines of demarcation and other matters decided at the last moment, the obtaining of which would have considerably delayed the transmission of the document:—

"Préambule:—Sa Majesté l'Empereur d'Allemagne, Sa Majesté l'Empereur d'Autriche-Hongrie, le Président de la République Française, Sa Majesté la Reine du Royaume Uni de la Grande Bretagne, Impératrice des Indes, Sa Majesté le Roi d'Italie, Sa Majesté l'Empereur de Toutes les Russies, Sa Majesté l'Empereur des Ottomans, désirant régler dans une pensée d'ordre Européen, conformément aux stipulations du Traité de Paris du 30 Mars, 1856, les questions soulevées en Orient par les événements des dernières années et par la guerre dont le Traité de San Stefano a marqué le terme, ont été unanimement d'avis que la réunion d'un Congrès serait le meilleur moyen de faciliter leur entente. A cet effet elles ont nommé les Plénipotentiaires dont les noms suivent, lesquels, après avoir échangé leurs pouvoirs, qui ont été trouvés en bonne et due forme, ont stipulé et adopté les articles suivants:—

"Article 1.—La Bulgarie est constituée une Principauté autonome et tributaire, sous la suzeraineté de S. M. le Sultan. Elle aura un gouvernement Chrétien et une milice nationale.

"Article 2.—La Principauté de Bulgarie sera limitée au sud par la chaîne des Balkans.

"Article 3.—Le Prince de Bulgarie sera librement élu par la population, et confirmé par la Sublime Porte, avec l'assentiment des Puissances. Aucun membre des dynasties régnantes des Grandes Puissances Européennes ne pourra être élu Prince de Bulgarie. En cas de vacance de la dignité Princière, l'élection du nouveau Prince se fera aux mêmes conditions et dans les mêmes formes.

"Article 4.—Une Assemblée de Notables de la Bulgarie, convoquée à Tirnovo, élaborera avant l'élection du Prince le règlement organique de la Principauté. Dans les localités où les Bulgares sont mêlés à des populations Turques, Roumaines, Grecques, ou autres, il sera tenu compte des droits et des intérêts de ces populations en ce qui concerne les élections et l'élaboration du règlement organique.

"Article 5.—Les dispositions suivantes formeront la base du droit public de la Bulgarie. La distinction des croyances religieuses et des confessions ne pourra être opposée à personne comme un motif d'exclusion ou d'incapacité en ce qui concerne la jouissance des droits civils et politiques, l'admission aux emplois publics, fonctions et honneurs, ou l'exercice des différentes professions et industries, dans quelque localité que ce soit. La liberté et la pratique extérieure de tous les cultes sont assurées à tous les ressortissants de la Bulgarie aussi bien qu'aux étrangers, et aucune entrave ne pourra être apportée soit à l'organisation hiérarchique des différentes communions, soit à leurs rapports avec leurs chefs spirituels.

"Article 6.—L'administration provisoire de la Bulgarie sera dirigée jusqu'à l'achèvement du règlement organique par un Commissaire Impérial Russe. Un Commissaire Impérial Ottoman, ainsi que les Consuls délégués *ad hoc* par les autres Puissances signataires du présent Traité, seront appelés à l'assister, à l'effet de contrôler le fonctionnement de ce régime provisoire. En cas de dissentiment entre les Consuls délégués, la majorité décidera; et en cas de divergence entre cette majorité et le Commissaire Impérial Russe ou le Commissaire Impérial Ottoman, les représentants des Puissances signataires à Constantinople, réunis en conférence, devront prononcer.

"Article 7.—Le régime provisoire ne pourra être prolongé au-delà d'un délai de neuf mois à partir de la signature du présent Traité. Lorsque le règlement organique sera terminé, il sera procédé immédiatement à l'élection du Prince de Bulgarie. Aussitôt que le Prince aura été institué, la nouvelle organisation sera mise en vigueur et la Principauté entrera en pleine jouissance de son autonomie.

"Article 8.—Les Traités de Commerce et de Navigation, ainsi que toutes les conventions et arrangements conclus entre les Puissances étrangères et la Porte et aujourd'hui en vigueur, sont maintenus dans la Principauté de Bulgarie, et aucun changement n'y sera apporté à l'égard d'aucune Puissance avant qu'elle n'y ait donné son consentement. Aucun droit de transit ne sera prélevé en Bulgarie sur les marchandises traversant cette Principauté. Les nationaux et les commerçants de toutes les Puissances y seront traités sur le pied d'une parfaite égalité. Les immunités et privilèges des sujets étrangers, ainsi que les droits de juridiction et de protection consulaires, tels qu'ils ont été établis par les capitulations et les usages, resteront en pleine vigueur tant qu'ils n'auront pas été modifiés du consentement des parties intéressées.

"Article 9.—Le montant du tribut annuel que la Principauté de Bulgarie paiera à la Cour Suzeraine, en le versant à la banque que la Sublime Porte désignera ultérieurement, sera déterminé par un accord entre les Puissances signataires du présent Traité à la fin de la première année du fonctionnement de la nouvelle organisation. Ce tribut sera établi sur le revenu moyen du territoire de la Principauté. La Bulgarie devant supporter une part de la dette publique de l'Empire, lorsque les Puissances détermineront le tribut, elles prendront en considération la partie de cette dette qui pourrait être attribuée à la Principauté, sur la base d'une équitable proportion.

"Article 10.—La Bulgarie est substituée au Gouvernement Impérial Ottoman dans ses charges et obligations envers la compagnie du chemin de fer de Roustchouk-Varna, à partir du jour de la signature du present Traité. Le règlement des comptes antérieurs est reservé à une entente entre la Sublime Porte, le Gouvernement de la Principauté, et l'Administration de cette compagnie. La Principauté de Bulgarie est de même substituée, pour sa part, aux engagements que la Sublime Porte a contractés tant envers l'Autriche-Hongrie qu'envers la compagnie pour l'exploitation des chemins de fer de la Turquie d'Europe par rapport à l'achèvement et au raccordement ainsi qu'à l'exploitation des lignes ferrées situées sur son territoire. Les conventions nécessaires pour régler ces questions seront conclues entre l'Autriche-Hongrie, la Porte, la Serbie, et la Principauté de Bulgarie immédiatement après la conclusion de la paix.

"Article 11.—L'Armée Ottomane ne séjournera plus en Bulgarie. Toutes les anciennes forteresses seront rasées, aux frais de la Principauté, dans le délai d'un an, ou plus tôt si faire se peut. Le Gouvernement local prendra immédiatement des mesures pour les détruire, et ne pourra en faire construire de nouvelles. La Sublime Porte aura le droit de disposer à sa guise du matériel de guerre et autres objets appartenant au Gouvernement Ottoman, et qui seraient restés dans les forteresses du Danube déjà évacuées en vertu de l'Armistice du 31 Janvier, ainsi que de ceux qui se trouveraient dans les places fortes de Schoumla et de Varna.

"Article 12.—Les propriétaires Musulmans ou autres qui fixeraient leur résidence personnelle hors de la Principauté pourront y conserver leurs immeubles en les affermant ou en les faisant administrer par des tiers. Une Commission Turco-Bulgare sera chargée de régler, dans le courant de deux années, toutes les affaires relatives au mode d'aliénation, d'exploitation, ou d'usage, pour le compte de la Sublime Porte, des propriétés de l'Etat et des fondations pieuses (vacouf) et les questions relatives aux intérêts des particuliers qui pourraient s'y trouver engagés. Les ressortissants de la Principauté de Bulgarie qui voyageront ou séjourneront dans les autres parties de l'Empire Ottoman seront soumis aux autorités et aux lois Ottomanes.

"Article 13.—Il est formé au sud des Balkans une province qui prendra le nom de 'Roumélie Orientale,' et qui restera placée sous l'autorité politique et militaire directe de S. M. Impériale le Sultan, dans des conditions d'autonomie administrative. Elle aura un Gouverneur-Général Chrétien.

"Article 14.—Les limites de la Roumélie Orientale seront . . .

"Article 15.—S. M. le Sultan aura le droit de pourvoir à la défense des frontières de terre et de mer de la province en élevant des fortifications sur ces frontières et en y entretenant des troupes. L'ordre intérieur est maintenu dans la Roumélie Orientale par une gendarmerie indigène, assistée d'une milice locale. Pour la composition de ces deux corps, dont les officiers seront nommés par le Sultan, il sera tenu compte, suivant les localités, de la religion des habitants. S. M. le Sultan s'engage à ne point employer de troupes irrégulières, telles que Bashi-Bazouks et Circassiens, dans les garnisons des frontières. Les troupes régulières destinées à ce service ne pourront en aucun cas être cantonnées chez les habitants; lorsqu'elles traverseront la province elles ne pourront y faire de séjour.

"Article 16.—Le Gouverneur-Général aura le droit d'appeler les troupes Ottomanes dans les cas où la sécurité intérieure ou extérieure de la province se trouverait menacée. Dans l'éventualité prévue la Sublime Porte devra donner connaissance de cette décision, ainsi que des nécessités qui la justifient, aux représentants des Puissances à Constantinople.

"Article 17.—Le Gouverneur-Général de la Roumélie Orientale sera nommé par la Sublime Porte, avec l'assentiment des Puissances, pour un terme de cinq ans.

"Article 18.—Immédiatement après la signature du présent Traité, une Commission Européenne sera formée pour élaborer, d'accord avec la Porte Ottomane, l'organisation de la Roumélie Orientale. Cette Commission aura à déterminer, dans un délai de trois mois, les pouvoirs et les attributions du Gouverneur-Général, ainsi que le régime administratif, judiciaire, et financier de la province, en prenant pour point de départ les différentes lois sur les vilayets et les propositions faites dans la huitième séance de la Conférence de Constantinople. L'ensemble des dispositions arrêtées pour la Roumélie Orientale fera l'objet d'un Firman Impérial, qui sera promulgué par la Sublime Porte, et dont elle donnera communication aux Puissances.

"Article 19.—La Commission Européenne sera chargée d'administrer, d'accord avec la Sublime Porte, les finances de la province jusqu'à l'achèvement de la nouvelle organisation.

"Article 20.—Les traités, conventions, et arrangements internationaux, de quelque nature qu'ils soient, conclus ou à conclure entre la Porte et les Puissances étrangères, seront applicables dans la Roumélie Orientale comme dans tout l'Empire Ottoman. Les immunités et privilèges acquis aux étrangers, quelle que soit leur condition, seront respectés dans cette province. La Sublime Porte s'engage à y faire observer les lois générales de l'Empire sur la liberté religieuse en faveur de tous les cultes.

"Article 21.—Les droits et obligations de la Sublime Porte en ce qui concerne les chemins de fer dans la Roumélie Orientale sont maintenus intégralement.

"Article 22.—L'effectif du corps d'occupation Russe en Bulgarie et dans la Roumélie Orientale sera composé de six divisions d'infanterie et de deux divisions de cavalerie, et n'excédera pas 50,000 hommes. Il sera entretenu aux frais du pays occupé. Les troupes d'occupation conserveront leurs communications avec la Russie, non seulement par la Roumanie, d'après les arrangements à conclure entre les deux Etats, mais aussi par les ports de la Mer Noire, Varna et Bourgas, où elles pourront organiser pour la durée de l'occupation les dépôts nécessaires. La durée de l'occupation de la Roumélie Orientale et de la Bulgarie par les troupes Impériales Russes est fixée à neuf mois à dater de la signature du présent Traité. Le Gouvernement Impérial Russe s'engage à terminer dans un délai ultérieur de trois mois le passage de ses troupes à travers la Roumanie et l'évacuation complète de cette Principauté.

"Article 23.—Les Provinces de Bosnie et de l'Herzégovine seront occupées et administrées par l'Autriche-Hongrie. Le Gouvernement d'Autriche-Hongrie ne désirant pas se charger de l'administration du Sandjak de Novi Bazar, qui s'étend entre la Serbie et le Monténégro dans la direction sud-est jusqu'au-delà de Mitrovitza, l'Administration Ottomane continuera d'y fonctionner; néanmoins, à fin d'assurer le maintien du nouvel état politique ainsi que la liberté et la sécurité des voies de communication, l'Autriche-Hongrie se réserve le droit de tenir garnison et d'avoir des routes militaires et commerciales sur toute l'étendue de cette partie de l'ancien vilayet de Bosnie.

"Article 24.—L'indépendance du Monténégro est reconnue par la Sublime Porte et par toutes celles des Hautes Parties Contractantes qui ne l'avaient pas encore admise.

"Article 25.—Les Hautes Parties Contractantes sont d'accord sur les conditions suivantes:—Dans le Monténégro la distinction des croyances religieuses et des confessions ne pourra être opposée à personne comme un motif d'exclusion ou d'incapacité en ce qui concerne la jouissance des droits civils et politiques, l'admission aux emplois publics, fonctions et honneurs, ou l'exercice des différentes professions et industries, dans quelque localité que ce soit. La liberté et la pratique extérieure de tous les cultes seront assurées à tous les ressortissants du Monténégro aussi bien qu'aux étrangers, et aucune entrave ne pourra être apportée soit à l'organisation hiérarchique des différentes communions, soit à leurs rapports avec leurs chefs spirituels.

"Article 26.—Les nouvelles frontières du Monténégro sont fixées ainsi qu'il suit:—Le tracé, partant de Linobrdo, au nord de Klobuk, sur la Trebisnica, descend vers Grand Carevo, qui reste à la Province d'Herzégovine, puis remonte le cours de cette rivière jusqu'à un point situé à un kilomètre en aval du confluent de la Cepelica, et de là rejoint, par la ligne la plus courte, les hauteurs qui bordent la Trebisnica. Il se dirige ensuite vers Pilatova, laissant ce village au Monténégro, puis continue par les hauteurs dans la direction nord, en se maintenant autant que possible à une distance de six kilomètres de la route Bilek-Korito-Gacko, jusqu'au col situé entre la Somina Planina, et le Mont Curilo d'où il se dirige à l'est par Vratkovick, laissant ce village à l'Herzégovine, jusqu'au Mont Orline. A partir de ce point, la frontière, laissant Ravno au Monténégro, s'avance directement par le nord-nord-est en traversant les sommets du Lebersnik et du Volujak, puis descend par la ligne la plus courte sur la Piva, qu'elle traverse, et rejoint la Tara en passant entre Crkvice et Nedine. De ce point elle remonte la Tara jusqu'à Rojkovac, d'où elle suit la crête du contrefort jusqu'à Siskojezero. A partir de cette localité elle se confond avec l'ancienne frontière jusqu'au village de Sekulare. De là la nouvelle frontière se dirige par les crêtes de la Mokra Planina, le village de Mokra restant au Monténégro, puis elle gagne le point 2,166 de la carte de l'Etat-major Autrichien, en suivant la chaîne principale et la ligne du partage des eaux entre le Lim d'un côté, et le Drin ainsi que de la Cievna (Zem) de l'autre. Elle se confond ensuite avec les limites actuelles entre la tribu des Kuci-Drekalovici d'un côté et la Kucka-Krajna ainsi que les tribus des Klementi et Grudi de l'autre, jusqu'à la plaine de Podgorica, d'où elle se dirige sur Plawnica, laissant à l'Albanie les tribus des Klementi, Grudi, et Hoti. De là la nouvelle frontière traverse le lac près de l'îlot de Gorica Topal, et à partir de Gorica Topal elle atteint directement les sommets de la crête, d'où elle suit la ligne du partage des eaux entre Megured et Kalimed, laissant Mrkovic au Monténégro, et rejoignant la Mer Adriatique au Krue. Au nord-ouest la tracé sera formée par une ligne passant de la côte entre les villages Susana et Zubci, et aboutissant à la pointe extrême sud-est de la frontière actuelle du Monténégro sur la Vrsuta Planina.

"Article 27.—Antivari et son littoral sont annexés au Monténégro sous les conditions suivantes:—Les contrées situées au sud de ce territoire, d'après la délimitation ci-dessus déterminée, jusqu'à la Boyana, y compris Dulcinjo, seront restituées à la Turquie. La Commune de Spizza, jusqu'à la limite septentrionale du territoire indiqué dans la description détaillée des frontières, sera incorporée à la Dalmatie. Il y aura pleine et entière liberté de navigation sur la Boyana pour le Monténégro. Il ne sera pas construit de fortifications sur le parcours de ce fleuve à l'exception de celles qui seraient nécessaires à la défense locale de la place de Scutari, lesquelles ne s'étendront pas au-delà d'une distance de six kilomètres de cette ville. Le Monténégro ne pourra pas avoir ni bâtiments ni pavillon de guerre. Le port d'Antivari et toutes les eaux du Monténégro resteront fermées aux bâtiments de guerre de toutes les nations. Les fortifications situées entre le lac et le littoral sur le territoire Monténégrin seront rasées, et

Above Portrait of Blowitz, inscribed Paris, 31 October 1878, by Anton von Werner.

Right Photo taken at the Ritz Hotel on the occasion of Blowitz's retirement in 1902 when his fellow journalists presented him with the statuette shown in the picture.

me if I would not have another cigar. He insisted on lighting it for me himself, and he held the match for about a minute. My cigar was lighted at last, and I went away.' We can almost see the glow of that cigar, and the glow of triumph as Blowitz walked away with enough material to fill his dispatches for months, and considerable status which encouraged other diplomats to confide in him.

What he wanted now was the text of the treaty. The delegates were due to sign it on Saturday 13 July.To get it in *The Times* of that day, scoop the world, astonish the delegates and make the name of Blowitz re-echo around the Chancelleries of Europe, he needed a copy by Friday. Even if he got it, he realized that the Prussian Post Office would almost certainly refuse to telegraph it to London before it was signed. So he laid his plans.

He called on the Belgian Minister in Berlin and told him that *The Times* was thinking of setting up a regular telegraphic service between Brussels and Printing House Square. On this pretext, he persuaded the Minister to give him a letter of introduction to the Belgian Director-General of Posts, instructing him to cooperate in what Blowitz described as a 'dummy-run' at very short notice.

A friendly diplomat agreed to give Blowitz a copy of the treaty on the Friday. He was probably one of the French delegation, which would have had the strongest motives for binding the Paris correspondent of *The Times* to the Quai d'Orsay with a favour of this kind. But his copy did not have the preamble, so Blowitz called on the French Ambassador, showed him that he had got hold of a copy of the treaty, and asked for the preamble. The Ambassador agreed to read it aloud to him once, and Superman Blowitz, with his phenomenal photographic memory, memorized it as it was spoken.

Blowitz then went through the motions of asking Bismarck for an advance copy of the treaty. Bismarck refused. But his refusal made it more difficult for him to give advance copies to the German press.

On the great Friday before the Congress ended, Blowitz pretended to leave Berlin in a huff. At Berlin's railway station he dictated the preamble of the treaty to his secretary from memory. Then he slit open the lining of the coat of his colleague, Mackenzie Wallace, and stitched the treaty inside it. As a precaution Blowitz travelled in a separate compartment and went to Paris. Wallace changed at Cologne for Brussels.

At 5 am in Brussels Wallace was, as expected, turned away by the telegraph clerk. So he woke up the unfortunate Director-General and produced the letter from the Belgian Minister. The French text with an English translation, 11,000 words, 57 out of the 64 clauses, was transmitted in time to appear in the later (mid-morning) editions of *The Times* just about at the time that the Treaty of Berlin was being signed. Telegrams from London carried the news back to Berlin. Blowitz had scooped the world.

THE TIMES leading article analysing the Treaty of Berlin, allowed itself to gloat, in the first paragraph, over Blowitz's astonishing scoop. Like all Blowitz's reports, the treaty was filed – and in this instance printed – in French (columns 5 and 6).
15 JULY 1878

With Gordon in Khartoum

In a dark corner of St Paul's Cathedral there is Hacks' Corner, containing memorials to famous war correspondents. One of them describes William Howard Russell accurately as 'the first and greatest of war correspondents'. Facing the bust of Billy Russell there is a tablet commemorating another foreign correspondent of *The Times*. His name is not so well known as Russell's. He died young, in the execution of his duty to the inky trade. But for a couple of years his exclusive reports in *The Times* were as sensational and as influential as anything that Russell filed from the Crimea. By one of the little accidents of journalism, he was the only journalist in Khartoum with General Gordon under siege. Gordon became one of the great martyrs of the imperial age. *The Times* correspondent was his prophet. His reports made Gordon a hero and brought down Gladstone's second government. His name was Frank Power.

Top Frank le Poer Power, the Consul and THE TIMES correspondent at Khartoum.

Below right General Gordon.

Opposite above Telegram sent to THE TIMES by Power.

Opposite below The printed text of the telegram.

Frank le Poer Power, son of a bank manager, was a restless and adventurous child of the Age of Imperialism. After leaving school, he obtained a commission in the Austrian army. But he soon chucked it, and became a cub reporter for the *Daily News*. In London he met Edmond O'Donovan, the war correspondent and trouble-shooter of the *Daily News*, who invited him to come with him to the little local difficulty that was brewing in Sudan.

Power was twenty-five when he arrived in Cairo with O'Donovan in June 1883. Britain's Sudanese connection was complex and glutinous. Egypt was ruled by an independent Khedive under the nominal control of Turkey but under the de facto imperium of Britain. Early in the nineteenth century Sudan had come under the rule of Egypt. But Egypt's authority was on the wane. The process was accelerated in 1881 when a holy man called Muhammad Ahmed ibn Abdallah announced that he was the Mahdi, the leader chosen by God to drive out the imperialist oppressors and bring in the reign of justice.

The Sudanese flocked to his banners, and in January 1883 his army had captured El Obeid, the capital of the province of Kordofan, within striking distance of Khartoum. The Egyptian authorities and their British advisers decided reluctantly and late that something had to be done, and dispatched a rag-bag force against the Mahdi, led by Hicks Pasha, an ex-Indian Army colonel. With him rode Power and O'Donovan. Power's opinion of the affair ironically coincided with that of Gladstone, the British Prime Minister, who saw the Sudanese as 'a people struggling to be free'. Power wrote:

> I am not ashamed to say I feel the greatest sympathy for the rebels, and every race that fights against the rule of Pachas, backsheesm, bribery, robbery, and corruption. It is the system, and not the Mahdi, that has brought about the rebellion. The rebels are in the right, and God and chance seem to be fighting for them. I hope they will hunt every Egyptian neck and crop out of the Sudan.

Power's account of Hicks Pasha's army is historically important. It is the only contemporary record of this large army that was about to march into the desert, in the traditional British square, and vanish off the face of the earth:

> We have here 9,000 infantry that fifty good men would rout in ten minutes; and 1,000 Bashi-Bazouk cavalry that have never learned even to ride, and these, with a few Nordenfeldt guns, are to beat the 69,000 men the Mahdi has got together. That Egyptian officers and men are not worth the ammunition they threw away is well known, and the few black regiments we have will be left to garrison this place, as the Arabs and townspeople fear them. Even our own officers and men (a cowardly, beggarly mob) believe that the Mahdi is a prophet, and are less than half hearted in this business, so that the ruffianly though brave Bashi-Bazouks and the niggers are the only men to be relied on.

Fortunately for him, Power fell ill and returned to Khartoum. Hicks Pasha, his army, and O'Donovan marched west of the Nile into the wastes of Kordofan and were never seen again. Nobody even heard of them for three months. Hicks is said to have died with his sword in one hand and his revolver in the other.

Power was stranded in Khartoum, the only journalist and pretty well the only Englishman there. He offered his services to *The Times* and was promptly signed up as its correspondent in Khartoum. His reports of the disaster that had wiped out Hicks Pasha's army and the deteriorating position of Khartoum were the only on-the-spot account, carried exclusively in *The Times*, and read with growing excitement, imperialist indignation and horror by the British public. Young Power suddenly found himself in a position of international importance. He and the garrison commander were the only people who had first-hand knowledge of what was going on. The British Government appointed Power its consul in Khartoum and instructed him to keep in close touch with its representatives in Cairo. Power's reports were gloomy: 'We have only 2,000 men to man four miles of earthworks and keep a rebel population of 60,000 Arabs quiet'. He repeatedly appealed for relief troops. With stiff-upper-lipped understatement Printing House Square and Whitehall gave Power permission to leave Khartoum if conditions grew dangerous.

The British Government had tried to wash its hands of responsibility for Sudan, hoping that the problem would go away. The destruction of Hicks Pasha's army also destroyed this policy. They either had to abandon Sudan or reoccupy it by force, and either policy was likely to cost British blood. Power's reports in *The Times* were inflaming public opinion dangerously to the view that something must be done. Gladstone decided reluctantly to send out General Gordon, hero of the Crimea, the Taiping Rebellion and Central Africa, to find a bloodless and liberal third way out of the corner. Gordon, with his military secretary Colonel Stewart, arrived in Khartoum in February 1884 and took charge.

<u>Telegraph</u>

<u>To Moberly Bell</u> via Berber *Send this*

<u>Cairo.</u> *C. G. Gordon*

Since last telegraph 21st April have been almost daily engaged with rebels who now thoroughly surround Khartoum. Gordon busily engaged laying out mines in front of works in all directions. Yesterday & today rebels came down to village opposite & fired heavily on palace we returned fire with artillery and musketry and on both occasions Arabs soon retreated. There was no loss on our side. The town is quiet, over half the population before the siege commenced went over to rebels thus weeding out all bad characters. Gordon issues rations to the poor. Food very dear, we have corn & biscuit for about four months. Gordon has issued paper money as our Treasure is still at Berber. The merchants accept it as money. All the arrears to soldiers can be thus paid off. Gordon has sent emmissaries to offer to all slaves of rebels their freedom if they abandon their masters and come in. If this takes, it will be a fearful blow to rebels. The general has hired the large Mission premises on the river and has moved all the ammunition there in case of attack with artillery on the fortifications it will be perfectly safe. A messenger from Seyid Mahomet Osman of Kassala who is an emir of Mecca and chief amongst the Musselmans in the Soudan came in bringing a letter. The Seyid says he has beaten the rebels round Kassala & he tells Gordon to be of good heart & he & all his men will come to his relief. In such respect is this man held that the rebels did not dare to stop the bearer of the letter. One of Nicks Bandsmen came in last night from Obeid. The Maidi has sent two guns forty boxes of shells & sixty remmingtons to be used against Salek Bey who is still holding out against the rebels at Mesalimia. This soldiers states that Slatin Bey at Darfour has not surrendered to the Maidi. The blue Nile is slowly rising and we hope that in ten or fifteen days the steamers will be able to smite the rebels hip and thigh. The health of the town is excellent & we three Englishmen here are well & hopeful. There are now arround the lines in addition to all other obstacles, such as crows-feet, broken glass, wire entanglements & cheveux de frise, three lines of land torpedos or percussion mines. They are enormously powerful and are much feared by the Arabs. We have no news what ever of the intentions of H.M.G. Learned today 27th April that a man with a post from Berber was taken by the rebels and killed

<u>Power</u> Times correspondent <u>Khartoum</u>

[Printed in *The Times* of 29 December 1884.]

LATEST INTELLIGENCE.

(From our Correspondents.)

EGYPT AND THE SOUDAN.

(By Eastern Company's Cables.)

KHARTOUM, April 2.

The position of affairs here is this :—The rebels, being gradually emboldened, are approaching the town on all sides. Khartoum for the present is safe, and pretty well provided.

The people are naturally asking, "Are we to continue for ever like this, or to be released by the English, the Turks, or the Egyptians ?"

It is reported that the Mahdi is sending artillery here from El Obeid, so that our steamers will be rendered helpless.

The total ignorance which exists among us as to the intentions of Her Majesty's Government is far worse than the certainty, however bad. The last news from Cairo was dated March 10. We have not learned that any help will be sent from without. It is now four months since the English Government heard of Hicks Pasha's disaster ; yet, except the sending of General Gordon, no step has been taken to relieve us.

Would it not be more honest of the Government, if it cannot carry out its self-imposed duty towards us by means of British troops, to hire Turkish regiments ? If England will not arrest the advance of the Mahdi, why not give £500,000 to the Turks to do so ? It would not cost more.

Again, if the Government has decided to do nothing, would it not be better to say so to the townspeople, instead of persuading them to hold out, day after day, and thus to jeopardize their chances eventually with the rebels ? General Gordon might tell them to make the best terms possible with the enemy, while we might try to get together the garrison, and attempt to escape, leaving the townspeople to their fate. The hope deferred of English intervention is making the people heart-sick.

It is just reported here that Salah Bey has captured the Sheikh El Obeid.

The rebels have not fired on the Palace to-day.

April 7.

Since I last telegraphed, the rebels have almost daily been engaged, principally by the steamers. Khartoum is at present the centre of an enormous rebel camp. The rebels' tents are within sight, and their bullets often strike or go over the palace, in which a man was thus killed last week. We have killed several of the rebels, but our store of Krupp ammunition is rather short. The situation is now very critical.

We are trying to run a steamer through the rebel lines to Berber. Yesterday, owing to the severity of the rebel fire, she had to return. The day before yesterday an attack of the rebels on Omdurman was repulsed. We have mined the plain in front of the fortifications.

I have had only two sources of hope in this crisis—first, the expectation of an English relieving column ; secondly, the plan of a retreat across the Equator. Because I am confident that General Gordon is abandoned by the Government, and that without Zobehr Pasha he can never beat the rebels, I fear that he will be driven to retreat by Central Africa. For to-day arrived an unciphered telegram sent from Sir Evelyn Baring to Berber, saying that no English troops would be sent to that place—in a word, clearly indicating that General Gordon and the others who have been faithful to the Government are thrown over.

To retreat on Berber is impossible. Sir Evelyn Baring's unciphered telegram to that place will quickly be spread abroad, and the Arabs will learn that the members of the English Government have turned down their thumbs while General Gordon is struggling here.

A retreat on the Congo will entail great hardships.

General Gordon, Colonel Stewart, and your Correspondent are in good health.

ALEXANDRIA, April 16.

An article published in the *Egyptian Gazette* summarizes intelligently what is the universal opinion expressed here as follows :—

"Is the government of Egypt to be conducted on English or on Egyptian principles ? This question should be answered carefully and candidly, without regard to personal interests, or sympathies, or previously declared principles.

"If we see fit to maintain the original policy of the government of Egypt according to English ideas, then we must logically insist that these ideas shall be carried out by Englishmen, without regard to the views of any Egyptian, however exalted in rank. If, on the other hand, we feel that the task is too large, and that we cannot accept the responsibility which it implies, then with equally little hesitation we should declare that we renounce our original intention. We should withdraw those Englishmen who thus become both useless and expensive, and should leave the entire government of Egypt to such advisers as His Highness may choose to call in."

A telegram from General Gordon to Sir Evelyn Baring reports that Salah Pasha is safe, but that he has failed in his attempt to capture the Sheik el Obeid. The spies report that the intended expedition of the Mahdi to Khartoum has been abandoned, owing to the existence of dissensions among his followers.

(By Telegraph.)

CONSTANTINOPLE, April 16.

Notwithstanding the decision of the Council of Ministers in the opposite sense, and contrary to the advice of Musurus Pasha, it has been decided to make another attempt to open negotiations with the British Cabinet regarding the Egyptian question, and a telegram has already been sent to Musurus Pasha, instructing him to propose to Lord Granville an exchange of views on the basis of his lordship's Note of December 28, 1882.

That Note, which was presented to the Porte on January 11, 1883, and communicated subsequently to the other Powers, enumerated and described the various questions of international interest and of internal administration with which the British Government had to deal, and indicated the solutions which his lordship considered to be best calculated to secure permanent tranquillity in Egypt. In a despatch to the British Chargé d'Affaires, which accompanied the Note and which was likewise communicated to the Porte, Lord Granville spontaneously recognized the special interest of the Sultan in the Egyptian question, and expressed a desire that his Government should have further information about the intentions of the British Cabinet, and should have an opportunity of expressing its own opinion regarding the questions at issue.

FRANCE.

PARIS, Wednesday, April 16.

It will be remembered that M. Savary, formerly a Deputy and Under-Secretary of State, was closely connected with the Banque de Lyon et de la Loire, the Union Générale of Lyons. M. Savary has turned up again in a new and more dramatic capacity. Last night a M. Lamy endeavoured to shoot him at a *café*, where he found him in company with his (Lamy's) wife. The attempt was not successful. The parties were arrested. After examination by the police commissary, M. Savary and Madame Lamy were set at large, and M. Lamy was sent to the House of Detention.

M. Savary and M. Lamy, it appears, were once partners at Lyons in a concern of some kind for using electricity called by an English name, and a very vague one—viz., "Electric Company." The company appears to have had misfortunes, and after its collapse Madame Lamy disappeared from her home, carrying off with her, according to her husband, his superfluous cash, and joined M. Savary in Paris.

M. Savary's version is that he was not Madame Lamy's paramour, but that he had met her at the *café* to inform her of the result of steps which he had taken on her behalf to some unexplained end. Whether M. Savary is guilty or not will, no doubt, appear in the sequel. In any case, he is the defendant in a suit for separation by his wife. M. Lamy has just lost one of his two children from an attack of croup. His wife is represented as being unusually good-looking.

A short time ago, as your readers will no doubt remember, Madame Sarah Bernhardt endeavoured to inflict personal chastisement on a fellow-actress, Mdlle. Marie Colombier, for the circulation of calumnious reports concerning her by the latter. Mdlle. Colombier recently published a volume, entitled "Sarah Barnum." A reply appeared entitled "Marie Pigeonnier," by an anonymous writer. Both books have given rise to criminal proceedings, and the legal authorities have decided on prosecuting Mdlle. Colombier as the author of the one, and the publisher and printer, in default of the author, of the other. It does not seem as yet clear on what ground the prosecutions are to take place.

The French Government has just, pursuant to law, decreed a pension of 3,000f. for the benefit of the widow and children of Prince Tamatoa (the brother of Pomare), who ceded the Society Islands to France. Tamatoa died on the 30th of September, 1881.

M. FERRY'S SPEECH AT PÉRIGUEUX.

PARIS, April 16.

The four Ministers left Périgueux at noon to-day, and will reach Paris at midnight.

M. Ferry's description at Périgueux last night of the state in which the present Cabinet found France was regarded by those who heard it as a sharp attack on M. de Freycinet. It is true that the latter was not M. Ferry's immediate predecessor ; for M. Duclerc came in between them, and, also, for a week or two, M. Fallières, now Minister of Education. But M. Ferry's animadversions were plainly directed against the Cabinet which held office during the spring and summer of 1883.

There is, no doubt, considerable truth in the charge of indecision which he launches against that Cabinet. Its foreign policy was certainly vacillating, the public works were nearly at a deadlock, and the magistracy and other questions seemed insoluble ; whereas the magistracy has now been remodelled, public works have been arranged, the Tunisian Protectorate has been definitively established, and the capture of Hunghoa has, according to M. Ferry, "ended the military period" in Tonquin. If both pictures are a little over-coloured, this is perhaps excusable in a Premier anxious to produce an effect.

It is, however, a singular thing that M. Ferry should have gone down south to glorify Gambetta, under whom he declined to serve in 1882, and to disparage M. de Freycinet, twice his colleague, and twice his chief. Though now, as it were, the head of the Gambettists, M. Ferry was never a Gambettist. He and Gambetta were colleagues during the War ; but Gambetta was mostly outside Paris while M. Ferry remained inside ; and afterwards there was no personal or political intimacy between them. M. Ferry never belonged to the Gambettist group, and when Gambetta, on the Senatorial rejection of *Scrutin de Liste*, suddenly clamoured for revision, M. Ferry, then Premier, at first gave the watchword, "Neither revision nor division ;" though he eventually endorsed a moderate programme of revision. If he is now at the head of a Cabinet which is more Gambettist than anything else, it must not be supposed that Gambetta's satellites really recognize him as a successor to that great man. There are men among them who consider themselves qualified for the leadership, and though M. Spuller seems content to bide his time and abstains from hampering the Cabinet, M. Paul Bert is a thorn in its side.

With M. de Freycinet, on the other hand, M. Ferry had more associations. They were colleagues under M. Waddington ; they remained so when the latter was succeeded by M. de Freycinet ; and though M. Ferry succeeded M. de Freycinet, he has in no way supplanted him, for he was not one of the three dissentients who occasioned his resignation. On Gambetta's fall, moreover, M. Ferry, though he had held the Premiership, did not deem it derogatory to serve again under M. de Freycinet, so that his last night's criticisms, if really aimed at the latter, recoil on himself as a member of the very Cabinet which he decries as settling nothing and not knowing its own mind. It is true, indeed, that M. Ferry during that period confined himself to his portfolio of Education, and was only subordinately responsible for general policy.

If, again, it is supposed that M. Ferry referred to the Duclerc Cabinet, his criticisms fall on his present colleague, M. Fallières, who was a member of that Cabinet. Thus M. Ferry's blows strike either himself, as M. de Freycinet's colleague, or his coadjutor, M. Fallières, as M. Duclerc's colleague. On the former theory, too, he attacks not merely an old colleague and chief, but the very man the dislike of the Chamber to whom is largely the cause of his own stability in office. The Chamber has inflicted, indeed, repeated minor defeats on M. Ferry, but it has refrained from overthrowing him, because it knows that he could only be succeeded by the Moderates, or advocates of Decentralization, and that M. Grévy would send for M. de Freycinet as their natural leader. Thus the very stability on which M. Ferry congratulates both himself and the Chamber is mainly due to M. de Freycinet, whom he is supposed to have attacked.

As to the future, M. Ferry's argument that this is a good time for revision because the country does not ask for it is somewhat paradoxical. It is obvious that if he succeeds in carrying a limited revision it will not satisfy or silence the Extremists, the only party clamouring for revision, and logicians will ask, Why, then, revise at all ? The only answer that can be given is that Gambetta, smarting under the Senate's rejection of *scrutin de liste*, pronounced for revision a few weeks after having deprecated it, that at the last elections the majority of the Republicans endorsed revision, and that the present Cabinet is pledged to propose it. It is a curious commentary on Gambetta's apotheosis that a moment of pique on his part should now be dooming the Republic to an ordeal to which it would not otherwise have been exposed.

THE UNITED STATES.

(By Anglo-American Cables.)

PHILADELPHIA, April 16.

The Pennsylvania Republican Convention to-day nominated Mr. Blaine for the office of President and Mr. Lincoln for that of Vice-President. The platform adopted advocates protection, and opposes any reduction of the tariff.

The general debate on the Morrison Tariff Reduction Bill is expected to continue for two weeks, or more, at intervals, when the vote will be taken on the question of striking out the enacting clause. This motion will, it is thought, be adopted by about 20 majority, thus defeating the Bill.

The heavy rains washed out the trestle bridges on the Western and Atlantic Railway, Georgia, yesterday. Two trains were consequently wrecked ; six persons being killed, and 18 injured. Two of those who lost their lives were burnt to death, the wreck of the cars having caught fire.

To-day's steamers took out $2,300,000 in gold, chiefly to the Continent.

(By Telegraph.)

GERMANY AND WESTERN AFRICA.

BRUSSELS, April 16.

It is announced that Dr. Nachtigall, now German Consul at Tunis, will, by order of his Government, proceed shortly to the West Coast of Africa to report on the measures which may be necessary to protect German interests in those regions.

AUSTRIA.

VIENNA, April 16.

The Emperor will leave on May 10 for Pesth. At the same time Her Majesty and the Archduchess Valérie will start for Gödölö.

As a question had arisen with respect to the right of Presburg to hold markets, the town authorities have furnished the following facts. The Emperor Sigismund in 1416 conferred on the town the right of holding markets on Thursdays all the year round ; the Emperor Joseph II. in 1784 gave it the right to hold a cattle market every Tuesday ; and the Emperor Francis in 1797 confirmed these charters. For some time only one market has been held each year, but it is not thought that by this neglect the privileges in question have been lost. The Hungarian Ministry of Commerce has sent one of its officials to Pressburg to superintend the necessary sanitary arrangements.

During May three repeating rifles, chosen out of 20, will be tried at the Army Musketry School in Bruck. Among them is the Bertalt pattern, by the chairman of the Spencer Arms Company.

THE AUSTRIAN CROWN PRINCE'S TOUR.

VIENNA, April 16.

The Crown Prince and Princess passed the town of Szegedin yesterday. The station was tastefully decorated. As an official reception had been declined, only the Sheriff and Burgomaster, in Hungarian national costume, were on the platform. Luncheon having been taken here, the journey was continued. At Temesvar a stay of eight minutes was made. Large numbers of the citizens had assembled, who greeted the arrival of the train with enthusiastic cheers, their Imperial Highnesses bowing repeatedly in return.

According to a telegram from Bucharest, the Crown Prince and Princess arrived in Bucharest at 6 a.m. this morning, and were warmly greeted by the assembled crowd.

CONSTANTINOPLE, April 16.

The extensive preparations made here for the reception of the Austrian Heir-Apparent and the Archduchess are nearly completed. A small palace has been constructed and furnished for them in the park adjoining the Imperial palace, and a long new street has been made to facilitate communication between the Austrian Embassy and the upper portion of Pera. In Broussa a palace has been repaired and furnished anew for their convenience, and a large sum has been expended in repairing the road between Broussa and Moudania.

AUSTRIA AND SWITZERLAND.

VIENNA, April 16.

The Swiss Federal Council has requested the Austrian Government, in view of the probable large export of cattle into Switzerland by the Arlberg Railway, to establish a common station for the inspection of beasts at Feldkirch, in the Vorarlberg. The Austrian Government has assented to this proposal.

AUSTRIA AND GREECE.

VIENNA, April 16.

The Greek Government having expressed a wish to conclude a Customs and Commercial treaty with Austria-Hungary, the Austrian and Hungarian Ministers of Commerce have set to work to draw up the main provisions to be included in such a treaty. The Greek Government especially desires a low duty on the importation of raisins.

RUSSIA AND THE VATICAN.

VIENNA, April 16.

The *Political Correspondence* states that after the lull of some months' duration, which followed the visit of the German Crown Prince to the Pope, the negotiations between Prussia and the Papal See have been resumed.

THE NEW RUSSIAN LOAN.

BERLIN, April 16.

The event of the day here is unquestionably the new Russian loan of 15 millions sterling, which derives political importance from the fact of the participation in it of the so-called "Seehandlung Societät," which is a Royal Prussian institution, and may be briefly described as a department of the Ministry of Finance. The Seehandlung's transactions are subject to the control and sanction of the Minister of Finance ; and as no Prussian Chancellor of the Exchequer would move in any matter of this kind without consulting Prince Bismarck, it is naturally and rightly concluded that the Chancellor not only is favourably disposed towards the Russian Government, but also has considerable confidence in its peaceful policy and in the stability of things in general in Russia. Prince Bismarck is much too farseeing a politician to furnish Russia with what might prove the sinews of war unless thoroughly convinced that this is not the end to which the Imperial borrower means to turn the money.

As for the loan itself, the amount is 15 millions sterling, 10 millions of which will be issued here, at Berlin, at the end of this month, probably on the 29th, after the Russian Easter holidays, in five per cent. (gold) bonds, in pounds, roubles, and marks, as in the Rothschild or Anglo-Russian loans. The other five millions have been reserved for the Imperial Bank at St. Petersburg. The firm of Bleichröder and Co. furnishes the money here (the 10 millions) as mandatory of the Seehandlung, and for its own account.

It may be mentioned that the Seehandlung has never before participated in a foreign loan, and that in the present case its participation is so complete that the coupons of interest on the Russian loan will be permanently payable in its bureaux. The Bourse here has been agreeably surprised by the transaction, and its satisfaction has been manifested by a decided rise in Russian securities of all sorts. Well may the semi-official *North German Gazette* express the prevailing feeling on the subject in the following words :—

"There is nothing, perhaps, that characterizes so clearly the thorough change which has taken place in the whole tendency of Russian policy as the fact that the announcement of a large Russian financial operation, which a few years ago would inevitably have caused deep disquietude, is now, on the contrary, regarded with confidence as a further step towards the internal consolidation of the Czar's dominions. And this impression is materially strengthened by the circumstance that the Seehandlung Societät in Berlin is one of the institutions with which the loan has been negotiated."

THE THREE EMPERORS.

VIENNA, April 16.

The various statements made with reference to an alleged intended meeting of the Emperors of Austria and Russia are premature. Should the Czar, however, in the ensuing summer, find himself near the Austrian frontier, the meeting may take place. As to a conference of the three Emperors, which is also spoken of as probable, there is certainly nothing in the political situation which would form an obstacle to it.

TURKEY.

(By Indo-European Telegraph.)

CONSTANTINOPLE, April 16.

Late this afternoon Aarifi Pasha, Minister of Foreign Affairs, was replaced by Assym Pasha, Minister of Justice, whose vacated post will remain unoccupied for the present.

(By Telegraph.)

VIENNA, April 16.

The allotments of the shares of the Turkish Tobacco Company in Vienna were made known last night on the Exchange. The subscribers receive the shares at 149fl. 25kr. in paper. About 20,000 shares were apportioned to Vienna. Of the 200,000 shares 30,000 were directly taken by the members of the syndicate and 90,000 were apportioned. The financial syndicate retains, therefore, 80,000, of which the Austrian Credit Anstalt will take 25 per cent. and the Ottoman Bank 50 per cent. The Turkish tobacco monopoly came into operation yesterday, and the company has already begun its business.

THE RELIGIOUS DIFFICULTIES IN TURKEY.

CONSTANTINOPLE, April 16.

The Grand Vizier still hopes that an amicable solution may be found for the question of the Greek Patriarchate, and he has accordingly given instructions that the local Press should refrain from exciting public feeling by discussing the subject. Meanwhile, it has been arranged that the Metropolitan of Ephesus shall fulfil temporarily all the functions of the Patriarch, so that the forthcoming Easter ceremonies, to which the common people attribute great importance, will be celebrated in the usual way. How the question will ultimately be solved it is impossible to predict, but it is certain that for the moment the Greek community have weakened their position by their internal dissensions. The Patriarch, it is stated, intends to insist that the accusations brought against him by some members of the Mixed Council shall be submitted to a competent tribunal.

In the Armenian community a similar excitement exists concerning the election of the Catholicos. The Catholicos, who is the highest dignitary of the Armenian Church, resides at Echmiadzin in Russian Armenia, but his spiritual jurisdiction includes the Armenian dioceses of Turkey, and these dioceses being more numerous than those of Russia, have hitherto had the preponderance at elections. In order to maintain this preponderance, the Patriarch of Constantinople had decided to hold a preliminary election here, and to send to the election at Echmiadzin two delegates bearing the unanimous vote of all the Turkish dioceses. As this procedure would render the election at Echmiadzin a mere empty formality, the Russian Government decidedly objects to it, and has formally declared that each delegate from Turkey will only be allowed to give one vote. The moderate party among the Armenians here is ready to make concessions, and anxious to obtain an amicable compromise ; but there is an extreme party, which condemns all conciliatory tendencies, and seeks to use the incident as a means of overthrowing their antagonists in office. The struggle between the two parties has already occasioned unseemly disturbances. When the council in which the moderate party has a majority attempted to hold a meeting with closed doors, the crowd broke into the council room, and after maltreating two of the members, compelled the others to hold the meeting publicly in the cathedral.

THE PROPAGANDÂ QUESTION.

MADRID, April 16.

There are not wanting indications that the sentence of the Italian tribunals respecting the property of the Propagandâ Fide is likely to excite considerable attention in the religious and political circles of this country. Had not the Holy Week festivities at Seville interfered, I understand that the Archbishop of Seville would have prepared a memorial to the King in favour of the Propagandâ Fide. The Archbishop of Valencia and four bishops of his province have already signed and forwarded a memorial, in which they appeal to Don Alfonso's penetration and elevated feeling to adopt the best course to aid the Pope against the unheard of aggression.

The Liberal newspapers express fears that a Government which contains an Ultramontane Minister—Señor Pidal y Mon—may further what they term the inconvenient and dangerous ideas of the clergy. The Cabinet maintains complete reserve as to its views, but in generally well-informed quarters it is asserted that the relations between Señor Pidal y Mon and Señor Canovas del Castillo have become rather strained.

ROME, April 16.

The *Osservatore Romano* announces that a legal notification of the judgment pronounced by the Court of Cassation was formally served upon the authorities of the Propagandâ at 10 o'clock this morning.

THE TURIN EXHIBITION.

ROME, April 16.

The Turin Exhibition, for which the municipality and citizens have subscribed 3,825,000f., will be a grand show of all that Italian hands and Italian soil produce, and will illustrate Italian enterprise, and demonstrate the progress of the arts and manufactures of the country to the present day. A novel idea in connexion with the Fine Art Section has been carried into effect, with a view to increase the general attractions of the Exhibition. Near to one extremity of the area, on the banks of the Po, over which the buildings and grounds extend, more than 9,000 square mètres are occupied by exact reproductions of 15th century buildings, of which remains are scattered over various parts of Piedmont. These are arranged in a group in the form of a feudal castle surrounded by its burgh, the original models for the edifices in which are to be found at Chieri, Bussoleno, Pinerolo, Avigliana, and other places, with curious varieties of construction in stone and terra-cotta.

The ancient castle is chiefly taken from the plan of the Château di Fenis, in the Val d'Aosta, with its round tower and picturesque courtyard. All the apartments have been furnished in the style of nearly five centuries ago, copied from authentic models and documents. With its occupants in the dress of the period, the structure should recall the life of those ancient days. The narrow and winding streets of the adjacent burgh have houses and shops, wherein the visitors will find the inhabitants, also in the dress of the time, represented pursuing their respective trades, in ceramics, copper work, the blacksmith's art, and others. In short, this section of the Art Department will present, as it were, a page of art history, an archæological study of Piedmontese monuments, and specimens of the productions of its mediæval arts and industries.

In the Modern Educational Department Rome will exhibit specimens of the progress of the pupils at the industrial schools here. Among objects worthy of notice will be found lace, embroidery, painted mirrors, and illuminations from the Female Professional School in the Via della Missione, and, above all, the artificial flowers for which this school is justly renowned.

CUBA.

MADRID, April 16.

The news received from Cuba *viâ* the United States contrasts strangely with that made public here from official sources. The Count de Valdosera, Colonial Minister, assures me this afternoon that the Government has exercised no reserve whatever as to what is passing in the island. The filibuster Aguero, whose extradition for various offences the Spanish Government unsuccessfully asked from the United States, has not increased the followers whom he had on landing in Cuba. On the contrary, his party, as already telegraphed, is split up, and flying from fastness to fastness in the mountains to escape the troops, who are in close pursuit.

HOLLAND.

BRUSSELS, April 16.

The Dutch journals state that the Queen of Sweden will arrive this week in Amsterdam; where apartments are also being prepared for the Empress of Austria, who desires to consult a Dutch physician.

THE SWISS COINAGE.

BRUSSELS, April 16.

The Swiss Government has applied at Paris for permission to issue 1,000,000f. worth of small silver coin. According to the Latin Monetary Union Convention, each of the States concerned can issue only 6f. per head of the population in small silver coin. For the circulation in Switzerland this amount is found to be insufficient. The Convention will terminate next year if it is not prolonged before the end of December next.

We have received the following telegrams through Reuter's agency :—

EGYPT AND THE SOUDAN.

CAIRO, April 16.

Sir Evelyn Baring to-day received the following telegram from General Gordon, dated 8th inst :—

"A spy from Salah Pasha on the Blue Nile reports that he is all right, and has 500 horsemen and 57 boat-loads of grain.

"Internal dissensions are rife in Kordofan, in consequence of which the expedition which the Mahdi was preparing against Khartoum has had to be abandoned. There seem to be two parties in revolt against the Mahdi.

"Salah's effort to capture the Sheikh El Obeid has failed.

"Kassala is all right and Sennaar also."

Zobehr Pasha received the following telegram from General Gordon this afternoon, dated April 7 :—

"I have appointed you Assistant-Governor-General of the Soudan. You will advise me on your arrival at Berber, and if possible I will send you two steamers. These with the other two steamers now at Berber you will provide with iron parapets in order to protect the troops on board. Take also as many as you can of the Galyieen tribe and make frequent skirmishes, but do not expose yourself."

The above telegram is unintelligible here because Colonel Stewart on General Gordon's own proposal has been appointed Assistant-Governor-General of the Soudan, and also because the Galyieen tribe have revolted. The telegram makes no mention of whether the disapproval of the British Government to the appointment of Zobehr Pasha as his successor was known to General Gordon.

FRANCE, CHINA, AND TONQUIN.

PARIS, April 16.

The French Government has received no information confirming the report that the French Admiral had taken possession of Amoy as a guarantee for the payment of a war indemnity to be demanded by France from China. The rumour is regarded in official circles here as wholly unfounded.

The *National* of this evening states that after the conclusion of military operations in Tonquin, General Millot will proceed with a detachment of troops to Hué, and will probably arrive there at the same time as M. Patenôtre. The journal adds that General Millot and M. Patenôtre will both sign the new treaty with Annam.

The *National* also says the statement that the French Cabinet had informed the Government of Pekin of its intention to demand a war indemnity is confirmed, but adds that up to the present China has made no reply to the communication.

FRANCE.

PARIS, April 16.

The strike among the coal miners in the Anzin district has now terminated. The *Petit Journal* to-day states that the miners' delegates decided yesterday by 25 votes against 15 to resume work to-day on the terms offered by the Anzin Company.

FRANCE AND RUSSIA.

PARIS, April 16.

Baron Mohrenheim, the new Russian Ambassador to France, will present his credentials to President Grévy on the 19th inst.

FRANCE AND SPAIN.

MADRID, April 16.

Referring to the report which has been circulated recently by several newspapers, that the chief of the Custom-house and the inspector of the station at Irun who took part in the dispute which occurred there between the French Ambassador and the Spanish officials in December last were about to be transferred to other posts, the Ministerial papers affirm that this incident has been completely settled, and that the French Ambassador has not demanded any satisfaction. They add that should the officials in question be transferred from their present posts this step will be adopted for the convenience of the public service.

THE EMPRESS OF GERMANY.

BERLIN, April 16.

The Empress is still suffering from a cold. As Her Majesty's indisposition has been accompanied by feverish symptoms, she will require special attention for some time.

GERMANY.

BERLIN, April 16.

It is stated that Prince Bismarck's plans for the re-establishment of the Prussian Council of State meet with some objections in the quarters where the decision rests on account of the exclusion of the official element. It is added that Prince Bismarck is desirous that a speedy decision should be arrived at with regard to his application to be relieved of his posts in the Prussian Ministry.

AUSTRIA.

PRAGUE, April 16.

The Socialist agitator Pokorny has been sentenced to six months' imprisonment for belonging to a secret society.

TURKEY.

ATHENS, April 16.

Intelligence from Constantinople states that the members of the International Commission of the Black Sea Lifeboat and Rocket Service will shortly meet to protest strongly against the refusal of the Porte to sanction the service regulations insisted upon by the Commission, and approved at the time by Mr. Goschen, but now finally rejected by the Porte.

There is no foundation for the report that the Porte has refused to sanction the appointment by the two Œcumenical Councils, of the Bishop of Ephesus as *locum tenens* of the Œcumenical Patriarch. The Porte, on the contrary, has approved the nomination, and submitted it to the Sultan, whose decision is shortly expected.

The Councils have resolved to authorize the Bishop to officiate at Easter in case the Sultan's sanction should not be received before then.

EASTERN ROUMELIA.

PHILIPPOPOLIS, April 16.

The agitation in favour of the union of Bulgaria and Eastern Roumelia continues. Aleko Pasha has requested to be recalled, stating that the provisional authority conferred upon him deprives him of the means of acting with energy.

Rumours are current that an agitation is being carried on for the purpose of provoking a rising on the Bulgaro-Roumelian frontier.

THE QUETTA RAILWAY.

SIMLA, April 16.

It is stated that the Indian Government has definitively arranged to proceed immediately with the construction of the Quetta Railway.

SOUTH AFRICA.

CAPETOWN, March 26 (*viâ* Plymouth).

It is reported from Zululand that five traders have been murdered.

All is quiet in Stellaland and everything seems to indicate a peaceful solution of the recently impending difficulties. Major Lowe has issued a reassuring proclamation at Taungs, Mankoroane's headquarters. Colonel Clarke, the British Resident in Basutoland, arrived at Maseru on the 18th inst., and at once assumed the duties of his office. Captain Blythe returns to resume the Chief Magistracy of the Transkei.

The Orange Free State Government has received a telegram stating that a great battle took place in Basutoland on the 23d inst. between Khetisa, Masopha, and Lerothodi.

The Farmers' Congress now sitting at King William's Town has passed a resolution declaring that it is not expedient to hand over the Transkei to the Imperial authorities.

The declared value of native gold sent from Pretoria *viâ* Kimberley, during the months of January and February is £8,680. As much more is known to have left by private hands.

THE PROPAGANDA QUESTION.

TORONTO, April 16.

The Roman Catholic Bishops in the province of Ontario have drawn up a petition to the Queen praying Her Majesty to direct steps to be taken for the protection of British subjects interested in the property of the Propaganda.

CANADA.

MONTREAL, April 15.

The Marquis and Marchioness of Lansdowne are now visiting this city.

NEWFOUNDLAND.

ST. JOHN'S, April 15.

Religious rioting has been renewed at Carbonear, in which the Catholics are reported to have been the aggressors. Armed Orangemen are now in possession of the town.

H.M. corvette Tenedos has been ordered to the place.

THE MEXICAN DEBT.

MEXICO, April 16.

According to the journal *Monitor*, the Governor of Fernandez, brother-in-law of the President of Mexico, is about to leave for Paris in the capacity of Minister, and will be intrusted with the duty of bringing about a settlement of the English debt. He is expected to start on May 8 next.

THE NEW ORLEANS EXHIBITION.

WASHINGTON, April 16.

President Arthur has issued an order relative to a Government exhibit at the International Exhibition to be opened at New Orleans in December next. The order says ;—"It is desirable that the Executive Departments should present such articles and materials as will illustrate the administrative facilities of the Government in time of peace and its resources in time of war, so as to demonstrate the nature of our institutions and their adaptation to the wants of the people." With the above object the President orders the formation of a Board composed of one member each on behalf of the Smithsonian Institute, the Department of Agriculture, and the Bureau of Education. This Board, when organized, will confer with the managers of the Exhibition.

THE UNITED STATES.

NEW YORK, April 16.

The men who have been on strike at the Fall River Mills are returning to work.

Engagements have been made for the shipment of nearly $3,000,000 in specie next Saturday.

THE QUEEN AND THE NATION.

Secretary Sir William Vernon Harcourt presents his compliments to the Editor of *The Times*, and, by command of the Queen, forwards the enclosed letter from Her Majesty for publication.

Whitehall, April 16.

"WINDSOR CASTLE, April 14, 1884.

"I have on several previous occasions given personal expression to my deep sense of the loving sympathy and loyalty of my subjects in all parts of my Empire. I wish, therefore, in my present grievous bereavement, to thank them most warmly for the very gratifying manner in which they have shown, not only their sympathy with me, and my dear, so deeply afflicted daughter-in-law, and my other children, but also their high appreciation of my beloved son's great qualities of head and heart, and of the loss he is to the country and to me.

"The affectionate sympathy of my loyal people, which has never failed me in weal or woe, is very soothing to my heart. Though much shaken and sorely afflicted by the many sorrows and trials which have fallen upon me during these past years, I will not lose courage, and with the help of Him who has never forsaken me will strive to labour on, for the sake of my children and for the good of the country I love so well, as long as I can.

"My dear daughter-in-law, the Duchess of Albany, who bears her terrible misfortune with the most admirable, touching, and unmurmuring resignation to the will of God, is also deeply gratified by the universal sympathy and kind feeling evinced towards her.

"I would wish, in conclusion, to express my gratitude to all other countries for their sympathy, above all to the neighbouring one, where my beloved son breathed his last, and for the great respect and kindness shown on that mournful occasion.

"VICTORIA R. & I."

NAVAL AND MILITARY INTELLIGENCE.

It is understood that on General Sir T. M. Steele surrendering the command of the Forces in Ireland next year he will be succeeded by General Prince Edward of Saxe-Weimer, who retires from the command of the Southern District at the end of the month.

The Tyne, troopship, which is on her way to Suakin from Malta with fresh crews for the recommissioning of the Briton and Ranger, is expected to return to Portsmouth on the 18th prox., after calling at the Mediterranean ports and Plymouth.

Her Majesty's troopship Crocodile left Port Said yesterday for Portsmouth.

The following appointments were made at the Admiralty yesterday :—John A. Robertson, staff-surgeon, to the Liffey, vice Conway ; John W. Davis, staff-surgeon, to the Heroine, vice Robertson ; Theodore J. Preston, surgeon, to Chatham Dockyard, vice Turgg ; James W. Watson, engineer, to the Jackal, vice M'Carthy ; and Charles Dawe, engineer, to the Asia, additional, for the Snake, vice Williams.

THE MILITIA.

Of the 172 regiments of Militia to be called out for training in the United Kingdom this year, over 80 will go into camp for the full period of 27 days. The preliminary training for 56 days of the recruits has now begun in the case of 69 regiments in great Great Britain and of 23 in Ireland. Only five corps are already out for regimental training, the principal part of this work being as usual reserved for the summer months. In Great Britain the total number of corps out will be 127—viz., 21 brigades of Artillery, three corps of Engineers, and 103 battalions of Infantry ; and in Ireland, 45—viz., 14 brigades of Artillery and 31 battalions of infantry. With the exception of four regiments, all the regimental trainings will be for 27 days. The exceptions are the Durham Artillery, who go to Dover for 34 days in June ; the Anglesey Engineers, 42 days ; the Hampshire Engineers, 56 days ; and the Monmouthshire Engineers, 41 days. Eight corps will proceed to Aldershot, and among the other camping places are Shorncliffe, Altcar, St. Anne's on Sea, Southport, Hounslow-heath, Leigh, Lanark Muir, the Curragh, Wicklow, Londonderry, Omagh, and Armagh. One brigade of Artillery, the Clare, will train at Portsmouth.

THE YEOMANRY CAVALRY.

The Secretary of State for War has approved of the undermentioned 39 regiments of Yeomanry Cavalry in Great Britain, numbering in all about 12,000 sabres, being called out for their annual training this year on the dates and at the places indicated :—Ayrshire, June 18 to 24, at Ayr ; Berks, May 19 to 26, at Newbury ; Buckinghamshire (Royal Bucks), May 15 to 24, at Buckingham ; Cheshire (Earl of Chester's), June 3 to 9, at Chester ; Denbighshire Hussars, May 31 to June 6, at Denbigh ; Derbyshire, May 5 to 13, at Derby ; 1st Royal Devon, May 7 to 14, at Teignmouth ; Royal North Devon Hussars, May 29 to June 5, at Barnstaple ; Dorset (Queen's Own), May 17 to 24, at Weymouth ; Royal Gloucestershire Hussars, May 15 to 22, at Cheltenham ; Hants, May 31 to June 7, at Winchester ; Herts, May 9 to 16, at Watford ; Royal East Kent (Duke of Connaught's Own) Mounted Rifles, May 15 to 22, at Margate ; West Kent (Queen's Own), May 17 to 24, at Gravesend ; Lanarkshire, June 11 to 20, at Lanark ; Lanarkshire (Queen's Own), June 19 to 28, at Hamilton ; Duke of Lancaster's Own, June 20 to 26, at Lancaster ; Lancashire Hussars, May 14 to 21, at Southport ; Leicestershire (Prince Albert's Own), April 28 to May 2, at Leicester ; East Lothian, July 9 to 15, at Dunbar ; Northumberland Hussars, August 1 to 8, at Newcastle-on-Tyne ; Southern Nottinghamshire, April 29 to May 8, at Nottingham ; Nottinghamshire (Sherwood Rangers), April 29 to May 6, at [illegible] ; Queen's Own Oxfordshire Hussars, May 2 to 9, at Banbury ; Pembroke, June 19 to 26, at Haverfordwest ; Shropshire, May 12 to 17, at Shrewsbury ; West Somerset, May 17 to 24, at Taunton ; Queen's Own Staffordshire, June 12 to 18, at Lichfield ; Loyal Suffolk Hussars, May 15 to 22, at Bury St. Edmunds ; Warwickshire, May 8 to 15, at Warwick ; Westmoreland and Cumberland, May 16 to 22, at Penrith ; Royal Wiltshire (Prince of Wales's Own), May 13 to 20, at Salisbury ; Yorkshire Hussars (Princess of Wales's Own), May 6 to 11, at York ; 1st West York, April 19 to 25, at Doncaster ; 2d West York, July 28 to August 3, at Harrogate.

The Middlesex, Montgomeryshire, North Somerset, and Queen's Own Worcestershire will train in the autumn ; the dates are not yet fixed.

Mr. Bright.—Mr. Bright has not yet been able to leave town for Bournemouth, in consequence of the inclemency of the weather. He is progressing, however, steadily.

Sir Michael Costa.—It was stated in Brighton last evening that no change had taken place in Sir Michael Costa's condition.

The Swiss Salvationists and their Persecutors.—According to an account which appears in the *Indépendant Bernois*, writes a correspondent, the scenes that lately took place at Montalchez (described in *The Times* of April 10) have had their counterpart at Neuveville (on the Lake of Neuchatel). On the evening of Saturday week a meeting of Salvationists held there was attacked by a band of ruffians, who broke the windows and *jalousies*, and forced their way into the room where the Salvationists were assembled and turned them out. On the Sunday an open-air meeting, held on a mountain in the neighbourhood, was attacked and dispersed, the worshippers being chased into the town, stoned, and beaten with sticks ; several of them were badly hurt. Almost at the same time a still more deplorable scene was enacted at Evilard, a village in the neighbourhood of Neuveville. A meeting held in a private house, and which ought, therefore in any circumstances, to have been inviolate, was invaded by a mob of half-drunken men, who committed the most disgraceful excesses. The house was bombarded with stones, the windows broken, the door forced, and the inmates beaten. One of the preachers was seized, laid on the ground, and an attempt made, which fortunately did not succeed, to force open his mouth and pour filthy water down his throat. In the end it was necessary to send to Bienne for a number of gendarmes to put down the disturbance, which did not finally cease until 1 o'clock the following morning. The victims belonged exclusively to the neighbourhood. There were no strangers among them.

He found Frank Power useful. He put the correspondent of *The Times*, old soldier of twenty-six, in charge of the paddle boats on the Nile that went on expeditions of reconnaissance and raiding for cattle and grain. He found Power even more useful in putting over to the British public the state of affairs in Khartoum and Gordon's view of what should be done, and in putting pressure on the Government to send relief or to get out. Dateline Khartoum, 17 April 1884, *The Times* carried this dispatch from Our Correspondent: 'Again, if the Government has decided to do nothing, would it not be better to say so to the townspeople, instead of persuading them to hold out day after day, and then to jeopardize their chances eventually with the rebels?' The wording is Frank Power's but the argument is Gordon's.

When Gordon could not make peace with the Mahdi, he fell back on the policy of finding an acceptable alternative native leader for Sudan. His choice fell on Zebehr Pasha who had previously been a successful military commander in Sudan. Unfortunately Zebehr was a notorious slave-trader, and his appointment would have shocked liberal opinion in Britain if it had leaked before it was a *fait accompli*. Gordon mistook the politicians' delay in replying to him as opposition to his plans, and finally losing patience, decided to make use of Power to press his views and demands. On 3 March Power sent a famous dispatch:

It is now admitted that Zebehr Pasha is the only man connected with the Sudan who is endowed with the ability and firmness necessary to head any government here. It is out of the question that General Gordon would leave Khartoum without first having formed a government which would in some measure stem the fearful anarchy that must eventually sweep over the Sudan. The arrival of Zebehr Pasha would draw over to his side the bands of rebels which are now scattered over the Sudan and his great knowledge of the tribes fits him more than any other man to take the place of the Egyptian Government. He would, of course, come here under certain stringent conditions. General Gordon has foreseen this ever since he left Cairo.

Right General Gordon, the moment before his assassination, January 1885. The painting is by G. W. Joy (City Art Gallery, Leeds).

Uproar and outrage back home. Power's message destroyed any hope of getting Zebehr's appointment through Parliament, and sealed the fate of Khartoum.

Gladstone, who did not want to shed blood in an imperialist adventure, preferred to treat Power's dispatches from the doomed city as sensationalism. He said in Parliament that it was farcical to treat Power's dispatches in *The Times* as 'virtually equivalent to an official declaration of policy conveying the mature conviction of General Gordon'. *The Times* defended its man in a leader:

Our Correspondent is one of the three Englishmen in Khartoum, General Gordon and Colonel Stewart being the two others, and it is a matter of moral certainty that his telegrams, even when he does not distinctly allege General Gordon's authority for his statements, represent the opinion of all three.

Gordon could not as Governor General state openly the desperate situation of Khartoum in case it caused panic. He had to keep a stiff upper lip. But he used Power to tell Britain the truth. The Prime Minister preferred not to listen.

On 1 April Power in Khartoum, Roland at Roncesvalles, blew a last blast on that dread horn: 'We are daily expecting British troops. We cannot bring ourselves to believe that we are about to be abandoned by the Government. Our existence depends on England.' They heard the trumpet in Printing House Square: 'If General Gordon be abandoned because he has not accomplished an impossible task, England will hold the Ministers of the Crown responsible for his life, and will exact the strict discharge of every fraction of that responsibility'.

By the end of August the telephone wires were cut. Gordon decided that Colonel Stewart and Frank Power should leave by river while it was still possible, to tell the world of the plight of Khartoum. On 10 September they sailed down the Nile on the paddle steamer *Abbas*, escorted by two large steamers. At Berber they sent the escort back. Between Berber and Merowe the *Abbas* struck a rock, and left Power and Stewart to continue the desperate journey in a small boat. A sheikh offered them camels to reach Merowe, where a troop of Bedouins under the command of Kitchener was encamped. The end of the story is told by a survivor:

Suleiman Wad Gam, being asked for camels, said that he would provide them, and invited Colonel Stewart and the two Consuls (Power and Herbin) to the house of a blind man, named Fakrietman, telling them to come unarmed, lest the people should be frightened. The camels were not given us. We all went unarmed, except Colonel Stewart, who had a small revolver in his belt. Presently I saw Suleiman come out and make a sign to the people standing about the village, armed with swords and spears. These immediately divided into two parties, one running to the house of the blind man, the other to where the rest of Colonel Stewart's party were assembled. I was with the latter. When the natives charged, we threw ourselves into the river. The natives fired and killed many of us, and others were drowned. I swam over to the left bank. The bodies were thrown into the river.

On 26 January 1885, two days before relief arrived, Khartoum fell and Gordon was slain. The Queen granted a pension of £50 a year to each of Power's sisters. Power's private letters were edited and published by his brother. They add vivid detail to his dispatches in *The Times* about a tragedy of Victorian imperialism that stirred the world and brought down a government.

The last reports filed by Frank Power, before he was killed at the age of twenty-four, pleading with the Government, through the columns of THE TIMES, to take some decisive action in Sudan.
17 APRIL 1884

Parnell: the most spectacular mistake

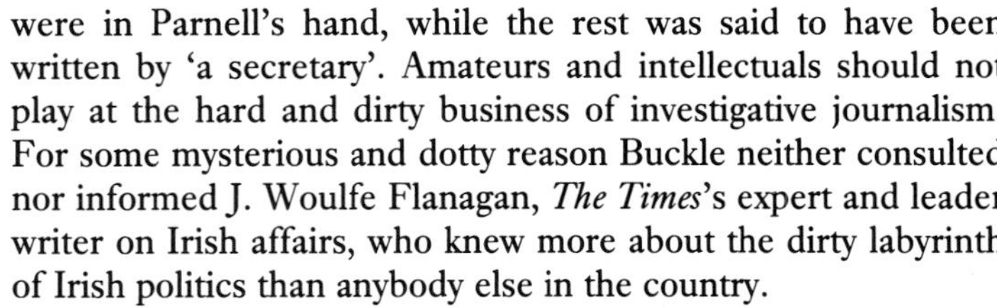

Daily journalism is a high-risk business. The haste to break the news before the opposition means that mistakes are inevitable. Even *The Times* has been known to nod. And when it nods, it nods Homerically.

The Parnell case was the most spectacular mistake *The Times* ever made. It destroyed the newspaper's reputation for infallibility. It cost a fortune and started the financial difficulties that eventually led to the sale of *The Times* to Northcliffe in 1908. It marked the final transition from the newspaper's radical beginnings to the camp of the conservatives: the heart of *The Times* no longer beat left of centre. It is a skeleton in the cupboard whose bones are still dusted down and rattled by the paper's detractors. The story reads more like a popular thriller than history.

In April 1886 Edward Houston, a chancer of a Dublin journalist, aged 23, called at *The Times* with a remarkable proposition. The editor, recently appointed, was George Earle Buckle, a brilliant scholar of Winchester and New College, but only just 30, and inexperienced. Houston said he could sell to *The Times* letters that implicated Parnell, the leader of the Irish parliamentary group in the Commons, in the Phoenix Park murders of 1882.

Houston refused to divulge his source for fear, he said, of assassination by the 'Invincibles', the terrorist gang responsible for the murders. In fact his source was Richard Pigott, proprietor of a shady Irish nationalist paper, and a notorious rascal: apart from being a newspaper proprietor he was a blackmailer, a writer of anonymous letters, a pornographer and an accomplished forger. Houston had already offered copies of the letters to W. T. Stead, editor of the *Pall Mall Gazette*, and a veteran connoisseur of scandalous scoops. Stead had refused to touch them.

Buckle was less prudent. He examined the letters; so did John Cameron MacDonald, the manager, and John Walter III, the proprietor. They came to the remarkable conclusion that they were genuine. Their belief was reinforced when they obtained Parnell's signature by advertising in the Personal Column for the autographs of famous men, including Parnell.

A more prudent or more cynical man than Buckle might have wondered why only the words 'Yours very truly' and the signature were in Parnell's hand, while the rest was said to have been written by 'a secretary'. Amateurs and intellectuals should not play at the hard and dirty business of investigative journalism. For some mysterious and dotty reason Buckle neither consulted nor informed J. Woulfe Flanagan, *The Times*'s expert and leader writer on Irish affairs, who knew more about the dirty labyrinth of Irish politics than anybody else in the country.

To add weight to its sensational 'scoop' *The Times* supported its publication of the Parnell letters with a series headed 'Parnellism and Crime'. When it reproduced the letters, it showed the importance that it attached to the story by making use for the first time of double-column headlines.

In the House of Commons Parnell described the letters as 'a villainous and barefaced forgery'. But many, including the Prime Minister, Lord Salisbury, could not believe that *The Times* was wrong. He accused Mr Gladstone of associating with 'allies tainted with the strong presumption of conniving at assassination'. As John Morley observed: 'They put their trust in the most serious, the most powerful, the most responsible newspaper in the world; greatest in resources, in authority, in universal renown'.

The Times challenged Parnell to sue. For a long time he made no move. But in 1888 a related libel action brought matters to a head and the Government agreed to set up a Special Commission, composed of three judges, to investigate all the allegations in the series of articles called 'Parnellism and Crime'.

The Times management made a poor showing at the inquiry. MacDonald, the manager, ageing and demoralized, left the impression that *The Times* was managed by a nincompoop. The handwriting expert was prevented from giving evidence by the absence of photographic copies of necessary documents. And the egregious Pigott was taken to pieces under cross-examination by Sir Charles Russell. In a dramatic coup he was trapped into showing that he himself made spelling mistakes that occurred in the letters.

John Morley describes the scene: 'The merciless hunt of an abject fellow-creature through the doublings and windings of a thousand lies. The breath of the hounds was on him and he could bear the chase no longer.' 'It was all very funny', wrote a more merciful observer; 'but I could not help recalling Becky Sharp's "it is easy to be virtuous on 5,000 pounds a year".'

The case collapsed. Pigott fled to Madrid, having quite characteristically made two qualified and contradictory confessions before he left. When the police caught up with him there, he blew out his brains.

The Times withdrew the letters unconditionally, but not the general allegations against Parnellism made in the articles. The Commission ruled that all the letters were forgeries, and exonerated Parnell from any part in the Phoenix Park murders. An Irish nationalist put the boot in to the solemn men who ran *The Times*:

> These men, with the salaries of the rich in their pockets and the smiles of London Society as their rewards, have been carrying on a deliberately planned system of infamous allegation against political opponents who have been striving to redeem the sad misfortunes of their country, in efforts to bring to an end a strife of centuries' duration between neighbouring nations.

The Commission sat for 128 days; more than 450 witnesses were examined; one counsel spoke for twelve days. The report, published in February 1890, filled more than 7,000 folio pages. The result for *The Times* was disastrous. The Commission cost the company over £200,000. But, even more expensive, the public belief in the paper's infallibility was shattered, and its trust in the paper's authority was weakened, temporarily at least.

Top The murder of Lord Cavendish and Mr Burke in Phoenix Park, Dublin, 1882.

Above The Tenniel cartoon, in PUNCH 1889, of THE TIMES's apology for publication of the Piggot letters. This parodies George Cruikshank's caricature of George IV as a repentant sinner draped in a sheet, from Hone's lampoon, THE QUEEN'S MATRIMONIAL LADDER, 1820.

Below Parnell in court.

One of the infamous TIMES articles on 'Parnellism and Crime', along with a facsimile of one of the letters alleged to incriminate Parnell in the Phoenix Park murders.
18 APRIL 1887

creditable to that party. The measure being rejected the Plan of Campaign was started in Ireland. It is not a combination to enable tenants to obtain a reasonable reduction, but it is a combination to enable tenants to withhold the whole rent of their landlord—just to accept absolutely and at their own discretion their own terms or to withhold the whole rent whether able to pay or not. It was not necessary for most men, Englishmen or Scotchmen, to be told by a Court of law that such a plan was an illegal plan. I think we had most of us arrived at that conclusion before it was arrived at by a Court of justice. But what is the action taken towards this Plan of Campaign by the Home Rule party? Mr. Gladstone himself has not permitted himself to say more about it than that he considers it to be a consequence of the action of the Government. Mr. John Morley has told us that however illegal, however unpatriotic the Plan of Campaign may be, in his opinion it is not more illegal or more unpatriotic than the conduct of certain landlords to exact their full rents without fulfilling their full duty. Sir William Harcourt has condemned it with his tongue in his cheek. He has said "It is a most illegal, most violent and illegal proceeding, and I object to violent and illegal proceedings (laughter); and so was Hampden's refusal to pay ship money, so was the throwing of the tea into Boston harbour," says Sir William Harcourt; "that was an illegal and improper proceeding, and I condemn it." (Laughter.) So Sir William Harcourt gave to it a sign of approval which is now extended by most of us to those proceedings to which he has referred. It is my opinion that this attitude of the leaders of the Liberal party is another discreditable incident which attaches to it. Mr. Goschen has spoken of the closure as being invented by a Liberal Government. Well, the responsibility of the closure was placed by the Liberal Government in the hands of the Chair, surrounded, however, with restrictions which made its operation almost impracticable, and the House of Commons in its present Session has undertaken to convert it from an impracticable into a practicable rule of procedure. (Cheers.) That initiative has been transferred from the Speaker to the leader of the House of Commons, and the initiative of the Speaker has been converted into a veto—in the opinion of most people not an increase but a diminution of responsibility. (Cheers.) But on the first occasion on which the Speaker has exercised that responsibility by refusing the veto in opposition to the closure, the leaders of the Liberal party thought it consistent with their duty, by ostentatiously leaving the House, to mark their sense of the want of impartiality which was exercised by him. The Criminal Law Amendment Bill has been introduced. Mr. Dillon immediately announced his intention, if the Irish people were ready to follow him, to lead them in armed insurrection. I am not aware that a single word has been uttered of condemnation, or even of deprecation, of that declaration by Mr. Dillon. Mr. Labouchere is an active member of the present Liberal party. He frequently takes part in the meetings of the party. He was one of the organizers of a meeting in Hyde Park, which has received the blessing of Mr. Gladstone himself. (Laughter.) Mr. Labouchere tells the people of England that rather than allow this Bill to pass they should resort to fighting in the streets. (Cries of "Shame.") He has told us in the columns of his paper that if he were in Russia he would be a Nihilist, and he has told us that if he were an Irishman and this Bill passed he would make war upon this country by such means as have always been open to oppressed nationalities. ("Shame.") These are the avowed, the published sentiments of one who is at present an influential member of the Liberal party. I think that I have said enough to show that the Liberal party as it exists at present has been greatly changed (hear, hear), and changed for the worse. ("Hear, hear," and cheers.) Evil communications have corrupted good manners. (Laughter and cheers.) I am not going to assume the part of a Pharisee, or to talk about the demoralization of party; but what I am bound to do is to speak a word about men and things as they appear to me; and I am bound to say that I do see some things—many things—in the present action and conduct of the Liberal party which do inspire me who behold them with alarm which is not limited to matters immediately connected with Ireland and the question of Home Rule. I see, or I think I see, in the conduct of the present Liberal party the toleration of doctrines which are doctrines of revolution, not of reform. ("Hear, hear," and cheers.) I see that an impatience of suffering, an anxiety to remove the evils which are among us, which have always been among us, is leading too many among them to look in the direction of those Socialistic or Communistic changes which have hitherto been condemned by the whole Liberal party, no less on account of their fallacy and on account of the ruin and the mischief which they would cause, than their morality. I see a toleration of those doctrines. I see also a toleration of violence—violence when used by people in the position of the Irish people, who can give any excuse for any grievance as a pretext for such a grievance. I see an indifference to law as law, if the laws ever appear to conflict with the theories or the dreams of the moment. Seeing all these things, I also see a disinclination to refuse to accept the decision of political questions expressed through the constitutional methods provided by our Constitution, even if it be through the extended franchise that is now enjoyed by the people of the whole country. (Cheers.) I see an inclination to transfer the decision and discussion of such questions from the Senate House to the streets and to public meetings. (Cheers.) I believe that all these things are departures from the former and the better traditions of the Liberal party. (Cheers.) If it be true that these things are to be seen in the present conduct of that party, then the issue, as Mr. Goschen has told you this evening, that is before us is something far wider than the Irish question (hear, hear), important as that question is. It is not a question only of the safety and the security of our fellow subjects in Ireland, dear as we conceive that question to be to the country's honour; it is a question of the maintenance of our system of Parliamentary government in England, and in Scotland, and in Ireland (cheers); and it is a question of the prosperity and, perhaps, even of the very existence of the millions of our fellow subjects (cheers) who depend for their daily bread upon the system of credit and of confidence which alone can be supported by the maintenance of law and of order. These are the issues which are now or may be very soon before us; and it is because it seems to me that the party in its present mood and under its present leaders underrate the gravity of some of the issues that are raised, because it seems to me to be led away from the old traditions of the party, and because the present Government is for the time being the representative of law among us, of order among us, and of the best traditions of our Parliamentary Government, I hold that it is the duty of every good citizen, and of Liberal Unionists above all, to continue to give in whatever way he is able, however humble his powers may be, his support to that Government which at present guides the affairs of this country. (Cheers.)

PRINCIPAL CUNNINGHAM proposed the toast of "The Ladies," which was replied to by Mr. GEORGE GOSCHEN.

Mr. WALTER THORBURN, M.P., gave "The Chairman," and the toast was cordially received. Before the company separated the National Anthem was played by a band in attendance.

THE BUCCLEUCH ENGRAVINGS.

The second portion of the fine collection of prints belonging to the late Duke of Buccleuch is now on view at Messrs. Christie's, and will be sold to-morrow and the following days. Although the interest shown in this part of the sale will not be so general as was the case with the last, where the lovely mezzotints after Sir Joshua Reynolds attracted so much notice, even from the unlearned, it is certain that the competition will be keener and the prices realized for many of the lots far beyond what was paid for the mezzotints. For this portion contains the famous collection of Rembrandt's etchings, the finest private collection in England, and one of the three or four finest in the world. Rembrandt's etchings are not for everybody; the taste for them is an acquired taste. But when acquired it will carry a millionaire to all lengths; will lead him to give six, eight, or twelve hundred guineas—sometimes even more—for a bit of paper seven or eight inches square, provided the print has the two essential qualities of rarity and fineness of impression. It is certain that this form of mania will be exemplified several times next week, for the Duke's collection includes a "first state" of the famous Hundred Guilder print, which was sold in times when prices were lower than they are to-day for over 1,100 guineas; it contains a fine impression of the "Burgomaster Six" (second state); first states of many of the fine Biblical subjects, such as "The Presentation in the Temple" (1,788); and superb examples of such rarities as "the great Coppenol" (2,025), the finest existing impression of the "Sylvius" (2,018), and first states of the "Young Haaring" (2,011), the "John Asselyn" (2,014), and many other of the portraits. The landscapes are equally fine, and the collection of them, as of the beggars and other subject pieces, is nearly complete. What adds to the interest of the collection is its *provenance*, for many of the prints can be traced back to Rembrandt's own day, and perhaps to his own possession. The Duke bought the collection (almost as it stands) from Messrs. Colnaghi some 30 years ago. Messrs. Colnaghi had it from Mr. John Heywood Hawkins, a celebrated collector; and before coming to him many of the prints had belonged to Baron Verstolk, to Wilson, and to Denon. Denon bought them at the sale of Zömer, a contemporary of Rembrandt's, who is believed to have had them from the master himself.

Besides the Rembrandts, the sale will include some fine Dürers, Marc Antonios, Ostades, &c., and a very curious book of portraits, the "Basiliologia," with 228 engravings after the works of the Passes, Delaram, Elstracke, and other old line engravers.

THE COMTE DE PARIS.—The Comte de Paris is among the passengers by Messrs. Donald Currie and Co.'s Royal Mail steamer Pembroke Castle, which left Lisbon at 2 p.m. on Saturday for Plymouth. The Pembroke Castle is expected to arrive at Plymouth early to-morrow morning.

THE LATE MR. NEWDEGATE.—The funeral of the late Right Hon. C. N. Newdegate, who represented North Warwickshire continuously for over 42 years, took place on Saturday, the remains being deposited in the family vault at Harefield, Middlesex. There was a preliminary funeral service at Arbury Hall, the Warwickshire seat of the deceased, on Saturday, and the service was attended by a large number of the tenantry and relatives and friends. On reaching Nuneaton the funeral *cortège* was joined by many gentlemen connected with various public bodies in the town and neighbourhood, and by tradesmen and others. The scene was a most impressive one, the shops being closed and blinds drawn down. Thousands of people had assembled in the street to see the long procession pass on its way to the railway station. The immediate circle of relatives and friends, with the tenantry and others stood bareheaded while the coffin, covered with magnificent wreaths, was removed from the hearse and placed in the train for conveyance to Watford.

PARNELLISM AND CRIME.

MR. PARNELL AND THE PHŒNIX-PARK MURDERS.

In concluding our series of articles on "Parnellism and Crime" we intimated that, besides the damning facts which we there recorded, unpublished evidence existed which would bind still closer the links between the "constitutional" chiefs and the contrivers of murder and outrage. In view of the unblushing denials of Mr. Sexton and Mr. Healy on Friday night, we do not think it right to withhold any longer from public knowledge the fact that we possess and have had in our custody for some time documentary evidence which has a most serious bearing on the Parnellite conspiracy, and which, after a most careful and minute scrutiny, is, we are satisfied, quite authentic. We produce one document in facsimile to-day by a process the accuracy of which cannot be impugned, and we invite Mr. Parnell to explain how his signature has become attached to such a letter.

It is requisite to point out that the body of the manuscript is apparently not in Mr. Parnell's handwriting, but the signature and the "Yours very truly" unquestionably are so; and if any member of Parliament doubts the fact, he can easily satisfy himself on the matter by comparing the handwriting with that of Mr. Parnell in the book containing the signatures of members when they first take their seats in the House of Commons.

We particularly direct attention to the erasure in the manuscript as undesigned evidence of authenticity, and should any questions be raised as to the body of the letter being in another handwriting, we shall be prepared to adduce proof that this peculiarity is quite consistent with its genuine character.

The body of the letter occupies the whole of the first page of an ordinary sheet of stout white note-paper, leaving no room in the same page for the signature, which is placed on the fourth page near the top right-hand corner. It was an obvious precaution to sign upon the back instead of upon the second page, so that the half-sheet might, if necessary, be torn off, and the letter disclaimed.

It is right and necessary to explain that the "Dear Sir" is believed to be Egan and that the letter was addressed to him in order to pacify the wrath of his subordinate instruments in the Phœnix Park murders—then (on May 15, nine days after the tragedy) still at large and undetected. The anxiety of the writer to keep his address unknown will be noted, and is curious in connexion with a belief prevailing at the time that Mr. Parnell was so impressed by the danger he had incurred by denouncing the assassinations as to have applied for the protection of the police on the plea that his life was in peril.

Mr. Parnell in this letter describes Lord F. Cavendish's death as an "accident," but he "cannot refuse to admit that Burke got no more than his deserts." That is his language to the "Inner Circle," but before Parliament, yielding to what he considered "the only course," or as it stands amended in the text "our best policy," he spoke on Monday, May 8, two days after the murders, as follows:—

Mr. PARNELL said he wished to be permitted to express, on the part of his hon. friends, on his own part, and, he believed, on the part of every Irishman in whatever portion of the world he might live, their most unqualified detestation of the horrible crime which had been committed in Ireland. (Hear, hear.) He could not now refer to the steps which the Government proposed to take. He did not deny that it might be impossible for the Government to resist taking measures such as had been mentioned by the Prime Minister. But he wished to express his belief that the crime had been committed by men who absolutely detested the cause with which he had been associated (hear, hear), and who had devised that crime and carried it out as the deadliest blow in their power against his hopes and the new course which the Government had resolved upon.

Particular attention may now be drawn to the wicked suggestion here made that the Phœnix Park crimes had been the work of the enemies of Parnellism and the League, "devised and carried out as the deadliest blow in their power against his hopes and the new course which the Government had resolved upon." Has that infamous accusation ever been recalled or even qualified, and to what benevolent construction of motives is a public man now entitled who made such a charge at the very time when he was smoothing down the "anger" of Egan's "friends" for denouncing them as murderers in Parliament?

To the country at large Mr. Parnell, Mr. Dillon, and Mr. Davitt addressed on the day after the murder the following manifesto:—

To the People of Ireland.—On the eve of what seemed a bright future for our country, that evil destiny which has apparently pursued us for centuries has struck another blow at our hopes, which cannot be exaggerated in its disastrous consequences. In this hour of sorrowful gloom we venture to give an expression of our profoundest sympathy with the people of Ireland in the calamity that has befallen our cause, through a horrible deed, and to those who had determined at the last hour that a policy of conciliation should supplant that of terrorism and national distrust. We earnestly hope that the attitude and action of the whole Irish people will show the world that assassination such as has startled us almost to the abandonment of hope for our country's future is deeply and religiously abhorrent to their every feeling and instinct. We appeal to you to show by every manner of expression that amidst universal feeling of horror which this assassination has excited. No people feels so intense a detestation of its atrocity, or so deep a sympathy for those whose hearts must be seared by it, as the nation upon whose prospects and reviving hopes it may entail consequences more ruinous than have fallen to the lot of unhappy Ireland during the present generation. We feel that no act has ever been perpetrated in our country during the exciting struggles for social and political rights of the past 50 years that has so stained the name of hospitable Ireland as this cowardly and unprovoked assassination of a friendly stranger, and that until the murderers of Lord Frederick Cavendish and Mr. Burke are brought to justice that stain will sully our country's name.

(Signed) CHARLES S. PARNELL.
JOHN DILLON.
MICHAEL DAVITT.

Here again the peculiar language employed will be noted. It is "the evil destiny which has apparently pursued us for centuries" which "has struck another blow at our hopes," &c.

Only a fortnight ago, on the first reading of the Crimes Bill, Mr. Parnell took occasion to refer to this manifesto in the House of Commons in the following remarkable terms:—

I do not believe you would ever have broken up that [the Invincible] conspiracy if it had not been for the denunciation of Mr. Michael Davitt, the member for East Mayo, and myself, issued after the crime in the Phœnix Park. It was the denunciation that shook that conspiracy and enabled the officers of the law in Ireland, by means of their secret inquiries and other agencies, to get under it and finally to break it up.

An interval of more than half a year elapsed between the Phœnix Park murders and the discovery of the perpetrators. In that interval, while "the stain on the name of hospitable Ireland," in spite of "the appeal" made in the manifesto, still adhered to it, Ireland's uncrowned king actually addressed to his trusted subordinate, the Treasurer of the Land League, Patrick Egan, the following extraordinary letter which tells its own significant tale.

In the facsimile which we place before our readers the paper lies open, the first page being to the right, and the fourth to the left.

Yours very truly
Chas. S. Parnell

15/5/82

Dear Sir,

I am not surprised at your friend's anger but he and you should know that to denounce the murders was the only course open to us. To do that promptly was plainly ~~[illegible]~~ ~~[illegible]~~ our best policy.

But you can tell him and all others concerned that though I regret the accident of Lord F. Cavendish's death I cannot refuse to admit that Burke got no more than his deserts.

You are at liberty to show him, this and others whom you can trust also, but let not my address be known. He can write to House of Commons.

MR. CHAMBERLAIN AT INVERNESS.

On Saturday evening Mr Chamberlain, M.P., accompanied by Mr. Jesse Collings, M.P., arrived at Inverness to begin his tour of investigation among the Highland crofters. The right hon. gentleman was met on the platform at the station by about a thousand people, the great bulk of whom indulged in continuous cheering while he walked to the station hotel. In the dining hall of this establishment about a hundred Unionists had assembled to present Mr. Chamberlain with an address, and he received a magnificent reception. The chair was occupied by Mr. Gavin Tait, chairman of the Unionist Association, and Mr. MacAndrew, Provost of the burgh. Provost MacAndrew introduced the deputation charged with the presentation of the address, which expressed deep sense and appreciation of the invaluable service rendered by Mr Chamberlain to the preservation of the unity and integrity of the United Kingdom of Great Britain and Ireland. It also expressed the cordial sympathy of the Liberal Unionists of Inverness with Mr. Chamberlain in the ordeal through which he had already passed in his advocacy of the cause.

Mr. CHAMBERLAIN, who was received with loud cheers, the audience rising, and waving hats and handkerchiefs, said:—Mr. Provost, Mr. Gavin Tait, and Gentlemen,—I thank you very sincerely for the very kindly welcome you have once more given me to your northern capital, and for the address with which you have just presented me and the assurance of support and sympathy it contains. (Cheers.) I was very proud to have conferred upon me the freedom of your Royal Burgh. I am prouder still of the qualification with which you invested me, now that I know that the majority of my fellow burgesses and fellow citizens share with me in their determination to preserve the integrity of the Empire. (Cheers.) I cannot help, as a Liberal Unionist, congratulating you upon the way in which you are at the present moment represented. (Cheers.) Mr. Finlay has made a great reputation for himself in the House of Commons, and the Liberal Unionist party has not produced any man who has shown greater force and logical argument in reference to this question than Mr. Finlay. (Loud cheers.) Mr. Gavin Tait has referred to the somewhat painful position in which we find ourselves. We are separated from old friends and colleagues; but, worse even than that, we are disappointed in our hopes and expectations. I cannot help contrasting the situation now with the situation as it existed when I last visited your town. We were then full of high hopes and expectations, we were on the eve of the election of a reformed Parliament, and we had the high expectation that the new Parliament would be able to give immediate attention to the pressing grievances of the nation. Now all that we had hoped, all that we had expected, has been laid aside and put upon the shelf. We are told that "Ireland blocks the way." I have again and again protested against that expression. It is not Ireland that blocks the way; the state of things in Ireland now is not different from what it has been for the better half of this century. I may almost say for several centuries before it. (Cheers.) We have had discontent and disturbances in Ireland, and never were discontent and disturbances more serious than when Ireland enjoyed an independent Parliament. (Cheers.) But on previous occasions the state of that country was not allowed to prevent the British Parliament doing its proper work and attending to the grievances of the British people. (Cheers.) I protest against its being supposed that there is anything very exceptional in the present situation which ought to make it difficult now. What prevents the British Parliament from doing its duty at the present time is not the Irish question; but the action of a section of the Liberal party. (Hear, hear.) There is another very serious feature in the situation to which sufficient attention has not been given—it is a state of things which has brought about demonstrations in politics and the degradation of our great assembly, so that its influence and usefulness are impaired and its character and dignity is lowered every day. (Cheers.) I have been reading as I came along, and I have no doubt you have seen it in the newspapers, a report of what occurred last night in the House of Commons. There was a scene of a character which is absolutely new to our great assembly (hear, hear), and which if allowed to continue will bring it down to a level lower than has been reached by any other representative assembly. (Cheers.) What happened last night? Colonel Saunderson, an Irish member, accused some of the Irish Nationalist members, and accused them truly ("Hear, hear," and cheers), of keeping company with men who are known to be murderers, or men who have connived at murder. (Cheers.) He accused them of that boldly and frankly in the face of the House of Commons, and thereupon several members flung an accusation—a violent and brutal accusation—at him across the floor of the House, and one member who is distinguished for that sort of thing became so violent that he had to be suspended. (Cheers.) Well, gentlemen, I say I think it is high time that the opinion of the people of Great Britain was made known about these scenes, and about the men who make them (cheers), and that the representatives of the people were informed that their constituents will not forgive any man who gives his sanction or encouragement to any of these scenes. (Cheers.) The violence of the scenes in the House of Commons and the conduct of particular members is due to the encouragement, the tacit but sometimes active encouragement, that they sometimes receive from members and even from leaders of the Liberal party. (Cheers.) Well, I say, I think you will fully agree with me that the state of matters we have to contemplate is not very satisfactory. How has it been brought about? What is the cause of the differences which have brought us to this pass? I should say that the cause is to be found, first, in the method in which the policy has been forced upon upon us, and, secondly, in the character of the policy itself. I say it is to be found in the method in which this policy was introduced, because the method is absolutely unparalleled in the history of this country. (Cheers.) Never before was it attempted to settle a great question—an extraordinary and almost revolutionary proposal—without discussion in the country and without a full knowledge of it. Take, for instance, the great case of the repeal of the corn laws. These laws were repealed almost suddenly by Sir Robert Peel under the pressure of famine, but the question of the repeal of the corn laws had been discussed beforehand for years and years in every town and county and village and hamlet in the three kingdoms; and before the repeal took place it was perfectly known that the vast majority of the people of the United Kingdom were in favour of it. (Cheers.) Take, again, the cause of education. Our national system of education was only established by the Imperial Parliament after years—after a generation—of discussion upon it. Or take the oldest and greatest of the reforms with which we are acquainted—the reform of the franchise. For nearly 20 years we had been discussing the importance, the necessity, and propriety of extending to the counties the franchise which had already been enjoyed by the boroughs. And it was not until all the arguments for and against the proposals were fully known to every man of intelligence in the kingdom that Mr. Gladstone found himself able or thought himself justified in bringing forward proposals in the House of Commons in order to give legislative effect to these reforms. (Cheers.) Why, I ask, was there a change in connexion with this question? Why was it sought at a moment's notice to force a revolution upon us? Why were we not taken into the confidence of our great leader? (Cheers.) You will recollect that so suddenly was this great matter brought forward that within a few months before the Bill was introduced into the House it was bruited about that there was some change in Mr. Gladstone's policy. The *Daily News*, the recognized organ of the Liberal party, completely contradicted the statement as an infamous libel—an invention of the Tories (laughter)—but within a few months of the time that this infamous libel was written it proved to be true and this great change had been effected. We know now what was in the mind of our late leader, and, as I say, without discussion and consultation we were precipitated into a controversy the evils of which I have attempted to describe. (Cheers.) Then, in the second place, the cause of our differences is to be found in the nature of the plan which was submitted to us. We were prepared—I think we all of us were prepared—to make large changes in connexion with the government of Ireland. (Cheers.) I myself, at all events, was prepared for the most extensive development of local liberties that was consistent with the interests of the Empire. (Cheers.) I stood as a Home Ruler upon that footing 12 years ago, when for the first time I solicited the suffrages of a constituency, and I have never wavered in my opinion that it is desirable to increase the local responsibility of Irishmen and that such a development of our local institutions would be an education of which they stand very much in need. (Cheers.) But it never entered into my conception—I could not have believed it possible—that an English statesman, the leader of the party to which I myself belonged, and whom I loyally followed for so many years, would be found prepared to press a measure for granting to Ireland a Parliament which, if not independent, was certain to become independent in a very short time afterwards. (Cheers.) That was not a proposal for Home Rule; it was a proposal for separation. (Cheers.) I have never denied that our opponents are perfectly sincere in saying that they do not intend separation. What I say is that I cannot understand how they can be so blind as not to see that, although they do not intend it, they are paving the way for separation by the policy they have put before the country. (Cheers.) As long as this is the policy of any section of the Liberal party or of its leaders, I say reunion is impossible. (Cheers.) But I am still not altogether despairing of reconciliation, though I confess that I have small hopes from the present leaders of the majority of the Liberal party. We have made every possible advance to them, we went further perhaps than was prudent in our endeavour to bring about some common ground of agreement, but they have been unable to meet us half way. What it was that prevented them from so meeting us I do not know. But there must have been some influences or engagements or alliances (laughter and cheers) which prevented that happy consummation which I believe they, as well as we, at one time desired. (Hear, hear.) I am persuaded that whatever the leaders may say, and whatever a small and violent section of the party may say, the great majority even of those who supported Mr. Gladstone's Home Rule Bill could not give it their entire and unquestioning support. How is it possible for them to have done so? We know as to almost every man among them that we can confront him with his own utterances a few months ago, which are in entire contradiction to the policy of the Bill. (Cheers.) And even at the last election, when this measure was before the country, there were very many Liberal members who, while promising a general support to Mr. Gladstone, declared that they would not support the Bill unless great amendments were made. (Cheers.) Well, then, here is our hope of union. I have ceased to appeal to the leaders; I have appealed to the more moderate men among the followers. I do not appeal to the extreme men, I do not appeal to the gentlemen who make a burlesque of politics. (Cheers.) I appeal to those who have seriously at heart the interests of their country (cheers), and I ask them—if they do not agree entirely with Mr. Gladstone's Bill, if they admit that amendments in it are necessary before it can be accepted by the country—I ask them now to formulate their own plan (hear, hear), and tell us what plan they have substituted for the plan which we have rejected, in order that we may loyally see whether it might not be possible under this new plan to come to an agreement. (Cheers.) Until they do so I can only say that the situation will remain as at present. (Cheers.) Our duty is clear, and that is—we shall fight out this quarrel even to the bitter end. (Cheers.) Mr. Tait has spoken of the ordeal through which some of us have had to pass. It is a very painful one, and one which no consideration would have induced us to accept but the consideration that the country itself, even its existence, or, at all events, its influence as a Great Power, was at stake. (Cheers.) For such a consideration as this we will not shrink or falter for one moment in our work. Be it for a longer or a shorter period we will continue on the lines we have worked out for ourselves, and we will give our consent to no proposal which does not fully and completely assure the union of the three kingdoms, the supremacy of one great Parliament, and the protection of minorities who have placed their confidence in our honour. (Cheers.) Until these conditions are secured we will not abate one jot of heart or hope, but steer straight forward. (Prolonged cheers.)

Mr. JESSE COLLINGS, on the call of the Chairman, also briefly addressed the meeting, which terminated with cheers for Mr. Chamberlain.

The right hon. gentleman dined with Provost Macandrew yesterday, and met a few prominent citizens. This morning he proceeds to Dingwall, and will drive through one of the crofting districts in his progress. At Dingwall he is to receive the freedom of the burgh, and will afterwards address a public meeting.

THE COLONIAL CONFERENCE.

A meeting of the Conference was held at the Colonial Office on Saturday, at 11 o'clock, under the presidency of Sir Henry Holland, when the following representatives were present:—Newfoundland, Mr. Robert Thorburn (Premier); New South Wales, Sir Patrick Jennings, K.C.M.G. (late Premier); Tasmania, Mr. Adye-Douglas (Agent-General), and Mr. John Stockell Dodds (late Attorney-General); Cape of Good Hope, Mr. Thomas Upington (Attorney-General); South Australia, Mr. John William Downer (Premier), and Sir Arthur Blyth, K.C.M.G., C.B. (Agent-General); New Zealand, Sir Francis Dillon Bell, K.C.M.G., C.B. (Agent-General); Victoria, Mr. Alfred Deakin (Chief Secretary); Queensland, Sir James Garrick, K.C.M.G. (Agent-General); Western Australia, Mr. John Forrest, C.M.G. (Commissioner of Crown Lands), and Mr. Septimus Burt; Natal, Mr. John Robinson.

The Earl of Onslow, Under-Secretary of State for the Colonies; Mr. Jenkyns, Parliamentary draftsman; Mr. F. F. Piggott, barrister-at-law; and Mr. Ilbert, C.I.E., were also present; and Mr. W. A. Baillie-Hamilton, secretary to the Conference.

A further discussion took place upon the questions of the enforcement of colonial judgments, bankruptcy proceedings, and winding-up of companies, and draft proposals for legislation in that direction were considered and settled.

The Conference will meet again at 11 o'clock to-day for the further discussion of the question of Australasian naval defence, when the First Lord of the Admiralty, with Admiral Sir Arthur Hood, K.C.B., and Vice-Admiral Sir A. Hoskins, K.C.B., will be present as before.

FOREIGN BRONZE COINS.

The Postmaster-General has issued the following notice:—

On and after Monday next, the 18th of April, and until Tuesday the 31st of May next, the above-mentioned coins will be received at all Post-offices in exchange for cash or stamps, at the following rates—viz., ten-centime pieces, 13 to the shilling; or five-centime pieces, 26 to the shilling.

No exchange to be made for a less sum than sixpence, the equivalent of which will be six and a half ten-centime pieces.

By command of the Postmaster-General.
General Post Office, April 16, 1887.

NOTICES.

PARNELLISM and CRIME—The Third Edition of a Reprint of the Articles under this head, recently published in The Times, is now ready, price One Penny.

A CANADIAN TOUR—A Reprint of the Letters from The Times Special Correspondent under this title is now ready, price 6d. Applications for copies to be addressed to the Publisher.

THE TIMES PARLIAMENTARY DEBATES, arranged in a convenient form for binding, will be issued every Monday during the sitting of Parliament. Price One Shilling, or 25s. per annum, post free. Annual subscription for bound volumes—half bound in morocco leather, £3 10s.; cloth, lettered, £2 10s. Vols. I., II., III., and IV. of the Commons and Vol. I. of the Lords now ready.

THE TIMES WEEKLY EDITION, price 2d., is issued every Friday morning, containing all that is of special or lasting interest in the editions of The Times of that and the five previous days, and printed in a form suitable for binding as an annual volume, or for postal transmission abroad.

THE MAIL, a reproduction of the substance of The Times, with the Latest Intelligence, appears on Monday, Wednesday, and Friday in each week. Price 2d.

Advertisers are requested not to send stamps. Post-office orders to be made payable to Mr. GEORGE EDWARD WRIGHT, at the Chief Office.

News Agents in the country can be supplied with papers from this Office, carriage paid to their railway stations, on condition of their selling at 3d. per copy.

The Times is sold for 3d. per copy at all railway bookstalls in England and Wales. Persons who cannot obtain it at that price are requested to communicate with the Publisher.

The Times will be forwarded by Inland Post to subscribers desirous of receiving it through that channel on payment of £1 quarterly in advance. Subscribers residing within the London Postal District have *The Times* delivered to them by the first post. Applications should be addressed only to the Publisher, at *The Times* Office.

TO CORRESPONDENTS.

No notice can be taken of anonymous communications. Whatever is intended for insertion must be authenticated by the name and address of the writer, not necessarily for publication, but as a guarantee of good faith.

We cannot undertake to return rejected communications.

Jack the Ripper: no gruesome detail spared

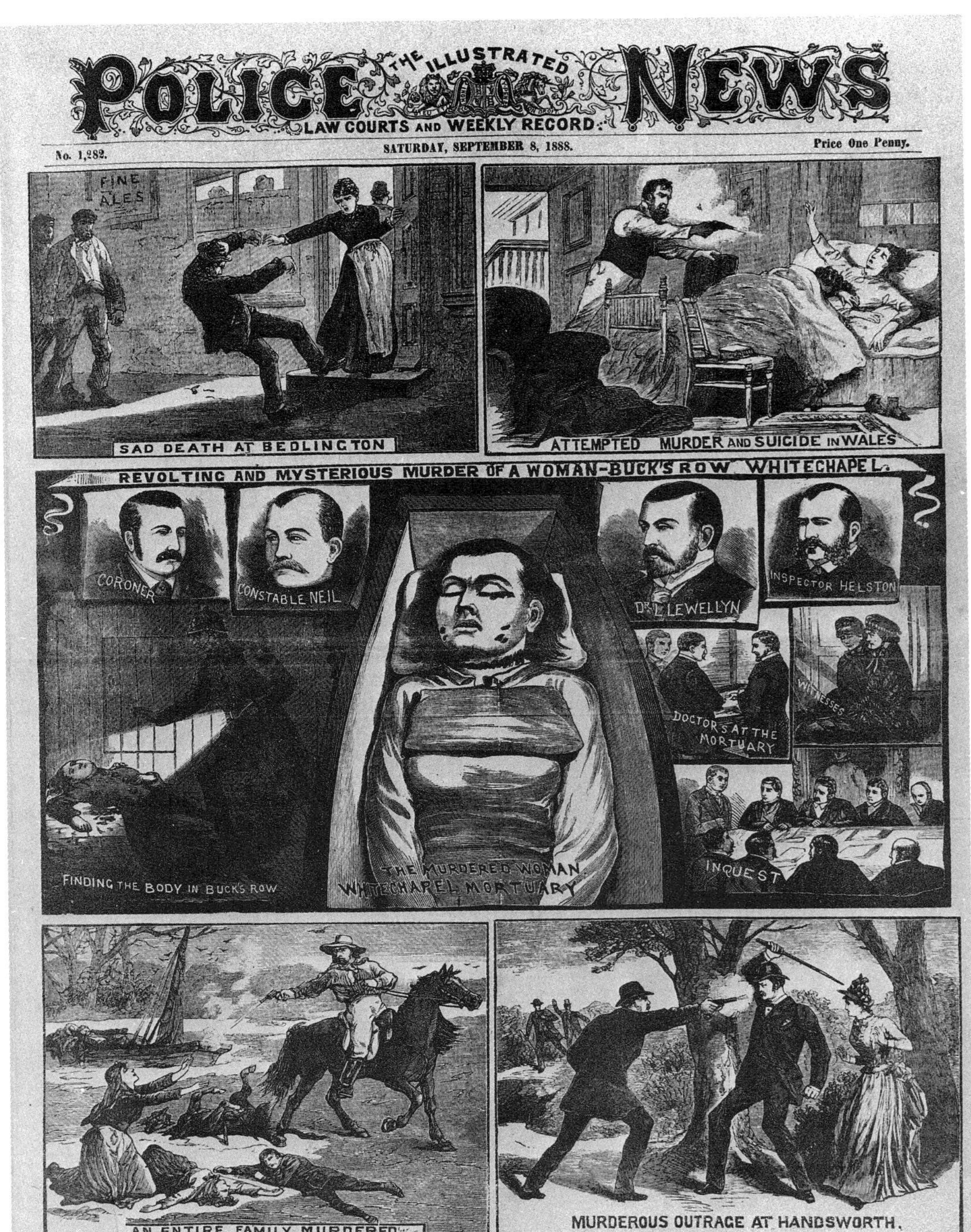

THE ILLUSTRATED POLICE NEWS
LAW COURTS AND WEEKLY RECORD.
No. 1,282. SATURDAY, SEPTEMBER 8, 1888. Price One Penny.

SAD DEATH AT BEDLINGTON

ATTEMPTED MURDER AND SUICIDE IN WALES

REVOLTING AND MYSTERIOUS MURDER OF A WOMAN—BUCK'S ROW WHITECHAPEL.

CORONER

CONSTABLE NEIL

DR. LLEWELLYN

INSPECTOR HELSTON

DOCTORS AT THE MORTUARY

INQUEST

FINDING THE BODY IN BUCK'S ROW

THE MURDERED WOMAN WHITECHAPEL MORTUARY

AN ENTIRE FAMILY MURDERED

MURDEROUS OUTRAGE AT HANDSWORTH.

Above The front page of THE ILLUSTRATED POLICE NEWS, a popular penny weekly of sensational crime reports. The middle section depicts the scene of the latest Ripper murder at Bucks Row, Whitechapel.

Below An engraving from THE ILLUSTRATED LONDON NEWS, 13 October 1888. Members of the local Vigilance Committee on the look-out for suspicious characters, at the time when the murders were 'painfully exciting the public mind'.

The Times has made and unmade many ministries. But it is an error to think of it as purely a political paper, thundering its prescriptions and denunciations from Printing House Square. As it happens, it took its famous sobriquet 'The Thunderer' not from its campaign for parliamentary reform or against the management of the Crimean War, but from a sensational scandal in high society.

In 1830 rumour was busy, first with the estrangement between a lord and his lady, and next with an illustrious duke by whom the lady was consoled. One Sunday afternoon Lord Graves was found with his throat cut, dead, with two razors beside the candles. In the absence of any letter, nosy gossips were divided on whether it was murder or suicide. They were disappointed when a short inquest was held early in the morning in order to avoid publicity for the relatives. *The Times* wrote a trenchant first leader arguing that such a hurried procedure was unwise in such a notorious case, and insisting that in any matter of life and death, inquiry could never be too careful, frank or open.

Opposition journals attacked *The Times* for being sensational and giving unnecessary pain. *The Times* defended itself. It said that it had received many letters charging it with deserting the popular cause in order to favour the powerful. 'When the Coroner's inquest, which should have elicited the truth, was curtailed of its fair proportions – then we thundered out that article in Tuesday's paper which caused so great a sensation.' It must be admitted that the sensation was chiefly journalistic. But rival newspapers picked up the notion of thundering to tease *The Times*. And the nickname of Thunderer caught on.

During the middle years of the nineteenth century John Thadeus Delane established *The Times* as the best mirror of events and as an unrivalled barometer of national feeling. He was fascinated by the great movements of politics and diplomacy. But he did not take a one-sided or high-minded view of the news and the responsibilities of *The Times*. Some readers liked to turn from perusal of the parliamentary debates (or even skip them altogether) to read about dishevelled lives that led to the divorce or criminal courts. Delane appreciated their interest and saw that it was well served. 'That was a good murder you had last week', he wrote to George Dasent, his assistant editor. Sex, money, violence and death are news, particularly for the British, and *The Times* has recorded crime – burglary, fraud, mugging, arson and murder – faithfully, often in great and gory detail.

Of all the good and juicy murders that have enlivened the pages of *The Times* and made the flesh of its readers creep with macabre pleasure, none can compare with its coverage of Jack the Ripper. Between August and November 1888, while the Ripper went about his business in London's East End, *The Times* published many thousands of words about the murders: on the false arrests, rewards offered, reported captures, ludicrous theories, and, inevitably, hundreds of letters from readers. There were even charts and plans for the simple-minded.

The reporters spared no gruesome detail. The report of the murder and mutilation of Mary Ann Kelly (opposite) ran to more than five thousand words. High-minded and fastidious readers have always complained about the vulgarity of the press. But much of the news *is* vulgar and sensational. Most news is bad news. If the Flying Scotsman left on time, had an uneventful journey and arrived in Princes Street on time, that was not news. If it crashed killing a hundred passengers, that was news, because everybody wanted to read about it. From the treatment by *The Times* and the letters it received, it is evident that its readers, the middle and upper classes, wanted to know every possible detail about Jack the Ripper, as they read the paper in their clubs and Victorian mansions. Let us not sneer at them. The same relish for horror and scandal is alive and flourishes today.

The Victorians may have justified their relish in the Ripper by the high moral tone of the paper's leading articles. Such events could not go unnoticed even at that august level. No fewer than six editorials appeared during the Ripper months. One of them took the literary approach: 'The mind travels back to De Quincey for an equal display of scientific delight in the details of butchery; or Edgar Allan Poe's *Murders in the Rue Morgue* recur in the endeavour to conjure up some parallel for this murderer's brutish savagery.' The leading article of 19 September was The Thunderer at its most Olympian:

> To detect the crimes and punish them is the first duty. But it is not the only duty. We have to consider how far our social organization is responsible for the preparation of the soil and atmosphere in which such crimes are produced. Social fellowship is, after all, the true remedy for social disease. The existence of an evil which produces such hideous results is an intolerable social reproach.

THE TIMES's ghoulishly detailed account of the discovery of one of Jack the Ripper's victims.
10 NOVEMBER 1888

LATEST INTELLIGENCE.

(From our Correspondents.)

THE SIEGE OF SUAKIN.

SUAKIN, Nov. 9.

Last night after dark about two hundred of the black battalion went out in four different parties to try and spike the enemy's guns, but failed. They were vigorously attacked by the enemy, but showed great courage, and had a hand-to-hand fight. Our losses included five killed and two wounded.

This morning large numbers of the enemy were seen in the direction of Hasheen and Handoub. There are in the trenches, it is believed, not less than 1,200 of them, with about 1,500 in the bush. Their loss last night was heavy. Two dead bodies of Arabs were brought in by the blacks.

General Grenfell will leave to-morrow morning for Suez direct.

*CAIRO, Nov. 9.

General Grenfell, who is now at Suakin, is in favour of a policy of passive resistance at that place.

THE EAST AFRICAN QUESTION.

BERLIN, Nov. 9.

The substance of my despatch last night, with a summary of a leading article in *The Times* referring to it have been telegraphed back to Berlin this evening in what appears to be so inaccurate a form as to call for a few words of supplementary explanation. What I meant to convey was that the commercial companies in German East Africa are at the present moment seriously considering the question of organizing a military or police force of their own to enter their service and make their authority respected, and are also pondering the feasibility, *faute de mieux*, of recruiting such a gendarmery, as it might be called, among some of the most suitable races of India, such as the Sikhs or the Mahrattas. This statement is the result of direct and authentic information.

There are two chief companies which are devoting themselves to the commercial exploitation of German East Africa—namely, the East African Company proper and the Plantation Company, the latter being in a manner the subtenant of the former, and I ought to have said that it is the Plantation Company which is primarily concerning itself with the idea of recruiting and embodying a gendarmery force of the kind referred to. Indeed, an agent of the company left for Zanzibar this very night, with the intention of crossing over to Bombay, should circumstances seem to demand it, and making local inquiries as to the feasibility of procuring the sort of men he wants. But it must not be assumed that the German Government itself has any direct finger in this pie. It seems to be the opinion of the Government that the task of repairing the East African Company's shattered position on the coast itself and in the interior is primarily the company's own affair; and it will meanwhile confine itself to its maritime operations, which are only calculated to help the several companies indirectly by striking a blow at their greatest enemies—the slave-traders. But if the companies are not to be annihilated altogether they must of necessity have the protection of some organized and self-supporting force of troops, police, or gendarmery—call it what you will—so as to render them independent of unwillingness, remissness, or even downright military impotence on the part of their natural protector and sponsor, the Sultan of Zanzibar.

To some minds here in Berlin the necessity for the creation of such a force appears to be all the greater, in view of the results that are not unlikely to accrue from the blockade of the coast, it being argued that a blockade in this case cannot differ in its effects very much from a bombardment, and that it would be wise to avoid the error committed by the English at Alexandria when they opened their guns on the town without at once landing a force to provide for its subsequent safety from the rebellious Egyptians. The analogy is not perfect, but there are certainly features of resemblance in the two cases. For these and other reasons, therefore, the German companies in East Africa are beginning to think very seriously of the expediency of organizing a protecting force of their own, and it is then but natural that they should look to India for the satisfaction, if possible, of their wants, seeing that Zanzibar itself, by frequent drafts on its resources of men, both of the porter and police kind, is no longer able to supply the wants of travellers and traders. One of the main obstacles, I believe, which impede the starting of the Emin Pasha expedition is the present hopelessness of procuring Panganis and others at Zanzibar, and the employment of European troops on such an enterprise is out of the question.

Whether or not the companies, with the Plantation Company leading the way, will make a serious effort to recruit men sufficient for their purposes remains to be seen, but in any case I repeat they are seriously considering the practicability of doing so, and meanwhile the Press friendly to their aims is beginning to discuss the subject in their interest. For example, the *Cologne Gazette* writes:—

"In the present altered circumstances the primary care of the East African Company is to recruit a colonial force of troops, such as will enable it to acquire the mastery over its territory which the Sultan does not seem able to assure to it. And this task will be all the easier of achievement seeing that on the one hand it can be powerfully supported on the coast by our German vessels of war, while on the other it will be greatly seconded by the common action of the Powers in repressing the slave-trade. It is true that the present troubles meanwhile hinder the company from buckling to the performance of this task; but they will not induce it to abandon its aim."

Similarly, an ex-Prussian officer at Zanzibar writes in detail to the *Kreuz Zeitung* on the "organization of a gendarmery in East Africa," and altogether there are manifold signs that some force of this sort, whether of native, Indian, or mixed elements, will now soon be called into existence as a defensive servant of the East African Company, and not as the military instrument of the German Government. There is one sentence in the letter of the Prussian officer at Zanzibar which deserves to be quoted:—

"The sudden abolition of slavery," says the writer, "would be a disadvantage to us, and a blessing to no one. On the other hand, the chasing of slave dhows, as it is practised by English vessels on our coast, is wholly to our interest, as it tends to counteract the depopulation of the country."

*ZANZIBAR, Nov. 9.

Her Majesty's ship Agamemnon is expected to arrive here on Tuesday next, and the international blockade is expected to begin forthwith.

THE EUROPEAN SITUATION.

VIENNA, Nov. 9.

About a month ago the *Correspondance de l'Est* published a letter from Rome, which stated that the Italian Government looked upon the Sultan as the enemy of the Triple Alliance. This was another way of hinting to the Sultan that he must look upon the Triple Alliance as inimical to him, and the letter therefore caused a great stir at the Porte. To-day the *Correspondance* prints a letter from Paris, which tries to attenuate the effect of the first, by declaring it to be notorious that Prince Bismarck regards Abdul Hamid with the fullest confidence; but the letter goes on to suggest that such is not the opinion of the Italian Government, although Signor Crispi, feeling that he had made a false step, in which Prince Bismarck would not follow him, was trying to conceal his real sentiments.

There is a Russo-French intrigue in all this, which ought to be divulged. When the first letter appeared in the *Correspondance de l'Est*, the *Oriental Express*, a newspaper which takes its inspiration from M. Hitrovo, the noted Russian Minister at Bucharest, attributed the authorship to Baron Blanc, the Italian Ambassador at Constantinople, whose diplomatic successes have rendered him particularly obnoxious to the Russo-French clique. The charge was a monstrous one, and evidently intended to bring Baron Blanc under the Sultan's displeasure, and to secure his recall. But on the 12th of October the *Levant Herald* denounced this manœuvre, and upon this the Russian and French Ambassadors complained of the journal, and demanded that it should be suspended. As the article in the *Levant Herald* had been submitted to official censorship before publication, and had received the *imprimatur*, the newspaper could not with any justice be suspended; but after the Porte had hesitated six days M. de Nelidoff went the length of saying that he should ask for his passports if the *Levant Herald* were not suspended; and suspended it accordingly was.

The sight of the Ambassador of a French Republic, governed by a Radical Ministry, busying himself to gag an English newspaper, has its humorous aspects; but there is nothing comical in the intrigue which was got up to ruin Baron Blanc's character. Fortunately, the Sultan appears now to have become aware of the truth, which is simply this—that the letter in the *Correspondance de l'Est* emanated from those who have most interest in maligning the objects of the Triple Alliance, and as M. Hitrovo was in Vienna at the time of its publication, it would not be at all surprising if that ingenious gentleman himself had been the inspirer of it. For the future it must be hoped that the Sultan will be proof against the arts by which M. de Nelidoff and Count Montebello are constantly endeavouring to work on his fears and suspicions. It is not forgotten in diplomatic circles how, on the 10th of April last, when Herr von Radovitz, the German Ambassador, was going to present his letters of credence to the Sultan on reappointment, Count Montebello sent M. Jarozinsky, one of the secretaries of his Embassy, to the Palace, to inform the Sultan that 8,000 Italian troops were going to spend the summer at Suez. This fiction greatly upset the Sultan, but it was simply a device to injure Baron Blanc and Sir William White in His Majesty's eyes; and, in fact, Count Montebello's diplomacy seems for ever directed to this object.

The Porte has sent no circular note to the Powers touching the rumours of a Russo-Turkish alliance, but a few days ago instructions were despatched to the Ottoman Ambassadors at Vienna, Berlin, London, and Rome, requesting them to say that the Sultan wished to maintain friendly relations with all the Great Powers, without entering into alliances. These declarations have since been made in Vienna by Sadoullah Pasha.

In acknowledging the decoration of the Osmanieh, in brilliants, bestowed upon him by the Sultan, M. de Giers has written to His Majesty saying that he hopes to see Russia and Turkey "enter into relations based on mutual confidence."

Prince Augustus of Coburg, an elder brother of Prince Ferdinand of Bulgaria, has been in Constantinople, and now proceeds to Sofia on a visit of some weeks.

*PARIS, Nov. 9.

The *Matin* to-day publishes a letter from M. Waddington, French Ambassador in London, declaring that, in contradiction to the assertions made by the journal on the 5th inst., he has never received any communication, either in writing or verbally, from M. Obroutcheff, whom he has not known during his tenure of office.

"There has never," adds M. Waddington, "been any question of an alliance between France and Russia," and he (the French Ambassador), has had, therefore, no cause to ask advice in London, or to address a communication to Berlin on the subject. If overtures of the kind described by the *Matin* had been made, he would have asked the advice of his colleagues, not of foreigners.

SERVIA.

VIENNA, Nov. 9.

Queen Natalie's appeals to the Œcumenical Patriarch of Constantinople and to the Synods of Greece and Russia against "the arbitrary and uncanonical" sentence of divorce pronounced against her by Archbishop Theodosius have been unofficially answered from Constantinople and Athens. The reply of both Patriarchs has been that they could not offer an opinion on the decrees of an independent Church. The Russian Synod, on the contrary, seems disposed to draw up a declaration against "the uncanonical nature of the sentence;" but this declaration will be in the form of a reply to the ex-Queen, and not a protest addressed to the Head of the Servian Church, as Queen Natalie desired.

*BELGRADE, Nov. 9.

At the opening of the Commission for the Revision of the Constitution, King Milan declared that this step was decided upon solely in the interests of the Fatherland and of his dynasty, so that when the Crown Prince ascended the Throne, and this, he added, might be soon, his Royal Highness would find a more favourable position than his father did.

FRANCE.

PARIS, Nov. 9.

The Revision Committee decided to-day by six votes to five that the new Constitution, when framed by a Constituent Assembly, should be submitted to a *plébiscite*. The Committee is thus playing blindly into General Boulanger's hands; but even should the Chamber prove equally infatuated, the Senate may be relied upon to veto the scheme.

The Prado case opened to-day with the evidence of Dr. Brouardel, who examined the body of Marie Aguétant after the murder. The wound in the neck, he said, had the appearance of having been made by pulling back the head, and cutting the throat from left to right. Death must have soon ensued; at most there would be from eight to ten minutes between the infliction of the wound and death. The throat once cut, the victim could utter no cry.

The servant of Aguétant described what she saw on the night of the crime. She could not identify Prado as the murderer.

The evidence thus far given in the Chambige case confirms the outline forwarded last night. The victim's husband, M. Grille, has testified that the compromising letters are forgeries. A policeman states that on listening at a keyhole he heard Chambige say to his (prisoner's) brother-in-law:—"I loved her; she did not love me: I have killed her."

RUSSIA.

ST. PETERSBURG, Nov. 9.

The condition of the Russian railways will, it is stated, be considered by a special commission. I understand that the resignation of Admiral Possiet, Minister of Public Roads, has been accepted, and that his successor will probably be General Annenkoff, of Transcaspian railway fame.

TURKEY.

CONSTANTINOPLE, Nov. 9.

General Valtinos and his suite, despatched by the King of the Hellenes to present the Sultan with an autograph letter and the insignia of the Order of the Redeemer, arrived here this morning. The General was received on landing with the customary honours. The members of the mission, who are to reside as guests of His Imperial Majesty at the Dolmabagtche Palace, will be admitted to an official audience to-morrow, and entertained at a Court dinner in the evening.

*Through Reuter's Agency.

FOREIGN AND COLONIAL NEWS.

We have received the following telegrams through Reuter's Agency:—

GREAT BATTLE IN THE SOUDAN.

TRIPOLI, Nov. 9.

Intelligence has been received here *viâ* Benghazi of a great battle having been fought in the Wadai country, which lies west of Darfur, between the followers of the Mahdi and the Sultan of Wadai's people. The Mahdists, to the number of 70,000, commanded by Gianuh, attacked the town of Wadai, but were repulsed with the loss of 3,000 killed.

The Mahdists, however, returned to the attack and captured Wadai, the Sultan flying to Mount Ghiri.

DEATH OF PROFESSOR BAMBERGER.

VIENNA, Nov. 9.

Professor Bamberger, the eminent physician, died in this city this morning.

ITALY.

ROME, Nov. 9.

A fire broke out to-day in a sulphur mine near Casteltermini, and four of the miners have been burnt to death. The flames had not been extinguished this evening.

NEW RUSSIAN CONVERSION LOAN.

BERLIN, Nov. 9.

The new Russian Four per Cent. loan, which is understood on the Berlin Bourse to have been contracted with an Anglo-French Syndicate, is intended for the conversion of the Five per Cent. loan of 1877 into Four per Cent. bonds.

COMMERCIAL INTELLIGENCE.

HONGKONG, Nov. 9.

Manchester goods dull; 8¼lb. shirtings, $225; 16-24 Taylor's twist, $94½. Tea.—Total export to date, 81,000,000lb. Exchange on London (four months' bank bills), 3s. 1⅝d.

NEW YORK, Nov. 9.

Cotton and Grain Statistics.

	1888.	Corresponding period last year.
	Bales.	Bales.
The week's receipts of cotton at all United States ports have been ..	271,000	301,000
Week's receipts Atlantic ports ..	147,000	145,000
Week's receipts Gulf ports	124,000	156,000
Week's receipts interior towns ..	157,000	216,000
Total since September 1	1,831,000	2,334,000
Week's exports to Great Britain ..	105,000	89,000
Week's exports to the Continent ..	45,000	104,000
Total since September 1	972,000	1,358,000
Stock at all ports..	650,000	776,000
Stock at interior towns..	260,000	357,000
	Bushels.	Bushels.
The export clearances of wheat from the Atlantic seaboard for Europe during the past week amounted to	10,000	670,000
The export clearances of Indian corn for Europe during the past week amounted to	550,000	450,000

THE MAILS.

Messrs. Donald Currie and Co.'s Castle packet Pembroke Castle, with mails and passengers for Cape Colony and Natal, left Dartmouth at 4 p.m. yesterday for Cape Town, calling at Lisbon and Las Palmas. Telegrams for conveyance to the South African colonies by this steamer should reach Lisbon not later that 10 a.m. on Monday, or Las Palmas not later than midnight on Wednesday next.

The Orient Line steamer Orient, from London, arrived at Port Said at 7 p.m. on Thursday, and sailed for Australia at 5 a.m. yesterday.

The National Line steamer The Queen, from Liverpool, arrived at Queenstown at 2 20 p.m. yesterday, and having embarked passengers, despatches, &c., proceeded for New York at 3 p.m.; all well.

The Anchor Line steamer Ethiopia, from Glasgow, arrived at Moville at 7 30 a.m. yesterday, embarked mails and passengers, and proceeded for New York at 2 15 p.m.

The Hall Line steamers Rufford Hall, from Kurrachee for Marseilles and Liverpool, and Aston Hall, from Bombay for Liverpool, left Port Said yesterday afternoon.

(From Lloyd's.)

ADEN, Nov. 9.—The Messageries Maritimes steamer Peiho, homeward bound, arrived here to-day.

BALTIMORE, Nov. 9.—The Norddeutscher Lloyd steamer Main, from Bremen, arrived here yesterday.

GIBRALTAR, Nov. 8.—The Norddeutscher Lloyd steamer Salier, from Bremen, passed here to-day.

GRAVESEND, Nov. 9.—The Harrison Line steamer Electrician, from Calcutta for Tilbury Dock, passed here yesterday. Messrs. J. T. Rennie and Son's steamer Dabulamanzi, for Port Natal, left here yesterday. The Clan Line steamer Clan Lamont, from Madras for Tilbury Dock; the Ocean Company's steamer Dardanus, from Shanghai for Albert Dock; the steamer Hildegarde, from Buenos Ayres for London Dock; and the steamer Chelydra, from New York for Millwall Dock, passed here to-day. The Orient Line steamer Lusitania, for Sydney, and the National Line steamer France, for New York, left here to-day.

KINGSTON, Nov. 7.—The West India and Pacific Company's steamer Texan left here to-day.

LISBON, Nov. 8.—Messrs. Lamport and Holt's steamer Laplace, from Liverpool for Brazil, arrived here to-day.

LIVERPOOL, Nov. 9.—The Pacific Steam Navigation Company's steamer Aconcagua, from Valparaiso, and the Liverpool and Maranham Company's steamer Brunswick, from Maranham, arrived in the Mersey to-day.

MALTA, Nov. 9.—The P. and O. steamer Massilia, from London for Sydney, has arrived here.

MARSEILLES, Nov. 8.—The P. and O. steamer Kaisar-i-Hind, from London for Naples, Aden, and Bombay, left here at 4 30 p.m to-day.

MONTEVIDEO, Nov. 8.—The Pacific Steam Navigation Company's steamer Patagonia, from Liverpool for Chili, arrived here to-day.

MONTREAL, Nov. 8.—The Donaldson Line steamer Concordia, for Glasgow, left here to-day.

NEW ORLEANS, Nov. 8.—The West India and Pacific Company's steamer Venezuelan arrived here to-day.

NEW YORK, Nov. 8.—The Wilson Line steamer Lydian Monarch, for Hull, left here to-day. Messrs. Lamport and Holt's steamer Horrox, from Rio Janeiro, arrived here on the 6th inst. Nov. 9.—The National Line steamer Egypt, from Liverpool, has arrived here.

PARA, Nov. 8.—The Booth Line steamer Lanfranc, from Lisbon, arrived here to-day.

RIO JANEIRO, Nov. 7.—The Shaw, Savill, and Albion Company's steamer Doric, from New Zealand, arrived here to-day, and left with passengers and the homeward New Zealand mails for London.

ST. VINCENT, Nov. 8.—The Houston Line steamer Hesperides, from Liverpool for River Plate, left here to-day. Nov. 9.—Messrs. Lamport and Holt's steamers Caxton, from River Plate and Brazil for Liverpool, and Pascal, from London for River Plate, arrived here to-day.

SHANGHAI, Nov. 8.—The P. and O. steamer Ravenna, from London, and the Norddeutscher Lloyd steamer Sachsen, from Bremen, have arrived here.

SUEZ CANAL, Nov. 9.—Messrs. Money Wigram and Son's steamer Kent, from Sydney for London, and the Messageries Maritimes steamer Ava, from Yokohama for Marseilles, have arrived at Suez. The P. and O. steamer Peshawur, from London for Bombay, left Suez this morning.

Outrage in Ireland.—A farmer named Myles M'Keown was found late on Thursday night in a field about half a mile from Newry with his skull fractured and several wounds on his face. He was unconscious when found, and now lies in the same state. The doctors believe that his recovery is impossible. No arrests have been made in connexion with the affair, nor is there at present any clue as to who his assailants may have been.

The Constitutional Union.—The annual dinner of the Constitutional Union will take place at the St. James's-hall on Wednesday next, when the Right Hon. E. Stanhope, M.P., will preside. The Lord Advocate for Scotland (Mr. J. P. B. Robertson, Q.C., M.P.) and Colonel Saunderson, M.P., will be among the speakers on the occasion.

The Weights and Measures Bill.—Yesterday Sir Michael Hicks-Beach, at the Board of Trade, received a deputation from the London Master Bakers' Protection Society, upon the clauses in the Weights and Measures Bill relating to the sale of bread. Mr. J. R. Kelly, M.P., and Mr. Whitmore, M.P., accompanied the deputation. Sir Michael Hicks-Beach, in reply, said that the principle of selling bread by weight ought to be maintained, and he wished to make it effective. The increase in the practice of delivering bread was an argument in favour of maintaining the obligation to carry weights and scales. If the existing law was not enforced in that respect, he would endeavour to see that the law should be enforced. He would, however, be prepared to consider any clauses submitted to him which would relieve bakers of the obligation of weighing bread when the purchaser did not require him to do so. He should not press clauses 28 and 29 of the Bill in their present form, and would be glad to consider any suggested amendments. He had received a suggested clause from the National Association of the trade, and he hoped the London Society would be able to agree with them upon some such clause. The question of considering the whole law with a view to amendment and consolidation was a very difficult one; it would be his duty to consider that matter, but he could not hold out any hope of being able to deal with it at any early date.

The Parcel Post.—Last night's *London Gazette* contains a Treasury warrant for the establishment of a parcel post with New Zealand. The rates of postage are the same as for parcels to the Australian colonies, viz.:—1s. 6d. for the first 2lb., and 9d. for each additional pound. It is understood that the first parcel mail for New Zealand will be despatched by the steamer which leaves the Thames on Thursday morning and is due to reach its destination about Christmas Day.

ANOTHER WHITECHAPEL MURDER.

During the early hours of yesterday morning another murder of a most revolting and fiendish character took place in Spitalfields. This is the seventh which has occurred in this immediate neighbourhood, and the character of the mutilations leaves very little doubt that the murderer in this instance is the same person who has committed the previous ones, with which the public are fully acquainted.

The scene of this last crime is at No. 26, Dorset-street, Spitalfields, which is about 200 yards distant from 35, Hanbury-street, where the unfortunate woman, Mary Ann Nicholls, was so foully murdered. Although the victim, whose name is Mary Ann (or Mary Jane) Kelly, resides at the above number, the entrance to the room she occupied is up a narrow court, in which are some half-a-dozen houses, and which is known as Miller's-court; it is entirely separated from the other portion of the house, and has an entrance leading into the court. The room is known by the title of No. 13 The house is rented by John M'Carthy, who keeps a small general shop at No. 27, Dorset-street, and the whole of the rooms are let out to tenants of a very poor class. As an instance of the poverty of the neighbourhood, it may be mentioned that nearly the whole of the houses in this street are common lodging-houses, and the one opposite where this murder was enacted has accommodation for some 300 men, and is fully occupied every night. About 12 months ago Kelly, who was about 24 years of age, and who was considered a good-looking young woman, of fair and fresh-coloured complexion, came to Mr. M'Carthy with a man named Joseph Kelly, who she stated was her husband, and who was a porter employed at the Spitalfields Market. They rented a room on the ground floor, the same in which the poor woman was murdered, at a rental of 4s. a week. It had been noticed that the deceased woman was somewhat addicted to drink, but Mr. M'Carthy denied having any knowledge that she had been leading a loose or immoral life. That this was so, however, there can be no doubt, for about a fortnight ago she had a quarrel with Kelly, and, after blows had been exchanged, the man left the house, or rather room, and did not return. It has since been ascertained that he went to live at Buller's common lodging-house in Bishopsgate-street. Since then the woman has supported herself as best she could, and the police have ascertained that she has been walking the streets. None of these living in the court or at 26, Dorset-street saw anything of the unfortunate creature after about 8 o'clock on Thursday evening, but she was seen in Commercial-street shortly before the closing of the publichouse, and then had the appearance of being the worse for drink. About 1 o'clock yesterday morning a person living in the court opposite to the room occupied by the murdered woman heard her singing the song, "Sweet violets," but this person is unable to say whether any one else was with her at that time. Nothing more was seen or heard of her until her dead body was found.

At a quarter to 11 yesterday morning, as the woman was 35s. in arrears with her rent, Mr. M'Carthy said to a man employed by him in his shop, John Bowyer, "Go to No. 13 (meaning the room occupied by Kelly) and try and get some rent." Bowyer did as he was directed, and on knocking at the door was unable to obtain an answer. He then tried the handle of the door, and found it was locked. On looking through the keyhole he found the key was missing. The left-hand side of the room faced the court, and in it were two large windows. Bowyer, knowing that when the man Kelly and the dead woman had their quarrel a pane of glass in one of the windows was broken, went round to the side in question. He put his hand through the aperture and pulled aside the muslin curtain which covered it. On his looking into the room a shocking sight presented itself. He could see the woman lying on the bed, entirely naked, covered with blood and apparently dead. Without waiting to make a closer examination he ran to his employer, and told him he believed the woman Kelly had been murdered. M'Carthy at once went and looked through the broken window, and, satisfying himself that something was wrong, despatched Bowyer to the Commercial-street Police-station, at the same time enjoining him not to tell any of the neighbours what he had discovered. Inspector Back, H Division, who was in charge of the station at the time, accompanied Bowyer back, and on finding that a murder had been committed at once sent for assistance. Dr. Phillips, the divisional surgeon of police, and Superintendent Arnold were also sent for. During this time the door had not been touched. On the arrival of Superintendent Arnold he caused a telegram to be sent direct to Sir Charles Warren, informing him what had happened.

Mr. Arnold, having satisfied himself that the woman was dead, ordered one of the windows to be entirely removed. A horrible and sickening sight then presented itself. The poor woman lay on her back on the bed, entirely naked. Her throat was cut from ear to ear, right down to the spinal column. The ears and nose had been cut clean off. The breasts had also been cleanly cut off and placed on a table which was by the side of the bed. The stomach and abdomen had been ripped open, while the face was slashed about, so that the features of the poor creature were beyond all recognition. The kidneys and heart had also been removed from the body, and placed on the table by the side of the breasts. The liver had likewise been removed, and laid on the right thigh. The lower portion of the body and the uterus had been cut out, and these appeared to be missing. The thighs had been cut. A more horrible or sickening sight could not be imagined The clothes of the woman were lying by the side of the bed, as though they had been taken off and laid down in the ordinary manner. While this examination was being made a photographer, who, in the meantime, had been sent for, arrived and took photographs of the body, the organs, the room, and its contents. Superintendent Arnold then had the door of the room forced. It was a very poorly furnished apartment, about 12ft. square, there being only an old bedstead, two old tables, and a chair in it. The bedclothes had been turned down, and this was probably done by the murderer after he had cut his victim's throat. There was no appearance of a struggle having taken place, and, although a careful search of the room was made, no knife or instrument of any kind was found. Dr. Phillips, on his arrival, carefully examined the body of the dead woman, and later on again made a second examination in company with Dr. Bond, from Westminster, Dr. Gordon Brown, from the City, Dr. Duke, from Spitalfields, and Dr. Phillips's assistant. Mr. Anderson, the new Commissioner of Police, Detective-Inspectors Reid and Abberline (Scotland-yard), Chief Inspector West, H Division, and other officers were quickly on the spot. After the examination of the body it was placed in a shell, which was put into a van and conveyed to the Shoreditch mortuary to await an inquest.

From inquiries made among the persons living in the houses adjoining the court, and also those residing in rooms in No. 26, it appears clear that no noise of any kind was heard. No suspicious or strange-looking man was seen to enter or leave the murdered woman's room, and up to the present time the occurrence is enveloped in as much mystery as were the previous murders. The man Kelly was quickly found, and his statement ascertained to be correct. After the examination the windows were boarded up, and the door padlocked by direction of the police, who have considerable difficulty in keeping the street clear of persons. Dr. M'Donald, coroner, in whose district the murder has happened, has fixed Monday morning for the opening of the inquest, which will be held at the Shoreditch Town-hall. It was reported that bloodhounds would be laid on to endeavour to trace the murderer, but for some reason this project was not carried out, and, of course, after the streets became thronged with people that would have had no practical result. The street being principally composed of common lodging-houses, persons are walking along it during all hours of the night, so that little notice is taken of any ordinarily attired man. The murderer, therefore, had a good chance of getting away unobserved.

With regard to Kelly's movements just before the murder, a report says that she was seen as usual in the neighbourhood about 10 o'clock on Thursday evening in company with a man, of whom, however, no description can be obtained. She was last seen, as far as can be ascertained, in Commercial-street about half-past 11. She was then alone, and was probably making her way home. It is supposed that she met the murderer in Commercial-street, and he probably induced her to take him home without indulging in more drink. At any rate, nothing was seen of the couple in the neighbouring publichouses, nor in the beerhouse at the corner of Dorset-street. The pair reached Miller's-court about midnight, but they were not seen to enter the house. The street door was closed, but the woman had a latchkey, and, as she must have been fairly sober, she and her companion would have been able to enter the house and reach the woman's room without making a noise. A light was seen shining through the window of the room for some time after the couple must have entered it, and one person asserts positively that the woman was heard singing the refrain of a popular song as late as 1 o'clock yesterday morning, but here again there is a conflict of testimony which the police are even now engaged in endeavouring to reconcile.

The same report, describing the removal of the mutilated body, says at 10 minutes to 4 o'clock a one-horse carrier's cart, with the ordinary tarpaulin cover, was driven into Dorset-street, and halted opposite Miller's-court. From the cart was taken a long shell or coffin, dirty and scratched with constant use. This was taken into the death chamber, and there the remains were temporarily coffined. The news that the body was about to be removed caused a great rush of people from the courts running out of Dorset-street, and there was a determined effort to break the police cordon at the Commercial-street end. The crowd, which pressed round the van, was of the humblest class, but the demeanour of the poor people was all that could be desired. Ragged caps were doffed and slatternly-looking women shed tears as the shell, covered with a ragged-looking cloth, was placed in the van. The remains were taken to the Shoreditch Mortuary, where they will remain until they have been viewed by the coroner's jury.

Mr. John M'Carthy, the owner of the houses in Miller's-court, who keeps a chandler's shop in Dorset-street, has made the following statement as to the murdered woman:—

The victim of this terrible murder was about 23 or 24 years of age, and lived with a coal porter named Kelly, passing as his wife. They, however, quarrelled sometime back and separated. A woman named Harvey slept with her several nights since Kelly separated from her, but she was not with her last night. The deceased's Christian name was Mary Jane, and since her murder I have discovered that she walked the streets in the neighbourhood of Aldgate. Her habits were irregular, and she often came home at night the worse for drink. Her mother lives in Ireland, but in what county I do not know. Deceased used to receive letters from her occasionally. The unfortunate woman had not paid her rent for several weeks; in fact, she owed me 30s. altogether, so this morning about 11 o'clock I sent my man to ask her if she could pay the money. He knocked at the door, but received no answer. Thinking this very strange he looked in at the window, and to his horror he saw the body of Kelly lying on the bed covered with blood. He immediately came back to me, and told me what he had seen. I was, of course, as horrified as he was, and I went with him to the house and looked in at the window. The sight I saw was more ghastly even than I had prepared myself for. On the bed lay the body as my man had told me, while the table was covered with what seemed to me to be lumps of flesh. I said to my man "Go at once to the police-station and fetch some one here." He went off at once and brought back Inspector Back, who looked through the window as we had done. He then despatched a telegram to Superintendent Arnold, but before Superintendent Arnold arrived Inspector Abberline came and gave orders that no one should be allowed to enter or leave the court. The inspector waited a little while and then sent a telegram to Sir Charles Warren to bring the bloodhounds, so as to trace the murderer if possible. So soon as Superintendent Arnold arrived he gave instructions for the door to be burst open. I at once forced the door with a pickaxe, and we entered the room. The sight we saw I cannot drive away from my mind. It looked more like the work of a devil than of a man. The poor woman's body was lying on the bed, undressed. She had been completely disembowelled, and her entrails had been taken out and placed on the table. It was those that I had seen when I looked through the window and took to be lumps of flesh. The woman's nose had been cut off, and her face gashed and mutilated so that she was quite beyond recognition. Both her breasts too had been cut clean away and placed by the side of her liver and other entrails on the table. I had heard a great deal about the Whitechapel murders, but I declare to God I had never expected to see such a sight as this. The body was, of course, covered with blood, and so was the bed. The whole scene is more than I can describe. I hope I may never see such a sight again. It is most extraordinary that nothing should have been heard by the neighbours, as there are people passing backwards and forwards at all hours of the night, but no one heard as much as a scream. A woman heard Kelly singing "Sweet Violets" at 1 o'clock this morning. So up to that time, at all events, she was alive and well. So far as I can ascertain no one saw her take a man into the house with her last night.

A correspondent who last night saw the room in which the murder was committed, says it was a tenement by itself, having formerly been the back parlour of No. 26, Dorset-street. A partition had been erected, cutting it off from the house, and the entrance door opened into Miller's-court. The two windows also faced the court, and, as the body could be seen from the court yesterday morning, it is evident that, unless the murderer perpetrated his crime with the light turned out, any person passing by could have witnessed the deed. The lock of the door was a spring one, and the murderer apparently took the key away with him when he left, as it cannot be found. The more the facts are investigated, the more apparent becomes the cool daring of the murderer. There are six houses in the court besides the tenement occupied by the deceased. The door of Kelly's room is the first on the right-hand side on entering from the street, and the other houses—three on either side—are higher up the passage.

The young woman Harvey, who had slept with the deceased on several occasions has made a statement to the effect that she had been on good terms with the deceased, whose education was much superior to that of most persons in her position of life. Harvey, however, took a room in New-court, off the same street, but remained friendly with the unfortunate woman, who visited her in New-court on Thursday night. After drinking together they parted at half-past 7 o'clock, Kelly going off in the direction of Leman-street, which she was in the habit of frequenting. She was perfectly sober at the time. Harvey never saw her alive afterwards. Joseph Barnett (called in other reports Kelly), an Irishman, at present residing in a common lodginghouse in New-street, Bishopsgate, informed a reporter last evening that he had occupied his present lodgings since Tuesday week. Previously to that he had lived in Miller's-court, Dorset-street for eight or nine months with the murdered woman Mary Jane Kelly. They were very happy and comfortable together until another woman came to sleep in their room, to which he strongly objected. Finally, after the woman had been there two or three nights he quarrelled with the woman whom he called his wife and left her. The next day, however, he returned and gave Kelly money. He called several other days and gave her money when he had it. On Thursday night he visited her between half-past 7 and 8 and told her he was sorry he had no money to give her. He saw nothing more of her. She used occasionally to go to the Elephant and Castle district to visit a friend who was in the same position of life as herself.

Another account gives the following additional details:—Kelly had a little boy, aged about 6 or 7 years living with her, and latterly she had been in narrow straits, so much so that she is reported to have stated to a companion that she would make away with herself as she could not bear to see her boy starving. There are conflicting statements as to when the woman was last seen alive, but that upon which most reliance appears to be placed is that of a young woman, an associate of the deceased, who states that at about half-past 10 o'clock on Thursday night she met the murdered woman at the corner of Dorset-street, who said to her that she had no money and, if she could not get any, would never go out any more but would do away with herself. Soon afterwards they parted, and a man, who is described as respectably dressed, came up and spoke to the murdered woman Kelly and offered her some money. The man then accompanied the woman home to her lodgings, which are on the second floor, and the little boy was removed from the room and taken to a neighbour's house. Nothing more was seen of the woman until yesterday morning, when it is stated the little boy was sent back into the house, and, the report goes, he was sent out subsequently on an errand by the man who was in the house with his mother. There is no direct confirmation of this statement. A tailor named Lewis says he saw Kelly come out about 8 o'clock yesterday morning and go back. Another statement is to the effect that Kelly was seen in a publichouse known as the Ringers, at the corner of Dorset-street and Commercial-street, about 10 o'clock yesterday morning, and that she there met her lover, Barnet, and had a glass of beer with him. This statement also is not substantiated.

A somewhat important fact has been pointed out, which puts a fresh complexion on the theory of the murders. It appears that the cattle boats bringing live freight to London are in the habit of coming into the Thames on Thursdays or Fridays, and leave again for the Continent on Sundays or Mondays. It has already been a matter of comment that the recent revolting crimes have been committed at the week's end, and an opinion has been formed among some of the detectives that the murderer is a drover or butcher employed on one of these boats—of which there are many—and that he periodically appears and disappears with one of the steamers. This theory is held to be of much importance by those engaged in this investigation, who believe that the murderer does not reside either in the locality or even in this country at all. It is thought that he may be either a person employed upon one of these boats or one who is allowed to travel by them, and inquiries have for some time been directed to following up the theory. It is pointed out that at the inquests on the previous victims the coroners had expressed the opinion that the knowledge of anatomy possessed by a butcher would have been sufficient to enable him to find and cut out the parts of the body which in several cases were abstracted.

The Whitechapel Vigilance Committee, who have recently relaxed their efforts to find the murderer, have called a meeting for Tuesday evening next, at the Paul's Head Tavern, Crispin-street, Spitalfields, to consider what steps they can take to assist the police.

A Mrs. Paumier, a young woman who sells roasted chestnuts at the corner of Widegate-street, a narrow thoroughfare about two minutes' walk from the scene of the murder, told a reporter yesterday afternoon a story which appears to afford a clue to the murderer. She said that about 12 o'clock that morning a man dressed like a gentleman came to her and said, "I suppose you have heard about the murder in Dorset-street?" She replied that she had, whereupon the man grinned, and said, "I know more about it than you." He then stared into her face and went down Sandy's-row, another narrow thoroughfare which cuts across Widegate-street. When he had got some way off, however, he looked back as if to see whether she was watching him, and then vanished. Mrs. Paumier said the man had a black moustache, was about 5ft. 6in. high, and wore a black silk hat, a black coat, and speckled trousers. He also carried a black shiny bag about a foot in depth and a foot and a half in length. Mrs. Paumier stated further that the same man accosted three young women, whom she knows, on Thursday night, and they chaffed him and asked what he had in the bag, and he replied, "Something that the ladies don't like." One of the three young women she named, Sarah Roney, a girl about 20 years of age, states that she was with two other girls on Thursday night in Brushfield-street, which is near Dorset-street, when a man wearing a tall hat and a black coat, and carrying a black bag, came up to her and said, "Will you come with me?" She told him she would not, and asked him what he had in the bag, and he said, "Something the ladies don't like." He then walked away.

A further report received late last night says:—"Not the slightest doubt appears to be entertained in official quarters that this fresh crime is by the same hand which committed the others. There is also, it is to be noted, a striking similarity in the period of the month in which the crime has been committed, for while two of the most atrocious of the other murders in the same district were committed on the 7th of the months of September and August, this was commenced or committed on the 8th—approximately the same period in the month. This would seem to indicate that the murderer was absent from the scene of these horrors for fixed periods, and that his return was always about the same time. The late storms might account for the crime on this occasion being a day later, the suggestion, of course, being that the murderer journeys across the sea on some of the short passages.

"Last night nothing further was known at Scotland-yard. In fact, all the inquiries centre in the east of London, whither have been sent some of the keenest investigators of the country. The murders, so cunningly continued, are carried out with a completeness which altogether baffles investigators. Not a trace is left of the murderer, and there is no purpose in the crime to afford the slightest clue, such as would be afforded in other crimes almost without exception. All that the police can hope is that some accidental circumstance will lead to a trace which may be followed to a successful conclusion."

The latest account states upon what professes to be indisputable authority that no portion of the murdered woman's body was taken away by the murderer. As already stated, the *post-mortem* examination was of the most exhaustive character, and the surgeons did not quit their work until every organ had been accounted for and placed as closely as possible in its natural position.

A man's pilot coat has been found in the murdered woman's room, but whether it belonged to one of her paramours or to the murderer has not been ascertained. Late yesterday evening a man was arrested near Dorset-street on suspicion of being concerned in the murder. He was taken to Commercial-street police-station, followed by a howling mob, and is still detained there. Another man, respectably dressed, wearing a slouch hat and carrying a black bag, was arrested and taken to Leman-street station. The bag was examined, but its contents were perfectly harmless, and the man was at once released.

The Salt Union.—Our Chester Correspondent telegraphs that Messrs. Brunner, Mond, and Co. (Limited), the alkali company of Northwich, have discovered a supply of brine at the Anderton Works capable of making several hundred thousand tons of salt per annum. This firm is at present the only powerful brine pumping competitor of the Salt Union in Great Britain. No agreement has been made by the union with them, though it was believed that an amicable understanding had been arrived at. The struggle between these two great concerns, if it becomes active, will be watched with interest.

The Iron Trade.—At Middlesbrough, yesterday, the market was quiet, and the tone was hardly so good as it was earlier in the week. Both makers and buyers are backward at entering into forward contracts. The favourable Board of Trade returns have somewhat strengthened the position of makers. For prompt f.o.b. delivery of No. 3 g.m.b. merchants quote 34s. 3d., or 3d. less than on Tuesday. Makers are still very firm, and hold out for 35s. Gellivara, the new brand of iron made from Swedish ore at Walker-on-Tyne, is now being offered for sale at 44s. 6d. for M. No.'s foundry, being about the same price as hematite, and is being used by some of the founders for the same purposes as best Scotch. The manufactured iron trade is active, and there are good inquiries in the steel trade. There is nothing fresh, and prices remain unaltered. Engineers and shipbuilders continue very busy. The coal and coke trades are firm.

Fall from a Train.—As the express train which left London at 12 10 yesterday was crossing the viaduct over the Mersey at Runcorn, a lady, whose name has not yet become known, fell from one of the carriages across the parallel metals. Some platelayers who were at work near the scene of the accident went immediately to the rescue and saved her from being cut to pieces by an up express then due from Liverpool. She was removed to the Widnes Hospital. At the time of telegraphing she was still alive, but she was terribly cut about the left side of the head and was quite unconscious. She is described as being well dressed and about 50 years of age. A massive gold bracelet was found on the line under the spot where she fell.

Respite.—A respite has been granted on behalf of the old woman Mary Boyd, sentenced to death at Glasgow for the murder of her grandchild, aged two years, at Dalry, Ayrshire.

Flora Shaw and the Jameson Raid

The Jameson Raid was a fiasco of British imperial policy in which *The Times* was dangerously involved. The protagonist at Printing House Square was Flora Shaw, the first professional woman staff correspondent, the first colonial editor of *The Times* and a fine crusading journalist. Her gender made her a *rara avis* of the inky trade. The black silk dress which she wore on her travels became as familiar a badge of office as Russell's commissariat cap in the Crimea. Her indiscretions caused *The Times* to be examined again before an official inquiry, within ten years of the Parnell affair. Her cleverness and loyalty before the inquiry enabled both her and *The Times* to escape without censure.

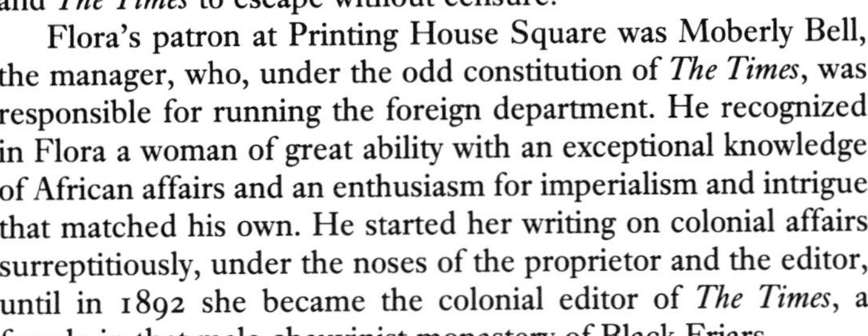

Flora's patron at Printing House Square was Moberly Bell, the manager, who, under the odd constitution of *The Times*, was responsible for running the foreign department. He recognized in Flora a woman of great ability with an exceptional knowledge of African affairs and an enthusiasm for imperialism and intrigue that matched his own. He started her writing on colonial affairs surreptitiously, under the noses of the proprietor and the editor, until in 1892 she became the colonial editor of *The Times*, a female in that male chauvinist monastery of Black Friars.

It was natural that Flora should be an ally and confidante of Cecil Rhodes, the founder of De Beers and The British South African Company, and by now the premier of Cape Colony[1]. His ambitions were not merely financial, just as Flora's were not merely journalistic. They both wanted to see British dominion extend from the Cape to Cairo. And they were both prepared to take unconventional steps to support this ambition.

They both supported the reform movement of the Uitlanders in the Transvaal. These white non-Boers, who were mainly British, worked in the diamond and gold mines and suffered many grievances under President Kruger (some legitimate, such as the absence of voting rights). The climax of their conspiracy came in the Jameson Raid on 29 December 1895.

Dr Leander Starr Jameson of the British South African Company staged a raid of about 400 troopers across the frontier into Transvaal to coincide with a rising by the Uitlanders. The rising never happened. The raid was a humiliating fiasco from the beginning. Jameson's men had been given thirty-six cases of champagne (more than a bottle per man) as 'a jumping powder' before they set out: a drunken trooper cut a wire fence instead of the telegraph wire to Pretoria, so that the news of their raid was quickly broadcast. Jameson and his men were captured. And back in London there was uproar, and demands to know what had been going on.

Above Flora Shaw, THE TIMES's first colonial editor and first full-time woman correspondent.

Below The Charge of the Three Hundred at Doornkop, by Captain Thatcher, 1896.

The answer was that behind the Jameson Raid lay an inextricable confusion of cables, advice, conspiracy and instructions, in which the clever colonial editor of *The Times* had played a leading part. The Government set up an official inquiry; and in February 1897 a Select Committee of the House of Commons began its hearings.

It emerged from the evidence that Flora Shaw knew that the Uitlanders in Johannesburg planned a rising, and that Jameson had a force ready if necessary to ride to their assistance. She made a good impression on the Committee, cool under cross-examination, and passing no blame back on her masters. She wore her famous black dress, with white lace and chiffonerie round the collar.

She disclaimed any knowledge that Rhodes had been stage-managing the rising from Cape Town. This was odd, since the South African Company had supplied her with a copy of its own code-book, and she had sent a number of telegrams to Rhodes urging action, saying 'delay dangerous'. Her editor knew nothing of these, though Moberly Bell knew. She had caused to be published in *The Times*, under the byline of Our Correspondent in Cape Town, the notorious 'women and children' letter. This was an appeal for help from Johannesburg, to be used by Jameson as a pretext for action. It was undated – Jameson simply had to add the date when the time came – and it ran:

> Thousands of unarmed men, women and children of our race will be at the mercy of well-armed Boers, while property of enormous value will be in the greatest peril. We cannot contemplate the future without the gravest apprehensions. All feel that we are justified in taking any steps to prevent the shedding of blood, and to insure the protection of our rights. It is under these circumstances that we feel constrained to call upon you to come to our aid.

When reading Flora's evidence one is constantly forced to doubt either her intelligence or her veracity. She was not stupid. Nevertheless, because of her personality and skill under questioning, she escaped blame and avoided implicating *The Times*. A minority report found Flora Shaw's memory 'somewhat defective'. The Committee was hunting other quarry than *The Times* anyway. Its report condemned the Jameson Raid, blamed Rhodes for everything except Jameson's crossing the frontier without orders, and exonerated the Colonial Secretary, Joseph Chamberlain. The fiasco of the Jameson Raid increased the tensions that led to the second Boer War.

On 11 January, *The Times* published exclusively the first official piece by the new Poet Laureate, Alfred Austin. It is about the Jameson Raid, and is a strong contender for the title of the worst poem ever written by a Laureate. The last verse goes:

> I suppose we were wrong, were madmen,
> Still I think at the Judgment Day,
> When God sifts the good from the bad men,
> There'll be something more to say.
> We were wrong, but we weren't half sorry,
> And, as one of the baffled band,
> We would rather have had that foray
> Than the crushings of all the Rand.

The Times paid Austin £25 for his poem. So inflamed was the jingoism of *Times* readers that the paper received numerous requests for permission to recite and reprint the lines, and even to set them to music.

[1] Cape Colony and Natal were the British possessions in South Africa; Transvaal and the Orange Free State belonged to the Boers.

Reports of the defeat of Jameson's raiding force only three days after it set out. The British jailed Jameson for fifteen months for his disobedience, irresponsibility and incompetence.
3 JANUARY 1896

LATEST INTELLIGENCE.

THE TRANSVAAL CRISIS.

DEFEAT AND SURRENDER OF DR. JAMESON.

SIR H. ROBINSON GOING TO PRETORIA.

The following telegrams were received at the Colonial Office yesterday evening :—

"From Sir Hercules Robinson to Mr. Chamberlain.

"January 2.

"Newton telegraphs that his messenger overtook Jameson ten miles on the other side of Klans river. Brought back verbal messages that the despatches had been received and would be attended to. The force was saddling up when messenger arrived, and at once proceeded eastwards. Jameson has thus received both my messages and has disregarded them.

"De Wet telegraphs this morning that it would have been impossible for him to have gone to Jameson and if it had been possible his mission would have proved futile as fighting commenced at 4 o'clock yesterday. He had been unable to obtain particulars from Joubert last night, and has heard nothing beyond the rumour this morning.

"*Cape Times* has telegram this morning as follows :—

"'Pretoria, Jan. 1.—Latest from Krugersdorp is that there has been hard fighting, the Chartered troops suffering heavily.'

"Will cable as soon as I learn anything authentic."

"Following message received from British Agent, South African Republic :—

'January 2.

'I have just seen the Executive General. He says as far as he knows Jameson has been driven from several positions. The burghers have 22 wounded prisoners, including three officers, and 20 other prisoners. Five dead bodies have been buried by burghers. Last information, fighting still proceeding. No force has yet moved out of Johannesburg to assist Jameson.

'Information received by Government of further British South Africa Company's forces mobilizing to enter Transvaal and a Kaffir commando within Transvaal on Bechuanaland border. The Free State ready to assist Transvaal if required.

'Jameson surrounded by large force close to Krugersdorp. Railway line between Krugersdorp and Johannesburg has been broken up.'

"Following telegram received from Acting President of Orange Free State to-day :—

"'I have the honour to inform your Excellency that 1,600 burghers have been commandeered to take up a position about 16 miles on this side of the Vaal River.'

"Following message received from British Agent in South African Republic :—

'Jameson's force surrenders.'"

The following official statement was issued yesterday afternoon :—

"The High Commissioner, Sir H. Robinson, is leaving this afternoon, with Mr. Chamberlain's approval, for Pretoria to deal with the situation in furtherance of a satisfactory and peaceful settlement."

Mr. Chamberlain yesterday sent the following telegram to Sir Hercules Robinson :—

"I regret that Jameson's disobedience has led to this deplorable loss of life. Do your best to secure generous treatment of the prisoners and care of the wounded.

"Telegraph names of killed and wounded, and let me know from time to time how the wounded are going on. This lamentable occurrence renders your presence in the South African Republic more desirable than ever. I presume that you are on your way."

JOHANNESBURG, DEC. 30.*

The situation is becoming hourly graver. Intense excitement prevails, and the exodus of women and children continues. There has been a considerable run on the banks. Large quantities of arms and ammunition are being secretly introduced in all parts of the Rand, and local stocks of arms and breadstuffs are being bought up. The enrolment of the Town Guard is proceeding. The tension at this moment is felt to be such that a casual fracas may result in an outbreak at any minute.

The tactics of the leaders of the National Union are still undefined. There is no active movement, apparent at least, on the part of the Boers. Local sympathies are much divided.

Influential deputations are visiting President Kruger to-day to discuss conciliatory measures with a view to the averting of a crisis.

A small meeting of Australians was convened at the Gold Fields Hotel to consider the question of protective measures. About 2,000 citizens attended, however, and the whole proceedings were excellently managed, order being thoroughly well maintained. A resolution, similar to that passed recently by the Mercantile Association, declining to take part in any revolutionary act, was adopted.

Meetings of the German and French residents have been held, at which it was resolved to instruct their Consuls at Pretoria to telegraph to Berlin and Paris respectively, urging the German and French Governments to make an official declaration of their interest in the Transvaal, with a view to their protection.

An exceedingly bitter feeling has been created against some German speculators here for circulating a petition to President Kruger assuring him of their loyal support. Only 20 signatures were obtained to the petition.

Public feeling has been greatly stirred here by the appearance of a number of Boers riding about the streets.

At the Standard Theatre, on Saturday night, during the performance of *Othello* before a crowded house, the orchestra played the "Volkslied," the Transvaal national air. The music was, however, drowned by a continued torrent of groans, hootings, and hisses. "God Save the Queen" was then given by the orchestra, and the whole house rose and cheered again and again until the last strain of the national anthem had died away.—*Reuter.*

[A portion of the above appeared in our Second Edition of yesterday.]

CAPE TOWN, DEC. 30.

The *Cape Times* says :—

"The advice to fold our hands and go on waiting upon good, kind Mr. Kruger, who is yearning to admit the Uitlanders to the franchise if only they would refrain from demanding it, is a joke which lapse of years has deprived of its pristine flavour. . . . The National Union are pledged to constitutional agitation. The Government has said that it will give constitutional agitation every fair facility of expression. Let it keep its word, and all will be well. It is simply a question of outfacing the obstructionist forces by a counter-show of moral force, fixedness, and unanimity. In Cape Colony, and we believe in the Free State too, it is recognized that the sympathy felt for the old burghers when they were struggling for enfranchised liberty, the truly democratic Republic, must to-day be given to those who make the same struggle for their rights, and must be taken from those who stubbornly refuse them."

The *Johannesburg Star* says :—

"The time for phrase-making has gone by, and the manifesto is a recital of galling, stimulating facts, eloquent in their brevity and pithiness. Our quarrel is not with the form of 'government. To stigmatize the leaders of the movement as 'flagomaniacs' is an insidious and wilful lie. It is an upheaval inevitable from within, and the political imbecility which continues to keep the safety-valve jammed down when one solid and guaranteed instalment of reform would set it free, will descend to all the posterity of the Boer as a national crime to be for ever held in bitter remembrance against the man who would not save his country when he could."

The *Cape Argus* says :—"There is something more than an ominous spirit of unrest abroad, and this it is that marks the difference between the present agitation and others in the past. The hour has arrived when the Uitlanders are prepared not only to make a stand, but to move forward. . . . They have a set purpose in view, and they are not to be turned by jeers or gibes, unmeaning promises, or scriptural metaphors. . . . Years ago we sympathized with the burghers in their gallant struggle for the independence which they now deny to others, and how has that sympathy been appreciated?"—*Our Correspondent.*

CAPE TOWN, DEC. 30.*

The *Cape Times*, in the course of an article strongly supporting the manifesto issued by the Transvaal National Union on the 26th ult., says :—

"The suggestion that workmen have something to gain from the enlightened fiscal policy of President Kruger and the Hollanders—some benefit which they imperil by standing firm with their employers on behalf of the common industry—is a suggestion which insults the intelligence of the Rand workmen. The demand made is right and just, and the danger increases with every day that it continues to be denied. . . . The Uitlanders' only danger—and it endangers the cause of peace proportionately, for how can they now recede?—is from themselves. For a few German Jews we can make allowance, but that Afrikanders and British colonists, with their traditions of freedom and cohesion, can betray the reform army by splitting its phalanx we cannot believe until forced to do so."—*Reuter.*

[The above appeared in our Second Edition of yesterday.]

*Delayed in transmission.

BERLIN, JAN. 2.

The announcement that the Chartered Company's forces had actually crossed the Transvaal frontier could not fail to aggravate the situation materially. The threatening attitude of the Uitlanders was already construed as evidence of a determination to subvert in the English interest the existing order of things in the Transvaal, and was held to justify an expression of serious concern on the part of Germany. The appearance on the scene in such circumstances of what is considered here to be practically a British force naturally strengthens the general conviction that the whole movement in the Transvaal has been prepared for a long time under influential auspices with the sole purpose of securing the immediate incorporation of the South African Republic in the British possessions. It affords at the same time much stronger grounds for intervention on behalf of the Boer Government than any mere internal disturbances.

The strain has indeed for the moment been slightly relieved by the assurance which Lord Salisbury gave yesterday to Count Hatzfeldt that her Majesty's Government disapproved Dr. Jameson's action, and that instructions had been telegraphed for the immediate withdrawal of the Chartered Company's forces from the Transvaal. But an exceedingly grave view of the situation is still taken in official circles here. The German Government does not, of course, question the good faith of the British Government, or the sincerity of its desire to arrest the progress of what is looked upon here as a regular filibustering expedition and a gross violation of international law. But what is questioned here is the determination of the British Government to maintain the Transvaal Convention of 1884 intact against the pretensions of the forward party in South Africa; and, subject to such modifications as President Kruger may be disposed to grant of his own free will, and with the consent of the existing Legislature at Pretoria, the maintenance, or, if necessary, the re-establishment of the *status quo* under that Convention is apparently the *minimum* satisfaction which the British Government is expected to give to the outraged feelings of Germany.

It is admitted that the occurrence of actual bloodshed would render the position an exceedingly difficult one for the British Government to deal with, and in view of the fact that the telegraph lines have been cut it is feared that an armed conflict may have already occurred. Apprehensions are also, if less openly, entertained that Dr. Jameson may not readily respond to the instructions addressed to him, even if Mr. Cecil Rhodes has nominally concurred in them. But it is contended that, whatever may have happened or may still happen, England has ample means of bringing to its bearings not only the Government of Cape Colony, but above all the Chartered Company, the existence of which depends solely upon the charter which it holds from the Crown. The withdrawal of the charter, with all the consequences which would ensue therefrom, is looked upon here as a weapon with which, if the British Government has an adequate sense of its responsibilities, Mr. Cecil Rhodes can at any time be brought back to an appreciation of international obligations in his double capacity as Prime Minister of Cape Colony and managing director of the Chartered Company in British South Africa. If the worst comes to the worst, the British Government would always have it within its power to prove by the resolute employment of such a weapon that it was no more willing to be an accessory after the fact than before the fact to the invasion of a friendly country by forces commissioned under the authority of the British Crown.

Though the German Government takes a very strong view of what it owes, not only to the material interests of its own subjects who are resident or whose capital is invested in the Transvaal, but to the kindred people who look to Germany for the protection of their national independence, it is not perhaps in that direction that the chief danger lies. It is scarcely probable that, whatever happens in the Transvaal, events will result in an open rupture between Germany and England, though such a course would doubtless find here many and exceedingly powerful advocates. But I am not speaking without authority when I state that as far as Germany is concerned the issue of this question may determine her whole policy towards England, whether it shall continue to be, as during the last six years at least, one of friendship and good will, or whether it shall be one of calculated hostility. Any tampering with the *status quo* in the Transvaal will be held to justify conclusively and irrevocably that growing distrust of England to which I have so frequently alluded.

British statesmanship has been for some time past suspected here of speculating for its own purposes upon the apparent division of Continental Europe into two irreconcilable camps, and of even encouraging that division in order to secure for itself greater liberty of action in other parts of the world. Even the action of British diplomacy in Constantinople in connexion with the Armenian question has been regarded mainly as an attempt to embroil the Continental Powers in the Near East, so as to give England an opportunity of regaining at her leisure the ground which she has lost in the Far East. But it is contended that the antagonism which undeniably exists between certain Continental Powers is, perhaps, not so profound or insurmountable as England believes, and she may some day be herself surprised to see how easily it might make room for a combination directed against herself. There are many weak points in England's armour, and if she is so strongly entrenched in South Africa that she can afford to play there a game of reckless defiance, she must not forget that in North Africa she occupies a position which is by no means so invulnerable. Nor is the Egyptian question the only one which might serve as a useful basis for composing at England's expense many of the differences which divide the Continental Powers. A penalty might thus be inflicted upon England much more effectively and easily than by any attempt forcibly to oppose her schemes of aggrandizement, *per fas et nefas*, in South Africa.

I have felt it my duty to place these views on record. It is useless for me to comment upon them, but it seems to me important that they should be known at the present juncture, as they are very widely entertained and shared in responsible quarters even by those who would be most reluctant to face the necessity of carrying them into effect, and of thereby practically reversing the whole course of Germany's foreign policy under the "Neuer Kurs." I will only add that these views, whatever misconceptions one must hope they are based upon, are not the outcome of any temporary petulance, but have been slowly and steadily maturing for a long time past. The events in the Transvaal have merely precipitated a crisis in our relations with Germany, of which premonitory symptoms have not been wanting.

On the other hand, there is every reason to believe that the German Government would welcome with proportionate satisfaction the evidence which her Majesty's Government is still in a position to give that these apprehensions are unfounded, and that there is no intention to disturb or to countenance any disturbance of the *status quo* in South Africa, or to extort from the Boer Government any concessions beyond those which might secure the redress of legitimate grievances without imperilling its real independence. Within those limits the German Government claims to have always been, and still to be, prepared to use its influence in Pretoria for a peaceful and satisfactory solution of the question, and the more settled the determination here to make that question the touchstone of Germany's policy towards England, the more favourably and effectually will a peaceful and satisfactory solution react upon the future relations of the two countries.

It can do no good at the present juncture to quote the bitter and violent language in which, unfortunately, the greater part of the German Press indulges to-day, though it is generally conceded that the official declarations both of Lord Salisbury and of the Colonial authorities at home and at the Cape are in themselves satisfactory. It is pleasanter to note that the *Frankfurter Zeitung* has once more justified its reputation for sober and well-informed treatment of foreign questions by publishing an article in which alone, as far as I know, in the German Press the claims of the Transvaal Uitlanders are discussed on their own merits in a critical but fair and dispassionate spirit.—*Our Own Correspondent.*

BERLIN, JAN. 2.

A telegram received to-day from Pretoria says :—"The British Agent here has telegraphed to the Governor of Cape Colony as follows :—'The Commanding General has positive information that 800 Bechuanaland troops, with six Maxim guns and four other cannon, have arrived in the neighbourhood of Rustemberg. They carry the British flag, and are on the march to Johannesburg. The President of the Republic requests me to inform you that the incursion of armed British subjects is a serious violation of the Convention, and that he is surprised that the British Government permits and does not prevent such serious acts. He hopes that you will immediately take steps to stop the intruders, as he cannot allow his—that is to say, the country's—rights to be violated in this manner. This might lead to serious consequences, for which his Government cannot be made responsible. I await your reply by return.'

"The reply was as follows :—'A rumour reached me to-day that Dr. Jameson with police troopers of the Chartered Company had entered the territory of the Republic and was marching upon Johannesburg. I have made telegraphic inquiry whether this is true. In any case I declare that, if the report is true, the step was taken without my sanction or previous knowledge, and that I have immediately telegraphed expressing disapproval of this action and have directed that the troopers should return without delay. Communicate this to the President.'"

The *National Zeitung*, in an article on the crisis in the Transvaal, says :—"Since the South African question has been raised on the English side and has been directed into a new course, it behoves other Powers to seize the opportunity to set forth the actual relation between England and the Transvaal with necessary and unmistakable clearness, and once for all to make it impossible for England to refer any more to the pretended dependence of the Transvaal."

The *Vossische Zeitung*, alluding to the same matter, repudiates the charge of presumption with which the English newspapers have received the expressions employed by the German Press. It then continues as follows :—"Germany needs no advice as to where her interests in South Africa begin and end, and if the Transvaal comes to Berlin for support she has a perfect right to do so. The Transvaal is not England's vassal. Mr. Chamberlain and the British Government do not share the standpoint of *The Times*. Sir Frank Lascelles has had repeated interviews with Baron Marschall von Bieberstein. In the Venezuela question German opinion took England's side. In the Transvaal question that is not so. It is to be hoped that no proofs of this beyond diplomatic representations will be necessary."

Other journals speak in a similar strain.—*Reuter.*

COLOGNE, JAN. 2.

The *Kölnische Zeitung*, commenting upon the news from the Transvaal to-day, says :—"The Chartered Company's invasion of the Transvaal is a breach of international law, which is the more serious since Mr. Rhodes, the Cape Premier, is at the head of the company, which, in spite of all denials, is exposed to the suspicion of having prepared this violation of the law long in advance. An increase of the political rights of the Uitlanders is a purely internal matter of the Transvaal, in whose independence several European Powers, and particularly Germany, are keenly interested. President Kruger has up to the present administered his difficult office in the interests of the country with great tact and skill, and it is to be assumed that he is, moreover, prepared to satisfy the legitimate interests of the foreigners permanently settled in the country. The Transvaal must resolutely quell the insurrection. There can be no question of considering the extension of political rights until law and order have been restored. Mr. Rhodes and his people, the instigators of this breach of the peace, will alone be held responsible for any bloodshed that may follow."

The *Kölnische Zeitung* regards Mr. Chamberlain's action in the matter with satisfaction, and adds :—"The British Colonial Minister, however, appears to have no confidence in his exorcism, for he accompanied it with injunctions to President Kruger for which there is no legal justification. Meanwhile the European Powers must take care that their interests and those of their subjects suffer no harm." The journal emphatically repels the pretension of *The Times* to allow no foreign intervention, and utters a warning against vain threats, which, it says, can only aggravate the situation unnecessarily. Germany, it continues, will, nothing daunted, stoutly protect her interests, and in no circumstances will she permit armed bands of Englishmen to violate the law of nations, in the maintenance of which Germany is interested. That this is so is proved by the steps taken by Germany, which are generally commended by the German people.—*Reuter.*

THE HAGUE, JAN. 2.

The *Handelsblad* and the *Rotterdamsche Courant*, the chief authorities upon colonial affairs in the Dutch Press, manifest a scepticism the reverse of complimentary in their reference to the invitation addressed from Johannesburg to Dr. Jameson and his followers, while the light in which the proffered intervention of the Government, as a means of bringing about a peaceful solution of the difficulty, is regarded here may be estimated by the concluding sentence of the article in the Rotterdam journal, which runs thus :—"And if England insists upon using compulsion it appears not improbable that Germany and even France, undeterred by the menaces of *The Times*, will lend their support to the oppressed State in its struggle against the British Empire."

In the same bellicose spirit a letter from a Herr Reesema, ex-correspondent of the Harling Committee of 1881, is published, which compares Dr. Jameson's 700 men to a band of medieval marauders, and declares that as their act of wanton aggression cannot possibly have the sanction of England, President Kruger's task is easier than it was in 1881, since he and his Boers will have to fight against robbers and not against England. At the same time the writer, somewhat inconsequently, sees fit to make an appeal to all the people of the Netherlands to send assistance to the Transvaal in men and money; congratulates it upon having gold in its coffers and upon the friendship of France and Germany; and trusts that upon this occasion the right will triumph once more over English greed of possession.

The animosity displayed by the Dutch Press in its comments on affairs in the Transvaal during the last few days has been singularly modified by the fact of Mr. Chamberlain's disavowal of the incursion of Dr. Jameson and his armed force into the Transvaal. The *Rotterdamsche Courant* says, however, that, though it is all very well to declare that the British Government and not the Chartered Company must settle the differences between the Boers and the Uitlanders, for this is the interpretation placed upon Mr. Chamberlain's telegram, England has not in reality the smallest right to meddle with the internal administration of the Transvaal. Attempts are also made to show that the Convention of 1884, which forbids the Boer Republic to contract an alliance with any other than the Orange Free State, does not preclude the former from appealing to a friendly Power in case of need.—*Our Correspondent.*

PARIS, JAN. 2.

The Cabinet Council to-day, according to a semi-official note, "was occupied with the situation in the Transvaal. The Government is attentively watching the progress of events, and is especially busied with the safeguarding of French interests. The Minister of Foreign Affairs has just appointed as Consul at Johannesburg M. Brochon, an engineer of repute, who by his standing and experience is better fitted than anybody at the present difficult moment to offer valuable co-operation to our Consul at Pretoria, M. Aubert, in the protection of French interests in the Transvaal."

The newspapers continue to reflect the serious interest felt here in the matter. The *Débats*, in an article entitled "The Invasion of the Transvaal," in which it states certain facts which it characterizes as "in themselves sufficiently edifying," puts to whom it may concern four questions :—"How does it happen (1) that the letter sent on Saturday from Johannesburg reached Dr. Jameson in time for him to set out on Sunday; (2) that Dr. Jameson had ready 700 armed men prepared for a campaign; (3) that these men were already provided with four days' rations—just the amount necessary to feed them on the journey from Mafeking to Johannesburg, which takes exactly four days; and (4) that it is known in London that the said Dr. Jameson was signalled on Monday at Malmain, in the Transvaal, and that no news from the said Jameson has come direct, who, moreover, it is feared, has not received the telegram recalling him?"

The fact that the telegraphs have been cut does not strike the *Débats* as having a serious bearing on any answer to these questions, for there is more than one line from the Cape to the Transvaal and to Mafeking, some passing by Bechuanaland and others across the Orange Free State. If we assume that the Cape High Commissioner and Mr. Chamberlain have been surprised by Dr. Jameson's extraordinary initiative, is it credible that he acted without receiving Mr. Cecil Rhodes's orders? "It is all very well to be a high official of the South Africa Company, but you do not in time of peace invade a civilized country without authority or without having received express orders."

The *Débats* does not go further than this. Its habitual weapon is irony. But the *Temps* is more outspoken. It characterizes Dr. Jameson's act as a filibustering expedition, land piracy, and deliberate brigandage of the first order, and it adds, "to allow such a precedent to be established would be to sanction the gravest blow dealt at national rights since modern Europe abandoned the system of letters of marque. Joint-stock wars, limited liability invasions, cannot possibly be tolerated in Africa any more than elsewhere." The *Temps* goes on to point out the extremely suspicious character of the alleged cutting of the telegraph wires, although it imputes to Mr. Chamberlain none but the sincerest motives. It even, unlike the *Débats*, exculpates Mr. Cecil Rhodes of any complicity. That statesman, it says, well knows that a war between the Boer and Anglo-Saxon elements would be the death-knell of his power, for, while in London the champion of indefinite colonial expansion, he is at the Cape almost the agent of the Afrikander Bund. He must regret, therefore, the folly of his subordinate, unless, "which no one has a right to affirm without irrefutable proofs, he has resolved to stake his all in the Transvaal on the English conquest and expropriation of the Boers from an El Dorado, of which the mineral wealth—this fatal gift cursed by all the burghers desirous of independence—leaves the placers of Mashonaland or Matabeleland far behind it."

The *Temps* adds that England cannot afford to allow Europe to have any doubt of its sincerity in all this business. It calls *The Times* adroit, but a bad adviser, for unctuously affirming that Mr. Chamberlain in recalling Dr. Jameson, who either has not received or has not obeyed the order, has done the Transvaal such a service that he becomes the necessary mediator between the burghers and the Uitlanders. This, it says, is to misunderstand the situation entirely. England has to save her honour. She has to repair this violation of territory. Indeed, certain equitable concessions, which the Transvaal might freely have granted, have now become impossible.—*Our Own Correspondent.*

THE VENEZUELAN COMMISSION.

NEW YORK, JAN. 2.

Late last evening the President gave out the names of his Venezuelan Commissioners. They are :—Justice Brewer, of the Supreme Court of the United States; Chief Justice Alvey, of the Court of Appeals of the District of Columbia; Mr. Andrew D. White, of New York; Mr. Frederic R. Coudert, of New York; and Mr. Daniel C. Gilman, of Maryland. This is the order in which they are named. How suddenly the President decided may be seen from the fact that two days ago no offer had been made to Justice Brewer. They are all men of character and standing. Whether they constitute a strong or an impartial Commission, or one which will command public confidence, is a question which takes a good deal of answering. There is even some question whether the President has a legal right to appoint United States Judges on such a Commission. Congress has set its face against allowing any official to draw two salaries. It is held by some that Justice Brewer and Chief Justice Alvey cannot serve, even if they draw no pay as Commissioners. It is held by many more that the judicial work of the Supreme Court ought not to be interfered with by the assigning of a Judge of that Court to other duties. These technical objections have weight, but the President has put them aside, and the American public will be likely to concern itself chiefly with the qualifications and duties of the Commissioners. There has been a strong hope that the President might so constitute his Commission as to make up to some extent for its organic onesidedness and for the irregularity of its origin. How far has he justified that hope?

Justice Brewer is a respectable member of the Supreme Bench. He would not be there if he were not a good lawyer. He is, or was, nominally a Republican. President Harrison appointed him to the Supreme Court in 1889. There are more distinguished members of that Court, but Justice Brewer is a good Judge. He comes from the State of Kansas, where, as throughout the West, somewhat extreme views of foreign affairs prevail.

Chief Justice Alvey, again, is a respectable Judge of the Court of Appeals of the District of Columbia, over which he has presided since its formation. President Cleveland appointed him. He is a Southerner, a Democrat of good repute in his district, and totally unknown to the country at large.

Mr. White, on the other hand, has a national reputation. He has had much to do with New York politics, has been United States Minister in Berlin and St. Petersburg, has a high and well-earned reputation as a diplomatist and perhaps a still higher as President of Cornell University, a post which he resigned in 1892 to go to Russia. By training and experience Mr. White is the best fitted of all five for the post, and is the only one of the five whom public opinion designated. He is a moderate Republican.

Mr. Gilman is another College President, Head of the Johns Hopkins University, Baltimore, which owes to him what Cornell owes to Mr. White—its existing organization and system. Outside of educational or University work Mr. Gilman is little known, except as a scientific and historical student. Among scholars his reputation is high. He has written a life of that President Monroe whose doctrine is now in dispute. His politics are doubtful Neither of Mr. Gilman nor of any one of these other three can it be affirmed that he has publicly taken sides in the present controversy, or that he is generally known to be for or against the President's policy or a friend or foe to Great Britain.

A very different account has to be given of the fifth member of the Commission. Mr. Coudert is a lawyer at the New York Bar, of great position and ability as such, with a large practice, and was junior counsel to the United States in the recent Behring Sea arbitration in Paris. He is a Tammany Democrat. Since the President sent his war Message to Congress Mr. Coudert has expressed himself on the subject of the Message and of Great Britain with great freedom. He was twice interviewed, and reports of these interviews appear in the *Herald* of December 18 and the *World* of December 19. Neither has been disavowed. Mr. Coudert treated the President's Message as an ultimatum to Great Britain. He spoke of her as disregarding the "notices" which she had received during the last ten years. To that there could be, he said, "but one result—an ultimatum such as she has now received in unmistakable terms." He added :—"One of the two nations must now give way or the most serious consequences ensue." He proceeded to argue that President Cleveland was "justified in taking the position indicated in his Message," because he had urged arbitration from the early days of his first Administration. Then comes this passage :—

"Far from acceding to this, Great Britain, as is not unusual when she is dealing with a weaker Power, enlarged the sphere of possible controversy by absorbing territory in addition to that which is in dispute. In 1885-86—that is, in one single year—she took possession of 3,300 square miles the title to which had always been in Venezuela. Not content with this, she found valuable lands which struck her fancy in another direction, and began to appropriate these. Where she intended to stop probably she did not herself know. She is accustomed to deal with large subjects in a regal way. The lion's paw is large and heavy, and woe to the weaker nation that feels its weight and its claws."

Lord Salisbury's discussion of the Monroe doctrine is then described as "humorous," and Mr. Coudert asks whether such an experienced statesman believed that he could "argue away a doctrine deeply embedded in the national heart." He continues :—

"Great Britain, less than any other nation in the world, has a right to dispute its necessity or its logic. She helped to plant the tree; she may not complain if she finds the fruit bitter to her lips. She intended it for Spain, but the people of the United States make no distinction of persons. That nation is their foe which will seek by violent means to despoil a sister Republic of this continent of territory lawfully belonging to its jurisdiction. It may seem a harsh doctrine; but this nation has never known any other. Great Britain has the rest of the world for her playground. Besides large slices of Asia and Africa, she has Gibraltar as a thorn in the side of Spain, Egypt wherewith to exasperate France, Malta as a souvenir of the Peace of Amiens—which she says Napoleon broke—and Cyprus as a new jewel in her crown. Were it not wise to look after what she has and leave America in peace?"

What I have quoted thus far is from the *Herald*. In the *World* Mr. Coudert speaks even more bluntly, saying that "England has been the bully of the world," and predicting that, in the event of trouble between England and the United States, France would seize Egypt and Russia Constantinople. Mr. Coudert moralizes further as follows :—

"England, of course, is responsible for the Armenian massacres. England will not permit Russia to seize Constantinople and wipe the unspeakable Turk off the face of the earth. Therefore thousands of Christians must suffer death. John Bull has no friends and Uncle Sam no enemies. If there should be trouble between America and England the sympathy of all Europe would be with us, and the hand of every European nation be raised against England. The English Government appreciates its friendlessness and helplessness, and because of that there will be no war."

Such is the language of Mr. Coudert, whom the President thinks a fit member of the Commission whose inquiry he said in his Message should be conducted "judicially." The Commission consists of five members, and Mr. Coudert may have a casting vote. It may rest with him to determine the boundary line beyond which the exercise of jurisdiction by England will be deemed "wilful aggression" to be resisted by the United States by every means in its power. It may rest with Mr. Coudert to determine the nature of the inquiry, and whether the Commission shall or shall not attempt to draw a boundary line. That contingency of war with England which the President created by his Message may, in fact, depend on Mr. Coudert's vote. It may be conceded that he would honestly endeavour to be impartial. What chances of success that endeavour would have may be calculated by the help of the declarations above given.

It is not yet known whether the President has defined anew the duties of this Commission. No new definition and no instructions have been made public. Its duties are to be collected from the Message and from the Act of Congress which sanctioned the Commission—"to report upon the true divisional line between the Republic of Venezuela and British Guiana." It may have a discretion of its own. It may be tied down by the President.

Owing, probably, to the lateness of the hour at which the news was received, no editorial opinion upon the Commission is expressed by any important morning newspaper in New York, except the chief Cleveland organ, which considers it "absolutely impartial." Nothing is said on the question of its legality, on the nature of its duties, on the omission of names which the public expected, or on the political complexion of the appointees. Mr. White is the only pronounced Republican. The one man whom the public wanted, and whose name would have given the Commission commanding authority, was Mr. Phelps. He was not asked. Mr. James C. Carter comes next. The President is said to have ruled him and others out because they had expressed opinions on the Monroe doctrine differing from his. For the reasons which I suggested yesterday President Cleveland may not have been able to secure men whose names would have been of themselves guarantees that the work of the Commission would be done impartially and wisely and with an intelligent effort towards a real settlement.

LATER.

An afternoon despatch from Washington professes to give an authoritative statement of the views of the Administration touching the Venezuelan Commission. According to this statement the Commission is to be absolute master of its own procedure, determining, among other things, the nature of the evidence to be taken and how the interested Governments may be represented before the tribunal. The State Department will give any assistance desired, but "will not allow itself to be placed in a position of taking sides as to the merits of the controversy between Great Britain and Venezuela. It will not undertake to present the Venezuelan case nor endeavour to offset any evidence that leads towards the British contention." It is hoped, says the despatch, that this will negative the assumption in Europe that the United States meant to constitute itself an arbiter.

This attitude is both new and unexpected, but if maintained consistently will tend to relieve the strain due to the former attitude of the same Department. Justice Brewer, however, has been interviewed, and says :—"The State Department has prepared certain features of evidence, regarded as essential, which would serve as a groundwork for investigation." When this has been gone over the Commission will determine what further steps are necessary, and will seek for the fullest information from all available sources, English included. Mr. Olney is reported as saying that the Administration will be entirely neutral and will not supervise or direct the Commission.

Mr. Coudert was asked to-day whether the interview in which he described England as the bully of the world was correct. He does not deny it. He adds, however, that he thinks the Venezuelan difficulty will be smoothed over, and says :—"It would be a strange thing if two of the greatest Powers of the world should go to war on a simple boundary dispute, the only difference between them being that one desired arbitration and the other did not." Most of the evening papers think the Commission fairly good; some say excellent; all treat it as having no other mission than to find out facts. Various Senators, including Messrs. Sherman and Chandler, praise it. Others regret Mr. Phelps's absence. Mr. Chauncey Depew declares himself greatly pleased. On the whole, the disposition seems to be to welcome the Commission as a way out of troubles the perplexity of which is now more keenly felt than ever. If it will serve that purpose the majority of Americans will readily condone mistakes in its conception or formation.

The New York Chamber of Commerce to-day adopted with but two dissenting voices the report of the Foreign Committee strongly censuring the President as having caused by his Message a sudden and deplorable check to the growing prosperity of the country. It holds him responsible for the loss caused by the rude derangement of business by the fall in value of merchandise and securities. It expresses profound regret that he should have suggested war as a possible outcome of a controversy "in which the American people have now, and probably can have, no more than a sentimental and passing interest." The Chamber pronounced strongly for the Monroe doctrine, "which still has the enthusiastic and unanimous support of the American people," and resolved :—

"That the Chamber of Commerce of the State of New York, being profoundly impressed with the gravity of the situation, which threatens the peace now and, happily, so long existing between Great Britain and the United States, appeals to the common sense and common interests of the people of both countries to avert the calamity of war by resort to arbitration or other friendly negotiation, which has so often been found to be a sufficient and satisfactory mode of settling international disputes and to which both Governments stand committed by profession, precedent, and the humanitarian spirit of the age."

This meeting was largely attended, and undoubtedly expresses with moderation the general feeling of the business community against the President's policy, which in private is commonly expressed with less moderation. It is now seen that there was no real reason for postponing this declaration. But one man spoke against it. Men like Mr. Charles Stewart Smith spoke for it with ability and deep seriousness. Ten days ago such a demonstration, which was then planned, would have been even more helpful than now, but it is still of great public service. It will not escape English attention that here, as yesterday in the Legislature of New York State and in Governor Morton's Message, arbitration is urged as the real method of settling the present controversy.—*Our Own Correspondent.*

INDIA.

CALCUTTA, JAN. 2.

The meeting of the Indian National Congress at Poona has excited but little interest, the comments of the Press being somewhat colourless. This is probably due to the absence of any burning question likely to lead to agitation, also to the number and length of the resolutions passed on subjects which are now threadbare. The subject of special verdicts from juries might possibly have attracted attention, but it is an open secret that the Government intends to abandon legislation in that connexion. The proceedings seem, on the whole, to have been singularly dull.

The accounts published of the durbar at Gilghit on December 31 show that Sir George Robertson was most successful in gathering together a large number of representative tribal chiefs now under the political control of the Gilghit Agency. The rewards given for loyalty during the Chitral outbreak confirm the Hindu-kush tribes in their loyalty and impress their neighbours, while the news of the durbar, with its military surroundings, should have a marked effect in the Indus valley, Chitral and the country southwards to the Punjab border. The Yasin province has now been formally placed under its own Governor, while the Mastuj and Ghizr districts have also been made small governorships, all in subordination to the British Agent at Gilghit, though no active interference will be attempted with the internal administration so long as a loyal spirit is shown. The *Pioneer*, commenting on the durbar, says that with this ceremony the hitherto somewhat intangible "influence" of the Gilghit Agency has at length assumed a form that will be understood and acknowledged, and, on the whole, probably welcomed, by all the borderland which has come under its keeping.—*Our Correspondent, by Indo-European Telegraph.*

CALCUTTA, JAN. 2.

The Bombay cotton-mill owners will recommend the Government to follow the same course as that indicated in Mr. Maclaren Morrison's resolution, adopted by the Bengal millowners, advocating the exemption from import duty of English cloth made from 20's yarn and under, and also 20's yarn and excising Indian-made cloth and bundled yarn over 20's.

The Press congratulates Mr. Morrison on having foretold a year ago that the result of the excise would be harmful both to Lancashire and India by developing the manufactures of China and Japan. The latter country, it is pointed out, will eventually supply its own requirements and secure the Indian market for counts above 20's.—*Reuter.*

AUSTRALIAN REVENUE RETURNS.

SYDNEY, JAN. 2.

The revenue returns of New South Wales for the quarter ending December 31 have just been issued. For the half-year from July to December the revenue amounted to £4,841,721, being an increase compared with the corresponding period of 1894 to the extent of £1,688. The financial year now ends on June 30 instead of December 31 as formerly.

The Treasurer estimated the revenue for the new financial year to be smaller by £260,000 than in 1894, so that the result for the first half-year is very satisfactory, especially in view of the abolition of a large number of custom duties on December 31.—*Reuter.*

PERTH, JAN. 3.

The revenue of Western Australia for the past quarter amounted to £449,764, or an increase of £120,270 as compared with last year.—*Reuter.*

THE ASHANTI EXPEDITION.

PRAHSU, DEC. 31.*

Sir Francis Scott and his staff arrived here to-day, all well.

John and Albert Ansah, King Prempeh's envoys, have sent on messengers to say that they cannot proceed, as they have been deserted by

Queen Victoria and 'the atrocious TIMES'

Above Queen Victoria and Prince Albert, 1858.

Below The splendid scene in Westminster Abbey at the coronation of Queen Victoria, from the painting by E. T. Harris. The Archbishop of Canterbury (Dr Howley) is shown about to crown the young Queen, who is holding the sceptre in her right hand.

Bottom The official invitation card which alone procured admittance to Westminster Abbey for the coronation of Queen Victoria in 1838.

Relations between Printing House Square and the Palace were turbulent during Queen Victoria's long reign. *The Times* was critical of the Queen on such matters as her Continental, particularly her Prussian, connections, the cost of marriage settlements for her children, the education of the Prince of Wales, and in particular her long seclusion after the death of the Prince Consort. For instance, on April Fool's Day 1864 the paper published as a sarcastic leg-pull: 'Her Majesty's loyal subjects will be very pleased to hear that their Sovereign is about to break her protracted seclusion'.

Albert's opinion had been strong: 'Soon there will not be room enough in the same country for the Monarchy and *The Times*'. Victoria did not expect criticism of the Monarchy or Her Government in the press, and expected Her Ministers to keep *The Times* 'straight'. She spoke of the 'atrocious' *Times*, and the need of 'a check on the reckless exercise of that anomalous power'.

In 1855, for example, she wrote to Palmerston complaining about the latest outrage from Printing House Square and demanding that he and his Ministers should break off all contacts with the paper. His reply is in the archives at Windsor. It runs, in part:

Viscount Palmerston presents his humble Duty to your Majesty and has had the honour to receive your Majesty's communication of the 6th instant. Viscount Palmerston was as disgusted as your Majesty was, at the articles in *The Times* to which your Majesty adverts, and he shewn [sic] to his colleagues in London your Majesty's letter. With Regard however to any practical Remedy there is much difficulty in finding any that would be immediately effectual. There is no Doubt some inconvenience in the admission of Editors and writers of newspapers into general society, but if they happen to be in a Position in Life which would naturally lead to their being invited, it would not be easy to exclude them merely on account of their Connection with a newspaper; and if they were not to be excluded entirely it is obvious that it would not be advisable to make their admission or exclusion depend upon the character of the last article in the Paper with which they may be understood or known to be connected. With regard moreover to *The Times* it is further to be considered that there is no one Person who writes or is answerable for all the leading articles in that Paper. There are many Hands employed in writing articles, and those only who are in the Confidence of the Editor can know who any given article was written by . . .

During the Crimean War, the reports and attitude of *The Times* had infuriated the Queen, but thereafter relations improved. The Queen sent a message appreciating 'the delicate and feeling

Lower Choir Gallery North Side A

THE CORONATION

of Her Most Sacred Majesty

VR

Admit

INTO WESTMINSTER ABBEY.

North Door

No. 117

Norfolk Earl Marshal

The first page of a very lengthy and stately report on Queen Victoria's coronation. The report is not without its lighter side: for example, the conversation of bystanders on the presence of a goose flying around the Palace (column 3), and their predictions that this omen betokened that Victoria 'would not long survive the ceremony'.
29 JUNE 1838

Page 74
Queen Victoria's death, announced with the sonorous pomp that might be expected, especially the report in column 6 of the Queen's last hours at Osborne.
23 JANUARY 1901

THE CORONATION.

From an early hour, indeed long before daylight, numbers of persons were to be seen gathering into little knots in the immediate vicinity of Buckingham Palace, and as the day advanced considerable additions to that number, as was to be anticipated, continued to be made until the hour of 8 o'clock had arrived, when the whole line on either side of the road leading up Constitution-hill from the New Palace, as well as the inner side of the iron railing which divides St. James's from the Green-park, was crowded with well-dressed persons, of whom a very large proportion consisted of ladies. Within the railing there were erected a series of platforms of various elevations, on which standings were obtainable at a charge of 2s. 6d. per head. This accommodation extended nearly from the Duke of Sutherland's residence up to the triumphal arch opposite to the entrance into Hyde Park, and, as far as we were enabled to see, not one was unoccupied. On either side of the arch, and on both sides of the gate, spacious galleries were erected, which were filled principally by elegantly dressed females, many of whom on the arrival of the youthful Sovereign took off their bonnets. It was impossible not to have anticipated where so great an assemblage had congregated that some disturbance would have occurred. Not so in this instance, however, for throughout the whole day not an angry word reached our ears, except such as were rendered necessary every now and then by persons planting themselves in the trees along the side of the roads. Then the commands of the police assumed somewhat a tone of that character.

In the course of the night a detachment of the Artillery from Woolwich had taken up their station in that part of St. James's Park immediately behind Marlborough-house, the residence of the Queen Dowager. About 7 o'clock the outer line of the footpaths up Constitution-hill were taken possession of by the 20th Regiment of Foot and the police. Shortly after the interstices between these official persons were filled up by a detachment of the Life Guards. The line towards the arch was made out by a portion of the Rifle Brigade. But so quiet, so peaceable, and so appropriately correct was the demeanour of the anxious spectators, that the presence of these authorities might have been safely dispensed with.

Before the clock had struck 9 placards were exhibited, communicating the information that the fireworks would not be let off in either parks until half-past 10 o'clock. The monotony which at all times attends the waiting for the commencement of the set out of a procession was yesterday but little relieved by casual occurrences. All was good humour, and it was evident, that so firm was the general resolve to be pleased, and to abstain from acrimonious conflict, that a total abandonment of the procession would alone have induced the slightest deviation therefrom.

One ludicrous circumstance occurred which may be worth mentioning. For some time a bird of large dimensions had been observed flying backwards and forwards, and then to hover over the Palace so frequently, as to call for the peculiar notice of a coterie of elderly ladies, who chanced to have esconced themselves in our own particular neighbourhood, one of whom, after much examination and apparent inward consultation, pronounced it to be a goose. To describe the instant expression of horror which rushed upon the faces of these ladies would be to attempt a task on which failure must attend. "What!" exclaimed they in one voice—"what! a goose; lor, you don't say so." "But I do," continued the first named, "and I am quite confident of it; it is a goose, poor dear soul." "Ay, ay, well may you say poor dear soul. Well, there's no saying anything for a certainty beforehand, is there? Who'd have thought it, that a nasty, ugly, long-necked (and here the lady somewhat stretched out her own neck, which could neither boast of plumpness nor of shortness) goose should have been fated to mar the happy events of this day! There will surely be some accident, or the poor dear soul, God bless her, will not long survive the ceremony." To this prediction the friends one and all assented with open mouths, one of them adding, that probably so lamentable a result might be averted, if any man would only shoot the wretch.

It should be here mentioned, that the whole of the eastern and northern sides of St. George's Hospital, as well as the fronts of the roofs of the houses at the upper end of Grosvenor-place, presented one mass of galleries, the majority of their occupants being members of the fair sex.

The roof of the palace itself, too, was thickly studded with spectators.

Soon after half past 9 detachments of the Blues and the Life Guards, accompanied with their respective bands, arrived opposite the entrance gate of the palace, and their appearance was quickly followed by that of 12 of Her Majesty's dress carriages together with the state coach. The carriages of her Royal Highness the Duchess of Kent, with those of their Royal Highnesses the Duke of Cambridge, Duchess of of Glocester, and the Duke of Sussex next reached the Royal residence in rapid succession. The whole of these vehicles drove into the court-yard.

During this proceeding the various foreign ambassadors formed into line in the Birdcage-walk. The equipages of these distinguished representatives of the foreign powers excited, as will readily be conjectured from a perusal of the following minute description of them, much admiration.

We give the notices of these splendid vehicles in the rotation they appeared in the procession:—

The Ambassador Extraordinary from the Sultan.—The carriage was drawn by two horses. The body painted a rich lake, with the rising sun and crescent richly emblazoned on the panels. The lining crimson and yellow silk, with rich festoons. The hammercloth blue, with gold and scarlet hanging. The centre scarlet velvet, on which is the rising sun and crescent with diamonds. The carving is very massive. The harness very handsome and elegant, with the rising sun and crescent and star, with trophies on the different parts to correspond. The coachman and footmen wore their usual European liveries.

His Excellency Marshal Soult (Duke de Dalmatia), Ambassador Extraordinary from France.—The carriage of this distinguished nobleman created by far more interest than that of any other ambassador. It was of French manufacture; the colour was a rich cobalt, relieved with gold. The panels were superbly emblazoned with the arms of his Excellency, at the back of which were the baton of a Field-Marshal. The only order was that of the Legion of Honour. It had side lights and four elegant lamps, ornamented with the ducal coronet, of rich chased silver. The raised cornice was also of silver, and it was higher and more elaborately chased than any other carriage in the cavalcade; at each of the four corners was a ducal coronet of large dimensions. The lining of the interior was of a rich nankeen satin, relieved with scarlet, and fitted up in quite an unique style. The hammercloth was of blue broadcloth, and trimmed with nankeen gimp and tassels. In the centre were the arms of his Excellency, exquisitely embroidered. The harness was ornamented with a most beautifully chased silver furniture. The liveries were of a drab colour, with a rich figured silk lace. It was drawn by two horses.

His Excellency the Duke of Palmella, Ambassador Extraordinary from Portugal.—The carriage was drawn by two horses. It is of a deep but very brilliant green, relieved with silver, on which is ornamental tracery of vermilion and a lighter green than the ground; the arms are richly emblazoned on all the panels; beneath those in the centre are the Duke's numerous orders. The loops are silver, with rich chased silver foliage, terminating with the coronet; a solid silver cornice surrounds the roof. The lamps are exceedingly rich, surmounted by the ducal cornet. The hammercloth is white, and in its character unique, and is remarkable for its elegance as well as its novelty. Between rows of rich lace is a deep gimp that, for its richness, might be taken for embroidery. In the centre are his Excellency's arms, richly gilt, within rich Genoa crimson velvet mantles, surmounted by the coronet. Theliming is of white satin damask, striped with rose-coloured satin, being drawn in the centre of the roof in festoons, the whole interior being finished with a white silk lace, figured with coloured roses. The harness is most richly embossed with silver, with waving plumes for the horses. The chasseur's uniform and servants' liveries are:—Chasseur's—green coat, trimmed on collar and cuffs with silver Russia braid, scarlet collar, cuffs, and turnbacks; trousers green, with broad silver lace down the sides, handsomely trimmed with silver Russia braid; silver cross-belt, sword, &c. Servants—coats of dark green, lined through with scarlet, laced richly with silver lace on edges, seams, flaps, and frames, with silver aiguilettes; waistcoats of scarlet, laced with silver lace; breeches, scarlet, with silver lace garters.

His Excellency Count Gustave de Lowenhielm, Ambassador Extraordinary from Sweden.—His Excellency's state carriage was drawn by two horses. The body is painted rich lake, with the arms and the different orders richly emblazoned on the panels. The lining is blue and yellow silk, with handsome festoons; the hammercloth is of white cloth, with gold fringe and hangings; the centre contains the arms and different orders of his Excellency, in chased gold, on crimson Genoa velvet, with rich lace fringe round the same; the carriage and wheels painted a rich cobalt blue, relieved with crimson and gold. The carving of the carriage is very massive; the harness is most splendid, with the arms richly embossed on different parts. The colour of the coats is crimson, trimmed with yellow, and laced in a most elegant manner with rich gold lace, which blends well with the waistcoats and smallclothes of white kerseymere; they are also trimmed with rich gold lace. The chasseur's dress is of green, of the most massive and splendid description, being laced in the richest manner with gold lace.

His Excellency the Marquis de Brignole, Ambassador Extraordinary from Sardinia.—His Excellency's carriage is of French manufacture. The body of a deep chocolate colour, relieved with white. On the panels the noble Marquis's arms are emblazoned in a beautiful style, to the garter of which are appended the various orders of his Excellency. It is the only carriage (excepting Marshal Soult's) that has side lights. It is particularly remarkable for its symmetry and chasteness. At each corner is an elegantly silver-mounted lamp, ornamented with his Excellency's coronet. The lining is of a rich figured crimson damask, the roof being ornamented with festoons of white satin; the whole is finished with a figured silk lace of crimson and white. It was drawn by two horses, their harness being ornamented with richly chased silver mountings. The liveries were a chasseur in a green uniform, with gold cross, belts, and lace; feather, blue and white. Footmen, &c. The coat is scarlet, the seams, lappets, &c., being covered with silk lace, with the arms of the marquis worked in colours. The waistcoats and breeches are white, trimmed with the same lace.

His Excellency Count Alten, Ambassador Extraordinary from Hanover.—The state coach painted olive green, relieved with white; the lining of rich drab silk with satin stripes; arms, supporters, and orders, emblazoned on panels, and handsome white hammercloths, with rich crimson and white fringe, and bullions, and embroidered arms and coronets. The liveries were white cloth, with crimson cuffs and collars, laced with silver; silver aiguilettes on the shoulders. The waistcoats white, laced with silver. The breeches of crimson plush, with silver garters. It was drawn by two horses.

His Excellency Prince Putbus, Ambassador Extraordinary from Prussia.—An elegant state coach of the first class, chastely painted the Royal yellow, relieved by a massy portion of gilding, picked out black, and edged with cobalt blue, decorated with heraldry painted on the doors in large mantles, in which are displayed his Highness's arms and foreign orders of knighthood, surmounted by a crown in the quarters. Both the back and end are also filled with emblazonry. The upper quarters are massively occupied by twelve stately elaborately chased head plates of his arms and orders; on the top of them is displayed a rich finished embossed cornice, gold relieved with rubies. The roof is elegantly and tastefully painted by being starred in gold, chastely studded and relieved with blue. The lining is a delicate and fine amber, in shades, the lace combining in relief our rose, shamrock, and thistle (not an unapt compliment.) The seat cloth is beautifully formed: it is of yellow velvet, tastefully and nearly covered with the richest lace, and having on the whole a fine effect. The carriage was drawn by two horses; harness ornamented with chased brass. His Highness had two chasseurs, in green and gold uniforms, with cocked hats, the feathers of which are yellow and green. The liveries were rich dark puce-coloured coats, covered with a heavy gold lace; waistcoats and breeches of yellow, with gold lace and garters.

His Excellency the Marquis de Miraflores, Ambassador Extraordinary from Spain.—The state coach is painted dark lake, and was drawn by four horses; the arms, with the different orders of his Excellency with supporters and rich mantling, beautifully emblazoned on the panels. The lining of rich crimson damask silk, bordered with white and crimson silk lace; the top beautifully worked and fluted in white satin. The footmen's standards and coachman's seat of solid carved work, richly gilt; hammercloth white, with gold-coloured fringe, and hangings, tastefully arranged in festoons. The harness is very elegantly ornamented with brass. The liveries were very neat, being white, trimmed with a figured silk lace.

His Excellency Baron van der Capellen, Ambassador Extraordinary from the Netherlands.—A state coach, painted an ultra-marine blue, relieved with orange, and lined with drab flowered silk and rich silk lace. Arms and supporters emblazoned on the panels in large crimson and fur mantles, surmounted by large coronets, and the stars of several orders displayed on the quarters; handsomely fringed hammercloth, with embroidered arms, and supporters, and richly chased lamps, surmounted by large brass chased coronets. It was drawn by six horses. The liveries were coats of the above beautiful blue, trimmed with silver lace, and silver epaulets; orange waistcoats and breeches trimmed with silver; hats with real ostrich feathers.

His Excellency Prince Schwarzenburg, Ambassador Extraordinary from Austria.—A state chariot of the most approved taste. The colour is yellow, relieved with blue. On the panels his Excellency's arms in a mantle, superbly emblazoned. Various orders are attached: among the most conspicuous is that of the Gold Fleece. The top is surmounted by a neat but tasteful silver cornice, with the coronet of the Prince at the four corners. The handplates are of silver. The hammercloth is of pale blue, trimmed in an elegant style with amber silk lace. In the centre are the armorial bearings of the Prince, of elaborately chased gold. The interior is lined with a rich blue water-silk damask. The carriage was drawn by two horses. The harness is beautifully finished, and although exceedingly rich and fully charged with arms, chased work, &c., at the same time is so *recherché* that any private gentleman might have used it without appearing to court attraction by any over display of ornament. The liveries.—Coats of imperial blue, lined with scarlet, decorated with a very small figured silver lace; waistcoat and breeches of scarlet, with silver lace trimmings. The chasseurs, an uniform of green, silver cross-belts, swords, &c.

His Excellency Count Stroogonoff, Ambassador Extraordinary from Russia.—The body of the state carriage is painted lake, with ornamental mouldings round the roof and framings, surmounted with coronets. The lamps embossed, and the body suspended by snakes issuing out of rushes, all richly guilt. The panels are embellished with his Excellency's arms, supporters (foxes), three crests on helmets, and the ribands and badges of the Russian St. Alexander and St. Wladimir, the lion of Belgium, the Greek order of Otho, and the medal to commemorate the campaign of 1812, in rich mantles, surmounted by the Count's coronet. The carriage is richly carved with oak branches, &c., painted vermilion and lake, and handsomely gilt. The lining is crimson figured silk, with gold-coloured lace and bullion trimmings, and relieved by the roof being white cloth embroidered with a wreath of oak, with the thistle and shamrock surrounding the rose. The seat-cloth is scarlet to match the livery, with gold-coloured lace and fringe with bullion drops, festooned and ornamented in the centre with his Excellency's arms in gold on a rich black Genoa velvet. The harness is very splendidly emblazoned with solid brass frames, the arms of the count being richly chased. Saddle-cloths of scarlet, laced with wide gold lace and black velvet. The bridle is mounted with gold. Rich crimson silk driving reins, with scarlet satin roses and ear-bows, the whole being of the most costly description. The terets are mounted with a massive coronet. The whip is embroidered with scarlet and white silk, and superbly mounted with gold. The state liveries of his Excellency are of the most splendid description. The colour of the coats scarlet, richly laced with a gold and silk lace. The arms and crest of Count Strogonoff embroidered on it; the lining yellow, and the cuffs and collars of black velvet. At each of the buttons on the cuffs and at the end of each loop of the lace is a handsome gold and silver tassel. The waistcoats are of yellow cloth, laced with the richest gold lace, 2¼ inches broad. The small-clothes of scarlet with a gold band. The whole of them are of the finest quality, and have a grand and imposing appearance. The carriage was drawn by two horses.

His Excellency the Prince de Ligne, Ambassador Extraordinary from Belgium.—The carriage is painted a deep lake, picked out with broad lines of gold, and edged with vermilion. The arms of the noble Prince are richly emblazoned on the panels; the roof ornamented by four gold coronets, one at each corner; the head plates are of brass, richly chased, and full mounted with brass; the seat cloth is drab, bound with a rich figured silk lace, nine inches wide, and ornamented with festoons and rosettes. The carriage was drawn by a set of six fine gray horses, four-in-hand and postilions, and was accompanied by two outriders on gray horses. The liveries were scarlet coat, with yellow collar, cuffs, and edging, richly laced with silver, and richly embroidered with silver lace front, back, and sleeves; a rich silver aiguilette and badge of the prince; yellow vest, richly laced with silver; yellow breeches, with silver garters. Postilion—scarlet jacket, with yellow collar and cuffs, richly laced all round, and embroidered with rich silver gimp, and badge on the arm; leather breeches. Footmen—Scarlet coat, with yellow collar, cuffs, and edging, richly laced all over with silver; yellow waistcoat, richly laced with silver; yellow breeches, with silver garters. They were very rich in their appearance.

His Excellency Count Ludolff, Ambassador Extraordinary from Sicily.—The carriage of his Excellency was the same that he has attended Her Majesty's Drawing-rooms in on ordinary occasions. It has, however, been slightly "touched up." The liveries were new, but of the same description that the Count uses on all state occasions in this country. In fact, there appeared to have been no preparations made by the Premier Ambassador Extraordinary.

The carriages of the resident Turkish, French, Russian, and Austrian Ambassadors, were those they are in the habit of using on state occasions, newly decorated for the day.

At a quarter before 10 o'clock the final formation of the procession was commenced, and after the necessary arrangements had been completed, it set out in manner following:—

Mr. Lee, the high constable of the city of Westminster.
A Squadron of Life Guards.
Under the direction of one of the Queen's Equerries, with two Assistants:—
Carriages of the Foreign Resident Ambassadors and Ministers, in the order in which they take precedence in this country.
The Chargé d'Affaires of Mexico.
The Chargé d'Affaires of Portugal.
The Chargé d'Affaires of Sweden.
The Saxon Minister.
The Hanoverian Minister.
The Greek Minister.
The Sardinian Minister.
The Spanish Minister.
The Minister from the United States.
The Minister from the Netherlands.
The Brazilian Minister.
The Bavarian Minister.
The Danish Minister.
The Belgian Minister.
The Wurtemberg Minister.
The Prussian Minister.
Carriages of the Foreign Ambassadors and Ministers Extraordinary, in the order in which they respectively report their arrival in this country.
Ahmed Fethij Pasha, Ambassador Extraordinary from the Sultan.
Marshal Soult, Ambassador Extraordinary from the King of the French.
The Duke de Palmella, Ambassador Extraordinary from the Queen of Portugal.
The Count Lowenhjelm, Ambassador Extraordinary from the King of Sweden.
The Marquis de Brignole, Ambassador Extraordinary from the King of Sardinia.
Count Alten, Ambassador Extraordinary from the King of Hanover.
The Prince de Putbus, Ambassador Extraordinary from the King of Prussia.
The Marquis de Miraflores, Ambassador Extraordinary from the Queen of Spain.
The Baron de Capellen, Ambassador Extraordinary from the King of the Netherlands.
The Prince Schwarzenburg, Ambassador Extraordinary from the Emperor of Austria.
Count Strogonoff, Ambassador Extraordinary from the Emperor of Russia.
The Prince de Ligne, Ambassador Extraordinary from the King of the Belgians.
Count Ludolf, Ambassador Extraordinary from the King of the Two Sicilies.
The Turkish Ambassador.
The French Ambassador.
The Russian Ambassador.
The Austrian Ambassador.
Mounted Band of a Regiment of Household Brigade.
Detachment of Life Guards.
Under the direction of one of Her Majesty's Equerries, with two Assistants:—
Carriages of the Branches of the Royal Family, with their respective Escorts.
The Duchess of Kent and Attendants, in Her Royal Highness's two Carriages, each drawn by six Horses; with her proper Escort of Life Guards.
The Duchess of Glocester and Attendants, in her Royal Highness's two Carriages, each drawn by six Horses; with her proper Escort of Life Guards.
The Duke and Duchess of Cambridge and Attendants, in his Royal Highness's two Carriages, each drawn by six Horses; with his proper Escort of Life Guards.
The Duke of Sussex and Attendants, in his Royal Highness's Carriage, drawn by six Horses; with his proper Escort of Life Guards.
Mounted Band of a Regiment of the Household Brigade.
Under the direction of one of the Queen's Equerries, with two Assistants:—
The Queen's Bargemaster.
The Queen's Forty-eight Watermen.

HER MAJESTY'S CARRIAGES,
each drawn by six Horses.

Two Grooms walking. — The First Carriage, drawn by Six Bays, — Two Grooms walking.
Conveys
Two Pages of Honour { James Charles M. Covell, Esq. / George H. Cavendish, Esq.
Two Gentlemen Ushers { Major Beresford. / Captain Green.
Two Grooms walking. — The Second Carriage, drawn by Six Bays, — Two Grooms walking.
Conveys
Two Pages of Honour { Charles Ellice, Esq. / Lord Kilmarnock.
Two Gentlemen Ushers { Charles Heneage, Esq. / The Hon. F. Byng.
Two Grooms walking. — The Third Carriage, drawn by Six Bays, — Two Grooms walking.
Conveys
Two Bedchamber Women { Lady Theresa Digby. / Lady Charlotte Copley.
Two Grooms in Waiting { The Hon. George Keppel. / Henry Rich, Esq.
Two Grooms walking. — The Fourth Carriage, drawn by Six Bays, — Two Grooms walking.
Conveys
Two Bedchamber Women { Lady Harriet Clive. / Lady Caroline Barrington.
Two Grooms in Waiting { The Hon. William Cooper. / Sir Frederick Stovin.
Two Grooms walking. — The Fifth Carriage, drawn by six Bays, — Two Grooms walking.
Conveys
Two Maids of Honour, { Hon. Miss Rice. / Hon. Miss Murray.
Groom of the Robes, Captain Francis Seymour.
Clerk Marshal, Hon. Colonel Cavendish.
Two Grooms walking. — The Sixth Carriage, drawn by Six Bays, — Two Grooms walking.
Conveys
Two Maids of Honour, { Hon. Miss Lister. / Hon. Miss Paget.
Keeper of Privy Purse, Sir Henry Wheatley.
Vice-Chamberlain, Earl of Belfast.
Two Grooms walking — The Seventh Carriage, drawn by Six ——, — Two Grooms walking.
Conveys
Two Maids of Honour, { Hon. Miss Cavendish. / Hon. Miss Cocks.
Treasurer of the Household, Earl of Surrey.
Controller of the Household, The Right Hon. G. Byng.
Two Grooms walking — The Eighth Carriage, drawn by Six Bays, — Two Grooms walking.
Conveys
Two Maids of Honour, { Hon. Miss Dillon. / Hon. Miss Pitt.
Two Lords in Waiting, { Lord Gardner. / Lord Lilford.
Two Grooms walking. — The Ninth Carriage, drawn by Six Grays, — Two Grooms walking.
Conveys
Two Ladies of the Bedchamber, { Lady Portman. / Lady Barham.
Two Lords in Waiting, { Lord Byron. / Viscount Falkland.
Two Grooms walking. — The Tenth Carriage drawn by Six Bays, — Two Grooms walking.
Conveys
Two Ladies of the Bedchamber { Lady Lyttelton. / Countess of Mulgrave.
Two Lords in Waiting { Viscount Torrington. / Earl of Uxbridge.
Two Grooms walking. — The Eleventh Carriage, drawn by Six Bays, — Two Grooms walking.
Conveys
Two Ladies of the Bedchamber { The Countess of Charlemont. / Marchioness of Tavistock.
Two Lords in Waiting { The Earl of Fingal. / Marquis of Headfort.
Two Grooms walking — The Twelfth Carriage, drawn by Six Blacks, — Two Grooms walking.
Conveys
The Principal Lady of the Bedchamber. } The Marchioness of Lansdowne.
The Lord Chamberlain, The Marquis Conyngham.
The Lord Steward, The Duke of Argyll.
A Squadron of Life Guards.
Mounted Band of the Household Brigade.
Military Staff and Aides-de-Camp, on Horseback,
Three and Three,
Sir R. Gardiner, Colonel Freemantle, Lord G. Russell,
Colonel Wynyard, Colonel Fergusson, Colonel Brotherton,
Sir A. J. Dalrymple, Sir J. H. Reynett, Colonel Smelt,
Colonel Arnold, Colonel Wemyss, Colonel Wood.
First and Principal Aide-de-Camp to the Queen,
Lieutenant-General Sir Herbert Taylor, G.C.B.,
attended by the Equerry of the Crown Stable, Sir George Quentin.
The Queen's Gentleman Rider, J. Fozard, Esq.
Deputy Adjutant-General, Major-General J. Gardiner.
Deputy Quartermaster-General, Colonel Freeth, K.H.
Deputy Adjutant-General, Royal Artillery, Sir Alexander Dickson.
Quartermaster-General, Sir J. Willoughby Gordon, Bart.
Military Secretary to the Commander-in-Chief, Lord Fitzroy Somerset, K.C.B.
Adjutant-General, Sir J. Macdonald, K.C.B.
The Royal Huntsmen, Yeomen Prickers, and Foresters.
Six of Her Majesty's Horses, with rich trappings, each Horse led by two Grooms.
The Knight Marshal, Sir J. C. Lamb, Bart.
Marshalmen in ranks of Four.
The First Exons of the Yeomen of the Guard, on horseback, Sir Thomas Curteis, Knight.
The Second Exon, Samuel Hancock, Esq.
The Third Exon, Captain William Bellairs.
The Fourth Exon, J. Nuttall, Esq.
One hundred Yeomen of the Guard, Four and Four.
The Clerk of the Check, James Bunce Curling, Esq.
Harbinger, Samuel Wilson, Esq.
Ensign Sir Thomas N. Reeve.
Lieutenant, Sir Samuel Spry, M.P.

THE STATE COACH,
Drawn by Eight Cream-coloured Horses,
attended by a Yeoman of the Guard at each wheel, and two Footmen at each door,
The Gold Stick, Viscount Combermere, — And the Captain of the Yeomen of the Guard, the Earl of Ilchester,
riding on either side, attended by two grooms each,
Conveying

THE QUEEN.

The Mistress of the Robes, the Duchess of Sutherland.
The Master of the Horse, the Earl of Albemarle.
The Captain-General of the Royal Archers, the Duke of Buccleuch,
attended by two Grooms.
A squadron of Life Guards.

The various members of the Royal family were loudly greeted as they passed in succession, and when the youthful Queen appeared the loudest plaudits rent the air. Not a male head remained covered, and loud were most of the assembled multitude in their wishes for Her Majesty's continued enjoyment of good health.

Her Majesty's State Hammercloth is covered with scarlet silk Genoa velvet, embroidered throughout with gold. The badges on each side and back, the fringes, ropes, and tassels, being of that valuable metal. We understand that it cost 1,000*l.*

His Royal Highness the Duke of Cambridge.—Two elegant hammercloths, made in the same style as those of His Majesty George III., in order to harmonize with the state liveries; they are composed of scarlet cloth, with several rows of rich purple Genoa velvet, edged with gold lace, and footmen's holders to correspond, with scarlet tassels, producing a beautiful effect.

HYDE-PARK CORNER.

This neighbourhood and the western portion of Piccadilly, though perhaps they did not present an appearance of quite so much splendour as may have distinguished other parts of the line, would yet have excited no small surprise and admiration on any occasion less remarkable than the present. The few tradesmen resident in that vicinity, following the example of their brethren in the other streets along which Her Majesty was to pass, had spared neither expense nor trouble to provide for the accommodation of their friends and connexions, as well as for that of their more welcome visitors, who paid 20s. or 30s. for seats. The awnings and balconies were for the most part decorated with much taste, and the effect was gay and showy, but on the whole inferior to other parts of the line. The nobility and gentry residing in this district had for the most part caused galleries and other accommodations to be erected for their friends and households to insure them an advantageous view of the procession. Amongst these may be enumerated the houses of Mr. N. M. Rothschild, Lord Willoughby d'Eresby, the Duke of Cambridge, the Earls of Cadogan, Rosebery, Coventry, &c. Upon the grounds immediately adjacent to the porters' lodges on either side of the gate at the top of Constitution-hill, there were raised very commodious galleries, protected from the weather, which were filled with hundreds of very respectable company. Soon after 6 o'clock in the morning Hyde Park-corner became a scene of the most animated and interesting character. The large galleries in front of St. George's Hospital afforded places to a vast concourse of company, and several of the houses along Grosvenor-place were occupied by numerous spectators. An inscription was placed on the front door of the hospital, stating that it would be closed during the day to all but cases of accidental injury. A large proportion of the military employed in the business of this splendid ceremonial passed either along Piccadilly or down Constitution hill, which of course much increased the bustle, the excitement, and the brilliancy of that neighbourhood. Horse Guards, Grenadier Guards, Hussars, Rifle Brigade, in succession attracted the attention and called forth the admiration of a multitude in whom 20 years of peace had not extinguished a sense of the gallant achievements which in times of danger had protected the independence and elevated the character of England. Before 8 o'clock the whole of the footways along Piccadilly and Constitution-hill were filled with a dense multitude, arrayed in their best attire, and fully resolved to enjoy to the utmost this universal holyday. At a very early hour a work of perfect supererogation was performed, namely, the watering of the roads, for there was quite enough of rain to prevent the least inconvenience from dust. The Rifle Brigade, mingled with police, lined the passage for the procession at this part of its course, the Horse Guards (red) being stationed at intervals of about 30 yards. Soon after 8 o'clock a few of the peers' carriages who possess the privilege of passing through that gate proceeded down the hill on their way to the Abbey, but from an early hour Grosvenor-place and Piccadilly were crowded with equipages, many of which were distinguished by greater splendour than perhaps was ever displayed on any similar occasion. At a quarter before' o'clock two of the Royal carriages, with six bays each, passed through on their way to the Palace, and this forming the earliest specimen of the procession, however insignificant in itself, appeared quite an event in the eyes of the excited crowd, whose chief amusement previously had been listening to the band of the Rifles, which was stationed outside the gate, and which played a little at intervals. The crowd here was more orderly and well regulated than we ever remember to have seen a London mob; it is, indeed, hardly fair to apply to them that designation, for it has very rarely happened that the pedestrians assembled to witness any public display presented so respectable an appearance. None of those practical jokes were played off that occasionally while away the time during which an idle multitude has to await the coming of the great event that has convened them. The occasional scream of a woman, arising from some groundless fear, a dispute now and then between a Park-keeper and a mischievous boy, or the freaks of a restiff horse, were the only interruptions that disturbed the general quietude which prevailed amongst the people up to 10 o'clock. One of the last-mentioned class of occurrences was very near being attended with unfortunate results. The horse of an officer of the Guards kicked rather viciously against the paling of the south-west corner of the gateway, and broke one of the iron rails, to the great terror, but not in the least to the injury, of the ladies stationed within the fence.

Soon after 9 o'clock all apprehension of rain seemed to disappear, and the confident expectation of a fine day to be universally indulged. At length the hour appointed for forming the procession approached, and every individual in the tens of thousands then assembled endeavoured to secure or retain a good position for seeing that which had induced him to forego a night's repose, and caused him to breakfast almost at supper time. Gradually the gorgeous procession advanced up the hill, and the discharge of a gun announced that the Queen had entered the state coach; the band of the Horse Guards played the national anthem, and the union of expectation and delight was apparent in every countenance. The carriages of the foreign ambassadors formed the first part of the line, and the taste displayed in these equipages was subjected to no measured criticism, it being universally agreed that the artisans of England, good in everything, were unequalled in coach-building, and that the taste of England was in this at least the true standard of excellence. The representatives of foreign potentates at this Court certainly never made a display of magnificence which even in the remotest degree approached that which graced the coronation of Queen Victoria, and those who questioned the chasteness or elegance of those equipages should recollect that no inconsiderable number of them were manufactured in London, and that their gorgeousness, remarkable as it was, could not be regarded as going beyond what the dignity and interest of the occasion required.

A few of the foreign Ambassadors were cheered as they passed through the gateway, the cheers given to the French Ambassador Extraordinary being by far the most marked; he and the Turkish Minister were considered the two great lions amongst the *corps diplomatique*.

The Duchess of Kent was the first of the Royal Family who passed through the gateway. Her Royal Highness very graciously acknowledged the cheers with which she was re-

CONTENTS.

LONDON, WEDNESDAY, JANUARY 23, 1901.

DEATH OF THE QUEEN.—Queen Victoria died yesterday evening at Osborne House. The first official intimation of the mournful event was a telegram from the Prince of Wales to the Lord Mayor, dated Osborne, 6 45 p.m.:—"My beloved mother, the Queen, has just passed away, surrounded by her children and grandchildren.—Albert Edward." The bulletins issued in the earlier part of the day had foreshadowed a fatal termination to her Majesty's illness. At 8 a.m. the physicians announced that the Queen showed signs of diminishing strength, and that her Majesty's condition had again assumed a more serious aspect. At noon there was a slightly more favourable bulletin, stating that there was no change for the worse in the Queen's condition. She had recognized the several members of the Royal family who were present, and was then asleep. At 4 p.m., however, there came the announcement that the Queen was slowly sinking, and at 6 45 the last bulletin, announcing that her Majesty had breathed her last at 6 30 p.m., surrounded by her children and grandchildren. Mr. Balfour, who had gone to Osborne in the course of the afternoon, telegraphed to the Earl of Pembroke, Lord Steward of the Household, that the Queen died peacefully at 6 30 p.m. The sad intelligence of the Queen's death spread rapidly over London and all parts of the kingdom, and was everywhere received with manifestations of the deepest sorrow. In reply to the Prince's message, the Lord Mayor telegraphed that he had received the announcement of the nation's great loss with profound distress and grief, and had communicated this most sad intimation to his fellow-citizens. Her Majesty's name and memory would live for ever in the hearts of her people. He desired to convey to the Prince and to all the members of the Royal Family the earnest sympathy and condolence of the City of London in their great sorrow. The Chairman of the London County Council announced at the close of the meeting yesterday evening the death of "the best loved and the most illustrious of all the Monarchs who have ruled in these realms," and said that in the name of the citizens of London he proposed to convey the respectful and profound sympathy of the Council to the members of the Royal Family. Similar expressions of sorrow and sympathy found utterance from public bodies in different parts of the country, and public functions and engagements of almost all kinds have been abandoned or indefinitely postponed. In all the colonies and dependencies of the Empire, in the United States—whose President addressed to the King a message of condolence immediately on receiving the news—and on the Continent the intelligence of the Queen's death has aroused feelings of keen sorrow and elicited expressions of profound admiration and respect for the departed Sovereign and sympathy for her people. (pp. 9, 11, and 12)

PARLIAMENT, in accordance with constitutional rule, will meet to-day, at 4 p.m. (p. 12)

THE REPORT OF THE SOUTH AFRICAN HOSPITALS COMMISSION was issued yesterday. While pointing out to what extent, and in what respects, complaints with regard to the care of the sick and wounded in the present war are well founded, the Commissioners are of opinion that, on the whole, it cannot be said that the medical and hospital arrangements have broken down. All witnesses of experience in other wars are practically unanimous in the view that, taking it all in all, in no previous campaign have the sick and wounded been so well looked after as they have in this. (p. 10)

THE LAW COURTS.—In the Queen's Bench Division of the High Court, yesterday, the trial of the action brought by the Columbus Company (Limited) against Birnbaum and Co. (Limited) to recover the price of certain advertisements inserted in a paper named *Commerce* was concluded. The jury were unable to agree on a verdict, and were discharged. (p. 17)

THE PEMBROKE ELECTION PETITION.—The trial of the petition presented by Mr. Terrell, Q.C., against the return of General Laurie for Pembroke and Haverfordwest Boroughs began yesterday at Haverfordwest before Mr. Justice Channell and Mr. Justice Darling. General Laurie has presented a counter-petition, alleging bribery, corruption, treating, &c., on behalf of Mr. Terrell. The arguments yesterday were devoted to the question of the position of the Haverfordwest freeholders, who, it was contended for the petitioner, had no right to be on the register at all. Their Lordships reserved their decision on this point till this morning. (p. 17)

CENTRAL CRIMINAL COURT.—Before Mr. Justice Wills, the trial of Benjamin Greene Lake, 62, solicitor, on charges of converting to his own use the money of clients which he held as trustee or as attorney, was concluded after occupying the Court for six days. His Lordship summed up at considerable length, dealing specifically with each of the four charges in the indictment. The jury, after a few minutes' consideration, found the prisoner guilty of misappropriating money belonging to three of the funds specified, but not guilty in regard to the fourth. His Lordship, in passing sentence, said he did not see how the jury could have arrived at any other conclusion than that embodied in their verdict. That a man in the prisoner's position should have done such things was terrible to think of, and must demand very condign punishment. Age, respectability, and a great reputation had unfortunately been great part of the stock-in-trade by which the prisoner's frauds had been committed. He sentenced the prisoner to seven years' penal servitude in respect of two of the offences, and to five years' penal servitude in respect of the third, to run consecutively—in all, 12 years' penal servitude. The prisoner thanked his Lordship for the infinite pains he had taken in the case, and said that if he were guilty, as his Lordship was bound to assume, the sentence was a right one. (p. 2)

CAPTURE OF AN ESCAPED CONVICT.—King, one of the convicts who escaped from Borstal Prison, Kent, some weeks ago, was recaptured in London yesterday morning. (p. 10)

THE WEATHER forecast for Southern England (London and Channel) anticipates for to-day north-westerly winds, fresh; colder; fair generally, but local showers in the early part of the day. (p. 13)

SPECIAL ARTICLES are published to-day on "Queen Victoria: Life and Reign" (pp. 3, 4, 5, 6, 7, and 8) and "The King: a Loyal Appreciation" (p. 10).

THE CITY.—The Money Market was quiet yesterday, with no material change in the rates for loans and discounts. Silver was fixed ⅛d. lower. On the Stock Exchange there was very little doing and in most markets the tendency was dull until towards the close, when there was some recovery owing to an advance in Consols, which closed a shade higher for the account than on Monday. American Railroad issues were well supported and left off at a considerable rise in many cases. The West Australian gold output for December is published. (p. 16)

THE WAR.—There is news of raiding by Boer parties in the vicinity of Johannesburg. The electric light works at Brakpan were attacked on Monday morning and much damage done to the machinery.—Skirmishing has taken place at two or three points in Cape Colony, and at Taungs and Boshof the invaders have suffered rather severely. The colonial Dutch are bringing in arms and horses to the authorities in large numbers. (p. 9)

The dreaded blow has fallen, and a world-wide Empire mourns its irreparable loss. Our beloved QUEEN, full of years and of honour, has passed to her rest. There are no words to express the general grief, the universal sense of national and personal bereavement, awakened by the event which it is our melancholy duty to chronicle to-day. For nearly sixty-four years QUEEN VICTORIA has watched, at first with conscientious diffidence, later with ever-maturing experience, but always with the sympathetic insight of a sensitive yet finely-balanced nature, over every development of national policy and destiny. Through that long period she has commanded the esteem of those who direct the affairs of the world, and has won the affection and the confidence of the vast majority, whose judgment must be formed upon general and external indications of character. Only a rare combination of sweetness and strength, only a subtle blending of the highest qualities of head and heart, can achieve that double success. This generation can never know, save in the most general and imperfect way, the extent of the beneficent influence wielded by the QUEEN at once over the great and over the lowly ones of the earth. The earlier years of her reign have so far passed into history that we know much of the inner life of politics which remains secret while the principal actors are alive. As regards the later portion of her reign we have no such materials, yet it was in that portion that her experience was ripest, her contribution to government most valuable, and her influence with the Sovereigns and statesmen who rule the world most firmly established. The condition of Europe when she ascended the Throne was one of extreme instability. A few years later it became one of turmoil and confusion, in which dynasties were overthrown and high potentates had to seek asylum. That the British Throne came through that troublous time, not merely unscathed, but with added prestige and security, must be held due in no small measure to the character of its occupant. Our own country by no means escaped the infection of the ideas that convulsed the Continent; nor was it exempt from the grave economic and social evils that formed a legitimate ground for discontent. There are few among us who can recall the attitude of the people towards the Monarchy in the thirties and forties, but all have material enough to show them how striking is the contrast presented by the state of public opinion at the present day. We must not forget that many causes combined to effect a fundamental amelioration of the social conditions, and that many minds contributed to the triumph of larger and nobler conceptions of government. But, if we have had orderly evolution where other nations have gone through devastating internal conflicts, if the Monarchy held its own while new buttresses were being built for its support, and if it now stands not only broad-based upon the people's will, but strong in the affections of kindred nations over sea, we owe these results, to a degree which it is hardly possible to overestimate, to the womanly sweetness, the gentle sagacity, the utter disinterestedness, and the unassailable rectitude of the QUEEN.

The nation owes her much more, though, for the reasons just alluded to, the proofs are not yet available in their fulness. Though always scrupulously careful not to overstep the limits marked out for her by the Constitution, the QUEEN has never forgotten the rights and duties that the Constitution confers and imposes. She has always played her part in Government as the Chief Magistrate of the nation, and has known how, when occasion demanded, to assert the rights of the Throne against a too autocratic Minister. By the extent of her family connexions and the friendly correspondence she maintained with Continental monarchs, she brought to bear upon international questions a kind of information which Ministers do not always possess, and a knowledge of personal equations which British Ministers, in the opinion of many, are not sufficiently careful to seek. The confidence inspired by her personal character enabled her on many occasions to use her intimate knowledge with effect in smoothing the rugged places of international relations, or in modifying a policy which through sheer inadequacy of information would have led to undesirable and undesired friction. History alone can do justice to her influence over the politics of Europe, but enough is known even now to assure us that, both by her informed criticism at home and by the deference paid to her abroad, she rendered from time to time very valuable services alike to her own country and to the peace of the world. There are yet other ways in which a Sovereign may profoundly affect, for good or bad, the fortunes of a nation. We have to thank the QUEEN for an influence of the most potent kind, consistently and vigorously used to enforce high ideals of social and personal virtue, of religious faith, and of the Christian life. Her own life was by choice, and as far as the necessities of her position would permit, one of almost austere simplicity and homeliness. Her Court has been absolutely unsullied by the vices which had come to be regarded as the inseparable concomitants of Courts, and if society at large has not quite reached her standard, at least it cannot plead the want of a shining example. In a yet larger sense the QUEEN has conferred an incalculable boon upon the nation. Her whole life, public and private, has been one great and abiding lesson upon the paramount importance of character. No lesson is more needed in days when superficial cleverness, or real ability untrammelled by scruples, too often fills the public eye by the meretricious aid of the self-advertisement which the QUEEN abhorred. Her triumphs have been won by sheer force of character. Though richly endowed with saving common sense, and with that sanity of judgment which is the highest of intellectual gifts, the QUEEN was not especially remarkable for high development of any specialized intellectual force. It was by the combination of sanity of judgment with inflexible integrity and unwavering grasp of the fundamental principles of conduct that she attained results far beyond the reach of the most brilliant intellectual endowments wanting that basis of character.

Epochs sometimes find names that do not very accurately fit them, but we can speak with singular accuracy of the Victorian age. So far as any period in the development of a nation can be taken out of its context and treated as a chapter by itself, the period covered by the reign of QUEEN VICTORIA can be so treated with quite unusual felicity. Her reign coincides very accurately with a sort of second renaissance, an intellectual movement accomplishing in a brief term more than had been done in preceding centuries. Since the days of ELIZABETH there has been no such awakening of the mind of the nation, no such remarkable stride in the path of progress, no such spreading abroad of the British race and British rule over the world at large, as in the period covered by the reign whose end we now have to deplore. In art, in letters, in music, in science, in religion, and, above all, in the moral and material advancement of the mass of the nation, the Victorian age has been a time of extraordinary activity. It is not easy without some concentration of thought to picture the transformation that has been wrought in the habits, ideas, and circumstances of the people of Great and Greater Britain since the QUEEN ascended the Throne. Nor is it easy, though the task is well worth attempting, to realize with any adequacy how differently that transformation might have worked out but for the personal character and example of the QUEEN, and the beneficence of the silent, persistent influence she exerted upon those who in turn influenced the shaping of events. There is much in what we see around us that we may easily and rightly wish to see improved. The *laudator temporis acti* may even contend that we have lost some things that had better have been preserved. But no permissible deductions can obscure the fact that the period in question has been one of intellectual upheaval, of enormous social and economic progress, and, upon the whole, of moral and spiritual improvement. It is also true, unfortunately, that the impetus has to some extent spent itself. At the close of the reign we are finding ourselves somewhat less secure of our position than we could desire, and somewhat less abreast of the problems of the age than we ought to be, considering the initial advantages we secured. The "condition of England question" does not present itself in so formidable a shape as at the beginning of the reign, but it does arouse the attention of those who try to look a little ahead of current business. Others have learned our lessons and bettered our instructions while we have been too easily content to rely upon the methods which were effective a generation or two ago. In this way the Victorian age is defined at its end as well as at its beginning. The command of natural forces that made us great and rich has been superseded by newer discoveries and methods, and we have to open what may be called a new chapter. But "the first of the new "in our race's story beats the last of the old." If we now enter upon our work in the spirit embodied in the untiring vigilance and the perpetual openness of mind that distinguished the QUEEN, if, like her, we reverence knowledge and hold duty imperfectly discharged until we have brought all attainable knowledge to bear upon its performance, her descendants will witness advance not less important than that of her long and glorious reign.

The grief which reigns to-day throughout the wide dominions of the Empire and in the hearts of many millions of men and women beyond our borders has hardly been paralleled in the history of mankind. The whole world feels that in the death of our beloved QUEEN it has suffered a loss which cannot be made good. Upon us, her subjects, the bereavement comes most heavily, but we have the consolation of knowing that men of all creeds and nations share our sorrow with their whole hearts. The death of those we love, however clearly we have foreseen it, always comes with something of a shock at the last, and, although the hopes cherished for the recovery of our venerable SOVEREIGN were very faint from the beginning, her illness has been so sudden and so brief that her people realize but imperfectly as yet the measure of their affliction. The first bulletin issued yesterday morning was ominous. There were symptoms, it reported, that the strength of the illustrious patient was waning, and the physicians declared that her condition had again assumed a more serious aspect. The statement published at mid-day could not allay the apprehensions caused by the earlier message. It merely affirmed that there had been no change for the worse in the past four hours and that HER MAJESTY was then asleep. At 4 in the afternoon the medical attendants announced that the QUEEN was slowly sinking, and at a quarter to 7 it became their duty to tell her sorrowing people that the best and best-beloved of English Sovereigns had breathed her last at half-past 6. Nothing can console the nation for their loss or greatly lessen the sorrow with which it fills, and will long fill, all hearts; but it must be to us some alleviation of our grief to know that the QUEEN we have loved and revered all our lives has had such an end as she would have desired and as we well may envy her. She has undergone no long illness, no weary and piteous process of slow decay, and apparently she has suffered little bodily pain. The form of the gracious and characteristic message, in which she intimated her purpose to allow the DUKE and DUCHESS of YORK to open the first Parliament of the new nation she has assisted to launch upon its course in the Pacific, showed that the thought of death was present to her mind some months ago, but up to last week she was in the fullest possession of her faculties of mind and body and was daily engaged in the business of her high office. Her long life of labour and of duty has ended with the "one "clear call" for which LORD TENNYSON prayed. She has died as she has lived, thinking and working for her people.

Nothing has endeared the QUEEN more to the hearts of her subjects than the strength and warmth of her domestic affections. From the nature of her malady there was reason to fear that she and her nearest relatives might have been deprived of the last consolation of a mutual recognition, and the dread that this might be so increased the bitterness of the general sorrow. It will be learnt with relief that they were spared this trial. The mid-day bulletin of yesterday states that HER MAJESTY had recognized the several members of her family who were gathered together at Osborne. The period of consciousness is hardly likely to have lasted very long, as we know that sleep supervened before noon, and it is said that the end came in sleep, but, however brief, it must have been and must be for the rest of their lives unspeakably precious to the children and grandchildren who were assembled round her bed. It was surrounded by her children and her children's children, that, as the PRINCE of WALES tells the LORD MAYOR in the simple and pathetic message in which he announced his Royal mother's death, the English QUEEN, whose first thoughts and feelings were ever for her English home, quitted this world. They and we have every reason to be grateful for the nature of the last scene of all. The end, we are assured, was absolutely peaceful and free from pain.

The universal and exceptional tokens of sympathy which are reaching us from all quarters of the globe show how deep is the impression left upon the heart and feelings of mankind by the goodness of our late QUEEN. It is the noble simplicity and purity of her life and of her aims which makes all the world feel the poorer for her loss. All peoples feel that in her they have lost a strong and constant factor making for good in the world, and the feeling is most just. QUEEN VICTORIA has been to two generations of men an example of moral excellence which has influenced their thoughts and their actions consciously and unconsciously. Where all nations join with us in deploring our irreparable loss, it would be invidious to choose out for special acknowledgment any single State. But there is one race whose love and sympathy in sorrow as in joy come home to us more nearly than those of all the rest. The great English-speaking Republic beyond the Atlantic has not failed to send to us, officially by the mouth of PRESIDENT MCKINLEY and unofficially by innumerable newspaper articles and other tokens of popular feeling, proof of how heartily and how profoundly it feels with us the grief we suffer to-day. Need we say for ourselves and for our Colonies how dear to us in such an hour is the fellowship in woe our American kinsmen so generously and so warmly tender us?

At a moment of acute and universal sorrow when the nation bows its head under a great and, as yet, imperfectly realized bereavement, natural feeling would prompt a reverent pause before we turn to the necessary business of the time. But a nation's grief for the loss of a beloved Sovereign admits of no such solace. The Throne is never vacant, and at the very moment of parting from our QUEEN we turn to acclaim our KING. He must at once take the oath as SOVEREIGN and will preside at a meeting of the Council, and this very afternoon Parliament, hurriedly summoned, will assemble to swear allegiance to the new monarch. He whom we have so long known as the PRINCE of WALES, and who has won for that title the affectionate regard of the country, now claims its homage as its rightful KING. He enters upon a great heritage of loyalty to the Throne established by his mother's long and beneficent reign, and he may count with certainty upon its transference to himself. The KING has undergone a long training in the best of schools and has proved himself the possessor of great natural aptitudes for the duties of Royalty, of which no inconsiderable share has fallen to his lot to discharge for many years past. Indeed, so great has been the part he has played in the State as PRINCE of WALES that, on ascending the Throne in his sixtieth year, he will exercise, at least in the ceremonial sphere, functions with which he is scarcely less familiar than if their actual discharge had been his for the ordinary lifetime of a generation. Endowed as he is with many of the most lovable and attractive qualities of his mother—with warm sympathies, with a kind heart, with a generous disposition, and with a quick appreciation of genuine worth—the nation is happy in the confidence that in spirit as well as in form it may count upon the maintenance of that conception of Royalty which is the only one that most of us have ever known. To these qualities the KING adds perfect tact, wide knowledge of men, and the business virtues of method, prompt decision, punctuality, and great capacity for work.

There is no position in the world more difficult to fill than that of Heir Apparent to the Throne. It is beset by more than all the temptations of actual Royalty, while the weight of counteracting responsibility is much less directly felt. It must be with a feeling akin to hopelessness that a man in that position offers up the familiar prayer, "Lead us not into temptation." Other men may avoid much temptation if they honestly endeavour to keep out of its way, but the heir to a Throne is followed, dogged, and importuned by temptation in its most seductive forms. It is not only the obviously bad that he has to guard against; he must also steel himself against much that comes in the specious garb of goodness and almost with the imperious command of necessity. The KING has passed through that tremendous ordeal, prolonged through youth and manhood to middle age. We shall not pretend that there is nothing in his long career which those who respect and admire him could not wish otherwise. Which of us can say that with even approximate temptations to meet he could face the fierce light that beats upon an heir apparent no less than upon the THRONE? As is pointed out in an Appreciation of the new KING which we print to-day, the PRINCE of WALES in all his public relations has been as unique among those who have occupied the same position as was his mother among Sovereigns. He has never failed in his duty to the THRONE and the nation. He has never followed the example of his predecessors by encouraging intrigues, or placing himself at the head of a faction. What is much more, he has shown a scrupulous care, worthy of his mother herself, never to overstep by a hairsbreadth the lines marked out for him by the Constitution, and never to compromise by any leaning to this party or the other the position which he expected one day to fill. To all the servants of the CROWN he has invariably shown equal and impartial courtesy and amiability. He has had and has used opportunities to serve the public in ways open only to one in his detached position, but with admirable discretion and perfect tact he has avoided the smallest appearance of service to a party.

In two things the KING is fortunate, as well as in his own character and the cordial affection it has inspired in the nation at large. He will have by his side a QUEEN who has also won the hearts of the people by her possession of all the qualities that go to make up womanly grace and worth. The PRINCESS of WALES from her arrival on our shores has been universally popular and beloved; and as QUEEN ALEXANDRA she will assuredly increase her hold upon the nation's affections by maintaining in her life and Court all the high traditions upheld by QUEEN VICTORIA. The KING again is happy, and the nation is also happy, in the fact that at his accession he has for chief adviser a Minister of LORD SALISBURY'S ripe experience, practised wisdom, high ability, and lofty character—a Minister who commands the unbounded respect even of his opponents, and whose reputation abroad is higher and greater than his countrymen possibly realize.

LA REYNE EST MORTE.

Mother of Mothers, Queen of Queens,
  Ruler of Rulers, Lord of Lords;
War harvests, but the Reaper gleans
  A richer prize than Swords.

God help our England, for we stand
  Orphaned of Her who made us one;
The Honour of the Fatherland,
  Her Hope, Her Trust, Her Sun.

Afar, where Summers burn and glow,
  The subject Peoples of our race
Shall see their stricken Master go
  With tears upon his face.

The Nation, at her dying, born,
  Shall weep beneath the Southern Cross,
And with her Mother-Country mourn
  Irreparable loss.

The scattered Islands of Her Realm
  Shall droop the emblem of Her sway
Who through the long years grasped the helm—
  Through the laborious day.

And flashing lights shall signal far
  Their tidings to the passing ships,
To tell the sinking of Her Star,
  Her sorrowful eclipse.

Oh Mother Queen! God's honoured guest,
  Who greatly welcomes those who bring
Thy great credentials; thine His rest!
  Amen. God save the King.

From The Times of 1801.

JAN. 23.

It is with satisfaction we learn, that a plan has been suggested by some Gentlemen in the City, of fitting out a considerable number of privateers for the purpose of cruizing against the trade of the Northern Powers, but more particularly that of the Danes and Swedes. This proposal has already met with such general encouragement, that there are strong grounds to believe it will be carried into execution. By the adoption of it, Government would be enabled to dispose of the whole of our naval force with full effect, and make every necessary provision for the defence of the United Kingdom. An association of a similar nature is also talked of among the Noblemen and Gentlemen of the country, unconnected with commercial affairs.

COURT NEWS.

(From the *London Gazette*.)
CHANCERY OF THE ROYAL VICTORIAN ORDER, ST. JAMES'S PALACE, JAN. 1, 1901.

The Queen has been graciously pleased to make the following appointments in the Royal Victorian Order:—

To be a Knight Commander.
Reginald Baliol, Viscount Esher, C.B.

To be an Honorary Member of the Fourth Class.
Lieutenant von Gerlach, Honorary Member of the Fifth Class.

Formal acknowledgment is made in last night's *Gazette* of addresses of condolence presented to her late Majesty Queen Victoria on the death of the Duke of Saxe-Coburg and Gotha and of Prince Christian of Schleswig-Holstein.

The Duke of Cambridge arrived in town from Paris about 8 o'clock last evening.

Prince Alexander of Teck arrived in London yesterday from White Lodge, Richmond.

Yesterday was the 70th birthday of Prince Christian of Schleswig-Holstein, who was born on January 22, 1831.

The Marquis of Salisbury arrived at King's-cross at 2 40 yesterday afternoon from Hatfield.

Viscount Cross left London yesterday for Eccle Riggs, Broughton-in-Furness, Lancashire.

The Master of Trinity Hall, Cambridge (the Rev. H. Latham), who was very ill on Sunday, was reported yesterday to have had an excellent night and to be generally better.

A bulletin issued yesterday morning states that Signor Verdi had an attack of apoplexy on Monday. The patient's condition yesterday, although less alarming, was still serious. The authorities and many of the inhabitants assembled before the composer's residence in Milan waiting their turn to ask for news and to sign the visitors' book. Many telegrams of inquiry have been received from abroad.

M. Paderewski arrived in Paris from Switzerland on Monday morning, and left in the evening for Berlin and Dresden to make final arrangements for the first representation of his new opera.

The council and ordinary general meetings of the Institution of Electrical Engineers called for to-morrow, January 24, will not be held.

Mr. Edward Beaumont, of Lincoln's Inn, has been appointed junior counsel to the Attorney-General in charity matters, in succession to Mr. Dibdin, Q.C.

Mrs. ten Thurn's dance for to-night at the Grafton Galleries has been postponed in consequence of the death of the Queen.

DEATH OF THE QUEEN.

It is with the most profound sorrow that we record the death of our much loved Queen.

Throughout yesterday the blow that has overwhelmed in grief the peoples of the British Empire was awaited with universal and almost breathless fear, which grew more tense and poignant as successive bulletins revealed its imminence. At 7 o'clock suspense was ended by the following message from the Prince of Wales to the Lord Mayor, which was instantly made public:—

"Osborne, Tuesday, 6 45 p.m.

"The Prince of Wales to Lord Mayor.

"My beloved mother, the Queen, has just passed away, surrounded by her children and grandchildren.

"ALBERT EDWARD."

Immediately afterwards arrived the final medical bulletin, couched in much the same words:—

"Osborne House, Jan. 22, 6 45 p.m.

"Her Majesty the Queen breathed her last at 6 30 p.m., surrounded by her children and grandchildren.

"JAMES REID, M.D.
"R. DOUGLAS POWELL, M.D.
"THOMAS BARLOW, M.D."

The following are the official bulletins which were issued earlier in the day:—

"Osborne House, Jan. 22, 1901, 8 a.m.

"The Queen this morning shows signs of diminishing strength, and her Majesty's condition again assumes a more serious aspect.

"JAMES REID, M.D.
"R. DOUGLAS POWELL, M.D.
"THOMAS BARLOW, M.D."

"Osborne, 12 o'clock.

"There is no change for the worse in the Queen's condition since this morning's bulletin.

"Her Majesty has recognized the several members of the Royal Family who are here.

"The Queen is now asleep.

"JAMES REID, M.D.
"R. DOUGLAS POWELL, M.D.
"THOMAS BARLOW, M.D."

"Osborne, 4 p.m.

"The Queen is slowly sinking.

"JAMES REID, M.D.
"R. DOUGLAS POWELL, M.D.
"THOMAS BARLOW, M.D."

A *London Gazette* Extraordinary, issued last night, contained the Official Bulletin announcing the death of the Queen which had been received by the Home Secretary.

The Lord Steward of the Household, the Earl of Pembroke, received the following telegram from Osborne from Mr. Balfour, First Lord of the Treasury:—

"The Queen died peacefully at 6 30.

"ARTHUR BALFOUR."

THE LAST HOURS AT OSBORNE.

(FROM OUR SPECIAL CORRESPONDENT.)

COWES, JAN. 22.

All day long the Angel of Death has been hovering over Osborne House. One could almost hear the beating of his wings, but at half-past 6 those wings were folded, and the Queen was at rest. To those who knew her Majesty best and most closely, as some of them have told me, the whole event seems incredible and unreal. To all of them the life of the Queen has seemed a part of the natural order of things, a thing as certain as the rising or the setting of the sun; and they are simply incapable of realizing what it means, and that feeling will be shared by almost all of those who were the Queen's subjects, but are now the subjects of him who was the Prince of Wales, and to whom no new title is likely to be generally applied until after the Queen's funeral. Foreseen and expected as the event has been, it is a shock now that it has actually come; and the effect of it has been to cause a feeling of stunned bewilderment, which seems for the present to drown all expressions of grief. Not that Osborne House is not full of sorrowful hearts, from the heart of the German Emperor, whose coming has been a real comfort to the Royal Family, to that of the simplest servant in the house. That feeling will extend over the country, and it certainly is felt by me in such measure as to render the task of writing very difficult indeed. The Queen is gone from her people full of years and honour. Their loss is irreparable, but they may take some comfort from the thought that for her the beautiful prayer of Tennyson has been exactly fulfilled. That which he wrote, in dedicating the "Idylls of the King" to the dead Prince Consort, in an address to the Queen, was:—

"May all love,
His love unseen, but felt, o'ershadow Thee,
The love of all Thy sons encompass Thee,
The love of all Thy daughters cherish Thee,
The love of all Thy people comfort Thee,
Till God's love set Thee at His side again."

All this might now be written with abundant and full truth in the past sense of a Queen without stain and without reproach, who has passed away full of years and honour.

Now for the necessary narrative of the events of the day. All last night the Queen lay in her bedroom in the pavilion in a very restless state. It was locked, the only persons allowed within being the doctors, the dressers, and two maids, who were under the superintendence of Nurse Soal, from the sanatorium on the estate. The early morning bulletin, which spoke of diminished strength, showed that the end was drawing near, and in the meanwhile all the members of the Royal Family who were within reach were summoned. The Bishop of Winchester, too, was summoned, and was with the Queen to the end. Before noon the flickering flame of life burned up more brightly for a moment, and her Majesty was able to recognize those who had been summoned to her deathbed. Then she fell asleep, but there manner in which the meaning and significance' of the marriage of the Prince of Wales had been brought out in *The Times*. In 1866 Delane turned down a scoop by refusing to publish a letter from the Queen's Private Secretary answering criticism of her seclusion: 'In the ordinary course it would appear in tomorrow's paper but I feel so strongly how much Her Majesty sacrifices by descending from her high position to answer a contemptible paragraph that I am most unwilling to publish it'.

In 1899 *The Times* showed self-restraint approaching anorexia by refusing a much bigger scoop. The Queen was so indiscreet as to send a telegram *en clair* to the Paris Embassy, expressing her horror at the verdict against Dreyfus. That great scoop-hound Blowitz, *The Times* correspondent in Paris, managed to get hold of the text and sent it in triumph to Printing House Square. *The Times* would not publish it. True, it was bound to leak out in Paris, as it eventually did. But the office explained to Blowitz: 'What we felt we could not do was to take the initiative of giving publicity to a private communication from the Queen'. Blowitz was disgusted – and he had cause to be.

In general relations between Victoria and *The Times* were healthily abrasive. *The Times* has never been a courtierly paper. But it did the old lady royally when she died.

She had been ill since the autumn of 1900, and on 15 January 1901 her condition was recognized as grave. *The Times* made its preparations, and the journalists encamped at the gates of Osborne House on the Isle of Wight, where she lay dying. Ten minutes after her death on 22 January, a message was read to them: 'Her Majesty the Queen breathed her last at 6.30 pm, surrounded by her children and grandchildren'. Pandemonium broke out. A stampede of journalists on bicycles hurtled down the hill to Cowes, to get to the telephones first, yelling as they pedalled: 'Queen dead! Queen dead!'

On the following day *The Times* published a 20-page paper, huge for the time, with thick, funereal, black column-rules to mark the passing of an age. From Osborne J. C. Vincent, a stringer (a freelance not on the staff), reported in prose a bit too purple for modern taste. Six pages of the issue were devoted to the life and reign of Victoria: a royal biography of 60,000 words, the combined work of T. H. (later Sir Thomas) Ward, a leader writer, and Brinsley Richards, a foreign correspondent.

The poem entitled 'La Reyne est Morte' seems bad enough to have been the work of the Poet Laureate, Alfred Austin. It was in fact the work of Henry Bell of Birmingham, an otherwise unknown figure in the archives of Printing House Square. The Poet Laureate's tribute appeared in *The Times* of the following day. From its opening line, 'Dead! And the world feels widowed!' it spelled out in detail for nearly a column the virtues of the 'Mother of the Motherland', 'The Lady of the World' and the 'Queen of Queens'. However, *The Times* did not manage to obtain the right to publish the less ceremonial, more charming verses by an unknown Hindu poet:

Dust to dust, ashes to ashes,
Into the tomb the Great Queen dashes.

Below Four generations taken at White Lodge at the christening of King Edward VIII in 1894: King Edward VIII (later, The Duke of Windsor), King George V, King Edward VII and Queen Victoria.

Right The mouth sagging, the eyes protruding and the grey hair swept back, Queen Victoria in 1897 could look back on a reign that had encompassed some of the greatest changes in Britain.

Bottom Queen Victoria's funeral. Procession entering Hyde Park, 3 February 1901.

Our Man in Morocco

Eccentricity is a valued element of the English idiosyncrasy – valued by the English at any rate. Journalism, because of its exhibitionist nature, attracts its fair share of eccentrics, adventurers and rascals. *The Times* has a notable gallery of them.

Take our man in Morocco at the beginning of the twentieth century, Walter Burton Harris. Walter Harris was the son of a London shipowner. He was educated at Harrow and then encouraged to travel by his father's business. By the time he was eighteen, he had already been round the world, and was a good linguist. At the age of 21 he accompanied a British diplomatic mission to Marrakesh. He spoke French and Spanish fluently and rapidly became fluent in Arabic, and in Moroccan manners. From Morocco he contributed several articles to *The Times*, and in 1906 he joined the staff as Our Special Correspondent in Morocco. Morocco was one of the last of the independent African countries remaining unorganized. The rivalry of the imperialist powers, and the adroitness of the Sultan, put the country at the centre of foreign affairs.

Harris was marvellously suited for the job in that dark and dangerous country. He had a naturally swarthy complexion, and walked barefoot and gesticulated in the Moorish fashion, as though to the manner born. He loved dressing up and was an expert at disguise. With his head shaven except for a lock of hair a foot long hanging from the crown, with turban, shirt and brown djellaba, and carrying a long native musket, he looked more like a fanatical Riff tribesman than the gentleman from *The Times*.

In his disguises he mixed with the natives in the souks of Marrakesh and the kasbahs of the Atlas Mountains, and knew more than anybody else in the world about what the Moroccans were thinking. He had private means, and an adventurous and eccentric temperament, both of which are distinct advantages for anybody working as a foreign correspondent for *The Times*.

He travelled all over Morocco; in those days unexplored by outsiders, it was wild and often dangerous. Harris's early exploits, the ride to Tetouan and the hazardous journey across the Atlas range, brought him fame among *Times* readers, and respect and popularity among the Moors. The British Government as well as *The Times* made full use of our Moroccan correspondent. For many years Harris sent the Foreign Office early and accurate information about what was going on behind the sand dunes. In 1894 the old Sultan died, and Harris carried a dispatch from the British Government to Fez – two hundred miles across wild and distinctly dangerous terrain.

The new Sultan was a young man who became a close friend of Harris. They were always playing tennis or bridge together, or going boating, to the intense suspicion of the French diplomats. Harris evidently had considerable influence over the young ruler, though he always denied it. He wrote: 'Over and over again I spent amusing hours in reading to the Sultan the absurd rumours in the French press of the supposed influence of *le correspondent* Harris'. Harris's diplomatic adventures provoked the French Chargé d'Affaires at Tangier to describe him as: '*Le fantaisiste correspondent du "Times", simple amateur de nouvelles sensationelles*'.

Harris was really better at adventures than politics. One of his most exciting was his capture by Raisuli, the rebel leader. Raisuli's stronghold was at Zinat, about twelve miles from Tangier. Harris dressed up and rode towards Zinat, hoping for another scoop. But he fell into an ambush, which was the sort of thing one was likely to fall into in Morocco. He was thrown into a small dark room:

> Light being admitted only by one small window near the roof, the first object that attracted my eyes was a body lying in the middle of the room, stripped of all clothing and shockingly mutilated. The head had been roughly hacked off, the floor all round was swimming with blood.

Harris spent nine days in the dungeon. He had it to himself after the corpse was removed. There was nowhere to wash or perform other bodily functions, and he was rapidly covered with vermin. He was fed once a day, if he was lucky. His life was threatened periodically. But eventually he was ransomed in return for twelve rebel tribesmen held in Moorish prisons.

A year later, in 1904, he was attacked in his house by brigands late at night. Bullets were flying everywhere. Harris was frightened to fire back in case he hit somebody, which would mean that he could no longer live in Morocco. The attackers shrank from making the final storming assault, so Harris and his servants managed to hold out until relief came with the dawn.

Harris was more than an eccentric adventurer. He made his life in Morocco, and enjoyed more than the bullets and the conspiracy. He had a passion for Moorish history and customs, and helped to restore old Moorish houses and gardens. After 1912 Morocco ceased to be a hot spot in international affairs, and the dispatches from Our Special Correspondent in Morocco became less politically important. He got less in the paper.

But Harris's writing never lost its wit and sense of the unexpected. In the thirties he travelled a great deal in the Near East, and sent many letters from there to the editor, gratis. The editor published them regularly in the correspondence columns, entertaining the readers and avoiding a fee. Subjects dealt with delightfully by Walter Burton Harris over the years included the etiquette of handshaking, pyjamas on board liners, a Berber chieftain's ingenuous request for a machine that would translate the wireless into Arabic, and currency and credit among the Yap Islanders of the Pacific.

Harris was an old pro. He was a good man to be in a tight spot with, though you could bet that afterwards he would get to the telegraph office or the runner with cleft stick first to scoop you. I sometimes detect his influence in Evelyn Waugh's novel *Scoop*. He was a real English eccentric and a true man of *The Times*. Appropriately, in 1918, the King gave Walter Burton Harris his licence to wear the insignia of Commander of the Shereefian Order of the Ouissam Alaouite, a suitably eccentric title conferred on him by his old friend the Sultan of Morocco, in recognition of his valuable services. His services to *The Times* were both valuable and amazing.

Above Tangier's tribute to Walter B. Harris, for many years Morocco correspondent of THE TIMES, who died 4 April 1933. The funeral took place at Tangier, and was a remarkable demonstration of the affection and esteem in which Harris was held.

Right Walter Harris, on left, with His Highness Mulai Ahmed, Shereef of Wazan, who arranged for his release from captivity in exchange for sixteen Moors. August 1903.

Walter Burton Harris's account of his ambush and capture by rebel tribesmen, and the negotiations for his release.
14 JULY 1903

THREE WEEKS' CAPTIVITY IN MOROCCO.

(FROM OUR CORRESPONDENT.)

TANGIER, JULY 6.

This afternoon, after exactly three weeks' captivity amongst the rebel mountaineer tribes, I was set at liberty in exchange for 16 of their prisoners who were in the hands of the Moorish authorities.

It was on Tuesday, June 16, that I was captured. Early on that morning the Sultan's troops had attacked and burned the village of Zinat, the stronghold of the bandit Raisuli. Hearing that a battle had taken place at that spot, situated some eight or nine miles away, I rode out toward the middle of the day in that direction, accompanied by my native groom, whose parents lived at Zinat, and who was most anxious as to the safety of his relations. Already the alarm had spread to the neighbouring villages, and we found the country round entirely deserted, the population having fled to the mountains of Anjera with all their cattle and as much of their goods as they could carry away. Although the attack of the Government troops had been made with the object of capturing Raisuli, the native cavalry had wandered far afield after loot, and a considerable number of cattle, &c., had been carried off from villages innocent of any rebellious intentions and in no way accessories to Raisuli's depredations.

I found it difficult on this account to obtain any accurate information of what had occurred, and a desire to do so, coupled with my groom's anxiety, persuaded me to approach nearer than was perhaps advisable to the scene of the morning's action. Skirting the stony hill on which Zinat is situated I entered the plain, crossed by small gullies, that lies to the south of the villages, and until within two miles of the place met with no incident worth recording. The whole country was absolutely deserted. Not a single person, not a head of cattle, was to be seen.

It was when we were crossing this plain that suddenly a volley was fired at us from men concealed in the brushwood and rocks of a small hill near by. The range was a long one, and though we could hear the bullets whizzing over our heads I do not believe that any passed us very closely. Setting spurs to our horses we cantered away out of range, and drew rein on an elevation in the plain in the midst of a field of corn. Turning to see what was happening, I perceived three or four natives a considerable distance away, who had taken off their cloaks and turbans and were waving to me to return. This waving of turbans is always in Morocco a sign of "aman" or safety, and I therefore waited for the men, who were moving quickly in our direction. Two alone approached us, both well known to me, and having arrived at the spot where we were stationed they apologized profusely for the mistake of their men in having fired, and begged me to return with them to Zinat to discuss the situation there. They were Anjera men from the neighbouring Román hills, who had not been present at the battle, but who had come down to Zinat as the irregular cavalry had carried off a considerable number of their cattle. They stated that they were desirous of knowing the intentions of the Moorish Government with regard to their tribe. If, they said, it was the Government's intention to attack them they were ready to resist; but, if the Moorish forces had been ordered merely to capture Raisuli and had looted their property without authority, they demanded the return of their cattle—a very reasonable demand. They added that they were afraid to proceed to Tangier to interview the authorities for fear of capture and imprisonment there, and asked me accordingly to take their message to the native officials, as on such occasions I had often done before. Under a promise of safety I proceeded with them in the direction of Zinat, having agreed that I should go to a spot near the hills where three or four of the headmen of the tribe were to meet me.

It was when proceeding in that direction that I was captured. We were crossing a small gully, thick with crimson-blossomed oleanders, when suddenly I discovered that I had fallen into an ambush. Flight was impossible, and as I was unarmed resistance was out of the question. From every side sprang out tribesmen, and in a second or two I was a prisoner, surrounded by 30 or 40 men, one and all armed with European rifles. I received no rough treatment at their hands, but was told that I was their prisoner and must proceed to Zinat. On arrival at the woods which surround the several villages which lie scattered on the Zinat hills messengers were sent to inform Raisuli of my capture, and in a short time I was taken to him. He was seated under some olive trees in a little gully surrounded by his men and by the headmen of the neighbouring tribes, who had collected on learning what had taken place. Raisuli received me pleasantly enough. I had known him in the days before he took to brigandage, and this no doubt stood me in good stead. He is a young man of handsome appearance, refined in feature and manner, and with a pleasant voice. He was dressed in the costume of the mountain tribes, a short brown cloak covering his white linen clothes and reaching only to the knees, with a turban of dark blue cloth. His legs were bare, and he wore the usual yellow slippers of the country. After a short talk with Raisuli, who narrated to me all that had taken place, he led me into what remained of his house, the greater part of which had been burned by the troops. Up to this time I had nothing to complain of in the attitude of the tribesmen, but a great number had collected in the vicinity, all anxious to catch a glimpse of the Christian captive, and not a few inclined to wreak summary vengeance on me for the devastation the Government troops had committed in the place. There was a good deal of hooting and cursing, but Raisuli's influence was sufficient for him to be able to hurry me through the crowd, now very threatening, and his own followers closed round me and guarded me from the mountaineers. It was an unpleasant moment, for I soon perceived that no authority existed over this collection of tribesmen, who numbered at this time perhaps 2,000—though by nightfall this number was probably doubled—and that there would be no possibility of protection did they proceed to extremes. It was with no little relief that I saw a small door opened in the remaining portion of Raisuli's house where I was pushed in. A moment later the door was closed again, but it seemed as though the crowd without would break it down. But Raisuli and his men, and a score of personal friends amongst the tribesmen, formed up against the doorway outside, and were able to dissuade the rabble from their intention of dragging me out.

The room in which I found myself was very dark, light being admitted only by one small window near the roof, and it was some time before my eyes became accustomed to the gloom. When I was able to see more clearly, the first object that attracted my eyes was a body lying in the middle of the room. It was the corpse of a man who had been killed there in the morning by the troops, and formed a ghastly spectacle. Stripped of all clothing and shockingly mutilated, the body lay with extended arms. The head had been roughly hacked off, and the floor all round was swimming in blood. The soldiers had carried off the head in triumph as a trophy of war, and they had wiped their gory fingers on the whitewashed walls, leaving bloodstains everywhere. However, I was not to suffer the company of the corpse for long, for half-a-dozen men came in, washed the body, sewed it up in its winding-sheet, and carried it away for burial, and a little later the floor was washed down, though no attempt was made to remove the bloody finger-marks from the wall.

Here I remained alone for some hours, and it was certainly an anxious time. I reviewed the situation quietly, and came to the conclusion that, in spite of the danger which I knew existed, I had much in my favour. The fact that the language of the people was almost the same to me as my own tongue was of great assistance, and amongst these mountain tribes I have a large number of personal friends, who, I believed, and rightly, would protect me as far as they were able. Unfortunately, few of my influential acquaintances amongst the mountaineers had arrived, though to my joy I learned, from the conversation of the guards outside the door, that they were expected during the coming night. I decided meanwhile to pretend absolute ignorance of any danger, and to talk of my condition as only one of a series of adventures that I have undergone in Morocco and elsewhere.

At sundown Raisuli and some of his men brought me food, and I had a long conversation with them. Raisuli was polite, but made no secret that he intended to make use of me, though he had not yet decided in what way. He, however, kindly informed me that, should the attack of the troops be renewed, I should be immediately killed. His career, he said, was practically finished, and his sole desire was to cause the Moorish Government as much trouble and humiliation as possible, and he argued that there would be no easier way to do this than by causing my death. However, he promised me, at the same time, that, provided no fresh attack was made upon the place, he would do his best to protect me. I was allowed to communicate with the British Legation, but was not aware till later that this letter never reached its destination, though the following morning I was in direct communication with his Majesty's Minister, and throughout my captivity no difficulties were put in my way in corresponding with the British Legation.

During the night a large contingent of the Anjera tribe arrived, amongst them several influential men on whose friendship I felt I might implicitly rely; and as a matter of fact I owe my release, and probably my life, largely to these men.

There is no need to give the details of the nine days that I spent at Zinat. Sufficient to say that I suffered very considerable hardship. Though never actually roughly handled, except for a few insulting blows with slippers, &c., my discomforts were extreme. During those nine days I was never able to wash; I never took my clothes off, with the result that I was smothered with vermin; once I went for 36 hours without any food, for none was procurable, as the village had been burnt, and during the whole time my life was threatened. My friends did what they could for me, but it was little they could do. There must have been some 4,000 tribesmen present, and they obeyed no one, and no one had any authority over them. It was a trying time, but my only chance lay in pretending to place implicit confidence in them, and thus gain time while the negotiations for my release proceeded. No words of praise are sufficient for the great tact displayed by Sir Arthur Nicolson, the British Minister, in conducting these negotiations. From the very beginning he realized the difficulties of success, and throughout, in every dealing that he had with the tribesmen, he showed the greatest tact and skill. He from the very commencement warned the Moorish Government not to take any steps to treat with the mountaineers, and conducted the entire proceedings himself, Mulai Ahmed, the young Shereef of Wazan, being the means of communication between the British Government and the tribesmen. These negotiations were doubly difficult owing to the fact that the mountaineers had no recognized chiefs and that many tribes were concerned. Yet, so ably were the negotiations conducted that throughout the whole proceedings the ignorant and fanatical tribesmen placed entire confidence in the Minister's word; and, though delays occurred, as they always do in Morocco, there was never a serious hitch.

The first demand made to me for my release was the removal of all Englishmen from the Sultan's Court. I naturally treated this as preposterous, and persuaded the tribesmen that it was mere folly to mention it. This was followed by other equally impossible conditions, which were likewise abandoned, and by the time that the British Legation was in communication with the tribesmen they had lessened their demands to the release of a certain number of tribal prisoners confined in the prisons of Tangier and Laraiche. Even in this respect their demands were excessive, and his Majesty's Minister wisely and rightly refused to negotiate the release of the 50 prisoners demanded, cutting the number to 12, which was, as a favour, eventually raised to 16.

The only time that I left my quarters for more than a few minutes together was on one occasion, a few days after my arrival, when I was taken down to a gully below the village to be shown the corpse of a Moorish cavalry soldier who had been killed during the engagement. In revenge for the beheading of the Zinat man who had been killed, the tribesmen had mutilated the soldier's body. It was a ghastly sight. The summer heat had already caused the corpse to discolour and swell. An apple had been stuck in the man's mouth and both his eyes had been gouged out. The naked body was shockingly mutilated and the finger tips had been cut off, to be worn, the tribesmen told me, as charms by their women. The hands were pegged to the ground by sticks driven through the palms, about a yard in length, bearing little flags. A wreath of wild flowers was twined round the miserable man's head, and the village dogs had already gnawed away a portion of the flesh of one of the legs. I was jokingly informed that that was probably what I should look like during the course of the next few days.

During the entire nine days that I was at Zinat I was no doubt always in danger, and certainly always in great discomfort; but I had used every opportunity to bring the friendly tribe of Anjera over to my side, and on the night of the ninth day my friends rose nobly to the occasion. They surrounded Raisuli's house and village with perhaps a thousand men, all armed and prepared, and demanded that I should be handed over to them, threatening that, if this were not immediately carried out, they would shoot or arrest Raisuli. It was a little *coup d'Etat*, and it was successful. In the middle of the night I was hustled out of the small room which I shared with a dozen guards, placed on the back of a mule, and carried off into the Anjera mountains by my friends of that tribe. For six hours we proceeded through mountain passes and thick brushwood, arriving soon after sunrise at the village of Sheikh Duas, one of the most influential of the Anjera tribesmen. It was a journey one will never forget—the darkness of the moonless night, the rough mountain tracks, the silence of the hundreds of armed men who accompanied me, and the intense relief that, even if my captivity was long protracted, I was amongst men who would, at any rate, protect my life. I was tired and weak. Nine days of constant strain, on a diet of inferior dry bread and water, with the necessity the whole time of pretending rather to enjoy the situation than otherwise, had worn me out. But from the friendly tribe of Anjera I received nothing but kindness—every word, every act of theirs was cheering and thoughtful—and, though life among them was rough enough in its way, I owe them a debt of gratitude that it will be difficult ever to repay. I remained 12 days at Sheikh Duas's village in the Anjera mountains, and throughout that period I never suffered an indignity or an insult from him or his people. A little room in his house was put at my disposal, and infinite pains were taken to render it clean and habitable. The best of such food as was procurable was given me—milk and cream cheese, and a rough porridge of sour milk and millet. His followers—for Duas is not above being a cattle robber on a large scale—helped me to pass my time pleasantly enough, and with them I explored the neighbouring mountains, and sat in the shade of the fruit trees of their little gardens listening to their local musicians or watching the ungraceful movements of their dancing-girls. I made friends there whose friendship I shall always value. I was treated as one of the tribe. I wore their dress, shaved my head, and conformed to all their customs; but above and beyond all my anxiety was at an end—I knew that I was out of grave danger.

Meanwhile the British Minister, ably assisted by the Shereef of Wazan, was carrying on the negotiations. Although I was now amongst friends these negotiations were delicate and difficult, for the Anjera tribe had given their word to the other tribes concerned not to release me until their prisoners were released, and these other tribes were constantly desirous of changing their conditions, and, owing to the distances which separated them, this necessarily meant delay. The very fact that I was now some 27 miles—a day's journey—from Tangier protracted the negotiations. Several times I seemed on the point of release, but some small hitch, unimportant it is true, would arise and a delay occur.

Except for this the time passed pleasantly, the scenery was delightful, and although it was the middle of summer the air was cool at this altitude. Little streams of water ran in every direction, and I was able to bathe and be clean once more. To all intents and purposes I was free to go where I pleased, and, though always accompanied by guards, so thoughtful and kind were they that one forgot that they were there to prevent my escape, and we all became the best of friends. Meanwhile the Shereef of Wazan spared himself no trouble. No sun was too hot for him to travel, no journey too tiring for him to undertake. He attended the tribal meetings and made known to the headmen the British Minister's intentions with regard to the tribal prisoners, orders for whose release had meanwhile been received from the Sultan. His Majesty's readiness to comply with Sir Arthur Nicolson's requests is deserving of all praise, for it must be remembered that the action of the rebels throughout was intended to humiliate the Sultan and his Government. What rendered the situation during my captivity, especially during the first part of it, doubly insecure was the fact that the tribes were in active communication with the pretender to the Moorish Throne—the leader of the rebellion—and it was proposed over and over again to send me to him as a useful hostage, and, had it not been for the friendship which existed between me and the Anjera tribe, a friendship of long standing, I have no doubt this proposal would have been carried out.

On Saturday, July 4, a large tribal meeting was held near Sheikh Duas's village, and during the usual wrangling which occurred on these occasions the Shereef of Wazan arrived, having travelled the 27 miles from Tangier that day, in spite of the heat of the July sun. His opportune presence settled my fate, and the negotiations were brought to a conclusion, not without considerable opposition. Yesterday a large contingent of tribesmen, the Shereef, and I, set out for Tangier, spending the night some 12 miles from that place. Even here a last attempt was made—an attempt that nearly led to bloodshed—to prevent my release, but happily unsuccessfully. This morning we moved down towards my own house, which stands alone, some two and a-half miles from the town. In a ruined fort a quarter of a mile from my villa a halt was made, and messengers were despatched to town with letters to the British Minister to release the tribal prisoners, who for the last week or so had been comfortably housed in the basement of the British Consulate, having been brought up from Laraiche in specially chartered steamers. Within an hour we saw the 16 prisoners arriving, and very shortly afterwards they were being welcomed by their friends. Lord Cranley, Mr. Wyldbore-Smith, Mr. Kirby-Green, and Mr. Carleton accompanied them on behalf of the British Legation, but no formal exchange took place. The moment the prisoners arrived I was free to depart, though the many adieux that I had to make with my mountain friends took some little time. We parted on the best of terms, and, wild and savage as the two hundred tribesmen looked, I could not but feel how great a debt of gratitude I owed them for having released me from the dangers and discomforts of my first days of captivity.

Nothing more remains to be narrated, except to mention over again the great tact with which His Majesty's Minister carried through the most delicate and difficult negotiations with an amalgamation of fanatical mountain tribes, who possess no authorized chief, and whose anti-European tendencies, especially at the present moment when rebellion is rife, are well known. In these negotiations he was most ably assisted by Mulai Ahmed, Shereef of Wazan, without whose religious influence communication with the tribesmen would have been most difficult. To them I owe the fact that I am to-day once more at liberty.

STOCKS AND SHARES.

MONDAY EVENING.

The next Settlement in Consols will begin on August 4 and end on August 6. The next Settlement in Railway and Foreign stocks, &c., will begin on July 27 and end on July 29.

The following is a statement of the opening and closing quotations of the undermentioned securities, together with the quotations at which they closed on Saturday and the prices at which they were made up at the last Settlement:

N.B.—In the case of railway and other securities whose issues quoted here are of more than one kind the prices given relate to the "Ordinary" stocks or shares unless otherwise specified. In the case of all securities the closing quotations are the latest obtained up to half-past 4 on all days except Saturday, when the latest prices are those obtained at 1 o'clock. For movements in prices which may take place after these hours refer[illegible]

In the subjoined official record of "business done" transactions marked thus * relate to small bonds, and those distinguished thus ‡ to an exceptional amount at special rates. Stocks and shares marked thus † have paid no dividend for the last two half-years and upwards:—

[The Money Market Article will be found on page 13.]

SIR JOHN FRENCH AT LEWISHAM.—Lieutenant-General Sir John French held, on Saturday afternoon, the annual inspection of the boys of the East London Industrial School, Brookbank-road, Lewisham, and also unveiled a tablet placed in the dining hall bearing the names of 35 old boys who took part in the South African War, and six of whom lost their lives. Sir John French said they were met to perpetuate the memory of not only comrades of the boys of that school, but also of his comrades. The memorial could not fail to be the greatest incentive to all of them to remember that their first duty was to their King and country. Parade and general inspection followed, and Sir John French, in an address to the boys, said three great attributes—loyalty, patriotism, and love of country—should be possessed by all. Without them no man could be great or good. All must possess them who wished to preserve our great Empire in the enjoyment of its present magnificence, power, and influential position in the world. They must also be prepared to meet the demands made upon them. They must be prepared to take their fair share, as every subject of the King should, in the advance of the Empire. Fire-escape practice and gymnastics were followed by inspection of premises and workshops.

NEW EXCURSION SERVICE TO BOULOGNE.—The General Steam Navigation Company opened their new summer passenger service from London to Boulogne on Saturday. It is intended to run a regular excursion service three times weekly during the season, leaving London-bridge at 10 a.m. on Mondays, Wednesdays, and Saturdays, calling at Greenwich Pier and Tilbury Pier (for passengers travelling via Fenchurch-street and other London, Tilbury, and Southend Railway stations). These boats will call both ways at Southend and Margate, thus giving an additional service to the one already run by the company to those places. The steamers will return from Boulogne on Sundays, Tuesdays, and Thursdays at 10 a.m. Special arrangements have been made for week-end tours and tourists generally, including hotel accommodation at Boulogne. On the occasion of her first trip on Saturday the Laverock carried over 80 passengers. The vessel was met on her arrival at Boulogne by M. Farjon, president of the Chamber of Commerce; M. Feuillade, secretary of the chamber, and several members of that body; and Mr. H. F. Farmer, British Vice-Consul, who welcomed the General Steam Navigation Company to Boulogne.

Trying to stop the rot

By the last decade of the nineteenth century, *The Times* was in a bad way. It was almost bankrupt because of the vast cost of the Parnell Commission, the dissipation of reserves, and the fall in advertising. Editorially it had become élitist and unadventurous. Circulation was falling. It was no longer required reading by the intelligent and the political. The later generations of proprietors, particularly the small proprietors, those multiplying beneficiaries of the first John Walter's will, were puny epigones of the founding fathers, being concerned only with the size of their dividends and not at all with the quality of their golden goose.

Moberly Bell, the manager, would try anything to stop the rot. He started a Special Publications Department, which originally published *The Times Atlas* and *The Times Law Reports*. They both made a modest profit. Then in 1897 Bell received a visit from two Americans, Horace Everett Hooper and W. M. Jackson. They were successful hustlers in modern methods of mass book-selling, and specialized in cheap reprints, direct selling by mail order, payment by instalments and high-pressure advertising. Hooper thought his methods would work in Britain and, with this in mind, he had bought the rights of the ninth edition of the *Encyclopaedia Britannica* from the publishers, A. & C. Black.

His proposal was to advertise extensively in *The Times*, which would offer the twenty-five volumes of *Britannica* for £14 instead of the usual price of £37. Subscribers would receive the full set on payment of the first instalment of one guinea. *The Times* would take the orders and receive a guinea for each set sold.

On 23 March 1898 the first page advertisement appeared in *The Times*. Day after day surprised readers were blasted with a barrage of novel advertising, exhorting them to 'Hurry! Hurry! Hurry!' to acquire 'learning, scholarship and general information'. In May the barrage intensified with the offer of revolving oak bookcases for only £3 to the first two hundred readers who applied.

The campaign paid off, exceeding Bell's wildest hopes. By 1905 *The Times* had made £108,000 out of the deal, and was able to pay its rapacious small proprietors an increased dividend.

Conventional British publishers were not pleased by the campaign. Hooper and Jackson were described as 'those alien Americans'. *Punch* mobbed up *The Times*:

> You are old, Father Thunderer, old and austere,
> Where learnt you such juvenile capers?
> It's part of the Yankee Invasion, my dear,
> To galvanize threepenny papers.

Bell was unmoved. To a critic in the office he replied: 'If *The Times*, in the interests of the country, is to carry on, it must be subsidized: the better a newspaper is, the fewer people there are to buy it'.

The ninth edition of the *Britannica* had been commissioned twenty years, and printed ten years, earlier. It was out of date. So Bell set up an editorial department in Printing House Square to produce a ten-volume supplement to *Britannica*. Together they became the tenth edition, published in 1903. It was a success both intellectually and commercially: by the end of the year sales had produced more than £600,000.

Horace Hooper was appointed advertising manager of *The Times*. The paper's monopoly of personal advertisements in the Agony Column, Sherlock Holmes's favourite reading, had dribbled away to *The Daily Telegraph*. Hooper greatly developed display advertising to take the place of the 'smalls', not without complaints from a number of the stuffier kind of reader who thought these big new ads vulgar and, worse, American. Circulation was still a problem. Older readers were dying and not being replaced by the younger generation, who were turning to something livelier.

Unfortunately, with their next plan to increase circulation, Bell and Hooper over-reached themselves. They started a lending library called *The Times* Book Club, with the object of increasing annual subscriptions to the paper. Subscribers to *The Times* became members of the Club, which not only lent them new books but also sold them relatively new books at second-hand prices. The costs would have to be carried by the increase in subscribers. But Bell hoped that the scheme would double the circulation of *The Times*, which would enable him to jack up its advertising rates.

Neither Bell nor Hooper understood the intricacies or the closed shop of the British publishing industry. The notion was to make up the library costs by selling off the books when the demand for them in the library had fallen off. The British Book Publishers Association deemed this to be an unBritish and unfair trade practice. So came about the Book War.

The Publishers Association drew up a new book agreement that bound its members not to sell books as second-hand until six months after publication. At the same time they refused to sell books to *The Times* Book Club except at full retail price. The battle was fought with extreme bitterness. George Bernard Shaw supported *The Times*. The publishers withdrew £10,000 worth of advertising from the paper. Reviews in *The Times* of books by the enemy firms asked subscribers 'to abstain from ordering the book as far as possible'.

Even *The Times* could not win a war over bookselling with the publishing industry of Britain. After eighteen months it capitulated, and signed the new book agreement. The prestige of *The Times*, or at any rate its face, had suffered. The desperate venture increased circulation a bit; but indirectly it sealed the fate of the Walter *Times*.

As reported in *The Times* of 18 July 1907, the High Court ordered that the partnership of *The Times* (i.e. the chief proprietors and the small proprietors) should be dissolved and *The Times* put up for sale. For the national institution to be sold was as embarrassing, and as entertaining to the malignant, as a dowager duchess taking up a new career on the music hall.

Hooper, however, remained with Moberly Bell, and advised him to perform one last piece of business that was to have portentous effect. He persuaded Bell to talk to Northcliffe. This was the first step to the purchase of *The Times* by its new proprietor, who was to bring it, wriggling and expostulating, into the twentieth century.

Hooper and Jackson, *The Times*'s American connection, were strongly disapproved of by many of the staff at Printing House Square. They may not have been dignified. Journalism is not a dignified trade. But they have a key place in the history of *The Times*. Without them The Thunderer would probably have died at the end of the nineteenth century.

Above Horace Everett Hooper, publisher of the ENCYCLOPAEDIA BRITANNICA 1898–1908, Advertisement Manager of THE TIMES 1906–8.

Right An advertisement for the first edition of THE TIMES ATLAS OF THE WORLD from THE TIMES of 22 August 1896. THE TIMES ATLAS was first published in 1895 and was an English translation of a German atlas. The next edition was published after the First World War by Lord Northcliffe, and was created by the Edinburgh firm of John Bartholomew and Son which has been associated with THE TIMES ever since.

THE EGYPTIAN EXPEDITION.

EGYPT—The SUDAN—The NILE VALLEY—ABYSSINIA.

ALL those who wish to follow the interesting and important events now taking place on the NILE, in ABYSSINIA, and ERYTHREA, should consult maps 103 105, and 106 of

THE TIMES ATLAS,

where all particulars will be found recorded with most detailed accuracy and precision.

REFER to THE TIMES ATLAS if you want to find ADIGRAT, ADOWA, AKASHEH, AMBUKOL, ASSAB, ASSUAN, BERBER, DONGOLA, ERKOWIT, KASSALA, GURA, HAIMAR WELLS (El Haimar), FERKAH, KOKREB WELLS, OBOK, SAGANA, WADY HALFA, WALKAIT, SUAKIN, and many other names daily referred to in the newspapers.

ALSO for the CARAVAN ROUTES, WELLS, OASES, WATER COURSES, and all other geographical details of Egypt, Sudan, and Abyssinia.

See THE TIMES ATLAS, pages 103, 105, 106.

SOUTH AFRICA.

THE TRANSVAAL and RHODESIA.

THE fullest geographical information with regard to events which are absorbing public interest in South Africa is to be found in

THE TIMES ATLAS, pages 104, 109, and 110.

THE TIMES advertising its Book Club in its pages. Also on the page (columns 1 and 2) is a report of some of the later discoveries made by Sir Arthur Evans in his excavations at Knossos.
15 JULY 1907

FURTHER DISCOVERIES IN THE PALACE OF KNOSSOS.

By Arthur J. Evans.

The great prehistoric Palace of Knossos is really inexhaustible. When in April last, in company of my experienced assistant, Dr. Mackenzie, I arrived on the site with the object of making supplementary investigations in the west wing for the final publication, neither he nor I had an inkling of the surprises that were in store for us.

The first object that called for serious attention led us somewhat away from the actual "House of Minos." About a mile to the north, on the way to the headland where a Royal tomb had already been excavated, a series of "Cyclopean" blocks had come to light that seemed to betoken the existence of a second great sepulchral chamber of a similar kind. These blocks, indeed, proved to have been removed from their original context, which still awaits discovery; but immediately below them were found two beehive tombs, cut out of the soft rock, in their form and certain features of their contents representing the old Minoan tradition, but belonging to a period about 800 B.C., when the Dorian settlement of a large part of the island was already an accomplished fact. The swords here were of the mainland type, iron succeeding the earlier bronze, and cinerary urns had replaced the earlier corpse burial; but the variety and invention displayed in the objects found, the continuity of many of the decorative motives as well as the appearance of the characteristic "stirrup vase," pointed to a distinct survival of the old indigenous element. In one tomb there were nearly a hundred vessels, and among them the more important cinerary urns presented quite a new and very elaborate style of Geometrical design. Their lids were surmounted by miniature vases, their bases were formed in a strange way by what might otherwise have been taken for curving handles, and several showed a novel form of polychrome decoration—in which a brilliant vermilion predominates—the colours in this case being imperfectly fixed and evidently intended for purely funereal use. On one of these vessels are sketched cult images of a goddess and a warrior god set on low bases. The most curious object was what appeared to be a small female idol wrought in iron.

But further researches in this later field had perforce to be postponed. Various supplementary trenches and pits that had been started in the Palace area itself were already producing important results. Beneath the pavement of the West Court, as remodelled in the latest Palace period, there opened out a circular walled area some 20ft. in diameter, descending about 12ft. to a cement floor. Its original purpose is uncertain, but its contents proved to be of the greatest archæological interest from the fact that, at the time when the West Court paving was extended over it, it was filled with a homogeneous mass of pottery and other *débris*, belonging to the first period of the later Palace, the "Third Middle Minoan" of my classification, the close of which seems to correspond with the XVth Egyptian dynasty. This period—in Egypt one of general depression and stagnation, due to the Hyksos domination—represents in Crete the high-water mark of the Minoan civilization. The art of this epoch —the close of which on any showing cannot be brought down beyond the 18th century B.C.— attains a naturalism never again achieved in the ancient world. A new and striking illustration of this distinctive quality came out, indeed, during the excavating of the Circular Area. A workman brought up to me what at first I took to be a fossil crab. It was only on observing the painted decoration on the back that I realized that this was, in fact, a hand-moulded relief belonging to some kind of clay vessel. Later on there came out parts of two other crabs—a "comb" or *pecten* shell, indistinguishable from the original—a limpet and zoophytes, all moulded in a similar fashion and apparently belonging to some kind of large basin, of which, however, only a part of the base was found. It looks as if the marine incrustations indicate its object, and that we had really before us part of a Minoan aquarium. The further occurrence in this same well-defined deposit of the remains of painted stucco—some of it with decorative reliefs—suggests that more of the Palace wall decoration than had been at first supposed may go back to the early period. Of special interest, too, were the feet and parts of the smoke-stained upper receptacles of a series of moveable plaster hearths such as were in use in the Palace. Some showed traces of painted borders; in one case a wave-ornament representing the antecedent stage of the very typical "wave" or "wave-and-star" border of the succeeding Palace period. But it is extremely interesting to note that this decoration in its later aspect reappears round the border of the fixed hearth in the Megaron at Mycenæ. This latter, therefore, declares itself as the lineal descendant of an older Minoan portable hearth, become fixed and of larger size in the Mainland hall owing to the greater winter cold. It is essentially a sister form, belonging to the same civilization, but modified by more northerly conditions.

Of the later painted decoration of the Knossian Palace, the weathering of the last few years has brought out some additional traces in the antechamber of the room to the throne. Here, above a border showing imitative blocks of veined marbles—a frequent dado design of the late Minoan period—the outline of a bull's foot has become distinctly visible, from which it may be inferred that the walls of this chamber were covered with some of the favourite scenes of the bull-ring.

It may be remembered that among the remains of wall paintings found in the rooms to the north of the Central Court were fragments of miniature groups, in which fashionably-dressed Court ladies took a prominent position, thronging the terraces and loggias of a great building (apparently the Palace itself) on either side of one of the characteristic small pillar shrines of the Minoan cult. With the skilled artistic help of M. Gilliéron, it has been possible for me to reconstruct the entire panel representing this subject. The small temple with its two lower wings and raised central cell rises in the centre above a low wall of large white blocks. This façade, from the crowds in front of it, was evidently the foreground of some kind of piazza, and the suggestion had long occurred to me that a shrine of this class might have actually overlooked the Central Palace Court. By a section of its west façade, moreover, some clear indications of the vicinity of such a sanctuary had already come out. Here, in a small rectangular bay, were found a remarkable series of seal-impressions showing a goddess on a lion-guarded peak with a typical Minoan temple in the background. In a chamber immediately behind this bay was made, moreover, the still more important discovery of the early Temple Repositories, containing the faience figures of a snake goddess and her votaries, and, amongst other cult objects—strangest of all—a marble cross.

But where was the shrine itself, as it must have existed in the latest days of the Palace?

The rains of successive seasons have now supplied the solution of the problem. On the slabs that mark the border of this very section of the Central Court, in an architectural interval between two large gypsum blocks, have become clearly visible the marks of the bases of two pairs of small columns, respectively indicating those contained in the sanctuary wings. It turns out, moreover, that the bay that contained the seal-impressions depicting the goddess and shrine actually corresponds with the interior of the northern wing. Between the two wings there is an interval in the façade representing the space occupied by the raised central cell, and an enigmatic rectangular recess immediately behind this now explains itself as the substructure of this central part of the shrine, which was evidently the real "holy of holies," designed for the custody of the images and fetish idols. In the basement part of this had been found during the first year's excavations remains of a gypsum chest filled with clay tablets inscribed with the linear script, and not improbably belonging to the temple archives. It has thus at last been possible to recover the actual plan of a Palace shrine of the same kind as that which the miniature wall painting depicts for us in all its brilliant colours surrounded by a fashionable congregation.

The supplementary probings and dissections of walls and floorings brought a further confirmation of the preponderantly religious character of this quarter of the Palace. Beneath the later stone benches and jammed into the wall-chinks of the neighbouring "Room of the Chariot Tablets" was found a series of stone libation vessels like those of the Temple Repositories, together with two high-pedestalled lamps of purple gypsum. Another discovery, due to the same exploratory methods, in the neighbouring "clay area" must be regarded as of first-rate architectural importance. It had been supposed theoretically that a broad flight of steps led up from the Propylaeum to the south of this area to a series of upper halls, of which the traces are still visible above the basement rooms of the west wing; but the earlier explorations had here come to a full stop, owing to the mistaken impression that the underlying *stratum* of Neolithic clay (in places some 25 feet thick) had here been reached. So far as concerned the slight ramp, representing the original ascent of the steps, this conclusion proved to be correct. But, on the east flank of this, the clay layer turned out to be only a shallow artificial platform due to later occupants of the site who had here built out of the stair foundations a hall, apparently of the mainland type. On removing this intrusive clay *stratum*, massive substructures forming a solid rectangular block became visible, which evidently belonged to a great supporting bastion of the original step-way, the exact dimensions of which can now be ascertained.

The analysis of some later structures to the west of this led to the detection of three more magazines, raising the total number of the magazines on this side from 18 to 21. By a singular piece of good fortune I am further enabled to chronicle a small find which has a direct and very interesting bearing on the contents of one of these magazines. A peasant hereabouts, while working in his field a short time since, had found an engraved Minoan bead-seal of hematite—probably derived from some ruined tomb in the neighbourhood of Knossos. Thanks to the very stringent and childish native law by which the authorities have power to confiscate even such minor relics, the seal had naturally found its way out of the country. In passing through Athens on my way out I saw the signet at an "antika" dealer's, and, recognizing its unique character, managed to secure it. Its main type—a bull with its head turned round—recalls the subject of a series of seal impressions from the Royal Lamb at Knossos, and is executed in the same bold late Minoan style. But the distinctive part of the device is that which fills the field above. Here are two guardian griffins on each side of a figure which I at once recognized as the ideograph of a kind of cereal that appears sometimes in connexion with a form of storehouse on a class of clay inventories specially connected with the Third Magazine—where, indeed, remains of burnt corn were also found. We have here, in fact, the actual signet of a Palace official —the steward of the Royal granaries.

But the great surprises of the supplementary excavations awaited us on the south and south-west. On these sides the whole Palace plan is nothing less than revolutionized. The line of gypsum wall, formerly regarded as the outer wall of the building on the south, proves to be not an outer wall at all, but the inner boundary of a spacious corridor that lay immediately within this face of the building. The real front wall on this side, forming the exterior boundary of the corridor, could be traced for a considerable distance west by means of its foundations and the blocks that had backed these. Towards the southern entrance the line of gypsum slabs that formed the central paving of the corridor had been preserved, showing a great resemblance to that which runs down the middle of the "Corridor of the Procession" leading from the West Court. A careful investigation further brought out the whole plan of the contiguous southern entrance, including, as in the case of the west portico, a small porter's lodge. Outside this southern gate was visible part of the pavement of an old roadway leading up the steep from the south-west. It seemed possible, therefore, that the point might be made out where this ancient roadline crossed the ravine of the small stream that runs below the Palace hill on this side. Some masonry existing at a likely spot near the stream turned out on investigation to be Roman—possibly the remains of an aqueduct. But a trench dug somewhat above this actually revealed an ancient paved way running towards the same point, but suddenly breaking off at what appeared to be the remains of a *tête de pont* that had been constructed at a time when the stream ran at a higher level and somewhat north of its present channel. The roadway thus struck ran in a more northerly direction than I had anticipated, suggesting that its principal connexion was rather with the Western Court than the southern entrance. Further trenches were therefore dug in the same line higher up the steep, with the astonishing result that a fresh series of Palace constructions came to light where, according to all our foregone conclusions, no Palace should have been. Exactly on the line followed, moreover, there opened a narrow passage, apparently leading from some postern-gate on the south-west, flanked on either side by bastions of good limestone masonry, rising in steps, and somewhat recalling those of the northern entrance. This passage must have opened on the West Court near its south-western angle. The lines all answer to the Palace orientation, and there can be no remaining doubt that a south-western quarter of the great building existed of which no account has hitherto been taken.

Simultaneously with this development, a very interesting phenomenon attended the excavations about the southern entrance. In examining the substructures of the porch here, a cutting appeared which proved to be part of the cupola of a huge beehive chamber excavated in the soft rock. It had been filled in with later *débris* and heaps of sherds going back to the time of the earliest Minoan Palace (Middle Minoan I.). Foundations belonging to the southern wall line had been sunk deep down into it, and a beautifully constructed terra cotta drain pipe—itself of very early date—carried through it. But the great cavity still continued widening and descending, and an exploratory shaft going down about 25 feet below the original summit of the vault still failed to reach the bottom. At this point I was compelled to break off work for the present season, but there can be little doubt that we have here to deal with a primitive beehive tomb belonging to a type of which two or three truncated examples had been found on the southern side of the island. It dates from a period that lies beyond the age of the Cretan Palaces, but, occurring as it does within the Royal precincts of Knossos, who shall say what revelations it may not offer?

For the present it has been necessary to bring the whole of the operations to a standstill, and, indeed, they had already extended far beyond the limits that I had set out for myself. Their net result is to show that an additional area of some 3,000 square yards must be added to the great Palace, to open up a series of unsolved problems of absorbing interest—among which not the least concerns the great primeval tomb—and to involve the organization of another great campaign before anything like finality can be attained. Some important development may also be expected on the north side, where supplementary excavation on a considerable scale is also necessary.

Bolingbroke Hospital.—On Saturday afternoon a new wing at Bolingbroke Hospital, Wandsworth-common, was opened for inspection. The institution is intended to be the general hospital for the south-western district, and when completed it will have 153 beds. The addition now completed consists of one of the three blocks which, with an administrative block, will form the entire hospital. The building has accommodation for two house surgeons and five nurses, and contains an operating room and wards for 17 beds, besides offices and stores. In every detail the utmost care has been taken to render insanitation impossible. The operating room, with its appurtenances and equipment, is regarded as not inferior to any in London. Natural ventilation is provided for throughout the building. The walls are tiled, all the woodwork is enamelled, and the flooring is polished. The roof is flat and has been asphalted; it will be used as a promenade for convalescents. The cost of the new building is about £25,000. A considerable sum is required to make up the total of £40,000 for the completion of the entire hospital.

THE UNREST IN INDIA.

(FROM OUR SPECIAL CORRESPONDENT.)

CHAIL, June 20.

Circumstances have so fallen out that the writer has found it expedient to visit a native State before proceeding to the capital cities of the Punjab. After the complexity of opinion existing in the summer seat of the Government of India, the restful atmosphere of the Patiala Hill station furnishes a mental sedative. It is always interesting to visit a native State; at the present moment it is more than interesting, it is instructive. In the native States more than anywhere else is to be found still that amenity of intercourse which in the past characterized the relations between European and native. Education, so perverted in other parts as to have become the root of all the present unrest in India, is here devoid of the poison of racial prejudice, and, consequently, in its development has not undermined the friendly instincts of a feudatory people. Such white men as the people see are the peers of the ruling Prince, and share the reverence in which his person is held. As long as the rulers of the native States evince no sympathy with the propaganda that has been fostered in Bengal the movement is shorn of much of its significance. And as far as can be seen at present the native States have no sympathy with the movement. Bengal itself can produce no leader who is likely to shake the loyalty of the ruling Princes. There may be powerful rulers who resent the strong Western hand that restrains their destinies, but such men do not look to the Universities and Bar libraries of Bengal for their emancipation. Bengal in itself possesses no equivalent of the feudatory overlords of the martial races of India. There is no Prince upon whose sympathy and magnetism they can rely. A scrutiny of recent speeches by Bepin Chandra Pal and his fellow-agitators would suggest that the Bengalis are not a little resentful of the attitude of the martial races and their chiefs. Bepin Chandra Pal notably has urged Mahomedans and Hindus to combine for the purpose of finding a leader, and has even suggested the Ameer of Afghanistan as a suitable personage. At Barisal he again returned to this theme—"The Napoleon of India would probably come from without her frontiers. Ameer Habibullah Khan might be the Napoleon of India and champion her cause. But ultimately the Indian Government was destined to be a Republic similar to the United States of America, with an Upper Chamber of feudatory chiefs and a Lower Chamber of the common people."

But the above, it may be contended, are merely the dreams of hot-heads in pursuit of "some few principles which they have chanced upon." If we go back to the genesis of the whole movement it can be traced in a great measure to a small society of *literati* bent on retaining the monopoly of subordinate Government appointments which they had hitherto enjoyed all over Bengal. That particular coterie of subtle-minded Hindus centred in and about Dacca (Bikrampur) saw in the proposed partition of Bengal a direct attempt to break Hindu predominance. The Babus at once became as a class the bitter opponents of partition. It meant for them not only a direct blow at their cohesion as a class, but a threat to their vested interests in Government appointments. Vanity and greed are amongst the less estimable characteristics of the educated Bengali, and partition, with the unpleasant prospects which it opened up, acted as an irritant to both. The medium through which the Bengalis gave expression to their hostility was the native Press, which they control. By means of the Press they succeeded in producing a paper boycott, a paper national fund, and a paper national unity. The question, therefore, which the Indian Government has to solve is whether there is any possibility of this "paper blockade" of the British Raj so influencing public sentiment in India that it will become really effective.

This brings us back to the evil soil in which the seeds of agitation have been sown. In what measure has the soil proved productive? As a coercive measure those authorities most competent to judge maintain that the *Swadeshi* movement has failed. But although its commercial aspect has to some extent dropped out of sight, its political aspect remains. Realizing its lack of stability on a commercial basis, its promoters have resorted to other and more dangerous devices, such as the widespread assertion that certain imported goods are subjected to processes offensive to the principles of Hinduism and Islam alike; that European salt has been purified with blood; European sugar with blood or bone charcoal. Also European piece goods are said to have been finished with a sizing compound derived from the fat of cows and pigs. Even these malicious attempts to play upon the religious prejudices of the people have been only partially successful. But *Swadeshi* paved the way for *Swaraj*—economic home rule for political autonomy, the boycott of British goods for the denunciation of British rulers. The Bengalis became the apostles of *Swaraj*, and, almost without exception, the entire native Press of the country adopted the new creed. Even then the dangerous character of this agitation was not recognized, until it had to be recognized also how very inadequately equipped we were to deal with it. So little support had been given to those who had realized from the first the danger of not dealing with it that we have had the edifying spectacle of *Jatra* (theatrical) companies touring the country enacting pieces written in support of the *Swaraj* doctrine; cheap actors playing in ridicule of the Government, and giving as the *pièce de resistance* of their *répertoire* sketches caricaturing the resignation of Sir Bampfylde Fuller, and representing the gradual conversion of Anglicized native officials to the *Swaraj* cause.

Encouraged by the supineness of the Government and its unconsciousness of the change which had come over their methods, the agitators embarked upon a progressive campaign, which at once swamped the Moderates and culminated in a propaganda to undermine the fidelity of the native States and the Army. How far this later phase of *Swaraj* has progressed it is impossible at the present moment to gauge. It is confidently believed that, in spite of extensive ramifications, the progress has been infinitesimal. But the two following points are of significance. The activity of an agitation, which originated three years ago in the vindictiveness of a small class of Bengal wire pullers, has been scientifically spread throughout the length and breadth of India. This agitation is at this very moment engaged in the dissemination of subversive doctrines that reach the ears of every class throughout India, and yet there exists no kind of machinery to check its operations beyond a drastic ordinance enacted almost a century ago.

TO THE EDITOR OF THE TIMES.

Sir,—Lord Curzon, in his striking review of Indian affairs at the Merchant Taylors' banquet recently given in his honour, dwelt with much force on the extent to which the disloyal movement was fomented by what he leniently termed "the incautiousness of a small knot of Englishmen," little known here at home, but whom their dupes in India imagined to be representatives of public opinion in this country. The late Viceroy abstained—no doubt for good and sufficient reasons of his own—from any comment on the far more mischievous effect of harassing questions repeatedly put in Parliament to the Secretary of State for India as to the measures he has been compelled to resort to for the repression of unrest and sedition. For weeks past Mr. Morley has been subjected to a captious catechizing of his action, coming not from obscure Anglo-Indians, but from well-known members, one of whom indeed has a long record of service in India and has held high office there; and this in the historically ominous year that completes half a century since the Mutiny, and is marked by the 150th anniversary of Plassey. It is difficult, it seems to me, to conceive anything more unpatriotic than the attitude thus adopted towards the statesman to whose hands the destinies of our great Eastern Empire are committed at a period of no little anxiety. There is no trace there of the spirit which, as Lord Curzon justly said, excludes with us all party feeling when we are face to face with a serious national emergency. Fortunately Mr. Morley may be trusted to show an undaunted front to what I venture to call pestilent criticism. India, we feel certain, is safe in his keeping and in that of Lord Minto, and reasonable men of all parties must rejoice at the unflinching firmness shown at this crisis, even as they cannot but commend the equally resolute manner in which Mr. Morley's colleague of the Foreign Office dealt with affairs in Egypt and his loyal support of his agents in the discharge of painful but unavoidable duties.

I have the honour to be, Sir, your obedient servant,

HORACE RUMBOLD, the representative of one severely wounded when on Clive's Staff at Plassey.

Travellers' Club, July 12.

MR. BALFOUR AND TARIFF REFORM.

Mr. Balfour addressed the following letter on Saturday to the secretary of the Western Counties' Tariff Reform Federation:—

4, Carlton-gardens, Pall-mall, S.W., July 13th, 1907.

Dear Sir,—I am obliged to you for calling my attention to the speech recently delivered by Lord Hugh Cecil at the Unionist Free Trade Club. But I am not sure that I quite understand on what grounds you think it is my business to explain it. It is a sufficient labour and responsibility to make speeches of my own, without taking upon myself the additional duty of commenting upon my commentators.

The policy which I advise the party to accept, and which, if I remain as leader, I shall endeavour to carry out, is, as every one is aware who has taken the trouble to read what I said at the Albert-hall a few weeks ago, to broaden the basis of taxation, to promote colonial preference, and to mitigate, as far as possible, hostile tariffs and illegitimate competition. So long as this policy itself be accepted, I have little inclination to quarrel over the name by which it should be described.

I remain yours faithfully,

Arthur James Balfour.

W. H. Williams, Esq.

ROYAL OPERA, COVENT-GARDEN. Proprietors, the Grand Opera Syndicate (Ltd.). TO-NIGHT, at 8, CARMEN: Mmes. Kirkby Lunn, Lejeune, Paulin, and Donalda; MM. Caruso, Gilibert, Crabbé, Zucchi, Navarrini, and Scandiani. Conductor, Signor Campanini.

HAYMARKET THEATRE. TO-NIGHT, at 9, "MY WIFE": Messrs. Aubrey Smith, A. E. Matthews, Holman Clark, H. Marsh Allen, Fred Lewis, Athol Stewart, H. de Lange, E. W. Tarver, P. Knox, C. Corwen, P. Clark; Miss Marie Lohr, Miss Millie Legarde, Miss Chevalier, Miss Walker, Miss Chatwyn, Miss Burt. At 8.30, MR. HENRI DE VRIES in "A CASE OF ARSON."

GARRICK THEATRE. THIS EVENING, at 8.30, THE WALLS OF JERICHO: Mr. BOURCHIER and Miss VIOLET VANBRUGH; Messrs. Eric Lewis, Cyril Keightley, Charles Goodhart, Whitby, Burchill, Imbert, Bristowe, Elliot, Carter, Cecil, Hilliard; Misses Pamela Gaythorne, Elfrida Clement, Nora Greenlaw, Welgall, Sumner, Killick.

CRITERION THEATRE (Piccadilly-circus). THIS EVENING, at 8.30, THE LIARS: CHARLES WYNDHAM and Miss MARY MOORE; Messrs. E. Kemble, Sam Sothern, Thalberg Corbett, Ellis Norwood, Bertram Steer, Reginald Walter, Herbert Dansey, J. White, J. Cabourn; Mesdames Granville, Spencer-Brunton, Dorothy Thomas, Catherine Dupont, Frances Vine.

NEW THEATRE. TO-NIGHT, at 8, THE SCARLET PIMPERNEL: Julia Neilson and Fred Terry; Messrs. J. Carter Edwards, Horace Hodges, Alfred Kendrick, Wigney Percival, Malcolm Cherry, D. J. Williams, Frederick Groves, W. A. Haines, Walter Edwin, Alan Borthwick, Euston Pickering, L. Rose Dunrobin; Misses Kathleen Doyle, Mary Mackenzie, Claire Pauncefort, Marion Sterling.

WYNDHAM'S THEATRE. THIS EVENING, at 9, WHEN KNIGHTS WERE BOLD: Mr. James Welch; Messrs. Grenville, Weir, Ford, Lane, Tully, Tomkins, Profett, Richardson; Mesdames Helen Palgrave, Winwood, Cordell, Mary Leslie, West, Chippendale, Hollingshead, and Audrey Ford. Preceded, at 8.15, by THE BOATSWAIN'S MATE.

VAUDEVILLE THEATRE. Lessees and Managers, A. and S. Gatti. TO-NIGHT, at 9, MRS. PONDERBURY'S PAST: Mr. Charles Hawtrey; Mesdames Marie Illington, Mona Harrison, Gwynne Herbert, Dorothy Hammond, and Billie Burke; Messrs. Charles Troode, Wilfred Draycott, Edwards Fitzgerald, Ernest Graham. At 8.30, THE ANONYMOUS LETTER.

SAVOY THEATRE. TO-NIGHT, at 8.25, IOLANTHE: Messrs. C. H. Workman, Harold Wilde, Frank Wilson, Overton Moyle, and Henry A. Lytton; Mmes. Clara Dow, Jessie Rose, Louie René, Ruby Gray, N. McLeod, V. Frampton.

THE PLAYHOUSE. TO-NIGHT, at 9, THE EARL OF PAWTUCKET: Mr. Cyril Maude, Mr. George Shelton, Mr. W. H. Post, Mr. Richard Sterling, Mr. Dore Davidson, Mr. John Harwood, Mr. Daniel McCarthy, Mr. A. Aspland; Miss Alexandra Carlisle, Miss Pollie Emery, Miss Elsie Ferguson, Miss Madge Titheradge. At 8.20, THE DRUMS OF OUDE.

PRINCE OF WALES THEATRE. THIS EVENING, at 8, "MISS HOOK OF HOLLAND": Messrs. G. P. Huntley, George Barrett, Herbert Clayton, F. Allandale, F. Pope Stamper, B. S. Foster; Mesdames Gracie Leigh, Eva Kelly, G. Brogden, G. Ivery, and Miss Isabel Jay.

TERRY'S THEATRE. THIS EVENING, at 8.30, MRS. WIGGS OF THE CABBAGE PATCH. Funniest Comedy in Town: Mrs. MADGE CARR COOK; Miss Louise Closser, Miss Bessie Barriscale, Miss Grace Griswold; Messrs. Frederick Burton, Forrest Robinson, and Entire New York Company.

LYRIC THEATRE. THIS EVENING, at 8, THE MERRY WIVES OF WINDSOR: Mesdames Euriquota Crichton, Rosina Buckman, Hilda Moody; Messrs. John Child, Lewys James, Charles Magrath, Charles Manners.

APOLLO THEATRE. THIS EVENING, at 8.15, TOM JONES: Miss Ruth Vincent, Misses Marie Daltra, Dora Rignold, F. Parfrey, C. Courtneidge, and Miss Carrie Moore; Mr. Dan Rolyat, Mr. Ambrose Manning, Mr. Jay Laurier, Mr. R. Crompton, Mr. J. Morley, Mr. A. Seames, and Mr. C. Hayden Coffin.

GAIETY THEATRE. TO-NIGHT, at 8, THE GIRLS OF GOTTENBERG: Mmes. May de Souza, Violet Halls, Olive May, Kitty Mason, Kitty Hanson, Wade, Cooper, James, and Gertie Millar; Messrs. George Grossmith, jun., Robert Nainby, Arthur Hatherton, Charles Brown, Evelyn Maxwell, Thorley, Bellamy, Grundy, Hale, Miller, and Edmund Payne.

DALY'S THEATRE. THIS EVENING, at 8.15, THE MERRY WIDOW: Messrs. Robert Evett, W. H. Berry, Lennox Pawle, Gordon Cleather, Fred Kaye, V. O'Connor, R. Roberts, and Joseph Coyne and George Graves; Misses Elizabeth Firth, Nina Sevening, I. Desmond, E. Welch, G. Lester, M. Russell, D. Dombey, D. Irving, F. Le Grand, A. Webster, M. Munro, A. Fraser, and Lily Elsie.

ALDWYCH THEATRE. TO-NIGHT, at 8.50, IN THE BISHOP'S CARRIAGE: Miss FANNIE WARD and Messrs. Frank Cooper, Charles Cartwright, Henry Vibart, Charles Collette, Arnold Lucy; Mesdames Agnes Hewitt, Edith Cartwright, Elspeth Dudgeon, Margaret Fuller. Preceded, at 8.30, by Mr. Charles Collette in a Musical Monologue.

DUKE OF YORK'S THEATRE. Lessee and Manager, Charles Frohman. TO-NIGHT, at 8.15, Griffith Humphreys; at 8.45, CHARLES FROHMAN PRESENTS GRACE GEORGE in DIVORÇONS: Miss Grace George, Mr. Frank Worthing, Mr. Douglas Gerrard, Mr. J. D. Beveridge, Mr. Max Freeman, Mr. J. W. Macdonald, Mr. Frank Collier, Miss Ruth Denson, Miss Ruby Ray, Miss Sadie Jerome, Miss Jane Corcoran.

COMEDY THEATRE. TO-NIGHT, at 8.30, THE TRUTH, by Clyde Fitch: Miss Marie Tempest; Mr. Allan Aynesworth, Mr. Dion Boucicault, Mr. Dawson Milward, Mr. Horton Cooper, Mr. Donald Calthrop; Miss Grace Lane, Miss Sybil Carlisle, Miss Rosina Filippi.

THE HICKS THEATRE, Shaftesbury-avenue. Sole Lessee and Manager, CHARLES FROHMAN. THIS EVENING, at 8.45, BREWSTER'S MILLIONS: Messrs. Gerald du Maurier, J. L. Mackay, Edward Sass, Clarence Blakiston, Louis Goodrich, F. Percival Stevens, G. Lestocq, C. Foote; Misses Mollie Lowell, E. D'Alroy, H. Thompson, K. Melrose, J. May, Beatrice Agnew. At 8.15, Hilda Trevelyan in The Dumb-Cake.

NOTICES.

The Times will be forwarded to subscribers within the United Kingdom on payment of £1, and within the Postal Union on payment of £1 6s. 6d., quarterly in advance. These rates give annual subscribers the privileges of The Times Book Club, at 376-384, Oxford-street, W.

Subscribers who fail to receive their copies regularly by the post and persons who cannot obtain The Times at all railway bookstalls for 3d. per copy are PARTICULARLY REQUESTED TO COMMUNICATE with the Publisher.

Advertisers are requested not to send stamps. Post-office orders to be made payable at the General Post Office to Mr. George Edward Wright.

THE TIMES can be obtained abroad in—

PARIS ...	The Times Office, 2, Chaussée d'Antin, M. Clautems, 30, Bd. des Italiens, and at the principal kiosques.
VIENNA ...	Haasenstein and Vogler.
BERLIN ...	Rudolf Mosse's Advertising Agency. Saarbach's News Exchange.
MAYENCE ...	Saarbach's News Exchange.
BOULOGNE ...	Merridew's Library.
NICE ...	Galignani's Library.
MILAN ...	Saarbach's News Exchange.
CANADA ...	F. S. Wright, The Times Agency, Stair Building, Bay-street, Toronto.
UNITED STATES	225, Fourth-avenue, New York.

Northcliffe to the rescue

The Times belongs to many different people. In the formal sense it belongs to its proprietor or proprietors, who pay the wages, carry the losses, take the profits and can sell or buy the national institution as a property. In a mystical sense it belongs to its readers, without whom it is dead: *Times* readers are more proprietorial than the readers of any other paper, loving its idiosyncrasies, objecting to changes and feeling bereft of any acceptable alternative when they cannot get hold of *The Times*. As a work of the mind, it belongs to the men and women who make it: the Black Friars, who, whatever their attitudes when they join the paper, quickly acquire the standards and traditions of *Times* Men, and the high opinion that the world would be better run from Printing House Square.

The Times is steered by all these and other interested parties. Even the editor is not an Island, entire of itself. He is not an autocratic emperor, but the head of a coalition of interests, opinions, arguments and pressures. Editorial freedom is not an absolute freedom to publish white for black and black for white: not for long, anyway. And editorial freedom comes more easily when it is based on commercial success. From the paternalist Walters to the *laissez-faire* Thomsons, owners of *The Times* have always taken a close interest in the contents as well as the balance sheet of the paper. It would have been odd if they had not. Editorial freedom is constantly being redefined and fought for in the hurly-burly and hustle to get tomorrow's paper out.

By the beginning of the twentieth century, the finances of *The Times* were unhealthy. None of the money-making sidelines had been sufficiently successful; and the growth of the popular press made the competition for advertising revenue fierce. Publishing *The Times* was no longer a licence to print money, as it had been fifty years before.

George Earle Buckle, editor since 1884, filled *The Times* with magisterial and scholarly articles on subjects of limited interest, such as Assyrian scripts. When he did get a big scoop, for example the exclusive news of the resignation of Lord Randolph Churchill given to him by Churchill himself, he seemed embarrassed, and published it as a small, separate paragraph on page 9. People spoke about the Gay Nineties. It was not an adjective that could have been applied to *The Times* in that *fin de siècle* decade.

Under Buckle *The Times* was reliable, authoritative, a little dull and extremely unprofitable. He claimed to have moved the paper from left of centre to right of centre: under Barnes and

Below Lord Northcliffe at Launceston, Tasmania, leaving the Town Hall after a civic reception given by the Mayor, 17 September, 1921.

In a dramatic bid to improve circulation figures, Northcliffe reduced the price of THE TIMES from threepence to a penny. This first penny issue carries an announcement to new readers (column 4) of whom there were many thousands.
16 MARCH 1914

The Times.

No. 40,472. (4.0 A.M.) LONDON, MONDAY, MARCH 16, 1914. TWENTY-FOUR PAGES (WITH FINANCIAL SECTION), PRICE 1d.

ADVERTISEMENT CHARGES.

BIRTHS.

MARRIAGES.

DEATHS.

IN MEMORIAM.

BY APPOINTMENT TO THEIR MAJESTIES THE KING AND QUEEN

SPRING RENOVATIONS

WITH THE ADVENT OF SPRING RENOVATIONS BECOME NECESSARY IN THE HOUSE—PAPERING AND DECORATING, RE-MAKING OF BEDDING, CLEANING OF BLINDS AND CURTAINS, RE-UPHOLSTERY OF FURNITURE, &c.

TO ENTRUST THE WHOLE OF THE WORK TO MAPLES MEANS THAT EVERY PART OF IT WILL BE CARRIED OUT BOTH SATISFACTORILY AND ECONOMICALLY.

Expert advice and estimates free

MAPLE & CO LTD

TOTTENHAM COURT ROAD

LONDON

PARIS BUENOS AIRES MONTE VIDEO

CARDINAL AND HARFORD

Specialize in importing Carpets. (They deal only in Carpets.)

They have their own permanent agents residing in all parts of the East, and consequently have a unique command of the Eastern markets.

CARDINAL and HARFORD (Est. 1792), The Levant Warehouse, 108-110, High Holborn, W.C., and 64, New Bond-street, W.

FURNITURE FOR CASH.

"The Practical Book of Furniture." (4th Edition), "The Practical Book of Furniture." (4th Edition) Free. Illustrated Schemes—

To Furnish a Flat for 60 Guineas.
To Furnish a House for £100.
To Furnish a House for £150.
To Furnish a House for £250.

WILLIAM SPRIGGS & Co., Ltd., 238-241, Tottenham Court Road, London, W.

COCKTAILS READY FOR USE.

MARTINI
MANHATTAN
DRY GIN
MAYFORT

Sample bottle free by post on receipt of 4s. 6d.
FORTNUM & MASON LTD.
182, Piccadilly, London, W.

CHOCOLATE TRUFFLES.
A SPECIALITY OF FORTNUM & MASON
MADE EVERY DAY.
2s. 6d. and 5s. PER BOX.
Post free on receipt of remittance
FORTNUM & MASON, Ltd.
182, Piccadilly, London, W.

HOSPITAL NURSES.

PERSONAL.

VARIETIES, &c.

TO NEW READERS OF "THE TIMES."

In consequence of the reduction of *The Times* to one penny, a great many readers are now seeing it for the first time. It is to those readers that the following notes are addressed, with the object of showing that *The Times*, in spite of the immense variety of subjects with which it deals, is better arranged and MORE EASILY READ THAN ANY OTHER NEWSPAPER IN THE WORLD.

In the middle pages of the paper, where it opens naturally, will be found—on the right hand an index and brief summary of the chief news, together with the leading articles; on the left hand the full record of some of the more important events of the day.

Immediately preceding this is the important page of Foreign and Imperial Intelligence, containing telegrams from *The Times* Correspondents in every quarter of the globe. Preceding this again are pages of miscellaneous general news, and, on the foremost pages of all, the daily Law Reports.

To turn to the other side of the central opening, there is a page devoted to Home news, and containing as a rule the more important political intelligence. Then comes a page of Court, social, and personal news, which is invariably the right-hand page immediately following the leading articles. Beyond this, again, when Parliament is in Session, is the Parliamentary Report, and last of all are the pages devoted to Sport.

Finance and Commerce form the subjects of a separate daily section of the paper, which is in itself a complete financial newspaper.

Reviews of books are published during the week and are afterwards collected, with much additional matter, in a separate Literary Supplement, published every Thursday morning at a penny.

Educational news is published daily, and an Educational Supplement is published at a penny on the first Tuesday of every month. There are many other special Numbers, such as the Empire Number and the Annual Financial Review, which are published from time to time during the year.

THIS ARRANGEMENT IS ALWAYS THE SAME, and it is because of it that *The Times* can claim, not only to deal exhaustively with a far greater variety of subjects than other papers, but to present them in the form most easily accessible to the busy reader.

CONCERTS, &c.

ROYAL COLLEGE OF MUSIC.

PATRONS' FUND.

GRAND IRISH FESTIVAL.

ROYAL CHORAL SOCIETY, ROYAL ALBERT HALL.

CONCERTS (continued).

CONCERTS (continued).

DANCING.

PERFECT WALTZ with REVERSE, BOSTON, ONE-STEP, and TWO-STEP GUARANTEED in FOUR PRIVATE LESSONS for £1 1s., and MAXIXE, TANGO, FURLANA or TA-TAO in three lessons, by

CHAS. D'ALBERT, LEADING TEACHER of SOCIETY DANCING, whose famous easy method has survived the test of years. CALL for lesson AT ANY TIME. EXPERT ASSISTANTS. 291-293, Oxford-street (next Bond-street Tube). Mayfair 5382.

DANCING.—MISS ALICE HALL, 22, George-street, Hanover-square, W. Valse, Boston, One-Step, TANGO, MAXIXE. Four private lessons, £1 1s. Practice Classes. COURT PRESENTATION LESSONS. 5463 Mayfair.

WARE'S SCHOOL of SOCIETY DANCING, Modern Gallery, 61, New Bond-street, W.—Furlana, Ta-Tao, Tango, Maxixe, Hesitation Valse, Boston, One-Step, &c.; four private lessons £1 1s. Boston, Tango, and Maxixe Class Monday and Friday Evening.—'Phone, Mayfair 3423.

ADVERTISEMENTS IN "THE TIMES."

Whilst "The Times" cannot guarantee the bona fides of every single advertisement that appears in its columns, the greatest possible care is taken to ensure that all advertisements inserted are trustworthy, and readers may, with an unusual degree of confidence, accept the statements made by any firm whose advertisements appear in these pages. The management invites correspondence with respect to advertisements which do not fulfil the spirit of the above assurance, and if upon investigation any reasonable complaint that reaches us is found to be justified such advertisements will not be allowed to appear in the future. Moneylenders' announcements are rigorously excluded.

Top George E. Buckle, editor of THE TIMES 1884–1912.

Centre NORTHCLIFFE TEACHING NEW TRICKS TO THE OLD PAPER AT THE PENNY PRICE, cartoon by Max Beerbohm.
Young Beerbohm, cartoonist, novelist, essayist, critic and dandy, had known the Harmsworths since staying at their home in 1896. Northcliffe sent him to Italy in 1906 on a roving commission to write articles for the DAILY MAIL. Although Max was most dissatisfied with the pieces published, it was the discovery of Italy that led to his determination to live there. He said later, 'many people have tried to make a success of me. It cannot be done. Lord Northcliffe was one of those who tried. He failed.'

Above Charles Frederic Moberly Bell, Manager of THE TIMES 1908–11.

Delane the paper knew where it was going, without working out where the centre was. Circulation fell. Moberly Bell, the manager, complained that 'people bought the cheap papers not because the price was low, but because their contents were low'. This was only partly true. *The Times* was extremely expensive at 3d; but its old-fashioned methods meant that it cost 6d to produce. Buckle himself aggravated the financial crisis, with all the high-minded unworldliness of a Wykehamist scholar, by publishing the palpably forged Parnell papers, so involving *The Times* in vast expense.

The constitution of *The Times* was complex. It was a co-partnership, with the Walter family as the chief proprietors. Under the will of John Walter I in 1812 shares in the *Times* partnership had been divided between a small number of beneficiaries. By 1900 the shares had been further subdivided so that there were about a hundred shareholders, known quaintly as the small proprietors. They became uneasy because they had an unlimited liability if *The Times* started making losses. They suspected the Walters, who never published their accounts, of feathering their own nest by charging exorbitant rents and printing costs. When dividends were good, little was heard from the small proprietors. As dividends shrank, they became restive. A guerrilla campaign against the Walter management of *The Times* was started, and was conducted with an obduracy and malignancy only found in a family quarrelling about money.

In 1905 a leader of the guerrillas applied for a transfer of *The Times* to a limited liability company. After two years of dissension and legal wrangling, the courts ordered the partnership to be dissolved and the paper sold. At this time the chief proprietors were Arthur Walter and his half-brother Godfrey. They wanted to sell the paper privately, with satisfactory guarantees that the new owner would not change the traditional character of *The Times*, which had become a national institution.

There were plenty of candidates for The Thunderer, not all of them with experience of running a newspaper. One of them was Lord Northcliffe (at that time, still Alfred Harmsworth), founder of the *Daily Mail*, the greatest popular journalist of the age. He was an erratic self-made man who changed the whole course of British journalism by making it both lively and prosperous. He was not likely to be approved of by the Establishment as owner of *The Times*: he had offered to buy a controlling interest in *The Times* as long ago as 1898, and had been turned down by the Walter family.

Godfrey Walter had a scheme to sell *The Times* to Arthur Pearson, founder of the *Daily Express* and owner of the *Standard*, the youngest and least successful of the 'Big Three' of popular journalism. The plan would have left the Walters with a stake in their family business.

By chance at a dinner party Northcliffe heard a hint of what was in the wind. He decided to play a forcing card that would stir things up. He instructed J. L. Garvin, the editor of his Sunday paper *The Observer*, to insert the following paragraph on 5 January 1908: 'It is understood that important negotiations are taking place which will place the direction of *The Times* newspaper in the hands of a very capable proprietor of several popular magazines and newspapers'.

Northcliffe calculated that this would cause an uproar. The City, the small proprietors and the Establishment would all jump to the conclusion that Northcliffe, a far bigger threat to them than Pearson, was the mystery buyer. There would be an outcry at the suggestion of *The Times* passing into the control of the rogue elephant leader of 'the yellow press'. He calculated right. There was uproar. Godfrey Walter panicked and instructed Buckle, against his better judgment, to insert a counterstatement in *The Times*. This stated that negotiations were in progress to turn *The Times* into a limited company under the chairmanship of Arthur Walter, with Arthur Pearson as the proposed managing editor.

This paragraph alienated everybody whose support the Walters needed. Buckle was unhappy about the part he had to play and began to work against them. The small proprietors saw the deal as just another example of the high-handedness of the Walters. The judge of the Chancery Court, who had to decide who should purchase *The Times*, considered that he was being treated with contempt.

And down at Printing House Square, the men and women who produced *The Times*, the Black Friars as Northcliffe came to call them, felt that they were being auctioned like cattle. In particular Moberly Bell, the manager of the paper, was outraged. He was an archetypal Black Friar. Were it not for his efforts and devotion to the platonic ideal of what *The Times* should be, the crisis in the affairs of Printing House Square would have arisen much earlier.

The Walters now had a bitter enemy in the camp. Moberly Bell was far more astute and capable than the whole of the Walter family working together. He had his hands on the levers of power at the paper. And he decided to oppose the Pearson deal. Accordingly, with reluctance, he decided to throw in his lot and the paper's with Northcliffe. He thought that he could ride the tiger by getting written guarantees from Northcliffe that he would maintain the independence of *The Times*.

Buckle had no enthusiasm for Pearson and was using his considerable influence around the London clubs to cabal against the deal. Arthur Walter began to wobble. Moberly Bell told him that he had found a secret purchaser who would guarantee to preserve the tradition and editorial independence of *The Times*. The second half of his statement was a triumph of hope over Northcliffe's track record.

The negotiations were conducted in cloak-and-dagger secrecy. The potential buyer was known simply as 'X', because, if his identity became known, the hostility that had been aroused against Pearson would be transferred to Northcliffe. When Moberly Bell met Northcliffe in secret, the latter said to him: 'Mr Bell, I am going to buy *The Times*. With your help, if you will give it me. In spite of you, if you don't.' 'I will help you', Bell replied, deciding to go for King Stork.

There were clandestine negotiations in a car in the suburbs. Eventually Pearson, who was no longer supported by the Walters, withdrew and the court directed the sale to Northcliffe. Bell had won, but at a cost. He presented the written guarantees, which he thought had been agreed orally, to Northcliffe. They were returned unsigned, with a letter requiring Bell's signature: 'It is understood that in the event of your acquiring *The Times* newspaper, I shall act as Managing Director for 5 years and carry out your absolute instructions'. If he refused to sign, Northcliffe said that he would withdraw immediately and completely from the negotiations.

Bell signed. On 29 April 1908 The Times Publishing Company came into existence. For a long time the name of the new owner was unknown to many in the office. At the time the sale seemed to many to be the unacceptable face of commercial journalism. But it underlined a truth that had never been forgotten by the less decadent Walters who owned the paper in earlier years: the independence of any newspaper of comment like *The Times* depends upon its commercial success. Without profits, you cannot be free.

Page 84
The first part of an article sent by Northcliffe from the Front during the First World War (column 6). On the same page (columns 1 and 2) is a leader supporting Northcliffe's line.
4 OCTOBER 1916

Page 85
THE TIMES announces the death of the man who had saved it from bankruptcy, and made it lead the field once again in journalism and printing.
15 AUGUST 1922

The Chief in charge

Like most men, Lord Northcliffe was an enigma. Born Alfred Harmsworth, he was a popularizer of genius, founder of the *Daily Mail* and a brilliant journalist for the rising educated middle and lower classes. He was an autocrat and a megalomaniac. He died raving mad, with (according to the house legend) the words 'Those damned Black Friars have beaten me' on his lips. He inspired enthusiasm and love. He was feared, hated and (much worse) disapproved of by shellbacks at Printing House Square. John Walter II and Northcliffe were the two greatest proprietors that *The Times* has yet had. They were dissimilar men, but they shared a certainty of what was right for *The Times*, and a determination to put it first.

After the cloak-and-dagger negotiations by which Northcliffe acquired *The Times* (see pp. 80–82), the national institution was moribund through senility. Circulation was down to 38,000. Both its production methods and its journalistic attitudes were fossilized from its great days in the nineteenth century. Somebody had to make these bones live. Northcliffe was the man.

Because of the prejudice, much of it snobbish, against the Harmsworth name and methods, the new proprietor trod gingerly into his new possession. He did not set foot in its offices for more than a year. For a long time he was known in Printing House Square as Mr X. He never met Arthur Fraser Walter, the chairman of the company of which Northcliffe had become chief shareholder. He did not touch the Ark of the Covenant of *Times* editorial policy, at first. But behind the scenes he got his hands on the machines and the account-books. Within five years he had replaced the antiquated Victorian machinery in the composing and press rooms with the latest technology and systems.

And gradually he transformed the appearance of *The Times*, so that it started to look like a newspaper instead of a learned journal. *The Times* before Northcliffe had paid no attention to layout, thinking it a little vulgar. One of Northcliffe's first appointments was to make one of the sub-editors responsible for the overall organization and planning of each day's edition: to regulate the amount of copy being sent to the printer, to co-ordinate the work of the editorial departments and to plan the layout and make-up of *The Times*. The fact that such an appointment was considered a dangerous innovation by the reactionaries shows how far *The Times* had ossified in its tradition.

Northcliffe respected tradition. He was a revolutionary with a sense of history, who knew that a daily newspaper, is only as good as its last issue. So he moved slowly. There was never any head-on opposition to his innovations or methods, but there was passive resistance and Fabian procrastination. Northcliffe, a man in a hurry, sometimes lost patience with the Black Friars.

Gradually the Old Guard retired. George Earle Buckle, editor for twenty-eight years, vacated the chair in 1912. Northcliffe appointed Geoffrey Dawson to succeed him, and gradually his young men of the new century replaced the Victorian old and bold. Editorially the blood was starting to flow again.

Commercially it was not. Drastic methods were needed to bring the patient back to life. Typically Northcliffe decided on the Napoleonic bold stroke. He lowered the price from 3d to 1d. The penny *Times* first appeared on 16 March 1914 (reproduced on p. 81). The nobs grumbled that this cheapened *The Times* to just any other paper. But circulation started to pick up and run at 145,000. The war later in the year pushed circulation up to 278,000 (wars and disasters are always good for the circulation of *The Times*: when the heavens are falling, people turn back to reliable old nurse).

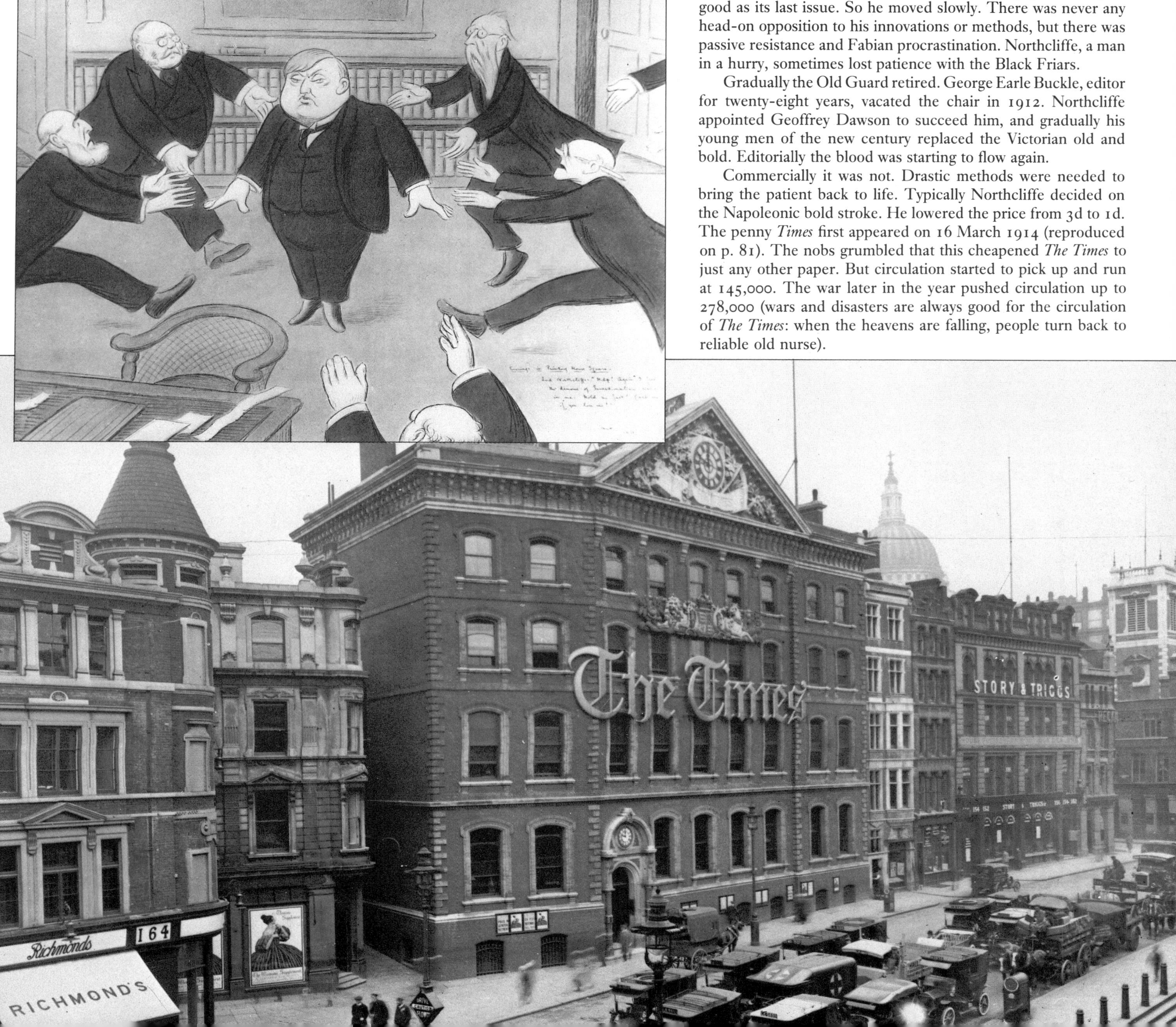

Below Max Beerbohm's cartoon: EVENINGS IN PRINTING HOUSE SQUARE. Lord Northcliffe: 'Help! Again I feel the demons of Sensationalism rising in me. Hold me fast. Curb me if you love me!'

Bottom THE TIMES building, 1921. Northcliffe added the giant letters.

WEDNESDAY, OCTOBER 4, 1916.

"THE TIMES" FUND.

Total to date £4,455,000 6 2

Owing to the pressure on our space the list of contributions to "The Times" Fund on behalf of the British Red Cross Society and the Order of St. John of Jerusalem is unavoidably held over. Subscriptions should be sent to the Chairman of the Joint Finance Committee,

Sir Robert Hudson,
83, Pall Mall, London, S.W.

The Medical Army.

Lord Northcliffe's vivid and detailed description of the Army medical service in France, which we publish this morning, will be read with deep interest. It is drawn from personal observation and is full of graphic touches which put the scene before our eyes. And the scene is one that ought to be put before us; no one can look on it without a thrill of admiration and gratitude. To those on the spot it is, no doubt, so familiar that they do not think of it, though the knowledge that medical succour is so close at hand and so efficiently organized must, if unconsciously, influence the fighting men and help to keep them in good heart. They know at least that if they are hit they will have every chance that human skill and kindness and courage can give them. We have believed that, too, at home, and it has comforted many an anxious heart. But it has been a vague belief. We have not known how the thing was done. The excellence of the medical service has been fully recognized in a general way from the first stages of the war. It has been known by its results, to which we have repeatedly drawn attention. Whatever else may have gone wrong in the war or fallen short of its purpose, this has not. It has exceeded expectation and accomplished wonders in the maintenance of health and the care of the wounded. The success was so complete and constant that it came to be taken for granted and people ceased to think of it. Every one with the slightest knowledge of previous campaigns knew that such success could only be achieved by masterly organization, and that behind the results there must lie a record of capable and devoted service unsurpassed by any other in the whole story of the war. But of the actual work we have heard very little, and the films only give a glimpse here and there. Now Lord Northcliffe has raised the veil and shown us enough to give substance and certainty to our comforting trust in the medical service. He has described the working of the machine and filled in the outline with details which enable us to realize, at least in part, what the task is and how it is performed.

No wonder he was impressed by what he saw and is full of admiration both for the organization and the *personnel*—the surgeons, stretcher-bearers and nurses, the Royal Army Medical Corps, and the great auxiliary societies of the British Red Cross and St. John. It is a most impressive story to read, from the regimental aid post—right up at the veritable "front," where the regimental surgeon and his stretcher-bearers have no more cover than the men actually fighting and are very little behind them—through the successive stages in the rear, down to the great hospitals on the coast and the hospital ship which takes those fit to travel across the Channel. Who says the British cannot organize? We are told that the position of each unit in the chain of medical service—the aid posts, dressing stations, collecting stations, clearing stations—is arranged as systematically as those of the military service. And the staffs, transport, and supplies must be organized with equal precision, or the whole machine would break down by its own weight. For it is on a prodigious scale. What Lord Northcliffe happily calls the medical army exceeds the whole British military forces overseas before the outbreak of war. One wonders where they all come from. Like the other Army, they come from all parts of the Empire and from all walks of civil life. The greatest call has been on the medical profession, because doctors cannot be improvised or trained in a short time. Lord Northcliffe awards them the palm of chivalry over all others for having left their lucrative home practices in a great rally of self-sacrifice. We do not deny these high motives. The medical profession has displayed surpassing devotion and courage and cheerfully paid a heavy—too heavy—toll of life, beside which pecuniary sacrifices are nothing. But they stand in a peculiar position, shared by nurses, but not by most of the civilians serving in the war. They are doing their own proper work in which they delight, and deriving from the due performance of function that happiness which it alone can give, as the greatest of philosophers taught more than 2,000 years ago in the most profound analysis of happiness yet given to the world. That does not lessen, it rather heightens, their merit, because their function is to relieve suffering, to save life and limb and senses, and to restore the sick and maimed to an active and useful life. These incomparable services have never before been rendered on so grand a scale or with such resources and such success. They are not confined to the organization described by Lord Northcliffe, but are applied with equal success to the still more important task of preventing disease and maintaining health. It is a notable fact that, in spite of all the privations and hardships of warfare, the rate of sickness in the Army in France is actually lower than the normal rate in peace-time.

Lord Northcliffe concludes his article with a significant reference to the aspirations of home-coming soldiers. We are glad to hear that they have learnt from their experiences in France to appreciate a rural life, and that they intend to fashion a changed England in which they will cultivate their own land, and live on it, as they have seen the French do. That is a consummation most devoutly to be wished; it would go far to solve some pressing economic and social problems which confront us in the future. And it is not owners of land who will put obstacles in the way of realizing it. The process of breaking up large estates and enabling tenants to become the owners of their holdings on easy terms was going on actively before the war. The opposition comes from theorists and politicians who are obsessed by the idea of small holdings under public ownership. That idea suits some conditions and some persons well enough, no doubt, but it has only a limited application. To suppose that the land of this country as a whole can be cultivated to the greatest advantage in that way is an error due to ignorance. We need here, and have room for, all types of cultivation—large farms as well as small holdings, and cultivating owners as well as tenants; but above all we need small cultivating owners. If the return of our soldiers results in a substantial increase of this class it will benefit the country all round.

Futile Blasphemy.

The German Crown Prince has been moved to adapt the Sermon on the Mount for the benefit of the American people. In the remarkable "interview" granted to a former American clergyman, which we published yesterday, he inquired, "Isn't there a book which says, "'Where the treasure is, there the heart "'is'?" "It is a pity," he added, "that "your treasure is not invested, during these "hours of world agony, in sowing the seeds "of preparation for the fruits of peace." It does not appear that the Crown Prince's "interviewer" revealed the identity of the Book or the context of the quotation. Possibly he was too much edified by the strange metamorphosis, or, rather, conversion, of the Crown Prince, by Allied arms, from lust of war to lust for peace. Otherwise he might have recalled references to "whited sepulchres" and to those who "outwardly appear righteous "unto men, but within are full of hypocrisy "and iniquity." "What a pity, what a pity "it is," exclaimed the Imperial Pecksniff, "all this terrible extinction of human life! "Is there one German general, one German "soldier, who does not bewail the dreadful "necessities pressed upon them by this combat? "Is there one who would not rather see all this "labour, skill, education, intellectual resource, "and physical prowess devoted to the task of "upbuilding and lengthening life?" He, the Crown Prince, is, moreover, a family man. He has a wife and children, and "it is no "happiness" to look forward to spending a third Christmas in the field. Of all the audacious utterances recorded in the "interview" this is perhaps the most daring. Does the Crown Prince imagine that his record as "a family man" is unknown in the United States? Can he suppose that his bellicose declarations, from the time of Zabern down to a few weeks since, have been forgotten? Is his contempt for the American public so colossal and so blind?

"We are all tired of the bloodshed. We "all want peace. England is the Power "responsible for the continuation of the "hopeless effort to crush us." Here we have the gist of the Crown Prince's plaint. Yet he has good words for England also. He trusts that he still has "many friends in "England." We can assure his Imperial Highness that he is mistaken—except possibly as regards the part of England covered by internment camps. "The Englishmen are "chaps who take sporting chances. . . . It "is a pity that all cannot be gentlemen and "sportsmen, even if we are enemies." But even a Hohenzollern Prince cannot be everything, however much he may twist and turn. We fear that to be a gentleman and a sportsman must always be beyond his reach. We prefer the utterance of the German officer who, in a burst of frankness, said:—"We shall never "be gentlemen, and you English will always "be fools." Yet, as the Crown Prince's declaration shows, it is possible not to be a gentleman and at the same time to be a fool. It is also possible to be gentlemen and at the same time to be sternly resolved, as the British peoples are, to see that the weak shall not be downtrodden, the helpless ravished and tortured, the unoffending assailed and robbed—even by pilferers of the Blood Imperial—without condign punishment being inflicted upon the guilty, and mankind being taught by its infliction to believe that there is a God in Heaven and righteousness upon the earth. "Where your treasure is, there will your "heart be also," says the Book to which the Imperial Pharisee blasphemously referred. The treasure of the British peoples, of their Allies, and, we believe, of the vast majority of Americans, is in the immutable principles of justice and liberty. There also is their heart. Neither calculated "squealing," of the kind which Mr. Lloyd George foresaw and denounced in advance, nor hypocritical bravado will deflect them by a hair's breadth from their purpose until it has been utterly achieved.

The Prime Minister and the Minister of Munitions had audiences of the King at Buckingham Palace yesterday.

POLITICAL NOTES.

ELECTORAL REFORM CONFERENCE.

THE SPEAKER TO PRESIDE.

It is understood that the Speaker of the House of Commons has consented to act as chairman of the Conference on Electoral Reform. The conference will be confined to members of the two Houses of Parliament selected by the Speaker, and the invitations were sent out in his name yesterday. The acceptance of the chairmanship by the Speaker will give the conference the best possible start. It ensures impartial dealing between the several parties interested. It marks the problems to be solved as primarily House of Commons questions. It is expected that the conference will meet at an early date, probably immediately after the reassembling of Parliament next week.

The conference is the outcome of a suggestion made by Mr. Long in the middle of August during a debate on the Special Register Bill, which is hung up *sine die*. The Prime Minister warmly endorsed the suggestion, and Mr. Long has devoted a great deal of time during the recess to carrying it into effect. It may be accepted that the conference will in the main follow the lines set out in *The Times* of August 22. The Government will not be represented in any way on the conference. It will include Parliamentary representatives of every political party and of every school of thought on electoral reform. The inquiry will be as wide as it can possibly be made. The four chief questions on which the conference will be asked to report are the following:—

1. Simplification of our registration machinery.
2. Changes in the franchise.
3. Redistribution of seats on an equitable and automatic basis.
4. Amendment of the Ballot Act to meet the grievance of the "absent voter."

The ideal aimed at is an agreed settlement on these questions, which have been the battledore and shuttlecock of parties for generations. Voting in the trenches, votes for unenfranchised soldiers and sailors, votes for women, a shorter qualification for the franchise, "one man, one vote," and "one vote, one value"—all such questions will be reviewed by the conference. The Ministerial view is that the Cabinet would accept an agreed settlement from the conference and present it to Parliament in a Bill. The conference will be somewhat larger than the Select Committee of 15 members which the House of Commons refused to accept from the Government in July. It will have all the help, in the way of staff and papers, that the Government, and especially the Local Government Board, the Department most concerned, can give it.

A DEPARTMENT WITH A FUTURE.

The Department of Labour Adviser to the Government, which is now installed in the new buildings which show such a handsome front to St. James's Park, is well worth watching. Its possibilities of development are as great as they are obvious. At present Mr. Arthur Henderson and Mr. G. H. Roberts have no executive powers, and act in a purely advisory capacity. Their primary function is to tender such advice to other Government Departments as will preserve industrial harmony during the war. This seems a limited sphere, but the two Ministers are quickly finding that their Department supplies a long-felt want. The practice of the Board of Trade has been never to intervene in an industrial dispute unless a strike or lock-out had been actually declared or its mediation had been sought by both parties. The new Department cuts in with expert advice before a crisis has been reached. Trade unions, quick to realize the value of the new Department, inform it of matters in dispute, and the machinery of Government is at once set in motion. It has already been called upon to deal with such matters as the objections of the boot trade to compulsory insurance against unemployment, the enlistment of skilled workmen, and some of the problems of demobilization. The Department is clearly capable of great expansion, and it is understood that a definite programme of work will shortly be submitted to the Prime Minister.

THE CLUBS' MOVING DAY.

Both the Constitutional and National Liberal Clubs will be in their new quarters in time for the reassembling of Parliament and for the quickened activity which the return of members from their constituencies entails. "Moving day" has been fixed in both cases for Monday next. It is expected that Mr. Bonar Law will take an early opportunity of addressing the members of the Constitutional Club in their new home at the Hotel Cecil. A political "house warming" at the Westminster Palace Hotel is also being suggested.

THE WAR COMMITTEE.

A meeting of the War Committee was held at 10, Downing-street, at 11.30 a.m. yesterday. The Prime Minister presided, and the following members were present:—Mr. McKenna, Mr. Montagu, Lord Curzon of Kedleston, Mr. Bonar Law, Mr. Lloyd George, and Mr. Balfour. The following also attended:—

Viscount Grey, Mr. Chamberlain, Mr. Long, Mr. Runciman, Lord Hardinge of Penshurst, Lord Newton, the Earl of Derby, Admiral Sir H. B. Jackson, General Sir W. R. Robertson, Vice-Admiral Sir H. F. Oliver, Sir T. W. Holderness, General Sir E. G. Barrow, Lieutenant-General Sir Nevil Macready, the Hon. Neil Primrose, Dr. Addison, Major-General F. C. Shaw, Mr. Kent, Lieutenant-Colonel W. Dally Jones, acting secretary, and Major C. L. Storr, assistant secretary.

HOW CARNOT "COMBED OUT."

TO THE EDITOR OF THE TIMES.

Sir,—Complaints are loud that numbers of men fit for active service are finding shelter in Government offices. The following passage shows that this abuse is no new thing, and tells us how "the organizer of victory" and his colleagues knew how to deal with it:—

[In 1795-6] they devoted the greatest attention to the execution of the laws relating to the young conscripts and compelled them with the greatest severity to rejoin the armies. They had caused the abolition of exemptions of all kinds, and they had constituted medical commissions in every canton to judge cases of [alleged] infirmity. Crowds of young men had thrust themselves into the Government Departments (*administrations*), where they robbed the Republic and showed the worst possible spirit. The most stringent orders were issued against toleration in the public offices of anybody except men who did not come under the conscription. (Thiers, *Histoire de la Révolution Française, Livre XXXII.*)

Yours faithfully,
ANTI-BUREAUCRAT.

SONS OF DECEASED OFFICERS.

TO THE EDITOR OF THE TIMES.

Sir,—The question of enabling sons of officers fallen in the war to be educated at the schools with which their families are connected is in the minds of many of us. So far as I understand, at least three organizations might be able to help—the Officers' Families Fund, the Pay and Pensions Fund, the Kitchener Memorial Fund. Old boys of the schools would no doubt be willing to do something, and probably governing bodies. House masters also could do a little, though not much in these days. Perhaps, too, grants might be made by the Board of Education, the county councils, or the Treasury. I would therefore beg to suggest that steps shall be taken to bring these various bodies into touch. A committee might be elected, a general scheme formulated, and definite offers of assistance invited. I write of boys, as I represent a boys' school, but the same might be done for girls.

I am, Sir, your obedient servant,
A. L. FRANCIS.

Blundell's School, Tiverton, Oct. 2.

DESPERATE VOLHYNIA BATTLE.

ENEMY'S OBSTINATE STAND.

1,000 MORE PRISONERS.

What is described by the Germans as the expected general attack on their positions in Volhynia is reported to-day from Petrograd and Berlin. The battle was fought on both sides of the main road from Lutsk to the enemy's fortified base at Vladimir Volynski, and it is represented by the Berlin authorities as an unusually desperate and costly affair for our allies. The Russian troops, they say, stormed their positions 12 times, and the Guard Corps 17 times, without effect. This is at variance with the brief Russian report, which mentions the capture of some of the enemy's positions in face of an extremely obstinate resistance. Neither side claims to have taken prisoners.

The third day of the fight on the Zlota Lipa yielded General Shcherbacheff another 1,000 prisoners, making a total of 5,000 for this successful operation.

Petrograd, Oct. 3.—The following official *communiqué* was issued here to-day:—

Dvinsk Front.—In the region east of Novo-Alexandrovsk [18 miles south-west of Dvinsk] towards 6 in the evening, the German troops, after artillery preparation, began to emerge from behind their barbed wire entanglements, but they were driven back by our fire to the trenches they had left.

The Centre.—On the River Servetch the enemy bombarded our positions in the Krinki-Ostashina sector [27-24 miles north of Baranovitchi in the centre], and at 1 o'clock in the morning showed a disposition to begin an offensive, which was completely checked by our fire.

Volhynia.—In the Zaturtsy, Volia Sadovskaia and Shelvoff regions [20, 20, and 24 miles west of Lutsk] fierce fighting took place, and our troops at some points took possession of certain positions of the enemy, who is offering an extremely obstinate resistance.

Galicia.—On the River Ceniowka [a tributary of the Zlota Lipa] and in the region of the heights on the right bank of the Zlota Lipa there was furious and ceaseless fighting.

On the Ceniowka the enemy, having brought up considerable reinforcements, launched a counter-attack, which we repulsed by our fire, inflicting heavy losses on him. Desperate fighting continues in this region.

Yesterday we took over 1,000 prisoners on this portion of our front. The total number of prisoners captured in this sector on September 30 and on October 1 and 2 is 5,000, including eight German officers and 600 soldiers.

Caucasus Front.—There is nothing important to report.—*Reuter.*

TWELVE RUSSIAN ATTACKS.

Berlin, Oct. 3.—German official report:—

Front of Prince Leopold.—From the Army Group of von Linsingen it is reported that the general attack expected west of Lutsk against the troops under Lieutenant-General Schmidt von Knobelsdorf, the groups under General von der Marwitz, and the army under von Tersztyanski commenced yesterday morning (October 2) after an extraordinarily intense artillery preparation.

From 9 o'clock in the morning the Russian troops were thrown forward with a prolific and inconsiderate use of men. The Russian Corps stormed 12 times, and the two Guard Corps 17 times. The 4th Army Corps, which was recently so heavily defeated near Korytnitsa [24 miles west-south-west of Lutsk] has apparently disappeared from the enemy line.

All the enemy attacks collapsed with the most exceptionally heavy and sanguinary losses. Where enemy detachments were able to penetrate into completely demolished trenches, as they did north of Zaturtsy [20 miles west of Lutsk], they were at once driven out by a counter-attack.

The Russian artillery by repeatedly directing its fire upon its own trenches forced the troops to advance or attempted to stem the returning waves and compel them to return once more to the attack.

It has been ascertained that the enemy who temporarily penetrated into some of our trenches killed our wounded who had been left behind. Our losses are comparatively small.

The success of the counter-attack made north of the Graberko [in North-East Galicia] has been extended. The number of prisoners brought in has increased to 41 officers and 2,578 men. The booty amounts to 13 machine-guns.

Front of Archduke Karl.—Continuing their attacks on the eastern bank of the Zlota Lipa, the Russians succeeded in advancing as far as the Lysonia height (south-east of Brzezany). They were driven back by German, Austro-Hungarian, and Turkish troops.

North of the Dniester a brief attack by a German detachment was successful.—*Wireless Press.*

MR. ASQUITH AND LORD MAYOR'S BANQUET.

WAR-TIME SIMPLICITY.

The Prime Minister, who has been consulted by the Lord Mayor Elect and the Sheriffs as to the celebration of Lord Mayor's Day on November 9 on the lines of last year, has intimated that he will be pleased to attend the banquet. He suggests, however, that in view of war conditions it should be of a simple nature.

The Lord Mayor Elect and the Sheriffs fully concur in this suggestion.

SUPPLY OF NURSES.

HOSPITAL MATRONS ADDED TO THE COMMITTEE.

The Secretary for War announced last night the appointment to the Supply of Nurses Committee of additional members representing the nursing profession, both military and civil. The committee was originally announced as having been appointed to consider the existing system of obtaining nurses for the hospitals for sick and wounded at home and abroad, and to make such recommendations as it may consider necessary for augmenting the supply.

The new members of the committee are as follows:—

Miss E. H. Becher, R.R.C., Matron-in-Chief, Queen Alexandra's Imperial Military Nursing Service.

Miss Sidney Browne, R.R.C., Matron-in-Chief, Territorial Force Nursing Service.

The Countess of Airlie.

Miss L. V. Haughton, Matron of Guy's Hospital.

Miss R. Cox-Davies, R.R.C., Matron of the Royal Free Hospital.

Miss C. Lloyd Still, Matron of St. Thomas's Hospital.

Miss A. McIntosh, Matron of St. Bartholomew's Hospital.

Miss A. M. Gill, R.R.C., Matron of the Royal Infirmary, Edinburgh.

Miss E. C. Barton, R.R.C., President, Poor Law Infirmary Matrons' Association and Matron No. 3 London Territorial General Hospital.

Lord Knutsford has withdrawn from the committee owing to inability to attend the meetings for some time.

The terms of reference are now officially given as follows:—"The committee have been appointed for the purpose of ascertaining the resources of the country in trained nurses and women partially trained in nursing, so as to enable it to suggest the most economical method of utilizing their services for civil and military purposes."

It should be noted that the committee has no power to deal with applications for employment.

As announced in *The Times* of September 16, the committee was at first composed of Mr. W. Bridgeman, M.P. (chairman), Lord Knutsford, Sir Frederick Treves, Hon. Francis Curzon, Mrs. Furse, Captain Harold Boulton, and Mr. E. W. Morris.

CONTRABAND LIST EXTENDED.

Proclamations published in the *London Gazette* of last night add to the list of articles to be treated as contraband of war, and also to the list of goods the importation of which is prohibited.

The additional articles to be treated as absolute contraband are insulating materials, raw and manufactured; fatty acids; cadmium, cadmium alloys, and cadmium ore; albumen; and waxes of all kinds. (Paraffin wax was already declared contraband.) Yeast is added to the conditional contraband list.

The importation into the United Kingdom is prohibited of aluminium powder; birds (live, other than poultry or game); manufactures of bone, horn, ivory, and celluloid; and cotton hosiery. The prohibition will not apply to such goods as are imported under licence of the Board of Trade.

By the same proclamation the prohibition of the import of oranges is removed.

SUBMARINES IN NEUTRAL PORTS AND WATERS.

ALLIES' WARNING.

The following Memorandum [Cd. 8,349] respecting the treatment of belligerent submarines in neutral waters has been communicated by the Allied Governments to the Governments of certain neutral maritime States:—

In view of the development of submarine navigation, and by reason of the acts which, in present circumstances, may unfortunately be expected from enemy submarines, the Allied Governments consider it necessary, in order not only to safeguard their belligerent rights and the liberty of commercial navigation, but to avoid risks of dispute, to urge neutral Governments to take effective measures, if they have not already done so, with a view to preventing belligerent submarine vessels, whatever the purpose to which they are put, from making use of neutral waters, roadsteads, and ports.

In the case of submarine vessels, the application of the principles of the law of nations is affected by special and novel conditions—first, by the fact that these vessels can navigate and remain at sea submerged, and can thus escape all control and observation; and second, by the fact that it is impossible to identify them and to establish their national character, whether neutral or belligerent, combatant or non-combatant, and to remove the capacity for harm inherent in the nature of such vessels.

It may further be said that any place which provides a submarine warship far from its base with opportunity for rest and replenishment of its supplies thereby furnishes such an addition to its powers that the place becomes in fact, through the advantages which it gives, a base of naval operations.

In view of the state of affairs thus existing, the Allied Governments are of opinion that—

Submarine vessels should be excluded from the benefit of the rules hitherto recognized by the law of nations regarding the admission of vessels of war or merchant vessels into neutral waters, roadsteads, or ports, and their sojourn in them.

Any belligerent submarine entering a neutral port should be detained there.

The Allied Governments take this opportunity to point out to neutral Powers the grave danger incurred by neutral submarines in navigating regions frequented by belligerent submarines.

August, 1916.

THE BURNT ZEPPELINS.

AMERICAN VIEW OF A PROBLEM SOLVED.

(From Our Correspondent.)

NEW YORK, Oct. 2.

The destruction of Zeppelins, since the latest successes of the British air defence forces, is coming to be regarded in America as a matter of course. All the newspapers publish prominently descriptive accounts of the doom of the latest German airship to be destroyed, and accompany these with brief chronicles of the destruction of other Zeppelins in the recent past.

The newspapers also reproduce with great satisfaction the *Frankfurter Zeitung's* mournful confession that Zeppelin attacks on England are becoming an affair of increasing difficulty and peril. Mr. von Weigand's report that super-Zeppelin raids are about to be begun with increased "ruthlessness" has evoked reminders to Germany that Great Britain seems to have solved the problem of the Zeppelins as ably as she solved the submarine problem.

The *Staats-Zeitung* publishes the news of the last attack on England with headlines of the largest size, and reserves its smallest type for the disclosure of the fact that another Zeppelin was burnt. The German-owned *Evening Mail* tries to discount a dispatch from its editor, Mr. McClure, affirming, on the strength of personal investigation, that the German Government's versions of the effect of Zeppelin raids on England is fantastically untrue. Mr. McClure tells his German readers:—

I am endeavouring to set forth the exact truth, not because what I write pleases me, but because I regard it as my duty as a good reporter to show the situation exactly as it is, especially in regard to peace.

To this the deputy German editor of the *Evening Mail* consolingly adds the lie that:—

Mr. McClure's dispatch was written before the recent Zeppelin raids, with their attending indisputable reports of heavy property damage and loss of life.

MAN-POWER AND IRELAND.

TO THE EDITOR OF THE TIMES.

Sir,—Your leading article upon this subject in *The Times* of to-day raises a question of very grave concern to all Irishmen who have at heart the interests of the Empire, of Ireland, and of the Irish Divisions fighting in the theatres of war.

The question of "man-power" is probably the most serious of those which at present confront the War Office. Our ammunition is assured. Our finances are equal to the strain. Have we and shall we have sufficient men in the field to carry on the work so gloriously initiated on the Somme in accordance with the welcome announcement of the Government's "fight to a finish" policy recently made by Mr. Lloyd George? I am well aware of the growing feeling that Ireland is not bearing her fair share in the supply of "man-power." I think in fairness to the different counties of Ireland the Government should publish a statement of the percentage of eligible men who have enlisted from each county. I have not the most recent figures, but I think it will be found to vary from 5 or 6 per cent. in some South and West counties to 25 per cent., or perhaps more, in the North-East.

When the Military Service Bill was before Parliament I on two occasions moved to include Ireland in its provisions, but on each occasion I was appealed to by his Majesty's Government not to carry the question to a division on the grounds of expediency—with the consequence that to my great regret we are now told that it will be impossible to keep up the Irish Divisions at the front. Anything more calamitous for the prestige of Ireland I can hardly imagine, and a more ignoble recognition of all we owe to the splendid and heroic work of our Irish Divisions cannot be conceived. Whether the Government are now in a position to announce a change of policy I do not know. The responsibility must rest with them, as they alone can judge of the feasibility of enforcing the Military Service Act in Ireland. But that some change must be made is apparent when you consider that there are at least 650,000 men of military age in Ireland, and that of these only about 100,000-120,000 have, as far as I know, enlisted.

Meanwhile what efforts are the Government making? How many eligibles are employed in the multitude of Government departments in Ireland, paid out of public funds? Has any pressure been put upon them? How much land has been purchased by the Government Departments since the commencement of the war at the public expense, and has any of this land been reserved for those who are willing to fight their country's battles? Or is it true that it has been, and is being, distributed to men who ought to be fighting, while none is reserved for the men in the trenches?

I think it will be found that Ulster has given more recruits than the three other provinces put together, and in addition has thousands of men working day and night on Admiralty and munitions work; but there is still the duty upon them to fill the gaps in the Ulster Division, overwhelmingly great, by reason of the imperishable glory won by their comrades on July 1. But many men in Ulster object to go and leave their places to be filled by men from the South and West, and by shirkers who will not do their duty. I have had many letters on this subject, and though I do not agree with the hesitation I entirely understand their feelings.

I believe, Sir, that in the near future it may be necessary to revise and extend the Military Service Act. We must have the men at all cost and at any sacrifice, and then what will be said in Great Britain, in Canada, Australia, New Zealand, and South Africa of a shirking Ireland which refused to hearken to the call of her own sons in the trenches?

Yours faithfully,
EDWARD CARSON.

5, Eaton-place, S.W., Oct. 3.

THE WAR DOCTORS.

THEIR LIFE UNDER FIRE.

BY LORD NORTHCLIFFE.

SOMEWHERE IN FRANCE.

Among the first forces mobilized by the Germans at the end of July, 1914, were the cinematographers and the artists. The German Empire has therefore a complete pictorial record of the war from its earliest days. We have lately begun to use the cinematograph. But we have not yet begun to enshrine by colour and canvas the lives of our men, and when we do send out a dozen of our best painters the War Doctor must be among the first to be made known and perpetuated.

We are so accustomed to consider doctors as part of our daily lives, or as workers in speckless and palatial hospitals, that we have hardly yet visualized the man who shares the hell of the front trench with the fighters, armed only with two panniers of urgent drugs, instruments, and field dressings, his acetylene lamp and electric torch. Most of us think of his war work as being accomplished at one of the great healing places at the Base.

If there be degrees of chivalry, the highest award should be accorded to the medical profession, which at once forsook its lucrative practices in London, or Melbourne, or Montreal, in a great rally of self-sacrifice. The figures of the casualties among them bring home to those who have only the big hospital idea of the war doctor, sad facts that should lead to due understanding of this not sufficiently known veritable body of Knights Templars in the Great Crusade. For the last three months in the Royal Army Medical Corps *alone*, I account them according to the figures published in *The Times* from day to day:—

Officers	**Killed**	**53**
„	**Wounded**	**208**
„	**Missing**	**4**
N.C.O.'s and Men (R.A.M.C. only).		
Killed		**260**
Wounded		**1,212**
Missing		**3**

* * * * *

I propose to set down the order in which our medical service arranges its chain of responsibility, premising my account by the statement that the medical army of to-day exceeds numerically the whole British military forces overseas before the outbreak of war.

It is a little difficult and complex to explain. I find that there is some confusion in the public mind as to the regimental work, that of the Royal Army Medical Corps, and their hand-maidens the British Red Cross Society and Order of St. John. But there is no confusion or overlapping in the zone of hostilities.

In the preparations for the great Battle of the Somme, Sir Douglas Haig, thorough in this as in every other detail, himself cooperated with the medical services in arranging his regimental aid posts, his casualty clearing stations, and the rest of them as systematically as his batteries, his ammunition "dumps," and his reserves.

First in the order of danger is the Regimental Aid Post, where the regimental doctor, with his stretcher-bearers, awaits, alongside the men who are to clamber "over the top," the bloody fruits of battle. In the early days of the war, before we had discovered the secret, or had the means, to blast our road into Germany by ceaseless shells, the Regimental Aid Post was, as a rule, in some deserted farmhouse as near to the front trench as possible. To-day, as we advance, our guns leave nothing standing, so that what was once perhaps a château is now only a stretch of rubble. There is therefore but little available cover for the doctors or the others before "consolidation."

The intensity of the French and German artillery at Verdun in March seemed to me then the limit of human capacity to produce noise and destruction. But the Somme bombardment actually furrows or flattens all before it. Verdun itself could not exist a week if exposed to the present French and British cannonade. Its intensity of sound is so great that at times the very earth shakes beneath one's feet.

The doctor has to-day probably only the shelter of one of our own trenches or any little part that may remain of a captured German trench. There is no other covering for him and his brave stretcher-bearers, who are at once his nurses and his orderlies. Happily not so many of these are fired upon by the enemy as heretofore; for, as the Prussians have realized that our artillery is the most deadly thing in the history of war, they have become a good deal more reasonable and human. Now that their own wounded greatly outnumber ours on almost every occasion, their doctors and stretcher-bearers often advance with a sheet or towel held high on a rifle as a flag of truce in order that they may collect their wounded and we ours. In the early days of the war similar suggestions on our part were haughtily and contemptuously refused. And so the advanced medical forces on both sides are at last sparing the wounded a good deal of the drawn-out horrors of "No Man's Land."

* * * * *

The fine young men with the English, Scotch, Irish, Canadian, and Australian accents who stand unarmed in these Regimental Aid Posts work with an intensity and celerity which eclipse even that of the surgeons in London's operating theatres.

The stretcher-bearers stagger in with their load. There is a lightning diagnosis, an antiseptic application, bandaging, a hastily-written label tied to the man's breast, and the wounded one is borne off and away in the open to the next stage, the Advanced Dressing Station,

DEATH OF LORD NORTHCLIFFE

PEACEFUL END TO LONG ILLNESS.

FUNERAL PLANS.

WESTMINSTER ABBEY SERVICE.

WORLD TRIBUTES.

We deeply regret to announce that Viscount Northcliffe died yesterday morning at his London residence, 1, Carlton-gardens.

The following announcement of his death was issued at mid-day by the doctors in attendance :—

Viscount Northcliffe died at twelve minutes past ten this morning. The end was perfectly peaceful.

P. SEYMOUR-PRICE.
HERBERT FRENCH.

FUNERAL SERVICE AT THE ABBEY.

BURIAL AT FINCHLEY.

The Dean of Westminster (Bishop Ryle) has communicated to Lady Northcliffe his desire that the funeral service for Lord Northcliffe before burial in St. Marylebone Cemetery, Finchley, shall be held in Westminster Abbey, and Lady Northcliffe has gratefully accepted the Dean's generous offer.

The Abbey service will be held on Thursday next and will commence at 12 noon. The greater part of the Abbey will be open to the public without tickets.

Seats in the Choir and Lantern will be reserved for relatives, personal friends, and others attending in a representative capacity. Application for tickets for these reserved seats should be made immediately to the Private Secretary, *The Times*, Printing House-square, London, E.C., and *not* to the Abbey clergy.

The interment in St. Marylebone Cemetery will immediately follow the Abbey service.

THE FATAL ILLNESS.

Dr. Philip Seymour-Price, the medical attendant, describes Lord Northcliffe's fatal illness as follows :—

The illness from which Lord Northcliffe suffered was infective or ulcerative endocarditis. It is probable that this fatal disease began insidiously months ago. In fact, it is not improbable that it started during his recent world tour.

The trouble made slow progress until some two months ago, when there was a considerable amount of fever, progressive weakness, and the heart was obviously becoming embarrassed. The patient's whole being was poisoned by the germ which was circulating in his blood. His condition steadily became worse.

Infective endocarditis is usually fatal. Very few patients recover from it, and in the case of Lord Northcliffe his extremely strenuous life, together with his war work, his world tour, his recent visit to Germany, and the noticeable loss of weight, had done much to undermine his constitution and had lowered his resistance to such an extent that the germ (streptococcus) was able to find its way into the bloodstream.

These germs exist ordinarily in the body, but it is easy to understand that, should they find their way into the bloodstream, the condition presents an extremely grave problem.

This was the situation that faced Lord Northcliffe's medical advisers on his return, obviously very ill, from the Continent.

Every treatment known to medical science has been tried, without success.

With characteristic energy and fortitude Lord Northcliffe put up a great fight. He was aware of his grave condition, but refused to yield to the enemy. He retained consciousness almost to the end.

THE CITY'S SORROW.

MESSAGE FROM THE LORD MAYOR.

We have received the following message from the Lord Mayor of London :—

LORD MAYOR OF LONDON.

"On behalf of the citizens of London, I desire to express the profound sorrow which the news of Lord Northcliffe's death has occasioned them. His great services to the Empire and his outstanding merit as a great and brilliant journalist are universally recognized and deeply appreciated.—JOHN BADDELEY, Lord Mayor of London."

ALD. SIR J. KNILL.

Sympathetic reference to the loss suffered by the country and English journalism in the death of Lord Northcliffe was made by Alderman Sir John Knill, the Acting Lord Mayor of London, in conversation with a Press representative at the Mansion House yesterday. Sir John Knill said :—

"I greatly regret to learn of the death of Lord Northcliffe. We had hoped that, though his illness was serious, he might yet have been spared to continue his work among us. But this, unhappily, was not to be. By the death of Lord Northcliffe English life and English journalism have been deprived of a great personality. A man of indomitable force of character and unbounded courage, he exercised a potent influence on the minds of men, and it is impossible to over-estimate the services he rendered to the country during the Great War. His family will be assured of the deep sympathy of the citizens in their and the country's great loss."

A MAKER OF NEW IRELAND.

LOVE FOR NATIVE LAND.

(From Our Own Correspondent.)

DUBLIN, AUG. 14.

Within three days two Irishmen who helped to mould Irish history have passed away. The wild Irish Republicans, and even some who support the Treaty, boast that Ireland is free today because England was beaten in the field of war. Of course, no sensible Irishman has any such illusion. The Treaty exists because British public opinion was converted to the necessity of an Irish settlement. No man played a greater part in that conversion than Lord Northcliffe. The news of Lord Northcliffe's death was received with genuine sorrow in the land of his birth. Those who knew him personally mourn the loss of a generous friend, who remained unspoiled by success and was singularly faithful to the comrades and associations of his early days. Lord Northcliffe paid his last visit to Dublin some years before the war, when he presided at a dinner, given in honour of his boyhood's friend, Mr. R. J. Mecredy. He made a charming speech, but it was in private conversation that he revealed his deep love for Ireland and his profound anxiety to serve her.

IRISH GIFTS.

Lord Northcliffe's achievements as a journalist and his great work in the European war are fully appreciated in his own country, but it is as an Irishman, endowed in a rare measure with the typically Irish gifts of courage and imagination, that his country will remember him. The young Irishmen to whom he offered a helping hand must be numbered in hundreds. The Irish policy of his newspapers in recent years has given invaluable support and encouragement to those who sought a sane and abiding solution of the national problem. All Irishmen, even those whom his independent attitude most often irritated, admired the high spirit in which he fought his battles and his catholic appreciation of what was good in the many Irish movements and policies of the last twenty years. They do not love him less because his faults, as well as his virtues, were the outcome of an Irish temper and an Irish vision. Rather were they proud of his wonderful success in life and of the great part which he played upon the stage of history during one of history's most tremendous periods. His career was a proof of the great things that character can achieve when it is backed by enterprise and industry, and one believes that his example will not be lost upon the Ireland of the coming days. Irishmen of all parties would have rejoiced if he had been spared to witness the secure establishment of the Free State and the beginning of a new era of progress in his native land. Like Mr. Griffith, however, he has died upon the threshold, but his country believes thankfully that the powerful influences and forces which he created will continue to work for Ireland's peace and progress.

WORLD-WIDE REGRET.

TRIBUTES FROM MANY LANDS.

We have received from many lands tributes to Lord Northcliffe. They include the following :—

THE AMERICAN AMBASSADOR.

Of the surprisingly few real personalities developed by the Great War, Northcliffe's will live in history as one of the three or four most vivid. It is not for an American to attempt to measure the value of his service to the Empire, but I may, I trust with propriety, bear testimony to the debt owed to him by the Republic for his unflagging endeavours in the interest of our common race.

It was a cardinal tenet of his faith that perpetuation of civilization could be assured only by mutuality of purpose and action on the part of our two countries, and he actually did more perhaps than any other one man, living or dead, to attain fulfilment of that noble aspiration.

America joins Britain in full sympathy at the loss of one of her greatest sons ; and I, in common with so many others who loved him for himself, grieve inexpressibly at the passing of a friend, dear and faithful for thirty long years.—GEORGE HARVEY, Dunkeld.

MR. HUGHES, Prime Minister of Australia.

A great and familiar figure has passed away. For the last eight or ten years Lord Northcliffe fought strenuously for the Empire. He was a great man in every respect. All who knew and loved the Empire deeply mourn his loss.

M. THEUNIS, Prime Minister of Belgium.

I am deeply grieved to learn of the death of so great a man as Lord Northcliffe.

MR. ISAAC F. MARCOSSON, the American Publicist.

"Deeply grieved to hear of Lord Northcliffe's death. It is an international loss ; sincere sympathy."

RUSSIANS IN LONDON.

Monsieur E. SABLINE, the former Russian Chargé d'Affaires in Great Britain, writes :—

"The Russian Colony in London has just learned, with feelings of the deepest regret, the sad news of Lord Northcliffe's death. Russians in England and those of my fellow-countrymen who are suffering in Russia will never forget the work of justice and compassion incessantly done by Lord Northcliffe on behalf of their country. In the name of the Russian Patriotic Organizations in London I beg to offer to those who worked with the Great Dead our heartfelt condolences."

REUTERS.

The Board of Reuters sorrowfully join with *The Times* in mourning the disappearance of an illustrious and romantic figure and a great genius from journalism and world affairs.—RODERICK JONES (Chairman).

Mr. ADAM MCCAY, President of the New South Wales Journalists' Institute, telegraphs :—"The Institute profoundly regrets the loss of a famous journalist and a great Imperial figure."

We have received a telegram from Mr. Bartolo, editor of the *Malta Chronicle*, associating that journal in the expression of world-wide regret at the heavy loss suffered by Lord Northcliffe's death.

On behalf of the Czecho-Slovak Legation, Mr. Jaroslav Cisar called at *The Times* Office to express the deep regret of the Government of the Republic for the death of Lord Northcliffe.

A biographical notice appears on pages 13 and 14, and Press and other tributes on page 15.

AMERICAN SORROW

A GREAT LOSS TO THE WORLD.

FRIENDSHIP FOR U.S.A.

(FROM OUR CORRESPONDENT.)

NEW YORK, AUG. 14.

The news of Lord Northcliffe's death has been received with the deepest feeling throughout the United States. The progress of his illness has been watched by the American people, among whom his name is a household word, with the most sympathetic interest. The news of his death was made public this morning by means of special bulletins placed outside the newspaper offices, a procedure adopted by New York newspapers only in most exceptional circumstances.

In the afternoon editions of the newspapers more detailed accounts of the circumstances of Lord Northcliffe's death appeared under heavy black headlines and were given precedence over even the news of the industrial crisis, which has reached an acute stage. Among many men in the forefront of American public life with whom Lord Northcliffe was closely associated, the news of his death has come as a stunning blow. The first of many expressions of appreciation which are reaching this office comes from Mr. Herbert Hoover, the Secretary of Commerce, who says :—

"The world has suffered a great loss in the death of the great and courageous journalist who served faithfully in building good relations between our two countries."

The President and Mr. Hughes, Secretary of State, have sent a joint message of condolence to Lady Northcliffe through the American Embassy.

Mr. E. R. Stettinius, one of the greatest of American bankers and partner in the firm of Messrs. J. P. Morgan, to whom I communicated the news this morning, said :—

"I am inexpressibly shocked and grieved."

The Pilgrims of America have addressed the following message :—

American Pilgrims, recalling the inestimable services that Lord Northcliffe had rendered in behalf of closer unity and cooperation of effort of the two great English-speaking Powers of the world—a cause which was, indeed, the keynote of his public policy and of all his personal relations—mourn his untimely death as the loss of a great and loyal friend of the United States and honour his memory.

Mr. Frank A. Munsey, proprietor of the New York *Herald* and many other newspapers and magazines, has furnished me with a copy of the leading article which will be printed to-morrow over his own signature.

In the death of Viscount Northcliffe (writes Mr. Munsey) the British Empire has lost its greatest single human force. There will be those who will say this tribute belongs to Mr. Lloyd George, not to Lord Northcliffe. But closer consideration of what makes for strength and power in men, of what makes for continued strength and power in nations, must in an impartial view endorse this utterance. . . . A great newspaper, the peerless newspaper of the world, whose roots dip deep into the centuries, in itself an enormous power, Lord Northcliffe owned and directed. Other newspapers owned by Lord Northcliffe were of matchless circulations and distinctive individualities—papers that cling closer to the bone and sinew of the human forces of the nation, and are in themselves an enormous power.

But greater than all these combined was the man Northcliffe, the creator of all this composite force except *The Times*, which became his through money of his own earning. There is continuity and perpetuity and grim strength to this kind of power that is above and beyond any power dependent on the suffrage of the people. . . . Lord Northcliffe's power had been recognized and had made itself felt throughout the British Empire, and with world scope, years before Mr. Lloyd George turned a wheel in national affairs. It perhaps is well within the fact to say that Lord Northcliffe had more to do with making Mr. Lloyd George Prime Minister than any other man or group of men. He brought all his resources to bear on dislodging the Asquith Government, which he believed wholly unequal to the vigorous prosecution of the war. He threw all his strength to Mr. Lloyd George. His work at this critical time in the life of his country, indeed throughout the war, was patriotic, untiring, powerful. No man gave of his energy and vitality more generously than he ; few men, if any, were in a position to be of the service to England and the Allies that Lord Northcliffe was with his great newspapers under his personal direction.

After reviewing Lord Northcliffe's career, Mr. Munsey writes :—

Lord Northcliffe's abilities radiated in many directions. He had the vision of the pioneer ; he was always a pioneer in the fields of his activities. He considered himself a Conservative, and had this strain deeply embedded in his nature, but his methods in all his undertakings were original, dramatic, daring. Making money with Lord Northcliffe as a boy was a necessity. A family of nine young children and a very wonderful mother came to him as a legacy from his dying father. Mere boy that he was, he accepted the stewardship with love, confidence, and zeal. It was a wonderful account he gave of this sacred trust. But Lord Northcliffe cared nothing for money for money's sake. He cared for it for what he could do with it. His passion was for constructive achievement, creation, the development of things. This dominating characteristic called for money to keep up with his expanding vision and fast broadening interests.

AN EDITOR'S TRIBUTE.

I have received the following message from Mr. John J. Spurgeon, editor of the Philadelphia *Public Ledger* :—

The death of Lord Northcliffe has removed the most picturesque and remarkable figure in the journalism of Europe and America. Few will dispute the fact that he wielded a power greater than that of any other private citizen in his time in his own or in any other country. He made and unmade Ministers. He put them down as easily as heads of great industries manipulate their subordinates. He rocked the Empire in the early dark days of the war by a single publication in *The Times* [a reference to the message about the shortage of shells], but this same publication perhaps saved the Empire, for it brought about a complete change in the methods of conducting the war. He saw his newspapers burned in the streets of London, but he lived to hear himself proclaimed as one who had done as much as any single individual to save the country.

Brilliant, daring, ruthless, hesitating at nothing when he believed himself right, Lord Northcliffe was perhaps the most feared man in England, yet multitudes of his countrymen regarded him as the country's greatest asset. He left his impression on the journalism of the world, yet the profundity of his mind had but barely started to produce. His career ended all too soon.

The New York *World* will publish a leading article to-morrow, in which it says :—

Lord Northcliffe was born for journalism as surely as Napoleon was born for war. It will be a generation before his influence upon political thought in Great Britain can be accurately measured. Americans can have only the kindliest feelings for the man himself. Few Englishmen ever understood the United States as well as he. None ever worked more ardently, more disinterestedly to promote British and American friendship. The United States was never a foreign country to him. When he was here he was a Yankee of the Yankees. Our manners were his manners, our customs his customs. He was hardly less at home in New York than in London. His was a short life measured by the accepted English standards, but it was a life that made much history, and only history itself will be competent to hold the scales.

LORD MANNERS TO MARRY.

It is announced in the Court columns on page 9 that Lord Manners is to marry Mrs. Claud Guinness in September. It is also announced that Lord Plunket is engaged to the widow of Captain Jack Barnato, R.A.F.

CONFERENCE FAILS.

"AGREEMENT TO DISAGREE."

BACK TO THE TREATY.

The Inter-Allied Conference came to a conclusion yesterday without any definite results having been arrived at, except the agreement to allow the next payment of £2,000,000 due from Germany to-day to be made within the next four weeks. This payment is what is known as a Clearing-House payment and is in respect of private claims as distinct from Reparations.

According to present arrangements, the French and Italian Delegations will leave London at 11 o'clock this morning.

The following is an authoritative statement on the course of the negotiations since Saturday :—

On Saturday evening the Experts' Committee was left wrestling with the proposals of the British Government, and no agreement was possible on the control of German State mines and forests, and there was some discussion about Clause 10 of the British proposals. [Clause 10 proposed a moratorium for Germany up to December 31, 1922, and the fixing of the annual payments thereafter at such an amount not exceeding 26 per cent. of German exports as the Reparation Commission might think proper, with a view to an early loan by Germany.] The main difficulty was over the mines and forests. Clause 10 was not in what the British Government regarded as final form, but it was useless to go on discussing Clause 10 when there was no agreement on the mines and forests. On Sunday, the Committee reported in the morning that they were unable to agree, and there were some conversations in London between M. Poincaré, M. Theunis, and Signor Schanzer ; and Signor Schanzer went to the country to discuss the position with Mr. Lloyd George.

Signor Schanzer's proposal was that the whole discussion should be adjourned until the various countries had carried out their funding negotiations with the United States and their delegations had returned ; and that then the questions of reparations and of inter-Allied indebtedness should be discussed together. It was understood on Sunday that M. Poincaré agreed to this suggestion and the British were ready to agree to it, leaving the date of the next meeting, of course, uncertain. When the Prime Ministers met yesterday morning, Signor Schanzer and Baron Hayashi (the Japanese Ambassador) being also present, Mr. Lloyd George began by saying that he had been very sorry to see some comment upon his absence in the country during the week-end.

The Prime Minister said that he hoped it had not in any way been misunderstood by his French, Belgian, Italian, and Japanese colleagues. As they knew, he had consulted them about going away before doing so. There was a strong feeling in this country against pressing public work on Sundays unless the situation urgently demanded it, and he had thought that it would be better, in the circumstances, not to press the experts too hard, but to leave them time to work out the matters which had been referred to them. He also thought that Ministers themselves would be better for twenty-four hours' reflection, which was often useful in the course of a heavy Conference. He had not gone away without consulting the others on this point and finding that they agreed with him.

The Ministers then discussed the suggestion which Signor Schanzer had taken to the country on Sunday, and M. Poincaré said that he was prepared to accept it on behalf of the French Government, provided there were no moratorium granted to Germany in the interim. All the other Governments represented thought this condition impracticable, and Signor Schanzer proposed that there should be a two months' moratorium ; but M. Poincaré said he could not accept an unconditional moratorium of any kind.

THE BRITISH PROPOSALS.

Mr. Lloyd George said that, so far as Great Britain was concerned, he saw no necessity for them there to decide upon whether there should be a moratorium or not. He was quite prepared to leave it to the Reparation Commission, which was the body set up by the Treaty of Versailles for dealing with exactly these differences ; he therefore repeated the proposals which the British Government wished to put forward, as follows :—(1) To adopt the Italian suggestion of an adjournment until the latter part of the year ; (2) to leave the question of whether there should be a moratorium or not to be decided by the Reparation Commission ; (3) to agree that the guarantees already demanded by the Committee of Guarantees and accepted by the German Government should be applied immediately ; (4) Great Britain would undertake to make no claim of interest or capital on the Allied debtors, pending the meeting at the end of the year.

These proposals were accepted, and supported strongly by all the Allies except M. Poincaré, who explained with much regret that he was unable to accept them. The position taken up by France was that there could not be any moratorium granted to Germany without fresh gages and guarantees.

Stating in brief again the British point of view, Mr. Lloyd George said that he could not agree to an adjournment without a moratorium, which would mean giving the Reparation Commission instructions that no moratorium was to be granted. The whole reason of the meeting at the present moment of the Allies was the general belief that Germany could make no more immediate payments. The British Government had always taken the view that this was a situation which should be dealt with in the first instance by the Reparation Commission as laid down in the Treaty of Versailles, and that an Allied meeting on the subject should not be held until the recommendations of the Reparation Commission were available. They had been discussing fresh gages and guarantees on the assumption that a moratorium was necessary, and it seemed quite idle to go back now and settle upon an adjournment with the moratorium absolutely barred. Great Britain thought that the gages and guarantees suggested by the Committee of Guarantees were quite adequate. Great Britain disapproved of the fresh gages and guarantees suggested, not out of any tenderness for Germany, but because she was convinced that these guarantees would defeat their own object.

Failing agreement, the British Government stood by the Treaty of Versailles, and had therefore suggested that the question of the moratorium should be referred to the Reparation Commission, as laid down in Article 234 of the Treaty. Or failing any agreement as to that, that the whole subject should be referred to the League of Nations under Articles 13 and 14 of the Covenant. As all these proposals had failed to secure assent, he was afraid that they must agree to disagree. All the others present took the same view, and M. Poincaré said that he would have to consider the situation with his Government.

AUSTRIAN PLEA FOR HELP.

Many of the delegates—including Mr. Lloyd George, Sir Robert Horne, Sir L. Worthington Evans, Sir Basil Blackett, and Sir Edward Grigg—were entertained at luncheon at the Italian Embassy. At 3.30 p.m. the Austrian Minister saw Mr. Lloyd George, and presented him with a Note with regard to the

(Continued at foot of next column.)

REBELS CAPTURE DUNDALK.

NATIONAL TROOPS SURPRISED.

DROGHEDA'S DANGER.

(FROM OUR CORRESPONDENT.)

BELFAST, AUG. 14.

The Irregulars brought off a big *coup* at an early hour this morning in Dundalk.

Shortly after 3 o'clock a large body of rebels entered the town and took the Free Staters completely by surprise. The latter made a stout resistance, and for a considerable period fierce fighting took place, but the Irregulars soon had full control of the town.

Ann-street police headquarters were first attacked, and the garrison made prisoners. The rebels then went to the gaol, and the prisoners, most of whom are Irregulars, were released. A state of terror prevailed in the town, and many of the inhabitants fled to Co. Armagh.

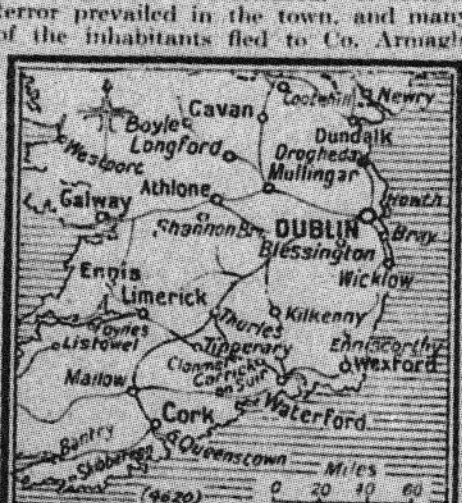

The railway station and the General Post Office were seized by the invaders, and the town was completely isolated, while strong patrols took charge of the main streets. It is reported, but the news lacks confirmation, that during the fighting five persons lost their lives and close on forty were wounded. Some of the banks were looted.

A party of Irregulars later in the day assembled a train, one wagon of which, it is stated, contained gelignite and bombs. The train proceeded in a southerly direction, and as telephonic, telegraphic, and rail communication between Belfast and places south of Dundalk was suspended in the afternoon, it is believed some bridges have been blown up and wires cut.

The usual afternoon mail train to Dublin, connecting with Kingstown and Holyhead from Belfast, had to be cancelled, while consignments of pedigree cattle for the Royal Dublin Society's Show, which opens to-morrow, were unable to get through.

DROGHEDA GARRISON PREPARED.

(FROM OUR OWN CORRESPONDENT.)

DUBLIN, AUG. 14.

The Irregulars at Dundalk seized trains and forced the railway workers to strengthen them with iron plates. One of these trains, filled with Irregulars, went off in the direction of Drogheda. The National troops there, however, were prepared for an attack. They tore up the railway lines outside the town in order to prevent the rushing of trains into the station, and posted men all about the town. It is believed here that no attack will be made on Drogheda before nightfall.

THE DUNDALK FIGHTING.

A Dundalk correspondent telegraphs :—

The first blow struck was at the military barracks, held by some two hundred men of the third Northern Division. Approaching the gate unobserved, some of the invaders placed bombs against it. The explosion shattered the gate to fragments, wrecked the guardroom, and damaged the houses in the vicinity. The garrison seemed to have turned out hastily to repel the intruders, and though they were outnumbered and surprised they put up a fight. Heavy firing continued, with almost incessant bomb explosions, for more than an hour. The garrison were eventually overpowered. It is stated that there were heavy casualties on both sides.

financial situation in Austria. This Note was the second addressed to Mr. Lloyd George as the chairman of the Inter-Allied meeting. The first had been received last week, and circulated to all the Delegations. The British Cabinet met immediately after, at about 4 o'clock, to receive the report of the Prime Minister, and unanimously upheld the line which he had taken. At 5 o'clock a plenary Inter-Allied meeting was held to discuss the Austrian Note. The general effect of the Note was to ask the Allies to guarantee a further loan to the Austrian Government of £15,000,000, and the Austrian Government declared that in the absence of such guarantees it would be obliged to declare its inability to continue its task. When the plenary Conference met, the Prime Minister read the Note, which had been circulated in translation, and said that he thought the Allies should not separate without giving their attention to this extremely grave situation.

It was difficult to know what more could be done, said Mr. Lloyd George, as Great Britain had already advanced £12,500,000 to Austria, without any appreciable effect in improving the Austrian situation. M. Poincaré and Signor Schanzer pointed out that France and Italy had given similar credits to Austria. France had given a credit of 55,000,000f. [about £1,000,000] this year, and Italy had given a credit altogether of 280,000,000 lire [over £2,800,000].

It was generally agreed that no Government was in a position to recommend to its taxpayers to incur any fresh burdens for the benefit of Austria until the situation there had been more thoroughly examined. All attached importance to such examination, and agreed that the Great Powers could not regard the collapse in Austria or the possible results with indifference. M. Poincaré suggested that as the League of Nations had already been engaged in investigating the Austrian position it might be invited to make this investigation complete. He knew that the League of Nations had no budget, but he thought that it might be able to suggest a programme of assistance to the Allies.

Mr. Lloyd George said that Great Britain would be very glad to adopt that suggestion, but he thought it would be only fair to inform the League that the Powers had all felt extreme difficulties in making any fresh subscriptions to Austria. It was no good making schemes based on the credits of other Governments when no such credits were obtainable. The League must take that into consideration and make the best recommendation it could. Every one agreed with that.

One other thing came up at the end of the meeting. Sir Robert Horne reported that the experts had come to a unanimous agreement on the Clearing-House payments and suggested that this report should be adopted by the Inter-Allied meeting. In brief, the substance of the report is that Germany shall make the next payment of £2,000,000, due on August 15, within the next four weeks ; that thereafter the agreement under which these payments are made should come to an end and that the different Governments should make fresh arrangements—separate arrangements—in the matter with Germany, subject in every case to the approval of the Reparation Commission.

M. Poincaré and M. Theunis both explained that they had adopted these proposals, which involved a real sacrifice of principle, for the sake of Allied unity. The Conference then broke up.

MENACING STRIKE DEADLOCK.

DANGERS OF U.S. RAIL DISPUTE.

(FROM OUR OWN CORRESPONDENT.)

WASHINGTON, AUG. 14.

When the full Congress meets again on Tuesday it will face an industrial situation of extreme gravity. The atmosphere at Washington is one of deep, unceasing anxiety, for every section of railway labour is now united in support of the shop-craft strike, rapid demoralization of the transportation system of the country seems unavoidable, and the coal strike is still unsettled. From what quarter relief may come none dares to predict.

In the week-end negotiations over the President's most recent settlement proposal the leaders of the four great railway brotherhoods appeared as representatives of the strikers, but, if by this show of solidarity it was hoped to influence the employers to abandon their stubborn refusal to permit the men to return to work with their seniority rights unimpaired, the gesture was in vain. The railway presidents all left Washington last night openly announcing their intention to fight to a finish. If they could carry their point on this matter of seniority they would have gone far to break the power of the unions, and they are grimly determined to hold on. They ask of the Government that it shall refrain from further attempts at settlement, confining its activities to the protection of citizens lawfully employed and to the prevention of interference with the carrying of mails, for with so much support and no more they believe they can break the strike.

The Labour leaders, on the contrary, spoke yesterday with ominous softness. They earnestly protested their desire for a settlement, and their willingness to aid the Government in reducing the annoyance and suffering of the general public to a minimum, and never a word of strike or walk-out did they breathe, but the fact to be remembered is that the direction of the negotiations has now passed from the hands of the shop craftsmen to the leaders of the four great brotherhoods—of engineers, firemen, trainmen, and conductors—who support the strikers at every point. In the hands of these great organizations lies the power to stop every train in the country, but it would obviously be poor policy, it would even be sheer madness, on their part to threaten such action in advance. There is a federal law which forbids interference with the transportation of mails, and not lightly would the brotherhood leaders brave a possible criminal charge of conspiracy.

ANOTHER WEAPON.

Moreover, there is another weapon to their hands, and this it is that the employers believe they will use—the plea that railway equipment is now so dangerously deteriorated that due regard for the safety of the travelling public and their own members should forbid its use. Already at many points engineers and conductors have refused to take out trains on the score of danger. These instances are likely to increase in number and to occur at vital points in the transportation system—or so the employers read the intentions of the Labour leaders—and it is prompt and vigorous action in each such case that the railways now ask of the authorities.

The deadlock seems to be as complete as it is fraught with danger to the country, and what Congress can do, or will try to do, remains to be seen. The employers will bitterly oppose any move towards Government operation of the lines. That, they believe, would be no more than a first step towards the concession of all the strikers' demand—ignominious surrender to the unions is the way they put it. However, Government working of the railways is the last thing President Harding wants. He has said that if the situation became much worse there would be no alternative to taking over some of the lines, probably a few coal-carrying lines, but he would take even this limited action *in extremis*. The Government may first adopt the method suggested by the employers—prosecution of the trainmen who interrupt the carrying of mails. This interruption has already been attempted in the case of the Santa Fé line, but the Department of Justice admits the difficulty of proving that the stoppage of trains on the ground of dilapidation and insecurity is not justified.

Congress is notoriously timid in cases such as the present. Its tendency is to pay any price for a solution. In 1916 it passed overnight a law making the adoption of an eight-hour rule obligatory upon the railways in order to avert an impending "tie-up," and there is certain now to be immediate talk of an assumption of control by the Government. This is just what the Labour leaders desire. They are all remaining in Washington in order, as they say, to be ready to testify before Congress if called upon, and all their influence will be exerted towards persuading legislators that the Government must take over the lines.

PRINCE OF WALES AND THE PRESS.

TO PRESIDE AT DIAMOND JUBILEE DINNER.

The Prince of Wales has accepted the invitation of the president and council of the Newspaper Press Fund to take the chair at the Diamond Jubilee dinner of the Fund, which will be held during the first fortnight in May next year.

ACCIDENT TO SIGNOR D'ANNUNZIO.

(FROM OUR CORRESPONDENT.)

MILAN, AUG. 14.

A serious accident occurred to D'Annunzio last night while he was walking in the gardens of his famous villa. He fell, severely injuring his head. At first the gravest fears were aroused, but the poet's condition subsequently improved, and although the doctors have not yet given a definite opinion, it is hoped that the patient is now out of danger.

MR. GRIFFITH'S FUNERAL.

(FROM OUR OWN CORRESPONDENT.)

DUBLIN, AUG. 14.

Great numbers of people to-day visited the Dublin City Hall where the body of Mr. Arthur Griffith lies in state. To-morrow evening at half-past 7 o'clock the body will be removed to the Pro-Cathedral in Marlborough-street. On Wednesday morning solemn requiem mass, at which Dr. Byrne, the Archbishop, will preside, will be celebrated. Afterwards the funeral will take place at Glasnevin Cemetery.

Mr. Churchill, who is abroad, on learning the news of the death of Mr. Arthur Griffith, telegraphed to Mr. Michael Collins and to Mrs. Griffith his deepest regret and sympathy in their heavy loss.

NAVAL A.D.C.'S TO THE KING.

The following officers have been appointed Naval Aides-de-Camp to H.M. the King, in the vacancies stated :—Commodore Alexander V. Campbell, D.S.O., M.V.O., vice Captain Richard Hyde, C.B., C.B.E., M.V.O., A.D.C., promoted to flag rank, July 24 ; and Captain George Trewby, C.M.G., D.S.O., vice Captain H. Ralph Crooke, C.B., A.D.C., promoted to flag rank, July 25.

I.C.S. RECRUITING.

THE "INDIANIZATION" CIRCULAR.

AN IMPARTIAL INQUIRY.

(FROM OUR CORRESPONDENT.)

CALCUTTA, AUG. 14.

The local Governments are considering the circular letters from the Government of India with regard to the Indianization of all the Indian services. The text of the circular contains no support for the allegation that the Viceroy favours speedier Indianization. The question is only an open one in the sense that the Government of India has invited expressions of opinion from the Provinces before considering the matter and sending its final dispatch to the Secretary of State. The inquiry has been undertaken in consequence of a resolution passed by the Legislative Assembly on February 11.

The Government of India suggests in the circular that the emergence of new factors may render necessary a revision of the existing orders in regard to the percentage of European and Indian recruitment. In the arguments advanced in favour of a radical modification of the existing policy, it is pointed out that any substantial falling off in the quality of the European recruits would obviously weaken the case for a strong European element, and that the attractions of the service are not so great, and the evidences of racial hostility may deter promising candidates from the adoption of Indian careers. The demand for the Indianization of services is wider and more insistent than the demand for self-government, and also more difficult to resist. The natural sentiment of the Indians is reinforced by financial considerations, for if the services were Indianized the scales of pay could be reduced. Moreover, the Indian Legislatures are pressing for rapid Indianization of the services.

Officers entering the existing services are entitled to remain for twenty-five to thirty years. It is possible, however, that twenty or twenty-five years hence conditions in India may render undesirable or impracticable the retention of a large number of European officers, and if recruitment on the present scale is maintained, Government may be faced with the necessity of retiring a great number of officers and paying them heavy sums in compensation. The presence of a substantial European element is already assured for some years to come.

That is the case for modification. On the other side, it is pointed out that the attractions of the services are still sufficient to draw men of the right stamp, and the burden of interpreting, guiding, and justifying policy will offer a stimulating field for intellect and character. Racial feeling may prove to be no more than a temporary phenomenon, and the Legislatures' demand for rapid Indianization may not continue. The risks inherent in a complete cessation of European recruitment are too great to be ignored.

Such are the arguments placed before the local Governments impartially, and the Government of India reserves its own conclusion until the Provinces have reported. Should the recruitment of Europeans be abolished, or largely reduced, extensive measures of reorganization will be necessary, involving, in all probability, the provincialization of the services.

In view of the erroneous statements which are circulating at present, it is necessary to emphasize that Government is merely consulting the Provinces, placing the facts and arguments before them. No policy has yet been framed, nor have any decisions been arrived at ; but the hope is strongly entertained in India that Parliament, with which the final power rests, will do nothing to hasten the extinction of the brilliant I.C.S.

BEVAN LEAVES VIENNA.

DUE IN LONDON TO-MORROW.

(FROM OUR OWN CORRESPONDENT.)

VIENNA, AUG. 14.

Gerard Lee Bevan, the former Chairman of the City Equitable Fire Insurance Company, left Vienna this morning at 7.15 by the Eastern express. If all goes well, he should be in Hamburg to-morrow morning in time to sail in the Caronia for Southampton.

He was driven handcuffed to the railway station. Here his Austrian police escort was joined by two English detectives, Inspector Smith and Sergeant Hipsly, who are travelling with him, and will take him over from the German police at Hamburg. Bevan appeared to be in good health, and before going into the train thanked one of the prison officials who was at the station for the considerate treatment he had received during his period of imprisonment.

A second-class carriage was reserved for him and his escort. Before the train started an English journalist handed Bevan a copy of a London newspaper, which he appeared to read with great interest.

Three second-class berths have been booked in the Caronia, which leaves Hamburg at 8 o'clock this morning and is due to arrive at Southampton some time to-morrow evening, so that there should be nothing to prevent Bevan's appearance before the Guildhall justices on Thursday morning if the train from Vienna is on time. It is due at Hamburg at 7.15 a.m., and as the Caronia sails punctually at 8 the margin of time is small ; but arrangements have been made by which the liner can be picked up at Cuxhaven, where the pilot is dropped.

The first hearing at the Guildhall will be short, only formal evidence being offered to justify a remand.

The vastly increased circulation overwhelmed the presses at Printing House Square, so the presses of the *Daily Mail* had to be called in to print the overflow. The printers there would cooperate only if *The Times* became unionized: *The Times* had been a non-union house for a century. Accordingly *The Times* Companionship, the old house union, passed into history and became a welfare club for men and women of *The Times*. Its influence was still potent: within living memory almost the first question that an applicant for a job at Printing House Square was asked was whether he sang tenor or bass (or, as it might be, soprano or alto), for the purposes of *The Times* operatic society.

By the beginning of the war that finally ended the Victorian Era, Northcliffe was in full control at Printing House Square. He was known as the Chief. He bombarded both the editor and the manager with streams of instructions and memoranda every day. Most of them were professional, constructive and practical. For example, one dated 27 January 1917:

> Today's *Times* came as a very great surprise to the Principal Proprietor. It contained a leading article which is practically a censure of the Women and National Service matter on the same page. It is halting and weak. It is exactly like one of those leading articles which brought *The Times* down to 27,500 a day, and necessitated the introduction of the Encyclopaedia and the Book Club.
>
> In future, when the Editor is away, I propose having a liaison between my other newspapers and *The Times* to prevent them contradicting each other as they do. This morning *The Times* not only contradicts its own news, but criticized my own newspapers of the two previous days. It is the sort of thing which cannot and will not happen again.
>
> Otherwise the paper was excellent, with some interesting articles.

The doctrine that the proprietor of a newspaper, particularly *The Times*, does not interfere with its editorial policy is a recent myth.

During the First World War Northcliffe's newspapers put in the field the most formidable concentration of political power since the Victorian heyday of The Thunderer. The *Daily Mail* with its circulation of nearly a million whipped up mass public opinion. *The Times* spoke authoritatively to the governing classes.

Take one famous example: the great shell scandal. In 1915 Colonel Charles à Court Repington, the military correspondent of *The Times*, filed a dispatch from France about the previously unsuspected shortage of high explosives. The *Daily Mail* picked up the scoop and waded in with:

> THE TRAGEDY OF THE SHELLS
> Lord Kitchener has starved the Army in France of high explosive shells

The campaign was considered unpatriotic by the simple-minded, though not by the poor bleeding Tommies in the trenches. The *Mail* was burned in the Stock Exchange, and *The Times* was banned in some service clubs. This trenchant and effective criticism of some aspects of the Government's handling of the war provoked a rival newspaper to comment: 'All Fleet Street knows which British journal has done most injury to the Allies, and has most unquestionably played the enemy's game. They would all point to *The Times*.' It was, of course, a recovery of the true traditions of *The Times*, when the Establishment complained about the paper, but trembled to read its leaders.

Northcliffe took the dignity of *The Times* very seriously, perhaps because the stuffy snubbed him for his popularization. When a leading firm of brandy-importers advertised in *The Times*, he sent a thunderbolt declaring that the paper was disgraced by accepting 'this page of barrels'. The quivering advertising manager reminded him that the paper needed money badly. The Chief replied: 'Your excuse is that of a burglar or embezzler: never take an advertisement because you want money'. On the other hand (and the Chief was a man of many hands), when an editor from Kansas criticized the front page of *The Times* for consisting of nothing but columns of classified advertisements, Northcliffe replied: 'Advertisements? They are the most important news. And where would you have it if not on the front page?'

Northcliffe was unique as a newspaper proprietor, in that he was also not just a journalist, but a great one. (As journalist, Beaverbrook was whimsical and unprofessional.) He raised the status of the inky trade. Under Northcliffe the reporter was better paid and got a sense of vocation. The days of Grub Street were left behind. When a scoop was missed because it broke on a Sunday and there was no money in the office to send a reporter, Northcliffe gave instructions that a hundred guineas in gold were to be kept at the front desk at all times for such emergencies. The instructions of the Chief were treated with such awe that this one was carried on long after his death.

His articles appeared frequently in *The Times* under the byline of Lord Northcliffe. In 1921 he went on a world tour, and wrote articles that display the range and touch of a true hack: rubber problems in Malaya, the court at Bangkok, surprises of sea travel, motoring in Palestine. Even without the ominous byline, they were Editor's Musts for publication, better than most other pieces in the paper.

In May 1922 he was off on his travels again, to Germany, Belgium and France, where he started to go mad in a spectacularly Napoleonic fashion, with hallucinations, conspiracy mania and megalomania. By June he was back in London. In August he died at the age of 57. One of his last thoughts was of the paper, and his reputation in the nearest thing in this world to the Recording Angel: 'In *The Times* I should like a page reviewing my life's work by someone who really knows, and a leading article by the best man available on the night'.

In the long eye of history, what were his achievements as proprietor of *The Times*? The better presentation of news, the importance of topicality, the introduction of features and other articles to appeal to women and the young, the improvement of the *Literary Supplement*, the introduction of the famous picture page and the equally famous fourth leaders . . . the list is so long that it gives the Recording Angel writer's cramp.

Above all, he saved *The Times* from death by arteriosclerosis. And by his will, which gave John Walter IV the option of purchasing his shares, he gave the paper a stable and independent future under a new proprietor trained to the new traditions of vitality and enterprise Northcliffe had introduced into Printing House Square. He may not always have been a comfortable proprietor to work for. But by God, he was good.

Below Lord Northcliffe with Mr Murayama owner of the ASAHI SHIMBUN, Japan's leading newspaper, November 1921. Northcliffe was on the world tour that preceded his death.

The Great War and the censor

It is generally agreed that the First World War was a turning-point. Old men say that those of us who were not there cannot imagine the *douceur de vie* of those golden years leading up to 1914. No doubt they had fortunate childhoods, and no doubt they are influenced by old men's nostalgia for the years when they were young. But the war was certainly a turning-point for *The Times*. It marked the transition into the new world of modern journalism, with the techniques of headlines, pictures, display and make-up. And in particular it gave Lord Northcliffe, the Chief, the chance to get a grip on the complacent old Establishment organ and shake it into new life.

Northcliffe started to take the daily conferences at Printing House Square. He had his own man, Geoffrey Dawson, as editor, and had got rid of most of the Old Gang. Sometimes he brought the editor of the *Daily Mail* with him, to coordinate the policies of his papers. He was not only dictatorial: he was quite often right. He was almost the only man in England who expected the war to last at least three years. The editor and everybody else expected a short, sharp war. He and *The Times* had been predicting war with Germany for ten years. Northcliffe knew Germany well. He opposed sending the British Expeditionary Force (BEF) to the Continent, but was persuaded to change his mind.

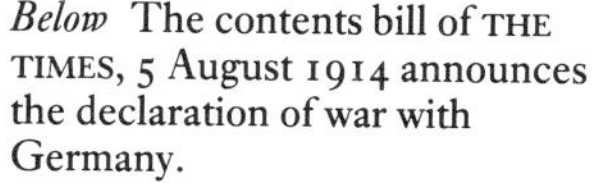

Below The contents bill of THE TIMES, 5 August 1914 announces the declaration of war with Germany.

Bottom Stretcher bearers carrying a wounded soldier through the mud of Flanders.

Times

AUGUST 5, 1914 1d.

BRITAIN AT WAR

War is a difficult time for newspapers, as for the rest of the country. On one hand, there is intense interest in the news, which is a matter of life and death not interest and titillation. On the other hand, other values supersede news values. In the new world of instant communications newspapers cannot discuss strategy in advance or criticize their own side in public with as much freedom as they have in peacetime. Keeping up national morale and propaganda are part of their function, as well as the journalistic functions of publishing the news as fast as possible, and commenting on it without fear or favour. In particular, censorship bites more than in peacetime.

In the First World War there was no nonsense about letting newspaper correspondents wander around the front line and discuss strategy and tactics with the generals in the manner of Billy Russell. There were only three sources of news from the BEF to start with: daily *communiqués* of inscrutable formality; the Commander-in-Chief's dispatches, which were high-sounding but vague; and stale news written up at General Headquarters (GHQ) by an official 'Eyewitness'. Eyewitness was in fact Colonel Swinton, the soldier-author, who wrote in peacetime under the *nom de plume* of 'Ole Luk-Oie'. His dispatches from France were described as hog-wash.

The strict official censorship probably harmed the British cause by encouraging complacency at home and discouraging potential recruits: nobody realized how badly they were needed. The Germans were much better at providing an efficient and vivid service of news about what was going on at the Front. They were, of course, winning at the time.

The Times tried to maintain its service of fast, exclusive news from its own correspondents. From Paris it organized a team of keen reporters, most of them young, to travel behind the Allied lines by car, bicycle or on foot, to get as near to the sound of the gunfire as they could and to pick up what news they could. One of them wrote home to Printing House Square in September:

> The best plan, I think, is to be as inconspicuous as possible and to go over the ground by train to a certain point and then by bicycle or on foot. This we have been endeavouring to do during the last few days with fair success. The principal thing is to keep rigidly away from the English who take a fiendish delight in arresting Correspondents; the French are much more reasonable.

Another wrote: 'So far as I can see the British are absolutely implacable as they are open neither to blarney nor logic; both ways in which the French can sometimes be moved'.

The Times's first big scoop came from one of these floating correspondents bicycling behind the lines at a venture. At the beginning of the war Arthur Moore, a staff reporter, had been sent across France and Italy to operate from Serbia. When he had got as far as Corfu he was recalled to go fishing for news behind the BEF. Bicycling around the back roads near Amiens,

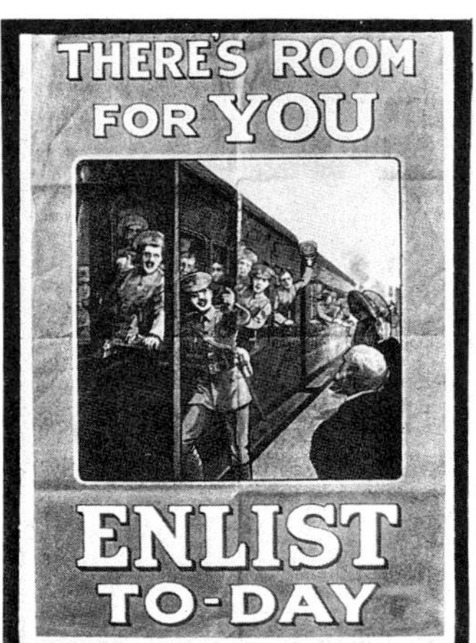

Top British troops on the Somme, 1916. The Somme offensive cost 600,000 British casualties.

Above Recruiting poster.

Moore rode into the thick of the chaos and confusion of a great battle. Scattered remnants of British forces were trying to rejoin their units. It was the British Fourth Division turning after the retreat from Mons.

Moore was greatly alarmed by what he saw and heard. It bore no relation to the official *communiqués*. Very early on the morning of 29 August he sat down and wrote a powerful piece that would have filled two columns of *The Times*. He sent it across to Printing House Square from Dieppe by a courier who arrived that evening.

The back bench (senior editorial staff) of *The Times* were also alarmed by what they read, and reckoned that not much of it would get past the censor. So they excised the more sensational passages themselves and sent it all off to the Press Bureau. After two hours it came back with the following note from the head of the Bureau:

PRIVATE

I am sorry to have censored this most able and interesting message so freely but the reasons are obvious. Forgive my clumsy journalistic suggestions but I beg you to use the parts of this article which I have passed to enforce the lesson – re-inforcements and re-inforcements at once.

F. E. Smith

In fact a number of the deletions made at Printing House Square had been reinstated with the annotation 'Stet F.E.S.' F. E. had also written in a few sentences in the last paragraph to stiffen the piece up.

The cautious men at Printing House Square were still uneasy about publishing a dispatch that seemed to them alarmist and possibly even unpatriotic. But they took the note from the chief censor as an instruction to publish, and went ahead in a special Sunday edition on 30 August. The article appeared under the bold and striking headlines:

BROKEN BRITISH REGIMENTS
BATTLING AGAINST ODDS
UNTARNISHED HONOUR OF OUR TROOPS
MORE MEN NEEDED

The article began by describing the previous day's Paris papers as 'like children's prattle, gleanings from the war-talk of their parents a week ago'. It appealed to the censor to let this report at least be published.

It went on:

It is important that the nation should know and realize certain things. Bitter truths, but we can face them. We have to cut our losses, to take stock of the situation, to set our teeth.

First let it be said that our honour is bright. Amongst all the straggling units that I have seen, flotsam and jetsam of the fiercest fight in history, I saw fear in no man's face. It was a retreating and a broken army, but it was not an army of hunted men. Nor in all the plain tales of officers, non-commissioned officers and men did a single story of the white feather reach me. No one could answer for every man, but every British regiment and every battery of which anyone had knowledge had done its duty. And never has duty been more terrible.

F. E. Smith had inserted his own surreptitious gloss at the end:

The British Expeditionary Force . . . has suffered terrible losses and requires immediate and immense reinforcement. The British Expeditionary Force has won indeed imperishable glory, but it needs men, men, and yet more men. The investment of Paris cannot be banished from the field of possibility . . . *Proximus ardet Ucalegon*. We want reinforcements and we want them now.

The Latin quotation, from *Aeneid* II, 311–312, 'The next door neighbour Ucalegon's house is already on fire' was in fact misquoted by the censor. The chaps at Printing House Square, who were good at that sort of Latin tag, rectified him.

The article outraged public opinion as unpatriotic and defeatist. The rival newspapers, rank with the stink of sour grapes, wrote of 'the great scandal' of the article. Questions were asked in the House. F. E. Smith, taking cover, answered ambiguously, disingenuously and downright duplicitously. He hinted that he had not had enough time to give proper attention to the offensive passages. In fact they had been with him for two hours, and he had written a private letter to the editor congratulating him on 'this most able and interesting message'. He told MPs that the article 'was clearly gleaned by the gentle*men* who wrote it from persons who had not been at the front, and who had given *him* a story disproportionate to the facts'. In fact he had written the most rousing part of the article himself.

The country needed to know that it was in a fight to the death, not a quick sporting walkover. *The Times*, with a bit of help from the censor, did a public service in breaking the news.

The front page of a special Sunday edition of THE TIMES, one of the rare occasions before 1966 when news reached the front page. Sunday editions were issued from the beginning of August 1914 till 6 December 1914, at 6 am, 11 am and 4 pm.
16 AUGUST 1914

Sunday Edition.

The Times.

No. 40,606. LONDON, SUNDAY, AUGUST 16, 1914. PRICE 1d.

THE EVE OF BATTLE.

NAMUR ATTACKED BY AIR.

INVASION OF LORRAINE.

RUSSIAN ADVANCE.

No fighting of any importance occurred in Belgium yesterday, though heavy firing is said to have been heard in the direction of Tirlemont.

The French military authorities have seized the opportunity offered by this lull to sum up in an official *communiqué* the results of military operations since war was declared. The main fact is that the German plan of a sudden stroke against the French frontier, directed through Belgium, completely miscarried. This gave time for the mobilization of the French Army to be brought to the utmost pitch of efficiency.

That accomplished, French troops, as we already know, entered Belgium in force, and their junction with the Belgian Army was effected with complete success.

Thus the hostile armies will enter upon the battle that is to come on terms of equality, so far as completeness of preparation goes. If the German plan of campaign had developed as it was expected to develop, the balance when the armies met would have been heavily in favour of the invaders. This has now been redressed.

There is sound sense in the warning of the French *communiqué* that different results may be expected in different parts of a line of battle which stretches across a front of between 300 and 400 miles. In Great Britain as much as in France it should be realized that initial success at one point will almost inevitably be compensated by temporary failure at another, and that the main issue will only be decided by a final readjustment of the position of the contending armies after fighting which will almost certainly extend over many days.

The map which we publish on page 2 shows in perspective the main area in which this gigantic battle array is set.

The French have retaken Blamont and Cirey, on the frontier of Lorraine, after a brilliant action in which a Bavarian Corps was put to flight.

Our Special Correspondent at Namur gives a vivid description of the bomb-throwing upon Namur by a German aviator.

The Russian armies are beginning to make themselves felt upon the frontiers of Austria-Hungary and Germany. The southern army of the Tsar has entered Galicia in three columns, which follow three separate lines of railway converging upon Lemberg.

In skirmishes which took place yesterday in Belgium French and German troops came into touch.

The Grand Duke Nicholas, General-in-Chief of the Russian Army, has issued a proclamation promising that if Russia is victorious the nation of Poland will be reconstituted by the restitution of those portions of its territory which for a century and a half have been in Prussian and Austrian hands. Poland will be granted local autonomy under a Lieutenant-Governor appointed by the Tsar, and she will have freedom for her own language and her own religion.

Austria-Hungary is reported to have asked Italy to allow the passage of Austrian troops through Italian territory in order to facilitate their progress to the French frontier. The Italian Government is said to have refused this request with indignation.

The German Government is credited with the intention of refunding to the late French Ambassador in Berlin £180 which he was compelled to pay for the special train by which he left the country.

Our Paris Correspondent states that the allied Powers have addressed further representations to Turkey insisting on the expulsion of the German crews of the Goeben and the Breslau.

We publish to-day more interesting extracts from the German Press.

The Prince of Wales's Fund had reached £1,100,000 at 2 o'clock yesterday.

BOMBS AT NAMUR.

ATTEMPT TO TERRORIZE THE TOWN.

MISSILES FROM AEROPLANES.

GERMANY WAGING WAR ON CIVILIANS.

(FROM OUR SPECIAL CORRESPONDENT.)

NAMUR, Aug. 15, 9 a.m.

A bomb has just fallen upon the roof of the railway station within a distance of 100 metres from the place where I was standing. Six or seven other bombs have also fallen in other quarters of the town. The platform of the railway station was covered with broken glass and a ticket collector had his hand burned, but no other damage was done. Luckily nobody was on the platform.

August 14.

This evening, at 6.30, a German aeroplane passed over Namur, and dropped three bombs, one after the other, on the town. The first two did no damage. The third fell on the side walk of the bridge d'Omalius and wounded five men, three of them very severely. When the bombs fell I was in the Place de la Gare, about 300 yards distant from the bridge.

The Plac was crowded at the time and every-one was gazing at the German aeroplane, and at a Belgian machine which was at the same moment coming down by a *volplane*. A slight flash was seen as the last missile left the aeroplane, but no one suspected what had happened. In a few minutes, however, an ambulance cart passed carrying one of the victims to the hospital, with the lower part of both legs completely shattered. When I reached the bridge the first thing that I saw was his straw hat torn to pieces lying in the middle of the road; on the pavement there was a big pool of blood, and a few fragments of cloth and flesh were blown in all directions by the force of the explosion.

If the object was to damage the bridge it completely failed. The only effect on the structure was a hole about 2ft. square and 8in. deep. In the cavity we found several bullets about the size of a sparrow's egg.

A DASTARDLY OUTRAGE.

Intense indignation is felt by the people of Namur at this dastardly outrage on a town which is not in state of siege, especially as from the point chosen for dropping the bombs the victims were almost sure to be civilians. But there is not the slightest appearance of panic, and the population are all going about their ordinary occupations.

So if the Germans wished to strike terror by what they have done they have utterly failed. The flash seen at the moment of the discharge seems to show that the bombs were fired from some kind of gun.

GERMANS AGAIN REPULSED.

3,000 REPORTED KILLED AND WOUNDED.

BRUSSELS, Aug. 15, 4.51 P.M.

A dispatch rider who arrived in Brussels from the Belgian outposts this afternoon informs me that the Belgians have gained another victory between Diest and Hasselt, resulting in a German loss of 3,000 men killed and wounded.

The Belgians are stated to have lost under 200 killed and wounded, and the Germans are now reported in retreat.—*Central News.*

FRENCH AND GERMANS IN TOUCH.

BRUSSELS, Aug. 15, 11.55 P.M.

An official *communiqué* issued this evening says that there was fighting to-day between French and German troops, the former having the advantage. Our allies are not far from us.

The forts are still holding out and do the maximum amount of damage to the Germans.

One of the German commanders who has bullet wounds in both legs continues at his post. He directs operations from a self-propelled invalid's chair. Many acts of heroism on the part of the Belgian troops during the fighting have been reported.

Entrenchments are being thrown up on the main roads round Brussels. These are for the reception of any of the enemy's cavalry detachments that may approach the capital. This step has been taken as a police measure, and not as part of the military operations.—*Reuter.*

FIGHTING NEAR TIRLEMONT.

BRUSSELS, Aug. 16, 12.35 A.M.

A dispatch from Tirlemont says that the sound of cannon has been heard from the direction of Bost and Hougaerde since 3 o'clock yesterday afternoon.—*Reuter.*

***Bost and Hougaerde are villages close to Tirlemont.

GENERAL VON EMMICH.

BRUSSELS, Aug. 15.

The death of General von Emmich, commander of the German forces before Liége, is confirmed. He will be succeeded by General Barwiz.—*Exchange Telegraph Company.*

BRUSSELS, Aug. 15.

There is no confirmation of the rumour that General Von Emmich, the German Commander in the attack on Liége, is dead. The rumour has been published in the papers here on the authority of an alleged refugee from Liége. There is no means of verifying it, and the report, which is not taken seriously here, is regarded as highly improbable.—*Reuter.*

THE DEFENCES OF NAMUR.

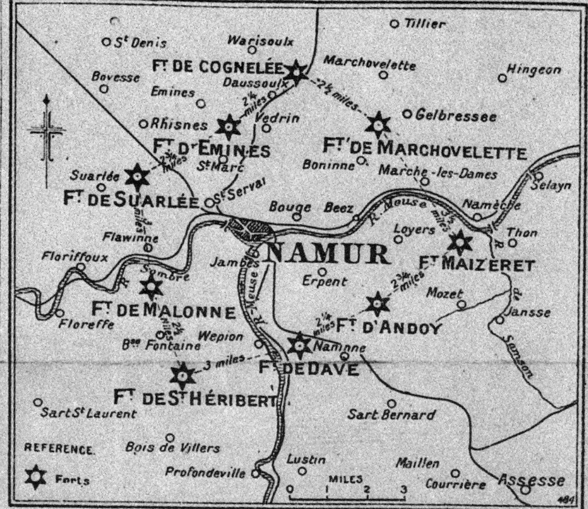

Namur, or *Namen* in Flemish, a town of 32,000 inhabitants, was important in the Middle Ages, but only became a fortress of the first class after 1692, when Louis XIV. caused it to be fortified by Vauban. King William III. took it in 1695, but the French regained it in 1702 for a few years. The citadel was abandoned as a military position in 1888, and the hill on which it stands made into a public park. At the same time the old fortifications were discarded in favour of the existing ring of detached forts, nine in number, which are at some distance from the town. They are all built on elevated positions.

THE EGHEZEE SKIRMISH.

SPIRIT AND DASH OF THE BELGIAN SOLDIERS.

(FROM OUR SPECIAL CORRESPONDENT.)

NAMUR, Aug. 14.

The engagement which took place yesterday morning a few kilometres from Eghezée was by no means such a big affair as the evening papers made out.

I have just visited the scene of the fight, and can give an exact account of what occurred. Soon after I turned off the main road from Brussels to Namur on to the side road leading to Eghezée I met a couple of Gardes Civiques of the Marie Henrietta corps, one mounted on a good-looking little horse captured from the Uhlans, the other on foot. They had left their quarters at Wavre this morning, in a motor-car, and at Eghezée each had picked up a horse left behind by the Uhlans. One of the horses had died on the road (we found him a few miles farther on) and his rider was stranded, but declined to go back with us to get his saddle for fear of drawing on us the fire of the Uhlans who are supposed to be in hiding in the district.

It is obviously part of the German scheme of invasion to terrorize the Belgians by these raids of Uhlans. The Commandant of Gens d'Armes at the village where we met the dismounted Garde Civique (we sent him in the car part of the way to his headquarters) was quite doubtful as to the wisdom of our going on to Eghezée, in case we might meet strolling bands of Uhlans by the way. His fears, however, proved quite groundless, and about half an hour after saying good-bye to him we came to the place where the Belgians had caught the Germans without having seen a trace of them.

The story of the fight was given me by a farmer in whose field it was fought. On Wednesday evening about 350 Uhlans rode up to his house, preceded by 60 cyclists, who had forcibly requisitioned three motor-cars, one of them belonging to a doctor of the Belgian Red Cross service. The German commandant, Colonel Hanstein, billeted himself for the night at the farm.

Early next morning a Belgian airman, flying low over the cornfield in which the Uhlans had parked their horses, drew their fire, and so revealed their whereabouts to some Belgian cyclist scouts of the 13th Regiment, who made off in the direction of the sound of the firing. The Uhlan cyclists, who were out scouting, saw them coming, and rode back as hard as they could to give the alarm. At once there was a general *sauve qui peut*. Most of the Germans were sitting quietly in the cafés of the village of Boneffe at the time, talking to the villagers. They rushed off down the road away from Eghezée leaving everything behind them, horses, rifles, mitrailleuse guns, and the requisitioned motor-cars. The few men who were looking after the horses in the cornfield let them loose, the bugler who was with the fugitives sounded a call to which they rallied, and as the pursuers, only about 30 in number, came round the corner of the road into view, the Uhlans threw themselves on to their horses and galloped off. The Belgians meanwhile dashed into a trench in a field of beetroot, about 500 yards off, which had been thrown up last week to repel the expected German advance, and opened fire on the horses and the retreating Uhlans on the road. They killed four or five men in the field, and about 35 more in the retreat, including an ober-lieutenant, and, it is thought, the colonel, and several of the horses.

When I reached the field the stiff carcasses of 17 of the Uhlan chargers were laying in a bunch where they had fallen. The villagers who had buried the dead Uhlans had tried to burn the bodies of the horses, but had only succeeded in partly charring one or two of them. When I came away they were just going to drag them into a deep trench, which they had hurriedly dug. Otherwise, except for a pile of torn coats and saddles and other equipment there was no sign of the rout.

Obviously it is absurd to describe this trifling engagement, in which one side did practically all the shooting, as a great victory. But it has its importance for this reason, that it showed once again the resolute courage of these daring Belgian soldiers.

CHASED IN THE ATLANTIC.

FRENCH LINER'S EXCITING VOYAGE.

(FROM OUR OWN CORRESPONDENT.)

PARIS, Aug. 15.

The French Transatlantic liner Lorraine has reached Havre after an exciting voyage from New York. She carried on board 450 French reservists. Before their departure they excited general enthusiasm in New York. The band at the restaurant they visited played the "Marseillaise" and "Carmagnolle," while ladies brought them cigars and cakes. Before leaving, Captain Maurras, commanding the ship, asked the officers and crew whether he should start in view of the danger of capture by German cruisers, and their opinion was unanimous in favour of the voyage. "Then I shall show the Prussians that I have good screws," replied the captain. The liner steamed out of harbour at midday on August 5, amidst a salute from the American forts and cheers from English and American crews on ships in the harbour, while tugboats in the bay greeted her departure with sirens. That evening she sighted the German cruiser Dresden, but managed to show her heels. Soon afterwards she intercepted wireless messages exchanged between two other German ships, Strassburg and Carlsruhe, which were waiting for her, but was able to escape them with the help of fog. These two vessels were about 25 miles away from the Lorraine, and as long as they remained within reach the voyage was exceedingly exciting, for it was understood from the intercepted wireless messages that they had received orders to sink her.

PURCHASE OF THE GOEBEN.

TURKISH EXPLANATIONS.

(FROM OUR OWN CORRESPONDENT.)

PARIS, Aug. 14.

Rifaat Pasha, the Turkish Ambassador in Paris, explains the purchase of the German cruisers Goeben and Breslau by Turkey by saying that his country was anxious to seize an opportunity of acquiring two units to assure the equilibrium of its naval forces with those of Greece.

You know [he said] that England at the beginning of hostilities requisitioned the two battleships which she found in her naval yards which were intended for us. This was a cruel disappointment, for the ships had been bought partially by public subscription. Our officers were particularly vexed. Greece has just added to her naval forces two battleships which were ceded to her by the United States. The Balkan equilibrium was upset. We should have been taken unawares, and we know by the experience of the last Balkan was how fatal is naval inferiority and that the war might have taken another turn if we had been stronger on the sea.

The Ambassador said that the German cruisers would remain in Turkey's hands, for she was resolved to keep them after having bought them with the sums due from England for the requisitioned battleships.

The Allied Powers cannot doubt our good faith in the circumstances, and ought to see in our action a measure of defence of a nature to prevent a European war from being complicated by a new conflict in the Balkans.

The Press Bureau states:—There is no reason to doubt that the Turkish Government is about to replace the German officers and crews of the Goeben and Breslau by Turkish officers and crews.

FIGHTING ON RUSSO-GERMAN FRONTIER.

ST. PETERSBURG, Aug. 15.

The following communication is published from the headquarters of the Russian Staff:—

On Wednesday last the Russians destroyed at 11 points the railway and telegraph lines between Tilsit and Schmalleningken. Towards the west of Vischyil, the Tilsit-Schmalleningken road has been damaged by German troops. Detachments of two German regiments, the 12th Lancers and the 9th Chasseurs, with guns, were discovered at Armouchinen, between Schirvinty and Kuzmen. The German troops avoided battle and retreated to the north-west.

Detachments of German infantry, with artillery and cavalry, were discovered at Markgraboff (Marggrabowa).—*Reuter.*

LIÉGE UNDER FIRE.

THE SUFFERINGS OF THE TOWNSPEOPLE.

SCENES IN THE STREETS.

(FROM OUR SPECIAL CORRESPONDENT.)

BRUSSELS, Aug. 14.

The story of Liége has been written so far as the purely military aspect of the case is concerned. But that is only half of the story. To the ordinary man it is not the military description of a siege that makes most direct appeal, but the more intimate story of the disruption of the lives of the townspeople, the civilians, the women and the children.

Such stories are now coming to hand, and they make terrible reading. They reveal war in all its naked horror, in all its unthinkable brutality. They show to what depths of despair innocent people may be plunged by this great plague, when it is carried to their doors and allowed to defile their hearths.

During the early days of the siege—that is to say, Tuesday, Wednesday, and Thursday of last week—it is clear that the people of Liége suffered very greatly. The noise alone was terrific; it never ceased. Right and left, north and south, the thunder of the cannon rolled with fearful menace, the rifles cracked fiercely, overhead the shells screeched and the bullets sang. An eye-witness has told me that it was like living in an inferno. Women and children, especially the latter, were terrified beyond expression; they hid themselves in their houses; many of them went down into the cellars and remained there without food, expecting every moment that their dwellings would be brought in ruins upon the top of them, entombing them.

EFFECT OF SHELL FIRE.

Nor was this apprehension foolish. Every now and then a shell would come screaming over the town and fall upon the roofs of the houses. It would explode with terrific force, shattering walls and floors and leaving a heap of ruins. From these houses one heard the screams of the injured and dying, the shrill alarm of little children; distraught women rushed out into the street. Several houses, moreover, took fire and were burned to the ground. Here, again, cruel scenes were witnessed, scenes which it is scarcely possible to think about. Some of the shells descended in the streets and were buried in the asphalt paving; when they exploded huge holes were blown out, rendering passage impossible and smashing the house fronts and balconies. Indeed, it is said that there was scarcely a single road in the town which escaped this terrible visitation.

When the bombardment began to grow less fierce the bolder citizens came out again into the streets. "The town," according to a refugee, "looked like a cemetery in which there had been an earthquake. The streets were torn up and full of wreckage. Thick columns of smoke rose from the smouldering houses; one saw other houses smitten to ruins scarcely a window remained unbroken. It was appalling."

BEHAVIOUR OF THE GERMANS.

And then, in small companies, the Germans who had succeeded in penetrating between the forts began to arrive in the town. The inhabitants, terrified anew, hid themselves once more. The German officers passed to one of the big hotels, "L'Hôtel du Phare," and took up their residence there. But so suspicious were they of the inhabitants that barricades were erected at all the principal entrances to the town and guards posted. The German soldiers forced an entry into many of the closed houses, in which they installed themselves, treating everything as their own property, and inflicting one knows not what shame upon their unwilling hosts. The house of one of the well-known doctors in Liége—Dr. Lenoir—was forced in this way, and his consulting-rooms occupied. The soldiers sat playing cards and smoking and drinking. They forced the townspeople to minister to their needs. An order, too, was issued that every Belgian should keep his door open day and night so that the conquerors should not be stayed if they desired to enter anywhere. Remember that the people of Liége had, most of them, their wives and families in the town, and consider what such an order means!

The ignorance of the German soldiery, too, was everywhere apparent. An officer who interrogated one of the Belgian refugees told him that he expected to leave next day for Paris, and this in spite of the fact that the forts were even then firing on his compatriots.

ATTACK ON SERVIAN FRONTIER.

TWO TOWNS OCCUPIED.

(FROM OUR CORRESPONDENT.)

SALONIKA, Aug. 14.

At 11 o'clock on Wednesday night an Austro-Hungarian force attempted to cross the river Save under cover of artillery fire. The Servians opened fire with their artillery and kept it up with excellent effect, the enemy being eventually compelled to retire in disorder. Twenty-five of the enemy, having failed to make good their escape, were left on the island of Tziganlia, and were taken prisoners and sent to Belgrade.

A large Austro-Hungarian force succeeded in crossing the Drina at Leshnitza and the Save at Shabatz.

The Servian artillery sunk a tug and a barge filled with soldiers between Belgrade and Semendria. At the same time an Austro-Hungarian force with a cavalry division was observed across the river and was dispersed with artillery fire. An attempt by the enemy to land a force across the Danube near Tekia failed completely.

The enemy continue to bombard Belgrade every night.

LORRAINE INVADED.

BRILLIANT FRENCH SUCCESS.

BOMBS ON METZ.

AN AIRMAN'S EXPLOIT.

(FROM OUR OWN CORRESPONDENT.)

PARIS, Aug. 15.

An important engagement has taken place in the district of Blamont, Cirey, and Avricourt, where the French troops encountered a Bavarian army corps. The villages of Blamont and Cirey and the heights beyond were carried brilliantly and whole columns of the Germans were driven back, leaving behind dead, wounded, and prisoners.

The French troops are continuing their advance into the Hautes-Vosges. The Germans are retiring into Upper Alsace. Thann has been recaptured by the French.

Prisoners declare that General Deimling, commanding the 15th Army Corps, has been wounded at St. Blaise, Vallé de Bruche.

To mark this exploit of the troops two French airmen left Verdun and, flying over Metz, dropped two bombs upon the Frascati hangars, where the Zeppelin airships are lodged. After being exposed to more than 200 shots fired by artillery the airmen regained Verdun in safety, having accomplished their mission.

A new German aeroplane, containing two officers, has been captured near Bouillon. The pilot was wounded.

Avricourt, in Lorraine, is shown on the map of the French eastern frontier. Blamont and Cirey are on the French side about six and 12 miles respectively S.E. of Avricourt.

A HISTORY OF THE WAR.

PUBLICATION NEXT WEEK.

The Times has in preparation a history of the present European conflict which will be published in weekly parts at a price of sevenpence.

The Times, on account of its great number of correspondents in the various European capitals, supplemented by an extra staff of experienced war correspondents now in the field, is in a position to obtain much special information of an exclusive character. For these reasons "*The Times* History of the War" will form the most complete record available of the present struggle. It will contain many important documents, maps, original photographs, and narratives of eye-witnesses. The first part, containing a summary of the critical events leading up to the crisis, will be published on *Tuesday, August 25.*

In order to ensure obtaining a copy of this important work an immediate order should be given to a bookseller or newsagent.

POLAND A NATION.

DECLARATION BY RUSSIAN GENERALISSIMO.

(FROM OUR OWN CORRESPONDENT.)

ST PETERSBURG, Aug. 14.

It is understood that an important document will be published shortly by the Generalissimo of the Russian Army, whereby Poland will be assured virtual autonomy. The Government printing offices are even now busy preparing copies of this document.

The Polish deputies have been consulted. Their great joy and satisfaction are difficult to describe.

ST. PETERSBURG, Aug. 15.

The following appeal has been addressed to the Poles by the Grand Duke Nicholas, Commander-in-Chief of the Russian forces:—

Poles.—The hour has sounded when the sacred dream of your fathers and your grandfathers may be realized. A century and a half has passed since the living body of Poland was torn in pieces, but the soul of the country is not dead. It continues to live, inspired by the hope that there will come for the Polish people an hour of resurrection, and of fraternal reconciliation with Great Russia. The Russian Army brings you the solemn news of this reconciliation which obliterates the frontiers dividing the Polish peoples, which it unites conjointly under the sceptre of the Russian Tsar. Under this sceptre Poland will be born again, free in her religion and her language. Russian autonomy only expects from you the same respect for the rights of those nationalities to which history has bound you. With open heart and brotherly hand Great Russia advances to meet you. She believes that the sword, with which she struck down her enemies at Grünwald, is not yet rusted. From the shores of the Pacific to the North Sea the Russian armies are marching. The dawn of a new life is beginning for you, and in this glorious dawn is seen the sign of the Cross, the symbol of suffering and of the resurrection of peoples.—*Reuter.*

THE SITUATION IN DALMATIA.

A REIGN OF TERROR.

Information from a trustworthy Dalmatian source describes, under date of August 3, the situation throughout the province as one of "misery and terror." Every male up to the age of 50 has been mobilized without regard to his fitness for military service. The object of this measure is to place the population under direct military control. Trade has ceased; communication between the islands and the mainland, and between the chief points of the mainland itself, is suspended; and food is becoming scarce.

At Ragusa the military authorities have arrested eight of the leading Slav notables, chiefly retired men of business unconnected with politics, and are holding them as hostages for the good behaviour of the population. An official warning has been issued that, if any damage is done to any Government property, the hostages will be hanged in the public square. Three of the hostages, MM. Banaz, Michitch, and Papi, are men of considerable wealth.

A Prime Minister unmade

Top Mr Asquith, the Prime M'nister, January 1913.
Above David Lloyd-George, Asquith's successor, who formed the new government when Asquith resigned in December 1916.

The Times has made and unmade many ministries. But only once has a Prime Minister resigned because of a leader in *The Times* – Dawson's leader of Monday 4 December 1916. The circumstances in which it came to be written are still hidden in mystery and conspiracy.

1916 was a bad year for Britain. The war was dragging on, with the appalling killing-morass of the Somme. Disappointment at Jutland; defeat in Mesopotamia; disaster at Gallipoli. Lord Kitchener had died at sea. People started to think, and say, that the Government might not be running the war very well. Because it was a Coalition Government, the main vehicle for such opposition was in the press rather than in Parliament. And the most powerful arm of the press was the Northcliffe newspapers. The grumbling and conspiring politicians knew that the support of the Northcliffe press was essential for the reconstruction of the Government that they all felt was needed.

The Prime Minister was Herbert Asquith, the great reforming Liberal statesman. But his powers were failing, and he was not temperamentally suited for the change of direction that was needed to get a grip on winning the war. Everybody concerned agreed that what was needed was a small inner war council or committee to coordinate and prosecute the daily fighting of the war. Not everybody agreed that Asquith should be a member of this war council, or whether he should resign.

An obvious successor to Asquith was Bonar Law, the leader of the Conservative ministers in the Coalition, a bitter and extreme opponent of Asquith's prewar Government; his support of the Ulster Unionists had aggravated the Irish constitutional crisis to near civil war in 1914. His backer and familiar was his fellow Canadian Max Aitken (later Lord Beaverbrook), at that time a backbench Tory MP, but busy secretly acquiring the controlling shares of the *Daily Express*, and becoming a press baron and mischief-maker. But Bonar Law shrank from the bitterness of another confrontation with Asquith in the middle of a mortal war. The other potential successor was Lloyd George, who had proved an energetic, imaginative and capable Minister of War, and who thought that there must be a quicker end to the war than the interminable blood-bath on the Western Front. These and other lesser conspirators gossiped and caballed.

Early in December the plot came to a head. Lloyd George submitted a proposal for a War Committee to the Prime Minister. There were to be only three members; Asquith himself was to be excluded. The Committee 'was to have full powers, subject to the supreme control of the Prime Minister, to direct all questions connected with the war'. Asquith accepted most of the proposals, but insisted on being chairman. Deadlock.

On Sunday 3 December Asquith and Lloyd George reached a compromise. It was that the Prime Minister would have supreme control of war policy, with the right to veto and the right to attend meetings of the War Committee (chaired by Lloyd George). But he would not be a member of it.

The top leading article in *The Times* of 4 December put a cat among these well-laid plans of mice and men. Dawson wrote that at last the country was within sight of a small War Council, the necessity for which had been 'steadily pressed in these columns for the last year and a half'.

> Of this Council Mr. Asquith himself is not to be a member – the assumption being that the Prime Minister has sufficient cares of a more general character without devoting himself wholly, as the new Council must be devoted if it is to be effective, to the daily task of organizing victory.

The Times continued that Mr Asquith's closest supporters, and others who had no politics beyond the war, must have convinced him that 'his own qualities are fitted better, as they are fond of saying, to preserve the unity of the nation (though we have never doubted its unity) than to force the pace of a War Council'.

It was savage, contemptuous and insulting. When Asquith read it, he jumped to the conclusion that he had been double-crossed by Lloyd George, who, he suspected, had spilled the beans about Sunday's agreement to Northcliffe or Dawson. Accordingly he revoked the agreement, and on Tuesday resigned, hoping to form a new Government without Lloyd George, and with himself as Prime Minister. In this hope he was disappointed. Asquith's credibility and credit were too far gone. It was Lloyd George who formed the new Government to win the war.

The question is which of the intriguers leaked or encouraged the leader that put the boot in. Historians have done minute textual research into the diaries to establish who saw whom at what moment of the fatal day. For example, Lloyd George met Asquith between 4 pm and 6.30 pm, and then returned to the War Office, where he saw Northcliffe. That night Northcliffe dined with Dawson before he wrote the leader.

Most of the participants left their glosses on the leader. On the day it appeared, Asquith wrote at once to Lloyd George:

> Such productions as the first leading article in today's *Times* showing the infinite possibilities for misunderstanding and misrepresentation of such an arrangement as we considered yesterday, make me at once doubtful as to its feasibility. Unless the impression is at once corrected that I am being relegated to the position of an irresponsible spectator of the War, I cannot possibly go on.

Lloyd George replied by return of messenger:

> I have not seen *The Times* article. But I hope you will not attach undue importance to these effusions. I have had these misrepresentations to put up with for months. Northcliffe frankly wants a smash. Derby and I do not. Northcliffe would like to make this and any other arrangement under your Premiership impossible. Derby and I attach great importance to your retaining your present position – effectively. I cannot restrain or, I fear, influence Northcliffe.

Dawson himself, in a memorandum, stated categorically: 'The leader was absolutely "uninspired". I had not seen, or held any communication with, Lloyd George himself for several weeks.'

An article of 12 December in the *Globe*, another of Northcliffe's armada of newspapers, ran:

> THE GREATEST DICTATOR – LORD NORTHCLIFFE'S SUPREME JOURNALISTIC FEAT
>
> Lord Northcliffe has just brought down the Asquith Cabinet. The fact remains that it was after reading the now famous leader in Monday's *Times* that Mr Asquith sent in his resignation. By that alone Lord Northcliffe has achieved probably the greatest feat in history. He has out-lioned all the famous lions of *The Times* itself.

According to A. J. P. Taylor in his biography of Beaverbrook, Wickham Steed (foreign editor of *The Times*) wrote to Lady Asquith in 1931 assuring her that Lloyd George was not guilty of inspiring the leader that caused Asquith to make a run for it.

Dawson may have written the famous leader off his own bat, having had no discussions with anybody. He was a secretive man. However, it would be interesting to have been a fly on the wall on the fatal Sunday when Lloyd George talked to Northcliffe, and later when Northcliffe dined with Dawson before he wrote the leader. Maybe they talked about the weather. I think that it is more likely, since they belonged to the chattering and opinion-forming classes, that they talked about the burning issue of the day. We shall probably never know. But we can confidently say that the leader of 4 December 1916 was the only *Times* leader so far that has led directly to the resignation of a Prime Minister.

The announcement of the formation of a small War Council, (column 4), along with the fateful and much debated leader (columns 1 and 2), one of the most famous and influential ever published.
4 DECEMBER 1916

MONDAY, DECEMBER 4, 1916.

"THE TIMES" FUND.

Acknowledged to-day.. £7,094 10 7
Total to date £5,366,677 11 6

Lists on page 4.

Towards Reconstruction.

Out of a welter of political speculation—some of it calculated, some of it merely misinformed—certain definite facts are beginning to emerge. The first is that MR. LLOYD GEORGE has finally taken his stand against the present cumbrous methods of directing the war. The second is that he has an alternative scheme of his own, which is not without support among his colleagues. The third is that we seem at last to be within measurable distance of the small War Council, or super-Cabinet for war purposes, which has been pressed in these columns for the last year and a half. On Friday, according to our Parliamentary Correspondent, MR. LLOYD GEORGE's decision took shape in the form of written representations to the PRIME MINISTER, and these have since been followed by personal discussion between them. The gist of his proposal is understood to be the establishment forthwith of a small War Council, fully charged with the supreme direction of the war. Of this Council MR. ASQUITH himself is not to be a member—the assumption being that the PRIME MINISTER has sufficient cares of a more general character without devoting himself wholly, as the new Council must be devoted if it is to be effective, to the daily task of organizing victory. Certain of MR. ASQUITH's colleagues are also excluded on the ground of temperament from a body which can only succeed if it is harmonious and decisive. On the other hand, the inclusion of SIR EDWARD CARSON is believed to form an essential part of MR. LLOYD GEORGE's scheme, and it is one which will be thoroughly understood. Since Friday, then, there has been in existence a political "crisis" of the first magnitude, if the word is applicable in these days to any domestic reconstruction. On Saturday MR. ASQUITH had a prolonged audience of the KING. There have been hurried journeys from distant parts of England and a protracted Sunday meeting of the Unionist members of the Cabinet. Not since the days when the Coalition was forming has any political situation produced such excitement or, we may add, such a general feeling of optimism. As we write on Sunday night the result of all these deliberations is still incomplete. But the essential facts remain as we have stated them, and there are good reasons for hoping that there are forces at work which will carry the necessary reform without interregnum or delay.

Obviously the first of these reasons is the character of the PRIME MINISTER, who has never been slow to note political tendencies when they become inevitable. The testimony of MR. ASQUITH's closest supporters—even more, perhaps, than the pressure of those who have no politics beyond the war—must have convinced him by this time that matters cannot possibly go on as at present. They must have convinced him, too, that his own qualities are fitted better, as they are fond of saying, to "preserve the "unity of the nation" (though we have never doubted its unity) than to force the pace of a War Council. Moreover, he can hardly fail to be profoundly influenced by the attitude of MR. BONAR LAW, who is believed to support MR. LLOYD GEORGE's proposals. We ourselves regard MR. BONAR LAW's attitude in this matter as the real point of decision between a friendly reconstruction and a further struggle with can only end in one way. If he holds, as the bulk of his former followers unquestionably hold, that the situation requires the sort of handling which is proposed; if he further holds that MR. LLOYD GEORGE is the man best fitted to preside over a real War Council; then he has a clear course before him. We may be allowed to add that he has also a great opportunity of re-establishing a personal position which has, perhaps necessarily, been obliterated by recent political events. It must be counted as fortunate that a period of quasi-opposition has never broken MR. BONAR LAW's old relations with SIR EDWARD CARSON. The latter—most unwillingly, we are sure, so far as his personal inclinations go—forms an essential part of MR. LLOYD GEORGE's scheme of reform. The two have always been congenial associates. They have something of the same resolution and fighting instinct. It is not unnatural that the one should turn to the other at a moment when he is staking everything upon an offer to reorganize the direction of the war. To such a combination MR. BONAR LAW can supply a real element of strength hereafter. What is perhaps more important, he can do everything at this particular moment to make it acceptable to the present Government and to the House of Commons.

It remains to say a general word about the action which MR. LLOYD GEORGE has taken. There are signs already of the inevitable suggestions that it is the outcome of an "intrigue," that it is inspired by personal ambition, that it is due to disagreement with the soldiers, or (by a curious contradiction) that it represents a "military revolution" against the civil power. We believe that every one of these suspicions is as utterly without foundation as the rest. If personal ambition counted for anything, no man in his senses would seek to gratify it at such a time by risking a great position, which is almost untouched by the general unpopularity of the Government. MR. LLOYD GEORGE, to the best of our knowledge, took his stand entirely alone so far as his colleagues in the Cabinet are concerned—a fact which itself refutes the tales of intrigue. Whether the War Office endorses his action we neither know nor care. It is clear at least that his Under-Secretary, LORD DERBY, is in full sympathy with him, and we infer from that important alliance that the bond of union between them is just a simple, patriotic anxiety to set things straight. But as for the soldiers, they are never greatly interested in Ministerial changes, and the present regime of the General Staff, under SIR WILLIAM ROBERTSON, has been almost quixotically correct in its complete divorce from politics. We imagine that all of them would privately take the view that great chances have been missed through weakness and vacillation in the supreme direction of the war. That is a view which is shared by many thousands of civilians. If the soldiers agree with them, it is they, after all, who have the best reason for grasping the disastrous effects upon next year's campaign of any further delay in solving the supreme, the critical, the still unsettled question of man-power. But the conception of MR. LLOYD GEORGE as a Military Dictator is a little too grotesque even for the most imaginative mischief-maker. His whole past belies it. His real defect in our opinion, even in the last few months at the War Office, has been too little, not too great, a power of sympathy with the military mind. In matters of the kind the simplest explanation is usually the best. This is by no means the first time in the last two years that MR. LLOYD GEORGE has been on the verge of a rupture with his colleagues. Once it was averted by the enforced surrender of the Government over the Military Service Bill. Once the Ministry of Munitions, and more lately the War Office, seemed to provide fresh opportunities, even under unsatisfactory conditions of useful individual service. But from the very beginning he has stood apart from the rest in his unmistakable enthusiasm for vigorous war. The Celtic temperament is apt to concentrate on a single passion, and MR. LLOYD GEORGE has somehow succeeded in impressing even the bitterest of his old opponents with his complete abandonment of every other thought beside the passion for victory. It was only a question of time before he found it impossible to work with the old digressive colleagues under the old unwieldy system. No elaborate theory is needed to account for his revolt. Nor, for the matter of that, is the country at large under any illusions about it.

A Humiliating Rebuff.

The news from Athens which we publish this morning will be received by the country with astonishment and indignation. Though full details are lacking, enough is known to make it clear that the Allies have again been betrayed and defied by KING CONSTANTINE and his Government. We are, indeed, assured that the Allied Governments are taking "concerted measures with a view to obtaining the necessary reparation for the attack "on the Allied troops," and that the Allied Ministers at Athens have been instructed to inform the Greek Government that "the matter is "now far more serious than a mere "question of handing over war material." It is added that the Greek Government will be required "to make amends corresponding to the gravity of the outrage "committed on the Allies." So far as is known, the position appears, briefly, to be that upon the expiration, on Friday last, of the ultimatum delivered by the French Admiral in the name of the Allies, three contingents of Allied troops were landed at the Piraeus and sent to Athens. Their strength appears to have been wholly inadequate to the task likely to await them. Their weakness is alleged to have been due to the childlike faith placed by the Allied representatives or commanders in KING CONSTANTINE's assurances that no disturbances were to be apprehended. On reaching their allotted positions, the British contingent found them held in strength by Greek forces. As instructions to avoid armed conflict appear to have been given to the Allied troops, the British contingent withdrew, but in the act of withdrawal was treacherously fired upon by the Greeks and suffered many casualties. It is not known whether the British contingent returned the fire. Simultaneously the French contingent, on reaching its positions, was received by KING CONSTANTINE's troops with machine-gun fire, to which a vigorous reply was made. Here also casualties were numerous. The Italian contingent was also fired upon, and had a sharp brush with the Greeks. Presently the guns of the Allied warships came into action, with the result that proposals for an armistice were made. It is not certain whether they proceeded in the first instance from the Allied Ministers or from KING CONSTANTINE. What is certain is that an armistice was concluded, on the basis of the withdrawal of the Allied contingents with the exception of a small force left to guard the Zappeion Camp, where French bluejackets have for some time been quartered. The most remarkable feature of these amazing events is that the Allied Ministers are said to have recommended their Governments to accept KING CONSTANTINE's offer of six batteries of mountain guns instead of the ten required, and to abandon the other Allied demands.

In the House of Commons on November 27 LORD ROBERT CECIL declared, on behalf of the Government:—"We shall never abandon "M. Venizelos. . . . I have assured the House "that we think it proper to protect the friends "of M. Venizelos from unjust and improper "attacks. When I say 'we' of course I mean "the Allies, not the British Government alone. "We are all agreed." Telegraphing on the same day, our Athens Correspondent said that "if the "threats of assault, pillage, and massacre against "the Venizelists are carried out, even in part, and "no counter-measures are taken in time, the effect "of this would be to weaken, if not altogether to "crush, the Venizelist Party, the members of "which would have to fear for their lives." Any measures of compulsion, he added, that may be contemplated to enforce the Allied demands, "ought to be preceded by measures for the protection of the Venizelists." These measures were not taken. If our information—which is borne out by that which DR. BURROWS furnishes in the powerful letter we print this morning—is accurate, the followers of M. VENIZELOS at Athens have suffered grievously at the hands of KING CONSTANTINE's troops. Whatever measures may be taken, it is clear that they must be prompt, drastic, and of such a nature as at once to restore the seriously-impaired prestige of the Allies, and to protect the Allied forces at Salonika from any further menace. It is also clear that it is for England, France, and Russia, as the protecting Powers of Greece, to deal with this grave matter, as they alone possess the requisite juridical standing. The whole story of our dealings with KING CONSTANTINE has been one long succession of incomprehensible blunders. This blundering must now cease, if the Allies are to retain any semblance of authority or influence in the Near East.

MAYFAIR FLOWER MAKERS.

HER MAJESTY'S GRACIOUS INTENTION.

An exhibition and sale of the Mayfair Flower Makers, which takes place at Messrs. Marshall and Snelgrove's next Wednesday and Thursday, is expected to attract large numbers to see the wonderful flowers made by British workgirls.

Her Majesty the Queen has graciously intimated her intention of paying an informal visit to the exhibition on Wednesday morning.

NEW MASTER-GENERAL OF THE ORDNANCE.

GEN. VON DONOP'S RETIREMENT.

The Secretary of the War Office announces that Major-General Sir S. B. von Donop, K.C.B., will to-day vacate the post of Master-General of the Ordnance and will be succeeded by Major-General W. T. Furse, C.B., D.S.O.

Our Parliamentary Correspondent says it is understood that Major-General von Donop is to be appointed Lieutenant-Governor of Jersey.

Sir Stanley von Donop, who was born in 1860, has been Master-General of the Ordnance since early in 1913. It will be remembered that in July, 1915, Sir H. Dalziel criticized the Ordnance Department in the House of Commons as having "let down" Lord Kitchener in respect of guns and high explosives, and he named Sir Stanley von Donop as being chiefly responsible. A few days later Lord Haldane, in a speech at the National Liberal Club, deprecating any search for scapegoats, defended Sir Stanley and attributed the deficiency in munitions to industrial troubles.

Major-General Furse is a brother of the Bishop of Pretoria and of the late Charles Furse, the painter. He was born in 1865, entered the Royal Artillery in 1884, and was A.D.C. to Lord Roberts when Commander-in-Chief in India. In the South African War he won the D.S.O. and five clasps, and in the present war he won the C.B., and was mentioned in dispatches. Major-General Furse has had long experience in various Staff appointments.

BEER AND ITS MATERIALS.

TO THE EDITOR OF THE TIMES.

Sir,—Your correspondent "Agricola" in a letter to *The Times* of to-day urges that materials used in the manufacture of beer could be economically diverted to the rearing of pigs, but he does not seem to have realized how much human food would be lost by the transfer. The food value of beer (*plus* milk and meat per cattle food) is more than half that of the brewing materials used, whereas the food-value of the pig-meat is less than one-fifth of that of the same materials. The total energy value as direct human food of the quantities quoted by "Agricola" is a little over four billion calories (4.15×10^{12}). In the form of beer (*plus* milk, &c., per cattle food) we receive upwards of two billion calories, whereas in the form of pig-meat we should receive at most 0.8 billion calories; *i.e.*, we should, by following "Agricola's" advice, experience a total loss of 1.2 billion calories—60 per cent. of the original beer value by the utilization of beer materials for pig-keeping.

I am not a pro-brewer, nor the reverse, but simply a student of physiology. The value of abstinence from beer (and spirits and champagne) under present conditions depends upon considerations other than those to which "Agricola" appeals.

Yours obediently,
A. D. WALLER.

University of London, Dec. 2.

PRODUCTION FROM THE LAND.

COMMITTEE TO HELP FARMERS.

An organizing committee has been formed of leading men interested in agriculture, with the object of bringing about at an early date a conference between the representatives of various interests in the land and to decide on a policy in the interest of the nation for increase of the food production. The committee consider that many questions upon which differences of opinion exist should be laid aside, and the movement should be concentrated upon the main question of how to increase the nation's food supply. The points under consideration are:—

(1) The immediate supply of the necessary machinery required for Spring work.

(2) The ample supply at a reasonable price of basic slag and other fertilizers.

(3) The transport and machinery, manure, &c., to be dealt with as urgent, as in the case of war material.

(4) The return to the land of necessary labour and better organization of labour conditions.

(5) A guaranteed minimum price where farmers undertake to increase the production of foodstuffs.

(6) Financial assistance to farmers, where needed, as in the case of munition manufacturers.

Among those who have joined the organizing committee or are otherwise interesting themselves in the movement are:—The Duke of Argyll, Lord Kenmare, Lord Dunraven, Colonel Marling, V.C., and Mr. Robert Sanders, M.P. Anyone interested in the movement is requested to communicate with the Secretary of the Organizing Committee, at 11, Waterloo-place, Pall-mall.

The King will hold a Council to-morrow.

RECONSTRUCTION.

PRIME MINISTER'S DECISION.

MR. LLOYD GEORGE'S STAND.

A SMALL WAR COUNCIL.

The following official statement was issued at 11.45 last night:—

The Prime Minister, with a view to the most active prosecution of the war, has decided to advise his Majesty the King to consent to a reconstruction of the Government.

From Our Parliamentary Correspondent.

The political storm, which had been gathering for some days, broke during the week-end. It took the form of a Cabinet crisis of unusual severity, and no final solution had been reached last night.

The facts are simple. For a long time Mr. Lloyd George is known to have been gravely dissatisfied with the dilatory and irresolute manner in which the Cabinet and the War Committee have directed the war. On Friday he informed the Prime Minister that he could not continue to remain a member of the Government unless the machinery for directing the war was drastically overhauled. Mr. Lloyd George, who made his representations in writing, proposed to Mr. Asquith that the War Committee should in future consist of only four members, and that it should have absolute control of the direction of the war. He suggested that the constitution of the War Committee should be as follows:—

Mr. Lloyd George	**A Labour Member**
Sir Edward Carson	**(possibly Mr. Arthur**
Mr. Bonar Law	**Henderson)**

These four men would, of course, have the active cooperation of Sir John Jellicoe and Sir William Robertson.

THE PRESENT WAR COMMITTEE.

The War Committee at present consists of seven members:—Mr. Asquith, Mr. Lloyd George, Mr. Bonar Law, Mr. Balfour, Mr. McKenna, Lord Curzon, and Mr. Montagu. It is a Committee of the Cabinet, and its decisions are subject to confirmation by the full Ministerial body of 23. While it is true that it controls the day-by-day conduct of the war without reference to the Cabinet, which almost automatically ratifies its acts, it has expanded, with its official advisers and regular Ministerial visitors, into almost as cumbrous a body as the Cabinet itself. We have, in fact, almost reached the position of seeing two Cabinets sitting side by side and taking a hand in the war.

The Prime Minister obviously needed a little time to consider this proposal, which involves at least three important departures from the existing policy.

(1) The withdrawal of certain prominent Ministers from the War Committee.

(2) The infusion of new blood, by the introduction of Sir Edward Carson and a Labour member.

(3) The transference from the Cabinet to the War Committee of independent control of the war in all its aspects, from the conduct of operations to such semi-domestic questions as supplies, blockade, food control, and man-power.

The Prime Minister did not reply until Saturday morning. Meanwhile, there had been some "kite-flying" in some of the London newspapers. It was said that the Prime Minister was considering a reduction of the size of the War Committee from seven to five members, namely, Mr. Asquith, Mr. Lloyd George, Mr. Bonar Law, Mr. Balfour, and Sir Edward Carson. The best commentary on this story is the fact that Sir Edward Carson has not been invited to join the War Committee, and had never heard of the project until he saw it in print on Saturday. Still the "kite" served a purpose. It distracted attention for a few hours from the real seat of the crisis.

The Prime Minister informed Mr. Lloyd George on Saturday that he could not accept his proposal as it stood. There the issue remained for a few hours, and the various parties went out of town, after the Prime Minister had had a long audience of the King at Buckingham Palace.

CONFERENCES YESTERDAY.

Yesterday found Ministers hurrying back to town for a series of important conferences. The Prime Minister returned from Walmer by motor-car. Mr. Lloyd George came up from Walton Heath. Lord Derby, who had intended to spend the week-end in Lancashire, had arrived from Knowsley on Saturday evening. Sir Edward Carson also returned from Birchington on Saturday.

In the morning the Unionist members of the Cabinet had a conference. Mr. Bonar Law presided, and all the Unionist Cabinet Ministers were present except Mr. Balfour, who was ill, and Lord Lansdowne, who was at Bowood.

In the afternoon the Prime Minister had interviews at 10, Downing-street with several of his colleagues, including Mr. Lloyd George, and Mr. Bonar Law.

At night matters stood thus. The Prime Minister had not accepted Mr. Lloyd George's proposal. He was prepared to accept a reduction in the number of the War Committee. The obstacles to a settlement were two:—

(1) The proposal that the War Committee should have unlimited power in the conduct of the war.

(2) Certain personal questions connected with the proposed additions to and exclusions from the War Committee.

It was made clear, however, to Mr. Asquith that Mr. Lloyd George did not stand alone. Mr. Bonar Law is believed to have given general support to his proposal. Both Mr. Lloyd George and Mr. Bonar Law particularly insisted on the need for associating Sir Edward Carson with the work of the War Committee. Sir Edward Carson's inclusion, in fact, may be taken as a proposal on which Mr. Lloyd George and those who are acting with him intend to insist.

LORD DERBY'S POSITION.

Lord Derby, too, has definitely associated himself with Mr. Lloyd George. He is prepared to support him even to the extent of resignation of his office, if a satisfactory settlement is not found. Lord Derby is indeed ready for any contingency. He has provisionally called a meeting of his Lancashire council for next Saturday, in order to explain in public any action which he may think it necessary to take.

The Cabinet as a whole have not so far been consulted. That may follow later, when the Prime Minister has taken a final decision. Meanwhile the crisis is acute, and the chiefs of the Ministry have reached, at all events, a temporary deadlock. The conversations between Mr. Asquith and his colleagues will be resumed to-day, and Mr. Lloyd George's scheme will be further discussed in the light of the events of yesterday and of a night's reflection. Proposals for an accommodation will doubtless be made, but this is an issue of principle on which there can be no real compromise. Either the old order will survive or a new one must take its place. Mr. Lloyd George is determined to fight the matter out.

Talk of resignations is premature. There have been no resignations so far, and there was some hope last night that there would be no need for them. But resignations there must be if the long-deferred issue is not settled with that wisdom and resolution which spring from the will to win.

In the circumstances of the time special importance attaches to the debate on man-power, which is fixed for Thursday in the House of Commons. The Unionist War Committee have sent an urgent "whip" to members on active service asking them to obtain leave, if possible, so that they may be present in the House during the debate.

To-morrow the House will discuss the Air Board crisis, which has not yet been solved.

NAMES OF ZEPPELIN DESTROYERS.

NAVAL AIRMEN REWARDED.

It was officially announced yesterday that the King has been pleased to approve the award of the Distinguished Service Order to Flight Sub-Lieutenant EDWARD L. PULLING, R.N.A.S., and of the Distinguished Service Cross to Flight Lieutenant EGBERT CADBURY and Flight Sub-Lieutenant GERRARD W. R. FANE, of the R.N.A.S., in recognition of their distinguished services on the occasion of the destruction of a Zeppelin airship off the Norfolk Coast in the early morning of Tuesday, November 28.

Flight Lieutenant Pulling was educated at St. Anne's, Redhill. On leaving school he became a telegraphist at Redhill post-office.

At the beginning of the war Lieutenant Cadbury left Trinity College, Cambridge, where he was studying for the law, and joined as an A.B. the crew of the *Zarifa*, a converted yacht manned mostly by Cambridge men. After nearly a year at sea he entered the R.N.A.S. and gained his pilot's certificate, and he has been stationed on the East Coast for nearly 18 months. He is the youngest son of Mr. George Cadbury, chairman of Messrs. Cadbury Brothers (Limited).

An appeal for less noise on "alarm" nights has been issued to the residents of a north Midland town by the authorities. Noises, it is said, impede signalling officers. The public are urged to cease banging doors, and persons in the open are asked to stop laughing and talking and to walk on the roadway for the sake of quietness.

NO TROOPS IN THE BRITANNIC.

The Secretary of the Admiralty made the following announcement last night:—

German wireless messages to the Embassy, Washington, are again promulgating mendacious reports, purporting to come from Rotterdam, that the hospital ship Britannic, recently sunk, had troops on board. A complete statement of all persons carried on board that ship was published on November 24.

As has been officially stated on several previous occasions, British hospital ships are employed *solely* in the conditions set forth in the Geneva and Hague Conventions, and they carry neither *personnel* nor material other than that authorized by those Conventions.

GREAT BATTLES IN RUMANIA.

So far as can be ascertained from official telegrams, the black line on the map indicates roughly the present front in Rumania. Very heavy fighting has taken place between Gaesti and Titu, and on the south and south-west of Bukarest, where Russian troops have come into action.

NEW THREAT TO BUKAREST.

THE ARGES CROSSED.

NEARING THE OILFIELDS.

RUSSIAN RALLY ON THE SOUTH.

The most imminent danger to Bukarest—namely, on the River Arges front, south and south-west of the city—has been relieved by the arrival of Russian troops, who, with the Rumanians, have driven back the enemy's main force and taken 26 guns. Elsewhere, however, Mackensen's forces are advancing with rapid strides, and in the middle course of the Arges, further north they broke through the Rumanian line. Altogether 9,000 prisoners and 64 guns are said to have been taken during the week-end.

The Russo-Rumanian success was achieved south-west of the city, where the enemy were within five or six miles of the forts. A late *communiqué* from Vienna, however, seems to suggest that our Allies' counter-offensive has been nullified by a fresh enemy advance. The position is left obscure, but it appears that the Russo-Rumanians sought to effect a turning movement in force, but were stopped and driven back.

At the same time, according to Vienna, German troops crossed the Arges west of Bukarest. If the statement is literally accurate and the Arges line is crossed in force at this particular point—the enemy were already over the river considerably higher up—the position is certainly worse. Failure generally on the Arges line would mean the loss of Bukarest, for the fortifications of the city, as the Rumanians announce in a semi-official statement to-day, were "suppressed" before the war, and the city has been left to the civilian population.

The enemy's greatest success was in the centre of Rumania on the road from Pitesti to Bukarest. Here, according to the enemy reports, the Rumanians accepted battle in the Arges sector, but their front was broken through, in spite of a desperate resistance. As a result the Rumanians announce that they are falling back from Gaesti on Titu, about 30 miles from the capital. Both these places are very near the oilfields—Tirgovistea, the nearest point, is about 15 miles away—which the enemy is also approaching from the north-west.

RETREAT FROM PITESTI.

BIG GERMAN DEFEAT.

RUMANIAN official reports:—

SATURDAY.

On the western frontier of Moldavia and the northern front of Wallachia there were infantry attacks and an artillery bombardment. Bad weather is hindering operations.

In the valley of the Dimbovitza our troops have retired towards the south.

WESTERN FRONT.—In the region of Pitesti [north-west of Bukarest] our troops have been violently attacked and obliged to retire slightly.

The violent combat on the Glavacioeul and the Neajloy [west of Bukarest] continues.

SOUTHERN FRONT.—In the Dobrudja we have violently attacked the enemy positions, and have reached their wire entanglements, which, at some points have been passed.

SUNDAY.

On the western front of Moldavia and the northern front of Wallachia there have been lively artillery and infantry actions. We attacked the enemy at various points, capturing from him 120 prisoners.

In the valley of the Dimbovitza there is no change.

WESTERN FRONT.—On the right wing the enemy is attacking with stubbornness our positions and has compelled our troops to retire towards Titu [halfway between Pitesti and Bukarest].

On the Glavacioeul our troops defeated a Turkish division in the region of Draganesti [42 miles west-north-west of Bukarest] and the main body of Germano-Bulgarian forces in the region of Ghimpati and Mihalesti [the latter six miles south-west of the Bukarest forts], driving them back towards the south. We have taken prisoners and war material, which have not yet been enumerated.

26 ENEMY GUNS CAPTURED.

RUSSIAN official reports:—

SUNDAY.

In the Arges Valley enemy attacks continue. In this region the fighting is assuming the character of a great battle. Under the pressure of the enemy, Rumanian troops, outflanked by cavalry from the south, are retiring in a south-easterly direction.

Rumanian operations south of Bukarest, with the assistance of Russian troops which have arrived, are successfully developing. Bulgaro-German troops have been compelled to retire, and we captured prisoners and booty not yet enumerated. As far as can be ascertained at the moment 26 guns were taken.—*Wireless Press.*

SATURDAY.

On the roads from Pitesti to Bukarest, in the valley of the River Arges, the enemy conducted a series of fierce attacks, and has compelled a portion of the Rumanian troops north of the Arges to retire slightly. All attacks south of this river were repulsed.

West of Bukarest, after persistent attacks, the enemy succeeded in pressing back the Rumanians towards the River Arges.

South of Bukarest all enemy attacks were repulsed, and by a counter-attack the Germano-Bulgarian troops have been driven from the villages of Comana and Gostinari [about 19 miles south and south-south-east of Bukarest], captured yesterday.

DOBRUDJA.—Our troops have gained possession of the western part of the Tchernavoda Bridge, and in the region of Kalakeui-Satiskeui [a line about 12 miles north of the Tchernavoda railway] have compelled the enemy to retire to the south from several heights.—*Wireless Press.*

RUMANIAN LINE BROKEN THROUGH.

9,000 PRISONERS AND 64 GUNS CLAIMED.

GERMAN official reports:—

SATURDAY.—Army Group of Field-Marshal von Mackensen. Fighting in Wallachia is developing into a great battle. The wing of our army breaking out from the mountains south-east of Campulung gained ground in the wooded mountains on both sides of the Dimbovitza sector.

In the River Arges sector, south-east of Pitesti, the Germans and Austro-Hungarians after stubborn fighting defeated and broke through the Rumanian Army which accepted battle here. The Bavarian Reserve Regiment No. 18, which has repeatedly distinguished itself, penetrated to one divisional head-

Votes for Women

Above A suffragette arrested.
Right Special prison accommodation for suffragettes.

It is no good pretending that *The Times* was in the vanguard of the struggle for rights for women. But neither was it among the diehards, resisting change in the last ditch. The paper that had thundered for reform in the early nineteenth century could see the justice of the case for women's suffrage.

It was Northcliffe who first directed *The Times* to write for women. For instance, in one of his famous memoranda of the day to the editor in May 1913 he laid down the law that *The Times* was deliberately to seek out women readers:

> As to the topicality, authoritative articles on Japan and California (you have printed many in the past), the Baghdad railway, British ministerial visits to Berlin, and official denials (Morley's, by the way, are just the same as Haldane's), new Polo legislation, the state of St Andrews Golf Course, where the championship is to be played (the *Daily Mail* have had a man up there reporting on every hole). However, the *mot d'ordre* for the next few months should be the season and topicality. Caruso's appearance on Tuesday is interesting. One rigid rule I would make for the future is that on the personal page there should be nothing like 'Scottish History Chair at Glasgow', which is of no interest to the distinguished Nuts and Flappers we are trying to pursue.

The Chief was clearly a difficult man to work for. His assessment of the interest of the Chair of Scottish History at Glasgow to *Times* readers may have been an underestimate. But he was a true magpie journalist: *Homo sum: humanum nihil a me alienum puto.* He wanted in *The Times* not just the red meat of politics, but also polo and California, Caruso and the season, nuts and flappers, and articles to interest even women – if you assume that intelligent women are interested in different things from men.

On the specific issue of votes for women, Woman Suffrage as it was called in those days, *The Times* took the unheroic line of St Augustine in regard to chastity and continence: it was a good thing in principle, but not yet. A century before, *The Times* had led the crusade for parliamentary reform. By the twentieth century it preferred to wait until public opinion was ready to accept the women's case.

Amendments were put down to the Franchise Bill of 1913 in order to give the vote to women. *The Times* argued with cowardly male rhetoric, I fear, in a leading article of 18 January:

> The amendments should be rejected, first and foremost, because the truly revolutionary proposal to abolish the distinction of sex in elections for Parliament has never been submitted to the country. The suffrage societies talk loudly of there being 'a strong demand' for the suffrage and 'a great body of opinion' in its favour; but the only way known to the constitution of making a demand effective is by taking the opinion of the electors upon it at a general election; and there has been no pretence of doing this, in the present case, at any time. Our second reason is that the exercise of the vote by women would be a danger to the country, nationally and internationally. Our third reason is that, as the militant campaign has shown, the wilder women, who can only too easily get a following among emotional or discontented members of their own sex, are one-sided, one-eyed, with no sense of the general interests of the country as compared with the fancied interests of themselves. Our fourth reason, which ought to be enough of itself, is that, since this agitation began, the opposition to it, not only among men, but among a vast number of quiet and reasonable women, who used to be silent and inarticulate, has become infinitely stronger and more determined.

Three days later the Prime Minister announced that there would be a free vote on votes for women. *The Times* was not amused:

> It is now proposed to decide the matter, not even upon a House of Commons estimate of its merits, but simply by a chance vote determined by all sorts of extraneous tactical and log-rolling considerations. The amazing thing is that so many Unionists should be eagerly aiding and abetting a procedure which cuts at the very roots of their professed principles.

The uproar by Conservatives against the Government for making grave constitutional changes without consulting the country was hollow: they too were foremost in advocating the same outrage. *The Times* concluded that Woman Suffrage 'would have to come, if it were decided by a genuine and incontestable majority of the British people that they ought to have it. Until then there is no right in the case.' Unless he held an election on the issue, Asquith would have on his hands 'another revolutionary measure'.

The Irish Crisis and the First World War postponed decision of the issue. Four years later the Speaker's Conference on Electoral Reform passed a majority resolution in favour of giving women the vote. *The Times* said that this was a sign of the times that could not be mistaken. The leading article ran:

> We have always regarded Woman Suffrage as one of the changes which are inherent in the circumstances of the war, though these circumstances are far too seldom understood or expressed. Nothing, for instance, could be more insulting to the patriotism of women than the suggestion, which is often put forward, that the vote is a fitting 'reward' for war-time work. Good work is its own reward. The real case for their enfranchisement in these days rests on the palpable injustice of leaving the women, who have become for the first time an essential factor in the national effort, to fight their industrial battles, hereafter without such help as the vote provides. And their case rests, further, on the value of their help in maintaining those far-reaching social reforms – in such matters as drink control, child welfare, education, and housing schemes – which the war has already brought about as emergency measures.

The Times was by definition a child of its times. It may have been slow. It may have been patronizing and pompous. But it usually gets round to grasping a moral issue by the right end.

A leading article on the 1913 Franchise Bill, in particular the amendments to enfranchise women. THE TIMES's position at this date was unequivocal: 'We urge the rejection of all these amendments'.
18 JANUARY 1913

SATURDAY, JANUARY 18, 1913.

SUBJECT INDEX.

Weather Forecast.

To-day's forecast for all districts of the United Kingdom except the Western Channel and Bay is wind between south and west, light to moderate generally, fresh locally; some rain, mist or fog in places, fair or fine intervals; rather milder.

TO-DAY'S NEWS.

Mr. Lloyd George on Insurance.

Mr. Lloyd George and the Liberal Insurance Committee were last night entertained at dinner at the National Liberal Club by the Chief Government Whip. Mr. Lloyd George said that the doctors' panels had been adequately filled, with the possible exception of the North of London, which must be very carefully watched. They did not want to trample on any one, but they were under an obligation in the name of the King to give free medical treatment to 1,500,000 workmen in London, and they meant to give it. (pp. 7 and 8)

Doctors and the Pledge.

The representative meeting of the British Medical Association specially summoned to consider the question whether the undertaking and pledge should be maintained or abrogated was begun yesterday at the Connaught Rooms. No decision was reached, and the meeting will resume its deliberations to-day. (p. 8)

Parliament.

The House of Commons was again in Committee on the Welsh Church Bill, and passed the 18th clause. (p. 11)

The Franchise Bill.

Our Parliamentary Correspondent states that Mr. Dickinson has put down an important modification of his amendment to the Franchise Bill to exclude Ireland from its operation. Mr. Pease has put upon the paper the closure resolution for the Bill. (p. 6)

The Wreck of the Veronese.

The work of saving the passengers and crew of the British steamer Veronese, which was wrecked on the Portuguese coast, is being carried on under great difficulties. A number of passengers have been landed, but several lives are known to have been lost. There were apparently some 219 persons on board the steamer. (p. 6)

The Religion of the Viceroy of Ireland.

The Church Association has sent to every member of the House of Lords a protest against the throwing open, in the Government of Ireland Bill, of the office of Viceroy to Roman Catholics. (p. 6)

Prince Albert's First Cruise.

Prince Albert, with other naval cadets, embarked at Devonport yesterday in the training cruiser Cumberland, which leaves to-day for a cruise in the West Indies. (p. 9)

King Edward's Hospital Fund.

The Prince of Wales has sent £100 to King Edward's Hospital Fund for London. The other children of the King have sent subscriptions of a guinea apiece. (p. 9)

Portsmouth Church Extension.

At the annual meeting of the Portsmouth Church Extension Association last night it was announced that the £50,000 for which the Bishop of Winchester issued an emergency appeal for the building of six new churches at Portsmouth was now assured. (p. 8)

Sir A. T. Quiller-Couch.

At Cambridge yesterday the complete degree of M.A. *honoris causa* was conferred on Sir A. T. Quiller-Couch, the new King Edward VII. Professor of English Literature. (p. 10)

Lord Durham and Political Parties.

Lord Durham, speaking at Darlington yesterday, advised farmers not to put their trust in politicians, whose convictions changed from week to week, but to support that Government whose performances were to their satisfaction. Farmers should consider what benefit they were to get from the Unionist policy of taxation which would raise the price of manufactured goods but not of farm produce or food. (p. 4)

Sir F. C. Gould on Drawing.

Sir F. Carruthers Gould spoke at the annual meeting of the Royal Drawing Society, which was held in the Guildhall Art Gallery yesterday. He commended the methods of the society and referred to the use he had been able to make of memorizing in his own work. (p. 9)

The University Franchise.

A special meeting of Convocation of the University of London yesterday, called to consider the Government Franchise Bill, resolved by a large majority that the University franchise is a beneficial element in the Constitution and should be continued. (p. 10)

Women as Barristers.

The proposed admission of women to the Bar was rejected by an overwhelming majority at the annual general meeting of the Bar yesterday. (p. 3)

The Estate Market.

Business at the Mart this week has been on a small scale, but many important investments are to be offered at an early date. (p. 12)

Fried Fish Shop: A Nuisance.

In the Chancery Division, before Mr. Justice Swinfen Eady, an interlocutory injunction was granted restraining the defendants' user of a fried fish shop on the motion of the owner of a house adjoining, a veterinary surgeon living at Dursley, in the county of Gloucester. His Lordship found that the odour complained of from frying fish was a nuisance at common law. (p. 3)

Sir Cornthwaite Rason's Affairs.

In the Bankruptcy Court, before Mr. Registrar Brougham, the hearing of an application for an order of discharge by the Hon. Sir Cornthwaite Hector Rason, late Premier of Western Australia, and subsequently Agent-General of the colony in London, who was adjudged bankrupt in October last, was concluded. The discharge was granted subject to a judgment's being entered for £2,000, of which £500 was to be paid before the order was signed. (p. 3)

Racing.

The Hurst Park January Steeplechases were begun yesterday. The Surbiton Handicap Steeplechase was won by Mr. H. Rich's Abbott's Choice, the Mole Maiden Hurdle Race by Mr. B. Parr's Bernstein, the Novices' Steeplechase Plate by Mr. P. Carr's Ballyhist, and the New Year Handicap Hurdle Race by Sir C. Assheton-Smith's Minstrel Park. (p. 12)

The Barnes Motor Accident.

At Mortlake Petty Sessions yesterday John William Sallows, motor-car driver, who was charged with the manslaughter on December 7 of Miss Chellingworth, was committed for trial. (p. 3)

City Intelligence.

For summary of to-day's City Intelligence see page 15.

IMPERIAL AND FOREIGN.

French Presidential Election.

M. Poincaré, the Prime Minister and Minister of Foreign Affairs, was yesterday elected President of the French Republic by a second ballot of the National Assembly at Versailles. The figures were:—M. Poincaré, 483 votes; M. Pams, 296 votes; M. Vaillant (Socialist), 69 votes. (p. 6)

The Powers and Turkey.

The Collective Note of the Powers was presented to the Porte yesterday by the Ambassadors. Our Constantinople Correspondent furnishes us with the text. Some of the reasons for the delay that has occurred are touched upon by our Berlin Correspondent. (pp. 5 & 6)

The Bulgarian War Losses.

In a telegram which has apparently been delayed for 11 days by the Censor, our Special Correspondent in Sofia reports that the Bulgarian war losses amount to 284 officers and 21,018 men already dead and 876 officers and 51,000 men sick and wounded. About 70 per cent. of the sick and wounded have recovered and many of them have rejoined their regiments. The cholera losses before Tchataldja were about 3,000 deaths out of 35,000 cases. (p. 5)

Russia and Mongolia.

The principal members of the Mongolian mission have had conferences with the Russian Ministers about the objects of their visit. Russians are interesting themselves in the establishment of a bank at Urga. (p. 5)

The Turco-Italian War.

The King of Italy has decided to hold a review in Rome of one company from every unit of the Army of Africa next Sunday. (p. 5)

Prince George of Bavaria.

The marriage of Prince George of Bavaria with the Archduchess Isabella Maria of Austria, which was solemnized last February, has been pronounced null and void. (p. 5)

Strike Riots in New York.

Riots occurred in several parts of New York yesterday as a result of encounters between the garment workers and the strike-breakers and police. Numerous arrests were made. (p. 5)

Women and the Franchise Bill.

Next week, at the fag-end of one of the longest and most exhausting Sessions on record, we are to have the Committee stage of a Bill which is intended to transform our whole Parliamentary franchise. On former occasions every such Bill has been almost the sole business of one Session, or even two; but that is not the method of a Government whose motto is "Let us legislate, legislate, for to-"morrow we die." A House and a country wearied of debates and of law-making are about to listen to the first serious discussion of a law which, if passed, will abolish every ownership qualification, will do away with plural voting, will put an end to University representation, and will establish universal manhood suffrage, subject only to six months' residence. Moreover, in spite of the precedent of the County Franchise Bill of 1884, it is not to be accompanied by any Redistribution Bill, though various amendments on this head are to be moved. We do not propose, however, to discuss these general aspects of the Bill at the present moment. To-day we may confine ourselves to the more novel feature of the coming debate—namely, to the various amendments which would in one form or another open the franchise to women. These amendments are four in number. The first, which is to be moved by SIR EDWARD GREY, and has the support of all sections of suffragists, proposes to omit the word "male" from the first clause of the Bill, thus changing "every "male person shall be entitled, &c.," into "every person." The second amendment, moved by the Labour Party, would substitute in the second section of this clause, for "a "person shall be qualified" "a person of "either sex shall be qualified," thus putting wives in the same position as their husbands, and daughters or sisters of full age on the same footing as their fathers or brothers. The third amendment, which comes next in order of comprehensiveness, bears the name of MR. DICKINSON, MR. ACLAND (a member of the Government), and others. It is known as the Norwegian amendment, because, as is the case in Norway, it enfranchises the wives of electors. Finally, the fourth amendment, which is to be moved by MR. ALFRED LYTTELTON, is practically identical with the Conciliation Bill of last year; that is to say, it proposes to give the Parliamentary franchise to women who at present possess the municipal franchise. It is needless to say that this approach of what may well be a decisive struggle in Parliament has roused both Suffragists and Anti-Suffragists outside into great activity.

Of itself, to carry SIR EDWARD GREY'S amendment would, of course, not settle the question, for the Law Courts have decided that in a Bill of this kind the word "person," if unqualified, means men only. But to pass it is essential, if the other amendments are to be discussed at all. It will therefore be debated at length, and will give the real opportunity for the discussion of the vital principle which lies at the root of the whole matter. If it is rejected the word "male" remains operative, and the question is settled for this Parliament; but if it is carried the other amendments are in order, and will take their turn. As to MR. HENDERSON'S and the Labour Party's amendment, which even MRS. FAWCETT'S societies think has "little chance of success," it is enough to say that it would at one blow enfranchise thirteen millions of women; in other words, an excess of about two millions over the whole male electorate, as it will be left by this Bill. The next amendment, that moved by MR. DICKINSON, with the support, as is generally understood, of MR. LLOYD GEORGE and the Radical suffragists, would enfranchise about six million women. Finally, in the event of either or both of these amendments being rejected, there comes that moved by MR. LYTTELTON, which is virtually the Conciliation Bill, rejected last spring by a majority of fourteen. This, which will enfranchise women who are Local Government electors—that is to say, women who are independent occupiers—would add to the register about one million and a quarter voters. Such, then, are the three alternative proposals to be laid before the House if, and only if, the Grey amendment is carried and the word "male" removed from Clause 1. If, on the other hand, as we have stated, and as we sincerely hope will be the case, that amendment is rejected, it is understood that the CHAIRMAN will rule the other motions out of order. But if they come on, it is well to ask what will be the probable action of existing parties, curiously divided and broken up as they are by the cross currents of this question. We may assume that, however strongly a Conservative suffragist may feel in favour of the abstract justice of "votes for women," he will not, in any circumstances, support either the Henderson or the Dickinson amendment, either of which would hand over England and Scotland to the government of numbers in a more unrestricted form than exists in any other great country. On the other hand, the Lyttelton amendment—the old Conciliation Bill—is regarded as a Conservative measure, and a large number of Unionists propose to vote for it on that ground. It is possible that an accession of the women who now have the municipal vote might strengthen the Conservative cause; but we believe that members who vote for the amendment on that ground would be acting under a fatal delusion. Things being as they are in the present House of Commons, it is certain that a clause so amended would not be allowed to stand. When the Bill came to the Report stage, MR. ACLAND, and probably MR. LLOYD GEORGE, would say "the larger amend-"ments having been defeated, we voted for "this one in order to get the principle of "woman suffrage admitted. That having been "secured, we now invite you, Mr. Dickinson, "or you, Mr. Henderson, to bring up again "your amendment, and the united Liberal "Party will vote for you." In that case it is easy to see that the danger would be extreme.

We urge the rejection of all these amendments, and of SIR EDWARD GREY'S first of all, for at least four reasons, to which it would be easy to add others. They should be rejected, first and foremost, because the truly revolutionary proposal to abolish the distinction of sex in elections for Parliament has never been submitted to the country. The suffrage societies talk loudly of there being "a strong demand" for the suffrage and "a great body of opinion" in its favour; but the only way known to the Constitution of making a demand effective is by taking the opinion of the electors upon it at a General Election; and there has been no pretence of doing this, in the present case, at any time. Our second reason is that the exercise of the vote by women would be a danger to the country, nationally and internationally. Our third reason is that, as the militant campaign has shown, the wilder women, who can only too easily get a following among emotional or discontented members of their own sex, are one-sided, one-eyed, with no sense of the general interests of the country as compared with the fancied interests of themselves. Our fourth reason, which ought to be enough of itself, is that, since this agitation began, the opposition to it, not only among men, but among a vast number of quiet and reasonable women, which used to be silent and inarticulate, has become infinitely stronger and more determined. Anti-Suffragists, as will doubtless be said on Monday at the Queen's Hall, not only by LORD CURZON, but by MR. HOBHOUSE, a Liberal Cabinet Minister, claim that the majority of the men and women of the country are with them, and that any General Election or any Referendum will show it. If these reasons are not enough to dissuade the House of Commons from yielding to a pernicious agitation and voting for one or other of the amendments, at least the Liberal majority is bound to pay some regard, in a matter of this immense importance, to the expressed opinion of their own PRIME MINISTER. MR. ASQUITH has described the grant of the Parliamentary vote to women as "a political mistake of a very "disastrous kind." He has also, it is true, given a pledge that the House shall be free to vote as it likes. It is free, but so is he—free to speak his mind, free to demonstrate, as we sincerely hope he will, the political and moral dangers to which the adoption of female suffrage will expose the country; and free to ask his followers, to whom he has, by the admission of both sides, rendered such signal services, not to impose upon him a new and most unwelcome burden.

M. Poincaré's Triumph.

The expected has happened and M. RAYMOND POINCARÉ has been elected President of the French Republic. His success is not only a great personal triumph, but also a victory for the more moderate and unaggressive elements of French Republicanism. On the first ballot he fell but eight votes short of the absolute majority necessary for election. On the second he had fifty-three votes more than the absolute majority, and 187 more than M. PAMS, his only formidable rival. The Socialists adhered to their own candidate, M. VAILLANT, on the second ballot, so that the only support, which the PRIME MINISTER can have received from outside the "groups of the "Left," must have come from Conservatives and Monarchists. The cries of the defeated "stalwarts," when the result was announced, show the interpretation which they would like to place upon it. It is, however, plain that the great majority of the President-Elect's supporters must have been Republicans of an orthodoxy which is above suspicion. As President of the Republic he will doubtless stand firmly by the principle he proclaimed when he took office as Prime Minister—the principle that he would not govern at all unless he had the support of those convinced Republicans who accept the institutions of the country as they are, including the separation of Church and State and the *idée laïque*. But institutions may be administered in a spirit of oppression or of conciliation, and numbers of the thorough-going upholders of the *idée laïque* who voted for M. POINCARÉ yesterday have been coming of late to believe that harsh treatment of the minority may be carried too far. In their hearts they agree with JULES FERRY that the danger is no longer to the Right but to the Left. They desire a President who will lend no countenance to Syndicalism, anti-militarism, and other movements, which aim, not merely at the Constitution, but at the framework of society and at the life of the nation. They abhor personal government as intensely as do the Combistes, but they have too much faith in the Republic to fear it. On the other hand, they believe that the presence at the Elysée of a "strong" President will increase the authority of the Government at home and the weight of France in the counsels of Europe. They were satisfied that M. PAMS, the candidate of the "advanced" Radicals, would not be such a President, and they expect that the PRIME MINISTER will. As the close friends of France, and her partners in the Entente, we most earnestly hope, for her sake and for our own, that their expectations will be fulfilled. A strong France is a European necessity, and there cannot be a strong France unless moderation inspires her policy at home as well as abroad.

The future, it is plain, must depend in large measure upon the spirit in which the beaten "groups" take their defeat. The vehemence with which they opposed M. POINCARÉ'S candidature, the bitterness of their language, and the indefatigable energy with which they strove to coerce him into a withdrawal reveal the intensity of the animosities that have long divided the Republican Party. The existence of these enmities has, indeed, been known for a considerable time. They date back to a period before the pressure of national opinion forced M. POINCARÉ as Premier upon the reluctant "stal-"warts" of the Left. The steadiness with which he has continued to advocate a return to *scrutin de liste* and the introduction of proportional representation has deepened their dislike to him. They have thriven very comfortably under the present system. It has assured their predominance in the Chambers. They are afraid of the wide constituencies and of the freer play of real opinion which the electoral reforms are designed to secure, and accordingly they hate the statesman who is pledged to these uncomfortable changes. Then they regard M. POINCARÉ as a man imbued with the old-fashioned prejudice that it is the duty of the executive to enforce the law, and no doctrine can be more repugnant to many of them. The resolution with which he has refused to submit to the dictation which M. CLEMENCEAU, M. COMBES, M. MONIS, M. CAILLAUX, and others sought to exercise over him, when they summoned him to renounce the candidature that has been so successful, will hardly abate the hostility of the leaders and manipulators of the groups. But these men and their followers are very powerful in the Chambers, and, should they decide to pursue their quarrel with the new PRESIDENT, they may make all attempts at "strong" government, and even at a tolerably effective government, difficult, if not futile. The Ministry must, of course, be reconstituted when the new PRESIDENT goes to the Elysée, and a good deal may turn upon the manner of its reconstruction. Should the ambitions ascribed to M. BRIAND and M. MILLERAND be satisfied, the Combistes will be able easily to find an issue on which the Socialists, who execrate both these statesmen as renegades, will join them. Not improbably they would then be in a position once more to overthrow Cabinets at their pleasure.

We may, however, hope that the patriotism, to say nothing of the intelligent sense of self-interest, of the "stalwarts," will induce them to defer, if not to forgo, a kind of vengeance which cannot be exacted without hurt and danger to France. Their leaders include men of high political intelligence, who must realize to the full how desirable it is that, in the present state of Europe, the Government of the Republic should speak with the authority of the Legislature and of the nation behind it. If they cannot renounce the personal and party revenges to which they feel impelled, they ought to see the expediency of postponing retribution on their adversaries until a more favourable time. Prudence may confirm the suggestions of patriotism. The way in which M. POINCARÉ "developed strength," as the Americans say, during the progress of the struggle is significant. As the head of the State he may develop more. He showed that he appreciated his own position very shrewdly in his reply to the Radical demand for his withdrawal. The attraction which he exercised over individual voters at Versailles is not unlikely to increase at the Elysée. Frenchmen, and particularly the ordinary run of French politicians, do not usually like to be "agin the "Government," especially if they suspect that the Government has the real sympathy of the nation with it. And the Radicals will remember that, if the Socialists hate M. BRIAND and M. MILLERAND, and do not love M. POINCARÉ, they are devoted supporters of M. POINCARÉ'S policy of electoral reform. The Combistes have unquestionably received a smashing blow. They must settle for themselves whether it is wiser to provoke a fresh encounter, or to seek an accommodation with their adversaries. There can be no doubt which course would best serve the interests of France.

The Modern Pilgrim.

Among the stepchildren of the Pilgrim Fathers the sense of ancestry is well developed. It is a pious and commendable trait, and an instinct which prompts large numbers to cross the Atlantic every summer and to visit the villages, manor houses, and churches wherein the future builders of New England lived and prayed. We are reminded of these annual migrants to our shores rather earlier than usual this year by the appearance of a little guide-book to some of the sites in England which are more intimately associated with the early history of the United States. "Meccas for Americans" is well illustrated, and has a cover ruddier than Baedeker. Here the cultivated American will find photographs of the homes of the WASHINGTONS, the FRANKLINS, and the PENNS, and many other honoured names of the founders of his nation. He will likewise find photographs, together with others which less directly concern him, of the Cabot Tower at Bristol; the birthplace of the "godfather of Virginia" at Hayes Barton; the houses in which the Great Lexicographer, the Father of Historical Romance, and the Bard of Erin were born; the birthroom of him who is above all the Bard; MOORE'S Beauty Spots; a distant prospect of Eton College; DISRAELI'S Home at Hughenden; the Roman Baths at Bath, where the common ancestors of two great peoples may have washed; WORDSWORTH'S Favourite Walk, GRAY'S nodding beech and babbling brook; also the brook of TENNYSON; and a view of Blenheim, famous for having obeyed two American duchesses, besides having been a haunt of CHAUCER. We cannot enumerate all the Meccas; but armed with this little book our pilgrims will be able to feel like those in GIBBON "from the remote and once savage "countries of the north" visiting "the foot-"steps of heroes, the relics not of superstition "but of empire."

To have sprung from the crew of the Mayflower is to boast of a nobler ancestry than the Norman. Our own Norman blood is so diluted that we hardly like to mention it; but to Americans who have no parallel to the old Devon distich:—

"Cruwys and Crocker and Coplestone
"When the Conqueror came were all at
"home,"

and can historically if not genealogically point to a definite band of founders, it is pardonable that they should look with interest and pride upon Brington, Groton, Jordans, Ecton, and other family homes still standing in the quiet countryside of England. And if Althorp and Blenheim can be associated, though only remotely, with them, what is more natural than the wish to pay a flying visit to those palaces also? Again, there is the call of literature. There is SHAKESPEARE; there is MILTON, who thought it not unworthy to insert into his text a reference to the American when alluding to the giant figleaves that clothed the first human pair; there are the JOHNSONS, BEN and SAM, as THACKERAY'S ambassador has long ago reminded us; and there is GRAY, perhaps the least American of all, whose "picturesque God's Acre," we are told, wears anything but the air of a "neglected spot." There might have been DICKENS, for he lectured in America, but Gad's Hill is not included among the Meccas. Neither are Oxford and Cambridge, though we have it on good authority that the latter, in spite of Emmanuel and the founder of Harvard, may be omitted if time presses; but Oxford on the Great Western Railway is the station for LAUD'S tomb, and LAUD, praise him or blame him as we may, was, as a modern historian observes, the founder of Anglo-Saxon supremacy in the New World.

In spite of ridicule and sarcasm, the tripper is becoming recognized as part of the order of things. A hundred years ago it was the countryman in town who provoked amusement; now it is the sightseer from another hemisphere. But it behoves us to tolerate his vagaries. He does not always travel thoughtlessly. He may be a pilgrim, and a pilgrim is not a synonym for a tripper. He may feel within him the stirrings of culture, a yearning after the well-springs of edification, a religious prompting such as inspired the medieval votary to visit the healing shrine. The desire of Americans to see England, now that travel is so easy, is thoroughly intelligible. They come to us by nature better prepared to appreciate what they see than we ourselves, for the most part, when we go on the Continent. GOETHE'S house at Frankfurt can never mean to us what Stratford means to the American. "The brook that babbles by" is as familiar to American ears as it is to ours, and if we are inclined to smile at Americans for going to see it, and even then, perhaps, to be disappointed at it, how many English people have not visited Vallombrosa, though at the wrong season for autumnal leaves, or have not quoted in ecstasy *te Lari maxime* on approaching Como in a prosaic railway carriage? We must be patient of the pilgrim at our gates, and regret rather that at so many Meccas he must meet only with disillusionment. For when a place becomes a Mecca it not infrequently loses its charm. The turnstile, the visitors'-book, the stall of light refreshments, and the rack of picture-cards may quench the enthusiasm of all but the most fervent Hadji.

MR. LLOYD GEORGE ON INSURANCE.

VINDICATION OF HIS SCHEME.

THE GOVERNMENT AND THE DOCTORS.

The Chancellor of the Exchequer was entertained at dinner last night at the National Liberal Club in celebration of the coming into operation of the benefits under the National Insurance Act. By a happy coincidence, entirely unpremeditated, as was stated, the event happened to fall on the 50th anniversary of Mr. Lloyd George's birthday. The invitations were sent out in the name of Mr. Illingworth, the chief Government Whip, "to meet the Chancellor of the Exchequer and the members of the Liberal Insurance Committee."

Mr. Lloyd George proposed the health of the Liberal Insurance Committee, and took advantage of the occasion to review the history of the measure, culminating in a glowing picture of the results which, in his opinion, it was destined to bring about. He taunted the Opposition with their attitude to the measure when they thought they saw an opportunity of making political capital out of it, and coming to practical results, already in sight, stated that there were more people in the employed classes insured than they anticipated. Some of the small shopkeeping class had been frightened, and had lost their chance which would have made an invaluable provision for them in after life. Up to the present 5,000 persons had received sanatorium treatment, and this year it was estimated that there would be nearly one million people who could claim maternity benefit, three and a half millions who would draw sickness benefit, and at least four millions who would receive medical treatment.

As to the doctors, Mr. Lloyd George said the panels were filled—adequately filled. There was only one possible quarter that they would have to watch very carefully, North London. They were under obligation, in the name of the King, to give medical treatment to one and a half million of workmen in London, and they meant to give it. Doctors who had come on to the panels would have every right to approach the Government if they found any grievance or difficulty in the actual working of the Act. But, he added significantly, it was impossible for him on behalf of the Government to offer any further inducement to persuade or cajole doctors who were not on the panel to come on. He gave the statistics of the doctors in relation to population in Kensington, Hampstead, and Shoreditch, and gloried in the fact that for the first time the poor man in Shoreditch could pay just as much for his doctor, by the aid of the State, as the most-well-off artisan in any part of the United Kingdom. In an eloquent concluding passage Mr. Lloyd George dwelt upon the preventive value of the Act. The Liberal Insurance Committee, he said, had laboured hard and so had he, and their work would never die.

Mr. PERCY ILLINGWORTH was in the chair, and among those present were Dr. Macnamara, Mr. Beck, M.P., Mr. Neil Primrose, M.P., Mr. Gulland, M.P., Dr. Addison, M.P., Mr. Cecil Harmsworth, M.P., Sir H. Raphael, M.P., Mr. Booth, M.P., Mr. Alden, M.P., Mr. Glyn-Jones, M.P., Mr. Edgar Jones, M.P., Mr. Chiozza Money, M.P., Mr. Higham, M.P., Captain Guest, M.P., Mr. Macpherson, M.P., Mr. Pringle, M.P., Sir Jesse Herbert, Mr. Godfrey Collins, M.P., Mr. Vivian, the Parliamentary Secretary to the Board of Trade, the Financial Secretary to the War Office, and Mr. Dawes, chairman of the London Insurance Committee.

The CHAIRMAN said it had been his desire to give some public expression to the profound thanks which were their due not only from the Liberal Party but also from his distinguished predecessor Lord Murray, whose absence they all deplored, and also on his own behalf, for the work they had done in connexion with the Insurance Act. If they were celebrating the demise of that Committee, for it had officially now ceased to exist, they were also celebrating the inauguration of a great social service, and by a happy coincidence, entirely unpremeditated, they were also celebrating the jubilee of the birthday of the Chancellor of the Exchequer. They offered him, not only on their own behalf but also in the name of many outside those walls, hearty congratulations, and they made their acknowledgments to him for the patience, wisdom, ingenuity, and, above all, the undaunted courage with which he had faced great obstacles and difficulties.

MR. LLOYD GEORGE'S SPEECH.

Mr. LLOYD GEORGE, who was very cordially received, said:—

I rise with very great pleasure to propose the health of the Liberal Insurance Committee, coupled with the names of Mr. Cecil Beck and Mr. Neil Primrose. They have been of invaluable assistance to the Government, and I certainly owe them a deep debt of personal gratitude for the assistance they have rendered to me. They helped the Government through one of the toughest and most baffling fights that the Liberal Party have ever been confronted with. I say it was baffling, because it was just like those old wars which we used to have two or three centuries ago which were not wars at all. Officially the nations were perfectly friendly. There was no declaration of war, and you had simply a sort of piratical expeditions against each other. And that is more or less the condition of things we had to deal with over the Insurance Bill. The official Tory Party did not until a very late period declare war. The Government offered them, when they introduced the Bill as a purely non-party measure, co-operation. They invited it. They made an offer which, I think, is perfectly without precedent in the history of any great measure introduced by any Government. They invited the Opposition to nominate a certain number of men to meet the Minister in charge, to confer with him about amendments and improvements of the Bill. They were offered the assistance of all the officials at the disposal of the Government, all the figures which they possessed, and anything they could command. I do not think there is a single precedent for a proposal of that kind being made by any Government to its political opponents in the House of Commons. It was rejected. I regret, in the interests of the public life, that it was rejected. There are very many great social problems which men of all parties feel acutely the need for dealing with, which they realize it is essential should be dealt with in the interest of the national health, the national prosperity, the national greatness, and the national existence of this country. I am perfectly certain there are men in all parties who are earnestly desirous of seeing these great problems dealt with effectively, wisely, and in a manner which would effect a permanent improvement in the conditions of life in the land, and I deeply regret that that offer was not accepted in order to set a precedent which in itself, I think, would have been one of the most fruitful precedents ever set by any Government. I made the offer. I was only one of the Ministers of the Crown, but it was made by the Prime Minister on behalf of the whole of the Government afterwards in the House of Commons. It was rejected, and the responsibility for the rejection of it must lie at the doors of the Opposition. (Hear, hear.)

ELECTIONEERING ADVANTAGES.

Why did they do it? Because, although at first they thought the Bill was a good one—their reception of it at first indicated that that was their honest and sincere opinion—there were indications that it excited a good many interests, that there were hostilities aroused, that there were suspicions and apprehensions and fears, which were quite natural, when you have got a great new idea of this kind, and they thought, "Well there is a certain electioneering advantage in turning this against the Government." I do not know of a case where a party so deliberately neglected a patriotic opportunity, and I am perfectly certain that Nemesis awaits them and every party that flagrantly disregards the obvious, clear, unmistakable path of national duty. They were clearly of opinion that from an electioneering point of view we had made a mistake. Mr. Bonar Law, with that recklessness which has characterized his oratory, ventured to express his belief that the Bill would never become law, that it would never come into operation. But he has said so many

THE TIMES Picture Page

The Times has always been a paper of the printed word for the reading and chattering classes. It is not always recognized that it has also led the world in the imaginative and artistic use of illustrations.

Woodcuts were used in advertisements as early as 1786. Fine drawings of ships, catafalques and housing schemes were published in the early decades of the nineteenth century. A spectacular example came on 7 April 1806, when the detailed ground-plan of a house was printed on the front page in order to illustrate a sensational murder. In 1817 *The Times* illustrated its political shift to becoming the leading campaigner for parliamentary reform by reproducing 'A view of the agricultural and manufacturing villages of unity and mutual cooperation', as envisaged by Robert Owen, the social reformer, early town planner and a founding father of English socialism. For Queen Victoria's diamond jubilee in 1897 *The Times* was the first newspaper to publish a colour plate of her; it was, however, one printed in Germany.

The first half-tone photograph was printed in *The Times* in 1914. The inspiration behind this advance was the new proprietor, the Chief, Lord Northcliffe, who had pioneered the picture paper in founding the *Daily Mirror*. He was determined to introduce pictures systematically into *The Times*: his stuffier readers, who already objected vociferously to black and white line drawings in advertisements, muttered that he was going to turn *The Times* into a 'threepenny *Mirror*'.

LONDON, MONDAY, APRIL 7, 1806.
Mr. BLIGHT's HOUSE.

Ground Plan of Mr. BLIGHT's House.

Above THE TIMES front page, 7 April 1806, gave an account of an indictment for murder at the Surrey Assizes. The engravings of the scene of the crime and a plan of the rooms were the first illustrations ever to appear in the paper.

Right Ulric van den Bogaerde, art editor of THE TIMES for 35 years, at work with Mr Grimwade, assistant art editor, at THE TIMES Picture Desk.

Northcliffe was lucky enough to find U. V. Bogaerde, a man skilled in the new technology of photography, an artist, and somebody who was always ready to try something new. Bogaerde's part in the history of press photography was as dramatic in its context as some of the parts that his son Dirk Bogarde has played on the screen. Bogaerde was installed in an iron birdcage in the basement of Printing House Square to experiment with mechanical screens and photogravure cameras. The work was so secret that only he and his collaborator had keys to the cage.

The First World War interrupted these pioneering experiments. After the war Bogaerde was employed as art editor and press photographer on Northcliffe's pet project, *The Times History of the War*, which ran to twenty-two volumes.

On 1 March 1922 the Chief, back from his world tour, decided to go ahead with his picture revolution at *The Times*. As usual he did so in a theatrical and imperious way that would have excited the admiration of that artistic Emperor Nero. He rang Bogaerde at eight in the morning and ordered him to prepare a full page of topical news pictures for publication in the next day's *Times*. The page proof, complete with captions, was to be submitted for approval to Lord Northcliffe at his house in Carlton House Gardens by midday. The proof was still wet, and Bogaerde was five minutes late. But the Chief approved, and ordered a full page of pictures in *The Times* every day from then on. Bogaerde obeyed orders (it was prudent to do so with the Chief) with the help of only one photographer and one printer.

Readers approved also. The addition of more staff and improved techniques made the pictures better. And *The Times* developed the practice of using fewer, but larger and better, pictures instead of a mass of small ones. By the early 1930s *The Times* was publishing large photographs of the English scene that excited the admiration not only of the general public, but also of artists. Roger Fry remarked that the pictures in *The Times* showed 'the unerring sense of interval [i.e. spacing] that marked the work of great landscape artists'. War, famine, pestilence and politics might rage on the news pages. On the picture page, especially on a Saturday, you could always be sure of finding a beautiful image, say, of swans on the Avon, or the hop-harvest in Kent. Bogaerde's title of art editor was serious, not journalistic hyperbole.

With Bogaerde as art editor *The Times* pioneered many firsts in the inky art of press photography: infra-red photography; a special lens that enabled a photographer to take a picture of a theatrical production during normal performance; colour pictures; and underwater photography.

Exhibitions of photographs from *The Times* were held at home and abroad. These were not just good for public relations, but were profitable. Thousands of prints were sold. Some of them are still asked for, forty years on. An admirer of the series that *The Times* ran on British trains wrote:

> I want to be the man who a week ago took that amazing picture of a locomotive at full bend. I understand that the photographer was on that train himself; or that strictly speaking only one of his toes was on it, the rest of him being hanging out. What I want to know is could I get his place as soon as he falls off? I am willing to take half his salary.

The writer signed himself Mr Anon. But then, Sir James Barrie was never a man to push himself forward.

The photographer's print is only the first step in the complex and hurried process of reproducing the picture in the paper. The supremacy of *The Times* pictures depended also on the work of the Process Department. Its staff of cameramen, artists and engravers were all exceptional craftsmen. The department was as zealous in its experiments and innovations as Bogaerde's. In 1955 an electronic engraver, the Klischograph, was installed in Process; in June of that year *The Times* published the first electronically engraved picture in a national newspaper. The old acid-etched plate took more than half-an-hour's work in Process: the Klischograph can have a block ready in about a quarter of an hour. An improvement of fifteen minutes is a lot in the daily hurricane of publishing a newspaper, and the new techniques allow news pictures to be fitted into the edition up to the last minute.

Speed, efficiency and economy take priority in industry, and newspapers are no exception. Older readers of *The Times*, however, regret that the machine has displaced the craftsman, and that Art has vanished from the pages of the paper.

The first picture page, which was so successful that it became a daily institution. Bogaerde was a pioneer and a perfectionist; one of his unfulfilled ambitions was to see his picture page in full colour. His successful experiments include infra-red photography and the development of techniques and equipment to reproduce subtleties of tone.
2 MARCH 1922

THE ARRIVAL OF THE ROYAL BRIDE AT SHIFNAL.

The three bellringers of Harewood Church, Yorkshire, on the Harewood estates, who rang the wedding peal.

Princess Mary and Viscount Lascelles photographed at Shifnal Station, where they received a joyous welcome on their way to Weston Park.

Villagers outside Shifnal Station, Shropshire, waiting to cheer the bridal pair on the arrival of the special train.

NOTABLE GUESTS AT THE ROYAL WEDDING.
(1) Admiral the Hon. Sir Edmund Fremantle. (2) Mr. Bonar Law (left) and Sir Eric Geddes.

Mary Elcock, aged five, an engine driver's daughter, with the bouquet which she presented to Princess Mary on arrival at Shifnal.

NOTABLE GUESTS AT THE ROYAL WEDDING.
(1) Mr. Winston Churchill (right) and Mrs. Churchill. (2) Left to right: Mr. Asquith, Lord Derby, and Mr. Austen Chamberlain.

(1) Princess Alice Countess of Athlone being presented with a bouquet when she opened *The Daily Mail* Ideal Home Exhibition at Olympia yesterday. On the right of the little girl is the Earl of Athlone. (2) Queen Alexandra, who was an early visitor to Olympia, inspecting the exhibits.

The memorial to Field-Marshal Sir Evelyn Wood was unveiled by Field-Marshal Lord Grenfell in St. Paul's Cathedral yesterday. (1) The Memorial Tablet. (2) Left to right: Mr. A. Wood (Sir Evelyn's grandson), Mrs. Hubert Balfour (daughter), Mrs. D. McGeogh, and Captain Arthur Wood (son).

One of the interesting features of the Ideal Home Exhibition at Olympia is the Royal Gardens which fill the annexe. Ten in number, they have been designed by Queens and other Royal ladies of Europe. A view of the Queen of Spain's garden is shown.

The King presenting his Challenge Cup to Captain Ayde, M.C., owner of "Gay Lally," at the Hunters' Show at the Agricultural Hall, Islington, yesterday.

A Rugby football match played in Paris between teams representing the Stade Francaise and Swansea resulted in a drawn game, each side scoring two tries (6 points). An incident in the match is illustrated.

THE PRINCE AT BHOPAL AND GWALIOR.

(1) The Prince of Wales, with the Maharajah Scindia, riding on the Royal elephant in the procession to the Palace on the arrival of His Royal Highness at Gwalior Station. (2) The Prince and the Begum of Bhopal proceeding to the Durbar Hall during the visit to Bhopal. (3) The scene in the Durbar Hall at Bhopal. The Begum is seen seated on the left hand of the Prince.

Some favourite photographs published in THE TIMES.
Left above
St Paul's in a blizzard.
Photographed by David Jones, 7 January 1969.
Left below
Sunset at Westminster.
Photographed by H. Warhurst in 1931.
Above
A night express at St Pancras Station, London.
Photographed by William Horton in 1929.
Right
Launching the Lizard lifeboat in rough seas.
Photographed by H. Warhurst in 1935.
Below
Tree felling at Hildenborough, Kent.
Photographed by William Horton in 1936.
THE TIMES sold prints of the photographs to readers, and this was the most popular.

Tutankhamun: Fleet Street scooped

The discovery of the tomb of Tutankhamun in November 1922 was one of *The Times*'s great scoops. It also caused a gratifying uproar in Fleet Street. Nothing is more enjoyable to the outsider than the sound of dog eating dog.

Howard Carter and Lord Carnarvon had been digging in the Valley of Kings near Luxor since 1914 in a search for a royal tomb. They were on the point of giving it up as a bad dig, when Carter unearthed a stone step . . . which led to a staircase of sixteen steps . . . which led to a sealed door bearing the royal name of Tutankhamun.

On 26 November, 'the day of days', they came upon a second sealed door. Carter made a tiny hole in the upper left hand corner. Using the candle with which he had tested for possible foul gases, he peered through the chink. His description of what he saw has become archaeological history:

> At first I could see nothing, the hot air escaping from the chamber caused the candle flame to flicker, but presently, as my eyes grew accustomed to the light, details of the room within emerged slowly from the mist, strange animals, statues, and gold – everywhere the glint of gold. For the moment – an eternity it must have seemed to the others standing by – I was struck dumb with amazement, and when Lord Carnarvon, unable to stand the suspense any longer, inquired anxiously, 'Can you see anything?' it was all I could do to get out the words, 'Yes, wonderful things'.

The report in *The Times* of the official opening caused immense excitement. The discovery of buried treasure, particularly if it includes gold and mummies from an immeasurable past, is such stuff as dreams of 'Hold the front page' are made on. Carter wrote sarcastically:

> Next came our friends the newspaper correspondents, who flocked to The Valley in large numbers and devoted all their social gifts – and they were considerable – towards dispelling any lingering remains of loneliness or desert boredom that we might still have left to us. They certainly did their work with some thoroughness, for each owed it to himself and to his paper to get daily information . . .

Accordingly, to channel the glare of publicity, Lord Carnarvon signed an exclusive contract with *The Times* in January 1923, whereby the paper was made the sole agent for distributing throughout the world the news, feature articles and pictures of Tutankhamun's tomb. *The Times* paid Lord Carnarvon £7,500 for this monopoly, and 75 per cent of the profits made from selling the news to other newspapers and agencies, all of whom were to be treated impartially.

The arrangement suited the archaeologists. Howard Carter concluded '. . . we in Egypt were delighted when we heard Lord Carnarvon's decision to place the whole matter of publicity in the hands of *The Times*'.

It also suited *The Times* to have exclusive rights to such a very *Times*-like story. It had made a similar contract for the (unsuccessful) Everest expedition in the previous year. Neither party expected to make money out of the arrangement: in fact, by September *The Times* had made a loss of £2,500 on it.

It did not, however, suit the rest of Fleet Street, which cried sour golden grapes, and denounced the arrangement as pure commercialism by both parties. The *Daily Express*, *Daily Mail* and *Morning Post* led a campaign of denigration. Carnarvon was represented as an archaeologist who preferred gold to the scholar's wreath of acanthus. The *Express* headlined a leader

The first report of the discovery of the tomb of Tutankhamun, sent 'by runner to Luxor', with a leading article in column 3. When the tomb was opened some weeks later, THE TIMES recorded: 'Whatever anyone may have guessed or imagined . . . they surely cannot have dreamed the truth as now revealed . . .'
30 NOVEMBER 1922

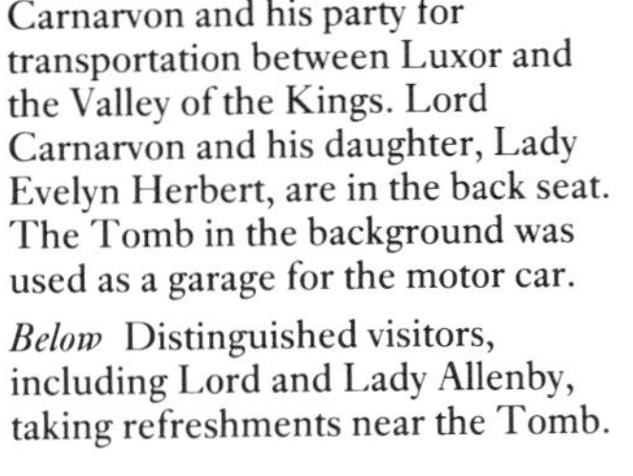

Right The motor car used by Lord Carnarvon and his party for transportation between Luxor and the Valley of the Kings. Lord Carnarvon and his daughter, Lady Evelyn Herbert, are in the back seat. The Tomb in the background was used as a garage for the motor car.

Below Distinguished visitors, including Lord and Lady Allenby, taking refreshments near the Tomb.

THURSDAY, NOVEMBER 30, 1922.

Weather Forecast.

England, S.E.—Wind westerly to south-westerly, mainly light; fair; mist in places at night; mild. (p. 14)

To-day's Times consists of 24 PAGES.

TO-DAY'S NEWS.

HOME.

The recent executions in Dublin were again discussed in the Southern Irish Provisional Parliament last evening. General Mulcahy, Minister of Defence, said the men were executed because they were part of a scheme which would destroy the national life. (p. 12)

The Minister of Labour invites the cooperation of the employers' organizations and the Trades Union Congress General Council in considering the question of unemployment insurance by industry. (p. 14)

The Burnham Committee has agreed that both panels should present a proposal for a temporary five per cent. reduction of teachers' salaries to their constituent bodies, in the hope that a satisfactory solution of the problem may be found. (p. 9)

When the trial of Gerard Lee Bevan was continued at the Old Bailey yesterday, the defence was opened, and Bevan went into the witness-box. His evidence had not concluded when the Court adjourned. (p. 5)

An exhibition of Japanese prints opens to-day at the British Museum. (p. 15)

Foot-and-mouth disease has broken out among cattle at Huntington, near Chester. (p. 12)

POLITICS.

In the House of Lords yesterday the Duke of Devonshire announced that a Bill dealing with the Canadian cattle embargo would be introduced this Session. There was a discussion on Mesopotamia and Palestine, and the Irish Bills brought up from the Commons were read a first time. (p. 7)

In the House of Commons statements were made with reference to France and Germany and the withdrawal of the British Minister from Athens. After the Irish Constitution Bills had been read a third time, the housing question was discussed. (pp. 7 & 8)

IMPERIAL.

The South Australian Government has been unable to obtain the passage of its Bill to bring an end to the system of compulsory arbitration in industrial disputes. (p. 11)

Mr. Albert R. Carman, editor of the Montreal *Star*, discusses the question of Canada and the Empire Bond. (p. 11)

FOREIGN.

The Lausanne Conference yesterday considered the question of the Aegean islands. A proposal for partial demilitarization of the southern group of the islands was opposed by the Turkish delegation, which desired complete demilitarization. (p. 12)

The Egyptian Cabinet, of which Sarwat Pasha was Prime Minister, has resigned. Nessim Pasha has undertaken the formation of a new Cabinet. (p. 12)

The Kemalists are exploiting the recent disturbances in Western Thrace to their political advantage, by alleging that they are a popular revolt against the Greek administration. (p. 11)

Lord Carnarvon and Mr. Howard Carter have made a remarkable discovery in the Valley of the Kings, where the Kings of the eighteenth Egyptian dynasty were buried (p. 13)

Our Paris Correspondent sends some details of the execution of the Greek ex-Ministers. (p. 12)

COURT AND PERSONAL.

The Prince of Wales will attend the eighth birthday celebration of "Toc H" at the Guildhall on December 15, and bestow the lamp of maintenance, the symbol of the society, on a number of branches. (p. 9)

LAW.

Summary of Law Cases will be found on page 5.

SPORT.

The Newbury Meeting was begun yesterday. (p. 6)

Kent beat Surrey in the Rugby Football County Championship at Richmond yesterday by nine points to three; and Oxford University beat Guy's Hospital at Oxford by thirteen points to none. (p. 6)

FINANCE AND COMMERCE.

In "City Notes" comment is made on:—The Coming Dividend Disbursements; Mexican Eagle Position; Three Bank Dividends; Welsh Tinplate Issue; Lord Furness on Steel Conditions; Another B.A.W.R.A. Protest; Brazil's Financial Burden; Britain Steamship Company's Accounts; and Port Authorities and Oil Waste. (p. 19)

Loans were in keen demand and up to 3 per cent. was paid. Silver recovered 3/16d. per ounce on Indian buying. The mark improved, but the franc again weakened, and New York reacted 5/16c. In stock markets home railway securities were buoyant. (p. 19)

A GREAT OPPORTUNITY.

M. Poincaré has intimated to the Prime Minister that he is ready to come to London on any day next week which may be arranged, and it is expected in Paris that Mr. Bonar Law will invite Signor Mussolini and M. Theunis to be present at their meeting. Consideration of the matters intended to be discussed at the Brussels Conference is, of course, the object of the proposed "conversations." We cannot doubt that M. Poincaré's offer will be gladly accepted, if indeed it has not been accepted already, and that the French Prime Minister will be in London within the next few days. Whether Signor Mussolini may be able to leave Italy at such short notice is perhaps doubtful, but his presence will add to the importance and to the weight of the gathering if he is able to attend. Like M. Theunis, who also represents Belgian interests in the problems to be debated, he will be warmly welcomed should he heighten the significance of the conversations by his presence. But while Italy and Belgium have serious interests in reparations, the chief burden and the chief responsibility rest upon England and upon France. Once again, as at the time of M. Poincaré's visit in the summer, a great opportunity is offered them. Once again it is for them to seize it greatly, as they failed to seize it last August. Again they have it in their power to make a real and comprehensive settlement of the inseparable questions of reparations and of Inter-Allied indebtedness in all their most important aspects. The conditions, indeed, are less favourable than they were four months ago, but with simplicity and earnestness of purpose, with largeness of vision and with firmness of resolve, the achievement is still possible. Every week adds to its difficulty; it may not be possible again. If the discussions are confined to secondary points—to debates upon longer or shorter moratoriums for Germany, or upon pledges to be exacted from her, or methods of execution to be employed against her in the event of her continued refusal to make reasonable exertions for the payment of her just debts—little good can come of the meeting. These points may have their importance in themselves, but no decisions merely upon them, if decisions were reached, would greatly promote a real settlement—a settlement which will lay foundations for the economic reconstruction of Europe and for the political security which only that reconstruction can bring. Shortly before the French Prime Minister came to London in the summer we indicated the general lines upon which a settlement of this kind seemed possible. It cannot deal with reparations alone; it must extend to the debts of the Allies to each other; it must include efficient supervision of German finance; and it must make available for a settlement the capital which Germans have fraudulently exported to foreign countries with the connivance of the German Government. When M. Poincaré last visited us he had a plan which is understood to have been based upon the simultaneous treatment of reparations and of Inter-Allied indebtedness, and to have proposed a reduction of Germany's obligations and an international loan. The scheme, unhappily, was never expounded by him. The Balfour Note "torpedoed" it before it could be produced, and M. Poincaré, instead of bringing it forward and leaving the British Government to accept the responsibility of rejecting it, kept it in his portfolio and confined his demands to matters of subordinate concern. We do not know whether he will come forward with such a scheme again, but if he were to do so we believe that it would meet with a truer perception of its worth and a more anxious desire to accept his views than prevailed in a section of the late Government last August. The Balfour Note affirmed the readiness of the Cabinet "to remit all the debts due to Great "Britain by our Allies in respect of loans, or "by Germany in respect of reparations," provided that "such a policy formed a part of a "satisfactory international settlement." But it made the extent of our remission of Allied Debts to us, and of our share of the German Reparation Debt, conditional upon the treatment by America of our debt to her. That made it worthless. We could not, without forfeiting our self-respect, seek to make a bargain of this kind with America, nor could France honourably join us in an attempt to put moral pressure upon America to accept it. Though public opinion here, including, as we know, the opinion of the Treasury and of the highest financial authorities in the City, immediately and strongly condemned that Note, M. Poincaré went back to Paris with his purpose unattained.

If the present Government understand the realities of the situation and have the courage to face them, they will repeat the offer of their predecessors without the condition. They will express readiness to remit the whole or a large part of the loans due to England from her Allies and the whole or a large part of the reparations due to her by Germany, "if "such a policy forms a part of a satisfactory "international settlement" for Europe. The loans, it is notorious, are practically worthless from a financial point of view, and our share of reparations is worth incomparably less to us than the advantages which we should derive from the early restoration of economic and political stability in West Europe. That is the great aim for all the Allies, for France and for Italy, as well as for ourselves. If we can get nearer to it by such sacrifices as these, and if by making them we should at the same time remove misconstructions and incipient doubts from the minds of our Allies, common sense bids us to make them freely and cheerfully. They must, however, form a part of a "satisfactory international settlement" so far as Europe is concerned. That is a *sine qua non* of any such concessions. Our debt to America, as has always been maintained in these columns, stands upon a wholly different footing. That we mean to pay, and that we have begun paying. To pay it is a matter of self-interest with us as a commercial nation, as well as a point of honour. These considerations do not apply to the debts of the Allies to us. What we want from them is their cordial and strenuous assistance in making the international settlement "satisfactory" in the widest and the truest sense. To achieve it may demand some sacrifices from them as well as from us, but it is worth achieving, for in it lies the peace of the world.

A Marvellous Discovery.

The earth holds in her recesses the rich memories of our race, and sometimes, as though the effort of the reflective and inquiring mind of modern man had suddenly flashed forth in a revealing intuition, a discovery comes that lights up the obscurity of the distant past. One such discovery we are privileged to record to-day. Our Cairo Correspondent tells us how, after sixteen years of patient toil and research, Lord Carnarvon and that distinguished excavator, Mr. Howard Carter, have been rewarded by a marvellous find in the Valley of the Kings near Thebes. All the mysteries of this famous valley had been disclosed, so it was thought, long since. Mr. Carter, with the pertinacity of the gifted archæologist who scents discoveries from afar, dug on persistently until at last, in the Royal necropolis of the Theban Empire, he came across some tempting signs below the tomb of Rameses VI. Lord Carnarvon went out from England, and he and Mr. Carter together opened the sealed doors of a hitherto unnoticed chamber. When opened this chamber revealed an amazing spectacle. There were gilt couches, inlaid with ivory and precious stones; innumerable boxes, inlaid and painted with entrancing hunting scenes; a wonderful throne; a chair encrusted with precious stones and adorned with Royal portraits; bituminized statues of a king, chariots, maces, a footstool, alabaster vases, and quantities of trussed duck and haunches of venison, left, according to the ancient custom, as provision for the great dead. Beyond the first chamber lay another chamber crowded with a confusion of gold beds, boxes, and alabaster vases, and beyond this, again, lies another chamber which may prove to be the actual tomb of the king whose funeral relics lie in bewildering profusion in the first two rooms. The name of the king who thus emerges in splendour from the dim past into the murky light of our troubled day is Tutankhamen, of the Eighteenth Dynasty, who reigned in Tel-el Amarna and Thebes over three thousand years ago. Little was known of him except that he claimed to be a son of the famous Amenhotep III., and that he married the daughter of that strange Pharaoh Akhenaten, who revolutionized the Egyptian religion by instituting in the worship of the rays of the sun a kind of monotheism, and at the same time promoted a remarkable artistic revival. Of Tutankhamen the chief fact hitherto attested is that in his reign the traditional religion, with its worship of Amen as the principal deity, once more claimed its own. He was, so to speak, the patron of a counter-reformation. Now, thanks to this remarkable discovery, we may perhaps learn more of the circumstances of this strange ebb and flow of religious emotion in the days when mankind was still young. And though the world is old now and restless still, with the craving for power and for a knowledge of great mysteries, even now when the Eastern lands are trembling between war and peace and a Europe undreamed of by the Pharaohs is wrestling with problems that would have been stranger to them than all their weird panoply is to us, that figure of the ancient king who thus suddenly steps out from oblivion has a permanent significance. On his footstool are figures symbolizing his lordship over Syria, and the peoples of Ethiopia owned his sway. Around him are the confused tokens of a reversion from a groping after new spiritual ideas to the comfortable forms of an ancient ritual. Through the ages the winds are blowing that disturb the spirit of man continually with the dream of power and comfort it with the hope of God.

Work and Maintenance.

In the course of the debate on the Labour amendment to the Address, to be moved to-day in the House of Commons by Mr. Clynes, Mr. Bonar Law will have an opportunity of explaining what steps the Government propose to take for the relief of the unemployed. While the efforts to browbeat the Prime Minister into receiving the deputation of the unemployed marchers have been in progress, he himself and the Cabinet Committee charged with the investigation of the whole question have been busily engaged, in cooperation with the Departments concerned, in deciding on the policy to be followed. That was obviously the first thing to be done. It was much more important, other considerations apart, that he should see the official representatives of the chief railway companies, and learn from them the outlines of the practical schemes, projected or already in operation, by which they hope to help, than that he should spend time in listening to the complaints and proposals of a set of men who, as he has pointed out to the London Labour Party, appear to be more interested in propagating Communism than in alleviating the lot of the workless. The justice of that criticism will be generally admitted. In refusing to lay their case before the Ministers of Labour and Health they not only committed a grave tactical error, but were unfaithful servants of the men whom they pretended to represent, and the only possible conclusion is that their real aims were those attributed to them by the Prime Minister. Fortunately, however, the care of the interests of the unemployed is in the hands of wiser men than these. Mr. Clynes's amendment expresses regret, first, that no proposal has been made for an adequate and equitable treatment of the victims of the policy which, he claims, has led to the present unexampled unemployment; and, secondly, that there are no signs of a change which will, on the one hand, enable European customers to buy British goods again, and, on the other, restore international trade and stabilize international exchanges. Stated in this way the twofold complaint of the amendment obviously leaves out of account the measures by which the Government propose to deal with the two main aspects of the unemployment problem. Until, therefore, Mr. Bonar Law rises to explain what these measures are the debate will serve mainly to bring before the House and the Government the views and suggestions of the Labour Party. In so doing it will fulfil a most useful and beneficial purpose, always provided that the Labour spokesmen, and, indeed, all who take part in the discussion, keep steadily in view the fact that this is no party question. It is a matter in which every member and every citizen is deeply and directly concerned, and its difficulties can be solved only by the generous and sympathetic cooperation of all parties in both Houses.

The amendment further claims that the adequate and equitable treatment of the unemployed is entirely a national obligation. If this is meant to imply that the whole burden of their relief should be transferred to the State it raises an issue about which there is bound to be controversy. But on broader lines there will be a general agreement in the House, as there is in the country, that, whatever may be found to be the best way of providing the necessary funds, the relief of the victims of unemployment is in the very highest sense a national obligation. For that purpose both work and maintenance must be provided. But work must come first. That, undoubtedly, will prove to be the guiding principle of the Government policy. They have to deal with an immense problem, and only by big measures can they hope to solve it. Our Labour Correspondent states that there is good authority for believing that it has been decided to keep the Cabinet Committee on Unemployment in permanent session until the end has been achieved. Meanwhile, there is every appearance that the steps which they are already prepared to recommend will go a long way to meet the difficulties which have to be faced. They are at least moving in the right direction. Besides big road and railway schemes, elaborated after consultation with the Ministry of Transport and the leading railway authorities, a comprehensive programme devised by the Office of Works, a fuller application of the Trade Facilities Act, and other plans the great virtue of which lies in the fact that they can be begun without delay, are features of the Government proposals which give colour to the hope that work rather than doles will be the groundwork of the relief measures in the immediate future. In connexion with the Trade Facilities Act, the provisions of which are to be renewed in a new Bill, the important announcement is made that a sum of £50,000,000, or double the amount previously taken under the Act, will be placed at the disposal of the Government for giving guarantees in respect of principal and interest. Looking further ahead, the Minister of Labour has addressed to the National Confederation of Employers' Organizations and the Trades Union Congress General Council a letter and memorandum, in which he invites their cooperation in considering whether, and how far, it might be desirable to establish an improved system of unemployment insurance by industries. This is a difficult question on which it will certainly be useful, whatever may ultimately be decided, to have the opinions of the two sections of the industrial organization of the country. But for the moment it is the emergency measures which must chiefly demand the attention of Parliament, and of these it is the schemes which can be started with the least delay that are the most important, in view of the urgent necessity of putting an end to the present distress.

Trustees or Vandals?

It is often difficult to decide the claims of historic interest and ancient beauty against those of modern utility. The issue has been raised once more in an acute form at Croydon, where for years there has been an agitation to demolish what is almost the sole surviving piece of dignified architecture in the place—namely, the red-brick Elizabethan hospital of Archbishop Whitgift's foundation—in order that an important but entirely modern thoroughfare may be widened. The other day, as we have shortly reported, the Croydon town councillors decided to pursue a long-canvassed scheme, and to seek Parliamentary sanction for it. A few courageous voices, it is true, were raised against the project, but the councillors, as a body, apparently show no appreciation for the past associations of their town, or for the intrinsic beauty of Whitgift's building. It must be allowed that the hospital stands in an awkward place, where there is a confluence of busy traffic, a tram-line, and a slope opposite the hospital which would make an alternative widening considerably more expensive. No one, however, who goes to Croydon can fail to perceive that here is a building which, in the interests of history and of beauty, ought to be preserved at any cost, and that its proposed erasure will become the concern of a wider public than the local. It is not as if Croydon were rich in antiquities, for the town has little now to remind its inhabitants of its not inglorious past. On the other hand, the buildings near the hospital are, even for a modern suburban shopping centre, singularly devoid of taste or meaning. It is against the general corruption of style in modern commercial architecture that many of the most thoughtful minds of the day are endeavouring to protest, and, in contrast with this degeneracy, every single example of older building, however plain, stands as an object lesson and a rebuke. But, as one town councillor said on Monday, "we "cannot see sentimental objections stand in the "way of the progress of a great town"; and, as another is reported to have said, the hospital, were certain "embellishments" taken away, "would be an extremely ugly building." If the former remark is brutally candid, the latter shows such a complete lack of discernment that it is to be hoped, for the sake of the town council, that the speaker is not truly representative of the æsthetic competence of that body. It would seem, however, that there has long been something highly distasteful in Whitgift's modest and well-proportioned quadrangle that challenges the town council to have done with it for ever. If it is to disappear, a remarkably well-preserved specimen of a collegiate building of that period, of which there are none too many, will be destroyed. Artistically it is much more worth saving than many ruins which are scheduled as ancient monuments, if only because it stands in the middle of commonplace surroundings, and puts to shame by its mere presence the gaudy products of modern commercialism. Though the traffic difficulty is not lightly to be dismissed, there ought to be ways of diminishing it, and if the town councillors could be induced to see the spiritual value of such a relic's continuance, they would not err in going about in the most circuitous ways in order to avoid the name of vandals.

The Minister of Pensions, Major G. C. Tryon, M.P., has appointed Mr. Charles Kenneth Murchison, M.P., to be his Parliamentary Private Secretary (unpaid).

NEW THAMES BRIDGE.

DISADVANTAGES OF ST. PAUL'S SITE.

CITY AND THE PURCHASED PROPERTY.

TO THE EDITOR OF THE TIMES.

Sir,—Whereas, on the immediate south of the City, three vehicular bridges cross the Thames, there is, at Charing Cross, the riverside centre of the vast traffic of Western London, no bridge across the river at all.

The necessity for one is evident; and, moreover, a magnificent bridge at this point would be a glorious memorial erected to the Great War. If, as seems possible, the decision to build the St. Paul's bridge may destroy the opportunity for beginning the Charing Cross bridge, then that decision will be a disaster.

I am, Sir, yours faithfully,
HAMO THORNYCROFT, R.A.
2, Melbury-road, W.

TO THE EDITOR OF THE TIMES.

Sir,—I have read the letter of the Chairman of the Bridge House Estates Committee of the Corporation in your issue of November 28. He is wrong in thinking that I did not appreciate the position of affairs, as stated in his letter, and I would suggest to him that a good deal of water has run under London Bridge since 1909, when the Corporation decided to take powers to build a new bridge over the Thames at St. Paul's.

What may have been desirable then may well require further consideration in the altered circumstances of to-day, especially with the object-lesson of Southwark Bridge before us, with its insignificant traffic, and bearing in mind that it is only 300 yards distant from the proposed new bridge. With regard to the expense which has been incurred in the preparation of plans and drawings, I think this is by no means wasted expenditure, as, without this research, it might not have been possible to ascertain the many difficulties and drawbacks incident to a bridge abutting on St. Paul's Cathedral but—as pointed out by Mr. Beresford Pite in his letter to you—entirely ignoring this great national monument, which, I understand, would scarcely be visible from the proposed bridge.

As to the fact that property of the value of over £1,000,000 has already been purchased to make the approaches, I have reason to believe that this property has considerably increased in value, and, consequently, no loss to the public would be sustained. I understand, moreover, that the Cathedral authorities are not in favour of the St. Paul's scheme, and, as a citizen, I am appalled to think what would be the effect of the introduction of a new line of intersecting traffic on the existing congestion at the west end of Cannon-street and Cheapside.

In any event, a little further delay will be hurtful to no one, and will give opportunity to all who are interested—which means all Londoners, and all who love London—to take stock of the situation as a whole, with a view to arriving at a right decision on the point now at issue, as to where the need for a new bridge is really greatest.

I am, Sir, your obedient servant,
WILLIAM H. DAVISON,
Citizen and Clothworker.
House of Commons, Nov. 28.

THE GROUNDS OF DIVORCE.

TO THE EDITOR OF THE TIMES.

Sir,—Lord Buckmaster states, in his letter in your issue of November 27, that anyone who wished to combat his views has had an equal opportunity to do so; so I trust you will allow me to do so.

We quite understand the difficulty he finds in treading "the labyrinth of ecclesiasticism" when he shows in his letter that he cannot even recognize a quotation from the Bible, and hunts in vain for it in a modern novel.

His arguments seem to be special pleading of the worst sort. For example, when he dwells on the sad case of a girl of sixteen, and her economic position, he does not seem to realize that a million women in England are in the same position because of the disparity of sexes. This appeal to our emotions is merely an argument for polygamy.

All these appeals to sentiment about "women chained to lunatics" are a mere blinding of judgment. The one and only issue is the right to re-marry; there is no chaining; the Church allows separation *a mensa et toro*.

Our objection to the extension of divorce with right to re-marry, which is the only point, may be summed up thus:—

(i.) Every quarrel would soon harden into an irrevocable separation, with no room for repentance and reconciliation. As at present, the binding life-long permanence of the marriage vow enables these matrimonial squabbles to be reconciled. One London magistrate told me that he never granted a separation order without sending the couple to talk matters over with the police court missionary. In one year he had 414 applications for separation orders; 381 of these were withdrawn after the interview. Only thirty-three out of 414 came into Court.

(ii.) With easy divorce every guest would be a possible rival. The power of suggestion is immense.

(iii.) No ideal can be maintained without the suffering of many individuals. A million soldiers laid down their lives to protect our home; and, for the same cause, another million are maimed, or crippled, or blinded, and have to face a life-long suffering. So, to maintain the sanctity and permanence of the marriage bond, a few must be content to endure a few years of celibacy till the death of their partner enables them to marry again. Millions live as celibates for worthy reasons—to maintain parents or invalid sisters. To maintain God's law of matrimony is worth much sacrifice.

Yours truly,
PAUL B. BULL.
House of the Resurrection, Mirfield, Yorks.

TO THE EDITOR OF THE TIMES.

Sir,—May I venture to claim the use of your columns in support of Lord Buckmaster's letter which you published on November 27?

In the debate upon the Matrimonial Causes Bill in the House of Lords on March 24, 1920, when supporting Lord Buckmaster, I drew attention to the following facts:—That his Bill was based upon the Report of a Royal Commission; that, in those countries where the Roman Catholic Church was the Church of practically the entire population, it was found desirable, for the welfare of the people, to legalize divorce; that divorce (although the law of this country) was at present most difficult in its operation for the working classes. None of these facts was controverted.

Has the question whether marriage is a divine institution or not anything to do with Lord Buckmaster's Bill, seeing that divorce is the law of the land and that the main purport of his measure is to place rich and poor upon an equal footing, as far as is possible, in the matter of divorce? As the representative for twenty-four years of a South London working-class constituency, I visited thousands of working-class homes, and I could multiply tenfold cases similar to those referred to by Lord Buckmaster.

In my opinion, if all the preventable misery, crime, and vice that exist in consequence of the defective state of our divorce laws were known to the public, the outcry for this necessary and long-delayed reform would be irresistible.

Yours faithfully,
RATHCREEDAN.
Bellehatch Park, Henley-on-Thames.

TO THE EDITOR OF THE TIMES.

Sir,—Lord Phillimore's letter in your issue of November 28 is less convincing than he must wish, in view of the prevailing impression that he is opposed to divorce on any grounds.

If this is the case, his detailed criticisms of Lord Buckmaster's examples of hard cases appear disingenuous. As no one can imagine Lord Phillimore being this, the appearance of it is to be deplored; but nothing is easier than for him to refute such an unjustified suspicion by writing again to disclose upon what grounds he considers divorce should be granted.

Yours faithfully,
CHRISTIAN.

AN EGYPTIAN TREASURE.

GREAT FIND AT THEBES.

LORD CARNARVON'S LONG QUEST.

(From Our Cairo Correspondent.)

VALLEY OF THE KINGS (by runner to Luxor), Nov. 29.

This afternoon Lord Carnarvon and Mr. Howard Carter revealed to a large company what promises to be the most sensational Egyptological discovery of the century.

The find consists of, among other objects, the funeral paraphernalia of the Egyptian King Tutankhamen, one of the famous heretic kings of the Eighteenth Dynasty, who reverted to Amen worship. Little is known of the later kings, including Tutankhamen, and the discovery should add invaluably to our knowledge of this period and of the great city of Tel-el-Amarna, which was founded in the fifteenth century B.C. by Amenhotep IV., the first of the heretic kings.

The remarkable discovery announced to-day is the reward of patience, perseverance, and perspicacity. For nearly sixteen years Lord Carnarvon, with the assistance of Mr. Howard Carter, has been carrying out excavations on that part of the site of the ancient Thebes situated on the west bank of the Nile at Luxor. From time to time interesting historical data were unearthed, but nothing of a really striking character was found, although Deir el Bahari

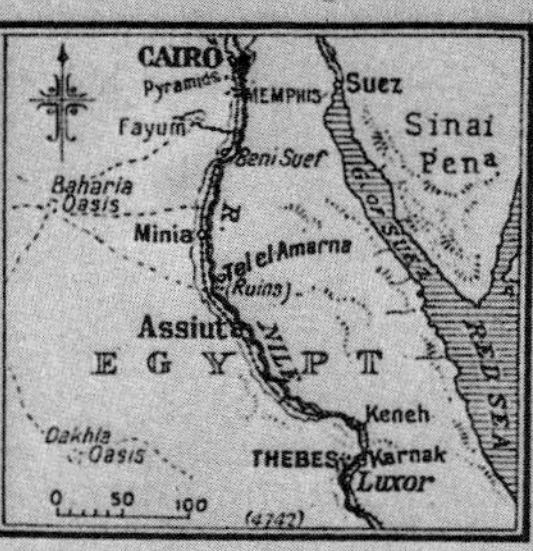

and Drah Abul Neggar were diligently explored. Seven years ago work was started in the Valley of the Kings, after other excavators had abandoned the Valley. Here, again, the excavators had little success. At times they almost despaired of finding anything, yet they did not lose heart.

The search was continued systematically, and at last the dogged perseverance of Mr. Carter, his thoroughness, above all his *flair*, were rewarded by the discovery, where the Royal necropolis of the Theban Empire was situated, directly below the tomb of Rameses VI., of what looked like a *cache*. Mr. Carter covered up the site, and telegraphed to Lord Carnarvon, who at once came out from England.

By this time news of the find had got about. The whole of Luxor, where every one down to the smallest urchin is an antiquity hunter, was agog. Great was the speculation in regard to the contents of the chamber. Would one of the missing kings be found inside? Was it the tomb of a queen or a high member of the Court of ancient Egypt (for the region is the burial place not only of many celebrated early Egyptian kings, but also of their wives and high officials)? Little, however, did Lord Carnarvon and Mr. Carter suspect the wonderful nature of the contents of the chambers—for there are more than one—as they stood outside. The sealed outer door was carefully opened; then a way was cleared down some sixteen steps along a passage of about 25ft. The door to the chambers was found to be sealed as the outer door had been, and, as on the outer door, there were traces of reclosing. With difficulty an entrance was effected, and when at last the excavators managed to squeeze their way in an extraordinary sight met their eyes, one that they could scarcely credit.

THE TREASURE WITHIN.

First they saw three magnificent State couches, all gilt, with exquisite carving and heads of Typhon, Hathor, and lion. On these rested beds, beautifully carved, gilt, inlaid with ivory and semi-precious stones, and also innumerable boxes of exquisite workmanship. One of these boxes was inlaid with ebony and ivory, with gilt inscriptions; another contained emblems of the underworld; on a third, which contained Royal robes, handsomely embroidered, precious stones, and golden sandals, were beautifully painted hunting scenes.

There was a stool of ebony inlaid with ivory, with the most delicately carved duck's feet; also a child's stool of fine workmanship. Beneath one of the couches was the State Throne of King Tutankhamen, probably one of the most beautiful objects of art ever discovered. There was also a heavily gilt chair, with portraits of the King and Queen, the whole encrusted with turquoise, cornelian, lapis, and other semi-precious stones.

Two life-sized bituminized statues of the King, with gold work holding a golden stick and mace, faced each other, the handsome features, the feet, and the hands delicately carved, with eyes of glass and head-dress richly studded with gems.

There were also four chariots, the sides of which were encrusted with semi-precious stones and rich gold decoration. These were dismantled, with a charioteer's apron of leopard's skin hanging over the seat.

Other noteworthy objects were Royal sticks, one of ebony with the head of an Asiatic as a handle in gold, another of the handsomest filigree work; also a stool for a throne with Asiatics carved on it, denoting that the King had placed his foot on the neck of the Asiatic prisoners taken in war. There were some quaint bronze-gilt musical instruments and a robing dummy for Royal wigs and robes.

There were also some exquisite alabaster vases with very intricate and unknown design, all of one piece, and some handsome blue Egyptian faience, and enormous quantities of provisions for the dead, comprising trussed duck, haunches of venison, &c., all packed in boxes according to the custom of the time. There were some remarkable wreaths, still looking evergreen, and one of the boxes contained rolls of *papyri*, which are expected to render a mass of information.

A further chamber revealed an indescribable state of confusion. Here furniture, gold beds, exquisite boxes, and alabaster vases similar to those found in the first chamber were piled high one on top of the other, so closely packed that it has been impossible to get inside yet.

Numbers of these treasures are in a fairly good state of preservation, but others are in a somewhat precarious condition. The greatest care is being taken in handling them, however, and there is every hope that under Mr. Carter's bitterly (and hypocritically) 'Tutankhamun Limited'. And the manager at Printing House Square, summoned to a meeting of the (then) Newspaper Proprietors' Association, defended the position of *The Times* vigorously. He said that he was 'rather surprised that it should have been suggested at this Council that private newspaper enterprise should be restricted – especially coming from the quarter it did'.

Most of the British press accepted the service offered by *The Times*. Those that did not rushed their own correspondents to Luxor. They included Arthur Weigall (himself an eminent Egyptologist) for the *Morning Post*, H. V. Morton (travel writer) for the *Daily Express* and Valentine Williams (creator of Clubfoot) for Reuters. *The Times* correspondent was Arthur Merton, who had broken the news of the discovery. In January 1923 he was joined by Sir Harry Perry Robinson from Printing House Square, whose duty was to run the news and picture syndication service.

Rivalry was bitter and jealous. Every day Merton's fellow journalists would meet in Weigall's room to discuss how to circumvent the exclusiveness of *The Times* agreement. It became nasty. One day Merton caught Mrs Valentine Williams peering surreptitiously over his shoulder while he was writing his message. He at once wrote on his pad: 'It is unladylike and rude to look over my shoulder'.

On the official opening day, 17 February 1923, Weigall and the Combine (as Perry Robinson described the opposition) were sitting on the parapet astride the tomb at 9 am, and did not leave until after 4.40 pm. Rumours ran through the press like scarabs through the funerary gear. At one point it was reported that eight mummies had been found. In spite of elaborate precautions, *The Times* was scooped by the opposition over the opening of the chamber.

The competition became even more acrimonious. Carter was a choleric man at the best of times. He became progressively angrier at being attacked in the press, at odds with the Egyptian authorities (incited, he said, by British journalists), and not receiving the support he felt entitled to from *The Times*. Merton was seconded to him as his publicity agent, becoming the sole channel between the archaeologist and the outside world. But matters did not improve.

The explosion came on 13 February 1924. Carter sent a notice to the Luxor hotels that he was closing the tomb to all visitors. The Egyptian authorities reacted quickly. When Carter went out to the tomb two days later, he found a guard of officials there with instructions to refuse him entry. *The Near East* periodical, commenting on the débâcle, said:

> Strained relations which may have been merely an incident were persistently made worse by the campaign waged by the British journalists and journals opposed to *The Times* publicity contract. The correspondents at Luxor have during two winters been deliberately trying to create around the question of the tomb the national prejudice. If all the facts of this campaign were made public they would throw much discredit on British journalism.

It is a measure of how far journalism has advanced, in one direction or another, that the conduct of rival hacks that seemed disreputable and reptilian in 1923 would seem perfectly normal to most journalists trying to get an exclusive today.

Howard Carter left Egypt, shortly after he had been locked out, in order to make a lecture tour in America. He returned to Cairo in December. A new Prime Minister was in office. His concern, and pressure from a number of people who had the interests of archaeology rather than newspaper scoops at heart, made it possible for the tomb to be reopened. On 10 October 1925 the last coffin in the sarcophagus was opened to reveal the mummy of Tutankhamun.

Below Native porters with guards removing the painted wooden manikin of Tutankhamun from the ante-chamber.

Below right The second stage in the demolition of the wall of the inner chamber. Howard Carter is seen inside and Mr Mace, of New York's Metropolitan Museum, is on the right. The shrine of Tutankhamun can just be seen, almost reaching to the roof.

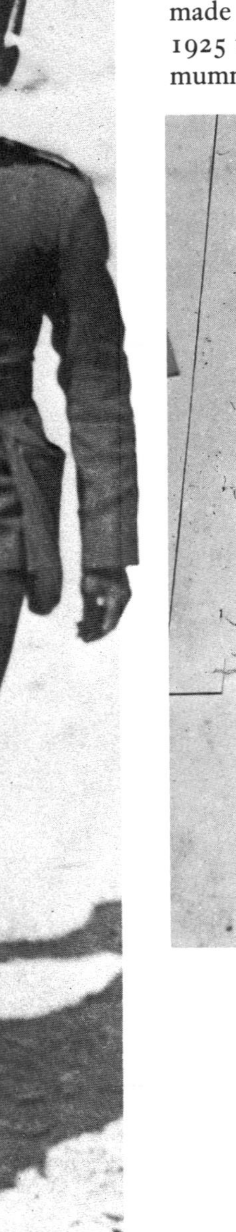

The General Strike: we thunder on

Until recent industrial troubles, *The Times* had never lost an issue. Through war and crisis, political upheaval and industrial difficulty, it was proud of its record of continuous publication since its foundation. It nearly lost an issue during the General Strike of 1926. But by remarkable efforts and luck it kept the thin black streak of printer's ink flowing.

The strike, which was in support of the miners, broke out a day before the agreed 'zero time', when printers at the *Daily Mail* took exception to an article that was to appear in the *Mail* on 3 May. The editor refused to alter the article. The printers walked out. And the General Strike was on.

The Government, unwisely in the view of *The Times*, made the stoppage at the *Mail* a *casus belli*, and refused last-minute negotiations with the strikers. On the following day Winston Churchill, Chancellor of the Exchequer, summoned the Newspaper Proprietors' Association to a meeting at the Treasury, and told them that it was essential that at least one newspaper was kept in publication during the strike. He offered them protection and moral support, but he had no skilled men to give them.

Major John Astor (later Lord Astor of Hever), chairman of The Times Publishing Company, went from his meeting with Churchill to address the Fathers of the Chapels (union branch leaders) at Printing House Square. His diary records that he told them:

'Situation beyond us. Part as friends and hope to meet as such before long. *The Times*, being above party or class, does not recognize the right of anyone to dictate policy or course of action and will carry on – so far and as long as possible – goodbye and good luck.' (Loud applause.) (Tongue in cheek?)

Right A food convoy passing the Mansion House, flanked by a company of special constables.

Below A London General Omnibus driven by a volunteer.

Far right The first issue of the BRITISH GAZETTE. Churchill, then Chancellor of the Exchequer, launched and edited this Government paper, which reached a circulation of 3 million within 8 days.

Monday 4 May was the last night on which *The Times* was published by normal means until the strike was ended. Emergency vans had been laid on in case the normal transport was strike-bound. But the edition was dispatched to the stations and wholesalers; the stand-by vans were used to take home the workers stranded at Printing House Square by the midnight stoppage of buses, trams and trains.

On Tuesday night, 5 May 1926, issue no. 44,263 was published (reproduced on the next page). Known familiarly by the staff as the 'Little Sister', it is the smallest issue of *The Times* ever published, and has become a collector's piece. It was produced by multigraph machines, which had been hurriedly installed in Printing House Square, on single sheets of paper, 13 × 8 inches, printed on both sides. Only 48,000 copies were run off, and they were sold out within hours in the London area. Later during the strike a further 10,000 were printed to complete sets and souvenirs for collectors.

The British Gazette

Published by His Majesty's Stationery Office.

No. 1. LONDON, WEDNESDAY, MAY 5, 1926. ONE PENNY.

FIRST DAY OF GREAT STRIKE

Not So Complete as Hoped by its Promoters

PREMIER'S AUDIENCE OF THE KING

Miners and the General Council Meet at House of Commons

FOOD SUPPLIES

No Hoarding: A Fair Share for Everybody

MILK DISTRIBUTION

Control of Supplies in the Metropolis

HOLD-UP OF THE NATION

Government and the Challenge

NO FLINCHING

The Constitution or a Soviet

COMMUNIST LEADER ARRESTED

Mr. Saklatvala, M.P., Charged at Bow Street

SEQUEL TO MAY DAY SPEECH

GOVERNMENT'S VIEW

THE "BRITISH GAZETTE" AND ITS OBJECTS

Reply to Strike Makers' Plan to Paralyse Public Opinion

REAL MEANING OF THE STRIKE

Conflict Between Trade Union Leaders and Parliament

By Wednesday night, by the recall of pensioners, the retraining of journalists, the retention of apprentices and the help of outsiders, *The Times* had got one rotary press running again. Thereafter it was able to publish a full-size, four-page paper throughout the General Strike. It was a remarkable achievement effected by a motley collection of people turning their hands to typesetting, foundry and press-machine work, working as readers and packers, and all the other mysteries of the inky trade. Working under the departmental managers were all types of people, from pensioners (the few skilled men) to company directors, including the directors of *The Times* itself, emulating John Walter II who had once set a late issue of *The Times* with his own hands. The machine room, under the direction of W. H. Tanner, a retired head of the department, was manned by a mixed company of chauffeurs, undergraduates, a sea captain and the sixteen-year-old son of the medical correspondent. As one account puts it: 'No wonder that Mr Tanner felt faint and had to have recourse time and again to restoratives'.

To keep *The Times* thundering the chairman recruited a number of his domestic staff from Hever Castle and his London house. The Establishment volunteered to help. Among MPs who turned out for the roughest and dirtiest jobs were Alfred Duff Cooper, Walter Elliot and W. S. Morrison (a future Speaker of the House of Commons). The arts were represented in the word-factory of Printing House Square by Lord David Cecil and A. P. Herbert. The ladies' list was headed by two duchesses, in charge of transport. Mistakes occurred. The sea captain, carried away by the rush of getting the edition out, one night poured a can of purple ink (intended for advertising posters) into the front-page ink-duct. There was no time to take it out, so a good

Page 102
The first strike issue of THE TIMES, also the smallest and briefest edition ever published. The genuine copies can be distinguished from the souvenir edition (produced later), because of the missing letter 'F' of 'Forecast' (column 1 top line).
5 MAY 1926

The Times

No. 44263 London Wednesday, May 5, 1926. Price 2d

WEATHER ORECAST. Wind N.E.; fair to dull; risk of rain N.Derbyshire and Monmouthshire.

THE GENERAL STRIKE.

A wide response was made yesterday throughout the country to the call of those Unions which had been ordered by the T.U.C. to bring out their members Railway workers stopped generally, though at Hull railway clerks are reported to have resumed duty, confining themselves to their ordinary work, and protested against the strike. Commercial road transport was only partially suspended. In London the tramways and L.G.O.C. services were stopped. The printing industry is practically at a standstill, but lithographers have not been withdrawn, and compositors in London have not received instructions to strike. Large numbers of building operatives, other than those working on housing, came out.

The situation in the engineering trades was confused; men in some districts stopped while in others they continued at work. There was no interference with new construction in the ship building yards, but in one or two districts some of the men engaged on repair work joined in the strike with the dockers.

Food - Supplies of milk and fish brought into Kings Cross, Euston and Paddington were successfully distributed from the Hyde Park Depot and stations. The Milk & Food Controller expects it will be possible to maintain a satisfactory supply of milk to hospitals, institutions, schools, hotels, restaurants and private consumers. Milk will be 8d. per gallon dearer wholesale and 2d. per quart retail today. Smithfield market has distributed 5,000 tons of meat since Monday

Mails - Efforts will be made to forward by means of road transport the mails already shown as due to be dispatched shortly from London. The position is uncertain and the facilities may have to be limited to mails for America, India and Africa.

At Bow Street Mr. Saklatvala, M.P., who was requred asa result of his Hyde Park speech on Saturday to give sureties to abstain rrom making violent and inflammatory speeches, was remanded for two days on bail.

Full tram and (or) bus services were running yesteday at Bristol, Lincoln, Southampton, Aldershot, Bournmouth and Isle-of-Wight, and partial services in Edinburgh, Glasgow, Liverpool, Leeds, Northampton, Cardiff, Portsmouth, Dover

Evening papers appeared at Bristol, Southampton, several Lancashire towns and Edinburgh, and typescript issues at Manchester, Birmingham and Aberdeen.

The Atlantic Fleet did not sail on its summer cruise at Portsmouth yesterday. The men went on shore duty.

Road and Rail Transport - There was no railway passenger transport in London yesterday except a few suburban trains. Every available form of transport was used. A few independent omnibuses were running, but by the evening the railway companies, except the District and Tubes. had an improvised service.

Among the railway services to-day will be 6.30 a.m. Manchester to Marylebone; 6.30 a.m. Marylebone to Manchester; 10. 10 a.m. Marylebone to Newcastle; 9 a.m. Norwich to London; 9 a. m. King's Cross to York; 3 p.m. King's Cross to Peterborough; 9 p.m. Peterborough to King's Cross. L.M.S. Electric trains will maintain a 40 minutes service. On all sections of the Metropolitan Railway except Moorgate to Finsbury Park, a good service will run to-day from 6.40 a.m.

The Underground hope to work a six minutes service on the Central London Line today from 8 a.m. to 8 p.m. between Wood Lane and Liverpool Street. The following stations only will be open:- Shepherds Bush, Lancaster Gate, Oxford Circus, Tottenham Court Road, Bank, Liverpool Street. A flat fare of 3d will be charged

The Prime Minister had an audience of the King yesteday morning.

There was no indication last night of any attempt to resume negotiations between the Prime Minister and the T.U.C.

The Government is printing an official newspaper, "The British Gazette" which will appear today, price 1d. It will be distributed throughout the London area. Volunteers for the London Underground Railways and for L. G. O. C. omnibuses should communicate with the Commercial Manager's Department. 55 Broadway, S.W.

The Prince of Wales returned to London from Biarritz last night travelling from Paris by air.

Below Office workers, and non-strikers waiting for transport home during the Strike.

Bottom Troops marching past the Mansion House, where the Lord Mayor took the salute, 19 May 1926.

many copies of the paper surprised the provinces by appearing with the front page printed in a rich sombre purple.

Throughout the strike the staff canteen was manned by volunteers. They sustained not just the amateur workers but also the pickets, who were given beer and sandwiches. The chairman noted that the pickets always touched their caps to him as he

passed their lines. In mid-week the chairman himself acted as cashier and paid out the wages.

The only rival publication to *The Times* during the General Strike was the *British Gazette*, the Government's official organ, masterminded by Winston Churchill and produced in the offices of the *Morning Post*. It was an unashamedly propagandist sheet. The greater part of its issues were thrust into houses or even left lying in bundles in the streets of London. As a newspaper it posed no threat to *The Times*. As a consumer of newsprint it was a real danger. On the second day of the strike *The Times* received a letter from the *British Gazette* commandeering on behalf of His Majesty's Government the whole of the newsprint of a certain size available to *The Times*. On 9 May formal notice was received from the Stationery Office commandeering newsprint. *The Times* was deprived of one quarter of its essential hoard of paper.

The strike continued until 17 May. Throughout it *The Times* maintained publication and never lost an issue. Circulation continually rose, and by the last day 405,000 copies were being printed. It received a compliment for its tenacity from an unexpected source. The *New Statesman* wrote:

> It was scandalous that *The Times* should have been deprived of its paper supplies in order to enable Mr Churchill to poison public opinion. We can only offer our gratitude and our congratulations to *The Times* for the struggle which it made in face of this robbery, and for the way in which it selected the comparatively small amount of news it was able to print, and maintained the best tradition of truthfulness and impartiality.

The Abdication crisis: spokesman or manipulator?

The Abdication Crisis of 1936 shook the British constitution. There have been persistent rumours ever since that *The Times* not only reported the news and commented on it, but was also secretly engaged in manipulating events behind the throne.

The chief rumour-monger was that evil imp, Lord Beaverbrook. In 1952, reviewing the latest volume of *The History of The Times* on the BBC, Beaverbrook alleged that Geoffrey Dawson, the editor of *The Times*,

> . . . first, was the most important factor – with the sole exception of the Prime Minister, Stanley Baldwin – in compelling the King to abdicate; second, Dawson did it by methods that many would condemn; and third, that he pursued his campaign against the King's marriage with a vigour that seemed more like venom.

Let us examine the evidence, rather than rumour.

Dawson was editor of *The Times* from 1912 to 1919, and again from 1923 to 1941. He was an Establishment figure: Eton, and Magdalen and All Souls, Oxford. His habit of mixing with the heart of the political and social worlds of his day has been compared to Delane's 'Swelling' activities (see p. 40). But Delane was never committed in a party political way to the extent that Dawson was.

The Prince of Wales met Wallis Simpson, the American socialite, in 1931. Gradually she and her husband became part of the Prince's social set. By 1934 careful readers of the Court Page of *The Times*, that coded noticeboard for the courtier classes, had noticed that Mrs Simpson had started to attend royal functions unaccompanied by her husband. The Prince's attentions towards her became a matter for gossip in high society.

The press was well aware of the situation, but found no cause to comment. Gossip columns were more respectful and less vicious in those days. In January 1936 George V died. Shortly after the accession of Edward VIII, Baldwin was already doubting whether the new King 'would stay the course'.

The crisis came with the news that Mrs Simpson was going to obtain a divorce from her husband. The case was down to be heard at Ipswich on 27 October 1936. Until then there had not been a peep in the British press about the affair. The Continental and American press had exercised no such discretion – the Americans in particular ran the scandal for all it was worth. William Randolph Hearst's New York *Journal* ran an article asserting that the King would marry Mrs Simpson eight months after the divorce.

Right The uncrowned King Edward VIII making his abdication speech.

Below Evening newspaper placards announced the abdication.

Newsagents in Britain refused to distribute American rags carrying such stories. But subscribers by mail-order received them, and the scandal was spreading. By now Dawson was receiving sacks of mail on the subject, particularly from the United States. A British subject living in America wrote saying that British prestige was suffering damage from the stories being published in the American press. He signed himself '*Britannicus in Partibus Infidelium*'. Dawson was so impressed that he gave copies of the letter to the King's Private Secretary and the Prime Minister. It has been alleged that Dawson concocted the letter himself. Not true. The original letter is in the archives at *The Times*.

On the curious incident of the mass silence of the British press, Dawson commented: 'There was in fact neither censorship nor collusion from first to last. The Prime Minister probably saw a great deal more of me at this time than he did of any other journalist: but that was due rather to an old friendship.' He said that 'in three or four conversations, of a purely personal character' with H. A. Gwynne of the *Morning Post* and Lord Camrose, proprietor of *The Daily Telegraph*, they had all agreed to report Mrs Simpson's divorce without comment. It was self-restraint as heroic as ordering bread and water in Maxim's. Beaverbrook persuaded the popular press to keep their mouths shut. The King telephoned Beaverbrook and asked him to help 'in suppressing all advance news of the Simpson divorce, and in limiting publicity after the event'.

After the divorce, Dawson spoke to Baldwin every day. In his diary Dawson wrote that Baldwin did not want 'any press comment at this moment which might weaken his position'.

Dawson may have been an élitist. But he had enough Grub Street instincts to be nervous of being scooped by the opposition newspapers with such a sensational story. He signalled his anxiety in two coded leaders. The first criticized the appointment of a new Governor General to South Africa, saying, 'The position of the King's deputy no less than that of the King himself must be kept high above public reproach or ridicule'. The second said: 'The House of Commons may well prove itself what the country has required: namely a Council of State which is able to demonstrate its solid strength in any crisis'. Beaverbrook described these leaders as 'intimidation in code': hyperbole was always the element in which Beaverbrook and his newspapers lived.

You cannot keep the dogs of Fleet Street chained for ever when a juicy hare is running away from them. The crisis broke. At a conference in Yorkshire the Bishop of Bradford delivered a speech, expressing his 'hope that the King was aware of his need for God's grace at his Coronation'. On the following day, 2 December, the *Yorkshire Post* broke the self-imposed embargo by

The unprecedented announcement of King Edward VIII's abdication. The first hint of what was afoot appeared in an insignificant paragraph in THE TIMES of 28 October that year, entitled 'Undefended Divorce Suit', which blandly recorded Wallis Simpson's divorce, forbearing comment.
11 DECEMBER 1936

THE KING ABDICATES

DUKE OF YORK ASCENDS THE THRONE

DECISION "FINAL AND IRREVOCABLE"

MR. BALDWIN'S NARRATIVE OF HIS EFFORTS

SUCCESSION BILL TO PASS TO-DAY

King Edward VIII announced his abdication to both Houses of Parliament yesterday.

At the end of questions, Mr. Baldwin rose from the Treasury Bench and walked to the Bar of the House. Turning and facing the Speaker, he announced, amid dead silence :—
" A message from his Majesty the King, signed by his Majesty's own hand."

After bowing to the Chair, he advanced and handed the message to the Speaker, who read it, as follows :—

After long and anxious consideration, I have determined to renounce the Throne to which I succeeded on the death of My father, and I am now communicating this, My final and irrevocable decision. Realizing as I do the gravity of this step, I can only hope that I shall have the understanding of My peoples in the decision I have taken and the reasons which have led Me to take it. I will not enter now into My private feelings, but I would beg that it should be remembered that the burden which constantly rests upon the shoulders of a Sovereign is so heavy that it can only be borne in circumstances different from those in which I now find Myself. I conceive that I am not overlooking the duty that rests on Me to place in the forefront the public interest, when I declare that I am conscious that I can no longer discharge this heavy task with efficiency or with satisfaction to Myself.

I have accordingly this morning executed an Instrument of Abdication in the terms following :—

> **" I, Edward VIII, of Great Britain, Ireland, and the British Dominions beyond the Seas, King, Emperor of India, do hereby declare My irrevocable determination to renounce the Throne for Myself and for My descendants, and My desire that effect should be given to this Instrument of Abdication immediately.**
>
> **In token whereof I have hereunto set My hand this tenth day of December, nineteen hundred and thirty-six, in the presence of the witnesses whose signatures are subscribed.**
>
> **(Signed) EDWARD R.I."**

My execution of this Instrument has been witnessed by My three brothers, Their Royal Highnesses the Duke of York, the Duke of Gloucester and the Duke of Kent.

I deeply appreciate the spirit which has actuated the appeals which have been made to Me to take a different decision, and I have, before reaching My final determination, most fully pondered over them. But My mind is made up. Moreover, further delay cannot but be most injurious to the peoples whom I have tried to serve as Prince of Wales and as King and whose future happiness and prosperity are the constant wish of My heart.

I take My leave of them in the confident hope that the course which I have thought it right to follow is that which is best for the stability of the Throne and Empire and the happiness of My peoples. I am deeply sensible of the consideration which they have always extended to Me both before and after My accession to the Throne and which I know they will extend in full measure to My successor.

I am most anxious that there should be no delay of any kind in giving effect to the Instrument which I have executed and that all necessary steps should be taken immediately to secure that My lawful successor, My brother, His Royal Highness the Duke of York, should ascend the Throne.

EDWARD R.I.

HISTORIC DAY IN PARLIAMENT

DIGNITY AND RELIEF

WESTMINSTER, THURSDAY

"Prayers are over." Never have the familiar words which precede the opening of business in the House of Commons sounded with more significance than to-day, when members assembled to hear that hopes and prayers for some decision other than that so strongly rumoured yesterday were doomed to disappointment. Relief that suspense was over was, however, clearly the universal sentiment, and though the House showed its views by its silences as well as by its applause there was strict observance of that dignity for which MR. BALDWIN—never so truly the representative of a united Parliament as on this day—made such an impressive plea.

The scene in the House itself reflected the fact that the occasion was historic. Every seat was filled. Members squatted on the steps of the gangways, stood in a serried crowd behind the Bar, and thronged the side galleries three deep. There was even a small overflow upon the steps of the Speaker's Chair. The Peers' Gallery was filled to overflowing, though all the more prominent peers preferred to attend the proceedings in their own House. In the Distinguished Strangers' Gallery was a representative assembly of diplomats, including the French and Belgian Ambassadors; and no member of the public fortunate enough to obtain a ticket had failed to use it.

THE KING'S MESSAGE

There was no attempt to curtail ordinary questions, and members even showed their state of tension by an unusual flood of supplementaries. But at 3.42 MR. BALDWIN, who had entered a few minutes earlier amid a general cheer, rose and strode down the House to the Bar. He turned about, and stood for a moment poised, with the fateful document clasped in his right hand. Raising it slightly, he declared in solemn and ringing tones, "A message from his Majesty the King. Signed with his own hand." A bow to the SPEAKER, and the PRIME MINISTER advanced to the table, passed to the left of it, and handed the paper to the SPEAKER, who rose to receive it. Members wearing hats uncovered their heads in sign of respect, and the SPEAKER, not without some traces of emotion, read the KING'S message renouncing his Throne.

It was received in dead silence, which testified better than movement or sound to approval of the inevitable. But when MR. BALDWIN rose in his place to move that the message be considered, the House gave him thanks in a deep cheer. His speech, by common consent a masterly and generous performance, won its triumph by its supreme simplicity. This was not thinking aloud, in spite of its improvisations, but the reflection of prolonged and unselfish effort.

Never, he said, amid loud assent, had a Prime Minister had to discharge so difficult and repugnant a task, and he proposed to discharge it with a plain statement of facts, helped by the permission of the King to reveal all the pertinent points in their conversations.

He recalled, at the very outset, his friendship with the King dating back to the happier years when the latter was Prince of Wales, and prefaced the whole story of these dark days with the unequivocal, and to him comforting, fact that this friendship remained unimpaired. The most telling proof of this was a later revelation of the King's repeated assertion, "We must settle this matter together. I will not have anybody interfering."

Then came the story. It began in mid-October, when Mr. Baldwin returned to "half-time" work after his long holiday. He found at once two disquieting things—a flood of correspondence from British subjects all over the world expressing uneasiness at the tales in the American Press, and the knowledge that Mrs. Simpson's divorce suit was imminent.

DUTY TO WARN THE KING

He decided that it was a duty, which could only fall on the Prime Minister, to warn the King as a counsellor and friend. Therefore on Sunday, October 18, without consulting any colleagues (an omission for which they had forgiven him) he asked for an interview—the first and only time when the initiative had come from him. The meeting took place on October 20 at Fort Belvedere; and MR. BALDWIN prefaced his account of it by an illuminating revelation of the consistent attitude of the King and of himself. He himself had taken the line that a servant was useless unless completely frank; and the King had never taken offence at anything thus frankly said.

On October 20, therefore, MR. BALDWIN told the King of the prevalent gossip, reminded him that, though the Crown had lost many prerogatives, the importance of preserving its integrity was greater than ever before, and observed that the respect for the Crown built up during three generations might much more swiftly be destroyed. He expressed the desire that these criticisms should have no cause to continue, recalled the bright hopes he had entertained of the new reign, and offered to help as a friend. He also pointed out the danger of the impending divorce case. He left the King to consider these observations, reported them to four of his senior colleagues, and felt relieved that the ice had been broken.

"GRIEVOUS NEWS"

A DECLARATION BY THE KING

Then came the second critical date—Monday, November 16. On that date, at an interview at Buckingham Palace, he spoke about marriage to the King for about 20 minutes. The need arose from the fact that in the interval a decree *nisi* had been granted to Mrs. Simpson.

He told the King that marriage with her could not meet with public approval, that the King's wife must be Queen, and therefore in his choice the voice of the people must be heard. The King said—on this November 16—"I am going to marry Mrs. Simpson, and I am prepared to go." Mr. Baldwin replied that this was grievous news, and that he must reserve comment. That same night the King told Queen Mary, and he told his brothers during the next two days.

The third date was November 25. Mr. Baldwin had had put before him the compromise suggestion of a morganatic marriage, and on this date the King asked him what he thought about it. He replied that in his view Parliament would never pass the necessary Bill; and the House in retrospect endorsed this view with an assenting cheer. But the King wanted the matter tested, and, though warned that it meant consultation with the full Cabinet and the Dominion Prime Ministers, expressed the desire that this should be done.

It was therefore done, and the results reported to the King on December 2. The King did not seem surprised at this, the only formal advice ever tendered to him, and, like a great gentleman, never referred to it again. At this interview MR. BALDWIN told him plainly what the alternatives appeared to be—namely, either to abandon his project or to abandon his Throne in the hope of later contracting his marriage, if it were possible.

FOUR CONSIDERATIONS

The next week, up to yesterday, was taken up by the struggle within the King himself. Laying stress on every favourable factor, MR. BALDWIN reminded the House that the King was no longer a boy, but a mature man, who had held fast to four considerations:—

(1) If he went, he would go with dignity.
(2) He would cause the least possible disturbance to his Ministers and his people.
(3) He would consider his brother in every possible way.
(4) He refused to countenance any conflict, and the idea of a King's Party was abhorrent.

In proof of this MR. BALDWIN read a rather pathetic note in pencil from the King himself, saying how dear had been his relations with his brother and how he knew what support and loyalty would be transferred to the latter.

Again MR. BALDWIN gave the King full credit for frankness when he might easily have concealed the whole matter for months. We must accept his view that he could not continue without the woman of his choice at his side. Indeed, MR. BALDWIN added, he had never wavered in his intention, and the delay in his formal decision was only because he thought he must weigh the representations made to him.

A whole host of figments disappeared when MR. BALDWIN described his own efforts to prevent this decision, and took comfort in the assurance from those in touch with the King that nothing had been left undone to prevent it. "Where I failed," said the PRIME MINISTER, "nobody could have succeeded; and those who know the King know what that means."

CABINET'S FINAL PLEA

So MR. BALDWIN came to the last date in the story—yesterday, December 9. In the morning the Cabinet received the King's formal decision. They replied, in a minute which MR. BALDWIN read out, expressing their profound regret and urging that he should change his mind even now. All was in vain, and the King refused. "None of us," said MR. BALDWIN, "will want to judge him. We are not judges."

The duty of Parliament was to close the ranks and do what he wished. Therefore he (MR. BALDWIN) appealed for dignity and for swift action upon the Bill to be passed to-morrow. He appealed for restraint and for a special thought for the "revered and beloved" Queen Mary. He appealed for concentration upon preserving the integrity of the Monarchy and for a rally of the nation behind the new King.

In a speech where every sentence told it is difficult to single out the most telling sentences; but the House showed its deep gratitude to the Prime Minister in every way open to an audience. MR. ATTLEE, who was cheered almost as loudly for his restraint and statesmanship during a trying time, suggested a suspension of the sitting, which the SPEAKER accepted without putting any question.

VIEWS OF THE HOUSE

LABOUR SUPPORT FOR NEW MONARCH

At 6 o'clock the House reassembled and heard with the keenest appreciation MR. ATTLEE'S considered comments. The LEADER of the OPPOSITION paid a warm tribute to King Edward VIII, and gave full weight to the view that the poor had lost a good friend. He wished the KING peace and happiness; but he also promised the new KING every possible help in a difficult task. The House broke into prolonged cheering, which was renewed for SIR ARCHIBALD SINCLAIR, who handsomely acknowledged that the idea of a morganatic marriage had been fantastic. He, like MR. ATTLEE, paid tribute to the way Mr. Baldwin had borne an unprecedented responsibility; he offered special sympathy to Queen Mary, and he expressed high hopes of the new KING and his Consort.

MR. CHURCHILL then, with some traces of nervousness, conciliated a formerly hostile House. He ruled out recrimination. He noted that there had never been any constitutional issue, and that the KING, by refusing to countenance any, had deserved well of his people. He justified his own plea for delay by pointing out that it had proved the decision to be free and uninfluenced. His own actions, Mr. CHURCHILL explained, had been due to affectionate loyalty to a friend of 25 years' standing from one who had stood by the side of Prince Edward when proclaimed Prince of Wales. The House clearly accepted what was a cross between an explanation and an apology.

After these responsible utterances, there was a little of the foam and bubble of irresponsibility. Mr. MAXTON announced that he had become a Republican. Mr. GALLACHER asserted that Mrs. Simpson's social set had been all too friendly with a foreign Power, and Mr. BUCHANAN declaimed against cant. But the debate was fittingly closed by the blind ex-soldier, SIR IAN FRASER, who, with sorrow for a lost comrade, promised the unbounded loyalty of ex-Service men to the new King.

The PRIME MINISTER, from whose shoulders many cares seemed to have fallen, then asked and obtained leave to bring in the Abdication Bill, and with a murmur of relief for a testing day well passed, the House adjourned.

IN THE LORDS

The scene in the House of Lords also reflected the character of the occasion. There was not a vacant seat, except on the Opposition benches, and the steps of the Throne were thronged with Privy Councillors and others whose privilege it is to attend there. The King's message was read by LORD HALIFAX, and the feature of the whole proceedings was the dead silence with which every reference to the King was received.

LORD HALIFAX'S speech reported only the final stages of the crisis and announced the assent of the Dominions to the proposed legislation. This assent was complete, except with regard to the Irish Free State, but a reassuring message had been received from Mr. de Valera saying that their Parliament would be summoned, if possible to-morrow, to make provision for the situation.

LORD SNELL and LORD CREWE both won general applause for their comments. Thus ended a day which reflected supreme credit on both Houses of Parliament and the democratic institutions for which they stand.

THE EMPIRE'S SORROW AND FAITH

WELCOME FOR THE NEW KING

The news of King Edward's decision to abdicate has been received in the Dominions with the deepest sorrow. In Canada, Australia, and New Zealand the Prime Ministers have made statements expressing the public emotion, and in all cities the people had shown that they held last-minute hopes that the King would take another decision.

"The news will be heard with profound regret by the people of Canada," said Mr. Mackenzie King in Ottawa. "With deepest sorrow in our hearts we bid Edward VIII farewell," declared Mr. Lyons in Canberra. "When he became King," Mr. Lyons also said, "we rejoiced that the one we knew so well, the one whose human qualities we admired so greatly, was the Prince who was to follow a Sovereign who had raised kingship to the highest pinnacle." Mr. Savage, the New Zealand Prime Minister, in a statement issued in Wellington, declared, "This is one of the saddest days in the history of the British people."

A CRISIS ENDED

In such terms do the Dominion spokesmen bid farewell to King Edward. At the same time other emotions are expressed. There is widespread feeling that the crisis which has gripped the British Commonwealth has ended. In India—where throughout the crisis the Press has made comments with dignity and restraint—the decision is appreciated as ending a crisis fraught with even greater dangers than have been exposed. In South Africa the decision is welcomed as being "the only possible course."

There is also praise for the action of Mr. Baldwin and for the attitude of the Parliament of Westminster—"worthy of the best traditions in its history."

Finally, there is a whole-hearted welcome for the new King and Queen. Mr. Savage's words again may be taken as typical: "The people of New Zealand, . . will honour and serve the King with all their traditional affection and sincerity." Or, among the newspapers, the Bloemfontein *Friend* may be quoted: "The Monarchy has gone through a purifying fire, and comes out of it stronger than before."

Messages from our Correspondents describing the reception of the news in the Empire appear on page 21. Foreign comment on page 15

TO-DAY'S BILL

SUCCESSION TO THE THRONE

DOMINION ASSENT

From Our Parliamentary Correspondent

Directly after the Prime Minister had presented His Majesty's Declaration of Abdication Bill to the House of Commons last night the text of it was available to members in the Vote Office and there was a rush to obtain copies.

The Bill is described as a measure "to give effect to His Majesty's declaration of abdication; and for purposes connected therewith," and the names of the following Ministers appear on the back of it:—The Prime Minister, Mr. Ramsay MacDonald, Mr. Chamberlain, Sir John Simon, Mr. Malcolm MacDonald, Mr. Elliot, Mr. Ormsby-Gore, Sir Donald Somervell, and Mr. R. A. Butler.

OPERATIVE CLAUSE

The Bill consists of two clauses, the first of which is the operative clause. It is in the following terms:—

WHEREAS His Majesty by His Royal Message of the tenth day of December in this present year has been pleased to declare that He is irrevocably determined to renounce the Throne for Himself and His descendants, and has for that purpose executed the Instrument of Abdication set out in the Schedule to this Act, and has signified His desire that effect thereto should be given immediately:

And whereas, following upon the communication to His Dominions of His Majesty's said declaration and desire, the Dominion of Canada pursuant to the provisions of section four of the Statute of Westminster, 1931, has requested and consented to the enactment of this Act, and the Commonwealth of Australia, the Dominion of New Zealand, and the Union of South Africa have assented thereto:

Be it therefore enacted by the King's most Excellent Majesty, by and with the advice and consent of the Lords Spiritual and Temporal, and Commons, in this present Parliament assembled, and by the authority of the same, as follows:—

1.—(1) Immediately upon the Royal Assent being signified to this Act the Instrument of Abdication executed by His present Majesty on the tenth day of December, nineteen hundred and thirty-six, set out in the Schedule to this Act, shall have effect, and thereupon His Majesty shall cease to be King and there shall be a demise of the Crown, and accordingly the member of the Royal Family then next in succession to the Throne shall succeed thereto and to all the rights, privileges, and dignities thereunto belonging.

(2) His Majesty, His issue, if any, and the descendants of that issue, shall not after His Majesty's abdication have any right, title, or interest in or to the succession to the Throne, and section one of the Act of Settlement shall be construed accordingly.

(3) The Royal Marriages Act, 1772, shall not apply to His Majesty after His abdication nor to the issue, if any, of His Majesty or the descendants of that issue.

CANADA'S REQUEST

The second clause declares that "this Act may be cited as His Majesty's Declaration of Abdication Act 1936."

A schedule to the Bill incorporates the terms of the Instrument of Abdication which Mr. Baldwin communicated to the House of Commons and which are set out on this page.

The Bill was eagerly studied by members of the House of Commons, who realized that at short notice the Government had been called on to frame a piece of legislation which has no parallel in modern political history. Special attention was paid to the reference to the Statute of Westminster and to the fact that under Section Four of its provisions the Dominion of Canada had requested and consented to the enactment of the Bill, and that the Commonwealth of Australia, the Dominion of New Zealand, and the Union of South Africa had assented to it. Section Four of the Statute of Westminster declares that:—

No Act of Parliament of the United Kingdom passed after the commencement of this Act shall extend or be deemed to extend to a Dominion as part of the law of that Dominion unless it is expressly declared in that Act that that Dominion has requested, and consented, to the enactment thereof.

The Statute of Westminster has been ratified by Canada, South Africa, and the Irish Free State, but not by Australia and New Zealand. In the opinion of the Government no further legislation will be necessary in Canada, but South Africa may require complementary legislation. It was hoped last night that before the Bill is passed through all its stages to-day information may be available as to the attitude of the Government of the Irish Free State.

ALL STAGES TO-DAY

The Bill deals solely with matters arising directly out of the Declaration of Abdication, and for the present the more difficult question of the revision of the Civil List and the financial support, if any, which is to be given to the outgoing Monarch is not touched upon. The broad effect of the Bill is to remove King Edward and his heirs, if any, from the succession to the Throne; to declare that, directly the Bill receives the Royal Assent, the member of the Royal Family next in succession to the Throne (the Duke of York) shall succeed thereto, and that the Royal Marriages Act, which empowers the Monarch to approve or disapprove the intended marriage of any member of the Royal Family shall not apply to King Edward after his abdication, nor to the issue, if any, of his Majesty or the descendants of that issue.

There is little doubt that both Houses of Parliament will be prepared to pass the Bill through all its stages to-day, for there is a general desire to respect the wish of the King that there should be no delay of any kind in giving effect to the Instrument of Abdication. One effect of the declaration in the Bill that when the Instrument takes effect "there shall be a demise of the Crown" is that all appointments made by King Edward will continue to have effect. Had this provision not been made there would necessarily have been some confusion and uncertainty.

AN I.L.P. AMENDMENT

The speeches of Mr. Maxton and Mr. Buchanan showed that the four I.L.P. members would oppose the Abdication Bill. Last night Mr. Maxton gave notice of the following amendment to the second reading:—

This House declines to give a second reading to a Bill which has been necessitated by circumstances which show already the danger to this country and to the British Commonwealth of Nations inherent in an hereditary Monarchy at a time when the peace and prosperity of the people require a more stable and efficient form of Government of a Republican kind in closer contact with and more responsive to the will of the mass of the people, and which fails to give effect to the principle of popular election.

KING EDWARD TO BROADCAST

A MESSAGE TO-NIGHT

It was announced at the end of the 9 o'clock news bulletin last night that the B.B.C. had been informed that it was King Edward's desire, immediately he has ceased to be King, to broadcast. The broadcast will be made by him this evening in the character of a private person owing allegiance to the new King.

Arrangements have been made for the King's message to be broadcast to every part of the world. It was not possible last night to state the exact hour at which the broadcast will take place, but it was hoped that, if the Abdication Act had been passed in time, the King would speak this evening at 10 o'clock. Should there be any alteration in these arrangements it will be announced from time to time to-day. After the King has spoken all B.B.C. transmitters will close down.

The B.B.C. announces that all its programmes for to-day, to-morrow, and Sunday are subject to alterations, which will be notified immediately details of changes become available. The scheduled programme for to-day has been revised.

A religious service, to be addressed by the Archbishop of Canterbury, will be broadcast from the concert hall at the B.B.C. on Sunday at 8 p.m.

THE NEWS FOR LISTENERS

Listeners to the wireless programmes heard without delay the news of the King's abdication. They had been warned at midday to expect an announcement two or three hours later. At 4 o'clock the broadcast music was cut off and the announcer said:—

"This is London. A quarter of an hour ago the Prime Minister came to the Bar of the House and handed to the Speaker a message from his Majesty the King."

The text of the King's message was read by the announcer. At 4.45 it was repeated, and a verbatim report of a large part of the Prime Minister's speech was read. During the rest of the day a single programme contained frequent news bulletins.

THE INSTRUMENT OF ABDICATION

SIGNATURE AT FORT BELVEDERE

The Instrument of Abdication was signed yesterday morning at Fort Belvedere by King Edward, with his three brothers as witnesses.

Throughout the day the neighbourhood was strangely deserted, no anxious crowds waiting round the gates. The King and his three brothers met just before 10 o'clock, the three Royal Dukes reaching the house within a few minutes of each other. About this time it was noticed that the standard of the Duchy of Cornwall, which had hitherto flown over the Fort when the King was in residence, was no longer to be seen.

Sir John Simon and Mr. Walter Monckton, K.C., Attorney-General to the Duchy of Cornwall, arrived at 12.55 p.m., and left again 50 minutes later.

Even when the news that the King had determined on abdication became known there was no gathering of people outside the King's house. Lord Louis Mountbatten was seen to leave, driving his own car. The Duke of York and the Duke of Gloucester left together, driving in the direction of Windsor. The Duke of Kent stayed till after 6 o'clock. After darkness fell Fort Belvedere was still deserted.

LONDON'S WELCOME TO THE DUKE

ENTHUSIASTIC CHEERS LAST NIGHT

The Duke of York returned to Fort Belvedere last night and dined with King Edward. He left the Royal Lodge, Windsor, by car at 6 o'clock, returning just after 9. About 11 he left the Royal Lodge again after spending some time with Lord Wigram, Deputy Governor of Windsor Castle.

Shortly after 11.30 his car was seen approaching his house in Piccadilly and the crowd, which had increased greatly when the theatres emptied, broke into remarkable scenes of enthusiasm. The car was surrounded by a throng of people, and for some time it was impossible for it to make any progress.

After the car had entered the yard outside 145, Piccadilly and the Duke was within the house, the crowd, by this time of tremendous size, began singing the National Anthem and "For he's a Jolly Good Fellow." Afterwards people called out "We want the King." Traffic was completely held up for some time. People in cars climbed on to the roofs of them, and from a number of omnibuses which had been caught in the stream of traffic people joined in calling out "We want the King."

KING EDWARD'S FUTURE

UNKNOWN DESTINATION

It is understood that King Edward will leave the country shortly after he has completed his abdication by giving his assent to the Bill which Parliament is to pass to-day. His signature of this measure at Fort Belvedere to-night will be his last act as King.

Late last night it was stated with authority that King Edward does not intend to go to Cannes, but his actual destination will be kept a close secret until he has left.

NO EDWARD VIII COINS

No King Edward VIII coinage will ever be in circulation. It had been expected that a proclamation, permitting the Mint to place the new coinage in circulation, would be issued before the end of the year, and that about two months later the coins would be available.

SCENES IN THE STREETS

QUIET CROWDS

NEWS RECEIVED WITH CALMNESS

The news of the abdication was received quietly in the streets of London, with no demonstrations or signs of marked popular feeling. There were assemblages throughout the day, ranging from fairly large crowds to small groups, outside all the buildings associated with the day's happenings—No. 10, the Houses of Parliament, and the Royal residences—but they were composed of people of the type which always gathers on the outskirts of great events. They stood stolidly waiting, or moved quietly if required, and the afternoon's tidings left them apparently undisturbed. Last night the crowds outside Buckingham Palace and the Duke of York's house and near Downing Street increased in size and were more demonstrative.

Early in the morning onlookers began to arrive in Downing Street, and by 10.30 there were some 200 of them. As the numbers increased the police moved them into Whitehall.

At 10.30 Sir John Simon went into No. 10, and at 10.50 Mr. Malcolm MacDonald, Secretary for the Dominions, followed. At 11.30 Mr. Walter Monckton, K.C., Attorney-General to the Duchy of Cornwall, and Sir Edward Peacock, Receiver-General to the Duchy, arrived.

IN PARLIAMENT SQUARE

As the time drew nearer for the Houses of Parliament to meet, another and larger crowd filtered into Parliament Square, pressing against the railings of Palace Yard and filing round the square under a dun sky, while the bells were pealed for a wedding at St. Margaret's.

When Mr. Baldwin left for the House he was greeted with loud cheers and an insignificant little burst of booing. Palace Yard was crowded with cars, and all the precincts of the House were packed with people. But Westminster Hall was empty, except for an occasional figure hurrying through.

There was no change in the demeanour of the crowds after the decision to abdicate became known, and no emotion was perceptible that could with any justice be described as a corporate reaction. Steadily moved on by the mounted police and the microphone, they filed along like somnambulists, staring up at the House. Some were indifferent and cheerful, others exchanged rumours. As dusk and the evening papers arrived the crowd thinned.

OUTSIDE THE PALACE

WAITING IN SILENCE

From morning to night small crowds lingered outside Buckingham Palace and Marlborough House. During the hours before the news of the abdication became known the gatherings were of people, mostly women, who collected to see possible movements of members of the Royal family, or of those who were passing between London and Fort Belvedere.

The largest assembly was that which stood until dusk against the railings of Buckingham Palace and afterwards was transferred to the steps of the Queen Victoria Memorial, and this was a silent grouping which did little but stare at a

Continued on page 18, column 4

ENTERTAINMENTS INDEX

(For details see page 14)

OPERA AND BALLET

Sadler's Wells	BALLET	8.30

THEATRES

Aldwych	AFTER OCTOBER	8.30
Ambassadors	THE TWO BOUQUETS	2.30 & 8.30
Apollo	HOUSEMASTER	8.30
Cambridge	NIGHT MUST FALL	8.30
Coliseum	THE DESERT SONG	8.15
Comedy	TO AND FRO	2.30 & 8.30
Criterion	FRENCH WITHOUT TEARS	8.40
Drury Lane	CARELESS RAPTURE	2
Duchess	MURDER IN THE CATHEDRAL	8.30
Embassy	ART AND CRAFT	8.15
Gaiety	SWING ALONG	8.15
Garrick	STORM IN A TEACUP	8.30
Globe	CALL IT A DAY	8.15
Haymarket	THE AMAZING DR. CLITTERHOUSE	8.30
Lyric	CHARLES THE KING	8.40
Mercury	PANIC	8.30
New	PARNELL	8.30
Old Vic	WITCH OF EDMONTON	8
Palace	THIS'LL MAKE YOU WHISTLE	8.15
Phoenix	HELL-FOR-LEATHER!	8.30
Playhouse	WHITEOAKS	8.30
Princes	THE FROG	8.15
Queen's	JANE EYRE	8.30
Royalty	MARIGOLD	8.30
St. James's	O MISTRESS MINE	8.30
St. Martin's	TILL THE COWS COME HOME	2.30 & 8.30
Saville	OVER SHE GOES	8.15
Savoy	YOUNG MADAME CONTI	8.30
Shaftesbury	LAUGHTER IN COURT	8.45
Strand	AREN'T MEN BEASTS!	8.30
Westminster	WASTE	8.30
Whitehall	ANTHONY AND ANNA	8.30
Wyndham's	MADEMOISELLE	8.30

CONCERTS

Grotrian Hall	MISS ISOBEL AND MR. G. FORREST NEILLANDS	8.15
Queen's Hall	LONDON SYMPHONY ORCHESTRA	8.15
Wigmore Hall	MR. NORMAN TUCKER	8.30

VARIETIES

Palladium	O-KAY FOR SOUND	6.20 & 9
Prince of Wales	ENCORE LES DAMES	2 to 11.30
Victoria Palace	LAUGHTER OVER LONDON	6.20 & 9
Windmill	REVUDEVILLE No. 85	1.30 to 11.30

EXHIBITIONS, &c.

Building Centre		10 to 6
Madame Tussaud's		10 to 10
Royal Agricultural Hall	SMITHFIELD CLUB CATTLE SHOW	9 to 8
Zoological Gardens		9 to sunset

PICTURE THEATRES

Academy	FREDLOS	1.30 to 11
Carlton	A WOMAN REBELS	10.45 to 11
Court	TELL ME TO-NIGHT	1 to 11
Curzon	MAYERLING	2.25 to 11
Empire	SING BABY SING	10 to 12
Everyman	STRICTLY CONFIDENTIAL	2 to 11
Forum	BED AND SOFA	1 to 11
Leicester Square	REMBRANDT	12 to 11
London Pavilion	COME AND GET IT	10 to 11
Marble Arch Pavilion	DODSWORTH	12.30 to 11.30
New Gallery	THE GREEN PASTURES	12 to 11
New Victoria	MAN WHO COULD WORK MIRACLES	12 to 11
Plaza	GO WEST YOUNG MAN	10.15 to 11
Polytechnic	AS YOU LIKE IT	2 to 11
Regal	GIRLS' DORMITORY	12.15 to 11
Stoll	THE DEVIL DOLL	11.45 to 11
Studio One	LA KERMESSE HEROIQUE	1 to 11
Tivoli	SABOTAGE	11.45 to 11

INSTRUMENT OF ABDICATION

I, Edward the Eighth, of Great Britain, Ireland, and the British Dominions beyond the Seas, King, Emperor of India, do hereby declare My irrevocable determination to renounce the Throne for Myself and for My descendants, and My desire that effect should be given to this Instrument of Abdication immediately.

In token whereof I have hereunto set My hand this tenth day of December, nineteen hundred and thirty six, in the presence of the witnesses whose signatures are subscribed.

SIGNED AT
FORT BELVEDERE
IN THE PRESENCE
OF

Edward R I

Albert

Henry.

George.

Above Geoffrey Dawson, editor of THE TIMES, 1912 to 1919 and 1923 to 1941.

Right The signed instrument of abdication.

Far right The Wedding of the Duke of Windsor to Mrs Wallis Simpson at the Chateau de Candé, France, 3 June 1937.

publishing a leader referring to the scandal in the American press. The London papers reported the Bishop's speech.

The King was convinced that he would be attacked in the press. In *A King's Story* he wrote:

> And because of the intimate association of Mr Baldwin, Archbishop Lang, and Mr Geoffrey Dawson, Editor of *The Times*, we had instinctively braced ourselves for an opening salvo from The Thunderer. In fact, rumour had reached us that *The Times* already had prepared a powerful and unfavourable editorial, and was only awaiting a signal to publish it.

The King instructed Baldwin to forbid any such leader in *The Times*. The Prime Minister explained that he had no control over the press. But he rang Dawson and asked whether the leader could be read over to him. Dawson sent him round a proof of the article.

On 5 December the King told the Prime Minister that he had made up his mind to abdicate.

In several leaders *The Times* set out its objections to the marriage, on the grounds of Mrs Simpson's two divorces. It attacked the notion of a morganatic marriage, which had been floated by Lord Rothermere and had found some support in Fleet Street. On this, *The Times* found it inconceivable 'that the Empire should accept a permanent statutory apology for the status of the lady whom the King desires to marry. The Constitution is to be amended in order that she may carry in solitary prominence the brand of unfitness for the Queen's throne.' Beaverbrook thought this leader insulting. On the other hand, his diarist and henchman Tom Driberg took the view that the leader protected rather than denigrated Mrs Simpson. A certain Delphic obscurity has at times been an element in *Times* leaders.

King Edward VIII abdicated on 10 December 1936. On the following day the leading article in *The Times*, written by Dawson, spoke of the King's qualities: 'Brave, completely free from pompousness, chivalrous, genuinely interested in the condition of the poor as he went about them'. Dawson did not pass over the King's defects: 'What seems almost incredible is that any man who was born and trained to such high responsibilities should sacrifice it all to a personal preference for another way of life. *Omnium consensu capax imperii nisi imperasset* – the well-worn quotation from Tacitus – is still irresistible.' The 'King's Friends' protested that this leader kicked a man when he was down. Now that the emotion has died down, it seems fair and honest comment.

The Abdication provoked more letters to *The Times* than any other single event: none was ever deliberately published; one in Latin nearly got in by accident, and another, quoting lines from Racine's *Bérénice*, found its way into the first edition, but was speedily removed from subsequent editions. After the Abdication, all the letters were read and analysed by a senior member of the staff. They show that at the beginning of the crisis readers were in favour of the King and his cause, but during the last few weeks, by far the greater number opposed the marriage.

That is a summary of the evidence. What part did *The Times* play in the Abdication Crisis? Conspiracy and collusion, or the traditional role of *The Times* as representative and leader of public opinion? Compton Mackenzie took the opinion that 'the Editor of *The Times* made himself responsible for the handling of the people'. In the long eye of history, fifty years after the constitutional storm, it seems absurd to suppose that anything written or done by Dawson and *The Times* played a decisive part in the Abdication of the King. From the very beginning, the King was determined to marry Mrs Simpson. Baldwin, supported by the Opposition, the Empire and the trade unions, was implacable in preventing the marriage. He took the view that public opinion would not accept a divorced woman on the throne of Queen Mary, Queen Alexandra and Queen Victoria. The business had the inevitability of a Greek tragedy. *The Times* played its customary role as spokesman of intelligent public opinion. But the King was going to have to go anyway.

Appeasement and other errors

It would be nice to pretend that *The Times* is infallible. Unfortunately it would not be true. The race of daily journalism to be first with the news means that occasional mistakes are inevitable. *The Times* has in its time committed some majestic and monumental mistakes. They range from misprints to false reports to mistaken policy.

THE TIMES DIARY

'When I had entered the back room in the Swiss bank, and turned the pages of those volumes, my doubts gradually dissolved. I am now satisfied they are authentic'

Secrets that survived the Bunker

by Hugh Trevor-Roper

Black Mark

In reserve

Marching orders

The classic misprint is said to have occurred in a report of Queen Victoria's visit to the Menai Bridge, in which the statement 'the Queen then passed over the Bridge' was corrupted to report the Queen doing something far more insouciant over the Bridge. It is also pure folklore that in the good old days any reader who spotted a literal in *The Times* was given a shilling. There have always been splendid misprints in *The Times*, as is inevitable in any publication that writes and prints as many words as are in three average novels in about twelve hours flat. There are more literals today because we are employing far fewer compositors and printers, and no longer employ the specialized cadre of marvellously precise readers and copy-holders.

Catastrophic false reports in *The Times* include the publication of the Parnell letters, which almost ruined the paper (see p. 66). Anybody who knew anything about Ireland could have seen that these letters, linking Parnell, an Irish MP, to a gang of terrorists, were crude forgeries. But the editor, infatuated with his sensational scoop, did not see fit to consult J. Woulfe Flanagan, *The Times*'s expert on Irish affairs, in case he spoiled a good story.

In the American Civil War, *The Times* supported the South almost until the bitter end (see pp. 53–5). The North was protectionist, the South was free-trading; and the huge Lancashire cotton industry depended for its raw material on the South. The coverage of the War between the States is not on the list of battle honours at Printing House Square. Leslie Stephen accused *The Times* of being 'guilty of a public crime'. He wrote that it had 'made a gigantic blunder from end to end as to the causes, progress, and consequences of the war'.

More recently *The Times* identified as the Fourth Man (who tipped off the spy Kim Philby that the security services were onto him) an inoffensive and much-loved Cambridge don who had just died. Any knowledge of Cambridge, or a single telephone call, would have demolished the story as nonsense. More recently still *The Times* identified a set of crude and banal forgeries as the Hitler Diaries, when a more sceptical and hard-nosed approach would have avoided considerable embarrassment.

When *The Times* gets things wrong, as is bound to happen in the hurly-burly of daily journalism, it has an honourable tradition of putting them right at once, and wearing sackcloth and ashes in print. Its corrections can sometimes be the most entertaining read in the paper.

But the most enduring policy stain on the leader page of *The Times* is its support for appeasement, which allowed Hitler to grow so big that he shook the world. Geoffrey Dawson, the editor, was one of a large group that included politicians of all parties who believed that the way to preserve the peace of Europe was to modify the harsh terms of the Treaty of Versailles in a spirit generous to Germany. If we treated the Germans decently, rather than squeezing the Huns till the pips squeaked, they would become peaceful. In the long eye of history, we can see the flaw in the argument: in Hitler we were dealing not with a rational being, but with a megalomaniac madman who wanted not peace but conquest. Only very few people recognized this at the time. This calamitous error of judgment has turned appeasement, which means no more than the irenic activity of seeking peace, into a dirty word.

The complex charges against *The Times* in the appeasement years leading up to the Second World War fall into two main groups. First, *The Times* is accused of suppressing or altering dispatches, particularly those from its excellent Berlin correspondent, Norman Ebbutt, so as to avoid irritating the Nazis. If true, it is a mortal sin of journalism. There is not much evidence for

Above right THE TIMES announces the Hitler diaries, the scoop that never was, 3 April 1983.

Below THE TIMES, Wednesday 15 June 1977, revived speculation about a 'fourth man' linked to the Soviet spies Burgess, Philby and Maclean. But the finger was pointed at the wrong man. THE TIMES scored a scoop, however, when Sir Anthony Blunt was exposed, November 1979.

Below right The first meeting of Neville Chamberlain and Adolf Hitler in Munich, 28 September 1938.

16 THE TIMES WEDNESDAY JUNE 15 1977

His political extremism was mixed with a passion for acting

The 'much loved Cambridge don' in the Philby affair

Burgess, Philby and Maclean : now the man who possibly guided them at Cambridge.

A misread and misunderstood agreement

What the Helsinki declaration was really all about

The Final Act is a vast, complex and finely balanced package conceding very few of the points the Soviet Union hoped to gain

DECLARATION OF PEACE AT MUNICH

FUTURE OF ANGLO-GERMAN RELATIONS

"THE DESIRE OF OUR TWO PEOPLES"

CONSULTATION HENCEFORTH, NOT WAR

Mr. Chamberlain, receiving representatives of the British Press yesterday before his departure from Munich, said :—

" I have always been of the opinion that if we could get a peaceful solution to the Czechoslovak question it would open the way generally to appeasement in Europe.

" This morning I had a talk with the Führer, and we both signed the following declaration :—

" We, the German Führer and Chancellor and the British Prime Minister, have had a further meeting to-day and are agreed in recognising that the question of Anglo-German relations is of the first importance for the two countries and for Europe.

" We regard the agreement signed last night and the Anglo-German Naval Agreement as symbolic of the desire of our two peoples never to go to war with one another again.

" We are resolved that the method of consultation shall be the method adopted to deal with any other questions that may concern our two countries, and we are determined to continue our efforts to remove possible sources of difference and thus to contribute to assure the peace of Europe."

PRAGUE ACCEPTS MUNICH PLAN

The Czechoslovak Government have accepted the Munich Plan for the transfer to the Reich of the Sudeten German territories. " I have taken the decision," said General Sirovy, the Prime Minister, " to save life and to save the nation. As a soldier I had to choose the way of peace."

CLOSING SCENES AT MUNICH

MR. CHAMBERLAIN ACCLAIMED

From Our Special Correspondent

MUNICH, Sept. 30

The Munich Conference closed to-day with the departure of Mr. Chamberlain for London by air at 2.20 p.m. Before he left the Prime Minister was able to make two announcements which justify high hopes that the Conference has not only banished the danger of war over the future of Czechoslovakia, but has opened up a new and better era in European relationships. The one was that the Czechoslovak Government had communicated through the British Minister in Prague their acceptance of the Four-Power Plan for the transference of Sudeten German territory to the Reich. The other [printed in full above] was that the heads of the British and German Governments had agreed upon a declaration committing each other to resolve their differences only by peaceful means.

Mr. Chamberlain left his hotel at 11.18 a.m. to take leave of Herr Hitler and have a final conversation, which it was known would touch on the general European situation. Apart from the two heads of Governments only Dr. Schmidt, the interpreter, was present. The conversation took place in Herr Hitler's private residence, in a long street in which there stands a statue of the Angel of Peace.

DEMOBILIZATION

The Anglo-German declaration was announced by Mr. Chamberlain to newspaper correspondents when he returned to his hotel at 1 o'clock. The Prime Minister added that although the question of military demobilization all round had not been discussed with Herr Hitler, he took it for granted that there would be a general demobilization. The impression in well-informed circles here is that Herr Hitler will order an immediate demobilization in the Reich as soon as he is convinced that the Czechoslovak Government genuinely desire and are in a position to carry out the terms of the Four-Power Plan of military evacuation.

The British delegation, which had been the last to arrive in Munich, was also the last to leave. Signor Mussolini departed by train at 7.40 a.m. with Count Ciano, the Italian Foreign Minister ; M. Daladier and his colleagues left shortly after 1 p.m. by air. They had taken leave of Herr Hitler after signing the Agreement in the early hours of the morning.

M. Daladier shortly before his departure had a long conversation with Field-Marshal Göring. An indication of the French Prime Minister's personal impression of Herr Hitler was conveyed by a remark made by him after the conversation. "That," he said, " is a man one can make politics with."

GERMAN TRIBUTES

Mr. Chamberlain, apart from the Führer, was the most popular of the visiting statesmen. His untiring efforts to reach a peaceful solution have captured the imagination of the German public. On leaving and arriving at his hotel to-day he received tremendous ovations. Men and women, uncertain whether to laugh or cry, insisted on shaking his hand, on thanking him, or pressing flowers on him. At the same time tribute was paid to Signor Mussolini for grasping at the opportunity of mediation offered him by Mr. Chamberlain, and to Herr Hitler for his readiness to make all concessions consistent with his undertaking to the German people that something practical would be done in the Sudeten German dispute by October 1.

Not least, a word of praise was offered to the Czechoslovak Government for accepting the Plan at short notice and obviating a local conflict which in the long run might well have involved other nations.

GERMAN CONCESSIONS

M. Masarik, of the Czechoslovak Foreign Ministry, and Mr. Ashton-Gwatkin, who was on the staff of Lord Runciman's mission to Prague, left Munich by air at 6 o'clock this morning for Prague to deliver the Four-Power Agreement to the Czechoslovak Government. From the Czechoslovak point of view the agreement represents a tremendous improvement on the demands presented by the Reich Government in their Godesberg Memorandum. The latter envisaged the complete military evacuation by October 1 of the whole Sudeten-German area arbitrarily determined by the Reich. The Four-Power Agreement provides for the evacuation over a period of 10 days of certain areas which have either been determined by the four Powers in conference or will be determined by the International Boundary Commission set up by the Conference. This Commission, which is composed of representatives of the Reich, Great Britain, France, Italy, and Czechoslovakia, will also determine the plebiscite areas, whereas in the Godesberg Memorandum the plebiscite areas were determined by the Reich and were thought by the Czechoslovak Government to have been adjusted so as to obtain in every case a German majority.

Under the Godesberg Memorandum also certain plebiscite areas would have been occupied by German troops immediately ; under the Four-Power Plan all plebiscite areas will be occupied by an international force, the composition of which will be decided by the International Boundary Commission.

TOKEN OCCUPATION

So far from demanding that the whole Sudeten German area be occupied by German troops on October 1, Herr Hitler, for the sake of agreement, has contented himself with what amounts to little more than a token occupation on that day. Territory No. 1, as it is called in the Agreement, is a strip about 45 miles long and 10 miles deep at the deepest point, adjacent to the Austrian frontier. The Germans are entitled under the Agreement to march in there at any time after midnight to-night. Mr. Chamberlain stated to-day, however, that the occupation will probably not begin until to-morrow night. That will give the International Boundary Commission time to supervise the Czechoslovak withdrawal, although, in fact, as there are no Czech troops and no fortifications in the district in question, withdrawal is not a difficult matter.

THE TIME-TABLE

The Agreement envisages the progressive evacuation by October 7 of four districts which together make little more than half of the Sudeten-German language area, and are substantially less than the districts marked red on the Godesberg map. They do not include the main Czechoslovak fortifications on the northern frontier. The programme is as follows :—

October 1 and 2.—Occupation of Zone No. 1. This is a small strip on the south-west frontier adjacent to Austria. The limit of the German advance is a line running roughly from Stubenbach by Krumau, south of Budweis, to Kaplitz and thereafter straight to the frontier.

October 2 and 3.—Occupation of Zone No. 2. A small strip on the northern frontier, including the two salients on either side of Zittau. The limit of the German advance is a straight line running roughly by Tetschen-Bodenbach and Reichenberg to the frontier.

October 3, 4 and 5.—Occupation of Zone No. 3. This is the large German " triangle " in the north-west. The line marking the limit of the German advance runs from near Waldmünchen, in Bavaria, by Kaaden to Ober-Leutensdorf. This zone includes Carlsbad, Marienbad, and Eger.

October 6 and 7.—Occupation of Zone No. 4. This is a small strip in Northern Moravia, east of Glatz. The line marking the limit of the German advance runs through Grulich, Zopiau, Freudenthal, and Jägerndorf.

The remainder of the predominantly German territory to be evacuated by October 10 will be determined by the International Boundary Commission.

CZECH CONSENT

There is every reason to believe that the Agreement involves no territorial cessions in addition to those to which the Czechoslovak Government have already assented at the request of the British and French Governments. If there is a weakness in the Agreement, it is that the necessity for doing something by to-morrow meant that the Czechoslovak Government were given no chance of making suggestions of their own, but could reply only " yes " or " no." On the other hand, as things have been arranged, it can scarcely be said that the transfer is being made under pressure of force. The arrangements for the evacuation and occupation, the determination of boundaries, the holding of plebiscites, and the settlement of all questions arising out of the transfer, are in the hands of an International Commission, on which, it may be noted, the British, French, and Czechoslovak Governments are in the majority. It is noticed also that the Agreement drops harsh clauses, such as the prohibition of the removal of livestock owned by persons who do not wish to be included in the Reich.

In general, the Agreement is regarded here as a triumph of common sense and good will, which owed not a little to the irresistible demand of world public opinion that the Czechoslovak dispute should not be permitted to plunge Europe into a catastrophic war.

MR. CHAMBERLAIN LEAVES

Mr. Chamberlain lunched at his hotel, which he left shortly afterwards for the Munich airport, amid yet another striking demonstration of enthusiasm from the crowds gathered outside. In spite of a thin drizzle, a large number of people had assembled at the airport to see the Prime Minister depart. Mr. Chamberlain, who had expressed his desire to be back in London without loss of time, walked briskly on to the landing-ground, where he was greeted by Herr von Ribbentrop, the German Foreign Minister, General Ritter von Epp, the Governor of Bavaria, Herr Siebert, the Bavarian Premier, and others. A guard of honour mounted by Herr Hitler's S.S. bodyguard stood at attention as the Prime Minister shook hands and stepped into his aeroplane. The machine took off amid loud and continued applause from the crowd, which was renewed again and again as it circled thrice round the airport before flying off in a north-westerly direction. Part of the British delegation followed a few minutes later in a second aeroplane.

FRANCE AND GERMANY

Field-Marshal Göring, in an informal conversation with foreign correspondents, made it clear that the Reich Government hoped the Munich Conference would prove to be the starting point of better Franco-German, as well as better Anglo-German, relations. The Field-Marshal, who acted as escort to M. Daladier during the Prime Minister's stay here, said that the solution of the Czechoslovak problem with the consent of France had removed the chief difficulty in the way of Franco-German understanding. He expressed his admiration for the French nation, and in particular for the French Army, whose worth he had tested by experience in the Great War. In the weeks and months to come, said the Field-Marshal, he could be relied upon to make and support all efforts to bring about the Franco-German understanding which had defied the efforts of all statesmen for centuries. The general public endorsed Field-Marshal Göring's remarks with shouts of " Heil Frankreich " as M. Daladier left Munich to return to France.

POLISH DEMANDS ON PRAGUE

A SHARP NOTE

FROM OUR OWN CORRESPONDENT

WARSAW, Sept. 30

The Polish Government are dissatisfied with the Czechoslovak reply to the Note of September 27, and at a meeting at the Zamek, which was attended by President Moscicki ; Marshal Smigly-Rydz, Inspector-General of the Forces ; the Prime Minister ; the Deputy Prime Minister and Minister of Finance ; and Colonel Beck, the Foreign Minister, it was decided to send by aeroplane another Note which is unofficially described as having " an ultimatum character." This Note reached Prague late to-night.

According to a statement released by the Polish Telegraph Agency this afternoon Czech soldiers committed an act of " provocation and aggression " by firing across the frontier on Wednesday night between the hours of 8 and 12. Special editions of the newspapers to-night announced that " the Polish Government will draw the necessary consequences from this act and place full responsibility on the Czechoslovak side."

The British, French, American, and German Ambassadors saw Colonel Beck this afternoon, no doubt to urge moderation and restraint.

Poland seems determined to enter the " land beyond the Olza " simultaneously with the entry of the German army into Sudeten territory.

The Soviet Government announced a week ago that their non-aggression pact with Poland would be denounced if Polish troops invaded Czechoslovakia.

COMPANY MEETINGS

Full reports of the proceedings at the meetings of Thos. W. Ward Limited, and Cohen, Weenen and Co., are published in our City columns.

OVATION IN LONDON

MR. CHAMBERLAIN'S HOMECOMING

CONGRATULATIONS OF THE KING

A cautious historian's comment on a former Prime Minister's achievement as a peace-maker in Berlin was that, without anticipating the verdict of history, it was but fair to place on record the claim of Lord Beaconsfield that he had brought back to his country " peace with honour." London last night anticipated the verdict of history on Mr. Chamberlain's work at the Munich Conference without any reserve, and the stirring welcome home which he received expressed in a most remarkable way the public gratitude to him for his successful efforts in the high cause of European peace.

For two hours before Mr. Chamberlain landed at Heston the narrow roads leading to the airport were made almost impassable by motor traffic and many thousands of people assembled as near as they could to the entrance to give him their greeting. Inside the gateway the road leading from the airport buildings was lined on each side by 120 boys from Eton College, who had on their own initiative sought and obtained permission to be there to cheer the Prime Minister on his return. On the aerodrome a number of distinguished people began to gather long before the air liner was due from Munich. The Lord Mayor of London (Sir Harry Twyford) was one of the first to arrive and soon afterwards there came the Lord Chamberlain, Lord Clarendon, Cabinet Ministers, High Commissioners for the Dominions, and the diplomatic representatives of France, Germany, Italy, and other countries.

LETTER FROM THE KING

The Lockheed air liner in which Mr. Chamberlain and his official advisers flew from Munich was sighted over the aerodrome at 5.38 p.m. against a grey sky from which there had just fallen a heavy downpour of rain. Two minutes later the machine had come to a standstill and the Prime Minister was standing at the cabin door smiling and waving his hat in response to the loud cheers that welcomed him back from his third and most memorable flight to Germany within 15 days.

As soon as Mr. Chamberlain stepped to the ground the Lord Chamberlain handed him a letter from the King. Then Lord Halifax shook him warmly by the hand ; and others who rushed forward to greet and congratulate him included the Italian Ambassador, Count Grandi, the French Ambassador, M. Corbin, the German Chargé d'Affaires, Dr. Kordt, and the Hungarian Minister, M. de Masirevich. Mr. Chamberlain had a cordial welcome from Ministerial colleagues, among whom were Lord Maugham, Mr. Hore-Belisha, Mr. Malcolm MacDonald, Captain Margesson, Mr. Geoffrey Lloyd, and Captain Harold Balfour. The Lord Mayor congratulated him on behalf of the citizens of London.

THE NATION THANKED

Then, amid continuous cheers, the Prime Minister stepped towards a microphone and spoke a message to the nation. He said :—

There are only two things I want to say. First of all I received an immense number of letters during all these anxious days—and so has my wife—letters of support and approval and gratitude ; and I cannot tell you what an encouragement that has been to me. I want to thank the British people for what they have done. Next I want to say that the settlement of the Czechoslovak problem which has now been achieved is, in my view, only a prelude to a larger settlement in which all Europe may find peace.

This morning I had another talk with the German Chancellor, Herr Hitler, and here is a paper which bears his name upon it as well as mine. Some of you perhaps have already heard what it contains, but I would just like to read it to you.

Mr. Chamberlain then read the joint declaration, and there was a further burst of cheering. There were more cheers as policemen made a way for him to his car, and the drive to London began to the singing of " For he's a jolly good fellow." As Mr. Chamberlain drove past the cheering Eton boys to the airport exit his car was surrounded by crowds who could not be held back by the police, and amid the enthusiasm many people tried to open the doors of the car to shake him by the hand.

Mounted police eventually made a way, and the Prime Minister drove slowly through the pressing and cheering crowds —among whom were hundreds of children waving tiny flags—towards London and the still greater welcome that was the acknowledgment of a victory gained for peace.

CROWDS AT THE PALACE

A BALCONY APPEARANCE

London's welcome reached its climax outside Buckingham Palace, where a crowd of several thousands had waited for over two hours. Indifferent to the heavy rain, they stood, densely packed, a happy throng, their hearts full of relief and a deep sense of thankfulness towards the man who had lifted a great weight of anxiety from their minds.

Mrs. Chamberlain arrived at the Palace at 6.15. The crowd cheered her loudly, and she smiled and waved in reply. She was conducted to their Majesties' private apartments, where she was received by the King and Queen.

Just before the Prime Minister arrived a rainbow seen over the rooftops was hailed by some as an omen. The rain ceased and soon distant cheering was heard, swelling to a roar as the homecoming Prime Minister approached. The crowd outside the Palace swept across the road leaving only a narrow lane for his car. Motorists sounded their horns in chorus as the Prime Minister, bare-headed and smiling happily, acknowledged the cheers. As the car drove slowly into the courtyard the crowd surged up to the railings, still waving and cheering, while members of the King's household and

Continued on page 14, column 5

JOY IN BERLIN

HOPE OF A BETTER UNDERSTANDING

FIRST FIVE-POWER MEETING

From Our Correspondent

BERLIN, Sept. 30

The " Commission of Ambassadors " which will arrange the details for the execution of the Agreement signed at Munich this morning met at 5 p.m. to-day at the Foreign Ministry, while outside in the Wilhelmstrasse newsvendors, crying : " Extra ! No more war with England ! " gave the Berlin public their first news of the joint declaration issued by Mr. Chamberlain and Herr Hitler this morning.

Germany was represented at this evening's conference by Freiherr von Weizsäcker, State Secretary at the Foreign Ministry, Great Britain, France, and Italy by their respective Ambassadors in Berlin—Sir Nevile Henderson, M. François-Poncet, and Signor Attolico—and Czechoslovakia by her Minister in Berlin, Dr. Mastny, who arrived here by air just before 6 p.m. So far as is known the full details of the Munich Agreement have not yet been received in Berlin, and it is therefore thought that the proceedings at this evening's conference will be limited to drawing up agenda and making arrangements for the future work of the commission.

Meanwhile the British Military Attaché, Colonel Mason-MacFarlane, is engaged in helping the War Office in London to draft operation orders for the speedy transfer to Czechoslovakia of the British troops who, together with a large contingent from the British Legion and possibly a similar body of French ex-Service men, will police the plebiscite areas before and during the poll.

PEACE WITH ENGLAND

The joint statement issued this morning by the Prime Minister and the Führer has come to the German people as another great and pleasant surprise in a day which is described here as one of miracles. The special editions of the newspapers containing this statement were snatched from the hands of their vendors as soon as they appeared on the streets of Berlin, and people stood in little groups smiling and peering over one another's shoulders to read the latest good news from Munich.

It is fully realized here that the declaration goes no further than to affirm the will for peace of Germany and Great Britain, and that it is in no way a formal undertaking, the jubilant headlines and the cries of the newsboys notwithstanding. But that does not matter. The Prime Minister of the country with which all Germans most desire good relations and their own Führer have solemnly declared their determination to seek peaceful solutions for the questions which remain to be settled between the two nations. That is good enough for the Germans, who hope that at last the moral isolation in which this country has stood for five years may be coming to an end and that a period of better understanding between the Reich and her neighbours has begun.

" HEIL CHAMBERLAIN "

The houses of the residential districts of Berlin were gay with flags this morning. Little cotton pennants and flags flew from the windows in the working-class districts and more pretentious banners in the fashionable quarters. The people had not been officially urged to decorate their houses, as is usual here, but hearing the news of the night's events at Munich had spontaneously expressed their joy and relief by putting out the flags that every German family possesses. As your Correspondent walked up Unter den Linden this morning an ex-Service man with a medal ribbon in his lapel hastened up to him and, grasping him by the hand, cried " Heil Chamberlain." This expresses the feelings of the German people well enough. Gratitude in the first place to Herr Hitler, but in an equal measure to the Prime Minister, without whom it is clearly realized peace would not have been saved.

When the news that agreement had been reached became known in Berlin the city abandoned itself to a joy which has not been felt here for many weeks. There were few noisy demonstrations of relief, but the people, who had been sitting tensely round their wireless sets, came streaming into the streets once the good news was known, and although pay day was still a day distant and the week's money running short in many households, the cafés and taverns did a roaring trade as the health of the four statesmen who had, in the now popular German phrase, " lifted a stone from the heart " of the German people, were drunk enthusiastically.

NEW METHODS

The Press to-day greets the agreement as a triumph primarily, as might be expected, for Herr Hitler, and secondly for Signor Mussolini, but also for the Prime Minister and M. Daladier. A new style of international politics, that of personal and frank discussion which Herr Hitler has always advocated, has, it is said, superseded the outworn " Geneva " method, and a new hope for European understanding has arisen as a result. German writers do not stint their praise for all who took part in the conference ; particular recognition is given to the work of the British Ambassador in Berlin, who in the past eventful week has done much to help bring about a successful settlement of the Sudeten German question.

The Commander-in-Chief of the Army, Colonel-General von Brauchitsch, to-day issued a general order, in which the troops who will to-morrow begin to enter the Sudeten German territory are instructed to maintain the strictest discipline, and to remember that the Army is the tool of the Führer and Supreme Commander and that the Sudeten Germans must be made to feel secure beneath the protection of the German Army.

ON OTHER PAGES

GROUP AT THE PALACE

REPRODUCTIONS TO BE ISSUED

The photograph of the King and Mr. Chamberlain with the Queen and Mrs. Chamberlain at Buckingham Palace last night, which is reproduced on page 16, will also be issued as a photogravure plate suitable for framing.

This plate will be ready by the middle of next week ; and the actual date of publication will be announced in *The Times*. The overall size of the plate will be 18in. by 15in. with an engraved surface measuring 10¼in. by 12¼in.

The plates will be obtainable by order from booksellers, newsagents, and bookstalls, also from *The Times* Book Club, 42, Wigmore Street, W.1, at 1s. each, or direct from the Publisher, *The Times*, Printing House Square, E.C.4, post free for 1s. 1½d.

To-day we also publish on pages 7 and 16 pictures in connexion with Mr. Chamberlain's visit to Munich and the extraordinary welcome accorded him on his return to London last evening. They include pictures of the scenes outside Buckingham Palace, in Downing Street, and at Heston.

On page 14 is a photograph of the declaration signed by Herr Hitler and Mr. Chamberlain yesterday in Munich.

SHARP RISE IN SECURITIES

RECOVERY IN STERLING

FROM OUR CITY EDITOR

So far as the City was concerned, the feelings of relief at the peaceful settlement of the Czechoslovak crisis were clearly reflected in a sharp, all-round advance of boom-like proportions in all classes of securities, in a further substantial recovery in the dollar value of sterling, in a material reduction in resales of gold by hoarders and others, in appreciably easier market discount rates, and in contradictory movements in the commodity markets, where the war commodity, wheat, suffered a further reaction, but rubber, which is more dependent on the continuance of peace, advanced sharply. Another direct result of the Prime Minister's achievement was a very material deflating of the high premiums which have recently been quoted for insurance against war risks on shipments of cargo, gold, &c.

Rises in the security markets were widespread and substantial, and in some cases prices were carried back to the levels prevailing before the gradual development of the crisis caused prices to begin to crumble. Leading British Government stocks showed gains of three points ; advances ranging in some cases from 10 to 20 points were recorded in Central European bonds ; and industrial, oil, and mining shares moved to materially higher levels. The day's business was considerable, and markets closed with a buoyant tone.

The change in the political atmosphere brought about by the Munich Agreement found immediate expression in the foreign exchange market, where from the outset there was a scramble to sell dollars, which had been the repository for nervous holders of sterling and other balances at the time of acute tension. The American exchange at one time reached $4.86, and though a reaction ensued the closing quotation of $4.82 represented a net movement on the day of over 6c. against dollars. The disappearance of war fears also had its effect in the bullion market, where the amount of gold dealt in was appreciably smaller, only £906,000 changing hands at the fixing, and the price was again lower at 144s. 1d. per oz.

The minimum rates for war risk insurance were lowered sharply in the London marine market yesterday. A new and temporary scale of rates is reproduced in our City columns.

QUEEN MARY

AN ATTACK OF LARYNGITIS

The following statement was issued from Marlborough House last night :—

Queen Mary is suffering from an attack of laryngitis and will be unable to fulfil her engagement at the West Herts Hospital, Hemel Hempstead, to-morrow. In consequence the Duchess of Kent will lay the foundation-stone of the children's ward and open the extension of the nurses' home on behalf of her Majesty.

END OF SUMMER TIME

CLOCKS TO BE PUT BACK TO-NIGHT

Summer Time ends to-night and Greenwich Time will be restored. The change officially takes place at 3 a.m. (Summer Time) to-morrow morning, when the clock will be set to 2 a.m., so that the hour 2-3 a.m. Summer Time will be followed by the hour 2-3 a.m. Greenwich Time.

All clocks and watches must be set to the correct Greenwich Time during the course of the night. Railways and other establishments where work continues during the night will no doubt make the change at the correct moment (3 a.m. Summer Time), but the public generally should alter their clocks before going to bed, so that they may be right in the morning.

Employers are asked specially to warn their workers to do this.

WINTER TIME NEWS BULLETINS

The B.B.C. announced last night that, beginning next Monday, the news bulletins will be read at the usual winter times, that is, at 6 p.m. and 9 p.m. in the National programme, and at 7.10 p.m. and 11.50 p.m. in the Regional programme.

OBITUARY

We announce with regret the deaths of Major-General T. H. Hardy, who served in India for over 30 years. A memoir will be found on page 15.

LORD STANLEY

It was reported yesterday that Lord Stanley had had a good night and that his condition was improving.

DEPRESSION IN PRAGUE

NO ALTERNATIVE

LOOKING TO A NEW FUTURE

Prague, Sept. 30.—The Czechoslovak Government have accepted the Four-Power Agreement signed in Munich. It was stated officially this afternoon that the Government, after considering the decisions taken " without and against them " at the Conference, had no other alternative but to accept them.

Earlier it had been officially stated in Prague that the Czechoslovak Government had received through Mr. Newton, the British Minister, a message from Mr. Chamberlain saying that he expected their reply by noon to-day. The Czechoslovak Government (the statement declared) expressed to Mr. Newton their amazement at being given such a short time to consider a matter of such historic importance and such a crushing responsibility.

Evacuation of Zone No. 1, on the southern frontier of Bohemia, begins to-night and will continue until Sunday. The evacuation of the other zones will be proceeded with systematically.

TO SAVE LIFE

Shortly after 5 p.m. the Prime Minister, General Sirovy, made a broadcast speech, in which he said :—

This is the most difficult moment in my life. I have taken the decision to save life and to save the nation. Superior force has compelled us to accept.

My duty was to consider everything. As a soldier I had to choose the way to peace. The nation will be stronger and more united. We have chosen the only right course.

The four Powers have decided to ask from us the cession of the German territories. We had to choose between a useless fight and sacrifices. We have accepted unheard-of sacrifices, imposed upon us. We have to choose between the death of the nation and cession of some territories. We shall accomplish the conditions imposed on us. The main thing is that we are remaining ourselves, and we must be united.

I am appealing to the people to maintain confidence in its leaders. Our State will not be the smallest. There are smaller States than we shall be. But an understanding with our neighbours will be easier. Our main concern must be to rebuild our State.

" WE SOLDIERS "

Immediately after General Sirovy's announcement General Krejči, Commander-in-Chief of the Army, made the following proclamation, which was broadcast :—

Soldiers, the Czechoslovak Government, under pressure of world events, was obliged to accept the transfer of various territories of our State. We soldiers, who were the pride of the nation until now, must remain so in the future. Western Europe has asked this sacrifice from us categorically in order to prevent world war.

In our oath we have promised the President of the Republic unconditional obedience. Destiny obliges us to fulfil this promise in the most painful circumstances. Our Chief Commander, the President of the Republic, the Prime Minister, and all the representatives of our State, anxiously aware of the enormous responsibility, could not have permitted useless losses which would have diminished the strength of our State. They have always had our confidence, and will have it in the future, because we are convinced that they have done everything that was humanly possible.

The true soldier must endure failure, for even in it there is a manifestation of true heroism. Our Army has not been vanquished. The Republic will need a strong Army. We are confident our nation will come happily out of the present difficulties. We soldiers will deserve it. Our Government will always find us ready for all sacrifices.

The Agreement was published here this evening. There were attempts at demonstrations, and Communists were extremely excited, but there are no serious disturbances, thanks to appeals for calm published by the Government, patriotic societies, and trade unions, and the authorities have the situation well in hand.

Depression prevails in the capital. All wireless programmes have been cancelled as a sign of national mourning ; only news is transmitted, a bulletin being sent out every half-hour.—*Reuter.*

its ever happening. The most damaging evidence is a letter that Dawson wrote on 23 May 1937 to the correspondent standing in for Ebbutt while the latter was away from Berlin:

> But it really would interest me to know precisely what it is in *The Times* that has produced this new antagonism in Germany. I do my utmost night after night to keep out of the paper anything that might hurt their susceptibilities. I can really think of nothing that has been printed now for many months past to which they could possibly take exception as unfair comment. I shall be more grateful than I can say for any explanation and guidance, for I have always been convinced that the peace of the world depends more than anything else upon our getting into reasonable relations with Germany.

It is clear that Dawson is referring to comment in leaders, not news: *The Times* published the bloody and sinister events of the rise of the Nazis as they happened. Ebbutt was a prolix correspondent and sometimes needed cutting, as journalists often do. Neither he nor any of his colleagues has suggested that his reports were deliberately emasculated. He was eventually expelled from Germany for his detailed and damaging reports of the persecution of the churches by the Nazis. A series of articles about the notorious concentration camp at Dachau, commissioned from the Munich stringer and prepared with difficulty and danger, was never published. That was a misjudgment – or was it something more sinister? But maybe the copy was not much good. Copy from stringers sometimes isn't.

The second major charge against *The Times* is that the leaders on appeasement probably strengthened Hitler's delusion that the British governing classes had gone soft and would never oppose him. But then he found support for those delusions in places as eccentric as debates at the Oxford Union. For example on 3 October 1938 Dawson wrote: 'The policy of international appeasement must of course be pressed forward. There must be appeasement not only of the strong but of the weak. With the policy of appeasement must go the policy of preparation – preparation not so much for war as against war.'

Probably the most damaging single leader during the appeasement years was published on 7 September 1938 at the height of the Czechoslovak crisis. Eduard Beneš, the Czech Prime Minister, was desperately negotiating to try to appease Herr Henlein, the leader of the Sudeten Germans. Dawson, just back from holiday, altered a leader to read:

> In that case it might be worth while for the Czechoslovak Government to consider whether they should exclude altogether the project, which has found favour in some quarters, of making Czechoslovakia a more homogeneous State by the secession of that fringe of alien populations who are contiguous to the nation by which they are united by race.

Right The Germans enter Sudetenland, October 1938.

Below The EVENING STANDARD 15 July 1939. Low's TOPICAL BUDGET cartoon shows the editor of THE TIMES and the Prime Minister in conference. Note all letters to the editor consigned to the waste-paper basket – except for one.

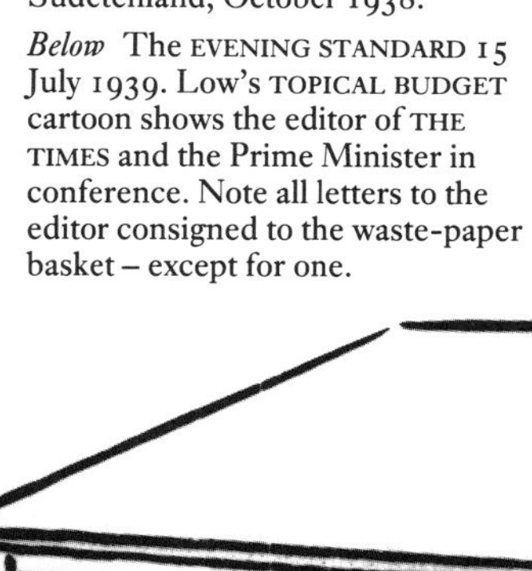

The Times was at this period widely regarded by foreign governments as the megaphone of the Government. It was not true, even then. But the Foreign Office issued an official statement saying that the suggestion in the *Times* leader that the Czechs might consider ceding land to the Germans in no way represented the view of the Government. Lord Runciman, on a mission of appeasement to Prague, wired London: 'Leading article in today's *Times* has added to our difficulties. It would be useful to caution them against adventurous speculation at a time when we are hoping to make some progress. The last paragraph of the article is a recommendation to an *Anschluss*.'

Claud Cockburn, who had worked for *The Times*, invented the term 'the Cliveden Set' to describe Dawson, Lord Lothian and other leading appeasers who regularly visited the Waldorf Astors at Cliveden. Cockburn alleged that the suggestion in the *Times* leader had been submitted to the German Embassy for approval. Dawson described Cockburn's allegation as 'a tissue of fabrication from beginning to end'.

The conspiratorial view of the appeasement years is of Dawson and *The Times*, the Cliveden Set and the rest of the Old Gang combining to hoodwink the public and turn a blind eye on Hitler, whom they hoped to use as a bulwark against the Antichrist of Communism. The truth is more complicated than the conspiratorial theory. It usually is.

Dawson thought that war was the most terrible catastrophe imaginable, and that it was worth doing anything to avoid it. He thought that Hitler was a rational being, and looked at the Nazis through rose-coloured spectacles. He did not vehemently support British rearmament, in case it annoyed the tiger. He preferred appeasement to war. These were terrible misjudgments. They were shared by most people in Britain, of all classes and parties.

Opposite page
The tragic irony of THE TIMES's jubilant and optimistic headlines can be seen only with hindsight, though correspondents abroad wrote privately to the paper advising against this stance. Douglas Reed, the Vienna correspondent, wrote on 16 March 1937: 'In my wildest nightmares I had not foreseen anything so perfectly organised, so ruthless, so strong. When this machine goes into action it will blight everything it encounters like a swarm of locusts.'
1 OCTOBER 1938

The Blitz: 'No interference with production'

Below Printing House Square after the air raid, as reported in THE TIMES.

Centre The staff of THE TIMES Intelligence Department (the library) clearing the wreckage after the air raid, 25 September 1940.

Bottom Col. J.J. Astor and Geoffrey Dawson in THE TIMES air raid shelter.

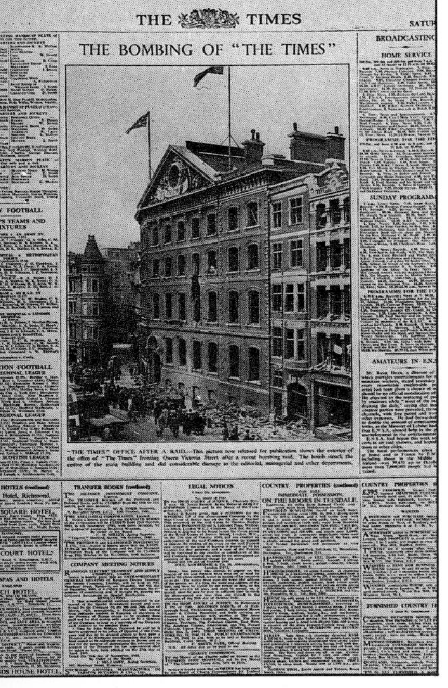

THE TIMES

THE BOMBING OF "THE TIMES"

"THE TIMES" OFFICE AFTER A RAID.—This picture now released for publication shows the exterior of the office of "The Times" fronting Queen Victoria Street after a recent bombing raid. The bomb struck the centre of the main building and did considerable damage to the editorial, managerial and other departments.

BROADCASTING

HOME SERVICE

SUNDAY PROGRAMME

AMATEURS IN E.N.S.A.

TRANSFER BOOKS (continued)

COMPANY MEETING NOTICES

LEGAL NOTICES

COUNTRY PROPERTIES (continued)

ON THE MOORS IN TEESDALE

FURNISHED COUNTRY HOUSES

SPAS AND HOTELS

The war with Hitler came closer to stopping the presses of *The Times* than libel of the Prince of Wales or the General Strike, the Parnell letters or bankruptcy, the small proprietors or failure to move with the times, or indeed any other event since 1785.

The Times was a national institution as well as a commercial organization. It was symbolic nationally that it should keep up its tradition of daily production. Accordingly emergency arrangements were made during the Second World War to print *The Times* if Printing House Square were to be knocked out of action. The presses of the *Evening Standard* were booked to print a sixteen-page issue of *The Times* in emergency. In case transport in London were immobilized at night, arrangements were made for an eight-page daily issue of *The Times*, and a sixteen-page weekly edition, to be printed at Kettering.

As in other firms and industries, many of the brightest and best of the Black Friars joined up and went off to fight Hitler. Many were killed. Others were translated overnight into war correspondents, with uniforms, accreditation, rations, and shepherding officers undreamed of in the pioneering days of Russell and Crabb Robinson.

At Printing House Square it was decided to carry on printing *The Times* through the air raids. The editorial staff were moved into the basement of the recently rebuilt building, beside the big presses and the foundry, and observers were posted on the roof to give warning of the approach of raiders. Tom Scott, of the night editor's staff, has left a vivid account of those frightening, troglodyte days and nights keeping The Thunderer thundering:

Living underground with the minimum of comfort was taking a heavy toll of Geoffrey Dawson's health. He was no longer young; he was no longer middle-aged. Night after night he tried to sleep in a very tiny room. What this 'bedroom' was originally used for I have no idea. Nevertheless, it was a cubby-hole that was much envied by other members of the editorial staff whose makeshift beds were on the basement floor. I suppose that Dawson could have gone home each night before the bombing began, but for reasons best known to himself he chose to stay on with us. But the conditions were obviously too much for him. Ultimately he could not suffer even lying awake on his bed in the cubby-hole; he would come out into the comparative wide expanse of the basement, his cloak – a kind of opera cloak – draped round his stooping shoulders, look around at the editorial bodies lying on the floor, many of them in most inelegant attitudes, and then make his way to the small bench that I used as a desk.

At that time in the mornings I was the only one of the editorial staff who was officially on duty. Dawson would sit opposite me and open the conversation with the same remark each night, or rather morning, 'Anything of importance happening?' He never at any time mentioned the bombing that was going on. I would give him a summary of the news that had come in since the first edition of the paper, which he had already read. He would listen closely, his bottom lip drooping as it usually did when he was listening to every word spoken to him.

After leading the rest of the nation down the primrose path of appeasement to the world bonfire, Dawson and his men at *The Times* had an obsession to keep *The Times* going through it all.

On the night of Wednesday 24 September 1940, the air raid alarm sounded at 8.22 pm; the All Clear was not given until 5.36

Column 3 announces the bombing of Printing House Square, two and a half weeks after the actual event, because of censorship regulations. THE TIMES buildings were also peppered with firebombs during the fire-raising raids in December 1940 and May 1941 – but damage was slight compared to this direct hit.
12 OCTOBER 1940

BLOW AT GERMAN OIL SUPPLIES

HAMBURG STORAGE TANKS DESTROYED

ENEMY BOMBERS SHOT DOWN AT DUSK

CANTERBURY CATHEDRAL GLASS BROKEN

The R.A.F. dealt their chief blow at German oil supplies on Thursday night. Oil tanks were blown up at Hamburg and fires started at several other places. Other raiders caused havoc at Kiel and at the docks at Wilhelmshaven.

London, Liverpool, and the north-east coast were raided last night. A squadron of Dorniers were intercepted by Spitfires when about to attack Liverpool and three were shot down after a chase over Wales.

R.A.F. ATTACKS ON SHIPPING

NAVAL PORTS BOMBED

The Air Ministry issued the following *communiqué* yesterday:—

Strong forces of R.A.F. bombers singled out oil targets in Germany for their main attack last [Thursday] night. At Hamburg oil storage tanks were blown up, and fires were started at Hanover, Reisholz, Gelsenkirchen, Cologne, Magdeburg, and Leuna.

In the face of intense anti-aircraft and searchlight activity warships were attacked at Wilhelmshaven and sticks of bombs fell across the harbour. At Kiel Krupps shipyards were heavily bombed and fires were started in the docks.

Shipping in the ports of Calais, Boulogne, Le Havre, and Brest was attacked in force, and at Cherbourg the coastal batteries were bombed. Other aircraft attacked shipping in harbour at Flushing and Amsterdam, as well as the docks at Den Helder.

The Fokker works at Amsterdam, factories at Bottrop, and a blast furnace at Oberhausen were bombed, and attacks were also made on railways at Soest, Hamm, and Gelsenkirchen, aerodromes at De Kooy, Kloppenberg, south-west of Bremen, and Osthein, in Bavaria, and on the seaplane base at Norderney.

All our bombers returned safely from these operations, in the course of which two enemy aircraft were shot down.

GREAT FIRES AT OIL PLANTS

ATTACKS ON SEVEN WORKS

Seven great oil plants at Hamburg, Hanover, Cologne, Magdeburg, Gelsenkirchen, Leuna, and Reischolz, with a combined annual output capacity of nearly 1,500,000 metric tons, were heavily attacked by separate raiding forces, says the Air Ministry News Service.

One of the heaviest blows was struck at the Rhenania Ossag mineral oil plant at Grasbrook, near Hamburg, which produces high-grade lubricant and has an annual output capacity of 400,000 metric tons. In a combined attack lasting for half an hour tons of high explosive and hundreds of fire bombs were unloaded on the refinery buildings and the adjoining storage tanks.

Eight large fires were counted in the factory area, and at the height of the raid a heavy explosion broke out near the centre of the plant.

At Hanover the Gewerkschaft Deutsche Erdol Refinery was the raiders' target. This great factory, which comprises three separate plants and produces benzine, fuel oil, petrol, and kerosene as well as lubricating oil. Numerous direct hits with high explosive bombs are reported to have been scored on the refinery, and fire bombs which fell close to the storage tanks started a number of fires. Violent opposition was also encountered by the raiding force which attacked the Rhenenia Ossafg oil works at Wesserling, near Cologne, and one heavy bomber was holed in 15 places by anti-aircraft shell splinters.

VIVID FLASHES

Parachute flares were used at Merseburg, near Leuna, to locate an important hydrogenation plant containing 140 manufacturing buildings which produces nearly half a million metric tons of benzine each year.

Later attackers reported heavy explosions and clouds of smoke billowing up from the works, and fresh outbreaks of fire.

Shortly after midnight more fires were started in an attack on the Braunkohlen benzine works at Magdeburg, and in a heavier attack on a large oil refinery at Gelsenkirchen violent explosions, followed by vivid blue and yellow flashes and outbreaks of fire, gave evidence of the extensive damage caused.

The seventh oil supply centre included in the night's objective was the Rhenania Ossag mineral oil works at Reisholz, near Düsseldorf. From shortly after midnight until nearly 2.30 yesterday morning this factory was repeatedly bombed by relays of raiders, and great fires, several of which were visible from over 60 miles away, were seen blazing in many parts of the works area.

The docks at Amsterdam were also subjected to harassing attacks. At Amsterdam bombs were seen to burst on a timber yard and on wharves. Another raider bombed the Fokker aircraft factory at Amsterdam, and a fire which engulfed a large building was later seen to be spreading rapidly.

The aerodromes in Germany and Holland were also attacked in the course of the night's operations. Other bombers continued the systematic hammering of the invasion ports. The raids lasted for about eight hours, and the main ports attacked were Cherbourg, Le Havre, Calais, and Boulogne.

The first bombs fell on Boulogne shortly before 8 o'clock, and the last on Cherbourg at 4 o'clock yesterday morning. During that long period much damage was done. At Boulogne many large-calibre bombs were seen to fall across the tidal harbour, the manoeuvring harbour, and the wet dock. Buildings were seen to be ablaze on the north-east side of the tidal harbour. Bombs were also dropped on a concentration of anti-aircraft guns at the mouth of the river south of Boulogne.

One of our heavy bombers returning to its base in the early hours of yesterday morning shot down an enemy machine in flames over Holland.

THREE DORNIERS DESTROYED

INTERCEPTED IN ATTACK ON LIVERPOOL

It was officially stated late last night that a number of Dorniers which attempted to attack Liverpool at about 6.30 last evening were intercepted by our fighters, chased over Wales, and three of them were shot down.

NIGHTS RAIDS ON LONDON

No searchlights were operated in the London area during the first few hours of last night's raid. Soon after the alert signal, bombs fell, and the raiders, flying high, were met by strong anti-aircraft fire.

Three bombs were dropped in quick succession in one London area, and the explosions were followed by the sound of falling débris.

When two high explosive bombs fell on villas in one district a family of four, including an elderly women who had been sheltering in the kitchen, were dug from the débris by neighbours. Apart from superficial injuries and shock, they were unhurt. Another family of four were injured and taken to hospital.

One bomb fell in a street, bursting a gas main, and one man in the street was killed. A.F.S. men dealt promptly with the fire.

Six raids were made by bombers on a north-eastern coast town last night. All the raiders were driven off by the fierce barrage from the ground defences. Bombs were dropped, but they fell in the sea, and there was no damage.

A North Wales coastal town had its first raid of the war last night. Two enemy aircraft were seen being chased by Spitfires.

The Air Ministry announced early this morning that reports received up to midnight show that eight enemy aircraft were destroyed during the day. Nine of our fighters were lost, but six of the pilots are safe.

BOMB-CARRYING FIGHTERS

DIVE ATTACKS ON THE COAST

The following Air Ministry and Ministry of Home Security *communiqué* was issued last night:—

Formations of enemy aircraft have crossed the coast of Kent on several occasions during the day. Most of them were fighters, and no heavy bombing attacks have been reported.

Bombs have been dropped at several places in Kent and Sussex and near the Thames Estuary. Casualties were not numerous, but a small number of people were fatally injured. Some damage was done to shops and houses, and at Canterbury windows in the cathedral were broken by a bomb which fell in the town.

Enemy aircraft also crossed the Dorset coast during the morning and again during the afternoon. On neither occasion did they penetrate far inland, and no casualties or damage have been reported from this area.

Five enemy aircraft have been destroyed to-day.

Five of our fighters have been lost; all the pilots are safe, though one of them is wounded.

Earlier yesterday the Air Ministry issued the following *communiqué*:—

It is now known that another enemy bomber was shot down on Thursday, making five enemy aircraft destroyed during the day. Our losses on Thursday were five aircraft, but the pilots of two are safe.

Three dive-bomb attacks were made by Messerschmitt 109s on a South-East Coast town during the morning. There were a few casualties, none of them fatal, but considerable damage was caused to property. One bomb fell on a sea wall, and the promenade and many houses and shops were damaged. Two bombs fell in a working-class area, wrecking many small houses, and one raider machine-gunned the streets.

BOMB NEAR CANTERBURY CATHEDRAL

WINDOWS BROKEN

Windows in Canterbury Cathedral were broken when a bomb dropped by a Messerschmitt hit a row of houses near the Cathedral. Two people were killed and some injured.

Before the outbreak of war steps were taken to safeguard the ancient glass and treasures of Canterbury. In August last year the valuable glass, which dates from the twelfth, thirteenth, fourteenth, and fifteenth centuries, was removed. Other precautions included the sandbagging and the shoring up of the roof of the crypt, and some of these protective measures aroused criticism.

The Dean, Dr. Hewlett Johnson, said that some very good examples of nineteenth-century window work were among the broken panes, particularly the work of the artist Austin. The protection of the roof of the crypt had been entirely justified, he said.

DAMAGE TO "THE TIMES" OFFICE

A HEAVY BOMB

NO INTERFERENCE WITH PRODUCTION

It is now permissible to publish the fact that recently *The Times* Office was heavily bombed and was much damaged. The part of the building which was struck is that facing Queen Victoria Street, Printing House Square, where stands what was the home of the Walter family in earlier centuries and the first home also of the newspaper they produced, escaped most of the surrounding destruction.

This destruction must have been greater but for the solid walls, the work of another generation, which defended the fabric on Queen Victoria Street. Windows indeed were smashed, the well-known clock disappeared, and there was some defacement; but the ancient red brick stood up well to the test of modern bombardment. The partial ruin of neighbouring structures showed how fierce the test had been.

Interior damage, however, was severe. Many rooms in the Editorial departments were reduced to chaos. The Managerial section fared almost as badly. But although the task of bringing order again from the mingled mass of masonry, broken glass, splintered furniture, and stored memoranda was great, it was tackled without delay and with a degree of success that would have seemed impossible at first to anyone contemplating the ruin.

TEST FOR A.R.P.

The air raid precautions taken long ago, including the special system of observation and warning, were ready for the call suddenly made upon them, hampered as they were by darkness. It is a happy fact that, though several of the staff had remarkably narrow escapes, none was more than slightly hurt.

The production of *The Times* was already in progress and was maintained without interruption. *The Times* of the following day was also published with no evidence whatever of the explosion or its consequences. Alternative plans and general good will sufficed amply to speed the work of rapid adaptation and to prevent any breach of continuity. Next morning it was noted by the public in Queen Victoria Street that above the ruins the two Union Jacks were flying as usual on their flagstaffs.

Pictures on pages 2 and 8.

PRIME MINISTER'S LETTER

The following letter has since been addressed by the Prime Minister to the chairman of *The Times* Publishing Company, Limited:—

10, Downing Street, Whitehall.
October 10, 1940.

My dear Astor,

Congratulations on the remarkable way in which *The Times* has carried on in face of all the damage and discomfort caused by the bombing of Printing House Square.

None of your readers could discover from the paper that your Editorial and Management departments have been destroyed.

The resourcefulness and adaptability of your staff are beyond praise.

WINSTON S. CHURCHILL.

Major the Hon. J. J. Astor, M.P.

ITALIANS ISOLATED IN E. AFRICA

SUPPLIES CUT OFF

FROM OUR SPECIAL CORRESPONDENT

CAIRO, Oct. 11

Every effort is being made by the Italians to get supplies to their besieged garrison in Italian East Africa.

Three routes are being tried. The first is a night-flying aeroplane that makes a 1,600-mile hop across the Sudan with mails and vital spare parts for aircraft and with staff officers and pilots. It carries just enough petrol to get across. The second route is by sea, either north from Madagascar or direct across the Indian Ocean to Italian Somaliland ports such as Mogadishu. Trading vessels, notably Japanese, have been observed in enemy ports. The third route is across Arabia to the Italian zone of influence round the Yemen and thence across the Red Sea by little native dhows.

Yet none of these ways can supply more than a trickle of goods to the Italians. They are dependent chiefly on rationing and the cutting down of all offensive action to a few scattered desert skirmishes and raids, chiefly on Aden.

Most of their ammunition, guns, and equipment in Abyssinia are out of date. We secured the cream of it when we captured two army supply ships in the Red Sea last June, but it is estimated that Italian East Africa has got supplies for months to come yet, and there is no present indication that the garrison is in danger of collapsing through a shortage this winter.

The Egyptian Consul in Addis Ababa, M. Albert Mansour, has arrived here after an 80-day trip. He wandered thousands of miles over East Africa by train, car, and aeroplane, and even on foot, while the Italians wrangled over his release. They sent him from one place to another while they debated what to do with him. At Asmara, capital of Eritrea, M. Mansour said, not a single day passed without the R.A.F. raiding some aerodrome, fuel dump, or military objective, but the residents had grown so sure that the R.A.F. was not after civilian objectives that they regularly climbed to their roof-tops to watch the bombing. Along the Sudanese border, he said, the British patrols were keeping the Italian garrisons in a state of alarm with their nightly armoured-car raids.

THE KING DELAYED BY TIME BOMB

When the King and Queen were motoring yesterday in a district outside London, traffic was held up while a small time bomb was exploded. The delay caused was only a few minutes, and immediately afterwards the royal car proceeded on its way.

MR. KENNEDY'S ESCAPE

Mr. Joseph Kennedy, the American Ambassador, escaped injury when two heavy bombs fell early yesterday in the grounds of the house in the country where he was staying. One bomb demolished some cottages on the estate, and 11 people who live in the cottages escaped with minor injuries. A 17-year-old boy was detained in hospital.

NAVY ATTACKS CHERBOURG

ASSAULT BY SEA AND AIR

GLARE SEEN FOR 100 MILES

The Admiralty issued the following *communiqué* last night:—

Heavy and light forces of the Royal Navy on Wednesday night carried out a bombardment of the enemy-occupied port of Cherbourg, where a concentration of enemy shipping had been detected by air reconnaissance.

The success of the bombardment was largely due to the excellent cooperation of the Royal Air Force, which assisted in reconnaissance and throughout the operation.

Our salvos were seen bursting effectively on the targets and very large fires resulted. These were visible from our ships on their way home at a distance of 40 miles.

Our ships met with no opposition from the enemy either during the approach or the bombardment. While returning from their bombarding positions our main forces came under fire from enemy shore batteries. No damage or casualties were, however, sustained. No naval opposition from the enemy was encountered, although it was known that enemy light forces were at Cherbourg.

"500 THUNDERSTORMS IN ONE"

BOMBARDMENT AS SEEN FROM THE AIR

The naval bombardment of Cherbourg on Thursday night was described yesterday by a Royal Air Force pilot who was operating in the area at the same time, states the Air Ministry News Service.

It was like hell let loose (a squadron commander said). As we went over the English coast the glare and explosions appeared to be so close that I imagined at first we must be off our course, but it was Cherbourg all right —about 100 miles away. Clouds drifting across the scene were silhouetted against the white glow of flares which dropped incessantly over the target area from other aircraft, illuminating the place. As we neared it, the enemy ground defences completed the effect with searchlights, "flaming onions," and light and heavy anti-aircraft fire.

We were over the target area when suddenly the Navy let fly. It was like 500 thunderstorms rolled into one. One of my pilots said that even the tornadoes he had experienced in the Pacific Islands came nowhere near it. Every cloud flamed bright amber colour, and we could see the bursts of the first salvo plumb in the docks. Until then the ground defences had been blazing away at us, but this sudden blast from the sea "foxed" them absolutely. They did not know if it was Christmas or Easter. The searchlights went quite drunk, waving aimlessly about the sky; the guns continued firing, but goodness knows what at. There was complete chaos down below. I said to my crew when we landed, "I have seen a few Fifths of November, but what about October 11?"

We were looking round for something left to bomb, and observed flashes from a coastal defence battery in action at Henneville; so we dropped our heavy bombs on that, starting a long fire.

GERMAN DESTROYERS ATTACKED

NIGHT RAID ON BREST

Raids by aircraft of the Coastal Command on Thursday night ranged from Den Helder on the Dutch coast down the Channel to Boulogne, Le Havre, and Brest.

The attack on German destroyers in the harbour at Brest was repeated for the second night in succession. Although weather conditions were difficult and anti-aircraft fire was intense, the pilots straddled the destroyers with heavy bombs and scored several hits.

Other salvos severely damaged workshops and storehouses on the shore. There were three heavy explosions in the dockyard at Den Helder after the Blenheim had let go its salvo. Other bombs fell on quays and set buildings ablaze. At Boulogne pilots saw their bombs burst amid a concentration of 30 to 40 small ships surrounding a larger vessel. At the end of this attack one Blenheim flew low and machine-gunned ships in the outer harbour.

WOUNDED AT CONTROLS

A Beaufort taking part in this raid was attacked just outside Boulogne by two Messerschmitt 109s. The first fire from the Germans put the Beaufort's rear gun out of action and jammed his undercarriage. A cannon shell blew a great hole in the cockpit and injured the pilot. He had five flesh wounds, but he stayed at the controls. The Germans continued the attack. Then a second Beaufort, returning from the raid, dived on the Messerschmitts.

"We gave one of them a sharp burst. At once both the Messerschmitts made off," said the gunner of the rescuing aircraft." By this time the wounded pilot was too weak to go on. He handed over the controls to the second pilot, who brought the aircraft safely to its base.

Blenheims which attacked Le Havre found the dock shrouded in mist. They selected one basin and bombed it accurately and systematically. "We had a tremendous reception," one pilot said. "The anti-aircraft fire was enough to cut us to ribbons. It seems miraculous that we all went through it and came back safely."

Another pilot said that the glare from the searchlights was so great that he could see four silhouettes from his aircraft above.

DAMAGE AT KIEL

Further blows were dealt on Thursday night at the German ports of Kiel and Wilhelmshaven by heavy bombers of the R.A.F.

Soon after darkness had fallen the raiders were on their way across the North Sea, and shortly after 9 o'clock the first of the heavy bombs had been dropped on the docks at Wilhelmshaven.

The raid lasted nearly two hours. Vigorous anti-aircraft fire and intense searchlight activity were encountered by the raiders, who attacked from varying heights. Most of the pilots and observers report having seen their bombs explode and others saw fires spring up in the target area. One burst was seen near the central floating dock.

One of our aircraft was attacked during the raid by an unidentified enemy machine. The rear-gunner returned the fire with such effect that the enemy aircraft was shot down and was seen by the air-gunner and wireless-operator lying in the sea 4,000ft. below.

At the same time as the raid at Wilhelmshaven the great strategic port at Kiel, 100 miles east across the Holstein Peninsula, was being battered by heavy bombers. Here, again, there was intense activity by anti-aircraft guns and searchlights. Most of the bombs were seen to burst in the target area and two huge fires were caused. These increased in volume, and when the raiders were on their homeward course over the North Sea and 70 miles from the target the flames were still seen lighting the eastern sky behind them.

NO BACKING DOWN TO JAPAN

AMERICAN STAND

PRESIDENT ROOSEVELT TO SPEAK

From Our Own Correspondent

WASHINGTON, Oct. 11

President Roosevelt, on the occasion of the tour of inspection of armaments which he is now making in Pennsylvania and Ohio, will speak to-morrow night at Dayton on the general subject of the defence of the Western Hemisphere. The speech, according to the White House, will be entirely "non-political," but by implication at least it can hardly fail to deal with the situation in Europe and Asia and to serve as a reply to attacks upon the Administration's foreign policy, made by the Republican candidate, Mr. Wendell Willkie.

What that policy is in regard to the Far East has, according to the syndicated column of Mr. Joseph Alsop and Mr. Robert Kintner, been conveyed in general terms to Congressional leaders "as authoritatively summarized." They say it is as follows:—

We are not going to fight Japan, but we are not going to back down in the Far East either. Possibly Japan will choose to attack us, because we have refused to back down. Then our course will be clear; but the possibility that Japan will so choose seems to be extremely remote.

Everything points to the correctness of this summary, but it will remain for the next week or weeks to indicate how much action "not backing down" may involve.

REMINDER TO THAILAND

The American Minister in Bangkok, Mr Hugh Grant, as a commentary on the demands for territorial concessions from Indo-China, has taken the opportunity to remind the Government of Thailand of the American desire for the maintenance of the *status quo*, and a few American aeroplanes, destined for Thailand, have been held up at Manila. The Chief of the Air Force of the Dutch East Indies is expected here shortly, and when asked whether he was seeking to purchase aircraft, Mr. Hull replied that he did not know, but that extensive sales had already been made to the colony.

These and other matters, like the dispatch of an anti-aircraft regiment of the National Guard to Hawaii, show how things are moving. Admiral Standley, former Chief of Naval Operations, speaking at Philadelphia last night, said that an American destroyer squadron should be sent to the Western Pacific, for "Japan will keep on moving until she finds we oppose her." But this—with the reservation that nothing is impossible—is merely an unofficial suggestion. Most Americans in the Orient are inclined to agree with Mr. Nathanial Peffer, who writes in the *New Republic* to-day:—

The Japanese must have a German victory. But this is far from saying that, on a German summons, they will go to war with America. . . . The last thing that the most heedless Japanese general wants is war with America.

RUMANIAN ASSETS

The American Treasury has "frozen" Rumanian assets in the United States, the extent of which is roughly calculated at $40,000,000 (£10,000,000). But Mr. Hull said to-day that Washington had "not thus far" urged American citizens to leave Rumania and other Balkan countries or considered the recall of the American Minister in Bucharest.

Incidentally, and "because of the present importance of Egypt" in international affairs, the War Department is sending a military attaché to Cairo for the first time since 1922.

It is generally believed here, and believed most strongly by those who have recently seen him, that Mr. Joseph Kennedy, the American Ambassador in London, intends an early visit to the United States. One correspondent to-day asked Mr. Hull bluntly whether there was truth in the report that this visit had been officially discouraged, because of Mr. Kennedy's "fears and glooms" and because their dissemination at home might affect the conduct of foreign policy. Mr. Hull replied smilingly that he knew nothing about it.

"JAPAN IS NOT COMMITTED"

PROFESSED RESERVATIONS ON NEW PACT

FROM OUR OWN CORRESPONDENT

TOKYO, Oct. 11

A diplomatic official to-day assured me that "Japan has not committed its destiny into Hitler's hands. We have not surrendered our autonomy in foreign policy. It is for the Japanese Government to decide what brings the treaty into operation." When asked to reconcile that statement with Article 3 of the pact, the official pointed to the word "attacked," and said that Japan retained the sole right to decide what constituted an attack in the terms of the alliance.

The evident implication is that there exists, besides the published text, some protocol allowing Japan a considerable friedom of interpretation. When asked to explain what tangible return Japan obtained for the obligation, which, however qualified, had already created intense suspicions, the official replied by describing the spiritual background of the treaty:—

Japan's primary object is victory in China. America and Great Britain oppose our new order and our policy there. They refuse to realize that Japan's prestige and her future in the Far East require a complete victory, which our military power will sooner or later achieve. Germany and Italy, like us, aspire to create a new world order. It is natural we should support each other. Further, it must be remembered that the face of Europe has been changed since the war began.

The meaning of this statement appears to be first that Japan has felt it necessary to abandon her isolation, and, secondly, the Japanese Government have been convinced that the Axis will be victorious. These explanations suggest that the treaty is less definite than it appears, but it must not be forgotten that the same internal forces which caused the treaty to be concluded will have the power of interpreting it when the time comes. Germany depends on them rather than on protocols. Meanwhile, Japan is serving the Axis by detaining the American Fleet in the Pacific, receiving in return diplomatic assistance in occupied Europe and certain munitions and technical aid.

ANOTHER V.C.

GALLANT ACTION IN SOMALILAND

The King has been pleased to approve of the posthumous award of the Victoria Cross, for most conspicuous gallantry on active service in Somaliland, to

WILSON, LIEUTENANT (ACTING CAPTAIN) ERIC CHARLES TWELVES, The East Surrey Regiment (attached Somaliland Camel Corps).

Captain Wilson was in command of machine-gun posts manned by Somali soldiers in the key position of Observation Hill, a defended post in the defensive organization of the Tug Argan Gap in British Somaliland.

The enemy attacked Observation Hill on August 11, 1940. Captain Wilson and Somali gunners under his command beat off the attack and opened fire on the enemy troops attacking Mill Hill, another post within his range. He inflicted such heavy casualties that the enemy, determined to put his guns out of action, brought up a pack battery to within 700 yards, and scored two direct hits through the loopholes of his defences, which, bursting within the post, wounded Captain Wilson severely in the right shoulder and in the left eye, several of his team being also wounded. His guns were blown off their stands, but he repaired and replaced them, and, regardless of his wounds, carried on, while his Somali sergeant was killed beside him.

On August 12 and 14 the enemy again concentrated field artillery fire on Captain Wilson's guns, but he continued, with his wounds untended, to man them.

On August 15 two of his machine-gun posts were blown to pieces, yet Captain Wilson, now suffering from malaria in addition to wounds, still kept his own post in action.

The enemy finally overran the post at 5 p.m. on August 15, when Captain Wilson, fighting to the last, was killed.

Further awards to members of the Navy, the Army, and the Royal Air Force appear on page 2.

MR. CHAMBERLAIN'S THANKS

"DEEPLY TOUCHED" BY SYMPATHY

A recording of a personal message from Mr. Neville Chamberlain thanking all who had written to him since his resignation from the War Cabinet was broadcast last night. He said:—

I hope in time to be able to reply to most, if not all, of them, but in the meantime I want to say how deeply my wife and I have been touched by this spontaneous and warm-hearted expression of sympathy and good will.

Most of my correspondents are quite unknown to me, but they express their gratitude for what I have tried to do, and by their regard for me, with such transparent and sometimes passionate sincerity, they have, indeed, lightened my affliction and made up for many disappointments. From the bottom of my heart I thank them.

There is one other note which runs through all my letters, and that is an unwavering confidence in ultimate victory. I share that confidence. It is not conceivable that human civilization should be permanently overcome by such evil men and evil things as we are fighting against, and I feel proud that the British Empire, though left to fight alone, still stands across their path, unconquered and unconquerable.

THE KING'S FUND

EXTENSION TO HELP CIVILIANS

An extension of the scope of the King's Fund to include civilians was announced by Sir Walter Womersley, Minister of Pensions, at Glasgow yesterday.

Sir Walter, sole trustee of the fund, which was established during the last War with subscriptions of over £1,500,000, said that he had considered at the outset of the war that the operations of the fund could be extended to include those who were not necessarily in the Services. The King gave his consent to the alteration of the Charter.

A cheque for £1,000 had been received from Mr. Henry J. Jourdain, whose son, Lieutenant E. P. R. Jourdain, was killed at Dunkirk. Mr. Jourdain was very concerned about those fishermen, yachtsmen, and boatmen who had assisted so heroically at the great evacuation, and thought it would be a good thing if a fund were started to give any assistance they might require. Mr. Jourdain's gift was in memory of his son, and although no public appeal was made other substantial sums had come in, and all had been set aside for the purpose.

Up to October 4 civilian pensions to air raid victims had been granted as follows:—Disabled, 291; widows, 402; dependents, 19. Civilian injury allowances to September 27 totalled 7,814. Officials were acting immediately in such cases, and pensions and allowances were being issued within a few days to prevent hardship.

WHAT TO DO WHEN CHALLENGED

ORDERS TO SENTRIES

FROM OUR AERONAUTICAL CORRESPONDENT

The form of challenge to be made by sentries and the correct answer are set out in Air Ministry Orders.

Any person approaching is to be challenged: "Halt, who goes there?" On receiving the answer "Friend," the sentry is to respond, "Advance one to be recognized." ("One" means one person.) If the party challenged consists of more than one person the challenge is to be repeated for each.

If a person challenged does not halt he is to be challenged in this manner: "Halt, or I fire." If he does not then halt he is to be challenged once more in this manner, but if he still does not halt and no means are available to stop him, the sentry is instructed to fire, aiming low to hit but not to kill.

Where a person who has been challenged can be stopped by some other means—such as by calling on the guard—the sentry is not to shoot.

U.S. COMMUNISTS' DILEMMA

DUCAL CONSENT NEEDED FOR WALL SIGN

FROM OUR OWN CORRESPONDENT

NEW YORK, Oct. 11

The American Communist Party has just been placed in the unhappy position of having to ask a Scottish duke for permission to advertise its virtues in Times Square.

Recently the party persuaded the owners of the hotel there to permit it to paint a sign on the side wall of the building, appealing for the election of Communist candidates for the Presidency of the United States and other offices. The owners soon afterwards regretted their decision, and had the sign painted out. The Communists then got a Court order requiring them to paint it again. The order stipulated, however, that, since the painters' scaffolding would overhang the adjoining property, the consent of the owner of that property must be obtained. The owner in question is the Duke of Roxburghe.

STRAITS GUN DUEL

A violent artillery duel between British and German guns was fought across the Straits of Dover by bright moonlight last night. There were apparently four enemy batteries in action. The biggest battery, of four guns, was at Wimereux, a battery of two guns was near Cap Gris Nez, and two others were east of Calais.

BRITONS IN RUMANIA

ADVICE TO LEAVE AT ONCE

CRITICAL PHASE IN RELATIONS

The British Government has instructed the Legation in Bucharest that in view of the uncertain conditions in Rumania all British subjects who wish to do so are advised to leave the country immediately, states a Reuter message from Bucharest.

Some British subjects are leaving this week-end, but it is probable that the majority will be accommodated on board a ship which is to leave Constanza for Istanbul on Monday evening.

From authoritative quarters in London the following statement has been issued:—

It is now possible to make a statement on the subject of the arrivals of German troops in Rumania. It has not been possible to do so hitherto owing to contradictory statements by the Rumanian Government and to the fact that telegrams from H.M. Minister in Bucharest were being held up.

Early in September a considerable number of German S.S. men in uniform arrived in Rumania. According to the Rumanian Government these men had been admitted in connexion with the evacuation of the German colony in Bessarabia. It was clear, however, both from the destinations to which the Germans proceeded and from the fact that they were accompanied by equipment, that the true object was to enable the Germans to occupy certain strategic points in Rumania.

There is reason to believe that an agreement was made with the German Government, even before General Antonescu assumed office, for the dispatch to Rumania of German armoured divisions.

On October 8 the news was received in London of the arrival of further German troops in Rumania. In reply to an inquiry for information H.M. Minister in Bucharest was informed by the Rumanian Government that Rumania would not be occupied by German troops and that no German "unit" had entered Rumania. The Rumanian Government's reply intimated that Rumania had the right to "procure where she can the material necessary for her armament and the technicians required for the instruction of her units." In fact, it seems that the material of two motorized and one armoured division are shortly to be imported.

"LARGE NUMBERS"

Sir Reginald Hoare, as the result of persistent requests, succeeded on October 9 in seeing the Rumanian Minister for Foreign Affairs, from whom he elicited the information that a very large number of "German instructors" were expected forthwith.

Sir Reginald Hoare saw the President of the Council the same day, and General Antonescu stated categorically that there were no German troops in Rumania, though, he added, that Germans, to the number of 3,000, were expected. General Antonescu described these men as "specialists, instructors, or technicians," but there are good grounds for believing that the men will be troops, that they will arrive very shortly, and that the numbers will be considerable.

Sir Reginald Hoare has made it clear to General Antonescu that, as he understands the position, the relations between Great Britain and Rumania have reached a critical point.

The arrest and ill-treatment of British subjects employed in the oil companies in Rumania have been the subject of the most vigorous protests by his Majesty's Government. The Rumanian Government have as yet to release all the British subjects concerned, but as a result of Sir Reginald Hoare's emphatic intervention his Majesty's Government have some reason to believe that the arrested persons are no longer in danger or discomfort.

GERMAN AEROPLANES OVER BUCHAREST

BOMBERS AND FIGHTERS

More than 150 bombers and fighters with both German and Rumanian markings were flying over Bucharest from 4.30 p.m. yesterday, states the British United Press in a message from Bucharest. Reports that 1,500 German aircraft and about 2,000 German tanks were on their way to Rumania were denied by the Rumanians and by both German and Italian sources.

Mr. Miller, the British employee of the Astra Romano Oil Company who was kidnapped last week by Iron Guard extremists and later handed over to the police, has now been passed on by the police authorities for Court-martial at the hands of a Military Tribunal on a charge of sabotage, states Reuter. He thus joins the five other British subjects in the military prison here who are awaiting trial on the same charge.

It is understood that the preliminary police report on Mr. Miller's activities exonerated him from the charge of sabotage, but the Director of Police refused to take the responsibility of releasing him with an order of expulsion from the country. Mr. Miller was therefore handed over to the military authorities.

The British Legation is taking every step possible to ensure that Mr. Miller and the five other British subjects are adequately defended and that the case should be heard as early as possible.

RUMANIAN DIPLOMATIST RESIGNS

Our Diplomatic Correspondent writes:

In London some Rumanian diplomatists are watching the events with the greatest misgivings. M. Dimancescu, Chancellor of Legation, has already resigned his post because, as he says, the present Rumanian Government has surrendered to a foreign Power. Others in the Legation are understood to be about to follow him if the breach between this country and Rumania becomes open.

MINESWEEPING TRAWLER LOST

The Board of Admiralty regrets to announce that H.M. minesweeping trawler Sea King (Temporary Skipper L. Rushby, R.N.R.) has been sunk by an enemy mine. The next-of-kin of casualties have been informed.

OBITUARY

We announce with regret the deaths of LORD MONSON and MR. H. M. J. LOEWE, Reader in Rabbinic at Cambridge University.

Memoirs and *The Times* List of Fallen Officers will be found on page 6.

BRITISH PRISONERS OF WAR

According to the official German News Agency, quoted by Reuter, British prisoners of war in Germany total 1,550 officers and 35,500 n.c.o.s and men.

Above May 1941, the Blitz on London. Building ablaze on Ludgate Hill, with St Paul's in the background.

Above right London carries on, 13 September 1940.

Right Col. J. J. Astor with THE TIMES unit of the Home Guard, July 1940.

Below From the left, John Walter, Geoffrey Dawson, Col. J. J. Astor, R. W. Cooper (war correspondent), R. Barrington-Ward (assistant editor), dining in the air raid shelter at THE TIMES.

on the following morning. It was a night of Inferno for the City. At 1.50 am a spotter on the roof reported to the Control Room that he 'did not like the sound of a plane coming in from the south west'. Then he and two others with him heard the whistle of bombs 'as close as breathing', and ducked. Printing House Square was heavily hit. There were about three hundred people in the building at the time, printing the next day's edition.

Dawson was asleep in his cubby-hole. This is what he recorded in his diary:

> A very noisy night. Retiring to my camp bed below about midnight. Two hours later there was a terrific and very near bang and a general buzz of excitement. I came up to find that two bombs had struck the front of the office. My own room was deep in glass and debris but otherwise intact. It was impossible to do much in the dark. Kent [the Manager] arrived to see to salvage, and John [Colonel John Astor, the Proprietor, who had been dozing in the Board Room] and I went home to sleep.

Nobody was killed. The Intelligence Department, which is how *The Times* grandiloquently and quaintly describes its excellent library, had suffered the worst damage. The streets of Blackfriars were strewn with the mountains of cuttings, files and other paper that are the fuel on which a newspaper runs. Underground, after an interval of eighteen minutes to get the lights back on, the presses started to roll again. *The Times* came out as usual.

No announcement of the hit was allowed by the censors in the British press until 12 October. Modern journalists, with their creed that the news must come first, have little notion of the rigours of censorship in the Second World War.

But the Germans knew, and showed what store they set on stopping *The Times*. On 27 September the German News Agency reported that Printing House Square had been hit and that *The Times* had been published in the provinces. On the following day the Germans changed their propaganda:

> One of the workshops for the distortion of the truth in London nearly disappeared from the surface of the globe. It is learned, in fact, that the administrative and editorial offices, as well as several storeys of the building occupied by *The Times*, have been heavily damaged by a bomb of a large calibre. Other printing offices in the City undertook the production of the paper.

Nice one, Goebbels. But not true.

The Prime Minister, Winston Churchill, wrote from Number 10 Downing Street:

> My dear Astor,
>
> Congratulations on the remarkable way in which *The Times* has carried on in face of all the damage and discomfort caused by the bombing of Printing House Square.
>
> None of your readers could discover from the paper that your editorial and management departments have been destroyed.
>
> The resourcefulness and adaptability of your staff are beyond praise.

The Everest scoop

Below Mount Everest flight. One of the machines at the base aerodrome, Houston.

Bottom View of Mount Everest from a survey station above the East Rongbuk Glacier, taken during the 1935 Reconnaissance Expedition.

The first ascent of Everest, published in *The Times* of 2 June 1953, was a great scoop and a symbolic British triumph on the morning of the Queen's coronation. The story of how *The Times* got the story is a classic of the inky trade.

The Times had been associated with earlier attempts to climb the highest mountain in the world, including the first one, led by Colonel Bury, in 1921, and the tragic one by Mallory and Irvine in 1924. The agreement then, and with later attempts, was to mutual advantage. *The Times* paid the Mount Everest Committee a fee for certain exclusive rights of publication and films of the expedition; it recovered some of its heavy expenses by the sale of rights to overseas and provincial papers.

The first member of the staff of *The Times* to travel with an Everest expedition was E. Colston Shepherd, the aeronautical correspondent, who went out with the Houston Mount Everest Flight Expedition in 1933. He seems to have been a useful man to have had on the team, for the official publication, *First Over Everest* (1933), describes him as being appointed 'Chancellor-of-the-Exchequer and Chief Major-Domo'.

The 1953 expedition led by Colonel (later Sir) John (later Lord) Hunt was in scale, preparation and cost the most ambitious ever mounted. Once again *The Times* secured first rights on reporting its progress. In addition, however, the office proposed that a member of its staff should accompany the expedition, to be responsible for sending back Colonel Hunt's articles, as well as his own dispatches. In the urgent application for the necessary visa, the foreign editor wrote that the *Times* man would be travelling not as a journalist but as 'a transport organizer'.

The staff-man chosen was James Morris, then 27, a sub-editor on the foreign news desk. The foreign editor commented, when the choice was made, 'I wish that Morris didn't look *quite* so pleased'. From the start it was obvious that, notwithstanding

THE TIMES

THE FIRST ASCENT OF

MOUNT EVEREST

SUPPLEMENT

LONDON JULY 1953 ONE SHILLING

ON THE SUMMIT

Tensing, photographed by his companion Hillary, at 11.30 a.m. on Friday, May 29, 1953.

Top Sherpa Tenzing on the summit, Friday 29 May 1953.

Above An advertisement from the special supplement published to mark the ascent.

Right Letter from the British Embassy, Katmandu, to THE TIMES outlining the codes to be used for success or failure.

c/o British Embassy,
Katmandu.
22nd May 1953

My dear Norman,

In my letter dated May 19, I enclosed a series of phrases, which (if you receive them) will bear the following meanings.

These phrases have been devised by Morris and myself to cover at least the two major eventualities of success or failure, since in certain sections of our route from him to you it has become impossible --- for reasons explained in my letter of May 19--- to use the words we had originally devised.

PLEASE ACKNOWLEDGE RECEIPT OF THIS LETTER BY CABLE, AS ALSO RECEIPT OF MY LETTER DATED MAY 19.

After receipt of this letter (or that of May 19, whichever is the earlier) you may at any time expect to receive, either direct or through the Foreign Office, a cable beginning

Either SNOW CONDITIONS BAD, meaning EVEREST CLIMBED

or, in the event of failure, beginning

WIND STILL TROUBLESOME meaning ATTEMPT ON EVEREST FINALLY ABANDONED AND WITHDRAWAL FROM MOUNTAIN UNDER WAY

Whichever of thes phrases is used will be followed by the names of the climbers who reached the highest point attained, using the following phrases for this purpose:

	meaning	
SOUTH COL UNTENABLE		BAND
LHOTSE FACE IMPOSSIBLE		BOURDILLON
RIDGE CAMP UNTENABLE		EVANS
WITHDRAWAL TO WEST BASIN		GREGORY
ADVANCED BASE ABANDONED		HILLARY
CAMP 5 ABANDONED		HUNT
CAMP 6 ABANDONED		LOWE
CAMP 7 ABANDONED		NOYCE
AWAITING IMPROVEMENT		TENSING
FURTHER NEWS FOLLOWS		WARD
ASSAULT POSTPONED		WESTMACOTT
WEATHER DETERIORATING		WYLIE

A SHERPA climber of any name (other than Tensing) will be represented by the phrase AWAITING OXYGEN SUPPLIES.

If the message records failure, i.e. begins WIND STILL TROUBLESOME,

The Times's first rights, other newspapers would be in the snow-field and the competition would be ruthless.

The plan was that messages would be carried by runner to Arthur Hutchinson, *The Times* correspondent in Delhi, who would be stationed at Katmandu. From there Hutchinson would cable them to Printing House Square.

The opposition were quickly at Katmandu. They included Ralph Izzard of the *Daily Mail* and Colin Reid of *The Daily Telegraph*. No news may be good news; but in a race for a big story no rival newsmen would have been even better. Morris eventually arrived at Namche Bazar (thirty miles south east of the 'Mother of Snows') to find that there was a police post with a wireless transmitter there. However, the dangers of messages being intercepted (two rival journalists had powerful receiving sets) or leaked by the staff at the post were too apparent. So Morris kept using runners to send his dispatches to Katmandu.

From Thyangboche James Morris with Charles Evans and Alfred Gregory set off for the mountain, and reached the expedition's base camp on the Khumbu Glacier. His first experience of mountaineering proper came with the climb into the Western Cwm up to 20,000 feet.

For the final assault he was sending regular dispatches home by his runners. The basic fee was £10–£15 if the arduous journey to Katmandu was done in eight days, £20 for seven days, £30 for six days. Not even a Sherpa Phidippides could do it in fewer than six days.

Towards the end of May everything was ready for the final assault. Although none of the rival journalists was on the mountain, Morris was worried about the security of communications through the Namche transmitter. The news that Everest had been conquered was bound to leak and deprive *The Times* of its exclusive.

A code for such circumstances had been arranged in London before he left. With a slight change it would still make sense to London when transmitted. 'Snow conditions bad' meant 'Everest climbed'. The code name for Hillary was: 'Advanced base abandoned'; Tenzing was 'Awaiting improvement'.

On 29 May Morris climbed up to Camp IV at the head of the Cwm at 22,000 feet. He found Hunt and most of the expedition assembled there. Morris wrote: 'I shall never, as long as I live, forget the transformation that overcame the camp when the summit party appeared and gave us the news of their victory . . . It was a moment of great beauty: a joy forever'.

The date was 31 May. 'In a moment of wild optimism', Morris thought, '*The Times* could conceivably print the news on the very day of Queen Elizabeth's coronation, June 2'. On that morning he had already climbed up from Camp III. However, he at once set off down the mountain as fast as he could, a reporter with a world scoop, slithering, often losing his footing, getting entangled with the ropes, and hovering on crevasses. At Base Camp he typed out the coded message: 'SNOW CONDITIONS BAD STOP ADVANCED BASE ABANDONED MAY TWENTY-NINE STOP AWAITING IMPROVEMENT STOP.' He handed it to a runner to deliver to the radio station at Namche Bazar. Thence it was transmitted to Katmandu. Across the wires the electric message came. The result is shown opposite.

On the eve of her coronation the Queen learnt of the success. And on 2 June the crowds who had lined the streets all night, waiting for the procession, read about it in *The Times*. Nobody could have put James Morris's part in that success and scoop better than the leader of the expedition, who in *The Ascent of Everest* wrote: 'At this time, the climax of the expedition, James was at the top of his professional form'.

James Morris's journalistic triumph: his scoop story of the successful ascent of Everest reached THE TIMES in time for publication on Coronation Day.
2 JUNE 1953

THOUSANDS SPEND NIGHT ON CORONATION ROUTE

PLACES TAKEN UP 24 HOURS IN ADVANCE

Thousands of people spent last night on the Coronation route, having taken up their positions yesterday in readiness for to-day's procession. They were not dismayed by showers of rain, and even sleet, against which many were poorly protected.

For to-day, cool, showery weather, with sunny intervals, is forecast.

Final preparations were made yesterday, including the completion of the decoration of the route with thousands of flowers, many of which had been flown from Commonwealth countries.

WORK IN ABBEY COMPLETE

EARL MARSHAL'S BROADCAST

The Queen will be crowned in Westminster Abbey to-day in the presence of her husband, the Duke of Edinburgh, the Great Officers of State, and an illustrious assembly; in the hearing, through the agency of broadcasting, of unnumbered millions spread over a large part of the world, and in the sight of another great aggregation of audiences within television range.

St. Edward's Crown will be placed upon the Queen's head by the Archbishop of Canterbury at about 12.30 p.m., towards the middle of a protracted service of rich imagery and deep spiritual significance. This moment of actual Coronation will be announced to the people outside the Abbey and in the streets by the firing of salutes of artillery at the Tower of London and in Hyde Park. Scenes of rejoicing will mark the event and the day throughout the Kingdom and Commonwealth and in many lands beyond.

The Duke of Norfolk, the Earl Marshal, in a statement broadcast last night, said that preparations for the Coronation were complete and the Abbey, in all its splendour, was ready. "To-night," he added, "I take over the keys, and they will be handed back to the Dean to-morrow evening."

Through streets lavishly decorated and lined with men and women of the services, the Queen and the Duke of Edinburgh will drive to the Abbey in the state coach, drawn by eight grey horses, by way of The Mall, Northumberland Avenue, and Victoria Embankment, leaving Buckingham Palace at 10.26 a.m. After the Abbey service they will drive back to the Palace by a much longer route, and for this return journey the state procession will be extended by the addition of contingents of the three services of the United Kingdom and detachments from the defence forces of the Commonwealth and Colonies.

45 MINUTES TO PASS

The return procession will take about 45 minutes to pass. Its head is timed to leave Marble Arch at 2.55 p.m.; the state coach with her Majesty and the Duke of Edinburgh leaves Westminster Abbey at about 2.50 p.m. and is due back at Buckingham Palace at about 4.30. The route will be:—Whitehall, Cockspur Street, Pall Mall, St. James's Street, Piccadilly, East Carriage Road, Oxford Street, Regent Street, Haymarket, Cockspur Street, and The Mall.

After the Queen has re-entered the Palace she will come out on the balcony to take the salute at 5.15 of a formation of 168 jet fighters of the Royal Air Force and the Royal Canadian Air Force flying across The Mall from right to left of her.

At 9 o'clock this evening the Queen will broadcast to her peoples in all B.B.C. services. Her address will be preceded by one given by the Prime Minister at 8.55 from Downing Street, and will set the seal on a memorable programme in the Home service, beginning at 8 o'clock, entitled "Long Live the Queen," in which a distinguished array of Prime Ministers and other statesmen and leading figures in the Commonwealth and Empire will speak.

UNDISMAYED BY RAIN

TRAFFIC STOPPED BY DENSE CROWDS

BY OUR SPECIAL CORRESPONDENT

Into a London transformed for pageant and carnival there streamed throughout the hours of light and darkness yesterday some of the great concourse that will be gathered to acclaim the Queen. A few had already gathered on Sunday evening. They mixed with the working millions and the sightseeing thousands and choked the pavements of the processional way. They overflowed on to the roads and stopped the traffic. They spread their blankets on the kerbs, set up their chairs, and looked down the long vista of their waiting hours undismayed.

In these matters figures hide a lot of guesswork, but an estimate by the police that by midday more than 5,000 intending spectators had begun their vigil in central London seemed not to lean towards exaggeration. By last night the total had grown by leaps and bounds, and many who thought they would be in good time for a commanding view found the front positions, and in some cases the second and third rows, already occupied and almost defensively entrenched.

Yesterday morning would have proved almost too late to be sure of room in the front row along the Mall, for by noon from the crowded railings of Buckingham Palace (where the guardsmen sentries patrolled inside the forecourt) to the nautically bedizened Admiralty Arch both kerbs were lined two and three deep by spectators, who lay at large on air cushions, blankets, and outspread newspapers. As the afternoon and evening hours wore on their ranks continually thickened, and towards dusk it began to seem that no space was left.

FAVOURITE CHOICE

If The Mall was the favourite choice, partly because of the long and broad processional prospect it will offer, the East Carriage Road through Hyde Park came next. Here, as in The Mall, to the agreeable setting has been added the boon of refreshment booths to supply the needs of the crowds during the long hours of their wait. All quickly found that the Park offered another comfort; they hired deck chairs, not only to sit in but to use as windbreaks.

The people were of many degrees and conditions, these thousands who foreran the millions, and they had been drawn from all parts of Britain, the Commonwealth, and the world outside the British family.

There were mothers, their backs propped against trees, with young children sprawled upon their laps asleep. There were older men and women who whiled away the minutes talking of other Coronations. There were abundant young people, contemporaries of the Queen, who conscientiously studied law and economics, made pencil sketches, or took down shorthand dictation one from the other until such time as it seemed good to sleep.

They were variously equipped. Many had canvas stools, some had sleeping-bags, others merely shrouded themselves in blankets. All had flasks and packages of sandwiches to supply the wants of at least 24 hours.

In the morning there came a sprinkling of rain in a wind that blew eagerly from the north to play the tyrant with the flags and banners. At noon the clouds parted and the sun shed comfort and grace upon the dripping mackintoshes and umbrellas, but the good spell did not last. As the afternoon turned to evening the sky dropped sleet which stung like small darts. But in spite of this and heavy showers, no inch of ground was yielded.

While the first crowds of the morrow sought their space to bivouac, the streets of central London were overwhelmed by sightseers. Always a crowd was gathered at Westminster Abbey, expecting not even some sudden second-best spectacle like a rehearsal, but imprinting the historic scene upon memory, detail by detail, colour by colour.

As the crowds jostled along the processional way, as the traffic stood halted and impatient to move, as the sky now threatened and then smiled, the last polish was put upon the beaming face of London. More flags were hoisted, more fabric draped upon the terraced stands that now seem meant for medieval tournament. Banks of flowers fresh from the nursery went into a thousand window boxes, and among them blooms flown from the Commonwealth and Empire.

Just before the Queen enters Westminster Abbey, in Parliament Square, she will pass a set-piece of floral homage from Australia, Bermuda, British Columbia, Ceylon, Hongkong, India, Jamaica, Malaya, Malta, Northern Rhodesia, Pakistan, South Africa, Tasmania, and Trinidad.

"CAMPING" ON THE PAVEMENTS

LONG WAIT BEGINS

BY OUR SPECIAL CORRESPONDENT

As night drew its cloak over London the human tide flowing into the city continued unabated. From buses, coaches, and underground stations the people streamed to join the thousands who had sought and secured vantage points all along the route during the earlier part of the evening.

The prospect of a showery if not thoroughly wet night did not daunt them, and cheerful crowds that had settled down for an all-night wait refused to move even for a heavy downfall of rain.

The wide pavements of the Mall, a premier position on the route, were solid with spectators at 9 p.m. Vehicular traffic was at a standstill, and a solid block of hurrying people, 10 or 12 deep, streamed from Trafalgar Square up the centre of the carriageway towards Buckingham Palace, seeking a place to squeeze in. Trafalgar Square was tightly packed. Family parties were camped on and around Nelson's column, and Landseer's lions each proudly bore six young people.

IMPROVISED SHELTERS

Preparations for the night were everywhere being made with all the ingenuity imaginable. Six umbrellas fastened together sheltered three times that number of people; groundsheets were contrived into a reasonable "night watchman's" shelter; a miniature bell-tent housed an astonishing number of children, and some students had seized small scaffolding poles left by workmen to erect a shelter for themselves and others. The cold, wet, and unyielding pavements were covered with groundsheets, sacks, rugs, blankets.

There was no lack of entertainment; accordions, banjos, and trumpets all were in use. Buskers and hawkers, hoarse with the unaccustomed lengths to which they could go, still plied their trades.

Conversation naturally turned on the weather. The great crowds had been soaked and were now nicely drying out. Would they be drenched again? A faint pink tinge in the evening sky was proclaimed a good omen. Friendliness and laughter were everywhere, and difficulties shared.

As darkness fell thousands still thronged in front of the Palace, waiting and hoping for a glimpse of members of the Royal Family. It was, perhaps, a vain hope last night, but to-day will be another story for the waiting thousands.

PALACE INVESTITURE

The Queen received Princess Margaret and Princess Marie Louise at Buckingham Palace yesterday afternoon and invested them with the insignia of a Dame Grand Cross of the Royal Victorian Order which they received in the Coronation Honours list.

Her Majesty also invested Sir Alan Lascelles, her private secretary, with the insignia of a Knight Grand Cross of the Bath, and Colonel Sir Dermot Kavanagh, Crown Equerry, and Sir Arthur Penn, treasurer to Queen Elizabeth the Queen Mother, with the insignia of a Knight Grand Cross of the Royal Victorian Order. General Sir Gerald Templer, High Commissioner for the Federation of Malaya, received the insignia of a Knight Grand Cross of St. Michael and St. George.

PRINCESS MARGARET AT THE ABBEY

Princess Margaret was given an enthusiastic reception by crowds gathered outside Westminster Abbey when she arrived there yesterday afternoon. She was met by the Earl Marshal. Later the Duke of Gloucester arrived with his two sons.

Princess Margaret remained at the Abbey for about half an hour. As she walked to her car near Dean's Yard the crowds, which had increased rapidly, broke through the police cordon and gathered around. With difficulty the police eventually made a way through to enable her to leave. The Duke of Gloucester and his sons left a few minutes later.

REGALIA TAKEN TO THE ABBEY

In a closed van, with one police car as escort the Coronation Regalia was taken from the offices of the Goldsmiths and Silversmiths Company to Westminster Abbey early yesterday. The Dean of Westminster, Dr. Don, was waiting at the cloisters entrance in Dean's Yard to receive the Regalia when it arrived there at 7.45 a.m. It was taken to the Jerusalem Chamber, where it will remain until this morning. A guard of eight Yeomen Warders was mounted.

The Regalia, which is normally kept at the Tower of London, was sent from there recently to the Goldsmiths and Silversmiths Company for cleaning and overhaul.

SUNSHINE AND SHOWERS

BY OUR WEATHER CORRESPONDENT

Cool, showery weather will continue in all districts to-day. During the afternoon and early evening some showers will be heavy and accompanied by hail and thunder, especially over the eastern half of the country. There will, however, be sunny intervals.

Coronation Gowns of the Royal Family, page 9.

A photograph showing the route followed by members of the British Everest expedition up the ice-fall (foreground), through the Western Cwm, and thence by the Lhotse face to the South Col (hidden by cloud) and the south-east ridge to the summit.

RECEPTION BY THE QUEEN

DELEGATIONS AT THE PALACE

The Queen, accompanied by the Duke of Edinburgh, received representatives of Commonwealth countries who are in London for the Coronation in the Throne Room at Buckingham Palace yesterday. Nearly 80 representatives were presented to the Queen, who afterwards moved informally among the company.

Sir David Maxwell Fyfe, the Home Secretary, Lord Swinton, Secretary of State for Commonwealth Relations, and Mr. Oliver Lyttelton, Secretary of State for the Colonies, were in attendance. Each Prime Minister was announced by the Lord Chamberlain and presented members of his delegation in turn.

Among those who attended were the Prime Ministers of Canada (Mr. St. Laurent), Australia (Mr. Menzies), New Zealand (Mr. Holland), South Africa (Dr. Malan), India (Mr. Nehru), Pakistan (Mr. Mohammad Ali), Ceylon (Mr. Senanayake), Southern Rhodesia (Sir Godfrey Huggins), Northern Ireland (Lord Brookeborough), and Malta (Dr. Borg Olivier). Sir Winston Churchill joined the Commonwealth Prime Ministers and the assembly also included the High Commissioners for South Africa, Ceylon, Australia, New Zealand, Pakistan, Canada, India, and Southern Rhodesia, and Mr. Bustamante, the Chief Minister of Jamaica.

The Queen later gave a luncheon for the Prime Ministers and other representatives. Members of the Royal Family present at the luncheon were Queen Elizabeth the Queen Mother, Princess Margaret, the Duke and Duchess of Gloucester, Princess Alice, Countess of Athlone, and the Earl of Athlone, Admiral Lord Mountbatten of Burma, and Lady Mountbatten.

When the Queen Mother and Princess Margaret left the Palace, people waiting outside swept across the road and impeded the progress of their car. Six mounted policemen had to clear a passage to allow it to drive up The Mall. The car was brought to a standstill two or three times and then moved forward at hardly more than walking pace until a way was cleared.

Picture on page 12.

REVIEW OF WORLD AFFAIRS

EXPECTED AGENDA FOR PRIME MINISTERS

BY OUR PARLIAMENTARY CORRESPONDENT

The Prime Minister will preside over the opening session of the Commonwealth Prime Ministers' conference at 10, Downing Street to-morrow. At this first meeting the Prime Ministers will agree on a general agenda for the conference, which is expected to last until June 9.

Two of the sessions are expected to be taken up by a general review of international affairs and a survey of the economic position of the Commonwealth in the light of developments since the last Commonwealth economic conference. The Prime Ministers will not be meeting to take policy decisions, which are for their individual governments, but it is generally felt to be most opportune that their presence together in London for the Coronation should occur at a significant juncture in world affairs. The conference, for example, will be of great value to the Prime Minister in enabling him to fortify himself with the views of the other Commonwealth Prime Ministers as a preliminary to his forthcoming meeting with President Eisenhower and the French Prime Minister at Bermuda.

The plenary sessions will be primarily devoted to matters of common concern in foreign, defence and economic affairs, but if the custom of previous meetings is followed, there should be some useful exchanges between individual Prime Ministers on topics of particular interest to themselves.

The Prime Minister will preside over the conference.

MAU MAU ACTIVITY INCREASING

FOREST GANG ROUTED

FROM OUR CORRESPONDENT

NAIROBI, JUNE 1

Military police and Kikuyu guards combined to crush a gang of terrorists in the bamboo forest of the Uplands district of Kiambu. At least 20 terrorists were killed and 15 wounded in 24 hours, and the remainder fled and were pursued.

The gang of 45 left Nairobi to join others in the forest. One prisoner declared that he and others were forced to join the gang in Nairobi, and said that they were half-starved and living on tree bark and roots. The Kikuyu guard first made contact with the gang after one of their number had been killed and four women kidnapped. In the same area security forces found another gang of 32 and killed four. Several loyalists, including women, had been killed or wounded.

It is officially stated that there has been a deterioration in the Meru district during the past month, and greatly increased Mau Mau activity.

BARCELONA FAIR

The Spanish Minister of Commerce opened the twenty-first annual sample fair at Barcelona yesterday.

CONTROL OF U.S. FOREIGN AID

STATE DEPARTMENT REORGANIZATION

PRESIDENT'S PROPOSALS

From Our Own Correspondent

WASHINGTON, JUNE 1

President Eisenhower to-day proposed to Congress a reorganization of the State Department which will bring under the department's authority all foreign economic assistance programmes, including the Mutual Security Agency.

For administrative purposes a new agency will be set up to control the activities of the various foreign aid programmes, but the Secretary of State will be directly responsible for all decisions on policy. The new agency will be called the Foreign Operations Administration and will presumably be presided over by Mr. Harold Stassen, the present mutual security administrator.

Another part of the plan will establish a new governmental body, the United States Informational Agency, to conduct all foreign information programmes, now divided between the State Department, the M.S.A., the technical cooperation programme, and the Voice of America.

MEETING A CHALLENGE

WASHINGTON, June 1.—In a message to Congress accompanying these proposals, the President said they were necessary to meet the challenge imposed by the nation's role of leadership in the non-Communist world.

"Our nation to-day is dedicated to international action in concert with other nations—through the United Nations and in regional arrangements with other nations—for collective security, for economic and social cooperation, designed to foster a community of world law," he said.

"We have come to know that national security entails mutual security with other free nations. And we have come to know that their freedom, in turn, depends heavily upon our strength and the wisdom with which we use it."

President Eisenhower said the reorganization would fix clearly the central responsibility for foreign policy below the President and group together other programmes, at present scattered, which implemented foreign policy. "Slackness, confusion, blurred authority, and clouded responsibility—any of these can defeat the noblest purposes of any foreign policy," he said.

A key point in the plan would be the creation of a separate agency "setting forth official United States positions for use abroad"—that is, presenting the official American view on a variety of questions.—*Reuter.*

MR. DULLES ON HIS TOUR

IMPORTANCE OF NEAR EAST PROBLEMS

WASHINGTON, June 1.—Mr. Dulles said to-night that the Government should pay more attention to the Near East and south Asia, where people suspected that the United States was trying to preserve the old colonial interests of Britain and France.

The Secretary of State was making a television broadcast on his recent 20,000-mile tour of 12 countries in the Near and Middle East. Referring to the Anglo-Egyptian dispute over the Suez Canal zone, he said: "The United States is prepared to assist in any desired way" towards a solution of the problem. He was convinced there was "nothing irreconcilable" between Egyptian sovereignty and the international concern over the future of the Suez base, which had an importance to western security.

He and the Mutual Security Director, Mr. Stassen, who accompanied him on his tour, had discussed the situation with General Neguib. "We asked, with some success, that there be further time to find a peaceful solution," Mr. Dulles added.

On the question of colonialism, he remarked that most of the people of the Near East and South Asia were "deeply concerned" about political independence for themselves and others.—*Reuter.*

COMMISSARS ABOLISHED IN YUGOSLAV ARMY

BELGRADE, June 1.—The official Yugoslav news agency, Tanjug, reports that Marshal Tito to-day issued an order abolishing the post of political commissar in Yugoslav Army units, military schools, and institutions. Instead of commissars, units will have an "assistant commander for political and cultural education."—*Reuter.*

OBITUARY

We announce with regret the deaths of COLONEL SIR GILBERT TANNER, D.S.O., T.D., for many years president of the Colne Valley Conservative Association; SIR PHILIP SMYLY, formerly Chief Justice of the Gold Coast; and MR. ALEX JAMES, the well-known International and Arsenal footballer. Obituary notices will be found on page 8.

THREE KILLED BY LIGHTNING

CRICKET PAVILION STRUCK

Three cricketers were killed and two seriously injured yesterday evening when, during a thunderstorm, lightning struck the home team's dressing room in the pavilion of the Co-operative Wholesale Society's soap works ground at Irlam, near Manchester. The team was playing against an Irlam district side. Players in the visitors' dressing room were unhurt.

The three killed were Ernest Taylor, aged 44, Herbert Vaudrey, aged 37, and George Perry, aged 31, all married men, and all from Cadishead. The condition of one of the injured, Kenneth John Townsend, of Flixton, was grave.

A flash, which enveloped several of the players, hit the corner of the pavilion where two pedal cycles were leaning. A hole was burned in the side of the building and a short length of wood ripped off. The window on the side where the home team was sheltering was smashed.

Within a few minutes two doctors, police officers, and ambulance men were at the scene. Taylor, Perry, and Vaudrey had apparently been killed instantly. Townsend was unconscious, and for the next two hours doctors, ambulance men, and police worked in relays in the pavilion, using oxygen to save his life. Eventually he partially recovered and was taken to hospital.

Mrs. Hope Robinson, aged 36, of Ilkeston, Derbyshire, was struck by lightning while playing golf at the Chesterfield course yesterday. She was taken to Chesterfield Royal Hospital, suffering from burns on her face and neck.

GALES CHANGE PLANS

Over 50 vessels of the Moray Firth fishing fleet sailed in heavy seas yesterday to take part in a review off Lossiemouth. The gaily bedecked vessels sailed in line astern out of port and past the reviewing vessel H.M.S. Welcome, a fishery cruiser, but so stormy was the sea that it was impossible for the reviewing party to board the cruiser. The ceremony took place from the pier.

What was to have been the chief feature of Llandudno's Coronation celebrations to-day—a fireworks display from the frigate Verulam anchored in the bay—has been cancelled because of a westerly gale. The ship has had to sail to safer waters and 70 officers and ratings are stranded on shore.

A 21-gun royal salute which should have been fired in mid-Mersey from the cruiser Sheffield to-day will now be fired instead in the Gladstone Dock, Liverpool, from the port side of the vessel. High winds last night prevented the cruiser from leaving dock.

STABBED GIRL FOUND DEAD IN THAMES

COMPANION MISSING

Detectives from Scotland Yard last night were investigating the death of Barbara Songhurst, aged 16, of Princes Road, Teddington, Middlesex, who was found stabbed to death in the Thames at Richmond yesterday morning, and also the disappearance of her friend Christine Reed, aged 18, of Roy Crescent, Hampton Hill.

Miss Songhurst, an assistant in a chemist's shop at Richmond, and her companion left Hampton for a cycle ride on Sunday, and were last seen together at Hampton.

Barbara Songhurst's body was found floating near Water Lane, Richmond. There was a wound on her forehead, but it was stated that death was due to three stab wounds in the back. Her shoes were missing.

Close to the towpath, near Teddington lock, and about a mile and a half from the point where the body was recovered, detectives found two pairs of girls' shoes. There was no trace of the bicycles.

Bloodstains on the verge of the towpath near the lock led police to the place they believe the girl was attacked and her body thrown into the river, on the ebb tide some time between 10 p.m. and 11 p.m. on Sunday.

Scotland Yard last night issued a description of Christine Reed. As the search for the girl continued police mowed grass near the towpath and police launches dragged the river.

ARRESTS BY EGYPTIANS IN CANAL ZONE

"SUSPICIOUS CHARACTERS"

CAIRO, June 1.—Egyptian authorities in the canal zone arrested more than 50 Egyptians and foreigners in Port Said, Ismailia, and Suez over the week-end. A spokesman of the Ministry of the Interior in Cairo to-night did not mention any charge of "intelligence with a foreign Power," as reported in certain Egyptian newspapers.

One source said the arrested people belonged to two categories—those considered "suspicious characters dangerous to public security" and those regarded as "super-patriot hotheads" who may precipitate incidents with unforeseeable consequences.

Members of the Government met to-day to discuss the latest developments in the canal zone in the light of "an important communication" from Washington.

Mr. Adlai Stevenson flew from Cairo to Fayid, in the canal zone, to-day.—*Reuter.*

EVEREST CONQUERED

HILLARY AND TENSING REACH THE SUMMIT

A message was received by The Times last night from the British Mount Everest Expedition, 1953, that E. P. Hillary and the Sherpa Tensing Bhutia reached the summit of the mountain, 29,002ft. high, on May 29. The message added: "All is well."

Thus the British expedition, under its leader, Colonel H. C. J. Hunt, has succeeded in its enterprise. Hillary, a New Zealander, was one of the members of the 1951 expedition which, under the leadership of Eric Shipton, found the Western Cwm and so discovered the southern route to Mount Everest, by which the success of the present expedition was made possible. It was Tensing who, with Raymond Lambert, on the first Swiss expedition of 1952 reached the record height of 28,215ft. on May 28.

If the plans announced were followed, Hillary and Tensing formed the second assault party in this season's attempt. They were using portable oxygen apparatus of the "open circuit" type. The first assault, made on May 25 with "closed circuit" apparatus by Bourdillon and Evans, presumably failed. Both were made from Camp VII—"that vital camp," in the words of our Special Correspondent with the expedition, "established on the bleak plateau on the South Col, at 26,000ft."—and the climbers must have returned safely on the day that they started.

INITIAL FAILURE

The failure of the first assault was not a surprise. The closed-circuit apparatus, in spite of various advantages over the other, was found to have certain definite disadvantages and is, in any case, less well tried. If the second, now successful, attempt had failed, a third was to have been made this season after a 10-day withdrawal to the Western Cwm. Had this in turn failed the arrival of the monsoon

E. P. Hillary

would have necessitated a postponement until the autumn. Plans for this eventuality had been made.

As reported in a message published yesterday, the timing of the assault was delayed, largely through obstacles, caused by bad weather, in the crossing of the difficult ice-covered Lhotse face, which leads to the South Col. This delay led to rumours in Katmandu—whence they were spread abroad—that the pre-monsoon assault had failed. Although there was some sickness among members of the expedition, as well as the obstacle of bad weather, there is no reason to think a withdrawal was contemplated at any stage.

JOINT SPONSORSHIP

The expedition was sponsored jointly by the Royal Geographical Society and the Alpine Club. The members are:—Colonel H. C. J. Hunt (leader), Major C. G. Wylie, W. Noyce, T. D. Bourdillon, A. Gregory, G. C. Band, R. C. Evans, E. P. Hillary, G. Lowe, M. Westmacott, Dr. M. Ward, Dr. L. G. C. Pugh, and T. Stobart.

Plans were made in the greatest detail in London and the expedition was armed with the latest equipment, much of it designed specially for this ascent. The party, most of whose members left England in the first days of February, established its base camp at Thyangboche, in Nepal, on March 26.

There followed a period of acclimatization and training. By mid-April a route was marked out through the ice fall and into the Western Cwm. A camp was set up on the Khumbu Glacier at some 20,000ft. by April 16, when the first tests of the oxygen apparatus were made. At that time May 15 was set as the target date for the assault on the summit.

SUCCESSIVE CAMPS

Plans were made for the establishment of eight successive camps, of which Camp I was the base camp on the glacier, Camp II was half-way up the ice fall leading to the Western Cwm, Camp III at the top of it, and Camp IV the advanced base. Camp V was a stores depôt at the foot of the Lhotse face, Camp VI was half-way up it, and Camp VII was on the South Col at 26,000ft. Camp VIII, perhaps never set up, was to be on the ridge between the Col and the summit.

The tactics of the assault were finally drawn up on about May 14, and the dates fixed for the two attempts were May 23 and 24. Bad weather, with heavy snowfalls, illness among members of the expedition, and a brief moment of reluctance on the part of the Sherpas, many of whom were also ill, conspired to postpone the attack. Because the long journey from the mountain to Katmandu could be covered only by runners on foot, several days had to elapse between the writing of dispatches and their arrival in London. The suspense has been rewarded, if only by the apt timing of the announcement of this great achievement on the eve of the Coronation.

Copyright

LONG RECORD OF ATTEMPTS

MOUNTAINEERS' ROLL OF HONOUR

FROM OUR SPECIAL CORRESPONDENT

BASE CAMP, KHUMBU GLACIER

With the conquest of Mount Everest, one of the great prizes of adventure has been won. Everything about Mount Everest is big, and its long record of victory over successive expeditions is of course due principally to its stupendous size. Here at the expedition's base camp at the head of the Khumbu Glacier the array of mighty peaks that surrounds the Everest massif is spread in panorama. To the south are the two fine summits of Taweche, and just across the valley to the west is Pumori, the noble mountain that George Leigh Mallory first saw and named. The twin peaks of Lingtren stand to the north, with the romantic pass of the Lho La which leads dramatically, between towering heights, into Tibet.

Above all these magnificent mountains, recognizably the greatest among the great, stands the summit of Everest itself, harsh and formidable; and down into the glacier around this camp tumbles the huge ice-fall of Everest, an extraordinary jungle of ice pinnacles and winding ice lanes that has become the staircase to the mountain's summit.

Another major problem of Everest concerns the weather. It is now generally accepted that at only two periods of the year can an assault on Everest reasonably be launched—in the lulls that generally occur, in May and September, before and after the monsoon.

Everest has proved so difficult an objective of adventure that the assaults that have been made on it during the past 30 years or so have acquired something of the nature of a campaign; each attempt has been a skirmish in battle rather than a complete battle in itself, and from each climbers have learnt more of the problems of the mountain and of the involved methods that must be adopted to solve them.

The campaign against Everest has fallen into two phases because of the mountain's theatrical situation across the frontiers of two "secret" countries—Tibet and Nepal. Before the last war Nepal was completely forbidden to foreigners, while the Dalai Lama, then the temporal as well as the spiritual ruler of Tibet, was sometimes willing to allow expeditions to Chomolungma, "Goddess Mother of the World," as Everest was known to his subjects.

THE RONGBUK ROUTE

The first seven expeditions to Everest, all British and all between the wars, therefore journeyed to the mountain from the north, starting from Darjeeling and travelling through the plains of southern Tibet to the Rongbuk glacier, which forms the northern highway to the Everest massif. The Lho La pass, high above the moraine hillock on which your Correspondent is sitting, would, if it could ever be crossed, lead a traveller from the south directly into the Rongbuk route of the early Everest adventurers.

The first expedition to Everest, mounted nearly seventy years after the discovery of the mountain as the world's highest, was a reconnaissance led by Colonel C. K. Howard-Bury in 1921. It was saddened by the death of one of its climbers, the celebrated Scottish mountaineer Dr. Kellas, who had a heart attack during the wearing approach march; but its members explored the approaches to Everest from north and east, and found what appeared to be a practicable route as far as the north-east shoulder of the mountain. Next year General C. G. Bruce, working on these findings, led an expedition which made the first assault on the summit. During it G. I. Finch and Captain Geoffrey Bruce climbed to 27,300ft. This expedition, too, was marred by death, for during a later attempt on the summit, just before the monsoon, seven Sherpa porters were killed in an avalanche.

Colonel E. F. Norton led the next expedition, in 1924, made famous and terrible by the disappearance on the high slopes of the mountain of two remarkable Englishmen, George Leigh Mallory and Andrew Irvine. The expedition began badly, with appalling weather. During the early weeks a Gurkha accompanying the party died of a clot in the brain, and a Sherpa porter of frostbite. But in May Norton himself reached a height of 28,126ft., climbing for the last part alone; and early in June Mallory and Irvine set off for a further assault on the summit in high confidence and good weather conditions. They were last seen at about 28,000ft., and it is not known how high they climbed.

AIR SUCCESSES

There were four full-scale expeditions to Everest in the thirties, besides successful flights over the summit made by British pilots, flying British aircraft, in 1933. In that same year Hugh Ruttledge led an expedition in the course of which F. S. Smythe, Wyn Harris, and L. R. Wager all climbed to about 28,100ft. In 1935 Eric Shipton led a reconnaissance to examine snow conditions and test climbers new to the Himalaya. In 1936 a second expedition led by Ruttledge was thwarted by bad weather, the monsoon arriving in the Everest region exceptionally early, and two years later the last attempt from the north, led by H. W. Tilman, was again defeated by the weather. In 1938 the lull before the monsoon never occurred.

Since the war the pattern of action against Mount Everest has necessarily changed. Entry into Tibet, now under Communist control, is out of the question for western climbers. In Nepal, on the other hand, changes of regime have led to an easing of restrictions on the entry of foreigners. British, French, Swiss, American, German, and Japanese expeditions have all been permitted to enter Nepal in recent years.

Tensing

The present expedition has enjoyed several advantages over its predecessors, although most of its climbers had little previous experience at very high altitudes—since the war there has not been a large reserve of experienced Himalayan mountaineers in England. First the weather—perhaps the most important and least foreseeable factor of all in an assault on Everest—has not been at its worst; the mountain has shown, in Mallory's words, "forgetfulness for long enough of its more cruel moods." The expedition's oxygen apparatus, after long years of hard trial and sometimes painful error, has proved more satisfactory than before. The Sherpa porters have improved in mountaineering skill and confidence. The *sahibs* enjoyed remarkably good health and fortune in the early weeks of the attempt.

But above all, as Colonel Hunt is first to emphasize, the 1953 expedition has been able to build upon the experience of others. Ten previous expeditions have learnt their lessons of Everest; at least 16 men have died in the learning. To-day, high above the rugged Nuptse ridge, Everest looks as surly, as muscular, as scornfully unattainable as ever; but after 30 years of endeavour the greatest of mountains is defeated, and many are the ghosts and men far off who share in the triumph.

Copyright

Man's Challenge to the Heights, page 7.

SYMBOL OF BRITISH ENDURANCE

N.Z. PRIME MINISTER'S TRIBUTE

Mr. Holland, the Prime Minister of New Zealand, who is in London for the Coronation, said last night: "Naturally I am exceedingly proud that a New Zealand member of this team has been the first Britisher to conquer the hitherto unconquerable Everest. What a grand achievement on the eve of the Coronation! And I would hope that this teriffic example of team spirit, endurance, and fortitude in this, our Coronation year, might be regarded as a symbol that there are no heights or difficulties which the British people cannot overcome. I cannot emphasize too strongly, however, that although a New Zealander is the first to conquer Everest this triumph has been made possible by the combined effort of a great many people, including the other members of the team and the organization behind them, and by the lessons learned from many previous attempts by many gallant men."

Winston Churchill and THE TIMES

Top Winston Churchill in the uniform of a 2nd Lieutenant, 4th Hussars, 1895.
Above Winston Churchill in 1923.

Relations between Sir Winston Churchill and Printing House Square had their ups and downs during the storm of the twentieth century. *The Times* had pioneered the idea of an independent newspaper that was a client of no party or politician, but spoke for Britain. Churchill took much the same view of his role. On occasions *The Times* and Churchill marched on the same side. More often they opposed each other. But they always respected each other as powerful and honourable adversaries.

Here is Winston on Lord Northcliffe during the world crisis of the First World War: 'Armed with the solemn prestige of *The Times* in one hand and the ubiquity of the *Daily Mail* in the other, he aspired to exercise a commanding influence upon events'. The solemn prestige and Churchill tended to find themselves opposed to each other during the years between the two wars. During the General Strike Churchill praised 'the most brilliant and courageous effort' of *The Times* in being the only national newspaper to keep on publishing. But he very nearly brought it to a standstill by requisitioning a quarter of its stocks of paper for the *British Gazette*, the Government giveaway sheet printed on *Morning Post* machines.

But the two conflicts in which *The Times* and Churchill found themselves directly opposed were the Abdication Crisis and the appeasement of Nazism (see pp. 104 and 107). Churchill regarded *The Times* as the voice of the blind and reactionary Establishment. *The Times* regarded Churchill as an irresponsible maverick. Neither pulled any punches.

Dawson described the King's party during the Abdication Crisis as 'the mischief-makers: a curious alliance of Churchill, Rothermere and Beaverbrook with all their papers, the *News Chronicle* representing the Liberal intellectuals, and of course Lady Houston and her *Saturday Review* reinforced by Oswald Mosley's Fascists, who were organizing demonstrations in the streets'. Dawson was, of course, a member of the Establishment and a friend of Baldwin's. His leader after the Abdication was high-minded and hard, but more generous to the King than he felt personally (see p. 106). The King's party described this leader as putting the boot in to a man who was down. To adapt another well-worn quotation, from Lucan, '*Victrix causa deis placuit, sed victa*' to Churchill. As far as there can be right and wrong in a complex historical conflict, *The Times* got public opinion right over the Abdication, and Churchill took the romantic but wrong road.

The roles were roughly reversed over appeasement. Churchill's was the voice crying in the wilderness about the blindness of the ruling class. 'Meanwhile most of the British Press, with *The Times* and the *Daily Herald* in the van, expressed their belief in the sincerity of Hitler's offers of a non-aggression pact.' It was a theme to which he returned *passim* in his articles and speeches of the late 1930s. Here he is in the House of Commons shortly before the earthquake: 'There was a sinister passage in *The Times* leading article on Saturday similar to that which foreshadowed the ruin of Czechoslovakia, which sought to explain that there was no guarantee for the integrity of Poland, but only for its independence'.

Churchill got Hitler right and *The Times* got him wrong, because Dawson, Barrington-Ward and the appeasement party in Printing House Square would go to any lengths to avoid the calamity of another world war. They were honourable men, but mistaken. Once they were proved wrong, they were generous to their old opponent. On the day after war was declared, Dawson welcomed Churchill into the Government in his first leader:

> Mr Churchill comes in now, as a matter of course, because he is a man of dynamic energy, most fertile imagination, and warlike temperament. These are qualities essential in a War Cabinet. They also provide sufficient reason why Mr Churchill was not invited to join in the Government during the period of negotiation. He himself bore witness yesterday that nothing has contributed so much to the strength of the British cause in this grave crisis as the conviction, shared with our people by the whole world, that war has been forced upon a Government completely unanimous and untiring in its pursuit of peace.

It would be wrong to pretend that *The Times* and Churchill saw eye to eye thereafter, throughout the war and the postwar years. They differed violently on matters as diverse as the need for a small War Cabinet, the need for reconstruction and a social revolution after the war, the wisdom of Britain sending armed aid against the communists in the Greek Civil War, and the right attitude for Britain to take towards Russia after the iron curtain had come down across Europe. On occasions tempers were lost and harsh words were spoken. Over the Greek Civil War, the Prime Minister attacked *The Times* in Parliament:

> How can we wonder at, still more how can we complain of, the attitude of hostile and indifferent newspapers in the United States when we have, in this country, witnessed such a melancholy exhibition as that provided by some of our most time-honoured and responsible journals (loud and prolonged cheers) and others to which such epithets would hardly apply? (laughter).

Churchill drafted a letter to send to the editor, with references to Munich, but was restrained by Brendan Bracken and Beaverbrook, who reminded him of the many times that the paper had supported him. Lightning still flew between the old adversaries in both directions. But they recognized that they were both on the same side, as they always had been, fundamentally: both *The Times* and Winston were passionate and strong-minded patriots. The editors and their senior assistants lunched and dined regularly with Winston to discuss high policy. He was always anxious to engage the solemn prestige of Printing House Square on the right side, i.e. his side, in any dispute of policy. Sometimes he got it, sometimes he didn't. *The Times* took its customary high-minded and magnificent view that the world would be best run from Printing House Square. Each respected the other. A few days before the 1951 election, Churchill said wistfully to his doctor, Lord Moran: '*The Times* is very favourable to me, more than it has been for a long time'.

When the old man died at last, at the bitter turn of the year into 1965, *The Times* honoured him with what will be its last full-scale funerary narrative. Television has made such magnificent written obsequies otiose.

Churchill died on 24 January 1965, in his ninety-first year. His death was not unexpected. For ten days and nights press and television had been keeping vigil outside his house in Hyde Park Gate in the bitterest winter for years. For the next week Churchill belonged to the media and the nation. He lay in state in Westminster Hall for three days: the first commoner to be given that melancholy honour since Gladstone. Every detail of the scene and arrangements for the funeral were described by *The Times* with a grandiloquent sonority that would have found favour with the marvellous old rhetorician himself. A whole page of the paper was devoted to reporting the speeches when the House of Commons paid tribute to its most famous member.

The funeral was on 30 January: a service at St Paul's, and then burial in the churchyard at Bladon, just outside the walls of Blenheim Palace, the ancestral home of the Churchill family. Thirty years before Churchill had described the funeral of his great ancestor, John the first Duke of Marlborough: 'His funeral was a scene of solemn splendour and martial pomp'. The description fits the events of 30 January 1965.

Winston Churchill's first term of premiership is announced (column 7). THE TIMES buried the hatchet. In Dawson's last leading article before his retirement, he wrote: 'So far as any man in the world can be regarded as indispensable, Mr Churchill has earned that much-abused title . . . He has the courage, the imagination, the power of leadership which are the attributes of a great War Minister' (8 September 1941).
11 MAY 1940

HITLER STRIKES AT THE LOW COUNTRIES

BELGIAN, DUTCH, AND FRENCH TOWNS BOMBED

HEAVY TOLL OF GERMAN AIR RAIDERS

ALLIES MOVING TO THE RESCUE

At dawn yesterday Germany invaded Holland, Belgium, and Luxemburg by air and by land.

The Dutch and Belgian troops are resisting stubbornly on the frontiers and at towns, such as Rotterdam, where German troops were landed by air.

The R.A.F. destroyed enemy troop-carrying aircraft at the Rotterdam aerodrome and on the beach near The Hague. The Dutch High Command states that more than 100 German aeroplanes were shot down by its forces. In an enemy air attack on Brussels aerodrome 37 persons were killed.

Several towns in France were also bombed and many civilians were killed. Forty-four German aeroplanes were sho. down on French territory.

In response to appeals from the three invaded countries, British and French troops moved across the Belgian frontier yesterday morning.

DUTCH RESIST FIERCELY

GERMAN LANDINGS BY AIR

From Our Special Correspondent

ROTTERDAM, MAY 10

The German military and air invasion of the Low Countries began before dawn to-day. Large numbers of aeroplanes crossed the frontiers and attacked the main aerodromes.

The Dutch High Command reports that the Dutch frontier troops are resisting on the Ijssel and the Maas, and that at least 70 German machines have been brought down. A late *communiqué*, announcing this news, states:—

The Dutch frontier troops are offering stubborn defence on the Ijssel and Maas. In spite of fierce German attacks our troops are maintaining themselves in Delfzijl.

Four German armoured trains have been put out of action. One of these was blown up with the railway line near Venloo.

At least 70 German planes have been shot down in attacks on Dutch aerodromes and while trying to land troops.

Small enemy forces are trying to maintain themselves inside the country, but are being fiercely attacked by our troops.

The first intimation of the invasion in Rotterdam came at about 4 a.m., when German aeroplanes appeared over the city and were fired on.

An earlier *communiqué*, announcing that German troops had crossed the frontier last night and that the Dutch frontier troops were resisting them, said that the demolitions which were planned for purposes of defence had been carried out, including the destruction of bridges over the Maas and Ijssel. Only at one point, at Arnhem, about 10 miles from the frontier, did the Germans succeed in reaching the Ijssel.

FIGHTING IN ROTTERDAM

It is learnt that two German aeroplanes were brought down near the oil tanks at Vlaardingen, between Rotterdam and the Hook of Holland. Two more are reported to have been brought down near Delft, and another near Waalhaven aerodrome, the airport of Rotterdam, to the south of the Maas. A few minutes before 5 a.m., a number of Dornier flying-boats alighted on the Maas, in the centre of Rotterdam, just south of the great road and railway bridges. Parties were landed, and seized the bridges without meeting with resistance. About the same time other German aircraft landed on the Waalhaven aerodrome, and took possession of it. Dutch troops are holding the north bank of the river, and judging from machine-gun fire some attempt was made between 8 a.m. and 9 a.m. to recapture the bridges.

A Dutch tank is reported to have crossed the road bridge and the woodwork of the bridge is on fire, but since that time firing has died down. Some German wounded are known to have been brought to a hospital on the south side of the river, but the situation is far from clear. Later in the morning two Junkers bombers were brought down in the centre of The Hague. They were carrying parties of soldiers equipped with folding bicycles. All the occupants, 17 in number, were killed.

The situation at Rotterdam this evening is an extraordinary one. Fighting is going on in the town itself, as well as round about it, yet in the central streets one would hardly be aware of it were it not for occasional bursts of machine-gun fire from the river front, where the Germans are installed at one or two points.

Having seized the bridges early in the morning, they pressed forward and occupied the Maas and the Bourse railway stations, both of which are near the river bank. They were driven out of the latter, and are reported to be surrounded in the former. The bridge, too, is said to have been retaken, but there is still a German machine-gun post in a strategical position on the Boompjes, the business section of Rotterdam's river front. This is all on the northern bank of the Maas. On the southern bank the Germans are strongly posted among the houses.

There are conflicting reports as to whether they are still in possession of the Waalhaven airport. Earlier in the day they were believed to be landing reinforcements there from aeroplanes which were being sent off in the direction of Dordrecht. There another batch of Germans is established, and hard fighting is said to be going on. Later in the day, however, the Waalhaven airport was reported to have been captured. Another detachment of Germans is installed in a factory outside Delft, between Rotterdam and The Hague, but they are understood to be surrounded.

"SITUATION IN HAND"

With small detachments of Germans scattered here and there about the country it is extremely hard to gain a clear picture of the position, but Dutch Army Headquarters in The Hague are satisfied that they have the situation in hand. Sporadic firing has been going on all day on the river front.

A Dutch destroyer came up the river this morning and backed into one of the harbour basins on the northern bank, whence she shelled the German machine-gun posts on the other side of the river. Four attempts were made to bomb her from the air, but without effect.

There is an air of Sunday evening calm in the main streets. People sit quietly outside the cafés enjoying their drinks, while a quarter of a mile away the machine-guns hammer away at intervals and soldiers are on guard at every street corner.

DUTCH CLAIM 100 GERMAN AIRCRAFT DOWN

A Netherlands *communiqué* issued early to-day stated that the number of German aeroplanes shot down over Holland now exceeds 100. In addition, 14 undamaged enemy aeroplanes fell into the hands of the Dutch at one of the reconquered aerodromes.

With the exception of one, the *communiqué* added, all the aerodromes temporarily captured by the Germans, are now held by the Dutch authorities again.

PARACHUTISTS IN BRITISH UNIFORMS

Reports reaching authoritative military circles in London state that about 200 parachutists in British uniforms landed at the airport of The Hague. Others in Dutch uniforms descended at Dordrecht. It is also stated that the Dutch Friesian Islands have been bombed and that parachutists have been landed.

A larger map of the Low Countries and Northern France appears on p. 8.

B.E.F. MOVES INTO BELGIUM

A WARM WELCOME

GERMAN AEROPLANES BEATEN OFF

The following *communiqué* was issued by G.H.Q. in France yesterday:—

"Leading elements of the B.E.F., in cooperation with the French Army, entered Belgium to-day.

"They were accorded a great welcome by the Belgian population."

From Our Special Correspondent

ON THE WESTERN FRONT, MAY 10

The British Expeditionary Force, in response to the appeal for assistance sent from Brussels, to-day moved over the Belgian frontier. The red and white poles spanning the roads near the Belgian Customs houses were raised, after presenting for many months a symbolic yet insuperable barrier. The British troops met with an enthusiastic reception from the Belgian population as they moved forward. Guns were decorated with flowers and the troops entertained to hurried refreshment as they pushed forward. German aeroplanes which attempted to molest the movement achieved few successes, although they caused some loss of life among civilians.

Already the troops, which for many months have been holding a strong defensive line just outside the Belgian frontier, have disappeared; they have moved on into the unknown.

TROOPS' CHANGED MOOD

Movements have been general to-day throughout the British zone. Lorries filled with troops are moving toward the forward areas, and from each lorry the muzzle of a Bren gun points skywards, warning fighters off the open roads. The mood of the British Expeditionary Force changed perceptibly to-day, and in place of dogged resolution, tinged perhaps with boredom, there are smiles and singing as the troops move off to the front.

The activities of the German reconnaissance aeroplanes throughout the day have been unceasing. The eighth air-raid warning to-day is sounding above the town in which I write. Throughout the day the sky was filled with the distant drone of aeroplanes. Several German machines have been brought down during the day, and the bursts of anti-aircraft fire scatter the raiders into flight.

HITLER IN CHARGE AT THE FRONT

GERMAN ARMY CLAIMS

A German Army *communiqué* states (according to Reuter):—

The Führer and Supreme Commander of the Army has gone to the Western Front to take complete charge of the operations of the forces there.

It was officially announced in Berlin last night that German troops had seized the town of Maastricht, crossed the River Maas at several points, and occupied bridges on the Albert Canal. They also claim to have captured Malmédy. In north-eastern Holland, German troops are stated to have reached the Ijssel.

BOMBS NEAR BASLE

FULL MOBILIZATION IN SWITZERLAND

FROM OUR CORRESPONDENT

GENEVA, MAY 10

The Swiss Federal Government this morning decided to mobilize the whole Army to-morrow morning and to cancel all leave.

A *communiqué* from the Swiss General Staff announces that at 5 o'clock this morning an unknown foreign aeroplane flew over Swiss territory and dropped 17 bombs on the railway near Délemont, south-west of Basle. Swiss neutrality was also violated by aeroplanes in several other regions on the northern frontier.

FRENCH CABINET CHANGES

FROM OUR OWN CORRESPONDENT

PARIS, MAY 10

The extension of the basis of the Cabinet to include two Right Wing Deputies, M. Marin and M. Ybarnégaray, was announced here early this evening, after a long series of conversations between M. Paul Reynaud, the Prime Minister, and political leaders.

BIG ATTACK BY R.A.F.

TROOP-CARRIERS DESTROYED

GERMANS BOMBED ON BEACH

The Air Ministry announced early to-day:—

German troop-carrying aircraft on the aerodrome at Rotterdam and on the beach near The Hague were attacked and destroyed yesterday afternoon by R.A.F. aircraft of the Bomber Command.

The raids, which were carried out by strong forces of our bombers, followed so quickly on the German occupation of the landing-ground that the enemy had had no time in which to establish an anti-aircraft defence system.

The only ground opposition came from the guns of stationary aircraft, and was ineffective. Enemy fighters, however, were active in force, and a number of combats took place.

The attacks on Rotterdam's former civil airport at Waalhaven began shortly after 3 o'clock yesterday afternoon. The airport's hangars, presumably fired by the Dutch before evacuation, were already ablaze when the first of the British bombers arrived over the aerodrome.

Attacks were concentrated on the large number of enemy aircraft, including 50 troop-carriers which were dispersed along the sides of the aerodrome, and numerous direct hits were noted until the pall of smoke over the aerodrome from successive bombing attacks became so dense as to make close observation impossible.

Four enemy aircraft were destroyed in one dive-bombing attack alone. Numerous fires were started and heavy casualties were inflicted on enemy personnel.

Ten enemy troop-carriers which had disembarked troops on the beach about eight miles north of The Hague were also attacked by a British bomber force in concert with long-ranger fighters. Flying low above the beach and firing with their front guns, the British fighters first attacked the line of stationary aircraft with devastating effect.

The bombers, attacking from a higher level, followed up the onslaught with salvoes of high explosive bombs. One salvo bursting 20ft. away from a troop transport was seen to lift the great three-engined machine bodily off the ground, and as it fell back it burst into flames. When the raiding forces withdrew two enemy aircraft could be seen half-submerged in the water, two more were in flames, and the remainder were riddled by bullets and bomb splinters.

AIR FIGHTING OVER WIDE AREA

ENEMY TROOPS BOMBED

The Headquarters of the British Air Forces in France issued the following *communiqué* last night:—

In the course of to-day's operations on the Western Front the Royal Air Force has been constantly in action.

Our reconnaissance aircraft have been operating over a wide area. Enemy troops have been attacked by our bomber squadrons. Wherever German bombers have been encountered our fighter squadrons have engaged them. Reports indicate that in the course of these combats numerous enemy aircraft have been destroyed.

Several of our aerodromes have been bombed. Little material damage has been done and no lives have been lost.

The Air Ministry announced last night:—

Royal Air Force aircraft have to-day undertaken offensive operations against aerodromes occupied by the enemy in Holland.

During last night an aircraft dropped several incendiary bombs in the country district in Kent. It has now been established by examination that these bombs were of enemy origin.

TOLL OF GERMAN RAIDERS

The first German attempts to bomb aerodromes and other objectives in the zone of the Advanced Air Striking Force of the R.A.F. in France were effectively frustrated by the co-operation between the British and French air arms and the ground defences. A number of enemy machines were shot down.

AIR BATTLES OVER NORTH SEA

An Air Ministry *communiqué* yesterday stated that while on patrol over the North Sea on Thursday aircraft of the Coastal Command engaged two enemy flying-boats, one of which was shot down and the other severely damaged. Another was shot down later by the same flight and a fourth damaged.

For about half an hour early yesterday morning a number of German aeroplanes circled over the Canterbury area. At intervals anti-aircraft fire could be heard. A heavy explosion shook houses in the village of Chartham and rattled windows in Canterbury itself. Later it was reported that four incendiary bombs had been dropped.

It is believed that the bombs fell in the extensive Pennypot Woods, a few miles from the village.

NEWS OF LANDINGS BY PARACHUTE

GUIDANCE TO THE PUBLIC

The Home Office asks members of the public to keep watch for enemy troops landing by parachutes and to report any such attempt at once to the nearest police station, giving the most accurate information possible as to the place and numbers of persons landing. The police will communicate at once with the appropriate military authorities. Any attempts would most likely be made during the hours of black-out, particularly at dusk or dawn, and in open spaces, especially near aerodromes.

OBITUARY

We record with regret the death of DR. W. BRADBROOKE, physician, antiquary, and genealogist.

A memoir and obituary notices of Fallen Officers will be found on page 9.

THE ATTACK ON BELGIUM

BRUSSELS BOMBED

FIERCE FIGHTING ON THE FRONTIER

From Our Correspondent

BRUSSELS, MAY 10

As M. Spaak, the Belgian Minister of Foreign Affairs, stated this afternoon in the Chamber, it was the sound of anti-aircraft guns firing at the German aeroplanes over Brussels that first announced to Belgium that Germany, for the second time in 26 years, had broken her promise to respect this country's neutrality.

The precautionary measures taken in the last few days in Holland and Belgium had caused no deep concern among the Belgian people. Ever since the war began 600,000 or 700,000 men have been mobilized to ensure the defence of the territory, and Belgians believed that their neutrality would be respected because it was well defended.

The Government, however, were better informed. A Cabinet Council assembled at 1 a.m., after news had been received during the evening that the German troops, immobilized for so long on their own side of the frontier, had begun to march at 9.30 p.m. This morning, at 4.30, the Ministers knew that Holland had been attacked. A few minutes later German aeroplanes appeared over Brussels, while the German armies had set foot across the frontier. The land forces, however, were at once held up in front of the demolition zone.

THE KING IN COMMAND

King Leopold, who, like his father, King Albert I, is Commander-in-Chief of the Belgian Army, proceeded immediately to General Headquarters to take over the direction of military operations. Meanwhile the Government issued the order for general mobilization and asked Great Britain and France to implement the guarantee that they had given to Belgium. At the same time King Leopold instructed his diplomatic representative in Berlin to present a protest to the German Government.

It was not till 8.30 a.m. that the German Ambassador in Brussels, Herr von Bülow-Schwante, asked for a meeting with M. Spaak, the Belgian Foreign Minister. At that moment hundreds of German aeroplanes had already bombed Brussels, Antwerp, and other Belgian cities, fighting had been going on for a long time at the frontier, and Belgium had learned from the bursting of German bombs and the rattle of machine-guns that Germany, more brutally and cynically than ever, had broken her pledged word. What passed at the interview between the young and energetic Foreign Minister and the German diplomatist was related by M. Spaak in his speech this afternoon in the Chamber. Knowing that nothing could excuse the German aggression, M. Spaak said to his visitor: "Let me speak first, Monsieur l'Ambassadeur," and in tones of cold contempt he declared that Germany, once more, had committed an aggression devoid of all justification.

BELGIAN MORAL FIRM

There are few people in the streets, and the public have in any case been asked to stay indoors. Anxiety, of course, is widespread, for there is hardly a Belgian home that has not a son or a husband at the frontiers, but, like all citizens of free countries, the Belgians know how to control their nerves in time of danger.

The Belgian troops have succeeded in blowing up in good time the roads, bridges, and passages which they had long ago mined in the "zone of destruction." On the other hand, Germany has shown once more that she uses her air force in one fell swoop against military objectives and against the civil population. They have bombed the aerodrome of Evere, the landing ground in particular of the aeroplanes of the Brussels-London line. In another raid 100 machines appeared over Brussels.

HOSPITAL BOMBED

At Antwerp a bomb partly destroyed the military hospital, and the railway station at Jemelle, at the junction of the principal lines connecting Brussels and Liége with the Belgian province of Luxembourg, was set on fire by German bombs.

The session of the Belgian Chamber this afternoon, during which M. Spaak spoke, did much to help Belgians to face with courage the imminent destruction of their country for the second time. In atmosphere it was strangely like a similar session on August 4, 1914, at which King Albert was present, but long before Parliament could assemble King Leopold had gone to join his armies.

In a speech in the Chamber General Denis, the Minister of National Defence, said that the Germans had failed in what appeared to be their primary objective—to destroy at a blow the Belgian aerodromes and the aeroplanes themselves.

The Germans had attacked the military aerodromes of Schaeffen, Evere, Nivelles, and Ostend. The buildings were badly damaged, but when it was realized that the attack was coming the precaution had been taken of withdrawing the machines, and they had been taken to other, unknown aerodromes. Only a small number of machines had been damaged, and only two destroyed. The Minister said that he regarded it as a great achievement that they had been able to prevent the Germans from carrying through their first move.

41 DEAD IN BRUSSELS RAID

BRUSSELS, May 10.—The number of victims in the German air raid on Greater Brussels is now stated to be 41 dead and 82 wounded.

Another air raid warning—the fourth during the day—was sounded at 10.55 p.m.—*Reuter.*

The German claim to have occupied five Belgian aerodromes is without foundation. Not one airfield has been captured. Parachute troops are being rapidly rounded up. Up to 6 o'clock last evening eight to 10 enemy aeroplanes had been brought down by anti-aircraft fire and by Belgian machines.

RACING CANCELLED

The stewards of the Jockey Club have obtained permission for the Newbury race meeting to be held to-day, but no other race meetings will be held until further notice. This applies also to National Hunt meetings.

Football and greyhound racing will not be stopped by the authorities to-day.

AIR RAIDS ON FRANCE

44 ENEMY MACHINES SHOT DOWN

From Our Own Correspondent

PARIS, MAY 10

It is officially stated to-night that 44 German aircraft were brought down on French territory to-day. The following is the text of the *communiqué*:—

The attack by German troops on Holland, Belgium, and Luxemburg was preceded by an aerial attack on a large scale during the early hours of May 10.

Besides the bombing attacks, many enemy detachments were landed by aeroplanes, or by parachute, in different points in Belgium and Holland.

In Holland especially these detachments tried to take aerodromes by surprise. On the whole they were successfully counter-attacked by the local troops.

The enemy's aerial attack, which began in the latter part of the night on French territory, was continued during the day. Some material damage of small importance was the only result of this bombing.

Our fighters and anti-aircraft came into action against these expeditions, and inflicted heavy losses on the German aviation. Forty-four enemy aeroplanes were brought down on French territory.

The Dutch, Belgian, and Luxemburg Governments having appealed to the Allies this morning, Franco-British troops at once responded to this appeal, and advanced on a front extending from the North Sea to the Moselle. Their progress continues in Belgian territory.

Sharp fighting has taken place in Luxemburg territory, where the German attack extends to the region of Sierck and slightly to the east of the Moselle.

PARIS GUNS IN ACTION

German aircraft claimed their first French civilian victims in the small hours of the morning when bombers attacked a number of centres—some of them open towns—including Nancy, Lyons and the adjoining airport of Bron, Lille, Colmar, Luxeuil, and Pontoise. No details of the raid are yet available, but it is known that civilians were killed and wounded at Nancy, and that several soldiers lost their lives at Lyons. Paris itself was awakened by an air raid warning at 4.50 a.m., and anti-aircraft guns opened fire, but so far as is known no bombs were dropped.

An official spokesman at the Ministry of War late to-night, giving a survey of the situation, mentioned Béthune, Chocques, Lens, Hazebrouck, Calais, Abbeville, and Laon as having been bombed, as well as the towns mentioned earlier. He said that in Holland flooding was proceeding.

To-day's bombing of open towns, added to the brutal assault on the Low Countries and Luxemburg, has set the seal on the resolution here to have done with German gangsterism once and for all.

"SOLDIERS OF FREEDOM"

This spirit finds reflection in the order of the day, short, simple, and dignified, issued this afternoon by General Gamelin, the Commander-in-Chief of the French Army:—

"The attack that we had foreseen since October was launched this morning. Germany is engaged in a fight with us to the death.

"The order of the day for France and all her Allies are the words: Courage, energy, confidence."

In a brief message of calm confidence, broadcast to the nation this evening, M. Reynaud said that this morning, between 7 a.m. and 8 a.m., the Allied soldiers, "the soldiers of freedom," had crossed into Flanders, the centuries-old battlefield, to meet the centuries-old invader.

22 KILLED AT NANCY

Twenty-two persons, including five women, were killed in the German air raids on Nancy yesterday, according to the French wireless (quoted by Reuter).

ENEMY BOMBING OF CIVILIANS

BRITAIN RESERVES RIGHT TO TAKE ACTION

The following statement was issued by the Foreign Office yesterday:—

His Majesty's Government in the United Kingdom, who in their reply of September 1 to the appeal of the President of the United States gave the assurance that their Air Forces had received orders prohibiting the bombing of civilian populations and limiting bombing to strictly military objectives, now publicly proclaim that they reserve to themselves the right to take any action which they consider appropriate in the event of bombing by the enemy of civil populations, whether in the United Kingdom, France, or in countries assisted by the United Kingdom.

ALLEGED BOMBING OF GERMAN TOWN

DENIAL IN LONDON

The official German News Agency (quoted by Reuter) stated last night:—

Three enemy aircraft bombed to-day the open town of Freiburg-im-Breisgau, which is completely outside the German zone of operations and has no military objectives.

The bombs landed in the inner part of the town and killed 24 civilians.

The German Air Force will answer this illegal action in like manner. From now on any further systematic enemy bombing of the German population will be returned by a five-fold number of German aeroplanes attacking a British or French town.

At the Air Ministry this morning it was stated that this report was untrue and "a further example of German mendacity."

R.A.F. LEAVE CANCELLED

It was learned at the Air Ministry yesterday afternoon that all leave from the R.A.F. had been cancelled and that all officers and men already on leave had been recalled.

IMPORTS FROM THE LOW COUNTRIES

The Board of Trade yesterday announced that it had, as a temporary measure, issued an open general licence authorizing the importation without further licensing of goods from Belgium and Holland. The new order comes into force immediately and will cover goods which have already been consigned.

⁂ An article on the industries of Belgium and Holland appears on page 3.

NEW PRIME MINISTER

MR. CHURCHILL ACCEPTS

WIDER BASIS FOR CABINET

LABOUR SUPPORT

From Our Parliamentary Correspondent

To make possible the formation of a new Government which will command the widest support in Parliament and the country Mr. Chamberlain last night had an audience of the King and tendered his resignation as Prime Minister. Mr. Churchill then accepted an invitation from the King to become Prime Minister and to form a new Administration which will include Ministers representing the Opposition parties.

The following statement was issued from 10, Downing Street:—

The Right Hon. Neville Chamberlain, M.P., resigned the office of Prime Minister and First Lord of the Treasury this evening, and the Right. Hon. Winston Churchill, C.H., M.P., accepted his Majesty's invitation to fill the position.

The Prime Minister desires that all Ministers should remain at their posts and discharge their functions with full freedom and responsibility while the necessary arrangements for the formation of a new Administration are made.

HELP OF OTHER PARTIES

It is believed that Mr. Churchill will be able to count upon the full support of both the Labour Party and the Opposition Liberals in establishing a new and more broadly based Ministry. To give the new Prime Minister full freedom of choice all other Ministers will resign, although they will retain their offices pending the appointment of the new Government. In an impressive final broadcast to the nation from 10, Downing Street last night (printed on page 3) Mr. Chamberlain mentioned that he had been strongly pressed by Mr. Churchill to remain a member of the War Cabinet, and had gladly offered to serve in that capacity.

Mr. Chamberlain went to see the King shortly before 6 p.m. after a meeting at 10, Downing Street of the War Cabinet, which was followed by a larger meeting of all Ministers of Cabinet rank. He remained at the Palace for about half an hour, and five minutes after he had left the King received Mr. Churchill. The German invasion of the Low Countries yesterday made it most urgently necessary in the national interest that a confused political situation should be ended at once, and that a Government which would have united support should be established to lead the nation at this critical time. Mr. Chamberlain's decision to resign was made known after the Labour Party had announced that they would join in the formation of a new Government "under a new Prime Minister who would command the confidence of the nation."

LABOUR IN CONFERENCE

The need for a new Administration in which the Opposition parties would share the responsibilities of leadership has been generally accepted, and Mr. Chamberlain's talks with Mr. Attlee and Mr. Greenwood on Thursday night, with Lord Halifax and Mr. Churchill present, were the first step towards achieving this object. At this meeting the Labour leaders were invited to state the conditions on which they would accept office in a reconstructed Government. They gave a preliminary indication that they would accept office in a new Government, but that they could not do so with Mr. Chamberlain as Prime Minister. They undertook to give a formal reply after consulting their colleagues of the executive committee of the Labour Party.

Yesterday morning, after news had been received of the invasion of Holland and Belgium, a meeting was held in London of the executive of the Parliamentary Labour Party. After this meeting Mr. Attlee and Mr. Greenwood issued the following declaration:—

The Labour Party, in view of the latest series of abominable aggressions by Hitler, while firmly convinced that a drastic reconstruction of the Government is vital and urgent, in order to win the war, reaffirms its determination to do its utmost to achieve victory. It calls upon all its members to devote all their energies to this end, and to stand firmly united through whatever trials and sacrifices may lie ahead.

The Labour leaders then left to attend the annual conference of their party at Bournemouth. A meeting of the Executive Committee of the Labour Party was held there yesterday afternoon, and a statement was afterwards issued, showing that the attitude adopted by Mr. Attlee and Mr. Greenwood, in response to Mr. Chamberlain's invitation, had been confirmed. The statement said:—

The national executive of the Labour Party have unanimously decided to take their share of responsibility as a full partner in a new Government, under a new Prime Minister, which would command the confidence of the nation.

OPPOSITION LIBERALS

Earlier in the day Mr. Chamberlain had seen Sir Archibald Sinclair, leader of the Opposition Liberals in the House of Commons. There was reason to believe that the Opposition Liberals also adopted the attitude that they would take part in forming a reconstructed Government under a new Prime Minister. They took the view, however, that it would probably be inadvisable to make the necessary changes in the Administration at this critical time, and that the introduction of new Ministers should be delayed till a more opportune time. On behalf of the Opposition Liberals Sir Archibald Sinclair issued yesterday morning the following statement:—

The German attack, aimed at Britain and France, has been launched with characteristic disregard of the rights of freedom of small nations through Holland and Belgium, whose forces are gallantly resisting the outrage. The assault must be broken by the skill and courage of the fighting Forces of the Allies, backed, in this as in other countries, by the firm will of a united people.

Recent events have proved the necessity for a prompt and radical reconstruction of the British Government; but the opening of the first critical battle in the West is not the moment. Meanwhile, let us all redouble our efforts in every sphere to defeat the enemies of freedom.

The events of that day were covered by six of the paper's staff. Their work can be recommended to any budding journalist as an example of the best stately writing of a vanished age. The composite piece opened: 'The long day had no beginning. It grew imperceptibly out of the third night of his lying-in-state.' The deputy news editor himself, whose whole life had been overshadowed by Churchill's, insisted on doing the early morning coverage from midnight onwards in Westminster Hall.

The Times's reports of the events of 30 January covered twenty-four pages, two of them describing the funeral under the heading THE NATION PAYS ITS LAST TRIBUTE, and two of them full of big, old-fashioned *Times* pictures. In addition *The Times* looked back into its own history and reprinted passages from its reports of the funeral of Wellington in 1852.

The cathedral service was described in splendour and solemnity. But humour kept on breaking in: 'High-ranking officers from Field Marshals downwards, many in greatcoats that seemed from their creases to have been in storage almost as long as their wearers'. As the royal families and the great and the good left, the anonymous correspondent from Printing House Square wrote: 'The captains and the kings had departed, but the glory – when would it ever fade away?' The Churchillian era moved slowly to an end as the people and the hacks bade goodbye to the great man. The great man himself, who loved a bit of stately rhetoric, would have thoroughly approved. He may have disguised it pretty effectively at times, but he was in fact a great admirer of *The Times*, which was why he was so irritated when it disagreed with him.

I dare say that if it were to happen again, *The Times* would cover it in much the same way. But it would need the death of a Churchill to bring that sort of tribute out of Printing House Square once again.

Right Winston Churchill and the Duke of Sutherland at Deauville, 1927.

Below The Prime Minister inspecting the ruins of the chamber of the House of Commons after it was completely destroyed during a heavy German attack on London the previous night, 14 May 1941.

Far right Winston Churchill inspecting the fleet at Spithead, 21 May 1937.

The first page of Winston Churchill's four-page obituary. The finest writing was reserved for the leader: 'There is a patriarchal grandeur and completeness about the life of Sir Winston Churchill such as the Chronicler saw in the career of King David, who had leapt into fame while still a stripling, . . had led a united people against overwhelming odds, had never faltered, never lost faith in their cause and their destiny, and came out with them at last into a little space of tranquillity before the end. He drank delight of battle, whether with shot or shell against the forces of tyrrany that he hated, or in the bloodless contests of the Parliament he loved. He is secure of his fame among the great deliverers. He belongs to his country; he belongs to the Commonwealth; he belongs to the world; and now he belongs to the ages.'
25 JANUARY 1965

No. 56,228 ROYAL EDITION

THE  TIMES

LONDON MONDAY JANUARY 25 1965

PRICE NINEPENCE

SIR WINSTON CHURCHILL DIES

Highlights of his Career

Born : November 30, 1874

Entered Harrow : 1888

Commissioned in the 4th Hussars : 1895

Escaped from the Boers : 1899

Entered Parliament : 1900

Under-Secretary of State for the Colonies : 1905

President of the Board of Trade : 1908

Home Secretary : 1910

First Lord of the Admiralty : 1911

Chancellor of the Duchy of Lancaster : 1915

Rejoined the Army in France : 1915

Minister of Munitions : 1917

Secretary of State for War and Air : 1919

Secretary for the Colonies : 1921-22

Chancellor of the Exchequer : 1924-29

First Lord of the Admiralty : 1939

Prime Minister and Minister of Defence : 1940

Leader of the Opposition : 1945

Prime Minister : 1951

Retirement from Office : 1955

Retired from Parliament : 1964

THE GREATEST ENGLISHMAN OF HIS TIME

WORLD LEADER IN WAR AND PEACE

Sir Winston Churchill, whose death in London yesterday is reported on the céntre page, led Great Britain from the peril of subjugation by the Nazi tyranny to victory; and during the last four years of his active political life he directed his country's efforts to maintain peace with honour, to resist another tyranny, and to avert a war more terrible than the last. In character, intellect, and talent he had the attributes of greatness.

An indifferent schoolboy, he was indifferent at nothing else which he attempted. Inheriting Lord Randolph Churchill's energy and political fearlessness, and being granted twice as many years, he carried to fulfilment a genius that in his father showed only brilliant promise. Leader of men and multitudes, strategist, statesman of high authority in the councils of nations, orator with a command of language that matched the grandeur of his themes, able parliamentary tactician, master of historical narrative, his renown is assured so long as the story of these lands is told.

The great war leader of his age, he lived through the fastest transformation of warfare the world has ever known, charging with the 21st Lancers at Omdurman in his youth, and in his old age arming his country with the hydrogen bomb.

He first entered Parliament in the sixty-fourth year of the reign of Queen Victoria. Sixty-four years later, in the thirteenth year of the reign of her great-great-granddaughter, he retired from it. Through more than half a century of British history there was not a year—barely a month—in which he was not actively and prominently engaged in public affairs.

Churchill's outstanding political virtue, which never deserted him, was his courage. There was the sheer physical courage which led him to seek more risks on active service before he was 25 than many professional soldiers know in a lifetime; and which gave him the will, when he was past 75, to overcome an affliction which would have laid other men low from the start. But there was moral and intellectual courage in equal degree. He served in Kitchener's Army in the Sudan—but attacked Kitchener publicly for his desecration of the Mahdi's tomb. He was returned as a Conservative in the "Khaki Election" of 1900—only to devote a passage in his maiden speech to a generous tribute to the Boers. No sooner was his maiden speech over than he shocked the Conservative front bench again by turning on one of his own party leaders, the Secretary of State for War, with a scorn which would have been startling even in a member of the Opposition.

Change of Party

He was still under 30 when, finding himself at odds with the tariff reform policy of Joseph Chamberlain, he crossed the floor of the House. So it continued all through his life—the habit of following his own judgment, his own intuition, and his own impulses. When he resigned from the Conservative "Shadow Cabinet" in 1931, as a protest against its attitude to India, he was acting with the same courage and independence which—they were inherited from his father—he had displayed from the very beginning. His independence frequently baffled his contemporaries, who tended to conclude, as did Margot Asquith in 1908, that he was a man of "transitory convictions". But the point is not that they were transitory but that they were his own. His mind was always restlessly surveying the political scene. He was for ever testing, courting, encouraging new ideas. No politician of this century has been less conservative and less hidebound.

This adventurousness, of course, had its disadvantages, of which his colleagues were often painfully aware. His mind never stopped roaming, and Asquith's Cabinet was described by one of its members as "very forbearing to his chatter". During the 1939-45 War—as the famous memoranda published as appendices to his history of *The Second World War* show—any question however trivial or however far removed from the central direction of the war might gain his attention. He seized on new ideas so indiscriminately that it became necessary for some of those closest to him to act as a sieve, and so prevent valuable time from being wasted on the wilder schemes. Yet, when the dross had fallen through, there remained in the sieve one or two nuggets. There is in Printing House Square a letter written early in the 1914-18 War by a high personage accusing Churchill of madness because of some impracticable scheme which he was pressing through in the face of much expert opposition. The "scheme" was the tank.

The independence of his ideas always made it difficult to define Churchill's political position. He was more of a Tory than a Conservative. The symbols of Toryism—Crown, Country, Empire—which might seem abstractions to some were to him realities. There was, indeed, always a personal element in the service he gave to his Sovereigns, which found quite different expressions in his attitude to the abdication of Edward VIII and in the tributes he paid when George VI died and Queen Elizabeth II was crowned. But it was a Toryism infused by another abstraction which to him was equally a reality: the People. He believed deeply that the People existed—not different and warring classes of people. In an earlier age he would have stood committed to the idea of the King and the People against the great Whig magnates—the cardinal principle of Disraelian Toryism. He was, in brief, a Tory Democrat, and in a speech to the Conservative conference in 1953 he proclaimed again the creed of his father, the first prophet of Tory Democracy.

Sense of History

Least of all was he a "Little Englander". No statesman has ever been more aware of his country's position in the world and its responsibility to the world. It was not merely his awareness of the facts of Germany's rearmament which made him speak so clearly from the beginning of the thirties; it was, even more (as befitted a descendant of Marlborough), his fundamental assumption that Britain was a part of Europe. He could no more have talked of Czechoslovakia as a far-away country than of Blenheim and Ramillies as far-away towns.

His politics were infused with a sense of history. It was a common gibe of his opponents that he lived in the past—that he was, in the words of Harold Laski, a "gallant and romantic relic of eighteenth-century imperialism". Nothing could be farther from the truth. He was as aware of the present, its opportunities and its challenges, as any of his contemporaries. But he drew from the past a profound conviction in the greatness of Britain, her people and her heritage. Romantic? It may be. But it was from this reserve that he drew the inspiration which he communicated to his fellow-countrymen in their and his finest hour. He was the symbol of British resistance, but of how much more as well. In his voice spoke the centuries which had made Britain as they had made him, and those who heard him in those days will never forget the echoes of Burghley, of Chatham, of Pitt, and countless more. "The last of the great orators to reach the heights."

The Right Honourable Sir Winston Leonard Spencer-Churchill, K.G., O.M., C.H., F.R.S., was born on St. Andrew's Day, 1874, at Blenheim Palace. He was the elder son of Lord Randolph Churchill and a grandson of the seventh Duke of Marlborough. His mother was the beautiful and talented daughter of Leonard Jerome, a New York businessman. Surviving her husband until 1921, she lived to see her son's fame firmly established.

Soldier and Journalist

The year had been an eventful one for Lord Randolph. Apart from his marriage and the birth of a son and heir, it had begun with his election as Conservative M.P. for Woodstock and included a maiden speech which drew from Disraeli, who had a good eye for a duke's son, a warm commendation. Lord Randolph's rise to power and influence was to be rapid, but his decline was even more rapid, and when he died in 1895 he left his son with memories of defeat and failure which carried a moral he was often to remember. Winston Churchill's education was conventional in its pattern; from a preparatory school at Ascot, to a small school at Brighton, to Harrow in 1888, and then, after twice failing to gain admission, to the Royal Military College at Sandhurst. But his verdict on Harrow was individual, for he left there, as he later confessed, convinced that he was "all for the public schools, but I do not want to go there again".

In 1895, soon after his father's death, he entered the 4th Hussars at Aldershot, and immediately obtained leave to go to Cuba for the *Daily Graphic* to watch the Spanish Army at work. While he was there he participated in the repulse of the insurgents who tried to cross the Spanish line at Trocham. After enjoying the London Season in 1896 he embarked for India, where he relieved the monotony of morning parades and evening polo by indulging his delight in reading. He was back in London for the Season in 1897, and then left in September to join the Malakand Field Force on the North-West Frontier of India. After being mentioned in dispatches for "making himself useful at a critical moment", he had to return to the 4th Hussars at Bangalore early in 1898, and there he occupied himself with the writing of his first history, *The Story of the Malakand Field Force*, which had considerable success at the time and is still consulted.

While he was at Bangalore he also wrote his only novel, *Savrola, a Tale of the Revolution in Laurania*, which he later urged his friends not to read. It contained, however, the sentence which seems to be as autobiographical as any he wrote: "Under any circumstances, in any situation, Savrola knew himself a factor to be reckoned with; whatever the game, he would play it to his amusement, if not to his advantage." During these early years Lieutenant Churchill, enjoying a liberty not likely to be granted nowadays to a serving officer, was able to combine the roles of a soldier and a newspaper correspondent, and it was as the representative of the *Morning Post* that at last, after three rebuffs from Kitchener, he joined the Sirdar's Army in Sudan. He reached Cairo in time to take part in the advance south into the Mahdi's country, and was present at the final victory at Omdurman.

Prisoner of the Boers

The strategy, tactics, and what a later generation has learnt to call the logistics of the campaign were set out by Churchill in *The River War, an Account of the Reconquest of the Sudan*, which was immediately successful when it was published in 1899. His early military writings showed a grasp, remarkable in a man of his years, of the operations of war, which was best revealed in the clear separation of the essential from the accidental. They were also distinguished by a dogmatic self-confidence which never hesitated in its criticism of senior officers. His outspokenness did not improve his prospects and he was doubtless wise to resign his commission after wearing the Queen's uniform for only four years. Moreover, his success as a journalist had enabled him to think of giving up the Army as a career, and he had even turned his attention to politics, addressing a Conservative garden party at Bath (his first political speech) and fighting a by-election (unsuccessfully) at Oldham.

It was as a correspondent, again for the *Morning Post*, that he left for South Africa within a fortnight of the outbreak of war in the autumn of 1899. There he met with sensational adventures very much to his taste. Taken prisoner on an armoured train expedition by a Boer by the name of Louis Botha he succeeded in escaping from the prison camp at Pretoria within three weeks, "jumped" a train, and after an extraordinary journey reached Delagoa Bay. He saw the campaign out until he could reenter Pretoria with the victorious Army, and when he returned to England he was received tumultuously at Oldham, where, in the "Khaki Election" of 1900, he won the seat from Walter Runciman. He was not yet 26, and contemporary accounts record that Joseph Chamberlain sat up and nudged his neighbour on the fron bench when, in his maiden speech, Churchill declared: "If I were a Boer fighting in the field—and if I were a Boer, I hope I should be fighting in the field. . . ."

Tariff Reform

Chamberlain was right to take notice: there was an ominous smack about the words, and in his first session in the House not only did Churchill speak vehemently against the Conservative Government's plans for Army reform—and their unfortunate advocate, Mr. Brodrick—but he voted against them as well. His unorthodoxy had deep roots He was at work on his life of his father, who had remained in a party with whose orthodox leaders he was at war and had suffered in the end only isolation and defeat. At the very beginning of his political career Churchill was in much the same position. He was as much a Tory Democrat as his father, in a party led by Balfour, who had always seemed to Lord Randolph to be the main opponent of Tory Democracy. Moreover, there was little intellectual adventure to be found in the Conservative Party of 1902, and Churchill, who always retained a great respect for the academic and cultured intellect, felt drawn to the company of Morley, Asquith, Haldane, and Grey.

Then, in the summer of 1903, Joseph Chamberlain made his great effort to revive protection—"playing Old Harry with all party relations", as Campbell-Bannerman excitedly remarked. With the Duke of Devonshire and Lord Hugh Cecil, Churchill declared himself a Unionist Free Trader, and by September, when it became clear that the Protectionists in the Cabinet had won, he was publicly exclaiming to a meeting at Halifax, "Thank God for the Liberal Party". Not unreasonably, the Oldham Conservative Association took exception to this and disowned him, and in the following year he crossed the floor of the House. How many who were there on that May 31, 1904, could foresee the irony in the incident as Churchill took his seat by the side of none other than David Lloyd George?

Before the end of 1905 Churchill had completed the life of his father. It stands, over half a century later, as one of the most brilliant political biographies of all time. The prose was perhaps never excelled by Churchill—later in his life the influence of the platform and the House of Commons made his prose too rhetorical—and the bringing to life of the political scene is so vividly and precisely done that the reader never loses his interest.

No sooner was this work of filial vindication done than Balfour—after months of trying to pacify his party and the House by "expressing no settled conviction where no settled conviction exists"—threw in his hand, and Campbell-Bannerman took office. Churchill accepted the office of Under-Secretary of State for the Colonies and was the spokesman of his department in the House of Commons. A month later, at the general election, Churchill was returned as a Liberal for North West Manchester—while Balfour was defeated in the adjacent seat. In the House it fell to him to maintain the Government's decision to grant full self-government to the annexed Boer Republics—a controversial issue—and he began to develop his parliamentary style in the thick of a major parliamentary battle. At the same time his mind was moving to a new outlook on home affairs. Before leaving the Conservative Party he had looked back to the time "when it was not the sham it is now, and was not afraid to deal with the problem of the working classes". Now he confidently declared that the Liberal Party's cause was "the cause of the left-out millions".

He was a Radical, describing the obstructive attitude of the House of

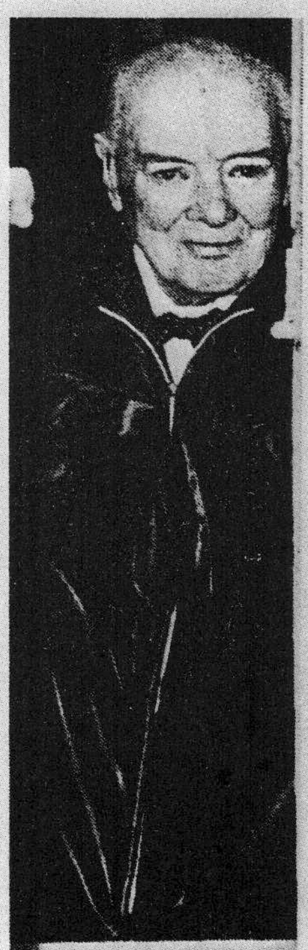

At Hyde Park Gate on his ninetieth birthday.

Lords as "something very like an incitement to violence". In 1908, when Asquith succeeded Campbell-Bannerman, Churchill was promoted to the Cabinet as Lloyd George's successor at the Board of Trade, having turned down the Local Government Board on the ground that he refused "to be shut up in a soup-kitchen with Mrs. Sidney Webb". Under the law then still in force his promotion forced him to submit himself for reelection and a tempestuous by-election ended in his defeat by Mr. Joynson-Hicks. But he was found a seat at Dundee, and he returned to London, his official career uninterrupted, to marry Miss Clementine Hozier.

In the political field he became a less conspicuous figure in the House of Commons, but in the country was second only to Lloyd George in his advocacy of the new Liberalism. A natural association developed between these two dissimilar men. Side by side they tried to check the rising naval expenditure, for, war-leaders though they were both to be, in 1908-09 their whole interest was focused on the first experiments in the "welfare state".

Bitter Attack

Churchill hesitated for a moment when Lloyd George introduced his People's Budget in 1909, but then threw himself into the fight in the country. Bitterly he denounced the House of Lords—especially the backwoods peers "all revolving the problems of Empire and Epsom"—and as president of the Budget League he enthusiastically praised the social policies which had made the Budget necessary. There were Conservatives who, though they could have overlooked his treason to his party in 1904, never could forgive his treason to his class, as they saw it, in 1909. They were later to have their revenge. He was now becoming—though still only 35—one of the leading members of the Government. In Cabinet, where one of his colleagues thought him "as long-winded as he was persistent", he distributed long memoranda to the rest of the members on all subjects—however far removed from the affairs of his own department. (In the Board of Trade he was teaching his subordinates the duties which now belong to the Ministry of Labour.) "Winston", recorded Grey, "will very soon become incapable from sheer activity of mind of being anything in a Cabinet but a Prime Minister."

After the bitter general election of 1910 Churchill was promoted to the Home Office, where his interest in the future welfare of prisoners helped to launch the movement for penal reform. But the most famous episode of his term at the Home Office was the Sidney Street "siege", which he characteristically insisted on witnessing personally. Germany's intervention in Morocco had made it imperative to put a term to the controversy over the British naval programme which was dividing the Liberal Party, and Asquith took what proved to be the decisive step of inviting the First Lord of the Admiralty (Reginald McKenna) and the Home Secretary to exchange offices. Churchill went to the Admiralty, with a mandate to maintain the Fleet in constant readiness for war with Germany.

Preparing for War

Germany's threat had completely changed Churchill's attitude to naval and military armaments, and he became (as 25 years later) a powerful advocate of preparedness, so much losing his interest in party differences and social policies that Lloyd George said he was apt to approach him with "Look here, David", and then "declaim for the rest of the afternoon about his blasted ships". In fact, the post exactly suited Churchill's temperament and gifts. His speeches in introduction of the Navy Estimates rank with Gladstone's Budgets as classical expositions of the relationship of policy to departmental practice. In the face of considerable service opposition he created a Naval War Staff. At weekends and when the House was in recess he familiarized himself with the work of the Navy, going everywhere, seeing everything, and exercising a magnificent judgment in his selection of officers.

When war came Churchill mobilized the Fleet on his own responsibility, forcing from Morley a sad reflection on "the splendid *condottiere* at the Admiralty". But two years later, when he was dismissed to satisfy the Conservative Party leaders, Kitchener took to him the personal message: "Well,

Haley: one of the great editors

Sir William Haley, editor of THE TIMES, 3 May 1966.

The Times is the best newspaper in the world. For many of us it is the only paper worth bothering with. Its editors are *ex officio* and often *per se* great men. Since Thomas Barnes was appointed in 1817 as the first editor in the modern sense, there have been only thirteen of them. Their whiskered faces hang in the editorial corridor like our corporate ancestral portrait.

When Sir William Haley was appointed editor of *The Times* in 1952, he was already a national figure, unlike his predecessors. For the previous eight years he had been Director-General of the BBC. He was asked why he had exchanged the vast empire of Broadcasting House for the little kingdom of Printing House Square. He replied 'Well, after all, it is the head of my profession'.

He entered the profession in 1920 as a telephonist at *The Times*, taking down copy from abroad. Two years later he married the girl to whom he had reported for duty, the foreign editor's secretary. The rising young man was sent to Brussels, where he reorganized the antiquated system of filing correspondents' copy to Printing House Square. Then he transferred to the *Manchester Evening News*. His single-mindedness, talent, some would say ruthlessness, pushed him to the top of the heap to become joint managing director of the *Manchester Guardian* group. He was appointed to the boards of the Press Association and Reuters. Thence to the top job at the BBC.

The Times was in trouble in 1952. It had not found a role or an audience after the war. Haley's predecessor, W. F. Casey, had been appointed as a stop-gap after the sudden death of Barrington-Ward in 1948. Casey was a first-class journalist but only a competent editor. Circulation had slipped to near the dangerous low-water mark of 200,000. Iverach McDonald, appointed foreign editor by Haley a few months after his arrival at Printing House Square, analysed the weakness in his autobiography, *A Man of The Times*:

> To our discredit, especially on the home side of the paper before Haley arrived, we often missed news that lay just below the surface. We were held back by fear of someone saying that we had manufactured it or got it out of proportion. Sometimes, quite simply, we did not go out to dig.

Haley changed all that. He was a Reithian figure, with a reputation as the only man in London with two glass eyes. Nothing escaped those formidable eyes. Every morning before he arrived at the office he would dictate over the telephone to his secretary a stream of memoranda expressing praise, criticism or displeasure over articles, pages, pictures and punctuation.

It was an autocratic regime. Editorial conferences were not seminars, or friendly gatherings, or gladiatorial contests, as they have been under other editors. Chairs were arranged as in a schoolroom, with the teacher sitting in front at the desk. The conferences were brisk, businesslike and laconic. Haley was not a man to waste words or time. Not everybody liked it. Prima donnas and strong individualists either left of their own volition or were informed that their departure would be in the best interests of the paper.

He was a man of steel. After he had rebuked an elderly journalist for some mistake, he asked him how much he was paid. When told (it was a pittance in those days), Haley observed icily 'Ah well, we cannot expect much for that, can we?' Margaret Allen, on her appointment as first woman deputy financial editor, said 'The City won't like it'. Sir William replied 'The City will have to put up with it'. From Sir William's style-book, in no circumstances to be taken out of the office: 'General statements are apt to be dangerous. For instance, "everybody is agreed that, etc." should be suspect, because the subjects on which everybody is agreed are indeed few'.

Under Haley's editorship, *The Times* extended its range of topics and treatment. He introduced factual guides of never more than half a column, and, as he himself said, 'in words of one syllable'. Profiles of men and women in the news combined curricula vitae with shrewd analytical notes, a bit like school reports. The headmaster was often writing the reports.

Haley was also a great writing editor. He wrote at least one leader a week. His Victorian moral drive showed in his leaders with their short sentences and sharp opinions: MORONS ON THE MARCH; IT *IS* A MORAL ISSUE. To a new, young leader writer, flushed with excitement and stammering to explain to the editor what line he had taken: 'I do not in the least care what line you have taken, Mr —, so long as you have taken 600 words and not a word more or less'.

Invited to claim his expenses after a month abroad visiting his foreign correspondents, Haley replied: 'There were no expenses: I stayed with friends'. A profile of a Royal Commission Chairman remarked that the famous judge 'will lose no sleep over any reactions to his work'. The proof came back, annotated in that big, bold hand in customary ink: 'No – this man is an insomniac'.To the obituaries editor: 'Let us not be snobbish about trade, Mr Watson'. To Louis Heren, offering a second bottle of Bernkasteler Spätlese between three of them on a festive occasion beside the Mosel: 'No; one is enough, Mr Heren'. 'This is my party' replied Heren, undaunted but aware of the risks, and ordered the second bottle.

He shared a passion for anonymity with his great predecessor, Thomas Barnes. There is no Thirty-Year Rule about Sir William's archives. He took the view that messages sent to him in confidence should remain confidential until the Last Trump; and there is some doubt whether they will be published even then.

He was the first editor of any newspaper to introduce the systematic confession of its errors in public. To show the standards of excellence that we were aiming at, the first correction we printed was not of an error of fact or a solecism, but of punctuation. It used to be the rule that we had to telephone the writers of letters we intended to publish in order to confirm their authorship. At nine o'clock one night the young Fred Emery, putting the Letters Page to bed, pointed out to Sir William up on the stone that he had been unable to get in touch with the author of the lead letter. 'Take it out at once' said the editor, causing chaos and half an hour's delay. When the page was finally away, Sir William said: 'Won't do that again, will you?'

He said that the role of *The Times* was to appeal not to the ruling class or any special group other than intelligent people of both sexes, and all classes and ages. He set up a committee to study the modernization, development and expansion of the paper. As a consequence, news replaced the Agony Column on the front page; a features department was set up, and Haley introduced a daily woman's page, a political cartoon and a diary.

Haley's leaders, such as IT *IS* A MORAL ISSUE, WHY THE £ IS WEAK or IT *IS* HAPPENING HERE, shook the country, rattled the Government and made *The Times* a trumpet in the land again. Their direct, forceful style, magnificently self-assured and sometimes wonderfully pig-headed, recaptured the vehement rhetoric of Thomas Barnes, his hero. In his farewell address to the Black Friars he said: 'There are things which are bad and false and ugly, and no amount of specious casuistry will make them good or true or beautiful'. He helped *The Times* to turn the corner, and circulation rose to more than 300,000 under his editorship. His potent spirit still stalks the corridors of *The Times*. He was one of the great editors.

One of Haley's renowned leading articles (column 2). Haley was a formidable organizer and administrator, as well as a great writing editor, with a vast capacity for work. Asked whether he had had a good weekend, he replied: 'Excellent. I read seven books, and reviewed four of them.'
18 MARCH 1963

MONDAY MARCH 18 1963

Special Articles:

Women's Topics:

Correspondence:

Index to Other Pages:

WEATHER FORECAST

A depression near W. Scotland will move slowly N. It will be mostly cloudy with rain at times over much of Scotland, although there will be bright periods with showers in parts of S. Scotland later. It will be cloudy with occasional rain in many areas of England, Wales and Northern Ireland at first. There will be showers and bright periods developing with some heavy showers and perhaps thunder. Temperatures will be near average.

Forecast for the period 6 a.m. to midnight:—

LONDON AREA, S.E. ENGLAND, EAST ANGLIA, CENTRAL S. ENGLAND, MIDLANDS, E. ENGLAND.—Mainly large amounts of cloud with occasional rain during morning; bright periods with showers later, risk of thunder; wind S. to S.W., fresh, becoming W., moderate; near average temp.; maximum temp. 52°F (11°C).

CHANNEL ISLANDS, S.W. ENGLAND, S. WALES AND MONMOUTHSHIRE.—Showers and bright periods, risk of thunder; wind S.W. to W., moderate or fresh; near average temp., maximum temp. 52°F (11°C).

N. WALES, N.W. ENGLAND, LAKE DISTRICT, ISLE OF MAN, CENTRAL N. ENGLAND, N.E. ENGLAND.—Mainly large amounts of cloud with occasional rain during morning, bright periods with showers later, risk of thunder; wind S. to S.W., moderate or fresh, becoming W.; maximum temp. 48°F (9°C).

BORDERS, EDINBURGH AND E. SCOTLAND, ABERDEEN AREA.—Mostly cloudy with occasional rain, bright periods with scattered showers developing later; wind S.E. to S., mainly fresh, becoming S.W. to W., moderate later; near average temp., maximum temp. 46°F (8°C).

OUTLOOK FOR TOMORROW.—Continuing changeable, sunshine at times but also showers or periods of rain.

SEA PASSAGES

S. NORTH SEA.—Wind S., strong to gale, veering S.W. and decreasing to moderate or fresh; rain or showers; visibility moderate or poor; sea rough, becoming moderate.

STRAIT OF DOVER, ENGLISH CHANNEL (E.).—Winds S. to S.W., veering W., moderate or fresh; showers; moderate visibility; sea moderate.

ST. GEORGE'S CHANNEL, IRISH SEA.—Wind S. to S.W., strong to gale, gradually veering W. and decreasing to fresh; rain or showers; moderate or poor visibility; sea moderate or rough.

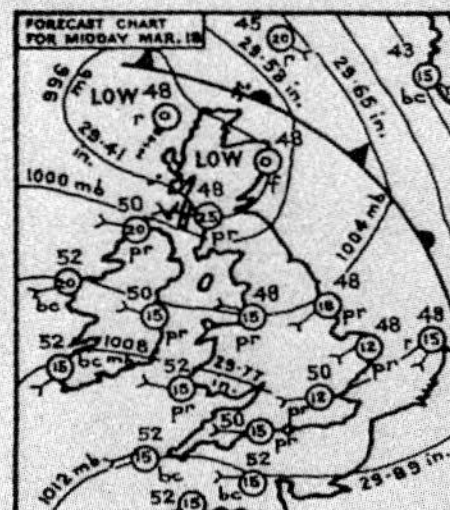

Atlantic Weather Chart—Page 9.

Sun rises, 6.9 a.m.; sets, 6.9 p.m.
Moon rises: 1.36 a.m. Moon sets: 10.8 a.m.
Last Quarter, 12.8 p.m.
Lighting-up time, 6.39 p.m.

High water at London Bridge, 6.18 a.m. and 6.42 p.m.; Dover, 3.29 a.m. and 4.1 p.m.

London (Kew).—Saturday temperature: maximum, day (6 a.m. to 6 p.m.), 54°F, 12°C; minimum, night (6 p.m. Friday to 6 a.m.), 46°F, 8°C. Rainfall (24 hours to 6 p.m.), 0.24in.

Barometer (at mean sea level) at 6 p.m., 1008.3 millibars (29.77in.), rising briskly. Sunshine (Kingsway) (24 hours to 6 p.m.), 7 hours.

YESTERDAY

London (Kew).—Temperature: maximum, day (6 a.m. to 6 p.m.), 54°F, 12°C, minimum, night (6 p.m. Saturday to 6 a.m.), 43°F, 6°C. Rainfall (24 hours to 6 p.m.), 0.02in.

Barometer (at mean sea level) at 6 p.m., 1009.2 millibars (29.08in.), falling slowly. Sunshine (Kingsway) (24 hours to 6 p.m.), 0.1 hour.

MIDDAY (G.M.T.) TEMPERATURES

ALGIERS	s.	73	JERSEY	r.	45
AMSTERDAM	c.	45	LISBON	d.	61
ATHENS	c.	61	LONDON	c.	52
BARCELONA	sl.	30	MADRID	c.	57
BERLIN	r.	36	MALTA	f.	61
BIARRITZ	c.	68	MANCHESTER	c.	48
BIRMINGHAM	c	50	N. YORK, E.S.T.	c.	51
BUDAPEST	f.	36	NICE	f.	57
COPENHAGEN	c.	30	OSLO	sn.	28
DUBLIN	r.	43	PARIS	c.	52
EDINBURGH	c.	48	STOCKHOLM	f.	32
FLORENCE	d.	50	VIENNA	sn.	34
GENEVA	f.	52	WARSAW	f.	32
GIBRALTAR	f.	64	ZURICH	s.	50
GUERNSEY	r.	45			

c., cloudy; d., drizzle; f., fair; r., rain; s., sunny; sl., sleet; sn., snow.

TODAY'S ARRANGEMENTS

Queen Elizabeth the Queen Mother, Princess Margaret and Lord Snowdon at Royal Film performance in aid of Cinematograph Trade Benevolent Fund, Odeon, Leicester Square.

Princess Royal opens W.V.S. Hellingly Club and canteen, near Hailsham, Sussex, 3.30.

Lord Mayor at Royal London Discharged Prisoners Aid Society annual meeting, Mansion House, 3.30.

Mr. Soames at Freedom from Hunger Campaign luncheon, Royal Commonwealth Society, 12.30.

Daily Mail Ideal Home Exhibition, Olympia, 10-10.

St. Michael's, Cornhill: organ recital, Dr. H. Darke, 1.

St. Martin-in-the-Fields: Rev. W. Rowett on "Hard sayings", 6.30.

Festival Hall: Haydn's *The Creation*, Harold Barnes conducts Barclays Bank Musical Society, 7.30.

Victoria and Albert Museum: exhibition of fans, 10-6.

S.P.C.K. Film Theatre: *The World Within*, Marylebone Road, N.W., 1.15.

British Museum (Bloomsbury): lectures, "Ancient Chinese bronzes", 11.30; "Aspects of graphic art 3: Rembrandt" (slides), 3.

United Law Debating Society: motion: "The right to strike should be restricted by legislation". Gray's Inn Common Room, 7.30.

Funeral: Lady (William) Fison, East Knoyle church, 2.

Memorial services: Major-General T. G. Dalby, Ugborough church, South Devon, 2.30; Mr. Wilfred Skinner, St. Mary-le-Strand, noon; Mr. John Spedan Lewis, All Souls', Langham Place, 6; Mr. P. J. S. Richardson, St Paul's, Covent Garden, noon.

IT *IS* HAPPENING HERE

The predominant note in the letters *The Times* has received about the two imprisoned journalists has been that of hostility to the press. The bitterness has gone far beyond what could be justified by a reasonable reading of the published proceedings of the Vassall tribunal. It has overflowed and at times sought to sweep away the principle at stake in these cases. They have broken the dam to a long pent-up, ever rising, flood of resentment against the practices of some newspapers. Intrusion, triviality, distortion, muck-raking, the inversion of values—the list of offences is long. They are real offences. The newspapers were warned years ago that if they went on the way they were going they would end by alienating those very sections of society upon whose good will the freedom and the working conventions of the press depend. This has now happened.

What makes the business so grave is the degree of ignorance, complacency, and apathy towards the particular dangers perpetually threatening every free society that now stands revealed. There really are people who believe that the encroachments of authority, the corruption of society, and maladministration can safely be left to the powers-that-be to put right. There seem to be even more who are convinced, though on what evidence is not clear, that after centuries of questioning, evolution, and amendment, the Law has at last reached so perfect a state that it must no longer, even on a matter of the deepest conscience, be defied. There is the assertion that such defiance can never be right. There are denials that our liberties can ever be preserved or enlarged by such means. And all this is taking place in a society that is supposed to be the most widely educated Britain has yet had, which has the means to be the best informed about the story of its past, and to which the crumbling of freedom among so many peoples during the past half-century should have taught inescapable lessons.

Part of the rot is shown by the accusations of exaggeration and hysteria against anyone who sees the issue in such terms. How ridiculous to imagine that in Britain anything could ever go seriously wrong. The truth is that in a quiet way very much is going seriously wrong. The Executive has taken over power from Parliament. It rules, or fails to rule, by a tacit agreement with outside forces in the community that *their* authority also shall not be challenged. The administrators at all levels decide more and more without the citizen having effective redress. Many ways of thought in the Law are restrictive, secretive, and hamper efforts to preserve the true public interest. And all these hazards are faced by a middle-class that, either through comparative affluence, weariness, or disgust, has thrown in its hand or lost sight of its responsibilities.

Grant all this—so runs a strong line of thought—that still does not give the press any position or competence to put things right. Who are journalists to regard themselves as the censors of power? Whatever may have been the role of newspapers in the past, they have long since forfeited any right to confidence or respect. Newspapers are now run to make money. New means of expression and communication have arrived that are more effective. Even if there used to be a convention whereby sources of information were preserved from disclosure it is now unnecessary and out of date.

The answers to these arguments are what they have always been. Journalists have no authority beyond that of other citizens. They do have in their hands an instrument which, when courageously and responsibly used, has so far proved in free societies to be the most effective in informing, in promoting discussion, in exposing error and malpractice, and in preserving liberties. Acting responsibly, moreover, is not a matter of obeying authority or accepting unchallenged what the lawyers say. It is to put first things first and to have a declarable reason for any challenge. Admittedly newspapers have to make money; Parliament was concerned not so long ago lest some of them could not make enough to survive. Some proprietors may put that object uppermost. (Let it be said there is as great a proportion of these in the provinces as in London.) That should not obscure the fact that the greater part of journalism does have an active conception of public service, and that is sometimes true even among those who have the oddest way of showing it. The new media have their attractions; their nature precludes them from fulfilling the role of the press. Satire is not enough. Authority will, for the time being at any rate, accept a few snooks as a cheap price to pay for the prohibitions it has been able to enforce in all countries without exception upon sound broadcasting and television.

The lesson of the events of the past month is that, in the final analysis, the only people who can preserve the freedom of the press are the journalists themselves. It will not be done by the Law or by Government; it cannot be done by Parliament. It is mistaken escapism to believe the responsibility can be concentrated in a Press Council. Neither taste nor ethics can be authoritarianly laid down. The way journalists behave, the spirit in which they go about their business, and the kind of business they go about are what will be decisive. This does not mean they can never be brash but must always be genteel, never rebellious but always docile. It does mean their seeming excesses should be for some discernible conception of the public good, and their manners be at least tolerable.

This is in essence one side of the contract a free society makes with its journalists. There is also the other. This is the recognition that the effective discharge of their duties, however self-chosen, depends upon certain freedoms or conventions, and among the most important of these is that journalists shall receive information from sources which they will withhold from all questioning because if there were ever the slightest doubt about this many other sources also would dry up. Far more serious than anything that has been uncovered about the behaviour of any journalist in the Vassall case is the inability of so many people to see this need, or to accept it as valid even when it is recognized. From the incredibly naive, who say that any source that will not bear disclosure is untrustworthy, to the ultra-sophisticated, who assert that it would be quite easy to pick and choose among the occasions when sources should or should not be revealed, there is all too wide a strand of opinion that cannot or will not acknowledge what is at stake. This is the preservation of the rights of every individual citizen against the usurpations of every form of authority, the ensuring of efficient and beneficent administration and of good government, and the defence of society against those forces that would corrupt it.

It is not an arrogant claim on the part of the press to have a role to play on this stage. Traditionally, and by the means at its disposal and the nature of its responsibilities, it has. Large sections of opinion would now apparently deny this, or would wish so to hobble the press as to make it ineffective. If some things that have happened have shown that a part of the press is sick, this desire, and so much acquiescence in it, shows much of public opinion is bemused. Never is a nation so vulnerable as when those sections of it which should be well informed and are inherently progressive lose their way because of the weeds.

An End to Discourtesies

It really is time that the British and French Governments stopped behaving to each other like schoolgirls after a tiff. It is childish and unbecoming; it does not represent public opinion in either country. The differences are much too serious for shows of pique. Many Frenchmen as well as British people sincerely deplore the manner in which PRESIDENT DE GAULLE broke off the Common Market negotiations, but that does not stop them from thinking the GENERAL was partly right in saying that Britain, with her overseas interests and traditions, was not ready to sink herself wholly in Europe. It is an occasion not for injured dignity but for recalling that in modern times European affairs have generally gone well when Britain and France have been together, and badly when they have been apart. There is plenty of opportunity for the diplomacy on which both sides pride themselves.

PRESIDENT DE GAULLE may have begun the tantrums on learning about the Anglo-American agreement at Nassau, but as soon as the British Government tried to be silly-clever by keeping PRINCESS MARGARET at home the dispute was put firmly on the wrong plane. Since then any act on either side—whether the Bidault broadcast or M. COUVE DE MURVILLE'S somewhat bleak declining of LORD HOME'S luncheon invitation—is taken by the other as a smack in the face. Denials of any such intention almost make matters worse. If British Ministers think that the five other members of the Community are cheering them on, or are anxious to put France permanently in a corner or to disrupt the Common Market, they are wrong. Let both sides stop it, and behave like friends and allies even though they cannot agree on European partnership.

The Old Guard Returns

MR. KOJO BOTSIO was dismissed from his post as Minister of Agriculture in Ghana in September, 1961, in the same purge which saw the political eclipse of MR. GBEDEMAH. In January, 1962, MR. BOTSIO was stripped of his party rights. In February, 1962, he resigned his parliamentary seat. Last May he began to return to favour as chairman of the National Council for Higher Education. In November he was nominated for a seat at a by-election. Now the wheel has come full circle and he is back in an important office as Foreign Minister. MR. KROBO EDUSEI, the present Minister of Agriculture, also began to go into eclipse in September, 1961, and seven months later was dismissed after publicity about his wife's purchase of a golden bed. His return to office was quicker, and he was appointed to his present post last September. What MR. EDUSEI and MR. BOTSIO have in common is their long connexion with the Convention People's Party, and the significance of MR. BOTSIO'S return to the Cabinet goes far beyond his personal political fortunes.

When the "old guard" went out of favour, *The Times* suggested that one explanation might be the need for a positive ideology which they were unable to provide, adding that it was disturbing to see men of experience dropped. Economically Ghana has passed through a difficult time, and in practice ideological fervour has proved to be no substitute for experience in the business of government—and certainly no great encouragement to potential investors. MR. BOTSIO'S appointment, like that of MR. EDUSEI, is a sign that PRESIDENT NKRUMAH'S current policy is based on a realistic assessment of the country's needs and a determined effort to fulfil them. There are other, less obvious, signs, like the recent decision to return responsibility for exchange control from the Bank of Ghana to the Ministry of Finance, which can be expected to interpret the regulations less rigidly and with more regard to the Government's policy of attracting investment. Taken together they indicate that the PRESIDENT, worried by the results of relegating the old guard, has been wise enough to seek advice from others besides the ideologists, and has felt himself strong enough to follow it.

Fair Enough

"I am still working out whether the questions were fair", a young Service man hoping to qualify as a Parliamentary candidate at a by-election is reported to have said after an interview, and he added handsomely enough "I think they were". The question of what, in its turn, constitutes a fair question is always a ticklish one and the human mind, from childhood days, has delighted in those that come under the heading of "trick". The answer to the conundrum "when is a door not a door?" was always guaranteed to bring down the house and although, strictly speaking, it comes in a different category, a good deal of more or less adult fun is still to be had with that form of words which infuriatingly demands "When did you stop beating your wife?"

Alice discovered to her cost how disconcerting rude, sharp-witted creatures can be when they apply to words and phrases that strict logic that seldom rules in normal life, and there is the ever-present temptation for the question asker to indulge in the same sort of perverted cleverness. He is liable, indeed, to set the worst type of all tests, that designed to find out not what the person being examined knows but what he does not know. Questions framed on this principle are calculated to inspire that passionate protest against the devious ways of authority which expresses itself in the simple eloquence of the phrase "It wasn't fair".

Yet many, it seems, are prepared to run the risk of exposing themselves to such a form of inquisition, for few forms of entertainment, if that is the right term, are as popular today as the "quiz". It is strange, incidentally, how the associations of the word have changed and now the vision it conjures up is less of a tall, slim, dandyish figure with a supercilious smile and that early nineteenth-century mingling of lorgnette and eye-glass than of a panel of celebrities indulging in a form of round game. There are multitudes of varying types of question from the idle to that which rates at 64,000 dollars, and it is as well to remember the proverb that runs "a fool may ask questions which forty wise men cannot answer". All, however, would probably agree that fair questions are those which find us ready and able to cope with them.

WARSAW UPRISING

Sir,—The year 1963 marks the twentieth anniversary of the Warsaw Ghetto Uprising, an epic of history, the memory of which it must be sadly said is fading from the minds of the peoples of the world.

In order to remind those who have forgotten and to inform those who did not or could not know of the infamies of Nazism, as well as to learn the lessons therefrom, the Memorial Committee, of which the undersigned are sponsors, has been established.

The significance of this year which marks the separation of a complete generation in time, from the heroic struggles of the Warsaw martyrs, is being commemorated on an impressive scale by the Polish Government, which has set up a committee to organize commemorative events under the leadership of the Chairman of the Council of Ministers, Mr. Josef Cyrankiewicz.

These events, beginning on April 18 next, will be attended by delegations of Jews and non-Jews from the United States, Brazil, France, Israel, and Great Britain. Among those who will form the British delegation are Dayan Rabbi M. Steinberg, a member of the Chief Rabbi's Rabbinical Court, the Rev. W. W. Simpson, general secretary of the National Council of Christians and Jews, and many other figures of note representing communities from all over the country.

We commend this Pilgrimage and ask those who wish to join to write to the Organizing Secretary, Mrs. L. Douglas, 17, Crooked Usage, Finchley, N.3.

We are, Sir, yours, &c.,

SAUL AMIAS; BOOTHBY; J. BRONOWSKI; MICHAEL CLIFFE; BARNETT JANNER; ISAAC LEVY; J. B. PRIESTLEY; SILKIN; †MERVYN STOCKWOOD; KENNETH TYNAN; TED WILLIS.

March 15.

LATE TO WORK

Sir,—Without detracting from Mr. Pollak's conclusions in his letter to you on March 14, it is necessary to correct a statement he made in the last paragraph.

Apart from the "munitions period" during the war, all subsequent productivity campaigns have sought to make factory (and office) staff work more effectively not harder. Many people are working too hard already, some on tasks which are not really necessary.

Part of the aim of the National Productivity Year is to broadcast the fact.

Yours faithfully,

A. D. C. CHAPLE.

64, Lee Park, Blackheath, S.E.3.

BRIGHTEST AND BEST?

Sir,—There is at present at each desk in the reading room of the Victoria and Albert Museum a little lamp which the reader can have on or off as he chooses. Unfortunately plans are afoot to remove these lamps and put in their place a strip of fluorescent lighting which will spread a glare over six desks, three a side.

The reading room of the British Museum has been spoilt by this lighting. Must it happen to the pleasant reading room of the Victoria and Albert Museum?

The reasons against this form of lighting are these: it is too harsh for reading by; it is a bad light for writing by—at least where creative writing is concerned for it inhibits the flow of ideas; there is little chance of having it off even on a bright day, someone is sure to want it on; in the case of the British Museum the fluorescent tubes are contained in ugly superstructures which spoilt the appearance of the reading-room.

Fluorescent lighting is doubtless suitable for the Ministry of Work's draughtsmen, but it is unsuitable as a reading lamp.

Why does the official mind automatically believe that something which is brighter is better. Must we be brighter? Can't we be dimmer?

Yours faithfully,

JOHN SYMONDS.

22, Well Walk, N.W.3.

A REASONABLE REWARD

SALARY SCALES FOR GRAMMAR SCHOOLS

TO THE EDITOR OF THE TIMES

Sir,—Many masters in this grammar school are grateful to the Minister of Education for his action in quashing the settlement arrived at by the Burnham Committee.

Grammar school masters, even with the existing differentials, are poorer than they were before the last war.

Only by improving the prospects will well-qualified men and women be attracted to the profession, and only in this way can the academic standard be maintained and eventually improved.

Many grammar school masters feel that their interests have not been adequately promoted on the Teachers' Panel of the Burnham Committee, which is dominated by the N.U.T., and welcome the committee's demise. They would urge a return to the practice, which prevailed until the Education Act of 1944, of separate negotiations to determine grammar school salaries.

Yours faithfully,

T. HILTON; H. R. THACKER; M. HOWARD-JONES; A. D. ALDERSON; K. J. STERCK; I. S. ANNETTS; T. W. FOSTER; R. W. BOOTE; A. J. HILES; J. B. CHAFFEY; A. W. OPENSHAW; E. B. SMITH; B. M. SMALLWOOD; B. S. VAIL; E. A. IREDALE; C. R. HEDLEY; M. R. OXFORD; R. E. GARTON; E. M. ROYDS-JONES; P. W. MOLLARD; G. C. THOMPSON; C. BRISCOE.

Price's School, Park Lane, Fareham, Hampshire, March 15.

Sir,—The excellent article by Mr. Chambers in *The Times* of March 12 on the deficiency of the negotiating machinery for teachers' salaries indicates, quite rightly, that salaries at the top of the profession must be high enough and be reached soon enough to attract the right sort of person.

Will, however, any reasonable standard of remuneration for male teachers ever be reached unless some form of dependants' allowances is introduced?

In the teaching profession the practice of equal pay for men and women has existed for some years. About 70 per cent of the profession are women, most of whom must consider themselves extremely well paid. The same certainly cannot be said of the 30 per cent of men, many of whom have wives and children to support. Why should all the women teachers' salaries be raised in order to obtain a reasonable remuneration for the family man?

Yours faithfully,

JOAN BULMER-THOMAS.

12, Edwardes Square, W.8.

PATIENT ISLANDS

Sir,—While on our island plantation of Mustique in the St. Vincent Grenadines, I read in the *Barbados Advocate* (January 5) where the Colonial Secretary, writing in his other capacity, was quoted from the Commonwealth Relations Office list as follows: "Britain has no desire to hold on to her remaining colonies a day longer than is necessary—politically they involve us in much unwelcome controversy, and economically we draw no profit from our sovereignty."

Sadly true no doubt but sadder still to taste its truth. The Windward and Leeward islands, the patient remnants of W.I. Federation, are negotiating anew with Barbados. So far the only indications for this Federation are that "H.M.G. would be prepared to consider to do what they consider equitable with regard to aid" (*Barbados Advocate*, January 16).

I fear lest "equitable" be taken to mean something not grossly less than the style to which they have long been accustomed. This is so inadequate today that many people have come here to support their own unemployed at home, largely the descendants of Africans who have worked for generations to foster British fortunes.

The resources of these islands, chiefly agricultural, have never been properly developed. For example, there is still no road round St. Vincent. Will they get this now? We have a responsibility before independence as well as after.

Aid to recharge should be granted now and a new status proffered such as "Associated Territories" to last until nationhood and the means to enjoy it are attained.

Otherwise hope and friendship will be lost. The gesture would cost little and is overdue.

Yours faithfully,

COLIN TENNANT.

9, Harp Lane, Great Tower Street, E.C.3.

FIGHT FOR GEORGIAN ROW

Sir,—It might appear from Mr. Leslie Bilsby's letter in your issue of March 16 that the developers for whom he writes have a monopoly of what he calls "the public weal", and that all others are either reactionaries of the right or anti-profit cranks of the left. Nothing could be farther from the truth. Those who seek to preserve Montpelier Row, and they include the L.C.C., which has placed a preservation order on it, do so only because it is worth preserving. The L.C.C. can hardly be accused of anti-development bias when one considers the widespread schemes for which it has been responsible since the war throughout the Greater London area, including Blackheath itself.

The paramount importance of preserving unspoiled the façade of Montpelier Row is that it is viewed not across the confines of a narrow street but from the noble expanse of London's historic approach by land from Dover and the Continent. The heath is still miraculously an undeveloped open space, with Greenwich Park to the north and elsewhere ringed by a frame of buildings, all in keeping one with one another, of which this Georgian terrace forms an essential portion. Replace part of a beautiful frame with a new section of incongruous design and not only will you ruin the frame but you will spoil the picture set within it. It is a picture of very real delight to countless visitors from overseas, as I know from my personal experience. It is something they regard as typical of England.

We who live in Blackheath and love it are not against development as such where it is needed, but we do, nevertheless, *pace* Mr. Bilsby, seek to hold on to that part of our heritage, whose retention is, as we believe, so clearly in the best interests of "the public weal".

Yours faithfully,

FRANK CARR.

10, Park Gate, Blackheath, S.E.3. March 17.

ONLY A LITTLE ONE

Sir,—Temporarily remote from a suitable library, I have been expecting that someone else would comment on two points in Sir Carleton Allen's letter in your issue of March 2.

First, "A public statement by a responsible guardian of the law that he proposes to select which felonies he will or will not prosecute seems to me startling, unprecedented and contrary to public policy." There is no difficulty in finding a precedent. The *locus classicus* is a statement by Sir Hartley Shawcross (as he then was) in the House of Commons on January 29, 1951 (Hansard, vol. 483, cols. 681-687). For a full appreciation of the principles involved the whole speech should be read, but the following extracts will suffice for present purposes:—

"It has never been the rule in this country—I hope it never will be—that suspected criminal offences must automatically be the subject of prosecution. Indeed the very first regulations under which the Director of Public Prosecutions worked provided that he should intervene to prosecute, amongst other cases: 'wherever it appears that the

Continued in next column

offence or the circumstances of its commission is or are of such a character that a prosecution in respect thereof is required in the public interest'. That is the dominant consideration." . . .

". . . the ordinary case is one where one has to review the evidence, to consider whether the evidence goes beyond mere suspicion and is sufficient to justify a man being put on trial for a specific criminal offence.

"In other cases wider considerations than that are involved. It is not always in the public interest to go through the whole process of the criminal law if, at the end of the day, perhaps because of mitigating circumstances, perhaps because of what the defendant has already suffered, only a nominal penalty is likely to be imposed. And almost every day in particular cases, and where guilt has been admitted, I decide that the interests of public justice will be sufficiently served not by prosecuting, but perhaps by causing a warning to be administered instead.

"Sometimes, of course, the considerations may be wider still. Prosecutions may involve a question of public policy or national, or sometimes international, concern. . . ."

"I think the true doctrine is that it is the duty of an Attorney-General, in deciding whether or not to authorize the prosecution, to acquaint himself with all the relevant facts, including, for instance, the effect which the prosecution, successful or unsuccessful as the case may be, would have upon public morale and order, and with any other considerations affecting public policy."

In the debate which followed, no one suggested that anything the Attorney-General had said was startling or contrary to public policy; indeed, there was no dissentient voice.

Secondly, Sir Carleton Allen suggests that, in considering whether to institute criminal proceedings, the discretion of the police is limited to deciding whether the evidence is sufficient to justify a prosecution. This suggestion cannot be accepted without challenging Sir Hartley Shawcross's statement, unless there is some ground for differentiating in this respect between the functions of the Attorney-General and those of the police, and so far as I know there is no fundamental difference.

The propriety of the pronouncement made by the Chief Constable of Southend is a different matter. Since its apparent effect was to restrict in advance the exercise in particular cases of a quasi-judicial function, it seems to be distinctly questionable.

Yours faithfully,

K. O. ROBERTS-WRAY.

The Old Golf House, Forest Row, Sussex.

Race Equality Stirs Again in South

From Our Washington Correspondent

The lonely flame of racial equality lit in Mississippi University last Autumn by Mr. James Meredith, the Negro student, was barely flickering when a new spark from South Carolina suddenly rekindled it. The registration of Mr. Harvey Gantt, a Negro architectural student, at Clemson College not only brought official desegregation to the last of the 50 states but it did so without the accompanying violence of last year. In Louisiana, meanwhile, an equally remarkable event took place. Tulane University, in New Orleans, a private institution under no legal obligation to desegregate, admitted 11 Negroes with a minimum of fuss or publicity. And Mr. Meredith announced that he would return for another term to the University of Mississippi.

In Alabama in 1956 the desegregation attempt by Miss Autherine Lucy, a Negress, was crushed before the example could spread to neighbouring states, but desegregation came to the state briefly and although Alabama is alone in having no desegregation in public education at present, Miss Lucy established the precedent which others are now trying to follow. Mr. Gantt's admission at Clemson College is proof positive of the value of responsible civic leadership which was negatively demonstrated in Mississippi. Yet, strictly speaking, it is a victory for expediency, economic and political, rather than for genuine integration. The state's executive, business and religious leaders, who counselled moderation, have not and will not give up their opposition to Mr. Gantt's presence and all that it stands for, but they are not prepared to risk the dislocation which would accompany another Mississippi incident.

ECONOMIC ASPECT

Too much cannot be expected, or claimed, as yet, but an encouraging start has been made—no troops, no helicopters, no marshals and above all no blood, no broken glass, no tear gas.

It has been suggested that South Carolina's aristocratic history and liberalism, contrasted with the frontier nature of Mississippi's beginnings, is responsible for its more graceful behaviour now. Perhaps so, but the more immediate reasons are economic. In the past four years South Carolina has attracted $850m. worth of outside investment and 57,000 new jobs have been created. Much might have been lost in an outbreak of chaos such as occurred in Mississippi.

The example of Georgia, where desegregation is proceeding rapidly, where the new Governor is a racial moderate and where a Negro sits in the legislature, provided a blueprint for success, and South Carolina's civic leaders have taken it up.

The prophet of this approach has been Mr. Ralph McGill, the editor of the Atlanta *Constitution*, who has used his columns to convert business and other leaders to moderation and the rule of law. He recently summed up the situation by saying: "Today the national conscience is committed to what we have called the American dream. There is much to be done. But it will be done." His confidence was confirmed at Clemson and just as Mr. Meredith, who was struggling with his personal decision, must have been encouraged, so the nascent moderate movements in Mississippi and Alabama may take heart. It will take time to loosen the grip of the White Citizens' Councils there, but the shock of Oxford, Mississippi, and the calm of Clemson have in their different ways contributed to the process.

ARTISTS HELPING

It is a far cry in Columbia, S.C., from the days of 1956 and 1957 when the legislature was commending the White Citizens' Councils, supporting the legal doctrine of interposition invoked by Governor Barnett in Mississippi, and banning a children's book about white and Negro fraternization. Then local authorities bought machine-guns with which to repel the expected federal invader. Now the new Governor, Mr. Donald Russell, has almost unanimous support for his policy of meeting legal obligations peacefully.

There are signs, too, that the new generation of Negro artists and musicians, whose predecessors were accused of deserting their own, are working actively for the Negro cause. Miss Leontyne Price, the Negro soprano, returned to her native Mississippi town recently to sing at a concert before a mixed audience, and Mr. Dick Gregory, the comedian who laughs at segregation for a living, is also active. He has helped his friend Mr. Meredith, and is organizing material assistance for Negroes who have been taken off the welfare rolls in Mississippi.

Governor Barnett is still breaking lances on behalf of states' rights and his own brand of constitutional government and it may be that, if he wishes, he will be able to exercise his oratorical powers in the Senate. He has an ally in the new Governor of Alabama, Mr. Wallace, whose inaugural address sounded so ominous that the Justice Department quickly took aerial photographs of the University of Alabama. Nevertheless, there is a firm belief among the enlightened politicians in the South that these men, who have been demonstrably unable to keep their promises, are gradually losing the sympathy of the voters. They point not only to Governor Russell in South Carolina but also to Governor Sanders, who came to power in Georgia in an election which saw the segregationist candidate finish a poor third.

LONG PROCESS

The tide of history is felt to be on the side of moderation in the South. It will be a long process by any reckoning and there will be some temporary setbacks, but the growing industrialization of the South is breaking down some of its regionalism and it is beginning to share with other areas the problems of urbanization, housing, mass transit and education, in all of which it is no more conservative than most other parts of the country.

If optimism is now possible, where before it was almost unthinkable, there is little cause for complacency and Mr. Robert Kennedy, the Attorney-General, has pointed out that the problems remain difficult, not only in the South with open discrimination but throughout the country where more subtle forms of the art are practised. It is the misfortune of the Negro and the Justice Department lawyer that the battle must be waged in the undramatic forums of lunch-counters, bus terminals, and classrooms, even though larger forces may be at work. Measured in these narrow terms, the Administration's policy of desegregation by litigation has had some success.

Mr. Kennedy has pointed out, with justifiable pride, that segregation on inter-state buses and trains has been ended. Whether this is due to his superior strategy or to the "Freedom Rides" of two years ago, it is a real achievement but it cannot deal with travel within each state. Here the responsibility falls to local Negro leadership, and it would be a lengthy process to repeat all over the South Dr. Martin Luther King's successful bus boycott in Montgomery, Alabama, which remains a monument to the efficacy of non-violence.

MONTHS TO FIGHT

Mr. Kennedy has brought new zeal to the tedious process of examining the voting rolls and bringing cases against discriminators or trying to persuade them to abandon the practice. The recent suit against Sunflower County, Mississippi, the home of the powerful Senator James Eastland, was a brave gesture but, apart from the evidence that other freedoms do not automatically follow the opportunity to vote, each case takes weeks to prepare, months to fight, and perhaps years to bear fruit.

The Attorney-General's boast that the number of school districts desegregated in the South rose last year from 912 to 972 was a proud one, but he was perhaps less than candid in making no reference to the 5,257 still to be tackled in Southern and Border states. This year the President has for the first time sought new civil rights legislation. His proposals were designed to facilitate Negro voter registration, guarantee equality in employment and assist schools which are desegregating.

OBSTACLES TO GROWTH

Sir,—Lord Brand says that "our great rise of prices here is undoubtedly due to the great pressure for constantly increased wages".

With the greatest respect I believe this to be a symptom rather than a cause while the underlying causes of the great pressure for more wages really are:—

(1) Constantly rising food prices due to agricultural protectionism. It is the price of food that moves the index and the index that moves wage-rates.

(2) The fact that employers can afford to pay more wages and stay in business due to the fact that they too are protected in the home market.

(3) The fact that whatever money is necessary to finance inflation is duly printed and put into circulation by the Bank of England as agents for the Treasury.

If I am right, inflation is not incurable. It requires only that some government should have the moral courage to administer the right dose. I believe the patient would respond.

Yours faithfully,

OLIVER SMEDLEY, Chairman, Free Trade League.

24, Austin Friars, E.C.2.

RARAE AVES

Sir,—The letters you published recently from the Archdeacon of Oxford and Prebendary T. F. Royds were of great interest, but the writers were wrong in relating them in any way to Lady Bridge's appointment.

The offices of Canon and Lay Canon are completely distinct. They have only two things in common, namely, that each is connected with a Cathedral, and each contains the word "Canon" in its title; but one might as well compare the Provost of a Scottish Burgh with the Provost of an Anglican Cathedral Church. The office of Lay Canon is of modern origin and its name is somewhat fortuitous. If, for example, it had been decided to name the office "Lay Deacon" the present correspondence would not have arisen, but perhaps one of your readers would have pointed out that there were already Deaconesses in the Church of England!

Nothing so far published disturbs the belief that Lady Bridge is the first woman in England to be appointed as a Lay Canon.

Yours faithfully,

TREVOR B. BIRKETT, Diocesan Registry, Portsmouth.

Crescent House, Queens Crescent, Southsea, Hampshire.

News on the front page

On 3 May 1966 *The Times* caused a sensation around the world by putting news on its front page, the traditional place for its famous Agony Column of personal advertisements. Television and radio were present to record the portentous event. The editor, a rigid upholder of journalistic anonymity, went so far as to appear on television. Fleet Street aired its opinions. Syndication carried the news around the world, so that small towns from the Mid-West to the Outback, and readers from China to Peru, were startled to learn that a faraway paper with a small circulation now carried news on its front page. In retrospect the uproar of news and comment seems disproportionate to the event. But it was a highly symbolic change: *The Times* was first and foremost a newspaper, not just a venerable institution, or a paper of record. Good judges thought that the change was forty years too late. *The Times* ought to have been first in the field, as it was in so many other innovations of journalism, typography and printing.

First night of news on the front page of THE TIMES, 3 May 1966. Left to right, the Hon. Gavin Astor (chief proprietor), R. Henry Smith (night production manager), Fred Park (works manager), William Haley, Lady Irene Astor, George Pope (general manager).

Personal announcements have appeared in *The Times* since it was first published as *The Daily Universal Register* (see pp. 130–1). In the eighteenth and early nineteenth centuries the front page usually carried a mixture of news and classified advertisements. By 1854 the tradition had been established that the front page was given over entirely to classified advertisements, including Births, Marriages and Deaths (irreverently known at Printing House Square as Hatched, Matched and Dispatched) and the personal notices. In 1886 it was labelled the Personal Column for the first time. Its popular name was the Agony Column, because many of the announcements consisted of heartrending cries for news of a lost son or lover; the actual origin of the sobriquet is lost in the mists of *Times*.

With the advent of news on the front page, the Agony Column and the rest of the classified advertisements were transferred to page 2 – a mistake of the first magnitude. Page 2 is an awkward place in a broadsheet paper for strap-hangers in the Tube, and other browsers, to get at. Shortly after he became editor in January 1967, William Rees-Mogg transferred classified ads to the back page, where they remained until the changes made by Harold Evans in 1981.

It was not the first time in the history of *The Times* that the front page had been given over to news and comment – see, for example, the facsimile pages illustrating the Battle of Trafalgar and the First World War (pp. 21 and 89). But now the change was to be permanent – and you cannot make changes in *The Times* without provoking comment. The paper belongs to its readers, as well as its proprietors, shareholders and journalists. A number of public figures gave their verdict on the change, including that eminent conservative, Earl Attlee: 'I don't like it'.

But *The Times* was anxious to reassure its readers that its essential nature would remain unchanged. A leading article on 3 May, headed MODERN TIMES, ran thus:

> The same people have produced today's issue as did yesterday's. They will produce tomorrow's. They will continue to have the same sense of responsibility and the same standards. They will at the same time use all their professional skill to make *The Times* more comprehensive, more interesting, more explicit, more lucid. *The Times* aims at being a paper for intelligent readers of all ages and all classes. The more it can have of them the better. Some people have expressed the dark suspicion that one of the reasons *The Times* is modernising itself is to get more readers. Of course it is. And we shall go on trying to get more readers for as long as we believe in our purpose.

It was unfortunate that the contents of the page on that first day of news on the front did not live up to the occasion. There was not a lot of news around on the night of 2 May. Accordingly a piece of 'informed' speculation that Nato's headquarters were to be removed to London was promoted to lead the page ('the splash', as it is called in the trade). This absurd *Times* 'scoop' caused ribaldry among its rivals. *Parturient montes, nascetur ridiculus mus*: after the brouhaha comes the anticlimax.

There was more to the changes of May 1966 than the transposition of pages and the putting of news on the front. The whole paper was reorganized. In particular, and most notable for professionals of the inky trade, Stanley Morison's classic Roman capitals for the headlines were dropped in favour of a mixture of capitals and lower case letters. Another portentous victim of the change was the royal coat of arms, which had been flown on the masthead of *The Times* since its foundation. Stanley Morison had wanted to get rid of it when he redesigned the typography of the paper in 1932, but the then proprietors were reluctant to assent to such a radical step.

The changes of 3 May had a dramatic effect on circulation – it had risen by 20 per cent after six months. Of all the many hundreds of letters that came into the office commenting on the changes, only one was printed. It came from Garter King of Arms approving the dropping of the royal coat of arms, 'for which there had never been any authority'. For the record: the royal coat of arms was put back on the front page on the wedding day of the Prince and Princess of Wales in 1981. It found favour with the then editor; to the extent that the paper took a step two hundred years backwards by displaying the arms used in 1792.

The last edition to carry advertisements and the Agony Column on the front page, ending a tradition that had lasted over 180 years.
2 MAY 1966

No. 56,620 ROYAL EDITION

THE TIMES

DIEU ET MON DROIT

LONDON MONDAY MAY 2 1966

PRICE NINEPENCE

CHARGES FOR ANNOUNCEMENTS

FORTHCOMING MARRIAGES (Court) .. (per line)
BIRTHS, MARRIAGES AND DEATHS .. (per line)
IN MEMORIAM .. (per line)
PERSONAL .. (per line)
PERSONAL TRADE .. (per line)
BOX NUMBERS .. (each)

Minimum—Personal 2 lines, other classifications 3 lines. Charges for other categories on request.

Telephone: CENtral 2000. Telex: 262622/3, or write to THE TIMES, Printing House Square, London, E.C.4. FRANCE—8 Rue Halévy, Paris, 9e. Tel.: Opera 037. Telex: 22193. U.S.A.—201, East 42nd Street, New York, N.Y. 10017. Telephone: 986-9230.

Inland and Air Edition subscription rates on request.

BIRTHS

BENNET.—On April 26th, 1966, to LINDA (née ...) and GLYN BENNET—a son (EDWARD JAMES). 11 ... Road, Bristol 8.

CHILVERS.—On April 30th, 1966, at Princess Christian Nursing Home, Windsor, to ROSEMARY and DONALD CHILVERS—a boy.

CLARK.—On April 27, 1966, at Queen Charlotte's Hospital, London, to MARY (née Andrews) and ...

MARRIAGES

DEATHS

DEATHS (continued)

THORESBY.—On 30th April, 1966, at his home, Halfpenny House, Hurley, Berkshire, MERVYN THORESBY, dearly loved husband of Pamela and dear papa of Nicolette and Gillian younger son of the late Dr. and Mrs. James Thoresby-Jones. Memorial service, Bisham Church, Wednesday, 4th May, at 4.30 p.m. Flowers to Sawyer Funeral Service, 32 West Street, Marlow, Buckinghamshire.

WATTS.—On April 29th, 1966, peacefully, at home, EDMUND HANNAY, aged 67, of Ashfields, Great Canfield, Dunmow, Essex, beloved husband of MARGARET WATTS. Cremation private on Tuesday, May 3rd. Flowers may be sent to Pickford, Brook House, Church End, Dunmow, Essex.

MEMORIAL SERVICES

IN MEMORIAM

BEAUTY AND FASHION

STEINER HAUTE COIFFURE

Gleneagles Hotel — Auchterarder 2231. North British Hotel, Edinburgh; Caledonian Hotel, Edinburgh — Waverley 7788. In fact you find elegant Steiner Salons almost everywhere—London, Manchester, Birmingham, Bradford, Cheltenham, Leeds, Hull, Dublin, Leicester, Ryde and of course around the world in Cunard and Royal Mail Ships.

HELANKA STRETCH SKI-STYLE PANTS, 22 to 32 waist. French, navy, brown and black, 65s. for average length, £4 for the taller woman, plus 2s. postage. Usual price £6 ... Guaranteed money refunded if not satisfied. Please state height when ordering.—MARGARET RUSSELL, 11, Chatsworth Parade, Petts Wood, Kent. Orpington 29078.

LONDON CENTRE for Modern Jewellery. Unique pieces, £3 to £800.—Ewan Phillips Gallery, 22a, Maddox Street, W.1. MAY. 4204.

SAUNA BATHS followed by revitalising body massage. Slimming and all beauty treatments. Fully qualified Beauticians and Physiotherapists. Salisbury House, Langton Green, Tunbridge Wells. Langton 2272.

SMALL WOMEN'S SHOES

STOCKED from size 1. Popular prices.—Weintrop, 71, Berwick Street, W.1. Postal service operated.

DIRECTORS AND PARTNERS

SURVEYORS, VALUERS & ESTATE AGENTS.—Well-known London W.1 firm will shortly have a vacancy for Junior Partner due to retirement of senior partner. Age 25-35. A.A.I. or A.R.I.C.S. General London experience or property connections essential.—Details of career in confidence, write Box C 1991, The Times, E.C.4.

BUSINESS OFFERS

PRE-BUDGET CARPET SALE

Carpets selling at GUARANTEED WHOLESALE PRICES direct from warehouse, only until stocks are cleared. Flawless hard-wearing WILTON CARPETS in 9 delightful shades selling at 31/6 a yard including free laying, normally retails at 55/- a yard (minimum 30 yards). "Royal Worster" velvet piled 100% pure wool Wilton in really superb colourings at 39/6 a yard including laying. This magnificent quality normally sells at 59/- a yard.

NEW CONSIGNMENT

Selling guaranteed HALF PRICE, 12 mixed bales of Persian carpets and rugs in really divine colourings in most sizes from £15-£300. Slightly damaged by minute hook marks, including Bokhara, Keshan, Tabriz, Hamadan, &c. Also a limited quantity of magnificent washed Chinese carpets and some outstanding off-white "Malabar" carpets in deep wool pile. Remember we will change any purchase right away. Terms by arrangement.

CARPET WAREHOUSE

8 Lexham Mews, W.8 (bottom of Allen Street), just off High Street, Kensington. Tel. WES. 4768, 6038. Open 10 a.m. to 7 p.m. Thursday, 8 p.m. SATURDAY, 10 a.m. to 1 p.m.

FOR MEN AT THE TOP . . . . . . TOP GIRLS

We specialize in supplying SECRETARIES and PERSONAL ASSISTANTS at executive level capable of taking full responsibility and ensuring the efficient smooth running of your office while you are engaged on more important business. For further information contact our department for EXECUTIVE SECRETARIES headed by Miss Neil.

NU-TYPE SEC. BUREAU

Executive Selection Division

119, REGENT STREET, W.1. REG. 4090.

Top Jobs for Top Girls, see page 2

TOP PEOPLE'S Secretaries are well placed; generally by STELLA FISHER BUREAU, 436, STRAND, LONDON, W.C.2. TEM. 6644.

AN INVESTMENT in the order of £2,500 by a youngish man of standing, in a small established firm of West End Wine Merchants would procure him a directorship, control over his capital, and a unique opportunity to learn the wine trade without leaving his present position, at any rate for some years. The applicant would be required to devote occasional evenings to the company's affairs and tastings and is requested to give some details of his background when replying.—Write Box C.1977, The Times, E.C.4.

YOUR PERFECT SECRETARY

We make secretarial recommendations only after visiting the employer in his own office to study his exact needs. In this way it is possible for us to select a senior secretary who will perfectly suit the employer in terms of ability, character and experience.

When you are next looking for a secretary, let us know at the outset. We will take the problem out of your hands by recommending for your final choice up to three secretaries who will perfectly meet your requirements. In the meantime may we suggest that you write to us for our leaflet.

NORTH & NEVILLE
Secretarial Consultants
37 Great Cumberland Place, London, W.1. Telephone Ambassador 2217.

(Continued on Page 2, column 2)

CLASSIFIED ADVERTISEMENTS on other pages

PERSONAL

£1,000 Reward

PERSONAL

PERSONAL

MOTOR CARS &c.

ON THIS . . . THE LAST DAY OF TRADITIONAL FRONT PAGE ADVERTISING IN THIS NEWSPAPER

H. R. OWEN LTD.
are proud to offer at
17 BERKELEY STREET, London, W.1. Tel.: MAY. 9060

1964 (August) BENTLEY S.3 Saloon; finished in Ming blue with off-white hide upholstery; fitted with electric windows and electric aerial; parking lights; lambswool rugs .. £4,850

1964 (January) ROLLS-ROYCE Silver Cloud III; finished in sage over smoke green with grey hide; electric windows; lambswool rugs .. £4,750

1963 (December) ROLLS-ROYCE Phantom V 7-Passenger Limousine; finished in midnight blue with brown hide to front and fawn West of England cloth to rear; full width occasional seats; one owner and only 4,000 miles .. £7,950

1963 (February) BENTLEY S.3 Saloon; finished in rouge irise with beige hide; electric windows; one owner .. £3,950

1962 (November) ROLLS-ROYCE S.C.II Saloon; finished in dawn blue with a black roof and blue hide; electric windows; 28,000 miles; one owner .. £3,950

1961 ROLLS-ROYCE S.C.II Long Wheelbase Saloon with division, finished in black with red hide; electric windows; one owner; 12,000 miles only .. £4,450

1960 (September) BENTLEY S.2 Saloon; finished in black over shell grey with red hide; 33,000 miles only .. £2,850

1960 (July) BENTLEY S.2 Continental 2-door Saloon by H. J. Mulliner; finished in tudor grey over black pearl with beige hide; electric windows .. £4,100

1960 (June) BENTLEY S.2 Continental 4-door Flying Spur by H. J. Mulliner; finished in Regal red with beige hide .. £3,975

1959 (April) BENTLEY S.1 Saloon; finished in blue grey with red hide and electric windows £2,150

1958 (September) BENTLEY S.1 Continental 4-door Saloon by James Young; finished in blue with scarlet hide .. £2,850

1956 (July) BENTLEY S.1 Continental 2-door Saloon by H. J. Mulliner with the now fashionable "Fast-back"; finished in dark metallic green with beige hide .. £2,450

1956 (April) BENTLEY S.1 Continental Convertible by Park Ward; finished in midnight blue with red hide and black power operated hood .. £2,650

1953 (April) BENTLEY "R" Type Saloon; finished in velvet green over Tudor grey, with red hide .. £950

AT

H. R. OWEN LIMITED
47 SLOANE STREET, LONDON, S.W.1. Tel. BEL. 8551

The following New and Used ASTON MARTIN CARS

New DB.6 Saloons with Vantage engine and colour to choice.

New DB.6 Saloons with standard engine and colour to choice.

New DB.6 Saloons with automatic transmission and colour to choice.

New DB.6 Volante in charcoal grey with red hood and hide.

New DB.5 Convertible in Platinum with red hide and many extras including chrome wire wheels; radio with twin speakers; electric aerial, Fiam horns; twin fog lamps, &c.

1965 (November) D.B.6 Saloon with Automatic Transmission, finished in Pacific blue with red hide; chrome wire wheels; heated rear window; radio; electric aerial; 5,000 miles only .. £4,695

1965 (November) D.B.5 Saloon in platinum with black hide and fitted with chrome wire wheels; heated rear window; radio and electric aerial; 6,000 miles only .. £3,650

1965 (October) D.B.5 Saloon in California sage with red hide; chrome wire wheels; heated rear window; one owner; 5,000 miles only .. £3,650

1965 D.B.5 Vantage Saloon finished in Dubonnet with natural hide; air conditioning; chrome wire wheels; heated rear window; radio; 15,000 miles .. £3,695

1965 (January) D.B.5 Saloon finished in fiesta red with black hide; chrome wire wheels; heated rear window; radio; 8,000 miles only .. £3,650

AT

H. R. OWEN LTD.
MELTON COURT,
27, OLD BROMPTON ROAD, S.W.7. Tel. KNI. 8451.

The following JAGUAR, DAIMLER, ROVER, FORD AND HILLMAN CARS ON SHOW

New JAGUAR 2.4 Saloon in silver blue with dark blue hide; overdrive; heated rear window; reclining seats.

New JAGUAR 3.4 Mk. 2 Saloon in Sherwood green with suede green hide; overdrive; power steering; chrome wire wheels; whitewall tyres.

New JAGUAR 3.4 Mk. 2 Saloon in golden sand with tan hide; overdrive; heated rear window; reclining seats.

New JAGUAR 3.8 Mk. 2 Saloon in opalescent maroon with black hide; overdrive and many other extras.

New JAGUAR 3.8 Mk. 2 Saloon in dark blue with biscuit hide; overdrive; heated rear window and reclining seats.

New JAGUAR 3.8 Mk. 2 Saloon in primrose with black hide; overdrive and many other extras.

New JAGUAR 3.4 "S" Saloon in dark blue with red hide; overdrive; power steering; heated rear window.

New JAGUAR 3.4 "S" Saloon in sand with tan hide; automatic gearbox; power steering; heated rear window.

New JAGUAR 3.4 "S" Saloon in dark blue with light blue hide; overdrive; power steering; heated rear window.

New JAGUAR Mk. X 4.2-litre Saloon in golden sand with black hide; automatic gearbox; electric windows; heated rear window.

New JAGUAR Mk. X 4.2-litre Saloon in silver grey with black hide; automatic gearbox; electric windows; heated rear windows.

New JAGUAR "E" Type 4.2-litre Fixed Head Coupé; Carmen red with black hide; chrome wire wheels; whitewall tyres; heated rear window.

New JAGUAR "E" Type 4.2-litre Fixed Head Coupé; dark blue with red hide; heated rear window; chrome wire wheels.

New DAIMLER 2½-litre V.8 Saloon; sand with red hide; power steering; heated rear window.

New DAIMLER D.R. 450 Limousine in black with electric division; heated rear window; alternator.

New DAIMLER D.R. 450 Limousine in black with dark blue upholstery; electric division; heated rear window; full width occasional seats.

New ROVER 3-litre Mk. III Saloon in light navy with blue upholstery; automatic gearbox; heated rear window; laminated windscreen.

New FORD CORSAIR V.4 G.T. in alpine green with green upholstery.

New FORD ZEPHYR V.4 Mk. IV in black cherry with black upholstery; whitewall tyres; column gear shift.

New HILLMAN SUPER IMP in spring yellow with black upholstery.

1966 JAGUAR E Type 4.2 fixed head coupé in silver grey with black hide; chrome wire wheels; heated rear window; radio; 3,000 miles .. £1,945

1966 JAGUAR 3.4 ... Type in white; with red hide; heated rear window; radio; electric aerial; many other extras; 3,850 miles only .. £1,765

1966 JAGUAR 3.8 S Type in silver blue with grey hide; automatic gearbox; radio; power steering, heated rear window; 6,000 miles .. £1,800

1965 ROVER 2000 in white; with black hide; heated rear window; safety belts; 8,000 miles .. £1,155

196- DAIMLER Majestic Major; dark blue with biscuit hide; power steering; radio; heated rear window; 8,000 miles .. £2,150

1964 DAIMLER 2½ litre V.8 in silver blue with dark blue hide; D1/D2 gearbox; radio; 11,000 miles .. £1,195

1963 MERCEDES Benz 300 S.E. convertible; dark grey with red hide; automatic; power steering; radio; 16,000 miles only .. £3,450

and also at our Showrooms at

RUSSELL MOTORS LTD.,
227, BROMPTON ROAD, S.W.3. Tel. KNI. 6692.

New AUSTIN COOPER "S" Type, 1,275ccs., in blue with white roof.

New MORRIS 1100 de Luxe in tartan red with grey upholstery.

New MG 1100 de Luxe in Connaught green with grey upholstery.

H. R. OWEN LTD.,
PROUD MEMBERS OF THE SWAIN GROUP OF COMPANIES

AGRICULTURE

3 lines 30s. (minimum)

Focus on Farming No. 522.

CRAFTSMEN

MOST of us have activities which take us into the country and we have all at one time or another stood in the doorway of the village smithy enthralled by the deft and speedy movements of the blacksmith. His firm handling of the horses, the ring of the anvil, and the acrid smell of burning hoof conjure up a never-to-be-forgotten picture. As he hammers the glowing horseshoe into its traditional form we are reminded that these pieces of hand-shaped metal are a symbol of good luck which is nearly as old as the craft of the smith himself which can be traced back to the second century B.C.

In the late Middle Ages it was customary to fix a horseshoe to the lintel of the door, either for the protection or good fortune of those within. Even church doors were sometimes decorated in this way and it is said that Nelson had a horseshoe nailed to the mast of H.M.S. Victory.

Where protection against the devil and other evil spirits was sought, the shoe was nailed convex side up. When required to bring luck, however, this was reversed so that the luck would not come out.

In many places the blacksmith's forge has, alas, been replaced by the spitting oxy-acetylene torch and broken machinery takes the place of the waiting horses. Nevertheless much of the skill and charm of the blacksmith's shop remain and although handmade horseshoes may one day be replaced by those mass produced in factories we still hold on to our memories of a past era.

MILNS of CHESTER
The Agricultural Seed Specialists

Whenever you see a fine field of corn or lush pastures, it is usually a sign that a wise farmer has been sowing MILNS SEEDS.
An illustrated Guide to Farm Seeds available free on request.

SHIPPING

3 lines 33s. (minimum)

SOUTH AFRICA
AUSTRALIA, NEW ZEALAND
ROUND-THE-WORLD

SERVING—Las Palmas, Cape Town, Durban, Fremantle, Melbourne, Sydney, New Zealand, Fiji or Acapulca, Rarotonga, Tahiti, Panama, Curacao, Trinidad or Barbados. One Class Tourist—Bookings to all ports. Also Round-the-World 75 days from £291.
s.s. "SOUTHERN CROSS"
*s.s. "NORTHERN STAR"
From Southampton—8 June, *15 July
7 Sept., *27 Oct., 8 Dec., *27 Jan., 8 Mar.

NEW ZEALAND via PANAMA—31 days
"GOTHIC" (First Class only) London 2 June
"CERAMIC" (First Class only) London 8 Sept.
SHAW SAVILL LINE (Dept. T.C.)
10, Haymarket, London, S.W.1.
(WHI. 1485), or Local Travel Agents.

GIBRALTAR, TANGIER, MOROCCO

Names that mean Winter Sunshine

P & O-Orient Liners offer the comfortable way to Gibraltar. Stay there awhile or wander on to Tangier, Marrakesh, or Spain's Costa del Sol.

Accommodation is available in sailings to Gibraltar between November and April next. Also many return opportunities.

Fares first class from £35, Tourist from £24.

For details see your Travel Agent now or write to

P & O-ORIENT LINES

14 Cockspur St., London, S.W.1. WHI. 4444

SOUTH PACIFIC
AUSTRALIA—NEW ZEALAND—FIJI
SAMOA—HAWAII—CALIFORNIA

Sail with Matson Lines around the ports of paradise, aboard
s.s. MARIPOSA s.s. MONTEREY
Sailings every three weeks from Sydney, Suva, Niuafo'ou, Pago Pago, Honolulu, San Francisco, Los Angeles, Bora Bora, Papeete, Rarotonga, Auckland, Sydney.
Full cruise, one-way or inter-port fares. All accommodation is first-class, air-conditioned and with private facilities.
See your Travel Agent or contact
MATSON LINES
UNITED STATES LINES
General Passenger Agents—Europe
50, Pall Mall, London, S.W.1.
WHItehall 5454

BLUE STAR LINE
TO
SOUTH AMERICA
LONDON via LISBON and CANARY ISLES
BRAZIL, URUGUAY, ARGENTINA
EXCLUSIVELY FIRST CLASS
ALL OUTSIDE CABINS
AIR CONDITIONED

ARGENTINA STAR ..	May 7	July 9	Sept. 24
URUGUAY STAR ..	May 22	July [illegible]	Oct. [illegible]
PARAGUAY STAR ..	June 4	Aug. 20	Oct. 22
BRASIL STAR ..	June 25	Sept. 10	Nov. 12

Round voyages throughout the year to warm, sunny South America.

Australia, South Africa, New Zealand and North Pacific Coast.

Passenger Office: Lower Regent Street, S.W.1. WHI. 2266. Branch Offices: Birmingham, Bradford, Glasgow, Liverpool, Manchester and ALL TRAVEL AGENTS.

SOUTH AMERICA
BRAZIL, URUGUAY and ARGENTINA
From London
Via Spain, Portugal and Canary Islands by modern 26,000-ton air-conditioned and stabilized passenger liners—
THE THREE GRACES

ARAGON	May 6	July 8	Sept. 16
ARLANZA	May 27	July 29	Oct. 7
AMAZON	June 17	Aug. 26	Oct. 28

1966 Edition of the SOUTH AMERICAN HANDBOOK Now Available. Price 20/-, by post 22/-

Apply LOCAL TRAVEL AGENTS or
ROYAL MAIL LINES LTD.
America House, Cockspur Street, S.W.1. TRA. 6271
Pacific Building, James Street, Liverpool, 2. CEN. 9251

U.S.A. & CANADA

SOUTHAMPTON—NEW YORK
QUEEN ELIZABETH (via Cherbourg) .. May 5
LIVERPOOL—QUEBEC and MONTREAL
CARINTHIA (via Greenock) .. May 11

CUNARD LINE

Pier Head, Liverpool, 3 (Liverpool: Maritime 3000); 15, Lower Regent Street, London, S.W.1 (WHI. 7890); 88, Leadenhall Street, London, E.C.3 (AVEnue 3010); or any Local Cunard Office or Agents.

KARACHI
City of London .. 4 May
ADEN AND MOMBASA
City of Pretoria .. 11 May
FAR EAST
City of Brooklyn .. 1 June
ELLERMAN LINES
29, Cockspur Street, London, S.W.1. Tel. WHItehall 5372
12, Camomile Street, London, E.C.3. Tel. AVEnue 4311
or Travel Agents.

SOUTHAMPTON TO U.S.A. AND CANADA
RYNDAM, to Quebec and Montreal .. MAY 10
NIEUW AMSTERDAM, to New York via Cobh MAY 11
MAASDAM, to New York via Galway .. MAY 14

SOUTHAMPTON—LOS ANGELES AND SAN FRANCISCO
STATENDAM .. SEPT. 1
Also sailings by cargo/passenger ships.
Consult your Travel Agent or
HOLLAND-AMERICA LINE
LONDON: 120, Pall Mall, S.W.1. WHI. 1972.
BIRMINGHAM: 47, Hagley Road, 16. Edgbaston 5706.
SOUTHAMPTON: 150, High Street. Tel. 29051.

Flotta Lauro/Lauro Lines
Monthly Sailings to
AUSTRALIA AND NEW ZEALAND
M/V Angelina Lauro
M/V Achille Lauro
Depart Southampton, May 16, June 18, July 22, Aug. 24, Sept. 28, October 30, December 5.
Sail down under in the superb luxury of these magnificent two-class Italian luxury liners. Excellent international cuisine. Gay night clubs. Elegant public rooms. Glorious swimming pools. First-class cabins have their own closed circuit TV and three-programme radio. Almost all cabins have toilet and shower/bath. Both ships are fully air-conditioned and fitted with Denny Brown stabilisers. Reduced fares for round trip. BOOK EARLY!
For full details apply your local travel agent or General U.K. passenger Agents.
E. H. MUNDY & CO.,
(Passenger Agencies) Ltd.
87, Jermyn Street, London, S.W.1. WHI. 5751.

JAMAICA BANANA PRODUCERS STEAMSHIP Co. Ltd.—Fast Direct Passenger Service.
LONDON TO KINGSTON
Apply to Kaye Son & Co., Ltd., 31-35 Fenchurch Street, London, E.C.3. Tel.: MANsion House 8711.

MOTOR CAR HIRE SERVICE

3 lines 45s. (minimum)

HARRODS CAR HIRE. Drive yourself or chauffeur-driven town or country, also lessons. HARRODS Ltd. (SLO. 1234), Knightsbridge, S.W.1.

ROAD TRANSPORT

3 lines 30s. (minimum)

JOSEPH MAY Ltd., the firm of experts specialising in skilful, economical Household and Office removals, 31-37 Whitfield Street, W.1. MUS. 2411.

Closure

Above Major Astor MP and Lady Violet Astor entertaining staff from THE TIMES at a garden party at Hever Castle. They are seen here talking to former members of the staff, associated with the 100th anniversary of THE TIMES.

Below New and old buildings of THE TIMES, 16 September 1962.

From 1785 until 1955 *The Times* was published every weekday, never missing an issue. Neither war nor strike, neither civil riot nor direct hit by a bomb in the Blitz, stopped the presses. John Walter II himself kept the wheels turning when his printers struck. During the General Strike *The Times* did not lose a single issue. As the newspaper became the greatest and most famous in the world, the people who worked for it became an élite band, who put getting the paper out above everything else. The printing and production departments actually called themselves a Companionship. Many had worked on the paper all their lives, as often their fathers had before them.

They may not have been paid as much as other workers in Fleet Street. Within living memory, a private income was a distinct advantage to anybody contemplating a career on *The Times*. Also within living memory, almost the first question asked a new recruit was whether he sang tenor, baritone or bass – for the operatic society. Every summer the entire staff went in special trains one Saturday to Hever Castle, the country home of the Astors, for the office dance and party, where managers danced with secretaries on the tennis courts, and where there were two classes of marquee – one for officers, one for other ranks. It was paternalistic and no doubt rather absurd. But those who worked for *The Times* believed that they sailed in a very special ship. They might be overworked, underpaid and exploited: but what mattered was getting *The Times* out.

From 26 March to 2 April 1955 there was an official national strike of all engineers and electricians, which silenced Fleet Street. The unthinkable happened. *The Times* along with the rest of the national press was stopped for twenty-six days.

The Times itself was strike-free until the Curse of the Thomsons struck in May 1968. Since then, through strikes both official and unofficial, both local and national, *The Times* had lost forty-one issues up to the closure from November 1978 to November 1979. Since the return to work in 1979, we have lost thirty issues. Losing an issue of *The Times* is a serious matter. The national debate falls silent. Deaths go unrecorded. Books go unreviewed. Law goes unreported. Letters that might have influenced affairs go unpublished. It is as though the Recording Angel himself had deserted his post in the heavenly carrel.

The causes of the closure of *The Times* for almost a year during 1978 and 1979, one of the longest industrial disputes in recent British history, are as complex as the causes of any great historical event, such as the Crimean War or the Fall of the Roman Empire. The immediate reason was the introduction of modern electronic typesetting technology (photocomposition) to replace that miracle of Victorian technology, the linotype machine. This revolution is changing the face of the printing industry; but in Britain it is a hard, bitter and slow revolution.

Other causes were gross and corrupt overmanning, wet and aloof management, low productivity, and powerful but fragmented unions pitted against a vast multinational corporation. In the 1970s there were eight unions and sixty-five separate chapels, or office branches, operating within the company, each fighting for its own members and trying to leapfrog the others.

Those of us who were there at the time believed that the move from Printing House Square to Gray's Inn Road was another fundamental cause. Down at Blackfriars we were proud to be *Times* men and women. Up at New Printing House Square, 'that snake-pit', the *Times* telephone operator sat next to *Sunday Times* operator who was being paid half as much again for doing the same job; printers compared pay packets with their counterparts on *The Sunday Times*; and avarice, envy, mistrust and bloody-mindedness set in.

By 1978 the pay of the staff of *The Sunday Times* and particularly of *The Times* was near the bottom of the Fleet Street league. There was dissatisfaction, disgruntlement and disruption. During the first three months of 1978 *The Times* lost four issues because of industrial disruption. It lost its full run of copies on twenty-one nights. Production of the weekly supplements had been disrupted on seven weeks, and of *The Sunday Times* on nine. The cost of this was about £2 million. Such losses, for a paper that was struggling to break even, were unendurable.

In April the management put forward its proposals for putting things right. These included the need to get the papers out without interruption; the establishment of a disputes procedure that would stick, and so avoid unofficial, wildcat stoppages by a few men which sabotaged the whole paper; the reduction of manning levels; and the introduction of photocomposition and new operating methods. Improved efficiency and productivity would enable the company, under the Government's restrictive pay policy, to put up wages. The management warned that if agreement had not been reached by 30 November, the company would suspend publication of *The Times* and *The Sunday Times*, and lay off the staff.

In retrospect the management's shopping list was too long and too complex for a single industrial negotiation. The arguments went on with chapels and unions all summer, and were most bitterly fought over the issue of the single keystroke, i.e. giving journalists access to the VDUs, so letting them set their articles in type without the help of a compositor. By 30 November only nineteen of the sixty-five chapels had reached agreement. In a signed article William Rees-Mogg, the editor, said that it

The last issue of THE TIMES to be published in the UK for almost a year. The closure, and the final settlement that brought it to an end, cost THE TIMES's owners about £40 million.
30 NOVEMBER 1978

Thursday November 30 1978
No 60,472
Price fifteen pence

THE TIMES

Fashion: Facing both ways, pages 10 and 11

Last-ditch Commons move to avert 'Times' suspension

As it became clear last night that this was likely to be the last edition of 'The Times' for some weeks, the Commons decided to hold an emergency debate today on the imminent suspension by the management of 'The Times', 'The Sunday Times' and the three supplements. Lord Thomson of Fleet, president of Times Newspapers, said there was no intention of closing permanently.

Ministers hold out little hope

By Fred Emery
Political Editor

The Commons is to hold an emergency debate this afternoon in a last-ditch attempt to avert, or at least defer, the suspension by Times Newspapers of its publications due at midnight.

MPs of both main parties last night reckoned the chances of success as slim. Ministers involved in continuing meetings with the management (there were no further meetings with the unions) held out scant hope of appealing to both sides to accept some form of arbitration, as had been rumoured.

However, one senior minister confided that if all the union leaders involved were to ask for such an arbitrator the Government would have to consider it urgently.

This is the first emergency debate to be granted by the Speaker since December 5 last year, when the Crown Agents scandal was also deemed a "specific and urgent matter" requiring urgent consideration. The only surprise in the Commons was that the Speaker declined, when urged by Mr Max Madden, Labour MP for Sowerby, to hold the debate last night rather than today.

Government whips, according to Mr Madden, had been ready to grant three hours last night, and had prepared themselves to lose no time on the scheduled debate, on the European Monetary System, by tabling a motion to allow it to contigue "open ended". The Speaker, however, does not give his reasons; although he gave an assurance that he had carefully considered the timing.

As it happened, Mr Madden was the loser in the race to apply for the debate. Mr Patrick Cormack, Conservative MP for Staffordshire, South West, had got his application in by 8.30 am and earned precedence. He will thus open the debate, and may also reply to it, thus giving the debate its tone.

He intends to call on the one union refusing to negotiate, the National Graphical Association, to agree to "substantial talks", in return for which the management, he hopes, might agree to "hold over" today's suspension deadline until after the weekend.

Mr Madden's approach would have been to try to bring pressure on ministers to persuade them to call on the management to abandon the suspension with the quid pro quo that all the unions, including the NGA, should agree to talk.

Mr Albert Booth, Secretary of State for Employment, who is believed to have some doubts whether the management has kept within the terms of the Employment Protection Act may be called upon to explain in his intervention today. Department of Employment officials are said to be in some confusion over the legal situation. If there has been a breach of procedure by the management, it was said, the matter will be for an industrial tribunal. For the Conservative Front Bench Mr James Prior, spokesman on employment, is expected to speak.

Mr Cormack, who describes himself as "a moderate-centre Tory", disclosed that he had discussed his ideas with Mr William Rees-Mogg, editor of *The Times*, and Mr Harold Evans, editor of *The Sunday Times*. They had all met at the dinner on Tuesday of the Institute of Journalists, of which Mr Cormack, an associate editor of the magazine *Time and Tide*, is also a member.

In moving his application, Mr Cormack was grave. "If the presses stop tomorrow there is no saying when or even whether they will roll again", he said. "The crisis itself and its possible consequences are incalculably important to everyone in this country, for the death or even lengthy silence of any of these papers would diminish all the freedoms we so rightly take for granted."

Many MPs stood to signify agreement when asked by the Speaker if Mr Cormack had leave of the House. Their number included Mr Michael Foot, Leader of the House, and Mr Booth. On the Government front bench, the Prime Minister sat impassively. Mr Denis Healey looked grim.

Mr Cormack says he regards his speech today as the most difficult of his life. He believes that the freedom of the press is fundamentally threatened unless there is proper respect by unions for procedures, such as those proposed for disputes by Times Newspapers' management.

He felt it paramount that the Commons should not watch while *The Times* went "quietly to sleep for a very long period when the House of Commons indulges itself debating matters of far less importance to society".

Last night he said that it would be "a tragedy of the highest order if intransigence persisted, and something that Hitler and those who went before had failed to halt was halted by a total unwillingness to discuss". He added: "It really is preposterous for any group to suggest that negotiations are under such duress that they cannot come to the talks. It cannot be said that the wildcat strikes which have created this situation ever took place after free and frank discussion with adequate notice being served".

Parliamentary report, page 8
Leadings article and letters, page 17

Management and unions dig in

By Paul Routledge
Labour Editor

This may be the last edition of *The Times* for many weeks, after the company's management and trade unions dug in last night for what promises to be a protracted dispute over wages, manning levels, unofficial strikes and the introduction of new technology.

Management sources privately estimate that *The Times*, *The Sunday Times* and the three associated supplements may be off the streets for two to three months after implementation of a seven-month-old threat to suspend publication of all titles until agreement is reached on a new industrial relations structure.

Dismissal notices to the company's 4,300 employees are likely to start going out from next Monday, although Lord Thomson of Fleet, chairman of the International Thomson Organisation and president of Times Newspapers Ltd, said in Toronto last night that there was absolutely no intention of permanent closure or sale of the newspapers (statement, page 2).

Lord Thomson said he intended to come to London next week to restate his position before the British public (Reuter reports from Toronto).

Efforts by MPs to get the Prime Minister to intervene culminated in the Commons last night. Earlier Mr Albert Booth, Secretary of State for Employment, held talks lasting about ninety minutes with Mr M. J. Hussey, chief executive and managing director of Times Newspapers, and Mr Dugal Nisbet-Smith, general manager.

But in the tense atmosphere at New Printing House Square it was widely expected that the management would proceed with its decision not to publish from tonight. That view was reinforced by Lord Thomson's comment that suspension "now seems probable".

His statement came after a day of worsening labour relations at Times Newspapers. Leaders of the National Society of Operative Printers, Graphical and Media Personnel (Natsopa) walked out of talks with the management, accusing it of "bad faith" and demanding talks with the company's main board. That proposal was rejected.

The National Graphical Association, whose members would be most affected by the company's aim to move to new printing technology, was still refusing last night to take part in talks until the management drops the closure threat.

Members of the National Union of Journalists employed on *The Times* will today be recommended to continue to negotiate on the management's proposals but to refuse to accede to them other than to sign a new disputes procedure.

There was intense interest in political circles and Fleet Street about the fate of *The Times* and its sister publications, but perhaps the best indicator came from a management circular to all members of the staff which sought to answer the main questions they have been asking.

In reply to questions about what the management is trying to do, it says: "Keep all the papers going with a secure future. This means stopping the damage caused by unofficial disputes, reducing manning in some departments through voluntary redundancy, and getting agreement for the introduction of new technology, new machinery in other areas and more flexible working. It is the

Continued on page 2, col 4

Mr Nixon in London: The beaming smile, the pendulous jowls and the glad hand of Mr Richard M. Nixon, thirty-seventh President (retd) of the United States, were fleetingly on view in London yesterday as their owner arrived to speak at the Oxford Union this afternoon (Dan van der Vat writes). The fact that he looks much older did not allay the strong feeling of *déja vu* among those who had not seen him in the flesh for a long time. Four years of virtual seclusion in disgrace after the Watergate scandal notwithstanding, Mr Nixon still does not travel, he campaigns. He began by shaking hands with a group of baggage handlers at Heathrow airport.

Fred Emery writes: Last night several Labou rand Scottish National Party MPs complained privately that Mr George Thomas, the Speaker, would be receiving Mr Nixon in the House of Commons, regardless of the fact that tthe United States House of Representatives Judiciary Committee recommended that he be impeached on three counts. The former president is the guest of the British-American parliamentary group, at the invitation of Mr Jonathan Aitken, Conservative MP for Thanet, East. And it was said authoritatively last night that it would be discourteous for the Speaker to have refused to see him. The Speaker is inviting him for drinks at 7 pm, on the ground that he is a "distinguished former statesman".

Dolphins fear cry of glass fibre whale

From Peter Hazelhurst
Tokyo, Nov 29

The prototype of a mechanical killer whale, designed to frighten dolphin away from Japan's fishing waters, appears to deceive the ocean's most intelligent mammal, when recorded cries of the whale are transmitted from within the equipment.

The black and white glass fibre model of a killer whale was tested for the first time yesterday. It was towed close to 15 dolphins, trapped in an enclosure in the bay of Taiji, near the southern tip of Honshu island.

At first the dolphins ignored the life-sized model of their feared natural enemy as it sidled up to the pen with its dorsal fin above the water.

Then engineers switched on recordings of the ferocious cries of the killer whale, magnified a hundredfold by electronic equipment, deep within the mechanical beast's fibre glass head.

When the plaintive deep bass cry of the killer whale echoed through the water, the dolphins showed immediate signs of insecurity. Squeaking in apparent panic, the 15 mammals grouped together, lashing the water into white foam as they swam round in a tight circle.

The cries of the killer whale were recorded in an aquarium in Toronto. Officials said the cries were expected to impress the dolphins because the recordings were made while the killer whale was hungry and searching for food.

As the model glided past the pen the electronic device was switched off and the mammals appeared to relax.

Mr Shinichi Yajima, an official in charge of the research programme, said: "They showed discernible signs of panic when the cries were turned on, but they were not perturbed by the silent model."

The mechanical whale was constructed at a cost of £8,500. The project was begun when the slaughter of 1,000 dolphin by Japanese fishermen off the island of Iki this year led to an international outcry.

Taken aback by the protests from Europe and the United States, Mr Takeo Fukuda, the Prime Minister, called for research to establish whether dolphin could be driven away from fishing grounds by more acceptable methods.

After eight months of work at the fishing agency's research laboratory the initial stage of the experiment appears to be successful.

The laboratory is now attempting to record distress signals of the dolphin. A scientist said: "If we can achieve this it will cause double panic."

Photograph, page 7

CBI shuns clash on sanctions

By David Felton

The Confederation of British Industry last night backed away from a major confrontation with the Government over sanctions on companies which breach the 5 per cent pay guidelines.

Instead of launching an all-out campaign against the Government, which some sections of industry had been hoping for, the CBI decided on a three-pronged plan of action to persuade the Government of the unfairness of sanctions.

The president's committee—the CBI's "inner cabinet" comprising 30 top industrialists—met in emergency session for 90 minutes in the wake of the announcement on Tuesday of sanctions against Ford which are expected to cost the company more than £60m.

The committee decided to lobby the Government and Opposition for an early parliamentary debate on sanctions and to seek counsel's advice on the legality of sanctions, particularly those covering export credit guarantees and temporary employment subsidies. Today Mr John Greenborough, the CBI president, is writing to the Prime Minister requesting an early meeting to discuss the whole question of sanctions and pay.

Earlier yesterday Mr Horace Cutler, Conservative chairman of the Greater London Council ordered an immediate study on the feasibility of changing the council's vehicle fleet from British Leyland to Ford to counter the Government's sanctions.

The GLC, which is the largest local authority in Britain, has 2,230 vehicles. The majority including 60 cars are made by British Leyland. The GLC spends £1m a year in replacing its fleet.

Donald Macintyre writes: Senior Transport and General Workers' Union officials are to meet the union's sponsored MPs to discuss possible concerted pressure on the Government to withdraw the Ford sanctions.

Meanwhile, the Government is to scrutinize the pay deal for 3,000 workers in British Oxygen gases division, with particular attention to the fact that while the company has put the increase on earnings at 9.5 per cent the TGWU has estimated it at closer to 17 per cent.

Mr Scott alleges he was seduced

From Michael Horsnell
and Trevor Fishlock
Minehead

Mr Norman Scott, a former model, said to be the target of a murder plot involving Jeremy Thorpe, the former Liberal leader and three other men, went into the witness box at Minehead Magistrates' Court, Somerset, yesterday and told his story covering 17 years.

According to Mr Scott, the story began in 1961 when Mr Thorpe drove him to the home of his mother, Mrs Ursula Thorpe, and seduced him.

After that Mr Scott, then aged 21, bought shoes, shirts, and silk pyjamas from Mr Thorpe's tailors, and, he said, was set up in a flat near Westminster, where Mr Thorpe visited him for sexual purposes.

The story continued, according to Mr Scott, with copies of the file he kept on the Thorpe matter being taken from him, one from his home, another by a ruse. It came to a head when, alone and frightened, he faced a gunman on Exmoor.

Mr Thorpe and Mr Scott were seeing each other for the first time for several years when Mr Scott, aged 38, of Chagford, Devon, entered the witness box.

He said he went to Mr Thorpe in 1961 at the House of Commons to seek help after falling out with his employer. He and his terrier, Mrs Tish, were taken to Mr Thorpe's mother's home near Oxted, Surrey.

Mr Scott said Mr Thorpe entered his room that night and gave him a novel about homosexual love, written by James Baldwin. It was "a beautiful story".

During the night, he added, Mr Thorpe entered the room, clad in pyjamas and dressing gown and began to talk to him, telling him he looked like a frightened rabbit.

Mr Scott said he started to cry because he felt someone cared about him and Mr Thorpe put his arms round him. Then, he alleged, Mr Thorpe kissed him and made love to him. "I was biting the pillow. I could not shout because I did not want to frighten Mrs Thorpe", he said.

That same night, he alleged, Mr Thorpe made love to him again. "I lay there and cried ... I thought I had come somewhere to be protected."

Mr Thorpe, he continued, told him to look for a room "which he wanted to be fairly near Westminster", saying that he would pay the rent until some insurance cards were sorted out. There, he said, Mr Thorpe visited him most evenings "ostensibly just to see me, but it was always the inevitable sex". Mr Scott said he had just wanted friendship but "it always came down to the wretched sexual bit and I hated it".

He said that when he said he wanted the affair to end and said he would show Mr Thorpe up in public, Mr Thorpe laughed and said: "You cannot hurt me, one of my greatest friends is the Director of Public Prosecutions." During the affair with Mr Thorpe, he said, he was called "Bunny".

On one occasion, he said, when a policeman called at Mr Thorpe's office in Bridge Street, the door was locked "and Mr Thorpe was making love to me".

Mr Scott told how on October 24, 1975, he was enticed on to Exmoor by Mr Andrew Gino Newton, the airline pilot who, the prosecution says, was hired to kill him. On the moor, he said, Mr Newton shot his dog, Rinka, but when the gun was levelled at him it failed to go off.

Full report, page 4

Envoy told talks onus is on Mr Smith

Dar es Salaam, Nov 29.—President Nyerere of Tanzania said today there was no point in holding an all-party conference until Rhodesia agreed to the main parts of an Anglo-American peace plan.

Dr Nyerere was talking to Mr Cledwyn Hughes, Mr James Callaghan's personal representative, who is due to visit Rhodesia next week on a tour aimed at setting up an all-party conference in Britain next year.

The Tanzanian leader, chairman of the group of five "front-line" black states which support the Patriotic Front guerrillas, told Mr Hughes that Mr Ian Smith, the Rhodesian Prime Minister, must be made to accept the main provisions of the Anglo-American plan before there could be a successful conference, a government statement said.

Those provisions had already been accepted by the Patriotic Front, Dr Nyerere said.

On arrival at Dar es Salaam yesterday, Mr Hughes said he would be willing to undertake "shuttle" diplomacy with Mr Stephen Low, the American Ambassador to Zambia.

Mr Hughes and Mr Low are to visit the four other front-line states—Zambia, Mozambique, Botswana and Angola—as well as Nigeria, South Africa and Rhodesia.—Reuter.

Our Salisbury Correspondent writes: The Rhodesian Parliament was today asked to vote another £18m for the conduct of the war, an increase of 7 per cent over the £254m originally budgeted for the current financial year. Rhodesia is now spending about £700,000 a day fighting the guerrillas.

Military headquarters meanwhile announced that guerrillas had murdered a white woman aged 60 and injured her husband. Fourteen guerrillas had been killed for the loss of three Rhodesian soldiers.

Algerian leader in deep coma

Algiers, Nov 29.—President Boumedienne of Algeria, aged 51, is in a deep coma today after suffering a relapse on Monday. Doctors, who had considered surgery to remove a suspected blood clot on his brain have decided on further tests.

They may try to get him to to the American body scanner, flown here on Monday, which can provide computerized pictures of the body.—Reuter.

Two defiant Labour MPs resign secretarial posts

By Our Political Staff

Two parliamentary private secretaries among the 39 Labour MPs who defied the Government whips on Tuesday and voted against the Redistribution of Seats Bill, to increase Northern Ireland's representation at Westminster, resigned their posts yesterday.

They are Mr Ivor Clemitson, MP for Luton, East, and Mr Bruce Grocott, MP for Lichfield and Tamworth, who were parliamentary private secretaries to Mr Albert Booth, Secretary of State for Employment, and Mr John Silkin, Minister of Agriculture, respectively.

Another Labour MP, who agreed with the objections made to the Bill by Mr Robert Mellish, MP for Southwark, Bermondsey, and others, was Mr Albert (Jock) Stallard, MP for Camden, St Pancras North. An assistant Whip, he abstained from voting.

Yesterday he had to answer for this to Mr Michael Cocks, Government Chief Whip, and was let off with a reprimand.

The Labour dissidents opposed the increase in the number of Ulster MPs at Westminster from 12 to 17 on the grounds that it was against previous declarations by Labour ministers and a concession to curry favour with the Unionists.

With Conservative backing, the Bill was given a second reading by 350 votes to 49.

The latest resignations come a few weeks after the dismissal of Mr Brian Sedgemore, MP for Luton, West, who was parliamentary private secretary to Mr Anthony Wedgwood Benn, Secretary of State for Energy, for his use of a confidential document in questioning Mr Denis Healey, the Chancellor, at a select committee hearing.

Healey pledge on EMS exchange rate

Mr Healey promised in the Commons that if the Government gets concessions enabling Britain to join the exchange rate regime of the proposed EMS the issue will be put to the House before January 1. He said that if the Irish Republic joined the regime and Britain did not, exchange controls would be introduced between the two countries **Page 2**

Soviet arms budget

The Soviet Union announced higher economic targets for next year's budget with defence spending held at 1977-78 levels. A rise of 4.3 per cent in the national income is planned, the Supreme Soviet was told **Page 6**

Open government

A committee representing the most senior grades of civil servants in Whitehall is to study open government. The Association of First Division Civil Servants is concerned about the implications of open government legislation for the traditional relationship between ministers and senior officials **Page 3**

Haven for refugees

The United States will admit an extra 21,875 refugees from Vietnam and Cambodia. It will also admit about 3,000 political prisoners on their release in Cuba, and is considering the admission of a further 1,000 victims of the Lebanon war **Page 7**

BL offers 17 pc rise

State-owned BL (British Leyland) offered its work force wage increases of around 17 per cent, the same as the controversial Ford settlement. BL says it does not expect any problems with the Government over the offer. BL shop stewards will decide today if it is to be put to a general ballot **Page 21**

Art buying by Japan

The Japanese Government has decided to spend £5.2m on buying outstanding European works of art and rare and valuable books. The planned purchases include paintings by Cézanne, Matisse, Picasso, Chagall, Henri Rousseau, Mondrian and Rubens. **Page 7**

Langtry letters sold

A group of Lillie Langtry's love letters, found in an attic in Jersey, were sold anonymously at Christie's for £8,000. The correspondence spans the period of her affair with the Prince of Wales, but is addressed to Arthur Henry Jones, who was secretly her lover **Page 19**

England win 1–0

A goal in the sixty-ninth minute by Steve Coppell gave England a fortunate 1—0 victory over Czechoslovakia, the European champions, at Wembley last night. England, who made six team changes, owed much to the goalkeeping of Peter Shilton. It was their eighth successive match without defeat **Page 12**

Fears for beef: Britain's farmers want a further devaluation of the "green pound". The Livestock Commission says beef output will fall again next year **3**

Tehran: Iran Opposition fails to agree on a new Prime Minister **6**

Normansfield's head gets dismissal notice

By John Roper
Medical Reporter

Dr Terence Lawlor, consultant psychiatrist in charge of Normansfield Hospital for the mentally handicapped at Teddington, was given three months' notice terminating his employment with effect from November 30, by the South West Thames Regional Health Authority last night.

The decision was announced after a private meeting of the authority yesterday to consider the report of the inquiry into the hospital, and its recommendations.

The report recommended that his contract should be ended and that he should never be given another job in the National Health Service. He has been suspended on full pay since the inquiry began two and a half years ago.

Normansfield visit, page 5

Berlin airlift of jeans approved by East Germans

Berlin, Nov 29.—American blue jeans went on sale in East Berlin yesterday and judging by the length of the queues along the pavements they met with instant success.

A total of 800,000 pairs will be put on the market by the end of the year, and according to a reliable source, jeans will also be on sale outside East Berlin later.

Despite the high price, £38 a pair, the demand so far is so great that each customer is being allowed to buy only one pair.

An American charter company, the "Flying Tigers", is bringing the jeans to Dresden and East Berlin in eight loads.

Smart East Berlin shops have also started carrying French ready-wear women's fashions. A wool coat costs the equivalent of nearly four months' salary.—Agence France-Presse.

was the first duty of an editor of *The Times* not to be the last one, but nevertheless, he believed that the policy being pursued by the management was the right one. 'In 1978 we have given our readers on *The Times* the least reliable service in the history of the paper; all the hard work of ninety per cent of the staff has repeatedly been destroyed by the unofficial and irresponsible action of small groups.' The leading article on the last day of publication was headed: 'There will be an interval'.

There is nothing more melancholy than a blacked-out newspaper. The journalists came in most days for gossip and the camaraderie of the Underground shelter. Nobody thought that the shut-down was going to last, and we kept on writing newspapers that were never published. Bernard Levin went to India, where he spent some time on an ashram. Many people wrote books. Eric Jacobs wrote a book about the *Times* dispute called *Stop Press*. The novel reviewers kept on reading the fiction of the week, and turning in their reviews for the spike. The literary editor of *The Times* hired himself out as a jobbing butler: his finest hour was serving champagne to a thousand gynaecologists and the Queen. A group of journalists put together a lively parody called *Not Yet The Times*, which sold 350,000 copies at 60p, and made a handsome profit.

As the months dragged on in stalemate and bitterness, it became apparent that the management's 'big bang' solution to the dispute (solving all the problems, overmanning, unofficial stoppages and the introduction of the new technology at a single stroke) was not working. To fly the flag of *The Times*, and to persuade the unions back to the negotiating table in a more conciliatory frame of mind, it was decided to print a weekly edition of *The Times* abroad in a foreign printing house.

With cloak-and-dagger secrecy, Frankfurt was selected. But the news leaked. Pickets gathered, and there was danger of a riot. About 10,000 copies of the international edition of *The Times* were eventually printed and sold in the United States and Continental cities, but not in the United Kingdom. And four middle-aged housewives in Germany, who spoke little English, demonstrated the new wave of the technology of photocomposition by setting the sixteen pages of this single edition with fewer misprints than a normal edition of *The Times*.

Negotiations resumed, and it was decided to set aside the issue of keystroking and take it up again after the resumption of publication. After apparently interminable ping-pong of negotiation between the competing unions and the management, it looked as though the papers would be closed permanently. There was one final ultimatum. After a frenzied flurry of negotiations, *The Times* resumed publication on 12 November 1979.

The dispute had turned the minds of the Thomson organization towards selling the papers if they could. It had been immensely costly in money and reputation to *The Times*. The only cold comfort was that it had demonstrated that there were a great many people in the country for whom there was no adequate substitute for *The Times*, who missed it terribly while it was away, and welcomed it back like a long-lost lover.

Top and right THE TIMES composing room, 1973.

Below THE TIMES machine room, March 1973.

Bottom right THE TIMES publishing room, 1973.

Royal events

Royalty is a government in which the attention of the nation is concentrated on one person doing interesting actions. A Republic is a government in which that attention is divided between many, who are all doing uninteresting actions. Accordingly, so long as the human heart is strong and the human reason weak, Royalty will be strong because it appeals to diffused feeling, and Republics weak because they appeal to understanding.

The sage Bagehot, of course. Too right, as usual, Walter.

About the most interesting action that royalty can do, apart from having a baby or dying, is getting married. Royal nuptials have always inspired *The Times* to exuberance of colourful writing and display. Because, unlike most news stories, you can see a royal wedding coming over the horizon for a long time, innovations of illustration, typography and display have been introduced for these splendid occasions. You can prepare for a royal wedding more than a day in advance. We did it for the weddings of Victoria and the Prince of Wales who became Edward VII. We did it again for the present Prince of Wales.

THE TIMES

Royal Wedding

The wedding of the Prince and Princess of Wales, at St Paul's, July 29 1981
A moment of personal dedication and public devotion in ten centuries of monarchy

Above The first colour front page of THE TIMES, on 30 July 1981, the day after the wedding of Prince Charles and Lady Diana Spencer.

Several newspapers, including *The Times*, regularly publish colour pictures in these brave new days of photocomposition and the new technologies of photography and printing. But the method is slow and specialized. The colour pictures are usually advertisements, strip cartoons or timeless photographs, say, of the local football side, wearing chemically livid strips, which can be printed well in advance and then inserted in the normal daily flood of newsprint.

On Thursday 30 July 1981 *The Times*, always a fugleman for the rest of Fleet Street in introducing new printing techniques, set another precedent by publishing a colour picture taken only twelve hours before. Nor did it hide its colour under a bushel, but gave the whole of its front page over to the colour picture. This was of the Prince and Princess of Wales waving to the crowds after their wedding from the steps of St Paul's Cathedral, just after noon on the previous day. How they brought the colour so fast on to the front page of *The Times* was an epic of the inky trade, depending on a lot of professionalism and not a little luck.

There were no means of printing original colour in the print-shop of *The Times* at Gray's Inn Road. The only way it could be done was to print the colour on newsprint reels at a specialist plant, and then feed these into the Gray's Inn Road presses carrying the ordinary run of paper, which would be running in spate that night anyway. The technique is normal in Fleet Street. But nobody had ever done it so fast, with a photograph taken on the previous day, and with communications in London jammed by the crowds.

It was decided that the simplest and quickest way to do the job was to wrap four pages around the ordinary *Times*. On the front was to be the big colour photograph of the Prince and Princess of Wales taken on their wedding day. That was the novel problem. The other three pages could be prepared in advance, or with less complex technology. Page 2 was given to black-and-white wedding pictures taken on the day. On the penultimate page we published a facsimile of *The Times* report of the last marriage of a Prince of Wales on 11 March 1863, when Delane was editor. The back page was given to a colour reproduction of Hayter's painting of Queen Victoria's wedding to Prince Albert and to purple prose appropriate to royal nuptials. If not easy on the night, pages 2, 3 and 4 were at least familiar techniques. Colour on the front would be a damned nice thing even in the hurly-burly of daily journalism.

East Midland Allied Press at Peterborough said that if we could get the colour separations of our chosen wedding photograph to them not later than 15.30 hrs, they would let us have the finished reels at *The Times* by around 22.30 hrs, in time for most of the nightly print-run. At a royal wedding in London everything goes like clockwork, but the clock is run by the police and it runs exceeding slow. The police timings meant that there would be less than two hours to take a photograph good enough to occupy the whole front page, develop it, select and scale it for the page, have the transparency broken down into colour separations, and get it to Peterborough – all this in a London congested to a standstill.

The printers at Peterborough had room for a helicopter to land. Rex Features, the processors of the film, and Keene Engraving, who were to produce the colour separations, thought that it could just be done, provided that everything went according to plan: a consummation devoutly wished but seldom achieved in the newspaper business. Plans went ahead in secret.

We then discovered that we did not have a good position inside St Paul's for a picture of the ring going on the bride's finger. On these spectacular media occasions, when the world's press and television are competing for pictures, places are allocated by rota. Those in a good position have a professional obligation to let the less lucky ones have copy transparencies. But with the world's press hustling impatiently for pictures on the royal wedding day, the best bet was that there would be a delay of at least two hours before we got the picture.

However, crafty foresight had booked *The Times* a window on the seventh floor of Juxon House on Ludgate Hill, overlooking the front steps of St Paul's. Experiments from there failed to bring in the goods. But the photographers had another rehearsal with a borrowed 800 mm Nikkor lens, and brought back black and white prints of something that might just fill the bill and the front page. After making as many safety nets for emergencies as possible and rehearsing it all, on the wedding day there was nothing to do but wait.

By 13.15, to cries of 'Here he is, here he is', the motorcyclist messenger in leathers and crash helmet panted to the picture desk at New Printing House Square, with eight frames of Ektachrome 400 taken while the Prince and Princess stood on the steps of St Paul's. The first one had the couple waving, but one face obscured; in the second they were not waving; the third had another part of a face obscured. But the fifth and sixth were excellent. The motorcyclist rushed them off to the engravers, and thence to Battersea Heliport.

The editor at the time, Harry Evans, a wizard for such spectacular photographical dramatics, suddenly realised that all the money and planning depended on a single motorcyclist finding his way through the dispersing crowds. A sub-editor told him: 'Don't worry, Harry; this is a day when *The Times* luck will count'. And it did. The plan was to run the edition as on a normal night with black and white (mono) pages only. Then when the colour reels arrived, to substitute on each printing machine a colour reel for one of the mono reels and feed the colour into the rest of the night's print.

The first lorry-load of colour reels arrived from Peterborough at 20.18, well ahead of time. Two hours later, as the other colour reels arrived, there were enough to stop printing the black-and-white only and make the switch to colour. It did not work. There was static in the newsprint and there was difficulty in registration. Finally at 01.30 am the first colour ran successfully, with excitement on every floor of the building. *The Times* put the rest of Fleet Street in the shade, as so often before. It sold 400,000 copies of its wedding issue in colour. It was very beautiful. It was a spectacular achievement. But it is the sort of exercise that a newspaper can afford to do only once in a blue moon.

Page 128
The first part of a weighty report of Queen Victoria's marriage to Prince Albert. The style of reporting royal events seems absurdly self-conscious and pompous today.
11 FEBRUARY 1840

Page 129
Part of the celebration of the marriage of Princess Elizabeth to the Duke of Edinburgh.
21 NOVEMBER 1947

TO CORRESPONDENTS.

We cannot insert the paragraph sent by a "Tauntonian," unless the writer will give us his name and address.

As we do not consider ourselves competent to pronounce an opinion on Captain Smith's invention, we cannot publish the letter on the subject except as an advertisement.

Will "Commodore" favour us with his name?

☞ The publication of *The Times* commenced at 7 o'clock yesterday morning, and finished at 9.

LONDON, TUESDAY, FEBRUARY 11, 1840.

In our last article upon the progress of Socialism, as developed by recent discussions in the House of Peers, we mentioned that my Lords Melbourne and Normanby, while attempting to vindicate their passive connivance at that progress, had given utterance to certain opinions, which, in our humble judgment, demand the serious attention of the country.

The office of a Cabinet Minister is, by universal consent, the most responsible that a man can hold. With the concurrence of the Sovereign, it is exclusively the province of Cabinet Ministers to provide for the judicial, ecclesiastical, diplomatic, and defensive service of the empire; and, although the ways and means cannot be obtained without the sanction of Parliament, yet, in order to preserve the functions and person of the Sovereign in the highest possible respect, the constitution has provided that the advisers of the Crown shall be solely answerable, not only for the application of those ways and means, but even for the exercise of the Royal prerogative itself. The appointment, therefore, of proper persons for public offices, the maintenance of a suitable protective force, the impartial administration of law, as well as the appliance of fitting moral agencies for upholding religion and order among the community—all these weighty obligations devolve entirely upon the executive Government: and so serious is the responsibility involved therein, that the Ministers of the Crown are not only required, on taking office, to swear the oath *de fidelo*, but for every abuse or neglect of their constitutional powers are amenable to inquiry and impeachment.

Now, as this accountability is manifestly of a mixed kind, implying subjection both to a divine tribunal and to a human one; and as the welfare of the community must materially depend upon the intelligent conscientiousness of those who undertake it, we humbly submit that, in the absence of a more direct reckoning, the declared sentiments of the Ministry in regard to their correlative obligations cannot fail to awaken in the public mind the gravest possible interest. What, then, are the views of Lords Melbourne and Normanby on this important point?

We begin with the noble Premier. On Tuesday last, when endeavouring to rebut the charge that Her Majesty's Ministers have been highly culpable in allowing Socialism to arrive at its present formidable strength, Lord Melbourne is reported to have acknowledged that, for his part, he did not know *what responsibility meant!* "The responsibility of man (said his Lordship) is an abstruse *metaphysical* subject, which I, for one, never understood."

Sorry should we be to put any construction on Lord Melbourne's words which they do not legitimately bear: but, as they were uttered with immediate reference to the Socialist dogma, that "all human actions are to be attributed to *necessity*," a dogma which, by denying the free agency and moral accountability of mankind, not only proclaims the day of judgment to be a bugbear, but declares that the penalties of human codes are an iniquitous persecution; so it is evident, that when the Whig Premier is pleased to speak of man's responsibility rather as an unintelligible metaphysical speculation, than as a divine and reasonable ordinance upon which, especially as incorporated and defined in British jurisprudence, this country depends for the moral rectitude both of its inhabitants and its *rulers*, his Lordship, while thereby putting in an extenuating plea for Socialism, shakes, to the extent of his indifferent authority, the very basis of our religion and our laws. The British fatalism of the Socialists, Lord Melbourne ought to know, involves practical issues very different from what were ever contemplated by the philosophical necessitarians of a former day. To what extent soever a distempered ingenuity may have taxed itself to contradict experience on the score of unrestrained and irregular impulses, it never was pretended that the community had no right to protect themselves, as far as possible, against individual determinations hostile to the common good. Proceeding upon the assumed injustice of our laws, the monstrous doctrine that a transgressor is not a proper object of punishment is peculiar to Socialism alone. And this, be it observed, is by no means a mere metaphysical abstraction—it is a great practical heresy, which, if extensively acted on, must demoralize the nation and plunge it into universal anarchy. Talk, indeed, of not understanding the responsibility of man! Gracious heaven, is it come to this, that such language shall be uttered by the Prime Minister of the Crown, who has sworn, as he shall answer to God and his country, that he will faithfully conduct Her Majesty's Councils, and administer with rectitude the executive department of the state!

If Lord Melbourne publicly proclaim that he does not, and never could, understand the responsibility of man, what is this but to declare, in effect, that as far as his Lordship's understanding goes, there is no difference between virtue and vice, or between religion and infidelity, or between Protestantism and Popery, or between allegiance and rebellion? Why, in point of fact, his Lordship's acknowledgement involves the very essence of Socialism itself: and, therefore, when we see such a sentiment avowed in high places, how can we wonder if multitudes of ignorant persons, believing the counter-denunciations which may have accompanied such an avowal to be nothing better than a convenient postern left open in case of need, shall exult in Lord Melbourne's virtual accordance with one of their most pernicious dogmas, and, cheered by the apologies of a titled amateur, shall become proficients in the entire course of nonsense and knavery inculcated by their professed Gamaliels?

Equally reprehensible in its own way, though certainly in some respects less offensive, is the distinction which my Lords Melbourne and Normanby attempt to set up between the public dissemination of unlawful opinions, and the actual perpetration of illegal deeds. "Opinions" (said the noble Viscount) "might be licentious or dangerous, but "he hardly knew that they could be illegal." Now, let us not be misunderstood upon this point. We freely admit that a man is at liberty to entertain what opinions he thinks fit; nor are mere opinions, as long as they are not rendered injurious to order, morality, religion, and the peace of society, properly cognizable by law. But between the unfettered enjoyment of one's private statements, and the active promulgation of those sentiments among large masses of the community, there is a very important difference. If a man be a blasphemer of the national faith, or maintain a grossly licentious theory of the appetites, or profess levelling notions on the subject of property, and, with these views, collects immense multitudes, practises upon their natural depravity, inflames them against the settled legislation of the country, and incites them to the hatred of Christian truth, then we say that such conduct is decidedly illegal, and ought to be visited with condign punishment. Lord Melbourne must not pretend that these pernicious *overt* movements ought to receive the same legal impunity as the caprices of private opinion. As far as regards the morals and well-being of society, which are the chief objects that render civil government at all desirable, the incendiary lecturers who go about from place to place endeavouring to disorganize our social structure and to corrupt the principles of the people, are, in our humble judgment, infinitely more criminal than the gangs who fire the farmer's stack-yard or steal the traveller's purse. We insist, then, that the *practices* of the Socialists, some of whose dogmas Lord Melbourne has roundly condemned, are replete with danger to the common interests of the country, and ought to be put down, as Carlile and Taylor were, by the strong arm of law. If this obvious duty be shrunk from by the Whigs, their sincerity, as professed Anti-Socialists, can receive no credit whatever.

"One of the worst features of the present Ministry is the want of fixed purpose, which paralyzes their supporters, who never know *how far they can rely on them*. Deliberation is very necessary; but there is a time for deliberation and a time for action; with *wise men* deliberation precedes action: but with *Ministers* action too often precedes deliberation. Lord John Russell might easily have known, and ought to have known, all the reasons for hesitating before the question came on first as well as now, and by shaping his course accordingly he would not have exposed the House and hon. members to the ridicule—we had almost said contempt—which must follow this lame and impotent conclusion after so much vapouring. We express ourselves strongly on this subject, because we are keenly alive to the injury which this course must do the Ministers. Irresolution is what is least forgiven in men in high stations. No man who appears to be always wavering himself can possibly inspire others with confidence. Well might Mr. Thomas Duncombe exclaim, 'Why, what was the whole question?' If the Duke of Wellington had first taken up his position at Waterloo, and then, when the enemy approached, begun to deliberate whether he had taken up the proper ground, the result of that day would have been very different. Oh, the curse of irresolution! We could forgive anything rather than the fault of men not knowing their own minds, and continually shifting their ground."

We copy the above passage from the leading article of a leading Ministerial print. The pressing occasion which has called forth this most just description of the character of the present Ministry, from one of its strongest supporters (the *Morning Chronicle*) is to be found in the announcement made on Friday last by Lord John Russell, that a bill is to be sought for from the Legislature for the settlement of the question of privilege, upon which we are told the majority of the house is all right, and the judges of the Court of Queen's Bench are all wrong—an assurance which, we confess, we should confide in more readily if we were to find that the usual course of questioning an unsound decision—by writ of error, when the House of Lords would probably call to its aid *all* the judges of the superior courts—were about to be resorted to. It was not, however, for the purpose of discussing the privilege question that we were induced to make the above extract from our contemporary. We alluded to it only as the immediate occasion seized upon by the Ministerial print in order to adduce its testimony to the character of the present Government; and, lest it should be supposed that there is, in the sketch thus drawn, aught of exaggeration produced by strong feeling on the particular subject, and also because we are prepared to find the parties very shortly "shaking hands" and exclaiming, with Peachum and Lockit, "Brother, brother, we are both wrong," for the reason which induced a reconciliation between those worthies, viz., that it was *against their interest* to quarrel, we propose to produce certain passages in the history of the Melbourne Administration, in proof of the charge that it is composed of men *not knowing their own minds, and continually shifting their ground;* and in corroboration of the above position, that "with *wise men* deliberation precedes action, but with *Ministers* action too often precedes deliberation."

The occurrences of the last and present month furnish a memorable instance in support of the *Chronicle's* view of this subject—the conduct of the Home Secretary with respect to the Newport traitors. The report of the decision of the judges on the point reserved at the trials at Monmouth was communicated to Lord Normanby on the 28th of January. It appeared from that report, that there was a great difference of opinion among those learned persons—so great, indeed, as, in our opinion, fully to warrant the determination not to subject the parties convicted to capital punishment. What was done by the Home Secretary? He wrote *the same day*, and after the receipt of that report, to the High Sheriff of the county of Monmouth, and directed that the prisoners should be "distinctly informed" that on the following Thursday "*the sentence of the law would be carried into effect*." The same high authority announced by letter to Lord Brougham on the 1st of February that the lives of the prisoners would be spared, and when communicating the intentions of Government to the House of Lords, he declared that *the sole reason* for this extension of the mercy of the Crown was the difference of opinion among the judges, of which this head of the department of justice in this country was fully apprised when he wrote the letter to the High Sheriff!

Where shall we find a better instance in support of the correctness of the position, that "with *wise men* deliberation precedes action, but with *Ministers* action too often precedes deliberation!"

But further, the Melbourne Ministry is composed of men "*not knowing their own minds, and continually shifting their ground.*" In support of this charge, which is as just as the preceding, the following *res gestæ et non gestæ* may be adduced:—The proceeding last session with respect to Canada, where, of *two* resolutions printed and announced for discussion, one was abandoned; the Bank of Ireland Bill, declared to be necessary for the public service, and then given up; in the session of 1836, the Church Discipline bill, described as essential to the best interests of the church, examined and discussed and carefully amended in the House of Lords, and then left "to lie on the table" in the Commons; and in another session, the church-rate question, where a resolution was carried, and then no further acted upon.

We might mention many other instances, but we deem the above sufficient for our purpose. On a future occasion we may, perhaps, proceed to show, that Ministers *deliberate, or pretend to do so*, when they should *act*.

Ministerial Malignity and Falsehood.—Even yesterday the Ministers would not suffer their scrubs to rest from lying and slandering. In the Palmerston print of last evening we find the following passage:—"The Dukes of Sussex and Cambridge, with the good sense and kind feeling for which they are distinguished, had consented, without hesitation, to the bill by which it was proposed that Prince Albert should rank before themselves. But the House of Peers, says *The Times*, 'would not perform an act of injustice to gratify the Queen's private fancy!' The Peers, forsooth, were trustees for the King of Hanover, who, though now an independent foreign potentate, will no more, it seems, concede his precedency than he will his annuity. Is there any apprehension that his Hanoverian subjects will relieve themselves from his rule, by compelling his Kingship to abdicate, as a punishment for substituting proclamations of his imperative will for the dominion of constitutional law among them! Whether Her Majesty will use her prerogative, and thus assign to her Royal husband that rank the indecent refusal of the Tory Lords succeeded in withholding from him previously to the marriage, we have no means of knowing. One thing is certain—or we have greatly mistaken the spirit which glows in the Royal bosom—that Her Majesty will allow no one to appear in her presence who will insult her feelings by obtruding their pretensions to precedency, and thus remind the Queen's husband that there are those to whom he must give place in his wife's Court." [We have already shown to our readers that the precedence asked for was precedence even of the *Heir Apparent to the Crown;* and that the Ministers themselves abandoned the request out of sheer shame, excepting, of themselves, the *Heir Apparent* from the clause. But they desired to give Prince Albert his precedence for his life, to which they saw symptoms of dissent in the Lords, and then they gave up the clause altogether, and set about such lies as the above. *Cupid* may bully and bluster as much as he pleases, but we tell him that the Queen has not the power to grant precedence for a longer period than her *own life.*]

Her Majesty's Privy Purse.—The only sum voted by Parliament for the Queen, over which Her Majesty personally has any control, is the 60,000*l.* for the privy purse. Out of this sum the Queen pays all the pensions that were granted out of it by George IV. and William IV., considering it more respectful to their memories to do so than to discontinue them, or to transfer them to the Civil List Pension Fund, which is made public by being laid annually before Parliament. Those pensions range through a variety of circumstances, from that of Mrs. Fox, the widow of Charles James Fox, who receives 500*l.* a year, to the servants of the late Mrs. Jordan, and amount in all to 10,000*l.* per annum. But these are far from being the only claims on the privy purse. Her Majesty, with kind consideration for the children of the late King, soon after her accession to the throne, granted from the privy purse no less a sum than 7,800*l.* per annum to the Fitzclarences. She gave also 3,000*l.* per annum to Sir John Conroy, and placed upon it some small pensions which the Duchess of Kent had hitherto paid. In fact, the fixed charities and racing plate paid annually out of the privy purse amount to 34,000*l.* per annum; which, substracted from 60,000*l.*, leaves only 26,000*l.* at Her Majesty's own disposal. Out of this comparatively small balance, the Queen has given away considerable sums in occasional charities, and has paid the remaining debts of the Duke of Kent, her father, to the amount of 50,000*l.* Her Majesty has at the same time patronized the arts, as far as her means would allow, though not certainly to the extent which she could have wished to do.—*Ministerial print.* [We should be glad to find this statement noticed by some competent person whose veracity could be relied on, and we think it quite sufficient to justify an application to Ministers in Parliament respecting its truth or falsehood. We can imagine nothing more disgracefully and unjustifiably shabby than to saddle the Queen with the payment of 3,000*l.* a year to Sir John Conroy. If he deserve a pension, the country, or the Duchess of Kent, certainly not the Queen, ought to pay it.]

The *Echo de l'Orient* mentions, that on the 7th ult. the Archduke Frederick of Austria was invited by Admiral Lassusse to visit his ship, the *Montebello*, of 120 guns, when a sham fight was got up for his Imperial Highness's amusement. The Archduke expressed himself highly gratified at so imposing a spectacle, and next day presented the Admiral with a fine ring in brilliants bearing his cipher, giving at the same time another to the captain of the Montebello, and a valuable watch to the second officer in command.

Amsterdam, Feb. 6.—The *Handelsblad* contains a long article on the bad management of the pilotage on the coast of Holland; the regulations are, it says, defective, and are not carried into execution. It says that the shipwreck of the Margaretha Johanna, Captain Schon, with a rich cargo from Batavia, was caused by the want of a pilot, and by the want of a buoy on a certain shoal, so that, misled by this negligence, he sailed directly upon the shoal, from which the buoy ought to have warned him.

Dutch Funds.—Amsterdam, Feb. 7.—Actual Debt, Two and a-half per Cent., 52¾ 53; Ditto, Five per Cents., 98½ 99; Amort. Synd., Four and a-half per Cent., 92¾ 93¼; Three and a half per Cent., 76½ 77; Commercial Company, Four and a-half per Cent., 175½ 176; New Ditto, Four and a-half per Cent., 100¼ 100¾; ditto 1837, Four and a-half per Cent., 100¾ 100¼; Loan of 1837, Five per Cent., 96¾ 97¼. Exchange on London, one month, 11 97½; two months, 11 87½.—*Dutch papers*, Feb. 8.

Prussian Funds.—Berlin, Feb. 4.—St. Schuld Sch., 4 per Cents., 104¼ 103¾; Prussian English Bonds, 1830, 4 per Cents., 103¾; 102 5-6ths. Exchange on London, three months, 6 21½.—*Prussian State Gazette*, Feb. 5.

The Hague, Feb. 6.—Yesterday evening the following unfortunate accident happened here. Count O'Kelly de Galway, formerly member of the High Council of Nobility, had been to an evening party at the Swedish Minister's on the Bezuidenhoutscheweg. His eyesight being bad, and the night dark, he fell into the water, and was drowned near the country-house of General Van der Bosch. The road being very lonely, where few people pass in the evening, nobody could go to his assistance.

The Hague, Feb. 5.—Yesterday his Excellency Baron de Bois le Comte, the French Ambassador, delivered to the burgomaster of the town the sum of 1,000 florins for the widow of the pilot, W. Kuyper, who unfortunately lost his life in saving the crew of the French ship Providence. We learn too, that the society of the province of Holland for the relief of shipwrecked persons has granted an annuity of 100 florins so long as she shall remain unmarried. Each child is to have 25 florins per annum till the age of 18. We hear that half the levy of 1839 on entering on the duty for 1840 will be sent home with unlimited furloughs.

Stealing a Banker's Parcel, value 6,000*l.*—In the early part of last week a parcel was received at the counting-house of Messrs. J. and J. Brocklehurst, in Milk-street, Cheapside, which had been forwarded from Macclesfield by the firm, and directed to be delivered to Messrs. Jones, Loyd, and Company, their bankers. A young man who acted as warehouseman and assistant-clerk in the office, seeing the parcel in the counting-house, and observing the direction, said he was going past the bank, and undertook to deliver it. No suspicion having been previously entertained of his honesty, he was allowed to take the parcel, but not returning in proper time, inquiries were made, and it was ascertained he had not been to the banking-house of Messrs. Jones, Loyd, and Co. at all, and, in fact, that he had absconded with the parcel. It was subsequently ascertained that he had proceeded by a steam-boat to Gravesend, and thence he posted to Dover. At the latter place he evinced considerable disappointment at being too late for the ordinary packet to Calais, and offered a large sum to be taken over in an open boat. The weather at the time was so boisterous that none of the boatmen could be prevailed on to take him. In a few hours after, however, the wind shifted a few points, and the boatmen undertook the task; and after 16 hours of desperate weather, and many hairbreadth escapes, he was landed at Calais, without a passport. Fortunately for the Messrs. Brocklehurst, the only immediately available property in the parcel was about 100*l.* in bank notes, which sum it must have cost the thief to reach Calais.—*Evening paper.*

At Ilchester, on Friday, as some workmen were pulling down an old house, they were nearly overwhelmed by a shower of silver pieces of the time of Elizabeth, Charles, and James II., which were contained in an ample canvass bag, of dimensions large enough to contain 40 pounds weight. Having burst, it is impossible to say how many it had contained. Several hundreds were secured by the owner of the premises, but the populace scrambled up the rest. Various conjectures are afloat, but we think the most rational one is, that the store was hidden during the Monmouth rebellion, and that the owner died on the field of battle.

CELEBRATION OF HER MAJESTY'S MARRIAGE WITH HIS ROYAL HIGHNESS PRINCE ALBERT OF SAXE COBURG AND GOTHA.

This most important and national event took place yesterday at noon, at the Chapel Royal, St. James's; and since the marriage of her Royal Highness the late Princess Charlotte of Wales, there has been no occurrence connected with the Royal family of England which excited so great an interest. It was known throughout the metropolis in the course of the last week that the celebration of the marriage would take place at noon, instead of an advanced hour of the evening, as was heretofore the custom with respect to Royal marriages. The knowledge of this fact brought many, many thousands from all sides of London into the Park at an early hour. Never did St. James's-park present such an extraordinary display—never was such an immense multitude assembled there since the rejoicings at the visit of the allied Sovereigns in 1814. As early as 9 o'clock considerable numbers had arrived in order to secure a good place from which to see the Royal *cortège* pass from Buckingham Palace to St. James's. By that hour the vicinity of Buckingham Palace, and all the avenues leading to both Palaces, were thronged. As the day wore on to noon, the assemblage between the back of Carlton-terrace and the foot of Constitution-hill had increased to a dense mass of very many thousands, through which it was difficult to keep open the carriage-way for that portion of the company who had the privilege of the *entrée*. The very lowering aspect of the weather seemed to have had no terrors for the visitors, male and female, young and old, who continued to arrive in masses, by which the space already described became, before 11 o'clock, thronged to most distressing pressure. Nor was this pressure diminished to any important extent by the smart showers which came down at intervals. As each successive group of visitors arrived they of course thickened the broad line of crowd at each side of the carriage-way between the two Palaces. Those whose stations were in the rear of this line soon got an opportunity of overlooking those in front by hiring standing room on some one of the many hundred chairs, tables, or benches, which were let out at various prices, from 1s. 6d. to 5s. each person. Many who could not afford or would not pay for such a luxury, succeeded in getting on the branches of the trees as well out of as in the line of the expected procession. The numbers who sought these commanding positions were so great in some of the trees that the branches gave way, and the parties came, not immediately to the ground, but on the heads and shoulders of the dense masses beneath them. We did not hear, however, that any persons were seriously hurt by those accidents. Many of them excited roars of laughter, from the efforts of those who had resorted to them to keep their places on the falling branches, or to secure more firm positions on the boughs above them. In the course of the morning the crowds in that part of the park situate between the back of Carlton-terrace and Marlborough-house were much amused by a marrow-bone and cleaver concert, got up in honour of the Royal nuptials, and we must do justice to those engaged by saying, that the effect of this rude music was by no means disagreeable. Soon after the firing of the guns, announcing the most important part of the ceremonial, the placing the ring on Her Majesty's finger, the whole mass of the visitors who had not obtained fixed stands rushed almost simultaneously towards Buckingham Palace, in order to have a view of Her Majesty and the Prince on their return. The pressure here became so great that it required the united and incessant efforts of the police and the Horse Guards Blue to keep the carriage way open. This necessary but disagreeable part of their duty was performed with much good temper, and in general was received with good humour even by those who appeared to suffer a little from it. The police regulations in this part of the park, and indeed in every part that we had an opportunity of observing, were admirably well arranged by the Commissioners Rowan and Mayne, and their directions were carried out by the force-officers and men under their command with great judgment and good temper. They had in some parts of the line an arduous and difficult task to perform; but we think that a great deal of their labour might have been saved by the erection of a strong barricade on each side of the line from Buckingham Palace to St. James's.

BUCKINGHAM PALACE (INTERIOR).

The officers of the household and the attendants of Her Majesty began to arrive at Buckingham Palace about half-past 10 o'clock. The Earl of Uxbridge, the Earl of Belfast, the Earl of Surrey, the Earl of Albemarle, Colonel Cavendish, Lord Alfred Paget, Sir George Anson, the Lord in Waiting, Ladies in Waiting, Maids of Honour, Bedchamber Women, Gentlemen Ushers, &c., were all assembled at 11 o'clock. After some little time had elapsed the ladies of Her Majesty's suite were summoned by the Master of the Horse, and handed into four of the Royal carriages by Colonel Cavendish (Clerk Marshal) and Lord Alfred Paget, and despatched to St. James's Palace.

At half-past 11 the six gentlemen composing the foreign suites of his Royal Highness Prince Albert and the Duke of Saxe Coburg Gotha mustered in the Grand Hall. They appeared in dark blue or green uniforms, and three of them took their departure in a Royal carriage for St. James's, accompanied by two Gentlemen Ushers of the Queen's household, to be in readiness to receive Prince Albert.

At a quarter to 12 the Royal carriages having returned, notice was given to the Royal bridegroom that all was in readiness for his departure. The Prince immediately quitted the private apartments of the Palace, and passed through the state rooms, into which a very few spectators were admitted. His Royal Highness was dressed in the uniform of a British Field Marshal, and wore no other decoration than the insignia of the Order of the Garter—viz., the collar, with the George appended, set in precious stones, the star of the order set in diamonds, and the Garter itself, embroidered in diamonds, round his knee. The Prince was supported on one side by his father, the Duke of Saxe Coburg Gotha, and his brother, the Hereditary Prince. The Duke was dressed in a dark-blue uniform, turned up with red, with military boots, similar to those worn by the Life Guards. His Serene Highness wore the collar of the Order of the Garter, and the star, and the star of the Order of Coburg Gotha. Prince Ernest wore a light-blue cavalry uniform, with silver appointments, carrying a light helmet in his hand. His Serene Highness wore the insignia of a Grand Cross of an Order of Knighthood. His Royal Highness Prince Albert was preceded by the Lord Chamberlain, the Vice-Chamberlain, the Treasurer and Controller of the Household, Lord Torrington (who wore the insignia of a Grand Cross of the order of Coburg Gotha, with which he has been lately invested), the Clerk Marshal, Equerries, Gentlemen Ushers, &c., the remaining portion of the foreign suite bringing up the rear. On descending the grand staircase, the favoured few occupying the Grand Hall behind the Yeomen Guard received the Prince with a loud clapping of hands, which his Royal Highness acknowledged in the most gracious manner. Indeed, to a group of ladies stationed close to the entrance, who were testifying their satisfaction, the Prince made his acknowledgements with an air of the most courteous gallantry. The Prince entered the carriage amid the sound of trumpets, the lowering of colours, the presenting of arms, and all the honours paid to the Queen herself. His Royal Highness, with his father and brother, occupied one carriage, and the attendants two other royal carriages. A squadron of Life Guards escorted the Prince to St. James's Palace. On the return of the Lord Chamberlain six of the Royal carriages were assembled, and his Lordship informed Her Majesty that all was ready. The Queen then left her apartments, leaning on the arm of the Earl of Uxbridge as Lord Chamberlain, supported by the Duchess of Kent, and followed by a Page of Honour. Her Majesty was preceded by the Earl of Belfast, the Earl of Surrey, Lord Torrington, the Earl of Albemarle, Colonel Cavendish, Sir George Anson, Lord Alfred Paget, Mr. Byng, and several other officers of the household. Her Majesty carried her train over her arm. The Royal bride was greeted with loud acclamations on descending to the Grand Hall, but her eye was bent principally on the ground, and a hurried glance around, and a slight inclination of the head, was all the acknowledgment returned. Her Majesty wore no diamonds on her head, nothing but a simple wreath of orange blossoms. The magnificent veil did not cover her face, but hung down on each shoulder. A pair of very large diamond earrings, a diamond necklace, and the insignia of the Order of the Garter, were the principal ornaments worn by the Queen.

The Duchess of Kent and the Duchess of Sutherland rode in the same carriage with Her Majesty, and the Royal *cortege* left the Palace at a slow pace under a strong escort of the Household Cavalry.

BUCKINGHAM PALACE (EXTERIOR).

This morning, at an early hour, every public approach to the Palace was crowded by numbers of Her Majesty's loyal subjects, anxious to obtain, if possible, a view of the bridal procession, and testify by their vociferous applause their perfect commendation of Her Majesty's choice of a royal consort. The court in front of the Palace was occupied by the Band of the Regiment of Blues and one or two companies of the Grenadier Guards, and the whole of the line thence to the garden-entrance of St. James's Palace was lined with Horse Guards and a strong corps of the police. The immediate road for the procession was kept clear with great difficulty, so numerous were the attempts from the pressure without to break in on the line and secure a position where a sight of the royal pair might be better had. The police, however, notwithstanding these ebullitions of "popular feeling," conducted themselves with great temper, and maintained order without any violent exercise of their supreme authority. Anxiously did the assembled multitude look for some signal of Her Majesty's departure from Buckingham Palace, and as carriage after carriage rolled down the Mall, carrying some of the honoured spectators to the chapel, the more impatient they became for the passing of the procession. 12 o'clock at length arrived, and his Royal Highness Prince Albert, attended by a small escort of Horse Guards, and accompanied by his father, the Duke of Saxe Coburg and Gotha, and his brother, Prince Ernest, then left the palace and proceeded to St. James's; but from the windows of the carriages being closed the royal party were only partially recognized, and passed along with but slight applause. At a quarter past 12, however, the band in front of the palace struck up the national air of "God save the Queen," and by the tremendous shouts which resounded through the park, it was proclaimed that Her Majesty had entered her carriage and was then proceeding to St. James's to plight her troth to his Royal Highness Prince Albert of Saxe Coburg and Gotha. As Her Majesty passed down the line she was most enthusiastically cheered, and appeared highly gratified by the loyalty which her subjects expressed, one or two ludicrous incidents amongst the crowd also exciting her smile; but her countenance was extremely pale, and appeared to betoken considerable anxiety. The *cortège* of Her Majesty was attended by a full guard of honour, but the carriages were drawn by only two horses each, and without the rich caparison which they usually wear on state occasions. The order of the carriages was thus:—

FIRST CARRIAGE.
Two Gentlemen Ushers.
Exon of the Yeomen of the Guard.
Groom of the Robes.

SECOND CARRIAGE.
Equerry in Waiting,
Hon. C. Grey.
Two Pages of Honour.
Groom in Waiting,
Hon. Major Keppel.

THIRD CARRIAGE.
Clerk Marshal,
Hon. H. F. Cavendish.
Vice-Chamberlain,
Earl of Belfast.
Keeper of the Privy Purse,
Sir H. Wheatley.
Controller of the Household,
Right Hon. G. Stevens Byng.

FOURTH CARRIAGE.
Bedchamber Woman in Waiting.
Captain of the Yeomen of the Guard,
Earl of Ilchester.
Master of the Buckhounds,
Lord Kinnaird.
Treasurer of the Household,
Earl of Surrey.

FIFTH CARRIAGE.
Maid of Honour in Waiting.
Duchess of Kent's Lady in Waiting,
Lady Charlotte Dundas.
Gold Stick,
Lord Hill.
Lord in Waiting,
Viscount Torrington.

SIXTH CARRIAGE.
Lady of the Bedchamber in Waiting.
Master of the Horse,
Earl of Albemarle.
Lord Steward,
Earl of Errol.
Lord Chamberlain,
Earl of Uxbridge.

SEVENTH CARRIAGE.
THE QUEEN.
The Duchess of Kent.
Mistress of the Robes.
Duchess of Sutherland.

By about ten minutes past 12 o'clock the whole of these carriages, with their respective occupants, had reached

ST. JAMES'S PALACE.

THE THRONE-ROOM.

On the arrival of the Queen at St. James's Palace Her Majesty was conducted to her closet, immediately behind the Throne-room, where she remained attended by the Maids of Honour and Trainbearers until the summons was received from the Lord Chamberlain conveying the intimation that everything was duly prepared for the Sovereign's moving towards the Chapel.

In this room the formal procession may be said to have been formed and marshalled.

PRESENCE CHAMBER.

In this room the principal individuals who were to fall into the different processions were congregated.

QUEEN ANNE'S DRAWING-ROOM.

Round the southern side of this room a gallery was erected, consisting of several rows of seats, each capable of accommodating a considerable number of visitors. Through this room the processions passed into

THE GUARD OR ARMOURY-ROOM,

in which a gallery on a smaller scale was raised. The procession progressed from this into the Vestibule, and from that down the

GRAND STAIRCASE,

opposite to which a gallery had been put up capable of containing about 150 persons.

THE COLONNADE.

Shortly after 9 o'clock the seats in the colonnade began to be taken possession of, and ere many minutes had elapsed there remained but few of the seats unoccupied, although there was an occasional arrival down to 11 o'clock.

At this hour the appearance which the scene presented was one of extreme animation, inasmuch as by far the greater portion of the assembled company was composed of elegantly, and in some instances brilliantly, dressed ladies. It were a matter of impossibility to enter upon an attempt to give anything like a minute detail of the attire either of the one sex or of the other, for it comprised every known colour, and embraced every description of style of make. The most conspicuous dresses were of light blue relieved with white, light green also intermingled with white, amber, crimson, purple, fawn, stone, and a considerable number of white robes only. Every lady exhibited a wedding favour, some of which were admirable specimens of a refined taste. They were of all sizes, many of white satin riband, tied up into bows, and mixed with layers of rich silver lace, others merely of riband intermixed with sprigs of orange-flower blossom, whilst were here and there to be seen bouquets of huge dimensions of riband and massive silver bullion, having in their centre what might almost be termed a branch of orange blossoms. Large as they were, however, they were not more so than the apparent devotion of their owners, if the anxiety with which they watched every movement of the officials passing to and fro, from the instant they entered the colonnade until the last of the "men of State" had quitted the scene, may be taken as a criterion.

It was remarked that "favours" did not form a very general appendage with the male branch of the spectators, notwithstanding there were many who had not failed to furnish themselves with this distinguishing emblem of the occasion. Some gentlemen there were, also, who did not even pay the respect to their Sovereign of providing court dresses. There appeared, nevertheless, to have been an unanimity of feeling with regard to the total banishment of black, except in a rare instance where a shawl or scarf of that hue was to be discovered.

The colonnade through which the procession passed to the chapel was not only excellently arranged, but was admirably lighted from the lanterns above and the windows behind. The seats, which were separated from the pillared colonnade by a dwarf railing, were covered with crimson cushions with gold-coloured borders and fringe. All the remainder of this temporary structure had the semblance of having been constructed of solid masonry. The floor of the colonnade was covered with rich Brussels carpet, which extended into the vestibule, up the grand staircase to the armoury, through the presence-chamber to Queen Anne's drawing-room, and thence to the ante-chamber and Throne-room, where Her Majesty and Prince Albert's portions of the procession were marshalled. The seats erected for the accommodation of the spectators were covered with crimson cushions and yellow fringe, thus sustaining uniformity throughout. They were railed off from the line of procession.

There were but few of the nobility or officers of state who entered the chapel by the colonnade or royal passage, but amongst that number were Earl Fitzwilliam and Earl Spencer, the Earl and Countess of Carlisle, the Duke and Duchess of Somerset, the Duke of Devonshire, the Marquis of Anglesey, the Marquis of Westminster, the Archbishop of Canterbury, the Archbishop of York, and the Bishop of London.

His Grace the Duke of Wellington also passed through the colonnade, and was most warmly cheered. The Duke slightly acknowledged the demonstration, and wended his way onwards to the place allotted for the occupation of the veteran warrior in the chapel.

Comparatively speaking, there was a scarcity of "rank" amongst the company in the colonnade. The only individuals of particular note upon whom our eye alighted were Sir George Murray, Mr. Sheil, and Mr. Charles Young. To the former of these gentlemen her Royal Highness the Princess Sophia Matilda of Glocester, from her place in the procession, spoke, whilst the Marquis of Anglesey stopped and shook hands most warmly with the gallant Baronet. Mr. Tennyson D'Eyncourt and Sir W. Brabazon were likewise occupants of seats in the colonnade, but, like the hon. and learned member for Tipperary, their presence was allowed to pass unheeded.

Of course, anticipation long postponed, and the virtue of patience, even within the walls of a Royal Palace, and upon such an occasion, became exhausted, and the slightest action or movement, however trifling, which tended to create a diversion, or to shed a new feature on a scene which had grown somewhat monotonous, was hailed as a species of Godsend, and accordingly the mere circumstance of the Rev. Lord Augustus Fitzclarence bringing forward one of the choir boys, a lad apparently of some 7 or 8 years of age, but particularly small, and examining his uncouth dress, gave rise to considerable merriment. The occasional passing to and fro of the macebearers—who, from their remarkable dress, namely, black, with large gold chains tied up on the shoulders with large white favours, excited a good deal of attention—was seized as a fitting opportunity to indulge in laughter.

But, looking at the mass which paraded the colonnade, we may say, that there were the burley Yeomen of the Guard with their massive halberts, and the slim Gentlemen-at-Arms, with their lighter partisans, perpetually moving up and down the corridor, proud of the notice they excited. There were also elderly Pages of State, and almost infantile Pages of Honour, officers of the Lord Chamberlain's-office, and officers of the Woods and Forests, embroidered heralds and steel-clad Cuirassiers, robed prelates, stoled priests,

MARRIAGE OF PRINCESS ELIZABETH: THE CEREMONY IN THE ABBEY

The scene in Westminster Abbey yesterday at the marriage of Princess Elizabeth, heiress-presumptive to the Throne, and Lieutenant his Royal Highness the Duke of Edinburgh, R.N. The bride, supported by the King, and the bridegroom with his groomsman, the Marquess of Milford Haven, are seen standing at the head of the steps to the sacrarium as the Archbishop of Canterbury performs the ceremony. In the group on the right are the Queen, Queen Mary, the Duke and Duchess of Gloucester, the Duchess of Kent, other members of the Royal Family and distinguished guests. In the group opposite them are Princess Andrew of Greece (mother of the bridegroom) and other relatives of the bridegroom. A staff photographer's picture.

The procession of the bride in the Abbey. Princess Elizabeth with her father entering the choir from the nave. Among the guests seen in the background are members of the diplomatic corps.

The bride and bridegroom waving to the crowd on leaving the Abbey in the glass coach after the ceremony.

A happy study of Princess Elizabeth and the Duke of Edinburgh leaving Westminster Abbey by the west door.

Agony Column

Some years ago *The Times* commissioned a famous firm of market researchers to conduct a survey into which parts of *The Times* were actually read. Readers were invited to tick little boxes to indicate that they read the various sections always, often, sometimes or never.

The secret exercise was depressing for the hard-working hacks who write the paper. The bits that they wrote were generally outscored by the bits that were provided gratis, such as letters to the editor, and the guest lists of memorial services and lunches at Downing Street on the Court Page. A significant number of readers returned their forms with no ticks on at all, indicating either that they bought *The Times* not to read, but to carry as a badge that they were top people, or that they refused to have any truck with such a piffling activity as market research. The latter is the alternative that I prefer.

The Agony Column, as it is jocularly known, scored very well in the poll of the market researchers, as any fool could have told them. The personal advertisements in *The Times*, providing keyholes through which to peep into the lives of the *Times*-reading classes in all their rich English eccentricity and incomprehensibility, have been a popular feature of the paper from its earliest days. The finest hour of the Agony Column was before May 1966, when it was banished from the front page. The splitting of it into a variety of commercial headings, with 'Announcements' to cover the odds and sods, has also reduced its rich and diverse idiosyncrasy.

LONDON, FRIDAY, SEPTE

A. B. is requested to MEET the PARTY he wrote to on the 18th inst. at the Jamaica Coffee-house, . Michael's-alley, Cornhill, THIS DAY, Friday, at 12 o'clock, recisely. Enquire at the Bar for C. D.

IF the YOUTH that left Islington on Sunday evening can remember that he ever had a mother, he is iformed he will soon be deprived of that blessing, except he umediately writes with particulars, or personally appears beore her. His friends will redress any circumstance, and settle very point to his satisfaction. —West Smithfield.

BIRD LOST.—LOST, on Blackheath, on Sunday evening, Sept. 2, a BROWN SPECKLED BIRD, he size of a Lark, and supposed to be a Bunting or Furze Lark; e is remarkably tame. Whoever will bring him alive and unirt, to Mr. Allen, Bookseller, Greenwich; or to Mr. Walker, ireen Man on Blackheath; or will give notice to either of hem where he may be restored, shall receive TWO GUINEAS Reward. No greater reward will be offered.

Above The Agony Column of Friday 21 September 1804.

Below An illustration to The Adventure of the Cardboard Box, by Conan Doyle, in THE STRAND MAGAZINE. The financial column of THE TIMES provided a clue to the contents of the packet sent to Miss Susan Cushing of Croydon.

Small advertisements appeared in *The Times* from the beginning. They were usually for situations wanted or on offer, and for lodgings required. Gradually human interest and English dottiness started to infiltrate commerce. On 18 December 1800 we read, with a romantic sigh:

A CARD – If the lady whom a Gentleman handed into her carriage from Covent Garden Theatre on Wednesday will oblige the Advertiser with a line to Z.Z. saying if single or married, she will quiet the mind of a young nobleman, who has tried, but in vain, to find the lady.

Similar short stories of lost love, whether inserted by true lovers, or white-slavers and other con-men, were to echo plangently through the Agony Column from then on. Another recurrent theme was the agony that created the sobriquet. An early example of this genre was published on 21 September 1804: 'YOUTH THAT LEFT ISLINGTON on Sunday evening: if the Youth can remember that he ever had a Mother, he is informed that he will soon be deprived of that blessing, except he immediately writes with Particulars, or Personally appears before her.' Gosh! Can she have survived until 7 November 1816 to insert the bitter question in the Agony Column: 'PHILIP – Would PHILIP like to hear of his MOTHER'S DEATH?'

"I FELL INTO A BROWN STUDY."

Agony is a superior sobriquet. It appeared as early as 1880 in *The Times* itself: 'A cryptogram in the Agony Column'. In 1930 Wyndham Lewis wrote in a letter: 'The Agony Column of *The Times* has echoed the rage of people who considered themselves to be attacked in *The Apes*'. All human life is in the personal ads: a secret history of love and hate, joy and sorrow, crime and madness, and other English obsessions, can be built up for the past two centuries from the names, initials and pseudonyms of the advertisers in the Agony Column. Many of the messages were in code, though generally not of a complexity that requires an Ultra machine to decipher it. Some years ago Printing House Square stopped accepting personal ads in code, unless a translation is provided. We are frightened of unwittingly publishing libel, obscenity or criminal communications.

Inevitably much of the history of the Agony Column has to be folklore: you cannot verify communications that were intended to be hermetic. There is a persistent office rumour that a sensational royal romance was conducted entirely through the Agony Column. Scotland Yard once trapped a blackmailer by inserting an answer to his coded message. During the First World War a female spy is said to have used the Agony Column to communicate in code with her network.

We may not at this late stage be able to unravel these secret communications, some of them ever better kept than the real colour of Ronald Reagan's hair. But there is no mystery about demonstrating the eccentricity of the Agony Column. You have only to read its lovers' messages on St Valentine's Day, covering the whole gamut from Yuk to Cuddly. It has been going on for ages. Note a classic entry as early as 1798: 'Wife sought by gentleman of excellent constitution, though afflicted with an incurable weakness in the knees occasioned by the kick of an ostrich'. I flickered and raised an eyebrow at an advertisement that appeared in 1960. It ran: 'Fire-eaters and sword-swallowers required, preferably with ecclesiastical experience'. Iconoclasts? Some sinister new cult? I investigated, and as Sherlock himself might have remarked, behind the most outwardly bizarre insertion in the Agony Column, my old friend, there lies a perfectly simple explanation. The fire-eaters and sword-swallowers with ecclesiastical experience were wanted by a theatrical firm casting extras for a thirteenth-century miracle play.

Such little snippets make news, if only of the Man Bites Dog silly-season sort. It is no secret that the other newspapers of Fleet Street read the Agony Column of *The Times* at once, when the first edition arrives in their offices late at night, trawling like Sherlock Holmes for the odder sides of human nature. There was such a scoop in the fifties, when somebody called Robert Cowell informed the world through the Agony Column of *The Times* that in future he wished to be known as Roberta Cowell. This broke the news of one of the first highly publicized sex-change stories, and the tabloids worked themselves into an orgasm of vulgar excitement about it. But the story appeared first, and more appropriately, in the Agony Column. In 1958 the press whipped itself into a frenzy of speculation about an announcement that the advertiser required a disused lighthouse. The explanation eventually turned out to be quite simple: a lady just wanted to get away from it all. In 1968 members of the MCC, unhappy with the way their club had handled the D'Oliveira affair, invited other dissidents to get in touch with the advertiser in the Agony Column, and started a story that ran and ran.

Nobody can properly taste the full flavour of English life, with all its sugar and spice, who does not read the Agony Column of *The Times*.

An historical article on historical entries in THE TIMES's Agony Column. More than seventy years ago, this article was bemoaning declining standards and priorities of contributors to THE TIMES. This pastime is as much a part of THE TIMES as the Agony Column itself.
25 JUNE 1914

"THE TIMES" AGONY COLUMN.

RECORDS OF A CENTURY.

FIGURES OF ROMANCE IN DISGUISE.

Since the days of Richardson and the *Liaisons Dangereuses*, dozens of novelists have adopted the epistolary method of telling a story; it has possibilities in the revelation of character, as Choderlos de Laclos best proved, perhaps, of all those who tried it successfully. We think, however, that nobody has yet written a novel all in agony advertisements from *The Times*. It would be worth trying; for what are those advertisements, in that celebrated column headed "Personal," but brief letters from one unknown to another, each unknown becoming better known as you read the column day by day? A history of the agony columns would contain, thus, a series of enigmatic romances, thrilling to the curious person with detective instincts. We imagine no better training for the ambitious inquiry agent.

Unfortunately, such an expert in agony would, we fear, miss to-day that *continuance* of correspondence, necessary if one is to piece together broken bits of the hearts that display their fractures. In old days, agonists went on, week after week—sometimes year after year—in pursuit of what they had lost, or what they hoped to gain. The most agonizing specimens were industriously collected, some years ago, in a small book which gave the best of them for the whole period between 1800 and 1870. During that time we can trace sets of appeals telling the same story under various disguises. With infinite patience, with an English obstinacy now rarer, apparently, than it was, half-hidden faces, separated fathers, prodigal sons, and the other eternal figures of romance, exhaled their flowery complaints in view of the public. It was possible, therefore, to gather a reasonable theory, from so much evidence, of the true state of the case concerning these sufferers. Nowadays, we fear that the agonist does not linger in his pain.

THE AGONY OF 1914.

A comparison of the old agonies with the advertisements of to-day has convinced us, too, that the personalities of the famous column tend more and more to be of a pecuniary, rather than of a passionate, order. If we were asked to compose a typical agony of the year 1914—more than a full century since the column started—we should give, in illustration, this:—

Professional man sick of living in town would like large house in country with large income to keep up same. O please help!

Or, again, this:—

Young man, weary of work in an office, seeks any sort of remunerative adventure. Would risk all, provided he got paid a lot. Good Alpinist. Can drive motor-car or motor-bicycle. Some experience of flying. Who will help?

Nevertheless, we cannot help regretting the obsolete agony. In an agony we like to find a paroxysm. It does'nt matter about the grammar, which is, we notice, frequently very bad from 1800 to 1870; what we seek is emotion, not good English. In those days, indeed, it was held no emotion ever could or should be English. That is why a fine paroxysm of 1851 reads thus:—

WILLIAM, thou wilt go to sea—thou shalt go; but O RETURN, and first receive the blessing of a heart-broken father, of a heart-broken Mother! O my son William, my son, my son William! Would God I had died for thee, O William, my son, my son!

It reads like a minor dramatist of the Mrs. Inchbald or Mrs. Centlivre period, or, later, of Arthur Murphy and "A Cure for the Heartache." In this manner, with bared neck and dishevelled hair, beating the breast did the Kemble rouse the pit. . . . But we doubt whether his poor mother "fetched" William by it. The boy had been reading nautical romances. Captain Marryat was but a few years dead. William's father, who was, no doubt, a Samuel-Butlerian father of the instructive type, made classical by James Mill, had warned the boy that if he ever so much as mentioned the sea to him again, he should receive the wrong end of a knotted rope on it. But we must not dream over William. Other advertisements invited the immediate return of other sons in a more modern and Shavian manner. As this, dated 1894:—

IF the YOUTH THAT LEFT ISLINGTON on Sunday evening can remember that he ever had a Mother, he is informed he will soon be deprived of that blessing, except he immediately writes with particulars, or personally appears before her.

That youth probably preferred to be deprived of that blessing of a mother, and we cannot help believing that it was the same youth who was appealed to, a few years later, by this—

PHILIP.—Would PHILIP like to hear of HIS MOTHER'S DEATH?

Perhaps! But we are sure he did not hear of it just then. His mother was waiting for him behind the door, and perhaps his uncle, too, for evidently the poor boy's father was no more. We trust Philip never went home. We always feel sympathy for the missing.

CIPHER AND EMOTION.

Such maternal, paternal, or filial agonies, however, have always been less common in the column than those simply sentimental. Many of these, during a half-century or more, were in cipher. Now only simple persons advertise in cipher. Whereas a pursuing parent might not discover an advertisement in full English, his attention, and, indeed, the attention of everybody, will inevitably be riveted and held by a jumble of capital letters, asterisks, and queries, or by such uncouth Irish-looking dialects as this, from one of the ciphered agonies of J. de W. in 1852:—

S. lmpi F. spl apkl. B. qkng. F. oing a Khq. 19th nhgm. oing. lqkh. hmig Fiffy migi.

We much prefer to see the sentimental appeal in full, or only hinting obscurely that it could say more than it does. For the courtly invitation of this type you have to go back to the Weber period and to glance over the columns between 1800 and 1830. At the very beginning, in 1800, you find this address to A CARD.

If the Lady who a Gentleman handed into her carriage from Covent Garden Theatre, on Wednesday, the third of this month, will oblige the Advertiser with a line to Z.Z. Spring Gardens Coffee House, saying if married or single, she will quiet the mind of a young Nobleman, who has tried, but in vain, to find the Lady. . . . The Lady was in mourning, and sufficiently cloathed to distinguish her for possessing every virtue and charm that man could desire in a female that he would make choice of for a Wife. . . .

The young Nobleman, as you see, had the familiar aristocratic ignorance of the ways of relative pronouns if not of Ladies, and we find ourselves hoping that his title proved sufficient allurement to the Lady "who" he loved at a distance. For another 50 years, the young Nobleman's emotional grammar set the tone of the column. "Amiable females" abound in it. In 1801 a gentleman tells one of them that he "will shortly be obliged to leave town in a few months," and we are not surprised when he adds that he is going to Ireland. In no better style, but with feeling as satisfactory, was "C.S." (in 1852) entreated to "leave off this cruel silence" and (in 1851):—

P.P.P. is implored, for mercy's sake, to write again. If not your wretched father will be a maniac and your poor unhappy mother will die broken-hearted.

THE CHANGE TO-DAY.

But we repeat—the essence of an agony is not style. It is not style that makes memorable the long correspondences of J. de W. and E. J. W.—the latter of whom used the column from 1851 to 1870. E. J. W. varies between finance—in cipher—and Colley-Cibberian turgidity of the "By Heavens, Madam!" sort. He appeals in bad English and worse French—never with sense, always with sensibility. Incomparable E. J. W.! You and such as you are dust and ashes, long ago. We shall not see the like of you in the agony column again.

We cannot show the change better than by giving a few extracts in chronological order:—

(1802) INCOGNITA'S elegant and well-composed EPISTLE, of the 19th instant, has had all the impression that possibly could be expected; another, with real name and place of abode, may be safely ventured. An immediate intercourse is earnestly requested by LEANDER.

(1826) I consent to any, every condition, rather than a continuance of this lengthened—this too justly-dreaded—separation.

(1846) With never-ending regret I own my rash error. The withdrawal of your future notice must seriously injure me, yet I deserve it, and humbly pray that He who knows to "err is human," will pardon me, soften your heart, and make you happy.

(1855) K. Spare the undeserving. Transgressors there may have been, 'tis true, but none so great I think as you.—A.Z.

(1860) GLEN.—SPECKLED FOWLS, buys—buy my mackerel!

(1870). You could not speak. It was too sudden. I am a good rider. Green is my favourite colour. I want money.

That, the last word of last-quoted agony of our little book, is precisely it. They want money. All do nowadays. Agonists such as E. J. W. knew of finer things. They wanted amiable females or lost children. We fear, from their continued appeals and final silence, that they got less than they wanted; while to-day, possibly, the numbers who "want money" get more than they deserve.

"PELLÉAS ET MÉLISANDE."

DEBUSSY'S OPERA AT COVENT GARDEN.

Arkel	GUSTAVE HUBERDEAU
Genevieve	LOUISE BÉRAT
Pelléas	J. MAGUENAT
Golaud	HECTOR DUFRANNE
Mélisande	LOUISE EDVINA
Yniold	SYBIL VANE
Un Medecin	GASTON SARGEANT

Conductor—GIORGIO POLACCO

There are just a few works which seem to have come into existence by a happy coincidence of thought and feeling between poet and musician rather than by the direct influence of the one upon the other. Debussy's musical setting of Maeterlinck's *Pelléas et Mélisande* is one of them.

The music is not primarily the outcome of the play; it is too thoroughly Debussy for that. One can imagine him with the music in his head or his heart, or wherever musicians keep their music before they write it, lighting upon the play and discovering it to be the verbal counterpart of the tone-poem he meant to write. And the extraordinarily subtle adjustment of the two seems to come naturally from this coincidence of feeling between the two artists. Debussy has never required the poet to give way to him; he was able to set the text as it stood save for the omission of the preliminary scene of the servants, which presumably was merely left out so that the opera might be of convenient length. On the other hand, we do not feel that the musician is consciously subduing his music for the sake of the words. He says all that he wants to say: at one moment an eloquent phrase on the flute, at another a long-drawn note on the double basses; or, again, an extraordinarily vivid crescendo leading from darkness to light, or a beautiful development of a leading theme, such as that associated with the elusive personality of Mélisande.

Elusiveness is the prevalent quality. Nothing must be too pronounced. Mélisande gazes into the depth of the well, Pelléas, forced by Golaud, peers into the dark waters beneath the vaults of the castle, and we, like them, seem to be looking at reflections, in which the outlines are never sharply defined. The singers and the players have to realize this. Mme. Edvina has done so to a great extent, and her great merit lies in her power of singing with a quiet mezzo-voce tone and the reserve which she shows in her acting. Mme. Bérat as Geneviève has this reserve by nature. She is never tempted beyond it. Some of the men in last night's performance were not equally successful. M. Maguenat's voice does not seem quite the right quality for Pelléas and M. Dufranne began by singing Golaud's first scene in a heavy and monotonous manner, which made it impossible to imagine that the little girl by the well was any enigma to him. He showed more sympathy and more resource in the later episodes, however. M. Huberdeau's Arkel was quiet and dignified; Miss Sybil Vane had to shout to make the voice of the child heard above the orchestra.

Signor Polacco showed in her scene, and sometimes elsewhere, too much of the impulsiveness which belongs to the Italian view of opera, but much of the orchestral playing under his direction was exquisite in its refinement of tone and phrasing.

"THE BELLE OF NEW YORK."

REVIVAL AT THE LYCEUM.

Ichabod Bronson	Mr. M. R. MORAND
Harry Bronson	Mr. HERBERT ST. JOHN
Karl von Pumpernick ..	Mr. LAURENCE CAIRD
"Doc" Snitkins	Mr. JOHN SANGER
"Blinky Bill" McQuirk. .	Mr. JOHNNY SCHOFIELD, Jun.
Kenneth Mugg	Mr. WALTER URIDGE
Count Ratsi Tattatoo ..	Mr. ERNEST GIFFORD
Count Patsi Tattatoo ..	Mr. T. O'BRIEN
Violet Grey	Miss DOROTHEA CLARKE
Fifi Fricot	Miss JULIA JAMES
Kissie Fitzgarter	Miss LILY GULLICK
Cora Angelique	Miss DOROTHY CRASKE
Mamie Clancy	Miss MAY RONAYN
Betty	Miss F. CAMERON

It came as something of a shock last night to realize that 16 years have passed since the April evening when Miss Edna May and her fellow-players first took the town by storm in that most successful of all American musical comedies *The Belle of New York*, and it is no disrespect to the excellent company which Messrs. Melville have got together for the revival at the Lyceum to say that at the outset last night the ghosts of the past hovered around on every side. There was not only the absence of Miss Edna May to deplore; death has lately laid low Mr. Frank Lawton, the whistler whose "Blinkey Bill" will long be a thing to remember, and many of the original company are scattered far and wide. But as the evening advanced the ghosts of the past receded into the background, for those memories could not be allowed to blind one to the all-round ability of the company of the present.

We imagine that this revival will be very popular. There was a tremendously enthusiastic audience last night, very different from that at the first night of the original production, when the theatre was by no means full. The quality of the musical comedy fare sent us from America has not improved in the meantime; one can think of *few* of the latter-day entertainments which will bear reviving 16 years hence. For the most part the company is an English one, but it has adopted the American method of plenty of restless bustle and noise, and its abounding vitality carries the production through.

Miss Dorothea Clarke, as the Salvation Army lassie, played in that arch and demure fashion which inevitably reminded one of Miss May, but the comparison was by no means to the newcomer's discredit, for she sang and acted the part in the pleasantest possible fashion. Miss Julia James, as "la Belle Parisienne," and Miss Dorothy Craske as the Queen of Comic Opera, were alike at their best, and Miss James's "When we are married" duet with Mr. Herbert St. John was quite the success of the evening. Then there are Mr. M. R. Morand, a sterling comedian, as Mr. Bronson, the president of the Rescue League, Mr. Laurence Caird as the polite lunatic with the one great ambition to kill Mr. Bronson, and Mr. Johnny Schofield, jun., excellent in every way, both as a whistler and an acrobatic dancer, as "Blinky Bill," whose untiring energy is only exceeded by that of Miss May Ronayn as a Bowery girl—for her enthusiasm for strenuous work is truly astounding. The whole production went with a fine swing.

BIG DRAPERY FIRE AT GUILDFORD.

Damage estimated at £20,000 was caused yesterday by fire at Messrs. White's drapery establishment, Guildford.

The fire totally destroyed the cutting-out room, four fitting rooms, and the contents of the basement storeroom. Considerable injury was also done to a fine oak-panelled Tudor showroom. The flames also damaged the Lion Hotel adjoining. Two fire brigades were engaged, and the fire appliances of the Friary Brewery were requisitioned. Most of the members of the Guildford Fire Brigade were at the National Fire Brigade Camp at Bournemouth.

CHARGES OF BIGAMY.

THE MARRIAGE OF A GIRL OF 14.

At the Central Criminal Court yesterday there were five charges of bigamy. In three cases the defendants were discharged, in one the defendant received a nominal sentence, and in one sentence was postponed.

Before the Recorder, EMMA JANET ELSIE RONDLE, on bail, pleaded "Not Guilty" to an indictment charging her with bigamy. The defendant, crying bitterly, said she thought her husband was dead when she went through the second marriage.

The RECORDER said it was an extraordinarily weak case. According to the evidence on the depositions, this girl, who was now only 21, was married seven years ago to a soldier. The soldier disappeared and had not been heard of for five years, and the defendant's mother believed he was dead. Then, on May 27, 1911, the defendant went through the form of marriage with her present husband.

Mr. F. J. Egerton-Warburton, for the prosecution, said he quite agreed the case was weak, and at the Recorder's suggestion he offered no evidence.

The jury found the defendant *Not Guilty*, and she was discharged. She left the Court with her mother.

EMILY MARY BUFFOY, on bail, pleaded "Guilty" to a charge of bigamy.

The defendant was married to her husband in 1899. In 1911 she went through the form of marriage with another man, her husband being alive. She now told the Recorder that the second husband was a lazy man and she had to work to keep his six children. He knew that she was a married woman and even when she was ill he remarked, "I won't get your insurance money if you die."

The RECORDER passed upon the defendant a nominal sentence of two days' imprisonment, which entitled her to be discharged at once.

GEORGE FARMER, a carman, pleaded "Guilty" to bigamy.

The defendant was married to his wife in 1896 and lived with her up to the time he was given into custody upon the charge. On March 23 he went through the ceremony of marriage with a young woman with whom he had become acquainted. When the defendant was arrested on the charge his wife was standing by the detective.

The defendant, who bore an excellent character, having been in one situation 20 years, said he must have been mad when he did this.

The RECORDER postponed judgment until the next sessions.

In the case of ANN ELIZA REGAN, on bail, who was charged with bigamy, no evidence was offered by the prosecution, and the jury found the defendant *Not Guilty*, and she was discharged.

FREDERICK WILLIAM BAKER, on bail, was found *Not Guilty* on a similar indictment and was discharged.

CHRISTIAN SCIENCE AND SHARES.

THE JURY SYSTEM.

Before the COMMON SERJEANT, FREDERICK SIMON GROSVENOR, 53, stockbroker, who was found *Guilty* at the April Sessions of fraud in connexion with the obtaining of a cheque for £2,000 from Captain Robert Gardiner, a member of the Christian Science community, in relation to a transaction in gold-mining shares, was brought up for sentence.

Mr. WILD, K.C., for the defence, said Grosvenor was a German who had been in England for 35 years, and had never previously had a charge against him. He had been adjudicated a bankrupt in 1898 and 1911, but was discharged each time.

The COMMON SERJEANT referred to the jury's disagreement in regard to another defendant, and said it illustrated the wisdom of the proposal that where one juryman stood out against the 11, if the Judge agreed with the 11 a verdict might be given.

Witnesses were called on behalf of the defendant to testify to his high character.

The COMMON SERJEANT said that no doubt according to the evidence Grosvenor was not the party most deeply concerned. He passed a sentence of six months' imprisonment in the second division.

A RUNAWAY MOTORIST.

MAXIMUM PENALTY FOR FAILURE TO STOP AFTER COLLISION.

At the Kingston-on-Thames County Police Court yesterday GEORGE VYVYAN DEAKIN, of independent means, staying at the Railway Hotel, Byfleet, was summoned for failing to stop his motor-car at Stoney-hill, Portsmouth-road, Esher, on May 25, after an accident in which a person was injured.

Thomas Hugh Roblou, in the service of Mr. Sopwith, the airman, said he was driving an A.C. two-seater car on the Portsmouth-road on May 25. At Stoney-hill he stopped to speak to a friend, and was restarting when he saw a Gordon Watney Mercédès car coming behind him. He waved to the driver to pass him on the left, but the car, which was going at from 40 to 45 miles an hour, swerved to the right and then to the left and hit Mr. Sopwith's car on the left-hand side, turning it completely over. The witness was thrown underneath the car, which was badly damaged, and the driver of the other car went on without stopping.

John Davis, a chauffeur, and Alfred Mead, both of whom saw the accident, said the driver must have known he had struck the small car.

A police sergeant said that at the Gordon Watney garage at Addlestone on the day after the accident the witness Roblou pointed out a Mercédès car which bore marks of having been in collision. On May 27, at the Railway Hotel, Byfleet, he saw the defendant, who said he knew nothing about it.

The defendant was sworn and admitted driving a Mercédès car on the night in question, but said that, so far as he knew, he was not concerned in the accident. The damage to his car was caused by a collision with a post outside the Blue Anchor at Byfleet.

The Chairman said the Bench were unanimous in convicting the defendant, who would be fined the maximum penalty of £10 and £2 17s. 6d. costs, and his licence would be suspended for six months.

THE POLICE COURTS.

ORDER AGAINST A PUBLISHER.

At Bow-street Police Court yesterday, before Mr. Graham Campbell, Mr. EVELEIGH NASH, publisher, of Fawside House, King-street, Covent Garden, was summoned for detaining certain letters belonging to Mrs. Maud Mary Chester ffoulkes, of Saville Court, Brompton-square.

Mr. Curtis Bennett, who appeared for the defence, said that he would consent to an order being made for the return of what was required. At the moment the letters had been lost, but he hoped they would be found, and, if so, they would be given up. In the alternative he was quite content that the magistrate should fix the value at the highest amount allowed by the Act—viz., £15.

Mr. Moseley, counsel for the complainant, said that his client did not want the money; she was very anxious to secure the return of the letters. The Magistrate.—They must be very valuable letters. Mr. Curtis Bennett.—My friend says so, and I should not like to dispute it.

The MAGISTRATE ordered the defendant to give up the letters or pay their value, £15, together with £2 2s. costs.

IMPOSITIONS ON MEMBERS OF PARLIAMENT.

Charges of imposition on Members of Parliament were investigated at the Westminster Court yesterday, when ALBERT ANDERSON, 46, *alias* Swift, of Rowton House, Newington Butts, pleaded "Guilty" to obtaining money by false pretences from Mr. G. C. Hamilton, M.P., and Mr. Rigby Swift, K.C., M.P.

Many letters to members of Parliament were produced, a common feature of them being alleged associations with the constituencies of the members. One letter to Lieutenant-Colonel Sykes, M.P., appealed for money to reach Knutsford for the funeral of a relative.

Mr. G. C. Hamilton, M.P., said he got a letter signed "A. Swift," the writer representing that he came from Altrincham, Cheshire, and making a piteous appeal to attend the funeral of a brother. The witness sent a sovereign, but comparing notes with another M.P. in the House, he found that they had both been swindled with similar letters in precisely the same strain, so he communicated with the police.

When the prisoner was arrested a letter was found from Mr. Rigby Swift, who sent a postal order for a sovereign. The prisoner was remanded for inquiry into other charges.

COMEDIAN SENTENCED.

At the Kent Assizes at Maidstone yesterday ADAM ARTHUR, professionally known as "Sandy McNab," 49, comedian, was charged with an offence against Margaret Mary Hemmingway, aged 13, at Sheerness.

The case for the prosecution was that the girl went from Glasgow, where she lived, to London with McNab and members of his company with the consent of her mother, and then proceeded to Sheerness, where the prisoner and the girl, who appeared to be stage-struck, stayed in lodgings.

He was found *Guilty* and sentenced to two years' hard labour, MR. JUSTICE DARLING remarking that if he could have given a heavier punishment he would have done so.

"COMMEM." AT OXFORD.

A FESTIVAL OF LEARNING AND GAIETY.

THE PUBLIC ORATOR'S JESTS.

(FROM OUR UNIVERSITY CORRESPONDENT.)

Commemoration, or "Commem," as the "gods" in the gallery prefer to call it, has once more come and gone. Every Commemoration has its individuality, but some have more than others.

In the old days a distinction was drawn between what was called a "grand" and an "ordinary" Commemoration. This year, until the last moment, the *Encaenia* bade fair to be "ordinary" and quiet, but the presence of Royalty makes grandeur, excitement, and attraction, and the list of Doctors, if small, is certainly interesting.

"Show Sunday" this year was rendered conspicuous by a "record." For the first time in history the sermon, an admirable and most appropriate one, was preached by the "Worshipful the Reverend the Mayor of Oxford," Mr. W. E. Sherwood.

THE NEW DOCTORS.

The theatre filled with Doctors and ladies, graduates and undergraduates and their fair guests, is always a stately and a pretty sight. The presentations were made by the Public Orator, Mr. A. D. Godley.

First came the young Duke of Saxe-Coburg, whose father, the Duke of Albany, is still remembered with pleasure and interest by older Oxford men. As the Orator said:—

Saxe-Coburg was hardly a foreign country, and the University both honoured the Prince for himself and revived in him the memory of his father.

Next followed the American Ambassador, Mr. W. H. Page.

England and America (said the Orator) had arrived at the hundredth year of unbroken peace. Cecil Rhodes had created a new tie between them, and Mr. Page, like his predecessor, was eminently qualified by his accomplishments for academic distinction.

Then all eyes turned to a figure of special interest, Lord Bryce, who for something like a quarter of a century, as many will remember, was himself the presenter for degrees on this occasion. The Orator spoke

of his manifold activity as professor, historian, diplomatist, and mountaineer. His candour had only increased his popularity as England's representative.

Next appeared a German jurist, Geheimrat Dr. Ludwig Mitteis, Professor of Law in the University of Leipzig, practical and a theoretical jurist. He was followed by Dr. Richard Strauss, who wore the gown, the most beautiful of all the Doctors' robes, of crimson silk and cream-coloured brocade, that of the Doctor of Music, *Doctoris non enarrabile tegmen*. Mr. Godley spoke of his well-known works *Elektra*, the *Sinfonia Domestica*, and the *Legend of Joseph* as revealing unknown and unsuspected harmonies and possibilities.

After presenting his last Doctor the Public Orator slipped round to the rostrum to deliver the "Creweian Oration" on the events of the year. These are always of a mingled strain, some glad, some sad. The shadow cast by the heavy and recent loss of the Senior Burgess could not but be felt.

THE CREWEIAN ORATION.

After paying the due tribute to the memory of Nathaniel Lord Crewe, the PUBLIC ORATOR said that he could not refrain from deploring the course of events, "quae neque laudari possunt neque praeteriri." The passage of the Parliament Act and subsequent political transactions, had brought Ireland to the verge of civil war; the country's only hope lay in rulers, if such could be found, even now, "qui patriam partibus anteferre possunt." In England, female criminals, "Furiae quaedam," were burning houses and churches; if imprisoned, they were ordered by Mrs. Pankhurst to obtain liberation by refusing food:—

"Furiarum maxima juxta
"Accubat et manibus prohibet contingere mensas."

Observing that in the midst of a crisis the University and the country had lost one of their wisest counsellors, the speaker eulogized the many-sided usefulness of Sir William Anson, that model of a good servant of Oxford and the State. Speaking of other losses among residents, he alluded to the renowned Latin scholarship of the late Professor Robinson Ellis, as well as that "mordax simplicitas" with which the Professor "res et homines velut imprudens acu tangebat"; to the learning and devotion of Canon Driver, the scientific and administrative ability and personal popularity of Professor Gotch, and the unostentatious virtues of Mr. W. H. Forbes. Many non-residents, too, had died, perhaps the most notable being Bishop Tucker, of Uganda, and Sir Hubert Herkomer, formerly Slade Professor, whose works are with us.

The Orator proceeded to welcome new holders of offices vacated by death or resignation. The new Vice-Chancellor, "nomine et ingenio validus," had succeeded, "laudando laudandus," to the Principal of Brasenose, whose "suavitas et constantia" in office would long be remembered.

On a brief survey of the University legislation of the past year, it seemed that the time occupied was more considerable than the results: "nunquam tantum temporis nihil agendo perdidimus." Changes in the constitution of the Hebdomadal Council had been defeated by habitual advocates of change; "adeo plerique jura aliena contemnunt, sua maximi aes'imant." The Responsions Statute, thought by some to facilitate the return of Astraea, had failed to please the University. There was a rumour of legislation conferring degrees on women: much good might it do them! "Quod si latum fuerit, utinam tam beatae sint illae quam se B.A. tas (aut etiam M.A. tas) fore existimant!"

Some allusion was made to changed methods of street traffic. Motor 'buses (Bi? or Bures?) had captivated the Oxford public, partly owing to the enterprise of a citizen, to whom the Orator appeared to refer in a paronomastic fashion. For a time "popellus nihil nisi Bos locutus est." These vehicles were now by law established, not without "pulveris exigui jactus," and a good deal of mud into the bargain.

The Orator concluded by congratulating the University on the continued residence of his Royal Highness the Prince of Wales. He had shared fully in its life, and whenever he left it he would carry with him its warmest wishes. It was enough for Oxford to have been allowed in some degree to assist in educating the Prince for the high duties of sovereignty.

The oration over, the recitation of prize compositions followed, ending, by custom, with the Newdigate poem on the touching and pretty story of the death of Sophocles, well rendered by Mr. R. W. Stirling, of Pembroke.

Then the Vice-Chancellor dissolved the Convocation, and the assembly streamed out. Not a few as they passed All Souls College—standing sad and silent, all its usual hospitalities omitted for the year—felt that for them at any rate Commemoration, and even Oxford, could hardly be the same again.

"INCIPIENT INSANITY."

TO THE EDITOR OF THE TIMES.

Sir,—In the article on "Incipient Insanity" in your issue of June 20 it is stated that "the sufferer himself is generally silent, he dare not clearly express his fears even to himself. He is ashamed to take counsel frankly with those who could help him." This is no doubt true in the majority of cases of incipient insanity, but it must not be forgotten that there are many, the subjects of mental disorder, who do appreciate their condition and who take counsel with their doctor. They are not insane in the legal sense of the word, but they are the subjects of a mental disease from a physician's point of view. If rich, the matter is not one of so great difficulty as if poor. To the latter no general hospital will open its doors, and the county asylum cannot assist them.

A simple measure which would certainly be very helpful is long overdue, namely, to add to the Lunacy Acts a clause permitting the public asylums to receive voluntary boarders. This is at present lawful as regards private asylums and registered hospitals. During the year 1912 there were admitted into the registered hospitals of England and Wales 918 certified patients and 228 voluntary boarders.

The "stigma" of being in an institution for the insane does not prevent those able to pay from applying for relief. Why should not the poor have the same opportunities?

I am, Sir, your obedient servant,
R. H. STEEN.
City of London Mental Hospital, Dartford, Kent.

THE COLLEGE OF THE "WEST COUNTRY."

SEXCENTENARY OF EXETER.

Exeter College, which is to-day celebrating its sexcentenary, has been pre-eminently in the truest sense the college of the "West Country." Founded in 1314 by Walter de Stapledon, Bishop of Exeter, Exeter has maintained through 600 years much of its original character. Its best historian significantly was a Cornishman, the late Rev. Charles William Boase, a pioneer in modern historical study and research. The object of the founder, as he tells us, was to pass a number of men rapidly through a university training for Holy Orders, and for five centuries and a half at least Exeter fulfilled this function. It has been a college remarkable for the number of its students as well as for their quality. Poorly endowed, it has encouraged them, like other Spartan mothers, to push their way in the world, and they have done so with success in every walk of life.

Few colleges with only 14 Fellows would have shown so many of eminent distinction in the early 'seventies, when the roll included Dr. William Sewell, the founder of Radley; Dr. Ince, late Regius Professor of Divinity; Mr. Boase himself; Dr. Jackson, until the other day Rector of his college; Mr. Ingram Bywater, the most learned Greek scholar in England of recent days; Mr. Henry Francis Pelham, afterwards President of Trinity and Camden Professor; Mr. Arthur Donkin, whose rare memory still lingers; and Sir Edwin Ray Lankester; while among the remainder the well-known "Tommy" Sheppard, Mr. C. E. Hammond, Mr. C. J. C. Price, Mr. P. F. Willert, and Mr. George Nutt, if a little less distinguished, were each and all men of mark.

A society which could display within a few years in its list of Honorary Fellows Lord Coleridge, Mr. Frowde, Sir Edward Burne-Jones, William Morris, Archbishop Temple, Bishop Ridding, Mr. H. F. Tozer, Professor Bywater, Professor Pelham, Sir Hubert Parry, and Sir E. Ray Lankester may well contend that its *alumni* will bear comparison with that of any foundaton of whatever character and size.

The college, too, has been strenuous in other directions. It is one of those which has been frequently and at different periods Head of the river and has produced not a few oarsmen of great note. If the colleges were to be "classed" by the number of University oarsmen they have produced, Exeter, the seventh in the total list, might claim to be in the first class.

Again, if she does not possess such large or ample grounds and gardens as some of her sisters, Exeter may still be called fortunate in her central and convenient situation, nestling under the shadow of the Bodleian, to whose outlook her beautiful Fellows' garden presents a delightful greenery.

The Hall has now been rendered singularly handsome and interesting by the embellishments of recent benefactors. Already one of the most spacious and imposing in Oxford, it has been converted, by the generosity of old members, into a beautiful memorial of the history of the college. Exeter now has "her prophets blazoned on her panes," and a splendid pageant and pictorial chronicle they form.

PRECEDENCE IN THE CITY.

A dinner was given last night by the Merchant Taylors' Company in honour of the Skinners' Company. In 1484 there was a dispute between these two Companies as to which should have precedence, and in April of that year Lord Mayor Sir Robert Billesden issued an award in settlement of the question, one of the articles of which was that each Company should invite the other to dine with them in alternate years. Last night it was the turn of the Merchant Taylors' Company to be the hosts. Mr. C. G. Kekewich (the Master) presided, and the Master (Mr. E. H. Cartwright) and the wardens of the Skinners' Company were present, the other guests including:—

Lord Aldenham, Mr. Justice Sargant, Mr. Justice Astbury, Sir Thomas Elliott (Master of the Mint), Sir Joseph Larmor, M.P., Sir Aston Webb, Sir Squire Bancroft, Colonel Sir Aubone Fife, Sir Melvill Beachcroft (Master of the Clothworkers' Company), and the Masters of other City Companies.

The CHAIRMAN, in proposing the health of the Skinners' Company, said he used to think it hardly possible that two Companies such as theirs should have quarrelled as to who should go first in the Lord Mayor's Show, but his opinion had lately undergone a change, for he had read in the papers of an attempt on the part of a corporate body created by statute only some 25 years ago to take precedence of the great City of London. After that one could believe anything.

The MASTER of the SKINNERS' COMPANY responded.

SOCIETY OF APOTHECARIES OF LONDON.—The diploma of the society, entitling them to practise medicine, surgery, and midwifery, has been granted to G. Mes and C. Ward.

The Skinners' Company have made a grant of 25 guineas to the general funds of the National Trust.

LIFE IN LONDON.

A COUNTY COUNCIL EPITOME.

THE MOVEMENT OUTWARDS.

The 23rd volume of London statistics published yesterday by the London County Council forms a valuable epitome of the life and administration of the County, and of those places which lie outside the administrative area and are designated "Extra London." The volume is admirably compiled and, particularly in the case of the vital statistics, illuminating comparisons are furnished with other English and European towns.

For some of the most interesting tables reference has been made to the Registrar-General's report on the Census of 1911. From this source material has been available to illustrate the general movement of population from the central to the more rural areas. It is noteworthy that in the decennium 1901-1911 there was a net loss by migration from the County of more than half a million persons. The figures show:—

Administrative County.—Net loss by migration, 553,200.

Extra London.—Net gain by migration, 363,000.

In spite of this migration the average density of population in London is approximately eight times as great, as that in Extra London, and those who have noted the effect of congestion of population on health will note the migration figures with satisfaction. It is particularly satisfactory to observe that the greatest losses by migration occurred in the most densely populated districts such as Stepney and Southwark.

Within the London area Hampstead has a death-rate of only 9·8 per 1,000. The highest figure is reached by Finsbury with 18·8. The rates for eight foreign capitals show that only two—Amsterdam (11·2) and Brussels (13·5)—have a lower death-rate than London.

It is interesting to note that of the population of London 30 per cent. were born outside the County. The foreigners in London number 153,064, of whom 56,016 live in Stepney. In view of this one may observe that Stepney holds the premier place for big families, with 4·46 persons on the average in each. The "occupations" volume of the Census shows that the chief industry in which London's foreigners engage is dress. More than 28 per cent. of the males employed in this industry are foreigners.

The facilities in London for open-air recreation are shown in a table of "parks and open spaces." Nearly 9 per cent. of the total area of London is occupied by open spaces, but the proportion varies very considerably in different boroughs. More than a quarter of the area of Westminster, 23 per cent. of Marylebone, and 18 per cent. of Hampstead is open space. On the other hand, Finsbury, Stepney, and Shoreditch, all of which have very high percentages of overcrowding, have each less than 2 per cent. of open space. While in Hampstead there is one acre of open space per 210 persons, Southwark has one acre for every 14,620 of population.

Advertising

The Times was founded as an advertising sheet. John Walter declared one of his objects as being 'To facilitate the commercial intercourse between the different parts of the community through the channel of advertisements'.

The great growth of advertising in the nineteenth century freed the press from political subsidy and venality. Because of its advertising *The Times* became free to publish what it wanted without having to please a paymaster. Advertisements made The Thunderer. Henri de Blowitz, the eminent *Times* foreign correspondent, by his trade inclined to prefer editorial copy to advertisements, observed: 'It is the English advertiser who permits the English journal to be so well edited, so well written, so high-minded'.

Below Mr Pickwick awards Erasmic membership of the Pickwick Club, September 1916.

Bottom Cigar advertisement spans four columns, alongside the Roll of Honour casualty lists, October 1916.

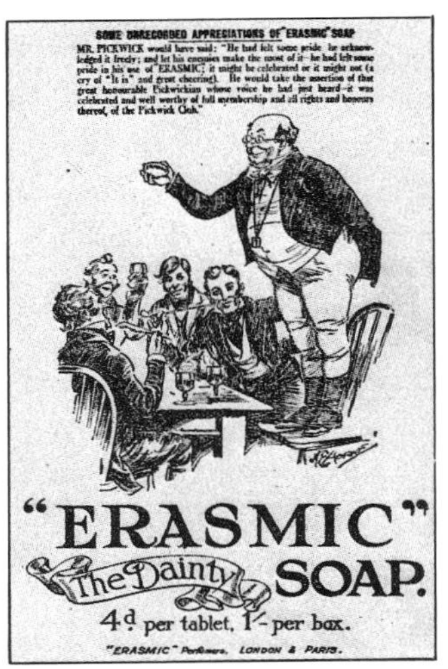
SOME UNRECORDED APPRECIATIONS OF "ERASMIC" SOAP

MR. PICKWICK would have said: "He had felt some pride he acknowledged it freely; and let his enemies make the most of it—he had felt some pride in his use of "ERASMIC"; it might be celebrated or it might not (a cry of "It is" and great cheering). He would take the assertion of that great honourable Pickwickian whose voice he had just heard—it was celebrated and well worthy of full membership and all rights and honours thereof, of the Pickwick Club."

"ERASMIC" The Dainty SOAP.

4d. per tablet, 1/- per box.

"ERASMIC" Perfumers. LONDON & PARIS.

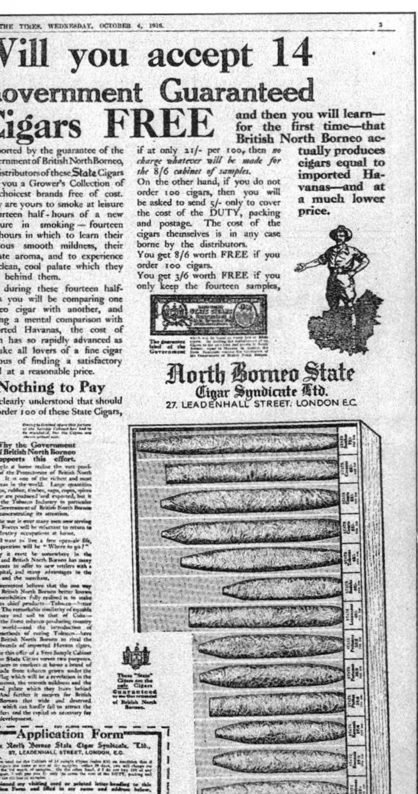
THE TIMES, WEDNESDAY, OCTOBER 4, 1916.

Will you accept 14 Government Guaranteed Cigars FREE

and then you will learn—for the first time—that British North Borneo actually produces cigars equal to imported Havanas—and at a much lower price.

if at only 21/- per 100, then *no charge whatever will be made for the 8/6 cabinet of samples.*

On the other hand, if you do not order 100 cigars, then you will be asked to send 5/- only to cover the cost of the DUTY, packing and postage. The cost of the cigars themselves is in any case borne by the distributors.

You get 8/6 worth FREE if you order 100 cigars.

You get 3/6 worth FREE if you only keep the fourteen samples,

Nothing to Pay

Why the Government of British North Borneo supports this effort.

North Borneo State Cigar Syndicate Ltd.

27. LEADENHALL STREET, LONDON E.C.

Application Form

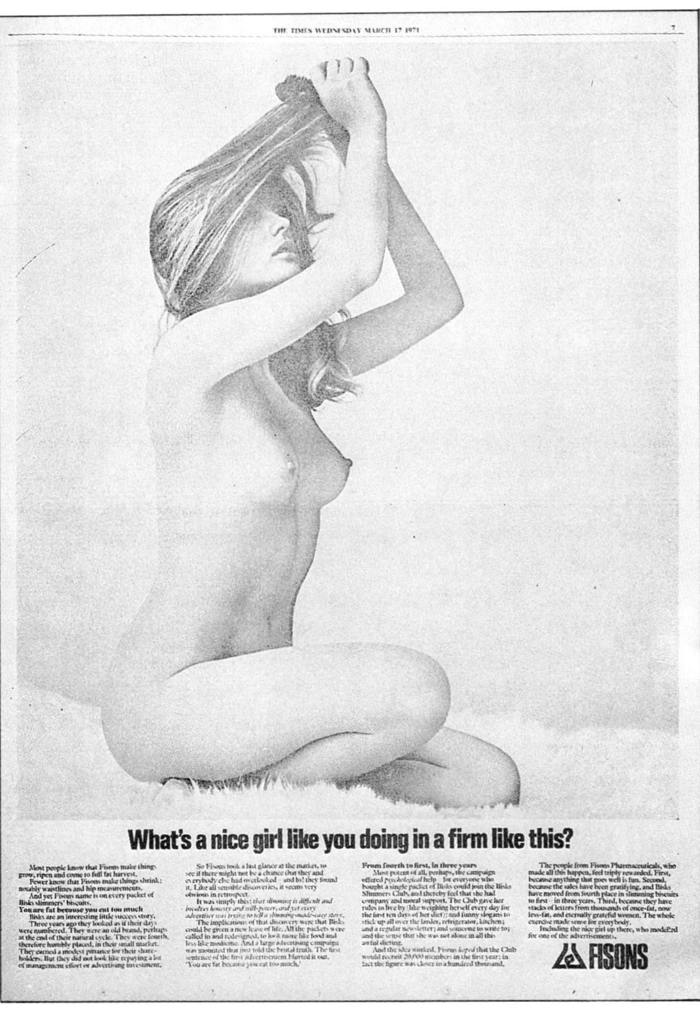

Above right First advertisement to feature a nude, 17 March 1971.

Right BEA, October 1947.

Far right Michelin, October 1947.

It was the ambition of newspaper proprietors, in those salad days as now, to fill their papers with advertisements. When John Walter went into journalism, his newspaper gave the theatres first position in column 1 on the front page, the royal theatres being put at the head of the first column (see p. 11). Astley's Amphitheatre was advertised, 'Capital fire-work entertainments, grand general displays of manly activity, on foot, on horseback or on the solid ground'. Other circus announcements followed. Booksellers', shipping and commercial notices, and official announcements of the Post Office, the Ordnance Office and other departments, made up the first page. As a rule the news occupied less than half the available space in the pristine *Times*. On special occasions, for instance an important trial or a particularly scandalous inquiry, advertisements were reduced to make space.

But on ordinary days the proprietor covered his first and fourth pages completely with advertising, and sprinkled ads throughout the two inside pages. The back page (page 4) generally consisted of notices of auction sales, of property advertisements, horses, carriages, and so on.

There was often a deficiency of 'ads', as they were called even in the eighteenth century. When this happened, the proprietor took the situation philosophically and stated in a conspicuous place in the paper that, owing to the arrival of an important foreign dispatch, he sadly had to disappoint his numerous advertisement customers whose announcements, they could be assured, would be printed as soon as the pressure of foreign intelligence was relieved. Another disingenuous device (not unknown today), resorted to for the sake of appearance and to encourage business by example, was to copy the advertising in a prosperous contemporary. It was better to give advertisements free than to have none. In an emergency Walter inserted the official announcements of the Victualling Office without authority, and by applying political pressure afterwards, brought the Minister to pay for the insertion.

By 1829 eight-page papers had often been published to contain all the ads, and *The Times* had become established as an advertising medium. On 1 January 1829 the first whole-page ad appeared. It was devoted to puffing Edmund Lodge's book *Portraits and Memories of the most Illustrious Personages of British History*. The occasion was deemed worthy of a puff in the news columns: 'A whole page of *The Times* today is filled with an advertisement containing a detailed description of one of those magnificent enterprises of individual labour and talent which so proudly distinguishes this country'. In the trade we call that 'a house job'.

On 29 December 1834 an advertisement consisting of more than five thousand names of merchants, bankers, traders, shipowners and other City businessmen occupied four pages, 'for the purpose of renewing the expression of our dutiful and loyal attachment to Your Majesty's Person and Crown'. It would have cost about £250.

The biggest advertisement yet to appear in *The Times* occupied nine full pages of the issue of 12 December 1910. It was not a riveting read, consisting of the numbers of Mexican Five Per Cent Loan Bonds, nearly ten thousand of them in all.

On 17 March 1971 *Times* ads broke another figure. Readers opened the paper to see an attractive girl in the nude (decorously sideways, not frontal) gracing all of page 3. The advertiser was the firm of Fison's. The company took all the display space in the paper that day to promote its full range of products: pig injections, insecticides, shampoo, fertilizers, and slimming biscuits, which must be taken to justify the naked lady. For full measure Fison's also took two large spaces in the Situations Vacant columns.

The advertising agency responsible for placing the ads wanted the nude to be in colour. But this was thought to be going too far, and the then editor firmly resisted the proposal.

Nevertheless, even in sober sub-fusc and white, the nude aroused plenty of publicity. Fleet Street and radio and television seized on this instance of *The Times* letting its knickers down. There were no letters of protest. The few that were sent to the editor on the subject were ribald. The phrase 'Topless People Take *The Times*' had a brief vogue. All copies of the issue were sold out, and for weeks after requests for copies were being received from many parts of the world. The model, Vivian Neves, was in the West Indies on 17 March. Like Byron, she awoke one morning and found herself famous.

A typical page of advertisements from the mid-nineteenth century, ranging from situations vacant to patent hair dye, guaranteeing 'No more green or purple dyed hair'.
14 JANUARY 1858

PIANOFORTES for the VACATION, to HIRE.—PEACHY's first-class.—73, Bishopsgate-street within.

PIANOFORTES.——CRAMER, BEALE, and Co. have a great variety by all makers, new and second-hand, for SALE or HIRE.—201, Regent-street.

PIANOFORTE.—For SALE, a decided bargain, a superior made 6¾-octave SEMI-COTTAGE, in neat rosewood case, with all the latest improvements. Price only 18 guineas; cost 35 guineas a few months back. To be seen at 122, Drummond-street, Euston-square.

PIANOFORTE.—An exquisitely beautiful two-pedal foreign walnut OBLIQUE GRAND, with Erard's patent check action, full compass, and quite new, for DISPOSAL, with unexceptionable warranty.—4, Great Marlborough-street, Regent-street, W.

PIANOFORTE.—A superior and remarkably fine brilliant-toned walnut COTTAGE, 6¾-octaves, carved front, and all latest improvements; only used four months; will be sold at a very low price for cash. So very superior a piano seldom to be met with. To be seen at Mr. Pain's, 1, Bishopsgate-street within, near Cornhill.

PIANOFORTE.—A lady, who has just given up her house, is desirous of DISPOSING OF a magnificent-toned ROSEWOOD OBLIQUE GRAND, (3 ft. 9 in. high, 5 ft. wide) full compass and nearly new. Worth attention. All the recent improvements. Address Zeta, or apply at 15, Frith-street, Soho, middle bell.

PIANOFORTE.—A fine brilliant-toned COTTAGE, in handsome walnut case, new only a few months ago, the property of a gentleman, who, having no further use for it, wishes to DISPOSE OF it. Apply at 28, Upper Montagu-street, Montagu-square, St. Marylebone.

PIANOFORTE for SALE, a bargain—a superior 6¾ rosewood Cottage, with fret work, carvings, metallic plate, reeded cheeks, handsome figured wood, with all the latest improvements, price 16 guineas, cash being wanted. Apply at 26, Southampton-street, Pentonville-road. Warranted.

PIANOFORTES for AUSTRALIA, the West Indies, and other colonies.—D'ALMAINE and Co.'s ROYAL PIANOFORTES, 6¾-octaves, all the latest improvements, mahogany, zebra, or rosewood. 25 guineas each. Warranted.—D'Almaine and Co., 20, Soho-square; established 1785.

PIANOFORTES and HARMONIUMS for SALE, also for Hire, from 10s. a month, with option to purchase by periodical payments if required. FREDERICK LYON warrants his pianos. Second-hands by Broadwood, &c. Harmoniums from 10 guineas.—26, Charles-street, Berners-street, Oxford-street. Estab. 1808.

PIANOFORTES, 17 guineas each, compass 6¾ oc-taves, rosewood cases, and elegant enough for any drawing room. These instruments combine every modern improvement, have the metallic plate and bolts, and are well adapted for extreme climates.—P. HOLCOMBE, manufacturer, 38, Berners-street, Oxford-street.

PIANOFORTES and HARMONIUMS.—GEO. LUFF and SON have the largest stock in London, for SALE or HIRE, with easy terms of purchase. Price from £10 to £100. Tuners sent on the shortest notice.—103, Great Russell-street, Bloomsbury, W.C.

PIANOFORTES for Government Employés, Clerks, and others. Hire saved by purchasing by instalments of not less than £5 per quarter. This offer not only guarantees the soundness of manufacture, but is the first of its kind. Supplied immediately (personal security only required) upon application to MOUTRIE and Co., manufacturers, King-street, Holborn, W.C. From 21 guineas for cash.

PIANOFORTES EXTRAORDINARY.—At MOORE and MOORE's, 104, Bishopsgate-street within. These are first-class pianos, of rare excellence, possessing exquisite improvements recently applied, which effect a grand, a pure, and beautiful quality of tone that stands unrivalled. Prices from 18 guineas. First-class pianos for hire, with easy terms of purchase.

PIANOFORTES, 15 guineas.—J. MANKTELOW's REGISTERED PICCOLO PIANOFORTE, warranted to possess the same action, tone, touch, and durability as the most expensive instruments. Every other description of cottage and piccolo pianofortes at greatly reduced prices.—12, Huntley-street, Francis-street, Tottenham-court-road.

COLLARD and COLLARD.—A first-rate ROSE-WOOD PICCOLO PIANOFORTE, by the abovementioned makers, with 6¾ octaves, and all the modern improvements, equal to new, to be SOLD, a bargain.—William Sprague, 7, Finsbury-pavement.

PICCOLO PIANO for immediate SALE, for 19 guineas. Three months' trial allowed if required. This is a very sweet and brilliant-toned rosewood piccolo, 6¾-octaves, with all the recent improvements, quite new. To be seen at Mr. Robinson's, 6, Francis-place, Stamford-road, Kingsland.

ERARD's PIANOS.—To be SOLD, at very advan-tageous prices, a splendid 7-octave PATENT REPETITION GRAND, of rich and powerful tone, cost 165 guineas, selected by Thalberg; and a first-rate Patent Oblique Cottage, cost 85 guineas. Both are in elegant cases, and like new in every respect, having been scarcely used.—Messrs. J. COOPER and Co.'s manufactory, 43, Moorgate-street, Bank. Also Three superior Semi-Grands, by Broadwood, &c., at low prices; and an elegant rosewood Cottage, price 25 guineas.

COTTAGE PIANO, an unprecedented bargain. Splendid rosewood case, beautifully carved, patent double-action, French fall, fretwork, metallic plate, three pedals, 6¾-octaves, and every improvement. It is sufficiently elegant for any drawing room, and the tone is powerful, rich, and brilliant. It has extra bolts and bracings for an extreme climate, and, from its soundness, strength, and many beauties, is well adapted for a professor. It has been in use only five months, but will be sold, through peculiar circumstances, for 27 guineas, less than half its original price. A warranty with it. To be seen at 322, Regent-street, nearly opposite the Polytechnic.

HARMONIUM for SALE, a bargain, very sweet and powerful toned, containing 10 stops—clarionet, flute, sourdine, bourdon, cor-Anglais, grand jeu, expression, tremulo, and two fortes. Apply to A. B., at the shoe warehouse, 18, Sun-street, Bishopsgate, E.C.

DEBAIN's superior HARMONIUMS.—(Fournis-seur de S. M. l'Empereur Napoleon III. et de S. M. la Reine d'Angleterre).—Entrepot, 41, Queen-street, Cannon-street west, St. Paul's, London.

THE NEW ALEXANDRE HARMONIUM for the DRAWING ROOM.—ALEXANDRE and SON have just taken out a new patent for the DRAWING ROOM HARMONIUM, which effects the greatest improvement they have ever made in the instrument. The drawing room models will be found of a softer, purer, and in all respects more agreeable tone than any other instruments. They have a perfect and easy means of producing a diminuendo or crescendo on any one note or more; the bass can be perfectly subdued, without even the use of the expression stop, the great difficulty in other harmoniums. To each of the new models an additional blower is attached at the back, so that the wind can be supplied (if preferred) by a second person, and still, under the new patent, the performer can play with perfect expression. The drawing room model is made in three varieties:—1. Three stops, percussion action, additional blower, and in rosewood case, 25 guineas; No. 2. Eight stops, ditto, 35 guineas; No. 3. 16 stops, ditto, Voix Céleste, &c. (the best harmonium that can be made), 60 guineas. Messrs. Chappell have an enormous stock of the six guinea harmoniums, and of all varieties of the ordinary kind, which are perfect for the church, school, hall, or concert room. Full descriptive lists of harmoniums and of pianofortes sent upon application to Chappell and Co., 49 and 50, New Bond-street, and 13, George-street, Hanover-square.

CHRISTMAS PARTIES.—The ROYAL CHORE-MUSICON, for quadrille parties, combining the effects of a small orchestra in a single instrument, at the command of one performer. For terms of hire, in town or country, apply to Robt. W. Ollivier, 19, Old Bond-street, where Mr. Charles Compton will exhibit the instrument daily, at 4 o'clock.

ORGAN.—For SALE, after the month of March next, a powerful BARREL ORGAN, having 12 stops, and playing 40 psalm and hymn tunes. For particulars apply to J. B., 53, Margaret-street, Cavendish-square, W.

A Superior FINGER ORGAN, by Bishop, for SALE. It consists of two rows of keys, 4½ octaves C to F, 8 stops with coupler, 3 composition pedals, swell throughout, and 3 appliances for blowing, in mahogany case, with silk and gilt front pipes; admirably adapted to a small chapel or drawing room. Terms and full particulars may be obtained, and the instrument seen, at Robert W. Ollivier's, musical instrument repository, 19, Old Bond-street, Piccadilly.

MUSICAL BOX DEPOT, 54, Cornhill, London, for the sale of SWISS MUSICAL INSTRUMENTS, made by the celebrated Messrs. Nicole, Frères, of Geneva. Large size, four airs, 14 in. long, £4; six airs, 18 in. long, £6 6s.; eight airs, 20 in. long, £8; and 12 airs, 20½ in. long, £12 12s. Containing selections from the most eminent composers, including popular, national, and operatic airs, together with hymns and other sacred music. Also a variety of Swiss musical snuff-boxes, playing two tunes, 14s. 6d. and 18s.; three tunes, 30s.; and four tunes, 40s. each. Printed lists of tunes, &c., may be had gratis and sent post free on application.

FURNITURE and PIANO, a bargain, fine walnut, warranted manufacture, nearly new, to be SOLD for half their value; consisting of a drawing room suite of chaste and elegant design, including a large size brilliant plate chimney-glass in costly unique frame, a magnificent cheffonier with richly carved back and doors fitted with best silvered plate-glass and marble top, superior centre table on pillar and handsomely carved claws, occasional or ladies' writing and fancy tables, six solid, elegantly carved chairs in rich silk, a superior spring stuffed settee, easy and Victoria chairs en suite, with extra lined loose cases, two fancy occasional chairs, and a handsome what-not. Price for the whole suite 46 guineas. The piano semi-cottage, nearly 7 octaves, of powerful and unusually brilliant and sweet tone, with all the most recent improvements, by an eminent maker. Price 20 guineas. N.B. Also a very superior Set of modern Dining Room Furniture, of fine Spanish mahogany, in best morocco, 40 guineas. To be seen at LEWIN CRAWCOUR and Co.'s, upholsterers, 7, Queen's-buildings, Knightsbridge, seven doors west of Sloane-street.

WRITING and LIBRARY TABLES, Bookcases, and every article of household and office furniture, of the best description, second-hand, for SALE, at PRIEST's extensive furniture warehouses, Tudor-st., Blackfriars-bridge, city. Established 35 years.

ELEGANT DRAWING ROOM FURNITURE.— All the newest and most novel materials for curtains and coverings, at CLEMENT, GEORGE, and Co.'s, cabinet, upholstery, carpet, and bedding manufactory, 33, Oxford-street, W.

SECOND-HAND FURNITURE.——ALFRED GREEN has several first-class articles taken in exchange in the course of business (including a splendid set of oak dining room furniture) to be disposed of very cheap, at his cabinet and upholstery manufactory and show rooms, 25, Baker-street, Portman-square, W.

WALNUT DRAWING-ROOM SUITE of FUR-NITURE, in first-rate condition, only used a few months, consisting of six superb cabriole chairs and spring-stuffed settee, and two easy chairs, en suite, covered in rich silk and chintz, loose covers, a fine walnutwood loo table on carved pillar and claws, occasional table, a 5-feet cheffonier with marble slabs and silvered plate-glass back and doors, and a large-sized chimney-glass in gilt frame; for 42 guineas. To be seen at R. Green and Co.'s, upholsterers, 204, Oxford-street, W.

EXTRAORDINARY DISPLAY of NEW and SECOND-HAND FURNITURE, covering a space of more than 20,000 square feet.—J. DENT and Co., proprietors of the Great Western Furniture Bazaar, 30, 31, 32, and 29, Crawford-street, Baker-street, beg most respectfully to invite attention of purchasers of any description of FURNITURE to their at present unrivalled stock, consisting of entire suites of drawing, dining, and bed room furniture, manufactured by the best houses in London, which they have just purchased from several noblemen and gentlemen leaving England, under such circumstances as enable them to offer any portion at less than one-third of its original cost. Every article warranted, and the money returned if not approved of.—Principal entrance, 29, Crawford-street, Baker-street.

MATTRESSES, warranted not to Wear Hollow in the Middle.—HEAL and SON have patented an improvement in the manufacture of mattresses, which prevents the material felting into a mass, as it does in all mattresses made in the ordinary way. The patent mattresses are made of the very best wool and horse-hair only, are rather thicker than usual, and the prices are but a trifle higher than other good mattresses. Their illustrated catalogue of bedsteads, bedding, and bed-room furniture contains also the prices of their patent mattresses, and is sent free by post.—Heal and Son, 196, Tottenham-court-road, W.

CHINTZES 3½d. per YARD, warranted fast colours at ALFRED GREEN's upholstery and general furnishing warehouse, 25, Baker-street, W. Being bought during the temporary panic they are equal to those usually sold at 9d. and 1s. a yard.

CARPETS.—VINCENT ROBINSON and Co., manufacturers and importers of Brussels, Turkey, Axminster, Tournay, Indian, Persian, and all other carpets in the best designs, and most moderate prices.—38, Welbeck-street, Cavendish-square.

CARPETS.——HARVEY, NICHOLS, and Co., Knightsbridge, have purchased an immense STOCK of BRUSSELS CARPETS, amounting to nearly £10,000, for cash. They are all first class goods, manufactured to order for one of the largest houses in New York, but, owing to the depression in the money market, were unable to fulfil their engagements. To be sold for cash only.

CARPETS.—Newest patterns and most elegant de-signs in tapestry.—Carpets, 2s. 4½d. per yard, patent felts, 2s. 3d., and every other article in furniture requisite for furnishing any class of house equally cheap. The whole warranted. The patent bedstead without a screw, 14s. 9d. each, full size. W. Waine, 3, 4, and 5, Newington-butts. N.B. An inspection of the extensive stock before purchasing elsewhere is respectfully solicited.

LONDON CARPET WAREHOUSE.—WAUGH and SON, 3 and 4, Goodge-street.

MAGNIFICENT BRUSSELS CARPETS, 3s. 3d. —MAPLES and Co., 145, Tottenham-court-road.

DIRTY TURKEY CARPETS, no matter how dirty or stained, pure washed, equal to new, by the METROPOLITAN STEAM WASHING and DYEING COMPANY, 17, Wharf-road, City-road, N. Lists forwarded on application to any part of England.

EIGHT HUNDRED PIECES of BRUSSELS, Tapestry, and Velvet Pile CARPETS, reduced 1s. per yard, at DRUCE and Co.'s, 58, 68, and 69, Baker-street. These are the most extensive show-rooms and furniture galleries in London, containing an unrivalled stock of cabinet furniture, bedsteads, and bedding, &c., with the prices marked in plain figures. A warranty for 12 months is given.

BRUSSELS CARPETS.—WILLIAM TARN and Co., Newington-causeway and New Kent-road, have purchased for cash, during the late commercial panic, several thousand pounds' worth of the best BRUSSELS CARPETS. The patterns and qualities are very choice, and the prices will be from 2s. 6d. to 3s. 9d. a yard, intended when in the looms, three months since, to realize from 3s. 6d. to 5s. a yard.

BENZINE COLLAS cleans and removes grease from gloves, silks, ribands, cloths, &c. In bottles, 1s. 6d., of all chymists and perfumers; and at the depôt, 114, Great Russell-street, Bloomsbury.

COALS.—Best Silkstone, 20s.; Wall's-end, 24s.; good kitchen coal, 18s.; small, 12s.; coke, 12s.—JOSEPH WOODWARD, Great Northern, 4, King's-cross.

COALS.——WIGAN's WALL's-END, thoroughly screened, at 24s. per ton (cash), equal to any charged 30s. per ton; Moira coal, for bed rooms, at 24s.—H. CASE and Co., Grand Junction-wharf, Paddington.

COALS, 21s.—LLOYD's superior large Wall's-end COALS, the most economical that can be obtained, only 21s. per ton, for cash on delivery; coke, 13s. per chaldron. Consigned solely to R. Lloyd, Bridge-wharf, Hampstead-road.

COALS, 21s.—Best Derbyshire, 21s.; Silkstone large house coals, 22s. per ton, delivered free. Also every other description of coals, at lowest prices. Cash only. Coke, 14s. Consigned to F. FILBELL, 11, Wharf, City-road.

COALS, 18s. per ton, Yorkshire; Derbyshire, 20s. 6d.; Silkstone, 21s. 6d.; Claycross, 22s.; best, 26s. Cash; and care should be taken to address T. JONES, Manager, Northern and Eastern Railway Coal-offices, 32, Great Marlborough-street, Regent-street, W., or 127, Albany-street, Regent's-park, N.W.

COALS, 21s.—By North-Western Railway.—SILK-STONE COALS, equal in quality to the best Wall's-end, 23s. per ton; best Derbyshire house, 21s. per ton; coke, 13s. per chaldron. Terms cash.—North-Western Railway coal office, Camden town.—RICKETT, SMITH, and Co. (late T. Whittle, Manager.)

COALS.—Great Western Railway.—Cash prices, de-livered within three miles of the station:—Best screened yard coal, as supplied to Her Majesty, 23s. per ton; second quality, 18s. per ton. All orders to be addressed to the Ruabon Coal Company (Limited), Great Western Railway, Paddington.

COALS.—North London Railway Coal Department. —Best Wall's-end, Lambton's, Hetton's, or Stewart's, delivered, thoroughly screened, at 27s. per ton; Russell, Hetton, or Cassop, 25s.; Silkstone, 22s.; best Derbyshire, 20s. Cash on delivery. All orders to be addressed to Messrs. PARRY, North London Railway Station, Caledonian-road.

COALS.—Sale for the year ending 31st December, 1857, 136,000 tons.—The best COALS for steam purposes are Lord WARD's Handpicked, 18s. 6d.; nuts, 16s. 6d.; cobbles, 14s. The best coals for domestic use are the Adelaide Main, 22s.; seconds, 19s.—For cash on delivery only. Sole consignee, WILLIAM PHILLIPS, 25, Coal Exchange, E.C. Merchants supplied.

COALS, best only, screened.—Rutland-wharf, Upper Thames-street; established 1730.—J. PERCIVALL and Co. (late Cundell and Percivall), importers of the best coals only. Present cash price 28s. per ton. Screened by hand and slates picked out. N.B. J. P. and Co. have vessels alongside their wharf direct from the collieries of the Earl of Durham.

COALS.—Best Coals only.—COCKERELL and Co., coal merchants to Her Majesty. Cash price, 28s. per ton, for screened, unmixed, best COALS, to which quality their trade has been exclusively confined for the last 24 years, always holding themselves liable to the forfeiture of £500 upon proof of a single transaction in other than the best Wall's-end coals.—13, Cornhill; Purfleet-wharf, Earl-street, Blackfriars; and Eaton-wharf, Belgrave-place, Pimlico.

COALS.——LONDON and NORTH-WESTERN COAL COMPANY are now delivering, for cash, their best COALS, 26s. per ton; best Silkstone, 22s. per ton; Derbyshire, 21s.; smokeless steam, 19s. The Company strongly recommend their best Silkstone, as being a cheerful, cleanly, and durable coal, equal in quality to any Newcastle seaborne coal, producing great heat, and very few ashes.—W. BETSON, Secretary, 5, Cardine-place, Camden-town.

COALS, 21s.—FINNEY, SEAL, and Co., the Metropolitan Coal Merchants.—Annual Sale Half a Million Tons.—Pinxton Wall's-end, 21s.; Silkstone, 22s.; Stewart's or Hetton's Wall's-end, 28s. per ton, delivered to any part of London north of the Thames for net cash on delivery.—The Great West of London Coal Depot, Paddington; Thornley-wharf, Regent's-park-basin; Victoria-wharf, Millbank, Westminster; Albert-gate Coal-office, Knightsbridge; and elsewhere.

COALS, by Screw and Railway.—LEA and Co., Highbury and Kingsland Coal Depots.—Hetton's and Tees, 27s. per ton cash—the best house coals, direct from the colliery to the Poplar Docks, by the screw steamers Cochrane, Hetton, and Killingsworth; or Russell's Hetton's Wall's-end (usually sold as best coals), at 26s. per ton. Delivered screened to any part of London. Highgate, Hornsey, or Edmonton, 1s. per ton extra.—Lea and Co., chief offices, North London Railway Stations, Highbury, Islington, or Kingsland.

COALS, per Great Northern Railway.—Prices of coals delivered for cash within five miles of E. and A. PRIOR's depot, King's-cross Station:—Earl of Durham's Lambton Wall's-end, 28s.; excellent seconds, much recommended, 26s.; J. and J. Charlesworth's best Silkstone, 22s. 6d.; J. and J. Charlesworth's Newmarket, bright burning, 22s.; J. and J. Charlesworth's Tapton, 21s.; best Victoria Hartley, 19s.; Baker's Hartley, 17s.; coke, 11s. 6d. per chaldron. Steam coals supplied per contract. The above qualities delivered at like prices from the wharfs at Bishopsgate, Nine-elms, Camden, and Mile-end. To ensure delivery of the description specified care should be taken to address orders direct to Mr. J. C. Matthews (the only authorized agent to Messrs. Prior,) 23, Pratt-terrace, King's-cross.

COALS.—Caution.—Great Northern Railway Com-pany.—The Directors consider it necessary to give this public notice, that the only authorized AGENT of this Company, to whom orders should be addressed for coal brought by this railway to London, is Mr. HERBERT CLARKE, at his offices, within the King's-cross Station, and that orders so addressed only will ensure the description and quality of coal consumers desire to have.

This notice is rendered necessary by, and to counteract the deception attempted to be practised by parties having offices in several parts of London, at which they advertise the sale of coals under the pretence of being the agents of this Company, and under the names of H. J. Clark, H. Clark, Henry Clark, &c.

Again, Mr. Herbert Clarke is the sole agent of the Company, and orders for coal should be addressed to him only, at this station, or to the undersigned. By order, J. R. MOWATT, Sec. Secretary's office, King's-cross Station, London, August 5, 1857.

COKE, 12s.—Best GAS COKE, delivered 12s. per chaldron; Barnsley House Coals, thoroughly screened, 20s. per ton. Cash on delivery.—RUSSELL and Co., 43, Skinner-street, Snow-hill, E.C., and Belmont Wharf, King's-cross, N.

FOUR FIRES for ONE PENNY.—The PATENT FIREWOOD can be obtained from any oilman or grocer in or near London, at 2s. per 100. Packed for the country, 500 for 10s. Lights instantly. No paper required. Manufactory, 18, Wharf-road, City-road, N.

FIELD's PATENT PARAFFINE CANDLES from IRISH PEAT, superior in appearance and illuminating power to any candles hitherto manufactured, at the same time burning much longer. J. C. and J. FIELD beg to intimate that these elegant candles may be obtained from them at 12, Wigmore-street, Cavendish-square; in Dublin, of James Lambert, 64, Grafton-street.

DAVIES's CANDLES, 6½d. and 7d.; patent wax or sperm, 1s. 1½d. per lb.; moulds, 8½d. per lb.; best sperm, 2s. transparent wax, 2s. 2d.; composite, 9½d., 10½d., and 11½d.; fine British wax, 1s. 8½d.; British sperm, 1s. 5½d.; yellow soap, 38s., 42s., 46s., 50s. per 112 lb.; mottled, 52s.; old brown Windsor, 1s. 9d. per packet; common brown Windsor, 1s.; honey, 1s. 4d.; white Windsor 1s. 4d. For cash.—At M. P. Davies and Son's, 63, St. Martin's-lane.

FALL in NIGHT LIGHTS.——PRICE's NEW NIGHT LIGHTS, Vauxhall night lights, Belmont night lights, 5½d. per box, or 5s. per dozen boxes; Child's night lights, Albert night lights, 6d. per box, or 5s. 6d. per dozen boxes; Price's genuine composite candles, 9½d., 10½d., and 11½d. per lb.; Belmont wax and sperm candles, 1s. 1d.; transparent wax, 1s. 6d. to 2s. 3d.; spermaceti, 2s. 2d.; genuine wax, 2s. 6d. per lb. Finest Colza oil, 4s. 9d. per gallon; sperm oil, 8s.; dips, 6½d. to 7d.; moulds, 8d. For cash only. Magnum soap tablets, 6d. each.—WHITMORE and CRADDOCK, city agents to Price's Patent Candle Company, 16, Bishopsgate-street within, E.C. Priced lists sent free.

COMPOSITE HOUSEHOLD SOAP, in half-pound pieces, cut, stamped, and dried by machinery, may now be obtained, in large or small quantities, of all respectable dealers in soaps; or it will be supplied as usual direct from the City Soap Works, London, in samples boxes of 209 pieces, for 52s., carriage paid and box free. N.B. This soap, in larger chests, is now in use in many of the leading public and charitable institutions, being found in all cases where economy and convenience are studied the best household soap ever offered to the public. None is genuine but that stamped D. and W. GIBBS, City Soap Works.

COLZA OIL, 4s. 6d. per gallon; dips, 7d.; sperm, 2s. 4d.; stearine, 1s. 1d.; Belgrave, 1s. 3d.; Price's composites 9½d. and 10½d.; soaps, yellow and mottled, 37s., 42s., 46s. per 112 lb.; greaves, 15s. per cwt. Carriage free within 10 miles.—W. YOUNG, 51, Park-street, Camden-town.

NUNN's VEGETABLE (COLZA) OIL, 4s. 6d. per gallon, refined by their peculiar charcoal process, by which all impurities are intercepted, and the illuminating power vastly enhanced, rendering it so highly valuable not only for the moderateur but also for any lamps in use at the present time. Supplied only by Thos. Nunn and Sons, 21, Lamb's Conduit-street, W.C.

THE HONEST GAS METER.—N. DEFRIES' celebrated DRY GAS METER is the best—nearly 80,000 in use, from 3-lights to 2,000 ditto. They have been successfully tested during the last 15 years by the public and all the principal gas companies, and pronounced a true measure. Observe the name of "N. Defries" on the badge. Office, 145, Regent-street; manufactory, Euston-road.

TEETH.——No. 91, Fleet-street.——AMERICAN MINERAL, the best in Europe, SUPPLIED only by Mr. PATERSON, Surgeon-Dentist. A single tooth, 5s.; a complete set, £5; without extraction of roots or any painful operation, which for appearance, durability, and comfort, cannot be surpassed.

TEETH.—45, Ludgate-hill.—Mr. ALBERT, Sur-geon-Dentist, supplies TEETH without extracting stumps or causing pain. A tooth 5s.; a set from £5. Teeth filled, 2s. 6d. Caution.—Mr. A. has no other establishment, having practised in the same house 24 years.

TEETH.—21, Ludgate-hill.—BELL and FRANCIS, Surgeon-Dentists.—Newly invented SELF-ADHESIVE TEETH, which do not require any wires or ligatures, and are fitted on the tenderest gums with absolute perfection and success. A tooth from 3s. 6d.; a set, £3 10s. Decayed teeth filled, 2s. 6d. Established 1801.

TEETH.——18, New Burlington-street.——Mr. ROGERS, the old-established dentist, continues to supply his improved artificial teeth, with flexible gums, which defy detection, no springs or wires, or any painful operation required; no extraction of roots or loose teeth, which, by Mr. Rogers's scientific improvements, are rendered sound and useful for mastication. Charges moderate.

TEETH.—Observe—30, Berners-street, Oxford-street, W., the original and oldest establishment of the name in London.—Messrs. MOSELY, Surgeon-Dentists, of 30, Berners-street, Oxford-street, W., sole inventors and patentees of the new soft composition for adding a natural or soft gum to the artificial teeth, by which means all pressure and the use of ligatures are avoided, and mastication and articulation perfected.

TEETH, 2s. 6d.—Messrs. READ, Surgeon-Dentists, 5, Holles-street, Cavendish-square, and 3, Broad-street-buildings, city, supply their improved incorrodible MINERAL TEETH, on the most tender gums, without extracting stumps, or any painful operation. An upper or lower set, on pure gold plate, £5; on platina, as durable as gold, £3 10s.; a single mineral tooth, 5s.; a complete upper or lower set of osonores teeth, £1 5s.; a tooth, 2s. 6d.; stopping, 2s. 6d. All teeth supplied warranted of the purest and best description, and unless perfect satisfaction be given no fee required.

TEETH.—Treasures of Art.—Dr. Edward Cock, of Guy's Hospital, and many other medical men of eminence, have recognized the diploma of Mr. ANDRE FRESCO, Surgeon-Dentist. His improved method of fixing artificial teeth on the most tender gums, without springs or wires resembles nature so perfectly as to defy detection, and from the flexibility of the material employed, loose teeth and roots are rendered firm and useful in mastication and articulation. Charges strictly moderate.—At 9, George-street, Hanover-square, and 513, Oxford-street, next Mudie's library.

TEETH.—No. 9, Lower Grosvenor-street, Grosvenor-square (removed from 61).—By Her Majesty's Royal Letters Patent.—Newly Invented Application of Chymically-prepared India-rubber, in the Construction of Artificial Teeth, Gums, and Palates.—Mr. EPHRAIM MOSELY, Surgeon-Dentist, 9, Lower Grosvenor-street, sole inventor and patentee.—A new, original, and invaluable invention, consisting in the adaptation, with the most absolute perfection and success, of CHYMICALLY PREPARED WHITE and GUM-COLOURED INDIA-RUBBER, as a lining to the gold or bone frame. The extraordinary results of this application may be briefly noted in a few of their most prominent features:—All sharp edges are avoided; no springs, wires, or fastenings are required; a greatly increased freedom of suction is supplied; a natural elasticity, hitherto wholly unattainable, and a fit, perfected with the most unerring accuracy, are secured, while, from the softness and flexibility of the agents employed, the greatest support is given to the adjoining teeth when loose, or rendered tender by the absorption of the gums. The acids of the mouth exert no agency on the chymically prepared indiarubber, and, as it is a non-conductor, fluids of any temperature may be retained in the mouth, all unpleasantness of smell and taste being at the same time wholly provided against by the peculiar nature of its preparation.

TOOTHACHE.—Mr. WATSON, Surgeon-Dentist (successor to the late Mr. Beacall), respectfully informs his patients and the public that he is now successfully treating this malady, when arising from decaying teeth, without having recourse to extraction or giving pain. Attendance from 10 till 4.—27, King William-street, Strand, W.C.

MR. ALFRED JONES, Surgeon-Dentist to their late R.H. the Princess Augusta and the Duchess of Gloucester, His Majesty Louis Philippe, and the ex-Royal Family of France, their Serene Highnesses the Princess Esterhazy and the Prince of Gonzaga, &c., may be CONSULTED upon every operation of dental surgery and mechanism, from 11 till 4.—64, Grosvenor-street, Grosvenor-square.

FOR STOPPING DECAYED TEETH.—Patro-nized by Her Majesty the Queen and H.R.H. Prince Albert.—Mr. HOWARD's PATENT WHITE SUCCEDANEUM, for filling decayed teeth, however large the cavity. It is used in a soft state, without any pressure or pain, and in a short time becomes as hard as the enamel, lasting for many years, rendering extraction unnecessary, and arresting all further decay. Sold by all medicine vendors. Price 2s. 6d.

BREIDENBACH's WOOD VIOLET SCENT, price 2s. 6d., genuine from the flower, by H. Breidenbach, perfumer to the Queen, 157 B, New Bond-street, W.

KISS-ME-QUICK.—PIESSE and LUBIN's new perfume for this festive season, distilled from fragrant tulips, 2s. 6d. bottle; three bottles in a pretty case, 7s. Entered at Stationers'-hall. Laboratory of Flowers, 2, New Bond-street.

RIMMEL's PERFUMED ALMANACK for 1858, just ready, price 6d., by post for 7 stamps, imparts a delightful scent to pocket books, card cases, desks, &c., and forms an acceptable present to friends at home and abroad. Sold by all perfumers, booksellers and chymists; and at the manufactory, 96, Strand.

AMUSEMENT for WINTER EVENINGS is abundantly afforded to all purchasers of one of MECHI's famous mahogany FOLDING BAGATELLE TABLES. Prices, complete with balls, bridge, cues, and mace, and directions for playing, six feet long, £3 15s.; seven feet long, £4 15s.; eight feet long, £5 15s.; eight feet six inches long, £8 10s.; nine feet long, £11 10s.; 10 feet long, £12 10s.; stands for ditto, with adjusting screw legs, 45s. to 70s. The stand is not absolutely necessary for playing the game, although its use facilitates (by ensuring an exact level) the interest of the play.—112, Regent-street, and 4, Leadenhall-street.

BARLOW's PATENT CASK STAND, a new in-vention, so admirably contrived that a full butt (as well as smaller casks) may be raised or tilted on it without labour or trouble. Its action is so impalpable that the sediment of the most limpid fluid by no possibility can be disturbed. Price 14s. Warranted to last half a century, and to repay its trifling cost a hundredfold. N.B. The patentee's name and address, James Barlow, 14, King William-street, Mansion-house, are on every article; all others are spurious. Engraving gratis.

INTERIOR DECORATIONS and PARISIAN PAPERHANGINGS, of the most tasteful and recherché description, plans of rooms taken, and designs made by experienced artists. Estimates free of charge. First-class work guaranteed. Every description of ornamental decorations and house painting. The prices are strictly moderate, and cannot fail to ensure orders.—C. NOSOTTI's interior decorating, cabinet furniture, and upholstery manufactory, 398 and 399, Oxford-street; established 1822.

FACEPOWDER.—SAUNDERS' FACEPOWDER, or Bloom of Ninon, beautifies the complexion; contains nothing injurious. Packets 6d., free for eight stamps. Superfluous hairs easily and effectually removed by Saunders' Oriental Depilatory. Packets 2s., free for 26 stamps.—J. Touzeau Saunders, 315 B, Oxford-street.

JAMES LEWIS's PATENT IODINE SOAP is recommended by the faculty in cases of chronic rheumatism, also for cutaneous affections. Sold by all respectable chymists in the kingdom, price 6d. and 1s.; at 66, Oxford-street, W. Wholesale at the manufactory, 6, Bartlett's-buildings, Holborn.

WHITE and SOFT HANDS throughout the winter. —The LONDON SOAP and CANDLE COMPANY, 76, New Bond-street, have prepared a new WINTER SKIN SOAP, which, by its early and continued use, will produce the softest of hands and the whitest of skin, even in the coldest weather and hardest water; it is agreeably perfumed, and beautifully soft in use. Sold in bars 1s. per lb. Sole depot.

A Beautiful COMPLEXION and a WHITE HAND.—DELL's ERNARDO is proved by upwards of 50,000 testimonials in its favour to be the most delightful and superior preparation extant, for its remarkable and unfailing success in rendering the skin soft, smooth, and delicate, and the complexion perfectly clear and beautiful, removing all redness, spots, freckles, and other disfigurements, &c. 2s., or sent free (with directions for use) for 30 stamps; double size, 3s. 6d., or 50 stamps. Sold only by Henry Dell, 76, Lower Thames-street. Packed and sent to all parts of the world on receipt of a remittance.

INDIA-RUBBER COMBS, by the Harburg Comb Company. A long experience has guaranteed the India-rubber Combs the vogue they enjoy in the whole world; they are by far the most superior combs, softer in use than tortoiseshell, yet not dearer than buffalo. Sole agents, BENDA, BROTHERS, 96, Newgate-street.

LUXURIANT WHISKERS, Moustaches, and Eye-brows, produced in a few weeks by the use of ELLIOTT's TONIC LOTION, the stimulative properties of which are unfailing in its operation. Thomas Elliott invites a trial from the most sceptical that they may be convinced of its infallible power. Price 3s. 6d., 5s. 6d., 10s. 6d., and 21s. Forwarded on receipt of postage stamps.—Thomas Elliott, hair grower, (first floor,) 51, Fenchurch-street.

W. WINTER's LIQUID HAIR DYE produces a natural and permanent colours, from the lightest brown to black, without any green, purple, red, or other extraordinary tints, unpleasant odour, or the least injury to the hair or skin, leaving the hair softer and more glossy than before the dye was applied. Invented and made only by Wm. Winter, 205, Oxford-street, near Portman-square, London, in cases at 5s. 6d., 10s. 6d., and 21s. Established 30 years.

NEW YEAR's GIFT for the TOILET.—The nume-rous cases of recovery of the hair, after having fallen off, or partial baldness, are truly astonishing. The testimonials of the efficacy of OLDRIDGE's BALM of COLUMBIA place its powers and virtues beyond all doubt or cavil. 3s. 6d., 6s., and 11s. per bottle. Sold by all chymists and perfumers, and by the proprietors, C. and A. Oldridge, 13, Wellington-street north, seven doors above the Strand.

HUBERT's ROSEATE POWDER is the most certain and elegant preparation for the removal of superfluous hair on the arms, neck, and face, so inimical to beauty. The genuine is perfectly innocent, is easy and pleasant to use, and has been prepared by and signed G. M. Hogard for 40 years. It is sold for the proprietor by Mr. Hooper, chymist, 24, Russell-street, Covent-garden, and 43, London-bridge, city; and by all perfumers; in packets, price 4s.; double ditto, 7s.; or by post free for 50 or 88 postage stamps.

CLOSE of HOLYDAYS.—The return of youth to their respective boarding schools induces a solicitude from parents and guardians for their personal comfort and attraction, and ROWLANDS' MACASSAR OIL, for accelerating the growth and improving and beautifying the hair, Rowlands' Kalydor for improving the skin and complexion and removing cutaneous eruptions, and Rowlands' Odonto, or Pearl Dentifrice, for rendering the teeth beautifully white, and preserving the gums, are considered indispensable accompaniments for the attainment of those personal advantages so universally sought for and admired. Caution.—The name "Rowlands" precedes that of the article on the wrapper or label of each. Sold by A. Rowland and Sons, 20, Hatton-garden, London; and by chymists and perfumers. Beware of spurious imitations.

BORACINE CREAM.—This is an entirely new and elegant preparation for cleansing and beautifying the hair, removing all scurf, dandriff, &c., giving a glossy and delightful appearance to the head; it is made entirely on chymical principles, being pure oleaginous and fatty matter, purified by a new process, and combined with a most soothing and novel ingredient yet known to scientific discovery. The sole inventors of this new and elegant pomade recommend its use from its peculiar influence in the growth, and obviating its natural decay. Parties are requested to observe their names and address as under:—RICHARDSON and Co., perfumers to the Queen and Royal Family, 30, Bishopsgate-street without, E.C. Price 1s., 1s. 6d., and 2s. 6d. per bottle. Kept by all chymists. A single trial will prove its efficacy.

NO MORE GREEN or PURPLE DYED HAIR.— Notice.—Any lady or gentleman who has been so unfortunate as to have their hair dyed any of the above named colours, now so common by the use of spurious imitations of HEWLETT's celebrated TYRIAN LIQUID, can have it restored, free of charge, to a natural shade of brown and black; and to prevent the pain and annoyance of having the hair turned all the colours of the rainbow, A. H. has resolved to charge the lowest possible price, having increased his number of rooms, and had them fitted up with every convenience. Gentlemen's hair dyed and kept in perfect order from 30s. to 2 guineas; whiskers, 1 guinea per annum; ladies' hair dyed and attended to, from 2 to 3 guineas per annum; this will include keeping the hair in perfect order to defy detection. Price for case, 5s. 6d., 8s., 12s., and 1 guinea.—5, Burlington-arcade, Piccadilly.

RESPIRATORS of every description, manufactured by W. B. ROOFF, 8, Willow-walk, Kentish-town. Price from 2s. 6d. Perfect and incorrodible, the result of nine years' experience. To prevent disappointment, each stamped "Rooff." Patronised by Government and hospital authorities. Sold by all chymists.

RESPIRATORS.—The ÆTHEREON is the only wholesome metallic respirator, as no injurious or corrodible metals, such as copper, &c., are used in its construction, and the harmless substitute is besides coated with gold or silver. By the use of the Æthereon in cold or foggy weather many severe colds and their more fearful consequences may be avoided. Sold by all chymists, price 5s. and 8s., and in the form of a gentleman's scarf, 12s. 6d. Wholesale agent, S. Maw, 11, Aldersgate-street, E.C.

IF you VALUE HEALTH and a GOOD FIGURE wear Dr. FITCH's PATENT CHEST-EXPANDING BRACES for both sexes. They prevent stooping habits, round shoulders, strengthen the lungs and voice, and assist the growth. Price from 5s. Also, his Abdominal Supporter, highly recommended for corpulency, pregnancy, prolapsus, umbilical hernia, and debility, which it instantly relieves, and cures. Price from 21s.—L. H. CHANDLER, removed to 47a, Welbeck-street, Cavendish-square, W. Prospectuses forwarded.

PATENT SELF-ADJUSTING TRUSSES.—— SALMON, ODY, and Co. most respectfully inform the public that their PATENT SELF-ADJUSTING TRUSSES afford more ease and security for the relief of Hernia than any other instrument for the purpose. They will answer for right or left side, requiring no under-strap or any galling bandage. A female attends by appointment from 10 till 2 o'clock.—292, Strand.

PRATT's ELASTIC STOCKINGS and KNEE CAPS are recommended by the most eminent physicians and surgeons as the best remedy for varicose veins, weakness of the legs, knees, and ankles. Price, thread, 4s. 6d. and 6s. 6d. each, silk 9s., 15s., and 16s. each. Also Pratt's new Truss for Hernia, approved by Her Majesty's Army Medical Board. Price 15s. and 30s. For an elastic stocking send circumference of calf, ankle, and foot, and length from below knee to ground; for a truss send measurement round the hips. Artificial legs upon a new construction.—PRATT, surgical instrument and artificial limb maker, 420, Oxford-st., London, 20 doors west of Tottenham-ct.-rd.

CORNS, Bunions, and Defective Toe Nails EX-TRACTED and CURED in one minute, without cutting or pain, by Mr. RENDALL, 85, Regent-street. Ladies attended by Mrs. Rendall if preferred. Terms 2s. 6d. to 5s. Mr. Rendall has testimonials from the Royal Family, which may be seen, with thousands of others from all parts of the kingdom, at his own house, 85, Regent-street.

CORNS and BUNIONS.—Mrs. HAYWARD, chi-ropodist, REMOVES CORNS and BUNIONS by an easy and simple method. She also attends carefully to painful or deformed toe nails. Terms 2s. 6d. to 5s. Mrs. Hayward is the sole proprietor of the celebrated Bunion Lotion for reducing bunions and other swellings of the feet or ankles; price 3s. 6d. per bottle. Mrs. Hayward attends persons at their own residences any hour before 12 at noon, and is at home from 12 o'clock until 5.—25, Marylebone-road, late New-road.

CORNS, Diseased Nails, &c.—Mr. EISENBERG, REMOVED from 14, Cockspur-street, to 10, Pall-mall east, five doors from the National Gallery.—Mr. Eisenberg, Surgeon-Chiropodist to His Imperial Majesty Napoleon III., and Author of "Diseases of the Human Foot," may be consulted daily from 10 till 5, for removing corns, bunions, or diseased nails, without cutting or the slightest pain. Mr. Eisenberg's system, completely different from ordinary treatment, is admitted by the first authorities to be the best that has hitherto been followed. N.B. 10, Pall-mall east.

POWELL's BALSAM of ANISEED, to be obtained of most of the principal chymists and medicine dealers in the United Kingdom, also in France, America, Australia, and New Zealand. Sold in bottles at 1s. 1½d. and 2s. 3d.

WHAT DISEASES ARE MORE FATAL in their consequences than neglected coughs, colds, or other affections of the lungs? The first and best remedy is KEATING's COUGH LOZENGES. Prepared and sold by Keating, 79, St. Paul's churchyard. Retail by all druggists. Ask for a 2s. 9d. tin.

THE SOMNAMBULE, ADOLPHE DIDIER, gives his MAGNETIC SEANCES and CONSULTATIONS for ACUTE and CHRONIC DISEASES, their Causes and Remedies, every day from 1 till 4.—19, Upper Albany-street, Regent's-park. Consultation by letter.

COCKLE's ANTIBILIOUS PILLS for Indigestion, Bilious, Liver, and Stomach Complaints. Prepared only by James Cockle, surgeon, 18, New Ormond-street, and to be had of all medicine vendors, in boxes, at 1s. 1½d., 2s. 9d., 4s. 6d., and 11s.

EXPORTERS of DALBY's CARMINATIVE, for cure of diarrhœa, dysentery, cholic, and cholera, provided free of extra charge, with directions for use in foreign language, upon applying to the proprietor, James Dalby; or to his agents, Barclay and Sons, 95, Farringdon-street, London. Price 1s. 9d. per bottle.

HOLLOWAY's OINTMENT and PILLS are astonishing remedies for scrofula and all skin diseases. As salt penetrates meat, so will this ointment reach the affected parts if rubbed in externally. Sold by all medicine vendors throughout the world, and 244, Strand.

MEASAM's MEDICATED CREAM, a certain cure for gout, rheumatism, burns, scalds, bruises, chilblains, old wounds, ringworm, erysipelas, all kinds of eruptions of the skin, &c., is as delicate in its use as eau de Cologne, it not being a greasy compound. Sold wholesale and retail at the warehouse, 13, Catherine-street, Strand, in pots, with full directions, at 1s. 1½d., 2s. 9d., 4s. 6d.; and in family jars, at 11s. and 22s. each; and by all medicine vendors.

PRICHARD's DANDELION, Camomile, Rhubarb, and Ginger PILLS. This excellent compound, skilfully adjusted, is an unfailing remedy for indigestion, constipation, liver and all stomach complaints, its action being so mild and certain cannot fail to restore health, and by continued use prove a most valuable medicine. Well adapted for emigrants. In bottles 1s. 1½d., 2s. 9d., 4s. 6d., and 11s. Prepared only by Mr. Prichard, apothecary, 65, Charing-cross; and of all medicine vendors; Constance, city agent, 37, Leadenhall-street.

DR. DE JONGH's LIGHT-BROWN COD LIVER OIL, prescribed with complete confidence and the greatest success by the faculty for its purity, speedy and uniform efficacy, entire freedom from nauseous flavour and after-taste, and marked superiority over every other variety, as the most effectual remedy for consumption, bronchitis, asthma, gout, rheumatism, sciatica, diabetes, diseases of the skin, neuralgia, rickets, infantile wasting, general debility, and all scrofulous affections. Sold only in imperial half-pints, 2s. 6d.; pints, 4s. 9d.; quarts, 9s.; capsuled and labelled with Dr. De Jongh's stamp and signature, without which none can possibly be genuine. Wholesale and retail depot, ANSAR, HARFORD, and Co., 77, Strand, W.C., Dr. De Jongh's sole British consignees.

A NEW DISCOVERY, whereby ARTIFICIAL TEETH and GUMS are fitted with absolute perfection and success hitherto unattainable. No springs or wires, no extraction of roots, or any painful operation. This important invention perfects the beautiful art of the dentist, a closeness of fit and beauty of appearance being obtained equal to nature. All imitations should be avoided, the genuine only being supplied by Messrs. GABRIEL, the old-established dentists, from 3s. 6d. per tooth, sets £4 4s. Observe name and number particularly.—33, Ludgate-hill, and 134, Duke-street, Liverpool; established 1804. Prepared white gutta percha enamel, the best stopping for decayed teeth, renders them sound and useful in mastication, and effectually prevents toothache. In boxes, with directions, 1s. 6d.; free by post, 20 stamps. Sold by most chymists in town and country.

LIVER, Nerves, Stomach, and Lungs Restored without Medicine.—DU BARRY's delicious health-restoring food REVALENTA ARABICA, cures speedily and without expense as it saves 50 times its cost in other remedies, indigestion, (dyspepsia) flatulency, phlegm, habitual constipation, all nervous, bilious, and liver complaints, dysentery, diarrhœa, acidity, palpitation, heartburn, hæmorrhoids, headaches, hysteria, neuralgia, debility, despondency, cramps, spasms, nausea and sickness, sinking fits, coughs, asthma, bronchitis, consumption, also children's complaints, and is admirably adapted to rear and strengthen delicate infants. Recommended by Drs. Ure, Shorland, Harvey, Campbell, Ingram, and 50,000 other respectable persons whose health has been perfectly restored by it, after all other means had failed. Satisfactory proofs of cure and references to respectable families, may be had gratis and free by post from Barry du Barry and Co., 77, Regent-street, London.

INFANTS' NEW FEEDING BOTTLES.—From the Lancet.—"We have seldom seen anything so beautiful as the nursing bottles introduced by Mr. Elam, of Oxford-street. Whether for weaning, rearing by hand, or occasional feeding, they are quite unrivalled."—BENJAMIN ELAM, 196, Oxford-street. 7s. 6d. The bottles and mouthpiece are stamped with my name and address.

WANT PLACES.—All letters to be post paid.

WET NURSE. Married, age 24. Child five weeks old.—E. H., 6, Acorn-street, Southampton-street, Camberwell.

WET NURSE, from the month.—S. S., Windle's, chymist, Maida-hill.

WET NURSE. Age 23. Very healthy. Good breast of milk. Second child, age two months.—Julia M., 9, Southampton-court, Tottenham-court-road.

NURSE (HEAD) in a gentleman's family, where there is one or two children. Experienced. Can take a baby from the month. Age 33. 3 years' character.—E. R., 6, Charles-st., Hatton-garden.

NURSE (UPPER), or Nurse to one or two children out of arms, a young person.—A. M., 21, Clerkenwell-green.

NURSE to two or three young children, or Housemaid. Age 23.—S. C., Clark's, 132, Jermyn-street, St. James's.

NURSE, or Housemaid. From the country. Age 22. Good character.—A. B., Hall's, 8, Minories, city.

NURSE. Trustworthy. Age 26. Very fond of children. Two years' good character.—A. J., 40, Bow-lane, Cheapside.

NURSE to one or two children, to wait on the lady. Age 26. Good character.—G. L., 2, Southampton-mews, Russell-square, W.C.

NURSE, a young woman. Can take a baby from the month or bring it up by hand.—M. S., Sear's, brushmaker, High-street, Stoke Newington.

NURSE to one or two children, in a nobleman's or gentleman's family. Age 23. Four years' unexceptionable character. Catholics preferred.—S. F., Brown's, 4, Goldsmith's-row, Hackney-rd.

NURSE in a gentleman's family, to take the first baby, or where there are two or three children. No objection to the country.—A. B., Mrs. Rhind's, 7, Sussex-place, Hyde-park-gardens.

NURSE in a nobleman's or gentleman's family. Can take an infant from the month or bring it up by hand. Good character. Long experience.—G. H., 62, Mount-street, Grosvenor-sq., W.

NURSE, or General Servant. Prefers the nursery. Can work well at her needle. Age 21.—M. R., 18, Paradise-street, Lambeth.

NURSE to an infant, and to do needlework to one or two children. Age 20.—E. M., Jobbins's, baker, High-street, Hampstead.

NURSE (SECOND), or to wait on one or two children, a French person, in her 17th year. Can speak English.—E. B., Pylewell's, Lymington, Hants.

NURSE (UNDER), or to take charge of one or two young children. Age 20.—E. C., Simmons's, 64, Edgeware-road.

NURSE (UNDER), or Under Housemaid. Good character. Been out before.—F. B., 32, Sherborne-st., Blandford-sq.

NURSE (UNDER), or to take charge of one or two children. Age 18.—E. G., 13, Park-road, near the common, Clapham.

NURSE (UNDER), or Under Housemaid in a gentleman's family. Well recommended. Age 16.—E. D., Lawson's, 19, Melton-street, Euston-square, N.W.

NURSE (UNDER), or in a gentleman's family. Age 16. Been out before. Highly recommended.—L. L., 68, Hamilton-terrace, St. John's-wood.

NURSE (UNDER), or Nursemaid in a small family. From the country. Understands dressmaking.—M. G., post-office, 313, Regent-street.

NURSERYMAID, or Housemaid in a gentleman's family. Age 18. Good character.—A. B., 2, Sherborne-place, Blandford-sq.

NURSEMAID or Under Housemaid. Age 19.—P. E., 61, Goswell-road.

NURSEMAID, or School-room-maid. Age 18. Clever at her needle. Good reference.—H. P., Clark's, news agent, Upper Sydenham, Kent.

NURSEMAID, or to assist another servant, a very steady and industrious young woman, from the country. Strongly recommended.—A. B., 5, Craven-buildings, Newcastle-street, Strand.

FEMME de CHAMBRE FRANCAISE, Protestante, âgée de 25 ans; sachant un peu l'Anglais. Faire les robes et coiffer. 1 an 10 mois de bon caractère.—M. L., 30, Gloucester-street, Queen-sq.

LADY'S-MAID. Understands hairdressing and dressmaking. Unexceptionable character.—J. K., 23, Gracechurch-street, city.

LADY'S-MAID, a Swiss Protestant. Speaks French and German. No objection to travel. Good references.—G. W., 7, Newman-street, Oxford-street.

LADY'S-MAID. Thoroughly understands her duties. Five years' good character. Age 33.—M. C., Mrs. Geddes', 7, Albion-place, Hyde-park-square.

LADY'S-MAID, or Young Ladies'-maid. Understands all her duties. Good character.—J. M., 16, Crawford-street, Portman-square.

LADY'S-MAID to an elderly lady or young ladies. Has been accustomed to travel. No objection to make herself useful.—E. W., 2 B, Wilton-road, Pimlico.

LADY'S-MAID, or Upper Housemaid. Accustomed to travel. Age 32. Good character. Elderly lady preferred.—C. A., No. 5, Mill-street, Hanover-square.

LADY'S-MAID. Experienced. Age 34. Perfectly understands dressmaking, hairdressing, and all duties required. Excellent reference.—A. B., 27, Pickering-place, Paddington.

LADY'S-MAID, or Young Ladies'-maid. Has a good knowledge of dressmaking, millinery, hairdressing, and getting up fine linen. Good reference.—C. P., Hunter's, perfumer, High-st., Clapham.

LADY'S-MAID. Thoroughly understands dressmaking and plain needlework. Has a knowledge of millinery and hairdressing. 10 months' character.—A. B., 8, Canterbury Villas, Maida-vale.

LADY'S-MAID, or Young Ladies'-maid. Understands dressmaking, hairdressing, and getting up fine linen. Age 25. Seven years' good character.—S. U., 9, Robert-street, Bedford-row.

LADY'S-MAID. Thoroughly understands dressmaking and hairdressing. Age 33. Two years' good character.—A. B., Salter's, 17, New-street, Dorset-square.

LADY'S-MAID, or Young Ladies'-maid. No objection to assist in the housework. Seven years' character. Age 28.—M. N., 17, Stanley-street, Paddington.

LADY'S-MAID. Would also take charge of one or two children out of the nursery. Well experienced.—M. A., Campion's, No. 38, Clipstone-street, Portland-place.

LADY'S-MAID in a nobleman's or gentleman's family. Age 29. Perfectly understands dressmaking, millinery, and hairdressing. 2 years' character.—J. L., 5, North-place, Hampstead-road.

LADY'S-MAID. Understands millinery, dressmaking, and hairdressing. Age 28. Good character. Country preferred.—M. H., the builder's, 22, Castle-street, Southwark.

LADY'S-MAID, or Young Ladies'-maid. Understands millinery, dressmaking, and hairdressing. Age 22.—A. M., 10, Bute-street, Old Brompton.

LADY'S-MAID, a native of Germany. Understands dressmaking, millinery, and hairdressing. Good character.—L. G., 3, Alfred-terrace, Queen's-road, Bayswater, W.

LADY'S-MAID (UNDER), or to wait upon young children. In her 18th year. Would make herself generally useful. Not been out before.—F. R., 21, Church-street, Soho.

YOUNG LADIES'-MAID, or Under Nurse. Understands dressmaking. Good character.—S. L., 14, Ebury-sq., Pimlico.

YOUNG LADIES'-MAID, or to wait on an elderly lady and do needlework. Age 22.—E. B., 39, Chester-st., Kennington-rd.

YOUNG LADIES'-MAID, or to wait on a lady. Two years' character.—A. Z., 2, Cole-street, Trinity-square.

YOUNG LADIES'-MAID, a young person, from the country. Perfectly understands dressmaking and hairdressing. Good character.—L. P., Wilson's, 37, Wigmore-street, W.

YOUNG LADIES'-MAID. Good dressmaker. Has not been out before. Well recommended. Wages no object.—H. H., Gate's, grocer, High-street, Guildford, Surrey.

SCHOOL-ROOM-MAID, or Nursemaid. Good references. Age 19.—A. B., 13, Store-street, Bedford-square.

NEEDLEWOMAN. Age 24. Three years' excellent character.—M. T., Bell's, 13, Upper Tachbrook-st., Pimlico, S.W.

NEEDLEWOMAN, and to wait on a lady. Good dressmaker. No objection to the country.—A. B., Mrs. Rhind's, post-office, Little Sussex-place, Hyde-park.

NEEDLEWOMAN, or Housemaid in a small family, where a footman or parlourmaid is kept.—A. H., Mrs. Rhind's, No. 7, Sussex-place, Hyde-park.

WARDROBEKEEPER in a gentleman's school, or anything similar. Trustworthy. Age 40. Good references.—M. J., 21, Token-house-yard, city.

A YOUNG PERSON to attend on young ladies, or Second Nurse. Good references.—C. F., 31, Carburton-st., Portland-pl., W.

A YOUNG PERSON, age 18, to assist where one or more servants are kept. Can work well at her needle. Not been out before. Good reference.—M. B., 18, Elder-st., White Lion-st., Nortonfalgate.

A YOUNG PERSON, to wait on a lady or children, or any light situation where trust and confidence are required. Good needlewoman.—A. B., Mrs. Johnston's, 33, King-street, Westminster.

A Married WOMAN, one or two sets of offices, within a mile of King's-cross.—R. B., Kaylen's, 5, Calthorpe-place, Gray's-inn-road.

A YOUNG PERSON, to wait on young ladies. Has not been out before. Wages a secondary consideration. Can assist in millinery and dressmaking.—E. B., 27, Duke-street, Stamford-street.

ATTENDANT on an elderly lady or invalid lady or gentleman. Good reference.—E. H., 23, Devonshire-street.

HOUSEKEEPER, or to wait on an invalid lady. Good reference.—J. S., 22, Lansdowne-road north, Notting-hill.

HOUSEKEEPER to a tradesman or widower, or to wait upon an invalid. Two years' character.—S. W., Mrs. Clapereau's, newspaper-office, High-street, Camden-town.

HOUSEKEEPER and GENERAL SERVANT to a single gentleman. Middle-aged. Town or country.—T. J., Hall's, 5, Halkin-terrace, Belgrave-square.

COOK and HOUSEKEEPER, or thorough Good Cook in a nobleman's or gentleman's family. Understands well the duties. Excellent character.—H. L., Attryde's, 36, Upper Seymour-st., Portman-sq.

COOK and HOUSEKEEPER to a single gentleman. No objection to chambers. Middle-aged. Four years' character. Town preferred.—A. B., 29, Bull and Mouth-street, city.

COOK and HOUSEKEEPER, or Cook where the lady is her own housekeeper and a kitchenmaid is kept. Good reference. Understands soups, made dishes, &c.—G. H., 98, Jermyn-street.

COOK and HOUSEKEEPER in a nobleman's or gentleman's family. 10 years' good character. Age 35.—A. D., Phillips's, No. 32, Store-street, Bedford-square.

COOK and HOUSEKEEPER. Age 38. Perfectly understands all kinds of soups, made dishes, ices, and confectionery. Wages £40.—G. P., 26, New-street, Brompton.

COOK and HOUSEKEEPER in a gentleman's family, where a kitchenmaid is kept. Understands the management of a large family. Good character.—B. L., 57, Mount-street, Grosvenor-sq.

COOK and HOUSEKEEPER in a nobleman's or gentleman's family, where a kitchenmaid is kept. No objection to a job by the week or month.—E. P., 179, Sloane-street, S.W.

COOK (PROFESSED). Understands her business in all modern cooking. No objection to a season engagement. 12 months' good character.—T. M., 11, Orchard-street, Portman-square.

COOK (PROFESSED), or Cook and Housekeeper to a single gentleman. One year and eight months' good character. No objection to a job.—C. P., 20, Princes-street, Cavendish-square.

COOK (PROFESSED) in a nobleman's or gentleman's family, where a regular kitchenmaid is kept. Good character. Would take a job.—M. P. A., 24, Seymour-place, Bryanston-square.

COOK (thorough), or Cook and Housekeeper, in a nobleman's or gentleman's family. Town or country. Age 38. Good character.—A. B., 9, Northumberland-street, Marylebone.

COOK (thorough GOOD), where a footman is kept. Two years' good character.—A. B., 21, South-street, Manchester-square.

COOK (thorough GOOD) in a gentleman's family, where a man-servant is kept. Good character. Age 30.—M. P., 5, Carburton-street, Berkeley-square.

COOK (thorough GOOD), where a kitchenmaid is kept or assistance given.—A. B., Hyde-park dairy, Park-side, Knightsbridge.

COOK (thorough GOOD) in a gentleman's family. Town or country. Understands baking and dairy.—M. A. E., 15, New-street, Old-street, St. Luke's.

COOK (thorough GOOD) in a gentleman's family. Good character. Age 30.—S. L., 2, Victoria-terrace, Adelaide-road, St. John's-wood.

COOK (FIRST-CLASS WOMAN) in a family hotel, or any respectable house of business where Sunday services are not always required.—X. C., 3, Polygon-mews, Euston-square.

COOK (GOOD), in a gentleman's family. Understands her business. Good character.—B. Y., 1, Charlton-st., Fitzroy-sq.

COOK (GOOD) in a house of business. Middle-aged. Good character.—J. T., Rose's, 352, Oxford-street.

COOK (GOOD). No objection to a job. Good character.—A. B., dairy, 72, George-street, Portman-square.

COOK (GOOD) in a small family. Middle-aged. Good character.—F. F., Pausey's, 9, Elizard-place, Brompton, S.W.

COOK (GOOD), where a man-servant is kept. Good character.—P. H., Miss Gillespy's, 5, Portsea-place, Connaught-square.

COOK (GOOD) in a gentleman's family. Five years' character.—M. O., 26, Medway-street, Horseferry-road, Westminster.

COOK (GOOD) in an hotel, tavern, or any house of business. Age 39. 11 months' good character.—M. C., 2, Burleigh-street, Strand.

COOK (GOOD), where a man is kept. Age 30. 16 months' good character.—E. T. W., 45, Upper Berkeley-street west, Hyde-park.

COOK (GOOD) in a gentleman's or tradesman's family, where a man-servant is kept. One year's good character.—S. P., Fernie's, 82, Edgeware-road.

COOK (GOOD) in a tavern or merchant's family. Very steady. Middle-aged. Excellent character.—C. D., 8, Thomas-street, Stamford-street.

COOK (GOOD) where a kitchenmaid is kept. Has just completed her business at the Travellers' Club.—M. S., 43, Albert-street, Bermondsey.

COOK in an hotel, where a kitchenmaid is kept. Thoroughly understands her business.—B. L., 23, Edward-st., Dorset-sq.

COOK in an hotel. Good character. Age 29.—A. B., 4, Charles-street, Portman-square.

COOK in a small private family.—H. D., 8, King-street, Kensington.

COOK. No objection to a job. Town preferred. Good character.—A. B., 19, Upper Rathbone-place, Oxford-street.

COOK in a gentleman's family. Good character. A short distance from town preferred.—P. S., 3, Maidenstone-place, Royal-hill, Greenwich.

COOK in a small family, General Servant to a gentleman, or in a house of business. Age 30.—E. F. C., 4, Edward-street, Wardour-street, Soho.

COOK and HOUSEMAID (two sisters), where a footman is kept. Three years' good character.—S. F., 9, Hatton-place, Edgeware-road.

COOK in a small family. Age 35. Town preferred. Good character.—A. R., 154, Prospect-place, Maida-hill, Edgeware-road.

COOK, or Cook and Housekeeper, in a gentleman's family. Understands soups, entrées, ices, confectionery, &c. Highly recommended.—A. K., post-office, Goswell-road.

COOK in a gentleman's family, a young person from the country. 5 years' good character.—S. B., 11, Paradise-street, High-street, Marylebone.

COOK (thorough GOOD PLAIN), where a man-servant is kept. Trustworthy. Good character. Town preferred.—A. M., 18, Paddington-street, Marylebone.

COOK (GOOD PLAIN), or General Servant in a small family, where a page-boy is kept.—J. W., 23, Belvidere-rd., Lambeth.

COOK (GOOD PLAIN), or Kitchenmaid, under a man-cook, in an hotel or tavern.—A. C., Dyers' Arms, Webb-st., Borough.

COOK (GOOD PLAIN). Middle-aged. Good character. E. C., Palmer's, Bell-green, Sydenham.

COOK (GOOD PLAIN) in a house of business. Age 29. Good character.—M. C., 37, South-street, Manchester-square, W.

COOK (GOOD PLAIN). Age 34. From the country. Good character.—A. B., Bailey's library, Brixton-rise, Surrey.

COOK (GOOD PLAIN). Middle-aged. 16 months' good character.—A. B., 67, Seymour-place, Bryanston-square.

COOK (GOOD PLAIN). Age 26. Good character.—M. K., 50, Vauxhall-street, Upper Kennington-lane.

COOK (GOOD PLAIN). Good character.—A. B., 51, Dorset-street, Manchester-square, W.

COOK (GOOD PLAIN) in a private family. Age 30. Good character.—Y. Z., 41, Mount-street, Lambeth.

COOK (GOOD PLAIN) and HOUSEMAID in a gentleman's family, two young persons.—L. G., post-office, Forest-hill, Sydenham, Kent.

COOK (GOOD PLAIN), or General Servant in a family of two, a country person. Age 30. 18 months' good character.—M. C., 3, Little Bride-street, Liverpool-road.

COOK (GOOD PLAIN). Middle-aged. Willing to make a family comfortable. 15 months' good character.—J. C., 15, Dorset-street, Clapham-road.

COOK (PLAIN), or General Servant in a small family. —A. B., 18, Marchmont-street, Brunswick-square.

COOK (PLAIN), or General Servant in a private or tradesman's family.—E. C., 7, Conduit-street west, Westbourne-ter.

COOK (PLAIN), or Kitchenmaid in a gentleman's family. Age 22. 14 months' good character.—A. M., 2, Hope-st., Hackney-rd.

COOK (PLAIN) in a small gentleman's or tradesman's family. Good character.—A. B., 21, Lower Oxford-street, Mile-end.

COOK (PLAIN) in a private family, in town. Two years and nine months' good character.—S. E., Castleman's dairy, Pitt-street, Fitzroy-square.

COOK (PLAIN), or Kitchenmaid in a private family. Age 22. Good character.—A. W., 40, Devonshire-mews west, Portland-place.

COOK (PLAIN), or Kitchenmaid, a young person from the country. 2½ years' good character.—M. C., 24, North-street, Manchester-square.

HOUSEMAID (UPPER), or Parlourmaid. 3½ years' good character.—C. L., 22, Lansdowne-road north, Notting-hill.

HOUSEMAID (UPPER), or Housemaid in a small family. Good needlewoman. Good character.—A. C., Faulkner's, 10, St. Alban's-terrace, Edgeware-road.

HOUSEMAID (UPPER). Thoroughly understands her business. Good character.—A. B., Knight's, 52, Upper Baker-street, Dorset-square.

HOUSEMAID (UPPER), where a footman is kept. Three years' good character. Tall. Age 30.—S. H., 27, Adam-street west, Edgeware-road.

HOUSEMAID (UPPER) in a nobleman's or gentleman's family. Age 29. Four years' character. Good needlewoman.—M. A. P., Andrew and Co.'s, 7, Conduit-st. west, Westbourne-ter., W.

HOUSEMAID (UPPER), or Housemaid where a footman is kept. Two years' character.—N. C., Wortley and Hanbury's, Upper Baker-street, Regent's-park.

HOUSEMAID (UPPER) and to wait on a lady. Age 30. Good needlewoman.—G. M., Bult's, 25, New Quebec-street, Portman-square, W.

HOUSEMAID (UPPER or TOWN) in a nobleman's or gentleman's family. Well recommended.—A. B., Buck's, 9, Castle-street, Long-acre.

HOUSEMAID (UPPER) in a nobleman's or gentleman's family. Good character.—E. W., 3, Shepherd's-court, Upper Brook-street, Grosvenor-square.

HOUSEMAID (UPPER) and to wait on a lady. Understands dressmaking, &c. 2 years and 9 months' undeniable character.—J. B., 6, Spring-street, Sussex-gardens.

HOUSEMAID (UPPER) in a nobleman's or gentleman's family. 12 months' good character. Age 32.—S. B., 6, Welle-street, Oxford-street.

HOUSEMAID (thorough) in a gentleman's family, where a footman is kept. Can get up fine linen.—E. F., 12, Spring-street, Hyde-park.

HOUSEMAID (thorough), where a footman or parlourmaid is kept. Two years' character.—M. C., Davies's advertising office, Maida-hill, W.

HOUSEMAID (thorough) in a gentleman's family. Can wait on a lady. Age 25. Good needlewoman. Good character. Town or country.—M. A., Hiscoke's library, Richmond, Surrey, S.W.

HOUSEMAID (thorough) and to wait on the lady. 3 years' good character. Can work well at her needle and get up fine linen.—F. W., Labram's, grocer, Frances-street, Tavistock-square.

HOUSEMAID, or Nurse in a gentleman's family. 14 months' good character.—E. L., 4, Upper Rathbone-pl., Oxford-st.

HOUSEMAID in a small family, where a parlourmaid or footman is kept. Age 24.—M. D., the library, 8, Spring-st., Hyde-pk.

HOUSEMAID where a footman or parlourmaid is kept. Good needlewoman.—A. M., Simmons's, 64, Edgeware-road, W.

HOUSEMAID in a tradesman's family, Nurse, or General Servant. Age 28.—E. G., 91, Grove-street, Camden-town.

HOUSEMAID. From the country. Can wait well at table. Good character.—E. L., 29, Upper King-street, Russell-sq.

HOUSEMAID in a house of business. Age 23. Good character.—H. B., 37, South-street, Manchester-square.

HOUSEMAID in a good family. 11 months' good character.—A. H., 17, Castle-street east, Oxford-street.

HOUSEMAID in an hotel. 2½ years' good character.—S. C., 42, Johnson-street, Seymour-street, Oakley-square.

HOUSEMAID, or Nurse, a German person. Good character.—M. D., 137, Salisbury-court, Fleet-street.

HOUSEMAID in a house of business. Age 25. Three years' character.—M. G., 6, Bell's-buildings, Salisbury-square.

HOUSEMAID in a small family. Age 24.—M. M., 1, Somerset-place, Denmark-road, Camberwell.

HOUSEMAID, or Chambermaid, in an hotel or club-house.—E. S., 52, Great Queen-street, Lincoln's-inn-fields.

HOUSEMAID, where a footman is kept. Good needlewoman. Age 26.—M. R., Robson's library, Lower Norwood, Surrey, S.

HOUSEMAID in a private family, where a footman is kept. Nine years' character.—E. B., Allchin's, 45, High-street, Marylebone.

HOUSEMAID in a gentleman's family, where a footman is kept. Good character.—F. H., post-office, Thayer-street, Manchester-square.

HOUSEMAID, where a footman is kept, or Second Nursemaid. Good needlewoman. From the country. Good character.—L. E., 23, Lucas-street, Commercial-road east.

HOUSEMAID, where a footman is kept. Age 36. A year and seven months' good character. Country preferred.—A. B., 4, Victoria-road, Pimlico.

HOUSEMAID in a gentleman's family. Good plain needlewoman. Can get up fine linen.—C. O., Dobson's, 40, John-street, Edgeware-road.

HOUSEMAID in a small quiet family, where a footman is kept. Good character. Age 24.—G. L., 2, Goding-place, Putney, Surrey, S.W.

HOUSEMAID, where a footman is kept. Can get up fine linen. Good needlewoman. Two years' good character.—A. U., 101, John-street, Windmill-street, Tottenham-court-road.

HOUSEMAID, or Chambermaid in an hotel or lodging-house. Has lived in a first-class lodging-house. Good character. Age 25.—J. L. P., 7, Russell's-buildings, High-street, Wapping.

HOUSEMAID in a nobleman's or gentleman's family, where a footman or page is kept. Age 25. Good character.—S. B., 54, Torrington-square.

HOUSEMAID in a small family, where a footman is kept and washing put out, in town. 18 months' character.—E. R., Webb's, 17, Leigh-street, Burton-crescent.

HOUSEMAID in a private family, where a footman is kept. Three years' good character.—A. C., 2, Arbour-street west, Stepney, opposite the Church.

HOUSEMAID in a small family, where a footman is kept. Age 26. Good character. To wait on a lady and do needlework.—D. G., 45, Cambridge-street, Hyde-park-square.

HOUSEMAID, where a footman is kept, or to wait on a lady. Good dressmaker and needlewoman. Three years' good character.—M. N., 9, Robert-street, Bedford-row, W.C.

HOUSEMAID. Age 26. 15 months' character. Can wait well at table, and fully competent to any duties.—R. S., Burnet's library, Camberwell-gate.

HOUSEMAID. From the country. Age 25. Good character. No objection to travel.—M. P., 25, Clift-street, New North-road, Hoxton.

HOUSEMAID, where a footman or parlourmaid is kept preferred. 14 months' good character.—S. C., grocer's, 15, Pratt-street, Camden-town.

HOUSEMAID in a small family, or where a footman or page is kept. Thoroughly understands her duties. Age 30. 14 months' good character.—S. S., post-office, Putney, Surrey.

HOUSEMAID in a gentleman's family, where a footman is kept. Age 27.—J. C., 34, Bloomfield-place, Grosvenor-mews, New Bond-street, W.

HOUSEMAID in a gentleman's family, where a footman is kept. Age 25. Perfectly understands her work. Two years' good character.—F. G., Brooke's, Wood-green, Tottenham.

HOUSEMAID where a footman is kept. Age 20. 12 months' good character.—A. B., Davidson's, 22, Devonshire-street, Portland-place.

Theatre

Right Playbill for Theatre Royal, Drury Lane, Thursday 17 October 1816. 'Mr Kean will appear this evening as the character of Shylock in Shakespeare's play of the Merchant of Venice.'

Below DURHAM MUSTARD TOO POWERFUL FOR ITALIAN CAPERS, OR THE OPERA IN AN UPROAR. The new Ballet and Opera productions of the 1797–8 season met with the protests of Bishop Barrington of Durham at the shameless display and apparent nudity of the dancers' flesh-coloured garments, and London lectures by Bishop Porterno on 'the growing relaxation of public manners'. The Bishop leaps across the orchestra and footlights as if to strike the dancers with his crozier crying 'Avaunt thee Satan, I fear thee not, assume whatever shape or form thou wilt I am determined to lay thee thou black Fiend.' The playbill on the wall, beside a satyr, announces 'The Divil of a Lover – He's much to blame', a musical farce and 'Peeping Tom', both performed in 1798. Caricature by Isaac Cruikshank, published 1798 and 1807.

The Times pioneered the concept of an independent press, free to say what it wanted without fear or favour, in fields other than politics. Freedom is indivisible. Take the theatre, for example. The theatre critics of *The Times*, from Hazlitt to A. B. Walkley, Charles Morgan and onwards, have been eminent literary figures who have helped to make and break reputations, and form the public taste. They also invented the remarkable doctrine that a critic should be free to give his honest opinion, rather than puffing friends of the proprietor and sniping at foes.

This was a novel doctrine at the beginning of the nineteenth century. The theatre was not respectable, and neither was journalism. Editors and hacks mixed with actors and playwrights in their green rooms, and published fulsome puffs in return for free tickets. They would publish your own review of a play that you had written yourself, if you wanted, and had slipped them something to make it worth their while. This vice is a pox on the face of journalism, which has not yet been completely eradicated, as can be seen from the activities of public relations officers who try to manipulate opinion in the press on every subject from politics to motor cars.

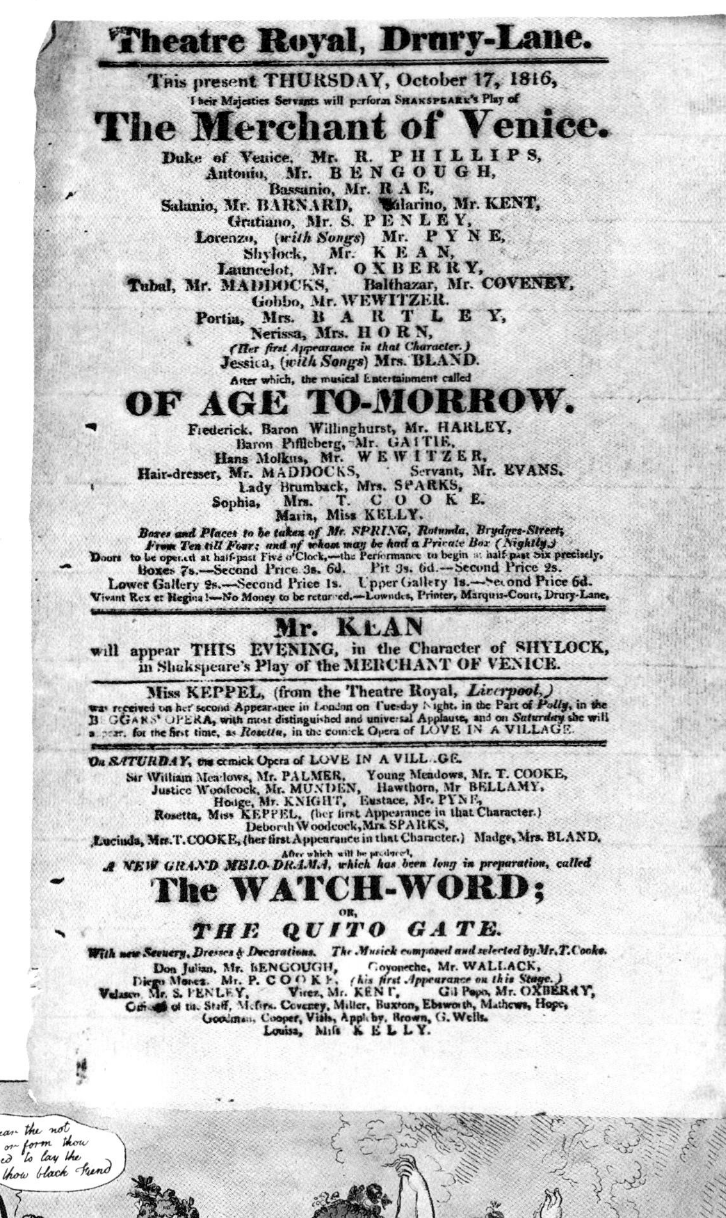

Theatre Royal, Drury-Lane.

This present THURSDAY, October 17, 1816,
Their Majesties Servants will perform SHAKSPEARE's Play of

The Merchant of Venice.

Duke of Venice, Mr. R. PHILLIPS,
Antonio, Mr. BENGOUGH,
Bassanio, Mr. RAE,
Salanio, Mr. BARNARD, Salarino, Mr. KENT,
Gratiano, Mr. S. PENLEY,
Lorenzo, (*with Songs*) Mr. PYNE,
Shylock, Mr. KEAN,
Launcelot, Mr. OXBERRY,
Tubal, Mr. MADDOCKS, Balthazar, Mr. COVENEY,
Gobbo, Mr. WEWITZER.
Portia, Mrs. BARTLEY,
Nerissa, Mrs. HORN,
(*Her first Appearance in that Character.*)
Jessica, (*with Songs*) Mrs. BLAND.
After which, the musical Entertainment called

OF AGE TO-MORROW.

Frederick, Baron Willinghurst, Mr. HARLEY,
Baron Piffleberg, Mr. GATTIE,
Hans Molkus, Mr. WEWITZER,
Hair-dresser, Mr. MADDOCKS, Servant, Mr. EVANS,
Lady Brumback, Mrs. SPARKS,
Sophia, Mrs. T. COOKE.
Maria, Miss KELLY.
Boxes and Places to be taken of Mr. SPRING, Rotunda, Brydges-Street; From Ten till Four; and of whom may be had a Private Box (Nightly.)
Doors to be opened at half-past Five o'Clock,—the Performance to begin at half-past Six precisely.
Boxes 7s.—Second Price 3s. 6d. Pit 3s. 6d.—Second Price 2s.
Lower Gallery 2s.—Second Price 1s. Upper Gallery 1s.—Second Price 6d.
Vivant Rex et Regina!—No Money to be returned.—Lowndes, Printer, Marquis-Court, Drury-Lane,

Mr. KEAN
will appear THIS EVENING, in the Character of SHYLOCK, in Shakspeare's Play of the MERCHANT OF VENICE.

Miss KEPPEL, (from the Theatre Royal, *Liverpool,*)
was received on her second Appearance in London on Tuesday Night, in the Part of *Polly*, in the BEGGARS' OPERA, with most distinguished and universal Applause, and on *Saturday* she will appear, for the first time, as *Rosetta*, in the comick Opera of LOVE IN A VILLAGE.

On SATURDAY, the comick Opera of LOVE IN A VILLAGE.
Sir William Meadows, Mr. PALMER, Young Meadows, Mr. T. COOKE,
Justice Woodcock, Mr. MUNDEN, Hawthorn, Mr BELLAMY,
Hodge, Mr. KNIGHT, Eustace, Mr. PYNE,
Rosetta, Miss KEPPEL, (her first Appearance in that Character.)
Deborah Woodcock, Mrs. SPARKS,
Lucinda, Mrs. T. COOKE, (her first Appearance in that Character.) Madge, Mrs. BLAND.
After which will be produced,
A NEW GRAND MELO-DRAMA, which has been long in preparation, called

The WATCH-WORD;
OR,
THE QUITO GATE.

With new Scenery, Dresses & Decorations. The Musick composed and selected by Mr. T. Cooke.
Don Julian, Mr. BENGOUGH, Goyoneche, Mr. WALLACK,
Diego Monez, Mr. P. COOKE, (*his first Appearance on this Stage.*)
Velasco, Mr. S. PENLEY, Virez, Mr. KENT, Gil Pepo, Mr. OXBERRY,
Officers of the Staff, Messrs. Coveney, Miller, Buxton, Ebsworth, Mathews, Hope, Goodman, Cooper, Vials, Appleby, Brown, G. Wells.
Louisa, Miss KELLY.

Durham MUSTARD too Powerfull for Italian Capers, or the Opera in an Uproar

In his autobiography, Leigh Hunt, the pioneer of candid dramatic criticism, described the craft at the beginning of the nineteenth century:

> Upon new performers, and upon writers not yet introduced, a journalist was more impartial; and some times, where the Proprietor for some personal reason grew offended with an actor, or a set of actors, a criticism would occasionally be hostile and even severe. Puffing and plenty of tickets were, however, the system of the day. It was an interchange of amenities over the dining table; a flattery of power on the one side, and puns on the other; and what the public took for a criticism of a play was a draft upon the box-office or reminiscences of last Thursday's salmon and lobster sauce.

It was a system unlikely to appeal to young John Walter II, with his high sense of the independence of the press. In 1805 he recruited Barron Field, another young man of twenty, as a new kind of candid theatre critic for *The Times*. Barron Field introduced his friend, young Thomas Barnes, to the paper. Barnes was already writing dramatic notices in the *Examiner* under the pen-name of 'Criticus'. His account of the first appearance of Edmund Kean as Shylock in *The Merchant of Venice* (Leigh Hunt was *hors de combat* in prison at the time) is one of the classic reviews of critical history, bearing comparison with Hazlitt's account of the same first night. It was a momentous introduction for *The Times*: Barnes went on to become its formative editor.

John Walter insisted that his young critics paid for their own theatre tickets and then wrote exactly what they thought of the piece. They followed his instructions with enthusiasm. For example, in its review of the past season at Covent Garden, published on 24 June 1807, *The Times* reported: 'Mr Reynolds's *Arbitration* was utterly contemptible; and Mr Lambe's *Mr H.* utterly damned. The musical pieces of the season bear an air of mediocrity in their language and of prettiness in their music: Mr Reynold's senseless pageant *The Deserts of Arabia*, a wretched pantomime called *The Enchanters*'. Warming to its theme, *The Times* carried on in the same piece to denounce *Peter the Great or Wooden Walls*, 'with its insipid songs and nauseous courtesies, by that ceaseless scribbler Mr Cherry. Mr Cherry is undoubtedly the lowest dramatist of this wretched day: Mr Reynolds can make a laugh sometimes, and Mr Thomas Dibdin can write a song; but Mr Cherry can do neither.'

The theatrical managers were appalled by such unprecedented plain speaking, and by the new breed of critic who could not be bribed, bought, flattered or frightened and who insisted on paying for his own tickets. They hit back in their poodle press at the 'damned boys' and 'supercilious lads' of *The Times*. Here is a good example of the counter-attack from the magazine called *Le Beau Monde* in its issue of January 1808:

> The writer who furnishes *The Times* with theatrical criticisms, (if that which is exhibited in utter contempt of critical principles can properly be termed criticism at all) is evidently a gentleman of much light reading. And, indeed, he attacks every individual who comes within his reach, with so sharp a superfluity of quotation that his writings make us sniff as furiously as a schoolboy does who has been cheated with mustard on his bread.

The *Satirist* of the same month wrote:

> Persons who judge impartially themselves, are apt to imagine, that the critiques they read in *The Times* are the result of great erudition, deep

Thomas Barnes's review (column 4) of Edmund Kean's debut as Shylock.
4 FEBRUARY 1814

...on the 16th ult. by a small party of British, ...being no troops in that quarter to oppose the ...Their contents, consisting, it is stated, of ...1600 cartridges, 30 camp kettles, several axes, ...&c. and about 300 pounds of lead, were carried ...by the enemy.

...Champlain squadron, under Commodore ...have put into the mouth of Otter Creek, ...Vt. for winter quarters.

PROCEEDINGS OF CONGRESS.

HOUSE OF REPRESENTATIVES.—JAN. 6.

LIEUTENANT-GENERAL PROPOSED.

Mr. [illegible], of N. D. offered for consideration the following Resolution :—

Resolved, That the Committee on Military Affairs be instructed ...into the expediency of empowering by law the President ...of the United States, by and with the advice and consent of the Senate, ...one Lieutenant-General to command the armies of ...the United States, with such powers and emoluments as may be ...expedient.

Mr. [illegible] said, in his opinion the result of the ...campaign had disappointed the expectations of ...the ...one. That opinion had been decidedly expressed ...by this house in its recent vote for inquiry into the ...causes which led to the failure of our arms. However ...it might be the opinion in this house, it was still ...so in the nation. He hoped and trusted the enquiry embraced in the resolution just alluded to, would ...be prosecuted as to shew where the blame really ...lay; that, if misconduct has taken place, it may ...be laid at the door of the person by whom it was committed—for as the matter now stands, no two persons ...in the House would agree on the causes whence this unexpected result had proceeded. But the inquiry, desirable as it is, though it may point out the cause of ...past failures, cannot operate any beneficial effect on ...the next campaign. The time, Mr. M. said, was fast ...approaching when that campaign ought to commence, ...and, so far as he had seen, no measure, the tendency of ...which was to render the ensuing campaign more successful than the last, had been adopted.

Mr. WRIGHT, of Md. said he did not rise to oppose the reference of this subject to the Military ...Committee, but he rose to put the Gentleman right ...as to the feeling of the house and of the nation, which ...he appeared so much to have misunderstood. Have ...the arms of the United States failed in the campaign? ...Have we not, on the contrary, been marvellously successful! We have gained a province taken from us, ...is that nothing! Lake Erie, a great inland sea, occupied by the enemy at the commencement of the campaign, and all its shores, are our's. We conquered and ...beat the enemy in that quarter; we reduced all the ...Indian tribes under the yoke of the United States, and ...compelled them to beg for subsistence for their wives ...and children from us. Here, there is a whole country ...emancipated from the British sway. Yes, Sir, we regained a province we had lost, and conquered all ...Canada, to the East end of Lake Ontario. Under a ...Pike did, we not succeed in taking York? Did we not ...lately succeed in every thing previous to the close ...of the campaign! On Lake Ontario, the great Yeo, ...who was to conquer us with so much facility, was ...driven into port; and we were in possession of all ...the waters of the Lake, with the exception of the ...water in the vicinity of the harbour of Kingston. ...Three weeks storm and rain washed our troops ...into general sickness and debility; and yet they ...proceeded on, and are now lying at the key of ...Canada, and ready to descend to Montreal the moment ...the season permits. No officer deserved condemnation ...till evidence appeared against him; and there was ...no evidence against the courage or conduct of our army, ...which had displayed, not *Roman* but *American* valour—so conspicuous, indeed, had been the courage displayed ...by both our army and navy, that he hoped the man ...who should hereafter speak of Roman valour, on this ...floor, would be considered as speaking of the *second degree*, and not the *first*!!!

This motion was agreed to without a division; and ...the resolution lies over for further consideration.

GOVERNOR CHITTENDEN.

Mr. SHARP, of Ky. after a number of introductory ...remarks, explanatory of the laws relating to the militia, ...which subject them, when in actual service, to the rules ...and articles of war, and place them during such time, ...in all respects, on the footing of regular troops, adverted ...to the recent proclamation of Governor Chittenden, of ...Vermont, calling the militia of that State from the position assigned them by military orders. This act, he said, ...was in direct violation of the statute which makes it penal ...to entice the soldiers in the service of the United States to ...desert. This act was done, too, at a critical time, and ...by a person standing in so conspicuous a station as to ...require particularly the punishment due to this offence. ...Mr. S. adverted to the peculiar state of the militia thus ...ordered home, on a frontier requiring their presence for ...its protection, and whence he said, from their character, they might indeed have been expected, being the ...descendants of the Green Mountain Boys, who so much ...distinguished themselves during the Revolution, under ...the illustrious Allens, to have voluntarily aided in the ...invasion of the territory of the enemy. Under these ...circumstances, and when their services were most needed, they were invited by Governor Chittenden, to desert ...their position. His conduct in this respect must meet the ...decided reprehension, not only of every member of this ...house, but of every good citizen in the nation. It ought, ...then, to receive legal scrutiny. His offence ought to ...be punished, lest our laws should be subject to the remark which was applied to Solon's—that they were ...like cobwebs, which entangled the weak, but which ...the strong could break through. To bring this subject ...directly before the house, he offered the following ...resolutions:—

Resolved, That the militia of any of these United States ...or the territories thereof, when lawfully employed in the service of the United States, are subject to the same rules and articles ...as the troops of the United States.

Resolved, That every person not subject to the rules and articles ...of war, who shall procure or entice a soldier in the service of the ...United States to desert, is guilty of an infraction of the laws of the ...United States, and subject to punishment.

Resolved, That his Excellency Martin Chittenden, Governor of ...the State of Vermont, by issuing his Proclamation, dated at Montpelier, on the 10th day of November, in the year of our Lord 1813, did ...entice soldiers in the service of the United States to desert—Therefore ...Resolved, That the President of the United States be, and he is ...hereby requested to instruct the Attorney-General of the United ...States to institute a prosecution against the said Martin Chittenden.

The Message was received from the *President*, and ...the House adjourned.

PORTSMOUTH, N. H. JAN. 1.

A Court-martial has been held on board the *Congress* ...this week, for the trial of Mr. William Harper, sailing master of the *Enterprise*, on a charge of cowardice ...in the action with the British sloop of war *Boxer*. ...Mr. Harper, we understand, repeatedly ordered the ...flag of the *Enterprise* to be struck in time of action. ...Captain Hull is President of the Court.

HIGH TREASON.—Last evening two persons were ...committed to jail in this town on the charge of high ...treason. They were apprehended in Berwick, in pursuance of a warrant from the Hon. Judge Story, by Mr. Thaxter, Deputy-Marshal, and conducted by him to this place. We understand that the charge alleged against them is supplying the British ships of Cape Harbour with cattle.—(*Boston Chronicle*).

NEW-HAVEN, JAN. 5.

Two persons have been detected in Fort Trumbull, New London, as spies (one of them dressed in woman's apparel), by a private in that fort. They had been on board of the American squadron and in fort Griswold. They were sent on board the frigate *United States*, Commodore Decatur. The one in woman's clothes proves to be the 2d Lieutenant of the *Ramilies*.

NEW YORK, JAN. 6.

At an early hour yesterday morning, five dwelling-houses, and St. George's Chapel (one of the finest Episcopal Churches in this city), in Beekman-street, and one dwelling house, and the African School, in Cuff-street, together with a number of work-shops and other small buildings in the rear, were destroyed by fire. The flames continued to rage with uncontrolled fury for several hours. The wind was high, and the flakes of fire flew in various directions, and to a great distance; and were it not that the roofs were covered with snow, which was then falling, an immense number of buildings must have been destroyed. Very providentially the steeple of the church fell within the building; had it fallen into the street, most probably many lives would have been lost.

THEATRE-ROYAL, DRURY-LANE.

THIS EVENING, WILD OATS.

To which will be added, THE CHILDREN IN THE WOOD.

To-morrow, The Merchant of Venice; after which (1st time), a new farce, in two acts, to be called Rogues All, or Three Generations. On Monday, The Devil's Bridge.

THEATRE-ROYAL, COVENT-GARDEN.

THIS EVENING, JULIUS CÆSAR.

Brutus, Mr. Kemble.

To which will be added, THE BEE-HIVE.

To-morrow, The Farmer's Wife, and the Miller and his Men. On Monday, King Henry VIII.; Cardinal Wolsey, Mr. Kemble; and the new Pantomime. On Tuesday, The Farmer's Wife; and Katherine and Petruchio. On Thursday, the Farmer's Wife; and the new Pantomime.

SANS PAREIL THEATRE, Strand.

THIS and TO-MORROW EVENING, a new Farsical Comic Burletta, in two Acts (written by Miss Scott), with new Music, Scenery, Dresses, and Decorations, called WHACKHAM and WINDHAM; or, The Wrangling Lawyers. Principal characters, Wilford Whackham, Esq. Attorney-at-Law, Mr. Meredith; Worrit Windam, Esq. Attorney-at-Law, Mr. Stebbing; Henry Windham, his Son, an Imitative Character, Mr. Campbell; Thomas Thresher, Whackham's Servant Man, Mr. Huckell; Quilldrive, Windham's Clerk, Mr. Haughton; Rebecca, Mrs. Daly; and Maria Whackham, Miss Scott. Previous to which, first time, a new Ballet Dance, called LOVE IN THE GROVE: or, The Merry Lasses. The principal characters by Mr. Flexmore, and the Miss Girouxs, who will introduce their admired Tamborine Pas De Deux. To conclude with an entire new Comic Pantomime, (written by Miss Scott), called The MAGICIANS; or, The Enchanted Bird. Clown, Mr. Flexmore; and Columbine, Miss Giroux. A new Mirror Dance, by Miss and Miss C. Giroux. Also her admired Skipping-Rope Hornpipe, by Miss Giroux. Immediately after the Burletta, Miss Browne will dance her much-approved Broad Sword Hornpipe.

For this Week only, the celebrated young SAUNDERS, and his Sister, whose pleasing Exhibitions have drawn forth such uncommon and enthusiastic applause, are engaged for six Nights only. The False Friend, and the Earls of Hammersmith, will (for the accommodation of those Ladies and Gentlemen who were last week disappointed of places) be repeated.

OLYMPIC THEATRE, Newcastle-street, Strand.

THIS and TO-MORROW EVENINGS will be presented, The FALSE FRIEND; or, The Assassin of the Rock. End of the first Piece, Miss Saunders will exhibit her wonderful Equilibriums on the Slack Wire, and, assisted by her Brother, will go through a variety of Feats and Dancing on the Tight-Rope, particularly that pleasing and astonishing Performance on the Double-Rope. In the course of the evening will be recited, 'Mary the Maid of the Inn,' by Miss Sydney; a Song by Mr. Pearman; and a Comic Song by Mr. Fitzwilliam. To conclude with, the grand serious Romantic, Operatic, Infantine, Heroic, Spectral Spectacle, entitled The EARLS OF HAMMERSMITH. The Band, which is select and complete, is led by Mr. Mountain. The whole under the management of Mr. Russell.

LONDON,

FRIDAY, FEBRUARY 4, 1814.

The public anxiety is naturally directed to the great events which are most probably in the very crisis of their development in France. It was yesterday reported, we know not with what truth, that BUONAPARTE had sent orders to SUCHET to evacuate Catalonia, and move with all speed upon Lyons which the latter accordingly undertook to do; but the Allies, aware of his intentions, prevented him by marching in force upon that city, into which they entered with the good wishes of the inhabitants, and after a very slight and ineffectual opposition by AUGEREAU.

The American documents the import of which we yesterday stated are this day laid before our readers. It will be seen that the letter of Lord CASTLEREAGH is plain and decisive, without losing any thing of that gentlemanlike tone which ought to prevail in the diplomatic intercourse of civilised nations. His Lordship states the entire readiness, and even earnest desire, of our Government to adjust all differences between the two countries, on principles of perfect reciprocity not inconsistent with the *established maxims of public law*, and with the maritime rights of the British Empire. The PRESIDENT, in his reply, abstains from appealing to maxims which he probably thinks antiquated,—maxims which certainly will not bear him out in his quixotic attempt to set up the rights of naturalisation against the duties of birth; but he says he is ready to treat on a reciprocity consistent with "the rights" of both parties. We suspect he has yet much to learn in the grammar of Rights, and that he has all the folly and jargon of the *Droits de l'Homme* school, in which he was educated, at the feet of that venerable Gamaliel JEFFERSON, still ringing in his ears. How comes it to pass, that the worthy citizens of America, who are certainly acute enough in matters of profit and loss, should be so excessively dull in detecting the metaphysical sophistry of a philosopher, who can do nothing but

Weave fine cobwebs fit for skull
That's empty when the moon's at full?

The nonsense which the PRESIDENT has talked on this subject of naturalisation is such as would disgrace a fifth-form boy at one of our public schools: and yet, forsooth, he is a Statesman!

The good manners of the PRESIDENT, too, appear to have been learnt in the French republican school. When the Jacobins pretended to open a negociation with us, it was always, as matter of course, prefaced by some insinuations of our "Punic faith," our insincerity, or the like. Exactly so does the PRESIDENT introduce his conciliatory letter. Lord CASTLEREAGH having told him that we were willing to enter immediately into a direct negociation, he surlily answers, he "sees with regret this new obstacle;" and then proceeds to fill half his letter with a long harangue on the disrespect we have shown to the Emperor of RUSSIA in declining his mediation. In the course of this argument, however, the learned PRESIDENT has certainly overshot his mark. He notices, that since the Emperor of RUSSIA "was engaged in war as an ally of England, it was his *interest* to promote peace between the United States and Great Britain." If our alliance rendered our interests of importance to Russia, the conclusion which the citizens of America must draw from this unlucky remark is, that the PRESIDENT's politics have placed his country in a most unfavourable situation. They must perceive how contemptible a figure their republic cuts in the eyes of Russia, and of all Europe, when compared with Great Britain: the one a sneaking vassal of a disgraced despot; the other, the steady, undeviating, and now proudly successful assertor of general freedom. Why did not Mr. MADISON render the interests of the United States as dear and as important to the Emperor of RUSSIA, as those of Great Britain are? Why? Because he could not do so, but by abandoning BUONAPARTE, and joining the sacred cause of nations, in which Great Britain stood so proudly eminent, and so conspicuous in her wisdom and valour. The drum and colours of a French Captain, the PRESIDENT could conscientiously follow; but to march under the Old British Union! the thought was too cutting. After this, it is ridiculous enough to observe his spaniel-like fawning on the Emperor of RUSSIA. "The offer of a mediation by one Power, and the acceptance of it by another, forms *a relation between them*, the delicacy of which cannot but be felt. Oh! yes. This is very intelligible. Mr. MADISON is willing that the relation between America and Russia should henceforth be the same as that which has hitherto existed between America and France. A very dignified profession of republican faith; but probably not altogether palatable to his countrymen, and possibly unacceptable to the Russian Sovereign himself.

General MAC LURE's account of the fall of Fort Niagara, we are sorry to observe, furnishes another instance of that readiness which has so frequently appeared in the American officers to censure and calumniate each other. The Commander of the fort he first accuses (upon mere surmise) of gross neglect; and then (upon grounds, perhaps, full as trivial) insinuates that he was guilty of direct treachery. After this, we pay the less attention to what he says of the inhumanities of the savages under British command. It is, however, somewhat curious to find, that the British officers were painted. It must be a critical eye, which, in the head of an engagement, could distinguish a true Indian from an Englishman painted to imitate an Indian; for such, we presume, is the meaning of the assertion. Major-General AMOS HALL affords us satisfactory intelligence indeed. The whole Niagara frontier now lies open and defenceless; and consequently the boasted victories of HARRISON in that quarter have been rendered wholly ineffectual and fruitless.

Extract of a letter from an officer on board his Majesty's ship *Albion*, off Nantucket, Dec. 11, 1813:—"We have this moment fallen in with a Russian ship from Rhode Island, bound to Liverpool, and from thence to Gottenburgh: her master states the information, that Commodore RODGERS sailed from Newport last Saturday evening, after having laid an embargo on all the outward-bound vessels the five days preceding. She contrived to elude the vigilance of our cruisers on this station, which is extraordinary, as we have seen and spoken with, in this week, his Majesty's ships *Ramilies, Loire*, and *Orpheus*; and there are smaller vessels cruising in shore."

WINDSOR, FEB. 3.

This morning proving remarkably fine, the QUEEN and Princesses AUGUSTA, ELIZABETH, and MARY, took an airing to Frogmore, where they partook of some refreshment, and returned to the Castle to dinner.

Last evening HER MAJESTY had a select party to tea and cards.

The apartments in the Castle, formerly belonging to the late Princess AMELIA, previous to her removal to Augusta Lodge, have been newly fitted up, in expectation of the arrival of the Duke of MECKLENBURG, the QUEEN's brother. His non-arrival is said to be owing to indisposition, and the inclemency of the season.

Yesterday at three o'clock, a Cabinet Council was held at the Foreign-office, which was summoned in consequence of the arrival of the dispatches brought by Lieutenant POGSON, on Wednesday evening, from America. It was attended by all the Cabinet Ministers except the LORD CHANCELLOR, who is still confined with the gout. The Council sat but a very short time; it was up in less than half an hour.

Lords LIVERPOOL and SIDMOUTH waited upon the PRINCE REGENT yesterday, at Carlton-house.

The pricking for the Sheriffs for the year ensuing will take place at the Privy Council to be held this day by the PRINCE REGENT.

Accounts from Bombay are said to state, that the troops of the Pacha of Egypt, after having entered Jeddia and Mecca without opposition or bloodshed, detached a force against Taif, the only place remaining in the hands of the Wahabees. The power of the Sect is, therefore, looked upon as annihilated in that part of Arabia.

LAW REPORT.

COURT OF KING'S BENCH, THURSDAY, FEB. 3.

REX V. WM. EARLE.

The ATTORNEY-GENERAL prayed the judgment of the Court upon this defendant, who had suffered judgment by default, on an indictment for a libel in *The Scourge* for the month of February, 1813, upon J. C. Burkhardt, of Northumberland-street, Strand, jeweller. The libel was signed "Censor," and (as far as we could collect) seemed to originate in the jealousy of an English against a German tradesman; Mr. Burkhardt having been employed, at the desire of the Duke of Sussex, to make the Mason's jewel which was presented to Earl Moira. The libel affected to give the history of the life of Mr. Burkhardt, and consisted of the lowest and most personal abuse. On the part of the defendant, affidavits were put in, which imported that the libel had been inserted as it was sent to the publication; and that no enquiry was made into its truth or propriety, till the editor was threatened with this indictment, when he offered to contradict and apologize for it. There was also an affidavit as to a negociation between the defendant and Mr. Hutchinson, solicitor for the prosecution, to compromise the indictment, upon withdrawing the plea of *Not Guilty*, and suffering judgment by default; to answer which affidavit, the Attorney-General now took leave of the Court. He proposed to Mr. Holt, for the defendant, to wave the present sufferance of judgment, and give the defendant leave to go to trial; but Mr. Holt declined this.

COURT OF CHANCERY, THURSDAY, FEB. 3.

Before the VICE-CHANCELLOR.—(MOTIONS).

BLISS V. GREEN.

This was a motion for an injunction to restrain proceedings at law upon the merits disclosed in the answer. The plaintiff, who was tenant of a copyhold estate belonging to the defendant, had some conversation with his landlord about the purchase of the property. After this the landlord caused his attorney to write a letter to the tenant, stating the terms on which he proposed to sell, and to this the tenant wrote an answer, accepting the terms, but referring it to the honour of the vendor to make a small deduction in the price; and stating, that before the admission of the purchaser in court, it would be proper to make inquiries as to a claim to the estate made by a third person. The landlord, however, went no farther with this transaction; but on the ground that the agreement was not complete, brought an ejectment to turn the tenant out of possession, and the tenant immediately filed his bill to restrain this proceeding.

The landlord, in his answer, insisted that his attorney had gone beyond his authority, in the terms of the letter which he had written, and that the reply of the tenant was but a conditional acceptance of the terms of the offer, and that therefore the agreement could not be considered as complete.

The VICE-CHANCELLOR thought there were sufficient merits, however, to call upon the Court to stay proceedings at law in the mean time, and therefore the injunction was ordered.

STEVENSON V. ANDERSON AND OTHERS.

Mr. Anderson, a London merchant, had sent to the house of Messrs. Goodhall, in Scotland, four Bills of Exchange to purchase linens for Anderson. Messrs. Goodhall did not purchase the linens, but a person of the name of Dicks, stating himself to be a creditor of Anderson, used arrestment in the hands of Messrs. Goodhalls, who after that sent the bills to Stevenson, their agent in London, to procure payment of the bills; and then Anderson brought his action of trover against Stevenson to recover the bills, upon which Stevenson filed his bill in Chancery to restrain this proceeding.

Mr. COOKE, upon this bill and affidavits, now moved for an injunction accordingly. Messrs. ROMILLY and TROWER, for the defendant, Anderson, opposed this, on the ground that it was no proper bill of interpleader, and that, therefore, no such motion could be made on bill and affidavits.

The VICE-CHANCELLOR stated, that his present impression was against the application. Goodhall had parted with the possession of these bills to his agent, after the arrestment, and therefore he might be responsible; but the proceeding now, he thought, if proper at all, ought to be instituted by Goodhall, and not by Stevenson. But he would not dispose of the matter absolutely, till he had an opportunity of reading the affidavits, and inquiring into the effect of a Scotch arrestment.

(N. B. By the law of Scotland, bills are not the subject of arrestment at all.)

DRURYLANE THEATRE.

Last night the character of *Shylock*, in the *Merchant of Venice*, was repeated at this theatre by Mr. KEAN, who has been for some time known on the provincial stage, though new to the metropolitan. So many first appearances have lately been made, and so much disappointment has generally been the result, that, we confess, we thought little was to be expected from Mr. KEAN. Our disappointment was in this instance of an agreeable nature. We have seldom seen a much better *Shylock*. If he be inferior to KEMBLE in those peculiarities which distinguish that great actor, and to COOKE, in the force which he, above most performers, could give to particular passages, he need have no fear of a successful competition with any other man on the stage who attempts the sordid and malignant Jew. He is not deficient in the knowledge of stage business, as it is called; his countenance, though not so strongly marked as might be wished, is yet sufficiently well-managed; his conception of the author is good; his gestures are natural to the sort of being he represents; his voice, though not powerful, is not unsuitable; and the points in the character which always must tell in skilful hands, were effectually given. His gabardine, and other articles of dress, prevent any observations on the fitness of his figure for other parts; but we can scarcely doubt that he will be found a considerable accession to the strength of the company at this theatre. He was very well received; but by an audience which could not boast of its number. Miss SMITH was rather wanting in feeling. WRENCH's *Gratiano* was like the *Gratiano* of most others, flippant and frivolous. We are aware we tread on sacred ground; but we must own that we think *Gratiano's* interruptions in the Senate scene, particularly in the received manner of making them, are no helps to the most important part of this fine play.

Extract of a letter from Lord WELLINGTON's army:—

"St. Jean de Luz, Jan. 16.

"Lord WELLINGTON's dispatches must have long before this time put you in possession of the official details of the actions of the 9th, 10th, 11th, 12th, and 13th of December. Since then the army has been, in a general sense, quiet; for we do not make any account of some little affairs of piquets on the right, such things not causing any general sensation in so large a body as that of our collective force, and indeed being seldom known through the full extent of the line. Since the actions of the five days just mentioned, the left column has been a good deal employed in throwing up field-works, and forming batteries, about two miles from Bidart, on the road to Bayonne. The object of these works is, I suppose, to give strength to our positions in case of any check on our advance; for I cannot think them designed as a security against a general attack from the enemy, as they have not shewn the least disposition to act on the offensive since the battles of the five days; although certainly suffering inconveniences in their present situation, which might tempt them to hazard an action, with a view to improve their circumstances, if they could entertain any hope of a successful result. The garrison, and inhabitants of Bayonne in particular, labour under many severe privations; one of the most distressing of which is, the extreme want of fire-wood, the only fuel of this part. Their communication with the Pyrenees, and the other woody districts, being completely cut off by the British and allied forces, who, besides the command of the carriage roads, have also the power of interrupting the navigation of the Nive and the Adour, no supplies of any extent can pass into the place. The greatest want felt in the place, according to the best information we can collect, is that of bread, or biscuit: a necessary, the privation of which the French can bear worse than any other people. They have corn and flour, we are told, in considerable store: but from the want of fuel to bake, they cannot make it into satisfactory means of sustenance. In order to procure a little supply for pressing use, they are obliged daily to pull down old houses for the purpose of converting the wood to the indispensable necessities of their cookery. Lord WELLINGTON's head-quarters are still at St. Jean de Luz. He goes out hunting occasionally, and appears to enjoy the pleasures of the chase like a true sportsman, as if he had not any other care on his mind. He enjoys excellent health and spirits. It is rumoured, that Sir JOHN MURRAY is immediately to be tried by a Court-martial; the trial, we understand, will take place here. Admiral HALLOWELL, who, it is understood, is to be the prosecutor, is expected here shortly. General DONKIN has been with us above a fortnight. Our communication with England is now frequent and regular, beyond any thing that we have experienced since our first coming to the Peninsula; and this, I assure you, is a great gratification—for besides the pleasure of constant domestic intelligence from our families, the eagerness with which we look for the newspapers, and devour their contents, is not to be described. Our communication with our friends in the Peninsula is become tedious and uncertain, in proportion as our intercourse with England is rapid and easy. With our friends in the general cavalry quarters, in the towns on the Ebro, we have less correspondence than with our friends at home; and with those at Madrid, Oporto, and Lisbon, we cannot exchange a letter in a month. The talk between our army and the enemy, whenever the sentinels or Officers find an opportunity for gossipping at a civil distance, which they are very fond of, turns all on peace. The French make no disguise of their being heartily tired of the war, and wishing very much for peace—Officers, soldiers, people, all."

In consequence of the severity of the weather, the river Tay has been completely frozen over between Perth and Newburgh. The intenseness of the cold there has been indicated by another circumstance. Wild swans have been observed on the open parts of the river below Newburgh. These birds pass the summer in Lapland, Iceland, anp other polar regions, and migrate to lower latitudes in winter. They are seldom seen, however, farther south than the lakes by which the Tay is fed.

At the General Quarter Sessions of the peace for the borough of Lynn, held before R. BEVILL, Esq. Recorder, Mrs. *Anne Clark* received sentence of death, for wilfully and maliciously attempting to stab her husband, Mr. W. CLARK, shipmaster, with an intent to murder him.

POLICE.

BOW-STREET.

Yesterday *James Savage*, the driver of an Hackney-coach, underwent a final examination, charged with stealing a box, containing bank of England notes and silver, to the amount of upwards of 1[illegible]., the property of Mary Williams. The substance of the evidence against the prisoner has been already detailed. The prisoner was committed for trial.

UNION-HALL.

John Verity, a young man of good address, was brought before Mr. BIRNIE, on charges of bigamy and fraud.

Mrs. Body, of Carrington-street, Mayfair, stated, that about three weeks ago the prisoner, who had represented himself as a man of family and fortune, and as holding the rank of Colonel in the army, married her daughter, he having at that time, and now, another wife, or wives, living.

Miss Ann Body, *alias* Verity, an interesting young woman, stated that she was married to the prisoner, at Newington church, on the 17th of last month.

Mr. Wm. Nichols, of Brentford, stated, that he had been informed by Mr. Cross, a gentleman residing at Brentford, that the prisoner was some time since married at Liverpool to his (Mr. Cross's) sister, who was still living.

Mr. Joseph Ridout, a grocer, residing at Ryde, in the Isle of Wight, stated, that in September last, the prisoner, who then represented himself as a man of fortune, and high rank in the army, purchased goods of him to the amount of 3l. and gave him in payment a draft on Sir James Esdaile and Co. for 10l. Mr. Ridout gave him the difference in cash; but on presenting the draft at Sir James Esdaile's, he was informed no such person as Colonel Verity did then, or ever had, kept cash with them.

Miss Ann Wild stated, that she resided at Wood-green, near Hornsey, with her mother. Some time since, the prisoner was introduced to them as a gentleman of fortune, and became intimate in the family. In conversation one day, Miss Wild accidentally mentioned that she had been obliged by necessity to pledge a gold watch for 9l.; the Colonel immediately intreated he might be allowed to redeem it for her, and took the duplicate for that purpose. The duplicate was given to him, but they had neither been able to obtain that or the watch since.

Glennon, the officer, stated, that in consequence of information he received from Mrs. Body, he went to the prisoner's lodgings at Newington; the gallant Colonel, however, having received some intimation of the honour intended him, had retreated to a neighbouring public-house, from whence he dispatched a messenger to his landlord, requesting he would convey some property to him left at his lodgings. Unfortunately for him, Glennon received the message, and determining to accompany the messenger in the character of landlord, the *unsuspicious* Colonel fell into the snare, and was taken prisoner. Several other charges are expected to be brought against him, and he was committed for re-examination.

CORONER'S INQUEST.

Yesterday an Inquest was held at the Middlesex Hospital, on the body of Edmond White, who was murdered on Sunday night, in St. Giles's. (This White was the man who lodged in the same house with *James Leary*.)

Patrick M'Carthy stated, that he lived in St. Giles's, and was a bricklayer's labourer; he knew the deceased, who was also a labourer; he was about 40 years of age, and a man of a quiet and peaceable disposition. On Sunday evening, about eight o'clock, witness was in a public-house, in St. Giles's; and in consequence of a riot in Bainbridge-street, he went to see what it was; and on going forward, he saw the deceased lying in the kennel, and a great many men beating him with sticks. Among them were Michael Regan, Patrick Regan, and Cornelius Callaghan, all labourers. Michael Regan struck the deceased a blow with a sword which he had in his hand; Patrick Regan also struck the deceased as he lay stretched out, with a stick, and also gave him a violent kick in some part of the body. Callaghan also struck the deceased a blow with a piece of wood he had in his hand.

William Pretty, House-surgeon to the Middlesex Hospital, stated, that the deceased was brought to the hospital about half past nine o'clock on Sunday evening, with a severe injury on the head; he died on Tuesday morning, and from a particular examination of the head, both at the time he was first brought to the hospital and since his death, witness was firmly of opinion that he died in consequence of the injury which he received in his head; there was a fracture of the skull, accompanied with depression of bone, a laceration of the membrane of the brain, and the brain itself much injured.

Margaret D[illegible]gine deposed, that the riot took place in a pot-house, in Bainbridge-street, where the deceased had been to pay his landlord some rent, and that she saw Michael Regan strike him with a sword, Patrick Regan, Cornelius Callagan, and Patrick Gallaugher, each struck him with sticks, and several others struck him, whose names witness did not recollect; but she should know them again, as she frequently saw them engaged in quarrels before.

Eleanor Harrington stated, that on Sunday evening she was in the Hare and Hounds public-house, in Buckeridge-street, and saw the deceased there. She asked him what brought him up from Saffron-hill at so late an hour? he was paying for a pot of beer, and had a purse in his hand with some money in it; he answered, that he came to pay his landlord, Martin Hearn, his rent. The deceased then asked witness to go with him to partake of a pot of beer; witness desired him to go before, and that she would follow shortly; he went out for that purpose, and witness shortly after followed. She heard a hallooing, and saw him two or three yards from the door of the Ship public-house, struggling to make his escape; and she saw Patrick Gallaugher come out with an iron bar in his hand; he gave the deceased a violent back-handed blow with it on the head: his hat fell off, and the deceased fell to the ground. Michael Regan then came up, with a piece of wood in one hand, and a cutlass in the other, and gave him a violent blow with one of them, but which witness did not know. Patrick Regan also came up with a large bludgeon, with which he also struck the deceased as he lay stretched under him. Many other persons also struck the deceased, whom witness did not know by name.

Martin Hearn stated, that he lived in Clarendon-square, Somers-town; he was acquainted with the deceased, who was always a quiet peaceable kind of a man; he was tenant to witness, and rented five small tenements, which witness built in New-court, Saffron-hill. The deceased did not come to pay his rent as stated by the other witnesses, only to excuse himself, he owing three weeks rent for them. On Sunday last witness went to the Ship public-house, in Bainbridge-street, kept by Owen Daly, where he was informed that two or three brothers, of the name of Norwood, who had a previous quarrel with another party in St. Giles's, were out that day providing men to fight the other party, and that there was to be a general fight. Witness, in consequence of this information, called on Mr. Chambers, the High Constable for the Holborn division. Witness informed him of it, and told him if he were to come and take some of the party into custody, it might put a stop to the fight. Mr. Chambers told witness to go back, and have an eye to them, and if he saw any thing serious likely to happen, to acquaint him with it, and that he would remain at home all the evening for that purpose. Witness returned to the Ship public-house, where he found some of the opposite party to that of the Norwoods: witness advised them to go home: there was a number of them, perhaps about a dozen; they had 7s. 6d. reckoning to pay, which the little girl was collecting; the reckoning might be about a pot a piece. Three women came in, two of whom witness understood to be wives of the Norwoods, and also a man of the name of Kelly, who immediately began a quarrel with Patrick Regan, who was there. A crowd was coming up from the end of Church-street, crying out huzza: a woman at the door called out "Here they come:" witness shut the door; a tall man on the inside pushed witness from the door, and put out his head, when he received a blow, which cut him so that his blood flowed down over the witness's breast; one of the men on the outside, who witness was informed was one of the Norwoods, had a shovel. They afterwards had a general quarrel on the outside; witness remained in at the time, and did not venture out: White, the deceased, was outside; he worked all that day with his master, until four o'clock, and then he asked permission to go to a funeral—a pretence, in order to come there; he did not come to pay rent; witness often blamed him for being among those parties.

The following questions were put to this witness by the Jury:—

Q. Do you know what views White had in coming to St. Giles's; did he come with an intention to fight?—A. I cannot tell.

Q. As you were not outside, how can you tell that White was with the outside party?—A. I do not know any thing of what passed on the outside.

A woman of the name of Norwood came forward to give her evidence, which went to state that the last witness, Martin Hearn, was the head of the other party, that he provided them with swords and sticks, and stood at the door to hand them arms as they went out.

The Jury returned a verdict of—*Wilful Murder against Michael Regan, Patrick Regan, Cornelius Callaghan, and Patrick Gallaugher.*

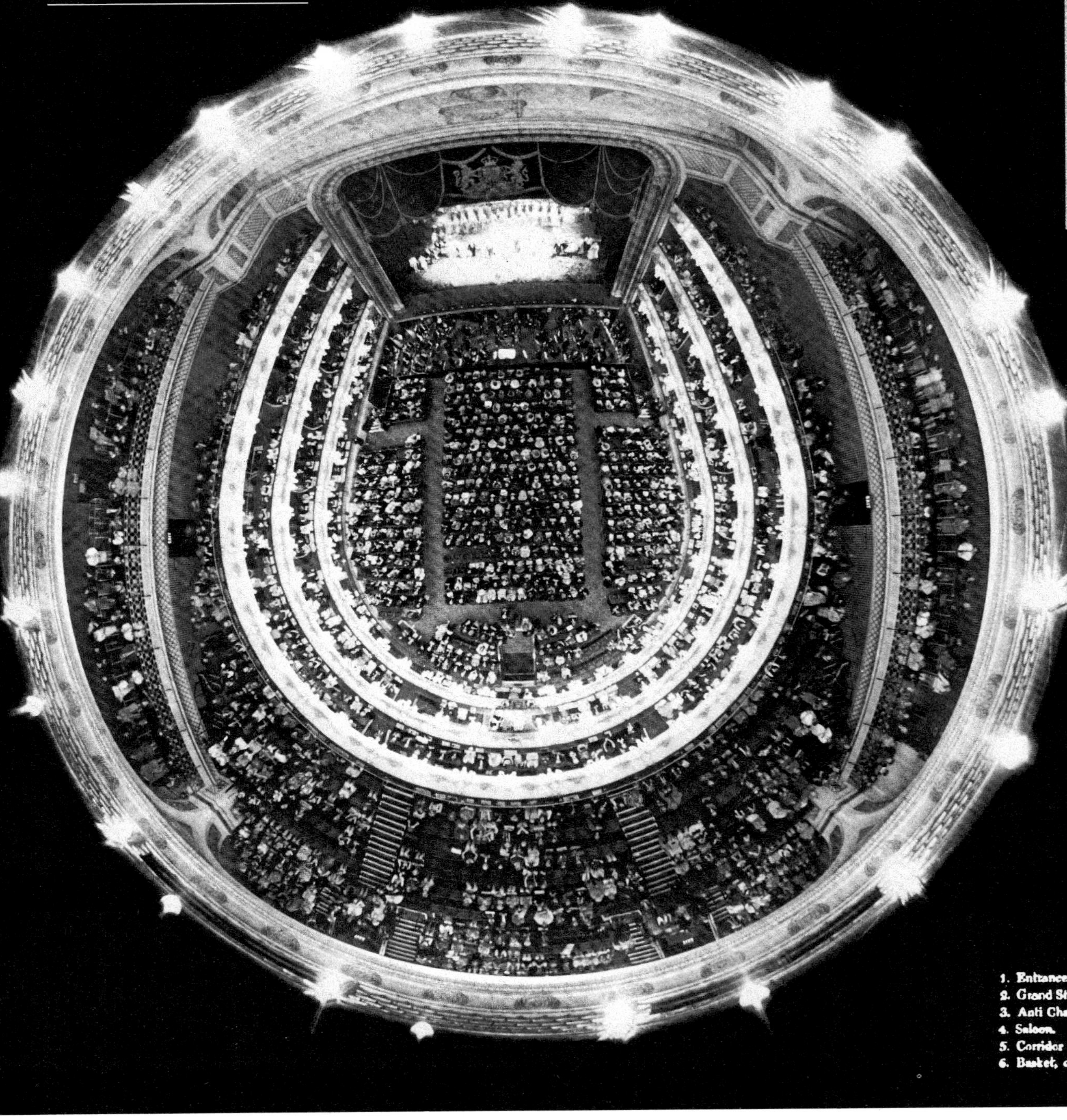

Of the INTERIOR of the Theatre, I send you a few particulars, accompanied by a sketch or two which may convey some idea of the plan. It is somewhat larger than the late house. The form is different from those hitherto built; it approaches nearly to the circle. The different forms of the antient, and of our modern Theatres, may be seen, by referring to the annexed figures. Those of the *antients* were semi-circular, as at A. The inside of the late *Drury Lane* is shewn by B. and that of the present *Opera*, between which and the *late Covent Garden* there was little difference, by C. The interior of the *new* edifice is represented by D. This figure gives the plan on the 3d tier, which is devoted to the private boxes, saloon, &c.

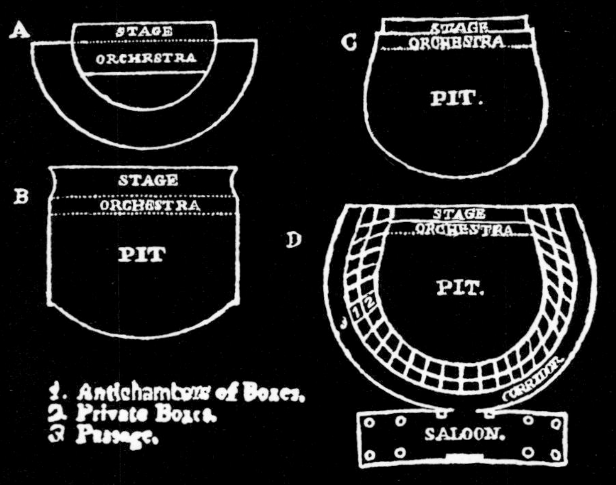

A STAGE ORCHESTRA

B STAGE PIT

C STAGE ORCHESTRA PIT.

D STAGE ORCHESTRA PIT. SALOON.

1. Antichambers of Boxes.
2. Private Boxes.
3. Passage.

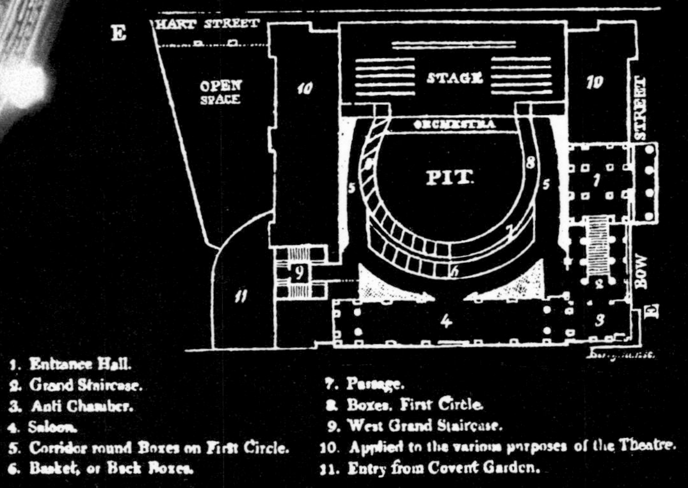

E HART STREET OPEN SPACE STAGE ORCHESTRA PIT BOW STREET

1. Entrance Hall.
2. Grand Staircase.
3. Anti Chamber.
4. Saloon.
5. Corridor round Boxes on First Circle.
6. Basket, or Back Boxes.
7. Passage.
8. Boxes, First Circle.
9. West Grand Staircase.
10. Applied to the various purposes of the Theatre.
11. Entry from Covent Garden.

Above A view of the Royal Opera House, Covent Garden, from the dome. Photo by Ian Bradshaw, 1969.

Above right Diagrams of Covent Garden Theatre that accompanied a description of the design and construction of the new theatre in THE TIMES, 1809.

Below The front of the Theatre Royal, Drury Lane, 1776. The Adams brothers' alterations to the interior and the façade were completed in 1775, the year of Mrs Siddon's debut. Garrick retired in 1776, and Richard Brinsley Sheridan took over as manager.

research and profound critical sagacity; it is therefore, our duty to undeceive them; for the critic, who disgraces his profession so completely as to oppose indiscriminately performers and writers only because they happen to be attached to a particular theatre [i.e. Covent Garden Theatre], deserves to be exposed, and, we trust, the circumstances we are about to state, will sufficiently elucidate the secret motives of its poignant satire and its piquant remarks.

Note the old-fashioned punctuation and the tone of baffled fury that the comfortable old arrangements had been broken for ever. It was untrue to suggest that *The Times* picked solely on Covent Garden: its reviews of contemporary plays at other theatres were just as beastly, when the critic felt that they deserved it.

Sheridan, the grand old man of the British theatre, entered the fray. He fell out with *The Times* because of John Walter's insistence, in his pursuit of independence, that theatrical managers pay the full rate for their advertisements, instead of the old gang's arrangement that theatrical advertisements went in the paper at cost, that is, at the price of the advertising duty only. Sheridan, whose natural element was hot water, wrote to John Walter Esquire Junior:

Dear Sir

I confess my surprise at being shown on my return today to Town a letter in your liberal Paper, containing a gross attack on me personally, and a very foul attempt to obstruct our endeavours to rebuild Drury Lane Theatre. The whole is a string of most impudent falsehoods. And addressing you, not as an Editor, but, on the footing of the fair and friendly intercourse, which, as a private man, I have always met you and your Father, I must regret, that you could have permitted the publications of such Libels. A proper answer will be sent; tho' not from me. And, I hope, I shall have the pleasure of finding you at home between three and four tomorrow.

In the struggle between poodle press and independence, the gods were on the side of the latter. The press was coming of age, led by *The Times*, and theatrical criticism was coming of age with it. Drama criticism may seem a comparatively small part of a modern newspaper; but it took more space in the early nineteenth century, and was one of the main features of a newspaper. If John Walter were going to succeed in his vision of an independent newspaper, he had to make his theatre criticism free from the old ring. He succeeded. In 1817 Hazlitt, the Moses of English theatre criticism, wrote:

I would advise any one who has an ambition to write, and to write his best, in the periodical press, to get if possible, a situation in *The Times* newspaper, the Editor of which is a man of business, and not of letters. He may write them as long and as good articles as he can, without being turned out of it.

It is not a bad primitive definition of the right relationship between the editorial staff and the management of an independent newspaper; a relationship that was forged in those brave young days, in the stalls as well as in the gallery of Parliament.

A review (column 2) of Henry Irving's production of HAMLET, with Ellen Terry as Ophelia, in which box-office arrangements seem to have made a greater impression than the production.
4 MAY 1885

THE QUEEN.

Escorted by the Trinity yacht Galatea, the Royal yacht Alberta, and the Admiralty yacht Enchantress, the Royal yacht Victoria and Albert, with the Queen and Princess Beatrice and Princess Louis of Battenberg on board, left Flushing at 8 55 a.m. on Saturday and arrived at Garrison Point Fort at the entrance to Sheerness harbour at 3 55 in the afternoon. The Galatea piloted the flotilla across the North Sea, but on nearing the English coast the Victoria and Albert steamed ahead of her consorts, and was safely moored alongside Port Victoria Pier before they entered the harbour. The Victoria and Albert was flying the Royal standard of England at the main, the Admiralty flag at the fore, and the Union Jack at the mizen, but, at the express wish of Her Majesty, who was desirous that no ceremony should be observed, no salutes were fired. [illegible] The river Medway in the vicinity of the pier was guarded by a detachment of the Metropolitan Water Police in boats, [illegible] The Queen and Princesses disembarked soon after 5 o'clock, and left Port Victoria Pier at 5 30 for Windsor. [illegible]

IRELAND.

DUBLIN, MAY 1.

The scene of greatest interest in Irish politics is now shifted to Rome, where the most influential dignitaries and exponents of Irish National opinion are now assembled. [illegible]

CORK, MAY 3.

At the Kanturk Petty Sessions on Saturday five young men, named Ryan, Bradley, Barrett, Carroll, and Thornton, [illegible]

WAR PREPARATIONS.

On Saturday Captain Brownlow of the Admiralty, with the view of meeting the requirements of the War Office, made preliminary arrangements for fitting out the 12 transports taken up on Thursday evening. [illegible]

THE THEATRES.

[illegible]

THE INVENTIONS EXHIBITION.

The ceremonial at the opening of the International Inventions Exhibition to-day will be of a simple character. Their Royal Highnesses the Prince and Princess of Wales will be received on their arrival at the main entrance in Exhibition-road, a few minutes before noon, by the Executive Council, who will have assembled in the new decorated vestibule. It is expected that the Duke and Duchess of Edinburgh and the Duke of Cambridge will also be present. A procession will be formed of the Executive Council and foreign Commissioners, and the Royal and illustrious visitors will be conducted to the Conservatory, where the formal proceedings will take place. The route will be through the new building called the North Court of the South Galleries as far as the door giving access to the octagonal pavilion erected last year for the water companies and now the Austro-Hungarian Court. Turning northward here the procession will pass into the South Central Gallery and up the east door, and along the garden terrace to the East Gallery, at the further end of which is the Chinese Court. Then by the East Arcade and Quadrant the Conservatory will be reached. Here a dais will be placed in the middle on the garden side, so that those season ticket-holders who are so fortunate as to get seats in the gallery will have a good view of all that passes. An address will be presented to his Royal Highness the President, who, after making a reply, will declare the exhibition open. The procession will re-form, and, leaving the Conservatory by the west end, will go by the West Quadrant to the West Gallery, the building in which the machinery in motion is put, and thence into the Central Gallery, containing musical instruments, turning southward again through the American Court, where a large stationary engine of 150-horse power, with a great fly-wheel 20ft. in diameter, made by Messrs. Hick, Hargreaves, and Co., of Bolton, is placed to drive the fine machinery of the Waltham Watch Company, which will certainly be one of the chief attractions of the exhibits from the United States. Crossing the South Central Gallery at its western end, where the furniture is shown, the Royal party will next be taken into the Old London Street, and after, perhaps, inspecting the tastefully fitted-up pavilion designed for the use of the Prince and Princess of Wales when they visit the exhibition, the procession will again advance southward until the long South Gallery is reached, through which the return to the principal entrance-hall will be made. Season ticket-holders who wish to go into the Conservatory Gallery, where there will be about 500 seats available, must enter by the principal door of the Albert-hall from Kensington Gore. Those who have received the tickets of special invitation, by which alone admission to the floor of the Conservatory can be gained, will find full directions as to the gates they should enter by in the official announcement published in the advertisement columns of *The Times*. Holders of season and other tickets who are content to see the procession passing through the buildings can enter either at the principal doors in Exhibition-road, by the Prince's-gate entrance, or from the west by the northerly entrance in Cromwell-road, but not by the south gates on that side.

Although any inexperienced visitor who strolled through the courts and galleries at South Kensington last week would suppose that the apparent chaos then prevailing could not possibly be resolved into order within the few days left before the opening, so energetically have the authorities worked that the arrangements will be found to be far more nearly complete than in the case of either the Fisheries or the Health Exhibition. The heaviest machines and engines are nearly all in place. Commanding the approach through the principal vestibule, and at the entrance to the long South Gallery, its prominent position, significant of the importance attaching just now to the art connected with war, is a long piece of ordnance—an eight-inch 14-ton gun of Whitworth steel, with smaller guns to the right and left, and other exhibits from the Royal Gun Factory at Woolwich. Beyond are railway locomotives and lofty signal-boxes, and further along steam-steering engines for ships, and various appliances of engineering construction. This long central gallery is, or seems to be, already nearly filled from end to end, though many smaller exhibits will be brought in to occupy vacant spaces at the sides during the next few days. In the south court of this gallery, newly constructed, and including the area last year occupied by the first-class dining rooms, are steam threshers and binders and drills, and other agricultural machines of all kinds.

Instead of the advertisements which last year covered the walls of the principal entrance-hall or vestibule, the panels will be filled with cartoons painted by Mr. Page and Mr. Nicholas, students of the National Art Training Schools, under the personal superintendence of Professor Chandler Roberts and Mr. H. Trueman Wood. These pictures, 20 in number, will illustrate the development of arts in ten classes of industries represented in the exhibition. Each group is shown in two stages of its progress, the earlier example being in nearly all cases taken from original drawings of the 16th century. On the right the series begins with a picture from Agricola's work, "De Re Metallica" (edition 1553), showing ore washing with primitive utensils and appliances. Next to this is a scene in Sierra Nevada, showing in the distance a high-trestled "flume," some miles in length, bringing water from the mountains, and in the foreground a miner directing an irresistible stream that washes away the face of the cliffs and with the detritus the coveted ore. Then there follow in couples pictures of the Catalan process of iron smelting, as practised in the 13th century, and a huge pear-shaped Bessemer converter pouring out its charge of molten steel; an ancient bridge from drawings by Leonardo da Vinci (1520), and the East River, or Brooklyn, Suspension Bridge at New York; George Stephenson's locomotive, "The Rocket" (1829), and its modern outcome; Miller and Symington's steamboat (1788), and a monster Atlantic "liner" of our day; an early weaving machine (from Jost Amman's *Stände und Handwerke*, Frankfort-on-the-Main, 1568), and a modern loom; the first known electrical machine, constructed by Otto von Guericke, and copied from his "Experimenta Nova," published in 1673, and a Gramme dynamo; a reproduction of a sketch in Biringuccio's "Della Pirotechnia" (1540) of the processes of boring and preparing a mould for cannon, and a Woolwich breech-loader; an early printing press (1520), and the Walter press in use at *The Times* Office; ancient clockmaking from Amman's work and a modern watch factory.

If the visitor is disposed to undertake his sight-seeing in a methodical way, he may, on emerging from the vestibule, turn to the right in order to make the circuit of the buildings, and then if his powers of attention do not begin to flag, he may, passing from the middle of the South Gallery northward, find his way into the gardens for fresh air and the more frivolous amusement of the promenade. Taken in this order the groups seen would present inventions in electricity, the most remarkable a sexduplex telegraphing system which has been worked in the United States on a line between the towns of Providence (Rhode Island) and Boston, six messages passing at the same time; gas, a department in which Messrs. Sugg and Co., and other friends of the gas companies, are preparing to show what the older illuminant can still do to hold its own against electricity; fuel, furnaces, &c., further along the eastern arcade, or, by a digression into the Eastern Annexe (at the end of which the Chinese Court and Restaurant remain looking very much as they did last year), educational apparatus, aeronautics, processes and machinery connected with paper, printing, and bookbinding will be seen. Continuing the tour into the East Quadrant, there will be found games (billiard tables, bagatelle boards, &c.), clothing, leather, and the machinery used in the preparation of these; and in the West Quadrant india-rubber, pottery and glass, and cutlery and ironmongery. On the West side is again the machinery in motion, the groups housed in the enlarged annexe being textile fabrics, machine tools, &c., hydraulics, while passing through the Aquarium into the Queen's-gate Annexe (where the Belgian exhibits were placed last year) the visitor will find carriage building and naval architecture exemplified. Leaving the Old London Street (newly paved with an ingenious imitation of cobble-stones and with herring-bone red-brick side paths) until the return, any one who, after the round suggested above, is still fresh enough in mind and body to see more, might pass from the north court of the long South Gallery into the octagonal pavilion which was erected last year for the water companies, and is this time allotted to Austria-Hungary. This gives access to the central block of buildings, where will be found the groups of chemistry (where side by side are the beautiful, but, as we are warned by medical authorities, dangerous dyes and antiseptic compounds), philosophical instruments, photographic apparatus, clocks and watches, jewellery, and furniture and fancy goods, and the courts assigned to the United States, Russia, France, Italy, Germany, Switzerland, Japan, and Siam.

The long and spacious building running across the gardens, and officially described as the Central Gallery, is given up to musical instruments. Nearly all the principal makers are to be found among the exhibitors, of whom some are going to considerable expense in the erection of ornamental stands. The walls will be decorated with appropriate designs from Messrs. Doulton's works, and with pictures and drawings illustrative of musical subjects. Messrs. Willis are putting up a large organ at one end, and Messrs. Walker one at the other end of the gallery, and there will be four large organs—two in the adjoining music room, in which two recitals daily will be given to permit exhibitors to have the quality of instruments tested. As proficient performers will be engaged, these morning and afternoon free concerts will doubtless form an attractive feature of the exhibition. Wind and stringed instruments will have their turn, and so will the drums. Among the novelties contemplated are historic concerts, at which the music of the Elizabethan and other periods will be rendered, with accompaniments on instruments of the time. The music room will contain seats for 400, and will hold 200 more. The King of Siam has sent over 19 performers of his Court band. They are expected on Saturday, but the instruments on which they are to play will not arrive until about the middle of the next month. For the historical loan collection, which promises to be wonderfully interesting, several gentlemen are engaged abroad in making selections from the possessions of those who are willing to lend. Mr. W. H. Weale has travelled with this purpose in Holland, Belgium, France, Germany, and Austria; Mr. Heron Allen has undertaken a similar mission in Italy, and Señor Riano in Spain. [illegible] a harp once played by Mary Queen of Scots (from the collection of Mr. Stuart, of Dalguise), the Indian instruments presented by the Rajah of Tajore to the Royal College of Music, some fine instruments from the Brussels Conservatoire, and pieces from the famous collections of M. Snoeck, of Renaix, and of M. Regibo will be among the treasures exhibited in the Albert-hall. Already the library is filled with these loans, and Mr. Maskell, who has the superintendence of the division of music, will have more than a sufficient number of such things to fill all the space at the disposal of the committee.

The Prince of Wales paid an informal visit to the Exhibition on Saturday in order to inspect and open the newly-constructed subway by which visitors travelling by the Metropolitan District Railway will be enabled to walk entirely under cover from the South Kensington Station of the underground railway into the Exhibition building. His Royal Highness was met in the vestibule of the main entrance of the Exhibition by the Duke of Edinburgh, Mr. J. S. Forbes, chairman of the Metropolitan District Railway, Sir Frederick Bramwell, chairman, and the Marquis of Hamilton, vice-chairman of the Executive Council, Sir Frederick Abel, C.B., Colonel Sir Francis Bolton, Mr. W. H. Preece, Professor Chandler Roberts, Dr. Stainer, and Mr. H. Trueman Wood; Viscount Gort, Mr. Murray, Dr. Wyld, and Mr. Isaacs, directors of the railway; Mr. Wolfe Barry and Mr. J. S. M'Cleary, the engineers, and Mr. Charles Lucas and Mr. Aird, the contractors for the subway; Mr. Hopwood, Mr. Alfred Powell, Captain Godbold, Mr. John Morgan; Mr. E. Cunliffe-Owen, secretary, Mr. Gordon Hake, the general superintendent, and Mr. J. Somers Vine, financial agent of the Exhibition. The Prince of Wales was conducted through the subway from the Exhibition to the railway station, a distance of about 400 yards. More exactly, the subway is 1,400ft. in length, 18ft. wide, and 11ft. high, lined with white glazed bricks, lighted throughout with incandescent electric lamps, and for a considerable portion of its course by windows on the side towards the Natural History Museum. Ventilation is further given by low grated shafts, which will form refuges for pedestrians at crossings in the roadway. About midway between the railway station and the Exhibition diverging subways will give access on the one side to the South Kensington Museum and on the other side to the grounds of the Natural History Museum. The work has been carried out with remarkable expedition, considering the nature of the operations, for it was not until the 6th of January last that a beginning was made.

Mr. J. S. FORBES, speaking at a luncheon which was given in the Exhibition vestibule of the subway on the return of their Royal Highnesses to the building, expressed the indebtedness of all concerned in the undertaking to the Prince of Wales for his attendance on that occasion and for the invaluable assistance he had been pleased to afford them in the inception of the enterprise, since, but for the intervention of his Royal Highness, it might never have been carried out at all. As some measure of the convenience this subway would afford to the public, he might mention that of rather more than four millions of visitors to the last Exhibition over three millions were conveyed by the railway. While greatly promoting the comfort of those passing between the Exhibition and the railway station, the subway, by relieving the street of congested traffic would, he believed, diminish the inconvenience which the inhabitants of the neighbourhood felt from the crowds entering and leaving the Exhibition. (Hear, hear.)

The PRINCE of WALES said,—I am very grateful to you, Mr. Forbes, for the very kind way in which you have proposed my health, and I beg to thank you, gentlemen, for myself and on behalf of my brother, for the reception you have given to the toast. It has afforded me sincere satisfaction to take part in this important work to-day, and to declare the subway open. It is very kind of Mr. Forbes to speak of anything I may have done with Her Majesty's Government in promoting the construction of this subway. I am glad to find that the obstacles, which I was afraid at first would be very great, have been overcome, and that the Board of Works has seen the advantage of having a subway like that which is opened to-day. (Hear, hear.) I entirely endorse the words which fell from Mr. Forbes as to the importance of this work, and I feel sure that not only will this Exhibition be greatly benefited by the subway, but also the permanent institutions at South Kensington. I only hope that it may be possible to carry the subway on to the Albert-hall, as this, I feel sure, would greatly increase the public utility of the work. (Cheers.) I thank you again for the way in which you have received the toast of my health, and I can assure you that it affords me great pleasure to do anything which I believe may be not only for the advantage of the people of this metropolis, but which may also conduce to the welfare of the country at large. (Cheers.)

His Royal Highness and the Duke of Edinburgh then left the Exhibition. Other toasts followed, the Marquis of Hamilton proposing "The Health of the Chairman of the Metropolitan District Railway Company."

ELECTION INTELLIGENCE.

BIRMINGHAM.—Mr. Broadhurst, M.P., has accepted the invitation addressed to him by the Liberal Committee of one of the seven divisions of Birmingham to stand as its Parliamentary candidate at the next election.

BRADFORD.—Strenuous efforts are being made to bring about a reconciliation between Mr. Forster and the Liberal Four Hundred of the borough, and it is hoped that he will be induced at the next election to come forward as a candidate for the Central Division of the borough. It is felt that a division in the Liberal ranks would be fatal to the interests of the party.

CUMBERLAND.—At a meeting held at Carlisle on Saturday a Conservative association was formed for the Northern Division of this county, and a provisional committee was empowered to take immediate steps to select a candidate. The candidate will probably be Mr. J. W. Lowther, the sitting member for Rutland, whose candidature for the Penrith Division of Cumberland was prematurely announced recently.

ESSEX.—It was announced on Saturday that Mr. J. Jackson, of Lexden Manor, has accepted an invitation to come forward as a Liberal candidate for the Harwich Division. Mr. J. Round, one of the present Conservative sitting members for East Essex, will be a Conservative candidate.

GLOUCESTERSHIRE.—Mr. A. B. Winterbotham, cloth manufacturer at Cam, near Dursley, has consented to contest the Cirencester Division of the county at the next election. Lord Moreton, who was the colleague of Colonel Kingscote, C.B., and was left the senior member for West Gloucestershire by the retirement of the latter, has written to his constituents expressing his determination not to offer himself again as a candidate for Parliamentary honours. His lordship's health is not equal "to the hours and duties of the House of Commons." The Liberal candidate for the Thornbury Division is not yet decided upon. Mr. B. St. John Ackers, junior member for West Gloucestershire, has been requested to contest the seat in the Conservative interest.

GLOUCESTER.—It is now decided that the Conservative candidate for the representation of the city of Gloucester will be Mr. W. K. Wait, a local corn merchant. He unsuccessfully contested the city in 1880, but had been twice previously returned as its member. Mr. Wait is to be opposed by Mr. T. Robinson, also a corn merchant, in the Liberal interest.

LANCASHIRE.—The Liberal Council for the Darwen Division of Lancashire have unanimously selected Mr. John Gerald Potter to oppose Lord Cranborne at the next election.

LEEDS.—On Saturday morning letters were received from Mr. Herbert Gladstone and Mr. John Barran. The former, writing from 10, Downing-street, Whitehall, stated that he accepted the invitation of a deputation from the Western division of Leeds, and he should be proud to offer himself as a candidate at the next general election. Mr. Gladstone accordingly declines to come forward for the Northern division of Leeds and also for the Eastern division, for each of which he had been invited to stand. Mr. Barran accepts the invitation to contest the Central division of Leeds.

NOTTINGHAMSHIRE.—At a meeting of Conservatives held at the George Hotel, Nottingham, on Saturday afternoon, it was decided to invite Dr. William Tindal Robertson to contest the Rushcliffe Division of the county in the Conservative interest at the next election, in opposition to Mr. J. E. Ellis, colliery proprietor, of Nottingham.

SHROPSHIRE.—Lieutenant-Colonel Kenyon Slaney, of Hatton-grange, Shifnal, Salop, has been selected as the Conservative candidate for the new Wellington Division of the county, and has issued an address to the electors. Mr. C. T. W. Forester, the Conservative member for the borough of Wenlock, which will lose its separate representation, has withdrawn his candidature for the Wellington Division in favour of Colonel Kenyon Slaney. The Central Liberal Council of the division will meet at Wellington to-morrow to select a Liberal candidate.

SOMERSET.—The Yeovil Working-men's Liberal Association unanimously resolved on Saturday night to discountenance Mr. George Mitchell's candidature for the Southern Division of this county, and to support the candidate selected by the delegates from the Liberal clubs affiliated to the Central Association.

WILTSHIRE.—The Central Liberal Association of the Devizes and Marlborough Division has chosen Mr. William Barber, Q.C., of Lincoln's-inn, Professor of Law of Real and Personal Property to the Council of Legal Education, as their candidate in opposition to Mr. W. H. Long, M.P., and Lord Henry Bruce, Conservative candidates.

THE MAILS.

The Royal Mail Company's steamer Don sailed from Southampton on Saturday, with the West India, Pacific, and Mexican mails, £2,452 in specie, 200 bottles of quicksilver, jewellery value £1,000, and a full complement of passengers and cargo.

Messrs. Lamport and Holt's steamer Pleiades sailed from Southampton on Saturday afternoon for Montevideo and Buenos Ayres, with passengers and a general cargo from London and Antwerp.

The Union Company's steamer Roman arrived at Southampton on Saturday morning from Hamburg, with outward cargo for the Cape of Good Hope and Natal.

The following mail steamships will leave Southampton during the ensuing week:—The Rhein (North German Lloyd) to-morrow, and the Ems (same line) on Thursday, with mails for New York; the Trojan (Union Company) on Thursday, with the Cape of Good Hope and Natal mails; the Tagus (Royal Mail Company) on Saturday, with the Brazil and River Plate mails; the Prinses Marie (Nederland's Company) on Saturday, with mails for Batavia and other ports in Java; and the Essequibo (Royal Mail Company) on Monday, with mails, &c., for Barbados. The following are expected:—The Hohenzollern (North German Lloyd) to-morrow, with mails from New York of the 25th ult.; the Orion (Lamport and Holt) on Wednesday, with mails from the River Plate and Brazil; the Elder (North German Lloyd) on Thursday, with 516 bags of mails from New York of the 29th ult., including the Australian and New Zealand mails *viâ* San Francisco; and the Werra (same line) on Sunday, with mails of the 2d inst. from New York.

The Hamburg-American Company's steamship Westphalia, from New York April 23, arrived at Plymouth at 4 30 p.m. yesterday. She brought 554 passengers and 85 bags of mails for England, France, and Germany. The Westphalia landed at Plymouth nine bags of mails and 17 passengers, and after embarking passengers for the Continent proceeded for Cherbourg and Hamburg at 4 55 p.m. On the 2d inst. the Westphalia spoke the steamer Moravia in lat. 49 58 N., and long. 11 32 W., steering west for New York.

The Allan Line steamship Corean arrived at Plymouth at 3 30 a.m. yesterday from London. Recently the company have arranged for several of their steamships to sail from London, and in connexion with that service it has been decided that they shall make Plymouth the last port of call. The Corean was the first ship to call at Plymouth, and judging by the number of passengers which she embarked there, this new departure of the company is likely to be attended with success. The Corean was timed to arrive at Plymouth on Saturday, but she was detained for 26 hours at Gravesend in consequence of having received peremptory orders from the Government to ship about 70 tons of ammunition for Montreal and a piece of artillery. Having embarked a number of passengers at Plymouth the Corean proceeded on her voyage at 11 a.m.

The Shaw, Savill, and Albion Company's chartered steamship Doric, from Wellington, March 22, Rio Janeiro, April 14, and Madeira, 28th, arrived at Plymouth at 4 30 p.m. on Saturday. The Doric made a good passage, her time being 41 days 11 hours, actual steaming time 39 days 10 hours. She met with fine weather throughout the passage, except when rounding Cape Horn, where she met with very heavy weather. She brought 101 passengers, 10 sacks of mails, three boxes of specie value £4,000, and a large cargo, including 16,000 carcases of mutton, and 4,300 bales of wool. Having landed 19 passengers, the mails, and despatches, the Doric proceeded for London at 5 15 p.m., arriving yesterday afternoon. Among her passengers were Lieutenant-Colonel Gamble and Mr. W. S. Allen, M.P. for Newcastle-under-Lyme, wife, and family, from Lyttelton.

The P. and O. steamer Bokhara will leave Gravesend on Wednesday for Gibraltar, Malta, Port Said, Suez, Aden, and Bombay. The same company's steamer Hydaspes will leave Gravesend on Wednesday for Gibraltar, Malta, Port Said, Suez, Aden, Colombo, Madras, and Calcutta. The Rome will leave Gravesend on Thursday for Malta, Port Said, Suez, Colombo, and Australia, direct. The Surat, from China and Bombay is expected to arrive at Plymouth about 6 a.m. to-morrow, and in London on Wednesday.

The Allan Line steamer Peruvian, from Halifax, April 25, *en route* to Liverpool, arrived at Moville at 9 55 p.m. yesterday with 16 cabin and 51 steerage passengers. The London mails were landed.

The Orient Line steamer Chimborazo, from Australia for London, passed Guia at 3 p.m. on Friday.

The Inman Line steamer City of Berlin arrived at Queenstown on Saturday, and proceeded for Liverpool at 10 15 p.m.

The Orient Line steamer John Elder, from London for Sydney, arrived at Melbourne on Saturday with the mails from London of 27th of March.

The Mogul Steamship Company's steamer Afghan, from the Clyde, left Shanghai on Saturday morning for Japan.

Messrs. Donald Currie and Co.'s Castle packet Drummond Castle, from Cape Town, *viâ* St. Helena, with mails and passengers from Natal and Cape Colony, arrived at Madeira at 2 a.m. on Saturday, and proceeded at 7 a.m. for Plymouth, where she may be expected on Wednesday morning.

The North-German Lloyd steamer Elbe, from Southampton on the 23d ult., arrived at New York at 8 a.m. on Saturday.

The North-German Lloyd steamship Werra left New York at 9 a.m. on Saturday, bringing the mails and a large number of passengers. She may be expected at Southampton on Sunday next.

The White Star Line steamer Britannic left New York for Liverpool at 9 30 a.m. on Saturday with 336 passengers.

The American Line steamer British Prince, from Liverpool, arrived at Queenstown at 8 30 a.m. yesterday, and having embarked passengers, despatches, &c., proceeded for Philadelphia at 9 55 a.m.; all well.

The National Line steamer Egypt, from New York, arrived at Queenstown at 6 35 a.m. yesterday, and having landed passengers, despatches, &c., proceeded for Liverpool immediately; all well.

(FROM LLOYD'S.)

ADEN, MAY 2.—The British India steamer Manora, from Calcutta for London, has arrived here.

AUCKLAND, MAY 1.—The Pacific Company's steamer Zealandia left here this morning with the homeward Australian mails *viâ* San Francisco.

AVONMOUTH, MAY 3.—The Anchor Line steamer Alexandria, from New York, arrived here to-day.

BALTIMORE, MAY 2.—The Johnson Line steamer Nessmore, left here to-day for Liverpool.

BARBADOS, APRIL 30.—The Royal Mail Company's steamer Medway, from Southampton, arrived here at 7 a.m. to-day.

BOMBAY, MAY 2.—The Hall Line steamer Wistow Hall left here this afternoon for Liverpool. The P. and O. steamer Malwa arrived here this morning from Colombo.

BOSTON, APRIL 27.—The Anchor Line steamer Caledonia, for London, left here to-day. MAY 3.—The Belgian White Cross Line steamer Pieter de Coninck, from Antwerp; and the Furness Line steamer Stockholm City, from London, have arrived here.

BRINDISI, MAY 3.—The P. and O. steamer Mongolia, from Alexandria, with the homeward India, China, and Australian mail, arrived here at 3 30 a.m. to-day. Letters may be expected in London about mid-day on Tuesday next.

CARDIFF, MAY 3.—The Bedouin Company's steamer Malek, for the Persian Gulf, left here to-day.

DARTMOUTH, MAY 3.—The Direct Line steamer Antilles, left here last night for the British West India Islands, with mails, passengers, and a full cargo.

DEAL, MAY 3.—The National Line steamer France, from New York for London; and the Furness Line steamer York City, from London for Halifax, &c., passed through the Downs to-day.

DOVER, MAY 2.—The Allan Line steamer Corean, from London for Quebec, passed here this morning. The Rotterdam Lloyd steamer Noord Holland, from Batavia for Rotterdam, passed here between 4 and 5 p.m. to-day. MAY 3.—The Belgian Red Star Line steamer Waesland, from Antwerp for New York, passed here this afternoon.

DUNGENESS, MAY 2.—The British and African Company's steamer Malemba, from the West Coast of Africa, passed here between 7 and 8 a.m. to-day for Hamburg.

GIBRALTAR, MAY 2.—The Glen Line steamer Glenfinlas, from Shanghai for London, has passed here. The Victorian Line steamer Glenmorven, homeward bound, arrived here to-day. MAY 3.—The Wilson Line steamer Cameo, from the Red Sea; and the City Line steamer City of Agra, from the Clyde for Calcutta, have passed here.

GRAVESEND, MAY 2.—The National Line steamer Denmark, for New York, left here yesterday. The Direct Line steamer El Dorado, from Barbados, the London Line steamer Salerno, from Newport News, and the City Line steamer City of Edinburgh, from Calcutta, passed here to-day for the docks. MAY 3.—The Royal Mail Company's steamer Derwent, from New York; Messrs. Angier Brothers' steamer Suppicich, from Jamaica; and the City Line steamer City of Oxford, from Calcutta, passed here to-day on their way to the docks.

HALIFAX, APRIL 30.—The Anchor Line steamer Australia, from London, left here to-day for Boston.

HULL, MAY 2.—The Wilson Line steamer Draco, from Bombay, arrived here yesterday.

LIVERPOOL, MAY 2.—The Johnston Line steamer Oranmore, from Baltimore, and the Hall Line steamer Rydal Hall, from Bombay, arrived in the Mersey to-day. The British and African Company's steamer Calabar, for Africa; the Dominion Line steamer Ontario, for Montreal; the Leyland Line steamer Virginian, for Boston; the Warren Line steamer Missouri, for Boston; the Guion Line steamer Nevada, for New York; the Johnston Line steamer Mentmore, for Baltimore; the Inch Line steamer Inchulva, for Bombay, *viâ* Cardiff; the Star Line steamer Mira, for Calcutta; Messrs Lamport and Holt's steamer Holbein, for Montevideo; and the Ocean Steamship Company's steamer Ajax, for Penang, left the Mersey to-day. MAY 3.—The White Star Line steamer Adriatic, from New York, arrived in the Mersey to-day. The Anchor Line steamer Hispania, for Calcutta, left the Mersey to-day.

MADEIRA, MAY 1.—Messrs. Lamport and Holt's steamer Euclid, from London and Antwerp, for Brazil and River Plate, arrived here to-day.

MALTA, MAY 2.—The P. and O. steamers Cathay, for Suez, Colombo, and Calcutta; Indus, for Suez, Colombo, and Australia, direct, both from London; and Parramatta, from Sydney for London, arrived here to-day. The Ocean Steamship Company's steamer Achilles, from London for Shanghai, has passed here. MAY 3.—The Queensland Line steamer Duke of Westminster, from London for Brisbane, has arrived here. The Bird Line steamer Avocet, from London for Calcutta, arrived off here to-day entering port.

MARANHAM, MAY 1.—The Liverpool and Maranham Company's steamer Braganza, from Liverpool, arrived here to-day.

NEW YORK, MAY 1.—Messrs. Lamport and Holt's steamer Donati, for Liverpool, left here to-day.

QUEENSTOWN, MAY 3.—The Cunard Line steamer Servia, from Liverpool, arrived here to-day, and proceeded at 2 p.m. for New York, after embarking mails and passengers. The Inman Line steamer City of Berlin, from New York, arrived here yesterday, and proceeded at 10 p.m. for Liverpool, after landing mails and passengers. The National Line steamer Egypt, from New York, arrived here to-day, and proceeded at 6 30 a.m. for Liverpool after landing mails and passengers.

RANGOON, MAY 1.—The Milburn Line steamer Port Adelaide left here to-day for Bombay.

SCILLY, MAY 2.—The Belgian steamer Jan Breydel, from New York for Antwerp, passed here at 7 p.m. yesterday.

SHANGHAI, MAY 2.—The Glen Line steamer Gleneagles from London arrived here this morning.

SINGAPORE, MAY 2.—The P. and O. steamer Rohilla, from Bombay, has arrived here.

SUEZ CANAL, MAY 2.—The Messageries Maritimes Company's steamer Oxus, from Marseilles for Shanghai, and the Clan Line steamer Clan Cameron, from the Clyde for Bombay, have arrived at Port Said. The Austrian Lloyd's steamer Orion, from Calcutta for Trieste, and the Union Line steamer Selembria, from Bombay for Havre, have arrived at Suez. The Anchor Line steamer Armenia, from the Clyde for Calcutta; and the Glen Line steamer Glenartney, from London for Shanghai, have arrived at Port Said. MAY 3.—The Orient Line steamer Potosi, from Sydney; the Queensland Line steamer Dorunda, from Brisbane; and the British India steamer Kerbela, from Bombay, all for London, arrived at Suez to-day. The Thames and Mersey Line steamer Gulf of Carpentaria, from Bombay for London, sailed from Port Said this afternoon. The Clan Line steamer Clan Cameron from the Clyde for Bombay, sailed from Suez this afternoon.

TOWNSVILLE, MAY 1.—The Queensland Line steamer Waroonga, from London for Brisbane, arrived here yesterday.

YOKOHAMA, MAY 2.—The Messageries Maritimes steamer Tanais, from Hongkong, has arrived here.

THE WAR IN THE SOUDAN.

TO THE EDITOR OF THE TIMES.

Sir,—The Soudan war has been announced as at an end, and in view of the debate which is to take place on it on Monday, and which will be the last occasion for public discussion regarding it, permit me to ask the Government through the columns of *The Times* a few questions, which it seems to me for English honour's sake are urgently in need of answer.

I have a double right now to ask them, inasmuch as Mr. Gladstone, in his speech last Monday, fully justifies me in all that I have for a year past been urging with regard to the injustice of the war. He admits, almost in so many words, that it has been causeless and objectless; and now, when I complain of it also on account of its exceptionally barbarous character, I feel that it can no longer be objected to me that the end has justified the means.

That the war has been barbarous beyond all modern precedent I think will be admitted when it is considered that it has been waged, not against a prince or a Government, but against a people, and that a pastoral people defending their flocks and herds, and the poor Nile peasants, with their water-wheels and gardens. There have been armies, indeed, in the field, but it is not they only that have suffered, and the armies have been wholly composed of volunteers, in large degree of fathers of families, in some instances of women and children.

I would divide my questions under two heads.

First, as to the physical wrongs done to these unfortunate tribes. I would ask is it true, or is it not true, that in General Earle's march from Korti the palm trees by the Nile were cut down and the standing crops destroyed? Is it true, or is it not true, that General Gordon, from his "pirate's nest," and after him Lord Charles Beresford, took down and burned for fuel the peasants' water-wheels, on which their whole existence depends? Is it true, or is it not true, that General Buller filled up the wells on his retreat through Bayuda desert? Is it true, or is it not true, that women and children have throughout the operations been made prisoners and kept in captivity as spies and on various pretexts. Are these things true? And is it known to the authorities that most of them are outrages on the immemorial rules of war obtaining in the desert? The destruction of the palms was wisely forbidden in the Koran at a time when the English were a tribe of rude idolaters; and women long before the Koran were granted chivalrous immunity by the Bedouin in their wars. Does the Government know that Lord Wolseley has left behind him famine in the land?

Again, is it true, or not true, that at Suakin money rewards have been offered to the so-called friendly tribes for every hand brought into the British camp—I mean the dead human hand, the hand with five fingers? I have it on authority I am quite unable to doubt that rewards were so offered last year, and I see this morning an account of a human hand having been thus brought into General Graham's camp. A pound was the sum named to me as having been paid last year officially for these trophies.

Again, is it, or is it not, true that a reward of £50 was offered for Ollivier Pain, dead or alive, as stated by one of your contemporaries, who gives the text of the proclamation, and explains that it was thought he might have some mission from the Mahdi—this at the very moment when Lord Wolseley had orders to forward all messages at once to Downing-street? Was this the way in which Lord Wolseley understood his instructions? And what crime had Ollivier Pain committed that a price should be set upon his head? Remember it is no longer a question of the Mahdi being an enemy of the human race.

Then, is it true, or not true, that the forced labourers asked about by Mr. Labouchere were supplied to the army by the Khedivial authorities, and were kept at their labours by the lash under British officers? The Government announced that they were paid. Perhaps. But were they lashed? I should like to be answered that—and also how many of them have been returned to their homes alive? How, also, about Lord Stanley's 500 Arab prisoners handed over by General Graham to the Italian garrison at Massowah? Truly if these things are true—and the Government has not denied them—Mr. Gladstone is right when he admits that we need not go to Khartoum to put down slavery.

In the second place, let me put a question or two about the moral wrong done to the Bedouin. Is there nothing atrocious—I use the word advisedly—in our having set tribe against tribe in our mistaken quarrel? Does the Government know nothing of the law of blood and the undying feuds they will leave behind them? Have they even thought of settling the account in money value before they go? Have they entered into any negotiation for their friendly tribes either with Osman Digma or the Mahdi? I remember learning, when I was a boy, a passage in Macaulay's Essays, where he speaks of the Red men being set to murder each other in the King of Prussia's quarrel on the banks of the Huron. In those days we called these things atrocious. Now they hardly excite a smile from an Under-Secretary.

Finally, let me ask—though there is no chance of its being answered—how many of the hundreds of thousands of pounds misspent have been spent in corrupting the Bedouin? Two years and a-half ago I made a protest in *The Times* against the wholesale bribery of the tribes by Lord Northbrook and Professor Palmer. Lord Northbrook denied the thing officially, but Professor Palmer's journal was soon afterwards published, proving the facts, and the authorities, naval and military, were far too well pleased with themselves on account of Tel-el-Kebir to keep up the pretence long. Lord Wolseley has always believed in money in war. I wonder whether he believes in it so implicitly now, and I should like to have a War Office opinion as to the real value of bribery with the Bedouin. My own experience is that the Bedouin cannot be bribed to any good purpose, and I hold it a crime to corrupt them. The whole desert south of Korosko is now corrupted by English gold for a generation—and with what result? You may treat the Bedouin with honour and they will serve you with honour; or you may treat them with coin and they will serve you with lying lips and a "fair pair of heels." I hope it will be elicited in Monday's debate what Major Kitchener's "intelligence" is valued at in the war accounts. I have heard of immense sums having been distributed by him in the early part of the campaign.

Before I finish, let me give you the true story of the betrayal of Khartoum, as it explains much that has been obscure, and points a moral. I have ascertained within the last few weeks that the principal agent in the surrender of the city was not Faraj Pasha, as originally stated, but a certain civilian exile from Egypt who had acted at one time under Arabi as Secretary of the Ministry of Marine. I know the history of this man well and can vouch for its accuracy, as I often heard it at Cairo when I was there. Four years or so ago Awwam was an honest and zealous *employé* in the Cadastral Survey under Sir Auckland Colvin—a service which of all others under the Control was the most inefficient, and is now acknowledged to have been so. Awwam, provoked at the waste and mismanagement, one day had the temerity to draw up a memorandum of what he knew and to send it to his chief. The answer was his dismissal. He then appealed to the native Press—for there was some liberty in those days—and his grievance made him a hero; and when Arabi came to power he gave him this place as secretary, which he held at Alexandria down to the bombardment. I never heard of his taking any prominent part in the politics of that eventful time, but on Sir Auckland Colvin's landing he was among the first persons arrested. Lord Charles Beresford tried him by one of his courts-martial and found him guilty of exciting to rebellion, or some such charge; he was handed over to the Circassian tender mercies, and, after 74 days in irons in the terrible Borgho prison, he was exiled to Khartoum. He was clearly a political prisoner if ever there was one; and when Lord Dufferin promised us the amnesty at the compromise of Arabi's trial, I wrote to him recommending Awwam's case to his special attention, and I have his answer, with a memorandum, curiously enough, by the very Sir Charles Wilson who afterwards was to reap such bitter disappointment at his hands. But Lord Dufferin declined to interfere, and Awwam was left at Khartoum to his revenge. On the 26th of January it was he who, with the English again at his gates, negotiated its surrender to its Arab deliverer.

I am your obedient servant,

WILFRID SCAWEN BLUNT.

Crabbet-park, April 29.

Parliament

For almost two hundred years *The Times* has been reporting the debates in Parliament. For most of that time, by so doing, *The Times* has deliberately been infringing parliamentary privilege. On 13 April 1738 the House of Commons resolved:

> That it is an high indignity to, and a notorious breach of privilege of this House, for any Newswriter of Letters or other Papers to give therein any account of the debates or other Proceedings of this House and that this House will proceed with the utmost severity against such offenders.

In the debate on the resolution one member protested indignantly that, if reported, 'Parliament when they did amiss would be talked of with the same freedom as any other set of men whatever'; and Sir Robert Walpole argued that reporting it would cause 'the House to be looked upon as the most contemptible legislative assembly on the face of the earth'. By cracking the shell of secrecy around what went on in Parliament, *The Times* helped to bring democracy to Britain, and made itself a power in the land.

Because reporting Parliament was illegal, for the first few decades of the nineteenth century *The Times* parliamentary report was taken down surreptitiously from the Strangers' Gallery. The reporter had to tip the doorkeeper to get a seat there. Gradually parliamentary reporting became accepted, though still illegal. By the middle of the nineteenth century the reporters had their own gallery, and even a room in the Palace of Westminster where they could transcribe their shorthand and check it against each other's.

From the beginning *The Times* made a feature of its parliamentary reporting under the heading 'Parliamentary Intelligence'. It recognized its importance by sacrificing advertising space for it. Good news sense, like good generalship, is concentrating your strength where it matters.

By the middle of the nineteenth century, commercial success enabled *The Times* to publish many more pages. A large share of them was given to Parliamentary Intelligence. Major speeches in the Commons and the Lords were reported *verbatim* and *ad nauseam*. The parade of serried columns with no leading, in small type and with tiny headings, make worthy but arduous reading.

In the circumstances it is not surprising that a disgruntled compositor who had just been given his cards managed to insert the malicious line: 'The speaker then said he felt inclined for a bit of fucking', at intervals throughout the report of an interminable speech by Sir William Harcourt, the Liberal politician, in 1882. What *The Times* apologized for as 'the gross interpolation' was spotted after only about a hundred copies had been printed. Most readers learnt of it only through the enigmatic apology.

Reporting Parliament, in an English way, became accepted, though still formally illegal; the first Press Gallery was opened in the Commons in 1835. In 1880 *The Times*, with blind eyes turned, installed in the Gallery a telephone connected to Printing House Square: at the other end sat an operator wearing headphones, who set copy as he received it. In the following year *The Times* got its own room in the Palace of Westminster. Thirteen full-time parliamentary reporters take down and sub the proceedings, often getting a more accurate version than *Hansard*. No matter how long either House sits, a parliamentary reporter of *The Times* is always present to report. In 1951 *The Times* introduced a new system of publishing Parliament in successive editions hot off the blabbermouth: a keyboard in *The Times* Room at Westminster controlling a code-perforating machine producing punched tape. The keyboard was connected to a Linotype machine in Printing House Square, where the tape cast lines of copy. Today photocomposition, photocopying and computer put the words of MPs into print almost as soon as they are spoken.

Below THE TIMES Room at the House of Commons, 22 February 1955.

Parliamentary reporters of *The Times* supply a daily edited and authoritative account of the words spoken. For almost as long, the parliamentary correspondent has sat beside the reporters, writing an impression of the day's events as if he were a theatre critic at a first night. It is a skilled and bitchy branch of the inky trade. As Kin Hubbard said: 'Nobuddy kin talk as interestin' as th' feller that's not hampered by facts or information'. In the trade the parliamentary correspondent's report is known as the Sketch. A famous *Times* political correspondent once described the Sketch as 'a descriptive piece in which somebody is licensed to describe Parliament in prose fit for the paintings of the Sistine Chapel'. He may have had in mind his colleague Sketch-writer, who wrote, after a general election: 'The real snag about the gaudy bird of promise – that avian strumpet which breeds astride the hustings every five years or so – is that the damned thing will moult as soon as you get it indoors'.

The Times probably employed the first Sketch-writer in the business (priority depends on what you count as a Sketch). Parliamentary debates were first summarized in a humorous and unkind way in the paper in 1831. The writer was Horace Twiss, KC and MP on and off. When he lost his seat, he wrote the first Sketches from the Gallery.

Asquith commended the Sketch in *The Times*: 'I suppose for one person who reads the report there are thousands who read the summary and the Sketch'. A Press Association Gallery reporter put the opposite, hard-news point of view:

> I came into the Gallery first in 1877, and the place is a very different place now. We are simply crowded out by Sketch-writers, and these gentlemen, who are rather lofty, have very little regard to the convenience of the reporter, thinking that they are a cut above him.

The Times invented both the hard-nosed report and the butterfly colour piece.

In the storms of the nineteenth century, no doubt the public queued to read column after column of parliamentary debate in *The Times*. The politicians certainly were always keen to see that they were well reported there. Disraeli's letters are full of complacent notes: '*The Times* report good'; 'Well reported in *The Times*'. In 1848, after a particularly important and prolonged speech, the old peacock wrote: 'I have no cause to complain of the reports. The version of *The Times* is almost *verbatim*, six first-rate shorthand reporters having been employed.'

You cannot please all Members of Parliament all the time. The Parliamentary Intelligence of *The Times* first formally fell foul of authority in June 1819, when it reported that George Canning had laughed during a speech by Joseph Hume, the famous Radical. Unfortunately Canning had not been present in the House at the time of his alleged laughter. He told the world so at length, and cried Breach of Privilege. The House ordered the printer of *The Times*, Charles Bell, to attend. He told the Speaker that he had obtained the offending paragraph from John Payne Collier, who had been skulking in the Strangers' Gallery. Collier spent a night in the custody of the Serjeant at Arms before being discharged with an official Reprimand from the Speaker.

The printer of THE TIMES, John Joseph Lawson, is called to the Bar of the House of Lords to answer a charge of libel. The proceedings are reported verbatim in columns 1 and 2 – and include a reprint of the offending paragraph.
20 APRIL 1831

The Times.

No 14,518. LONDON WEDNESDAY, APRIL 20, 1831. PRICE 7d.

PARLIAMENTARY INTELLIGENCE.

HOUSE OF LORDS, Tuesday, April 19.

Earl SPENCER said he had to present a petition from the county of Northampton, which had been agreed to at a public meeting convened by the High Sheriff. The petition was in favour of the measure of reform now before the other house, and the petitioners prayed that their lordships would pass the measure when it came up to them. The petition was signed by the High Sheriff. The noble earl presented a similar petition from Towcester, Northamptonshire.

The Duke of RICHMOND presented a petition from a hundred in the western division of the county of Sussex, in favour of the reform bill.

The Earl of WESTMORLAND said, he felt himself in a very disagreeable situation, from his not having been present when the petition from the county of Northampton was presented. He knew very well that the course he was now pursuing was somewhat irregular, but he would attempt to bring himself into order by moving that the petition be taken into consideration at a future day. In the first place, he wished to tell their lordships that he did not concur in that petition; and, secondly, he wished to rescue the gentry of the county of Northampton, generally, from the discredit of having supported a petition in favour of a tyrannical and arbitrary measure. (A laugh, and cries of "hear, hear.") Yes, he intended to be heard; noble lords might take his word for that. The objections to that measure were of a grave character and so numerous, that he could not deal with them properly except in a speech too long for an incidental discussion of this kind. He therefore would only say that he did not concur in the measure, and endeavour to rescue the gentry of the county from having concurred in it. He thought the measure was both a revolution and revolutionary. He held that there were two principles which could not be violated without departing from the constitution. The first was, that no man could be divested of a legal right except a known crime had been proved against him; the second was, that the poorest man in the land, however low he might be, was quite as much entitled to the protection of the laws as the richest person in the country. These were principles in which he had been brought up, and he would ever stand up in defence of them. And yet this measure was one which went to the disfranchisement of all the people of England who happened not to be freeholders or not to come within the favoured and arbitrary limits of the measure. This he contended to be contrary to the British constitution. He thought that the people were stamped with the mark of degradation by this bill. As to the disfranchisement of the close boroughs, he did not think that, consistently with the British constitution, that thing could be done. "Nec meus hic sermo," said the noble lord; "it is the argument of Junius, and let those who find fault with it, find fault with Junius, not with me." Junius argued the question of the close boroughs very fairly and very well. First, he (Junius) put the objection, and dealt with the anomaly; but then, on t'other side, he said, "Now I don't know, perhaps I should like to disfranchise them; but then if I were to allow that, how do I know that you or I will not be disfranchised next?—if I allow the principle, I cannot tell how far it may be carried." He contended that the Parliament deserved gratitude, not degradation in the eyes of the people. They had removed 25,000,000*l.* of taxes: they had repealed every law against the liberty of the subject: and they had abolished every sort of division and distinction amongst all classes of His Majesty's subjects. This was what the Parliament had done, and he believed that the people were grateful for it. He thought that this was a sufficient excuse for his not having joined in that petition, which the noble earl had thought proper to present in his absence. It was a mistake to say that the petition was signed by the High Sheriff; it was signed by the High Sheriff's deputy, and the High Sheriff himself was not present at the meeting. This meeting was called by certain persons in the great hall, which was a place larger than that house; there were a great number of persons present; a great disturbance ensued. The Sheriff adjourned the meeting into the open air, and then, in consequence of ill health being unable to attend, left his under-sheriff to perform the business. One party got up this petition; another party met at one of the inns and signed a declaration, in which they expressed their alarm at this measure, and protested against it. Now what he must take the liberty of saying was this,—namely, that in the hall the voice of the meeting was against the petition, and that, with the exception of about 30, all the gentlemen of the county of Northampton who were present went and signed the protest. As many as 50 of the gentry and clergy, and about 400 other persons, signed the protest. He said, therefore, that the petition did not at all express the sense of the county.

Earl SPENCER (who spoke in so low a tone that his observations were very indistinctly heard below the bar) said, that he should not have presented the petition in the absence of the noble earl, if he had known that the noble earl wished to be present at the presentation of it. He came down at the usual hour, and presented the petition in the regular way; and as the noble earl had not favoured the meeting with his company, and still less with the expression of those opinions to which he had to-day given utterance, it was not unnatural that he should not have supposed the noble earl to be very much interested in the petition. (Hear.) The petition had been sent to him from the Under Sheriff with a letter, in which it was said, that the High Sheriff requested he would present it to their lordships. Whatever might have been the prayer of a petition so forwarded to him, he should, if it were respectfully worded, have felt it his duty to present it. With regard to the meeting, it had certainly been held in the Town-hall at first; but any one who had seen the Town-hall would know that it was nothing like so large as that house, and, on this occasion, it had somehow or other been filled, before the doors were opened, with persons whose conduct plainly showed that they were there for the purpose of exciting a disturbance. An adjournment to the Market-place was carried; and then a party absented themselves from the meeting, and drew up a declaration which, he was informed, had been carried round the town and signed by the lowest persons. To that he did not object,—for he agreed that the lowest had just as good a right as the highest had to the expression of their opinions; but he contended that those who had remained with the meeting that was presided over by the regular authority, ought to be considered as the meeting, and that the petition which had proceeded from them ought to be considered as the petition of a meeting of the county regularly advertised, and convened with the usual formalities.

After an interchange of a few observations between the Earl of WESTMORLAND and Earl SPENCER, which were not audible below the bar,

The Earl of WINCHILSEA said, that he did not rise to occupy their lordships with his opinions about Parliamentary reform, or about the bill on that subject before the other house of Parliament; but connected as he was with the highly respectable county of Northampton, and with the highly respectable gentlemen who signed the requisition, he did feel himself called upon to vindicate those gentlemen from that unjust aspersion which the noble earl had cast upon them, in accusing them of having lent their support to a tyrannical and revolutionary measure. (Hear.) He deprecated violent language alike on both sides, upon a measure in which the country was so deeply interested (hear); and he was extremely sorry that the noble earl should have characterised such a measure as tyrannical and revolutionary. (Hear, hear.) Still more did he regret that the noble earl should have aspersed honourable men by saying that they were tyrants and revolutionists, which was the plain consequence of the accusation that they had supported a tyrannical and revolutionary measure; for, whatever might be the warmth of the noble earl's attachment to the constitution, the noble earl's character was not, and could not be, higher than the character of many of those upon whom he had cast this aspersion. For his own part, he gave to every man who differed from him on constitutional questions the fullest credit for being actuated by no other motive than the welfare of his country. He should always do so, and he hoped that others would do the same. He would not trouble their lordships then with any observations upon the bill; nor should he have addressed their lordships now at all, but that he felt himself called upon to relieve a respectable body of men from an aspersion, which he trusted that the noble earl himself would, upon reflection, regret that he had cast upon them.

THE TIMES NEWSPAPER.

The Earl of LIMERICK said—Presuming, my lords, upon the very kind indulgence which I received at the hands of your lordships yesterday, when I brought before your lordships what I conceived to be a breach of the privileges of your lordships' house, I am induced to entreat your lordships to indulge me now for one or two minutes, and I promise not to detain your lordships longer. Having already stated to your lordships, fully and unreservedly, my opinion upon the subject in question, it would be at once bad taste and bad sense if I were to travel into the matter again; and I rise now to assure your lordships that I have no personal feeling whatever with regard to the transaction. True it is, my lords, that I considered that it was through me that the dignity of your lordships' house was attacked,—but it was in consequence of the attack upon that dignity, and not in consequence of what was said of me personally, that I brought the matter under the notice of your lordships. These were the grounds upon which I acted, and if I had it to do again, I would do precisely as I have done. My lords, I have endeavoured to save your lordships some time and trouble by looking into the precedents which have been followed upon similar occasions, or to which similar occasions have given rise; and I find that in early days very severe penalties have been inflicted upon persons who have been guilty of such an offence as that which I conceive has been committed in the present instance. However, my lords, I am no advocate for violent measures or for severe penalties in any case. (Hear, hear.)

The LORD CHANCELLOR here interrupted the noble earl, and said—I am sure, my lords, that the noble earl means nothing but what is quite right in the course which he is now pursuing; but allow me to suggest to your lordships, that that course is not consistent with the order of your lordships' proceedings. Your lordships yesterday agreed to an order,—namely, "That the printer of *The Times* newspaper do attend this house to-morrow at 4 o'clock." Now that order is peremptory (hear, hear); and I take it that in the first instance your lordships must be informed whether that order has been complied with, and whether the person is in attendance. (Hear, hear.) With this, I apprehend, your lordships must commence your proceedings in this matter, unless the noble earl intends to move that that order be discharged, and that I do not understand to be the noble earl's intention.

The Earl of LIMERICK.—Certainly, my lords, I have no such intention, any more than I have the intention of pursuing any course which is inconsistent with the order of your lordships' proceedings. I will therefore very shortly bring my observations upon the subject to a conclusion. My lords, I have no personal feeling in the matter. I took it up solely for the sake of the house, and with the house I now leave it.

Mr. Pulman, the Yeoman-Usher, here appeared at the bar, and said—"My lords, the printer of *The Times* newspaper is in attendance."

The LORD CHANCELLOR.—Let him be brought to the bar.

Mr. Lawson then appeared at the bar.

The LORD CHANCELLOR.—What is your name?

Mr. Lawson.—John Joseph Lawson.

The LORD CHANCELLOR.—Are you the printer of *The Times* newspaper?

Mr. Lawson.—I am, my lord.

The LORD CHANCELLOR.—Look at the paper which will be handed to you, at the paragraph which will be pointed out to you. (Here Mr. Courtenay showed Mr. Lawson *The Times* newspaper which contained the paragraph complained of.) Are you the printer of the paper in which that paragraph is inserted?

Mr. Lawson.—I am, my lord.

The LORD CHANCELLOR.—You may withdraw.

Mr. Lawson having withdrawn from the bar, one of the clerks of the table read the following paragraph:—

"Yet mean, cruel, and atrocious as every civilized mind must consider the doctrine, that Ireland has no need of poor laws, or some equivalent for them,—hateful and abominable as is such a screen for inhumanity,—there are men, or things with human pretensions, nay with lofty privileges, who do not blush to treat the mere proposal of establishing a fund for the relief of the diseased or helpless Irish with brutal ridicule and almost impious scorn. Will any man credit that an Irish absentee lord could say what he is reported to have uttered in the House of Peers last night, when Lord Rosebery presented a petition, praying that a compulsory tax on land might be introduced into Ireland, towards alleviating her poor? We shall not name him,—because the House of Lords is armed with a thing called a 'Bar,' and other disagreeable appendages. But there are members of that house who surprise nobody by declaring their indifference to 'popular odium,'—especially when they are at such a distance from Ireland as to ensure the safety of their persons."

After the reading of the above paragraph there was a short pause, and then

Lord WYNFORD rose and said, "My Lords, I for one beg leave to express my obligation to the noble earl near me, for having brought this matter under the consideration of your lordships, and"—

Here there arose a murmur in the house. We heard the word "bar," and we suppose that some noble lord must have moved "that the bar be cleared," for Mr. Courtenay, leaving the table, desired the messengers to clear the bar. All the strangers below the bar, not excepting the reporters, were then put out of the house. The members of the House of Commons, who were standing at the foot of the throne, were allowed to remain.

[After a short interval, in which their lordships determined that the paragraph was a false and scandalous libel, Mr. Lawson was again called in.

On his being placed at the bar, the LORD CHANCELLOR informed him, that the house had determined that the paragraph, which had appeared in the paper of which he was the printer, was a false and scandalous libel, and that their lordships were then ready to hear any thing which he might have to urge in his defence.

Mr. Lawson commenced by expressing his regret that there should have appeared in *The Times* newspaper, of which he was the printer, any paragraph calculated to give offence either to their lordships in general, or to the noble earl in particular. Their lordships must be aware that owing to the rapidity with which a journal like *The Times* must be printed, and the multiplicity of articles which necessarily found their way into it, it was almost impossible for him, using every diligence in his power, to peruse every separate paragraph which appeared in the paper. The paragraph, of which their lordships complained, had found its way inadvertently into the paper, and he had only to repeat his deep regret that it had done so.

Mr. Lawson was again ordered to withdraw, but shortly afterwards was recalled to the bar, when several questions were put to him by several of their lordships, through the Lord Chancellor. He was asked, whether he had the supreme control of the paper of which he was the printer? He replied that he had not. He was then asked, if he knew who had? He replied that he considered himself to be holding a confidential situation in *The Times* newspaper-office, and that he therefore could not answer that question without a breach of trust to his employers, and a loss of character to himself.

The LORD CHANCELLOR then informed Mr. Lawson that he was not bound to answer any questions unless he pleased. It would be enough for him to state to their lordships that he declined answering any question to which he had an objection. At the same time, he must inform him, that their lordships would form their own opinions as to his reasons for not answering such questions as might be put to him. Was he (the Lord Chancellor) to understand that he (Mr. Lawson) declined to answer the last question?

Mr. Lawson.—Certainly.

A noble lord then asked whether a gentleman, whose name he mentioned, was not the editor of *The Times* newspaper.

Mr. Lawson replied, that this was only another mode of putting to him the last question; and therefore, with all respect to their lordships, he must decline giving any answer to it.

Mr. Lawson was then asked whether he was the person whose name was entered as the printer at the Stamp-office. His reply was in the affirmative. Certain questions were then put to him respecting the proprietors of the paper, whose names were entered at the Stamp-office; but his reply was, that he did not know who they were. He was then ordered to withdraw.

Lord WYNFORD then moved, "That John Joseph Lawson, having admitted himself to be the printer of a false and scandalous libel, which had appeared in *The Times* newspaper of the 16th instant, be committed to Newgate during the pleasure of the House, and that he also pay a fine of 100*l.*, as a penalty for publishing the aforesaid libel."

The motion was resisted by the LORD CHANCELLOR, the Duke of WELLINGTON, the Marquis of LANSDOWNE, and Earl GREY. The House was about to divide on the motion, when, on the amendment of a noble lord, it was carried, that Mr. Lawson should be committed to the custody of the Usher of the Black Rod, and that he do attend their Lordships to-morrow morning at 10 of the clock.

The determination of their Lordships was then communicated to Mr. Lawson, who was conveyed, in the custody of two messengers of the House of Lords, to Oliver's Coffee-House, where he now remains.]

It is obvious that we cannot vouch for the exact correctness of all the passages within brackets.

CIVIL LIST.

When we were readmitted to the bar, we found Earl GREY on his legs, moving that the house resolve itself into a committee on the civil list bill. Their lordships were no doubt aware, that hitherto it had been customary for their lordships to vote, under the head of the civil list, not only all the personal expenses of the Monarch, but also many of the civil expenses of Government. It had been the custom, not only in the reign of George III., but also in that of George IV.; and the total amount of the sums voted for the civil list of the late monarch, including the personal expenses of the King, and the civil expenses of his government, amounted to 1,056,000*l.* In the civil list proposed by the late government, it was intended to make some alteration, and to separate from the personal expenditure of the King part of the expense of the civil government. It was intended to transfer part of the expenses which had been previously charged on the civil list to the consolidated fund, and to vote them in future annually with the estimates. It had been proposed to separate from the civil list, the salaries of the Judges, of the Lord Chancellor of Ireland, of the Speaker of the House of Commons, and of some other offices, which were to cease with the lives of their present holders. The amount of the salaries of these offices in England and Ireland together, was 63,389*l.* This sum was to be separated from the civil list, and was to be transferred to the consolidated fund, and voted along with the ordinary estimates of the year. Besides, there were to be taken from the civil list 30,000*l.*, which was paid for our consular establishments; 13,040*l.* paid for expenses in Scotland, for prosecutions, &c. &c.; and 7,513*l.* paid to dissenting ministers in England,—amounting together to 50,553*l.* Now, this sum, added to the former sum of 63,389*l.* which he had before mentioned, gave a total of 114,000*l.* (so Earl Grey said) which was in future to be separated from the civil list. It was then proposed by the late Government, to vote for the civil list of His Majesty, comprising the personal expenses of the Sovereign and part of the expenses of his civil government, a sum of 970,000*l.*, which, added to the 114,000*l.* already mentioned, made all the expenses of the civil list proposed by the late Government 1,084,000*l.*, which was 100,000*l.* less than the civil list voted to his late Majesty. It had been proposed by the present Government to carry still further the principle of separating the expenses of the Government from the expenses necessary to enable the King to live in that comfort and splendour to which no king had a better title than the gracious sovereign at present on the throne. For this purpose it was proposed that in the bill which he now moved to have referred to a committee, there should be nothing contained except what related to the personal expenses of His Majesty. The reasons for making this separation he would state at a subsequent period. At present it would be most convenient to show how the civil list proposed by the present Government would operate in comparison with that proposed by the late Government. It had been proposed, in the first place, to transfer to the consolidated fund a considerable part of the pensions which now existed, and were hereafter to be reduced. Secondly, it was proposed to transfer to the same fund the salaries of the judges, the diplomatic salaries, and the salary of the Lord Lieutenant of Ireland, amounting in all to 382,249*l.* It was also proposed to vote in the committee of supply the sum of 30,000*l.* proposed by the former Government, for the salaries and expenses connected with the Board of Works. It was also proposed that the salaries of ambassadors, of the Lord Privy Seal, &c. amounting to 171,000*l.*, should be voted in supply. The noble earl, after pointing out the difference of expense in the plan of the civil list proposed by the late, and in that proposed by the present Government, observed, that the real difference of expense was not more than 21,000, a saving which arose from the reduction of some offices, and the calling in of some pensions. He could not state that there was in this respect any great saving at present, but there would eventually be a large saving. He then proceeded to explain the reductions which the present Ministry intended to make in the pension list. The late Government had intended to reduce it from 150,000*l.* to 140,000*l.* The present Government intended to reduce it, not to 140,000*l.* but to 75,000*l.*; so that there would eventually be a saving in this respect of 65,000*l.* At the same time there would be a great diminution in the amount of pensions which Government would have the power to grant. The noble earl then entered into various details to prove the point; and, after dilating upon it for some time, said, that he would now proceed to state what the different articles were which formed the 510,000*l.* which made up the civil list. That list was to be divided into five classes. The first class contained the privy purse for the King, and the allowance for the establishment of the Queen. The sum fixed for the privy purse was 60,000*l.*, a sum which he was sure that their lordships would not think too large, when they heard that it was the same amount as that which had been appropriated to this purpose ever since the year 1779. The allowance for the Queen's establishment was 50,000*l.* He was sure that it would not be necessary for him to vindicate the amount of that sum: on the contrary, he felt that he had rather occasion to lament that it was not larger, when he recollected that when the late Queen Charlotte first came to this country her allowance was fixed at the same amount, and that in the year 1786 it had been raised to 58,000*l.* He would take that opportunity of stating the indignation which he felt on hearing last night of the shameful manner in which her illustrious name had been made the subject of attack. He felt the greater indignation, because he knew that there was not the slightest shadow of foundation for the malevolent imputations which had been made against her. (Hear, hear.) He felt that he had occasion to regret that this sum was too little, rather than occasion to apologize for its being too much. Here also he must say, that the means which had been granted to all former Queens had not been granted to her present Majesty, to provide for the expenses incident to her exalted station. He lamented that the usual sum had not been granted to Her Majesty for an outfit, as she had every thing to provide for her exalted position in the country, and as she could not provide for them at all without anticipating much of her ordinary revenue; the present Government proposed to grant 60,000*l.* for the privy purse, and 50,000*l.* for the Queen's allowance, making 110,000*l.* in all. The second class comprised the salaries of the great officers of the household, amounting to 130,100*l.* Here he must observe, that the committee to which the estimates of the civil list had been referred, after examining into the subject, had proposed that this grant be reduced 119,000*l.* (A noble lord expressed his surprise at this statement.) He begged pardon, he meant that it be reduced to 119,000*l.* Now this would have reduced the general estimate of the civil list to 498,000*l.* But when it came to be considered in the other house of Parliament, the house would not accede to the recommendation of the committee, but left the civil list at the amount of 510,000*l.*, originally proposed. The third class comprised the expenditure in the department of the Lord Steward, of the Lord Chamberlain, of the Master of the Horse, &c., and for that expenditure 180,000*l.* was provided. He was happy to say that upon an examination into this subject by the committee, it appeared that there could be no reduction made in the amount of expenses incurred on account of His Majesty's personal comfort, beyond that which had been made before this Government entered into office. The next class comprised the Royal bounties and charities, for which 23,000*l.* was provided; and the fifth and last class included the pensions, in which there had been a reduction made, which brought the sum provided for them down from 140,000*l.* to 75,000*l.* The comparison, then, between the estimates of the two governments on these five classes stood thus:—For the first class both governments had set aside a sum of 110,000*l.*; for the second class the late government had set aside 140,546*l.*; and the present government 130,000*l.* Now the difference on this point did not arise from any saving which had been made to the public, but from the transfer of several items to the consolidated fund. For the third class, which consisted of the bills for the departments of the Lord Steward, the Lord Chamberlain, the Master of the Horse, &c., the late Government proposed 210,500*l.*, and the present Government proposed 180,000*l.* But this difference was not occasioned by any saving made to the public. For the fourth class the same charge was made in both. For the fifth class, which contained the pensions, the late Government had made a provision of 140,000*l.*; the present Government had reduced it to 75,000*l.*; so that, adding up the amount of each separate vote, the late government made a provision of 624,600*l.* for the civil list, and the present Government a provision of 510,000*l.*, leaving a difference of 114,000*l.* between the two. This was not all made up of savings: the great advantage of it consisted in the reduction of the pensions, which he had already described. This was the general statement which he had to make of the provisions for the King under the present civil list bill. The noble earl then proceeded to point out the advantages which he conceived would arise from separating the personal expenses of the Monarch from the civil expenses of the Government. The separation would remove all doubt from the public mind as to the portion of the civil list which was actually required for the expenses of royal state. There would he a great advantage in this; for the country would then know what portion of expense was furnished for the support of the comfort and the splendour of the Monarch, and thus a stop would be put to the cruel misrepresentations which had so long been circulated on that subject. He thought that when the amount of the pensions were taken into consideration, and it was considered that 510,000*l.* was all the sum set aside to pay them, and to support the royal dignity, no one would think it too much, as compared either with the provision made for former sovereigns of England, or with that made for the other sovereigns of Europe. Besides, in separating the civil expenses of the Government from the civil list, there was this further advantage, that you brought them under the control of Parliament, and enabled Parliament to deal with them as circumstances might require. The result of the new arrangement proposed by the present Government would be, that there would be of that portion of public money formerly voted to the civil list no less than 553,000*l.* withdrawn from it, and placed under the control of Parliament; whereas, under the system of the late government only 114,000*l.* of that sum would have been rendered subject to the same control. There was only one other point to which he wished to call the attention of their lordships, and that was that the reduction on the pension list was only available to 65,000*l.* a-year. He knew that it had been made a reproach to the present Government that the amount of that list had not been reduced at once from 150,000*l.* to 75,000*l.* His answer to that reproach should be very brief. He did not mean to deny that, technically speaking, the pension list, having been granted during the late King's life, only ceased with him, and might be discarded instantly. But he thought that it would be a harsh, and, though not an illegal, an inequitable mode of proceeding so to deal with it. He was not bound to defend the manner in which the pensions on that list had been granted. He had no interest in any of them. Whether they had been granted improperly or not, he could not tell; he only knew that there were circumstances attending some of them which excited great distrust in the public mind. He thought, however, that it would be invidious to go into a minute inquiry into the circumstances which had attended the granting of each pension. Though they were not legally pensions for life, the understanding that they were granted for life was so general, that it would be injustice, or something like injustice, to take from individuals that provision to which they had been accustomed to think themselves entitled as long as they lived. He therefore thought it better that the public should suffer the payment of these pensions for a time, than that it should be guilty of any conduct which bore the appearance of injustice, and which would have the effect of placing his Majesty in such a situation as would compel him to take away such pensions as his father and his brother had granted, as they expected, for the lives of the present holders. That was the reason why the Government had thought that it ought not to reduce the pension list at once to the amount at which they had determined to fix it eventually. The noble earl concluded by moving that this bill be now committed.

The Duke of WELLINGTON explained at some length the principle on which he had drawn up his plan of the civil list, and observed that that plan was intended to enable the Sovereign, so far as it was practicable, to defray all the expenses necessary to be incurred in supporting the dignity and splendour of the Crown, without having them mixed up with the expenses of his civil government. Certainly the Crown had enjoyed great advantage in supporting its dignity and its efficiency, so long as the system of supporting itself on its hereditary revenues remained in practice. That system was departed from at the commencement of the reign of George III., and a further departure from it had been made since, into which he would, with their lordships' permission examine presently. From the accounts he had seen of the hereditary revenues enjoyed by George II., he had reason to believe that if they were now enjoyed by they Sovereign, and employed in defraying the civil expenses of the Government, and the dignity and splendour of the Crown, they would amount to a sum larger than would be necessary to meet those expenses, notwithstanding the increase which had been made in them by the increased salaries of the Judges, the increased number of the public offices, and the vast increase of the Royal Family. He believed that the hereditary revenues of the Crown, independent of its droits and its West India duties, amounted to not less than 850,000*l.* a year. He made this statement, because it was important that their lordships should recollect it, and that the public should know, that notwithstanding the expenses of the sovereign were great, the sovereign had as much right to the sum which he had mentioned as any of their lordships had to their estates. The system of giving the sovereign the amount of certain taxes for the support of his civil government was first departed from in the reign of George III., when a fixed sum was appointed instead of it for his support. In process of time the expence of the civil government increased, and the civil list became in debt. The consequence was, that in 1815 an inquiry was made into the circumstances which had caused that increase of charges. What was the course then adopted by Parliament? It was to bring certain charges,—as, for instance, the charges for ambassadors,—under the annual vote of Parliament, and the object was to avoid thereby the fixing of any fresh debt, for which no estimate could be previously made, upon the civil list. In 1820 it was determined that nothing should be brought before Parliament in connexion with the civil list that was not a casual expense, and for which a regular vote could not be submitted. The late Government had proposed that a portion of the sums previously charged upon the civil list should be transferred to the consolidated fund; he alluded to the salaries of the Judges, the Lord Chancellor, and the Speaker of the House of Commons. He could not but complain of the salaries of the great officers of Government being subjected to annual discussion in Parliament. He wished to place these salaries upon the consolidated fund, to prevent the possibility of the country being left without a proper and efficient administration of public affairs. He would not leave the Government to the chance of being impeded by a small majority in a committee of the House of Commons, which, according to the proposed plan, might diminish the salaries of public officers at pleasure. At the period of the revolution there were long discussions on the subject of the hereditary revenues of the Crown, and the provision for the Sovereign, but no one had ever dreamt of separating the Crown from the civil government, in making a provision for royalty. The plan of separation was one of modern invention: he objected to it altogether, because by possibility it might place the Crown in a situation such as it ought not to be placed in, by depriving it of the assistance of a public officer, whose salary might be lost by a single vote in a committee of supply. (Hear, hear.) Further, he was of opinion that the repairs, alterations, and other expenses of the Royal residences, limited as they were to a certain sum, ought to be placed under the control of the Treasury, and should not be left to an annual vote of the House of Commons. The noble earl was mistaken in supposing that the saving upon Scotch and Irish pensions would amount to 4,000*l.* a year. He (the Duke of Wellington) could only make the amount of saving 2,000*l.* [Earl Grey intimated that he had stated it at the latter sum.] He entirely agreed with the noble lord in the propriety of abstaining from disturbing pensions, many of which had been well deserved, although a few might have been granted on insufficient grounds. The noble duke proceeded to allude to two pensions granted by his late Majesty to two near relations of his own—one after the battle of Salamanca—the other after that of Vittoria; and added, that he felt deservedly proud of this favour graciously vouchsafed by his Sovereign. Parliament might take away such marks of approbation, but resign them he never would. He repeated his expression of the pain which he felt at seeing the expenses of the Sovereign detached entirely from those of the civil government, and the latter left, in point of fact, entirely at the mercy of the chance of a single vote in a division of the House of Commons. One word with respect to the discontinuance of the office of auditor of the civil list: he assured the noble lord that unless he had some person in the Treasury to perform the duties of that office, the civil list must get into debt. The noble duke then went on to object to the proposed reduction in the salaries of the great officers of the Government, and observed that at the existing rate of salaries, unless a first lord of the Treasury (and the remark would apply to other officers) possessed a large private fortune, he must be ruined in consequence of the heavy expenses entailed on him by his situation, and the inadequacy of the sum allowed for the maintenance of those expenses. In proof of this, he might instance the cases of three prime ministers, Mr. Pitt, Mr. Perceval, and Mr. Canning, all of whom had been ruined by being in office. He himself had proposed a provision for the family of Mr. Canning in consequence. So much on the subject of the higher offices in the Government. With respect to some of the smaller offices held by members of the House of Commons, there were few in which, on gentlemen accepting them, it did not take the entire of the first year's salary to defray the expenses of re-elections, patents, &c. How could it be pretended, when such was the case both with respect to the higher and lower offices of Government, that the salaries of public men ought to be reduced? The Parliamentary business of the Government in the House of Commons was greater than could be at present performed by the members of Government; for instance, hardly a committee sat in which it was not desired to have a person connected with Government as chairman or member of it. Such being the case, he objected to the reduction in the number of Government officers (the Vice-Treasurer of Ireland being one), as well as to the diminution of the salaries of office.

Lord GODERICH admitted the expenses incident to the holders of official situations were very great. There were many expenses which it would be impossible to enumerate; but for many years Parliament had proceeded cutting down the salaries of minor offices, and it would not be either fair or decent if they did not now proceed to deal with the salaries of places of greater consequence; and as the former had been reduced on account of the alteration effected by a change in the currency, the latter ought not to escape similar treatment. The noble viscount proceeded to say, that he could not see in the separation of the expenses of the crown from those of the civil government, any thing calculated to degrade the Sovereign, or impede the business of the state. Besides, although it was perfectly true that certain portions of the salaries of civil officers had been paid out of the civil list, it was equally undeniable that other portions of them were differently provided for, so that the present arrangement was not so novel in point of principle as the noble lord appeared to suppose. In conclusion, he expressed his conviction that no difficulty would be experienced in consequence of the abolition of the office of auditor of the civil list.

Lord ELLENBOROUGH was satisfied that when the noble earl opposite came to reconsider the subject, he would find that he could make no reduction in the expenses of the Board of Control, as had been proposed. He could assure the noble lord that the salaries of the clerks in that office were at present too low, and that the general strength of the department required to be augmented. He regretted that the expenses of the Crown were in future to be exhibited as a specific annual charge, distinct from the civil government of the state. This was not the time when such an experiment ought to be made. He objected to the plan of placing under the control of Parliament a large number of matters formerly charged upon the civil list—matters closely connected with the civil government, and in relation to which the utmost inconvenience was to be apprehended from taking annual votes of the House of Commons. He believed that the best reformer in pecuniary matters was an honest government acting under the control of Parliament. A popular assembly was rarely just or wisely economical in financial matters; it was often extravagant, and frequently its proceedings were not equitable.

The Earl of CARNARVON did not blame ministers for having adopted a course of retrenchment in relation to the salaries of office, for after all that had been said on the subject of economy, they never would have received credit from the public for integrity of purpose if they had taken a different course. But he believed that the country would be a loser and not a gainer by the proposed change, for it was clear that public men could not support the dignity of office on the present official salaries, and the result of any further reduction of emoluments would be to compel the sovereign to choose his servants from the opulent part of the aristocracy without reference to ability for the discharge of public duties. It was not from ministers that observations such as this could be expected. He thought it his duty, then, as an independent member of the house, to state his objections to the proposition for the reduction of salaries. In doing so, he did not wish to throw any difficulties in the way of the details of the present measure, but he did feel it to be his duty to express his disapprobation in relation to this part of the plan of His Majesty's Government.

The house then went into a committee, and the clauses of the bill were agreed to without any amendment.

The house having resumed,—

A NOBLE LORD presented a petition from the corporation of the city of Hereford, praying that no infringement might be made on their elective privileges: also a petition from the same place, for the abolition of slavery; and a like petition from Sutton. Also a petition from Hereford, against so much of the beer bill as permitted the consumption of beer on the premises where sold.

Lord BEXLEY presented a number of petitions, from various places, against negro slavery.

Adjourned.

HOUSE OF COMMONS, Tuesday, April 19.

This being the day appointed to ballot for a committee to decide on the merits of the Coleraine election petition, the gallery was not opened until 4 o'clock. (We understand that it is not the intention of the parties to prosecute the petition.)

PARLIAMENTARY REFORM.

The CHANCELLOR of the EXCHEQUER said, he rose to present a petition from the clergy, gentry, freeholders, and other inhabitants of the county of Northampton, in favour of Parliamentary reform. He felt it necessary, in presenting this petition, to make a few observations, with reference to the circumstances under which it was agreed to. There were now gentlemen in the house who were present at the meeting in which the petition was proposed and acceded to, who, if he did not state the facts accurately, could correct him. The meeting was convened on Thursday last, by the High Sheriff, in consequence of a numerously-signed requisition which had been forwarded to him. The party which was opposed to reform, and that which was in favour of it, severally made considerable exertions to secure a majority. The two parties in the county were of nearly equal strength. He believed that the majority of the country gentlemen, though he lived on the best terms with them, were adverse to his political opinions; and therefore he imputed his return for the county rather to feelings of private friendship than to any approbation of his political sentiments on some particular points. In order to oppose with effect the petition which he was about to present, many of the gentry invited to the meeting individuals who were connected with them in various parts of the county; and that it should not be a dry invitation, they gave to these persons, as he had been informed, a breakfast. The county meetings were usually held in the Shire-hall; but when the sheriff arrived there to preside over this meeting, there was a vast deal of noise, which was continued for an hour and a half or two hours, to so great a degree that no human being who might desire to deliver his sentiments could make himself heard. At length a motion was made by an honourable relative of his, to adjourn the meeting to the open air, on the Market-hill; and another proposition was made to dissolve the meeting. The question was put, and the sheriff decided that the motion in favour of adjournment was carried. Those parties who were opposed to the petition declined attending the meeting in the open air. They went to an inn, and there drew up and signed a protest against the proceedings. The Under Sheriff, the High Sheriff himself having declined presiding, took the chair at the meeting on the Market-hill. It was, he contended, a regularly convened county meeting, at which there were about 3,000 persons present, who agreed to this petition. He therefore had a right to say that this was a petition of the county in favour of the reform measure now under consideration. It might be said that the meeting was not attended by many respectable persons; but to this he would answer, that there were present at the meeting individuals who were as respectable as any in the county. But it ought to be observed, that at meetings held out of doors, and even at meetings held within doors, persons in the lower class of life would be present. But he thought the petition which had been agreed to at this meeting went to prove, that no re-action on the question of reform had taken place in the county of Northampton. As to the names signed to the protest, he was bound to say that many of them were those of persons of the highest respectability, several of them his own personal friends. But there were also the names of others, who could not, on account of rank, object to those who were present at the out-door meeting. He saw amongst the signatures to the protest that of a chimney-sweeper and of a post-boy. Those persons certainly had a right to state their opinions, and he only mentioned the circumstance as a set-off against any charge of want of respectability which might be alleged against the meeting out of doors.

Mr. CARTWRIGHT said, that during the 35 years in which he had been connected with the county, he had never known the adjournment of a meeting from the Shire-hall to the open air. There was sufficient room in the hall for 200 persons more than attended. At 12 o'clock, when he entered the hall, there was scarcely a soul there. Under all the circumstances, he must, therefore, contend that this was not the petition of the county of Northampton. It did not, he was confident, express the sense of the resident clergy, gentlemen, and freeholders, of Northampton. As he had said before, he never knew an instance of a meeting being held at Northampton in the open air, except on one occasion, when the noble lord made his triumphal entry into Northampton, and stepped from his chariot into a waggon for the purpose of addressing the populace. That was the only time when such an occurrence had taken place in Northampton for 35 years. If the noble lord would examine the names appended to the protest, he would at once perceive that a great majority of the clergy and gentry of Northampton were opposed to the present plan of reform. Those who signed that paper admitted that some reform was necessary in the representation of large and populous town, although they could not give their sanction to such a measure as was now proposed.

Mr. VERNON SMITH explained the part which he had taken at the Northampton meeting. In his opinion the adjournment to the Market-place was proper. At the time that the adjournment was moved, the hall was as full as it possibly could be, and a vast number of people were congregated outside.

Sir G. ROBINSON (we believe) said, that he could see no reason for the adjournment of the meeting. The freeholders, and all those who were concerned with the meeting, could hear much better in the hall than in the open air; besides, it was pouring torrents of rain at the time when the adjournment was carried. He firmly believed, that there was no proposition against which his constituents entertained a stronger objection than they did against this bill. He had not before expressed his opinion on this question, and therefore he would make one remark before he sat down. He had heard many gentlemen in that house state that they were friendly to moderate reform, but that they would nevertheless vote for the second reading of this bill. He had told his constituents that he also was friendly to moderate reform; but no gentleman to whom he had made that declaration had called on him to support a measure of so sweeping and comprehensive a description as the present. He was quite convinced, that if the hon. member for Middlesex had proposed such a measure a twelvemonth ago, it would have been denounced by many of the present ministers as dangerous to the constitution. He would not withhold his support from any moderate plan of reform which was likely to be beneficial to the country, but he never would vote in favour of the present bill.

The CHANCELLOR of the EXCHEQUER said, if the people of Northamptonshire were adverse, as had been said, to the bill now before Parliament, it was rather strange that they should sign a petition in its favour.

After a few words from Mr. CARTWRIGHT and Mr. V. SMITH, the petition was ordered to be printed.

The CHANCELLOR of the EXCHEQUER presented a petition from the nobility, gentry, justices of the peace, and heritors of the county of Perth, in favour of reform; and a similar petition from Towcester, in the county of Northampton.

Mr. W. DUNCOMBE presented a petition from the mayor, aldermen, and burgesses of Leeds, in Common-hall assembled, against the plan of reform proposed by ministers.

The Hon. MEMBER presented similar petitions from the towns of Doncaster, Bradford, and Barnsley.

Lord MORPETH admitted the petition from Doncaster was respectably signed, but he had been requested by very intelligent correspondents in that town to state, that the petition did not speak the sense of the great body of inhabitants.

Mr. W. DUNCOMBE said, that certainly no public meeting had been held for the purpose of debating this petition. That course had not been pursued, because, if it had, the other party would have attended, and would have overwhelmed those who were friendly to moderate measures by their clamour.

Mr. SYKES said he was informed that the petition from Barnsley did not contain the opinion of one-twentieth of the population.—Laid on the table.

Mr. LITTLETON said, he rose to present a petition, which he had had for some time in his hands, emanating from a most respectable meeting of the inhabitants of Staffordshire, regularly convened by the High Sheriff. It was a petition of very great importance with respect to the rank and property of those by whom it had been signed. He believed that every populous and wealthy parish in the county had sent two petitions to Parliament on the subject of reform; the one calling for some measure of reform, and the other approving of that which was proposed by the Government. There was not one manufacturing parish with which he was acquainted in that county that was not unanimously favourable to the bill. There might be some few persons who entertained fears and scruples on the subject, but the general feeling was decidedly in favour of the measure. He concurred in the opinion of the petitioners, and he would sacrifice his own private opinion on some minor points, in order to secure the great object which ministers had in view. (Hear, hear.)

Mr. C. PELHAM was adverse to the bill, which would diminish rather than increase his constituents.

Sir C. MORGAN said, great praise was due to the Marquis of Cleveland, whose name was affixed to this petition, as a reformer, when the house recollected the way in which he had dealt with his boroughs.

Mr. J. CAMPBELL said, that the freemen of Stafford had acted in the most independent manner. They did not insist on retaining exclusive rights. No; they came forward fairly, and said, "Let our townsmen be admitted to the same privileges which we enjoy."

The petition was then read: amongst the signatures to it were those of the Earl of Shrewsbury and Lord Gower.

Sir C. MORGAN said, that as the owner of many boroughs, the Marquis of Cleveland had conducted them in such a manner as laid the foundation of the present bill.

Lord J. RUSSELL said, that the noble marquis who had been alluded to, used his boroughs as other borough proprietors did—to support his own political opinions.

Colonel DAVIES said, that the noble marquis could not be accused of tyrannous conduct, with reference to his boroughs, for he believed that a gentleman who sat for one of those boroughs would vote this evening against the bill.

After a few words from Mr. LENNARD, Mr. LABOUCHERE, General GASCOYNE, Mr. PORTMAN, Mr. KEMP, and Sir H. HARDINGE, the petition was ordered to be printed.

Mr. LITTLETON presented a petition from a parish in Staffordshire, against the law of settlement by hiring and service; also a petition from Burslem, against certain parts of the beer bill, and a petition from a Protestant dissenting congregation, for the abolition of slavery.

NEWFOUNDLAND.

Mr. ROBINSON postponed the presentation of a petition from Waterford, relating to Newfoundland, to Thursday, and his motion on the state of that colony to the 24th of May.

REFORM BILL.

Lord JOHN RUSSELL moved the order of the day for resuming the adjourned debate on the question for going into the committee on this bill.

Mr. BULWER opened the discussion in a speech of some length, but from the tone in which parts of his remarks were given, and the noise that prevailed in the house, the hon. member was very imperfectly heard in the gallery. We understood him to say, that he would not enter into the discussion as to the number of members which should constitute the house. That, however, would make no difference as to the general character of the measure; but he hoped that the right hon. gentleman opposite would meet in a spirit of conciliation and compliance the wishes of those who desired to make modifications in the bill, where those modifications did not trench on the general principle of the bill. He could not support the amendment of the hon. and gallant member for Liverpool, for that would be to admit that England, Scotland, and Ireland, were separate kingdoms, instead of being one united empire. He admitted that the Parliament had as much right to take away from or add to the number of members for Ireland, as it had to give a member to York or any other county. When he saw the increasing wealth and population of Ireland, he would not say a word of Scotland, for she was able to take care of herself, but when he saw the increasing wealth and population of Ireland,—he thought the increase of the number of representatives for that country very judicious, and in his opinion any alteration of the bill in that part would be very injurious. The hon. member then adverted to the speech of the hon. member for Newark, and contended that that speech would go against any reform whatever. They were not however now called upon to decide the question whether there should be a reform. That had been decided ages ago. The very principle which established our constitution admitted that it might be improved, and it was absurd to suppose, that while a change was taking place in every thing around us, the system of representation should alone remain stationary. Though he approved of the principle of reform, he thought it would be better if it did not go the length proposed in the total disfranchisement of so many small boroughs. There were certain small evils in a state which it was much better to bear, because they were often made a barrier to prevent greater evils. He would preserve some of those small boroughs, to prevent the influence of popular passion. He thought, therefore, that the noble lord might have effected a great improvement in the representation without going to the extent of taking away so many small boroughs. At the same time he was aware that the particular circumstances in which the country was placed,—the excited state of the public mind, the state of Europe generally, so many states of which had succeeded in changing their government altogether, or introducing extensive alterations of their system,—all these facts considered, he admitted that it was necessary to bring forward such a measure, not as would have satisfied the country in ordinary circumstances, but such as was calculated to sooth an excited and discontented people: for he very much doubted whether such a measure as would easily pass that house would be at all sufficient to satisfy the country. One of the objections to the measure was, that the approbation given to the measure by large mobs or meetings at Manchester, and by the hon. member for Preston, showed its democratic character, and he owned that at first he participated in some degree in the feeling of alarm which was then occasioned. He had since, however, learned from the hon. member, that he did not consider that the bill went far enough, and he owned that he considered it as an argument in its favour that it did not meet the views of that hon. member and of those who joined with him in his notions of reform. He took it for granted that those who were opposed to, as well as those who supported, reform, had the same object in view—that of preventing revolution. They were all agreed as to the end, but differed only as to the means; one party thinking that the concession of power to the people to the extent proposed by this bill would be itself a revolution; the other, that if such power were not conceded, a revolution must be the consequence. Now let the house consider what were the opinions of that class of reformers who did not think this bill went far enough. The hon. member then proceeded to say that the opinions of one part of the press—those small periodicals which were published in defiance of the stamp acts, and had escaped the notice of the Attorney-General, were opposed to the bill, because it did not go far enough, and because they hoped that by the rejection of this, Parliament would at length be obliged to concede that more extended reform which they desired. He read an extract from one of these cheap publications, called *The Poor Man's Guardian*. When he found all those republican writings opposed to the bill, he thought it ought to be a reason for supporting it, because it would have the effect of destroying the influence of those parties. But while he admitted the danger of going too far in concession, he could not shut his eyes to the still greater danger of refusing any. What, he asked, had caused the late French revolution? Was it the moderate and conceding plan of Casimir Perier, or the obstinacy of Peyronnet and Polignac? After adverting to the consequence of resistance to the public feeling in the cases of Louis XVI. and Charles X., the hon. member observed that we lived in times when public opinion was every thing, and when even the prerogatives of the Crown, aided by the power of the sword, would not balance the scale against the feelings of the people. Liberal concession, then, in such a time, was sound policy. In giving his support to this bill on these grounds, he did so (as we understood the hon. member) at the sacrifice of private feeling. He was not there the nominee of any person in the sense of being an organ of his opinion. The noble lord to whom he more immediately owed his seat would not require that his opinion should be merely the organ of that which he himself entertained on this important question, and would not in any manner restrict his vote.

Mr. J. CAMPBELL said, that if any thing could, more clearly than another, show the necessity of the bill before the house, it would be what had just fallen from the hon. member who last addressed it, who had openly avowed that he owed his seat in the house to the influence of a peer. In the purer times of the constitution such an avowal would be sufficient to unseat a member, but we had now got so much accustomed to these matters, that our feelings were not at all affected by them. A predecessor of the right hon. gentleman in the chair had declared, that practices were now openly avowed, with respect to seats in that house, which were sufficient to make our ancestors turn in their graves; yet now an hon. member talked of owing his seat to a peer just as he (Mr. Campbell) should talk of his constituents. This subject had been already been so fully discussed, that he could not hope to give any thing new on it. He would therefore confine himself to the amendment of the hon. and gallant member for Liverpool. The hon. and gallant member for Liverpool had a great objection to diminish the numbers for England and Wales. He wished that number should be 513, no more or less. For his part, he saw nothing so peculiar in the number of 513 that we should adhere to that number in preference to any other. Lord Coke found a great and peculiar advantage in the number of 12. There were 12 tribes of Israel, 12 apostles, 12 disciples, 12 signs of the zodiac, 12 months in the year, and equally conveniently there were 12 judges. (Hear, and a laugh.) But by what similar standard he could try the number of 513 he did not know. If the hon. and gallant member had confined himself to the limitation of the number of members for Scotland to 45, and for Ireland to 100, he might have something like a case to go upon; though, having looked at the acts of union with each of those countries, he saw nothing in them to prevent an addition to the members of either. The hon. and learned member then referred to the correspondence between the Scotch and English commissioners, to show that the number of members for Scotland was not then definitively arranged, but that it was left open to future discussion. He contended that it was absurd to suppose that an increase of members should not be made if the wealth and population of the country greatly increased. The three countries, though they had at one time a hostile feeling to each other, and had separate interests, were now united as one, with one common interest. He then went on to show, that the number of 513 members for England and Wales arose from the great abuse of the power of the Crown, in issuing writs for members to serve for different towns before unrepresented. Under the Tudor sovereigns 154 members were added to the house, not allotted to the great towns, which then began to appear, such as Wakefield, Halifax, and Manchester, but to small places in the county of Cornwall. In Henry I.'s time no more than 12 members were sent to Parliament from the county of Cornwall, but at present no less than 42 were returned by different places in that county. If hon. members were to examine the schedule A of the reform bill, they would find that the majority of the places mentioned in that schedule were first summoned to return members to Parliament under the reigns of the Tudors. The borough of Aldborough was not larger at the time it had the privilege given to it of returning members than at present. It was, therefore, only by an abuse of the King's power that such places as that were summoned to return representatives. The writs that were issued for them could not be considered in any other light than as transferable writs. Hon. gentlemen had all heard of a case, which was argued before the House of Lords, in which it was contended that the possession of a barony gave a right to the possessor of a seat in the House of Lords. Lord Eldon, who was at the time Lord Chancellor, asked Lord Brougham, who was one of the counsel in the cause, whether an assignee, upon obtaining possession of the property, would have a right to sit in the House of Lords? Lord Brougham replied, that he would have such a right; and supported his assertion by saying that there were other and as great anomalies in the constitution. Now it might be the constitution of the House of Lords, that some peerages were transferable, but it was not the constitution of the House of Commons that writs should be transferable. The House of Commons was intended by the constitution to represent the people, and be returned by the people; and the true principle of the constitution was laid down in the writs issued by Edward I. The hon. and learned gentleman here read an extract from one of those writs, in which it was directed that all the people should have a voice in the election of their representatives. He admitted that in those summonses the principle of universal suffrage was laid down, and upon him and upon those who objected to universal suffrage was cast the *onus* of proving that universal suffrage would lead to inconvenience. He was prepared to show that universal suffrage would lead to great inconvenience, monstrous ruin, and universal destruction. But still there was a medium between universal suffrage and giving the right to particular individuals to return members to that house. He saw no reason why the numbers of that house should not be reduced, and he could not agree with some hon. members in thinking the hon. and gallant general's motion of little importance. If, however, that motion should be agreed to, he hoped that the reform bill would still be allowed to pass, for he was confident that great benefit would be conferred on the country by that measure.

Mr. FANE thought that system of representation the best which ensured the best government, and secured for the people equal laws, impartial justice, and equal rights. These advantages were maintained in our present representative system and responsible executive. In all human institutions there must always be some defects; but instead of trying to remove faults where he found any, the noble lord opposite had offered a visionary scheme of his own in exchange for that system which had elevated the kingdom of England to such a pitch of grandeur and happiness. He believed, that if His Majesty's ministers had proposed a moderate and temperate measure of reform, the opposition to it would not have been violent; but their plan was so immoderate, that he could not conceive how any person who was attached to the constitution could give it his support. The noble Lord opposite (Lord J. Russell) had stated, that three years ago not many petitions had been presented on the subject of reform, but that since that time such a change had taken place in the minds of the people, that the table of the house was now covered with reform petitions. He (Mr. Fane) asked what had occurred in England to produce that change? Nothing had occurred in England; but in France a revolution had taken place. (Hear.) The French had expelled an imbecile monarch; and immediately this country became affected with the French epidemic. We, though under circumstances diametrically opposite, were for imitating the example set by the French. Their charters were violated, and they revolutionized to get a constitution; but we were to revolutionize to subvert one. The house had been told much of the necessity of reform, but little of its benefits. Would reform, he asked, ease the burdens of the people, and effect reduction? It would not. He that told the people that reform would alleviate their distress, only deluded them. (Hear.) If the people chose to have colonies, they must keep up an army,—if they would have commerce, they must have a fleet to protect it,—if they would have a monarch, they must have a civil list,—if they would have a church, they must pay tithes,—and last, not least, if they would retain the national honour, they must pay the national debt. By reform the people of England meant reduction of taxes (hear); by reform the faction meant the violation of national faith, and the overthrow of church and state. The faction used reform as the hon. and learned member for Waterford did the repeal of the Union as the means to a good end. By reform the faction hoped to effect a change of government; but whoever attributed any desire to the people of England for the subversion of the Government libelled them. There was at present a great call for a cheap Government, but the people might learn from the history of their own country how little they were likely to obtain that object by violent changes. Charles I. unjustly took 200,000*l.* from his people. For that offence he was brought to trial and suffered. The country, in the mean time, was afflicted by all the miseries of civil war, and at length submitted to Cromwell, who extracted 2,000,000*l.* from the pockets of the people. So much for reform procuring a cheap Government. The advantage of the present system of representation was, that all the different interests of the country found advocates within the walls of that house; but this proposition of the noble lord would exclude from the enjoyment of the elective franchise all the labouring classes, who were thus held out as unworthy to participate in the councils of the country. There were but two bodies in the country who would, under the provisions of the reform bill, enjoy the elective franchise,—the higher classes, and the householders paying above 10*l.* a-year. He did not believe that representatives chosen only by those two bodies would be able to conduct the affairs of the country advantageously, or preserve the national faith. Locke, on Civil Government, stated that the power derived from the people was strictly and positively granted for the purpose of making laws, and not legislatures; and that the legislature had no power to place its authority in other hands but those in which it was vested by the people. The number of the members to be returned to Parliament by England, Scotland, and Ireland was settled at the time of the respective unions. With respect to the proportion of the representatives, the noble lord, the Paymaster of the Forces, had quoted a passage from one of Mr. Pitt's speeches to serve his own purpose. The passage quoted by the noble lord was as follows:—"Considering the question in this point of view, I really think the precise number of the representatives not a matter of great importance." Now he would quote the passage immediately following to serve his (Mr. Fane's) purpose. "At the same time," said Mr. Pitt, "when it is necessary that the number should be fixed, it is necessary to have recourse to some principle on which to found our determination." He only hoped that some hon. member would bring the question of the proportion of the representation fairly before the house; for he thought that its being introduced under the disguise of the reform bill was an insult to the three united kingdoms. The noble lord opposite last night exclaimed in a tone of indignation, disclaiming the charge of partiality in the concoction of the reform bill which had been brought against government, that he did not envy the heart of that man who could entertain such suspicions. (The Chancellor of the Exchequer intimated dissent from the statement of the hon. member.) All he would say was, that he envied not that man his heart who had conceived the present reform bill. (Laughter.) He thought it would lead to great corruption and the vilest traffic. (Hear.)

Mr. WILBRAHAM said he was determined to give the motion of the hon. and gallant general his decided negative. He was neither jealous of the Irish Catholics nor the Scotch members, and he thought the business of the house would be better done by a considerable diminution of its numbers. He had always entertained opinions favourable to Parliamentary reform, and he had therefore no opinions to retract, nor inconsistencies to account for. He had always considered that the corrupt manner in which members were returned for certain boroughs as a great evil, and a cause of that discontent which had lately manifested itself in the country. But he was free to confess that when he first entered the house he took his station among those who were called moderate reformers, and would have been glad to see the representation amended by the transfer of the franchise of corrupt boroughs to populous places. But when he saw the cloak that was thrown over corruption in that house,—when he saw the moderate proposals of the noble lord, the member for Tavistock, uniformly rejected, and when he saw how the franchise of East Retford was disposed of, he then began to despair of measures of moderate reform, and he was convinced that nothing but a great and comprehensive scheme of reform would effect the object he had in view. (Hear, hear.) He need not, therefore, say how much he was delighted with the plan of the noble lord. It was a glorious measure, and worthy of those from whom it proceeded. (Hear, hear.) It struck deep at the root of corruption, and maintained every interest in the state except the interest of the boroughmonger. (Hear, hear.) The house had heard a good deal of late about revolutionary measures, and charges had been made against gentlemen for being democratic. He did not think the course of truth was promoted by employing injurious epithets, nor personal virulence. He would, therefore, abstain from such a course; and endeavour to call the attention of the house to what he conceived would be the practical effects of the reform measure. In the first place he found 44 members were to be given to great commercial places, and he was sure that they would return gentlemen as well educated, and as much attached to the constitution, as any he saw around him. One difference, however, between these members and some of the gentlemen in that House would be, that they would know something about the interests of their constituents; and of these particular arts and mysteries which they had been sent to Parliament to represent and protect. (Hear.) With respect to the eight members allotted to the districts round the metropolis, it was impossible for him to say what would be their character; but considering the great wealth and splendour of some of those places, he could not think that those who possessed that property would be desirous to throw every thing into confusion. The measure also provided, lest there

Below 'The Lords meet for the Despatch of Business'. PUNCH cartoon of the House of Lords by John Leech, 1845. The Lords were televised at work for the first time in 1985.

Bottom Inauguration of THE TIMES teleprinter typesetting service at the House of Commons. Mr Speaker taps a message on the teleprinter machine as the Hon. J. J. Astor looks on, 5 June 1951.

THE LORDS MET FOR THE DESPATCH OF BUSINESS.

Overnight *The Times* published an apology, which one member judged more offensive than the original paragraph.

On 16 April 1831 it was the turn of the Lords to take official exception to the report in *The Times* of their proceedings. The debate was about a petition on the Poor Laws in Ireland, and *The Times* report was splendidly opinionated: 'There are men or things who do not blush to treat a fund for the relief of the diseased or helpless Irish with brutal ridicule'; 'Will any man credit that an Irish absentee Lord could say what he is reported to have uttered in the House of Peers last night?'

The Earl of Limerick took the attack to be directed at him, not unreasonably, since he was the only speaker in the debate on the petition. He claimed Breach of Privilege, and asked that the editor should be ordered to attend the House. The Lord Chancellor, Lord Lyndhurst, was uneasy about the affair. He said that the printer of a paper was the only person legally liable in such cases, and, 'as it was impossible to avoid voting such a publication as that just read to be a Breach of Privilege, the case would be like a hundred others. After a long debate, every man would be anxious that the whole affair should end.'

The printer of *The Times* was John Joseph Lawson. He was ordered to attend the Bar of the House on 19 April. There he refused to answer the question: 'Who has supreme control of *The Times?*' On the following day he presented a petition expressing guarded regret at having given offence. Several Lords suggested that he should be committed to Newgate. In the event, after spending two nights in the custody of the Serjeant at Arms, he got off with a fine of £100 and a Reprimand from the Woolsack. The Lord Chancellor had a point: the House of Lords had spent two days on a relatively minor matter without in any way curbing the impertinent presence of *The Times*.

The right to report Parliament was being fought for and won. In 1833 Daniel O'Connell, the great Irish Catholic campaigner, complained in his customary vehement manner that he had been misreported in *The Times*. Remarkably the Gallery reporters of *The Times*, who were illegal eavesdroppers, made public reply in a letter in their paper on 26 July: 'We have deliberately resolved not to report any speech of Mr O'Connell until he shall have retracted, as publicly as he made, the calumnious assertion that our reports are designedly false'. It was a high and mighty threat from people with no standing. The letter was signed by the eleven reporters headed by John Tyas, the famous reporter who had covered Peterloo for *The Times*.

O'Connell moved that Mrs Anna Brodie (one of the many minor co-proprietors of the paper), James Lawson and John Joseph Lawson should be called to the Bar of the House of Commons. Mrs Brodie was later excused, on gallant chauvinist grounds. O'Connell admitted that his aim was not to punish the printers but to unmask the proprietors and shut them up. During the debate one MP observed handsomely that he had made inquiries about the reporters from *The Times*, and 'he had good reason to believe that they were gentlemen of education and integrity'. Sir Robert Inglis complained bitterly that he had spoken half a dozen times and had never been reported in *The Times*. He admitted that not everything could be reported, but grumbled that 'it often happened that debates of importance were sacrificed to make way for the description of a milliner's fancy'. (Members of Parliament still think that what they say is the most important news in the world.)

A Mr Harvey declared that he had once gone into the Reporters' Gallery and asked why the reports of the speeches in *The Times* had so little similarity with the speeches he had heard made in the House. One of the reporters replied: 'If we stated to the public one half the nonsense which is spoken in the House, we should soon write ourselves out of existence'. Joseph Hume made the revolutionary and sensible proposal that authorized reporters ought to be appointed to report Parliament. O'Connell lost his motion by 105 votes.

In 1847 the Lords again had a go at *The Times*. Another Irish peer, the Marquess of Westmeath, objected to the report in *The Times*: 'The Marquess of Westmeath complained of the ridicule with which his proposal had been received'. He complained that *The Times* was as unscrupulous as the *Sun* at putting words in his mouth, asserted that 'the composition of that newspaper is almost illiterate and bad English', and moved that the printer be called to the Bar. Lord Brougham soothed him: 'He had himself long suffered under a misrepresentation by the Press, and he found that the more frequently he contradicted it, the more constantly it was repeated'. Westmeath did not press his motion.

The printer of *The Times* was summoned to the Bar of the House of Commons twice more before the battle to report Parliament was formally won. For nearly two hundred years the Houses of Parliament insisted that the Press Galleries were illegal and were allowed to operate only on magnanimous sufferance. At last in 1971 a motion was passed that: 'The House will not entertain any complaint of Breach of Privilege in respect of the publications of the debates or proceedings of the House'. Parliamentary reporters ceased to be Strangers in the House and came in out of the cold. The long battle had been won.

Top Sir Edward Carson, later Lord Carson.

Above Cartoon from VANITY FAIR of John Walter III, 10 September 1881.

Below The Law Courts in The Strand, 1860.

Law

The Times has a unique relationship with the law. It is the only newspaper whose Law Report can be cited in court. For several weeks, until one or other of the series of law reports is published, the only report of a new decision is the one in *The Times*. The Law Report in *The Times*, written and edited by barristers, is a branch of the law. It is also often highly entertaining. On the other side of the bench, *The Times* has both prosecuted and defended itself against prosecution in some notable court cases.

The Times found news in the courts from the beginning. On 24 February 1785 it reported two cases at law in its four small pages, one case of assault, the other of debt. During that first year of its life it reported 60 cases in detail; four years later the number had risen to 200; and a hundred years later *Palmer's Index* lists over 1,500 detailed law reports in *The Times*.

In 1884 the Incorporated Council of Law Reporting for England and Wales decided that the profession could use an official supplement to its own law reports. Accordingly, in November 1884, *The Times Law Reports* began to appear as a separate publication. To begin with they were simply reprints of the condensed reports that had appeared in the daily paper. But gradually they expanded into verbatim transcripts of judgments.

Their weekly appearance gave them a head start in competition with other official reports. They were highly thought of in the profession. On one occasion counsel remarked dismissively of a case, 'It was reported only in *The Times Law Reports*'; the Master of the Rolls interrupted him at once: 'They are excellent reports, especially of cases decided in this court'. The barristers who wrote them were more than once commended from the bench. A high compliment was paid to them many years ago: at the conclusion of counsel's arguments the judge asked the *Times* law reporter if he would write the judgment. The *Times* man, who was in his spare time one of the best lawyers in the Temple, accepted the invitation and a judgment was delivered that is still quoted.

In 1952 *The Times Law Reports* ceased as a separate publication, and their function was taken over by the Incorporated Council of Law Reporting. The daily Law Report in *The Times* continues its unique chimera existence as part journalism and part law.

By their nature newspapers tend to become involved in the law as parties to litigation as well as reporters of it. *The Times* is no exception. In the first year of its existence *The Times* was sued. A certain John Bell brought a suit against John Walter, the proprietor, and his infant printing house, alleging that Walter had defaulted from an agreement to print logographically *An Apology for the Life of George Anne Bellamy*, 'replete with anecdotes which no doubt were *all true*'. Lord Mansfield ruled: 'There is no colour of an agreement between Bell and Walter – the plaintiff must be non-suited'. Four years later Walter was less successful when he found himself in the dock for criminal libel against the Prince of Wales and the Duke of York (described on p. 15).

In 1891 a proprietor of *The Times* found himself in court again. John Walter III appeared before the Lord Chief Justice and Mr Justice Mathew. The plaintiff, one Rumney, in pursuit of a libel action against *The Times*, was demanding that the newspaper inform him of its circulation. On being refused the information, Rumney obtained a judge's order for it. Walter appealed. Precedent supported Rumney's case and Walter's appeal was dismissed. But Rumney was refused costs, with the Lord Chief Justice describing his case unkindly as 'frivolous and ridiculous'.

In the following year John Walter III was back in the Chancery Division, this time as plaintiff, bringing a copyright action against the proprietor and publisher of the *St James's Gazette*. The case concerned the pirating of an article by Rudyard Kipling, and occupied two days. The lengthy judgment was given in favour of *The Times*, though a technicality deprived John Walter of some of the costs.

In 1908 there was a famous case. John Murray had published *The Letters of Queen Victoria* in three volumes at £3 3s. *The Times* reviewed the book on the day after publication. Its anonymous critic (John Bailey) was flattering, not to say courtierly, about the book, but mentioned in his review that it was expensive. A few days later *The Times* was ill-advised enough to publish a long letter of 1,500 words following up the review. The writer stated in the course of his letter: 'Her letters are part of the national archive of our time. Mr Murray has exploited Queen Victoria for his own enrichment; in thirty-two pieces of silver.' The editor, the libel lawyer and the back bench (senior editorial staff) must have been sleeping to let that one through.

The letter was mainly concerned with money, the costs of book production, sales and so on. The ammunition in the letter had been supplied by Horace Hooper of the *Encyclopaedia Britannica*, who was the manager of The Times Book Club. But the trigger had been pulled by a certain Mr Ross, an employee of the Book Club, who had signed the letter as Artifex.

The libel was so gross that the case did not have any special legal interest. But it brought the legal heavyweights to battle: each side engaged two KCs and a junior. F. E. Smith led for Murray, and Sir Edward Carson for Walter and *The Times*. On the bench was Mr Justice Darling, the witty and literate lawyer who could be relied on to raise a laugh in even the dustiest passages of the law. The hearing lasted two days. On the third Darling summed up, referring to the parties as 'national institutions'. He described the case as 'almost a quarrel between Magna Carta and the Bill of Rights'. The jury took only thirty-five minutes to find Walter guilty of libel and award £7,500 damages.

There was a happy sequel. Later in the year the King expressed a 'command' that a new and popular edition should bring Queen Victoria's letters within reach of all of His Majesty's subjects. John Murray in conjunction with *The Times* published an edition at 6s. More than 100,000 copies were sold.

The Times was sued for libel again in 1921. Alfred Warwick Gattie, managing director of the New Transport Company,

THE LETTERS OF QUEEN VICTORIA

A SELECTION FROM HER MAJESTY'S CORRESPONDENCE BETWEEN THE YEARS 1837 AND 1861

PUBLISHED BY AUTHORITY OF HIS MAJESTY THE KING

EDITED BY ARTHUR CHRISTOPHER BENSON, M.A. AND VISCOUNT ESHER, G.C.V.O., K.C.B.

IN THREE VOLUMES

VOL. I.—1837-1843

LONDON
JOHN MURRAY, ALBEMARLE STREET, W.
1908

Above Title page of THE LETTERS OF QUEEN VICTORIA, first published by John Murray in 1908.

claimed damages from *The Times* for falsely and maliciously publishing a leading article about him and his scheme of transport. The case did not occupy much of the time of Mr Justice Coleridge and a special jury. The jury intimated that the action was frivolous, and awarded judgment with costs to the defendants.

In 1936 *The Times* was back in court as defendant in a libel case. The plaintiff was Captain Cuthbert Reavely, a professional singer and actor, who claimed that he had been libelled in *The Times*'s criticism of a performance of *Elijah* at the Albert Hall. The piece had been under the byline of Our Music Critic, who was at that time H. C. Colles, but it had in fact been written by his deputy Frank Howes. Misled by the anonymity of *The Times*, the singing Captain sued Colles, but then dropped his action against the music critic, leaving *The Times* as the only defendant.

On the ghastly night in question Mendelssohn's music had been performed in the Albert Hall not as an oratorio, but as a pageant with scenery, costumes and dramatic poses. Captain Reavely played the part of Ahab. He had only one line to sing: 'Art thou Elijah? Art thou he that troubleth Israel?' Having sung his line, he had to remain on stage for nearly an hour, mute, but according to the Captain, 'he had to act during the whole of that time'.

The Times did not care for the spectacle and said so with vim and acerbity. In *re* the part of Ahab, the critic wrote: 'The conflict between Elijah and Ahab is stultified by the physical appearance of a King who can only make gestures of impotent annoyance'. He described the singing of Captain Reavely's moment of glory as 'unsteady in declamation'.

Captain Reavely stated that 'anyone reading the article in *The Times* would consider him wholly inadequate both physically and histrionically'. The paper pleaded fair comment. The case was tried before Mr Justice Swift and a special jury. Mr Lawton appeared for Captain Reavely; *The Times* had a cohort of counsel, led by Sir William Jowitt KC.

It was a good libel action, as these things go. *The Oxford English Dictionary* was brought in to help the court with the definition of oratorio. The judge had his *bons mots*: 'I believe that everybody who reads *The Times* has a charitable mind'; 'Do you happen to know whether any of the angels has brought a libel action?'

When the plaintiff had finished his evidence, Mr Justice Swift said: 'I confess I cannot see anything for *The Times* to answer'. The jury agreed with him.

In 1952 *The Times* was in the dock. The prosecutor was the Crown, and the trial was heard in the Central Criminal Court. The Tronah Mines Ltd had placed an advertisement in *The Times*, in consequence of which the paper was charged with incurring expenses with a view to promoting or procuring the election of the Conservative candidate in the Cities of London and Westminster in the General Election. The company and its secretary were also charged.

The arguments were important, long and inspissated. The report took up columns and columns in the Law Report. The result was a formal verdict of Not Guilty.

In 1963 *The Times* appeared for a change as plaintiff in a libel action. The paper considered that it had been libelled in a book about smoking published by Penguin. The author, a doctor, had suggested that the editorial content of *The Times* on the effects of smoking on health was motivated by tobacco advertising and a desire not to offend those with interests in the tobacco industry. Penguin withdrew the allegation and the affair was settled as amicably as is possible with the ferocious English laws of libel.

In 1971 Bernard Levin wrote a characteristically sprightly article entitled 'Profit and Dishonour in Fleet Street', referring to matters at the *Daily Mail*, his former employer. Lord Rothermere and others issued a writ against *The Times*, its editor and Levin. An order was made by a Master that the action should be tried by a jury. Mr Justice Ackner allowed the plaintiff's appeal that the action should be tried by a judge alone. Two years and many pounds after the offending article appeared, the Court of Appeal sat for two days on *The Times* appeal against the ruling of the High Court. Once libel gets in the hands of the lawyers, there is no end to the time and grief and cost of it.

The Times pleaded justification and fair comment on a matter of public interest. The plaintiffs alleged that the defendants wrote and published the article with actual malice. *The Times* wanted trial by jury: plaintiffs argued that the trial would require prolonged examination of documents (its list of them covered seventy-seven pages), and asked for trial by judge alone. The appeal of *The Times* was allowed on the ground of the national importance of the case, with one of the three Lords Justice dissenting.

In the end, after the deployment of so much preliminary legal heavy artillery, the case was settled out of court. The settlement was given a prominent place in the Law Report of 10 April 1973. *The Times* and other defendants

> acknowledge that the charges are unjustified. They have signified their willingness publicly to apologize for the serious damage done to the plaintiffs. It was never the intention of the defendants to impugn the personal honesty or integrity of the plaintiffs, or to suggest that the true reason for the closure [of the *Daily Sketch*] was the personal enrichment of Lord Rothermere or the Honourable Vere Harmsworth.

In 1976 the Downing Street press officers of the Prime Minister, Harold Wilson, took offence at a piece in the linguistic series entitled New Words for Old. It dealt with the value word Truth, and suggested, in its customarily light-hearted way, that Truth meant little more than the official line put out by party press officers.

Downing Street took umbrage, and at first broke off relations and sent *The Times* to Coventry, refusing to speak to lobby correspondents, and even to supply the list of those who had dined at Downing Street the previous night, for the Court Page. A senior executive from Printing House Square had to go to Number 10 in the office Rolls to collect the New Year's Honours List: and he had to go round to a side door.

After six months the press officers decided to sue for libel. William Rees-Mogg, the editor, said that he would fight the case to the House of Lords, calling as witnesses the Prime Minister, most of his Cabinet, and Marcia Williams, among others. *Times* counsel, James Comyn QC, rubbed his hands, puffed one of his chain of cigarettes and said: 'It will be a grand case, and I shall be proud to represent you. But it is my duty to warn you that it will be the most expensive litigation this century.' 'Never mind,' said the intrepid editor, 'we shall proceed.'

In the spring of 1977 Harold Wilson resigned. There was less glamour in taking on a former Prime Minister on the issue of whether his press officers were professional fibbers. So *The Times* settled, and paid the press officers £100 each.

Any newspaper worth its ink has occasionally to tread near the edge of libel in the search for truth. It is a perilous part of its function that *The Times* has been fulfilling since the eighteenth century. The peculiar function of *The Times* is to be gamekeeper as well as poacher; to be an official record in its Law Report, as well as to debate, argue, and mine for the truth and for good law in its other columns.

An official TIMES Law Report on a libel case in which THE TIMES itself was the defendant.
10 APRIL 1973

Law Report April 9 1973 Queen's Bench Division

Libel action over Levin article settled

Rothermere and Others v Times Newspapers Ltd and Others
Before Mr Justice Eveleigh

The settlement was announced of a libel action brought over an article published in *The Times* on March 19, 1971.

Mr David Hirst, QC, said that he appeared with Mr T. H. Bingham, QC, for the plaintiffs. Mr James Comyn, QC, and Mr Peter Bowsher represented the defendants.

Mr Hirst said: "There are three plaintiffs. The first is Viscount Rothermere, Chairman of Associated Newspapers Group for 38 years until his retirement in January, 1971. The second plaintiff, the Honourable Vere Harmsworth, is the son of the first plaintiff; he has been a Director of Associated Newspapers for many years and became Chairman upon the retirement of his father. The third plaintiff is Associated Newspapers Group Ltd, a public company whose main business is the publishing of newspapers which include the *Daily Mail*.

"There are also three defendants. The first is Times Newspapers Ltd, publishers of *The Times* newspaper. The second, Mr William Rees-Mogg, is the Editor of *The Times*. The third, Mr Bernard Levin, is a journalist, formerly employed as a columnist on the *Daily Mail* and now employed in a similar capacity on *The Times*.

"On March 8, 1971, the management of Associated Newspapers announced plans for a radical reorganization of the business of the company whereby publication of the *Daily Sketch* was to cease, and it was to be merged with the *Daily Mail*: the most stringent economies were to be effected and a large number of employees of the company were to become redundant.

"On March 19, 1971, there was published in *The Times* an article written by Mr Levin, entitled in most editions "Profit and Dishonour in Fleet Street", which castigated in the most extreme terms the plaintiffs' conduct concerning the reorganization just mentioned.

"These serious allegations contained in the article were quite unjustified. Associated Newspapers had in recent years suffered severe losses in publishing its national newspapers. Such losses could not be allowed to continue without serious detriment to the future business of the company, its many public shareholders and the security of the majority of its employees. From the late autumn of 1970 onwards all feasible courses and remedies open to the company had been the subject of the most intense and anxious consideration. Economic advice had been sought from an independent and eminent consulting firm. This advice was to the effect that the company should curtail its publishing activities to an extent considerably greater than that eventually decided upon by the plaintiffs. Far from being made to increase the plaintiffs' personal fortunes or corporate wealth, the cuts made were those regarded as the minimum necessary to put this public company on a sound financial basis. The redundancy of many employees was regarded as the unavoidable price to be paid for the continued employment of the much greater number who were to remain. These decisions were implemented after full consultation with the unions by Mr Harmsworth, who was present and spoke at the meetings with staff representatives where the decisions were fully explained. They were made after much heart searching and with the greatest reluctance by all concerned in the management of Associated Newspapers, who treated the redundant employees with generosity. It must be a matter for much regret in the circumstances that such serious charges should have been made against Lord Rothermere and Mr Harmsworth.

"The defendants have, since this action was brought, had the opportunity fully to investigate the true facts, and as a result they acknowledge that the charges were unjustified. They have signified their willingness publicly to apologize for the serious damage done to the plaintiffs. They have agreed to indemnify the plaintiffs against their costs. They have undertaken to publish no similar libels of the plaintiffs. They have agreed to publish the text of this statement with the same prominence as the offending article. The plaintiffs are not insisting upon the payment of the substantial damages to which they are advised they are entitled and on these terms the plaintiffs are prepared to pursue the action no further.

"There is one further matter that I would mention to your Lordship. At the pleading stage of this matter an allegation of express malice was made based, inter alia, on the contention that by reason of his previous employment by the plaintiffs the Managing Director of Times Newspapers Ltd, Mr M. J. Hussey, must have known that the picture of the plaintiffs' conduct and business as presented by Mr Levin's article was false. However, the plaintiffs now accept that Mr Hussey was in no way concerned with the writing or publication of the article and that he did not see the article prior to publication. Since this allegation of malice received some publicity at a time when the case was before the Court of Appeal on an interlocutory point, the plaintiffs have thought it right to place on record that, in the light of the assurances to which I have referred, the allegation of malice against Mr Hussey is withdrawn."

Mr Comyn, on behalf of all the defendants, said: "I endorse unreservedly all that my learned friend has said. While the article complained of was very critical of aspects of the closure of the *Daily Sketch* and its merger with the *Daily Mail*, it was never the intention of the defendants to impugn the personal honesty or integrity of the plaintiffs, or to suggest that the true reason for the closure was the personal enrichment of Lord Rothermere or the Honourable Vere Harmsworth. The defendants are happy to make this plain in terms and to withdraw any such suggestions, and to take this opportunity of apologizing to the plaintiffs and expressing their appreciation of the fact that the allegation in the pleadings against Mr Hussey personally has been withdrawn."

The record was, by leave, withdrawn.

Solicitors: Swepstone, Walsh & Son; Charles Russell & Co.

John Davies, Cabinet Minister for Europe, on the first 100 days

Dynamic change, not disarray in the EEC

There is nothing magical about 100 days, as Napoleon and others have found out. But it is perhaps long enough to have got some kind of a feeling of what the Community is and not too long for the sense of adventure to have become dulled. The novelty of being "in", and in to stay, is in fact still vivid.

There is, too, a not unnatural tendency, as the newcomers, to be a little critical of what has already been achieved and perhaps a little overconfident of what is going to be. The Community we have joined is not just an agricultural policy on the one side and a customs union on the other. It is certainly deeper and more significant than that would imply and both depth and significance have strengthened with our joining. It is in a curious and ill-defined way the guarantee of peace in Western Europe after centuries of war: defence and security are not written into its treaties but they lie at the heart of its existence.

We have joined something more than a common agricultural policy and a customs union: something even more than a great sheaf of objectives set by the 1972 summit. We have joined a union of nations who have by uniting greatly enhanced their own security and their own prosperity. And we have joined them for the self-same reasons. We seek security and prosperity: we believe that we can contribute to both as we hope to be advantaged by both.

The manner of our joining has not made dramatic headlines: it is all too easy to think that it has been very unspectacular and humdrum—and so in a way it has. But not entirely. The adaptation to a new way of regulating affairs even in rarified fields of activity presents real problems. To be doing so at a time when major changes are taking place in habits and attitudes internally as well makes those 100 days exceptional. We are merging a wholly different social, professional, fiscal, political and even legal system with our neighbours at a time when our own system is in a phase of profound change.

We have undoubtedly made a vigorous beginning. We named two Commissioners of outstanding reputation and with strong political backgrounds. We recruited a group of parliamentary delegates of obvious quality—unhappily representing as but a part of our political spectrum. We devised our own way of seeking homogeneity in the handling of government policies as they affected our Community interest. In all these things we struck our own note, seeking to learn from others but not necessarily to copy them. We have certainly marked our individuality upon the enlarged Community—not always to our own or our partners' satisfaction.

But we are there as a cogent factor with new ideas and different habits and our own mode of expression. Nobody ever thought that Britain could insert herself in the ranks without some consequent trauma; but it has been one of vitality and innovation, not of disturbance and disarray.

The Community as a whole has been humming away at a very high rate of revolutions and in every part of its machinery. The strain is very great.

The dynamic activity of the Commission is evident to all. The Parliament has been flexing its muscles and measuring its potential. The Council of Ministers—that extraordinary multiple unity—has repeatedly been in session in its many guises—foreign ministers, agricultural ministers, finance ministers, social ministers, atomic ministers, transport ministers—arguing away night and day with unfailing courtesy, unflagging resilience and at times with decision.

Less in the public eye but central none the less to the whole process have been the permanent representatives and their staffs: they are the catalysts between naked national policy and the overall Community purpose. Behind this complex pattern of Community effort there has been a matching analysis of national interest to feed into the Community policy making: the analysis calls for frequent inter-country discussion seeking support,

We cannot be sure that its undeniably laborious and cumbersome method of decision making is equal to the strain

moulding national ideas to multi-national accord, trading lesser interests for greater. In our first 100 days the momentum has been terrific—we are assured abnormally so. In that same 100 days two members have been through general elections: one has formed a new government after weeks of effort: one is still working on a caretaker basis.

This widespread and intense activity has largely been deployed on new fields of action initiated by the summit meeting of last October—but not all of it. The continuing need to maintain the agricultural system whilst constantly reshaping it to meet new pressures and demands has, as ever, been a major generator of work. The sudden crisis in the world monetary system have called upon the Community to react urgently and out of phase with the intended programme. The steepening and threatening trend of inflation has demanded immediate attention.

But the crises have not held back the main flow of work. The elaboration of negotiating mandates for the enlarged Community to update and rearrange its internal trading relationships has been proceeding apace. New deals with the members of EFTA who have not become members of the Community including the last-minute refuser Norway; with Cyprus, with Uruguay, with Iceland. Negotiations in view with India and Brazil; with the diverse countries of the Mediterranean; with the associated and associable countries of Africa and the Caribbean and elsewhere; with the Asia Commonwealth; with the state-trading countries; and of course, most important of all with the whole trading world in the so-called GATT multilateral this autumn.

In another field of work—regional policy—the preparation of a new dimension to the Community's range has been pressed forward.

In yet another, the intense and complicated problem of translating the broad concept of economic and monetary union into a reality has been exercising the minds of experts throughout the Community. We shall begin to be seeing the results of their deliberations very soon now.

Matching them have been the equivalent efforts made in the fields of social policy, of science and research policy, of industrial policy, of energy policy, of environmental policy and of others still.

The great problem that is now posed is whether the Community can cope with that output. We cannot be sure that its undeniably laborious and cumbersome method of decision making is equal to the strain which it is now being called upon to bear (though the apparent inertia is deceptive; at times things move apace). No one should be too critical of what it has achieved to date, bearing in mind that everything of real importance has had to achieve a consensus amongst the original members before it could emerge as the Community.

But the weight of demand has been stepped up to a level never previously even contemplated, and the decision making process has itself been made more complex by the addition of three new members. In addition, the increased membership and the widened range of activity entails an imperative demand for greater democratization of the whole, and that certainly does not make decisions easier or quicker to take. Yet without it the human face of the Community will not be seen and if it is not, all the skills and expertise in the world will not allow it to fulfil its main purpose.

Certainly the most pressing problems are these: to bring on the one hand the meaning of the Community home to its peoples, on the other to translate that meaning into action. If these can be attained, then the present objectives add up to a reshaping of our lives and of our continent of a quite unprecedented kind. It means the reemergence at long last of a truly European personality.

The next 10 years can see a veritable transformation of life in Europe as a springboard to an epoch when the Continent will have redicovered its genius and reshaped it to the needs of its peoples and of a modern world.

The effort and the will to bring about that transformation is needed now.

Putting our worst fears in black and white

Bernard Levin

A week or so ago, a man found lying hurt on the pavement explained his injuries by saying that he had been "mugged" by two coloured youths. A few days later, he admitted that he had not been attacked at all, and that he had hurt himself by falling out of his car. The psychological need in him that led him to concoct a false tale of assault does not here concern me. The parts of his story that I wish to use today as my starting-point are that the two imaginary assailants were *coloured*, and were *youths*, and that he had been *mugged* by them.

The ready combination of these three elements in the mind of a man seeking an identity and role for his imaginary assailants strongly suggests that they came from a stereotype that he had accepted unthinkingly, indeed unconsciously. But "acceptance" implies a donor. From where did he get that stereotype, and what are the implications for us all in its existence?

These questions seem particularly urgent today, in the light of Mr Enoch Powell's latest race-speech, but they have, of course, been urgent for a long time, and certainly since well before Mr Powell realized what precious political metal there might be for him to mine in matters racial. As long ago as April, 1966 (and I can hardly have been the first to point it out), I wrote an article in which I drew attention to the fact that "The first British-born generation of the children of the big post-war wave of coloured immigration will be coming to manhood and womanhood within the next few years . . . " and speculated on some of the problems that approaching maturity would bring with it. "Our responses to our fellow Britons with black faces", I wrote, "are going to be very different from what they are to their parents or grandparents. What is more, we . . . will, if we are sufficiently far-sighted and intelligent, be able to look on our coloured compatriots with eyes unclouded by guilt. . . ."

Clearly, we were *not* sufficiently far sighted and intelligent, for although we certainly look on our coloured compatriots without feelings of guilt, too many of us look on them with such carefully-fostered feelings of fear and resentment that we have failed almost entirely to accept and assimilate them as—given the right kind of understanding leadership—we might have done. Instead, we have allowed race relations to deteriorate into a condition of such squalor that it is not considered extraordinary, let alone disgraceful, for Mr Rippon—a member of the Cabinet—to remain a member of a political organization (the Monday Club) which apparently sees nothing wrong in associating with the National Front, provided that such comradeship does not go so far as to permit the support of National Front candidates against Conservative ones. Indeed, the situation is even worse than that, for one can now read serious discussions of whether, if the current election for Chairman of the Monday Club should result in the victory of the candidate who favours even closer association with the National Front, Mr Rippon will *or will not* resign.

Now the other side of the state of affairs implied by the man who invented a mugging and attributed it to two imaginary coloured youths is the state of affairs in which it might easily have been true. We have allowed the growth of a black urban group of young people whose disaffection from the society of which they are part is almost complete, and, in the case of too many of them, probably irreversible. The recent reports in The Times Diary on the relations between coloured communities and the police revealed how bitter was their distrust of "the law", how certain they were that the police were against them, planted drugs on them, assaulted them. What is more, such a state of affairs would be horrifying even if there were not the slightest shred of any justification for it, for its suggests that the black communities need scapegoats to justify their condition just as much as the white communities do to explain theirs.

For just as bad housing, inadequate education, the lack of recreational facilities and the shortage of jobs other than the most menial, though endemic in many areas with large coloured populations, are not *caused* by the coloured presence, however convenient it is for the resentful and deprived among the white population to believe that they are (and, it must be added, however convenient it is for the Government to allow such myths to be believed), so it is not a conspiracy by a malevolent white society that narrows the horizons of coloured people. Both the one and the other are caused by the same sets of conditions—economic, social, historical—and the solution to both must be sought in the eradication of those conditions.

Yet the solutions are *not* sought there; they are sought rather in the treatment of race as an almost exclusively political question, so that—because politics is always at the front of the stage while social questions of a far more fundamental kind are only dimly to be seen at the back—not only is the racial situation itself made worse, but the pressure to relieve the conditions in which racial "problems" flourish is seriously weakened.

Let us take one obvious, and timely, illustration of this. Mr Powell is constantly harping on the fact that the British people were never consulted on the question of coloured immigration into Britain. He knows perfectly well, however, that "consultation" of the kind implied is not, and never has been, part of our constitution. Whether it should be, and if so how it can be introduced, is an important question; but thinking about it is more difficult, and less politically rewarding, than to suggest an evil and many-tentacled conspiracy forcing black neighbours upon unwilling white Britons. Similarly, it is easier, and pays better in terms of political support, to suggest that London suburbs are becoming more heavily black-populated because of the same conspiracy than to examine the world-wide phenomenon of intra-urban population-shifts, and thus admit that it is taking place for reasons largely unconnected with race or colour, let alone with the thrusting of mythical excrement through imaginary letter-boxes by fabulous immigrants.

After all, even if we were to accept Mr Powell's statistical claims without question, they would still amount to a coloured population, in years to come, of something like 5 or 6 per cent of the total. How have we managed to get a triviality like that so hideously and dangerously out of proportion? The easy answer is that though the total spread evenly throughout the country might be negligible, its concentration in a few urban centres is dreadful and insupportable. It isn't; but why should it be thought so, and why should so much effort go into making it thought so, and indeed to making it actually so? More to the point, why should the effort succeed? No doubt if there were no deeply buried racial fears beneath our consciousness, Mr Powell would never have raised his banner ("Without an audience", says the proverb, "dogs do not bark"), but the fact is that having raised it he found people flocking to it. Why?

For an answer, we must return to the man who invented the story that he had been mugged by two coloured youths. He had reached for the stereotype because, beset as we all are by the huge, impersonal forces and processes that shape our lives, he had found it necessary to reduce them to a couple of identifiable enemies, and to colour them black. But the huge, impersonal forces are not going to become less huge or less impersonal as the years go by. If there is already, because of these forces, an entirely new dimension of resentment to add to the old ones of dreary living conditions and low income, resentment will grow rather than diminish in the coming years, and the tensions between scapegoat and scapegoat-seeker will grow worse. That they have already become as bad as they are is the result of a confidence-trick, but not the one of which Mr Powell accuses successive Governments. Apparently insoluble problems existed; their solution was sought in the irrelevant and diversionary restriction of the numbers of coloured immigrants. The problems were not solved by this, so the conclusion was drawn: restrict the numbers further. Still the problems were not solved, and again the cry went out: tighten the tap yet more! It was tightened yet more, and still the problems were not solved—indeed, they grew worse. Sooner or later, we will have to recognize that the disease and the cure have nothing to do with each other.

The fact that such recognition has, for many people, by now been rendered virtually impossible is not primarily the fault of Mr Powell, though he has certainly helped to bring such a state of affairs about. The real culprit is, again, Government, though—again—not for the reasons Mr Powell gives. The fault lies in a wholly contradictory dual approach that has bedevilled our race relations for more than a dozen years, and that consists of the pretence that it is possible to combine on the one hand increasing restrictions on the numbers of coloured immigrants allowed in, together with continuous talk of the "problems" and "difficulties" that this "wave" (or even "invasion" or "assault") has caused, and on the other hand a call for fair and equal treatment of the coloured minority. This is not a plea for a return to the "open door" policy. But if you behave and talk as though a black man were some kind of virus that must be kept out of the body politic as far as possible, and discussed in terms of the ill effects it is having as it multiplies in the national bloodstream, together with calls for the production and use of more powerful antibiotics to counter its dire effects, then it is the shabbiest hypocrisy to preach racial harmony at the same time, for the two themes are totally, and obviously, incompatible.

This, if you like, is the real deception, the real concealment, the real cowardice, the real failure, of successive Governments. But there are no votes in saying so. Instead, Governments, local authorities, Churches, social workers, have joined in the call for a non-existent panacea called "integration", and have called upon the immigrant and coloured communities to take the first step in its direction by dissolving their differences in the warm welcome of the native population, the better to ingratiate themselves with their "hosts".

It's nonsense, isn't it? We inevitably—not deliberately, except in the case of an obvious few, but inevitably—encourage hostility to coloured people (and not merely to immigrants, but to their British-born children—or offspring, as Mr Powell would call them when he is not calling them piccaninnies), and then expect them to take us seriously when we say that if only they will stop having steel-band parties or cooking curry we will welcome them into our midst and encourage them to marry our daughters. But the truth is that the only concession acceptable in the kind of climate that we have created is for the coloured people to turn white, and not even giving them a bath in Brobat will bring that about.

The fact is, of course, that the disparity between the indigenous community on the one hand and the immigrant community and its indigenous-born generations on the other, is so great in terms of numbers, economic and political power, psychological security and every other kind of social strength and cohesion, that it must be, and can only be, from the white majority that the first, major concession must come. And that concession, of course, is no more and no less than a genuine recognition of equality, and a genuine abandonment of unjust discrimination. Mr Powell has now taken to declaring, in tones of horror and amazement, as though he has just discovered the fact and as though it was yet another proof of the indelible depravity beneath a black skin, that coloured immigrants, and even their children, do not regard Britain as home, but still think of the country from which they or their parents came as their true home. What the devil are they supposed to feel—that home is the country whose leaders talk as though they are some kind of infection, and where Mr Powell—and others far more extreme than he—campaign unhindered and almost unrebuked for their further restriction and ultimate extrusion? What is all that supposed to give them—a feeling of security?

One essential truth embedded in this question—embedded so deep it has become invisible—is that the great majority of immigrants came to Britain to work, and in the great majority of cases because they had been recruited to do a specific job. The proportion of unemployed coloured people has never been significantly higher than of the population as a whole, and until the very recent upturn in unemployment (now falling again anyway), it was clear that without the coloured worker there would be a substantial labour shortage, and in some industries a catastrophic shortage. Moreover, immigrants have tended to settle in the places where the demand for their work existed, and that has meant in the big cities where the rapidly expanding service industries needed their labour. But when have you heard a Prime Minister, or a Home Secretary, or a Minister of Employment, say so?

We have got to face the fact that there has now grown up in Britain a generation of coloured people who simply will not accept the words of Esau from the mouth of Jacob. Either we abandon the fatal duality in our attitude to them, or they will turn to the *ignis fatuus* of Black Power on the one hand, and of sullen and vicious alienation from our society on the other. This is overwhelmingly a white society, and it will remain so even if Mr Powell's most lurid and gleeful nightmares come true. So it is from within the whiteness of our society that the new, healing attitude must come, and come soon. Otherwise, those who pretend falsely to have been mugged by coloured youths will sooner or later seem, amid the cries of those who actually have been, even more eccentric than they are.

The Times Diary

In search of the true nut cutlet

For veteran London vegetarians, life has never been the same since the demise of Shearns in Tottenham Court Road. There you could get proper vegetarian meals delivered by long-serving waitresses to tables bearing tablecloths. Nowadays vegetarian food is served mainly at restaurants with faddish names, where you eat off scrubbed wooden tables and have to squeeze on to slim benches alongside dieting secretaries in a hurry.

Worst of all, I was told, you can no longer get nut cutlets. My reporter, checking this out at some London wholefood restaurants, found it to be entirely true. What you get instead now are nut rissoles. The restaurateurs say the ingredients are the same—peanuts and cashews, herbs, optional cheese, carrots, cabbage, onions, egg, breadcrumbs and perhaps a hint of leek.

Fans of the true nut cutlet, unmollified, say they do not taste the same at all. And then, they add, what about nut sausages, or mushroom and chestnut ragout flavoured with Marmite? When that was the dish of the day at Shearns you would be hard put to get a table at all, with or without a cloth.

Lilian Schofield, managing director of Wholefood, in Baker Street, says cutlets and the like went out when people stopped trying to make everything sound like meat. "Why should they imitate it?", she asks. Vegetarianism is no longer considered merely the poor cousin of a meat diet.

Wholefood, Cranks and the Nuthouse are among the many restaurants that make their own rissoles to eat there or take away. Their average price is 10p. The two tested, from Cranks and the Nuthouse, were quite different.

The Cranks one was like a flat potato cake with finely chopped ingredients and rather dry. The taste of carrot vied with the nuts. In the Nuthouse they serve rissoles like small tubs, made of coarsely chopped nuts and vegetables. They are wetter and there seem to be more vegetables than nuts.

As for the waitresses and the tablecloths, Lilian Schofield says: "In the days of Shearns everyone had waitresses and tablecloths. Your waitresses were 30 shillings a week and thought themselves lucky to be in work. You could pay a girl £35 a week to be rude to your customers these days."

And if you do not like the scrubbed tables, you can always take your food back in a bag and eat it off a tablecloth on your office desk.

In the last few days I have been on four short flights of about an hour each. All have taken off about half an hour late, generally because of the late arrival of the incoming aircraft. So why not schedule all flights a half hour later if they rely on incoming aircraft? This would save much unnecessary waiting and irritation.

Angry chefs

The staff of the Imperial Hotel, Torquay, have just completed their gala weekend and rounded off their series of gastronomic events for this year. They were aggrieved at my report of French dissatisfaction with their interpretation of the gastronomic specialities of the Moulin du Maine Brun, Angoulême. They bridled particularly at the suggestion that they were all in the habit of downing tools and going home at 9.30.

The Imperial's Chef Duncombe says his assistant chefs normally leave at 9.45, but the kitchens are always open another hour, and all this goes by the board for gastronomic weekends, when they sometimes have to work right through the night. "It is also a very different thing turning out 1,000 meals a day to five-star hotel standard instead of 50 *à la carte* dinners in France. My men put in a lot of professional, hard work and what they accomplished was no mean feat."

To show there were no hard feelings towards the French, the Moulin's *selle d'agneau sauce chevreuil* was featured in the gala weekend, representing the best recipes from the winter gastronomic season.

Inappropriate

Oxford opera lovers resorted to conduct more often associated with Italian audiences last week. Their slow hand-clapping and derisory catcalls, though, were directed not at the Sadler's Wells Opera and its performers, but at the filmed commercials screened during the interval at the New Theatre.

The dramatic tension of *La Traviata* on Friday was broken between Acts II and III for a filmic eulogy to Mr Burt's jeans, complete with beautiful young people and some suggestive unzipping. There were also advertisements for Bacardi and Coke, Guinness, Babycham, and a plant hire firm.

Alfred Hattersley, the manager of the New, says he has had several personal calls and letters of complaint. He says: "the contract to screen commercials is quite a new one, and the income it provides is very important to the future of the theatre.

"To keep the place open to stage opera we have to get as much money as we can. However, I have collated all the representations I have received, and have sent them to the appropriate director at head office in London with a request for an urgent discussion."

Fashion note

In *The Sunday Times* last week Nicholas Tomalin noted how the gap between dinner wear and an ordinary men's suit was narrowing. I was able to take advantage of this phenomenon in Luxembourg at the weekend, when I discovered on arrival that the final of the Eurovision song contest was a black tie affair.

I used my wide-lapelled blue corduroy suit (made in Poland, £20 off the peg at Alexander's New York). I bought a fashionable wide black velvet ready-made bow (£2.50) in downtown Luxembourg and wore it with a pale blue long-collared shirt.

It thought it was most dashing and I was planning to use the same ensemble for supper with the French ambassador next week. But the man from *The Sun* said it looked a bit coarse. "Too much corduroy and not enough velvet", was his tactful way of putting it. So I suppose I shall have to resort to Moss Bros after all.

Eating daisies

Something else from the contest which was squeezed out of the Diary yesterday. The Portuguese song had an unusual political message which stood out among the generally soupy romantic lyrics. It is by Jose Carlos Ary dos Santos, a poet of Leftist persuasion. Here are two verses:

"Fare thee well my hippy-lazy hero,
Fare thee well my belle,
If you want some old and queenish cheerio
You can go to hell.
Fare thee well my bunny-girl of joy,
We don't want to play playboys.

Fare thee well my sugar-sugar-daddies,
Fare thee well my ladies,
Fare thee well all easy moneymakers,
Who are eating daisies.
Fare thee well you fat old profit-takers,
You will never have us on."

And it ends viciously: "And then big brother said that this song must not go on."

Bombs and birds

Tom Harrisson can fairly be counted among the last of the great British polymaths. An ornithologist, explorer, anthropologist, archaeologist and pioneer of social observation, he now spends most of his time in Brussels, with the occasional trip to his favourite stamping ground in Borneo.

In the current *New Statesman*, Harrisson has written a letter asking for help with a book he is writing about air raids in the Second World War, and their side effects. The book will be based largely on the documents and on-the-spot reports of Mass-Observation, which he founded in 1937 through the same journal's letters column.

Ten years ago Harrisson lived in a rambling wooden house in Sarawak with his German-born wife, several Dayak retainers, five tortoiseshell cats and three orang-outangs. This month Roger Berthoud ran him to earth in Uccle, a prosperous suburb of Brussels, with a Belgian wife, their own tennis club in the garden and an impressive collection of artefacts

Discussing his air raid study, he said: "We had 500 people writing diaries for us and another thousand answering questions on all sorts of subjects—what people were talking about in the pubs and so on". Mass-Observation, then carrying out research on the effect of air raids on the morale of sailors' wives in ports, sent in teams of observers after and even during bombing raids.

His chief impression was of the enormous resilience of the victims. "It's impossible to bomb people's hearts, as Vietnam has shown once again."

Harrisson has the same resilience. He was the first white man to be dropped into the interior of Borneo in 1944, to rally and lead the tribesmen. He stayed there for more than 20 years as an ethnologist.

From Brussels, he tries to keep both Britain and Borneo in focus. He returns to Borneo every year and has recently written a paper on the eating habits of the local birds.

PHS

Top Ferdinand Eber, roving war correspondent, arrived in Sicily as Garibaldi began the invasion, reported the capture of Palermo, and was appointed General in command of a brigade of the insurgents.

Above centre TIMES correspondents meeting in the Far East, 1909. Valentine Chirol, Foreign Editor, left, F. Brinkley, Tokyo Correspondent standing, and G. E. Morrison, Correspondent in China, right.

Above Louis Heren, the journalist who started as a messenger boy with THE TIMES and finished as deputy editor, pictured here reporting on the Israel War of Independence, 1948.

Right J. D. Bourchier, TIMES correspondent in the Balkans. An Irish classical scholar and former Eton College schoolmaster, who supported the Bulgarian and Greek struggles for independence from Turkish rule. Bourchier was deaf and it was said to be a common sight in the gardens of the Royal Palace in Sofia to see King Ferdinand of Bulgaria shouting state secrets into Bourchier's ear trumpet. Painting by N. Michailouz, 1908.

Some of Our Own Correspondents

War is one of the most terrible of human activities, and early news of war sells papers. *The Times* established its predominance in the newspaper market during the Napoleonic wars; during war and rumour of war circulation still shoots up. And there have always been journalists prepared to march towards the sound of the guns, notebooks at the ready.

Crabb Robinson was appointed the first foreign correspondent in 1803. Foreign implied war correspondent in those troubled times. As such Old Crabby reported the Battle of Friedland, the Treaty of Tilsit and the Peninsular campaigns. He was the first of the honourable cohort of *Times* war correspondents who in the line of duty suffered hardship, danger and occasionally death to get the news back to Printing House Square first, and to open the eyes of the British public to the virtues and failings of their armies.

The job of the foreign correspondent of *The Times* is not just to cover wars and other hard news, but to provide running assessments of how his adopted country is moving politically, socially, culturally, and in every other way, just as diplomats send their reports back to the Foreign Office. He must travel widely in the country of his posting, and not take the capital city as the sole source of ideas and action, nor merely report what the native newspapers are saying.

Many of these foreign correspondents of *The Times* became great men abroad, with quasi-diplomatic status, because of their influential connections back home at Blackfriars. Examples are Blowitz in Paris, Chenery in Constantinople, Bourchier in the Balkans, Harris in Tangier and George Morrison in Peking. The irony was that their names were quite unknown to the ordinary reader in the United Kingdom, who knew these great men only by the byline From Our Own Correspondent, which they made the proudest byline in the annals of journalism.

Some of them became so influential in their adopted countries that they went native. In Bulgaria Bourchier became so close to the Government that a stamp was printed depicting him in Bulgarian national costume. In China Morrison became adviser to President Sun Yat Sen. *The Times* disapproves of such dalliance. It takes the view that its servants should have no room for any loyalties other than to Printing House Square.

Suspicion that foreign correspondents might go native, or become *plus royaliste que le roi*, caused *The Times* to institute the practice of sending out a special correspondent. This special correspondent was sent from Printing House Square to take an alternative and possibly corrective view of some foreign country or situation.

Both these special and our own permanent correspondents abroad were expected to file news and feature material. They were also expected to send home detailed confidential memoranda on affairs that would be indiscreet to publish in the paper, for the off-the-record information of the editor and his leader writers.

War is nothing but the continuation of politics with the admixture of other means. Foreign correspondents as well as the gungho professional war correspondents were always called upon to expose themselves to the dangers of shot and shell. They still are. Crabb Robinson and Billy Russell were lucky to get away with their lives. So were Louis Heren and Bob Fisk. Frank Power had his throat cut by the banks of the Nile, and Frank Riley was murdered in 1927 during the civil war in China. Numerous others have been killed and wounded in the service of Printing House Square. But as far as we can tell, only one war correspondent of *The Times* has become a General in a war that he was reporting – so far.

His name was Ferdinand Eber, a Hungarian who wrote English like a native, and spoke it like a Hungarian. His long career as war correspondent for *The Times* was both picturesque and picaresque. Eber was an old *condottiere*. He was the prototype war correspondent who got a charge out of the sound of gunfire. In the Crimea after the Battle of Inkerman, Russell exclaimed to his colleague Eber, 'God! Wasn't it an awful day!' Eber, who was eating his supper out of an old newspaper, looked up and said: 'Awful? No, a most bewdiful day: fine baddle as ever vos. No men ever fide bedder. De Generals should all be shot.'

He rattled around the wars and trouble-spots of the world for *The Times*, and with the luck of the old warhorse correspondent, arrived in Sicily in May 1860, at the same time as Garibaldi and his Thousand invaded to begin the Risorgimento. Eber filed a full account of the landing and capture of Palermo in *The Times* of 9 June: 'An epic poem could be written about what the 1,062 Italians and five Hungarians did in Sicily'.

The trouble was that Eber preferred fighting to filing even an epic poem. He had applied to Garibaldi for a commission, and had been appointed General commanding a brigade in the insurgent army. His dispatches to Printing House Square dwindled and fell silent.

Mowbray Morris, the manager and accordingly marshal of foreign correspondents, wrote his errant war correspondent a desperate letter on 1 August:

> What are you about? Everybody can describe the Battle of Melazzo but you, whose special duty it was to describe it. Surely you do not think that we sent you to Sicily to liberate the island, or even to describe it. Rumour says you are engaged on the one, and your own letters show how much attention you have paid to the other. It is not my wish, nor have I any right, to interfere with your sympathies or your ambition. If you desire the fame of a patriot and liberator, and choose to fight for Italy in the service of Garibaldi – do so – but at least be candid and say what you are about, and do not leave me in a state of uncertainty. This cannot go on – and I must call upon you to make your election between *The Times* and your other masters whoever they may be. We cannot have half a service.

The new General resigned neither his military nor his journalistic appointment. He had missed the Battle of Melazzo, being engaged on his military duties in central Sicily. But he pieced together a belated but stirring account of the battle, which filled five columns of *The Times* on 4 August. And he carried on roving around the world for *The Times*; and full of blood and battles was his age. He was a grand old war hack, who 'saith among the trumpets, Ha, ha; and he smelleth the battle afar off, the thunder of the captains, and the shouting'. And he usually managed to file his copy eventually, also.

An on-the-spot report from Ferdinand Eber of Garibaldi's campaign in Sicily.
9 JUNE 1860

THE INSURRECTION IN SICILY.

(FROM OUR SPECIAL CORRESPONDENT.)

PALERMO, MAY 28, MORNING.

Fatigued as I was I slept the whole night through, but people who did not assure me that the bombardment from both Castle and ships was more furious than during the day. Otherwise the night passed quietly enough, a few random shots by outlying posts forming the only interruption. I was just getting up in the morning when I was attracted by running and shouts in the street below. I looked out and saw two persons running through the street, waiving their handkerchiefs and shouting "*Viva la libertà!*" I could not at first understand their tardy enthusiasm, but when I was told that they were some of the political prisoners just set at liberty I could understand this unexpected burst of *evvivas*, which, I need not say, found considerable echo on all sides. Several hundreds of these people were running about the streets, a loud testimony to the Bourbon rule. The troops which had occupied the prison of the Vicariato and the barracks close by had evacuated the spot, were embarked in boats, and taken across to the Castello. The communication between the troops in the Castello and the Piazza Reale was thus cut off.

The next news was that the troops which had been posted in Monreale had been withdrawn towards the town. They were seen descending the road in the early morning and going towards the Royal Palace, augmenting the number of those stationed there by several thousands. This scattering of the Royal forces was one of the most important objects in Garibaldi's marches. The Neapolitans, knowing the hatred of the people and the numerous bands bent on doing mischief, never dared to move except in large masses. Wishing to guard the position of Monreale, they had sent from 4,000 to 5,000 men there. They had another body quite equal to this disposed along the road from Parco to Piana, as they thought, in pursuit of Garibaldi. They required a strong garrison in the citadel and on the road to the Mole, so that comparatively little remained for the defence of the town itself.

This morning two Neapolitan steamers came in, the Capri and another, both full of troops, who are supposed to intend landing somewhere or other. They are troops sent off before the catastrophe could have been known at Naples. They seem undecided what to do under the circumstances, for if they chose to land they might easily do so under the fire of the citadel. There is comparative stillness this morning. Not a shot has been fired from the ships, and the citadel is likewise more moderate in its exertions.

NOON.

I have just returned from head-quarters in the Piazza del Pretorio, where the mystery of the silence of the ships has been explained to me. Admiral Mundy sends his Flag-Lieutenant, Mr. Willmot, every day three times on shore to communicate with Mr. Goodwin, the Consul, and know everything that is going on. This morning Mr. Willmot had another mission. The Neapolitan Commodore called on board the Hannibal very early to ask for the Admiral's good offices, in order to effect a suspension of arms with General Garibaldi, and obtain from the latter permission for two general officers from the forces in the Royal Palace and outside of it to traverse the town and communicate with the Admiral. Admiral Mundy answered that he would not consent to be the mediator in any kind of negotiations unless the fire from the ships and the citadel first ceased. The Commodore promised immediately to cease firing from the vessels, but said that he could not pledge himself to put an end to the fire of the citadel, as the General commanding there was not only not under his orders, but was, on the contrary, his superior officer; but that he would do his best to persuade the commander of the citadel to follow his example and cease firing. On this the Admiral promised to send the message of the Commodore to General Garibaldi. The Commodore kept his word, and his ships have not fired a shot since; but it seems his persuasive powers were lost on the commander of the Castello, for he continues shelling from time to time, but rather mildly in comparison with yesterday. The message of the Commander seemed to prove, better than even the abandoning of the position towards the Mole and the great military hospital with 700 sick and wounded, that things were not looking very promising for the Neapolitans. Yet, in spite of this, General Garibaldi, with his usual magnanimity, consented immediately to make an armistice, to stop his career of victory, and to allow the Generals to pass through the town. Nay, he despatched orders immediately to cease hostilities all along the line of attack, and sent a message informing the Neapolitan Commodore of it through the Admiral. It was carrying generosity rather too far. However, it is Garibaldi's nature to have faith in the cause he fights for, and to be magnanimous even to his enemies.

Besides the Neapolitan commanders there seem to be others, too, who think that the victory is on Garibaldi's side. After writing a few lines in the morning I sauntered into the town, my first object being, of course, to go to head-quarters. I had taken up my own quarters in the Hotel of the Trinacria, just opposite to the French Consulate. When I came out of the door I saw a gentleman in a blue coat and brass buttons marked with the Imperial eagle of France, talking to mine host, who immediately presented to me the gentleman with the brass buttons as the Chancelier of the French Consulate, who wished to see General Garibaldi, and asked me, as I was going that way, to take charge of him. I consented, and off we went. All along the road the Chancelier displayed a very inquisitive turn of mind, asking me what the number of Garibaldi's force was, whether he had possession of the town, whether he was well provided with ammunition, and all kinds of other indiscreet questions, which I answered in my best diplomatic manner. He informed me that he had something very particular to communicate to the General, and I entertained him with accounts of the bombardment, showing him the traces of it, and expatiating about the infamy of it, and the pitiable figure the representatives of the "civilized" nations played in the whole affair. Thus we arrived at the Piazza Pretorio and found the General on the platform of the large fountain. I presented my companion, who took Garibaldi aside and congratulated him, in the name of his Government, on the happy success of his expedition, assuring him of the sympathies of France, and displaying great eloquence, which I suspect was lost on the straightforward soldier in his red flannel shirt, who, although no diplomat, has a keen appreciation of human nature.

The taking of Palermo has had decidedly its effect on the country around. There is no end of the *squadre* which are approaching in all directions and hovering about the Regii. As soon as these latter had left Monreale the insurgents in the neighbourhood descended to occupy it as well as San Martino. All about Piana and Corleone they are swarming and skirmishing, so that the column of 1,500 or 1,600 men which has been sent in that direction is rather compromised. They hoped to destroy Garibaldi and his partisans, and the fate they prepared for them may await themselves.

But while thus the general march of events is decidedly favourable I must say the Palermitans are scarcely up to the mark. They are all well-intentioned, but they are distressingly indolent, and want that general co-operation which is most calculated to insure success. There is no initiative or activity on their part, and their sole occupation seems to be to invent and spread rumours. Not a quarter of an hour passes without some fellow or other coming in out of breath and announcing the advance of the Royal troops; now they are from one, now from the other side. Above all, horses and cavalry seem to be the nightmare of the Palermitans. They see the solitary regiment of Neapolitan cavalry everywhere. It is in vain that their noses are thrust against the barricades with which the whole town is blocked up, they *will* see the cavalry. But, although they are thus haunted by the Royal troops, few seem to think that they ought to do something for themselves—making preparations for the defence of their houses and streets, and being always ready to meet an attack. It never occurs to them, as it did to the Lombards last year, that it is their duty to think day and night how to alleviate the sufferings of those who bleed in their cause. It is not the want of will, but a deficiency in acting otherwise than by order. The only thing which they do spontaneously is to cry "Evviva," and promenade the streets eager for news and gossip.

The irregulars are decidedly improving. They are getting a taste for barricade and street fighting; they still blaze away their ammunition in a frantic manner, but they are beginning to keep to their posts and even to advance, if not too much exposed. This is our advantage in these street fights; the longer they last the more they increase the confidence of the irregulars and destroy the discipline of the regular troops.

Every hour brings new proofs of this in the shape of prisoners and deserters from the Neapolitan forces. With those taken in the hospitals there must be above 1,000. There is an order from the General to treat them well, and there is no animosity prevailing against them, but so much the greater is that against the *sbirri*, spies, and "*compagni d'armi*," a kind of local police, who have committed great horrors. They are picked out everywhere, and brought up in gangs of five and six to the committee trembling for their lives; but only one of them has been killed hitherto, having been taken in the act of firing at those who wanted to arrest him.

The ceasing of the bombardment, or rather the diminishing of it, has brought people out into the streets again.

EVENING.

When I went to Head-quarters in the afternoon, I found every one in a state of great indignation. Long after Garibaldi had sent his consent to a suspension of arms, the bombardment from the Castello was continued. Nay, the Neapolitans had continued firing on the advanced posts, although strict orders from Garibaldi had prevented the patriots from answering. Taking advantage of this quiescence on the side of the latter, the Neapolitans had burnt some houses and taken possession of some barricades which flanked theirs in the Piazza Reale. Several Cacciatori were killed and wounded. The General was on the point of addressing a letter to Admiral Mundy, complaining of this breach of faith, when Lieutenant Wilmot called again on the part of the Admiral at 6 p.m., saying that as no answer had arrived from the Commodore he thought the General liberated from his promise. On this the order was given to retake the lost positions. A couple of Orsini's shells were thrown, and soon dislodged the Royalists. Half an hour afterwards Lieutenant Wilmot called again. The Commodore had sent his answer, which was to the effect that the two Neapolitan Generals asked for the protection of the British flag in their passage through the town. The Admiral categorically refused, on which the Commodore declared that all negotiations were at an end.

The impression gained by this answer was that the whole negotiation was merely a feint to gain time and prepare for some movement. Every moment fresh reports came in stating that the whole Neapolitan fleet was in movement, with the exception of the Ercoli, the frigate which had been shelling the town yesterday. The two steamers with troops, after landing five boatfuls of their cargoes in the Castello, went off, one of them towing a gunboat, and the other two merchant vessels. The general impression is that they meditate a landing of the rest somewhere, and a general attack. I must say it looks to me rather like a preparation for departure and embarkation of the troops. However, all preparations are made for their reception, should they attempt an attack.

MAY 29, MORNING.

The night passed quietly—so at least I am told, for I slept without waking once. The whole of the Neapolitan fleet left during the night, going out straight to sea, but in the morning the Commodore's vessel was seen to the east, in the direction of Termini, the very place where the Neapolitan troops embarked in 1848.

The bastion of Montalto, close to the Royal palace, has been evacuated by the Neapolitans, who left behind a large 32-pounder gun. The force which occupied the Finanze has sent an officer as *parlementaire* to offer to retire. The condition proffered by Garibaldi was that they should lay down their arms. They refused to do this, and the 32-pounder is being prepared to make them understand the necessity of such a step. The fort has, besides, its water and its provisions cut off, so there is no doubt that it will soon be brought to reason.

The supposition that the movements of the Neapolitan fleet are calculated rather to ensure the safety of the Neapolitan troops than to do damage to the patriots is gaining ground every moment. Just when I was at the Pretorio one of the captains of squads stationed outside made his report,—the Neapolitans cut off from communication outside, as well as from the sea-shore. San Martino, La Favorita, Monreale, Parco, as well as the district towards the sea-shore, are all full of guerillas, harassing the Royalists day and night. They are massed in Porazzo and Santa Theresa, and have been trying to make a forward move both yesterday and this morning towards Olivuzzo, in the direction of San Martino and La Favorita. This is probably a feint, while their real intention is to operate on the opposite side, where their shot went.

While I was with the General a letter arrived from Corleone by which he was informed that the Neapolitan Colonel commanding the column sent there was inclined to come over if his rank was confirmed to him. He is surrounded on all sides by guerillas, his road cut off, and he has a considerable force before him. The answer was, of course, an acceptance of his proposals, which came in an indirect way.

The proposal does not surprise me. Yesterday several officers came in in plain clothes and gave themselves up. I saw about 60 or 70 prisoners and deserters in one place, who all wished to have arms and become soldiers of Italian independence.

But with all this it would be desirable that the Palermitans did more, and the *squadre* too. The first seem only busy with their *evvivas*, and the latter, like true Bashi-Bazouks, with wasting their ammunition.

6 P.M.

About 3 p.m. one of those panics suddenly broke out again which occur every moment, and serve more than anything else to demoralize the town and the *squadre*. The steamers which had gone off yesterday came back, and the rumour was that they were disembarking their troops before the Porta dei Greci;—great running and movement, great confusion, all caused by a column of dust on the road running along the sea-shore. In the afternoon there was some heavy firing, both towards the Piazza Reale and to the left of it, where the Neapolitans have a bastion which flanks the palace and is itself defended from the Castello. All yesterday and to-day the object on that side was to get possession of a cluster of houses, so as to isolate that bastion and force them out of this as from that of Sant'Agatha. The town is too large, and Garibaldi's immediate followers are too few to be sent everywhere, and too precious to be exposed except in the greatest necessity. Thus it is the *squadre* who form the mass in most places. While ammunition lasts all goes well; but unfortunately, blaze away as they do, a couple of hundred cartridges would not be sufficient for one of them. I really think they are worse in this respect than the Bashi-Bazouks. Well, the ammunition being exhausted on that point just at the moment the Royalists made a move in advance, one party of *Picciotti* fell back in one of the streets, and thus allowed the Royalists to shut in a street of houses in which another party of them was still holding out.

Garibaldi was at dinner when the news arrived. There had been so many rumours of an advance of the Neapolitans during the day that the first impression was that this was merely another of those wild rumours; but Captain Niva, who brought it, was one of the Garibaldians, and there could be no doubt about its truth. One street or one house is no great object in a town like Palermo, which has many more of them than can be well defended, but so much the more important was the moral effect of losing a portion already once held. With his usual *coup d'œil*, which I begin to think looks like inspiration, Garibaldi felt this. He jumped up from his chair, saying, "Well, then I suppose I must go there myself." He saw it was one of those moments when the chief must be at the head of his troops to restore their confidence. He went downstairs, and took with him whatever he found on the road to that exposed point, and proceeded to retake the lost ground.

His presence not only soon checked the advance of the Royalists, but made them likewise lose the advantage they had gained a moment before. With that marvellous ascendancy which he exercises over those around him, he succeeded in a short time in making the *Picciotti* fight, and even in animating the population which had remained in the houses.

In spite of the urgent entreaties of his followers not to expose himself he remained in the open street, without any shelter, haranguing and encouraging the men; the enemy seeing this, [illegible] from behind the barricade. One of the *Picciotti* was shot through the head just before Garibaldi, who, seeing him falling, held him up for a moment; and Colonel Turr, at his side, got a ricochet ball against his leg as he took hold of the General and dragged him by main force under shelter. But the effect was produced. One rush brought the party close enough to throw one of Orsini's shells, which prostrated seven or eight men. The bugler, who is always at Garibaldi's side, sounded the charge, and the Neapolitans ran. The sound of this bugle seems to act formidably on the nerves of the Neapolitan troops; they know they have to do with Garibaldi's men, and at Calata Fimi they ran before even the charge took place.

The two steamers, which had troops on board, have anchored, and have begun to disembark them at the Castello under cover of the men-of-war, which have their broadsides turned towards the town, ready to bombard. This shows that the Neapolitans have not given up the game, but hope to regain the ground they have lost. These troops are not Neapolitans, but speak German; some say they are Bavarians. Whether their presence will restore the *morale* of the Neapolitan troops remains to be seen.

MAY 30, MORNING.

The troops which were disembarked last night went out of the Castello towards the Mole, and then, by a circuit, rejoined, as it seems, the troops on the other side. This looks as if they were anxious to hold their ground in and about the Royal palace, rather than to make an attack on the town.

The news from the country could not be better. Everywhere the people are rising and the troops withdrawing. On the evening of the 23d General Affan di Heisla abandoned Girgenti, leaving the civil authorities to their own devices. As soon as the troops left the population hoisted the Italian flag. A committee was formed, and a national guard. The cries were, as everywhere else, "*Viva l'Italia*," "*Viva Vittorio Emmanuelle*," and "*Viva Garibaldi*." The civil authorities were respected, and although the prisoners, 200 in number, were let out, no disturbance occurred. The whole province there, as everywhere else, is following the example, rising, instituting a committee, and arming itself. The province of Catania has risen, with the exception of the town, which is still held by the military as well as that of Trapani. And all this occurred before the taking of Palermo, the news of which event has not yet had time to produce its full effect. If the Neapolitans ever again get possession of Sicily, the Sicilians deserve to be ruled for ever by King Bombino.

The Neapolitan fleet has not fired a shot since the morning of the day before yesterday, when Admiral Munday spoke his mind on the subject to the Commandore, so that one-half of the misery has been spared to the Palermians. But the Castello is incorrigible; whenever it hears a noise or sees a movement in any part of the town down comes a shell. If it were possible to miss I dare say they would, but this cannot be expected in these narrow streets. The houses are, for the most part, so badly built that one shell is sufficient to make them a heap of ruins and bury the inmates. Whole families have thus disappeared, and hundreds of inoffensive people been killed and wounded. The fleet fired about 80 or 90 shells the first day; as for the Castello, it must have thrown more than 300.

The first day Garibaldi addressed a protest to the commanders of the foreign men-of-war against this cowardly inhumanity; but they cannot interfere directly without instructions. It is to public opinion in Europe that the appeal must be made. Let it decide whether a Goverment which resorts to such means is worthy to exist.

The Parliament of Great Britain is assembled, let it take the matter in its hands. If a convict who has committed manslaughter or burglary becomes an opprobrium in the eyes of men, surely the bigoted idiot who massacres in this way hundreds of defenceless people to revenge himself of his own impotence deserves to be branded with infamy!

9 A.M.

Just at this moment a flag of truce has come in from the Royal Palace with the following letter directed to General Garibaldi:—

"The Command-in-Chief of the Armies and Naval Stations beyond the Faro, Palermo, May 30, 1860.

"General,—As the British Admiral let me know that he would receive with pleasure on board of his vessel two of my generals to open a conference with you, of which he would be the mediator, if you allowed them to pass through the lines, I beg you to let me know whether you assent, and if so to indicate to me the hour at which the armistice is to begin. It would be likewise advantageous that you allowed the two generals to be accompanied from the Royal Palace to the Sanità, where they would embark.

"Waiting for your answer, I have the honour to be,
"To his Excellency General Garibaldi." "LANZA."

To this letter the answer was, that General Garibaldi would have no objection to meet the two generals on board the Admiral's vessel; that he would send round orders to all the line to cease firing; that the armistice was to begin at noon, and that at 1 p.m. they should meet on board the Admiral's ship. Colonel Turr, the Inspector-General of the national forces, sent the letter of Lanza on board the Hannibal by Mr. Wilmot, the flag-lieutenant.

12 30 P.M.

If a man is found to have taken in confusion his neighbour's cloak it may pass for a mistake; but if that same man is found on the very next occasion in the same position it is time to cry "Stop thief!" and collar the individual. When the Neapolitans asked for an armistice, and General Garibaldi sent accordingly the order to all the line to cease firing, they not only continued shelling, but tried to take advantage of the cessation of the fire to gain a better position. To-day they not only tried, but actually gained a considerable advantage. In order to cease firing at noon and begin the armistice, Garibaldi had begun to send round the line about an hour before. Just about the same time a Neapolitan column appeared on the very same road by which Garibaldi had entered. It was provided with artillery, and began to advance from the Ponte dell' Amiragliato, where they had been stationed, towards the Porta di Termini. In vain was the white flag denoting an armistice exhibited, not only did the firing continue, but the citadel began sending its shells in the same direction. Several of the officers mounted on the top of the barricades, and tried to inform the Neapolitans of the armistice. They were received with rifle shots, and Colonel Carini besides others was wounded. The Garibaldins still stuck to their instructions, and did not return the fire. Message after message came to Garibaldi that they must fire or else abandon their position. The general was just on the point of taking the resolution that the armistice was broken, when two Neapolitan officers came in as *parlementaires*. They excused the affair as a misunderstanding, and that the column had not received the orders about the armistice. They were sent in front to stop the fire and arrest the advance. Curiously enough, during all this time the shelling from the citadel went on also, and surely the citadel could not be supposed to be without news of the armistice! Just at 12 the news came that the column of the enemy had penetrated into the town. Garibaldi immediately, as he did yesterday, collected his reserves, and marched on. It was quite true, and Lieutenant Wilmot, R.N., who had come on shore to bring the Admiral's consent to the conference on board, found himself in the midst of the advancing column of Neapolitans and the men of Garibaldi. A shell fired at the same time from the Castello burst close to him, the Neapolitans levelled their muskets, and it was with considerable danger that he at last reached Garibaldi. It was five minutes past 12. Mr. Wilmot brought the Admiral's consent to an interview on board, and a few minutes after two Neapolitan officers arrived to say that it was all a mistake, that the column had not received the orders.

The Admiral's boats are to be ready at a quarter past 1. I must say if I had been Garibaldi I should not have listened to any proposals before the column coming from outside had given up the positions out of which it had cheated his troops. But Garibaldi is incorrigible in his magnanimity. I am waiting to hear what passed on board, and hope to be able to tell you of it before the mail closes and Her Majesty's ship Intrepid starts.

4 P.M.

The conference on board is not over yet, and all the boats are assembled round the Hannibal. The town is in a most excited state, the impression having got abroad that the Neapolitans intend offering a capitulation and free retreat to Garibaldi. It is in such moments that you see of what stuff a population is made, and certainly that of Palermo is not of the stuff of which heroes and martyrs are made. Instead of throwing themselves into the houses nearest to the points occupied by the enemy, they run about the streets discouraging each other.

4 30 P.M.

The conference is just over. Garibaldi has come on shore, and is gone to the Palace with the two Neapolitan Generals. The French mail starts, and I must send off my letter without being able to give you the details of the conference. The report is, however, that an armistice is concluded till to-morrow at noon, and that it is, above all, with the view to provide for the great number of wounded that the Neapolitans asked for an armistice.

At any rate, you will not have long to wait for a final decision one way or the other; it must come in a few days. Neither party can hold out much longer. An epic poem could be written about what the 1,062 Italians and five Hungarians did in Sicily during these last 20 days; how they fought, how they marched, how they bore fatigue. If every Sicilian was ready to do the thousandth part of what they did, there would be no more fighting required. As for pay, the very word is unknown; most of those who came have means of their own, never ask for anything except ammunition, live on what they can buy, and seem almost to have forgotten what sleep is. The only drawback is that they were only 1,062 at landing, and that those who think themselves great in the Italian cause thought it their duty this time to impede most effectually all reinforcements. If one was ill-natured, one might almost suppose that they thought it a good opportunity to get rid of Garibaldi, but they may find themselves mistaken.

SARDINIA AND SICILY.

(FROM OUR OWN CORRESPONDENT.)

TURIN, JUNE 5.

The second expedition, which was to leave Genoa yesterday, has been put off for several days; its leaders are anxious to fit it out with all such means as may give it the greatest efficiency. Garibaldi's enterprise had been so imperfectly matured that, far from taking with him wherewith to arm the Sicilian insurgents, that daring chieftain had barely 1,000 muskets for the use of more than 1,400 of his followers; and, although he supplied himself with ammunition at Talamone, his riflemen found themselves without percussion caps at Calata Fimi, and had to betake themselves to their bayonets, in their inability otherwise to avail themselves of their pieces. Medici and Cosenz, Malenchini and Michele Amari, with many other illustrious patriots, have engaged to take part in this second expedition; and they are bent on avoiding Garibaldi's oversights—those oversights which not all men are able to make up for by transcendant daring and unfailing strategy. It seems, also, that Medici and his friends are tarrying at Genoa till they succeed in establishing so sure a communication with Garibaldi as may enable them to effect a landing at the most seasonable moment, and at the most opportune spot. The forces these Argonauts have assembled are considerable. They will embark 5,000 or 6,000 men; they employ two large steamers belonging to the defunct Transatlantic Company, and they have also chartered two English steamers. There is but little mystery or reserve about their doings. "Hit him hard—he has no friends," is the motto with respect to the King of Naples; he has put himself and his Government without the pale of civilized Europe; the common law of nations does not apply to him. Funds are freely collected here as well as in England to wage war against him; and the Sardinian Government dare not, even if they were inclined, interfere with those who are employing such funds in raising men and arms and ships to compass the tyrant's overthrow. It is thought, however, that this second expedition has been stayed by a positive veto of France. The armistice at Palermo gives rise to a variety of surmises. The most probable conjecture is that which attributes to Garibaldi a design to win over a part, if not the whole, of the native Neapolitan troops. He handles them very tenderly, it may be observed, in his orders of the day; he praises their valour, even to the disparagement of the Austrians whom he was confronting last year, and who, he says, never offered so stubborn a resistance as he met with on the part of the men who disputed the narrow gorges at Calata Fimi against him; he testifies all his heartfelt regret that Italians should have to imbrue their hands in Italian blood, and looks forward to the day in which all the members of the same Italian family shall join their efforts against a common foreign enemy. The armistice of the 28th of May, the proffered capitulation allowing the Neapolitans to leave Palermo with all the honours of war, unless they are the result of a lack of ammunition, are proofs of a moderation on the part of Garibaldi which his admirers are fain to ascribe to deep designs. Some defections in the Neapolitan troops have already occurred. We are now to see the effects of the generosity of an enemy who, as yet, only appeared in the eyes of those troops as formidable. The behaviour of Italian soldiers under despotic rulers is something about which no safe reckoning can be ventured upon. The Tuscan regiments last year espoused the national cause to a man; those of the Duchess of Parma were disbanded, and were neither for nor against their country; while, on the other hand, those of the Duke of Modena followed their Prince in his flight, and continue, most of them, faithful to him till such day as it may suit him to release them from an allegiance which burdens him with the charge of their keeping. The King of Naples had, however, two regiments of Swiss and Bavarians at Palermo—two regiments, that means about 6,000 men. These will, in all probability, stick to their colours to the last; but they may also overawe and control their Neapolitan fellow-combatants, so as to compel them to do their duty in spite of themselves.

On Saturday last La Farina left, alone, in a small English steamer, for Sicily. He is supposed, of course, to go with the intent of lightening the burden of the Dictatorship which Garibaldi took upon himself in Palermo. Should the capital be rid of the Neapolitan troops, the war would necessarily be carried to Messina, Catania, or the coasts of Calabria, and the Liberator must leave the civil government in the hands of a Prime Minister well inclined, no less than able, to second his designs. La Farina is a moderate patriot, Piedmontese and Cavourian to the backbone. His departure could not take place without a perfect understanding between him and the great statesman at the head of the Sardinian Government. Garibaldi himself is stanch to the King, and bent upon carrying the immediate and unconditional annexation to Piedmont of any part of those southern kingdoms he may happen to snatch from the Bourbon. The original insurrectional Sicilian movement was, undoubtedly, in a national constitutional sense; the insurgent chiefs invariably declared for Victor Emmanuel and Italian Union; but Garibaldi himself left Genoa in a state of real or apparent enmity with Cavour. He professed to act in the King's name, and to have the King's warrant for all his doings; but, at the same time, he disavowed any connexion with the King's advisers, and spoke in no measured terms of their faint-heartedness and duplicity. Under Garibaldi, again, are Sirtori, Nino Bixio, and many others known as Mazzinian, or at all events ulta-democratic partisans. The Mazzini party here in Piedmont, and still more in Genoa, show little scruple in taking upon themselves all the credit of this great Sicilian movement. Garibaldi himself is by them designated as a Mazzinian, such being the fate of all those who, no matter for what purpose or from what circumstances, were ever for one moment brought into contact with that body. Bertani, one of Garibaldi's bosom friends, with a great many others, have set themselves up here and everywhere in Italy, collecting funds and mustering men and arms, apart from at least, if not in open opposition to, that National Society which acted under the leadership of La Farina, and enjoyed the more or less open patronage of Cavour's Government. Some apprehension was entertained, in short, that the revolution in the South might be turned by the Mazzinians to their own purposes; and unquestionably, as I have often told you, such ground as Victor Emmanuel loses in Italy is won by Mazzini. The Sicilians are the last people in Italy to dream of a republic; still no one can say what a people may do who are driven to their wits' end, and who have not the wisest of leaders at their head.

It is in consideration of all these contingencies that La Farina came to the sudden resolution of going to Sicily. It was felt to be of the utmost importance that Garibaldi should have other advisers by his side than Sirtori, Bixio, and other daring young enthusiasts, who are so much more fit to upset a State than to set it up. It is Count Cavour himself who goes to Sicily with La Farina. The great weapon wherewith the Mazzinians fight their battles now-a-days is the principle of Italian unity; to the attainment of that end Cavour and La Farina are also working. But they think of the differences they have to settle with the Pope, with France, and Europe. Bertani and his friends laugh all such doubts and misgivings to scorn; they are ready to attack the Pope simultaneously with the Bourbon, and think little of a war in which they might have France and Austria arrayed against them. At the same time with La Farina several Mazzinian chiefs—it is said Mazzini himself—proceeded to Sicily.

FOREIGN INTELLIGENCE.

FRANCE.

(FROM OUR OWN CORRESPONDENT.)

PARIS, FRIDAY, JUNE 8, 7 A.M.

It is now pretty certain that the great Powers have declined to interfere between the King of Naples and the Sicilians. In the despatch from the French Government in reply to the application to the Emperor Napoleon, the French Minister is reported to have said that, between the cowardice of a capitulation and the barbarity of a bombardment, advice was impossible, and that there only remained to express regret that the Neapolitan Government did not follow the advice given to it for the last ten years. Had it done so, Southern Italy would have acted as a counterpoise to Northern Italy; whereas now the North threatens to swallow it up entire.

Letters received in Paris to-day announce that the Sicilian insurgents have obtained possession of Girgenti, the chief town of the province, situated 70 miles south-east of Palermo. When Garibaldi was apprised of this fact he sent an extraordinary commissioner there to organize a Provisional Government and to direct the insurgents, so as to combine their operations with his own.

The commissioners appointed to trace the boundaries between the newly annexed provinces of Savoy and Nice and Piedmont are said to have suspended their sittings, from which it is inferred that, should Sicily be annexed to Piedmont, which is more than probable, the Emperor Napoleon would demand a further accession of territory—where is not stated.

The Council of Commerce held three sittings last week, which make 13 devoted to an inquiry into the state of the iron manufactories. A great number of manufacturers have already been heard by the Council. The attention of the Council has been first directed to the various branches of the iron trade, but particularly to the important and difficult question of steel. The Council enters into the most minute details of the several questions proposed for its consideration, and studies with untiring attention the various interests affected by the Treaty of Commerce of the 23d of January last. All the representatives of the different industrial interests connected with the iron trade have had an opportunity of expressing their opinions with the utmost freedom, and of entering into whatever details they thought proper. Some of the depositions lasted as long as two hours, and were listened to by the Council with an attention which never flagged. Several of the deponents have spoken in the highest terms of the courteous bearing of all the members of the Council, and especially of the kind manner in which the interrogatories were conducted by the President, M. Rouher. Thirteen sittings, each of five or six hours, have already been devoted to the inquiry into the industries connected with the production and manufacture of iron, and the Council has already heard 150 persons. For this important branch of the national industry three distinct series of questions were drawn up, and are not yet exhausted, at least so far as concerns the numerous manufactures employing iron and steel. A strictly logical order has been followed, beginning with the natural ores, and proceeding to their successive transformations, in which labour and skill constantly increase the value of the products. These different industries still occupy the attention of the Council. The first series of questions embraced ironstone; pig, bar, and sheet iron; old iron, cast and wrought, and scoria. The inquiry bore upon everything connected with their importation into France. In the second series, which is also exhausted, the questions related to all kinds of iron castings, wire, sheet iron covered with tin, lead, copper, or zinc, and also to steel. The third series comprises all the manufactures in which iron and steel are employed.

It is announced that it is intended to restore to the Rue de la Chaussée d'Antin the name of Rue du Mont Blanc, which it received by a decree in the year 1792, when Savoy was first annexed to France. This is the eighth time within less than 200 years that the name of this street has been changed. It was first called Chemin de la Chaussée de Gaillon, next Des Porcherons, then Rue de l'Hotel Dieu, and finally Rue de la Chaussée d'Antin. It took the name of Rue de Mirabeau in 1791 from the great orator, who died there in the house now bearing No. 42. There are still some men living who recollect to have seen the two following verses, by M.J. Chenier, inscribed in letters of gold on a black marble slab inserted in the front wall—

"L'âme de Mirabeau s'exhala de ces lieux ;
"Hommes libres, pleurez ! Tyrans, baissez les yeux."

But the tyrants of 1793, who did not readily "cast down their eyes," passed a sponge over the inscriptions, scraped the walls of the house, and substituted the name of Mont Blanc for Mirabeau. This street is further celebrated for having been the residence of many celebrated persons, and among them of the Empress Josephine previous to her marriage with General Bonaparte, of Cardinal Fesch, the uncle of Napoleon I., and of General Foy.

The annexed provinces of Savoy and Nice are being occupied by troops. One battalion of the 90th Regiment of the Line is quartered at Nice, and the two other battalions of the same regiment between Villafranca, Menton, and Monaco. The 18th and 26th Regiments of the Line, which served in Italy during the late campaign, have gone to Chambery. The 14th battalion of Riflemen has marched for the same destination. The regiments selected to garrison the other towns in Savoy will shortly take possession of their new quarters.

The delivery in Paris of London papers and letters is becoming more irregular. The London papers, due in Paris at 7 on Wednesday evening, were not delivered until past 12 yesterday, and the London papers of Thursday evening were not delivered here until 6 p.m. yesterday.

The Three per Cents. closed on Friday at 68f. 30c., coupon, detached for the end of the month, and the Four-and-a-Half per Cents. at 96f. 25c.; Orleans Railway Shares, 1,330f.; Great Northern, 977f. 50c.; Strasburg, 597f. 50c.; Paris to Lyons and the Mediterranean, 870f.; Western of France, 570f.; Bordeaux and Cette, 516f. 25c.; Lyons and Geneva, 407f. 50c.; Bank of Crédit Mobilier, 660f.; Austrian Railways, 512f. 50c.

Cours Authentique.—PARIS, June 6.—Cash Prices.—Four-and-a-Half per Cents. (not reimbursable for 10 years), 96f. 96f. 5c. 10c.; Three per Cents., 69f. 95c. 70f. 69f. 95c. 70f. 70f. 5c. 70f.; ditto, New Loan, Certificates of 500f. and under, 69f. 95c.; Bank of France, 2,820f. 2,830f.; Crédit Foncier, 880f. 882f. 50c.; ditto, Obligations of 500f., Four per Cents., 486f. 25c. 485f.; ditto, Three per Cents., 448f. 75c.; ditto, Tenths, Four per Cents., 98f. 75c. 97f. 50c.; ditto, Tenths, Three per Cents., 92f. 50c.; Promissory Obligations of 1,000f., Three per Cents., 1,015f.; Crédit Mobilier, 667f. 50c. 668f. 75c.; Discount Bank, 675f.; Piedmontese Five per Cents., 84f.; Austrian Five per Cents., 81½; Spanish Three per Cents., Interior Debt, 46¾ ½ ⅝; ditto, Passives, 16; Belgian Four-and-a-Half per Cents., 96½ ⅜ ½ ⅝; Roman Loan, 80. Exchange on London, at sight, paper, 25f. 12½c.; money, 25f. 10c.; three months, paper, 24f. 90c.; money, 24f. 87½c.

Cours Authentique.—PARIS, June 7.—Cash Prices.—Four-and-a-Half per Cents. (not reimbursable for 10 years), 96f. 10c. 20c. 25c.; Three per Cents., shut the 6th at 70f.; ditto, June 22, 68f. 60c. 55c. 50c. 45c. 40c.; ditto New Loan, Certificates of 500f. and under, 68f. 50c.; Bank of France, 2,830f.; Crédit Foncier, 880f.; ditto, Obligations of 500f., Four per Cents., 486f. 25c.; ditto, Obligations of 500f., Three per Cents., 450f.; ditto Tenths, Four per Cents., 98f. 75c.; ditto Tenths, Three per Cents., 92f. 50c.; Crédit Industriel et Commercial, 506f. 25c. 507f. 50c.; Crédit Mobilier, 670f. 667f. 50c. 665f.; Discount Bank, 675f.; Piedmontese Five per Cents., 84f. 25c. 84f.; ditto, Three per Cents., 53f.; Austrian Five per Cents., 81¾ 82; Spanish Three per Cents., Exterior Debt, 1841, 48; ditto, 1852-6, 47¾ 48; ditto, Interior, 46¾; ditto, Deferred Converted Debt, 37¼ ⅜; ditto, New Passive, 16; Belgian Four-and-a-Half per Cents., 96¾; Roman Loan, 81. Exchange on London, at sight, paper, 25f. 12½c.; money, 25f. 10c.; ditto, three months, paper, 24f. 90c.; money, 24f. 87½c.

TURKEY.

(FROM OUR OWN CORRESPONDENT.)

CONSTANTINOPLE, MAY 30.

The attitude of Russia does not appear to me necessarily to lead to the inference that anything like immediate dismemberment of the Ottoman Empire is intended. To enable us to form something like a correct estimate of the measures recently adopted by the Government of the Czar, it is necessary first to determine what degree of intimacy exists between France and Russia,—to what extent they have a mutual understanding as to the affairs of Turkey. I need scarcely repeat that, without some well-defined plan arranged with France, Russia would not venture at the present moment to push matters to extremity with this country. The line taken by M. de Lavalette becomes, therefore, a question of the utmost importance. No doubt, after all that has happened, it would be a matter of little surprise should it ultimately transpire that the real policy of the French Government is the reverse of that which might be inferred from the assurances and the actions of its agent in Constantinople. The manifestation by the French Ambassador of goodwill towards Turkey may be regarded with some suspicion; it nevertheless serves to show either that the alliance between Russia and France is not so close as there are some grounds for believing it to be, or that both countries regard the time for action as not yet come. There is therefore some satisfaction in being enabled to state that since I last wrote it has come to my knowledge that M. de Lavalette and our own Ambassador have acted in unison on the subject of the Russian demand for a mixed commission to inquire into the state of the Slavonic provinces, and that Russia has in consequence somewhat modified her tone. It is now resolved that a native commission shall be sent into those provinces to correct all administrative abuses, and to devise and report upon a scheme for future improvement. Another commission, clothed with similar powers, will also be sent into Syria, where scarcely any government at all can be said to exist.

On Sunday evening last Mehemet Ruchdi Pasha was superseded in the office of Grand Vizier, Mehemet Kiprisli Pasha having been appointed to succeed him. In order to give greater prestige to the commission to be sent into the European provinces, his Highness the Grand Vizier has been appointed as its president. During his absence from Constantinople Aali Pasha will perform the functions of First Minister. Suliman Pasha has, I am informed, been appointed to preside over the labours of the Syrian commission. It is to be hoped that this nomination will not be confirmed, inasmuch as it is difficult to say what are his qualifications for the office.

The Russian Minister having acquiesced in these arrangements, it would seem that there should, for the time, be no further cause of anxiety; yet it is a fact that the *corps d'armée* of Bessarabia has been considerably augmented. The troops whose appearance on the Pruth created such excitement in Europe have been in Bessarabia for the last six months at least. It now appears, however, that there is a very large additional force on the Dniester. Common report fixes the total number of men which Russia now has in this province at 80,000; from 60,000 to 65,000 would probably be much nearer the mark. The French Government having shown no disposition to join in any scheme of present aggression, it is to be presumed that these troops have been concentrated on the confines of the Turkish territory merely with a view to giving greater weight to the Russian demands on the Porte. A great Roman Catholic movement has taken place during the last 12 months in Bulgaria, Macedonia, and Candia; and Russia may probably have felt that it was necessary to make some counter-move to maintain what prestige the Crimean war left her. Conversion to the Roman Catholic and Greek churches is simply understood in this country to imply the acquisition of French or Russian protection. When France happens to be the country on which the Porte looks with peculiar dread, the protection of the French Ambassador will avail most; and then Roman Catholicism will spread. Russia knows this, and does not fail to perceive that sixty or seventy thousand men in Bessarabia may exercise no small influence on the consciences of men and prevent further secessions from the orthodox church; hence possibly the move she has lately made. When Lord Stratford de Redcliffe the other evening presented to the House a petition from the Evangelical Alliance on behalf of the Protestants of Turkey, he spoke of a desire which had "sprung up for a purer Christianity;" and to this he ascribed many of the secessions from the Catholic and Greek churches to Protestantism. His Lordship cannot but be aware that by far the greater number of these converts are utterly incapable of defining the differences which exist between the several churches. Modesty alone could have prevented his informing the House that, in the case of these Protestants, the protection of the English Government, or rather that of Lord Stratford de Redcliffe himself, formed a prominent article of their new belief.

Omar Pasha arrived in Constantinople on Saturday last.

COURT CIRCULAR.

The Queen will hold a Privy Council this day (Saturday) at Buckingham Palace.

Her Royal Highness the Duchess of Kent visited the Queen yesterday at Windsor Castle.

Her Majesty the Queen and his Royal Highness the Prince Consort left Windsor Castle for Buckingham Palace at 25 minutes before 4 o'clock yesterday afternoon, accompanied by his Majesty the King of the Belgians, the Prince Alice, Prince Arthur, the Princesses Helena, Louise, and Beatrice, and the Count of Flanders.

The Royal suite consisted of the Countess of Desart, Lady Caroline Barrington, the Hon. Lucy Kerr, the Hon. Mary Bulteel, Lord Camoys, the Hon. M. Sackville-West, Major-General the Hon. Charles Grey, Major-General Seymour, Lieutenant-Colonel the Hon. D. de Ros, Colonel Count de Moerkerke, Dr. Koepl, Major Burnell, and Major Elphinstone.

The Royal party proceeded to the station of the Great Western Railway at Windsor, where a guard of honour of the Coldstream Guards was on duty. The Queen was conveyed by a special train to town.

Her Majesty was escorted by a detachment of Light Dragoons from the Paddington terminus to Buckingham Palace, where the Queen arrived at 25 minutes before 5 o'clock, and was received by the Earl of St. Germans, Viscount Sydney, Viscount Castlerosse, and Major-General Wylde.

Prince Leopold arrived at Buckingham Palace yesterday afternoon, from Windsor Castle.

The Prince Consort rode on horseback yesterday afternoon, attended by his Equerry in Waiting.

The Queen and Prince Consort, accompanied by the King of the Belgians and the Princess Alice, honoured the performance at the Olympic Theatre with their presence last evening. In attendance were the Countess of Desart, Hon. Lucy Kerr, Lord Camoys, Major-General Seymour, Lieutenant-Colonel the Hon. D. de Ros, Colonel Count de Moerkerke, and Dr. Koepl.

His Royal Highness the Prince of Wales, attended by Major-General the Hon. R. Bruce and Lieutenant-Colonel Keppel, left Windsor Castle yesterday and returned to Oxford.

Their Royal Highnesses the Duchess of Cambridge and the Princess Mary, attended by Lady Geraldine Somerset and Lieutenant-Colonel Home Purves, left Windsor Castle yesterday for their residence at Kew.

His Royal Highness the Duke of Cambridge, attended by Colonel Tyrwhitt, left Windsor Castle yesterday and returned to London.

Prince Louis and Prince Henry of Hesse, attended by Baron Van der Capellan, left Windsor Castle for London yesterday morning.

Viscount Palmerston left Windsor Castle on Thursday afternoon and returned to town. The other visitors staying at Windsor Castle took their departure yesterday.

A deputation of steamtug owners had an interview with Sir G. C. Lewis yesterday at the Home-office. The deputation consisted of Messrs. Charles C. Nelson, London; J. Stewart, engineer, Blackwall; W. Watkins, W. B. Caulfield, Daniel Barker, J. Spicer, J. Mitchell, R. Ross, W. Williams, E. Williams, D. Oates, J. Lawson, J. Watson, J. F. Nelson, I. J. Middleton, J. Eckin, and W. T. Phillips. The deputation was accompanied by Sir James Duke, M.P., Lord Holmesdale, M.P., Sir Charles Napier, M.P., Mr. A. S. Ayrton, M.P., and Mr. A. Kintrea, Parliamentary Agent.

General Dupuy, Minister from the Republic of Hayti, had an interview with Lord John Russell yesterday at the Foreign-office.

A meeting of the Finance Committee of the Royal Commission for the Exhibition of 1851 was held yesterday at the Privy Council-office. There were present Earl Granville (Chairman), Lord Overstone, the Right Hon. R. Lowe, M.P., Sir Alexander Spearman, Mr. T. Baring, M.P., Mr. W. Coulson, Q.C., Mr. C. W. Dilke, Mr. T. F. Gibson, and Mr. Edgar Bowring (Secretary).

Despatches were sent from the Colonial-office yesterday to the Governors of Canada, the Falkland Islands, and the Bahamas. Despatches were received from the Lord High Commissioner of the Ionian Islands.

THE LATE VISCOUNT HINTON.—A handsome stained glass window has just been placed in the south wall of the Church of St. Mary Magdalene, Taunton, in memory of the late Viscount Hinton, colonel of the 1st Somerset Militia. The expense has been defrayed by the officers of that regiment. The window is a three-light, and contains full-length effigies of three of the warriors of the Old Testament—Joshua, David, and Gideon, under elegant canopies. Underneath are panels illustrative of Joshua's vision of the captain of the host, David slaying Goliath, and Gideon breaking down the idol. The following is the inscription:—"In memory of Vere, Viscount Hinton, late Colonel of the 1st Somerset Militia, son of John fifth Earl Poulett. Died 29th of August, 1857. Placed by brother officers." The tracery consists of angels holding Christian armour. The designers were Messrs. Clayton and Bell, of Cardington-street, London.

IMPUDENT ROBBERY.—On Wednesday morning last, about 6 o'clock, an impudent thief walked into the Castle Hotel, Windsor, and proceeded up the principal staircase to the bedroom of Sir John Thorold, and stole from the dressing-table a gold watch and chain, several valuable rings and pins, nine sovereigns, and some silver, with which he got clear off. He was respectably dressed in black, and had dark moustachios and whiskers. The barmaid, seeing the fellow enter the hall of the hotel so early in the morning, locked the bar door and followed him upstairs, but as he entered the bedroom she considered he was one of the gentlemen who attended the races and had taken the apartments for the week. Sir John was awake at the time, and thought it was his valet who had entered the room, and therefore the rogue quietly left it, and coolly following the ostler, who at the time was going downstairs, made [illegible]. Information was given to the borough police, and [illegible]. By some fortunate oversight the thief left on the table a diamond pin worth 60 guineas.

Assassinations

Top Assassination of President Lincoln, 15 April 1865.
Above Assassination of Spencer Perceval, 11 May 1812.

The Times has always been hot on death: not just death in the Obituaries and Personal columns, but death as in Battle, Murder and Sudden Death. It is hard to find a single early issue in which there is not an account of some gruesome killing, told with relish and at length, tucked away in the closely packed columns of political and financial news. Assassination rather than murder made the front page. And the two centuries of *The Times* have been rich in assassinations, from Spencer Perceval, the only British Prime Minister to have died by assassination, to the Kennedys, Martin Luther King and all the other sensational killings of our bloody century. You can, if you want, trace two hundred years of *Times* history in blood.

The unusual word 'assassination' comes from the Arabic for 'hashish-eater'. In Muslim history the assassin was a fanatic sent by the founder of his sect, the so-named Old Man of the Mountain, to murder either Crusaders or the leaders of rival Muslim sects. He went about his dirty business in a hashish-drugged state. The present distinction between murder and assassination is a fine one, to exercise philosophers, lawyers and lexicographers. A dictionary of law defines assassination thus: 'Murdering a person by lying in wait: in modern times the term is frequently applied to the open murder of great personages from political motives'. Journalism distinguishes between murder and assassination according to their victims. When a nobody is killed, that is murder; when a somebody, whom we have all heard of, is killed, that is dignified with the more portentous word, assassination. When beggars die, the papers call it murder. The heavens themselves thunder forth the death of princes and presidents as assassination. Following a case in the Queen's Bench Division in 1881, it was held to be a misdemeanour for a newspaper to exult over an assassination (in this case that of the Tsar of Russia), and to express the hope that it was not the last.

A century before this judgment, *The Times* anticipated the misdemeanour with bells on. On 13 July 1793, as every schoolboy knows, Jean Paul Marat, the vet who had become a Jacobin leader, was stabbed to death in his bath by Charlotte Corday. In its issue of 23 July *The Times* printed an extract from the proceedings of the National Convention in Paris giving dramatic details of the assassination:

> At these words she plunged this knife into his bosom. (Cambon shews the instrument). Marat had only time to say, *I am dying*. His servant entered the room, and made a cry: people ran to her assistance. This new Tisiphone went out with audacity; she was stopped. She might have assassinated herself, but she did not. When we told her that she would lose her head upon the scaffold, she looked at us with a smile of mockery.

Note the use of short sentences for rhetorical effect when describing assassinations, a trick of that first great journalist, Tacitus.

Two days later *The Times* published a short paragraph that exulted over the assassination: 'Divine vengeance overtook him in the midst of his sins, and he fell by that instrument of sudden death with which he had been accustomed to arm others for similar purposes. May every Republican Tyrant meet with a similar fate.'

For the assassination of Spencer Perceval, shot at Westminster by a mad bankrupt, *The Times* of 12 May 1812 laid on outrage rather than exultation, with a trowel:

> From our report of the Parliamentary proceedings of the two Houses will an indignant and sorrowful nation learn the occurrence of one of those horrible events with which the annals of Great Britain have not often been stained, – the murder of Mr Perceval, the Prime Minister of these realms; a man, who, in his personal intercourse, gave offence to no one . . .

To find a precedent for the assassination of a Prime Minister in office you would have to go back to Thomas à Becket, which would be cheating.

The assassination of Abraham Lincoln gave *The Times* the chance to change its policy on the American Civil War – not before time. It had supported the South (see pp. 53–5), and its criticism of Lincoln had been patronizing, élitist, chauvinist and abusive. On 27 April 1865 *The Times* reported the sensational assassination. John Wilkes Booth had shot Lincoln in Ford's Theatre, Washington, and, as all assassins should, had flourished a dagger after the shot. *The Times* made amends for its previous treatment of Lincoln with a warm appreciation of his work: 'He was as little of a tyrant as any man who lived'.

After Lincoln, assassination became a deplorably common way of making a political point. Two more Presidents of the United States, a Tsar of Russia, a President of France, and the Kings of Portugal and Greece were assassinated before that day in June 1914 at Sarajevo, which is blamed as the trigger of the First World War. The Great Powers were already hurrying down the primrose path to the world bonfire when a student, Gavrilo Prinzip, a Serbian nationalist assassin, pulled the trigger. But even without the power of seeing the bloody future, *The Times* recognized the assassination of Archduke Francis Ferdinand and his wife as a portentous event, pregnant with doom, and devoted nearly two pages to it and the background.

On 24 August 1922 *The Times* reported the assassination not of a prince, but another man of the people like Lincoln, under the headline IRELAND'S LOSS. General Michael Collins, head of the Irish Free State Provisional Government, was ambushed and died fighting near Brandon, County Cork. Ireland was a problem for *The Times*. The Parnell forgeries (see p. 66) lay heavy on the folk memory of Printing House Square. For a number of years it had been trying, with some success, to bring impartiality into its leading articles, as far as that is possible in Irish affairs.

In June and July 1919 a series of ten big articles considered at length and in depth and with wisdom the many problems facing Ireland. They were written by R. H. J. Shaw. On Ulster Shaw wrote: 'Ulster must stay part of Ireland: justice to her claims does not require obedience to her dictation'. Just before the assassination of Michael Collins in 1922 *The Times* had become involved in Ireland by the sword as well as the pen. Arthur Kay, one of its two correspondents in that most distressful country that ever yet was seen, was kidnapped by the IRA. Michael Collins had arranged his release. Shortly after, this hero of the Irish struggle for independence was ambushed and shot.

On 30 January 1948 Mahatma Gandhi was shot by a Hindu fanatic. *The Times*, which had been as critical of Gandhi over the years as it had been of Lincoln, said that the shot 'robbed the Indian peoples of a unique guide along the paths of peace'. Apart from selling papers, assassination brings the best, or at any rate the *gravitas*, out of Printing House Square.

When Kennedy was killed in Dallas on 22 November 1963, the world saw the terrible and banal scene over and over again on television before they read about it in their *Times* the following morning. The treatment has changed over two centuries, as it has for Martin Luther King, Indira Gandhi, and all the forthcoming assassinations in our terrible century. There are bigger headlines, pictures, more display, more background, since *The Times* can no longer expect to be the first to break the bloody news in this electronic age. But it still treats assassination seriously, as the incalculable aberration that can tilt the balance of history.

A report of the assassination of President Abraham Lincoln, whom William Howard Russell described as 'not . . . what – according to the usages of European society – is called a gentleman'.
27 APRIL 1865

Page 148
The assassination at Sarajevo of Archduke Francis Ferdinand of Austria and his wife, the event that precipitated the First World War.
29 JUNE 1914

TE EGRAPHIC DESPATCHES.

AMERICA.

ASSASSINATION OF PRESIDENT LINCOLN.

OFFICIAL REPORT.

The following official telegram from Mr. Secretary Stanton has been received by the United States' Legation in London:—

(*Viâ* Greencastle, *per* Nova Scotian.)

"Sir,—It has become my distressing duty to announce to you that last night his Excellency Abraham Lincoln, President of the United States, was assassinated, about the hour of half-past 10 o'clock, in hi private box at Ford's Theatre, in the city. The President about 8 o'clock accompanied Mrs. Lincoln to the theatre. Another lady and gentleman were with them in the box. About half-past 10, during a pause in the performance, the assassin entered the box, the door of which was unguarded, hastily approached the President from behind, and discharged a pistol at his head. The bullet entered the back of his head and penetrated nearly through. The assassin then leaped from the box upon the stage, brandishing a large knife or dagger, and exclaiming '*Sic semper tyrannis!*' and escaped in the rear of the theatre. Immediately upon the discharge the President fell to the floor insensible, and continued in that state until 20 minutes past 7 o'clock this morning, when he breathed his last. About the same time the murder was being committed at the theatre another assassin presented himself at the door of Mr. Seward's residence, gained admission by representing he had a prescription from Mr. Seward's physician which he was directed to see administered, and hurried up to the third story chamber, where Mr. Seward was lying. He here discovered Mr. Frederick Seward, struck him over the head, inflicting several wounds, and fracturing the skull in two places, inflicting, it is feared, mortal wounds. He then rushed into the room where Mr. Seward was in bed, attended by a young daughter and a male nurse. The male attendant was stabbed through the lungs, and it is believed will die. The assassin then struck Mr. Seward with a knife or dagger twice in the throat and twice in the face, inflicting terrible wounds. By this time Major Seward, eldest son of the Secretary, and another attendant reached the room, and rushed to the rescue of the Secretary; they were also wounded in the conflict, and the assassin escaped. No artery or important blood-vessel was severed by any of the wounds inflicted upon him, but he was for a long time insensible from the loss of blood. Some hope of his possible recovery is entertained. Immediately upon the death of the President notice was given to Vice-President Johnson, who happened to be in the city, and upon whom the office of President now devolves. He will take the office and assume the functions of President to-day. The murderer of the President has been discovered, and evidence obtained that these horrible crimes were committed in execution of a conspiracy deliberately planned and set on foot by rebels under pretence of avenging the South and aiding the rebel cause; but it is hoped that the immediate perpetrators will be caught. The feeling occasioned by these atrocious crimes is so great, sudden, and overwhelming that I cannot at present do more than communicate them to you. At the earliest moment yesterday the late President called a Cabinet meeting, at which General Grant was present. He was more cheerful and happy than I had ever seen him, rejoiced at the near prospect of firm and durable peace at home and abroad, manifested in a marked degree the kindness and humanity of his disposition, and the tender and forgiving spirit that so eminently distinguished him. Public notice had been given that he and General Grant would be present at the theatre, and the opportunity of adding the Lieutenant-General to the number of victims to be murdered was no doubt seized for the fitting occasion of executing the plans that appear to have been in preparation for some weeks, but General Grant was compelled to be absent, and thus escaped the designs upon him. It is needless for me to say anything in regard of the influence which this atrocious murder of the President may exercise upon the affairs of this country; but I will only add that, horrible as are the atrocities that have been resorted to by the enemies of the country, they are not likely in any degree to impair the public spirit or postpone the complete and final overthrow of the rebellion. In profound grief for the events which it has become my duty to communicate to you, I have the honour to be

"Very respectfully, your obedient servant,

"EDWIN M. STANTON."

[A portion of the following appeared in our Third Edition of yesterday:—]

(By British and Irish Magnetic Telegraph.)

(FROM OUR OWN CORRESPONDENT.)

(Per the Nova Scotian, *viâ* Greencastle, April 26.)

NEW YORK, April 15, 11 a.m.

President Lincoln is dead. He was shot through the head while at Ford's Theatre, at Washington, shortly before 11 o'clock last evening, and died at 22 minutes after 7 this morning.

The assassin procured admission to the President's private box on the pretence of being the bearer of despatches from General Grant, and deliberately shot him from behind with a common one-barrel pistol. He jumped from the box to the stage, flourishing a dagger, and exclaimed "*Sic semper tyrannis.*" He then made his escape through the back entrances to the stage, and got off before any one had presence of mind to pursue him.

About the same time an attempt was made to assassinate Mr. Seward by a man who appeared at the house of the Secretary, and demanded to be shown to his room under pretence of giving personal instructions respecting the use of some medicine of which he was the bearer. Upon being refused, he thrust the doorkeeper aside, and proceeded to Mr. Seward's chamber, at the door of which he met Mr. Frederick Seward, whom he felled with a blow from a bludgeon. He then entered the chamber, knocked down Major Seward and two attendants, and stabbed the Secretary several times in the breast, neck, and face, and escaped.

The physicians assert that the wounds are not necessarily fatal, but in consequence of Mr. Seward's previous weak condition, from the results of his accident, it is not expected he can recover.

Mr. Frederick Seward's skull is badly fractured, and one of the attendants is believed to be fatally injured. An actor named J. Wilkes Booth, together with his horse, has disappeared from his home, and is supposed to be the assassin of the President. A letter found in his trunk makes it evident that the assassination was planned previous to the 4th of March, but was not carried into effect owing to the faintheartedness of the accomplice, who is supposed to have made the attack upon Mr. Seward.

The calamity has excited intense indignation and horror in this city.

Business is almost wholly suspended.

1 o'clock.

General Anger, Military Commandant at Washington, has offered a reward of $10,000 for the apprehension of the assassin.

Booth, the supposed assassin of President Lincoln, has been arrested. Secretary Seward's condition is unchanged; that of his son Frederick is critical.

Vice-President Johnson received the oath of office as President of the United States from Mr. Chase at 11 o'clock. He simply said, "The duties are mine; I will perform them, trusting in God."

There have been private sales of gold at 155 to 160.

April 14.

Mr. Stanton announces that, after mature consideration and consultation with General Grant upon the results of the recent campaign, the Department has decided to order the immediate stoppage of all draughting and recruiting, the curtailment of purchases of arms and other war *matériel*, the reduction of General and Staff officers to the actual necessities of the army, and to remove all military restrictions upon trade and commerce, so far as may be consistent with public safety. General Grant arrived in Washington yesterday, and re-occupied his head-quarters there. He is asserted to have assured Mr. Stanton that the military expenses can be immediately reduced to the extent of $1,000,000 per diem without infringing upon necessary efficiency.

Reports of General Lee's movements are contradictory; one states that he has gone to consult with General Johnston; another that he is *en route* for Weldon, North Carolina; while a third declares that he is adjusting his affairs at Richmond, preparatory to an immediate departure with his family for Europe.

The *Tribune's* correspondent with the Potomac Army writes that the Army of Northern Virginia at the time negotiations for its surrender were pending was estimated to number upwards of 30,000 men, but that the prisoners actually on parole will not exceed 8,000; the remainder, he states, on the authority of Confederates, upon learning that their surrender was meditated, immediately left the ranks, most of them with the determination to join General Johnston, in North Carolina.

The Navy Department has decided to dispense with the services of the strikers in the Brooklyn Navy-yard. They have, consequently, been discharged.

The leading citizens of Richmond and many members of the Confederate Legislature of Virginia, on the 11th, with the concurrence of General Weitzel, summoned a meeting to consider what steps could be taken to restore peace to the State. Upon the project being made known to Mr. Stanton he prohibited the meeting, and removed General Weitzel from command.

This being Good Friday, there has been no meeting of the Stock or Gold Boards. Prices on the street were:—Gold, 146. Exchange, 109½, in gold.

United States' Sixes, 1881, Coupons, 108½; Five-Twenties, Coupons, 107; Ten-Forties, Coupons, 93.

New York Central, 101½; Erie, 70¾; Illinois Central, 114.

Cotton, 33c. Breadstuffs unsettled, and irregular. Provisions firmer. Coffee quiet. Sugars improved.

(REUTER'S TELEGRAMS.)

(Per the Nova Scotian.)

NEW YORK, April 15, Noon.

Wilkes Booth, the assassin of President Lincoln, is the brother of Edwin Booth, and is known as a rabid Secessionist.

According to the latest reports he has been arrested, and Mr. Frederick Seward is dead.

General Sherman moved in three columns from Goldsborough on the 9th inst. Johnston evacuated Raleigh, and moved west of the town, leaving it in possession of Hampton's cavalry. Johnston is reported to have gone to Greensborough.

Mobile papers of the 4th inst. confirm the capture of Selma, Alabama, with 23 guns and a large amount of property. The Federals opened a furious fire on the defences of Mobile on the 4th, exploding a magazine in Spanish Fort. The amount of damage done is unknown. The siege continues. Two tin-clad gunboats have been destroyed by torpedoes.

Thomas, with a large force, is expected on the north side of Mobile.

Wilson's cavalry is overrunning Alabama, and is also moving towards Mobile.

It is rumoured that Mr. Adams will be recalled from London to take charge of the State Department.

President Davis issued a proclamation, dated Danville, April 6, announcing his purpose to continue the war and never submit to the abandonment of one State of the Confederacy. The proclamation was issued some days before Lee's surrender.

It is said that the Governor of North Carolina will shortly convoke the Legislature to repeal the Secession Ordinance, and restore the State to the Union.

Business is almost entirely suspended on account of Lincoln's assassination.

The Stock and Gold Boards will not meet to-day. Gold is selling in the streets at 151½.

1 p.m.

Andrew Johnson was sworn in as President by Chief Justice Chase at 11 o'clock this morning. Secretary M'Culloch, Attorney-General Speed, and others were present.

Johnson said, "The duties are at present mine. I shall perform them. The consequences are with God. Gentlemen, I shall lean upon you. I feel I shall need your support. I am deeply impressed with the solemnity of the occasion and the responsibility of the duties of the office I am assuming."

Johnson appeared remarkably well, and his manner created a very favourable impression.

The whole of New York is draped in black, and there is general mourning throughout the country.

(By Submarine Telegraph.)

THE PAPAL STATES.

We have received the following telegram from our correspondent at Rome, *viâ* Naples:—

"ROME, April 25.

"M. Vegezzi had another audience with the Pope on Sunday evening, which lasted for two hours.

"The Bishops already appointed in the former dominions of the Pope will be allowed to assume office without taking the oath of allegiance.

"Bishops who have been exiled or imprisoned are allowed to return at their own pleasure.

"The Pope admits the right of the King of Italy to appoint Lombard and Piedmontese Bishops, according to ancient rights."

(REUTER'S TELEGRAMS.)

FRANCE.

PARIS, April 26.

All the Paris evening journals express a feeling of horror at the assassination of President Lincoln.

The *Patrie* publishes a despatch from Rome stating that the Pope yesterday received the extraordinary Mexican mission.

3 30 p.m.

The Bourse has been firm.

Rentes closed at 67f. 40c., or 5c. higher than yesterday.

THE KING OF THE BELGIANS.

BRUSSELS, April 26.

The King was in a very low state last night. This morning, however, His Majesty's condition was more favourable, and has continued so during the day.

THE ITALIAN PARLIAMENT.

TURIN, April 26.

To-day the Chamber of Deputies approved by a large majority the articles of the Bill relative to the suppression of religious corporations.

The Senate was engaged in the discussion of the Penal Code.

OVERLAND MAILS.

The Peninsular and Oriental Steam Navigation Company have received the following telegram:—

"GIBRALTAR, April 25.

"The Delhi, with the heavy portion of the Calcutta and China mails, left here at noon to-day. She may be expected at Southampton on the 30th inst.

"The Pera, from Southampton the 20th inst., reached Gibraltar this day at 1 a.m., and left at 5 p.m. for Alexandria."

SECOND EDITION.

THE TIMES-OFFICE, Thursday Morning.

(REUTER'S TELEGRAMS.)

ROME.

PARIS, April 27.

The *Moniteur* of to-day says:—

"Despatches received here from Rome justify us in the belief that the negotiations between Cardinal Antonelli and Signor Vegezzi for the arrangement of the difficulties relative to the installation of the Italian Bishops are proceeding favourably."

SPAIN.

MADRID, April 26.

To-day, in the Senate, Senor Corradi said, in a speech upon the question of Santo Domingo:—

"Before peopling Santo Domingo, let us people and civilize our Spanish provinces. We shall not lose strength or prestige by abandoning that island. We shall, on the contrary, gain moral force by bestowing upon the Cubans the political rights enjoyed by Spaniards."

The Alcades of Madrid have resigned.

The Government has received a telegram from Paris, announcing the assassination of President Lincoln.

EXECUTION OF LEDUC.

(By Submarine Telegraph.)

(FROM A CORRESPONDENT.)

BOULOGNE-SUR-MER, April 27.

Leduc, who murdered his two children last November, was guillotined this morning on the Place Impériale.

ELECTRIC TELEGRAPHIC DESPATCHES.

(FROM OUR OWN CORRESPONDENT.)

AUSTRALIA.

FALMOUTH, Thursday Morning.

The ship Scottish Chief, of St. John's, N.B., 1,053 tons, Captain Dennehy, arrived off this port last evening from Melbourne, and proceeded for London, after obtaining some fresh supplies.

Her date of sailing, the 23d December; rounded Cape Horn 29th January, and crossed the Equator on the 13th March.

Her cargo consists of 3,940 bales of wool, and she has on freight 4,635 ounces of golddust, and three cabin and 12 steerage passengers.

She experienced strong southerly winds until she rounded New Zealand; the prevailing winds were then S.W. In lat. 56 S., long. 111 W. to 79 W., passed an immense number of icebergs, and for three days the ship was surrounded by ice; since leaving 44 S. had light easterly winds, no S.E. trades; crossed the Equator with light winds from the east; moderate N.E. trades; parted from them in lat. 25, long. 45 N., since then light easterly winds, and a quantity of calms. The prevailing winds since leaving the Tropics have been north, south, and east due north.

(By Magnetic Telegraph.)

GRAVESEND, Thursday Morning.

Arrived, April 26.—Wilhelmina, from Porto Rico.

Arrived, April 27.—Carl Frederick, steamer, from Demerara; Earl of Auckland, steamer, from Rotterdam; Panther, steamer, from Boulogne.

DEAL, Thursday Morning.

Passed.—Henry, for Quebec; John Gilpsick, for Boston; Palawan, for Sydney—all from London.

THE WEATHER.

METEOROLOGICAL REPORTS.

Thursday, April 27, 9 a.m.	B.	T.	W.	F.	Ex.	D.	I.	R.	S.
Nairn	30·11	51	W.	2	4	W.	c. f.	—	1
Aberdeen	30·07	54	W.N.W.	3	7	W.	b. c.	—	3
Leith	30·09	55	W.	2	5	N.W.	b.	—	1
Ardrossan	30·15	55	N.N.W.	4	5	W.N.W.	o. c.	—	2
Greencastle	30·20	49	N.	1	2	S.W.	o. a.	—	1
Valentia	30·09	53	N.W.	1	2	W.S.W.	b.	—	1
Cape Clear	30·10	55	S.E.	3	3	S.E.	m. b	—	2
Liverpool	30·20	49	N.W.	1	3	W.N.W.	o.	—	1
Holyhead	30·16	46	W.N.W.	4	4	N.W.	c. f.	—	2
Penzance	30·15	50	E.	0	2	S.	b.	—	2
Brest	30·08	70	E.	2	2	N.E.	b.	—	4
L'Orient	30·04	66	N.E.	3	2	S.	b.	—	2
Rochefort	30·01	57	E.	3	2	N.	b.	—	2
Plymouth	30·13	50	Z.	0	3	S.	f. b.	—	1
Weymouth	30·15	58	Z.	0	1	S.W.	b.	—	1
Portsmouth	30·15	53	E.S.E.	2	2	S.W.	c. b.	—	1
London	30·16	59	Z.	5	2	N.	b.	—	—
Yarmouth	30·12	49	S.W.	2	4	N.E.	c. b.	—	6
Scarboro'	30·12	54	N.E.	1	1	S.	c. b.	—	1
Shields	30·04	53	N.W.	2	2	E.N.E.	c.	—	2

Explanation.

B.—Barometer corrected and reduced to 32° at half-tide level, each 10 feet of vertical elevation causing about one-hundredth of an inch diminution, and each 10° above 32° causing nearly three-hundredths increase. T.—Thermometer exposed in shade. W.—Wind, direction of true—two points left of magnetic. F.—Force (1 to 12—estimated). Ex.—Extreme force since last report. D.—Direction of upper force. I.—Initials:—b., blue sky; c., clouds (detached); f., fog; h., hail; l., lightning; m., misty (hazy); o., overcast (dull); r., rain; s., snow; t., thunder. R.—Rainfall, snow or hail (melted), since last report. S.—Sea disturbance (1 to 9). Z.—Calm.

Probable.

Friday.	Saturday.
On Northern Coasts.	
W. to N. and back, moderate to fresh; generally fine.	N.N.W. to W.S.W., fresh; in places some rain.
Western.	
N.W. to N.E. and back to W., moderate to fresh.	As above.
Southern.	
Variable, light, to N. and W., moderate; fine.	N. to W. and S.W., moderate to fresh; showers in places.
Eastern.	
N.E. to N.W. and S.W., variable, moderate; fine.	As next above.

Northern = Scotland. Western = Ireland, Wales, and adjacencies. Southern = English Channel and Bay of Biscay. Eastern = Eastward England and North Sea.

Wind and Weather Reports, Thursday, April 27.

(By Electric and International Telegraph.)

Belfast, N.W.; dull.	Greenock, W.; fine.
Brighton, S.E.; fine.	Hartlepool (West), N.E.; fine.
Cardiff, E.; fine.	Hull, S.W.; fine.
Deal, W.; fine.	Milford Haven, E.; fine.
Dublin, —; dull.	Queenstown, E.; fine.
Dundee, W.; fine.	Ramsgate, W.; fine.
Falmouth, calm; fine.	Swansea, calm; fine.
Gravesend, N.E., fresh.	

STOCK EXCHANGE.

Thursday, 12 Noon.

Consols for Money	90¼
Ditto, Account (May 9)	90⅜

Church of England Scripture Readers' Society.—The May meeting of this society was held yesterday at the Hanover-square-rooms, the Rev. the Bishop of Winchester in the chair. The Chairman, in opening the proceedings, remarked that he took a part some twenty years since in establishing the society, assisted by the late Bishop of London, and supported by the late Archbishop of Canterbury. After a year's trial the society was brought before a general meeting of bishops, and was generally approved, and since then it had gone on increasing year by year until now it had 139 grants of readers in 102 of the parishes and districts of the London and Winchester dioceses, thereby aiding in the spiritual support of 1,117,220 persons. The operations of the society had hitherto been confined to the dioceses of London and Winchester, and he considered it a most gratifying fact, as showing the interest taken in the society, that it was now proposed to extend it so as to include the archdiocese of Canterbury in the diocese of Rochester. The progress of the society might be seen in the receipts, which in the first year amounted to 3,488*l.* 8s. 6d., and had gradually increased until now they amounted to 12,589*l.* 14s. 2d. The Secretary read the annual report, giving instances of the manner in which the operations of the society had been carried out, and showing that it had been assisted by the Bishop of London's Fund. Mr. Thomas Chambers, the Common-Serjeant, moved the first resolution, approving the report, [illegible]

ASSASSINATION of PRESIDENT LINCOLN.

THE HOUSE OF COMMONS AND THE NEWS FROM AMERICA.

On receiving the melancholy intelligence of the lamentable occurrences in the United States, the Members of Parliament assembled, consisting of gentlemen of all parties, immediately signed the following address of sympathy to the resident American Minister, and to whom it was presented at 6 o'clock yesterday evening:—

"We, the undersigned, members of the British House of Commons, have learnt with the deepest horror and regret that the President of the United States of America has been deprived of life by an act of violence; and we desire to express our sympathy on the sad event with the American Minister now in London, as well as to declare our hope and confidence in the future of that great country, which we trust will continue to be associated with enlightened freedom and peaceful relations with this and every other country.

"London, April 26."

The intelligence of the assassination of President Lincoln and of the attempt to assassinate Mr. Seward caused a most extraordinary sensation in the city yesterday. Towards noon the news became known, and it spread rapidly from mouth to mouth in all directions. At first many were incredulous as to the truth of the rumour, and some believed it to have been set afloat for purposes in connexion with the Stock-Exchange. The house of Peabody and Co., American bankers, in Broad-street, had received early intelligence of the assassination, and from there the news was carried to the Bank of England, whence it quickly radiated in a thousand directions. Meanwhile it was being wafted far and wide by the second editions of the morning papers, and was supplemented later in the day by the publication of additional particulars. Shortly after 12 o'clock it was communicated to the Lord Mayor while he was sitting in the Justice-room of the Mansion-house, and about the same time "the star-spangled banner" was hoisted half-mast high over the American Consulate at the corner of Gracechurch-street. The same flag had but a few days before floated in triumph from the same place on the entry of the Federals into Richmond, and still later on the surrender of General Lee. Between 1 and 2 o'clock the third edition of *The Times*, containing a circumstantial narrative of the affair, made its appearance in the city, and became immediately in extraordinary demand. A newsvendor in the Royal Exchange was selling it at half-a-crown a copy, and by half-past 3 o'clock it could not be had there for money. The excitement caused by the intelligence was manifest in the public streets, and the event was the theme of conversation everywhere. The revival of the affair of the Road-hill murder, which in the earlier part of the day had created a profound sensation, sank into insignificance in comparison with the interest and astonishment excited by the news of the tragedy at Washington. A photographer in Cornhill, "taking time by the forelock," exhibited *cartes* of the deceased President in his window, inscribed "the late Mr. Lincoln," and accompanied by an account of the assassination cut from the second edition of a contemporary. Throughout the remainder of the day the evening papers were sold in unexampled numbers, and often at double and treble the ordinary price, all evincing the universal interest felt in the astounding intelligence.

LIVERPOOL, April 26.

The reading of the telegram announcing the assassination of President Lincoln produced a general expression of horror and disgust on the Liverpool Exchange to-day. At first it was alleged that the assassin was a Confederate, but the Southern men indignantly repudiated the imputation, and some of them who had known Booth positively asserted that he was an abolitionist of the Johnston and Butler school, and had been known to be mad for some months. The flags on the Town-hall and Exchange-buildings were hoisted half-mast, and in the course of the day a proposal to hold separate meetings of the Northern and Southern men for the purpose of expressing their abhorrence at the crime met with general acquiescence. The effect of the news on 'Change was a rise in cotton and the Confederate Loan, and a decline in Federal securities.

MANCHESTER, April 26.

Such a state of excitement as was produced by the news of President Lincoln's assassination this morning was never witnessed here before. On the Exchange and everywhere the general expression was one of reprobation and horror that such a crime should have been committed. The news put a stop to all business, and the day has passed away in mere talk and excitement.

BIRMINGHAM, Wednesday Evening.

The news of the assassination of the President of the United States has produced a profound sensation here, and as much of sympathy, consternation, and dismay as can be conceived; in fact, as to all of these feelings, second only to one other calamity which might have afflicted this nation and the world. It was a little past 12 o'clock when the first telegram was received here announcing this sad occurrence. Like all other bad news this spread rapidly, and in less than half an hour the Exchange, where the telegrams were posted, was thronged with persons in whose faces were depicted an expression of the deepest anxiety. Very many were reluctant to believe the news, and in a state of feverish and eager desire clung to the hope that the telegram was some stock-jobbing trick or fraud for some sinister purpose; and in these times when so much is done for the sake of creating a sensation, or for some more unworthy end, it is no wonder that even the public should at length have been taught to be cautious, and be reluctant to swallow the highly-spiced dishes set before it.

Nearly three hours passed away without the receipt of any confirmation of the first telegram, and hope was reviving when the full details of the appalling tragic occurrences just perpetrated at Washington came to hand. There was no face in which grief was not depicted, no sentiment uttered but that of abhorrence at these foul crimes. Of the truth of that the American people may rest assured, so far as this town is concerned, for although there has always been a strong feeling of sympathy here for the Southerners, and never more so than during the last hours of the gigantic efforts of the noble-hearted Lee and his valiant soldiers, there is nothing but detestation at the foul murder with which this fratricidal war has been crowned.

The Mayor was absent in London when this afflicting news was received, but his worship was immediately telegraphed to by Mr. Alderman Hawkes, with the view of some immediate expression in reference to this untoward event by the people of the town.

Wilkes Booth, the assassin of President Lincoln, is said to be the son of an English tragedian, whom some of our theatrical readers may, perhaps recollect. He (the father) is thus described in the *American Encyclopædia*:—

"Booth, Junius Brutus, an English tragedian, born in London, May 1, 1796, died on the passage from New Orleans to Cincinnati, December, 1852. After fulfilling engagements at Deptford, near London, and other places, and even performing at Brussels, in 1814 he made his *début* at Covent-garden Theatre, in London, as Richard III. His personal resemblance to the crookbacked tyrant conformed exactly to the traditions of the stage, and his personification of the character was in other respects so striking that he competed successfully with Edmund Kean, then just rising into fame. The managers of Drury-lane induced him to act there in the same plays with Kean; but when, after a few nights, he was again announced at Covent-garden, his appearance was the signal for a serious theatrical riot, which resulted in driving him for a time from the London stage. In 1821 he made his first appearance in the United States, at Petersburg, Virginia, and in New York, at the Park Theatre, in the succeeding year, on both of which occasions he assumed his favourite character of Richard III. From that time until the close of his life he acted repeatedly in every theatre in the United States, and, in spite of certain irregular habits, which sometimes interfered with the performance of his engagements, enjoyed a popularity which a less gifted actor would have forfeited. During the latter part of his life he resided with his family at Baltimore, making occasional professional excursions to other cities. He had just returned from a lucrative tour to California when he died. The range of characters which Booth assumed was limited, and was confined almost exclusively to those which he had studied in the beginning of his career. He is most closely identified with that of Richard, in which, after the death of Edmund Kean, he had no rival. Among his other most familiar personations were Iago, Shylock, Hamlet, Sir Giles Overreach, and Sir Edmund Mortimer. In his peculiar sphere—the sudden and nervous expression of concentrated passion—as also in the more quiet and subtle passages of his delineations, he exercised a wonderful sway over his audience, and his appearance upon the stage has been known to awe a crowded and tumultuous house into instant silence. His presence and action, notwithstanding his short stature, were imposing, and his face, originally moulded after the antique type, was capable of wonderful expression under the influence of excitement. Several of his children have inherited a portion of his dramatic talent, and are now prominent actors on the American stage."

[illegible]

THE AMERICANS IN LONDON.

TO THE EDITOR OF THE TIMES.

Sir,—I shall be much obliged if you will state that a meeting of the Americans in London will be held at this Hotel to-morrow, at 12 o'clock, with reference to some appropriate expression of sentiment concerning the lamentable intelligence from the United States.

Very truly yours,

FERNANDO WOOD.

Grosvenor Hotel, Pimlico, April 26.

PRESIDENT ANDREW JOHNSON.

(From *Ripley and Dana's Cyclopædia.*)

Johnson, Andrew, a United States' senator from Tennessee, born in Raleigh, North Carolina, December 29, 1808. When he was four years of age he lost his father, who died from the effect of exertions to save a friend from drowning. At the age of 10 he was apprenticed to a tailor in his native city, with whom he served seven years. His mother was unable to afford him any educational advantages, and he never attended school a day in his life. While learning his trade, however, he resolved to make an effort to educate himself. His anxiety to be able to read was particularly excited by an incident which is worthy of mention. A gentleman of Raleigh was in the habit of going into the tailor's shop and reading while the apprentice and journeymen were at work. He was an excellent reader, and his favourite book was a volume of speeches, principally of British statesmen. Johnson became interested, and his first ambition was to equal him as a reader and become familiar with those speeches. He took up the alphabet without an instructor, but by applying to the journeymen with whom he worked he obtained a little assistance. Having acquired a knowledge of the letters, he applied for a loan of the book which he had so often heard read. The owner made him a present of it, and gave him some instruction on the use of letters in the formation of words. Thus his first exercises in spelling were in that book. By perseverance he soon learned to read, and the hours which he devoted to his education were at night after he was through his daily labour upon the shopboard. He now applied himself to books from two to three hours every night, after working from 10 to 12 hours at his trade. Having completed his apprenticeship in the autumn of 1824, he went to Laurens Courthouse, South Carolina, where he worked as a journeyman for nearly two years. While there he became engaged to be married, but the match was broken off by the violent opposition of the girl's mother and friends, the ground of objection being Mr. Johnson's youth and the want of pecuniary means. In May, 1826, he returned to Raleigh, where he procured journey-work, and remained until September. He then set out to seek his fortune in the West, carrying with him his mother, who was dependent upon him for support. He stopped at Greenville, Tennessee, and commenced work as a journeyman. He remained there about 12 months, married, and soon afterwards went still further westward, but failing to find a suitable place to settle he returned to Greenville and commenced business. Up to this time his education was limited to reading, as he had never had an opportunity of learning to write or cipher, but under the instructions of his wife he learned these and other branches. The only time, however, he could devote to them was in the dead of the night. The first office which he ever held was that of alderman of the village, to which he was elected in 1828. He was re-elected to the same position in 1829, and again in 1830. In that year he was chosen mayor, which position he held for three years. In 1835 he was elected to the Legislature. In the Session of that year he took decided ground against a scheme of internal improvements, which he contended would not only prove a failure, but entail upon the State a burdensome debt. The measure was popular, however, and at the next election (1837) he was defeated. He became a candidate again in 1839. By this time many of the evils he had predicted were fully demonstrated, and he was elected by a large majority. In 1840 he served as Presidential elector for the State at large on the Democratic ticket. He canvassed a large portion of the State, meeting upon the stump several of the leading Whig orators. In 1841 he was elected to the State Senate. In 1843 he was elected to Congress, where, by successive elections, he served until 1853. During this period of service he was conspicuous and active in advocating the Bill for refunding the fine imposed upon General Jackson at New Orleans in 1815, the annexation of Texas, the tariff of 1846, the war measures of Mr. Polk's Administration, and a homestead bill. In 1853 he was elected Governor of Tennessee after an exciting canvass. He was re-elected in 1855 after another active contest. At the expiration of his second period as Governor, in 1857, he was elected United States' senator for a full term, ending March 3, 1863.

A SLIGHT MISTAKE CORRECTED.

TO THE EDITOR OF THE TIMES.

Sir,—In your report of the Permissive Bill Banquet in the Free Trade Hall last week you slightly err in respect to what Mr. Pope said relative to the "district of 47½ square miles, with a population of 9,500, and no public-house." Mr. Pope did not say that the district included Dungannon, but that it was bounded on one side by the borough town of Dungannon. The district is in the Dungannon union, and the inaccuracy of the report forwarded to you is easily accounted for. But the substantial facts are not affected, in any way, by the error. The Dungannon magistrate who writes you cannot but know these facts. I enclose you the *Alliance News'* report of Mr. Pope's exact statement.

Very respectfully,

THOS. H. BARKER, Sec. United Kingdom Alliance.

Manchester, April 25.

The Works of the late John Leech.—Second Day's Sale (Yesterday).—The attendance was equally numerous as on the preceding day, and the sketches, single drawings, and political cartoons, brought very high prices. Of the first named the following were the more important:—231 and 3. Sketches for cartoons, one slightly coloured, "a Railway Collusion;" "June;" "the Honeymoon," &c.—14 guineas (Campbell). 234. "A Foolish and a Betting Man—a Foolish and a Better Man;" and three other subjects, in a single frame—19½ guineas (ditto). 236 and 7. "Picked up on the Beach," "Quite a New Sensation," and seven others—19 guineas (Griffin). 238. "Grandmamma is supposed to have given Master Tom some Plums," and three others, in one frame—10½ guineas (Vokins). 239. A fact.—(Short-sighted Officer) "Sergeant, get that man's hair cut," and three other subjects—11½ guineas (Campbell). 240. "A Delicate Proposition," and five other subjects, in one frame—12 guineas (Martin). 241. "A Hint to the Commissioners," and seven small sketches, in a single frame—11 guineas (Eaton). 242. "A Very Great Man," and five other subjects—10 guineas (Davidson). 245 and 246. "Distressing Situation of a Sentimental Gentleman." "Who would not be a Riding-master?" "Private Theatricals," and four other subjects—12 guineas (Martin). 253. "When it is very foggy in London it is delightful at Brighton," and five other subjects, in one frame—11 guineas (Campbell). 254-6. "The Confirmed Bachelor," "No Doubt of it," "Domestic Bliss," "Preparing for the Derby,"&c.—14½ guineas (O'Neill). 262 and 4. "What Master Tom did after seeing the Pantomime," "An Ornament to Society," and ten other subjects—18*l.* 7s. 6d. (Griffin). 265 and 6. "The Christening of Jones's First," "Something in That," "A Little Shooting in Ireland," "The Bois de Boulogne," and four others—12½ guineas (Colnaghi). 271 and 2. "The Sea-side—a Sou'-wester," "Suburban Felicity," and four others—11½ guineas (Goldsmid). 274 and 5. "Evening Party in Sebastopol," "The Fun (?) o the Fair," &c.—11 guineas (O'Neill). 279 and 80. "Real Tragedy," "A General Election," and six other subjects—10 guineas (Lucas). 281 and 2. "One Good Turn deserves another," "Nothing like Horse Exercise," and nine other subjects—10½ guineas (Ditto). 284. "The Mermaid's Haunt," and two other subjects, in a single frame—29 guineas (Lucas). 287-8. "Positive Fact," "Our Used-up Man has a few Friends to Breakfast," and seven other subjects—12 guineas (Ditto). 291. "The Pic-nic overtaken by the Tide," and four other subjects, in one frame—10½ guineas (Eaton); 297 and 300. "Aquatics; a comfortable Ran-dan;" "Mr. Briggs has gone to the Exhibition, a Boy holds his Horse in the meantime;" and three other subjects—10½ guineas (Cooke). 303-4. Officer (loq.) "Well, my fine Fellow, so you have been in the regular Army?" "Artificial Ice," and five other subjects—10 guineas (King). 305. "The Mistletoe Bough," and three other subjects in one frame—11 guineas (Lucas). Single Drawings.—309* and 310. "The Dog Days," and "Mrs. Muggins at Chobham"—10 guineas (Born). 311-13 "Upon Tree," "The Meet and the Winner"—17½ guineas (Lucas). 315, 316. "Butterfly Hunt," and "A Surprise"—11*l.* 10s. (Lucas). 321-3. "Ware Hare," and "A Hunting Sketch"—12*l.* (Colnaghi). 325-7. "The Huntsman's Return," and "The Parade, Brighton"—14*l.* 5s. (Ditto). 328. "Exmoor Ponies"—10 guineas (Orridge). 331. "A Cavalier"—17½ guineas (Snooks). 332-3. "A nice bracing Day at the Seaside," and "Scene in a Park," hounds running—16*l.* (J. E. Millais). 334 and 336. "Chamber Practice," and "Sporting Intelligence, Hunting, from our own Correspondent"—12 guineas (Lord G. Fitzgerald). 337. "Delicate Compliment"—10 guineas (Ditto). 340-1. "Pheasant shooting," "A Warm Corner," and "Fly Fishing"—10 guineas (Gladwell). 341A. "The Beach; a Sketch for warm Weather"—20½ guineas (Burton). 343-4. "What's to be done in July?" and "A Mount in the Midlands, April, 1862, Delicious"—13½ guineas (Colnaghi). 347. "Putting his Foot in it"—6½ guineas (Snooks). 349-50. "Delight of the Hon. T. Rasper, who has promised himself a Day with the Pytchley," and "Doing it Thoroughly"—13½ guineas (Colnaghi). 351-2. "A hot chestnut is a very good thing after dinner, but it is not so pleasant just as the fox breaks," and "Our little friend Tom Noddy determines to have a day's hunting in a fresh country"—13½ guineas (Ditto). 353. "Hold hard, Master George"—10½ guineas (Ditto). 354A. "Brighton and Back"—19½ guineas (Money). Illustrations to Facey Romford's Hounds, &c.—356-5. "Romford disturbs the dignity of his huntsman," "Fresh as a Four-year-old, and a pretty Present for a Master of Hounds," "Muggington on Placid Joe, late Pull Devil and Simon Heavyside and his Hounds"—25½ guineas (Johns). 360. "Let me try, then," said Lucy, "and the View"—15½ guineas (Johns). Political Cartoons.—365 and 8. "The Only Competent Person" and "Duty"—10 guineas (A. Lewis). [illegible] Life of Mr. Briggs, and the highly important Albums of the great artist.

NAVAL AND MILITARY INTELLIGENCE.

We have received the following letter from our correspondent, dated Malta, April 22:—

"There is little to report of either naval or military news since the departure of the last mail on the 17th inst. Her Majesty's ship Himalaya went round from the Great into the Marsamuscetto harbour yesterday and leaves to-day with the 7th Royal Fusiliers for Quebec. The Victoria, 102 (flagship of the Commander-in-Chief), and the Enterprise, 4, ironclad, have been out for a cruise, and have returned into port. The Surprise, 4, leaves to-day for Tunis. The Royal Oak, 35, ironclad, was inspected the day before yesterday by the Commander-in-Chief. The result, I believe, was very satisfactory. The Swedish corvette Gefle, Capt. Pattersen, left on the 11th inst. for Tunis and Cadiz. Mr. F. R. Drummond Hay, Consul at Crete, will, it is said, succeed Col. Herman as Consul-General at Tripoli, and Mr. Charles Dickson, at present Consul at Souchum-Kaleh and Redout-Kaleh, will take the place of Mr. Drummond Hay at Crete. Mr. Andrews, engineer and general superintendent of the Mediterranean Extension Telegraph Company, left Malta on the 17th inst. to repair the Corfu and Otranto cable."

The Adjutant-General, Sir James Yorke Scarlett, has promulgated a circular memorandum, addressed to general and other officers commanding on stations at home and abroad, dated Horse Guards, 5th of April, 1865, containing the following extract of a letter from the War-office, dated the 29th of March, 1865:—

"The Secretary of State for Foreign Affairs has notified to Earl de Grey that the Governments of Austria and Prussia have determined to grant a provisional national flag to the Duchies of Schleswig-Holstein and Lauenburg until the definite settlement of the constitution of these territories, and have requested Her Majesty's Government to recognize the flag in question, and to grant ships bearing it the same rights which were accorded to the ships of the Duchies previously to their separation from Denmark. Her Majesty's Government have now agreed to recognize the flag provisionally, saving the rights of the States of Holstein and Schleswig and of the German Confederation, and only till the definite constitution of the Duchies concerned. This flag will have the colours blue, white, and red, in horizontal stripes, and will be distinguished from the Mecklenburg flag, which has the same colours, by a yellow field placed on the blue field next the flagstaff."

An order was promulgated yesterday to the troops at Portsmouth by Major-Gen. Lord William Paulet, K.C.B., Lieutenant-Governor of Portsmouth and Military Commander-in-Chief of the South-west District, from the Horse Guards, dated April 24, in which the Field-Marshal Commanding-in-Chief expresses his satisfaction at the very creditable state in which he found the troops under Lord W. Paulet's command at the late inspection, and requests that he will make this known to the commanding officers of regiments serving in his district.

The hired transport Shannon, Capt. Daniels, 1,232 tons burden, having embarked the A and B batteries of the C brigade, now amalgamated with the Royal Horse Artillery, from Her Majesty's Indian service, sailed from Calcutta on the 14th of January, and arrived yesterday at Woolwich. The Shannon (one of Green's first-class ships) made the Royal Arsenal pier at 12 o'clock, at high tide, and immediately commenced landing the troops and baggage, under the superintendence of Capt. Nangle, Deputy-Assist. Quartermaster-General, which was effected with the utmost order and expedition. In less than an hour the whole of the troops and baggage were on shore, and at 1 o'clock the Shannon was under way to the East India Docks to clear out her cargo, which consists of indigo, raw silk, saltpetre, &c. The health of the troops was remarkably good. One death only occurred during the voyage, the result of a severe attack of dysentery. Before leaving the ship the officers expressed their thanks to Capt. Daniels for the uniform kindness and attention which they had all received at his hands, and which had made the passage, they said, most agreeable. For some days after her departure from Calcutta, and until nearing the Western Islands, the Shannon had most favourable weather, but she was afterwards constantly becalmed and experienced a succession of head winds. On entering the Channel she was again detained by the fog, and was obliged to anchor one night off Dover, and also on Tuesday night at the mouth of the Thames. After disembarking, the troops were drawn up under the open shed facing the landing-place in the Arsenal, and awaited the preparations necessary for taking over the barrack quarters. At 3 o'clock Major-General E. C. Warde, C.B., Commandant, rode down the Arsenal, attended by his personal Staff, consisting of Capt. Williams, A.D.C., Brigade-Major Hay, and Capt. Nangle. He was accompanied by Col. Gambier, C.B., Deputy-Adjt.-General; Col. Huyshe, commanding the C Brigade; Col. Anderson, C.B., commanding the 4th Brigade, Royal Artillery; Lieut.-Col. Reilly, C.B., B Brigade, Royal Horse Artillery; Major-General Sandham, R.E., Royal Military Academy; and others. They were there joined by the regimental and bugle bands of the Royal Artillery, by whom they were escorted to the garrison. The bronzed appearance of the men bespoke a long residence in India. On their arrival on the Royal Artillery parade they were inspected by General Warde, and formed three sides of a square, when the General informed them that he had taken the opportunity of meeting them on their landing, and, from the favourable report which had been forwarded to him of their conduct in the field, as well as their general behaviour in quarters, he was proud to welcome them as comrades and brothers to join the Royal Artillery, of which regiment they now formed a component part. His despatch, he said, informed him that up to their embarkation at Calcutta they were all men of high soldierly bearing, and as such he was happy to receive them as members of the Royal Artillery—the honour and glory of the army. He had full confidence, he said, in their determination to maintain intact the high reputation they had brought with them from their distant home, and he should merely caution them to resist the temptations which were constantly thrown in the way of soldiers. The men were then dismissed to quarters.

The ship Roxburgh Castle, 1,121 tons, Capt. C. Dinsdale, whose arrival in the Channel from New South Wales was announced in *The Times* of Tuesday, arrived at Spithead yesterday morning, and anchored for the purpose of disembarking the Royal Artillery. She has brought to England the following officers and men belonging to the 3d Battery of the 12th Brigade:—Capts. Lovell and Smith; Lieuts. Greer, Larcom, and Hallett; Assist.-Surgeon Milburn, 60 men, 14 women, and 36 children. The troops will disembark this morning and will be placed in quarters in Blockhouse Fort—the western battery at the mouth of Portsmouth harbour—the Artillery at present stationed there removing to Sandown, Isle of Wight. As soon as the disembarcation of the troops has been effected the Roxburgh Castle will resume her voyage to London, to deliver her colonial cargo.

The ship St. Lawrence, 1,200 tons, Capt. Toynbee, from Calcutta for London, also put into Spithead yesterday morning to discharge her Government freight of troops, consisting of Major M'Neil, Royal Artillery; Capt. Clarke, 7th Dragoon Guards; Capt. Murphy, 52d Regiment; Capt. Gould, 97th; Lieut. Seagrim, 23d; Col. Money, Mrs. Money and children, Madras army; Major and Mrs. Garth and family, Mrs. Colonel Priestly and family, and upwards of 300 time-expired men and invalids, from various regiments serving in India, together with a proportionate number of women and children. The St. Lawrence was towed into Portsmouth harbour yesterday afternoon by the Thames steaming Victor, and will disembark her troops this morning alongside the dockyard, when the invalids will be sent on by Government steamer to the Royal Victoria Military Hospital at Netley, and the time-expired men to the depôts of the regiments to which they belong.

The iron frigate Warrior, 40, was yesterday admitted into the steam basin of Portsmouth dockyard from her harbour moorings, and it may therefore be reasonably hoped that no time will now be lost by the authorities, either at the Admiralty or at Portsmouth, in bringing forward this fine frigate for recommission as rapidly as possible.

The following appointments were made yesterday at the Admiralty:—Commander Henry W. Mist to be inspecting commander in the Coastguard, vice Brown; Lieuts. G. Robinson, E. C. Drummond, N. S. F. Digby, and F. C. de Lousada to the Caledonia; J. Whittall, paymaster, to the Winchester; and Henry S. Lauder, assist.-surg., to the Gleaner.

MORALITY IN CUMBERLAND AND WESTMORLAND.

TO THE EDITOR OF THE TIMES.

Sir,—I have just seen in a leading article in *The Times* some remarks on a few suggestions of mine relative to illegitimacy in the northern counties, and I shall feel obliged if you will kindly insert these few words, as the writer seems partly to have misunderstood my meaning—partly, I fear I may have expressed myself imperfectly. I am understood to suggest that employers of farm-servants should refuse to employ the parents of illegitimates. What I certainly meant to say was that they should refuse to employ them at once and without question, and should not treat a man of known profligacy or a woman of known frailty just as they would others of spotless character; in fact, that they should require a certificate of good conduct extending over a reasonable time, which I imagine most prudent householders in London would require.

To make "ruin" the inevitable doom of frailty and not allow a *locus pœnitentiæ* would be preposterous, and as cruel as it would be foolish.

Then, he says, that I am "shocked to observe that neighbours speak gently of a young woman's fall, and that she may be forgiven and look forward to a good place."

God forbid that I should either entertain or express any such feelings. I heartily agree with what appear to be the writer's own sentiments [illegible]

April 25. J. PERCIVAL.

AUSTRIAN HEIR AND HIS WIFE MURDERED.

SHOT IN BOSNIAN TOWN.

A STUDENT'S POLITICAL CRIME.

BOMB THROWN EARLIER IN THE DAY.

THE EMPEROR'S GRIEF.

The Austro-Hungarian Heir-Presumptive, the Archduke Francis Ferdinand, and his wife, the Duchess of Hohenberg, were assassinated yesterday morning at Serajevo, the capital of Bosnia. The actual assassin is described as a high school student, who fired bullets at his victims with fatal effect from an automatic pistol as they were returning from a reception at the Town Hall.

The outrage was evidently the fruit of a carefully-laid plot. On their way to the Town Hall the Archduke and his Consort had narrowly escaped death. An individual, described as a compositor from Trebinje, a garrison town in the extreme south of Herzegovina, had thrown a bomb at their motor-car. Few details of this first outrage have been received. It is stated that the Archduke warded off the bomb with his arm, and that it exploded behind the car, injuring the occupants of the second carriage.

The author of the second outrage is stated to be a native of Grahovo, in Bosnia. No information as to his race or creed is yet forthcoming. It is presumed that he belongs to the Serb or Orthodox section of the Bosnian population.

Both criminals were immediately arrested, and were with difficulty saved from being lynched.

While this tragedy was being enacted in the Bosnian capital, the aged Emperor Francis Joseph was on his way from Vienna to his summer residence at Ischl. He had an enthusiastic send-off from his subjects in Vienna and an even more enthusiastic reception on reaching Ischl.

SCENE OF THE MURDER.

(FROM OUR SPECIAL CORRESPONDENT.)

SERAJEVO, JUNE 28, 9.30 P.M.

To-day at 9.50 a.m. the Imperial train conveying the Archduke Francis Ferdinand and his Consort arrived here from Ilidzhe. After inspecting the troops on the Filipovitch parade ground the august visitors drove in a motor-car along the station road and the Appel Quay to the Town Hall.

The first attempt, when the bomb was thrown, took place at 10.15, as the car was driving along the Appel Quay, just before reaching the Chumuria Bridge. An Aide-de-Camp seated in one of the motor-cars which followed the Archduke's car was wounded in the neck by fragments of the bomb and several passers-by also received slight injuries.

The perpetrator was arrested. He is a young printer, 20 years of age, Nedjeliko Cabrinovitch by name, and a native of Herzegovina, belonging to the Serb-Orthodox faith.

When the motor-car conveying the Archduke and his Consort reached the Town Hall his Imperial Highness said to the Mayor:—"What is the good of your speeches? I come to Serajevo on a visit, and I get bombs thrown at me. It is outrageous."

When the procession drove back from the Town Hall the second attempt was made. At 10.40, as the Heir-Apparent's motor-car reached the corner of the Appel Quay and of the Franz-Josefsgasse, another bomb was thrown at the car by Gavrilo Prinzip, a Bosniak High School student, also belonging to the Serb-Orthodox faith. This bomb did not explode.

Thereupon the assassin fired three shots from a pistol. The first shot hit the Archduke in the neck, the second hit him in the leg, and the third hit the Duchess of Hohenberg in the lower part of the body.

General Potiorek, chief of the Administration, who was sitting in the Archduke's motor-car, escaped injury. The perpetrator was seized by the crowd and severely mauled.

The Archduke and the Duchess of Hohenberg were rapidly conveyed to General Potiorek's official residence. Both were past all human aid and received the last Sacrament. The Archduke expired a few minutes after his Consort.

The town has been plunged into the deepest mourning. The national flags have been hauled down, and black emblems have been hoisted in their stead. Several suspicious-looking persons have been arrested. The approaches to the Palace are barred and guarded by the military.

HEROISM OF THE DUCHESS.

(FROM OUR OWN CORRESPONDENT.)

BERLIN, JUNE 28.

The news of the assassination of the Archduke Francis Ferdinand and the Duchess of Hohenberg was made known here by extra editions of the newspapers at about 5 o'clock this evening. The version published here states that the Duchess attempted to shield her husband by throwing her own body in the way of the assassin's bullet.

The utmost horror and consternation have been aroused by the crime, which is a terrible blow to the ally of the Dual Monarchy. No one has yet attempted to gauge its possible effect upon the stability of Europe, and the diplomatic world is almost stunned.

OFFICIAL REPORT OF THE CRIME.

POPULAR INDIGNATION.

ATTEMPT TO LYNCH THE ASSASSIN.

(FROM OUR OWN CORRESPONDENT.)

VIENNA, JUNE 28.

The hand of the assassin has once more descended on the reigning House of Austria-Hungary and added yet another to the list of terrible tragedies which have befallen the House of Hapsburg.

The Archduke and his Consort were paying an official visit to Serajevo at the close of the manœuvres of the 15th and 16th Army Corps, which had been taking place in the neighbourhood. They arrived at the capital early this morning from the little bathing resort of Ilidzhe, which had been their headquarters during the last few days, and to which they were to have returned this afternoon before leaving for Vienna in the evening.

The account of the crime given by the Austrian Official Telegraph Agency, which is being distributed by the newspapers on typewritten sheets in the Vienna streets this afternoon, is as follows:—

"As his Imperial and Royal Highness the Archduke Francis Ferdinand, with his Consort, was proceeding this morning to a reception in the Town Hall, a bomb was hurled at his motor-car. His Imperial and Royal Highness warded off with his arm the bomb, which exploded after the Archducal motor-car had passed. Count Boos Waldeck and the Aide-de-Camp of the Governor, Lieutenant-Colonel Morizzi, who were in the next car, were slightly wounded. Of the public six persons were injured, some slightly, some severely. The man who threw the bomb was arrested. He is a typographer na med Cabrinovitch, from Trebinje.

"After the reception in the Town Hall, the Archduke continued, with his Consort, his drive through the town. A student named Prinzip, belonging to the highest class in the public school (gymnasium), a native of Grahovo, fired several shots at the motor-car with a Browning pistol. The Archduke was hit in the face and the Duchess was wounded by a shot in the abdomen.

"The Archduke and the Duchess were taken to the Konak (Governor's Palace), where they succumbed to their injuries.

"Prinzip was arrested. Both he and the man who threw the bomb were almost lynched by the infuriated crowd."

EVIDENCE OF A PLOT.

At the hour of telegraphing, 7.45 p.m., the above is practically all the information received here concerning the crime. The fact that the fatal shots were fired after a first attempt had failed would seem to indicate, however, that it was not merely a mad act on the part of a hot-headed student, but was the result of a regularly laid plot. Whether the circumstance that the first would-be assassin comes from Trebinje, in Herzegovina, and the second from Grahovo, in Bosnia, implies that both were participators in a movement spread over the two provinces cannot yet be determined. The judicial inquiry will no doubt make this clear.

The first news was received here early this afternoon, but it was not for some hours that the general public learned from the typewritten sheets that the Heir-Apparent and his Consort had been murdered. To the natural shock caused by the news of the perpetration of such a crime is added a feeling of surprise that he who was widely supposed to favour the formation of the Southern Slav subjects of the Monarchy into a third State on an equal footing with Austria and Hungary, and his Consort, who was herself a member of a Bohemian and therefore a Slav family, should have been the victims of a Slav assassin.

ASSASSIN'S STATEMENTS.

9 P.M.

The latest reports received here from Serajevo represent the assassination to have had its mainspring in the Pan-Serb agitation. Cabrinovitch, who is stated to have tried to escape by jumping into the river, is reported to have affirmed in examination that he had received the bomb from Belgrade, while Prinzip stated that he had been for some time in the Servian capital and for nationalistic reasons he had made up his mind to assassinate at the first opportunity some important Austro-Hungarian personage. The supposition that the crime is the result of a plot is strengthened by a report that close to the place where the assassination took place a second unused bomb was found.

On the preceding page will be found:— Memoirs of the Archduke and the Duchess. Photograph of Serajevo.

AUSTRIAN EMPEROR AND THE NEWS.

A TRAGIC CONTRAST.

RETURN TO-DAY FROM ISCHL.

(FROM OUR OWN CORRESPONDENT.)

VIENNA, JUNE 28.

The Emperor, who went to Ischl yesterday for his annual summer change of air, was informed immediately of the double assassination. The first person to express condolences to his Majesty was the Duke of Cumberland, who drove over in a motor-car from his residence at Gmünden. The Emperor is expected to be back in Vienna at 6 o'clock to-morrow morning. Three children of the Archduke are staying at the Castle of Chlumetz in Bohemia, whither the Duchess of Hohenberg's brother-in-law, Count Wüthenau, at once proceeded to break the news to them.

In Vienna the flags are being flown at half-mast on the public buildings and the foreign Embassies, but there is little trace of public excitement.

VIENNA, JUNE 27.

The Emperor Francis Joseph left here at 8.10 this morning for Ischl, where he intends spending the summer. The route to the railway station was gaily decorated and lined by an enormous crowd, which heartily cheered his Majesty.

At the station the Emperor was welcomed by the Burgomaster and the members of the Municipal Council. The Burgomaster expressed the great joy which his subjects felt at the recovery of their Sovereign, who was looking well and hearty and appeared to be in excellent humour. The Emperor, in reply, said he was deeply touched by the expressions of love and loyalty he had received. The Imperial train steamed out of the station amidst the enthusiastic acclamations of the public and the playing of the National Anthem.—*Reuter.*

KING GEORGE'S SORROW.

A WEEK OF COURT MOURNING.

The King commands that the Court shall wear mourning for one week for His Imperial and Royal Highness the late Archduke Franz Ferdinand of Austria-Este, K.G., the mourning to date from Sunday, the 28th inst., and on Sunday, July 5, the Court to go out of mourning.

The Lord Chamberlain is commanded by the King to announce that the State Ball arranged to take place this evening is postponed on account of the lamentable death of the Archduke Franz Ferdinand of Austria-Este, K.G., and of the Duchess of Hohenberg.

The members of the Royal Family were inexpressibly shocked yesterday afternoon by the receipt of the news of the assassination. During the evening Commander Sir Charles Cust, Equerry-in-Waiting to the King, called at the Austrian Embassy on behalf of his Majesty to request that an expression of his deep sympathy and that of the Queen be forwarded to the Austrian Court.

The shock which the news caused to the Royal Family was the more profound because the Archduke and the Duchess had so recently been their guests.

THE NEW HEIR-PRESUMPTIVE.

A POPULAR PRINCE.

The Archduke Charles Francis Joseph, who now succeeds his uncle, the late Archduke Francis Ferdinand, as Heir-Presumptive to the Hapsburg throne, was born on August 17, 1887. He is the eldest son of the late Archduke Otto, the younger brother of the Archduke Francis Ferdinand, and of the Archduchess Maria Josepha, sister of the Duke of Saxony. His father, who died of an incurable disease in November, 1906, had been a brilliant officer, and was the handsomest of the Hapsburg princes. His mother, the Archduchess Josepha, supervised his education with the utmost care, and sought as far as possible to correct any unwelcome tendency that he might have inherited. He grew up a shy, simple youth, indistinguishable from the mass of young Archdukes, and scarcely appeared in public until his marriage, on October 21, 1911, to the Princess Zita of Bourbon Parma. This marriage, which the Emperor promoted, was extremely popular in Austria, both on account of the youth of the Archducal couple and of the winning character of the bride. It was hailed, moreover, as affording a promise of an eventual return to a more direct line of succession than the transmission of the Crown from uncle to nephew. This promise was fulfilled in November, 1912, by the birth of their son, the youthful Archduke Francis Joseph Otto.

Immediately after his marriage the Archduke Charles Francis Joseph was sent with his cavalry regiment to Kolomea, a garrison town in the extreme east of Galicia. He marched with the regiment across the whole of Galicia, and gained great popularity with the Polish and Ruthene population. At Kolomea his boyish simplicity and the girlish charm of the Archduchess Zita won all hearts; and when they left the Galician garrison to take up more responsible duties in Vienna—where the Emperor Francis Joseph fitted up for them the old castle of Hötzendorf, near Schönbrunn—they had become the most popular of the younger members of the Imperial family.

TRAGEDY OF A ROYAL HOUSE.

THE AFFLICTED EMPEROR.

SUCCESSIVE STROKES OF FATE.

"Then I am to be spared nothing" was the cry of anguish wrung from the Emperor Francis Joseph by the murder of his wife. And fate seems again to answer "nothing."

After all the awful blows that have fallen upon him as a Sovereign and as a man, it was fondly hoped by all who have watched the vicissitudes of his troubled life that the head of the House of Hapsburg, the oldest of European Sovereigns, might be suffered to close his days in peace. It was not to be. At 84 years of age, after a reign of 66 years, as he had barely recovered from a long and dangerous illness, the hand of destiny implacable has fallen upon him once more. And the stroke is the more terrible because it is of the same kind as those which have so often visited him. Brother, son, and wife were torn from him, one after the other, by violent and sudden deaths. Now the pistol of a Slav assassin has taken the nephew who was to succeed him and the mother of that nephew's children. There are men and women in all states of life to whom fate seems ruthless, showering upon them one pitiless blow after another. But few amongst these children of misfortune can have had to suffer a succession of calamities so grievous as the stricken old man who sits upon the proudest Throne on the Continent. The hearts of all nations and of all sorts and conditions amongst them must go out to him in this latest visitation, this "sorrow's crown of sorrow," in the late evening of his life. Since the guillotine left the daughter of Louis XVI. a lonely orphan in the Temple, reft of father, mother, and aunt by the executioner's axe, and of her boy brother by the brutalities and the neglect of her gaolers, we can recall no history so tragic and so pathetic as has been this.

MAXIMILIAN OF MEXICO.

Francis Joseph had suffered much as a Sovereign before he was called upon to bear the first of the yet crueller sorrows of his domestic life. This is not the time to dwell upon the crushing disasters of Magenta and Sadowa; upon the rich provinces lost; the hereditary position in Germany forfeited; the proud ambitions and large hopes disappointed and defeated; the harassing internal troubles which followed the campaigns against France and Savoy in Italy and against Prussia in Bohemia. It was when the first bitterness of the day of Königgrätz and of the treaty with the conquering Prussians was past that the terrible news of Maximilian's death came from Queretaro. That the Emperor's brother would lose the crown he had gone out to seek had long been recognized. His Empress, the unhappy Charlotte, had come back to Europe in the summer of the war with Prussia, on her vain pilgrimage to seek support for her husband. He had been implored to abandon an enterprise that had become hopeless, but with mistaken chivalry he would not renounce the task he had undertaken. Only those who knew the ferocity of party passions in Mexico had foreseen what his doom must be when he fell into the hands of Juarez. The story of his end has been often told. The treachery which helped to bring about his capture; the tranquil dignity he showed in his captivity and at his so-called trial; the cold and implacable malignity with which Juarez rejected all the many appeals made to him for mercy; the death scene when the descendant of Maria Theresa and the kinsman of Marie Antoinette showed his savage persecutors that he knew how to die as a Christian and as a Hapsburg; the brutal refusal of his murderers to deliver his dead body until their pride and vanity had been assuaged by repeated petitions—all these details of that sad end to a young and brilliant life are well known. The widow, whom he had dearly loved, and whose high spirit had largely moved him to accept the fatal Crown, was driven out of her mind by the frightful strain she had undergone, and yet haunts the world a lunatic, tormented, it is said, by lucid intervals in which all the dread past is again before her.

Then the House of Austria was left free for a space from visitations of the more awful kind, though minor troubles and scandals afflicted it. In January, 1889, a yet darker and more appalling calamity came upon it. On the morning of January 30, the news of Prince Rudolph's mysterious death was spread about in Vienna. He was found dead in his bed at a hunting-lodge which he used to visit. Doubt as to the nature of his death was removed by a note which he had written to a friend the day before. "I could not do otherwise," it said. Why, in the flower of his youth, but a few years after his marriage, this brilliant and accomplished prince—courtier, soldier, and statesman, with many gifts and acquirements, with refined and educated tastes and the keenest interest in everything, felt compelled to take his own life, is one of the secrets that are reserved for the future.

THE MURDER OF THE EMPRESS.

Again the sword was suspended over the head of the Hapsburgs and of their chief. In September, 1898, he was already advanced in years. He was making ready to keep his jubilee in a couple of months' time. On the 10th of the month a telegram came from Geneva with the news that his wife, the beautiful and fascinating Elizabeth of Bavaria, had been stabbed to death by an Italian Anarchist named Luccheni. The Emperor had loved her dearly. The story of their engagement at her father's mountain home is one of the prettiest of Court idylls. They had had their differences, but his affection and his respect for her were deep and abiding. Now she was stricken down by an empty-headed enemy of society, who had chosen his victim almost by chance. He had been an Anarchist since he was 13, and he was indifferent, he declared, as to what "head of a State" he killed. Chance threw in his way the beautiful Empress—"a woman" as her husband piteously said, "who never hurt a soul, and only did good all her life." This seemed to have filled up the measure of his sorrows. No man has ever possessed the royal gift of self-control more fully than he. But the murder of his wife, coming after the suicide of his only son and the "execution" of his brother and playmate was almost more than he could bear. "I pray the Almighty for power to fulfil what I have been called to perform" were amongst the words in which he revealed to his people the spirit in which he suffered. In the same spirit, we doubt not, he will face this latest trial which has been inflicted upon him—a trial awful in itself, and the awfulness of which is enhanced manifold by the dark shadows of all the calamities that have gone before it. "God has given him the qualities needed to meet all turns of fate," wrote the mother who knew him well, when he was yet untried. His trials have been fearful, but he has met them all with the courage and the magnanimity of the greatest of his great House.

LINER ON THE ROCKS OFF DONEGAL.

ALL PASSENGERS SAFE.

MESSAGE FROM THE CAPTAIN.

The Anchor liner California, which was on a voyage from New York to Glasgow, ran on the rocks at Tory Island, off the Donegal coast, yesterday afternoon. It is understood that she had about 1,000 passengers on board, but the latest news received early this morning is that, although the position of the liner is serious, no lives have been lost. The accident occurred during a thick fog.

In reply to a wireless message from *The Times*, Captain Coverley, of the California, at 2.20 this morning sent the following details of the accident:—

California ran ashore, Tory Island, in fog about half mile from lighthouse. Did not hear foghorn blowing. Quiet sea. No danger. Three men-of-war and steamer Cassandra standing by to transfer passengers.

COVERLEY, Master.

The California went on the rocks with such force that the lower part of her bows was badly stove in and two front holds soon filled with water. She is in five fathoms of water forward and seven fathoms aft. Another steamer is standing by. There was no panic, and news has been received in Londonderry that the landing of the Irish passengers may be expected before noon to-day.

The news of the stranding was caught by the Malin Head wireless station and the entire torpedo boat destroyer flotilla on duty off the Ulster coast, looking for gun-runners, was called up and wireless orders were given to all the destroyers from the cruiser Hecla in Lough Swilly to hurry with all speed to the scene of the accident. Subsequently, orders were received by all telephone and telegraph stations on the coast from Bangor to Bunbeg, Co. Donegal, to keep offices open all night. By 11 o'clock six destroyers were making for Tory Island.

PLAN OF THE TOWN OF SERAJEVO.

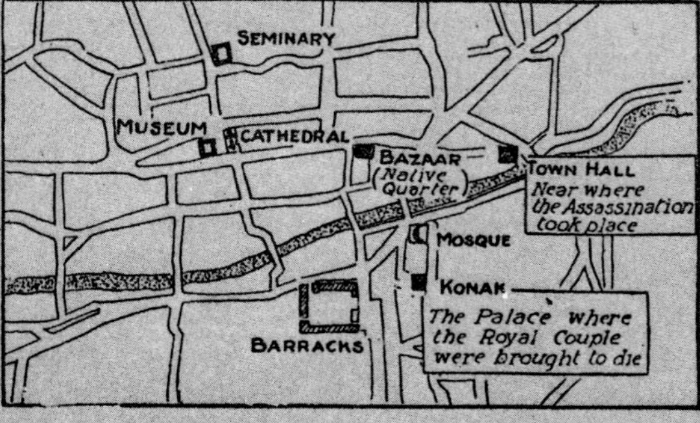

Silly season

his opinion, the city of Dublin supported no hospital by voluntary contribution; the inhabitants were too poor. In 1853 the grant was increased in consequence of the dearness of provisions.

Mr. Stanley, registrar of the Meath Hospital; Mr. Matthews, registrar of the Cork-street Hospital; and Dr. Thomas Brady, of the King and Queen's College of Physicians in Ireland, gave further evidence to a similar effect, and the committee adjourned.

CLOSING OF THE LYCEUM THEATRE.—Although the usual bills and advertisements were issued on Saturday for a performance at this theatre the house was closed in the evening, an announcement being posted up at the different entrances to the following effect:—"Royal Lyceum Theatre, under the management of Madame Vestris.—The public is respectfully informed that the theatre will be closed this evening."

BALLOON ACCIDENT.—An accident, the consequences of which are expected to be fatal, took place at Cannes on Sunday last. A M. Despleschin, of Nice, had announced his intention of making an ascent in a balloon, and two gentlemen, M. Hardy, of Cannes, and M. A. de Sorr, a literary man from Paris, had made arrangements to accompany him. These two gentlemen had taken their seats in the car, M. Despleschin not having yet entered it, when some person in the crowd, anxious to see the balloon start, cried out "Let go." The man who held the ropes, thinking that the order had come from the aeronaut, obeyed, and the balloon rose rapidly into the clouds, and disappeared. M. Hardy and M. de Sorr are both entirely ignorant of the management of a balloon, and it is feared that they have been carried out to sea. Up to the 2d no intelligence had been received of them.—*Galignani's Messenger*.

Above 9 May 1854
Below right 18 September 1856

The Times is the paper of record. It has a duty to inform, to instruct and to thunder. But it has never thought, because it is serious, that there should be no more cakes and ale. It also has a duty to entertain. Readers, even *Times* readers, cannot stand to attention on the intellectual and political parade ground all day. One of the peculiar delights of *The Times* has always been the incidental snippets of inconsequential and absurd information with which it has stood easy from the heavy stuff.

The great S. J. Perelman used to read *The Times* every day, wherever he was, as a constant source for his humorous pieces. He said of the Law Reports in *The Times* (the only newspaper reports that may be cited as authority in a court of law): 'The further you get, the more they resemble *Alice in Wonderland* crossed with a D'Oyly Carte operetta'. The funny bits, reflecting the celebrated English talent for eccentricity, come in unexpected places. Every year on the Ides of March somebody pays to insert in the Personal Column a moving memorial notice for Julius Caesar; similar pious memorials are put in on the appropriate days for Byron, Charles I and many others. The dining lists, engagements, school notices and other paid advertisements on the Court Page are shining examples of British snobbery, and accordingly British humour. The bottom right-hand corner of the Letters Page is a notorious nest for cuckoos, home for the dotty and the potty, and material for sociologists and psychoanalysts of the British humour.

Item, 11 October 1973:

Sir,

Amongst the memorable notices displayed by London Transport and recently reported by your readers, let this one find a place:

Gents and lift out of order
Please use the stairs.

If you go back to the end of the last century, you will find readers much exercised about when precisely, pray, the new century would begin. Item, 2 January 1900:

Sir,

It is known that Julius Caesar was killed on 15 March, BC 44, that Augustus died on 19 August, AD 14, and that the period between these two dates was 57 years, five months, and some few days. It is obvious that there is no room for a year 0 – either BC or AD. Our century has yet a year to run.

Tacitus, Boethius, Shakespeare, Richard Brinsley Sheridan and Goethe were other witnesses cited as evidence in this controversy, which, like the best *Times* funnies, was treated with high seriousness and came to no definite conclusion.

From the beginning Printing House Square had a taste for extraordinary and hilarious news stories from around the world, reported in a style as po-faced as the high politics in the adjacent column: we call them Fillers these days.

For example, 28 October 1858:

A young man named Power, residing at Castlecomer, went a few evenings ago to fly what he termed a Spanish kite, of very large dimensions. Having adjusted the cord and tail, it rapidly ascended with a brisk breeze until it had taken the full length of the cord, which became entangled round Power's hand. The wind increasing, he was drawn a distance of nearly half a mile in the greatest agony, the cord cutting into the bone. The Rev. Mr Penrose, the protestant curate of the parish, seeing the man running and shouting, at one time raised off the ground for a distance of some perches, and again running along at full speed, perceived that he was dragged by the kite, and followed him as fast as he could; but being unable to come up with him, he shouted at the top of his voice to 'Let go; there was a man killed in a thunderstorm by the lightning of a kite.' When Power heard these words, he shouted with redoubled vigour, but could not extricate himself until, after the distance mentioned, he was stopped by a high stone wall, the top of which, being coped, cut the cord and set at liberty the kite and the owner, who was almost lifeless with fatigue and fright.

The Victorians had better accidents than we do. The compiler of a collection of bizarre and amusing Victorian accidents taken from NIBS (News In Briefs) in *The Times*, published in 1984, observed that the Victorians, to judge from the reports in *The Times*, lived in a world infinitely more hazardous than ours.

Poisons were freely available, guns were universally owned, gunpowder was used to clean kitchen stoves, horses were continually running off with their carriages, thunderstorms were thought to strike people down with an electric fluid, and, at the theatre, the footlights were still naked flames. And we have not even considered the dangers of kite-flying. Paradoxically, the antholo-

I remain, Sir,
AN INDIAN SUBALTERN OF FIFTEEN YEARS.

A REGULAR FIX.—During a thunderstorm in the town of Berne, says the *Albany Knickerbocker*, the electric fluid struck an apple tree, against which a young man named Lawrence was leaning. It split the tree from top to bottom, making a gap sufficiently large to let Mr. Lawrence slip in about a foot, immediately after which it sprung to, and held him as tight as if he had been in a steel-trap. Before he could be extricated a resort to axes and crowbars became necessary. This is probably one of the tightest places that Mr. Lawrence ever got into.

[Advertisement.]—"Romance and Reality," price 2s.; cloth, 2s. 6d.; by Miss Landon (L. E. L.) is the title of the new volume of Ward and Lock's "Standard Novels." "Romance and Reality" was Miss Landon's first production of prose fiction, and was most successful, and no wonder, for it combines in one happy mixture the romantic, the high life, the common life, the satirical, the historical, and the other attributes of the best works of its class. Lately published in this series:—"Maid Marian and Crotchet Castle," by Peacock, price 1s.; "Stanley Thorn," by the author of Valentine Vox, 2s.;

gist observed, the Victorians of the Fillers in *The Times* seem to have been more reckless, more carefree, more enterprising than us. In those old columns you will meet people who carry nitric acid in their pockets, drink unknown substances with dire effects, shoot themselves with their own guns, and go bathing when they cannot swim. You will find the bizarre and the poignant, absurd feats, miraculous escapes, and monumental bad luck stories. Above all, you will find a delight in prurient detail that is ill-concealed.

I am sure that this is right: part of the attraction of those old Fillers was that they made our flesh creep. Item, 26 July 1851:

As an omnibus was on Wednesday passing along the Place de la Bastille volumes of smoke suddenly issued from it, and the passengers were observed to descend in terrible confusion. In the interior was a man who was rolling about in terrible suffering. This man, it appeared, had imprudently placed a bottle of nitric acid in his coat pocket, and a jolt of the vehicle caused the bottle to break. The liquid spread over him, and occasioned the smoke.

In a moment his clothes were reduced to cinders, and his flesh was horribly burnt. A lady seated next to him had her silk gown entirely destroyed, and she was besides slightly injured. One person had a bundle of chymical matches, which caught fire. The flames extended to the vehicle and did it considerable damage. When the passengers descended, the man who had the nitric acid was conveyed to the Hospital of St Antoine. He was in an alarming state, and his flesh fell from him.

Or take the extraordinary and horrible occurrence reported, with relish, on 27 August 1847:

On Friday last, shortly after daylight, two men, living at Sedlesham, near Bognor, Sussex, were engaged in netting small fish for bait. One of them named Jeffreys, having caught some small soles, was, according to custom, about to lay hold of one with his teeth, in order to draw it through the mesh, when it made a sudden effort to free itself from his grasp, and darted through the mouth into the larynx, with its head in the gullet. The fins being extended transfixed it in that situation. The man became totally overpowered, and the attempts of his companion to withdraw it were unavailing. Medical aid was sent for (a distance of four miles) but when the medical man arrived he found life totally extinct, and declined operating to remove the fish, judging it necessary not to interfere before an inspection had been made by the coroner and jury. The breadth of the fish was about three fingers, and it continued to flicker for many hours. This ill-fated individual was a young man, and has left a wife and three children to deplore the loss. A small subscription has been raised at Bognor for the widow, and it is hoped that the humane will forward to her donations, which may be conveniently effected by enclosing postage stamps.

There is nothing restrained about horror stories in *The Times*. They rise up and grab the reader by the throat like a clot of blood, or a flapping sole. But the classic *Times* silly season stories should combine information with entertainment and oddity. As the poet Horace remarked about his contemporary journalists: '*Et prodesse volunt, et delectare poetae*'. Hacks want to instruct as well as amuse.

One of the most amusing and instructive *Times* excursions in recent years has been on the subject of the design and performance of the ancient Greek trireme. It raged in the correspondence and news columns throughout the summer and autumn of 1975.

Below 2 October 1872
Below right 17 February 1969

rate himself. Mr. Macpherson, of Blairgowrie-house, said that Protestants generally would be deeply indebted for the exposure the Bishop had made of the ritualistic practices in St. Ninian's Cathedral, and the sooner those who were in favour of them went to the Church of Rome the better. The proposal to give a vote of thanks to the Bishop ultimately fell to the ground.

AFTER EDGAR POE.—The *Nord* is responsible for the following account of a horrible accident which has just happened at Montrouge. A M. Dumas, residing there, an agent of manufacturing chymists in Rouen, has kept for the last three months a black ape, which had been brought to him from Africa. It was M. Dumas' custom every evening before going to bed to take a glass of *eau sucrée*, into which he put a little orange water. The monkey, which was in the bedroom and saw him do this, is believed to have formed the purpose of repeating the act. M. Dumas had just received from his employers a specimen of nitric acid which he was to sell to a retail dealer in Paris. After having opened and examined the bottle, he prepared his glass of sugar and water, went to bed, and fell asleep. The monkey then poured the contents of the bottle into the glass and retired. Feeling thirsty during the night, M. Dumas rose and swallowed the poison. He died shortly afterwards, having suffered the most excruciating agony. The *Siècle* adds to what is stated above, that when the neighbours came in, the monkey was seen with the empty bottle in its hands.

were unable to walk after a car crash.

Beetles as thieves: Seven horned beetles held by the police in Belo Horizonte, Brazil, as accomplices in pilfering, are reported to have died of starvation. The beetles were trained by bus drivers to steal plastic tokens out of the fare boxes, according to the alleged confession of one of 17 drivers accused.

Delayed in transit: A card posted in 1907 at Vatournanche, in north Italy, has arrived at its destination, the mountain village of Etroubles, 34 miles away.

Cricket deaths: Two Trinidad policemen have died of heart attacks while listening to radio commentaries on the West Indies Test series with Australia.

Blind climbers: Eight young blind men have scaled a 60ft. rock face and made a descent by rope

Right 9 August 1955

The swamps of East and Central Africa are of vast extent. Permanent drainage and dry cultivation are not the only or necessarily always the best method of exploiting them. Very little is known of their basic chemistry and biology, and the object of the investigation is to contribute towards the framing of long-term policy.

BULLET THROUGH BRAIN CAUSED A HEADACHE

FROM OUR CORRESPONDENT

PRETORIA, AUG. 8

"A million-to-one chance" is how doctors describe the escape this weekend of a young African who was shot through the back of his head by a revolver bullet which emerged above his eyes without doing more than give him a headache. Doctors say the bullet passed between the lobes of the brain as it "breathed." After being shot, the native walked some distance and an hour of two later made a statement to police in hospital. He also identified his assailant. To-day he was progressing well.

It was an interesting though not topical subject discussed with high solemnity and complete frivolity. Its nature brought in such obsessive *Times* readers as ancient mariners, classical scholars, meteorologists and old-fashioned English eccentrics. It generated enough material to produce a small book. And as usual its results were inconclusive. On 4 October the President of Wolfson College, Cambridge, summed up the progress so far:

Sir,
Thank you for giving space to such a fascinating and instructive correspondence. May I try to cast the account? All good men seem to agree on the following:

1. That oared ships did not go into battle under sail;
2. That the Greek trireme used full oar power, to produce up to 11½ knots in short bursts, only in battle or in emergency;
3. That oared ships did not put to sea when the wind was unfavourable, rowed out of harbour and then either hoisted sail or continued rowing according to the state of the wind;
4. That a trireme's speed in still water under oar can be credibly calculated to have been five to six knots with one division rowing, a little more with two;
5. And that this calculation does not conflict with Xenophon's '120 nautical miles under oar in a long day'. The word he uses can only mean the hours of daylight. So, with 15 hours of daylight plus one hour of twilight at latitude 42 degrees on midsummer day, the speed works out at seven knots and a half, but there would have been little help from the current for the last 103½ miles. According to the Navigation Department of the National Maritime Museum, Black Sea currents run counter-clockwise, but through the Bosphorus there is a north–south current because of the seventeen inch difference in levels at each end.

The later MSS of Xenophon have a variant reading 'a *very* long day', which suggests that the scribe shared your correspondents' feeling that Xenophon was exaggerating a bit. Etesian winds blowing with the current through the Bosphorus would have kept a galley in port.

There the trireme matter rests for the moment. But not for long; not for long.

Women

Top 9 October 1916
Above 3 January 1921
Right 1 March 1922

The Times is the newspaper for intelligent people of all ages, classes and genders. It has been reluctant to devote special pages to 'women's' topics, or to make a special effort to attract female readers. At least one of the great editors went on record as holding that there was no distinction of sex among *Times* readers: they were all simply intelligent people.

Consequently the researcher who looks for material on women's pages or women's affairs in the archives of *The Times* will find slim pickings. But if he perseveres, and reads the files of back numbers of the paper, he will find that from an early date *The Times* has devoted space to the frivolities of fashion and frills, buttons and bows, cooking and household matters. In 1804, on the first day of the month or thereabouts, there were regularly several paragraphs on fashion, including accounts of fashionable gatherings as well as what the well-dressed *Times* reader was wearing. The pieces were headed by a wood-engraving of a cherub pierced by Mercury's staff and carrying a peacock's feather. The cherub, presumably, was for love and beauty, the peacock for vanity, and Mercury must have been included as the patron of pickpockets, thieves and the rest of the rag trade.

Below the cherub was the inscription FASHION, a word to make subsequent *Times* patriarchs bristle. In February 1804, the month and year in which Immanuel Kant and Joseph Priestley (the discoverer of oxygen) died, in which Blake published *Jerusalem* and Beethoven the Eroica, in which Bonaparte had himself crowned as Emperor Napoleon of France, and foreign affairs looked threatening apart from all that, *The Times* fashion column laid down that the well-dressed *Times* reader, or at any rate his wife, should be wearing that month:

FULL DRESSES – A Turkish robe of fine, plain or worked muslin.

PROMENADE DRESSES – A short round dress of white muslin with a pelice of fawn colour Georgian satin cloth.

HEAD DRESSES – A white lace veil placed to fall over the left shoulder, and ornamented with a wreath of minionet.

GENERAL OBSERVATIONS – The prevailing colours are scarlet, blue, and yellow.

It all sounds deliciously Jane Austen. But it was also the sort of stuff that provoked a later *Times* reader to ask: 'After all, what is fashion? From the artistic point of view, it is usually a form of ugliness so intolerable that we have to alter it every six months.'

After this promising start, *The Times* did not keep up with the fashion. During the Victorian era, when the paper rose to the peak of its influence, we can find little evidence of efforts to make an especial appeal to women. It was left, as were so many things, to Lord Northcliffe to persuade his editorial staff to take some interest in feminine affairs and give some space to them. Soon after his arrival in Printing House Square, the Chief realized that *The Times* was lagging far behind the times in recognizing the changing pattern of British life, in particular in noticing that women were taking a more active role in public and social affairs, or at any rate were pressing to do so.

On 1 October 1910 a Women's Supplement was issued gratis with *The Times*, but the announced intention that it should be followed by others was not fulfilled. Nevertheless the paper continued to give an increasing amount of space to the activities and imagined interests of the female sex. In addition to his countless problems and pursuits, Northcliffe found time to send a memo reminding his managing director that *The Times* must interest women, otherwise the paper would attract no West End advertising. When that advertising did appear, the Chief kept his eagle eye on it to see that it was properly reproduced. On one occasion Northcliffe complained that the fine lace-work on line-drawings of some frocks in an advertisement was 'all smudged'. 'What woman,' he demanded, 'is going to buy goods of that appearance?'

The first Woman's Page in *The Times* started on 15 November 1937 and appeared once a week on Mondays until 1940, when it was discarded because of the wartime shortage of newsprint. Between the wars *The Times* also dealt exhaustively with the Ascot fashions: although it did not appear on the Woman's Page, every June in the twenties and thirties saw lengthy and tedious descriptions of dresses worn in the Royal Enclosure at the famous race meeting. Often Ascot fashion occupied a whole page.

The Woman's Page reappeared after the Second World War, in September 1955, in the same format and day of the week as previously. Newspapers are creatures of habit. In spite of their passion for the news, they cling to the old familiar ways of presenting it.

In May 1966 *The Times* introduced not merely news on the front page, but also the startling innovation of a daily Woman's Page. It was edited by a lively and irreverent young woman who is said, according to Printing House Square folklore, to have got the job on the strength of her *bon mot*, when being interviewed by the editor, that '*The Times* is the tribal noticeboard of a dying race'. The page was transformed into a lively and disputatious forum that delighted thousands of new readers and alarmed some of the older fogies.

These pioneers led the way to the state of play today, when the title of Woman's Page has been discarded, on the reasonable grounds that men as well as women are interested in fashion, babies, cooking and other 'women's' topics. These subjects are treated on general feature pages, where men and women are treated as people rather than opposing sexes, all interested in the little bits of life. The columns have marched a long way from the early fashion and the tribal noticeboard. Today they deal with fashion (male as well as female, and indeed unisex) and the matters of the kitchen, as they have since *Times* began. But today they give more space to the problems and stresses of the modern age: drugs, birth control, abortion, menstruation, the menopause (male as well as female), the one-parent family, homosexuality, medical problems that you never realized you had until you read about them. They are all grist to the mill of the old, really very old, women's columns of *The Times*.

A monthly column of Fashionable Intelligence, which included chic social events, as well as a prescription for stylish dress for the season.
2 MARCH 1804

Page 154
The first daily fashion page, another of Haley's innovations on the day that news was introduced on the front page.
3 MAY 1966

DURHAM ELECTION.

As we expected, a sharp contest is likely to take place at Durham. Mr. WHARTON, who was thrown out of his seat by the Freemen's Petition, reached the city with a new writ last week, accompanied by a person of the name of TWEDDEL, whom he introduced to a meeting of the Freemen at the Town Hall, as a proper man to represent them. The Corporation was neither pleased with the new candidate, nor the manner of bringing him forward; and therefore called a subsequent meeting for the purpose of proposing a gentleman, the result of which was, that Mr. SHAFTOE, of Whitworth, should be invited to come forward on the occasion, to oppose Mr. TWEDDEL. Mr. SHAFTOE's answer was, that he wished to decline the honour intended him. The respectable body of Freemen were by no means satisfied with the reply, and held another meeting to deliberate further on the business, when it was agreed upon to make a second application to Mr. SHAFTOE. They accordingly sent him a petition, signed by upwards of 260 respectable Freemen. This proceeding had the effect, and Mr. SHAFTOE declared his intention of offering himself a candidate for the city on Monday last, when shouts of joy resounded in every quarter of the Market-place. Soon after Mr. SHAFTOE had made his intention known, Mr. GOWLAND, whose father had formerly spent vast sums in Durham election contests, arrived there with a view of offering himself; but on learning what had taken place with respect to Mr. SHAFTOE, he shook hands with that gentleman, wished him success, and cheerfully offered him his support. The poll opens this day.

A number of persons who have never been heard of in the British Navy, have of late been raising their voices against the FIRST LORD of the ADMIRALTY, and complaining of the public naval defence. The venerable and heroic Earl knows well how to laugh to scorn these puny whipsters. They are something like a flotilla of Boulogne gun-boats collected round a British seventy-four; and it is very likely some honest man may think with very little better intent.

It is a remarkable circumstance, that neither Mr. SHERIDAN nor Mr. ERSKINE were in their places in the House of Commons, either on Monday or Wednesday.

Some of the suggestions thrown out by Mr. PITT, in Monday's Debate, seem deserving of consideration, which we are by no means prepared to say of all. The line that he took was judicious, though his speech was, as we expected, strongly tinctured with hostility towards the present Government. In the Debate on Wednesday, he paid many compliments to Mr. FOX, from which we leave the Public to draw their own inferences.

Colonel EYRE's manly speech in Wednesday's Debate, was highly creditable to him as an independent Country Gentleman. Mr. FOX seemed to take great pains to do away the impression which it made on the House.

It was pretty well understood, before the Debate took place on Monday, that Sir ROBERT LAWLEY, Sir H. MILDMAY, or some member of Mr. CANNING's little junto, was to move the question of adjournment.

It was not a little remarkable, that even Mr. FOX appeared less anxious to press the question of adjournment on Monday, than his new allies on the Bench below him. What if Mr. WINDHAM should turn Jacobin, and Mr. Fox Aristocrat!! "*Prisca redit Venus*" is, we understand, to be the motto of this disgusting union.

The Electors of Westminster have an undeniable right to applaud their Representative, in some men's view of the subject, as he would leave the inhabitants of towns out of the way of military fatigues. It is the regular army; and the armed *peasantry*, who are to do the business; but no shopkeepers.

Several Ladies of *ton* have lately been seen on horseback, dressed in pelices. Considering, however, their former excellence in equestrian exercises, it must be allowed they had *riding-habits*.

It is not a very gratifying spectacle, to see men of high rank and consequence in the State, sitting on a *coach-box*, and driving their horses; though at the same time, it must be admitted, that nothing is more proper than for persons of exalted station to attend to their *carriage*.

Lord and Lady MIDDLETON arrived in town yesterday.

The Countess of SHAFTESBURY is confined by illness, at her house in Lower Seymour-street.

Count BEAUJOLOIS has taken up his residence at MACDONAGH's Bath Hotel, in Bury-street, St. James's.

We are happy to say that all the differences in the Southwark Corps have at length been amicably adjusted.

The Volunteers who since the 1st of November, have at different times been placed on permanent pay and duty, amount to 23,792, exclusive of commissioned and non-commissioned officers.

Wednesday a large tender conveyed from the *Enterprize*, off the Tower, a great number of impressed seamen and volunteers, for the ships fitting out at the Nore.

PUBLIC OFFICE, BOW-STREET.—Yesterday *William Morgan*, the driver of a hackney-coach, was examined before Sir RICHARD FORD and Mr. ROBINSON, on a charge of wilfully driving his coach against a chair, in which the Duke of PORTLAND was returning from the Opera on Tuesday night last, whereby the chair was broken to pieces, and his Grace's life much endangered. By the testimony of the chairmen, it appeared that as they were crossing Piccadilly, they observed the prisoner driving his coach furiously towards them, when one of them called out to him to stop, but he paid no attention to it, and continued his course, and in a moment the pole struck the glass of the chair, which it shattered to pieces, overturned the chair, and threw down the men, who, as well as his Grace, were in the utmost danger of being trampled to death by the horses; however they fortunately escaped with little injury. The fact being so very clear, the prisoner was ordered to find bail for the assault, and in default was committed to prison. *Thody, Reynolds*, and *How*, the persons in custody on suspicion of divers forgeries, were again examined before Mr. KINNAIRD, when several other persons who had been defrauded by them appeared, and the prisoners were remanded.

ST. JAMES's, March 1.

Lord AMHERST, } in Waiting.
Mr. FANE, }

Among the persons of distinction who left their cards were:—

Foreign Ministers—Spanish, Portuguese, American, Danish, Bavarian, Neapolitan, and Turkish.

Duchess Dorset.

Dukes—Bedford, Athol, and Montrose.

Marchionesses—Buckingham and Downshire.

Marquisses—Salisbury, Cornwallis, Hertford, Lorne, and Thomond.

Countesses—Uxbridge, Rosslyn, Cholmondeley, Bridgewater, Rothes, and Fortescue.

Earls—Dartmouth, Aylesbury, Morton, Chesterfield, Harcourt, Camden, Spencer, Pomfret, Stair, Coventry, Portsmouth, Winchelsea, Temple, Carlisle, Errol, Caernarvon, Bristol, Limerick, Darnley, Malmesbury, Effingham, Mount Norris, and Fortescue.

Bishops—London, Winchester, St. Asaph, Hereford, Ferne, Durham, and the Rev. E. Legg.

Ladies—Huntingfield, Walpole, Howard, Campbell, Reed, Cornwall, Dacre, C. Herbert, Alvanley, Bishop, Douglas, Folkes, Bankes, Bradford, C. Somerset, Castlereagh, Melville, Buxton, Walsingham, Radstock, and M. Parker.

Lords—Falmouth, Sydney, Wentworth, Walsingham, Cremorne, Huntingfield, Northwick, Boston, Yarborough, Selsey, Stopford, Morpeth, Porchester, Henley, Auckland, Whitworth, Radstock, Boringdon, Newark, Brome, Hinchinbrook, L. Gower, C. Somerset, Bayning, Minto, Soudes, Folkestone, Carleton, Gray, and Hotham.

Sirs—H. Strachey, H. Hill, W. Elford, W. Curtis, W. Geary, C. Cave, W. Dolbin, P. Hales, R. Anslie, J. Colleton, J. Harrington, C. Morgan, R. King, J. Wrottesley, and R. C. Glynn.

Admirals—Nugent, and Milbank.

Generals—Rainsford, Ross, Balfour, Ogilvy, Bertie, Craig, Stuart, Tarleton, Leeland, and Walpole.

Colonels—Gray, Dalrymple, and Macguire.

Mistresses—Barrington, Yorke, C. Yorke, Fisher, Bragge, Brown, Mainwaring, Blackburne, Law, R. Benyon, Lawrell, Lisle, Bridgman, Simpson, Freemantle, Bland, Randof, and Sutton.

Misses—De Gray, Vanneck, Louth, Cornwall, Banks, Addington, Hussey, Law, Courtney, and Chester.

Messrs.—Abbot (Speaker), Angerstein, Cooper, Smyth, Golding, Egerton, R. Walpole, Adams, Bragg, H. Addington, Fordice, Bootle, Tierney, Brown, Sloan, G. Vansittart, N. Vansittart, Poole, Howard, G. Villers, H. Lascelles, Stratton, Gray, Windham, Canning, Reynolds, Lawrell, Rose, Sargent, Wm. Dundas, Cameron, Corry, the Recorder, and the two Sheriffs of London.

COUNTESS OF CHOLMONDELEY's ROUT.

Her Ladyship gave a grand rout to about 300 of the *haut ton*, on Wednesday evening. Nearly one hundred excuses were sent in consequence of indisposition; the company, notwithstanding, consisted of as fashionable an assemblage as any that has met this season. Amongst the persons of distinction present were—

Duchesses—Bolton, and Dowager Leeds.

Marchionesses—Salisbury, Bath, and Downshire.

Countesses—Jersey, Fortescue, Ashburnham, Bristol, Darnley, Dowager Buckinghamshire, Clare, Cardigan, and Carlisle.

Margravine of Anspach.

Ladies—E. Fortescue, G. Cecil, two Thynnes, Folkes, De Dunstanville, Manners, Hort, Graves, Stewart, Cranley, Townsend, Morpeth, H. Cavendish, Amherst, Auckland, Castlereagh, L. Corry, L. Brome, Perth, Rumbold, Walpole, Wynne, Boston, E. Stratford, Cornewall, J. Harrington, Croftons, Banks, Langford, Melbourne, E. Howard, and J. Howard.

Mistresses—Fane, Grigg, Pierrepoint, Sturt, Duff, Orby Hunter, Banks, Wheeler, Wortley, Rigby, North, Tarleton, Erskine, Barry, Davidson, Vaughan, Walker, Walpole, Montello, Weddell, Crow, Bouverie, W. Freemantle, and Brown.

Misses—Two Croftons, Crow, Banks, Richards, Cornewall, Hervey, W. Wynn, Walpole, two Rumbolds, Hussey, Mure, Folkes, Manners, Monk, Hanson, Whitbread, Coleman, Broderick, Methuen, Craven, two Edens, two Townsends, two Norths, Barry, Drummond, Vaughan, and Bennett.

Earls—Jersey, Westmoreland, Bristol, and Darnley.

Lords—Dungannon, Cowper, Graves, G. Seymour, Langford, Amherst, Borringdon, Auckland, Chetwynd, Boston, Sydney, Villiers, Newark, St. Helens, Clonmell, and Harewood.

Sir W. W. Wynne.

Portuguese Ambassador.

General Stanhope.

Colonel Bligh.

Baron Armagh.

Messrs.—T. Hope, Gregg, Skeffington, Orby Hunter, Wheeler, Jenkinson, Coleman, Lascelles, Wortley, K. Cravan, Rigby, B. North, Davidson, T. Grosvenor, D. North, G. Cholmondeley, Bouverie, W. Irby, Blunt, M. Lewis, and Freemantle.

LADIES' CONCERT.

The first Ladies Concert of Vocal and Instrumental Music, was held last night at Mrs. BENYON's, Grosvenor-square, which was attended by nearly 200 subscribers of fashionable celebrity.—The following were the selections for the evening, under the direction of Mrs. KING:—

ACT I.—Sestetto—*Mozart*. Song, Signor ROVEDINO—*Cimarosa*. 'Vado in giro nei palchetti.'—Duetto, Sig. VIGANONI and Mrs. BIANCHI—*Paesiello*. 'Ah! momento fortunato.'—Concertante, Horns, Messrs. PETRIDES.—Song, Miss MISSENDEN—*Boyce*. 'Softly rise, O southern breeze.'—Terzetto, Signor VIGANONI, Signor ROVEDINO, and Miss MISSENDEN—*Mozart*. 'Ah Taci ingiusto core.'

ACT II.—Concerto Clarionet, Mr. W. MAHON.—Song, Mrs. BIANCHI.—*Handel*. 'Angels ever bright and fair.'—Song, Signor VIGANONI—*Sarti*. 'Bella bea cui degl' anni.'—Echo, Horns—*Petrides*.—Song, Mrs. BIANCHI—*Bianchi*. 'Nel silenzio i mesti passi.'—Quartetto, Signor VIGANONI, Signor ROVEDINO, Miss MISSENDEN, and Mrs. BIANCHI—*Guglielmi*. 'Perfido! a questo eccesso.'

MOZART's Sestetto was performed in the first style of excellence; the first Violin, by SALOMON. The Duetto "*Ah momento fortunato*," was given with great effect, by Sig. VIGANONI and Mrs. BIANCHI, who was introduced to the Ladies Concert for the first time last evening. Dr. BOYCE's Song, "Softly arise, O southern breeze," was happily executed by Miss MISSENDEN.—Mrs. BIANCHI's Song in the second Act, "Angels ever bright and fair," was given with taste, and went off with great *eclat*. The whole performance was such as to excite the admiration of the company.

LONDON FASHIONS FOR MARCH.

FULL DRESSES.—1. A round dress of Egyptian brown or puce coloured sarsnet. The body made quite plain, very low in the back and over the bosom. Sleeves of white satin trimmed with lace. Cap of white satin or muslin, trimmed with pink and black velvet; a bunch of heron feathers fixed on the left side; white shoes, swansdown muff and tippet.—2. A robe of slate coloured sarsnet, with sleeves of lace and muslin, or worked muslin; a lace tucker drawn across the bosom. A turban of slate coloured satin to match the dress, ornamented with pearls or diamonds and heron feathers. White shoes.—3. A robe of white satin trimmed with swansdown; white tippet. A Spanish hat of black velvet turned up on one side, and ornamented with a black feather.—2. Round dress of white or coloured muslin, with a fur tippet. The hair dressed and ornamented with an elegant tiara and combs.

HEAD DRESSES.—1. A cap of white crape, trimmed round the front and to the top of the crown with white lace; a bunch of roses in front.—2. A hat of pink crape trimmed round the front, and ornamented with flowers.—3. A cap of buff satin trimmed with pink and black velvet, and a deep lace border.—4. A cap of white crape, trimmed with white ribbon and a bunch of flowers.—5. A cap of buff satin, with a large twist of white crape round the front, and a very long end on the left side; a bunch of roses in front.—6. A turban of yellow crape; the crown flat with a very large twist round the front, ornamented with pearls and yellow feathers.—7. A turban of blue crape and white satin, ornamented with blue feathers.—8. A hat of Etruscan silk, ornamented with a willow feather.—9. A cap of white crape, ornamented with pink lillies. A lace border.

GENERAL OBSERVATIONS.—The prevailing colours are Egyptian brown, buff, and pink. The dresses still continue to be made very low, and lace is introduced into almost every part of them. Turbans are much worn. The hair when dressed without a turban, is in large bows; and ornamented with pearl or diamond combs. Large silk shawls of a new fabric, in imitation of leopard's spot, are much worn, for the Opera and Play. Black velvet pelices, and spencers, continue to form the walking-dress.

SHIP NEWS.

PLYMOUTH, *Feb.* 28.—Arrived the *British Fair* cutter, of 14 guns, Lieut. PRICE, Commander, with dispatches from Lord NELSON, whose fleet she left cruizing off Majorca, at which time the Toulon squadron had not sailed, though they were apparently all ready for a start the first favourable opportunity; sailed from Gibraltar 18 days since, from whence she also brought dispatches, the whole of which were forwarded last night to the Admiralty.—Arrived the *Sirius* frigate from the Channel fleet.

PORTSMOUTH, *Feb.* 29.—Sailed the *Montague* man of war, to join the Channel fleet; and *Eurydice* frigate for Yarmouth.—The *Charlotte* schooner is appointed convoy for Guernsey.

Yesterday morning early an alarming fire broke out at the house of a foreign artist, in Winchester-street, Paddington. The flames were first discovered at the top of the house, by some men who were going to work, and who gave the alarm to the family. The fire raged violently from the upper part of the house, while three children attracted the notice of the spectators, in momentary expectation of being lost in the flames: they were, with difficulty, rescued from their awful situation; soon after which two of them expired in excruciating agony, and the other is not expected to survive. By the arrival of the engines the fire was subdued, after having burnt the upper part of the house.

MARRIED.

Yesterday, at St. George's, Bloomsbury, Richard Boulton, Esq. eldest son of Henry Boulton, Esq. of Thorncroft, Leatherhead, Surrey, to Miss Carolina Shubrick, third daughter of the late Richard Shubrick, Esq.

DIED.

On Thursday, the 16th inst. at Brill, after a few days illness, the Rev. Joseph Laurentius Littlehales, LL.D. Rector of Grendon Underwood, and Curate of the perpetual Curacy of Brill and Boarstall, in the county of Bucks, and one of his Majesty's Justices of the Peace for that county.

CORN-EXCHANGE, Wednesday, Feb. 29.

We had not many fresh samples of Wheat; fine was 1s. dearer. Ordinary had scarce any buyers, Prime Dantzic fetched about 60s. per quarter. The supplies of Barley were very large, which caused a decline of 1s. per quarter. Malt cheaper, and but little sold, expecting it lower. Peas, with Beans of each kind, at little difference. Not having many Oats they sold at an advance of 1s. Flour in good supply, fine American 32s. per barrel.

Wheat, - - -	26s 36s a 54s 0d	Beans, - - - - -	30s a 36s 0d
Fine ditto, - - -	55s a 56s 6d	Tick ditto, - - -	27s a 32s 0d
Barley, - - - - -	17s a 21s 6d	Oats, - -	17s a 19s a 23s 0d
Malt, - - - - - -	47s a 54s 0d	Poland ditto, - -	24s a 25s 0d

PRICE OF STOCKS.

3 p. Ct. Red. Ann. shut	Short Ann. shut
3 p. Ct. Cons. Ann. 55 ½ ⅝	Imp. 3 p. Ct. 54 ⅞
4 p. Ct. 72 ⅞ 73 ½ 73	Imp. Ann. 9 7-10ths
5 p. Ct. Navy 88 ¾ ⅞	Omnium 3 dis.
5 p. Ct. 1797 94 ¼ 95 94 ⅞	Lottery Tickets, 17l. 8s.
L. Ann. shut	Cons. for Acc. 56 ⅛ 56

Last Price.—Cons. for Mon. 55 ⅞—Do. Acc. 56—Omnium 3.

HAZARD, BURNE, WARNER, and Co.
STOCK-BROKERS, No. 93, Royal Exchange.

WANT PLACES.

AS HOUSEKEEPER to a single Gentleman or Lady, or as COOK in a small Family, a middle-aged woman. Direct, post-paid, to A. S. No. 4, Printing-house-lane, Water-lane, Blackfriars.

AS LADY's MAID, a young Person, who understands mantua-making and getting up fine linen, works well at her needle, &c.; wishes to travel; has no objection to live in the country. Direct to A. B. at Mr. Hale's, Shoemaker, No. 1, Cleveland-street, Fitzroy-square.

AS UPPER HOUSEMAID, or HOUSEMAID in a small genteel family; no objection to wait at table, and can have a good recommendation from her last place. Direct, post-paid, to T. B. No. 84, Great Tower-street.

A STEADY MIDDLE-AGED MAN, in a Merchant's Counting-house, or on a Wharf; has been many years used to the water-side business on a wharf: can be well recommended, and give security if required. No objection to superintend a warehouse. Direct for I. H. at Mr. Collins's, No. 23, St. Thomas's-street, Southwark.

SALES BY AUCTION.

Superb Collection from the Borghese, and other Palaces.

MR. CHRISTIE has the honour to acquaint the Nobility, Public, and the Cognoscenti in particular, that he will submit to Sale by Auction, THIS DAY, at the Great Room, in Pall-Mall, one of the most superb assemblages of ITALIAN PICTURES, ever brought to this country, the whole recently consigned from Rome. This collection is composed of chef-d'œuvres, selected from the treasures of the Borghese, Colonna, Doria, Aldobrnadini, Ghigi, Cavalieri, Rospigliosi, and Bolognetti Palaces, most of them actually painted for these several families, as shall be made appear to the purchasers by original documents and papers. Among them are the following inestimable:—A Crucifixion, with the Virgin of St. John (upon a Tabernacle) painted by M. Angelo Buonarotti, for the Oratory of the Cavalieri Palace, the Virgin, Infant Christ with St. John, St. Catherine and a Bishop, by Titian; an Assumption of the Virgin, Palma the younger; Christ taken down from the Cross, Bramante; the Marriage of St. Catherine, J. Romano; and a Descent from the Cross, Lud. Carracci, all from the Borghese Palace. A Magdalen Guido, from the Pallazzo Ghigi, the Visitation of St. Elizabeth, by Al. Buonvicino, from the Aldobrandini, and a view of Prince Colonna's Palace at Genezerario, by Claude, from the Colonna Palace.

It is hoped the short time allowed for making known the sale of this collection, will not prevent its recommending itself to the notice of the public, who may be assured that a similar exhibition and sale have never before been witnessed in this country. May be viewed 3 days preceding.

Capital Italian Pictures.—By Mr. CHRISTIE,
At the Great Room, Pall-mall, THIS DAY, March 2, at 12,

A Capital and singularly valuable COLLECTION, being a select Consignment of the very superior Class of PICTURES in the great Italian Schools, unique in point of rarity and excellence. Among them the connoisseurs will recognise the celebrated Holy Family by Andrea del Sarto, not long since imported from Italy; a picture that, for design and execution, may be deemed the finest of his works, equal to Raphael; a Nymph reposing in a landscape, Titian, one of his very finely coloured pictures; an Entertainment by Grotto, a noble Landscape, with the Temptation of our Saviour, from the Jesuits Church, at Rome, S. Rosa, particularly commended by Vatari, and others, capital and rare, in the finest preservation. Also an Assemblage of capital Italian, French, Flemish, and Dutch Pictures; including a noble picture of the Master by Giorgione; a Holy Family, a chaste and elegant composition, P. Veronese; the well known Jupiter and Amalthea by Jordaeus, from the collection of the late Sir Gregory Page, a chef d'œuvre, and others of distinguished merit. May be viewed 2 days preceding the sale, when catalogues may be had in Pall-Mall.

To Architects, and others.—By Mr. CHRISTIE,
At the Great Room, in Pall-Mall, on Wednesday, March 7, at 12 o'clock, by order of the Executors,

THE capital SET of highly-finished VIEWS of DUBLIN, the original drawings in water-colours, which have furnished the plates for that admired work, entitled, "Views of the City of Dublin, by the late ingenious and scientific Artist, James Malton, Esq. deceased;" together with the Copper-plates, Impressions, and Letter-press of that and his other popular works, viz. On Cottage Architecture, Ornamental Villas, the Painter's Maulstick, Stonehenge, and others on Geometry and Perspective. Also, his Collection of Architectural Designs, Studies, and Models, Books of Architecture and Prints, Sketches and Views from Nature, and a choice assemblage of original Drawings, by the late R. Hamilton, Esq. R. A. hitherto reserved from public sale.—May be viewed 2 days preceding, when Catalogues may be had in Pall-Mall.

Elegant Furniture, Portland-Place.—By Mr. CHRISTIE,
On the Premises, on Thursday, March 9, and following day, at 12,

ALL the neat and singularly elegant HOUSEHOLD FURNITURE, large French plate glasses, and other effects, the property of J. L. GREFFULHE, Esq. removing from No. 33, in Portland-place, the corner of Devonshire-street. The Furniture comprises drawing-room suits of fine cotton, made up in the most fashionable style, large ottomans, &c. en suite; large French plate glasses, excellent mahogany dining-room furniture, capital bedding, and various effects; the greatest part nearly new, and in the neatest condition.—May be viewed 2 days preceding the sale, when catalogues may be had in Pall-Mall.

By LEIGH, SOTHEBY, and SON,
In York-street, Covent-Garden, THIS DAY, March 2, and the 4 following days, (Sundays excepted) at 12 o'clock,

THE LIBRARY of a CLERGYMAN, lately deceased, consisting of a good Collection of Books, in Divinity, History, Voyages and Travels, Natural History, Classics, Natural Philosophy, Mathematics, Poetry, and Miscellanies.—Catalogues at the place of sale.

SALES BY AUCTION.

Genuine and Prime Constantia Wine from the Cape,
By Mr. H. PHILLIPS,
At his Great Room, No. 67, New Bond-street, To-MORROW, March 3, at 1 o'clock,

ONE Hundred and Eleven Dozen of Pint Bottles of RED and WHITE CONSTANTIA WINE, of pure and unadulterated quality, rich and highly flavoured, the property of a GENTLEMAN, lately returned from the Cape, and by whom it was purchased of Mr. Harry Claete, the proprietor of the great Constantia Farm at the Cape. The most unequivocal proof of the genuine purity and superior excellence of this wine, as also of its being the real produce of the vineyard, are deposited in the hands of Mr. Phillips. It will be allotted in small parcels, and samples may be had, upon paying for, at Mr. Phillips's. Catalogues may be had at the York Hotel, Bridge-street, Blackfriars; Mr. Lloyd's, Bookseller, Harley-street; and as above.

Cellar of French and Foreign Wines, London Particular Madeira, &c.—By Mr. H. PHILLIPS,
At his Great Room, No. 67, New Bond-street, To-MORROW, March 3, at 1 o'clock, and following day,

A CELLAR of choice and excellent WINES, in wood and bottles, of approved vintages, and warranted fine qualities, comprising London Particular Madeira, 4 pipes, in the Hon. East India Company's Vaults; Old Port, 140 dozen; New Port, 223 dozen; Claret, 3 hogsheads and 12 dozen; Constantia, red and white, 40 dozen; and Sherry, 86 dozen, together with about 112 dozen of Champagne, Burgundy, Bucellas, Lisbon, Calcavella, Noyeau, red and white Coniac Brandy, &c. —Samples may be had 3 days preceding the sale, upon paying for as above, with catalogues, which may be had at the York Hotel, Bridge-street, Blackfriars; and at Mr. Lloyd's, Bookseller, Harleys-treet.

Ladies Wardrobe of elegant Laces, Veils, Muslins, Long Cloths, Shawls, &c.—By Mr. H. PHILLIPS,
At his Great Room, No. 67, New Bond-street, on Tuesday, March 6, at 12 o'clock,

A LADY's WARDROBE of elegant LACES, VEILS, CLOAKS, beautiful India Muslins, Long Cloths and Shawls of rich Patterns, Feathers, Cornelian Necklaces, Pearls and Jewellery, the genuine property of a Lady of Rank, deceased, removed from her residence, Kensington. The principal part whereof are new and of very superior description, and of beautiful patterns.—May be viewed the day preceding the Sale, and Catalogues had at the York Hotel, Bridge-street, Blackfriars; Mr. Lloyd's, Bookseller, Harley-street; and No. 67, New Bond-street.

Farm and Estate, High Suffolk.
By Mr. H. PHILLIPS,
At his Great Room, 67, New Bond-street, on Wednesday, March 7, instead of the 28th instant (as before advertised) at 12 o'clock, unless previously disposed of by Private Contract, of which timely notice will be given,

A Valuable and desirable ESTATE, known by the name of HILL FARM, consisting of a Farm House, with out-buildings and other conveniences, and 92 acres (more or less) of rich land, 42 acres of which, or thereabouts, are meadow and pasture land, and the remainder arable; about 12 acres are copyhold of inheritance, and the remainder freehold. The above estate is situated partly in the parish of Hoxne, and partly in the parish of Horham, in the county of Suffolk, and exclusive of 1 field, containing about 4 acres, lies in a ring fence, and is now in the occupation of Mr. ROBERT WILSON, as tenant, by lease for a term of which 17 years were unexpired at Michaelmas last, at the annual rent of 100l. To be viewed by leave of the tenant. For further particulars, or to treat by Private Contract, apply to Messrs. Tahourdin, Solicitors, Argyll-street, of whom printed particulars may be had; also of the tenant, on the premises; at the White Hart Inn, Scole; and of Mr. Phillips, 67, New Bond-street.

Clocks, Watches, and Time Pieces.—By Mr. H. PHILLIPS,
At his Great Room, 67, New Bond-street, on Thursday, March 8, at 12 o'clock,

THE genuine and valuable STOCK in TRADE, comprising a variety of capital and excellent gold and silver stop watches and chronometers, hunting watches, elegant musical and plain clocks and time-pieces, dials, &c. by that esteemed maker, Mr. JAMES TREGENT, retiring from business, and removing from his magazine, Cranborne-street, Leicester-square. And a small collection of prints, in port folios, intended for exportation. May be viewed 2 days preceding the sale, and catalogues had as above; at the York Hotel, Bridge-street, Blackfriars; and at Mr. Lloyd's, bookseller, Harley-street.

Compact Residence, Blackheath.—By Mr. H. PHILLIPS,
On the Premises, Grote's-buildings, Blackheath, on Monday, March 12, at 12 o'clock,

A Compact LEASEHOLD HOUSE, with convenient and well arranged suits of domestic apartments and offices, coach-house and four-stall stable, excellent kitchen garden well cropped and planted, and small pleasure garden and spacious fore-court, fenced by iron pallisadoes and gates, the property and late residence of WM. INNES, Esq. deceased. The Premises are pleasantly and airily situate on the South-side of Blackheath, about 4 miles from London; are held on lease for 23 years, at a low annual rent of 40l.—May be viewed by tickets, to be had of Mr. H. Phillips, No. 67, New Bond-street.

Pipe of Madeira, Port, Sherry, &c.—By Mr. H. PHILLIPS,
At his Great Room, No. 67, New Bond-street, on Wednesday, March 14, at 1 o'clock, by order of the Executors,

THE CELLAR of genuine and excellent WINES of the late Mr. WM. CONSTABLE, of Sackville-street, Jeweller, deceased, principally imported by himself, comprising a Pipe of choice and highly-flavoured Madeira, and about 120 dozen of Old Port, Sherry, Madeira, and Lisbon, and a few dozens of English Fruit and made Wines, which, with the foreign, are esteemed of superior qualities. The delivery to the purchasers will be from the private residence of the late Mr. Constable. —May be tasted at the time of sale, and Catalogues had as above; at the York Hotel, Bridge-street, Blackfriars; and at Mr. Lloyd's, Bookseller, Harley-street.

Modern Furniture, Church-End, Willsden.
By Mr. H. PHILLIPS,
On the Premises, on Monday, March 15, and following day, at 12,

ALL the genuine and modern HOUSEHOLD FURNITURE, pier and chimney glasses, mirrors, pictures, prints and china; farming and gardening implements; a mangle; and a variety of valuable and useful effects. The Furniture comprises excellent four-post and field-bedsteads, rich cotton and dimity hangings, seasoned and prime bedding, an assortment of mahogany domestic furniture, set of parlour chairs, covered with red morocco, drawing-room suite, carpets, culinary; and every requisite article of furniture.—May be viewed Friday and Saturday preceding the Sale, and catalogues had on the premises, at the York Hotel, Bridge-street, Blackfriars; and at Mr. H. Phillips's, 67, New Bond-street.

Leasehold Cottage, Church End, Willsden.
By Mr. H. PHILLIPS.
On the Premises, on Monday, March 15, at 12 o'clock.

A Compact COTTAGE HOUSE, with roomy stabling, standing for carriages, large barn, and every requisite domestic and farming office, fore court, kitchen garden, and pleasure ground, late in the occupation of EDWARD GIBBONS, Esq. together with fifteen acres of rich meadow and pasture land; the situation is pleasant and retired, at Church End, Willsden, Middlesex, about 4 miles from London, held by lease for about 15 years, at 50l. per annum.—May be viewed, and printed particulars had on the premises; at the York Hotel, Bridge-street, Blackfriars; and of Mr. H. Phillips, 67, New Bond-street.

Freehold Land, Thorpe, Surrey.—By Mr. BALDWIN,
At the Swan Inn, Chertsey, Surrey, on Wednesday, March 14, at 3 in the afternoon, (if not disposed of by Private Contract, of which due notice will be given)

FORTY-ONE ACRES (more or less) of FREEHOLD ARABLE and MEADOW LAND, situated in Thorpe-fields and Norlands, in the parish of Thorpe, in the county aforesaid, now in the occupation of Mr. Richard Reeves, tenant at will. The above Estate consists of some of the best arable land in Thorpe-field; and of that well-known good meadow land, in Norlands. An early inclosure being about to take place, the purchaser will become entitled to all the advantages thereof, and a proportionate share of the common land of the parish, which has ever been considered exceeding good.—For particulars, apply to Mr. Cole, Attorney, at Windsor, who is authorised to treat for the same, or Mr. Baldwin, Chertsey.

Grove House and Land, Tooting, Surry, with immediate possession.—By Mr. SAVILL,
Early in April, (unless an acceptable offer is previously made)

THE remaining Term of Lease of Grove House; situate at the extremity of Lower Tooting, on the Epsom Road. The residence is replete with suitable apartments to accommodate a large and respectable family; in complete repair and perfect order; is delightfully placed in a full grown shrubbery and pleasure ground, ornamented with lofty trees, double coach-house, excellent stabling for 6 horses, paved yard and out-offices, a beautiful paddock, and 3 inclosures of rich and fertile arable and grass land, containing 46 acres or thereabouts. The kitchen gardens at an agreeable distance from the dwelling, are enclosed with lofty brick walls and oak fence; the ground is abundantly cropped, and the walls covered with prime fruit-trees; a commodious farm-yard, with bailiff's cottage, barn, granary, cow-house, calf-pens, pig-sties, cart-house, and stack-yard. Tickets for viewing, and further particulars may be had of Mr. Savill, Aldgate High-street.

THE TIMES TUESDAY MAY 3 1966 FASHION FOR WOMEN 19

NEW READERS START HERE

For the first of the new daily women's pages the theme is fashion; and the fashion is suits. Now that May is here, the suit really does become a feasible fashion proposition, because the gap in temperature between outdoors and indoors has narrowed until you can move freely from one to the other without adding or subtracting clothes in order to be comfortable. The usual problem with a suit is that if you are warm enough in it in the street you swelter indoors and are forced to peel off the jacket, revealing what appears to be a separate outfit—sweater and skirt or blouse and skirt—which is frequently not formal enough for, say, a lunch engagement.

The ideal suit is one that can accommodate a sweater or shirt for more treacherous days, but is also cut to allow you to wear it on its own when heat or occasion requires. Warm days call too for a skirt that is easy to move around in, pleated perhaps for extra coolness and crisp appearance.

Women are buying more clothes, and cheaper clothes, these days. Whereas "one good winter coat" used to be the rule, many girls now buy two or even three, and several summer coats too. The fashion page will therefore generally show several items of the same genre so that readers on the lookout for a specific type of garment will be able to get an idea of what is available in that type, and at what price range. The merchandise will always justify its price—if it is expensive it will be because experience has shown that a satisfactory similar garment is not available any cheaper.

It is fashionable just now to use young-looking models in photographs—10 years ago it was the more sophisticated types such as Barbara Goalen who made teenagers wail that there were no clothes around for them.

The answer is simple. Take no notice of the face, if it is not your age group. Just look at the clothes in a detached way. If the knees worry you, remember that sample clothes are always made to be worn just a little more extreme than they will be by women who ultimately buy them.

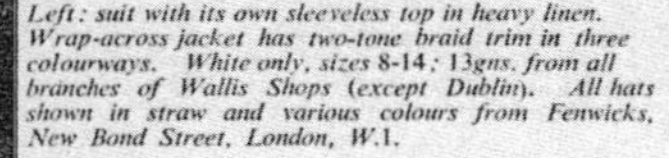

Left: suit with its own sleeveless top in heavy linen. Wrap-across jacket has two-tone braid trim in three colourways. White only, sizes 8-14; 13gns. from all branches of Wallis Shops (except Dublin). All hats shown in straw and various colours from Fenwicks, New Bond Street, London, W.1.

Above left: suit in lightweight wool, collarless and long-jacketed, fastens with demure bow. In blue, orange, lemon or pink. Sizes 10-14; £13 2s. 6d. from all branches of Richard Shops—or write to Mail Order Dept., Richard Shops, 364 Kensington High Street, London, W.14.

Above: suit that is really matching separates, in linen-look fabric. Jacket £4 19s. 6d., pleated skirt 4gns. Both in sizes 10-18; choice of six colours. From Peter Robinson (London and Sheffield), Riceman's (Canterbury), Kempthornes (Richmond), Kendal Milne (Manchester), Darlings (Edinburgh).

Photographs by Barry Lategan

Drawings by Alan Cracknell

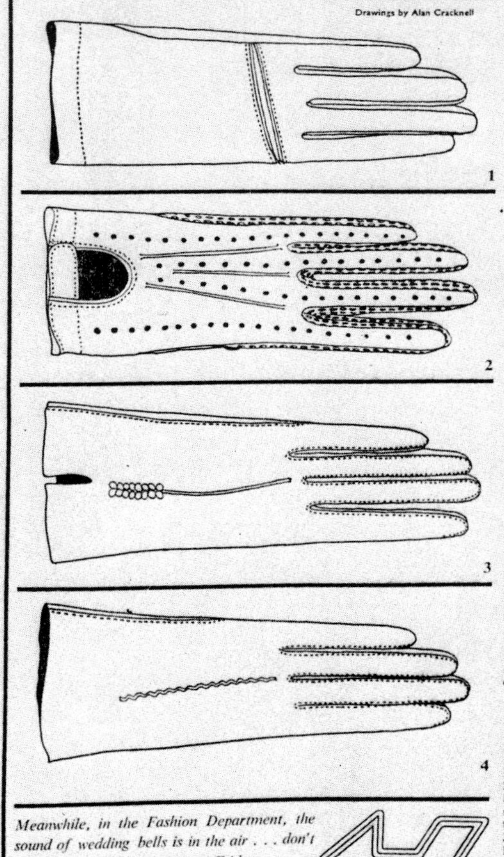

Death to the long white glove?

Very short white gloves have long been the prerogative of American business girls and Minnie Mouse. Over here, the longness and paleness of gloves was almost a status symbol.

At the last Paris Collections, however, one fact emerged with chalk-white clarity: that the new sleeve length, which ends just above the elbow—in many cases with a turn-up cuff—needs just the shortest ever white gloves to balance it.

Once your eye has grown accustomed to seeing a slice of bare arm between glove and cuff, even with longer sleeves the effect is much younger and prettier now.

Gloves are one of the things that should always be of the best quality you can afford; pale gloves particularly should always be in glacé leather or suede. Now that the finest leathers are washable, pale gloves are no longer the preserve of the fortunate few who could afford to have them cleaned after every wearing—and could afford enough pairs not to go bare-handed while they were away.

When buying gloves, always stipulate that they must be washable—Pittards guaranteed leathers, for example, are excellent. Wash your gloves carefully and *frequently* in a special shampoo such as Five Star, and don't panic when they dry out after the most gentle handling looking like wizened Chinaman's skin. Remain calm, stretch the leather carefully between your fingers, and the colour miraculously reappears. White gloves are especially alarming to wash, but they really do come up chalky again.

And, by the way, that old-fashioned implement of the dressing table, a glove stretcher, is invaluable for moulding washed leather gloves back into shape.

1. Knuckle-bender style glove by Kir has elasticized wrist for closer fit. 2gns.
2. String sides and perforated cut-out back—ideal for hot weather driving or sporty occasions. Elasticized wrist has tab velcro-d fastening. By Kir, 2gns.
3. Formal soft town glove by Milore has minuscule embroidery near wrist. About £3 5s.
4. Classic casual glove, handstitched. By Milore, about £3 5s. 0d.
All gloves in pale leathers, guaranteed washable, by Pittard.

Meanwhile, in the Fashion Department, the sound of wedding bells is in the air . . . don't miss the next fashion page on Friday.
Tomorrow: the women's page will be interviewing people in the news.

Invective

It would be romantic to pretend that all good men have always recognized the shining merits of the great newspaper. It would not be true. Any newspaper that impudently set itself up as an independent fourth estate of the realm, with its own opinions on affairs of state which it proclaimed loudly and with devastating effect, was bound to attract opposition and invective from those who thought they had a monopoly on statesmanship. *The Times* annoyed the great and the good into paroxysms of indignation, so that they gave the appearance of having contracted rabies. On occasions this is still its function. Of all papers *The Times* has a tradition to question received wisdom, to champion the unfashionable, to say the unsayable.

Right From its first year of publication THE TIMES made a practice of reviewing the annual exhibition of art at the Royal Academy. Often a notice would be spread over two, or even three days. An article in 1823 on the arts stated 'we will most liberally praise the praiseworthy, but we cannot give up the privilege of using the rod' – a stricture, obviously taken to heart by this reviewer, 4 May 1841.

means the sort of personage intended by the author of the fairy tale. The picture is nevertheless a work of very high merit.

No. 125. " Portrait of Miss Milman," H. P. Brigge, R.A.—This is a huge unmeaning portrait, occupying the space that should be left for better pictures.

No. 176. " The Seat of Prince Albert of Cobourg, near Cobourg," J. M. W. Turner, R. A.—Here is a picture that represents nothing in nature beyond eggs and spinach. The lake is a composition in which salad oil abounds, and the art of cookery is more predominant then the art of painting.

No. 206. " To arms, to arms, ye brave," W. Etty, R. A.—Mr. Etty should know better than paint such nonsense. Here is a parcel of half naked people struggling and tussling, without any motive, and exposing their persons in a way that calls for the interference of the police.

No. 223. One of those grand and correct representations of the Templar of Upper Egypt. By Mr. D. Roberts, R. A.—It is a very noble picture.

No. 242. " Poor Law Guardians." C. W. Cope.—This is

Right below Prince Lieven was the Russian ambassador in London 1812–34. His wife acquired some fame and considerable criticism for her political influence – a practice which received short shrift from the editor of THE TIMES, Thomas Barnes, as his leading article demonstrates, 23 May 1834. The princess maintained her contacts with England after her departure; her letters to Palmerston spanned the years 1828–56.

it could not make him great.

The recall of Prince LIEVEN, or, rather, of Madame la Princesse, is an "event." We cannot say of her Serene Highness that the "petit nez *retroussé*" has occasioned much mischief, whatever her organs of speech or her implements of writing may have done; nor indeed is it quite credible that the cause commonly assigned for this earthquake in the diplomatic world should be the true one—viz. Her Highness's appetite for meddling in politics, and assuming the direction of every Cabinet in Europe, because any time for almost these 20 years she had given abundant provocation of that kind. There never figured on the Courtly stage a female intriguer more restless, more arrogant, more mischievous, more (politically, and therefore we mean it not offensively) odious and insufferable than this supercilious Ambassadress. She fancied herself "a power." She was, however, more frequently a dupe, the dupe of her own artifices reacted upon by those of others. Her Serene Highness would have put down this journal—would she not? She would have flung us bodily into the Thames on more than one occasion, as a certain illustrious ex-Minister, no doubt, could testify. But, alas! the Thames is not the Neva. In England no fine lady can command a public functionary to administer the knout to those poor wretches who may happen to offend her—at any rate, Count MATUSCHEWITZ has some claim to an additional decoration. He has at last, and after a long struggle, well executed his *delicate* task.

Those who have attacked *The Times* form a formidable batting team. Their invective is nearly as good as the Commination prayers in the Prayer Book for Ash Wednesday.

In 1846 Prince Albert, the Prince Consort, called *The Times* 'that wicked paper' and suggested that it could be 'got over by giving it exclusive information'. Like many politicians Albert could not conceive of a paper that took its own line in the national interest, without favouring friends or attacking enemies in high places. Delane was one of the first journalists who could not be bought, even by exclusive information. Royal disapprobation of *The Times* was aggravated by the line the paper took in the Crimean War. Buckingham Palace considered it unpatriotic. In fact, the patriotism that saved the Army was shown by Printing House Square.

The politicians were as alarmed as the Palace by the unbiddable independence of the new power in the land. In 1856 Lord John Russell wrote to Clarendon: 'For me who have had my full feast of office it does not much matter, but if England is ever to be England again, this vile tyranny of *The Times* must be cut off'. Russell had been part of the Ministry that had been forced from office during the Crimean War, largely by the thunderbolts from *The Times*. Other less interested parties believed that *The Times* had urged the policy that eventually brought victory, saved the remnant of an army, and brought down a Ministry that would never have won the war. A proposal was made in the City for a public testimonial. Delane declined the honour: 'We can neither claim nor accept any other reward than that which we derive from the belief that we have done the best in our power to merit the favour which the public has so long bestowed on us'. Lord John Russell recognized the dangerous omnipotence of the new power:

> The railway of revolution is made, & it only remains to run a train along it. If you see the evil as I do & many others do, the remedy is in your own hands & Palmerston's; do not make yourselves like poor foolish Molesworth the unconscious tools of a domestic revolution.

The Times was abused from all sides of the political turmoil, by the radicals as well as the reactionaries. It is a sign that the paper is doing its job when zealots of all parties and opinions find it worthy of much improvement. William Cobbett, the great rural riding pamphleteer, coined the epithet 'the bloody old *Times*', deeming Printing House Square insufficiently sympathetic to his crusade for the rural poor and against corruption and greed in high places. The Chartists adopted his slogan. One of their pamphlets declared: 'The bloody old *Times* has such a reputation for unmitigated falsehood and scurrility that the phrase "I'll *Times* you" has become equivalent to "I'll grossly abuse you"'.

The Times was not on the side of the Chartists, at best admitting grudgingly: 'Some decent fellows have, indeed, been induced to join the Chartists'. It came as something of a surprise, therefore, when the Chartists supported the proprietor John Walter II in his first campaign for election to Parliament, at Nottingham in 1841. They turned out in force to an anti-Poor Law meeting convened by him, and turned it into a universal suffrage meeting. *The Times*: 'One of the most disgusting and disgraceful scenes it has ever been our lot to witness'. Chartist paper: 'The most glorious of all glorious victories of the glorious Chartists'.

One of the Chartist leaders explained to Walter why they were supporting him: 'Sir, don't have a wrong idea of the reason why you are to have Chartist support. We mean to use your party to cut the throats of the Whigs, and then we mean to cut your throats also.'

PARLIAMENTARY INTELLIGENCE.

HOUSE OF LORDS, SATURDAY, MARCH 22.

The house sat this day for the purpose of receiving several bills from the Commons, and to forward the bills on the table a stage.

The Earl of SHAFTESBURY took his seat on the woolsack at a quarter past 4 o'clock.

The Lambeth Water-works Bill, the Henfield-road Bill, and the Exeter Market Bill, were read a second time, and ordered to be committed.

Mr. BERNAL, Mr. G. W. WOOD, and other members of the House of Commons, brought up a copy of the report of the committee on the Liverpool Freemen Disfranchisement Bill. The same hon. gentlemen also brought up the Pension Duties' Bill, the Qualification Indemnity Bill, the Smuggling Act Amendment Bill, the Consolidated Fund Bill, and the Northern Union Railway, which bills were severally read a first time.

The house then adjourned to Monday, at half-past 12 o'clock.

HOUSE OF COMMONS, SATURDAY, MARCH 22.

The SPEAKER took the chair at 4 o'clock; there were about 50 members present.

Mr. MILLS brought up the report of the committee on the Brixton Canal-navigation petition.

Mr. J. O'CONNELL brought up the report of the committee on the Dublin and Kingstown Railway petition.

Mr. G. W. WOOD moved the third reading of the Northern Union Railway Bill.—It was read a third time and passed.

Mr. POTTER presented a petition from the Company of Proprietors of the Birmingham Canal-navigation, against the Birmingham and Bilston Railways Bill.—Referred to the committee.

Mr. MILLS brought up the report of the committee on the Carnarvonshire railway petition.

THE PENSION DUTIES BILL.

On the motion of Mr. SPRING RICE, this bill was read a third time and passed.

TITHES—MINISTERIAL PROPOSITION.

Mr. S. RICE moved that on Monday next the house should go into committee on the subject of tithes in England and Wales.—Agreed to.

The same hon. Gentleman gave notice of the intention of Lord Althorp to submit to such committee of the whole house certain resolutions with a view to the commutation of tithes. (Hear.)

POOR-RATES.

Lord NORREYS presented a petition from Thame, in Oxfordshire, complaining of the present burden of poor-rates, and praying the house to adopt some remedial measure.—Laid on the table.

DISSENTERS' DISABILITIES.

Mr. HALL presented a petition from the Protestant Dissenters of Newport, praying to be relieved from all existing disabilities; and one from the Protestant Dissenters of Monmouth, to the same effect.

Mr. GASKELL presented a similar petition from the three congregations of Protestant Dissenters of Wakefield, in Yorkshire.

Mr. M. A. TAYLOR presented a similar petition from the Protestant Dissenters of Sudbury.

Mr. THICKNESSE presented a similar petition, most respectably signed by 2,800 Dissenters of all denominations of the borough of Wigan, the prayer of which was supported by Mr. POTTER.

Mr. SCHOLEFIELD presented a similar petition from the ministers and congregation assembling at Ebenezer Chapel, Birmingham, in which they complained heavily of the injustice of any compulsory payment for the support of a church whose tenets they, from conscience, disavowed. As a proof of the willingness to maintain their own church decently and becomingly, the petitioners stated that in a period of 20 years they had spent between 20,000*l.* and 30,000*l.* on their own place of worship, and in the erection of schools for the moral and religious culture of their children.

All these petitions were laid on the table.

THE BRIGHTON GUARDIAN.

Colonel EVANS presented a petition from a place the name of which we could not hear, praying for an amelioration of the sentence passed on Mr. Cohen, for a libel published in the *Brighton Guardian*; and for an alteration of the law under which his conviction took place.—Laid on the table.

THE STAMP ACTS.

Mr. MURRAY presented a petition from the merchants and traders of Leith, praying for an alteration of the present Stamp (Receipt) Acts.—Laid on the table.

PARLIAMENTARY RECORDS.

Mr. MURRAY presented a petition from the provost and magistrates of Leith, praying that the house would be pleased to forward to the chief magistrate of each district of the kingdom, copies of all reports, bills, and other documents printed or passed by that house, in order that the people might have a more speedy and correct knowledge of the laws they were called upon to obey.—Laid on the table.

INLAND NAVIGATION OF IRELAND.

Mr. JOHN O'CONNELL brought up the report of the committee on the bill for improving the navigation of the rivers, lakes, and estuaries of Ireland.

REGISTRATION OF VOTERS.

Mr. BAILLIE presented a petition from the governors of the poor of Bristol, praying to be relieved from the responsibility and expense of the registration of voters.

OBSERVANCE OF THE SABBATH.

Mr. THICKNESSE presented a petition from the mayor, magistrates, and inhabitants of Wigan, praying for such an amendment of the law as would insure a decorous observance of the Sabbath.

Colonel EVANS presented a petition from certain master bakers of Westminster, praying for a protection from labour on the Sabbath-day.

Mr. SINCLAIR presented a petition from a place in Scotland on the same subject.—Laid on the table.

WEAVERS.—BOARD OF TRADE.

Mr. MAXWELL presented petitions from several bodies of handloom weavers in Lanark, Renfrew, and other parts of Scotland, praying for the establishment of Boards of Trade, and for such other relief as their destitute condition required and the house could supply. The petitioners also prayed that some means should be devised by which they might be enabled to send their children to school. The hon. member heartily supported the prayer of the petitioners, and trusted the house would see the necessity of complying with it.—Laid on the table.

MESSAGE FROM THE LORDS.

Mr. BERNAL moved that the message sent by the Lords on the previous day be read, which was done, and the house in reply directed the hon. gentleman to carry to them the reports applied for.

SOUTHWARK WATER-WORKS.

Colonel EVANS brought up the report of the committee on the petition for the Southwark Water-works, and obtained leave to bring in a bill for carrying the project into execution. The bill was accordingly brought in and read a first time.

BURIAL-GROUNDS.

Mr. S. RICE moved for returns of the several sums expended by parishes in England and Wales in the purchase of land for the formation or extension of burial-grounds, with a statement of the sources from whence the same were derived.—Ordered.

CHURCH PATRONAGE (SCOTLAND).

Mr. SINCLAIR, in presenting a petition from a parish in Aberdeenshire against the present system of church patronage in Scotland, said that it was stated in a letter which he had received from a most respectable quarter, that unless this all-important question were speedily settled, the church of Scotland would be in great danger.

Mr. MURRAY presented a similar petition from Leith.

They were referred to the committee now sitting.

The house adjourned at half-past 4 o'clock to Monday at 12.

PARLIAMENTARY NOTICES.

HOUSE OF COMMONS.

NOTICES OF MOTIONS, AND ORDERS OF THE DAY, WHICH NOW STAND FOR THE ENSUING WEEK.

MONDAY, MARCH 24.—ORDERS OF THE DAY.

1. House-tax repeal bill—second reading.
2. Illegal securities bill—further consideration of report.
3. Bribery at elections bill—further consideration of report.
4. Hertford borough bill—further consideration of report.
5. Supply—report.
6. Supply—committee.
7. Exchequer of receipt bill—further consideration of report.
8. Hemp and flax bounties—report thereon.
9. Ways and means—committee.
10. Stafford borough disfranchisement bill—third reading.
11. Tithes commutation—committee thereupon.

NOTICES OF MOTIONS.

1. Mr. Clay—to present a petition from persons in the parish of Wapping, praying that they may be permitted to bake biscuits for ships' use in bond. (Morning sitting.)
2. Mr. Hutt—to present a petition praying for a repeal of the duty on the export of coals. (Morning sitting.)
3. Mr. C. Grant—petition of East India Company on equalization of duties. (Morning sitting.)
4. Mr. Spring Rice—select committee on House of Commons offices.
5. Colonel Evans—to bring to the attention of the house the case of —— Bodkin, and others, now under protracted imprisonment in consequence of certain illegal and irregular proceedings which have taken place at the Clerkenwell Sessions, under the Middlesex justices.
6. Lord Viscount Althorp—to move resolutions regarding the commutation of tithes.
7. Mr. Alderman Wood—to refer the petition of Mr. Swift on the subject of the Glasgow lottery to the select committee; also, that Mr. O'Connell, member for Dublin, and Mr. H. B. Curteis, member for East Sussex, be added to the Glasgow lottery committee.
8. Mr. C. Buller—return of all livings whereof the whole or any portion of the tithes are in possession of the dean and canons of Windsor; of the amount annually received from each by the said dean and canons; of the names and residences of the persons performing the clerical duty in each; of the amount paid to such persons by the said deans and canons; and of the amount made up to the said officiating persons from other sources.

Last day for reading private bills the first time.

TUESDAY, MARCH 25.—NOTICES OF MOTIONS.

1. Sir S. Whalley—to present a petition from the vestrymen of St. Pancras against the proposed salary of 1,200*l.* a-year to the chairman of the Middlesex sessions. (Morning sitting.)
2. Mr. T. Attwood—to present a petition from Henry Dundas Perrott, late a lieutenant in the Royal Navy; also another petition from the freeholders and inhabitant householders of St. Leonard's, Shoreditch, praying for an inquiry into his case. (Morning sitting.)
3. Sir H. Verney—to present a petition from the borough of Buckingham, complaining of certain grievances which interfere with the privileges of election. (Morning sitting.)
4. Mr. Robinson—select committee to consider the expediency of a revision and such a commutation of taxes as may afford relief to the labouring and productive classes, and equalize the pressure by a more just distribution of the public burdens, so that the interest of the national debt and the necessary charges for the public service, after making every practicable reduction, may be raised with the least injury to the industry and improvement of the country.
5. Mr. Brocklehurst—select committee to inquire into the constitution of the South Sea Company, with a view to pay off or transfer the funds of the said company to the consolidated fund, and to provide for the payment of the dividends thereon by the Bank of England.
6. Mr. Lennard—return of the number of persons in England and Wales who received sentence of death in the year 1833 [illegible]
7. Colonel Williams—[illegible]

[illegible]

ORDER OF THE DAY.

Roman Catholic marriages (Scotland) bill—committee.

WEDNESDAY, MARCH 26.—ORDERS OF THE DAY.

1. Highways Bill—second reading.
2. Felons' property bill—second reading.

NOTICES OF MOTIONS.

1. Mr. Ewart—return relating to the official document entitled the Custom-house Bill of Entry.
2. Mr. Ewart—bill for abolishing capital punishment in cases of letter stealing and returning from transportation, and in certain cases of burglary.

FRENCH PAPERS.

(From *Galignani's Messenger* of Thursday.)

The regiments sent to the frontiers of Spain immediately after the death of Ferdinand VII. are about to return into the interior of the country, and some of them have already commenced their march.

According to the *Vapor* of Barcelona, the recent acts of the Spanish Ministry bearing a liberal colour, the disquietude of the patriots has ceased, and their ardour for the public weal is greater than ever. Every one is now anxious to enroll himself in the Urban Militia, and the alarm entertained relative to the freedom of the press has been dissipated.

The *Augsburg Gazette* of the 16th inst. contains the following extract of a letter of the 12th from Frankfort-on-the Maine:—"Letters from Vienna state that the affairs of Switzerland occupy much attention there, and that resolutions will be passed for the removal of the Poles and other political exiles from that country. These resolutions will be afterwards sanctioned by the Diet, and then announced to the Swiss Confederation in the name of all the Governments of Germany. Such overtures can but be agreeable to the Confederation, it being its interest to remain on friendly terms with the neighbouring States, and to rid itself of those troublesome guests, whose sole occupation is to create discord and disturbance, not only within but without that country. It must be seen, however, whether the federal Government possesses force enough to clear its territory, or whether it is swayed by terror of the faction that pointed out Switzerland as an asylum to the Poles. If it be so weak as not to be able to carry into effect the wishes of the neighbouring States, as also its own, the opinion at Vienna is, that it would be better at once to break off all intercourse with a country where there appears to be no Government, and where party spirit alone seems to reign, rather than lose time in useless remonstrances. Then, as in similar cases, diplomatic relations with Switzerland will first be broken off, and afterwards a military cordon will be established, to prevent anarchy spreading to the adjoining States. These measures will not fail in their effect; Switzerland will see its real interest, and the Swiss Government will have a fair opportunity of appealing to the good sentiments of the people. In the mean time, it is to be hoped that there will be no occasion to proceed to these extremities, strong, coercive, and remedial measures being now under consideration at Vienna, relative to Switzerland, from which country, it is evident to all, the spirit of propaganda set up there must be expelled. The Genevese must be convinced how fatal to their interests the presence of these foreign adventurers must be, and to what lengths a mistaken philanthropy may lead." This paper has the following from Berlin, dated the 9th inst.:—"The self-styled Germanic Popular Assembly at Paris is carrying on its intercourse with this country by means of unpaid letters. Several of their correspondents, supposed to be their friends, have given over their letters to the police. Numerous letters of this kind from a native of Cologne, now a private tutor at Paris, have been handed over to the authorities of Rhenish Prussia. When the police, by the mildness of its measures, receives such support from the people, it has nothing to fear, and can only feel obliged to the propagandi for this mode of making known its design." The *Gazette* has the following from Constantinople, dated the 18th ult.:—"The army is being considerably reinforced. The motive for so imposing a force at this moment is unknown. It may be a source of uneasiness to the Pacha of Egypt, but his attention is absorbed by that country, and he has his eyes fixed on Arabia. We hear that there is much discontent throughout Egypt and Syria, partly produced by foreign influence. The armament of the Porte therefore surprises us so much the more. It is true England and France are taking steps to renew the difficulties relative to the treaty of July, but it is not easy to connect the military equipments with this subject, as it is not likely that the employment of force will be requisite therein. It creates astonishment that the very limited finances of the country should be wasted upon an excessive army. Besides, it was not a memorial, but a note, which the British Ambassador presented to the Porte at the beginning of the month relative to the treaty with Russia. The French Ambassador presented a similar remonstrance, even more moderate than that of the British representative. It is not known what the Porte will do; it is supposed, however, as heretofore, the Ottoman Government will declare it regrets not being able to comply with the wishes of the two maritime Powers, and retract engagements that have been solemnly contracted. This is all that can be said. It then remains for England and France to take it ill, or to allow things that are accomplished to remain so. Prudence will doubtless dictate the latter course. It is still singular to see France and England, whose interests are so opposite, so firmly united against the advancement of Russia. We think it will only tend to strengthen the Porte's reliance on the Cabinet of St. Petersburgh. In the Seraglio there is, before all things, a respect for power, and this will be shown to Russia in proportion to the apprehension she inspires. The old traditions, relative to the light hair that is one day to put an end to the Ottoman empire, have lost their influence. They are forgotten, or no longer applied to Russia, who was a friend in need; the same prejudice exists in Europe against red hair; an old Turkish proverb says—'Trust not the red.' Reinforcements of the British station at Malta are spoken of; we heard of such once before, but they led to no result. No power has cause to dread a war so much as England; any war would be European, and would soon be changed from a war of interests into one of principles." The *Gazette* quotes the funds at Vienna, on the 11th inst., Five per Cent. Metallics, 97 11-16; Ditto, Four per Cent., 88⅞; Bank Actions, 1,250.

The *Berlin State Gazette* of the 14th inst. quotes Prussian Four per Cents., 98¼ 98; Ditto, Five per Cents. (1822), English Loan, 103.

The *Suabian Mercury* gives the following, under date of Berlin, March 5:—"It is announced that Prince William, the King's brother, is about to be appointed Governor of the fortress of Mentz, but it is probable a Vice-Governor may be named at the same time. The Diet of Brandenburg is said to be so fully occupied that it frequently sits for eight hours together. Dr. Julius, whose philanthropic exertions for the improvement of prisons are well known, will take his departure next week for America, going first to England and returning by France, in order to gather in his way every valuable information he can collect on the subject which so much interests him."

The *Leipsic Gazette* contradicts the news of a commercial treaty of union for the whole of Germany. Austria, it says, can, without inconvenience, remain in her actual position.

The *Turkish Gazette* of the 4th ult. contains a firman, appointing Selim and Osman Pachas, who, it is known, have quitted the Egyptian service, Pachas with two tails, and Generals of regular troops. This firman is remarkable, because it throws a light on the relations of the Porte with Egypt. It appears that the Porte dares not openly justify the treason of Osman, for fear of awakening the resentment of Mehemet Ali.

The following is an extract of a letter from General d'Uzer, Commander at Bona, dated February 23:—"The Ramadan has just terminated by the usual horse races, but this year they have been more numerous and brilliant than in 1833. The whole population of the town and of the neighbouring tribes were assembled. The magnificence which the natives displayed in horses, arms, costumes, and ornaments, was excessive. The part which the neighbouring tribes took in these fêtes is a fresh proof of the confidence with which we have inspired the Arabs, and there is reason to hope that the tranquillity we enjoy will induce new tribes to shake off the yoke of the Bey of Constantine, and rally under our flag. A circumstance worthy of remark is, that in the time of the Turks many highway robberies were always heard of, and now these crimes are extremely rare."

M. Pitrat, editor of the *Gazette du Lyonnais*, a legitimatist journal published at Lyons, has signified to the collectors his determination not to pay taxes. He founds his refusal upon the oath imposed upon the electors. The prefect of the Rhone has consequently ordered his goods to be distrained for the amount, and sold in the Place de Montazet on the 20th (this day).

(From *Galignani's Messenger* of Friday.)

The *Madrid Gazette* of the 11th instant contains the following decree:—"Being desirous by all legal means of consolidating the national credit, which is the basis of the prosperity and glory of the country, I have ordained—1. That for the present all provisions made for Prebendaries, Canons, and all other ecclesiastical benefices, except for those who have the cure of souls, for the Prebends *de officio*, and the Presidents of Chapters, shall be suspended. 2. The product of these vacant benefices shall be exclusively appropriated, according to the bulls of the Pope, to the liquidation of the public debt. 3. Notwithstanding the enactment of Art. 1, I reserve to myself the power of recompensing eminent services rendered to the church or the state. You will take this for granted, and provide for its execution.—Signed by the hand of the Queen at the Palace, this 9th March, 1834.—To Don Nicolao Maria Garelly." "This determination," says a letter which communicates the above decree of the Government, "shows that it is convinced of the necessity of having recourse to the immense wealth possessed by the Spanish clergy, whose resources may relieve the Treasury, and at the same time diminish the elements of civil war, by taking from the priests the means of influencing the populace in favour of Charles V. The decree at the same time shows that M. Martinez de la Rosa entertains a statesmanlike notion of political economy, by doing everything in his power to give confidence to the public creditors of Spain, and dissipate the fears excited by the report of M. Gargollo."

The *Augsburg Gazette* of the 17th inst. contains the following extract of a private letter of the 10th from Mentz:—"The office of Governor of the Fortresses in our city devolving on Prussia in October next, the King's son, Prince Frederick of Prussia, who has property in our neighbourhood, has been appointed to fill it. General Muffling is spoken of as Vice-Governor. Count Mensdorff will continue to act as Governor on the part of Austria until the term of that power ends; he will then quit our city, much to the regret of the inhabitants, to take on him the Government of Bohemia."—The *Gazette* quotes the funds at Vienna, on the 12th inst., 5 per Cents., Metallics, 97 7-16; ditto 4 per Cents., 88 1-10; Bank Actions, 1245 1-10.

The *Berlin State Gazette* of the 15th inst. quotes Prussian 4 per Cents. 98¼ 98; ditto, 5 per Cents., 1822, English Loan, 103.

The *Nuremburg Correspondent* of the 16th inst. has the following, of the 10th, from Vienna:—"The Emperor's health continues to improve. As soon as spring weather has set in, His Majesty proposes to travel, visiting the Tyrol, to inspect the new fortress erecting there, then descending into Lombardy, where he intends to fix his residence, by turns, at Milan and Venice. In July His Majesty will return to the baths of Hellenellen. The young Queen of Hungary has been in a suffering state for some time past. The Congress at Vienna proceeds slowly, being obliged to communicate [illegible] all eyes were turned upon it; now it may be compared to a virtuous housewife, of whom so little is known that nothing is said of her. The *Giovane Italia* has again proclaimed its existence by an assassination at Parma. Recent events in Savoy [illegible] The uncertainty [illegible] Mehemet Ali and his warlike son do not trouble themselves about [illegible]"

The *Frankfort Gazette*, of the 17th inst., says [illegible] announces that the Grand Duke of Nassau had summoned the States to meet at Wiesbaden before the end of this month. The Grand Council of Berne, in its sitting of February 28, abolished all the stamp duties on the journals and every other species of periodical publication, and further decreed that such journals and writings should be conveyed by the post throughout the canton without any charge whatever for postage.

The *Tribune* announces that its number of yesterday was not seized, but that M. Lionne, its responsible editor, has been summoned to appear before the Court of Assizes on the 31st inst., to answer for the publication of an article instigating to the commission of three different crimes, not followed with effect.

FRENCH FUNDS.—PARIS, March 20.—Five per Cents., 104f. 80c. 85c. 80c.; Four and a Half per Cents., 99f. 90c.; Four per Cents., 94f.; Three per Cents., 78f. 65c. 70c. 65c. 60c. 55c.; Bank Actions, 1,795f. 75c. 1,797f. 50c.; Rente de Naples, 94f. 90c. 85c. 80c. 70c.; Roman Five per Cents., 95¼ ½ 95 95¼; Rente d'Espagne, Five per Cents., 28¾ ⅞ ¾ 28 27¾ ⅞ ¾; Rente d'Espagne, Three per Cents., 41 41¼ 42¼ 42 41¾ ⅞ ¾ ⅞ 42 41¾ [illegible]; Royal Spanish Loan, 81¼ ⅜ 82 81¾; Rente Perpetuelle d'Espagne, 66¼ [illegible] 66¼ [illegible]; Belgian Loan, 100¼. Exchange on London, one month, money, 25f. 25c.; three months, money, 25f. 12½c.—*Cours Authentique*.

FRENCH FUNDS.—PARIS, March 21.—Five per Cents., 104f. 85c. 80c. 70c. 75c.; Four per Cents., 94f.; Three per Cents., 78f. 45c. 50c. 45c. 40c.; Bank Actions, 1,800f.; Rente de Naples, 94f. 70c. 65c. 75c. 65c. 60c. 55c.; Roman Five per Cents., 95¼ 95 95¼; Rente d'Espagne, Five per Cents., 28 27¾ [illegible]; Rente d'Espagne, Three per Cents., 40¾ ¾ 41 40¾ 41 41¼ ½ ¾ 41¾ 42; Royal Spanish Loan, 81¼ ¼ ½ 82 81¼; Rente Perpetuelle d'Espagne, 66 65¾ [illegible] ¾ 65 65¾; Belgian Loan, 1831, Five per Cents., 100¼ ¾; Haytian Loan, 275f. Exchange on London, one month, money, 25f. 25c.; three months, paper, 25f. 15c.; money, 25f. 15c.—*Cours Authentique*.

FLANDERS MAIL.

BRUSSELS, MARCH 20.

The official bulletins of the health of the Prince Royal, published yesterday evening and this morning, state that he is getting better.

In order to dispel the fears manifested by our Chamber of Commerce and other persons on the intention of the Government to obtain iron from England for the construction of the intended rail-road, the Minister of the Interior gave, in the sitting of the 17th, detailed statements proving that we have ourselves iron in abundance. The quantity which the several farmers, &c., in Belgium can produce in one year is 18,700 tons. Of this quantity there is a regular demand for 9,700 tons, leaving 9,000 tons to be disposed of annually. There will, therefore, be much more than will be required for the rail-road. As for the locomotive machines, waggons, &c., there will be found in the country mechanics as well able to make them as in England; however, by way of precaution, we shall procure from that country the most perfect models.

Yesterday evening again some groups of young men were seen parading the streets of several quarters of Brussels. Patrols of the garrison were on foot at the same time. No disorder took place.

The inhabitants of Brussels accused of disorderly conduct the evening before yesterday have been confined in the Petits Carmes.

A letter from Arlon of the 17th of March says—"I am just informed, but cannot answer for the truth of the statement, that there has been a rencontre between a Prussian and a French patrol at Frisange, and that some musket-shots were exchanged between them."

The *Observer*, of Hainault, says—"We are informed that for this week past a red flag has been flying on the heights of Fleurus, with the following inscription:—'No iron rail-roads.' There is great fermentation in the neighbourhood."

The Chamber continues its endless discussion on the iron rail-road. M. Eloy has spoken vehemently against the project: his main argument was, that the iron rail-road would afford the means of importing foreign iron into the heart of the country. Truly the Chamber wastes its time and that of the country. It is even now impossible to predict when this general discussion will come to a conclusion.

MARCH 21.

The bulletins of the health of the Prince Royal yesterday evening and this evening state that it continues to improve.

Papers containing threats against the Catholic clergy have been posted up this week, as well as the week before, in several places at Mechlin.

The Government now knows that a corps of 35,000 Dutch troops, which may be assembled in 48 hours, to form an army of operation, is cantoned on the frontier between Bois-le-Duc and Helmont. Every branch of the service, including the *ambulances*, is prepared and complete. We do not know whether the Minister of War has made the arrangements which prudence dictates under such circumstances. We do not think it necessary to dwell on the danger of relying on the treaty which King William signed with England and France on the 21st of May last. If he should violate it, and prompt success should crown his boldness, Europe, in its present situation, would soon forget this violation of a treaty, which, after all, would only replace affairs in the same state as in 1815. Belgium would pay more dearly than ever for the blind confidence which it places in England and in France, which are at present so much taken up with their domestic concerns that they neglect abroad (in the East for instance) interests of far more importance to those two Powers than those which would attach them to our country, if a war were necessary to maintain it even in the wretched condition in which they have placed it, for their own advantage.—*Courrier Belge.*

At the conclusion of the sitting of the Chamber to-day, the President announced that Messrs. Gendebien and Puydt were the only remaining speakers on the list for the general discussion of the project of the iron rail-road, and they will be heard to-morrow.

BELGIAN FUNDS, BRUSSELS, March 21.—Actual Debt, 2½ per Cent., 51½; Rothschild's Loan, 5 per Cent., 97½; Loan of the City, 1832, 4 per Cent., 94½.—*Brussels papers*, March 22.

ST. PETERSBURGH, MARCH 4.

In order to promote the maritime trade of the Black Sea, His Majesty has ordered guilds of seamen to be formed for 10 years at Alechky, in the government of Taurida, and at Nicopolis, in the government of Catherinoslaff. These guilds, or companies, are to be wholly exempt from taxes and military service, and to consist of persons who voluntarily offer themselves, and engage to do all that their new profession requires. That they may acquire the necessary practical knowledge, they are to serve five years on board the Imperial fleet in the Black Sea, especially on board small ships and transports, where the duty is more like that on board merchantmen. At the expiration of these 5 years they are to receive from the Naval Board certificates as qualified seamen.—*Frankfort papers*, March 19.

TO THE EDITOR OF THE TIMES.

Sir,—In the discussion last night in the House of Commons on the subject of Dissenters being obliged to pay church-rate, as reported in your journal of this day, the member for Boston (Mr. Wilks) is made to say that the Dissenters do not so much object to it as a pecuniary obligation, as in point of principle.

Without stopping to set down the aggregate amount paid annually by Dissenters in this way, permit me to say that I think the hon. member is in error.

As regards myself, I desire only to state the fact, that, as a householder of this city for 20 years—15 in the ward of Bridge, and 5 in that of Candlewick—I have had taken from me upwards of 178*l.* in the name of church-rate. I speak only of the money.

I am, Sir, your obedient servant,

Great Eastcheap, March 19. W. TATCHELL.

THE KING'S THEATRE.

The Last Five Nights of the Season.

THIS EVENING, and every evening during the Week (Good Friday excepted), Mr. C. H. ADAMS will deliver his LECTURE on ASTRONOMY, to be illustrated by the most extensive transparent apparatus ever exhibited in this country. At intervals Mr. Cruse will perform appropriate music on Mr. Green's Royal Seraphine. Doors open at half past 7, begin at 8 precisely. Boxes, First and Second Tier, 4s; Third Tier 2s. Pit 1s. Private and family boxes of Mr. Seguin, at the Opera-office, in the Haymarket, daily.

THEATRE ROYAL, DRURY-LANE.

On EASTER MONDAY, RICHARD THE THIRD. Duke of Glocester, Mr. Macready; Earl of Richmond, Mr. Cooper; Elizabeth, Mrs. Faucit; Lady Anne, Miss Taylor. To conclude with (1st time) an Easter Folly, entitled ANSTER FAIR; or, Michael Scott, the Wizard.

THEATRE ROYAL, COVENT-GARDEN.

On EASTER MONDAY, GUSTAVUS THE THIRD; or, The Masked Ball. Gustavus the Third, Mr. Warde; Colonel Lillienhorn, Mr. Templeton; Captain Ankarstrom, Mr. H. Phillips; Count de Horn, Mr. Seguin; Count Ribbing, Mr. Wilson; Oscar, Miss Shirreff; Christian Engleheart, Mr. Bedford; Madame Ankarstrom, Miss Inverarity; Arvedson, Mrs. Fitzwilliam. To conclude with DER FREISCHUTZ.

This Week.

THEATRE ROYAL, ADELPHI.

THIS EVENING the entertainments will commence with an act selected from Mr. YATES'S REMINISCENCES. After which, Mrs. YATES'S DELINEATION of the PASSIONS. Mr. John Reeve will give a grand serio-comic, scena buffa al affectuoso, maestoso, spiritoso, pomposo, entitled Il Gran Maestro Signor Strutto. Tableau, CALYPSO AND HER NYMPHS. Telemachus, Miss Daly; Calypso, Mrs. Love. Old Friends with New Faces, Character Portraits of living and departed Actors, by Mr. Yates. The BATTLE OF THE AMAZONS. To conclude with THE ARTIST'S DREAM, or Fairy Visions, by Mr. H. Childe.

Madame Vestris.

ROYAL OLYMPIC THEATRE.

French Plays.

The Nobility, Subscribers to the French Plays, and the Public, are respectfully informed, that this THEATRE will OPEN on Wednesday, the 2d of April, with a variety of ENTERTAINMENTS, the performers selected from the principal theatres of Paris and the Continent. In the course of the season several performers of celebrity will appear. Private boxes 4, 3, and 2 guineas each. Stalls 10s. 6d. Boxes 6s. Pit 3s. 6d. Applications to be made to Mr. Last, at the box-office in Wych-street, from 10 till 5 o'clock.

SURREY THEATRE.

For the BENEFIT of Mr. RAYNER.

OPEN for THIS EVENING only. Mrs. Waylett with four Ballads. Mr. Hunt, Mr. Edwin, Mr. Morley, Mr. Williams, Mr. Forrester, Mr. Vale, Mr. Rayner, and Mr. W. H. Williams; Mrs. Vale, Miss Julia Dunbar, and Mrs. Embden, with the Glee Singers. Mr. Bangs on the Symphonion, the Polish Brothers, and a phalanx of concentrated talent of harmony and sweet sounds. To begin at a quarter before 7.

TO CORRESPONDENTS.

"ARCHIMEDES" should give us his real name.

"A. B. C." is not the person alluded to, *his* letter however shall appear, if we can find room for it.

☞ The publication of *The Times* commenced at 8 o'clock on Saturday morning, and finished at half past 9.

LONDON, MONDAY, MARCH 24, 1834.

It will be seen that the Ordnance Estimates passed the House of Commons on Friday evening without any attempt at a division, and indeed without a particle of objection except from Mr. JOSEPH HUME, who made a rambling speech on the occasion, but does not seem to have produced a single convert to his suggestions. At the same time we are bound to state, that there seems to us to be considerable justice in the censures of the hon. economist upon that most improvident and stupid practice of keeping on hand an enormous quantity of old and perishable—nay, indeed, half perished stores, for which there is no immediate use whatever, and of which a supply to almost any conceivable amount might be had by contract from private manufacturers, in a country where such masses of capital are employed, so as to meet a war demand, the most extensive and sudden that could be contemplated. Why should the Ordnance retain in depôt a quantity of muskets amounting to near 1,000,000—of a description, moreover, no longer answering the wants of the British army, as not possessing the modern improvements in such weapons—when, from the proceeds of their sale to foreign countries, a sufficient, though inferior number of new arms, might be fabricated without expense to the public, and better adapted to the existing practice of war?

While on this point of military equipment, we may just remark the slovenly and inefficient manner in which the business of our Ordnance service has long been carried on, when, as an experienced officer assures us, the British musket, among a people too so skilled in every hardware manufacture, is in one essential part of it, viz., the *lock*, inferior to almost every other in Europe; few of our Tower-proof muskets being useable, from the excessive coarseness and difficulty of the lock-springs, until they have been worked upon by the regimental armourers at the expense of the officers in the command of companies. Surely there is money enough paid by Government, as well for the workmanship as for the repair and preservation of muskets, to justify us in demanding that they should be of at least the average quality distributed to the other European troops. We likewise agree with Mr. HUME as to the good consequence of sweeping away the accumulation of old stores—in diminishing the (apparently) enormous expense of the Storekeepers' department at home, and in some of our foreign possessions. Less, however, need be said by way of insisting on increased economy in this department, as Mr. HUME admitted that the present Administration is not to blame for the injudicious management alluded to, and Colonel MABERLY states that the above-mentioned sources of inconvenience and expense are in a rapid course of diminution. The reduction as compared with last year's estimates is about 80,000*l.*, and since the accession of Lord GREY'S Government the saving has been nearly four times as much.

Lord PALMERSTON some days ago was not very signally successful in defending his foreign policy relative to the East of Europe; and one feature certainly in the badness of his case was the unfortunate choice he had made of diplomatic agents, or the lamentable weakness with which he had succumbed to the choice made for him by others of the Cabinet.

Now look to the west of Europe—the extreme west; and what indication can we find in Lord PALMERSTON of a more discriminating judgment, or of a more manly resistance to the encroachments attempted on his patronage as Minister for Foreign Affairs? Lord PALMERSTON being responsible for the success of his diplomacy, ought to have his free agency in the proper conduct of that diplomacy undisturbed; for in this, as in all cases, it is but fair that power and responsibility should be united, understanding that the former is in no case to be abused. We must take for granted, therefore, that the selection of his subordinate functionaries is Lord PALMERSTON'S own; and in the case of Portugal, what is that selection? We have heard a great deal more than his Lordship is aware of as to proceedings at Lisbon,—more, indeed, than a regard to the public interest and to private confidence will at this moment permit us to promulgate. Suffice to say at present, that if this Government be sincere in its professed good wishes to the cause of Donna MARIA, it ought to appoint as its Ministers and servants to her Court persons imbued with similar feelings, and earnest and anxious NOT *for the triumph of the usurper* MIGUEL, but for that of the lawful QUEEN and of the constitutional monarchy. At a crisis like that under which Portugal is just now suffering, nothing can be of more essential urgency than to choose as members of our mission there, *none* but friends to the QUEEN. And has such a principle of nomination been observed? Has it not, on the other hand, been grossly violated? Who are the three Secretaries of Legation at Lisbon, and how are they regarded by the heads of HER MAJESTY'S Government? They are, one and all rank Tories. Mr. GRANT, Mr. CHESTER, and Sir ALEXANDER MALET (the latter lately the Conservative candidate for a western borough), are all rank Tories. They are one and all members of, or biassed towards, that faction which has laboured with indefatigable and disgraceful zeal for the overthrow of that Sovereign whom the KING and Parliament have recognised as the intimate ally of the British nation, and for the defeat of that policy which has been espoused and maintained by the most cordial approbation of the United Kingdom. Such are the Secretaries, and who is their Chief? Lord HOWARD DE WALDEN—a man (to say the least) of no political sympathies with the Government which employs him. Is this wise of Lord PALMERSTON? And it is not the first time we have called his Lordship to account on the same subject. Let him revise his diplomatic list. It is a bad one; it is fit only for Schedule A, with two or three exceptions. We do not mean to offend Lord PALMERSTON—far from it; but even should his Lordship take offence, we cannot help it: we must do our duty. His Lordship may not relish this unceremonious snubbing. He once hinted to the Duke of WELLINGTON that in such and such cases "he might be under "the necessity of resigning." "Well, my Lord," replied the pithy soldier, "what then?"

On Saturday we noticed Sir THOMAS DENMAN'S rumoured elevation to the House of Lords; but highly as we thought, and think, of the CHIEF JUSTICE, and warmly as we felt disposed to express that opinion, it was impossible for us as honest men to do otherwise than state our strong repugnance to any augmentation of the legal peerage, even in the person of a learned gentleman, in favour of whose upright, manly, and amiable character the suffrages of the whole community are united. We have reason to think that the promotion which we would fain have discredited is actually on the eve of taking place. We are in nowise led to any change of sentiment on this important subject of the too frequent introduction of professional persons into the House of Peers, having no other claim to that honour than their occupancy of an eminent judicial office. On the general ground of inexpediency, of cheapening the highest dignity in the realm, of ruining respectable private families by entailing on them a rank which for more than one generation they are seldom able to support, and thus making nobility corrupt by making it dependent, it is difficult, we conceive, for two reasonable men to differ in opinion, and on such considerations we must abide by the judgment which was plainly enough intimated in last Saturday's *Times*. But facts are now enumerated which, while they seem to exculpate Ministers from any voluntary adoption of a practice much to be deprecated, appear to form a justification of the measure on principles of pure necessity. It is well known that the Tories have, for factious purposes, been encouraging and bringing forward loud complaints of the disappointment attributed by them to Scotch suitors, touching a delay in hearing their appeals from the Court of Session. Lord BROUGHAM, within these few days, told his mind on the matter to Lord ELLENBOROUGH, and administered to that conscientious Peer a degree of satisfaction with regard to the ostensible subject of his remonstrance, which mayhap was more than the noble complainant had bargained for. The LORD CHANCELLOR has been singularly destitute of all active or useful co-operation from his legal brethren, members of the House of Lords, since his accession to the woolsack. Lord LYNDHURST has been strenuously, and, no doubt, laudably exerting himself in the business of his own proper Court of Exchequer, and somehow or other has had no time to do any thing (at least, if any thing, it has been very little) in the trial of appeals before the Lords. Lord WYNFORD'S sufferings from gout are such as, in spite of his zealous anxiety to be useful, not to admit of his Lordship's sitting frequently; so that, in fact, unless the LORD CHANCELLOR were to abandon his own court of equity, and let its business run to absolute neglect, it would be impossible for him alone to get on rapidly with appeals from Scotland. And if he were, as he ought not, to prefer the House of Lords, and to postpone the Chancery, what would the Tories, or, more important still, what would the country say to it? Under these circumstances, and in submission to a strong necessity, though in deviation from the rules of abstract policy, this expedient of calling up the LORD CHIEF JUSTICE has, we presume, been resorted to; so that Lord ELLENBOROUGH at least, and his hypothetical Scotch clients, will have sufficient reason to be grateful.

We have received the Paris papers of Thursday and Friday, which, though they contain the debates of the Chamber of Deputies on Wednesday and Thursday, have not yet brought us the conclusion of the discussion on the bill for regulating or suppressing political societies. The numerous amendments proposed, in which our readers could find no interest except after a more extensive development than we have room to give them, had not been disposed of on Thursday evening, and the debate was therefore adjourned to the following day.

We allude again to the subject in this stage of its progress, merely from regard to a new fact introduced into the controversy by M. PRUNELLE, the Mayor of Lyons. That honourable Deputy, who proceeded from Paris to Lyons during the late *strike*, seems to have acquired an extensive knowledge of the objects and designs of the union of workmen by which that strike was directed. He stated that the Society of *Mutualists*, or the association for mutual aid, consisted of 3,000 members, and that through its intervention the Lyons workmen had lately stood out for a rise of wages. This association disclaimed all connexion with politics; but their papers and orders of the day showed that political societies had proposed a junction with them and with the disaffected operatives. One of these orders of the day recommended "to the brethren, to be on their guard "against attempts made to introduce the printed papers of "the Society of the Rights of Man into their lodges," and made the chiefs of these lodges responsible for the execution of this command. The hon. deputy inferred from this and other facts, that the political clubs of Paris had endeavoured to take advantage of the social discontents of Lyons to convert a dispute about wages into an insurrection against the Government. The Trades' Union had expelled some of these political agitators from their lodges, declaring that they were desirous to avoid politics; but the very fact that, upon so insufficient grounds, they had interrupted the labours of 60,000 people for 10 or 15 days, showed that they had been excited by political theories, or encouraged by political agitators. The hon. member ascribed both their opinions on state politics, and their notions on the unlimited powers of their masters to increase their wages, to their ignorance; but thought that they would not have behaved as they did, unless their heads had been filled with republican or Saint Simonian doctrines.

This society of *Mutualists* is said to be very formidable. It is composed, like the trades' unions of this country, of a certain number of lodges; 12 of these lodges correspond with a central lodge, and these central lodges again are connected with a common centre, which is called the executive council. The authority of this executive council governed for ten days more than 50,000 workmen in and about Lyons with absolute sway.

It is further stated by the same hon. deputy, that, though about 4,000 of the foremen of the different workshops were opposed to this tyranny of the executive council, they could not at first overcome it, or resist its interdiction of labour. They even denounced 33 of its ringleaders to the KING'S *Procureur*, but no legal proceedings were taken against them. This inaction appeared to M. PRUNELLE to be injudicious, but both the local law officers of the Crown and the general Government seemed unwilling to interfere.

This last observation called up the Minister of Trade, who justified the conduct of the Government by saying that judicial proceedings against the council of the *Mutualists* would have brought on a collision between the people and the military force, which would certainly have been useless, and might have been sanguinary. All that the authorities, therefore, thought themselves justified in doing was to watch over the public peace—to refrain from active interference in settling the question of wages—to collect a sufficient force to restrain every attempt at plunder or violence—to assure the masters, that, whatever course they should pursue, they might rely on finding protection, and therefore to request them to wait the result, if they chose to hold out against the demands of their workmen, without terror or alarm. The effect of this forbearance was the return of the men to their work after about a fortnight's *strike*, without any disturbance of public order or any promise or expectation of increased wages.

From this statement of facts, of which we can entertain no doubt, two important inferences may be drawn by the foolish and unthinking members of our own trades' unions, and by the abettors of the existing Derby *strike*. The first is, that they are as likely to be the dupes of mischievous political plotters as the clubs or lodges of the silk-weavers of Lyons; and the second, that they are as certain to meet with signal losses and final discomfiture. The working population of Lyons, it will be remembered, rose against their masters on a demand for higher wagers in November, 1831. Their unanimity was then so great, their discipline so perfect, and their numbers so overwhelming, that they conquered and disarmed the National Guard, composed of the shopkeepers and manufacturers—that they drove out the large garrison force from the city, and stood out against large reinforcements of troops sent from the neighbouring departments—and that they usurped the civil and military authority of the place, holding unequivocal dominion in the second chief manufacturing town of France for more than a week. Much blood was shed on the occasion, and great alarm was felt for the result over all the kingdom. But what was the fruit of this bloodshed and of these apprehensions? Nothing but loss to the workmen, who were obliged, after suffering great privations, to return to their work on the old terms. Within these last six weeks other combinations have been formed in the same city; and without the commission of the same violence, a cessation of all labour has been successfully enforced by the executive council of the trades' unions. What again, in this second instance, has been the result? Why, after the loss of 10 days or a fortnight's wages, the 50,000 workmen of Lyons, commanded to desist from their work till their masters should raise their wages, are compelled by want and threatened starvation to come back, and to solicit employment from their masters at the old terms. In both cases they have had an overwhelming physical force in their favour,—in both cases they entered into a competition with the capital of their employers in circumstances which must have intimidated the latter into a compliance with their terms, if, as they supposed, the amount of wages was dependent alone on their arbitrary regulation—and in both cases after exhausting the amount of their funds and the resources of their ingenuity, and after enduring the greatest hardships and privations, they found that their masters were as necessary to them as they to their masters.

Can the formidable experiment be tried on a grander scale, or in more favourable circumstances, by any trades' unions in this country? Let those who would counsel a great strike, or who have ruined the poor men at Derby by their pernicious aid, answer the question.

We have received, by the Victoria, which arrived at Liverpool late on Saturday night, New York papers from the 25th ult. to the 2d instant. The files from the 17th to the 24th have not yet arrived. We have not room to-day for extracts, but the contents of these papers are not important.

We are concerned to learn that the infant son of the King and Queen of Belgium is very seriously indisposed, although the papers received to-day express hopes of his recovery. Dr. Clarke left London for Brussels the night before last to give his advice on this afflicting occasion.—*Globe.*

The sixth report of the committee on public petitions has just been printed, from which it appears that the total number of petitions presented in the House of Commons this session, to the 7th of March inclusive, is 885. Of these petitions no less than 192 are from Protestant Dissenters, praying for relief from their grievances, and the signatures to these petitions amount to 31,900. The number of petitions from Ireland for the entire abolition of tithes is 113, to which 84,849 signatures are attached; there are 70 petitions for a repeal of the legislative union, with 58,164 signatures; 49 in support of the established church, with 7,285 signatures; 32 petitions for the better observance of the Sabbath, with 9,357 signatures; 13 petitions, with 104,180 signatures, for a repeal of the corn laws; and 61 petitions, and 15,063 signatures, praying that no alteration may be made in those laws; the petitions complaining of agricultural distress amount to 34, with 8,920 signatures; the number of petitions against the system of lay patronage in the Church of Scotland is 50, to which 50,730 signatures are attached.

EARL FITZWILLIAM.—We find by letters received from this nobleman, that he is favourable to the redress of the Dissenters' grievances, except on two very important points, viz., their exemption from church rates, and the admission to graduate at the Universities. We regret that this excellent nobleman should not see the propriety of relieving Dissenters from an unjust and vexatious burden, and of admitting them to the advantages of the great national seats of learning.—*Leeds Mercury.*

The Archbishop of Canterbury has presented the Rev. Edward Churton, Head Master of the Hackney Church of England School, to the rectory of Monk Hely, in Suffolk.

The following is a summary of the entries in the Civil Registers of Algiers, since its occupation by the French, so far as relates to the European residents:—

	Births.	Marriages.	Deaths.
1830, last six months	5	0	6
1831, ————	44	3	118
1832, ————	139	21	304
1833, first six months	129	18	96
Total	317	42	524

LIVERPOOL CORN EXCHANGE, Friday.—We have few fresh arrivals of grain since Tuesday, which, with what is offering from granary, formed a good selection of samples for this day's market. The advices from Mark-lane and other quarters not being of a character to enliven our trade, caused a considerable indisposition amongst the millers and dealers to enhance their stocks. Wheat even of the finest quality would not reach our quotations, and secondary qualities were quite unsaleable. Oats sell very slowly, and barely maintain their value, whilst Barley and Malt are quite neglected. Since the last sales of bonded sour flour on Tuesday, nothing further has been done in this or any other kind of grain under lock. Flour and oatmeal without change in value.

LIVERPOOL COTTON MARKET, Saturday.—The cotton market this week has been unsettled: up to Wednesday the demand was very good, and ⅛d. per lb. on common and fair qualities of American was realized, without change in other kinds; yesterday there was less doing, and consequently less of steadiness in prices; to-day there has again been an increased inquiry, but only sufficient to barely support the above advance. Speculators have taken 1,500 American, 1,000 Surat, 200 Pernambuco, and 50 Bahia, and exporters 500 American and 500 Surat. The import this week is 6,191 bags, and the sales are 21,190 bags—viz., 250 Sea Island, 14½d. to 20d.; 20 stained ditto, 11½d.; 8,900 Boweds, 8½d. to 9d.; 5,690 New Orleans, 8d. to 9½d.; 2,000 Alabama, &c., 7½d. to 9d.; 810 Pernams, 10½d. to 11½d.; 700 Bahia, 9½d. to 10d.; 700 Maranham, 9d. to 11d.; 40 Demerara, 10d. to 13½d.; 110 Egyptian, 13d. to 14d.; and 1,800 Surat, 5½d. to 7½d. per lb. The sale to-day amounts to 1,500 bags, at previous rates.

LIVERPOOL, Saturday Evening.—Arrived the Victoria, from New York, sailed the 2d instant; Catherine, from Savannah; Integrity, from Jamaica; Broad Axe, from Bilboa; Catherine Angelina, from Amsterdam; Cervantes and George Canning, from London; Vrow Elizabeth, from Havre; Diligent, from St. Michael's; Industrie and Johanna Gertrude, from Rotterdam; Elida, from New Carleby. Off the port, the Harmony, from ——. Arrived yesterday the Palestine, from New Orleans; Aries and Noble, from Mobile; Dependent, from Charleston; Red Rover, from Gallipoli; Cuba and Robert Finnie, from Antwerp; Petrus Lodovicus, from Dordt; Albertina and Johanna, from Rotterdam; and Marianne, from Dantsic and Portsmouth.

A singular fatality is attached to the riches of Ali Pacha, as well as to the persons who were destined by him to enjoy them. At the period when he quarrelled with the Porte, and was expecting an attack the issue of which might be fatal to him, he sent all his treasures to Corfu, directing that in case of his death they should be divided between his two sons, Mouctar and Veli, and in case of their death, among his grandchildren, and finally, on failure of them, between Sir Thomas Maitland and Sir Frederick Adam. Mouctar and Veli have both been killed, all the grandchildren have perished, and Sir Thomas Maitland is no more. Sir Frederick Adam alone survives. Years have passed since these treasures were conveyed to Malta, and there they still remain, deposited in the Government Palace. By a singular accident, while they were lowering the chest from the ship that took it to Malta into a barge moored alongside, the ropes broke, and it fell into the sea, but the Maltese divers, after great difficulties, succeeded in recovering and bringing it to land.—*Temps.*

A young gentleman of the name of Harrison, who for some time past been residing at the Rainbow Tavern, Covent-garden, on Friday committed suicide in his bed-room by shooting himself through the abdomen. When the waiters and gentlemen in the house burst open his door, on hearing the report of the pistol, the unfortunate man was found lying on the floor on his back, and he died before a surgeon could arrive.

Below KLADDERADATSCH, the Berlin journal of political graphic satire, displayed the right-wing extremes of German Nationalism, and was virulently anti-British from the 1890s on. Cartoon by Arthur Johnson.

Back in the blue corner, Queen Victoria was not amused. She sent a letter, drafted in the Prince Consort's own hand, to her Prime Minister, Lord Palmerston, from Balmoral on 6 October 1855:

The Queen has been as much disgusted with the late atrocious articles in *The Times* on the Army in the Crimea, the King of Prussia, the late promotions etc etc as she understands the Cabinet to have been in London. Ld Panmure speaks even of the desire evinced in different quarters to establish an Anti *Times* League – The Queen believes this would but aggravate the evil like any repressive laws, but she would put it to Ld Palmerston, whether it is right that the Editor, the Proprietor and the Writers of such execrable publications ought to be the honoured and constant guests of the Ministers of the Crown? Their introduction into our higher society and political Reunions to the extent to which it is now carried and the attention which is publicly shown to them there, is the most direct encouragement they could receive, adding both to their importance and power for mischief. Their exclusion from these circles would on the other hand, without being a direct attack, mark fitly the disapproval of their acts and operate as a check on the reckless exercise of that anomalous power the danger of which to the best interests of the country is so universally admitted. Ld Palm: would perhaps show this letter to his colleagues.

In the debates on the Address on 3 February 1852 *The Times* was attacked vehemently and at length by the Prime Minister and the Leader of the Opposition for its unfriendly attitude to Louis Napoleon of France, which was causing trouble (see p. 44). In a famous leader Delane defined the freedom of the press: 'We hold ourselves responsible, not to Lord Derby or the House of Lords, but to the people of England, for the accuracy and fitness of that which we think proper to publish'.

As the century rolled on, the politicians had to resign to living with this 'anomalous power' that had sprung up among them. But it did not make them love it. *The Times* was publicly denounced as 'that arch-liar: I am no more impressed by press attacks than by the barking of a dog; but I am surprised that a newspaper like *The Times* allows itself to be so badly served all the time'. That *Times* piece, on the Boxer Rebellion in China in 1900, clearly drew blood. Haldane told Metternich that *The Times* was 'incorrigible'. Gladstone wrote: 'The insolence becomes more and more a national evil'.

There is material to make a large and lively book out of attacks on *The Times* over the past two centuries. It would include the cartoon from the famous German magazine *Kladderadatsch* on the news of Lord Northcliffe's appointment as Director of Propaganda in Enemy Countries in 1918. It shows Satan welcoming the Chief aboard, clutching a copy of *The Times* and saying: 'Welcome, great master. From you we shall at last learn the science of lying'. It would include a long chapter on Appeasement, in which many notable critics, most with hindsight, a few at the time, identified *The Times* as the stooge of Government and creature of the Cliveden Set. This chapter would include the whole speech to the Commons by Winston Churchill during a debate on the European situation on 3 April 1939. Churchill took a characteristically robust view of the pretensions of *The Times*, once describing its 'solemn prestige': he did not mean it kindly.

It would contain harsh attacks and violent invective against *The Times* in every year of its two hundred years of history. In August 1984 Michael Foot wrote a powerful letter attacking 'the rising note of hysterical hate' that he detected in *Times* coverage of the miners' strike, declaring that *The Times* would bear much of the responsibility if it took a long time to restore a decent democratic tone to debate in the country, and asserting that the only war going on in the country, encouraged by *The Times*, was the class war, the old pastime of the upper classes.

The Times is not always right. It is not carved on tablets of stone. But it is a healthy thing when it is vehemently attacked by the powerful and the eloquent. It is a sign that it is performing its true function of joining in the national debate at the highest level. The time to worry would be if the great stopped attacking *The Times*, either because it was in their pocket or because they had fallen asleep while reading it.

THE TIMES was frequently scornful about Lord Palmerston. The second leader (column 4) shows The Thunderer railing against the Foreign Secretary.
24 MARCH 1834

Book reviews

Top George Eliot, novelist. Photo by Mayall, 1858.

Above William Thackeray, painted by E. Edwards *c.* 1863.

Below THE TIMES was quickly off the mark with its notice of VANITY FAIR, 10 July 1848 – hardly surprising considering that the book had been appearing in monthly parts since January 1847. The review ran to nearly a column and was probably written by Samuel Phillips – a versatile gentleman who from 1845 to 1854 combined the post of art critic with that of reviewing fiction and biography.

In the admirable management of the opposite qualities in one individual lies the secret of Mr. Thackeray's pathos. His ordinary vein is the gravely satirical; but when he chooses to abandon the quiet smile his pathos is at once striking and profound. There is no attempt to force the sentimental—not the slightest approach to the maudlin, but the touches of tenderness seem naturally to belong to the characters and to the texture of the work. Mr. Thackeray owns a world of kindly sympathy, a feeling that, while there is a hollowness in so much apparent virtue and grandeur, there is often something good beneath a coating of vice and repulsiveness. The tenderness that comes over the brutal, selfish old father whose son is killed in battle, is an excellent specimen of his talent for the pathetic. There is nothing more disgusting in a book than a scene in which the domestic affections are badly managed. A clumsy dealer in the sentimentalities of the hearth is not only unskilful, but is invariably obtrusive; palpably showing you that he is labouring with all his might and main to bring the tears into your eyes that he may dim your perception of his own weakness. But Mr. Thackeray's pathos has an effect that is really refreshing. Having dubbed the whole social structure by the name of *Vanity Fair*—having gravely shown how great is the disproportion between inward werth and outward show, he might leave an uncomfortable misanthropic impression, were it not that he never loses sight of the better traits of human nature; and it is precisely because his pathos is so natural, and flows forth so unobtrusively, that it is so irresistible in its effect. It reminds one of the exquisite touches which occur in Fielding's *Amelia*.

A comparison between Mr. Thackeray and Fielding is frequently made, and has probably arisen, not from a merely accidental resemblance, but from an actual adoption of Fielding as a model by the author of *Vanity Fair*. Not only is the disposition to detect the motives of men under their acts common to both writers, but the affinity is still preserved in that grave tone of irony of which Fielding was so great a master, and which he is said to have borrowed from Cervantes. Mr. Thackeray's mock reverence for the humbug he lashes is sustained with a perseverance that is truly wonderful. To sneer at the worship of vanity he does not linger outside, but he boldly enters the temple, sits down among the most ardent devotees as if he were himself a fanatic, and punctiliously follows the ritual. He is an adept in knowledge of all those

The Times, originally founded to advertise a new printing process, has always taken an interest in the world of books – although the hard men of journalism have always considered book reviews wasteful of space. On 17 January of that first year 1785, *The Times* devoted a column of its very limited space to reviewing *Recherches sur les Origines, l'Esprit et le Progrès des Arts de la Grèce*. On balance it was a favourable review, though it did not name the author, and included some magisterial qualifications: 'We have observed the author to be too cautious . . . we only lament . . . we are sorry that the limits of a newspaper cannot admit of a further review of the above learned work'.

Advertising must have been slow. A few days later a whole column of the infant four-page *Times* was used to review the pamphlet *On the Nature and Principles of Public Credit*. It does not sound a lot of fun. On 16 February of its first year *The Times* announced on its front page:

> Besides moral and political essays, historical anecdotes, and the earliest intelligence of what passes, *The Daily Universal Register* proposes on the beginning of every month to publish a *characteristical catalogue* of such books and pamphlets as have passed critical observation or *the fiery ordeal of reviewers*.

Ten books were listed every month, each being given half a dozen lines of comment. The variety was eclectic: *State of Prisons in England* by John Howard; a version of the work of Metastasio ('translation tolerable'); a monograph on subalterns' pay ('several inaccuracies mark this work'); and *The Works of John Fothergill* by John Coakley Lettson, whom Printing House Square found 'inattentive to the force of terms in the English language'.

Barnes was a friend of such literary contemporaries as Leigh Hunt, Lamb and Macaulay; but books did not receive a lot of attention during his term as editor. He probably summed up his attitude in a review of Lady Blessington's *Two Friends* in 1835:

> We are not in the habit of noticing the novels which are issuing in an almost continued stream from the press – not, certainly, that we undervalue a species of literature adorned by Fielding and Smollett or Scott and Edgeworth – but because we have little time for amusing ourselves with any romance except the extravagant romance of political life.

Delane, not as bookish as Barnes, gave much more space to reviews. He did of course have more space to give. He tended to review books during the parliamentary recess, and did not care a jot whether the book was hot off the press or old, only that it was an important book, worthy of major notice in *The Times*.

And there were some important books around. Take 1859, half way through Delane's editorship: *The Times* reviewed books ranging from Tennyson's *Idylls of the King* and George Eliot's *Adam Bede* to James Stuart Mill *On Liberty* and Darwin *On the Origin of Species*. The anonymous reviewer got Darwin right. He concluded that, whether or not the theory would survive the uproar it had aroused, a great work had been given to the world.

On 21 March 1840 *The Times* set out on the first lap of its longest book review. The book under review was *The Oration of Demosthenes Upon the Crown* by Henry, Lord Brougham. Henry, a former Lord Chancellor, had been a friend of Barnes for many years, but had fallen out with him. On that first day *The Times* devoted three columns to tearing the book apart and doing a dance of derision on the pieces: 'There is not one single page in which there are not, on an average, three or four blunders, which would be unpardonable even in a stripling of fourteen'. Five days later *The Times* returned to the attack with another two columns about 'the foul, wallowing, boisterous and unEnglish translation'. Three more columns of invective on 28 March; three more on 3 April; two more on 4 April. In all the review ran to 20,000 words: longer than the book itself. The anonymous critic with the sledgehammer was Joseph W. Blakesley, later Dean of Lincoln, for many years book reviewer for *The Times*.

In a token gesture to the equality of the sexes, *The Times* used an occasional woman reviewer, anonymous as always. The society beauty Caroline Norton sometimes reviewed a book: in a letter to the editor she observed that *East Lynne* was 'a mere amplification of a story of mine ages ago'. The novels of her cousin, Sheridan Le Fanu, were reserved for Mrs Norton's log-rolling attention. This goes against purist modern literary editor's practice, which rules that one should never review a book by a friend.

Novels by Disraeli got good reviews in *The Times*. *Coningsby* was awarded eight columns in 1844: its political theme coincided with the dominant interest of *The Times*, and it is possible that Disraeli was considered a useful contact, though such considerations should not affect the length or friendliness of a review.

On the other hand, Dickens was given generally unfavourable reviews. *The Chimes* was blamed for stirring up discontent among the poor, and thereafter it was downhill. The *Christmas Story* was castigated for excessive sentimentality, and *The Cricket on the Hearth* was described as 'a twaddling manifestation of silliness almost from the first page to the last'. Let us hope that it was mere coincidence that by now Dickens was editing the aggressive rival newspaper, the *Daily News*.

Thackeray was given a glowing review of *Vanity Fair*, but was thereafter given a hard time by the *Times* critics: *Esmond* was described as a bad pastiche, 'a very questionable and cracked specimen of old China'. *The Times* judged *Jane Eyre* coarse and a work of genius for the first two volumes, but bookseller's stuff for the third. *Shirley* was 'at once the most high-flown and the stalest of fictions'. *Wuthering Heights* was mercifully not reviewed. Trollope fared pretty well. Hardy's *Far From the Madding Crowd* was well received, with the complaint that its language was trying to imitate George Eliot. Of all the great Victorian novelists, Eliot got the best press in *The Times*. *Adam Bede* was judged to have placed its author overnight among the masters of the art.

In 1897 Printing House Square began publication of a weekly called *Literature*, price 6d, to survey systematically the products of the publishers. It was not a success, except that it was a rude forefather of *The Times Literary Supplement*. In January 1902, a free *Literary Supplement* appeared in *The Times*, which then consisted of eight pages. The original idea was that this would appear occasionally to review books for which the main paper could not find space. It was such a success that it was soon appearing weekly. With characteristic and endearing eccentricity, Printing House Square selected its naval correspondent to edit it.

In March of that year Northcliffe reduced the price of *The Times* from 2d to 1d and introduced his other changes. He wrote: 'Book reviews must go in certain places, say between Parliament and Sport. And the advertisers will want their adverts next to them. And *The Times* analysis of new books must appear daily, bit by bit.'

This policy of regular reviewing continued until the Second World War, when the shortage of newsprint killed it. It was not until 1952 that books started to be reviewed regularly again. On 17 February 1955 the Books Page, roughly as we know and love it today, appeared for the first time. These days, with about 40,000 new books published every year, and much competition for space in *The Times*, even if a new Dickens or Lord Chancellor on Demosthenes were to publish, he would have to be content with a notice of a thousand words – and not a word more.

This lengthy and glowing review of George Eliot's ADAM BEDE appeared at a time when novels did not often receive the attention of THE TIMES. In the last sentences of the review, the question is raised whether Mr George Eliot is male or female, 'since none but a woman's hand could have painted those touching scenes . . .'
12 APRIL 1859

ADAM BEDE.*

There can be no mistake about *Adam Bede*. It is a first-rate novel, and its author takes rank at once among the masters of the art. Hitherto known but as the writer of certain tales to which he gave the modest title of "Scenes," and which displayed only the buds of what we have here in full blossom, he has produced a work which, after making every allowance for certain crudities of execution, impresses us with a sense of the novelist's maturity of thought and feeling. Very seldom are so much freshness of style and warmth of emotion seen combined with so much solid sense and ripened observation. We have a pleasant feeling of security in either laughing or crying with such a companion. Our laughter shall not be trifling, and our tears shall not be maudlin. We need not fear to yield ourselves entirely to all the enchantments of the wizard whose first article of belief is the truism which very few of us comprehend until it has been knocked into us by years of experience—that the world is wide, and all the human heart is one. All the novelists and all the dramatists that have ever lived have set themselves to exhibit the difference between man and man. Here, they seem to say, are circumstances precisely similar, and yet mark how various are the characters which grow out of these circumstances. The Pharisee in the Temple felt that he was different from other men, thanking his God for it; and which of us, in the immaturity of experience, is not forced chiefly to consider the differences between ourselves and other men, often utterly forgetting the grand fact of an underlying unity? Here we see monsters, and there we see angels, alien faces and inaccessible natures. It is only after much beating of the head, long intercourse with society, and many strange discoveries and detections, that the truism which we never doubted becomes a great reality to us, and we find that men's hearts resemble one another even as face answers to face in a glass. It is in the enunciation of this difficult truism that Mr. Thackeray differs from all previous novelists. It is the supreme motive of all that he has written, and the key to all the criticism that has been poured upon him. There is not a page of his works in which we do not hear the author exclaiming, "You see all these people that appear to be so different; I tell you they are all alike. You despise that wretch—thou art the man. See what a monster I have painted;—I am that monster. Good friends, let us all shake hands; external differences are very well and very amusing, but I beseech of you to think less of the external differences than of the prevailing identity. We shall have less of laughing at each other and leering each other to pieces when we come to recognize that there is no inherent distinction between Tyburn Jack and the Lord Mayor, between Sally, the cook, who looks after the dripping and thinks tenderly of the policeman, and the great lady intent upon pin-money and wondering whether Arthur is going to offer his arm to the supper-room. People are bad, no doubt, but they are no worse than we are; we think too well of ourselves—we give fine names to our own faults, we find excuses for our errors. Pray let us give the fine names all round; let us think kindly of others; let us excuse our neighbours; let us not condemn the world wholesale." With regard to which philosophy two things are to be noted,—the first, that, whether true or false, it is the reverse of uncharitable; it is the expression of a warm human sympathy; as a matter of fact, it is but a secular rendering of the deepest sentiment of Christianity—the sense of personal unworthiness in the presence of God, which teaches us the weakness of our nature, and how near the very best of us are of kin to the chief of sinners and the most degraded of beings. The second, that a novelist, writing in accordance with this philosophy, has a most difficult task to perform. It is comparatively easy to draw a character so long as we dwell mainly on points of difference and contrast. But when the object is to touch lightly on mere peculiarities, and to dwell mainly on those traits which we have all in common, and which, therefore, are anything but salient, the difficulty of the task is enormously increased.

We do not mean for one moment to detract from Mr. George Elliot's originality when we say that after his own fashion he follows this difficult path in which Mr. Thackeray leads the way. He has fully reached that idea which it is so easy to confess in words, but so hard to admit into the secret heart, that we are all alike, that our natures are the same, and that there is not the mighty difference which is usually assumed between high and low, rich and poor, the fool and the sage, the best of us and the worst of us. In general, it is only matured minds that reach this state of feeling—minds that have gone through a good deal and seen through a good deal; and our author has precisely this broad sympathy and large tolerance, combined with ripe reflection and finished style, which we admire in Mr. Thackeray. Here the comparison ends. Mr. Elliot differs so widely from Mr. Thackeray in his mode of working out the philosophy which is common to both that some of our readers may wonder how we could ever see a resemblance between him and the great painter of human vanities and weakness. Whereas Mr. Thackeray is, to the great disgust of many young ladies, continually asserting that we have all got an evil corner in our hearts, and little deceitful ways of working, Mr. Elliot is good enough to tell us that we have all a remnant of Eden in us, that people are not so bad as is commonly supposed, and that every one has affectionate fibres in his nature—fine, loveable traits, in his character. The novel before us is crowded with characters, but they are loveable. It is true that one individual is guilty of seduction, that another is guilty of murder, and that a third is a greedy old miser, but the author finds good in them all and lets them off easy, not only with pardon, but in the two former cases loaded with affectionate sympathy. If in this way he has gone to an extreme, it is a fault which most persons will readily forgive, since it enables them to think better of poor fallen human nature. How kindly he excuses that selfish old Squire who has not a thought for one human being apparently! "I believe," says his grandson and heir, "if I were to break my neck he would feel it the greatest misfortune that could befall him, and yet it seems a pleasure to him to make my life a series of petty annoyances." Then says the parson, with his kindly philosophy, and with a phrase which puts a fine gloss on all manner of selfishness, "Ah, my boy, it is not only woman's love that is *ἀπέρωτος ἔρως*, as old Æschylus calls it. There's plenty of 'unloving love' in the world of a masculine kind." The ingenuity with which the kindhearted Squire is thus made to fit into a new and improved edition of human nature, gilt-edged, is characteristic. Mr. Thackeray, on the contrary, would have made us unwilling to condemn the man by showing us that we, too, have our selfish fits, and that especially the grandson who makes the complaint is longing for the death of the useless old Fogie. But, although tending to such opposite results, the principle upon which both novelists work is the same. Here is a sentence which Thackeray himself might have written:—"Before you despise Adam as deficient in penetration, pray ask yourself if you were ever predisposed to believe evil of any pretty woman—if you ever could, without hard headbreaking demonstration, believe evil of the one supremely pretty woman who has bewitched you. No; people who love downy peaches are apt not to think of the stone, and sometimes jar their teeth terribly against it." We might quote a long passage to a similar effect from the first chapter of the second volume, but it will be sufficient to give one sentence in which the author represents human affection as triumphing over every obstacle of mental deficiency and personal appearance. After mentioning the ugly fellows with squat figures, ill-shapen nostrils, and dingy complexions, whose miniatures are kissed in secret by motherly lips, he says:—"And I believe there have been plenty of young heroes, of middle stature and feeble beards, who have felt quite sure they could never love anything more insignificant than a Diana, and yet have found themselves in middle life happily settled with a wife who waddles."

The story is simple enough, and, as far as the mere skeleton is concerned, soon told. For the sake of introducing a fair young Methodist who has the gift of preaching, the date of the incidents is thrown to the end of last century, but the time is not strictly observed, and we are not very much surprised to be informed that Bartle Massey "lighted a match furiously on the hob," which is far from being the only anachronism in the tale. Mrs. Poyser, the chatty wife of a well-to-do farmer, is the pivot on which the plot revolves. She is the chorus who is continually intervening with her opinions. As far as conversation goes, it might be important to mention that she has a husband, and that her husband has a father; but the story is not affected by such trivial circumstances. She has two nieces, however, Hetty and Dinah, who are of the utmost importance, for they supply the motives of all the action in the novel. Hetty is a thoughtless little kitten; her cousin Dinah a lovely Methodist, who goes preaching. Now, Adam Bede, the carpenter of Hayslope, the hero of these volumes, and a very noble character, was deeply in love with Hetty, who, however, is seduced by Captain Donnithorne, the young Squire. When he leaves her in order to join his regiment at Windsor he writes a letter to her, stating that in consequence of the difference of their positions it would be impossible for him to marry her, and she at once consents to marry Adam Bede. But as the wedding-day approaches so also approaches the hour of her shame, and she flies from her friends,—flies alone to seek out the Captain who had promised to be her friend in trouble. After a weary journey, the greater part of the way on foot, she arrives at Windsor, but only to discover that the Captain has gone with his regiment to Ireland, and nothing remains for her but to trudge back. She trudges back, body racked with pain and mind with anguish; she tries to commit suicide, but has not the courage; she at length gives birth to a child among strangers; she exposes the child in order to get rid of it; she is tried for its murder; she is transported; and she dies in exile. The Captain is very wretched, contrives to save her from the gallows, which was the punishment of her crime, and then himself goes away to drown his sorrow in the war with France. Adam Bede is long broken-hearted, but in the end marries the other niece of the Poysers, Dinah, the gracious young Methodist, and the story ends with his happiness. There is not much of a story it will be seen. The great charm of the novel is rather in the characters introduced than in the action which they carry on. All the characters are so true, and so natural, and so racy that we love to hear them talk for the sake of talking. They are so full of strange humours and funny pretty sayings that we entirely overlook the want of movement in the story. Besides which, when the dialogue ceases, the author's reflections are so pointed, and his descriptions are so vivid, that we naturally think more of what we have than of what we have not. There is not a character in the novel which is not well drawn, and even if the portrait is but a sketch still it is a true one. We have not mentioned the name of Mr. Irwine, the parson, who is very carefully drawn, nor of his mother, who is touched off in a more rapid manner; and yet the former is a very important personage in the dialogue, and is a fine moral influence throughout the tale. He is a very favourable specimen of the moral preachers of the close of last century, and the author has placed him in contrast to the more Scriptural style of which Dinah Morris, the young Methodist, is the representative. He sympathizes strongly with both, but leans most to the side of those moral teachers who have been somewhat harshly judged he thinks. Comparing Mr. Irwine with the curate of an "evangelical" turn who succeeded him, he makes Mr. Poyser pronounce this judgment:—"Mr. Irwine was like a good meal o' victual; *you are the better for him without thinking on it;* but Mr. Ryde is like a dose o' physic; he gripes you and worrets you, and after all he leaves you much the same." Irwine is a noble man, with a fine presence and a kindly, catholic nature. He was a silent influence, who did not trouble his parish much with theological "notions," but gave them the example of a kind heart, and demanded from them the reward of honest lives. "It's summat like to see such a man as that i' the desk of a Sunday," says that rattling Mrs. Poyser. "As I say to Poyser, it's like looking at a full crop o' wheat, or a pasture with a fine dairy o' cows in it; it makes you think the world's comfortable-like." The tolerance with which an author who is able to conceive the character of Dinah Morris, and to sympathize with her religious views, is thus pleased to regard a very opposite type of the religious character—a type which many worthy people, no doubt, would be disposed to brand as utterly irreligious, is one of the finest things in the novel, and affords a very good illustration of the tendency of the author to beat down all external differences, and bring into the light the grand points of genuine resemblance. You fancy that there can be nothing in nature more diverse than the spiritually-minded, praying, and preaching Dinah Morris, and the carnally-minded, easy, gentlemanly Mr. Irwine. I tell you, again and again, says Mr. Elliot, that there is no difference between them.

It will be evident that in order to establish the identity of man with man an author must travel a good deal into the region of latent thoughts, and unconscious or but semi-conscious feelings. There is infinite variety in what we express; there is a wonderful monotony in that great world of life which never comes into the light, but moves within us like the beating of the heart and the breathing of the lungs—a constant, though unobserved influence. It is in this twilight of the human soul that our novelist most delights to make his observations. Old Lisbeth Bede says of her son Adam, who is continually visiting the Poysers with the object (unknown even to himself) of seeing Dinah Morris:—"Eh, donna tell me what thee't sure on; thee know'st nought about it. What's he allays going to the Poysers' for, if he didna want t' see her? He goes twice where he used t' go once. Happen he knows na as he wants t' see her; *he knows na as I put salt in's broth, but he'd miss it pretty quick if it warna there.*" It is to the world of thoughts indicated in Mrs. Bede's very homely remark that the author has turned his chief attention. Like Mr. Thackeray, he takes a peculiar pleasure in showing the contrariety between thought and speech, the heart within and the mask without, which we call a face. He is always showing that we are better than we seem, greater than we know, nearer to each other than, perhaps, we would wish. It is a fertile theme of immense interest, and through the three volumes the author has handled it with rare skill. His dissection of all the motives at work in Arthur Donnithorne's mind when he is pleased to trifle with the affections of Hetty is very masterly—how he was tempted, how he struggled with the temptation, and what a strange under-current of feeling was carrying him on to his purpose, while he took note only of the feeble ripple on the surface. In the case of poor Hetty we have a similar analysis, but one still more difficult, owing to the utterly thoughtless character of the girl. She, perhaps, might be accepted as a fair example of the truth of Pope's very unjust saying, "Most women have no characters at all." Not that she is unreal—she is drawn to the life; but she is one of those who are so much less than they seem to be, whose most significant acts mean so little, that it is not easy to fix upon any central principle in their nature, any strong point of thought, or word, or act which belongs to them. "Hetty's face had a language that transcended her feelings," says the novelist.

"There are faces which nature changes with a meaning and pathos not belonging to the single human soul that flutters beneath them, but speaking the joys and sorrows of foregone generations; eyes that tell of deep love, which doubtless has been and is somewhere, but not paired with these eyes—perhaps paired with pale eyes that can say nothing; just as a national language may be instinct with poetry unfelt by the lips that use it."

All through the work the same train of thought runs, and at the very opening of the novel we have a curious illustration of it in a remark uttered by Joshua Rann, the parish clerk. "Joshway," as he is called by the people around, is a most imposing fellow, whose views of religious questions may be summed up in his own petty criticism:—

"Them Methodisses make folks believe as if they take a mug o' drink extry, an' make theirselves a bit comfortable, they'll have to go to hell for 't as sure as they're born. I'm not a tipplin' man nor a drunkard—nobody can say it on me; but I like a extry quart at Easter or Christmas time, as is nat'ral when we're goin' the rounds a-singin', an' folks offer't you for nothin'; or when I'm a-collectin' the dues; an' I like a pint, wi' my pipe, an' a neighbourly chat at Mester Casson's now an' then, for I was brought up i' th' Church, thank God, an' ha' been a parish clerk this two an' thirty year: I should know what the Church religion is."

The observation to which, however, we particularly refer was made on the occasion of a crowd collecting on the village-green to hear the young Methodist preach. Many were the comments, more or less appropriate, of the village worthies on the audacious act which Dinah Morris was about to commit, but, surely, if there was one comment more unmeaning than another, it was that of old Joshway, who in a resounding voice exclaimed, "Sehon, king of the Amorites; for His mercy endureth for ever; and Og, the king of Basan, for his mercy endureth for ever." Mr. George Eliot points out, with great gusto, the unconscious associations which led to this extraordinary speech—how Mr. Rann felt the necessity of maintaining the dignity of the Church, how, further, he felt that this dignity was bound up with his own sonorous utterances of the responses, and how, in accordance with this theory, he volleyed forth a quotation from the Psalm of the previous Sunday, in order to give a practical illustration of the Church's dignity.

The gem of the novel is Mrs. Poyser, who, for that combination of shrewd remark and homely wit with genuine kindliness and racy style which is so taking in Mr. Samuel Weller, is likely to outvie all the characters of recent fiction, with the single exception of the hero we have named. Mrs. Poyser, in her way, is as amusing as either Mrs. Gamp or Mrs. Nickleby, and much more sensible. Wife of a rough and ready farmer, she is a great woman. She is the firstling of the author's mind, which he is not likely to surpass, even as that glorious Sam Weller, the firstling of Mr. Dickens's pen, has not been outshone by any successor. Mrs. Poyser pervades the novel. Her wisdom is always coming out either spoken by herself, or quoted by somebody else, or mentioned by the author. On one occasion, the author, unable to express himself in his own words, introduces Adam Bede to express the thought in his words, and Adam Bede, finding his own language inadequate, is obliged to fall back upon the expressions used by Mrs. Poyser, whom accordingly he quotes. "You're mighty fond o' Craig," says Mrs. Poyser to her husband, speaking of a certain Scotch gardener; "but for my part, I think he's welly like a cock as thinks the sun's rose o' purpose to hear him crow." This is the Poyser style, a good pungent style, remarkably effective when it is necessary to scold her husband, to subdue her nieces, or to lash the maids. It is a fine thing to hear her out of the goodness of her heart and the fulness of her wisdom abuse her whole household. One poor maid breaks a jug. How they all catch it, as if there never happened such an event before! In the midst of her storming, she herself breaks a jug, and instantly we are entertained with the philosophy of jug-breaking, from which it is to be gathered that there is a fatality in jugs, and that they fly out of one's hands with a determination to be broken, no matter how tight they are held. Her style runs into proverbs. "Folks must put up wi' their own kin, as they put up wi' their own noses—it's their own flesh and blood"—she says. "If the chaffcutter had the making of us, we should all be straw, I reckon," she says again. "I'm not one o' those as can see the cat i' the dairy, an' wonder what she's come after" is another of her sayings. "Ah, it's fine talking, it's fine talking. It's hard to tell which is Old Harry when everybody's got boots on" is also hers. Of mankind she says, "The men are mostly so slow, their thoughts overrun 'em, an' they can only catch 'em by the tail. Howiver, I'm not denyin' the women are foolish; God Almighty made 'em to match the men." She adds a little further on, "Some folks' tongues are like the clocks as run on strikin', not to tell you the time o' the day, but because there's summut wrong i' their own inside." A good homely woman, it will be observed, who knows how to keep her own, and doing her duty well, has a wonderful supply of self-complacency. "Eh," she says to her husband, after a day of pleasure, "I'd sooner ha' brewin' day and washin' day together nor one o' these pleasurin' days. There's no work so tirin' as danglin' about an' starin' an' not rightly knowin' what you're goin' to do next; an' keeping your face in smilin' order, like a grocer o' market day, for fear people shouldna think you civil enough. An' you've nothin' to show for't when it's done, if it isn't a yallow face wi' eatin' things as disagree." This husband to whom she talks has a character different from hers, but he has caught up her style of conversation, and often when he is speaking we fancy it is Mrs. Poyser, until she breaks in with her more rattling, clattering tones. "I'm no friend to young fellows amarr'in' afore they know the difference atween a crab an' a apple; but they may wait o'er long," says Mr. Poyser, in terms which make us fancy that it is his wife who speaks. "To be sure," strikes in Mrs. Poyser, "if you go past your dinner time, there'll be little relish o' your meat. You turn it o'er an' o'er wi' your fork, an' don't eat it after all. You find faut wi' your meat, an' the faut is all i' your own stomach." In some respects, also, Mrs. Poyser is repeated in another good lady with a querulous twist in her,—old Lisbeth Bede, mother of Adam. When her husband is dead, Adam proposes to go to the village to have the coffin made, fearing that if he worked at it himself it would pain his mother. "Nay, my lad, nay," Lisbeth cries out in a wailing tone, "thee wotna let nobody make thy feyther's coffin but thysen? Who'd make it so well? *An' him, as know'd what good work war*, an's got a son as is th' head o' the village, an' all Treddles' on too, for cleverness." "Very well, mother," says Adam, "if that's thy wish I'll make the coffin at home; but I thought thee wouldstna like to hear the work going on." Then comes the reply:—"An why shouldna I like it? It's the right thing to be done. An' what's likin' got to do wi't? It's choice o' mislikins is all I'n got i' this world. One mossel's as good as another when your mouth's out o' taste. Thee mun set about it this mornin' fust thing. I wunna ha nobody to touch the coffin but thee." She refuses even to let her other son, Seth, a good young fellow of the soft species, assist Adam. "Thee wast often angered wi' thy feyther when he was alive; thee must be the better to 'm, now he's goe'n. *He'd ha thought nothin' on't for Seth to ma's coffin.*"

We might go on quoting these speeches until at last we transfer half the novel to our columns. The hero of the work, Adam Bede, is not so remarkable for his speeches as for what he does. He speaks out in a strong, manly way, but not very often with that sharp epigrammatic force which is so characteristic of Mrs. Poyser, Lisbeth Bede, and the schoolmaster, Bartle Massey, who, by the way, has met with a disappointment in early life, and has ever since been a womanhater, as will be seen in the following profound remark:—"Nonsense! it's the silliest lie a sensible man like you ever believed, to say a woman makes a house comfortable. It's a story got up, because the women are there, and something must be found for 'em to do. I tell you there isn't a thing under the sun that needs to be done at all, but what a man can do better than a woman, unless it's bearing children, and they do that in a poor make-shift way; it had better ha' been left to the men—it had better ha' been left to the men." The speeches of Seth Bede and of Dinah Morris, though excellent as illustrations of character, are, like those of Adam, not of the epigrammatic sort. Dinah's sermon is very fine, and she herself is a most beautiful piece of portraiture—a perfect chrysolite. The minor sketches are superabundant; they crowd the canvass. We have not here one great and real character in the midst of a mob of lay figures. The subordinate personages are in their way quite as well pictured as the leading ones. The whole work, indeed, leaves upon us the impression of something highly finished and well matured, and we close the volumes wondering whether the author is to do better in his next novel,—curious, also, to know who the author really is. Nobody seems to know who is Mr. George Eliot, and when his previous work appeared it was even surmised that he must be a lady, since none but a woman's hand could have painted those touching scenes of clerical life. Now, the question will be raised, can this be a young author? Is all this mature thought, finished portraiture, and crowd of characters the product of a 'prentice hand and of callow genius? If it is, the hand must have an extraordinary cunning, and the genius must be of the highest order.

* *Adam Bede*, by George Elliot, author of *Scenes of Clerical Life*, 3 vols. W. Blackwood and Sons.

UNIVERSITY INTELLIGENCE.

CAMBRIDGE, April 11.

The following have been elected Fellows of St. John's College:—

The Rev. Thomas George Bonney.

Mr. Richard Horton Smith.

Mr. Alexander William Potts.

The Lady Margaret's Professor of Divinity purposes to lecture in the Arts' School on Pastoral Theology on Mondays and Saturdays in the Easter Term, commencing on Monday, May 2, at noon.

The Professor of Arabic has given notice that he proposes to commence his lectures on Tuesday, May 3, and to continue them on Fridays and Tuesdays during the term.

SUBJECTS.

Arabic, 10 a.m.—The Moallakah of Lebid; the Koran.

Syriac, 11 a.m.—The New Testament; the Ecclesiastical History of John, Bishop of Ephesus.

EXPIRING LAWS.—The Select Committee have reported a long list to the House of Commons of expiring and temporary laws. They include the Income-Tax Act, which will come to an untimely end on the 6th of April, 1860 (curiously enough on Good Friday). The Militia Act will expire on Lady-day, 1861. The Act for the government of the new colony of British Columbia will come to an end on the 31st of December, 1862.

Letters to the editor

'Could not this outrage be averted? There sprang from my lips that fiery formula which has sprung from the lips of so many choleric old gentlemen in the course of the past hundred years and more: "I shall write to *The Times*".' (Max Beerbohm, *A Letter That Was Not Written*, 1914.)

It is a matter of chagrin as well as pride to the professional journalists who write *The Times* that the most famous page in the newspaper is the one written by its readers, the Letters Page. A market survey conducted by management consultants in the 1960s indicated that it was (*pace* the crossword and Deaths) the page that most readers turned to first. The letters columns are compulsory reading for the other night editors of Fleet Street: many a good story has been picked up from a letter in the paper's first edition. Letters to *The Times* are the stadium in which the intelligentsia and the eccentric classes parade their hobby-horses.

The Times has always published letters from its readers. In the early days correspondence was published under the heading 'Letters to the Conductor'; and later, 'Letters to the Printer'. Writing to *The Times* is an institution as old as the paper – and not just a national institution, but an international one. Statesmen, scientists, men of affairs, and artists from all the old worlds and the new world have contributed. But in spite of the uninformed rumour that you have to be a member of the Athenaeum, or at least of Parliament, to have your letter published, by far the most frequent contributor is the ordinary man or woman in the street, unknown to wider fame. About ninety thousand letters are addressed to the editor every year. Many are called, but few are chosen: the average number printed at present is thirteen a day.

Below Cartoon in PUNCH by George du Maurier, *c.* 1890.

THE TIME-HONOURED BRITISH THREAT

Indignant Anglo-Saxon (*to provincial French innkeeper, who is bowing his thanks for the final settlement of his exorbitant and much-disputed account*). "Oh, oui, mossoo! pour le matière de ça, je *paye!* Mais juste vous regardez *ici*, mon ami! et juste—vous—marquez—mes—*mots!* Je *paye—mais je mette le dans la 'Times!'*"

It is scarcely possible after two hundred years to establish definitively which topic excited the greatest number of letters to *The Times*. The Irish question in the nineteenth century, and the Navy programme and food tax policy in the early twentieth century filled acres of space in the newspaper. But what can be stated with certainty is that during the last sixty years there has been no postbag to equal the one that arrived during the Abdication crisis. Oldest inhabitants of Printing House Square speak with awe, and possibly hyperbole, of having to force their way into the Letters Room over piled sacks of mail. It may have been unique. Its treatment certainly was, for not one letter about the Abdication was deliberately published (see p. 106). Geoffrey Dawson, the editor, used the letters merely to give him an indication of the progress of public opinion.

For the record, and as a curious footnote of history, it can be revealed that one letter about the Abdication, from 'XY', did find its way into *The Times*; the editor removed it after the second edition. Its arrival there is inexplicable, especially since *The Times* does not usually publish anonymous letters. It can now be revealed that 'XY' was a young man of the Establishment, a scholar, an explorer and a writer of wit, who had connections with *The Times*.

When a selection of letters to *The Times* was published under the title *The First Cuckoo*, the reviewer in the *Jerusalem Post* wrote: '*The Times* correspondence is the last resort of the piquant, the idiosyncratic, the nutty, the dotty and the potty'. Taking a less narrow view, the French Academician Jean Dutourd wrote: '*Quel document sur Albion! Quelle mine pour les historiens et les sociologues! Et aussi quelle source de poésie pure!*'

Before the Second World War the column was largely the enclosure of the Establishment (a sloppy term that for these purposes includes the rural rector as well as his bishop, the landed as well as the titled gentry, the country solicitor as well as the eminent KC). For the past forty years or so the column has been opened to a far wider public, not as a matter of policy but because that is where the good letters are coming from. One can speculate that this is because of a wider and improved system of education, and because of the proliferation of problems of a local and social nature. Not just a magic circle, but all intelligent people like to think that they have a hand in running the country these days; and that often means writing to *The Times*.

Probably the grandest letter to *The Times* was the one from a Queen of Great Britain. Following criticism by *The Times* of her three years of mourning seclusion since the death of the Prince Consort, Queen Victoria wrote in her own hand to rebut the criticism (see opposite page). She employed her private secretary General Grey to take her letter addressed 'To the Editor of *The Times*' to Printing House Square. Delane decided to publish it under Court News rather than on the Letters Page.

The Government and Court were shocked at this constitutional innovation. Lord Clarendon wrote to his wife:

> It has produced a very painful impression, and is considered very *infra dig.* for the Queen. It is her own writing, and Grey took it straight from Windsor to Delane. By chance he met Puss [Granville] on the way, who urged him to consult some of the ministers before the Queen so committed herself, but he would not hear of it. Lady Palmerston told me that Pam had made up his mind to speak to her on the subject; but I am sure he won't.

If the editor were asked what quality he most favoured in his correspondents, he would probably reply 'brevity'. The most common reason for the rejection of a letter for publication is overwriting. The late Colonel Wintle was a percipient man when he wrote to the editor: 'Sir, I have just written you a long letter. On reading it over I have thrown it into the wastepaper basket. Hoping this will meet with your approval, I am Sir . . .'

On 18 June 1940 a letter that had never been intended for publication appeared at the head of the column (see opposite page). The interest and sympathy 'An Airman's Letter' received was so overwhelming that *The Times* reprinted it as a pamphlet, and thousands of copies were sold for charity. To this day enquiries are still received about it.

A selection of letters to the editor. Top left, a letter from Queen Victoria, dated 6 April 1864, and to the right of it a letter written by an RAF pilot to his mother. The others illustrate the range of passion and eccentricity from the famous and the unknown that characterise the Letters Page.

THE COURT.

An erroneous idea seems generally to prevail, and has latterly found frequent expression in the newspapers, that the Queen is about to resume the place in society which she occupied before her great affliction; that is, that she is about again to hold levees and drawing-rooms in person, and to appear as before at Court balls, concerts, &c. This idea cannot be too explicitly contradicted.

The Queen heartily appreciates the desire of her subjects to see her, and whatever she *can* do to gratify them in this loyal and affectionate wish she *will* do. Whenever any real object is to be attained by her appearing on public occasions, any national interest to be promoted, or anything to be encouraged which is for the good of her people, Her Majesty will not shrink, as she has not shrunk, from any personal sacrifice or exertion, however painful.

But there are other and higher duties than those of mere representation which are now thrown upon the Queen, alone and unassisted—duties which she cannot neglect without injury to the public service, which weigh unceasingly upon her, overwhelming her with work and anxiety.

The Queen has laboured conscientiously to discharge these duties till her health and strength, already shaken by the utter and ever-abiding desolation which has taken the place of her former happiness, have been seriously impaired.

To call upon her to undergo, in addition, the fatigue of those mere State ceremonies which can be equally well performed by other members of her family is to ask her to run the risk of entirely disabling herself for the discharge of those other duties which cannot be neglected without serious injury to the public interests.

The Queen will, however, do what she can—in the manner least trying to her health, strength, and spirits—to meet the loyal wishes of her subjects, to afford that support and countenance to society, and to give that encouragement to trade which is desired of her.

More the Queen *cannot* do; and more the kindness and good feeling of her people will surely not exact from her.

24 JANUARY 1933

is now up to the batsmen to kill the two-eyed stance.

I am yours faithfully,

R. H. LYTTELTON.

GREY WAGTAIL IN ST. JAMES'S PARK

TO THE EDITOR OF THE TIMES

Sir,—It may be of interest to record that, in walking through St. James's Park to-day, I noticed a grey wagtail running about on the now temporarily dry bed of the lake, near the dam below the bridge, and occasionally picking small insects out of the cracks in the dam.

Probably the occurrence of this bird in the heart of London has been recorded before, but I have not myself previously noted it in the Park.

I am your obedient servant,

NEVILLE CHAMBERLAIN.

37, Eaton Square, S.W.1, Jan. 23.

P.S.—For the purpose of removing doubts, as we say in the House of Commons, I should perhaps add that I mean a grey wagtail and not a pied.

7 APRIL 1911

TO THE EDITOR OF THE TIMES.

Sir,—Of all the varying symptoms of madness in the life of modern nations the most dreadful is this prostitution of the conquest of the air to the ends of warfare.

If ever men presented a spectacle of sheer inanity it is now—when, having at long last triumphed in their struggle to subordinate to their welfare the unconquered element, they have straightway commenced to defile that element, so heroically mastered, by filling it with engines of destruction. If ever the gods were justified of their ironic smile—by the gods, it is now! Is there any thinker alive watching this still utterly preventible calamity without horror and despair? Horror at what must come of it, if not promptly stopped; despair that men can be so blind, so hopelessly and childishly the slaves of their own marvellous inventive powers. Was there ever so patent a case for scotching at birth a hideous development of the black arts of warfare; ever such an occasion for the Powers in conference to ban once and for all a new and ghastly menace?

A little reason, a grain of commonsense, a gleam of sanity before it is too late—before vested interests and the chains of a new habit have enslaved us too hopelessly. If this fresh devilry be not quenched within the next few years it will be too late. Water and earth are wide enough for men to kill each other on. For the love of the sun, and stars, and the blue sky, that have given us all our aspirations since the beginning of time, let us leave the air to innocence! Will not those who have eyes to see, good will towards men, and the power to put that good will into practice, bestir themselves while there is yet time, and save mankind from this last and worst of all its follies?

Yours truly,

JOHN GALSWORTHY.

.. Addison-road, W., April 5.

AN AIRMAN TO HIS MOTHER

THE FIGHT WITH EVIL

"MY EARTHLY MISSION IS FULFILLED"

Among the personal belongings of a young R.A.F. pilot in a Bomber Squadron who was recently reported "Missing, believed killed," was a letter to his mother—to be sent to her if he were killed.

"This letter was perhaps the most amazing one I have ever read; simple and direct in its wording but splendid and uplifting in its outlook," says the young officer's station commander. "It was inevitable that I should read it—in fact he must have intended this, for it was left open in order that I might be certain that no prohibited information was disclosed.

"I sent the letter to the bereaved mother, and asked her whether I might publish it anonymously, as I feel its contents may bring comfort to other mothers, and that every one in our country may feel proud to read of the sentiments which support 'an average airman' in the execution of his present arduous duties. I have received the mother's permission, and I hope this letter may be read by the greatest possible number of our countrymen at home and abroad."

TEXT OF THE LETTER

Dearest Mother,—Though I feel no premonition at all, events are moving rapidly, and I have instructed that this letter be forwarded to you should I fail to return from one of the raids which we shall shortly be called upon to undertake. You must hope on for a month, but at the end of that time you must accept the fact that I have handed my task over to the extremely capable hands of my comrades of the Royal Air Force, as so many splendid fellows have already done.

First, it will comfort you to know that my role in this war has been of the greatest importance. Our patrols far out over the North Sea have helped to keep the trade routes clear for our convoys and supply ships, and on one occasion our information was instrumental in saving the lives of the men in a crippled lighthouse relief ship. Though it will be difficult for you, you will disappoint me if you do not at least try to accept the facts dispassionately, for I shall have done my duty to the utmost of my ability. No man can do more, and no one calling himself a man could do less.

I have always admired your amazing courage in the face of continual setbacks; in the way you have given me as good an education and background as anyone in the country; and always kept up appearances without ever losing faith in the future. My death would not mean that your struggle has been in vain. Far from it. It means that your sacrifice is as great as mine. Those who serve England must expect nothing from her; we debase ourselves if we regard our country as merely a place in which to eat and sleep.

History resounds with illustrious names who have given all, yet their sacrifice has resulted in the British Empire, where there is a measure of peace, justice, and freedom for all, and where a higher standard of civilization has evolved, and is still evolving, than anywhere else. But this is not only concerning our own land. To-day we are faced with the greatest organized challenge to Christianity and civilization that the world has ever seen, and I count myself lucky and honoured to be the right age and fully trained to throw my full weight into the scale. For this I have to thank you. Yet there is more work for you to do. The home front will still have to stand united for years after the war is won. For all that can be said against it, I still maintain that this war is a very good thing; every individual is having the chance to give and dare all for his principle like the martyrs of old. However long the time may be, one thing can never be altered—I shall have lived and died an Englishman. Nothing else matters one jot nor can anything ever change it.

You must not grieve for me, for if you really believe in religion and all that it entails that would be hypocrisy. I have no fear of death; only a queer elation. . . . I would have it no other way. The universe is so vast and so ageless that the life of one man can only be justified by the measure of his sacrifice. We are sent to this world to acquire a personality and a character to take with us that can never be taken from us. Those who just eat and sleep, prosper and procreate, are no better than animals if all their lives they are at peace.

I firmly and absolutely believe that evil things are sent into the world to try us; they are sent deliberately by our Creator to test our metal because He knows what is good for us. The Bible is full of cases where the easy way out has been discarded for moral principles.

I count myself fortunate in that I have seen the whole country and known men of every calling. But with the final test of war I consider my character fully developed. Thus at my early age my earthly mission is already fulfilled and I am prepared to die with just one regret, and one only—that I could not devote myself to making your declining years more happy by being with you; but you will live in peace and freedom and I shall have directly contributed to that, so here again my life will not have been in vain.

Your loving Son,

A WORDSWORTH SONNET

TO THE EDITOR OF THE TIMES

Sir,—Another apposite quotation from the past is provided in Wordsworth's sonnet, "November, 1806," which runs:—

Another year!—anoth...

Parker.

rane, M.P., and Lady Cochrane, Sir G. Bartley, M.P., and Lady Bartley, Sir J. Dimsdale, M.P., and Lady Dimsdale, Sir E. Reed, M.P., Sir T. Wrightson, M.P. and Lady Wrightson, and Sir G. Parker, M.P., and Lady Parker.

SUMPTUARY REGULATIONS AT THE OPERA.

TO THE EDITOR OF THE TIMES.

Sir,—The Opera management at Covent Garden regulates the dress of its male patrons. When is it going to do the same to the women?

On Saturday night I went to the Opera. I wore the costume imposed on me by the regulations of the house. I fully recognize the advantage of those regulations. Evening dress is cheap, simple, durable, prevents rivalry and extravagance on the part of male leaders of fashion, annihilates class distinctions, and gives men who are poor and doubtful of their social position (that is, the great majority of men) a sense of security and satisfaction that no clothes of their own choosing could confer, besides saving a whole sex the trouble of considering what they should wear on state occasions. The objections to it are as dust in the balance in the eyes of the ordinary Briton. These objections are that it is colourless and characterless; that it involves a whitening process which makes the shirt troublesome, slightly uncomfortable, and seriously unclean; that it acts as a passport for undesirable persons; that it fails to guarantee sobriety, cleanliness, and order on the part of the wearer; and that it reduces to a formula a very vital human habit which should be the subject of constant experiment and active private enterprise. All such objections are thoroughly un-English. They appeal only to an eccentric few, and may be left out of account with the fantastic objections of men like Ruskin, Tennyson, Carlyle, and Morris to tall hats.

But I submit that what is sauce for the gander is sauce for the goose. Every argument that applies to the regulation of the man's dress applies equally to the regulation of the woman's. Now let me describe what actually happened to me at the Opera. Not only was I in evening dress by compulsion, but I voluntarily added many graces of conduct as to which the management made no stipulation whatever. I was in my seat in time for the first chord of the overture. I did not chatter during the music nor raise my voice when the Opera was too loud for normal conversation. I did not get up and go out when the statue music began. My language was fairly moderate considering the number and nature of the improvements on Mozart volunteered by Signor Caruso, and the respectful ignorance of the dramatic points of the score exhibited by the conductor and the stage manager—if there is such a functionary at Covent Garden. In short, my behaviour was exemplary.

At 9 o'clock (the Opera began at 8) a lady came in and sat down very conspicuously in my line of sight. She remained there until the beginning of the last act. I do not complain of her coming late and going early; on the contrary, I wish she had come later and gone earlier. For this lady, who had very black hair, had stuck over her right ear the pitiable corpse of a large white bird, which looked exactly as if some one had killed it by stamping on its breast, and then nailed it to the lady's temple, which was presumably of sufficient solidity to bear the operation. I am not, I hope, a morbidly squeamish person; but the spectacle sickened me. I presume that if I had presented myself at the doors with a dead snake round my neck, a collection of blackbeetles pinned to my shirtfront, and a grouse in my hair, I should have been refused admission. Why, then, is a woman to be allowed to commit such a public outrage? Had the lady been refused admission, as she should have been, she would have soundly rated the tradesman who imposed the disgusting headdress on her under the false pretence that "the best people" wear such things, and withdrawn her custom from him; and thus the root of the evil would be struck at; for your fashionable woman generally allows herself to be dressed according to the taste of a person whom she would not let sit down in her presence. I once, in Drury Lane Theatre, sat behind a *matinée* hat decorated with the two wings of a seagull, artificially reddened at the joints so as to produce an illusion of being freshly plucked from a live bird. But even that lady stopped short of the whole seagull. Both ladies were evidently regarded by their neighbours as ridiculous and vulgar; but that is hardly enough when the offence is one which produces a sensation of physical sickness in persons of normal humane sensibility.

I suggest to the Covent Garden authorities that, if they feel bound to protect their subscribers against the danger of my shocking them with a blue tie, they are at least equally bound to protect me against the danger of a woman shocking me with a dead bird.

Yours truly,

G. BERNARD SHAW.

THE TIMES LIST OF
NEW BOOKS and NEW EDITIONS.
*** This column is restricted to books published during the last six months.

31 OCTOBER 1949

Yours faithf...

NOËL NEWSOME.

Medhurst Row Farm, Edenbridge, Kent.

THE DEATH OF A MOUSE

TO THE EDITOR OF THE TIMES

Sir,—Several years ago I bought a very ingenious mousetrap which actually caught one mouse. The cheese was placed in a cage approached through a small doorway. When the mouse had entered, the door automatically closed behind him. When, bored with trying to get at the cheese, he sought to depart, the only way open was up a sloping tunnel. At the top he came out on to a platform, which tipped over under his weight and deposited him in a tank of water. As the platform returned to level, it released a catch which opened the front door for the next victim. It is only fair to the mice to say that the one caught by this apparatus was too young to know any better.

Yours faithfully,

C. J. JEFFRIES.

Colonial Office, Church House, Great Smith Street, S.W.1, Oct. 28.

The Court Page

It is an axiom of the inky trade of journalism that royalty is the next best thing for selling newspapers, after baby polar bears and other small cuddly animals. That is why Fleet Street decorates its front pages with pictures of Princess Di and the Queen Mum with banal and remorseless regularity. There may even be some truth in the axiom. Not all the axioms of journalism are necessarily mistaken, though many of them are.

From the beginning *The Times* has catered for the public interest in the doings of its royalties. For example, in its first issue it noted: 'Yesterday their Majesties came from Windsor, and last night honoured the Theatre with their presence'. Thereafter such royal itineraries appeared daily, though they were not always so courtierly – for instance in the thunderous valedictory leader on the morning after the death of George IV. It was not until the 1830s that royal comings and goings acquired the title of the Court Circular, by which they are still known.

Over the past two hundred years the procedures have been majestically formalized and dignified, as trivial matters to do with princes tend to be. The Court Circular is the responsibility of the Lord Chamberlain's department, and is delivered daily from St James's Palace on exceedingly stiff, yellow and expensive paper. A full grammar of the correct style and form of the Court Circular would take more space than it would be worth, and would try the patience of the reader. But the text is a wonderful exercise of nice pedantic and courtierly discrimination over titles and tittles, discernible only by the professional Court Circular watcher. Thus the official members of the royal family get a capital T for their precedent definite articles, as in Queen Elizabeth The Queen Mother. Her Majesty, of course, gets capitals for Her Majesty. Lesser breeds without the inner circle get no capital: the Duchess of Kent. He is The Prince Andrew, because he is a son of the Sovereign; but plain Prince Michael of Kent, because he is only a grandson of George V.

Above Debutantes about to be presented at Buckingham Palace. The Misses Phyllis and Kathleen Tew in their car in the Mall, 19 May 1931.

Similar subtle discrimination is indicated in the degree of grief that the Court Circular attributes to the Queen when there is a death in the family. Let us assume that the deceased is the child, or has married the child, of A (with a capital A, as, no doubt, the Court Circular would have it) – of A Sovereign: then the Queen is said to have 'received' or 'learned' the news with 'great' regret. If the deceased is only a grandchild or other more distant relation of A Sovereign, the Queen receives the news with plain regret. When the Queen's mother-in-law, Her Royal Highness Princess Andrew of Greece, died in December 1969, the Court Circular reported that the Queen had 'heard' the news with great regret. This unusual rubric enabled the cognoscenti to infer that Princess Andrew had died upstairs at Buckingham Palace, so enabling the Queen to hear rather than receive the news.

When the Court Circular states that 'The Queen has arrived at Windsor Castle', it means that the Queen and her Court have moved into official residence there, not that they have dropped in on a whim. It no longer breathlessly records the Queen's every visit to polo matches and other minor social and recreational events. By golly, it did for Queen Victoria.

The importance of the Court Circular to the paper of record was recognized by the addition of the royal coat of arms. There has been a running argument for two centuries about whether *The Times* has any right to carry them. The Palace, the Earl Marshal and the Lord Chamberlain take the view that the royal arms are private property, and that *The Times* is pirating by printing them. For a time they prevailed upon William Rees-Mogg, while he was editor, to remove the arms from the masthead. The hard men of journalism say that the royal arms are national as well as private property, and that anyway they are striking emblems of newspaper design. In these deep waters, all that can be said with certainty is that the royal arms printed in *The Times* are often anachronistic to the trained eye of a royalty watcher. Those on the front page in 1984, for example, were first used by *The Times* in 1792, and are dynasties out of date.

The Court Circular is a minefield for the unwary. It is a part of the paper that a small elite of the readers turn to first, and they have jealous eyes. Woe betide the untrained sub-editor who does not recognize the significance of the Court arriving at the Palace of Holyroodhouse, and fails to register the momentous event by putting the royal arms of The Queen of Scotland at the top of the Court Circular.

It was that great professional popularizer Northcliffe who tidied and systematized the Court Page. Headlines were made bolder. The items were arranged systematically. And the Court Circular came to roost in a regular space. And other features, many of which remain today, were introduced to give the Court Page of *The Times* the flavour that we know and love: obituaries, engagements (in which the style for titles and form is as rigorous as the Court Circular), marriages, university news, the list of dances at the beginning of the Season (which actually ended in 1958, with the last presentation parties for debutantes, but nobody has noticed yet), catalogues of those who were lucky (or unlucky) enough to dine at Downing Street last night. Northcliffe introduced on the Court Page a columnar article, generally of a light-hearted or off-beat nature, and usually sent in by amateur writers. This article was known in the office as the Court Pager. These little essays were in the best tradition of English belles-lettres, and were often charming and sometimes hilarious. A list of some of their titles gives the idea: Model policemen, Russian china figures, Birthdays in Cos, A ramble in the foothills of the Himalaya, Lambing time in New Zealand, Taking a choir to Holland, Home woodlands. Many of them represented that old English art form, which generations of children have been made to produce on the first day of term, 'What I did in the holidays'.

The Court Pager and the Fourth Leader were discarded when news was moved on to the front page. Although they were much regretted, the humour of the times and of *The Times* had shifted so that it was no longer possible to write, or to read, such pieces with the high seriousness required by the genre. The disappearance of the Court Pager left more room for death. And obituaries started to cover a wider area of the dead, memorializing not just the great and the good, but anybody who had an interesting or unusual life.

Market research indicates that the Court Page is one of the best-read parts of the paper. Irreverent young journalists on *The Times*, who call it the boneyard and grumble when their stories end up on it, are misguided. It generally manages to give a uniform selection of the comings and going, the wooings and dyings, of people of all sorts and conditions, from Service appointments to the Church of England and Oxbridge results (only first class degrees from other universities). School announcements about the arcane goings-on at St Cake's next term are a minor branch of English poetry. Hopeful lawyers queue outside Printing House Square on the nights that the Bar exam results are published on the Court Page to get the first intimation of triumph or disaster. The one thing that cuts a swathe through the Court Page is a State Visit, with columns of space occupied by interminable lists of who sat in which carriage, and whither the Sovereign's Escort. But every syllable of the Court Circular has to find a place under the royal coat of arms.

The Court Circular describes the start of a state visit by the King of Norway.
6 JUNE 1951

COURT CIRCULAR

BUCKINGHAM PALACE, JUNE 5

The King of Norway arrived in London this afternoon on a visit to The King and Queen at Buckingham Palace.

The Norwegian Royal Yacht "Norge," conveying The King of Norway to England, was met in the North Sea by a Naval Escort of British Destroyers and an Escort of Aircraft of the Royal Air Force.

Monsieur V. Bommen (Chef du Cabinet), Monsieur I. Smith-Kielland (Maréchal de la Cour), and Captain O. Malm (Aide-de-Camp) are in attendance upon His Majesty.

A salute was fired at Sheerness Centre Bastion by No. 223 Independent Maintenance Battery, Royal Regiment of Artillery, under the command of Captain H. E. Cooper.

Upon arrival off the Great Nore, the "Norge" was boarded by Admiral Sir Cecil Harcourt (Commander-in-Chief, The Nore) and proceeded up river escorted by two Motor Torpedo Boats.

As the "Norge" entered the Pool of London a salute was fired from the Tower of London Saluting Battery by "A" Battery, 1st Regiment Honourable Artillery Company (R.H.A.), under the command of Major G. Buchanan.

The Duke of Gloucester, on behalf of The King, drove by motor-car to Westminster Pier, embarked in the Royal Barge, and proceeded down river to the "Norge," moored at the Battle Bridge Buoys.

His Royal Highness went on board to welcome The King of Norway on behalf of The King and Queen.

The Duke of Gloucester was accompanied by His Excellency the Norwegian Ambassador (Monsieur Per Preben Prebensen) and presented the Earl of Eldon (Lord in Waiting to The King) and Colonel Sir John Aird, Bt. (Extra Equerry to The King), who have been specially attached to The King of Norway.

His Majesty, with His Royal Highness, embarked in the Royal Barge and proceeded to Westminster Pier, and was met upon arrival by The Queen and by The Princess Elizabeth, Duchess of Edinburgh, The Princess Margaret, and The Duchess of Kent.

The following were also present at the Pier:—Field-Marshal the Viscount Alanbrooke (His Majesty's Lieutenant for the County of London), the Right Hon. C. R. Attlee, M.P. (Prime Minister), the Right Hon. Herbert Morrison, M.P. (Secretary of State for Foreign Affairs), the Right Hon. James Chuter Ede, M.P. (Secretary of State for the Home Department), the Right Hon. the Lord Mayor and the Sheriffs of the City of London, Admiral of the Fleet the Lord Fraser of North Cape (First Sea Lord of the Admiralty and Chief of Naval Staff), Field-Marshal Sir William Slim (Chief of the Imperial General Staff), Marshal of the Royal Air Force Sir John Slessor (Chief of the Air Staff), the Right Hon. Sir John Anderson (Chairman of the Port of London Authority), Air Marshal Sir Basil Embry (Air Officer Commanding in Chief, Fighter Command), Major-General Julian Gascoigne (General Officer Commanding London District), Sir Harold Scott (Commissioner of Police of the Metropolis), the Right Hon. the Chairman of the London County Council, and the Mayor of the City of Westminster.

A Guard of Honour of the 2nd Battalion, Coldstream Guards, with the State Colour of the Regiment, the Band of the Regiment, and the Drums of the Battalion, under the command of Major R. D. Dobson, was mounted on the Embankment.

The King of Norway was conducted to his carriage by the Duke of Beaufort (Master of the Horse) and accompanied by The Queen, with The Princess Elizabeth, Duchess of Edinburgh, The Princess Margaret, and The Duke of Gloucester drove to Buckingham Palace, a Carriage Procession having been formed in the following order:—

FIRST CARRIAGE
THE KING OF NORWAY
THE QUEEN
The Duke of Gloucester

SECOND CARRIAGE
The Princess Elizabeth, Duchess of Edinburgh
The Princess Margaret
The Master of the Horse

THIRD CARRIAGE
The Countess of Halifax
His Excellency The Norwegian Ambassador
Monsieur V. Bommen
The Earl of Eldon

FOURTH CARRIAGE
Monsieur I. Smith-Kielland
Captain O. Malm
Colonel Sir John Aird, Bt.
Colonel F. F. B. St. George, The Life Guards

MOTOR-CAR
The Lady Margaret Hay
Lieutenant-General Sir Frederick Browning
Captain the Lord Plunket

A Sovereign's Escort, with two Standards, under the command of Major the Viscount Dillon, Royal Horse Guards (The Blues), was furnished by the Household Cavalry, and The King's Guard of the 3rd Battalion, Grenadier Guards, with The King's Colour and Band of the Regiment and the Drums of the Battalion, under the command of Major R. Steele, was mounted at Buckingham Palace.

The route of the Procession was lined by contingents of the three Services.

The Lord Chamberlain, the Lord Steward, and the Ladies and Gentlemen of the Household in Waiting were in attendance in the Grand Hall, Buckingham Palace, upon the arrival of The King of Norway.

His Majesty's Body Guard of the Honourable Corps of Gentlemen at Arms, under the command of the Lord Shepherd (the Captain), and The King's Body Guard of the Yeomen of the Guard, under the command of Major-General Sir Allan Adair, Bt. (the Ensign), were on duty in the Grand Hall.

The King of Norway drove to Westminster Abbey this afternoon, where His Majesty laid a Wreath on the Grave of the Unknown Warrior.

His Majesty subsequently visited Queen Mary at Marlborough House.

The King and Queen gave a Dinner Party this evening in honour of The King of Norway, at which Queen Mary, The Princess Elizabeth, Duchess of Edinburgh, The Princess Margaret, The Duke of Gloucester, Princess Astrid of Norway, The Duchess of Kent, the Lady Patricia Ramsay and Admiral the Hon. Sir Alexander Ramsay, Princess Alice, Countess of Athlone, and Major-General the Earl of Athlone, Princess Marie Louise, the Marquess and Marchioness of Carisbrooke, Vice-Admiral the Earl and the Countess Mountbatten of Burma, and the Duchess of Beaufort were present.

The following had the honour of being invited:—

SUITE OF THE KING OF NORWAY

Monsieur V. Bommen (Chef du Cabinet), Monsieur I. Smith-Kielland (Maréchal de la Cour), Captain O. Malm (Aide-de-Camp), the Earl of Eldon (Lord in Waiting), Colonel Sir John Aird, Bt. (Extra Equerry).

AMBASSADORS

His Excellency The Brazilian Ambassador and Dona Isabel Moniz de Aragão, His Excellency The Norwegian Ambassador and Madame Prebensen, His Excellency The Danish Ambassador and Countess Reventlow, His Excellency The Swedish Ambassador.

MEMBER OF THE NORWEGIAN EMBASSY

Monsieur S. B. Hersleb Vogt (Counsellor) and Madame Vogt.

THE CABINET

The Lord Chancellor and the Viscountess Jowitt, the Prime Minister and Mrs. Attlee, the Secretary of State for Foreign Affairs.

SPECIAL INVITATIONS

The Archbishop of Canterbury and Mrs. Fisher, the Right Hon. The Speaker and Mrs. Clifton Brown, the Duke and Duchess of Buccleuch and Queensberry, the Marquess and Marchioness of Salisbury, the Marquess and Marchioness of Linlithgow, the Countess of Eldon, the Earl of Halifax, Field-Marshal the Viscount and the Viscountess Alanbrooke, Marshal of the R.A.F. the Viscount and the Viscountess Portal of Hungerford, the Lady Priscilla Aird, the Lord and the Lady Maclay, the Lord and the Lady Leathers, the Lord Goddard (Lord Chief Justice of England), the Lord and the Lady Altrincham, the Lord Brand, the Lord and the Lady Citrine, Admiral of the Fleet the Lord Fraser of North Cape (A Lord Commissioner of the Admiralty and Chief of Naval Staff), the Hon. Thomas and Mrs. Brand.

The Right Hon. Winston Spencer-Churchill, M.P., the Right Hon. Sir Alexander and the Lady Theodosia Cadogan, the Right Hon. The Lord Mayor and the Lady Mayoress, Sir Edward and the Hon. Lady Bridges, Admiral of the Fleet Sir John and Lady Cunningham, Marshal of the R.A.F. Sir John Slessor (Chief of the Air Staff) and Lady Slessor, Field-Marshal Sir William Slim (Chief of the Imperial General Staff) and Lady Slim, Admiral Sir Patrick and Lady Brind, General Sir Andrew and the Hon. Lady Thorne, Sir Gilmour and Lady Jenkins, Sir Laurence and Lady Collier, Sir George and Lady Ponsonby, Lady McMorrough Kavanagh, Sir Frederick and Lady Godber, Sir Archibald and Lady Forbes, Captain Sir Geoffrey de Havilland, Sir Gerald and Lady Kelly, Sir Ellis and Lady Hunter, Mr. Cameron and the Lady Hermione Cobbold, Captain and Mrs. Robert Dormer, Mr. Olaf Hambro.

THEIR MAJESTIES' HOUSEHOLDS IN ATTENDANCE

THE KING'S HOUSEHOLD

The Earl of Clarendon (Lord Chamberlain), the Duke of Hamilton and Brandon (Lord Steward), the Duke of Beaufort (Master of the Horse), the Right Hon. Sir Alan Lascelles (Private Secretary), Lieut.-Colonel the Hon. Sir Piers Legh (Master of the Household), Lieut.-Colonel Sir Terence Nugent (Comptroller, Lord Chamberlain's Office), Colonel Sir Dermot McMorrough Kavanagh (Crown Equerry), Major-General Guy Salisbury-Jones (Marshal of the Diplomatic Corps), Captain the Lord Plunket (Equerry in Waiting), Group Captain Peter Townsend (Deputy Master of the Household).

THE QUEEN'S HOUSEHOLD

The Dowager Duchess of Northumberland (Mistress of the Robes), the Countess of Halifax (Lady in Waiting), the Lady Katharine Seymour (Lady in Waiting), Lieut.-Colonel the Earl of Airlie (Lord Chamberlain to The Queen).

QUEEN MARY'S HOUSEHOLD

The Dowager Lady Ampthill (Lady in Waiting), Major the Hon. John Coke (Equerry in Waiting).

THE DUKE OF GLOUCESTER'S HOUSEHOLD

Sir Godfrey Thomas, Bt. (Private Secretary).

Madame Hägglöf, the Secretary of State for the Home Department, and Mrs. Herbert Morrison had the honour of receiving invitations, but were unavoidably prevented from obeying Their Majesties' commands.

During Dinner The Princess Elizabeth, Duchess of Edinburgh, on behalf of The King, gave the Toast of The King of Norway, to which His Majesty made a reply.

A detachment of The King's Body Guard of the Yeomen of the Guard was on duty.

The String Band of the Welsh Guards, under the direction of Captain F. L. Statham (Director of Music), and the Pipers of the Scots Guards played selections of music during and after the Dinner.

The Princess Margaret this afternoon re-opened Cecil Sharp House, 2, Regent's Park Road, the Headquarters of the English Folk Dance and Song Society.

Her Royal Highness was present at the Golden Jubilee Ball of the Victoria League which was held at the Hurlingham Club this evening.

Miss Jennifer Bevan was in attendance.

CLARENCE HOUSE, JUNE 5

The Lady Margaret Hay has succeeded Lady Palmer as Lady-in-Waiting to The Princess Elizabeth, Duchess of Edinburgh.

ST. JAMES'S PALACE, JUNE 5

The Duchess of Gloucester to-day visited York, where Her Royal Highness carried out a number of engagements in connexion with the City's Festival Celebrations.

Major Michael Hawkins was in attendance.

King Michael and Queen Anne of Rumania have left London.

Mr. and Mrs. Anthony Galliers-Pratt's permanent country address is now Whitwell Hall, Whitwell-on-the-Hill, Yorkshire (telephone: Whitwell-on-the-Hill 33).

Commander and Mrs. Allan Noble have moved to 45, Chelsea Square, S.W.3 (telephone: Flaxman 9395), which is now their permanent address.

The Very Rev. Dr. W. R. Inge is 91 to-day.

Lady Marling, wife of Sir John Marling, gave birth to a son in London on Saturday.

LUNCHEONS

HIGH COMMISSIONER FOR INDIA

The High Commissioner for India gave a luncheon to Maulana Abul Kalam Azad, Minister for Education, Government of India, at India House yesterday. Among those present were:—

The French Ambassador, the Turkish Ambassador, the Nepalese Ambassador, the Afghan Ambassador, the Iranian Ambassador, Sir Dhiren Mitra, Mr. D. N. Chatterjee, Professor Humayun Kabir, Lieutenant-Colonel C. L. Pasricha, Mr. N. N. Masud, and Mr. A. J. Kidwai.

THE INDONESIAN AMBASSADOR

The Indonesian Ambassador, Dr. Subandrio, gave a luncheon at the Dorchester Hotel yesterday in honour of the Indonesian Parliamentary delegation who are on a visit to this country.

CHARTERED INSTITUTE OF SECRETARIES

The president, Sir Edward Wilshaw, and council of the Chartered Institute of Secretaries yesterday entertained oversea members of the institute from Australia, South Africa, Canada, and New Zealand at a luncheon at Tallow Chandlers' Hall, E.C.4.

AT HOME

THE EGYPTIAN AMBASSADOR

The Egyptian Ambassador was at home yesterday to members of the Anglo-Egyptian Society on the occasion of their annual general meeting.

DINNER

VICOMTESSE OBERT DE THIEUSIES

The Belgian Ambassador and Vicomtesse Obert de Thieusies gave a dinner party last night at the Belgian Embassy. The guests included:—

The Netherlands Ambassador and Mme. Michiels van Verduynen, Marquis Rossi-Longhi, Earl and Countess Beauchamp, Baroness Ravensdale, Lord and Lady Iliffe, Colonel the Hon. J. J. and Lady Violet Astor, Lady Crosfield, Brigadier and Mrs. T. D. Daly, Mr. and Mrs. J. B. Rickatson-Hatt, Mr. and Mrs. Henry Tiarks, Group Captain H. Southey, Mrs. M. L. Arnold, Major and Mme. J. Ceuppens, and M. A. De Staercke.

SERVICE DINNERS

D BATTERY, R.H.A.

The annual dinner of D Battery, Royal Horse Artillery, took place last night at the Royal Artillery Mess, Woolwich. Lieutenant-General E. F. Norton presided, and the guests were General Sir Hubert Gough and Major-General Geoffrey Brooke.

MOUNTAIN ARTILLERY DINNER CLUB

The annual dinner of the Mountain Artillery Dinner Club was held at the United Service Club last night. General Sir John Brind presided.

FORTHCOMING MARRIAGES

THE HON. ROBIN WARRENDER AND MISS G. E. ROSSITER

The engagement is announced between Robin Hugh Warrender, third son of Lord Bruntisfield and Dorothy Lady Bruntisfield, and Gillian Elisabeth, only daughter of Mr. Leonard Rossiter and Mrs. Elisa Rossiter, of 26, Lowndes Street, S.W.1.

MR. A. D. HAYDON AND MISS B. M. BAILIE

The engagement is announced of Anthony David, son of Mr. and Mrs. D. P. Haydon, of Harborne, Birmingham, and Barbara Maryanne, daughter of Mrs. A. C. Bailie, of Johannesburg, and the late Mr. J. H. Bailie.

CAPTAIN G. J. F. HOLDEN AND MISS K. M. O'NEILL

The marriage will take place shortly between Captain George James Forster Holden, Royal Engineers, son of Mr. and Mrs. James Holden, of Tulse Hill, London, and Kathleen, younger daughter of Mr. C. T. O'Neill, M.C., and Mrs. O'Neill, of Kingston, Surrey.

MR. H. O. JONES AND MISS M. M. M. CADMAN

The engagement is announced between Humphrey Owen, only son of Mr. and Mrs. A. E. Jones, of Dan y Blorenge, Abergavenny, Monmouthshire, and Margaret Marian Metcalf, elder daughter of Mr. and Mrs. H. W. Cadman, of Knole, North Park, S.E.9.

MR. P. A. LEDWARD AND MRS. B. GRAY

The engagement is announced of Philip Archibald, only son of the late Archibald Prentice Ledward, and of Mrs. Ledward, of Hill Cottage, Harrow, and Brenda, younger daughter of William C. Hamilton, of 20, Queenhithe, E.C.4, and 20, Manor Court, Southgate, and of the late Mary Grace Hamilton.

MR. G. LONG AND MISS A. H. WALKER

A marriage has been arranged, and will shortly take place, between Gerald, son of Mr. and Mrs. F. H. Long, of York, and Anne, elder daughter of Mr. and Mrs. Ralph Walker, of Sheriff House, Rugby.

MR. T. G. MATTHEWS AND MISS S. A. HOYLE

The engagement is announced between Trevor Gilbert, only son of the late Mr. H. W. Gilbert Matthews, and of Mrs. A. Matthews, of Glencroft, Furness Vale, and Stella Ainley, younger daughter of Mr. and Mrs. Philip N. Hoyle, of Kirklees, Buxton.

MR. J. A. C. MAULE AND MISS K. L. A. TUCKEY

The engagement is announced between John Arthur Carteret, son of Mr. and Mrs. H. C. Maule, of Parkstone, Dorset, and Kathleen, daughter of Mr. and Mrs. C. O. Tuckey, of Bournemouth.

CAPTAIN F. DE R. MORGAN AND MISS H. E. RAIKES

The engagement is announced between Captain Francis de Riemer Morgan, M.C., The Buffs, elder son of Major-General H. de R. Morgan, D.S.O., and Mrs. Morgan, of Llandefaelog House, Brecon, and Hilda Elined, second daughter of Major-General G. T. Raikes, C.B., D.S.O., and Mrs. Raikes, of Treberfydd, Bwlch, Breconshire.

MR. B. D. NAYLOR AND MISS E. J. WEST

The engagement is announced between Basil Drummond, younger son of the late Mr. N. Naylor, and of Mrs. Naylor, of 42, Leonard Court, Edwardes Square, London, W.8, and Elizabeth June, only daughter of Mr. and Mrs. Reginald E. West, of Tideway, St. Margaret's Bay, Kent.

LIEUTENANT (L) J. C. PARKER, R.N., AND MISS S. M. G. EDWARDS

The engagement is announced between John Clifford, son of Mr. and Mrs. W. H. Parker, of The Hawthorns, Gerrards Cross, and Shirley, daughter of Lieutenant-Colonel C. L. Edwards, Royal Marines (retd.), and Mrs. Edwards, of 303, Keyes House, Dolphin Square, S.W.1.

MR. L. PERKS AND MISS HARDY

The engagement is announced from Capetown of Lionel, son of Lieutenant-Colonel and Mrs. F. J. Perks, of Chiswick, and Jill, elder daughter of Mr. G. T. Hardy, of Port Said, and of the late Mrs. B. M. Hardy.

MR. J. M. WILLIAMS AND MISS A. J. M. HOLMAN

The marriage arranged between Mr. John Williams and Miss Jenefer Holman will take place at Mawnan Parish Church on Saturday, June 16, at 2.30 p.m.

MR. G. P. WRIGHT AND MISS J. KENNEDY

The marriage arranged between Mr. Godfrey Peirse Wright and Miss Jean Kennedy will take place at the Cathedral Church of St. Mary and All Saints, Salisbury, Southern Rhodesia, on August 4, 1951.

CAPTAIN D. A. BARKER-WYATT, R.E., AND MISS J. E. G. ANDREWS

The engagement is announced between Captain Desmond Alfred Barker-Wyatt, R.E., younger son of Mr. and Mrs. J. H. G. Barker-Wyatt, of Stoke Bishop, Bristol, and Jancis Edith Gillian, younger daughter of Brigadier R. W. Andrews, D.S.O., M.C. (late R.A.), and Mrs. Andrews, of Hambledon Lodge, Child Okeford, Dorset.

MARRIAGES

LIEUTENANT-COLONEL C. M. KIRBY-SMITH AND MISS A. D. PLAISTED MCCAMMON

The marriage took place quietly yesterday at St. Saviour's, Walton Street, Chelsea, of Lieutenant-Colonel C. M. Kirby-Smith, R.A. (retd.), son of Mr. H. Kirby-Smith, of Oxford, and the late Mrs. Kirby-Smith, and Miss Ann Davis Plaisted McCammon, daughter of the late Lieutenant-Colonel T. V. Plaisted McCammon, 5th Royal Irish Rifles, and the late Mrs. McCammon. Prebendary H. J. R. Osborne officiated. The bride was given away by Sir Lynden Macassey. Major-General H. A. Hounsell was best man. A reception was held at the Basil Street Hotel.

MR. D. WYNN-WILLIAMS AND MISS A. NETTLEFOLD

The marriage took place on Saturday, June 2, at St. Michael's, Chester Square, of Mr. David Wynn-Williams and Miss Anne Nettlefold. The Rev. F. H. Gillingham officiated. The bride was given away by her father. Mr. George Wynn-Williams was best man. A reception was held at Londonderry House.

MR. C. J. BROOKS AND MISS P. B. MATTHEWS

The marriage took place quietly on June 2 at Holy Trinity, Brompton, between Mr. Christopher John Brooks and Miss Patricia Beverly Matthews.

CHRISTENING

The infant daughter of Dr. and Mrs. John Ley Greaves was christened Elisabeth Anne Fiennes by her uncle, the Rev. Geoffrey Twisleton-Wykeham-Fiennes, at East Worldham church on June 3. The godparents are the Rev. Geoffrey Twisleton-Wykeham-Fiennes, Mr. F. Fitzherbert-Wright, Miss M. Skrimshire, and Miss E. Collier-Green.

BRIDGE

EARLY LOSERS

BY OUR BRIDGE CORRESPONDENT

There are times when the declarer in a difficult contract in planning his play can see that he can only succeed if the important missing cards are exactly where he would like to have them.

In a recent congress teams match North dealt at Game All:—

North: S.—Q.J.10.7.5.4. H.—Q.J.8. D.—Q.9. C.—J.7.
West: S.—A.K.2. H.—9.5. D.—K.6.3.2. C.—10.8.6.4.
East: S.—9.8.6.3. H.—K.6.3. D.—J.8.7.4. C.—9.5.
South: S.— —. H.—A.10.7.4.2. D.—A.10.5. C.—A.K.Q.3.2.

At several tables the contract was Six Hearts by South. At one table, on the lead of the king of spades, South, after much thought, decided that he could set up dummy's long spades if, in addition to the knave of clubs, he could find two trump entries in dummy. This plan failed, for, after ruffing three spades in his own hand, he could only enter dummy by using his last trump to ruff, thus leaving East with a trump.

Another declarer with the same lead adopted a more simple course. It required only the king of diamonds to be with West and the king of hearts with East, so on ruffing the first spade he led a small diamond to the queen. West played the king, and the queen of diamonds became an entry to enable the declarer to lead hearts through East's king. The two kings being just where he wanted them to be, this line of play succeeded.

Declarers naturally dislike losing tricks early in the play but it is often necessary to do so, while full control is held of all suits, in order to prepare the way for what comes later.

North dealt at Love All:—

North: S.—A.K.5. H.—A.9.8. D.—8.7.6. C.—A.4.3.2.
West: S.—8.7.3.2. H.—J.7.6. D.— —. C.—K.Q.J.10.9.8.
East: S.—Q.10.9. H.—Q.10.3.2. D.—J.10.4.3. C.—7.6.
South: S.—J.6.4. H.—K.5.4. D.—A.K.Q.9.5.2. C.—5.

South was the declarer in a contract of Six Diamonds and West led the king of clubs which was taken by North's ace. The two of clubs was returned and South discarded a heart. Taking with the eight, West led the queen of clubs, East discarded a heart and South ruffed. The ace of trumps was led and West discarded a club.

North took the next trick with the king of spades and led the seven of diamonds on which East played the ten and South the queen. West discarded a club. North was put in with the ace of spades to lead the eight of diamonds. East played the four and South the nine. West discarded a spade. The king of diamonds drew East's knave, and West and North each discarded a spade. The position now was

North: S.— —. H.—A.9.8. D.— —. C.—4.
West: S.— —. H.—J.7.6. D.— —. C.—J.
East: S.—Q. H.—Q.10.3. D.— —. C.— —.
South: S.—J. H.—K.5. D.—5. C.— —.

The lead of the five of diamonds now squeezed both opponents.

PROBLEM No. 969

North: S.—A.K.5.3. H.—Q. D.—8. C.—10.6.2.
West: S.—9.6.4. H.—9.5. D.—A.10.7. C.—Q.
East: S.—J.10.7. H.—10.6.2. D.— —. C.—K.9.5.
South: S.—Q. H.—K.8.4. D.—J.3.2. C.—8.7.

Spades are trumps. South to lead, and North-South to make 7 tricks.

CENTRAL SCHOOL MATINÉE

YOUNG ACTORS ON TRIAL

The annual *matinée* by students of the Central School of Speech Training and Dramatic Art was given at the New Theatre yesterday. It was a reminder that there are two ways of showing off young actors: in parts they can act and in parts they cannot act yet. The second course, that adopted by the Central School yesterday, is probably the wiser course.

The five acts or long scenes which formed the programme were a fair specimen of the kind of drama which an actor in the better sort of theatre might be required to play. *Crime Passionel, The Gioconda Smile, An Ideal Husband,* and *Captain Carvallo* all offer him great rewards for his pains. Mr. Coward's *Home Chat* was perhaps a bit stiff. Being itself a work of inexperience it calls for a resourcefulness which experience alone can offer; and it was only in this play that the actors fared ill, all except Mr. Robert Chetwyn, who looked volumes. The other works produced some commendable attempts, or, rather, in showing actors and actresses reaching out for effects as yet beyond them some actors and actresses with possibilities. Mr. Hugh David, as M. Sartre's dictator, Miss Laura Stevens, Mr. Louis Smith, and Miss Janet Smith in Mr. Huxley's horrid drama, and Mr. David, Mr. Stephen Hancock, and Mr. Chetwyn in Mr. Cannan's witty and romantic comedy, were of particular interest. But the Wilde play brought forth what was perhaps the most striking apparition of the afternoon. Miss Patricia Keevney, who played Lady Markby, was naturally much too young for that amusing chatterbox, but what a clever simulation of a witty woman!

PLAY BY RONALD FIRBANK

The Princess Zoubaroff, the one published play by Ronald Firbank, is to be produced at the Watergate Theatre on Friday. The princess, it may be recalled, founded a new religious order for her friends in Florence, and, among other things, started a distillery for a new liqueur known as "Yellow Ruin." The play is set in the twenties and considerable trouble has been taken, it is said, to get authentic costumes of the period. The scenery has been made of plastic glass.

DR. G. M. TREVELYAN

Under the age limit set by the statutes, Dr. G. M. Trevelyan will cease to be Master of Trinity on June 30. After that date all letters or other communications addressed to the Master will be opened by the appropriate officers of the college. The address of Dr. and Mrs. G. M. Trevelyan will then be 23, West Road, Cambridge (telephone: 56704).

The Archbishop of Canterbury and the Bishops of Derby, Lichfield, Bradford, Bristol, and Southwell were among those present yesterday at a centenary luncheon at the diocesan training college at Derby and a thanksgiving service in the cathedral.

The King of Norway with the Queen, Princess Elizabeth, Princess Margaret, and the Duke of Gloucester, on their arrival at Buckingham Palace.

SALISBURY CATHEDRAL

"OUR LADY'S TUMBLER"

BY RONALD DUNCAN

FROM OUR DRAMATIC CRITIC

SALISBURY, JUNE 5.

The twelfth century French legend of Our Lady's Tumbler has a rounded loveliness, but it is brief, as brief as an anecdote. All that the tumbler has to offer the statue is his professional skill which was never of much worldly account and is no longer what it was; but it is the offering of a humble heart and the statue makes a miraculous sign.

The anecdote lends itself to literary extension, as Anatole France showed in a few exquisite pages, but much less readily to the requirements of a play. There is the danger that the taking simplicity of the miracle will be spoiled by the comparatively rough spade work needed to prepare the stage for it. Mr. Ronald Duncan meets this danger by discovering a simplicity of style which matches the simplicity of the theme. He sets the story in the cathedral of a monastery on the feast day of the Blessed Virgin. We are shown the offering to the statue of a rose, an anthem, and a poem. The rose is lovely; the anthem beautiful; and the poem is as good as Mr. Duncan can make it and there is only the gentlest of hints that perfect as these offerings are they are the offerings of imperfect human hearts.

The Brothers are artists, just a little puffed up with pride in their own accomplishment. But these preliminaries to the legendary situation successfully hold the audience and it is oddly enough the situation itself which first breaks the tension. There is something too much of the bespangled tumbler's performance but the tension is renewed before the end and the final scene is extremely impressive.

The play was given in front of the chancel screen of the cathedral. Mr. Cecil Beaton had arranged eight tall black candle holders on either side of a statue of the Madonna set against a blue and gold background—a simple and entirely satisfactory arrangement. A choir drawn from the Salisbury Music Society and the cathedral choristers sang in the south transept, and the audience sat on seats built up to a high rake along the nave. The play was admirably performed by the Salisbury Arts Theatre Company under the imaginative direction of Mr. Peter Potter. Mr. Donald Eccles, Mr. Paul Lee, Mr. Colin Ellis were the competing Brothers and Mr. John Humphrey was the head of the community who conducted the ceremonies from the pulpit. It was a well balanced group of performances and Mr. Charles Hubbard playing the tumbler was very effective and would be more so if his tumbling were a little curtailed.

FESTIVAL MUSIC

BERLIOZ'S REQUIEM

Of all the concerts that bear a special festival label the performance of Berlioz's Requiem "Grande Messe des Morts" at the Albert Hall last night displays it in the largest type.

Symphonies, programmes of Purcell, and new contemporary items may occur at any time; but not this monster score, for it bars itself from common use, first by demanding a load of apparatus and, secondly, by depending upon a big manner to provide bigness of music, which only adds a load of dullness to most of its pages.

Without wearing Berliozian spectacles it is not easy to discover within this series of highly original exteriors anything comparable to the visionary themes by which Bach, Beethoven, and Verdi encompass a world with a phrase. Berlioz tries to make our heart miss a beat or throb at double pace with his awed murmurs, sudden clamours, and parchment thunders; but with recollections of the modern choral turba and orchestral expressionism the most one does is to raise an eyebrow or enjoy a thrill of sound. Taken as a sound-picture the Requiem is immensely good in parts, one of its best parts being the steady piece of musical construction that is allied to the words of the *Lacrymosa*. Last night the performance was not more than half-powered. But there was a distinct gain in placing the four brass bands on the fringes of the platform instead of at four points of the compass in the auditorium. Their close-fitting harmonies in the *Tuba Mirum* produced the most magnificent noise of its kind that has been heard in the Albert Hall for just over three weeks. Sir Malcolm Sargent, in charge of the B.B.C. choir and orchestra, managed his scattered forces and the composer's marks of expression very skilfully.

MME. CAROSIO

Complaint has been made that the Festival Hall does not flatter this or that sort of music. Nor does it, but it tells the truth about consummate art, and a singer who, like Mme. Margherita Carosio, has no technical flaws to conceal may well prefer truth to flattery. For no small vocal inflection is lost; the ringing tone is not taken from the voice but its purity and warmth, complementary qualities rarely combined, stand revealed in their beauty. Last night she sang a programme of Italian songs and arias to the piano accompaniment of Mr. Herbert Greenslade. Bellini and Donizetti came first and provided the vehicle for all those graces of singing which reconciled the eighteenth century to a good deal of music that was by nature insipid but which contented the Italians for another century. Her second big group consisted of modern songs, including examples of the atmospheric song which Pizzetti and Respighi were concerned to adopt from France and Germany. Pizzetti's "I Pastori," though owing something to Debussy, was such a modern Italian song and found Mme. Carosio equally capable of interpreting it as she had been of Donizetti's "Rapito il cor" with its cascades of liquid sound. Some of the other modern songs showed too much influence of Puccini, but Mme. Carosio almost persuaded us that their sentimentality was harmless.

LISZT-SCHUMANN RECITAL

Mr. Pierre Bernac and Mr. Dorel Handman joined forces in the Wigmore Hall last night, the former to sing songs and the latter to play piano-sonatas by Liszt and Schumann. Schumann admired Liszt's playing without reserve; "the instrument," he said once, "glows under his hands." By that standard Mr. Handman's performance of the B minor sonata might be thought to lack fire, though the hushed beauty of his reflective playing was some compensation for missing virtuosity. More Eusebius than Florestan, he gave a sensitive and intimate account of Schumann's own G minor sonata. The artistry of Mr. Bernac's singing is well-known, but last night he tended to distract attention from its many beauties by an unsteadiness in the shaping of the vocal lines. The *Liederkreis*, Op. 39, was rather uniformly sombre, and Mr. Bernac's head-tone, lovely in *mezza-voce*, was sometimes too much uncovered.

PURCELL

The Royal Hospital at Chelsea, to some minds Wren's masterpiece, was completed in the year 1692; in that year Purcell wrote his tremendous St. Cecilia Ode "Hail Bright Cecilia." The two works of art came together last evening when the music was heard in the chapel of the Royal Hospital. That may have been a felicitous piece of programme-building, but coincidence was also at work, when the sun's rays caught and spotlit the harpsichord as Mr. Thurston Dart rolled brilliant, darkling, chords round the building during "Saul and the Witch of Endor," and when the choral cry in the Cecilia ode, "one perfect harmony," died away as the clock struck the hour on the keynote of the last chord. "Tis Nature's Voice" sang Mr. Alfred Deller and we were inclined to agree with him, though Purcell must have been having a quiet joke at his own expense when he set those words for his own falsetto voice. It was a fascinating programme containing, as it did, the magical six-part In Nomine, the Fantasia on one note, and the Bell Anthem (performed with string accompaniment), as well as the items already named. Miss Elsie Morison, Mr. Rene Soames, Mr. Gordon Clinton, and Mr. Hervey Alan also gave of their best.

FREEDOM OF CITY OF LONDON

Among applicants for the freedom of the City of London, submitted by the Chamberlain to the Court of Aldermen yesterday, were Lady Mountbatten of Burma and Lord Cottenham. Lady Mountbatten applied through the Shipwrights' Company and Lord Cottenham through the Coachmakers' and Coach Harness Makers' Company.

Obituary

MR. KOUSSEVITSKY

A CONDUCTOR OF GENIUS

Mr. Serge Koussevitsky, for a quarter of a century conductor of the Boston Symphony Orchestra, died on Monday night at the New England Medical Centre at the age of 76 after a short illness, according to our New York Correspondent.

It would be wrong to say that Koussevitsky graduated from a string-bass player to a conductor, for his talents in both directions seem to have developed not only at the same time but at a very early age. He was already a sufficiently accomplished player of his unwieldy instrument at the age of nine to play in the theatre orchestra of his native town and some two years later actually conducted it. Nevertheless, he first achieved a reputation outside Russia as a double-bass player and his virtuosity on that instrument was first demonstrated to London audiences in 1907 in a series of recitals at the Wigmore (then the Bechstein) Hall. In the course of the next year, however, he conducted the London Symphony Orchestra in a Beethoven programme which proved to be the precursor of many other fine performances not only of Beethoven but of modern Russian and Finnish music.

Though when his interpretations were first heard in western Europe their passionate and romantic aspects were most prominent to audiences, his insistence on clarity of line and meticulous control of speed and dynamics were later recognized as the chief instruments whereby a singularly lofty and penetrating mind achieved interpretations of the great works of orchestral literature of a quality seldom equalled. It is the ideal of the conductor to persuade all the players to perform like virtuosos; then he can feel that his vision can be realized. It was Koussevitsky's greatness that, having the vision, he could persuade those under his direction that their every semiquaver was an essential ingredient in the grand design of the composer.

Serge Alexandrovitch Koussevitsky was born at Tver on July 26, 1874, and studied the double-bass under Rambauseck at the Philharmonic School, Moscow. His reputation as a virtuoso on that instrument dates from 1896, but his attraction to the orchestra caused him to study conducting first in Russia and then under Nikisch at the Berlin High School. Like Berlioz, however, his genius was of the intuitive kind which owes little to teaching and he formed his own orchestra, which toured Russia with great success, interpreting such modern composers as Scriabin and Sibelius. He also founded a music-publishing house, but this was confiscated after the revolution and his orchestra was scattered. Though he accepted the invitation to take charge of the State orchestras, he was not happy in Russia and finally left in 1922.

Between 1922 and 1924 he conducted in London, Rome, Berlin, Paris, and Barcelona and then became conductor of the Boston Symphony Orchestra. The reputation of that orchestra rose to unprecedented heights during the quarter of a century he had charge of it and there is no doubt that his work there had a profound effect on the musical life of the United States. Meanwhile, he had founded the Berkshire Music Centre at Tanglewood, Massachusetts, and continued to direct it after his retirement from his post as conductor of the Boston Symphony Orchestra in 1949. His conducting of Beethoven's Ninth Symphony at the Albert Hall last year was greeted with tremendous enthusiasm and there must be many who regret that he had to cancel, owing to ill-health, the European tour he had planned for this year.

SIR GEOFFREY BRACKEN

Sir Cecil Brackenbury writes:—

Permit me to correct a statement made in your obituary notice of my friend Sir Geoffrey Bracken, who was a member of the Governor's executive council when I was Chief Secretary to the Government of Madras. While in no way wishing to belittle Sir Geoffrey's deep understanding of the Nationalist movement and his sympathy with its constitutional progress, I think it is due to him to say that he was always correctly attired when attending meetings of the Legislature and was never known under any circumstances to have donned the insignia of the Indian Nationalists.

After his time, when there was a Nationalist Government, the Prime Minister, Mr. C. Rajagopalachari, presented me with a length of khaddar cloth to be made into a suit. Complimentary presents of khaddar cloth were made by other Congress leaders to high officials, including, I believe, some Governors of Provinces, but probably not for wearing apparel. I venture to think your mistake arose out of the similarity of Sir Geoffrey's name to mine.

WILLS AND BEQUESTS

MRS. FRANCES ISABEL SEDDON, of Fitzjohns Avenue, N.W.3, left £110,625 (duty paid, £54,982).

She left £1,000 to the Converts Aid Society and £500 to the Catholic Truth Society.

LADY FLEMING, of the Convent of the Good Shepherd, Iden Manor, Staplehurst, Kent, widow of Sir Francis Fleming, K.C.M.G., left £6,746.

She left £1,000 to the Superioress of the Convent of the Good Shepherd, Iden Manor, and a further £50 for charitable purposes.

Other wills include:—

KUBLIN, Mr. Woolf Walter, of Mount Street, W., managing director of the Britannia Electric Lamp Works, Limited, Sunbeam Road, N.W. £66,299

SMITHWHITE, Mr. James, of Esher, Surrey, retired stockjobber (duty paid, £69,618) .. £149,305

The late Mr. Frank Barrington Deacon, whose name was published under "Wills and Bequests" on June 4, was formerly of Messrs. Deacons, solicitors, of Hongkong, and not of Deacons and Co., Limited, exporters.

BROADCASTING

HOME SERVICE

330m.

6.30 a.m., Band. 6.55, Weather. 7, News. 7.15, Programme Parade. 7.50, Religious Talk. 7.55, Weather. 8, News. 8.10, Programme Parade. 8.15, In the Kitchen. 8.20, Music. 9, Recital. 9.30, American Commentary. 9.45, Schools. 10.15, Service. 10.30, Music While You Work. 11, Schools. 12, Records. 12.25, "My Friends the Braithwaites." 12.55, Weather.

1, News. 1.10, Reports from Abroad. 1.30, Rhythm Band. 1.55, Cricket. 2, Schools. 3, Two Plays: "Lady in a Cage," and "The Man from Kilsheelan." 4, Debussy. 4.15, Any Questions? 5, Children's Hour. 5.55, Weather.

6, News. 6.15, Sport. 6.20, Records. 6.45, Henry Hall's Guest Night. 7.30, English Cathedral Music. 8, The Dome of Discovery. 8.15, Discussion on the art and personality of Burns. 9, Big Ben Minute: News. 9.15, Special Correspondent. 9.30, We Beg to Differ. 10, Chamber Orchestra. 10.45, To-day in Parliament. 11, News.

THE LIGHT PROGRAMME

1,500m. and 247m.

9 a.m., News. 9.10, Housewives' Choice. 9.55, Hymn and a Prayer. 10, Theatre Organ. 10.30, Music While You Work. 11, Mrs. Dale's Diary. 11.15, On With the Dance. 11.30, Tourist Trophy: Motor-cycle Races. 11.45, Yesterday in Parliament. 12, Tourist Trophy. 12.10, R.A.C. Rally. 12.15, Organ. 12.45, Welsh Orchestra. 1.45, Listen with Mother. 2, Woman's Hour. 3, Music. 3.30, Forces' Educational Broadcast. 3.45, Tourist Trophy. 4, Dance Music. 4.15, Mrs. Dale. 4.30, Tourist Trophy. 4.45, Grieg. 5.45, Theatre Orchestra. 6.15, One Night Stand. 6.45, The Archers. 7, News. 7.25, Sport. 7.30, Keep Smiling. 8, "1066—And All That." 9.30, Have a Go! 10, News. 10.15, Topic for To-night. 10.20, Orchestra. 11, A Book at Bedtime. 11.15, R.A.C. Rally. 11.20, Melody. 11.56, News.

THE THIRD PROGRAMME

464m. and 194m.

6 p.m., New Music. 6.40, Talk by Mr. Osbert Lancaster. 7, Purcell. 8, Professor E. H. Carr on "The New Society." 8.45, Bach. 9.10, Talk by Sir Thomas Beecham on "A Mass of Life." 9.30, Hardy's "The Dynasts." (Part 3). 11.5, Brahms.

TELEVISION

3, Country Dish. 3.30, "The Paris Metro." 5, For the Children. 8, Newsreel. 8.15, Olympic Gymnastics. 8.30, Picture Page. 9, Here's Howard. 9.30, "Prelude to Progress" (film). 10.5, News (sound only).

S.S.A.F.A. BALL

The Lord Mayor and the Lady Mayoress will be the guests of honour at a ball to be held at the Dorchester Hotel on Monday, July 9, in aid of the Soldiers', Sailors', and Airmen's Families Association. Drinks beforehand will be free and there will be a four-course dinner. Trumpeters of the Life Guards will play a fanfare; the Scots Guards will play for reels during the evening; and the other dancing will be to Carroll Gibbons's band.

MEMORIAL SERVICE FOR ADMIRAL TYRWHITT

A memorial service for Admiral of the Fleet Sir Reginald Tyrwhitt will be held in Westminster Abbey on Friday, June 22, at noon. Friends who wish to attend should apply for tickets by telegram or letter to the Secretary of the Admiralty (Memorial Service) before Saturday, June 16. Dress for officers will be monkey jackets with medals, sword, one neck decoration and up to two stars of orders. Mourning bands will not be worn. Retired officers may wear uniform if desired.

Obituaries

An obituary in *The Times* is the final status symbol in this world, and the last word until the Recording Angel gives his report. There is the famous folklore of the occasion when *The Times* made a mistake and published somebody's obituary before he died. The subject of the death notice read his own obituary over breakfast, and choked. In some agitation he telephoned his best friend and quavered down the telephone: 'I say, Reggie, have you seen this morning's *Times*?' There was a long pause. Then Reggie replied: 'Yes, I have, dear boy. And would you mind telling me where you are speaking from?'

The Obituaries Department keeps about 10,000 obituaries on file, waiting for the occasion when they will be needed. Some are written by specialists on the staff. Most are written by knowledgeable outsiders who usually know the subject well, but not too closely. The posts of obituaries editors for *The Times* at Oxford and Cambridge are positions of power, and are closely guarded secrets known to everybody who matters in the universities. The identity of authors of other unsigned articles in *The Times* is kept secret for thirty years. The authorship of obituaries is embargoed for a century.

Nubar Gulbenkian, an Armenian, son of the oil millionaire Calouste, fought a bitter feud with his father. He was anxious to find out what side of the dispute the obituary in *The Times* was going to take. He made a habit of taking senior members of the staff of *The Times* to lunch at the Ritz, and offering them £1000 for a premortuary view of his obituary. He never saw it. When it appeared in 1972, the obituary took a balanced and magisterial view of the affair.

From the beginning *The Times* has published obituaries. Some of the earliest were notices of people who were put to death during the French Revolution. But until the latter half of the nineteenth century obituaries were not systematically organized, or consistent in coverage or quality. On more than one occasion *The Times* simply plagiarized a death notice from another paper, if it did not have one of its own.

Delane was the first editor who took a particular interest in obituaries. He used to give the death of a famous person his personal attention. Delane recognized that the death of a great man is an event that seizes the public's mind. He remarked to a colleague: 'Wellington's death will be *the only topic*'.

Delane started the practice of getting obituaries ready in advance and having them standing in type for the fatal occasion. But then (as now) the paper could be caught napping by an unexpected stroke of death. A member of the staff was instructed at 5 pm to write an obituary of the Italian statesman Cavour before the paper went to press.

The obituaries of *The Times* are a prime source for scholars and researchers. Contributors to the *Dictionary of National Biography* are advised in their 'Notes' to begin their research with *The Times* obituary.

For many years the style of a *Times* obituary has been formalized. The introductory paragraph summarizes the principal achievements of the person's life. This leads on to details of the subject's parentage, birth and education. His or her life's work is then dealt with in more detail. And the notice closes with any honours and decorations received, marriage and children. The formula suits statesmen, civil servants and servicemen. But it is not so suitable for the dishevelled lives of today's film and pop stars.

The Times has always tried to cast its net wide, to include not just politicians and the like, but anybody who has led an interesting life or contributed something to the world. One of the most famous and moving was the obituary of La Belle Otero, the celebrated nineteenth-century courtesan. Nevertheless, it is a mark of distinction to have one's obituary published. The deaths of Nazis, notorious murderers and other villains whose lives have damaged the world are recorded in the news pages, not as obituaries.

It is a puzzling question, not beyond all conjecture: who earned the longest obituary in *The Times*? The paper of the nineteenth century, with its parsimonious attitude to pictures and headlines and its long columns of closely set type, had more space for the illustrious dead than today's paper can spare. Many of the eminent Victorians scored more than 10,000 words of obituary. Kaiser Wilhelm I was disposed of in about 15,000 words. But it is hardly surprising to find that Queen Victoria won the prize with 60,000. It is a record that is unlikely to be surpassed. In recent times the longest obituary has been 13,500 words for Sir Winston Churchill (see p. 19).

Mistakes over death are more embarrassing even than mistakes about the living. Because a telephone call to the newsroom was misheard, Lord Bessbough being heard as Lord Desborough, the latter was able to read his own obituary in the paper. *The Times* had to 'tender our sincere apologies' on the subsequent day. Desborough lived to a ripe old age, having anticipated things by seeing his own obituary in print.

The Times had more excuse for killing off its special correspondent in Peking – the celebrated Dr George Morrison – since he had indeed been wounded during the Boxer Rising, during which he played a vigorous part in the defence of the British legation. The generous two-column obituary published prematurely in *The Times* prompted a friend to say to Morrison: 'The only decent thing they can do now is double your salary'.

Right Obituary in THE TIMES of La Belle Otero, the famous courtesan of the 1890s, 13 April 1965.

Obituary

LA BELLE OTERO

COURTESAN OF THE GAY NINETIES

La Belle Otero, one of the last of the famous courtesans of the Gay Nineties, died in Nice on Saturday. She was 97.

At the height of her fame in the carefree years between the dawn of the twentieth century and the outbreak of the First World War, La Belle Otero was reputedly the possessor of a sizable fortune, in addition to a fabulous hoard of jewels showered upon her by her royal and aristocratic lovers. Yet for the past 40 or so years she had lived in more than modest circumstances in a small furnished flat in Nice, gradually selling her jewels, as she had already dissipated her fortune, to pay her gambling debts. For, despite the many famous men who had figured in her spectacular life, the green baize tables of the casinos were her one great lasting passion.

Her origins were obscure. She was born Caroline Puentovalga in Cadiz in 1868. It is believed she was carried off at the age of 13 by a cabaret dancer, and that a year later she married an Italian tenor who quickly lost whatever fortune he possessed at the baccarat tables.

Soon after that, under the name of La Belle Otero, she made her debut as a dancer at night clubs in Monte Carlo. And, at least for the next 30 years, she never looked back. In an epoch of famous courtesans she was among the half-dozen who enriched the chronicles of the time. Legend places among those who shared her favours, and contributed handsomely to her fortune, King Edward VII, the Grand Duke Nicholas, the Kaiser, King Alfonso, Aristide Briand, Gabriele d'Annunzio and many, many others. She visited St. Petersburg: she made a triumphal tour in the United States, and she was acclaimed wherever she went, not so much on account of her talent, for that was slender, but because of her beauty, her vitality and what, in these days, one would call her sex appeal.

Stories about her abound. One concerns her rivalry with another famous beauty of the day, Emilienne d'Alençon. It was the fashion for the well-known courtesans of the day to appear on special occasions—a gala at the Paris opera house for example—weighed down, as it were, by all the jewelry they possessed. It was a sort of competition. On one such night La Belle Otero waited until all her bejewelled sisters, particularly the Alençon, had taken their seats to make her entry in a simple unadorned black dress—followed at a distance by her Swiss maid carrying an immense heap of jewels on a tray.

She was indeed the idol of the nineties: a few years ago a film of her life was made: it was a poor shadow of the reality.

SIR SIGMUND DANNREUTHER

Sir Sigmund Dannreuther, C.B., who was Deputy Secretary of the Air Ministry from 1923 until his retirement in 1934, died on

On THE TIMES's Obituaries Page, disparate people often share the honours, as on the page opposite where the lives of King Ibn Saud and Dylan Thomas are among those commemorated.
10 NOVEMBER 1953

Obituary

KING IBN SAUD

MAKER OF MODERN ARABIA

King Ibn Saud, whose death is reported on another page, was the greatest figure in the Arab world in this century and for most of his life and his reign was a firm friend of this country.

The Wahabi King, Abdul Aziz Ibn Abdur Rahman Al Faisal, commonly called Ibn Saud, King of the Hejaz and Nejd and its dependencies, was born at Riyadh about 1880. His father, the Emir Abdur Rahman, was the youngest of four sons of the Emir Faisal who reigned over Nejd from 1834 to 1867. On Faisal's death his two elder sons, Abdullah and Saud, plunged the country into civil war, as the result of which Hasa was occupied by the Turks in 1875 and Riyadh itself by Ibn Rashid in 1891. Abdur Rahman went into exile with his family, first at Bahrein and later at Kuwait, where the young Ibn Saud came under the influence of the astute Sheikh Mubarak Ibn Sabah, at a time when the Persian Gulf was a focus of international rivalries. From this period Ibn Saud imbibed a conviction that the friendship of Great Britain was essential to the prosperity and independence of Arabia. The lawful pretender to the Wahabi throne was Abdul Aziz, son of Saud, but it was Abdur Rahman who in 1900 took the first step towards unseating the usurping dynasty of Ibn Rashid Emir of the Shammar. After the defeat of his attempted invasion he formally relinquished his rights and obligations to his son Abdul Aziz, whom he was destined a quarter of a century later to see the recognized king of the greater part of Arabia.

CONQUEST OF RIYADH

In 1901 Abdul Aziz Ibn Saud launched out into the desert on a desperate venture with a force of 200 men, including his cousin, Abdullah Ibn Jiluwi, who afterwards became his Governor of Hasa. Leaving the bulk of his force a day's journey distant, he entered Riyadh by night in January, 1902, with 15 men and forced an entry into a house opposite the fort, the gate of which he watched till dawn. Immediately the Rashidian governor issued from its portals the watchers rushed out and cut him down. Ibn Saud was immediately proclaimed ruler of Nejd, and the next few years were spent in the recovery and consolidation of the outlying provinces. In 1904 the Turks sent a force to assist Ibn Rashid to defend himself against the growing power of his rival, but the battle of Bukairiya, at which Ibn Saud was wounded, decided the issue and the Turkish forces withdrew under safe conduct leaving Ibn Saud master of the Qasim.

At the desert watering of Artawaya there was founded in 1912 the first of the Ikhwan colonies, the prototype of some hundred or more settlements which sprang up during the next 15 years all over Nejd. The nucleus of each colony was a mosque and ecclesiastical establishment subsidized by the State, and the essential features were agriculture and the mixing of hitherto antagonistic tribal elements in a common brotherhood. Each colony became in effect a section of the Wahabi standing army and a monument to the political genius of Ibn Saud. Having thus built up his administration on firm foundations Ibn Saud turned his attention to Hasa where the Turks had ruled since 1875 and drove them out.

OPERATIONS AGAINST IBN RASHID

During the spring of 1914 Captain W. H. I. Shakespeare, British Political Agent to Kuwait, had visited Ibn Saud, and soon after the outbreak of war in Europe he was again sent to Riyadh to secure the Wahabi ruler's cooperation against the Turks. Ibn Saud undertook military operations in the Shammar against Ibn Rashid, who had sided with the enemy, and in January, 1915, an indecisive battle was fought at Jarrub, in the course of which Shakespeare was unfortunately killed. The British authorities then decided against further activities in the Wahabi country and Ibn Saud, who concluded a treaty of friendship with Great Britain in December, 1915, at Uqair, remained quiescent and increasingly nervous at the position which the Grand Sherif of Mecca, King Husein, was making for himself in the west with the assistance of Lawrence and others.

In spite of all British efforts to foster friendly relations between the Hashimite King Husein and the Wahabi ruler, obvious rivals for the ultimate hegemony of Arabia, the bitterness between the two rulers increased as the 1914-18 War progressed. Early in 1919 King Husein persuaded Lord Curzon and the British Government to adopt his view of the controversy and to authorize him to occupy Khurma. Ibn Saud, with threats of the stoppage of his annual subsidy of £60,000 and of the displeasure of the British Government, was ordered to relinquish the village, but with characteristic energy in defence of his rights against all encroachment he placed himself at the head of his army and marched west. The Hejaz was in a ferment of anxiety and Taif, the summer capital, was evacuated, but, characteristically again, Ibn Saud, having vindicated his position and annexed Turaba, returned to Riyadh. During the next three years Ibn Saud steadily pursued a policy of expansion, adopting the offensive as the best means of defence against the declared designs of the Hashimite Court. Meanwhile the nomination by the British Government of Hashimite Sherifs to the thrones of Transjordan and Iraq came as a bitter disappointment to him.

The stage was now set for a final settlement with the Hejaz, and the first step in this direction was the Conference of Kuwait (1923-1924), convened by the British Government and rendered abortive by the obstinacy of the Hashimite representatives, who demanded the setting back of Ibn Saud's

frontiers to the 1915 position. The die was thus cast for war, and in September, 1924, the Wahabi army advanced on the Hejaz. Mecca was occupied in October and the siege of Jeddah began in December. During 1925 the whole of the Hejaz was gradually overrun, and in October Sir Gilbert Clayton, on behalf of the British Government, visited Ibn Saud in his camp in Wadi Fatima to negotiate the treaties of Babra and Hadda, by which outstanding questions with Iraq and the boundary of Nejd and Transjordan were satisfactorily settled.

TREATY OF JEDDAH

In May of the same year Sir Gilbert Clayton again visited the Wahabi King to negotiate the treaty of Jeddah, by which the complete independence of the dual monarchy of the Hejaz and Nejd was formally recognized. In the winter of 1927-28 the Wahabi King again visited his central dominions and was actively occupied in the task of settling an unfortunate outbreak of Ikhwan fanaticism on the Iraqi-Nejd frontier, caused by the mistaken belief that the Iraqi Government had violated its treaty obligations by building a police post at the desert walls of Busaiya, 70 miles from the frontier. British aeroplanes were sent into Nejdi territory to bomb the Mutair Beduin by way of reprisals for their attack on Busaiya. Throughout this incident the Wahabi King retained his equanimity, endeavouring, by protest against the unnecessary intervention of the British and Iraqi Governments as well as by action to restrain his Beduin subjects from giving further cause for provocation, to transfer the dispute from the battlefield to the conference chamber.

Meanwhile prospectors had been busy in the Arabian peninsula and rich deposits of oil were suspected if not proved. A less far-seeing sovereign might have allowed merely commercial considerations to prevail, especially in view of the keen competition for concessions. Ibn Saud, however, true to the policy he had pursued all his life in his foreign relations, preferred to lease what were afterwards discovered to be very rich deposits indeed to predominantly Anglo-Saxon interests. As early as 1933 he had awarded the oil concessions of the eastern part of his kingdom to the Standard Oil Company of California, which was later joined by the Texas, Standard Oil of New Jersey, and Socony-Vacuum companies. Production, begun in 1936 with 2,600 metric tons, had risen by 1949 to 23 million metric tons. Thus a ruler whose total revenue in 1917 had been some £100,000 now enjoyed a revenue of not less than £30m. Such an increase was indeed beyond the dreams of avarice, and Ibn Saud was able to tell the American business men in 1941, who had acquired further concessions, that two years before the Germans and Japanese had been bidding frantically for concessions. "The Japanese," he said, "offered me twice as much for one-third of what you now obtain." During the whole period of the 1939-45 War Ibn Saud remained the firmest of the friends of Great Britain in the Middle East, though many attempts were made to undermine his loyalty.

THE ARAB LEAGUE

The Zionist claims to Palestine were never admitted by Ibn Saud, though his distrust of the Hashimites led to a rather lukewarm support of the Arab League. The comparative ineffectiveness of the league cannot, however, fairly be placed only on Ibn Saud's shoulders. The question of leadership was involved and there were three claimants, none of whom was disposed to forgo his claim. Ibn Saud could fairly claim that he was by right of achievement the greatest man in the Arab world. The Hashimites could claim that as descendants of the Prophet, and for hundreds of years the guardians of the holy places, they were entitled to lead, while Egypt, as the most settled and progressive State, felt that the leadership ought to be hers. In spite of visits of courtesy the rivalry remained and effectively prevented the emergence of any broad body of policy. Nevertheless, the league was more than once a useful weapon in the armoury of peace and the idea underlying it permitted in 1948 the first friendly meeting for over a quarter of a century of Ibn Saud and the late King Abdullah of Transjordan, then the most capable living member of the Hashimite house.

These contacts continued under King Abdullah's son and grandson. Towards the close of Ibn Saud's life the cordiality of his relations with Britain was temporarily overcast by his effort to assert his sovereignty over the Buraimi oasis, which the British-protected Sultan of Muscat also claimed. Fortunately the dispute, which was, on the whole, conducted temperately, seems unlikely to cause a serious breach of good understanding.

Personally a man of commanding presence and of a stature exceptional in Arabia the Wahabi King was remarkable for a gentle and equable temperament capable of sudden transition under provocation to heights of indignation truly majestic. Uxoriously inclined, he took the fullest advantage of the social code of Islam—often for purely political purposes—to marry frequently and to divorce freely. He is believed to have had no fewer than 150 wives, by whom he had a large number of acknowledged children. His fortitude in the field of battle was only equalled by his equanimity in the council chamber and his long reign bids fair to establish itself in history as the Golden Age of modern Arabia.

PROF. W. M. ROBERTS

Professor Walter Meakin Roberts, O.B.E., who died recently at Farnham in his seventy-eighth year, was the last of a long line of distinguished Professors of Mathematics at "The Shop"—the Royal Military Academy, Woolwich, which closed down in September, 1939.

Among his predecessors, to name only a few, were Thomas Simpson, Christie—who collaborated with Michael Faraday (also a member of "The Shop" staff) in electro-magnetism—Barlow, and Sylvester. "Bill" Roberts, as he was affectionately named, in his generation was no less distinguished than these great mathematicians. He gave devoted and outstanding service to "The Shop" for 35 years and added to the prestige of that famous institution by the fine quality of his teaching, his judgment and perception in many matters related to the development of young men from the status of gentleman cadet to that of officer, and by his infectious enthusiasm.

Before joining the staff in 1904 he had been a scholar of Corpus Christi College, Oxford, had won both the junior and senior mathematical scholarships awarded by the university, achieved a first in the Final Honours School of Mathematics, and had taught for a few years at St. David's College, Lampeter. While at Woolwich he was the author of text-books and publications in his subject, and for many years was honorary treasurer of the Mathematical Association. In 1930 he was appointed O.B.E.

During the 1914-18 War, when the subject of mathematics was temporarily removed from the syllabus of "The Shop," Roberts, then 40 years of age, volunteered for the Army and served as a private soldier, and later as a commissioned officer, in the Royal Artillery. He saw active service in France and returned to "The Shop" after the war with the rank of major. Again, in the more recent war, and by then 60, he volunteered for service and was granted a commission in the Royal Regiment. He was with the R.A. O.C.T.U. and finally the R.E. O.C.T.U. until he retired at the age of 65.

"Bill" Roberts contributed much to "The Shop" in many of its activities, quite apart from his contribution to the teaching of mathematics, and perhaps particularly to athletics, in which in his earlier days he had been a skilled performer. He assisted in the coaching of the G.C.s, and played an important part in the formation of the Milocarian Club. He was also a well-known mountaineer and a member of the Alpine Club.

Possibly the most prominent feature of "The Shop" was the spirit of loyalty which was engendered among the staff and in the large number of gentlemen cadets who graduated from it. In no small degree did "Bill" Roberts foster and add to this spirit. His passing has brought great sorrow to his many friends and to generations of officers of the Royal Regiment, the Corps of Royal Engineers, and the Royal Corps of Signals. He is survived by his wife, who nursed him devotedly through a crippling illness of three years' duration.

COLONEL H. S. KAYE

Colonel Harold Swift Kaye, D.S.O., M.C., died on Friday night at the age of 71. Educated at Harrow and Sandhurst, he obtained a commission in the 1st Battalion, The King's Own Yorkshire Light Infantry in 1901. During the 1914-18 War he attained the rank of lieutenant-colonel and was in command of the 5th Battalion, The York and Lancaster Regiment, and later the 17th Battalion, The London Regiment. He was awarded the D.S.O. and the M.C.

After retiring from the regular army in 1919 he commanded the 4th Battalion, The King's Own Yorkshire Light Infantry, at Wakefield, until 1924, when he was promoted colonel and retired.

Colonel Kaye will be well remembered for his connexion with the Yorkshire county cricket club, of which for some years he was captain. He was also a proficient boxer, winning the army officers' lightweight and welterweight boxing championships on several occasions. He was chairman of Marshall Kaye and Marshall Limited, woollen manufacturers, of Ravensthorpe, Dewsbury. He leaves a widow, a daughter of the late Surgeon Vice-Admiral Sir James Porter, two daughters, and a son.

LIEUT.-COL. F. E. PACKE

Lieutenant-Colonel the Hon. N. G. Bligh writes:—

May I write a word of tribute to a very gallant friend who has just passed away, Lieutenant-Colonel Frederick Packe, C.V.O., O.B.E.? Throughout the last war he continued to live in his charming house in London surrounded by the things he loved, and in spite of near misses by bombs and increasing lameness owing to his previous wounds, in addition to his other duties, he went daily, with difficulty, to his City office. He retired only a year ago. Painful illness and almost total blindness had latterly incapacitated him, and prevented him from enjoying pictures and other beautiful things that he loved so much, and I feel sure that he was glad to go. He was a man of quiet courage and endurance, great charm, and cultivated taste, and is a sad loss to his many friends.

Dr. Ralph Grange Watkin, Ph.D., a former member of the staff of Tokyo University, where he made a study of Japanese art, has died in retirement at his daughter's home at Sunderland. He also worked at Breslau University, and when he returned to this country in 1906 he taught at the Haberdashers' Aske's School, London, until 1934.

MR. DYLAN THOMAS

INNOVATION AND TRADITION

Mr. Dylan Thomas, the Welsh poet and story writer, died yesterday in New York at the age of 39.

Dylan Marlais Thomas was born at Swansea in 1914. He was educated at Swansea Grammar School, where his father, who died last year, was senior English master. He began writing early, and at the age of 12 he was able to show his parents and his friends poems which seemed to have no direct ancestry in English poetry. These poems already bore the marks of that strong individuality in pattern-making and choice of language which was to distinguish him from all his fellow-writers in maturity.

He had developed at school a passionate feeling for language which was sharpened and intensified by an acute destructive judgment. He took no reputation for granted. He approached the great masters of his art with an impudent suspicion, because, from the first, he distrusted the academic approach. Yet, when they had walked with him through the furnace of his own imagination and emerged unscathed, there was no man who loved them more. Indeed, no poet of the English language has so hoodwinked and confuted his critics. None has ever worn more brilliantly the mask of anarchy to conceal the true face of tradition. There was nothing God ever made that Dylan Thomas, the revolutionary, wanted to alter. The careful compounder of explosive imagery believed only in calm.

At the age when Rimbaud wrote his poems Dylan Thomas had left school and was working as a reporter for the *South Wales Evening Post*. His first poems, apart from those which had appeared in the school magazine, which he edited, were printed in the *Sunday Referee*. He had also at this time begun to write short stories. Then, finding newspaper work and his own writing incompatible, he left the newspaper and lived for a time in London, sharing a flat with two of his Swansea friends. Here his literary work continued, and he developed rapidly his researches into the power of language. He directed his various gifts to the concentration of verbal energy in a pattern at once musical and compact. His poems reflected the fiery, Blake-like passion of his vision, while his early stories explored the relation between immediate reality and archetypal symbols.

THE EARLY POEMS

When in 1934 Dylan Thomas's first book, *Eighteen Poems*, was published, its impact was immediate and profound. It was at once realized by discerning readers, among whom Edith Sitwell was one of the first, that this poet had created an idiom; that he had disturbed the roots of our language in an organic way and given it a new vitality. There was nothing stale or imitative in the book: the poems were fastidiously worked; they were poems of a man who had listened, not once but a hundred times, to the minute effects of words. It is true that still, in 1936, when this was followed by *Twenty-One Poems*, the poet had not yet found his most permanent and compelling medium of expression. Yet there was nothing topical in his work. The most mistaken of his admirers were those who loved it for its novelty. It was, even in its first phases, an ancient poetry, not rejecting antiquity for the present but seeking, with every device of language, the ancestry of the moment.

"THE MAP OF LOVE"

If the poetry of his first two books had been admired for the wrong reasons the poems printed in his third book, *The Map of Love*, could hardly suffer the same fate. Whereas the first book leaves an impression that the poet could extend his stanzas from the fund of invention and verbal felicities at his command, and that the same prescription could produce new poems, there is no such impression left by the poems in *The Map of Love*. Each is an experience perceived and controlled by the religious sense and each answers its own questions. He has pared his imagery without losing any of its force; and these poems close with the statement at the end of the poem for his twenty-fourth birthday:

In the final direction of the elementary town
I advance for as long as forever is.

The Map of Love contained also a set of stories which were clearly the work of the same hand, and these were followed two years later by the humorous stories, in quite a different vein, which Dylan Thomas collected under the title *A Portrait of the Artist as a Young Dog*. These stories, about the poet's own boyhood, written from direct experience in Swansea and the Gower peninsula, may seem to some to carry the fault of exaggerated statement, but they are as true to life as his own personality was to his friends.

INNOVATIONS IN THE STANZA

It is, however, upon the poems in *Deaths and Entrances* (1946) and the few poems of the slim volume *In Country Sleep*, published in America in 1951, that his reputation as one of the greatest masters of English poetry is likely to rest. In these Dylan Thomas has not only used to perfection the idiom he himself created but has invented stanza forms which are themselves organic and which redouble the force of the entire poem. These poems form the final section of his *Collected Poems*, published last year.

During the war Dylan Thomas, who was always interested in the cinema, made several documentary films. His book, *The Doctor and the Devils*, published earlier this year, is the first instance of a film-script being printed before any film of it has been made. Among his unpublished works are several poems and a radio play, a part of which was printed in the half-yearly Italian review, *Botteghe Oscure*. The scene of this play is a Welsh village, and parts of it have been performed in New York.

GIFT FOR MIMICRY

In recent years Dylan Thomas had made several tours of American universities, giving readings of poetry and lectures. His reading of poetry, and particularly of his own poems (which he confessed that he did not like reading) was unrivalled; and he was almost equally accomplished in reading humorous scripts of an unparalleled adjectival richness, which were among the most popular wireless features of our time. His gift of mimicry could make each character of his stories distinct and unforgettable. He loved people. He did not write only for the few but also "for the lovers. . . . Who pay no praise or wages Nor heed my craft or art."

Dylan Thomas had intended, before returning to England from this last tour, to work with Stravinsky on the *libretto* of an opera. It is likely that by his death the world has lost a masterpiece. What it has not lost is the work of a poet who was able to live Christianity in a public way, and whose work distilled it—a poet narrow and severe with himself and wide and forgiving in his affections. Innocence is always a paradox, and Dylan Thomas presents, in retrospect, the greatest paradox of our time.

He married, in 1936, Miss Caitlin Macnamara, who survives him, together with two sons and a daughter.

COL. H. C. McWATTERS

Colonel Herbert Claude McWatters, D.S.O., died in hospital at Evesham on Saturday at the age of 75. Born in 1878, he was educated at Clifton and the Royal Military College, Sandhurst, and entered the Indian Army in 1900. His services during the 1914-18 war were mentioned three times and he was awarded the D.S.O. in 1917. He was mentioned again in dispatches during the operations in 1919-20 against the Afghans. He leaves a widow.

PROF. W. LEYHAUSEN

Our Bonn Correspondent reports the death at the age of 65 of Professor Wilhelm Leyhausen, widely known as "the father of the Delphic idea," for whose services to the art Delphi made him an honorary citizen in 1927. He filled the chair for rhetoric in the Friedrich Wilhelm University of Berlin, and after 1945 M. François-Poncet, who had known Professor Leyhausen before the war, invited him to Mainz, where he founded the International Delphic Institute in conjunction with Professor Gustave Cohen, of the University of Paris. It was also due to his initiative that the "Delphiad" was established as a kind of Olympiad of the spirit. "Delphiads" have been held at Mainz, Freiburg, Verona, and Lyons.

Lady Sinclair, wife of Lord Sinclair, died on Sunday at her home near Dalry, Kirkcudbrightshire. She was Violet Frances, daughter of Mr. J. M. Kennedy, M.V.O., and her marriage took place in 1906.

MR. J. V. KITTO

THE HOUSE OF COMMONS LIBRARY

Mr. J. V. Kitto, C.B., C.B.E., formerly Librarian of the House of Commons, died yesterday hardly more than a week before his seventy-eighth birthday.

John Vivian Kitto was born on November 17, 1875, the son of the late Prebendary J. F. Kitto, sometime vicar of St. Martin-in-the-Fields. He was educated at Trinity College, Glenalmond, and Balliol College, Oxford, where he took a second class in modern history in 1899. For a time he thought of pursuing an academic career and was successively a schoolmaster and history lecturer. However, he seized the opportunity of joining the library staff of the House of Commons, which satisfied his strong historical sense and academic attitude to life and in 1908 he was appointed assistant librarian. Sir Henry Campbell-Bannerman was then Prime Minister and before Kitto retired from his post eight other Prime Ministers were to govern the country.

During the 1914-18 war he served in the Royal Garrison Artillery and on demobilization returned to his seat in the Members' Library from which, indeed, the gravest political crisis or the most exciting incident in or near the House could hardly stir him. He was fond of cataloguing the excitements that had taken place within a few yards of his chair, which his conscientious attention to duty had caused him to miss and he used to ruminate on the book he could have written, if he had witnessed them and had kept a diary. Yet, as he said, it would probably have contained so much parliamentary scandal that he would have been frightened to publish it after all.

When in 1937 he was promoted to the post of librarian, he had long made up his mind to reorganize the library, which then wore the aspect of the kind of library to be found in the country house of an impecunious gentleman of the middle of the nineteenth century. Then came the war of 1939 and his ideas had to remain in cold storage. In 1945, however, he pointed out to a Select Committee that the library required £15,000 spent on it at once and that its annual allocation was a mere £1,200. In the course of the next year he retired and the scheme he had done so much to initiate was carried out by his successor, the late Hilary St. George Saunders, under the supervision of Lord Ruffside, then Mr. Speaker Clifton-Brown.

He married in 1908 Nettie Catherine, daughter of Lieutenant-Colonel H. Ryves, and there were two children of the marriage, a son and a daughter.

COL. L. C. JACKSON

Colonel Lambert Cameron Jackson, C.M.G., D.S.O., formerly Chief Engineer of Western Command, died at his home near Alton, Hampshire, on Saturday at the age of 78.

He was born on September 28, 1875, and was educated at Clifton and the Royal Military Academy, Woolwich. Gazetted to the Royal Engineers in 1895, he was employed on survey duty on the frontier between the Sudan and Abyssinia in 1899-1900 and was then sent to South Africa where he won the Queen's medal with three clasps, and the King's medal with two clasps. In 1903-04 he served on the Anglo-German boundary commission working in the neighbourhood of Lake Chad and was then placed in charge of the military survey of the Orange River Colony. He returned home in 1909 to take up an appointment at the War Office and then attended the Staff College, Camberley, from which he graduated in 1913.

He served throughout the 1914-18 war on the Western Front, was mentioned six times in dispatches, was given the brevet of lieutenant-colonel, and was awarded the D.S.O. in 1917. After working as a G.S.O.1 at the G.H.Q. of the Army of the Rhine in 1919 he was sent out to fill a similar position in the Burma Division in 1920, but he was soon promoted to the appointment of Assistant Quartermaster-General at Army Headquarters, India, and held that post until 1924. Then for some three years he was Deputy Chief Engineer at Eastern Command, and in 1928 returned to Germany as Chief Engineer of the Army of the Rhine. His last post, which he held from 1930 to 1932, was Chief Engineer, Western Command, and while in the appointment he served also as A.D.C. to the King.

He married in 1910 Olive Margaret, the third daughter of the late Sir Howard Elphinstone, V.C., K.C.B., C.M.G., who survives him, together with two sons of the marriage.

MR. WILLIAM MILBURN

Mr. William Milburn, F.R.I.B.A., principal of Messrs. William and T. R. Milburn, architects and surveyors, of Sunderland, who designed the Dominion Theatre in London, has died in hospital at Sunderland at the age of 68. During his career he earned many distinctions, including the Saxon Snell Prize of the Royal Institute of British Architects in 1908 and two years later the institute's Godwin Bursary. He was elected F.R.I.B.A. in 1926, and in 1932 was chairman of the Durham and Northumberland branch of the Chartered Surveyors' Institution. The following year he became president of the Northern Architectural Association, an office held previously by both his father and uncle.

WESTERN SOCIETY'S SYMBOLIC HERO

INVINCIBLE TECHNICIAN "LOSING CONFIDENCE"

FROM OUR CORRESPONDENT

EDINBURGH, Nov. 9

Professor A. J. Toynbee, in the seventh of his Gifford lectures in the New College, Edinburgh, to-night, stated that every society at every stage of its history needed a symbolic hero to embody in a national form the present goal of the society's endeavours.

The western society's ideal figure in the Middle Ages and in early modern times was that of the inspired saint. In the late modern age the west had substituted for this the figure of the invincible technician, not the abstract scientific thinker, but the practical man who increased mankind's wealth and power by extending the limits of human control over non-human Nature. In the seventeenth century the technician stole the role of western hero from the theologian because, by comparison, the technician seemed harmless, but in the nineteenth century, as the progress of western technology gathered momentum, the technologist came to be valued in the west for his now apparently unlimited power.

WANING POPULARITY

Down to the dropping of the two atomic bombs on Japan in 1945 it was taken for granted that the western technologists' power was a beneficent force which could work only for the good of the human race. Since 1945 the western technician had begun—like the western theologian after the sixteenth-century wars of religion—to lose his popularity, and, what mattered more, his self-confidence. He was now also losing the intellectual freedom that was an indispensable condition for success in his work. "As for the release of atomic energy, this has made the western public suddenly see the western technician in the new light of a criminal who has unbottled the jinn that might destroy human life on earth. More than that, the technician himself is now wondering whether he may not really have been guilty of this crime. At any rate he has realized that the power which he has been capturing from Nature for mankind is a morally neutral force that can be used for evil as readily as for good.

Atomic science had become enslaved to governments in two ways: its apparatus was too costly to be financed by private enterprise; and its products were engines of such tremendous power that the governments that had financed them were guarding the knowledge of them as a state secret—for their own use in possible future warfare against one another.

"This twentieth-century iron curtain that has now descended, in the west as well as in Russia, upon scientific research is a deadly blow to experimental science," Professor Toynbee said, "for the lifeblood of science since the close of the seventeenth century has been its freedom to exchange information and to publish it. Is technology going now to suffer the eclipse that overtook theology 300 years ago? And, if so, is religion going to return again to the west through a scientific door?"

City

Top Thomas Alsager, first City editor of THE TIMES.

Below PUNCH cartoon: PORTRAIT OF THE RAILWAY PANIC, 1846.

Below right Stock Jobbers, *c.* 1790.

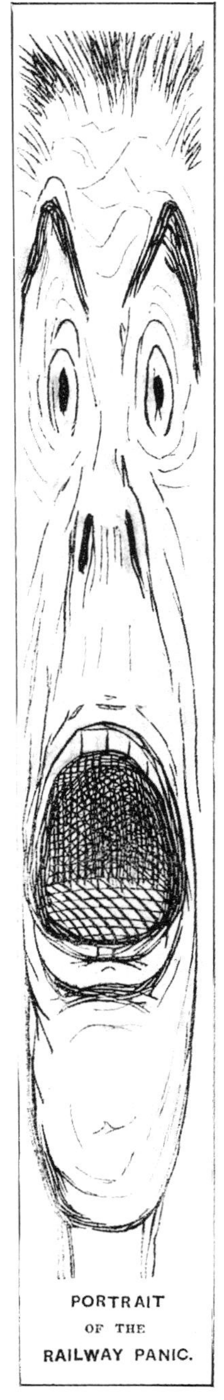

From its birth *The Times* was concerned with the City of London, and its financial and business activities in the Golden Square Mile, which was then in the process of becoming the financial capital of the world. In his Prospectus To The Public, published in the first issue of *The Daily Universal Register*, John Walter declared: 'A due attention should be paid to the interests of the trade, which are so greatly promoted by advertisements'. Walter asserted that the great object of his new paper would be: 'To facilitate the commercial intercourse between the different parts of the community through the channel of advertisements; to record occurrences and to abridge parliamentary debates'.

Performance was not as grand as prospectus: it seldom is in human affairs. On that first day *The Daily Universal Register* carried a dozen lines of Stock Prices, and that was about it. For the next forty years that amount daily was the sum total of City and financial news in *The Times*: there were other things going on in the world – wars, Napoleon, the Reform Act, to name but a dozen. And there were only four pages to report it all in. In the 1820s an article headed 'Money, Market, and City Intelligence' started to pay proper attention to Mammon.

In 1840 its City reporting got *The Times* into hot water, not for the last time. The paper's Paris correspondent made a surreptitious journey to Brussels, and reported from there an ingenious swindle of forging the newly introduced letters of credit. *The Times* carried the report under the explicit headline: EXTRAORDINARY AND EXTENSIVE FORGERY AND SWINDLING CONSPIRACY ON THE CONTINENT. It named the forgers, led by Alan Bogle. Bogle sued. His solicitor explained to *The Times*: 'The libel was so utterly destructive of all reputation, that before admitting it to a place in your journal you were bound to satisfy yourself that it did not implicate a perfectly innocent individual'.

The case was heard over two days in August 1841. *The Times* devoted two pages to a full report on both days. Judgment was given for Bogle. *The Times* recorded the dramatic moment: '"We find for the Plaintiff: One Farthing damages." A titter went through the court.' *The Times* was ordered to pay the costs of the action. In gratitude for the exposure of the fraud, Glyn's and the other banking houses of the City subscribed £2,700 for *The Times*. *The Times* gratefully but proudly declined to accept it, so it was used to found *The Times* Scholarships at City of London School and Christ's Hospital. Memorial tablets were put up at Lloyd's and one now stands in the foyer of the *Times* building.

The first City editor was Thomas Massa Alsager, a manager of *The Times*, and an enthusiastic amateur musician who was proficient on all the instruments in the orchestra. At the private concerts at his house Beethoven's great Mass and other works were performed for the first time in Britain. Alsager introduced the daily money article, and established a *Times* office in the City. It lasted there until 1922.

In 1845 *The Times* joined battle in its City pages with the railway monopolists. The public had run mad with the delusion that everybody could make a fortune from the development of railways. Share-pushers, who had no intention of putting the money anywhere near a railway, were raking it in. *The Times* thundered: 'Whence is to come all the money for the construction of the projected railroads?' And answered that only a certain amount of the vast money invested by the gullible public was ever going to see a return. In November it published a Supplement that demonstrated that on paper more money had been invested in railways than there was money in the country. It predicted trouble. There was. *The Times* offended influential and greedy people, and lost advertising and circulation. It was accused of making false announcements of amalgamations of the railway companies in order to depress shares. And it was accused of not being disinterested when it puffed one particular railway company, a director of which was William Delane, treasurer of *The Times* and father of the paper's great editor.

The City office of *The Times* must be, like Caesar's wife, above suspicion. M. B. Sampson, head of the City office for twenty-five years, fell from grace in 1875, when it was discovered that he had been reimbursed by a company promoter for some speculative losses that Sampson had suffered in the company. From then on Printing House Square kept a closer eye on what was going on at its City office. Arthur Crump succeeded Sampson. Delane once told Arthur Fraser Walter, the proprietor, that he had had occasion to reprimand Crump for using the vile new word, contango. Delane added: 'I did not love Sampson, but he kept us clear from slang'.

The Supplements started to accept company meetings as paid advertisements. *The Times* itself had always refused to do so, insisting instead on sending one of its reporters to company meetings at considerable expense. The argument was that if you printed as an advertisement the company's own report, the directors would choose to publish only those parts of the meeting that they thought fit to print: in other words, puffs and propaganda, not news. *The Times* took the austere view, as it had with Parliament, the theatre and all other aspects of life, that it preferred its own to the official version.

In 1967 the new owners of *The Times* introduced a separate Business News inside the main paper. Some thirty journalists were added to the City staff to produce it. It was a separate section with its own title page, causing some confusion to readers, who waded through the main paper and then found themselves having to start again at the beginning, with a second lot of leaders, features, letters, news and diary. The strategy was to engage *The Financial Times* head on, on its home ground. But in the event, it proved a horrendous and costly mistake. It boasted some exclusive stories and some highly intelligent City journalists. But in general the City did not care for its breezy approach to finance and commerce, and stuck to its old Pink 'Un. And commuters in the morning rush hour had to wade, thigh-deep, through discarded copies of the Business News of *The Times* to get to their trains. In 1970 *The Times* took Business and City News back into its proper place, as a proud and authoritative part of the main paper.

An account of the court proceedings against Alan Bogle, through whom THE TIMES exposed a piece of financial skulduggery.
18 AUGUST 1841

SUMMER ASSIZES.

HOME CIRCUIT.

CROYDON, MONDAY, AUG. 16.

BOGLE V. LAWSON.

We resume our report of this case, of which we yesterday gave the opening speeches both for the plaintiff and the defendant. After Sir W. Follett had closed his address to the jury, he then proceeded to call the following evidence:—

Mr. George Carr Glyn sworn, and examined by Mr. PLATT.

You are a partner in the banking-house of Glyn, Halifax, and Co.?—I am.

In the course of business of your house has it been the custom to grant letters of credit to persons going on the continent?—It has been our practice.

Will you be so kind as to look at that? (A letter of credit was here handed to the witness.) Is that a letter of credit granted by your house?—It looks like one signed by Mr. Halifax. (This was a genuine letter of credit granted to Mr. Nicholson.)

(Another document, purporting to be a letter of credit, was now handed to the witness.) Examine that signature there, and say whether you think that is a genuine document?—I doubt its being genuine.

What makes you doubt its being genuine?—The signature is very stiff; the handwriting is not so free as Mr. Halifax generally signs.

(A second document of a similar description to the last was then handed to the witness.)—That is very like his common signature.

Have you got your book with you in which entries are made when letters of credit are granted?—I have. (Produces it.)

By Mr. THESIGER.—Are the entries made by yourself?—No, they are not.

By Mr. PLATT.—Do you know whether you granted a letter of credit to Mr. Nicholson?—I know we did.

By Mr. THESIGER.—How do you know?—By the fact of the handwriting.

Do you know by any other way?—I do not. The entries are made by one of our clerks.

Examination by Mr. PLATT continued.—What was the course pursued when letters of credit were granted?—We issued these general letters of credit for the purpose of meeting the travelling expenses of families visiting the continent. They presented them at any of the bankers' mentioned in our letter, and obtained money upon them.

On the granting of those letters what was the course pursued in your house?—The entries were made by a particular clerk, whose business it was to transact that part of our business.

Have you got the bills drawn by Nicholson against that letter of credit?—No, I have not.

Is it the course of the clerk to make an entry?—It is.

Are you in the habit of seeing this book in which the entries are made?—Day by day.

Are you enabled in the course of business to know whether these entries are correct?—I don't doubt it; I know they are correct.

By the COURT.—Do you ever check it yourself by the letters of credit?—We do, my Lord; the partner checks, and also sees that the party has given the signature for the purpose in the book I hold.

Refer to Mr. Nicholson's signature.

By Mr. THESIGER.—Do you know the signature of Mr. Nicholson?—I have accepted bills drawn by him.

Did you see Mr. Nicholson sign that book?—No.

By Mr. PLATT.—Have you acted on bills of exchange with that signature?—We have.

Have you with your own hand accepted such bills?—I have.

Is that the signature of the gentleman on the faith of whose signature you accepted those bills?—This, to the best of my knowledge and belief, is the signature of Mr. Nicholson.

Whence did those bills come which you accepted?—I cannot state.

By the COURT.—How long is it since you began to accept bills for Mr. Nicholson?—Several years.

By Mr. PLATT.—Have you accepted bills with that signature lately?—No, I have not. Mr. Nicholson is gone abroad.

The bills so accepted you have paid?—We have.

Mr. THESIGER objected to this line of examination.

Sir W. FOLLETT.—My learned friend has a perfect right to make any objection he chooses, but this is not one which is tenable on legal grounds. We are seeking to prove that he gave a letter of credit to Mr. Nicholson. I propose to do that by requesting the gentleman to turn to one of his books which is regularly kept in the bank, to which he has constant access, and into which he looks every day. The entries were made, not in his own handwriting, but in that of his clerk acting under his inspection. I submit that he has a right to look at that book to see whether he ever granted such letter of credit.

The CHIEF JUSTICE.—The objection is twofold—first, as stated by Sir W. Follett, and secondly as to the handwriting of Nicholson.

Sir W. FOLLETT.—The book itself is evidence, because Mr. Glyn states that he would act on that book, and that he pays the bills on the faith of those entries.

The CHIEF JUSTICE.—I am of opinion that we should have the clerk.

By Sir W. FOLLETT.—You have accepted bills for Mr. Nicholson?—Yes.

Have you paid them?—They have been paid at our house, not by me individually.

What number of clerks would it be necessary to send for?—Four or five.

What is the name of the clerk who made this entry?—Swinyear.

Is he in London?—He is.

(A letter of credit was here handed to the witness.)—This is in favour of Robert Nicholson, and is marked No. 490.

How many partners in your house sign these letters of credit?—The whole of the house, six partners. This is very like Mr. Halifax's writing, but looks stiff.

Form your belief whether it is or not?—I think I should have paid on it.

From your belief in the similarity of the writing?—Yes.

Setting aside all you have heard about a conspiracy, would you believe it to be his handwriting?—I should believe it to be Mr. Halifax's handwriting, but stiffer than usual.

Mr. Halifax is not here?—He is abroad.

See if you have got the name "Count de Pindray?"—I don't see any such name.

(The second letter of credit was here handed to the witness.)—You consider that to be in the handwriting of Mr. Halifax?—If this had been presented, I certainly should have paid on it.

Is that No. 570?—Yes.

Did the same clerk always make the entries?—He was sometimes absent.

Who made them then?—Henry Wellington.

Cross-examined by Mr. THESIGER.—When you first looked at the first letter of credit produced by you, you said "I doubt that it is genuine?"—I doubt, the handwriting being so stiff.

Does that doubt still exist?—Not to the same extent, upon comparing it.

What with?—With my recollection of Halifax's handwriting.

Do you still waver as to its being a genuine signature?—It is impossible for me to say whether or not.

Question repeated?—I still think the signature of that letter is not like Mr. Halifax's usual handwriting; it is more stiff.

Does that induce you to doubt that it is genuine?—I should pay on that letter if it was placed before me.

What induced you to say you doubted its genuineness?—In looking again at that letter I see the handwriting of our clerk, and the number inserted by him.

I am speaking now of Mr. Halifax's signature. On that alone being presented, would you have paid it?—If that letter was presented to me for payment, I would have paid, although having a doubt on my own mind that it was as free as his usual handwriting.

Question repeated.—I doubt whether I should pay it.

The other letter of credit produced is more like Mr. Halifax's common signature?—Yes.

How many of those letters of credit on the average does your house issue in the year?—Some 300 or 350.

Signed by the different partners?—By whomever may be in attendance.

Do you require the signature of the party to whom you give the letter?—We do, both in our book and in the letter. It goes with the letter presented by the party to whom we give the letter of credit.

Do you advise your correspondent abroad of those letters of credit?—Not of letters of credit of that description. They were issued for the convenience of persons travelling abroad.

Do you send the signature to your correspondents?—Not by post, but in the letter which the party takes with him to the bank.

You make the person fill in his name in the body of the letter?—In our presence; or if not, he must send us a letter stating that he has done so.

By Sir W. FOLLETT.—You said there was some of the handwriting of your clerk in the letter?—Yes, the word "*Monsieur*," the figures "1,500," and the words "*quinze cent livres*." That is in the handwriting of Swinyear.

Besides the number in the corner?—Yes; and the date.

The bearer puts in his name after "*presenté par*?"—Yes.

(The letter of credit in favour of the Count de Pindray was here handed to the witness.)—Is any of this in your clerk's handwriting?—No.

Have you any customer of that name?—No.

You don't know such a person?—I never heard of him.

Sir W. FOLLETT said that he would send to town for the clerk to prove his handwriting in Nicholson's letter.

The CHIEF JUSTICE.—I have no objection.

Sir W. FOLLETT.—With respect to the other, is it necessary that we should have the clerk to prove that no letter of credit was issued?

The CHIEF JUSTICE.—The book will prove that by the fact of the non-entry.

Mr. THESIGER.—I admit that.

Sir W. FOLLETT.—Then as to this being an imitation of the signature of Mr. Halifax, turn to the book, and say whether you gave any letter of credit to a person named Dr. Coulson?—I find no such name.

By Mr. PLATT.—Does any appear to have been granted to a person named Perry?—There's no such entry.

Any one to a person named Ireland?—None.

Any to a person named Pipe?—Not any.

Any to the Countess de Vandec?—There is no entry in that name.

Any to Marie Rosalie Josephine Desjardins?—No entry in that name.

Do you know anything of these bills of exchange? (Five of those documents were here handed to the witness.)—No, I do not.

How many bills are there?—Five.

Do they appear to be all drawn by the same person?—They purport to be so.

Had the person there described any credit at your house?—He had not.

Cross-examined by Mr. THESIGER.—Look to that book, and say whether Count D'Arjuzon had any account at your house?—He had.

When?—The letter of credit was issued to him, as far as this book tells me, on the 7th January, 1840.

The usual course of your letters of credit is for twelve months?—Six months.

The number of this letter of credit is 523?—Yes, and the amount 150*l.*

What was done upon this letter of credit?—I have got an entry here; the 3d of February, 100*l.* was paid, and on the 5th of February, 45*l.*, leaving a balance of 5*l.*

Drawn where?—This book does not give the particulars.

When were these sums drawn?—The date I mentioned is the date of the acceptance.

By Sir W. FOLLETT.—Have you any credit there to the Marquis de Bourbel?—None.

Is it usual to return your letters of credit?—We always enjoin it on our friends, but they don't always do it; it is the usual practice.

Mr. PEACOCK was then proceeding to put in the depositions of two witnesses examined by commission in Belgium, when

Mr. THESIGER objected to their being received, as being the depositions of parties suffering punishment under a criminal conviction, and now in prison.

Sir W. FOLLETT contended that the depositions could not legally be excluded.

The LORD CHIEF JUSTICE.—It is not a judgment in our English courts. However disqualified in Belgium, he is not disqualified here. The only disqualification in point of law here attends the sentence of a criminal court in this country.

Mr. THESIGER.—I have here a copy of the judgment pronounced upon him.

M. Delhauche and an interpreter were here sworn.

Sir W. FOLLETT objected to the evidence of this witness being received, the commissioners having been regularly empowered by the English judges.

The LORD CHIEF JUSTICE.—I will take a note of your objection.

M. Delhauche was then examined by Mr. THESIGER, through the interpreter; and deposed that he was an *avocat* practising in the Belgian courts. He handed in a copy of the judgment pronounced upon William Perry and Angelina Pipe by the Court of Appeal, which he stated that he had examined and compared with the original. It was sealed by the authorities, and signed by the president. It was a true copy of the judgment in the case of the two prisoners mentioned. The judgments of the Court of Appeal were kept in the *greffe* (register), and it was there that he examined it. By the 23th article of the penal code of Belgium, persons imprisoned for forgery and such offences were prohibited from giving evidence till the period of their punishment expired. The date of the judgment was the 19th of February, 1841. Perry was sentenced to 15 years' hard labour, and the female to 12, and both to public exposure.

Cross-examined by Sir W. FOLLETT.—They were likewise sentenced to be branded. They were condemned to *travaux forcés*. Every person so sentenced was prevented by the article to which he alluded from giving evidence in a court of justice. He was also disqualified from carrying arms. [When this question was put to him, the witness caused some amusement by the energy with which he exclaimed, "*Diable! non, il est degradé!*"] A person in this position was incapacitated from serving in the army or fleet. He could, however, give evidence by *simple renseignement*, the meaning of which was, that when a convict was suffering under a criminal sentence, the president of the court had a discretionary power of causing the prisoner to give his evidence without being sworn. He had carefully compared both judgment and copy. He had read over the original with the *greffier*, who read the copy. The disqualification was the result of the prisoner being condemned to an infamous penalty.

The copy of the judgment was then read by the clerk, who also read the depositions of the witnesses examined in Brussels.

William Perry's deposition was as follows:—

"To the first interrogatory I say,—I am an engraver and printer, and carried on that business at No. 5, Upper Rupert-street, Haymarket, in London, in 1839, and up to March, 1840.

"To the second interrogatory I say,—I know the Marquis de Bourbel. I was employed by him, in the way of my trade, profession, and business, and otherwise, about the middle of February in the year 1840, at his house 100, Quadrant, Regent-street, London. I first printed him 100 portraits, then some card plates, then nearly 300 of those letters of credit."

"To the third interrogatory I say,—I arrived at Calais, I think, on the 28th of March, 1840, in company with the Marquis de Bourbel and the woman Angelina Pipe. I did not know the object of their journey at that time, nor of their so accompanying me.

"To the fourth interrogatory I say,—The same day we left Calais for Dunkirk. We slept at Dunkirk that night, and the following morning started by diligence for Ostend, in company with the Marquis de Bourbel and Mrs. Angelina Pipe. On Sunday, the 29th of March, we arrived at Ostend, and remained there till the following Tuesday. I met there Mr. Frederick Pipe, the husband of Mrs. Angelina Pipe, the Baron d'Arjuzon, his lady, the Baroness, two servants and a little child; the man servant was named Antonio, and the maid Annette.

"To the fifth interrogatory I say,—No letter of credit was delivered to me at Aix-la-Chapelle or Ostend, but a letter of credit was delivered to me at Liege by the Baron d'Arjuzon, about half-past 9 on the morning of Monday, the 20th of April, 1840, to go to Nagelmacker and Co., and there to ask for 500*l.*; the letter of credit was forged, but I did not know it was forged at the time of the presentment. I returned it after I came out of the bankers to the Baron d'Arjuzon. It appeared to be signed by Glyn, Halifax, Mills and Co., and had a stamp upon it.

"To the sixth interrogatory I say,—On the 21st of April, 1840, I presented a letter of credit to the bankers, Nagelmacker and Co., at Liege."

Mr. THESIGER objected. It was not specified in any way to what letter the witness alluded.

Sir W. FOLLETT.—We will prove that presently.

Upon the clerk reading the words in Perry's deposition, "I demand 500*l.*,"

Mr. THESIGER objected to this evidence being received; and the Court took a note of the objection.

Mr. Andrew Kirwan was sworn and examined by Sir W. FOLLETT.—

You are a barrister?—Yes.

Did you act as a commissioner to take the evidence of Perry?—I did.

Did you inspect and copy the alleged letters of credit found in his possession?—They were shown to me by the *greffier* of the Cour d'Appel at Brussels, who refused to part with them, they being in the custody of the Court.

Was that the court in which the prisoners were condemned?—It was.

Did you take copies of them?—I did.

Were they copied in his presence?—Yes; he had both the original and a copy of them.

Those which you now hand me are correct copies?—They are.

The reading of Perry's deposition was then proceeded with, as follows:—

"I returned the letter to the Baron d'Arjuzon; it was filled up for 800*l.* I demanded 500*l.* on it. At the time I did not receive anything, in consequence of not having my original passport. I was obliged to go to Brussels to obtain the passport, and on the Wednesday following, having obtained it, I went again to the banker, and he paid me 100*l.* I drew one bill of exchange in favour of Nagelmacker and Co. for 100*l.*, and which is the bill now produced to me in my examination. The said letter was forged; it appeared to be signed by Glyn, Halifax, Mills, and Co.; there was what is called a dry seal on it. I received the letter of credit from the Baron d'Arjuzon. I gave the money I received upon it to the Baron d'Arjuzon. It was partly engraved and partly written. I printed the impression from engraved plates by order of the Marquis de Bourbel at the end of February, 1840, at a house in Lisson-grove, London. I do not know who engraved the plates; they were already engraved when I went to print them.

"To the seventh interrogatory I say,—On Tuesday, the 21st of April, I presented another letter of credit to Messrs. Engler and Co., bankers at Brussels. I also returned that letter of credit to the Baron d'Arjuzon. It was filled up for 1,500*l.* It was forged. It purported to have been signed and sealed by Glyn, Halifax, Mills, and Co. I received it from the Baron d'Arjuzon. I demanded and received upon it 750*l.* from one of the persons in the office of Engler and Co. I drew two bills of exchange in favour of Engler and Co. for sums amounting together to 750*l.* upon Glyn, Halifax, Mills, and Co. These are the bills now presented to me in the custody and from the hands of the *greffier* of the Cour d'Appel at Brussels, and shown to me at this my examination. I gave the 750*l.* to the Baron d'Arjuzon. The letter of credit was partly engraved and partly written. I printed the impression from engraved plates, by order of the Marquis de Bourbel, at the end of February, 1840, at a house in Lisson-grove, London. I don't know who engraved the plates. They were already engraved when I went to print them.

"To the eighth interrogatory I say,—I presented a letter of credit to Messrs. Agie and Co., bankers at Antwerp, on Thursday, the 23d of April, 1840. It was the same which I had previously presented to Engler and Co., and I demanded of Agie 500*l.* upon it.

"To the ninth interrogatory I say,—I presented a letter of credit on Friday, the 24th of April, to De Meulemeester et Fils, bankers at Ghent. It was the same which I had previously presented to Nagelmacker and Co. at Liege, and I demanded of De Meulemeester et Fils 100*l.* upon it.

"To the tenth interrogatory I say,—The Marquis de Bourbel employed me about the middle of February, 1840, to work off impressions from three engraved plates, and I worked off nearly 300 from all the three plates, each piece of paper containing an impression of all the three plates. The Marquis de Bourbel supplied me with the three plates for that purpose. I have seen four impressions in the possession of the Baron d'Arjuzon at Antwerp, on the continent of Europe.

"To the eleventh interrogatory I say,—The document now produced and shown to me, and marked 'A,' corresponds as to the paper and copper-plate printing thereof with the letters of credit mentioned and referred to in my answers to the fifth, sixth, seventh, eighth, and ninth interrogatories respectively, and differs therefrom as to the written matter contained therein.

"To the twelfth interrogatory I say,—The engraved part of the said document marked 'A' was worked by me for the Marquis de Bourbel, and was last seen by me in his possession—I mean previously to its being exhibited to me to-day, together with the other impressions I worked off for him. I do not know with certainty by whom the stamp with which the said document was marked was engraved or made; it was engraved by the order of the Marquis de Bourbel; it was engraved for the Marquis. The reason I know that it was engraved by the order of the Marquis is, that he sent me with a letter to an engraver named Palmer, and that I got a seal from Palmer in a letter or parcel: I know it was a seal, for I felt it. I am positive it was, I have had so many seals in my hands. It was a piece of thin whity-brown paper.

"To the thirteenth interrogatory I say,—I never heard the Marquis de Bourbel and Alexander Graham, when in conversation together, mention the plaintiff, Allan George Bogle. On the road between Liege and Antwerp Alexander Graham told me—"

Mr. THESIGER objected to this evidence being received. Any declaration as to what a third party had done was inadmissible.

Sir W. FOLLETT.—This is a disclosure of the mode in which the conspiracy was carried on. It is a statement as to an act done by one of the conspirators for the purpose of inducing the witness to go and present one of these forged letters of credit.

Sir W. FOLLETT then put in a bill of exchange, dated the 22d of April, 1840, Liege, for 100*l.*, drawn by J. W. Ireland upon Glyn and Co., at 30 days after date, No. 551, and another for 100*l.*, dated 24th of March, 1840.

To Mr. Glyn.—Would the numbers refer to the number of the bill, and the date of the letter of credit?—Generally, not invariably.

Sir W. FOLLETT then put in another bill for 400*l.*, bearing date the 22d of April, 1840, in favour of Messrs. Glyn, together with a bill of 540*l.*, dated the 24th of March, and another for 350*l.*, dated in Brussels the 22d of April, 1840.

The Clerk then read the deposition of Angelina Pipe, as follows:—

"To the first interrogatory,—I was resident in Lisson-grove, London, some time in the month of March, 1840, when I left England for Calais by the persuasion and at the instigation of the Marquis de Bourbel, my husband, who with Thomas William Perry, otherwise William Perry, otherwise Thomas William Ireland, accompanied me upon my voyage, and I believe the expenses were paid by the Marquis de Bourbelle.

"To the second interrogatory,—I know the Marquis de Bourbel, the Baron Louis D'Arjuzon, Frederick Pipe, *alias* Coulson, Alexander Graham, Thomas William Perry, otherwise William Perry, otherwise Thomas William Ireland, and Marie, commonly called the Baroness D'Arjuzon.

"To the third interrogatory,—I did in or about the latter end of March, in the year 1840, travel from Calais to Dunkirk, from Dunkirk to Ostend, and from Ostend to Aix-la-Chapelle. At Dunkirk I met my husband, the Marquis de Bourbel, but no other person. At Ostend I met the Baron D'Arjuzon and Marie, his woman, commonly called the Baroness D'Arjuzon, a child, and two servants. At Aix-la-Chapelle, after we were there a fortnight, I met Alexander Graham. I did not learn the object of their being there, except that Perry told me at Liege that the Baron D'Arjuzon and Graham were fraudulently drawing money from bankers.

"To the fourth interrogatory,—At Antwerp, on or about the 22d or 23d day of April, 1840, the Baron D'Arjuzon made an application to me, and said, 'I have got something I want you to present which will put money into your pocket.' The Baron did not say what it was, nor do I know, for I did not even take it into my hand. I told him if he would give me 50,000*l.* I would not have any thing to do with his proceedings. The Baron D'Arjuzon did not otherwise than as I have before stated hold out to me any expectation of benefit or reward if I would present any letter of credit.

"To the fifth interrogatory,—I was not present at the presentment of any letters of credit by the said Thomas William Perry, otherwise William Perry, otherwise Thomas William Ireland, to any persons whomsoever.

"To the sixth interrogatory,—After I left Aix-la-Chapelle I travelled to Liege, Brussels, Antwerp, Bruges, Ghent, and Ostend, on the continent of Europe.

"To the seventh interrogatory,—I was arrested at Ostend on the 25th day of April, 1840; previous to the time when I was arrested, Perry asked me to lend him my small basket, which I did, and he afterwards gave it to me again with something in it tied up in a handkerchief of his. Perry did not say what it was, but I afterwards learned, when the parcel was opened by the maritime bailiff, that it contained notes and gold. I had two half-sovereigns of my own in my pocket when I was arrested, but no money besides; I had an opportunity of throwing the basket into the sea, but did not do so, not knowing then what was in it.

"To the eighth interrogatory,—Except as I have stated in my answers to the 1st, 2d, 3d, 4th, 5th, 6th, and 7th interrogatories, I do not know nor am I in any manner acquainted with any undertaking, transaction, or business in which the persons named in the second interrogatory or any of them were engaged between the time of my arrival at Calais and that of my arrest at Ostend.

"To the ninth interrogatory,—I am not acquainted with the handwriting of the Marquis de Bourbel, and the paper writing mentioned in this interrogatory not being produced to me upon this my examination, I am unable to say whether I do or do not believe the same to be in his handwriting.

"And to the last interrogatory,—I do not know of any other matter or thing, nor have I heard, nor can I say, anything touching the matters in question in this cause that may tend to the benefit or advantage of the defendant besides what I have been interrogated unto."

Mr. Kerrich was then called and sworn, and examined by Sir W. FOLLETT.

I believe you have carried on the business of banker at Florence?—I have resided at Florence for some years.

You were, I understand, in partnership with Messrs. Bogle and Macarthy?—Yes, I was.

When did the partnership commence?—It commenced on the 14th of November, 1837.

When did you first become acquainted with Mr. Bogle?—I knew Mr. Bogle at Florence in 1835. He was then residing there. Mr. Bogle was first clerk to Mr. Johnston, and subsequently he entered into business on his own account.

Do you know Mr. Graham?—I became acquainted with Graham in 1835.

Did Mr. Cunningham Graham carry on business at Florence?—No.

Or his son?—No.

I believe Mr. C. Graham married the mother of Mr. Bogle?—He did.

After you entered into partnership with Mr. Bogle, did you see Mr. C. Graham?—I saw him from time to time.

Where?—I saw him at the bank.

Did you visit him?—I did, at his house, on several occasions.

I perceive by these papers that you have been in communication with Glyn and Co.?—Yes.

Were you acquainted with Mr. R. Nicholson?—Yes.

What did Mr. Nicholson do?—He brought to me a letter of credit from the house of Glyn and Co.

I wish to direct your attention to this letter (handing one to the witness). Will you look at that letter, and tell me whether it is the same that was presented to you?—It is the same letter.

In what mode did you make the payments to Mr. Nicholson?—I made the first payment on the 18th of November, 1839; and the second in January, 1840.

No payment, I believe, was made between the dates you mention?—None whatever.

When you made the first payment, did Mr. Nicholson leave the letter of credit with you?—He did so.

Where was that letter kept?—It was preserved carefully in a tin box.

Where was that tin box kept?—During the hours of business it was on my desk.

Did the box contain other papers besides the letter of credit to which you refer?—It contained other documents with that letter.

It is not usual to leave letters of credit with the bankers to whom they are presented?—It is not the ordinary practice.

In this case the ordinary course was departed from?—It formed an exception to the usual practice.

I suppose Mr. Bogle was quite aware that you kept the letters?—He was.

Do you remember Mr. Bogle making any allusion to the letter?—Mr. Bogle applied to me for the letter of credit.

At what time? Will you have the goodness to specify the time as accurately as you can?—He applied to me about December or January.

At what period?—I mean either at the latter end of December, or end of January, 1839.

Did Mr. Bogle tell you for what purpose he wished the letter?—He did not say what he wanted the letter for.

Did you, when the application was made, make any observation to Mr. Bogle on the subject?—I did; I asked him if it was his intention to draw again.

What was Mr. Bogle's reply?—He said, "I don't know," or some such words.

What course did you pursue with regard to the application?—I gave Mr. Bogle, as he requested, the letter of credit.

How long did he keep it?—He kept the letter for three hours at least.

The letter was then returned to you by Mr. Bogle?—It was.

Mr. Nicholson did not draw again?—No.

After the letter was returned to you what did you do with it?—I put it carefully in a tin box.

Are you acquainted with the Marquis de Bourbel?—I am slightly acquainted with the Marquis.

At what period did that acquaintance commence?—It commenced about the 9th of March, 1839.

How did you become acquainted with the Marquis de Bourbel?—I was introduced to him by Mr. Bogle.

What did the Marquis do?—He opened an account with the house at that time.

Are you aware where the Marquis resided?—He resided at that period partly at Florence, and partly at his villa or some such place, at Leghorn.

Do you know when the Marquis left for England?—I do not know exactly, but think about September, 1839.

Did you see him after that period?—I saw him at Florence on the 21st of April afterwards.

I believe you know a person called the Count de Pindray?—I did.

When did you see the Marquis?—I saw him on the 21st of April in Mr. Bogle's room at the bank.

Have the kindness to describe the room?—The room was situated immediately opposite to my own, where I and Mr. Macarthy sat. The room is divided in the centre by a glass partition. There is a hole in the centre, through which the money is put on a marble slab.

Is it the custom for persons to be in the room with the person who pays the money?—It is not usual.

Where did you see the Marquis?—I saw him in the open part, early in the morning, when I first came to the bank.

At what time?—At 10 o'clock.

What are the banking hours?—The bank opens at 10 and closes at half-past 3 o'clock.

Did you leave the Marquis there?—No, I did not.

What were the Marquis and those who were with him doing?—They were all transacting business together.

What became of Mr. Bogle?—I left him there, and went to my own room.

When did you see Bogle after that?—I went back in half an hour to Bogle's room, and found the Marquis there. He was then inside.

Was Bogle there?—He was.

Did you go into the room?—No.

Why not?—The door was locked.

Then you failed in obtaining admission?—I could not get in. I tried the door, and found it locked.

What course did you pursue?—I returned.

Are you certain that Mr. Bogle and the Marquis were there?—I saw them both.

In what way?—Through the glass.

Did you go again?—I went a second time.

Had he left?—No, he was still there. Bogle was there for two or three hours.

When did that occur?—On the 21st of April.

Did you see him leave the bank?—I did not.

Did not the Count de Pindray present a letter of credit?—He presented a letter of credit on the 21st of April.

Be so kind as to examine this letter (handing one to witness), and tell me if it is the same document presented to you at the time you have just specified?—I have examined the letter, and it is the same document.

Was any one there when the letter of credit was presented?—Mr. Bogle was in the bank at the time—the Count presented the letter to Mr. Bogle.

Did Mr. Bogle introduce the Count to you?—He did so.

What did you do with the letter?—I examined the signature.

Was it your duty to do so?—It was my province to examine the signatures of all letters of credit.

What was your impression upon examining the signature?—I thought immediately it was a letter from Glyn and Co.

Did you put any questions to the Count de Pindray?—I asked him several questions relating to his leaving England.

Were his answers satisfactory?—They were satisfactory.

How much money did he obtain?—The sum of 200*l.*

When was the letter of credit brought to the bank?—On the next day.

Where were you at the time?—I was not there.

When you went to the bank on the following day did you see any one there, and whom?—I found the Count de Pindray, Mr. Bogle, and Mr. Macarthy there.

What was the Count's business?—He was anxious either to have the bills returned to him, or to have them destroyed, or to restore the money.

Did he assign any reason for so wishing?—He said it was in consequence of the authenticity of the letter having been doubted.

Did he say by whom it had been questioned?—He did not to me.

Did the Count say anything else?—He was very indignant. He thought it hard that his honour should be doubted.

Are you aware who it was who doubted his honour?—I heard from Mr. Macarthy, who doubted the authenticity of the bill.

What statement did Mr. Macarthy make to you?—I was told by Mr. Macarthy that the Count had tried to obtain money from Mr. Phillipson of the city, who had doubts of the authenticity of the letter.

Did Mr. Bogle make any observation?—He made none whatever.

What did you do with the letter of credit?—I examined again the signature of the letter of credit, and compared it with the letter of credit to Mr. Nicholson.

What was then your impression of it?—I still thought that it was genuine.

What was done with the money and bill?—The 200*l.* was returned to the bank, and I tore up the bill in the Count's presence.

Who made the entry on the bill in your hand?—I did.

What is the entry?—It is, "The above payment cancelled by the express wish of the drawer. Signed, Bogle, Kerrich, and Co."

What did the Count de Pindray do with the paper?—He took it and went away with it.

What became of the Count?—I did not see him afterwards.

Examine that signature, and tell me whose it is?—The signature is my own, and the entry is by my clerk.

When did you hear of the conspiracy?—I did not hear of the conspiracy until I received a communication from the English Minister.

When did you receive that communication?—On the 9th of May. I received certain documents at that time from the Minister.

Will you examine these papers (some documents were handed to the witness), and tell me if they are the same that you received?—The witness, after examining them carefully, said that they were the same.

Did you receive a letter from Oppenheim and Co. on the same day?—I did.

On seeing the name of Bogle mentioned in the documents received from Mr. Fox, now Lord Holland, who was then Minister at Florence, did you endeavour to find Mr. Bogle?—I did. I went to several places after the bank was closed.

Where did you find him?—I found him at his own house in Florence on Saturday.

Did you read the paper to Bogle?—I did so.

Did you read to him the whole of these documents?—Yes.

Did you read to Mr. Bogle the passage in the documents wherein his own name was mentioned?—Most certainly.

The following document was then handed in to the court by Sir W. Follett, and was read:—

"DUPLICATE OF A MINUTE IN THE REGISTRY OF THE TRIBUNAL OF FIRST INSTANCE SITTING AT BRUSSELS, IN THE PROVINCE OF BRABANT.

"Examination of Thomas William Ireland by the Maritime Bailiff of Ostend, the 27th of April, 1840.

"Your name?—Thomas William Ireland.

"Your age?—30 years.

"Where were you born?—In London, Oxford-street, 408.

"Where is your domicile and habitual residence?—Upper Rupert-street, Haymarket, No. 5, London.

"Are you married?—Yes.

"At what period did you for the first time come to the continent?—I arrived in Calais on the 28th of March from London.

"Were you in the company of any one else, and if so, what were their names?—I was with the Marquis de Bourbel and a woman named Augustine Mawberg.

"Where did you become acquainted with those persons? What were their projects? Had you known them before?—Declares that he had a shop, and was a printer and engraver without means of support, not being able to supply his wants. That the Marquis de Bourbel engaged him a month previous to his arrival with him at Calais to work for him, and as to the woman, or girl, Mawberg, she accompanied the accused (Ireland), and the Marquis as interpreter, because she spoke French well.

"Where did you go to after your arrival at Calais; were you still in company with De Bourbel and the girl Mawberg? What stay did you make at Calais; and have you seen De Bourbel present any false letters of credit?—The same day to Dunkirk by the diligence, and in the same company. I had not nor had De Bourbel then made any use of the false letters of credit, of which I affirm that De Bourbel was the bearer to the number of about 50 or 60, and of the value, I should presume, of from 20,000*l.* to 25,000*l.* sterling.

"From Dunkirk where did you go?—We did not stop at Dunkirk; we continued our route by diligence for Ostend, where we arrived on Sunday, the 29th of March last.

"Where did you lodge at Ostend with De Bourbel and the woman Mawberg?—At the Hotel d'Allemagne, kept by Augustus Clacy.

"How many days did you stay there?—From Sunday, the 29th of March, until Tuesday, the 31st.

"You tell me of Dr. Coulson and the Baron de Castel, who had already arrived in Ostend previous to your arrival there from Dunkirk?—It was arranged between De Bourbel, De Castel, and Coulson to meet at Ostend. He is ignorant of what passed between them, and declares that the woman Mawberg lived formerly with Coulson.

"Where did you go after leaving Ostend?—To Aix-la-Chapelle by the railroad.

"Have you attempted to make use of the forged letters of credit in your journey from Ostend to Aix-la-Chapelle?—No, we only stopped at Liege for supper.

"Memorandum.—Here the accused Ireland declares, that during his aforesaid stay at Ostend he received one of the forged letters of credit, of which De Castel was the bearer, and was ordered by the Marquis de Bourbel to present it to the banker J. B. Brasseur, of Ostend; that he refused to do so, having burnt the letter of credit.

"When did you arrive at Aix-la-Chapelle?—The 1st of last April, accompanied by the Baron de Castel, his wife, and the woman Mawberg, and two servants in De Castel's service. De Bourbel quitted Ostend with Coulson on Monday, the 30th of March.

"How many days did you stay at Aix-la-Chapelle, and what employment, what occupation, and what attempts took place and were made?—With the abovenamed persons, we remained at Aix-la-Chapelle from the 1st to the 19th of April; no attempt was made, nor any presentment of false letters of credit to procure money. Declares that De Castel and his wife or concubine lived in a splendid style and spent largely. He (Ireland) could not easily see Castel, who wished to avoid him. Ireland was destitute of funds, as well as the girl Mawberg, with whom he was then living.

"Where did you go to after leaving Aix-la-Chapelle on the 19th of April?—To Liege, where I arrived on Monday morning, the 20th of April, with De Castel, who had left his wife at Aix-la-Chapelle with the servant.

"Did you endeavour to raise any money with your forged letters of credit, and how long did you stay at Liege?—I received from De Castel, in the street where the banker Nagelmacker resides, a false letter of credit for 800*l.* sterling. I presented the said letter, demanding the first time 500*l.*, which were refused, because his passport was not regular. I presented it again the next day, and received from M. Nagelmacker 100*l.*, 80*l.* of which were delivered over to De Castel, and 20*l.* were given to him for his trouble.

"In what species of money were you paid the 100*l.*?—In gold, in pieces of 10 florins.

"Did you retain the letter of credit for 800*l.* presented by you to Messrs. Nagelmacker?—Yes.

"From Liege where did you go?—To Brussels, where I presented a forged letter of credit for 1,400*l.* to Messrs. Engler, of which I received 750*l.*, partly in gold and partly in Belgian bank-notes.

"What did you do with this sum of money, and how was it divided between you and your accomplices?—I received from De Castel 20 per cent. on the 750*l.*; the remainder he kept himself.

"From Brussels where did you go?—To Liege, and thence to Antwerp.

"What did you do at Antwerp?—I presented to M. Agie the same letter of credit for 1,400*l.* which I had presented to Mr. Engler. M. Agie refused to give me any sum of money on it, as that letter was not confirmed by the London banker.

"What did you do with this letter after the refusal of M. Agie?—I burnt it at Antwerp.

"Why did you burn it?—That it might not be put in evidence, which might have compromised me, knowing it to be false.

"From Antwerp where did you go, and who were the persons who accompanied you?—To Ghent, with the woman Mawberg.

"What steps were taken by you at Ghent?—I presented to M. Meulemeester a letter of credit for 800*l.* sterling, the same which I had presented to M. Nagelmacker, and on which I had obtained 100*l.* M. Meulemeester refused it, saying he had no letter of advice. I then went to Ostend, where I was to make use of the same letter of credit, but did not, having burnt it. He was arrested on Saturday, April 25.

"Who remitted you the letters of credit, and how and for what sums?—I received one for 1,400*l.*, and another for 800*l.*, from the Baron de Castel.

"Where and on what day did you quit De Castel?—At Antwerp, on Thursday last, April 23.

"Where do you think he is gone?—He went immediately with a man named Nicholson to Aix-la-Chapelle to continue their criminal work—they were then to go on the Rhine and into Germany.

"Had they passports and under their real names?—Their passports were under the names of De Castel and Robert Nicholson; their real names were, the former Baron d'Arjuzon and — Graham, an English or Scotchman, whose father is well off and living at Florence; he seems also to be a great swindler.

"Where did you last see De Bourbel?—At Ostend, at the Hotel d'Allemagne, on the 30th of March.

"Do you think De Bourbel had anything to do with this gang?—He is the principal author and actor in reality; but he does not make himself known. It is he who caused the plate to be made; but I do not know by whom. He also paid in London all expenses; he engaged me to accompany him after I had thrown off at London at one time 175 letters, and at another time 30—in all 205. I am a printer by trade; De Bourbel furnished the press, which belonged to him, and he left it in London; but I cannot say in what street or house. I know, however, and confess that it was in De Bourbel's house No. 100, Quadrant, Regent-street, that I printed the letters.

"When Bourbel quitted Ostend where did he go to?—He went off to Calais and from there to Paris, where he was to wait for the correspondence of his accomplices, to repair afterwards to Leghorn. He speaks English well. I have learned nothing more of him, but he was continually corresponding with De Castel, or rather Baron d'Arjuzon.

"Of what use to you were the tools that I found on your person when arrested?—They belong to me; I am an engraver as well as printer.

"You have spoken to me of a Dr. Coulson, what has become of him?—He accompanied De Bourbel to Italy to operate there. They (the accomplices) have separated into several countries, in order to use their forged letters.

"You have spoken to me in your first and second examinations of a certain Bogle, a banker of Florence, and correspondent of the banking house of Glyn, Halifax, Mills, and Co., of London?—Yes, I will tell you what I know. I heard young Graham say in conversation, 'Mr. Bogle will have his share easily, for he had nothing to do for his pains.' Bogle is the brother-in-law of Graham, having married his sister. N.B. Observe that Graham, sen., his son, and son-in-law, are all sharers of the spoil, forgers, and swindlers. The bank of Bogle enjoys great credit.

"Did you see De Bourbel at Antwerp?—No, he did not go there. I only saw him at Ostend, and knew him in London.

"What passport had De Bourbel?—I cannot say, but it was under his real name, in order that he might be supposed unknown in the fraud, though in reality the inventor. The orders emanated from him, and all correspondence with the accomplices—viz., Graham, the younger, *alias* Nicholson, Arjuzon, *alias* De Castel, and Frederick Coulson.

"What age is De Bourbel, his height, his dress?—He is 40 years of age, light hair, fine stature, wears a great coat of kid skin, his complexion pale, and of agreeable physiognomy.

"Where did you exchange the 250*l.*, the share you received, into the sovereigns and English bank-notes that I found on your person?—At Antwerp, at a money-changer's on the Place de Mein, for sovereigns and English bank-notes.

"Where were you to address any correspondence you might, or ought, to have sent to De Bourbel?—At Mr. Skinner's, poste restante, Leghorn, and also to De Bourbel himself, poste restante, Leghorn.

"I am certain you have also taken a false name in your passport?—Yes, my name is William Perry, living in London, as it is written at the bottom of the first page.

"Do you think that the woman Mawberg (Lenoq) is initiated in all your acts and those of your accomplices?—She was present at all our conversations and interviews, for some of us not speaking any thing but English she served us as interpreter of the French.

"Thus closed and completed at the house of the Maritime Bailiff, admitting that the translation made into English by Professor Addamson, as well of the questions as of the answers, is in all things agreeable to my declaration.

"Ostend, April 27, 1840. "LANNE ADDAMSON,
"THOMAS WILLIAM IRELAND.

"The accused, Ireland, was to address his letters to Graham thus:—'Alexander Spiers, Esq., aux soins de Messrs. A. & W. Galignani, Paris;' and for the Baron de Castel, 'To Baron D'Arjuzon, Post Restante, Paris.' Graham, called Nicholson, and D'Arjuzon were to meet in Paris on the 1st or 2d of May next."

Mr. Kerrich's examination continued by Sir W. FOLLETT.

Did you read the part of the document which referred to Mr. Bogle himself, as well as the part relating to Graham?—Yes.

What did Bogle say?—I do not recollect his precise words. He appeared greatly distressed; so much so that it was painful to witness.

Did he deny the truth of the statement?—He did not. He expressed something.

What kind of expression did Mr. Bogle use?—He said he was ruined.

How long did you remain with him?—Some length of time.

Did you leave him at home?—No.

Where did you go?—I went to the ambassador's, to leave the papers.

Did you see the ambassador?—I did not.

Did you go to Bogle's house?—I went to Bogle's mother's house.

Did you leave him there?—I did.

When did that occur?—On Saturday, the 9th of May.

At what hour?—A quarter after 12 at night.

When did you see Mr. Bogle again?—I saw him again on Monday. I saw him at his own house.

What was he doing?—He was in bed.

At what hour was that?—Between the hours of 11 and 12.

Who was with you at the time?—Mr. Macarthy.

What transpired?—I talked a great deal to him on the subject of the business.

What did Bogle propose to do?—He proposed an immediate retirement from the firm.

Did anything else transpire?—Yes, Mr. Bogle made a decided declaration never to enter the bank again.

Had you or Mr. Macarthy proposed such a step to him?—Decidedly not.

What did you say when Mr. Bogle announced his intention?—I begged him to reflect on the step he was taking. Mr. Bogle asked me to take the keys of the bank.

Where were they?—They were in some part of his room.

Was he in bed during the whole of the time?—He was.

I believe you found the keys in an adjoining room?—I did.

Did he at that period talk of getting up?—No.

What was done with regard to the partnership?—A notice of dissolution was signed at that time, prepared by Mr. Macarthy.

Where is the notice?—It is at Florence.

Who signed it?—Mr. Bogle and all signed the paper on the 12th of May.

Did Mr. Bogle go to the bank after that notice of dissolution was signed?—He only made his appearance once after that at the bank.

What did he state?—He said that he had received an order from the police commanding him to leave the country in five days.

Did Mr. Bogle, in consequence of that order, make any request?—He did; he asked us to assist him in obtaining from the Minister permission to remain a short period longer in the country.

Who went to the Minister to make his request?—To the best of my belief, Mr. Macarthy did.

Did you make any observation to Bogle about his not leaving his bed?—I did so.

What did you say?—I asked him why he did not get up and show himself at his usual places of resort.

What was his reply?—He said, "I cannot, I have not spirits."

Did he go out?—Yes, in a carriage.

Did he obtain from the Minister what he wished?—I imagine he did.

Why do you think so?—Because Bogle did not leave Florence until the 28th.

Did you see him at Florence on the 28th?—I cannot say that I did.

During the time that Bogle was at Florence what documents did he receive?—He received a document addressed to Bogle, Kerrich, and Co., with the postmark of "Algiers" upon it.

What did you do with it?—I took it myself to Mr. Bogle. The inner packet was addressed to Mr. Bogle, and was, to the best of my belief, marked "Private."

When did that occur?—It took place whilst Bogle was at Florence.

Did you receive any other packets?—I did; one was dated on the 8th of June, and the other on the 17th of the same month.

How were they addressed?—The outside was addressed to Bogle, Kerrich, and Co., and the inner one to A. Bogle, Esq., and marked "Private."

Sir W. FOLLETT (handing a packet to the witness).—Examine that packet, and tell me if that is one that was received?—Yes, it is.

Is that the other?—It is.

Did any other packets arrive of the same character?—Others arrived on the 8th and 17th of June. I opened the outer, but not the inner, envelopes.

Do you know M. le Mezurier, the banker at Rome?—I do.

Had you any communication with him on the subject of the conspiracy?—I had.

When did you show him the letter?—I did not show it to him at first, but did so at the end of the conversation.

Did you make any remark upon the handwriting?

Mr. THESIGER objected to the question.

Sir W. FOLLETT.—Did you, in consequence of what was said, go or send to the English Minister?—I did.

Did the English Minister attend at the bank?—He did not; I went to him; M. le Mezurier was present.

What did you find in the letter?—The documents which are now in the court.

Do you know the family of Graham?—I do.

When did they leave Florence?—On the 29th or 30th of May.

Before they left did they send anything to your bank or house?

Mr. THESIGER.—Who brought them to the bank and house?

Mr. Kerrich.—They were brought by a common porter.

Sir W. FOLLETT.—Was there a lathe amongst them?—Yes.

What portion of Graham's family did you see prior to their leaving Florence?—I saw Mr. Graham and Miss Graham.

What did Miss Graham tell you?—She instructed me to take great care of the things that had been sent to the bank and house.

What things were they?—A great variety of things.

Where did you see the things?—I saw them at Mr. Graham's, in Miss Graham's presence. I did not see the lathe there.

You received all the things that were consigned to you?—I did.

The tracing machine was put away at your bank with the other things, I believe?—Yes.

Do you know a person of the name of Roster?—I do.

What transpired between you and Roster?—I had some conversation with him on the subject the evening afterwards, when Bogle had left Florence.

What did that conversation induce you to do?—It led me to examine the things committed to my charge.

Did you not find among the things this machine? (A machine was placed upon the table which had been used by the conspirators for the purpose of forging the signature.)—I found that tracing machine (pointing to the one on the table.)

Was Roster with you when you instituted the examination and made the discovery?—Yes. I directed his attention to the machine.

For what purpose do you think such a machine was constructed?—To the best of my belief for the object of tracing.

Did you examine the machine again?—I did so, with Roster, in the month of June.

That was after Bogle left Florence?—Yes, after he had left.

Did you make any experiments with the machine in the presence of Mr. Roster?—I did not in his presence.

Did you see Mr. C. Graham or his son after that time?—I did not see either of them.

Are you confident of that?—I am.

Where did Mr. Bogle represent he was going after he left Florence?—He told me that it was his intention to visit England.

Did he say anything of Mr. Cunningham Graham, or his son, or where they were?—He did not.

Cross-examined by Mr. THESIGER.—You say that you are acquainted with Mr. Graham's family?—Yes.

With Mrs. Graham, and the two Misses Graham?—Yes.

Did you live in the same house with them?—No, but I did not reside at any considerable distance.

Did you not see the Marquis de Bourbel in 1839?—I did not.

During the time that the Marquis de Bourbel resided at Florence, did he not move in good society?—No, he did not.

Did you ever meet Mr. Cunningham Graham or Mr. Bogle at Court?—I did not go to Court.

You say that you were in the habit of visiting at Mr. C. Graham's?—I did not visit him very frequently.

You have stated that the banking-house was divided into two compartments—one in which Mr. Bogle sat, and the other which you and Mr. Macarthy occupied?—Yes.

If I understand you correctly, you state that it was Mr. Bogle's particular duty to attend to the cash department?—Yes; the checks were always presented to Mr. Bogle.

It was his duty to examine directly all bills and letters of credit?—Yes.

I understand that it was the custom for a number of loungers to assemble at Mr. Bogle's?—Yes, it was too much the custom to do so.

I suppose they met for the purpose of reading the papers?—Yes.

Had you seen the Marquis de Bourbel often at the bank?

Sport

Englishmen treat their sport more seriously than politics or religion. Accordingly sport has always had a prominent place in *The Times*. Indeed, it gave what some might consider a disproportionate amount of space to sport, considering that for many years *The Times* consisted of only four pages. In 1785, the first year, when *The Daily Universal Register* was an advertising sheet rather than a newspaper, we still found room to cover a number of cricket matches. There was a report of coursing. There was a stirring account of 'a pitched battle between Mendoza, the noted fighting Jew, and a tailor of the Borough'. In 1787 we reported golf for the first time, with details of a match for a Silver Club at the links at Leith.

Below Mendoza, known as 'the fighting Jew', was English boxing champion from 1791 to 1795. He wrote a pamphlet, 'The Art of Boxing', in 1789.

Bottom Derby horses in training, 1929.

But racing took the pride of place, with frequent reports of meetings from as far away as Catterick Bridge. As time went on, the Turf was increasingly noticed. Delane took a personal interest: he was a fine all-round athlete, who preferred riding to reading books. He was a frequent visitor to the races at Ascot, where he had a house, and *The Times* reflected the interest of its great editor.

Cricket is not merely a sport and an art, but a very English idiosyncrasy (see also p. 170). As such, it attracts more letters in that pavilion of national idiosyncrasies, the Letters Page of *The Times*, than all other sports combined. Many of them have a passion that the English reserve for matters of national importance, such as royalty, cruelty to animals and how one should eat eggs.

You might suppose that a campaign to reform the lbw law would be a dry topic, of interest only to insiders and inswingers. But not at all. Here is F. G. J. Ford – 'six feet two of don't care' our cricketing correspondent called him, because of his insouciant approach to batting – driving and hooking in the correspondence columns of *The Times* on the subject of the parsimonious pad-play that made the change necessary: 'the evil microbe', 'the *fons et origo mali*', 'this curse of modern cricket which has eaten into the very soul of the game and cast a slur upon the moral value of the very word "cricket"'. He demanded that prodding forward with one's pad be stamped out 'like an earwig under the boot'.

The Times in the early nineteenth century is a record of, among other things, the Englishman's passion for gambling. Betting on walking matches was common, and earnestly reported. More unusually there was a full and bloody report of odds laid on a fight between a monkey and a number of dogs: 'In the space of a minute most of the dogs have been disabled from loss of blood'. A hurdle race between a bay mare and 'Thomas the Salopian runner' was good for 400 words, or about a twentieth of the editorial space. The horse won.

By the middle of the nineteenth century *The Times* had established the tradition that it was a paper of record for everything that could be called sport, even billiards. As an example of sporting articles in *The Times* let us select the classic account of the fight between Tom Sayers and John Heenan, the American champion, on 17 April 1860. It lasted 2 hours 20 minutes, ending in a draw when the ring was invaded by spectators.

It was the last great prizefight before the Queensberry Rules came into effect and (in the opinion of the Old Guard) made boxing a wet and unEnglish pastime. The fight took place at an 'unknown' location near Farnborough. *The Times* used the adjective deliberately because the fight was against the law, and spectators and reporters had to avoid the vigilance of the police. Over two thousand people turned up, including many of the aristocracy and upper classes, reporters and the gentleman from *The Times*.

The Times had taken a keen interest in fighting since Thomas Barnes became editor.

> When he [Barnes] was at Cambridge, having had lessons from a boxer, he gave himself airs, and, meeting a fellow in a field who did not make way for him, as he expected and thought due to a gownsman, he challenged the man; accompanied by a smile and a tap on the shoulder, he received the answer: 'I am Cribb, my lad'.

Tom Cribb was one of the punching fathers of British pugilism. Barnes took him back to his rooms and gave him a wine supper.

The name of the boxing correspondent of *The Times* at the Sayers–Heenan fight is unknown. He had after all been breaking the law. He was probably one of Delane's bright young men who could turn his pen to anything. He clearly had a high-flown literary style. Where else but in the columns of The Thunderer could the report of a prizefight begin: 'Time was when the Championship of England was an office which conferred honour on the highest, when "Marmion, Lord of Scivelhaye, of Tamworth tower and town" held a grant on condition of doing battle in single combat'?

That is what is called in the trade a delayed or teasing intro. Those were spacious and leisurely days, my masters. The writer went on to fill three full, unleaded columns of *The Times*, no headlines, hardly any paragraphs, with his report. After forty-two rounds and about six thousand words it came to its end: 'At length the police forced their way to where they were fighting, in a space not much larger than an ordinary dining-table, and the referee ordered them at once to discontinue'.

The fight might have finished. The interest of *The Times* in it had not. On the following day it returned to the subject with a monumental leader of more than two thousand words. It managed to bring in Darwin, the Quakers, Rousseau, heraldry, and much other matter not obviously associated with pugilism. The fight was used as a peg on which to hang a moral lecture on the shortcomings of men and nations: 'Yet what is competition but a fight in which the laws of fair play are often disregarded?' The last word on the subject (for the time being) was written by Tom Sayers, the champion, himself. It is an example of his sportsmanship, and a tribute to the sporting instincts of *The Times*.

The report of the last great prize fight before the introduction of the Queensberry Rules. The fight attracted great popular attention, and despite its illegality was thoroughly reported.
18 APRIL 1860

SECOND EDITION.

THE TIMES-OFFICE, Wednesday Morning.

TELEGRAPHIC DESPATCHES.

The following telegrams have been received at Mr. Reuter's office :—

FRANCE.

"PARIS, APRIL 18.

"The *Constitutionnel*, in an article signed by M. Boniface, says it is authorized to declare that the pamphlet, "*La Coalition*," is entirely the work of a private individual, who has, neither directly nor indirectly, been inspired by Government."

SPAIN.

"MADRID, APRIL 18.

"The report that Ortega had been executed is untrue."

The letter of our Paris correspondent, dated yesterday (Tuesday) evening, had not arrived when our Second Edition went to press.

SWITZERLAND.

(FROM OUR OWN CORRESPONDENT.)

GENEVA, APRIL 15.

When Parliamentary Government was in its most brilliant epoch in France, and the eloquent speeches pronounced from the tribune of the Chambre des Deputés were admired by the continent of Europe, some enthusiasts began an agitation to abolish the sentence of death, and Victor Hugo, the exile of Jersey, then in the zenith of his glory, wrote his famous pamphlet, "*Les Derniers Jours d'un Condamné*," in which he applied all the power of his fertile imagination to paint the moral tortures of a man condemned to death and awaiting his execution. That impotent struggle against an inevitable fate approaching nearer and nearer; those long hours of exhaustion and lethargy after the mental strife—the glimpses of hope reviving again the desperate struggle for life, and soon again eclipsed by the gloom of despondency; those moments of wild rage against his own impotence and the whole world, and all the while Time, the implacable and irrevocable, passing away unheeding his torture, and bringing nearer and nearer the fatal moment.

There is a good deal of analogy between this desperate but impotent struggle painted by the pen of Victor Hugo and the situation of Switzerland for the last week or so. When the Swiss were first roused to the consciousness of their impending fate they determined to risk everything rather than to submit to it. It was the resolution of despair. Troops were called out, an extraordinary meeting of the Federal Assembly convoked, full powers and unlimited credit given to the Federal Council. At the same time energetic protests were addressed to the great Powers, and their intervention invoked. This appeal to others seemed most natural in an affair which interested others as well as Switzerland, and only few remarked that these preparations for self defence in the same breath with asking for the assistance of others could not but produce a false position and paralyze one effort by the other. It was as if the prisoner condemned to death had been at the same time meditating to break the bars of his dungeon and expect from others his delivery. He risked to fail in both. The two were in contradiction. There was indeed one way to get out of this seesaw, and this was to act in the first instance and expect and trust to the approval and support of others. Such decision implied the risk of being abandoned, but it offered likewise the chance of rousing the Powers more effectually than by any protests, however energetic. Every day brought fresh proofs that the French Government, unmindful of its promises, was working to get possession of the disputed districts, deciding thus the question beforehand in its own interest. Its agents, scattered all over the country and aided by the interested support of the *employés*, and with the connivance of the Sardinian Government, were destroying, one by one, the chances of a vote in favour of Switzerland, and there were many, especially in the neighbouring cantons, who saw but one way to destroy this entangled net, and that was to break through it by occupying militarily the Chablais and Faucigny before it was too late. Trusting to assurances from abroad, the Federal Council shrunk before so great a responsibility, and thus the favourable moment was lost. Aware of this circumstance, the French lost no time in taking advantage of it; step after step they advanced, unheedful of the energetic but impotent protests of Switzerland, which accompanied them. Under the plea of evacuating Italy the French troops crossed, company by company, the Mont Cenis, and established themselves at Chambery, occupying thus the country under false pretence. Under the plea of relieving the National Guard of the fatigues of active service, one post after another passed into the hands of the French troops. The whole country, north as well as south, was inundated by secret agents in disguise; hosts of *commis voyageurs*, with articles unprecedentedly cheap, were trying practically to convince the people of Savoy of the advantages of a union with France. To crown all, M. Laity, the Imperial Commissioner, undertook his Easter tour. Things being thus prepared, the day of voting was fixed, and in this voting only the alternative given to say "Yes" or "No" to the union with France. That is no alternative at all. Sardinia having renounced solemnly its rights, Switzerland being altogether left out of the question, the "No" has no meaning at all; it is the unknown, and vague, and uncertain. Besides this, it is easy to throw obstacles even in the way of those who would still prefer this "Nothing," as the Germans would say, to a union with France. In all well-regulated countries printing licences are given and withdrawn by the Government *ad libitum*, and it is scarcely probable that any printer will feel inclined to sacrifice his licence to his patriotic feelings. This is rather serious in a country where reading and writing have by no means become the common property of the masses. In six days the voting takes place, and not even the most sanguine can have the smallest doubt about its result. The Annexionist Committee in Chambery has called upon the municipalities and Syndics to make the communes vote *en masse*, enjoining the former to take matters into their own hands in case the Syndics were refractory. M. Laity has officially announced that the Chablais and Faucigny are to have their commercial zone like the Pays de Gex; Thonon is promised a Lyceé, with 50 gratuitous bourses for young men of the country; Annecy shall have its railway and stud,—in one word, nothing has been neglected to bring home to the Savoyards all the advantages of a union with France, while everything has been done to make it clear to them that they have no other chance left. The vote being thus made sure of, the civil occupation of the country will be a natural corollary of it.

And while this is going on at their gates the Swiss suffer all the tortures of the condemned, as painted by Victor Hugo. Protest comes after protest, and note, memoranda, and confidential missions never ceasing. Every new step made by France causes a fit of rage, every symptom of goodwill on the part of the Powers is a new glimpse of hope; and in the meantime this every day more hopeless struggle wears out the excitement, and leaves a feeling of despondency behind it. A few days more, and the French will be masters of Savoy; and no one flatters himself that the Powers will go to war to take away the neutralized parts of it. People begin to feel almost ashamed of the martial preparations which led to so little result, and if they could make the troops still remaining under arms disappear unperceived they would do so willingly. Above all, the military feel their false position, drilling on the Plainpalais, while a few miles off the French go on annexing as if Switzerland did not even exist. Such a position cannot but have a bad effect on the spirit of the troops and officers, calculated as it is to impair their self reliance.

For the last few days the assurances from abroad seem to give a little more hope; but they scarcely go far enough to contemplate even the possibility of an energetic support of the claims of Switzerland to the Chablais and Faucigny; and, I repeat it nothing is done to guarantee the neutrality, and to guard against future encroachments, unless this claim is recognized as valid. Let any one take up a map and see the position of Geneva, the Pays de Vaud, and the Vallais of the disputed districts belong to France. Every one can see what the Sous-Prefect of Gex openly says, that before six months are over Geneva will be French. Even an unmilitary man, who will take a tour from Douvaine by Annemasse to St. Julien on one, and from Gex to the Rhone on the other side, can see that a defence of Geneva is out of the question; it would be merely sacrificing the forces which would be called upon to do it.

THE INDIA MAILS.

The Peninsular and Oriental Steam Navigation Company have received the following telegram this morning (Wednesday) :—

THE BOMBAY MAIL.

"The Ottawa arrived at Suez on the 10th April.

"The Valetta arrived at Marseilles on the 18th, at 6 a.m. The mails leave for London at 10 a.m.

"The Euxine was at Alexandria on the 12th; expected at Malta on the 17th, and at Southampton on the 27th instant."

THE OUTWARD CALCUTTA AND CHINA MAILS.

"The Pera arrived at Malta on the 12th, at 3 p.m., and sailed for Alexandria on the 13th, at 10 a.m.

"The Panther arrived at Malta on the 14th, at 9 p.m., and sailed at midnight for Alexandria.

"The Alhambra left Malta for Corfu on the 14th, at midnight.

"The Colombo, with the London mail of the 20th-27th February, reached Point de Galle on the 26th March, *en route* to Calcutta."

ELECTRIC TELEGRAPHIC DESPATCHES.

(FROM OUR OWN CORRESPONDENT.)

SOUTHAMPTON, WEDNESDAY MORNING.

Wind N.E.

Arrived, April 17.—Hunghorn, from Christiana; Charlotte, from Guernsey; Branch and Waterwitch, from Sunderland; Ann, from Middlesborough; Duke of Cornwall, steamer, from Dublin.

Arrived, April 18.—New York, steamer, from Bremen.

Sailed, April 17.—Northumberland, for Cardiff; Duke of Cornwall, steamer, for London; Dispatch, steamer, for Jersey; Atrato, steamer, for St. Thomas; Tagus, steamer, or Lisbon; La Poule, for Cherbourg.

(BY SUBMARINE AND BRITISH TELEGRAPH.)

GRAVESEND, WEDNESDAY MORNING.

Wind N.E.; tide 2 hours' flood; weather strong.

Arrived, April 17.—Ceylon, from Wilmington; Planet, from Singapore; Neptunus, from Wismar; Apollo, from Griefswald; Peter Megge, from Middelharnis; Vrow Pretbeika, from Middelharnis; Industry, from Jamaica; Hans Thorwold, from Hermosund; Thea, from Gravelines; George, from Faro; Christiana, from Engelholm.

Sailed.—Banshee, for Corfu; Prospero, for Bermuda.

DEAL, WEDNESDAY MORNING.

Wind N.N.E.; strong.

Passed.—Emperor, for Quebec; Water Nymph, for Port Phillip; Glenshee, for Mauritius—all from London; Sylph, screw steamer, from Bordeaux, for London.

STOCK EXCHANGE.

WEDNESDAY MORNING, 11 O'CLOCK

Consols for Money	...	...	... 94⅛ to 94⅜
Ditto, May 9	...	...	... 94⅜ to 94½

SHIP NEWS.

LONDON, April 17.—Wind at noon, N.E. to E., strong breeze, and fine clear weather. The Tre Emanuele Raseto, with a cargo of barley, &c., sailed from Malta on the 27th of November for the United Kingdom, and has not since been heard of.

BRISTOL, April 17.—Wind at noon, E., strong; fine.—Arrived, the Blossom, from Barbadoes—the Figlio Alessandro, from Odessa—the Horizonti, from Samarang—the Alma, from Cork—the Queen, from Hayle—the Tom, from Watchett. Sailed, the Louisa, for Quebec—the Louisa, for Cork—the Geelong and the Eaglewing, both for Cardiff—the Henry Southan, for Padstow—the Princess Royal, for Bideford.

VESSELS SPOKEN WITH.

The Phaeton, from Liverpool for Valparaiso, April 6, 45 N., 12 W.

The William Jackson, of Bristol, steering S.E., Jan. 20, 33 S., 60 W.

The Scotland, of Beaton, steering S.E., Feb. 23, 11 S., 35 W.

The Gertrude, of London, for Calcutta, March 7, 3 S., 29 W.

The Webster, from New York for Liverpool, March 22, 40 N., 71 W.

The Coronella, from Liverpool for Bahia, March 6, 47 N., 12 W.

The Beicarris, from New Orleans for Liverpool, March 25, 27 N., 83 W.

The Judith and the George Green, both from New Orleans for Liverpool, March 19, off Hatteras.

The Callender, from New Orleans for Liverpool, March 23, off Key West.

The Anna Maria, from Madras for London, Feb. 17, 34 S., 25 E.

The Tudor, from London for Algoa Bay, Feb. 18, 36 S., 20 E.

The Lillies, from Bombay for Liverpool, March 2, 15 S., 7 W.

HIGH WATER AT LONDON-BRIDGE THIS DAY.

Morning .. .. 16 min. after 12 | Afternoon .. .. 34 min. after 12

THE CASE OF THE CURATES.

TO THE EDITOR OF THE TIMES.

Sir,—As you have allowed the holders of small incumbencies and our foreign chaplains to state their grievances in your columns, will you kindly allow a poor curate to state the peculiar hardships which recent legislation has entailed upon the unbeneficed clergy?

I ask for this indulgence the more confidently because the letter of "E. L. C." has already elicited a reply, whereby a remedy has been made known for the grievance which he complained of, and because I can also point out a method by which the hardships which I wish to bring before the public notice might in a measure be alleviated.

In former days, before the passing of the Act for the abolition of pluralities, 100*l.* a-year and a house was no difficult thing for a curate to meet with. An incumbent with three or four parishes, situate, perhaps, many miles apart, could necessarily only reside in one of them. The others supplied homes for married curates. But these sole charges are yearly becoming scarcer, as the Plurality Act comes more into operation and each parish has its resident incumbent. My own sad experience will show clearly how this is the case, and, alas! it is no solitary instance. I am a married curate, with a family of several very young children. I have been in Holy Orders 12 years, during which time I have had to move my furniture five times, owing to the death, resignation, or return of the incumbents. Not one plurality charge have I been able to meet with in all that time. I am now under marching orders again. The utmost that my diocesan, whom I have just returned from consulting, can offer me at this moment, after looking out for me for the last 12 months, is 80*l.* a-year and a house.

I have advertised my requirements, I have searched through advertisements for vacancies, and I cannot meet with anything higher than 80*l.* a-year and a house.

Now, as this is the result of the Act for the abolition of pluralities, surely the framers of that Act did not foresee how their remedy of an abuse would press hard upon the already poor curate, or they would have provided some compensation for the change it was to produce in his circumstances. A very simple compensation was at hand. A rule might henceforth have prevailed that every fifth Crown or Chancellor's living should be placed in the bishop's hands for them to bestow on some pains taking, long-serving curate. This would have held out some ray of hope over the now cheerless path of the poor curate who has no "friend at Court" to procure him a living, and who has sometimes, as I have now, to search the length and breadth of the land for a house and 100*l.* a-year.

The Government of the day, whether Whig or Tory, would have been no loser by thus benefiting a large and loyal, a grateful, and, let me add with all humility, an influential class.

Allow me to ask—Is it too late or impossible to adopt this remedy now?

Oblige me by inserting this letter in an early number of *The Times*, and thus help to make known the hardships of the POOR MARRIED CURATE.

April

TELEGRAPHIC DESPATCHES.

[A portion of the following appeared in our second edition of yesterday :—]

The following telegrams have been received at Mr. Reuter's office :—

FRANCE, SAVOY, AND SWITZERLAND.

"PARIS, TUESDAY, APRIL 17.

"M. Thouvenel has informed the representatives of the Powers who signed the Final Act of Vienna of the nature of the reception France will give to the circular note of the Swiss Federal Council of the 5th of April respecting the convocation of an European Conference.

"It was not until the King of Sardinia had formally taken possession of Lombardy and the treaties of Zurich had been signed and ratified that France and Austria jointly addressed an invitation to the Powers who had signed the treaties of Vienna to assemble at a Conference, in order to make known to them the territorial arrangements which had resulted from the cession of Lombardy to Piedmont, which cession was freely consented to by Austria. No Power having then objected, France will follow the same course. When, therefore, the cession of Savoy and Nice, freely consented to by Piedmont, shall have been sanctioned and ratified by universal suffrage of the inhabitants, and by the vote of the Sardinian Parliament, France will take possession of those provinces. Immediately afterwards she will consent to the assembling of a Conference for the purpose of receiving a communication of the treaty concluded on the 24th of March last between Napoleon III. and King Victor Emmanuel.

"France will likewise be willing that the said Conference shall examine the following question,—'In what manner are the rights of France, irrevocably acquired through the cession of Savoy and Nice by the King of Sardinia, to be reconciled with the guarantees stipulated by the treaties in favour of Switzerland?' It being, however, well understood that the Conference shall leave the treaty of the 24th of March intact.

"The *Moniteur* of this morning gives the following as the definitive result of the voting in the city of Nice :—

"For annexation 6,810

"Against 11

"The *Constitutionnel* denies the existence of direct negotiations between France and Switzerland on the question of the neutralized districts of Savoy, and adds that the negotiations are only between the Powers who signed the treaties of Vienna.

"Baron Monrad, who arrived here last week from Copenhagen, was received on Sunday by the Emperor at a private audience, and left again yesterday evening to resume his functions as Minister of Public Instruction at Copenhagen.

"Baron Dirkink Holmfeld, formerly Danish Ambassador, also left yesterday evening for Copenhagen. He was previously received at a private audience by the Emperor, who presented him with the Grand Cross of the Legion of Honour.

"3 25 P.M.

"The Bourse has been very dull and heavy. Rentes closed at 70f., or ¼ lower than yesterday.

"The pamphlet *La Coalition* originates from a Government source, although it has been denied."

"BERNE, TUESDAY.

"There again appears some probability that the Conference will take place.

"England proposes Brussels as the place where it should be held, while France insists upon Paris, in which she is supported by Russia."

"GENEVA, APRIL 17.

"General Canrobert, accompanied by several officers of Engineers, has visited the fort of Les Rousses, on the frontier of Switzerland.

"The Canton de Vaud has been supplied with war *matériel*.

"The English Government has given encouraging assurances to the Federal Council."

RUSSIA.

"GENEVA, APRIL 17.

"Prince Gortschakoff, in his reply to the note of Switzerland, identifies Russia with the other Powers who signed the treaties of 1815, and who recognized the inviolability and neutrality of Switzerland. In this note the Prince also states, that it is the true political interest of Europe to preserve Switzerland from all foreign influence. But France having manifested an intention of negotiating, either with the great Powers or the Swiss Confederation, and the Federal Council having expressed a similar desire, Russia gives her complete adhesion to the assembling of a Conference, being convinced that the Federal Council does not doubt her solicitude to efficaciously insure the neutrality of Switzerland."

THE KINGDOM OF THE TWO SICILIES.

"MARSEILLES, TUESDAY.

"The direct steamer from Naples arrived this evening, and brings advices from that city to the 14th inst.

"It is asserted that on Thursday last a large bomb was thrown before the Palace. The explosion shattered all the windows. No person was injured.

"The revolutionary attempt of the 8th at Messina commenced by the killing of two sentinels.

"The movement was less serious than reported by the passengers of the Meandre, which remained at a great distance from the spot where the combat took place.

"Flying columns were pursuing the bands of insurgents, who had taken refuge in the mountains.

"It is certain that no preparation had been made to pass the Roman frontier, unless an attack were made against Rome by Piedmont.

"Intelligence from Rome adds that the Pope had resolved to take no initiative in a war in the Romagna, and that General Lamoricière would only concentrate a corps in Umbria between Rome and Ancona."

"MARSEILLES, APRIL 17.

"The official Neapolitan journals from the 10th to the 13th inst. inclusive say nothing of the popular movement at Messina. Private letters merely state that the attempts to surprise the military posts at Messina had been repelled, and that the agitation was less at that place than at Palermo.

"10,000 men were pursuing the insurgent bands.

"Since the insurrection commenced the Government has sent into Sicily four battalions of Infantry, two battalions of Artillery, and a regiment of Lancers. The Governor of Sicily had written that no more reinforcements need be sent, his forces being sufficient."

CENTRAL ITALY.

"FLORENCE, APRIL 17.

"The King and Count Cavour have been received with enthusiasm."

"NAPLES, APRIL 14 (*viâ* GENOA).

"The insurrection has spread to Trapani, where the Provisional Government and the National Guard have joined the insurgents. The Royal troops still occupy Palermo, which is destitute of everything. Great activity prevails in the arsenal at Naples. The embarcation of troops for the provinces continues. The agitation is increasing. The *corps d'armée* in the Abruzzi has been recalled."

"TRIESTE, TUESDAY.

"The *Trieste Zeitung* says:—'According to authentic private information from Messina to the 9th, the Austrian Consul had quitted that city on board an Austrian merchant vessel.

"'A bombardment of the city was expected in the course of the 9th.'"

THE FIGHT FOR THE CHAMPIONSHIP.

Time was when the Championship of England was an office which conferred honour on the highest, when "Marmion, Lord of Scrivelbaye, of Tamworth tower and town," held a grant of the lands of the Abbey of Polesworth on condition of doing battle in single combat against all knightly enemies of his King. The fashion of this office, however, has passed away with the days of chivalry, and lance and battle-axe have been laid aside to become mere things of show and no more used by men. The Dymocks are still extant, but the modern Champions of England know them not, and the pageant warrior who threw down the gauntlet to some hundred ladies and gentlemen in Court dress at a coronation has been succeeded by a race of brawny and muscular fellows, men who "mean fighting, and nothing but it," and who vie with the *athletæ* of old in their rigidity of training and immense powers of endurance. At first there was no lack of Royal patronage for the new race of champions. In Broughton's last prize fight he was backed by the Duke of Cumberland, who almost acted as his second, and few great battles took place at which one or more of the sons of George III. were not present. Sir Thomas Apreece nearly always seconded Gully, until that champion retired from the ring, and having realized a large fortune, sat in the House of Commons as member for Pontefract. In those days a noted bruiser was thought good company for any man, and we hear almost without surprise how, about 40 years ago, Lord Camelford "assisted" Belcher when he fought Bourke in the churchyard of St. George's, Hanover-square, in the presence of some 10,000 spectators. Those were the "good old days," the "palmy days" of the ring, about which the sporting journals are always so pathetic as having gone by,—we are glad to say, never to return. He would be a bold peer indeed who would have seconded Sayers yesterday as Lord Deerhurst used to second Spring; and what would be said now of a cathedral town offering, as of old, 500*l.* to the combatants to beat themselves almost to death within its reverend precincts? The new Police Act has been the death of pugilism. Its greatest professors now lead a hole-and-corner life while training, or issue forth their challenges in mysterious terms. From this rapid downfall it has been just now for a time arrested by the first attempt to carry off the Champion's belt into another country,—and, of course, that country was America. There is no disguising the fact that this challenge has led to an amount of attention being bestowed upon the prize ring which it has never received before; and, much as all decent people disliked the idea of two fine men meeting to beat each other half to death, it was nevertheless devoutly wished that, as somebody was to be beaten, it might be the American. There is no doubt that Sayers had the good wishes of nine-tenths of the community. There seemed something almost patriotic in its way for a man of his light weight to encounter a brawny giant, who describes himself as being "half horse, half alligator, and a bit of the snapping turtle," and who, in addition to all these qualities, has proved himself to be as clever and formidable a prize fighter as ever entered the ring. We need scarcely enter on any recapitulation of the events which led to this match, all of which may be summed up in the few words, that Sayers holds "the belt" as the Champion of England, and in virtue of his office, while he retains it, is bound for three years to accept all challenges, no matter from whom. This challenge accordingly came from America on Heenan's part, and, in spite of the immense natural advantages of his challenger, Sayers was bound at once to accept it. All relating to the day and place fixed for the match was, of course, kept a profound secret, as the police, to do them justice, left no means untried to prevent its taking place. Nevertheless, in spite of all precautions, a special train was hired, which started from London-bridge at 4 a.m. yesterday morning. The train was one of immense length, containing some thousand persons, all of what are called the upper classes, though each person was muffled up to the eyes in shawls and wrappers, so that it was hard to say whether your *compagnon de voyage* was or was not the redoubtable Sayers or Heenan himself. All along the line police were posted, with mounted patrols, at regular distances; but the train turned off at Reigate, and after a long run came out in the Farnborough station, close to Aldershott. In an instant after, all were out in the fields, following the men who with the ropes and stakes led the way across what turned out to be a most difficult piece of country. There seemed a constant succession of double hedges and ditches, which were crossed at last more or less successfully, until a rather narrow stream, or very broad muddy ditch (the Blackwater), which divides Surrey from Hampshire, brought all to a full stop. A few venturesome spirits essayed to leap this, but their success was not such as to encourage others, inasmuch as most contrived to light in the very middle of the water, and those who did gain the opposite bank had only to jump back for their pains, as the ring was formed on the Hampshire side after all.

The instant the enclosure of ropes and stakes, 24 feet square, was formed, Sayers stepped into it, and was cheered tremendously. Heenan, who followed, was greeted in the same manner, and the two men, who there for the first time met, warmly shook hands, and then stepped back to take a long and careful survey each of the other. There was a toss for corners, which Heenan won and chose that in which he would have the highest ground, and with his back to the sun, leaving Sayers the spot where the glare was full in his face. Umpires for each man were appointed, and a referee for both, and these preliminaries over Heenan proceeded to strip to his waist. It seemed impossible to restrain a murmur of admiration at the appearance which he then presented. In height he is about six feet two, with extraordinarily long arms, deep chest, and wide and powerful shoulders. His appearance yesterday was truly formidable. Exercise and long training had developed the immense muscles of his arms and shoulders till they appeared like masses of bone beneath the thin covering of skin. There seemed not an ounce of superfluous flesh. His ribs showed like those of a greyhound, save where they were crossed by powerful thews and sinews, and as he threw up his long sinewy arms and inflated his huge chest with the morning air he looked the most formidable of the tribe of gladiators who have ever entered the arena. Every movement showed the sinews and muscles working like lithe machinery beneath their thin fine covering, and every gesture was made with that natural grace and freedom which always seem to belong to the highest development of physical power. Sayers looked at him long and earnestly, and as one who saw in his every movement a dangerous customer, and he too stripped in turn. The contrast between the men was then still more marked than before. Sayers is only about five feet eight; his chest is not broad, nor are his arms powerful, and it is only in the strong muscles of the shoulders that one sees anything to account for his tremendous powers of hitting. Sayers, too, looked hard as flint, but his deficiencies in regard to his antagonist in height, weight, and strength, and above all, length of arm, made it almost a matter of surprise how he could hope to contest with him at all. When to these disadvantages are added the superior height of the ground on which Heenan stood, and the light of the sun full in Sayers's eyes, it will be seen how tremendous were the obstacles with which he had to contend. As far as training went, however, the utmost had been done for both, and it would not be a lost lesson if some of our young volunteers imitated the boxers in these respects. Their whole system of training may be summed up in two or three words—moderation in eating and drinking, exercise, and constant use of the sponge bath and rough towels. With these aids any man can train; without them he can do nothing. Heenan's skin yesterday was, as we have said, fair and white as marble—Sayers's as dark as that of a mulatto; and the "fancy" leant strongly to the opinion that the former was too delicate, and would bruise too much—and this was true. As the men stripped the spectators sat down outside the ropes, about six feet distant, in an outer ring, in which were gentlemen of all ranks—members of both Houses in plenty. Authors, poets, painters, soldiers, and even clergymen were present.

There was a minute's pause after the final shaking hands, when the seconds retired and left the antagonists face to face at last. Both instantly put themselves into position—the right hand held close across the body, the left advanced at length, and kept moving gently out as if to feel its way. The immense difference between the height, weight, strength, and length of arm of the men was now more than ever manifest, and the disadvantages under which Sayers laboured appeared to many to be too much for him. The sun shone bright and full in his face, so as almost to blind him; yet Sayers seemed cool and confident, and smiled coolly as he ventured in reach of that tremendous muscular arm. Both seemed very cautious. The feints were quick and constant, and as each avoided the other with more or less agility neither could help laughing. At last Sayers caught a slight blow on the mouth, which he returned heavily, drawing first blood from Heenan, amid shouts of congratulation. Both seemed still more cautious, and after much sparring and warding off an intended blow with the speed of thought, both stopped and looked at each other with hands down. After a little rest, they again sparred and closed, when Sayers gave his adversary some heavy body blows, and got down easily.

Each man was instantly attended by his seconds, who carefully sponged his body and face, and rinsed out his mouth with a little cold water. Again they advanced. Each seemed then to know his antagonist better; the sparring was quicker, and the huge muscular arm of Heenan went backwards and forwards with immense rapidity. Three times he hit at Sayers, but out of distance, and apparently as if to put the Champion off his guard; at last he darted forward like lightning, and dealt Sayers a blow in the mouth which sent him reeling. Tom, however, as if to show how little he cared for it, at once ventured close to his huge antagonist—too close as it proved, for the long arm of Heenan was shot out like a dart, and with a heavy blow on his forehead Tom was knocked almost into his own corner. There were great cheers at this, and though Heenan seemed very pleased, Sayers took it as a matter of course, and went back to his corner, apparently unconcerned. Here he was sponged for a minute, and returned with a deep red lump across his forehead, and his mouth slightly disfigured, though with far less punishment in appearance than could have been expected, owing to his skill in jumping back ere the blow reached, and thus weakening half its force. He was smiling, and seemed quite at ease as he again approached the American in his own corner, who was very careful not to leave it, in order to keep Sayers with the glare of the sun in his face. This seemed to perplex Sayers much, and he again presented an opening, of which the Benicia Boy instantly availed himself, and with one blow dashed Sayers to the ground. Again there were tremendous cheers for Heenan, and ironical congratulations to the Champion in the young novice he had met with. Those who had backed Sayers seemed rather depressed; the betting gradually became even, Heenan being almost as much in favour as the Champion. There were loud cries of "Time," at which Heenan advanced to the centre of the ring, and waited for Sayers, retiring as the latter advanced, till the American again had the benefit of the higher ground and the sun in Tom's eyes. Sayers now found it was useless attempting outfighting with a man of such enormous strength and length of arm as the American, he therefore tried to dash in and got a slight blow at Heenan, who returned it with a very heavy one, which sent Tom staggering back, and after some further exchanges, all in favour of the powerful young American, Sayers got down.

Again the men were attended to, and again Sayers came forth, much marked and with a heavy cut over his eyebrow, to cope with Heenan in his own corner. This time the sparring was so long and cautious that at last both men put down their hands and laughed. Again they began, and after a few feints Heenan dashed out his left and for the fourth time fairly struck Sayers to the ground with a very heavy blow. The effect of these repeated blows seemed almost greater on the spectators than on Sayers. The latter tried to treat them lightly, but around the ring a very different opinion was entertained, and Heenan was backed to win, and was cheered and encouraged to the utmost. Both men were duly wiped down, and Sayers's head and face, which were now smeared with blood and heavily bruised and bumped, was held close pressed between cold sponges to keep down the contusions, which had now altered his deep sallow hue.

Shouts now went round the ring that Sayers had virtually already lost, and indeed the punishment he had received was so much more severe than that bestowed upon his tall, wiry antagonist, who seemed always smiling and always fresh, that matters really began to look serious for the Champion, and almost to warrant the belief that "the belt was going to Troy." Apparently roused by these shouts to stronger efforts, Sayers came on again, and, watching his man cautiously, stepped back from a dreadful blow aimed at him, sprang in before the American could recover himself, and gave Heenan a terrific smash full in the eye, splitting up the cheek and sending his huge antagonist reeling like a drunken man back into his corner. The effect of this blow was so tremendous that even before half a minute had elapsed Heenan could scarcely be recognized as the same man, so swollen, disfigured, and blood-stained were his features. There were loud cheers for Sayers, who went up to Heenan's corner and peered into his face with a curious, half-puzzled expression, as if he too was astounded by the effects of his own handiwork. Sayers now let no time slip, but catching a most formidable blow of Heenan's on his right arm, again dashed in, and gave in return a still worse blow to the American, following it up with another, which seemed to smash his nose, and almost knocked Heenan off his legs in turn, so that he required the most careful attention from his seconds to make him fit for the next round.

The betting now changed again, and if Sayers was not a decided favourite, there at least seemed nothing to choose between the two. All the rounds had been long and cautiously fought, but the hitting had been dreadful, and both men began to show signs of fatigue, and after long sparring, in the seventh encounter, both paused, rested, and at last retired to rinse out their mouths, which were very bloody, with water. As they came up again Sayers at once dashed in and gave another terrific blow to Heenan, which sent the blood pouring down over his broad chest, and seemed to make his huge form tremble like a child's. Heenan paused for a moment and then darted in, but Sayers got under his guard, closed, and, after giving him some heavy body blows, both fell, Sayers under.

It had been noticed in the last two rounds that Sayers made not the least use of his right hand, with which in all his previous contests he had administered such terrific punishment that a full blow from it may almost be said to decide the fate of a battle. The reason of this was now painfully apparent on his again stepping into the ring. In stopping one of Heenan's tremendous blows it is supposed that one of the bones of his right arm was broken. Certain it is that the limb was frightfully swollen, and so powerless that he could only manage to support it across his chest. From this time, therefore, Sayers fought the rest of the battle with his left hand, only seeking every opportunity to ease the evident pain of the injured limb by opening the hand and resting it on his chest or ribs. He, however, advanced smiling, as did also Heenan, though the features of the latter were so distorted and swollen that it was hard to say what he was doing. Sayers, notwithstanding the loss of his right arm, still pushed in, and gave the American another fearful blow, which sent him staggering back to have the blood wiped from his gashed features, while Sayers as usual pried in with a curious look to see what mischief he had done. The blow, however, though dreadful to look at, seemed to have no effect on the strength of the gaunt iron frame of the American, who was quickly out, and after some slight sparring again launched forth his powerful arm, and striking Sayers on the nose with a blow that was heard all over the meadow, he felled him like an ox. This round lasted 13 minutes, and the men seemed so distressed at its close that each had to be carried to his corner. The seconds had much to do with sponging their faces and washing over the marks of their wounds, though some of Heenan's seemed too deep to be meddled with in this way. Time was loudly called by the umpires, and the American instantly rose; Sayers was much longer coming up, though he seemed almost fresher of the two, but not nearly so strong. As soon as Sayers was in reach Heenan gave him a heavy blow over the eye, and almost immediately after a still more fierce one on the mouth and nose, which now in poor Sayers seemed all knocked into one. There was slight sparring and both exchanged hits, all the profit in this unpleasant species of barter being on the side of the American. Sayers drew back to spit the blood from his mouth, and was laughed at by some of Heenan's supporters. An imprudent ebullition, inasmuch as Sayers seemed stung by the taunts of the Americans, and again springing in, gave Heenan a blow which sent him tottering back, following it up with another and another, and a fourth tremendous one in the mouth. Heenan seemed staggered by these fearful visitations, and reeled like a drunken man, leaving himself so unguarded that if Sayers had had the use of his right arm the fight would have ended there and then. As it was, however, Sayers dared not trust himself in the grip of an antagonist so immensely his superior in height, weight, strength, and length of arm, and he could only follow up his advantage by giving another heavy blow with his left in the mouth, and a most tremendous smash into the American's ribs, which sounded all over the meadow as if a box had been smashed in. In a minute after, however, Heenan came up trying to laugh, but only to receive a still worse blow in the face, which covered him with blood, and sent Sayers himself reeling back from the force of his own blow. There was a short pause, during which Tom, as usual, scanned curiously the dreadful effect of his hitting, and both went at it again, each exchanging heavy blows till both were covered with blood—especially the Benicia Boy, who in the end rallied and hit out fiercely, knocking Sayers down with an awful smash. The powerlessness of Sayers's right arm was more than ever manifest in this round, which lasted nearly 20 minutes. He seemed unable even to move it from his side, and it was fortunate indeed for him that Heenan himself makes very little use of his right. Both men now seemed much distressed, and Heenan presented an awful sight. His face was gashed with apparently very deep flesh wounds, and the whole of the right side of his face, eye, nose, and mouth was simply one huge blue lump. Sayers, too, was badly punished about the mouth, but his face and head, though bloody, swollen, and much discoloured, were almost natural when compared to those of his antagonist. Both were very slow to the call of time. The Benicia Boy was first out. Sayers then came out, and Heenan at once, bringing his gaunt muscular left into play, reached over Tom's guard like lightning, and knocked him down with a tremendous blow. Again Sayers was out, though weak, and Heenan rushed to force the fighting; each hit the other hard, and after a slight struggle Sayers got down, laughing. Another round followed with much the same result as to hitting; but in the close Heenan lifted Sayers from the ground with ease and flung him down heavily. Sayers was evidently distressed, and had not the least chance in closing with his powerful antagonist. Again there was a little struggle, and Sayers at last got a heavy blow on Heenan's left eye, the only one with which he could now see, receiving in return a blow in the chest, when he managed to get down. Both were very slow in coming up again, and Sayers being dodged round as usual, with his face to the sun, seemed dazzled; again the terrific long arm of the Benicia Boy came in, and Sayers was knocked down and apparently half stunned. He required much care from his seconds before he came up again, though when he did so it at once seemed to revive all his vigour, for he made straight at Heenan and dealt him a blow in the face that was heard all over the field. His antagonist seemed nothing loth to close for all this, and gave Sayers almost as bad a blow in return, till they both closed, when Sayers had all the best of it, and, for the first and only time, threw Heenan heavily.

In a minute both, though distressed, were at it again, and Heenan, with a fearful blow, knocked Sayers half across the ring. Another round ended, after a few exchanges, with the same result, except that Sayers was even harder hit, and seemed quite stunned.

Strange to say, after these tremendous rounds Sayers still came up fresh, and showed not half the awful marks of punishment visible all over Heenan, who was now a disgusting object. His left hand was much swollen and puffy, and his left eye was fast threatening to close as irremediably as his right had done long before. His friends shouted to him from all parts of the ring to go in and finish Sayers by closing with him, as the latter could now only use one hand; but Heenan in turn was getting cautious, and did not seem to like the look of running into Sayers, who, always cool and wary, never now threw a chance away. Several rounds were fought after this with success more or less varying, each taking and giving heavy blows, and writhing his battered face into such contortions as might pass for smiles. In all the closes Heenan's immense strength prevailed, and he threw the Champion easily till in both the 21st and 22d rounds Sayers was knocked off his legs. Still he came up gaily, though carefully, and generally managed in most of the struggles to give one or more of his heaviest blows on Heenan's left eye, which was now almost gone like the other. The scene gradually became one of the most intense and brutal excitement. There were shouts to Heenan to keep his antagonist in the sun,—to close with him and smash him, as he had only one arm, while the friends of Sayers called to him to take his time, as the American was fast blinding and must give in. The bets were even on both men, and then again varied with every round. When Sayers was knocked down almost senseless under a tremendous blow there were cheers from the Americans till the fields echoed again, which were retorted by the English whenever their Champion sent his huge opponent reeling back from the tremendous blows which were always dealt on the eyes. At this time several policemen came upon the scene, and did their best to force their way into the ring; but the crowd, which now amounted to some 3,000, kept them back by rushing on the ropes, shouting and cheering the combatants to the utmost. During all this the men fought on with varying success, the heavy "thuds" upon the face of one or the other being clear above all the din. Sayers seemed getting weaker each time he was knocked off his legs, and Heenan more and more blind. It appeared all a chance whether the English Champion would be struck senseless or Heenan remain sightless, and at his mercy. Sayers now tried getting away, and leading his opponent round the ring. In one of these runs he got a heavy blow on the neck, which enabled his antagonist to overtake him, when they closed, and Sayers fell, Heenan striking him a heavy blow on the head while on the ground. An appeal of foul play was made, but it was overruled, as the blow was supposed to be struck in the heat of fighting, and Heenan, it was truly said, could scarcely see whether his antagonist was up or down. The fighting was still very quick, Heenan almost as strong as ever, and, though apparently much distressed, trying to get it over before he quite lost his sight. In the 38th round Heenan got Sayers's head under his left arm, and, supporting himself by the stake with his right, held his opponent bent down, as if he meant to strangle him. Sayers could no more free himself than if a mountain was on him. At last he got his left arm free, and gave Heenan two dreadful blows on the face, covering them both with the blood, but Heenan, without relaxing his hold, turned himself so as to get his antagonist's neck over the rope, and then leant on it with all his force. Sayers rapidly turned black in the face, and would have been strangled on the spot but that the rules of the ring provide for what would otherwise be fatal contingencies, and both the umpires called simultaneously to cut the ropes. This was done at once, and both men fell heavily to the ground, Sayers nearly half strangled. The police now made a determined effort to interfere, which those present seemed equally determined to prevent, and the ropes of the ring having been cut the enclosure itself was inundated by a dense crowd, which scarcely left the combatants six square feet to fight in. Umpires, referees, and all were overwhelmed, and the whole thing became a more close mob round the two men fighting. After this four other rounds were fought, in the midst of this dense mass of partisans of either side, who, however, allowed the men to fight in the fairest way they could, consistent with their having hardly any room to fight at all. This, however, was, on the whole, unfair to Sayers, whose only chance now lay in avoiding the tremendous blows of his antagonist, against whom he contended with only one hand, and who, though now as blind as a bat, was still possessed of nearly all his immense strength, and, to a little man like Sayers, very nearly as formidable as ever. In these rounds sometimes Sayers got awful blows upon the head and body, and sometimes he managed to give in return his tremendous lunges full in the disfigured face of his antagonist. At one time caps were thrown up, and cheers given for Heenan as having won, when he knocked down Sayers, who would spring to his feet and give the American such staggering blows that he in turn was hailed as conqueror. At length the police forced their way to where they were fighting, in a space not much larger than an ordinary dining-table, and the referee ordered them at once to discontinue. To do them justice, both seemed very willing to leave off, and Heenan was so blind that in the last round he could not see Sayers, but hit his unsuspecting second a tremendous blow in the face, which knocked him head over heels. Both men then left what had been the ring, Sayers, though much blown and distressed, walking firmly and coolly away, with both his eyes open and clear. His right arm, however, was helpless, his mouth and nose were dreadfully beaten, and the side of his head and forehead much punished. Heenan was almost unrecognizable as a human being, so dreadful had been his punishment about the face and neck. Yet he was still as strong on his legs, apparently, as ever, thanks to his perfect training, and, after leaving the field of battle, he ran as nimbly as any of the spectators and leaped over two small hedges. This, however, was a final effort, and he almost instantly after became so utterly blind that he was obliged to be led by the hand to the train.

How the fight would have terminated but for the interference of the police it is now literally quite impossible to say or even speculate. At any moment Sayers might have got a blow which would have struck him almost senseless; while if Heenan could have closed with him the Champion's chance would have been, perhaps, a poor one. On the other hand, Sayers was carefully avoiding this, and Heenan's sight was so far gone that in two or three minutes more he would have lain at the mercy of a child. As matters now stand, the fight is adjourned *sine die*, and the only impression left is one of astonishment that Sayers, with one arm, should have so long contended, with success, with such a formidable antagonist, and that Heenan should have borne his terrific punishment without his strength or courage to fight giving way.

STATISTICAL SOCIETY.—A meeting of this society was held last evening at their rooms in St. James's-square, at which Colonel Sykes presided. A paper was read by Mr. Newmarsh, one of the honorary secretaries, on Indian currency and banking. After taking a general review of the principles of banking and of the monetary systems that had been pursued both in this country and in India, Mr. Newmarsh made particular reference to the plan of finance proposed by Mr. Wilson to be established in the latter country, to which he entertained a strong objection because it proceeded upon the principle of separating the banking department from the issuing department. During the last 40 years they had had the experience of four panics—viz., in 1825, 1837, 1847, and 1857; and his belief was that in 1837, especially, the country was saved because the Bank of England was a bank of issue as well as a bank of deposit. It was his firm belief that if they separated the function of issue from the function of banking, they would have no means at a moment of crisis of saving the country. The hon. gentleman urged many other objections to Mr. Wilson's scheme, and dwelt with much earnestness on the injurious effect it would have upon discounts and the monetary operations in India. Colonel Sykes took a favourable view of Mr. Wilson's financial plan, and thought that if the substitution of a paper for a metallic currency could be effected, it would be a great benefit to the people of India. A discussion ensued, in which Mr. Hodge, Dr. Hyde Clarke, Mr. M'Pherson, Mr. Fawcett, and Mr. Jellicoe took part; and the question which engaged their attention was, whether it would be advantageous that the existing banks in India should be allowed to issue notes in combination with the functions of a banking department, or whether the whole financial and monetary system of India should be vested in the Government. The proceedings of the evening closed without any formal result, it not being in accordance with the rules of the society to come to any resolution on questions discussed.

Cricket

Heaven knows when cricket started. I doubt whether we should go into it here. The word may be derived from the Old French word *criquet*, a kind of club, perhaps used in a ball game. You could go for the version that it comes from the Flemish *Krick*, a stick, or from the Old English *cricc-crycc*, a crutch or staff. Romantic historians notice a game called *creag*, played by Prince Edward and chalked up in Edward I's accounts for that year. Manuscript illustrations from the thirteenth and fourteenth centuries have been taken to represent early cricket. If put to it, I will cite the early medieval stained glass window in Gloucester Cathedral, taken as inchoate golf or hockey, to be a chappie playing an early form of straight drive. Papist wild boys point to a decretal of Pope Gregory IX (*circa* 1230), which has an illumination showing a boy with a straight club and a ball, and an older man showing a stroke with a long stick.

To be boring about it, there is no sensible evidence until the middle of the sixteenth century. At that point a record of the Borough of Guildford refers to a game of 'creckett' played by pupils of the Royal Grammer School, Guildford, played *circa* 1550.

By the time that *The Times* arrived on the scene, cricket was an essential part of the English idiosyncrasy. By 22 June of its first year, 1785, *The Daily Universal Register* was already bossing the world about how to conduct itself, and taking the high and mighty line that cricket, like everything else, would be best conducted from Printing House Square:

> It is recommended to the Lordling Cricketers who amuse themselves in White Conduit Fields, to procure an Act of Parliament for inclosing their play-ground, which will not only prevent their being incommoded, but protect themselves from a repetition of the severe rebuke which they justly merit, and received on Saturday evening from some spirited citizens whom they insulted and attempted *vi et armis* to drive from the footpath, pretending it was their bounds.

The first report of a cricket match was printed in July 1785. It lasted three days and a thousand pounds were wagered on the result: contrary to wet views, betting has always played a large part in cricket. The contestants were the White Conduit Club and the Gentlemen of Kent. The captain of the former club was the Earl of Winchilsea, *honoris* if not fine cut *causa*. He led his side to victory by 306 runs: Kent made only 28 in its second innings. These were stirring times, my masters.

The White Conduit Club, though strange, is a great name in cricket. The club played at Islington, and it employed Thomas Lord. With the support of that honourable straight driver, Lord Winchilsea, Thomas Lord eventually bought the sloping patch of turf known around the cricketing world with affection, and irritation, as Lord's.

On 2 May 1786 *The Daily Universal Register* reported with more hope than prescience that *le criquet* had caught on across the Channel. It said that a cricket match had been played by some English Gentlemen in 'the Champs Elyes' (jolly well *sic*): 'His Grace the Duke of Dorset was, as usual, the most distinguished for skill and activity. The French, however, cannot imitate us in such vigorous exertions of the body.' The French had other things about to occupy them.

In 1786 we also reported that the Star and Garter Club met Kent at cricket in Pall Mall. The game began with the odds of six to four in favour of Kent. The betting rapidly changed to five to one on their opponents, who finally won by five notches. Purists may whimper that cricket is about straight bats or straight arms or stiff upper lips. What it is actually about is betting.

On 29 May 1787 *The Times* advertised on its front page that a match was about to be played 'in the new cricket ground in the New Road, Mary-Le-Bone'. The teams were to be Essex and Middlesex. Alas and dammit, the sports editor of the day chose to ignore the game. A month later White Conduit Club met an All-England Team in a three-day game for a thousand guineas a side. England won by 246 notches: those were the days. 'Two thousand people present conducted themselves with utmost decorum. The utility of the batten-fence was evident, as it kept out improper spectators. A very good collation was spread out under a covered recess.'

The White Conduit Club was merged into the Marylebone Cricket Club. *The Times* missed the portentous event. However, in 1788 some cricket was reported that seemed as significant at the time: FOUR MEN WITH TOTAL AGES OF 297 YEARS PLAY AT ALFRISTON; MAIDS WIN MATCH AGAINST MARRIED AT COBHAM; on 9 September the *double entendre* cricketing headline, YOUNG GENTLEMAN CRITICIZED FOR PLAYING WITH OWN LAMPLIGHTER.

After those primitive days, cricket took hold of *The Times*. The Walter family were cricketers. In the 1880s they started a series of cricket matches, under the patronage of *The Times*, between Bearwood, the Walter family home in Berkshire, and the employees of the paper. The ghastliness continued, astonishingly and touchingly, until the Second World War – even under the proprietorship of Lord Northcliffe, who detested cricket.

Northcliffe's successor, Major J. J. Astor (later Lord Astor of Hever), was more of a cricketer. He played for Eton, and carried on playing after the war, in spite of and quite regardless of having lost a leg in action. The dear old fellow was President of the MCC in 1937, the club's 150th anniversary. *The Times* celebrated the event with a Special Supplement.

Cricket is as English as *The Times*, and *vice versa*. You can trace the history of English cricket, if you have a mind for it, from the White Conduit Club to Kerry Packer, and from W. G. Grace to bloody Boycott and Botham, in the columns of the old organ. So long as England stands, there will be chaps playing cricket, and *The Times* droning on about them.

Right Mary-le-Bone Cricket Club, 1809. The Club had two home grounds on the northern outskirts of London, at Dorset Square and then St John's Wood, before settling finally on the present site of Lord's in 1815. The game too has changed somewhat over the last 200 years. Although the game was played in whites, the outfits appeared to be considerably more elegant, and the players less well protected. The bat had a more generous striking surface; there were only four balls per over, each run was called a notch, and the umpire at the batsman's wicket placed himself precariously behind the wicket keeper.

The LAWS of the NOBLE GAME of CRICKET.

as revised by the Club at St. Mary-le-bone.

THE BALL muſt weigh not leſs than Five Ounces and a Half, nor more than Five Ounces and Three Quarters. At the beginning of each Innings either party may call for a New Ball.

THE BAT

Muſt not exceed Four Inches and One Quarter, in the wideſt part.

THE STUMPS

Muſt be Twenty-four inches out of the ground, the BAILS Seven Inches in length.

THE BOWLING CREASE

Muſt be in a line with the Stumps, three Feet in length, with a RETURN CREASE.

THE POPPING CREASE

Muſt be Three Feet Ten Inches from the Wicket, and parallel to it.

THE WICKETS

Muſt be oppoſite to each other, at the diſtance of Twenty-two yards.

THE PARTY WHICH GOES FROM HOME

Shall have the choice of the Innings, and the pitching of the Wickets, which ſhall be pitched within Thirty Yards of a center fixed by the Adverſaries.

When the Parties meet at a Third Place, the Bowlers ſhall toſs up for the pitching of the Wickets, and the choice for going in.

It ſhall not be lawful for either party during a Match, without the conſent of the other, to alter the Ground, by rolling, watering, covering, mowing, or beating. This rule is not meant to prevent the Striker from beating the ground with his Bat near where he ſtands during the Innings, or to prevent the Bowler from filling up holes, watering his ground, or using ſawduſt, &c. when the ground is wet.

THE BOWLER

Shall deliver the Ball with one foot behind the Bowling Creaſe, and within the Return Creaſe, and ſhall bowl four Balls before he changes Wickets, which he ſhall do but once in the ſame Innings.

He may order the Striker at his Wicket, to ſtand on which ſide of it he pleaſes.

THE STRIKER IS OUT

If the Ball is bowled off, or the Stump bowled out of the ground.

Or, if the Ball, from a ſtroke over or under the Bat, or upon his hand, (but not wriſts) is held before it touches the ground, although it be hugged to the body of the Catcher.

Or, if in ſtriking, or at any other time while the Ball is in play, both his feet are over the Popping Creaſe and his Wicket put down, except his Bat is grounded within it.

Or, if in ſtriking at the ball he hits down his Wicket.

Or, if under pretence of running a Notch, or otherwise, either of the Strikers prevent a Ball from being caught, the Striker of the Ball is out.

Or, if the Ball is ſtruck up, and he wilfully ſtrikes it again.

Or, if in running a Notch the Wicket is ſtruck down by a throw, or with the Ball in Hand, before his Foot Hand or Bat is grounded over the Popping Crease. But if the Ball is off, the Stump muſt be ſtruck out of the ground.

Or, if the Striker touches or takes up the Ball while in play, unleſs at the requeſt of the other Party.

If with his foot or leg he ſtops the Ball, which the Bowler in the opinion of the Umpire at the Bowler's Wicket ſhall have pitched in a ſtraight line to the Wicket, and would have hit it.

If the Players have crossed each other, he that runs for the Wicket which is put down, is out; if they are not croſſed, he that has left the Wicket which is put down, is out.

When a Ball is caught, no Notch to be reckoned.

When a Striker is run out, the Notch they were running for is not to be reckoned.

If loſt Ball is call'd, the Striker ſhall be allowed four, but if more than four are run before loſt Ball is call'd, then the Striker to have all they have run.

When the Ball has been in the Bowler's or Wicket-keeper's hands, it is conſidered as no longer in play; and the Strikers need not keep within their ground, till the Umpire has called PLAY, but if the player goes out of his gronnd with an intent to run before the ball is delivered, the Bowler may put him out.

If the Striker is hurt, he may retire from his Wicket, and have his Innings at any time in that Innings.

If a Striker is hurt, some other Perſon may be allowed to ſtand out for him, but not go in.

If any Perſon ſtops the Ball with his Hat, the Ball is to be conſidered as dead, and the oppoſite Party to add Five Notches to their Score; if any are run, they are to have five in all.

If the Ball is struck up, the Striker may guard his Wicket either with his Bat or his Body.

In single Wicket Matches, if the Striker moves out of his ground to strike at the Ball, he shall be allowed no Notch for ſuch ſtroke.

THE WICKET KEEPERS

Shall stand at a reaſonable diſtance behind the Wicket, and ſhall not move till the Ball is out of the Bowler's hand, and ſhall not by any noiſe incommode the Striker; and if his hands, knees, feet, or head, be over, or before the Wicket, though the Ball hit it, it ſhall not be out.

THE UMPIRES

Are the sole judges of fair and unfair play, and all diſputes ſhall be determined by them; each at his own Wicket: but in caſe of a Catch, which the Umpire at the Wicket cannot ſee ſufficiently to decide upon, he may apply to the other Umpire, whoſe opinion is conclusive.

They ſhall allow Two Minutes for each man to come in, and Fifteen Minutes between each Innings; when the Umpire ſhall call *Play*, the party refusing to Play ſhall loſe the Match.

They are not to order a player out, unless appealed to by the Adverſaries.

But if the Bowler's ſoot is not behind the Bowling Creaſe, and within the return Creaſe, when he delivers the Ball, they muſt, unasked, call *No Ball.*

If the Striker runs a ſhort Notch, the Umpire muſt call *No Notch.*

The Umpire of the Bowler's Wicket, ſhall be first applied to decide on all Catches.

The Umpires are not to be changed during the Match, but by the consent of both Parties.

BETS.

If the Notches of one Player are laid against another, the Bets depend on the First Inning, unless otherwiſe ſpecified.

If the Bets are made upon both Innings, and one Party beats the other in one inning, the Notches in the First Inning ſhall determine the Bet.

But if the other Party goes in a ſecond time, then the Bet must be determined by the number on the Score.

Published by John Wallis, 13, Warwick-Square, London.

A day for Englishmen to be proud of is recorded here – Australia were all out for 78 runs.
25 JUNE 1968

ROYAL EDITION
TUESDAY JUNE 25 1968
NO. 57,286 NINEPENCE

THE TIMES

DE KAT'S FULL STORY, WRITTEN SPECIALLY FOR THE TIMES, P. 10

LOCOMEN'S BAN BOUND TO CAUSE GREATER CONFUSION TODAY

Anxious commuters studying the notice board at Cannon Street station, London, last night.

Government refuses to interfere

The situation on the railways is expected to deteriorate sharply today after yesterday's decision by the Associated Society of Locomotive Engineers and Firemen to join the work-to-rule from midnight last night.

Main line services, most of which ran yesterday with only minor delays, are likely to suffer widespread cancellations, and Southern Region commuters, who were the worst affected yesterday, face far greater disruption today as a result of the decision by the drivers' and firemen's union.

Mr. Marsh, Minister of Transport, said yesterday that he would not interfere in the dispute. The railways' management were on their own and could expect no help from the Government.

Sir Henry Johnson, chairman of the Railways Board, said last night: "The Aslef decision will complicate the situation further. It must be worse tomorrow. We are hoping all the time that we shall find a way out."

Police shut station gates

BY A STAFF REPORTER

In spite of conspicuous little knots of police in all the London main line stations, last night's rush-hour passed without serious incident. A senior police officer at Victoria said it had gone exceptionally well.

The worst crowd scenes occurred at Cannon Street, where at one point early in the rush-hour police closed the station gates because of the crush inside. But this was a temporary measure, and the press of angry bowler hats soon thinned out. Ironic cheers greeted each train announcement.

The information clerk at Cannon Street said no one had been particularly rude, though his colleague showed me that he had kept a poker under the counter.

West End theatregoers ignored the curtailed train timetables and many theatres reported full houses

Because of the railwaymen's dispute *The Times*, in conjunction with other newspapers, has had to make alternative arrangements for distribution. We apologize if copies are received late in some areas.

yesterday in spite of their being warned to take trains getting them home by 10 p.m.

But theatre managers fear that if late trains continue not to run audience figures will be hit.

A spokesman for the London Palladium said: "I don't think it has fully sunk in yet that some people may have difficulty getting home. If the present situation continues some theatres could certainly feel the pinch."

More time for GCE exam

The University Entrance and School Examinations Council at London University said yesterday that it had advised schools whose pupils arrived late to sit their G.C.E. examinations that they should be allowed extra time so that they had the full three hours for the papers. Special consideration would also be given to such papers, an official said.

Five thousand railway workers and their wives and families might be forced to make fresh travel arrangements for their annual holiday, which starts this weekend, because of the work to rule by their colleagues. The men, who make and service locomotives at the Crewe locomotive works, have been told that the traditional special trains laid on for the West Country and other holiday centres might have to be axed.

Regular rail commuters at Bromsgrove, Worcestershire, received telephone calls from their local station yesterday telling them that their train had been cancelled.

Mr. Michael Abbott, secretary of the Bromsgrove Passenger Action Committee, said he thought it was a "very nice gesture".

'Not according to rule'

Yesterday was not without its flashes of humour. A train from Littlehampton to Victoria had made one of its many extra stops and was pulling out of a station when the brakes were suddenly applied. Passengers saw the guard, who had almost missed the train, running along the platform shouting at the driver, "This is not according to rule".

The smallest public railway in the world, which operates between Hythe and Dungeness, Kent, was running to time. A spokesman for the company which runs the mini-sized trains said: "Our men are quite independent . . . it's business as usual for us."

ASLEF BETRAYS A NOTE OF REGRET

By MICHAEL BAILY, Transport Correspondent

Announcing Aslef's decision to bring forward its go-slow a week, Mr. Ray Buckton, assistant general secretary, said after a three-hour meeting at the union's headquarters at Hampstead yesterday: "My executive have given very serious consideration to all the circumstances. They are very firm in their attitude that our just claim for an increase in rates of pay should be considered as separate and apart from the efficiency and productivity jobs.

"If the board say there is extra money for our people in these pay and efficiency talks, then we fail to see why they cannot indeed make a proposal to give a percentage to our member grades, even if this is subsequently to be taken into consideration in the finalization of pay and efficiency talks."

Apparently betraying a note of regret over yesterday's decision, Mr. Buckton said Aslef would try not to worsen the difficulties of commuters and business people, but with about 60 per cent of rest days being worked, Southern Region was bound to be badly disrupted.

The first day of the go-slow went off a good deal more smoothly than had been expected. Some overnight expresses were cancelled, and commuters, especially on the Southern Region, suffered overcrowding and irregular services. But the main flows of both passengers and freight were successfully moved, and traffic in London was not badly obstructed by commuters taking to their cars.

Sir Henry Johnson, British Railways chairman, said during the afternoon that the effects so far had not been as bad as had been feared. It appeared that there was little working to rule, although the men's refusal to work overtime and on rest days was obviously having its effect.

In a statement on the B.B.C. programme *The World at One*, Sir Henry said he could offer little hope of an early end to the dispute while the railwaymen demanded an increase across the board.

Michael Thomas writes:—One reason why services were not even worse affected yesterday was simply that more than two-thirds of the men defied their union's instructions and worked overtime or on their rest days as usual. Only a handful worked to rule in the sense that they carried out their duties in an abnormal way.

The British Railways Board may consider today whether to suspend the railwaymen's guaranteed week agreement. This would make it possible to send home men left without work by the industrial action of others and save the cost of their wages.

Sir Henry Johnson, chairman of the board, said last night that disciplinary action could not be taken against men for working to rule or for declining to volunteer for overtime, but it could be taken against any man who refused to obey legitimate instructions.

New proposals on train manning, an issue which reached deadlock in the productivity negotiations, were sent to both unions yesterday with an invitation from British Railways to discuss them today. Affecting some 80,000 footplatemen and guards, they would cost £2m. a year to introduce, but this would be offset by savings. One proposal is that drivers' milage bonuses should be replaced by a flat weekly allowance. Another attempts to break the deadlock over the manning of locomotives by men apart from drivers.

Even if talks take place on these proposals they are unlikely to settle the main dispute, which is over the unions' demand for an immediate all-round increase without productivity conditions.

Southern Region cuts, page 2.

Railways must act alone, Marsh says

FROM OUR CORRESPONDENT—Carlisle, June 24

Mr. Marsh, Minister of Transport, said here today that he will not interfere in the railway dispute. He told a press conference that the Government could no longer interfere in British Railways affairs.

"The situation is totally different from any previous dispute", he said. "The management of British Railways must deal with this dispute. They are on their own. They can expect no help from the Government.

He added: "At the very time when British Rail has a shiny future, it is faced with a dispute which can not only damage it financially but which can have very serious implications indeed for the people who work for British Rail."

Earlier Mr. Marsh had opened a £100,000 extension to the seat-belt manufacturing plant of Kangol Magnet Ltd. in the city.

Our Political Correspondent writes:—

Tory backbenchers protested in the Commons yesterday when a private notice question on the disruption of rail services addressed to Mr. Marsh was answered by Mr. Carmichael, one of the parliamentary secretaries. Mr. Peter Walker had put in the question half-way through the morning. By that time Mr. Marsh was flying to Carlisle.

Nor could the question be passed to Mr. Swingler, Minister of State, Ministry of Transport. He was in Lancashire for the day, speaking in the Nelson and Colne by-election campaign.

Without the facts, several parliamentarians on both sides of the House thought Mr. Marsh had his priorities wrong, for the question dealt with what the Ministry is doing "to minimize inconvenience to public and industry".

Mr. Carmichael made a holding statement decribing the day's events, and did not allow himself to be drawn into controversy about the dispute.

Mrs. Castle, Secretary of State for Employment and Productivity, went to 10 Downing Street last night to discuss the work-to-rule with Mr. Wilson, but Government quarters went out of their way to emphasize that the discussion did not presage any possibility of Government intervention to bring about a settlement on terms that conflict with incomes policy. Mr. Wilson and Mrs. Castle are said to be standing firm in their view that the Government's incomes policy has been brought under direct challenge and they have no intention of surrendering to the pressure from the railway unions.

Parliamentary report, page 14.

HOW THE AUSTRALIANS WERE SKITTLED OUT AT LORD'S

England dismissed Australia for 78 in their first innings at Lord's yesterday. Good fast bowling supported by magnificent close-catching combined to put out the Australians for their lowest score in a Test match in this country since 1912. At the close of play Australia had scored 50-0 in their second innings. Report page 15.

W. M. Lawry, c. Knott, b. Brown 0

I. R. Redpath, c. Cowdrey, b. Brown 4

R. M. Cowper, c. Graveney, b. Snow 8

K. D. Walters, c. Knight, b. Brown 26

A. P. Sheahan, c. Knott, b. Knight 6

I. M. Chappell, l.b.w. b. Knight 7
G. D. McKenzie, b. Brown 5

J. W. Gleeson, c. Cowdrey, b. Brown 14

B. N. Jarman retired hurt 0

N. J. N. Hawke, c. Cowdrey, b. Knight 2
A. N. Connolly, not out 0
Extras 6
Total 78

Gaullists may get back with clear majority

From CHARLES HARGROVE—Paris, June 24

The victory of the Gaullist party in the first ballot of the French parliamentary elections yesterday could turn into a landslide in the second vote next Sunday. Even on the most conservative estimates the Gaullist majority in the new Assembly will be much more substantial than it was in the last.

The Government can even look forward to the possibility of having an absolute majority in its own right without having to rely on the qualified and critical support of M. Giscard d'Estaing's Independent Républicans.

On the first vote the Government has recovered three-fifths of the seats it held in Parliament, with another 333 to be filled. Very few of its candidates have failed to obtain the 10 per cent of votes cast in the first ballot that they need to remain in the second, and a substantial number are very well placed to win under mutual withdrawal arrangements which will be struck with Independent Republican candidates.

A new development came tonight when M. Pompidou suggested a similar arrangement to candidates of the centre—offering to withdraw the Gaullist candidate if the centrist had emerged in a better place in the first ballot whenever there was risk that a communist might win.

He went even further. He said that he was prepared to withdraw the Gaullist candidate in favour of a better placed candidate of the centre even if there were no communist threat.

M. Pompidou said: "I think that such a union for the second ballot is made all the more necessary because we know how decisive the second ballot is, that it is never settled in advance, and that the experience of the past few years, particularly of last year, shows that hopes formulated after the first ballot can sometimes be disappointed."

He added that he hoped that the electorate "remains vigilant and on the alert, and that no one imagines the game is won; and that on June 30, in the evening, and only then, Frenchmen may quietly and optimistically think about their holidays."

The Gaullist leaders are remembering March, 1967, when through over-confidence they lost in the second ballot much of the ground they had won in the first.

They also wish to avoid provoking the voters into switching their support between now and next Sunday through fear that the Gaullist party might emerge too powerful and therefore insensitive to the need for reform.

The victory is remarkable for a party which had been in power uninterruptedly for 10 years and for a leader aged 77. The Gaullists undoubtedly cashed in handsomely on the climate of fear engendered by demonstrations, riots, and strikes; and the Opposition's clumsy and ill-timed bid for power before it had in fact been relinquished.

The party kept before the electorate the spectre of further disorder and unrest if the opposition came to office. It wen back many votes from the centre which last time, in protest against its style of government and its refusal of discussion, had gone to the left. These elections have proved once again, as in 1848, 1871 and on other occasions throughout recent French history, that in times of stress the reaction of this country is overwhelmingly conservative, and that the chance of the left only comes in times when the voters feel that the institutions and the foundations of the social structure are not threatened.

Swing from left

But this does not altogether explain the extent of the Gaullist success. The failure of the opposition to propose a convincing alternative also played a part. Many votes won by the Gaullists were communist or left-wing votes.

The danger would be for Gaullism to imagine that it was back in the halcyon days of 1962, with its absolute "unconditional" majority, and to act as though the events of last May had merely been an unpleasant episode which yesterday's poll had effaced. Half of France still supports the Opposition.

Gaullist gamble pays off, page 6; leading article, page 11.

Inquiry over bank chief's salary

BY OUR POLITICAL STAFF

Payment of a £4,279 increase in director's remuneration to Mr. Jocelyn Hambro chairman of Hambros Bank is being investigated by the Department of Employment and Productivity. Mr. Walker, Parliamentary Secretary to the Ministry, said in the Commons yesterday.

He told Mr. Allaun, Labour M.P. for Salford East, that the Prices and Incomes White Paper made it clear that the principles of the policy applied to directors' remuneration.

"The Government expect directors to show the same sense of responsibility towards these principles as is being asked of wage and salary earners", he said. "We will be keeping the question of directors' remuneration under close review, as details become increasingly available through the operation of the Companies Act, 1967."

Mr. Allaun said in his question that the chairman of Hambros had a rise of from £20,866 to £25,145 a year in the past 12 months, besides share dividends.

Business News, page 21.

Police alerted by strike ship

FROM OUR CORRESPONDENT

DOVER, JUNE 24

For five hours today members of the crew of the Israel ship Avocadocore (18,433 tons) argued with officials as the vessel lay at anchor in the middle of the fog-shrouded harbour at Dover. Police stood by on shore.

The ship, sailing to Bremerhaven with a cargo of fruit was diverted to Dover to land eight members of the crew who were refusing to take orders. But when the ship was preparing to leave Dover the crew were still on board.

After immigration officers went out by launch to board the ship a radio message asked Kent police to stand by. The message said some of the seamen were armed with knives and wire hawsers. A convoy of vehicles took police to the pierhead, but they were later withdrawn.

13 die in Swiss rail crash

FROM OUR CORRESPONDENT

GENEVA, JUNE 24

Thirteen people were killed and 119 injured, some seriously, when two trains collided head-on on a single-track stretch of the main line from Lake Geneva to the Simplon tunnel today.

Picture, page 7.

Woman's body near camp

FROM OUR CORRESPONDENT

GUILDFORD, JUNE 24

A murder hunt began tonight after the body of a woman in her early twenties had been found naked and mutilated on a track near the Women's Royal Army Corps depot at Guildford, Surrey. She had been strangled and also attacked with a blunt instrument.

Joan de Kat in the fishing boat to which he was transferred after leaving the Jagona at Skagen.

Saved sailor slips quietly ashore

SKAGEN, DENMARK, June 24.—M. Joan de Kat, the French yachtsman saved from the Atlantic by an international rescue operation, slipped quietly ashore here today.

M. de Kat, a 27-year-old artist whose trimaran Yaksha broke up in mid-ocean while he was taking part in the single-handed transatlantic yacht race, was picked up by the Norwegian cargo ship Jagona.

He came ashore today in a fishing boat.—*Reuter.*

Alone on the Atlantic, page 10.

Hancock dies in Sydney

SYDNEY, Tuesday morning.—Tony Hancock, the British comedian, was found dead today in a flat in the Sydney suburb of Bellevue Hill. Police announced his death but gave no further details.

Mr. Hancock, who was 47, had his greatest success in a B.B.C. television series *Hancock's half-hour.*—*United Press International.*

On Friday, Tony Hancock's wife was granted a decree *nisi* in the Divorce Court in London, on the grounds of cruelty and adultery.

ON OTHER PAGES

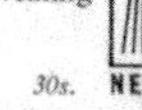

Crossword

The Times crossword is one of the most famous features of the paper, and a tribal shibboleth of the English intelligentsia. There are harder crosswords published: not many. But no other puzzle combines the wit and exactitude of *The Times* crossword with the literary references to an old-fashioned English gent's education. It is essential for the solver to have read Shakespeare and Lewis Carroll; it is a help to know one's classical mythology; and one needs a wide general knowledge in the liberal arts.

The clue to one of the famous early punning puzzles was: It is topping to kiss a monkey. The answer was: Apex. Other famous recent clues were: (7 letters) (a blank with no clue). The answer was: Missing. Then there was the clue: o (8,6). The answer is: circular letter.

The first crossword appeared in *The Times* on 1 February 1930. It followed a letter from Lieutenant Commander A. C. Powell, noting that a crossword had appeared in the weekly edition of *The Times*, and asking 'Would it not be an additional attraction if the same crossword were reproduced in your daily edition?' It was introduced, and there was the customary uproar from diehards, that it was a sign of *The Times* going to the dogs and pandering to the frivolous. But the crossword became a national institution.

Above Adrian Bell, crossword editor, 1980.

Below THE TIMES/Cutty Sark crossword competition.

For a number of years the crossword floated backwards and forwards in the paper. But in 1947 it settled finally in the bottom left-hand corner of the back page. This was largely because of its popularity as a solace for commuters in their daily passage to work, like one of the more crowded circles of Dante's *Inferno*: they could do the crossword while strap-hanging without trying to unfold the paper. In 1981 when the Information Service was introduced there was a proposal from the designers to run the clues horizontally at the side of the puzzle; the plan was rejected when it was pointed out that this spread the puzzle across four columns, making it impossible for any strap-hanger to do the crossword on the Tube.

What is special about *The Times* crossword? The first crossword editor, Ronald Carton, drew a corner of the veil from the tabernacle in a letter to the management during the war. The management wanted to cut the length of clues in order to save space during the paper shortage. Carton spoke up for England:

The clues are the flesh and blood of the crossword; if they are emasculated they lose their outstanding *Times*-y character and essence. I greatly fear that our team will be discouraged when they see their best quips, their salty aphorisms, their topical thrusts, their pertinent comments, their apt quotations pruned of the phrases that gave them point and savour. The puzzles will be drained of their vitality. They will become dull, and, whatever criticisms may have been passed on them by slow-witted solvers in the past, they have never been rated dull.

The team of about eight compilers follow no printed rules. But some customs of house style are observed. Words with unpleasant or rude associations (e.g. leprosy, semen, prick, carcinoma, incontinent) are banned. The names of living persons are avoided. Both compiler and editor rigorously scrutinize the clues for the faintest hint of *double entendre*: the ingenious wits that attempt the crossword can spot a rudeness in the most innocent clue. Sometimes a news story breaking has made a clue in tomorrow's crossword into bad taste overnight. During the war the lunatic fringe detected from the clues that the compilers were crypto-Nazis, or even sending messages to Berlin.

Over the years readers have tried to explain the British passion for *The Times* crossword. Some have commended it as gymnastics for the intelligence; others have considered it a useful exercise in English idiom and idiosyncrasy for foreign students. One reader claimed it was a sovereign remedy for sea-sickness.

The most famous correspondence on the crossword began in 1934, when Sir Josiah Stamp informed the readers of *The Times* that he had completed the crossword in fifty minutes. Sir Austen Chamberlain was quick off the mark in claiming to have knocked nine minutes off Sir Josiah's time, 'and I had wasted time badly over one of the anagrams'. He added that he understood that M. R. James, the Provost of Eton, measured the time he needed for boiling his breakfast egg by that needed for solving the crossword; and the Provost hated his egg hard-boiled.

P. G. Wodehouse protested that 'To a man who has been beating his head against the wall for twenty minutes over a single anagram it is g. and wormwood to read a statement like that of the Provost'. Another brutally honest writer to the paper confessed that after sixteen years of unsuccessful efforts, he had at last managed to finish a crossword: in three weeks. The ability to fill in 225 squares, minus the blanks, at the drop of a hat between stations is not universal.

Since 1970 there has been an annual competition, with about two thousand entrants competing to beat the clock and each other at solving *Times* crosswords. The Old Guard, I dare say including the Provost of Eton, think that the idea of doing the crossword as a competition is vulgar and trivial.

In a correspondence on the Letters Page in 1969 about the difference between a human brain and a computer, a Member of Parliament wondered wistfully how many possible ways there were, using all 26 letters of the alphabet, of filling the empty squares in that day's crossword puzzle. He wrote: 'It will greatly cheer us to learn how many millions of other possibilities the brain needs to reject in order to select the one correct one which gives us lesser mortals such intense satisfaction'.

You do not wonder things like that on the Letters Page without getting a prompt answer. A reader wrote in that the answer to the question was 26^{120}, which is, approximately, 24873 followed by 222 noughts (0s). Should anybody cavil because this calculation included solutions in which every letter was the same, the ingenious reader included a puzzle with just such a solution. All across: Gently to Annoy. All down: Used in golf. The solution consisted entirely of the letter T, viz.

Across: Tease.
Down: Tees.

Generally the crossword evokes wit and humour. On one occasion we received a letter that led every compiler to feel that the toil of composing cryptic clues had been worthwhile.

Sir, Can you find space in *The Times* for a sincere and grateful vote of thanks to your admirable and ingenious puzzle inventor? Through some sad and lamentable days of sorrow and bereavement they have been a veritable anodyne to the painful thoughts and memories.

The first TIMES crossword, compiled by Adrian Bell. The clues are simple compared to those of recent years.
1 FEBRUARY 1930

Parliament

CANAL BOATS BILL

SECOND READING IN THE COMMONS

MAJORITY OF 116

HOUSE OF LORDS

FRIDAY, JAN. 31

LORD PONSONBY, in the absence of the Lord Chancellor, took his seat on the Woolsack at 11 o'clock.

A message was brought up from the Commons desiring consideration of their amendments to several of the Lords' amendments to the Unemployment Insurance Bill. [This business has been set down for Monday.]

Their lordships rose immediately.

HOUSE OF COMMONS

FRIDAY, JAN. 31

The SPEAKER took the Chair at 11 o'clock.

CANAL BOATS BILL

Mr. GOSLING (Whitechapel, Lab.) moved the second reading of the Canal Boats Bill, which provides that on and after the first day of next year no child under the age of 15 years shall reside or travel on or in a canal boat. Speaking of the supporters of the Bill, he said that they included many of the men who were engaged in the actual working of the boats. The National Society for the Prevention of Cruelty to Children strongly supported the measure, because they could find no adequate way of providing for the education of the children or for the prevention of child labour in canal boats except by removing the children from them altogether. The children did not remain in one place long enough to get hold of. The education authorities could not afford staff enough to trace the boats about. He invited hon. members to go to the nearest available spot and, taking the children at haphazard, to find out whether any of them had a vestige of education. Many years ago power was given to companies and corporations to spend money to provide education and rest schools. They did not do so, but since this Bill had been before the House they had been falling over each other and saying what they were willing to do. He asked the House not to believe them. What was at the bottom of all this was child labour. (Cheers.) With regard to the suggestion that a floating school should be provided, he said that such a school on a canal boat must be of the size of a canal boat; but if it were bigger it could not get about. Sanitary arrangements were impossible, and where was the playground? The essence of canal life was keeping on the go.

LETTERS IN "THE TIMES"

He asked members to get out of their minds what some silly fools had been writing to *The Times* and other papers about these children. The children wanted to go to school. Employers asked how they were going to train people for the boats if the children were taken out of them. He did not wish to say that canal boat navigation was not skilled, but it was the lowest skilled of all navigation on the inland waterways of the country. It had been admitted on behalf of the Canal Association that canal children were not educated. If that was so, why did the association allow it to go on? (Cheers.) The Wolverhampton Education Authority had passed a resolution expressing the opinion that these canal children could not receive anything approaching an adequate education unless it was made illegal for them to live on board the boats during term time. The N.S.P.C.C. had made an investigation on this subject. They found that in the boats visited there were 1,649 children of school age. The education of 79 of these was described as good; in 301 cases it was fair; in 314 cases poor; in 703 cases practically nil; and in 252 cases the children had never attended school. Of those classed as good or fair practically all had at one time or other lived ashore.

The same representative of the Canal Association whom he (Mr. Gosling) had already quoted had stated that if some part of the family were to live on shore it meant taking the women off the boats and a very great increase in the cost of transport. He (Mr. Gosling) did not admit that. He was prepared to sit down with the owners and reconstruct the working of the boats. To say that they could not be worked without women and children was too silly. (Cheers.) The men who worked the barges which came from the Medway into the Thames left their women and children at home. Quite a number of canal boat owners would not allow children on their boats. (Cheers.) Children were passed from one boat to another according to whether there were more or less than were needed. He knew that there were cases where a man and wife would work two boats and borrow the children to make up the crew. That must be known to the owners of the boats. This was, therefore, not only a question of education but also of child labour. There was no factory inspection of these boats and therefore no limitation on the hours of labour. London refuse was being taken to the dump on these boats. Was it necessary for women and children to live in a dust-cart? (Cheers.)

Mr. SEXTON (St. Helens, Lab.), who seconded the motion for the second reading, said he had had seven years' experience of a ship's forecastle, and, bad as it was, it was palatial compared to the living quarters on canal boats. He wished that some of those who were objecting to the provisions of the Bill would visit Lancashire, and see where the canal passed for miles under a city and where the occupants of the canal boats had to use their feet to push the boats along. Children were born there and lived there, and those things were done so that profits might be made out of the labour of women and children.

MOTION FOR REJECTION

SIR H. NIELD (Ealing, U.) moved the rejection of the Bill. He said there was a danger of allowing legislation to proceed on grounds of sentiment. No doubt, very much could be said of the undesirability of women and young children living on barges of the character which had been described, and particularly on barges that conveyed the refuse of metropolitan boroughs. He thought women and children were not allowed to go on such barges.

Mr. GOSLING said that was the custom at that very moment.

SIR H. NIELD.—Then I say it should not happen: it should be stopped. Do not let it be supposed that any of those who are opposed to this drastic Bill would defend a thing of that sort. Proceeding, Sir H. Nield said that Mr. Gosling gave credit to those who were engaged in educating the children who went on canal boats and who were doing that work largely voluntarily, but he did not give altogether a fair account of what was being done. There had been no organized outcry against the conditions of their life by those engaged in canal boat traffic.

Mr. ALPASS (Bristol, Central, Lab.).—What about the slaves? They did not complain of their conditions.

SIR H. NIELD.—If it is the suggestion of the hon. member that the conditions of these people are equivalent to the conditions of slavery his interruption will do his cause not good, but harm. (Hear, hear.)

Mr. ALPASS.—My suggestion is that the slaves did not support the agitation to set them free. (Hear, hear.)

SIR H. NIELD said that what the canal boat people protested against was not the hardship of their conditions, but against any attempt to break up their family life. Clergymen intimately associated with them bore testimony to the healthy, moral, and happy conditions of family life on the canal boats, and that the lack of educational facilities for the children was largely imaginary. Nor was it true that the children were being exploited. He himself had travelled in a canal boat from Birmingham to see the conditions of the life. The boat people had no knowledge of the purpose of himself and his companion on the journey. There were young children on board. They were not working, they were running about at play. He saw nothing beyond the opening of a gate to allow the boats to pass through and similar light services of the kind.

The report of the inspector of canal boats to the Ministry of Health for 1928-29 dwelt on the increasing and successful efforts that were being made to educate the children; the parents, recognizing the advantage of better education for the children, being anxious to avail themselves of the opportunities now available. The inspector also called attention to the increase of motor canal boats, with the result that the individually owned and worked boat, common 20 years ago, was now to be found only in out-of-the-way districts. The companies, which owned a large number of boats, carried out the law regulating the conditions of the life. Cases of neglect that had to be brought into Court were few. The inspector also stated—referring to what he called the impression which seemed to prevail that children on canal boats were put to tasks beyond their strength—that his experience was that the parents were solicitous for their children's welfare and looked after them properly. Was the House prepared to take the view that the family life of these honest, hard-working folk must be broken up now when great changes in modern transport were in contemplation in, at least, the case of the Grand Junction and the Regent's Canals, which might result in the disappearance of the barge altogether?

EDUCATIONAL ASPECT

Mr. BEAUMONT (Aylesbury, U.), in seconding the motion for rejection, said that the matter dealt with by the Bill was obviously one that needed attention, but, like so many other proposals of admirable and well-meaning people, the promoters of it had allowed their zeal to outrun their discretion. The Bill laid down that no child under the age of 15 should reside or travel on or in a canal boat. That was a very drastic proposal. It meant that no child home for holidays would be allowed to go even for a few days' trip with his or her father in such a boat. (Ministerial cries of "No" and "that's not in the Bill.") That would be the effect, if it was not the actual proposal, of the Bill. The Bill would put upon the mother the hardest choice a married woman could be called on to make—namely, whether she would live with her husband or with her children. It would put on these canal boat people, whose wages were all too small, the necessity of keeping up two establishments, and it stood to reason that the homes they would be able to keep up would be among the cheapest. (Hear, hear.)

There was no doubt, whatever that, on the educational side of this question, the promoters of the Bill had a very good case. He was not going to dispute the submission that these canal boat children should be sent to school like any other children, and if the Bill had only gone as far as the Chamberlain Report he would not have opposed it. But it went much farther, for it took away the children, not only before they were of school age, but also during their holidays from school. No one could justify that on the ground of education. There were other and less drastic means of dealing with the educational aspect of this question. There was a clause in the Act of 1921 dealing with these children which said, in effect, that in the case of non-attendance at school, the education authority in which the barge was registered might prosecute, but that a certificate might be given to that authority that the child was receiving education in a school under any other authority. If that provision were applied, he believed it would solve the question. But if he were wrong in that view, they had the Chamberlain Report, which recommended that these children should not be allowed to live in the barges in school terms. That was a much better and less drastic provision than that of the Bill.

If he could get from the promoters or the Government a definite undertaking that they were prepared to accept amendments along the lines of the Chamberlain Report, confining the Bill to children of school age, he, personally, would not vote against the second reading. In the absence of such an undertaking he would oppose the Bill at every stage.

Mr. WEST (Kensington, N., Lab.) said that the fact that, according to figures, 75 per cent. of these children really had no education disposed of the argument that family life was to be broken up because "the child suffered from an imaginary lack of education." It might be true that, as a correspondent in *The Times* had said, these children were more cheerful and healthy than those living in tenement houses. It might be true that life on these barges, with their horrible cargoes of filth and garbage from the London streets, was not so bad as life in the tenement slums of Paddington, but the remedy was, not to keep the children on the barges, but to get better conditions in these tenement houses. (Hear, hear.) Sir P. Lidiard, in a letter to *The Times*, said:—"If you banish the children from the barges you banish the wives, and if you banish the wives, what is likely to happen? The saying (no doubt as a generality quite unjust) that the sailor has a wife in every port is sufficient evidence of the danger to which I need not further allude, except as an ex-Mayor of Paddington, to assure members of the House of Commons that it is a very real danger." Imagine a gentleman taking a statement and admitting that it was probably unjust and untrue, and saying that because of that, if they took the wives away it would be bad from a moral point of view. As to the assurance that the danger was a very real one, he did not believe it. When they had to deal with a woman and five or six children, sometimes girls and boys, of 15, 16, or 17 years of age, there was graver danger from the moral point of view in perpetuating the existing conditions than in removing the children, and he hoped the mother too, and trying to get for them decent homes near the place where the husband had to work. (LIEUT.-COLONEL FREMANTLE.—"It is not proposed to deal with children of 17 and 18, but to leave them on the boat.") Half a loaf was better than no bread. The Bill proposed to keep children away up to 15 years of age. He supported the Bill.

SIR J. WITHERS (Cambridge, U.) said he would be prepared to go the whole way in the Bill, so far as education was concerned. But what were they going to do? If 1,000 children would on January 1 next be taken from their fathers and mothers they would have to provide boarding schools. He would be prepared to vote for those schools. Unless, however, something of the kind was included in the Bill, the measure seemed to him impracticable. He could not vote for it unless the Government were going to bring in some proposal to deal with the children in a practical way.

Mr. MANDER (Wolverhampton, E., L.) supported the Bill, but said that before it was passed it would have to be amended drastically. To suggest that any person who allowed a child of 14 to travel in a barge for a day should be liable to two years' hard labour was ridiculous. What converted him to the support of the Bill was the document sent round in opposition to it by the Canal Carriers' Association and the Canal Association. Why should these children be deprived of the opportunities which all the other children of the country had of getting instruction and making the best use of the talents with which they had been endowed? No industry should be carried on if it inflicted hardship or suffering or real disadvantage on its employees and their children. (Cheers.) It had been said that if the children were removed from the boats they would live in slums on shore. The remedy for that was to see that the slums were cleared away, as he hoped the Government intended to do.

MAJOR LLEWELLIN (Uxbridge, U.) said that the offences dealt with under this Bill could not be compared with those under the Children Act, and the penalties imposed by that Act were therefore quite inappropriate in this instance. Legislation of that character, if it were not very carefully scrutinized in that House, might do irremediable harm to a large number of people, and it was such legislation, put forward without full consideration, which brought the criminal law into disrepute. The ground, as he understood it, upon which the Bill was chiefly supported was that there was lack of educational facilities for the children. On that ground he went the whole way with those who were pressing the measure. But how could that question be dealt with on the drastic lines of the Bill? It could be dealt with on the lines of the Neville Chamberlain Report, which proposed to make it an offence for a child to live on a barge during school terms. The Bill, however, while imposing large penalties, proposed for the educational offence merely a penalty of 20s. On the ground of education, there was no need to separate young children up to the age of five years from their fathers. He suggested that some sort of boarding school should be established, and that the mothers should have the choice of staying with their husbands or with their children. Those people would deserve allowances just as much as naval officers if by statute their children were taken out of the barges.

GOVERNMENT'S ATTITUDE

Miss LAWRENCE, Parliamentary Secretary, Ministry of Health (East Ham), who intervened briefly to explain the Government's attitude to the Bill, said she wanted in the first place to clear up a matter of fact. Unfortunately, there was no doubt that children lived on barges that carried refuse. That had been mentioned in the reports of the inspectors of the Ministry of Health, and it had been discussed in the Report on Public Cleansing in London. One of the recommendations of the inspectors was that children should not be allowed on barges where refuse was carried. Proceeding, Miss Lawrence said the debate had revealed an extraordinary amount of consent in the House that something ought to be done. There had been no root-and-branch opposition to the Bill. There was a general feeling that the House was dealing with a very great evil, but that members were not altogether at one on how to deal with it. The promoters of the Bill, with whom she had been in consultation, desired two objects—the complete rooting out of child labour and the giving of complete educational facilities to the children. If those two objects were provided for, the promoters of the Bill were willing to discuss the means. She asked the House to pass the Bill with an enormous majority, as the second reading would mean that something would be done.

LORD E. PERCY (Hastings, U.) said the Bill proposed to deal with a very special class of workers whose conditions of work and life were very peculiar. It did not propose to spend a single penny of public or private money in providing any special school accommodation for the children, or any special housing accommodation for the family. It confined its prohibitive provisions to certain practices. Certain things which admittedly needed remedy were left untouched. For instance, there was nothing in the Bill which would prevent a woman in an advanced state of pregnancy from being confined on board a barge. Another feature of the Bill was that its penalties were to be imposed, not on the employer of labour on the barges but on the family who refused to have its life regulated. Its prohibitions had not been recommended by any Government. No mention had been made by the promoters of the Bill of the report of the Committee on life and conditions of canal boats over which Mr. N. Chamberlain had presided. That report showed that the health conditions were not bad. But the grounds for the prohibitions asked for in the Bill were really not that the conditions on the boats in regard to health, decency, and morals were worse than in the slums, or that there were no legislative enactments against child labour on the boats. The real reasons for the Bill were that the provisions against child labour were difficult to enforce, and that health conditions were difficult of control by Government inspectors. Therefore the Bill amounted to this—that the population of this country, as a matter of principle, should live where they could be properly inspected by the public authorities, where the sanitary inspector could have access to their homes at any hour of the day, and where the inspectors of the Home Office and the Board of Education could prevent child labour. Did hon. members recognize this new principle that was being introduced by the Bill? The old principle was that the school must be brought to the child, that no parent was to be compelled to send his child to school unless the local authority provided a school within comparatively easy distance of his home. The new principle was that parents should not be allowed to live in places that were not within easy reach of a proper school. The school system was being reorganized. It depended upon being able to get a senior school at a reasonable distance for the children. If they were going to introduce this new principle, they might have it applied far beyond the range of canal-boat children and on other than educational grounds. That was an extension of the recognized powers of compulsion which the country ought to refuse to accept. (Hear, hear.)

Nothing short of a Select Committee would induce him to do otherwise than oppose the second reading of a Bill which was, on the face of it, a frank attempt to deal with a complicated social problem by a very sweeping measure of prohibition and entirely indiscriminate compulsion without consideration of the consequences. There was a proposal made to the Chamberlain Committee that boarding accommodation should be provided in selected centres for these children and that facilities should be offered to parents to send their children to such schools. That proposal was turned down on the ground that it would force a local authority to go to great expense to provide that accommodation and that there was no guarantee that parents would be sufficiently responsible to send their children to the schools when provided. He believed that, if this accommodation were provided and that if they conducted a campaign of advice among parents, they would get them to send their children to school, for it was fatuous to suppose that working-class parents were not as keenly interested in their children being educated as the parents of any other class. That, he believed, was the way in which the State in these days ought to go. He knew it was expensive, but if they were serious in their view of these terrible evils, then let them put up the money which would solve them in the way that was most acceptable to the parents involved, and not try to get rid of the extra expense by passing a sweeping measure of compulsion which took no account of the conditions of the children or the self-respect of the parents. (Hear, hear.)

POSSIBLE AMENDMENT

SIR D. MACLEAN (Cornwall, N., L.) said that it had been recognized for nearly a century in civilized countries that no parent could now do what he liked with what he called his own and that children were citizens from the day of their birth and belonged to the community in which they were born. As far as practicable they were to have an equal opportunity of discharging their citizenship and service to the nation. The Bill as it stood was rather a steep order. It was rather a strong thing to say that anybody responsible for a child travelling, for however short a time on a canal boat should come within the scope of section 12 of the Children Act, 1908, with all its penalties. He could say with the assent of the mover that in Committee the promoters of the Bill would be willing to accept an amendment to limit the application of the Bill to children of school age. The criticism with regard to penalties ought to be fully and fairly met.

LORD E. PERCY asked whether there would be an amendment that application should be limited to the school term and should not extend to holidays.

SIR D. MACLEAN said he would deal with the matter in a moment. As to the position with regard to education, it had been stated that the total number of children who suffered from lack of education was about 1,000. He feared that was a serious under-estimate of the position. The Chamberlain Committee said they were quite clear that there was only one satisfactory method of providing for the education of canal boat children, and that that was to keep them off the boats altogether during school term. Not a single member would say he dissented from that. The educational case was overwhelming. Want of education practically tied these children down to the occupation of their fathers. In Committee, he would point out, the promoters of the Bill would be compelled to conform to the general wishes of the House.

MAJOR LLEWELLIN asked whether the right hon. gentleman would allow young children to reside on the boats and travel with their parents on school holidays.

SIR D. MACLEAN said that personally he would not have the slightest hesitation in agreeing to that.

DR. HASTINGS (Reading, Lab.) said that it seemed that a very strong case could be made on grounds of health and general well-being for the exclusion of children of all ages from canal barges. Though it was very difficult to show from statistics that the health of the children of bargees was bad, it was known that bargees as a class did suffer very much from respiratory diseases and pneumonia, which was no doubt connected with their life in ill-ventilated cabins.

LIEUT.-COL. FREMANTLE (St. Albans, U.) said that the problem of the children of bargees was a small one compared with the 700,000 children in the schools on shore. He realized the point about the smallness of the canal boat cabins, and the fact that the boats offended against the ordinary canons of sanitation and housing. But hon. members made a great mistake in saying that the life of these people was mainly lived in the cabins of their boats. It was an open-air life, and, from the point of view of health, their life compared very favourably with that of people in towns. There was no case for the Bill on the health side; the practical aspects were the questions of child labour and education. Was child labour on the barges really a serious problem? The work performed by the children was slight and could not be economically replaced by adult labour. To speak of child labour in this connexion was to apply a stigma to conditions to which it did not apply. The real danger in schemes of social reform was allowing the appeal to be made to the heart instead of the head. There was no case in the Bill on the score of health nor of child labour, and, so far as education was concerned, it was stated in reports that the children on the barges showed a remarkable degree of intelligence and great brightness. The Bill contained no practical measures; it merely suggested the forcible removal of children from their families. That was a tyrannical proposal which would mean that children would be sent to over-crowded tenements.

The DUCHESS of ATHOLL (Kinross and West Perth, U.) said she rose to support the Bill, and in doing so found herself in the novel position of disagreeing with her late chief, the ex-President of the Board of Education. While she was at the Board of Education she made a personal investigation of conditions on the canal boats, and particularly to satisfy herself as to the education of the children. She must say she was amazed at some of the statements on the subject that appeared in the Press. She knew something of the admirable work that was done at the canal school at Paddington, but she thought any visitor to schools attended by canal children would find that only a fraction of the children who ought to be there were there, and that those who attended were educationally backward. Things could not be otherwise, having regard to the life the children lived, travelling backwards and forwards in the boats. There had been an improvement in the general level of education since the Chamberlain Committee reported; but on the other hand the problem had increased in size, for while the number of canal children returned in the Chamberlain Report was 1,100, the latest return furnished by local education authorities gave the number as 1,700, and that, it was understood, was not complete. She was thankful that even among the opponents of the Bill there was a large measure of agreement that the education of the children must be improved. She agreed that it would be better to bring about improved conditions by general consent and good will rather than by compulsion, but she thought it strange to find Lord E. Percy opposing compulsion having regard to the fact that a compulsory system of education had been set up by the State.

Her investigations had opened her eyes also as to some of the disadvantages of life on the canal boats. She found that the cabin in which the boatman, his wife, and some of the children lived and slept was considerably less in size than the table of the House of Commons; that it had no window for ventilation, only a hatch. The report of the Chamberlain Committee had pointed out how undesirable a place such a cabin was for a woman to be confined in. Nor was it easy for her to get the medical attendance which a woman in her situation required. As to the question of child labour, she had heard from boatmen and boatwomen of such work as driving horses, opening and closing locks, and heavy work of the kind being done by small children, and she had herself seen children under 12 engaged in such hard work as pushing the heavy beam at lock gates. That work was still going on, and, though it might not assume very large proportions, its existence was established beyond doubt. Lord E. Percy had referred to the proposal which was put before the Chamberlain Committee for the provision of boarding accommodation, but she understood that when that proposal was put before a large body of parents it was rejected. These parents were very keen on the education of their children, but they did not want to be separated from them, and, if the children had to go on shore to get education, she believed that a great many of the mothers would go with them. A great many of these people were willing to make the sacrifice involved in sending their families ashore and in engaging a mate or other help to assist them in running the boat, and she had heard them complain that it was only a minority who were being helped by their families. She believed that there were less than 500 families who were so helped, but it did not mean, if all the mothers involved went on shore, that 500 houses would have to be found in Paddington, or Birmingham, or elsewhere. These 500 families were to be found in some 28 districts up and down the country, so that it was really a smaller practical problem than many people seemed to imagine. She did not think that the Bill, as drafted, gave a long enough time for arrangements of this kind to take place, and she thought the promoters would be wise to allow a longer time, and also to make the penalties for a contravention of the law less severe. (Hear, hear.) She felt as strongly about family life as anyone in the House, but she would point out that if the whole of these 500 families went on shore, the mothers would only be in the same position as the wives of fishermen, of sailors, and of commercial travellers. (Hear, hear.)

After the closure had been agreed to without a division the second reading of the Bill was carried by 180 votes to 64—majority, 116.

A motion to refer the Bill to a Select Committee, moved by COMMANDER SOUTHBY (Epsom, U.), was negatived by 158 votes to 44—majority, 114.

The House stood adjourned at 20 minutes past 4 o'clock.

DIARY OF THE WEEK

Following is a record of the business done in both Houses of Parliament during the past week:—

HOUSE OF LORDS

MONDAY.—Road Traffic Bill agreed to on Report.

Unemployment Insurance (No. 2) Bill read third time.

TUESDAY.—Following Bills read second time:—Portsmouth Corporation, Shoreham Harbour, Birkenhead Corporation, Epsom Rural District Council, Guildford Rural District Council, Leicester Corporation, London County Council (General Powers), and Southampton County Council (Bursledon Bridge).

Commons' amendments to Arbitration (Foreign Awards) Bill agreed to.

WEDNESDAY.—Following Bills read second time:—Bootle Corporation, Lancaster Corporation, Shakespeare Birthplace, &c., Trust (Amendment), Southport Corporation, and Wakefield Corporation.

Debate on the Attorney-General's dictum as to the meaning of the word "Parliament."

THURSDAY.—Boston Corporation Bill read second time.

Debate on transferring land in payment of death duties.

HOUSE OF COMMONS

MONDAY.—Consolidated Fund (No. 2) and Poor Law Bills read first time.

Following Bills read second time:—Bristol Corporation, Chester Water, Coventry Corporation, Croydon Corporation, Derby Corporation, Great Western Railway, Kingsbridge and Salcombe Water Board, London Midland and Scottish Railway, Manchester Corporation (General Powers), Metropolitan Railway, North Cheshire Sewerage Board, Nottingham Corporation, Reading Corporation, Rochdale Corporation, Stockton-on-Tees Corporation, Tees (Newport) Bridge, and Tees Valley Water.

Optional Clause ratified.

Committee appointed to consider report of Select Committee of 1920 on Ministers' Remuneration.

Supplementary Votes for Ministry of Labour and Beet-Sugar Subsidy agreed to on Report.

Land Drainage (Scotland) money resolution agreed to on Report.

TUESDAY.—Mock Auctions Bill read first time.

Following Bills read second time:—Children (Employment Abroad), Collecting Charities (Regulation), Borough Market (Southwark), Bournemouth Corporation, Brighton and Hove Gas, Bristol Cattle Market, Barnley Corporation, East Surrey Water, Kingston-upon-Hull Corporation, Leeds Corporation, Manchester Extension, Southend-on-Sea Corporation, Southern Railway, South-

(Continued at foot of next column)

THE FINANCIAL OUTLOOK

MR. SNOWDEN ON HIS POLICY

NO RAIDS ON CAPITAL

Mr. Snowden, Chancellor of the Exchequer, speaking last night at a dinner of the Leeds Chamber of Commerce, referred to the weekly returns of national receipts and expenditure as being not very encouraging. He said:—

I am a very stern constitutionalist, and it is the invariable constitutional practice not to disclose the Budget until it is opened in the House of Commons. If Budget secrets were disclosed in advance, then the Budget would be knocked into smithereens; but there are some things in regard to the financial situation as it may be at the end of the financial year in March which I ought to be able to make public property. The weekly returns of the revenue receipts and expenditure are being followed with very keen interest, and I regret to say that so far they are not of a very encouraging character. Two months remain before the end of the financial year, and the bulk of the revenue from the main sources has still to be realized, and I don't know what may happen in regard to receipts from income-tax, which is collected mainly during the next few months. Unless there is a considerable improvement it is not unlikely that we shall find at the end of the year that the Budget estimates of 12 months ago have not been realized.

OVER-ESTIMATION

I ventured a criticism upon these estimates last April, and some of the items did appear to me to err on the side of over-estimation. It seemed to me that at the time the Stock Exchange boom of the previous year was on the wane, and therefore the yield from stamp duties would not be realized during the current 12 months. That has turned out to be the case, and the yield will probably be several millions short of the estimates. Another item which in recent years has been a growing item has not been living, or rather dying, up to expectations—the estate duty. The falling-off in this is probably accounted for to some extent by the fall of values, especially of Stock Exchange values. Therefore I regret that I am not in a position to-night to express myself in very sanguine terms about the revenue side of the account at the end of next March.

I see in the newspapers every day criticisms about the "orgy of extravagance" in which this Government is indulging. Apparently I, in the matter of national expenditure, am like a dead Scotsman—I am a rigid economist—and I am unwilling to give my approval to any item of national expenditure which is not absolutely necessary. This criticism is not altogether unfounded. It is like the story of Mark Twain's death; it is grossly exaggerated. It is quite true that we have to meet items of expenditure, some of them of very considerable amounts, but practically, with the exception of one item only, the whole of that is to meet commitments on which the country had already entered.

UNEMPLOYMENT INSURANCE

The only additional item of expenditure which will result from the legislation of this Government at the present time is that involved in the Act improving the widows', orphans', and old-age pensions scheme. Practically speaking, the only increase in expenditure which will fall this year is the additional payment to the Unemployment Insurance Fund. In view of the very unintelligent observations which have been made by bank chairmen in speeches during the last few days I feel bound to make a full explanation of this increased expenditure. It will impose an increased burden on the Exchequer of about £8,500,000, and next year it will be about £14,000,000. I hope, however, that there may be an improvement in trade resulting in a reduction of unemployment which will not make necessary the expenditure of the full provision we have made next year.

The national finance of this country will have to pay its way. I shall commit no raids. I shall not live out of capital, and I shall not take out of capital to meet current and recurrent expenditure, and treat it as ordinary revenue. That can be done once or twice, perhaps three or four times, but the day comes when the expenditure must be met. That day has come. In the last four years there have been raids of capital to the extent of £50,000,000 used as revenue in order to avoid imposing taxation. The statutory Sinking Fund has not been met to the extent of £30,000,000. Twenty-two and a half million pounds of Budget surplus which ought to have gone into debt reduction was put into suspensory account in order to meet the prospective cost of the derating scheme. The cost of the derating scheme has not been provided out of all revenue. Next year I shall be able to meet that cost out of the suspensory fund, but the following year it will be necessary to find ways and means of raising an additional sum of £15,000,000.

RECOVERY OF TRADE

I will sanction no expenditure, especially at a time like this, which I do not believe to be imperatively necessary. There are many things I should like to do, but we must wait to do many things we should like to do until we are in a position better to afford them. Our main consideration at the moment is that the State should use all the power it has to help the restoration and increase the prosperity of industry. Nobody has a greater personal interest in that than the Chancellor of the Exchequer, because it is through the prosperity of industry that the national revenue can be secured. And, therefore, the responsibility of the Chancellor of the Exchequer, when he is faced with the imperative need of raising revenue, is to do it in such a way as will rather be a help and encouragement to industry than an additional burden upon it.

I do not see that in the immediate future any very considerable reduction of expenditure can be made, except perhaps on one or two items. Since we came into this room to-night (added Mr. Snowden, looking at his watch) we have spent £18,000 upon our armaments. We are spending upon armaments about £120,000,000 a year. The only other item I can see in the future with a possibility of some considerable reduction is the War Debt, which is costing us £350,000,000 a year, absorbing more than the yield of the income-tax and supertax.

If we can get trade prosperity, if we can get—as I hope and believe we shall get before very long—cheaper money rates, then, I think, it will be possible to make some impression upon the huge volume of our national debt, and by then it will be possible to reduce taxation. The great concern of the Government, and particularly the Chancellor of the Exchequer, should be the recovery of trade, and I do want to protest against the expression of pessimism, which is far too widespread to-day. It is doing incalculable harm, not only in our own country, but to a far greater extent abroad. The state of our trade to-day is certainly not so black as it is painted in some quarters. There is a bright side of the trade situation in this country. Last year the exports of coal rose by 20 per cent., and the signs of advance are still not lacking.

We now have the Coal Bill. That Bill is being criticised on the ground that it will mean an increase in the price of coal. The purpose of the Bill is to help the reorganization of the coal industry and to put it on an economic basis, and we believe that the proposals which we are making will have that result. I do not believe that the effect of this Bill will be to increase the price of coal. I believe that the reorganization will effect economies which will enable men to work half an hour less in the working day without an increase in prices. . . .

This is still the most wonderful country in the world. There is plenty of life in the old dog yet. The only thing it lacks is more pluck. We are without those great resources of wealth which most countries have. We have to import a great deal of what is the foundation of our industries and then find a market for the finished articles across the seas. We are doing that, and we are maintaining at any rate our weight.

Staffordshire Mond Gas, South Yorkshire and Derbyshire Gas, Stockport Corporation, and Stoke-on-Trent Extension.

Coal Mines money resolution considered in Committee.

WEDNESDAY.—Fancy Jewellery (Standard Trade Descriptions) Bill read first time.

Debates on Empire Free Trade and Insurance for Agricultural Workers.

THURSDAY.—Consolidated Fund (No. 2) Bill read second time.

Lords' amendments to Unemployment Insurance (No. 2) Bill considered and certain of them disagreed with.

Coal Mines money resolution withdrawn and resolution (No. 2) read second time.

FRIDAY.—Canal Boats Bill read second time.

CHESS IN THE HOUSE OF COMMONS

AN ANGLO-AMERICAN TROPHY OF 1897

(FROM OUR CHESS CORRESPONDENT)

The House of Commons can now safely claim to be in possession of another very interesting chess souvenir—the set of Persian chessmen presented by the late Mr. Arthur Walter of *The Times*, as a prize for the winning team in the match by telegraph between the House of Commons and the American House of Representatives, on May 31 and June 1, 1897.

This match was due to the initiative of the late Sir John Henniker Heaton, who was primarily responsible for chess being introduced into the House of Commons. The British players were in Committee Room 12, and the House of Representatives players in one of the rooms at the Capitol, in Washington. I do not know if any of the American players still survive, but of the House of Commons players only one is still alive, Mr. (now Sir Horace) Plunkett. He led the House of Commons team on that occasion, and had the honour of defeating the Hon. Richmond Pearson, who was responsible for the arrangements on the other side. The match was drawn with a score of two and a half games all, a contingency not provided for when the trophy was presented.

In a letter to the Hon. Richmond Pearson, published in *The Times* of June 3, 1897, Mr. Henniker Heaton, as he then was, wrote:—

"My dear Sir,—At the conclusion of our friendly contest, the success of which is so largely due to your energy and devotion, I beg, on behalf of the British team, to tender our sincere congratulations to our honourable opponents. The match will always be remembered on this side of the water as one of the most interesting events in the jubilee year, and an event which demonstrates *urbi et orbi* the cordiality of feeling between the United States and the United Kingdom has rightly its place—a high one—in the history of that great celebration. . . . The interest aroused here, and indeed all over the Continent, has been unprecedented. . . . We all felt that, under the guise of a game, a great event was being accomplished and a serious yet kindly lesson was being given to the World. . . .

"Another problem remains. What is to be done with the magnificent board and men presented by Mr. Walter, of *The Times*—himself an enthusiastic chess player? Neither side is entitled to it, and the contingency was not foreseen. I venture to propose arbitration, if the precedent would not affront or compromise any of our friends on your side.

"I have the honour to be your faithful servant,

"J. HENNIKER HEATON."

The recovery of the House of Commons chess cup, mentioned in *The Times* of May 17, 1928, revived the memory of the Trophy of 1897, and it was ascertained, thanks to the efforts of Sir Richard Barnett, that the House of Commons did possess a set of chessmen which might well be the set in question. Beyond that nothing was certain. It so happened, however, that a colleague in Printing House-square placed in my hands a few days ago a cutting from the journal entitled *Lords and Commons*, dated March 25, 1899, containing an interview with Mr. Henniker Heaton in which mention is made of the intention of the Chess Committee of the House of Commons to entertain Mr. Walter—"the donor of the Challenge Trophy so keenly contended for by Members of the Popular Assemblies in this country and America."

It would appear that a return match for the Trophy was projected, as Mr. Henniker Heaton said, "Of course, Mr. Walter's Trophy must be tournamented for again. We cannot leave the question of the superiority between American and English chess-playing legislators at a 'tie.'" And later on: "Equally naturally, I take as keen an interest in the approaching contest for Mr. Walter's beautiful Trophy—which consists, by the way, of a superb Persian board and set of men—as I did in the contest of two years ago." For some reason the return match never materialized, but here was evidence that the Trophy had not left the House of Commons, besides providing a means of identification.

By the courtesy of Sir Assheton Pownall, I was enabled to inspect the set of chessmen yesterday, and of its identity there can be no doubt. It is in ivory, red and white, and the carving of the figures is clearly Persian. Sir Assheton Pownall is not certain where the board is, and that may be less easy to identify.

LARGE FLOUR MILL TO CLOSE

It was officially stated at Hull yesterday that Messrs. Spillers, Limited, have found it impracticable, economically, to manufacture at York the quality of mill products required by modern trade conditions. They have decided, therefore, to cease manufacturing at York and to supply their customers' requirements from the company's more modern flour mills elsewhere. The statement added that Messrs. Spillers will make every effort to minimize the local hardship involved in their decision to close the York plant. The plant in question is the flour mill known as Leetham's Mill, York.

MUNICIPAL ROAD TRANSPORT

MR. MORRISON AND THE HOUSE OF LORDS

Speaking at South Hackney last night, Mr. Herbert Morrison, the Minister of Transport, said that on Tuesday the House of Lords would give the Road Traffic Bill a third reading, thus completing, at any rate for the time being, their consideration of this great measure of road reform.

The Bill, which the Government had every intention of passing into law, would secure the more effective control of motor traffic, and, while coming down heavily on the reckless driver, would protect the considerate motorist against the fear of frivolous prosecutions. Compulsory third party insurance would substantially eliminate the scandal of no compensation being paid in a number of cases of death or personal injury as a result of motor accidents. The provisions for fundamental reform in the licensing of public service vehicles would enable us for the first time, so far as it was possible and within the limitations imposed by private enterprise, to secure a nationally co-ordinated system of road passenger transport. Related to this part of the Bill were the original provisions enabling local authorities, after obtaining the licence of the area Traffic Commissioners, to operate omnibus services without going to Parliament if they already possessed some statutory transport powers. Unfortunately, the House of Lords, at a moment when it was exceptionally unrepresentative, struck out that part of the Bill at the behest of certain vested interests who were anxious that the local authorities should not appear before the Traffic Commissioners on a basis of equality with private undertakers.

The Lords had raised the bogy of municipal trading as a smoke-screen to hide the character of the influences which had led to their action, in spite of the fact that Parliaments of all political complexions had repeatedly conferred transport powers on municipalities. Mr. Scurr would bring forward, next Friday, a Municipal Omnibuses Bill, and in any case the Government was not done with the matter yet. Municipalities of all political views were demanding justice in this matter and, provided they made their influence felt, they would yet secure the predominance of public over private interests. By their action on this matter and on the Unemployment Insurance Bill the Lords were in danger once more of becoming the victims of illusions as to aristocratic power, and were in a fair way to raise once more the issue of the Peers versus the People. If they did, they would be beaten even more decisively than they were before.

BRITISH TRAMWAYS

INCREASED EXPENDITURE AND LOWER RECEIPTS

A return issued by the Ministry of Transport, giving particulars of the accounts and statistical returns of the tramway undertakings in Great Britain for the year ended December 31, 1928, for companies, and March 31, 1929, for local authorities, is now on sale at the Stationery Office, price 10s. 6d. In addition to summaries of the year's results, the return contains full particulars regarding the capital, income and expenditure, volume of traffic, and operating results of each undertaking.

Comparative figures are as follows:—

—	1928-29	1927-28	Increase (+) or Decrease (−)	
	£	£	£	Per cent.
Capital expenditure at end of period	100,498,735	99,913,760	+ 584,975	0·59
Gross receipts ..	27,067,214	27,751,504	− 684,290	2·47
Working expenditure ..	21,479,735	21,943,147	− 463,412	2·11
Net receipts ..	5,587,479	5,808,357	− 220,878	3·80
	No.	No.	No.	
Passenger journeys	4,623,258,679	4,705,842,932	− 82,584,253	1·75
Car miles	396,295,085	396,554,545	− 259,460	0·07

The return also gives particulars of the working of trackless trolley undertakings in Great Britain. The number of passenger journeys during the year was 99,065,544, compared with 80,112,970 in 1927-28, an increase of 23·66 per cent.

THE LORD CHIEF JUSTICE IN CORNWALL

The Lord Chief Justice (Lord Hewart) paid his first official visit to Cornwall yesterday, when he opened the Winter Assizes at Bodmin. In his charge to the Grand Jury his LORDSHIP said he could not congratulate them on the lightness of the calendar in the same way as he had been able to do in the three other assize towns he had visited on the Western Circuit, because there were 18 or 19 cases, several of them of a repulsive nature. At the conclusion of the Grand Jury's deliberations the FOREMAN (Mr. Percival Williams), on behalf of his colleagues, said they assured his Lordship of their hearty appreciation of the honour conferred on the county by his personal visit. It was a matter of very rare occurrence for a Lord Chief Justice to visit such a remote county as Cornwall. His LORDSHIP, in reply, said it was a great delight to him to come there at any time, and his only regret was that he had not been able to come earlier.

CROSSWORD PUZZLE NO. 1

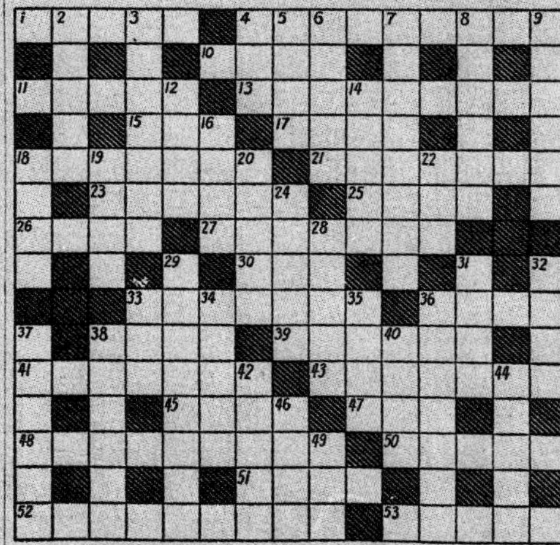

ACROSS

1 Spread unevenly.
4 Part of a Milton title.
10 A month, nothing more, in Ireland.
11 He won't settle down.
13 22 down should be this.
15 Cotton onto, so to speak.
17 Head of a chapter.
18 Denizen of the ultimate ditch.
21 Frequently under observation.
23 What's in this stands out.
25 Flighty word.
26 If the end of this gets in the way the whole may result.
27 Retunes (anag.).
30 This means study.
33 Simply enormous.
36 There's a lot in this voice.
38 This elephant has lost his head.
39 A turn for the worse.
41 Done with a coarse file.
43 Red loam (anag.).
45 This rodent's going back.
47 Makes a plaything with its past.
48 Wants confidence.
50 A mixed welcome means getting the bird.
51 This girl seems to be eating backwards.
52 The men in the moon.
53 A pinch of sand will make it dry.

DOWN

2 Heraldic gold between mother and me.
3 Out of countenance.
4 Upset this value and get a sharp reproof.
5 Intently watched.
6 In some hands the things become trumpets.
7 A religious service.
8 This horseman has dropped an h.
9 Sounds like a curious song.
12 This ought to be square.
14 Momentary stoppage.
16 Written briefly.
18 Calverley's picturesque scholars carved their names on every one.
19 Site of 45 across.
20 Precedes advantage.
22 Parents in a negative way.
24 Used to be somewhere in France.
28 Happen afterwards
29 Climbing instinct in man.
31 A terrestrial glider
32 The final crack.
33 The little devil's on our money.
34 Simplest creature.
35 Time measurements.
36 Jollier than 4 across.
37 Ladies in promising mood.
38 Presents are commonly this.
40 Gets the boot.
42 Hail in Scotland may mean tears.
44 Works, but usually plays.
46 She's dead.
49 Only a contortionist could do this on a chair.

The second crossword puzzle in this series together with the solution of puzzle No. 1, will appear in *The Times* on Monday.

Index to THE TIMES

The Times is the great paper of record. It is the best available account of what went on in the world on a particular day until we get the definitive report by the Recording Angel, when the crooked facts shall be made straight, and the rough places plain. Other publications eventually record some of the categories dealt with by *The Times* in more detail: *Hansard* on Parliament, the Law Reports, *The Annual Register* for some of the statistical information about foreign countries, *The Dictionary of National Biography* on death. But *The Times* publishes first. And no other publication attempts to keep such a comprehensive record of such a wide range of the day's events, from latest appointments at the universities or in the City or the Services, to reviews of new books and first nights, to dispatches and think-pieces from home and abroad. Back numbers of *The Times* are a treasure house for historians, and anybody else who wants to recapture a fact or a flavour of the past on a particular day. But the treasure house is not much use without a key. Agreeable as it may be, few people have the leisure to browse through files or microfilms of *The Times* hoping to find what they want by serendipity.

More than a hundred years ago somebody recognized that with a key he could unlock this great national treasury of record. His name was Samuel Palmer, a London bookseller and bibliophile. He sold a great many copies of *The Times* at home and abroad every day. And he reckoned that he could make money by compiling and selling a guide or index to back numbers.

His suggestion got a dusty answer from Printing House Square. Mowbray Morris, the manager, thanked him coldly and ended his letter by saying, 'Our own arrangements within this office have for many years made us independent of all assistance from without in the matter of an index'. Mowbray Morris was boasting on thin ice, as well as being pompous. His famous arrangements consisted of a manuscript index, haphazardly maintained only since 1865, for office use. It was not much good for finding what you wanted in a hurry.

Palmer was not fobbed off. He set to work compiling his own index to *The Times*. The first volume, covering the period October to December 1867, appeared in the following year and was well received in the literary and academic world, and in Fleet Street. Even *The Times* allowed it faint praise: 'It is indexed upon a plan at once simple and clear'.

Carried away with enthusiasm for his project, Palmer decided not only to index current issues of the paper as it was published, but to work his way backwards through the files to 1785, indexing as he went. His assistants started working on back numbers in the British Museum, while also keeping up with the current quarterly volumes of Index. Palmer set the type in his own office, and printed his Index there on his private press. He persisted in trying to interest *The Times* in its index. In 1881 John Macdonald, the new manager, was constrained to turn him off again: 'I must think that you do not need at this later date to be told once more that the proprietors of *The Times* are not disposed to buy your Index from you. Your persistence in inviting them to do so must remain fruitless.'

Palmer was not a man to be discouraged from his magnificent obsession. He died in 1899, by which time his Index had got back as far as 1824. His son carried on the family business until June 1941, when *Palmer's Index* ceased publication. By then the retrospective volumes had got back to 1790.

Palmer was quite right in his belief that an Index to *The Times* would be a valuable tool of scholarship and research. But the Index he produced is actually not much good. He was working on a shoestring and could not afford to be lavish. So only one slip for each entry was his rule: there was no cross-referencing. No modern indexer could work such a primitive system.

But the main reason that *Palmer's Index* is difficult to use is that he indulged his fantasy in his choice of headwords and subjects. Until a researcher has become accustomed to Palmer's little ways, his Index will be no use to him. For example, one of Palmer's favourite words was EXTRAORDINARY. Under it in his Index you will find such diverse entries as EXTRAORDINARY ESCAPE OF A BOY AT ERITH STATION FROM A BULL BEING ON THE LINE and EXTRAORDINARY MARRIAGE ADVENTURE. A good rule for using Palmer is: when in doubt, look under EXTRAORDINARY.

An accident in a factory, at sea or in the hunting field was catalogued by Palmer under ACCIDENTS. However, if somebody was killed in the street, the event was indexed under STREET ACCIDENTS. You will find no entries under MUSIC in Palmer. And this is odd because *The Times* devoted considerable space to music in the nineteenth century. If you want to find it, look under THEATRE, where Palmer, for reasons that seemed good to him, decided to index all concerts, operas and such cattle.

Palmer's Index is a constant source of curiosity, as well as a muddy well of information. Consider such entries in the Index as: PRACTICAL SUGGESTION ON GRATEFUL OFFERINGS; ELEVEN INDIANS AND ONE CANTEEN; FEMALE BLONDIN LEAVES HOSPITAL ON CRUTCHES. It may not be history, but by God it makes you want to look it up. The entry, ABODE OF BLISS, A GAMEKEEPER'S AFFAIR, suggests *Lady Chatterley's Lover.* Look it up and you will find that the entry refers to a gamekeeper who had been trespassing on the estate of a landowner called Bliss.

It may not be a perfect Index. But it was the only guide to the news of the eighteenth and nineteenth centuries. It has done worthy work in its time. The Institute of Criminology at Cambridge used *Palmer's Index* to trace almost a thousand early leading articles on crime and the law in *The Times*. It is an interesting Index, but it needs to be used with discretion.

Since 1905 *The Times* has published its own *Official Index*, recording itself as well as everything else as it comes out. From 1973 on the Index has included all *The Times Supplements* and *The Sunday Times*. For a while it was published quarterly. Then the increase in news forced it to appear every two months. Today it comes out once a month, with an annual cumulative volume.

There are subscribers to the Index all over the world, and their numbers are increasing. It goes mostly to other newspapers, libraries, colleges and universities. With microfilm of back numbers of *The Times* students can read about great events as they seemed to the men from *The Times* at the time. Today's news has become history by the time it has been recorded.

Even today the researcher needs to look out for pitfalls when using a newspaper index. Language in a newspaper changes even faster than elsewhere – as its name suggests, a newspaper is interested in new things. For example, *The Times Index* of 1930 refers to: TURF; MOTOR ACCIDENTS; and WIRELESS. Today it catalogues the same topics under: HORSE RACING; ROAD ACCIDENTS; and BROADCASTING.

We must not be too unkind to Samuel Palmer. He was a pioneer, and a servant of the Recording Angel. Indexing is a tricky business because the indexer cannot possibly know what is going to interest those who are going to use his index, years and maybe centuries later. Palmer's quirky ghost still haunts some modern compilers. Item, from the index to James Braid's *Advanced Golf* (1908): WIND, PLAYING IN, STIFF SHAFTS FOR DRIVERS WHEN; and ENJOYMENT OF GAME, MOST FROM BEST. Item, from the index to the *Crowther Report* (1959): CAMBRIDGE (see under OXFORD).

A typical page from Samuel Palmer's Index to THE TIMES listing various calamities reported in THE TIMES from 1 October to 31 December 1867. Inset: Palmer's title page.

8 PALMER'S INDEX TO "THE TIMES" NEWSPAPER. [Oct. 1 to

Abyssinia (*continued*).
—— Two Italian Staff Officers to attend the Expedition, 23 *n* 12 *b*
—— Value of Kroomen in the intended Expedition, 1 *o* 9 *b*
—— Viceroy of Egypt and the Expedition, 5 *n* 9 *f*
—— Ways and Means for the War, 29 *n* 7 *a*
—— What has become of the Expedition, 1 *n* 8 *d*
—— Zoologists for the Expedition, 22 *n* 10 *b*
Accidental and Marine Assurance Company, 28 *o* 5 *a*—30 *o* 7 *a*
ACCIDENTS:—
Accident in a Hunting Field, near Falkingham, 16 *n* 9 *c*
——— to a Cab at Peckham, 3 *d* 7 *f*
——— to a Cab in Stoke Newington Road, 22 *n* 5 *d*
——— to a Fruit Schooner off the Tyne, with Loss of Life, 7 *o* 10 *c*
——— to a Gentleman and his Groom, 22 *n* 5 *d*
——— to a Volunteer at Rugeley, 21 *n* 6 *f*
——— to Mr. Gladstone, 30 *d* 7 *a*
——— to Mr. Greaves, near Chesterton, 28 *o* 7 *e*
——— to the *Germania* 17 *o* 7 *d*
——— to Sir Thomas Biddulph, 30 *n* 12 *c*
——— to the Empress of the French, 7 *o* 10 *c*
——— to the Royal Cortège, 30 *n* 12 *c*
——— to the *Summer Cloud* 15 *o* 9 *d*
—— Boiler Explosion near Leeds, 31 *d* 10 *b*
—— Bursting of a Reservoir at Kelso, 17 *d* 7 *f*
—— Collision in Belfast Lough, 18 *o* 1 *a*
——— near Carrickfergus, 17 *o* 7 *d*
——— off Hastings, 21 *d* 5 *d*
—— Death from the bursting of a Boiler, 22 *o* 10 *d*
——— from Morphia, 23 *d* 9 *f*
—— Destruction of the *Danish Queen* by Fire, with Loss of Life, 15 *o* 7 *d*—8 *n* 7 *c*
—— Discovery of a Body in the Mersey, 5 *o* 10 *d*
—— Explosion and Loss of Life at the Highbury Coal Depôt, N.L.R., 8 *o* 7 *f*
—— Explosion of Gas in Dublin, 15 *n* 7 *e*
—— Family Poisoned at Wolverhampton, 15 *o* 9 *f*
—— Fatal Accident at a Stone Quarry, near Liverpool, 23 *n* 12 *d*
——— at Biarritz, 19 *o* 10 *a*
7 *b*
s, 18 *d* 9 *b*
f
rbour, 8 *n*
n 7 *d*
7 *b*
d 9 *f*
—11 *o* 10 *c*
7 *f*
ry Square,

Accidents (*continued*).
—— Fatal Gun Accident at Birmingham, 13 *n* 7 *e*
——— at Chatham, 10 *d* 10 *b*
——— at Kimside Moor, 31 *o* 7 *c*—2 *n* 7 *b*
——— by a Clergyman's Son, 23 *d* 5 *f*
——— in Berkshire, 19 *n* 7 *f*
——— in Cornwall, 8 *n* 9 *d*
——— Life-boat at Gorlestone, 23 *d* 10 *d*—25 *d* 7 *f*
——— Wagon, to the Son of Dean Green, 26 *d* 7 *b*
—— Fearful Explosion at Woolwich, and great Loss of Life, 7 *o* 10 *e*—11 *o* 7 *e*
—— Gun, at Bideford, 31 *d* 4 *f*
—— Land Slip at St. John's Wood, Loss of Life, 29 *o* 7 *e*
—— List of Accidents in the Streets, 16 *o* 7 *e*
—— Ship Burnt in Leith Docks, 2 *o* 9 *b*
—— Shooting Accident at Great Yarmouth, 15 *o* 7 *f*
—— Singular Accident at Foxearth, 15 *n* 4 *e*
—— Steam-boat Collision on the Thames—Inquest, 5 *o* 7 *a*
—— Terrible Steam-vessel Explosion in the Mersey, 30 *n* 9 *e*
—— Three Men suffocated in a Well, 18 *d* 9 *f*
—— Two Men killed by a Boiler Explosion at Bradford, 7 *n* 5 *f*
—— Two men shot near Whitehaven, 19 *d* 11 *f*
Accidents, Mining:—
—— at Shank-house Pit, Cramlington, 2 *n* 12 *b*—6 *n* 10 *f*
—— Boiler Explosion in the Odessa Colliery, 13 *n* 3 *f*
—— Disgraceful Accident in Breconshire, 22 *n* 5 *d*
—— Fatal at Basford Coal Mine, 22 *o* 7 *d*
——— at Old Mill Colliery, Barnsley, 19 *n* 9 *b*
——— at the Hoosac Tunnel, Massachusetts, 6 *n* 7 *e*
——— Explosion at the Bwllfa Steam Colliery, 28 *d* 10 *c*—30 *d* 9 *c*
——— Fire in Moorsely Down Pit, 9 *n* 9 *b*
—— Ferndale Colliery, 15 *n* 8 *e*—18 *n* 7 *b*
——— Explosion, 9 *n* 9 *b*—11 *n* 7 *e*—12 *n* 6 *d*—13 *n* 7 *f*—14 *n* 9 *f*—15 *n* 8 *d*
—— Fire-damp at St. Etienne, 24 deaths, 14 *o* 7 *d*
——— Explosion at Blangy, 18 *d* 10 *b*—20 *d* 10 *c*
——— near Stourbridge, 12 *n* 9 *b*—14 *n* 9 *b*—6 *d* 10 *a*
—— Inspectors' Reports on, *n*, 15 *n* 4 *e*
—— Oaks Colliery—*See* OAKS.
—— Violent Explosion, 6 *n* 7 *a*—7 *n* 6 *b*—9 *n* 7 *f*
Accidents, Railway:—
——— at Bletchley Junction, 25 *d* 9 *c*—27 *d* 4 *c*—30 *d* 4 *f*
——— at Buttevant, 11 *o* 9 *a*
——— at Dalston Station, N.L.R., 11 *o* 5 *f*
——— at Peterborough, 25 *n* 6 *e*
——— near Rosegill Colliery, 11 *d* 10 *c*
——— on the L. & N.W. near Shrewsbury, 4 *d* 10 *f*
——— on the Lyons Railway, many injured, 7 *o* 8 *b*
——— on the N.W. Railway, from Manchester, 18 *o* 7 *e*
——— on the S.E. Railway, 8 *o* 7 *f*
——— or Suicide on the North Woolwich Railway, 4 *o* 8 *f*
——— to the Royal Train at Ealing, 18 *n* 9 *b*

TO THE

PROPRIETORS AND EDITORS OF "THE TIMES" NEWSPAPER,

THE MOST IMPORTANT AND INFLUENTIAL JOURNAL

IN THE WORLD,

WHOSE MORAL INFLUENCE DIRECTS THE MINDS OF THE PEOPLE, THE SENATORS,

AND THE GOVERNMENT OF THE NATION:

This Index,

WHICH ATTEMPTS TO CLASSIFY AND ARRANGE THE IMMENSE MASS OF INFORMATION

CONTAINED IN ITS COLUMNS, IS DEDICATED,

WITH EVERY RESPECT, BY

SAMUEL PALMER.

Upper Holloway, Jan. 1, 1868.

INDEX

THE Universal DAILY Register

Printed Logographically. By His Majesty's Patent

SATURDAY, JANUARY 1, 1785. [Price Two-pence Halfpenny.]

SHIPPING ADVERTISEMENTS

To the Public.

WEDNESDAY, JUNE 29, 1785.

THIS DAY IS A HOLIDAY AT ALL THE PUBLIC OFFICES.

THE TIMES OR DAILY UNIVERSAL REGISTER

PRINTED LOGOGRAPHICALLY

TUESDAY, JANUARY 1, 1788. (Price Three-pence.)

The Times.

Price Three-pence. THURSDAY, JUNE 12, 1788.

The Times.

WEDNESDAY, FEBRUARY 4, 1789. PRICE 3d.

The Times.

LONDON, WEDNESDAY, JULY 18, 1832.

The Times.

LONDON, SUNDAY, AUGUST 16, 1914.

THE DEFENCES OF NAMUR.

LIÉGE UNDER FIRE. THE SUFFERINGS OF THE TOWNSPEOPLE.

LORRAINE INVADED. BRILLIANT FRENCH SUCCESS. RECAPTURE OF THANN.

ATTACK BY AIR.

The Times

London Wednesday, May 5, 1926. Price 2d

Wind N.E., fair to dull; risk of rain.

Evening papers appeared at Bristol, Southampton, several Lancashire towns, Edinburgh, and Tyneside.

The Times

LONDON, SATURDAY, OCTOBER 1, 1932

PERSONAL

CLUB ANNOUNCEMENTS

CONNOISSEURS' GUIDE

CHEPSTOW RACE CLUB.

THE TIMES

LONDON MONDAY OCTOBER 3 1932 PRICE 4d

PERSONAL

BUSINESS OFFERS

CLUB ANNOUNCEMENTS

CHEPSTOW RACE CLUB.

THE TIMES

BRITAIN AT WAR: LATEST NEWS

LONDON MONDAY SEPTEMBER 4 1939 PRICE 2½d

DEATHS (continued)

PERSONAL

EMERGENCY ADDRESSES

PUBLIC APPOINTMENTS

DOMESTIC SITUATIONS VACANT (continued)

MARRIED COUPLES AND MENSERVANTS

APPOINTMENTS & SITUATIONS VACANT

THE TIMES

WEDNESDAY JUNE 13 1984 (20p)

Outlook bleak for coal board's talks with miners

By Paul Routledge, Labour Editor

Takeover talk at Fleet St papers

By William Kay, City Editor